Panzer Regiment 8

Panzer Regiment 8 in World War II

Poland • France • North Africa

Kevin Fish

Schiffer Military History
Atglen, PA

Dedication

Dedicated to my late grandmother
Carolyn Burnett Kane
1903-1988

Cover Photo
The crew of the II./*Abteilung* command panzer in November 1941, after the Crusader battles. *Hptm* Wahl, standing, and *Olt* Hess second from the right. (Hess)

Book Design by Ian Robertson.

Copyright © 2008 by Kevin Fish.
Library of Congress Control Number: 2008934419

All rights reserved. No part of this work may be reproduced or used in any forms or by any means – graphic, electronic or mechanical, including photocopying or information storage and retrieval systems – without written permission from the copyright holder.

Printed in China.
ISBN: 978-0-7643-3087-2

We are interested in hearing from authors with book ideas on related topics.

| Published by Schiffer Publishing Ltd.
4880 Lower Valley Road
Atglen, PA 19310
Phone: (610) 593-1777
FAX: (610) 593-2002
E-mail: Info@schifferbooks.com.
Visit our web site at: www.schifferbooks.com
Please write for a free catalog.
This book may be purchased from the publisher.
Please include $5.00 postage.
Try your bookstore first. | In Europe, Schiffer books are distributed by:
Bushwood Books
6 Marksbury Avenue
Kew Gardens
Surrey TW9 4JF, England
Phone: 44 (0) 20 8392-8585
FAX: 44 (0) 20 8392-9876
E-mail: Info@bushwoodbooks.co.uk.
Visit our website at: www.bushwoodbooks.co.uk
Free postage in the UK. Europe: air mail at cost.
Try your bookstore first. |

Contents

	Author Notes and Acknowledgements	6
	List of Maps and Illustrations	8
	Foreword	9
	Prologue	10

Part I

Chapter 1:	The Early Years, 1936-1939	12
Chapter 2:	The Polish Campaign, September 1939-May 1940	22
Chapter 3:	The French Campaign, May-July 1940	34
Chapter 4:	Between Campaigns, August 1940-April 1941	61

Part II

Chapter 5:	North Africa, May 1941	70
Chapter 6:	The Summer Battles, June-September 1941	83
Chapter 7:	The Crusader Battles, October-November 1941	102
Chapter 8:	Withdrawal from Cyrenaica, December 1941	128
Chapter 9:	Back from Tripolitania, January – April 1942	145
Chapter 10:	Gazala and Tobruk, May-August 1942	154
Chapter 11:	The Battle of Alam Halfa, August-September 1942	178
Chapter 12:	The Battle of El Alamein, October-December 1942	192
Chapter 13:	Fighting for time in Tunisia, January-February 1943	217
Chapter 14:	The Final Battles of the Afrika Korps, March-April 1943	241
Chapter 15:	The End in North Africa, April-May 1943	254
	Epilogue	261
Appendix 1:	German Award Definitions	262
Appendix 2:	Regimental Commander and Award Holders	263
Appendix 3:	Glossary	264
Appendix 4:	The Regimental Role	266
Appendix 5:	Rank Equivalent Guide	276
	Notes	277
	Bibliography	285
	Index	288

Author Notes and Acknowledgments

Since a very early age I have always aspired to write a book and record for the sense of history some of the events that took place during the Second World War. This book has truly allowed me to do just that, in addition to providing me a sense of accomplishment and fulfilled my primary goal of giving something back to the subject that has captured a large part of my life. Over the years I have collected and read many books, and have taken from them many of the things that I have found to be most interesting to me the reader; I hope that what is and has been interesting for me will also be for you the reader. Being a self proclaimed history buff and amateur in book writing I hope that I have done a decent job of capturing the way of life in a German panzer regiment, and explained those events in a clear and concise manner that is easily understood by all.

As this is my first such book project, many may find fault with it, and that is just fine by me, as long as the criticism is not heaped on those that have assisted in the book in any way. The reader will find that in many portions of the book there is exacting detail, while in others it is quite scarce; this of course is due to the lack of personal accounts or battlefield reports. I feel that over the past few years I have been able to compile most of the remaining records dealing with this Regiment, and feel that what is written on these pages is the truth and fact. The reader will notice that many of the veteran accounts and after action reports have a good sense of bravado, and it is important to understand that these accounts were written by men that believed in their cause and survived the bloody battles, and earned the right to be a bit boastful of their achievements. It has not been my intension to slander or hype any of the participants; I have attempted to keep an open mind and reported the events as they happened, and have attempted to cover the Regiment's entire combat record and mix that record in with the overall historical context of the time. Where appropriate and available, a veterans' accounting of the situation has been inserted into the text in order to give the reader the view from the man on the ground. It must, however, be remembered that some of these accounts were written or given well after the event occurred, and at times can seem a bit confusing. That being said, it has amazed me how some of the surviving veterans still have a keen mind and attention to detail after well over 60 years. I have found that the individual and company war diaries kept on that actual day or written just after events took place are the most accurate of all the material I have come across, but at times, they too can lead to a false sense of location and events. In order to keep a bit of the German flavor, I have chosen to use various German terms and words, as I feel they give and best describe and assist the reader in keeping track of the Regiment in the battles and actions it participated in.

As this book focuses on one particular regiment, I have chosen to use that word as a title and abbreviated the full title, as it saved space. I have also chosen, in many places, to use the word British as opposed to Commonwealth or Dominion Troops or Forces, as again it saved space and allowed the text to flow. I have not intentionally attempted to offend the Australian, New Zealanders, Indians, South Africans, nor any other commonwealth troops who served with the British Army and Air Forces in North Africa. The same apology must be made to the men of the various German formations that served in North Africa with the *Deutsches Afrika Korps*, as again I have found it easier to use the more liberal term D.A.K. when describing certain German actions. It is important to point out that the true and accurate D.A.K. was composed of the 15th and 21st Panzer Divisions, but here you will see the liberal use of the word to describe the actions of other units like the 90th Light "Afrika" Division and other formations that served alongside these two panzer divisions. As for a number of locations, especially in Poland and Africa, I have attempted to use the more common name and location. In numerous locations in Poland and North Africa I have placed the Polish or Arabic name next to the one that can be found in many present day maps and correspond to the older ones. I feel that this allows the reader more specific detail to better follow along with the storyline and relate to where the Regiment was located, even in areas where I have omitted map coverage. During the many years of reading and writing about the Regiment I have read through so many accounts that any failure to give proper literary credit where it is due is my fault alone, and I apologize for any copyright infringements that I may have made, as they were made totally unintentionally.

As with any book of historical fact, there are a lot of people, organizations, and agencies to thank, and if I have failed to do so, I offer you my sincerest apologies. This book has been a pure joy to undertake; not only has it helped my German language skills, but it has literally brought me closer to my neighbors and the community in which I live. First and foremost I want to thank my lovely wife Tatiana, who always believed in my ability to accomplish this task and supported me through the difficult periods. She was my primary translator, and without her help none of this would have been possible. Secondly I would like to thank all of the veterans and families of the Regiment whose story I am telling. Each one

Author Notes and Acknowledgments

of you have made me feel so welcome, and opened not only your homes to me and my family, but the extremely difficult past. My special thanks goes to the veterans: Willi Bassler, Hans Bennemann, Helmut Bleiber, Wilhelm Bühler, Hermann Eckardt, Dr. Klaus Foerster, Wilhelm Hagios, Gotthilf Haidt, Fritz Haustein, Kurt Kathe, Gerhard Kienzle, Hans Killermann, Erich Kuch, Max Lebold, Wilhelm Ludwig, Dr. Dieter Maisch, Hans Mayer, Ernst Rummler, Wolfgang Schefold, Horst Sonnenkalb, and Gerhard Weidelener. As some of you are now gone, I am truly sorry that I could not have finished this book quicker so that you could have seen it. To General Heinz-Felix Beckmann, who not only served in the *Abteilung* which was reborn of the Regiment after its capitulation in Africa, but whose article that first appeared in 1994 in *Die Schwartz Beret* got me started. It was his article which laid the basic ground work and gave me a starting point with which to begin and pursue this dream of mine. My many thanks to you and the effort and guidance you've given me. To the family and friends of the Regiment: Wolfgang Boger; Willi Poppenberger; Frau Dorrit Halverscheidt, wife of the late Karl Halverscheidt and presently the president of the regimental association; and Frau Traut and Frau Weber, the two daughters of the late *Oberst* Friedrich Haarde. The von Heydebreck family, Karen Ryan, Martin Deppe, and others whose names I may have forgotten. Many thanks to Hans-Jürgen Sostmann who helped me greatly by allowing me a first look at any new material, and his wife, who was able to keep my son Nikolai busy during my visits with them, I cannot ever begin to thank you enough. To Ludwig Bauer for fulfilling my request with his gracious foreword. Many thanks to Major Bill Linn (U.S. Army) for all your help and mentorship with setting things up and getting me focused on the little things that I had overlooked, and to MSG Johnny Hasselquist (U.S. Army) and others for their time in providing me translation assistance. Major (Ret) Frank Golding, for the gracious loan of some of the pictures of Walter Spohn. My thanks to the ladies of the Böblingen Stadt Archives, Frau Conny Wenzel and Frau Schimdt, and at the Koblenz Archives, Frau Martina Caspers. At the U.S. National Archives (NARA) my thanks to the men, women, and students for all their assistance and patience during my visits. Many thanks go to Dr Eckert Guth, who performed some of the research for me when I was behind schedule. To my editors, Bob Biondi and Ian Robertson, thanks for your trust, help, and encouragement, and a special thanks to Tom Houlihan, my graphic artist, who on short notice bailed me out by taking on the map design project and made this book so much better. To all those helpful and in most cases anonymous names from the various internet websites which assisted in translation of German words and abbreviations, thanks guys, your help was and is greatly appreciated.

List of Maps and Illustrations

Map 1. The Invasion of Poland – September 1939.
Map 2. The Invasion of France - May 1940.
Map 3. The Sedan Bridgehead.
Map 4. The Invasion of France: Breaking the Weygand Line. June 1940.
Map 5. The Mediterranean Theater of Operations.
Map 6. Battleaxe: 15-17 June 1941
Map 7. Operation Crusader, Phase 1: 19-22 November 1941
Map 8. Operation Crusader, Phase 2: 25-26 November 1941
Map 9. Operation Crusader, Phase 3: 27 November-7 December 1941
Map 10. Cyrenaica, January – April 1942
Map 11. The Battle for Gazala
Map 12. The Fall of Tobruk, 20-21 June 1942
Map 13. The Battle for Alam Halfa, 30 August – 3 September 1942
Map 14. The Battle for Alamein, 24 October – 3 November 1942
Map 15. Retreat to Tunisia
Map 16. Tunisia 1943
Map 17. Operations in Southern Tunisia, 14-15 February 1943
Map 18. Kasserine Pass, 13-18 February 1943
Map 19. The End in Tunisia

Foreword

By Ludwig Bauer, former *Leutnant* and winner of the Knights Cross with Panzer Regiment 33 of the 9th Panzer Division.

To bind wreaths for victorious armies, to tell the coming generations about their deeds on memorials of stone has been a common custom. However, regiments that despite heroic performance of their duty went under in the wake of their defeat are soon forgotten. It is therefore even more impressive how the development and fate of the former Panzer Regiment 8, of the former German Army, is illustrated in this book. Remarkable first, because the Regiment shows, in an exemplary manner, what the just formed German panzer weapon during the Second World War managed to accomplish. Impressive also that the author does not belong to the generation of the grandchildren whose interest is not without saying anymore, but belongs to the armies to which the remnants of the Regiment capitulated in 1943. The book on one hand is evidence of the expertise and the objective judgment of the author, but it also sets standards for the noble fairness and the great respect which an American non-commissioned officer and amateur historian can have for the soldierly accomplishments of the former German soldiers even after sixty years.

To accept the request for a foreword is at the same time an honor and duty for me. I have always found myself in similar situations like the comrades of the Panzer Regiment 8 when I was a young soldier and officer of the German tank forces. I believe, therefore, that I can permit myself to give a few words about the military and human accomplishments that stand the somber facts. Panzer Regiment 8 was one of the founding regiments of the German tank forces and played an instrumental role in its development. The limitless, always evident suitability for all attack and defensive tasks was based, besides on an excellent, always regenerating training, especially on the virtues of this Wurttembergisch Regiment: Duty, Honor, Loyalty, and love for the fatherland, as the basis of the soldierly community and exemplary comradeship of all ranks in conjunction with a discipline strong of character. The regiment fought until the end in May 1943 in all variants of tank warfare. It always fought with bravery, but also with all the highs and lows of war, and always and again with severe losses. It was quite possible the first tank detachment in history that accomplished the coup to capture the fortress of Brest-Litovsk. In the offensive of 1940, the Regiment was part of the forces that within 10 days pushed 400 kilometers from the borders of Western Germany to the English Channel. This would be a great feat even under today's conditions. However, then there was not the high technology of today. Tank warfare dominated in Africa with its marked form of fast wide sweeping movements, violent tank duels, and war of attrition. Later, when the Panzer Abteilung was reformed, it fought in the unprecedented tough and hard defensive battles on the German Eastern frontlines, and finally in the end in the area around Berlin. The Regiment fought in the spirit of good German soldierly tradition: always fair, heroic, and without fanaticism, believing in a good cause namely to serve the protection of the fatherland. The soldier experienced the horror of mercilessness of the modern war, but politics were always far removed from the knowledge of a front line unit. The attitude of the men was especially fueled by the feeling of the double duty for the fatherland and comrades. These ties kept them together in battle and also later as prisoners of war. It is now on the survivors and the later generations to honor this memory. As one of the ones who can still give witness, I want to thank the author of this book for not only the competent quality of his work, but also for the important contribution in keeping alive this memory.

Ludwig Bauer 2005

Prologue

On a rainy Thursday in September 2002, I sat behind a group of elderly men and women with a few of their relatives and escorts on a less than perfect U.S. Army bus as we drove around the grounds of Panzer Kaserne. I noticed that they all were very excited, and were constantly looking out the windows and speaking as if they were on a grammar school field trip. The members of this group belonged to the Panzer Regiment 8 Kameradshaft and were touring the kaserne in order to determine a new location for a monument.

Some 60 years prior to this visit, two members of the 6th Company had fallen in the campaign in Poland, and in order to remember these two men, their company had placed a small stone plaque near the company barracks with their names on it. The stone remained in place for many years, and like many things of today fell into a state of disrepair. Now, after all these years, members of the 1st Battalion, 10th Special Forces Group raised some concern over this broken stone and approached the base housing engineer, and with him decided that it was time to give this stone its proper place on the newly renovated kaserne. For these veterans and families a quiet corner of the kaserne, under the trees and away from the daily activities, seemed like a perfect place to relay the stone. But then there was the suggestion of using a more visible spot in the new and expanded parking lot on one of the beautiful green islands with bushes and trees. At this suggestion the bus became quite loud and the sense of excitement grew when the group realized that the engineer was not asking them to hide the stone away in a shady corner of the kaserne.

As I sat in the back and watched the veterans, now all in their 80s, I understood what we were doing for this group and what it meant to them not to have to hide their war service. This was not like in America, where we are proud of our veterans and their service, and proudly erect and display battle monuments and statues dedicated to them. Our actions here today were almost unheard of in post war Germany. The stigma of National Socialism had scared this country, its people, and its veterans for generations. There are very few memorials to their service, and their reunions occur in quiet locations and are low key events that revolve around a short religious service and lunch. We were not here this day celebrating Nazi Germany, but remembering soldiers, which it seems that only other soldiers, regardless of which side they fought on, can do. Indeed, many German veterans were party members and followed Adolph Hitler's promises for a return to power and glory, albeit many never envisioned it would lead these proud men and, in some cases, women down a road to destruction and ruin. But for many of these veterans they were just soldiers doing their duty for their country and, more importantly, for one another. As I spoke to them in my broken German, I produced a small pamphlet book about the German *Afrika Korps* and Rommel that contained a few pictures of some of the Knights Cross winners. I was thinking oh, maybe they will remember Rommel from their time in Africa. As the gentleman in front of me scanned through the booklet he motioned to the older man sitting next to him and turned to me, and informed me that the older man sitting there was one of the Knights Cross winners. I could see the resemblance immediately, and sure enough this was Hermann Eckardt, the last surviving member of Panzer Regiment 8 to be decorated with the Knights Cross for bravery in action. As my excitement began to grow the short bus ride ended and we all got off the bus to pose for a few pictures beside the flag pole; we parted company with the group, and an invitation quickly followed to join them that afternoon at a local café for some further talk. And so began my relationship and friendship with many of these veterans, which in turn led me to write and document the proud history of their Regiment that at one time was feared by many in the desert wastes of North Africa, and was known as Rommel's Swabian mailed fist and the true striking power of the German *Afrika Korps*.

I hope you enjoy their story.

Part I

1

The Early Years
1936-1939

In September 1916, the British *Fourth Army* set in motion the first tank attack of the modern age near the French town of Flers. The idea of an armored fighting vehicle mounting machine guns and cannons, and designed to break through the wire and trenches of the German positions, was the idea of British *Colonel* E. D. Swinton, then serving with the *British Expeditionary Force* (B.E.F.) in France.[1] Better known as a tank, in order to keep the idea and design a secret, those first tanks went forward in an attempt to support the infantry as they advanced. That first attack did not go as well as some had expected, because many of the tanks became bogged down in the wet, muddy, shell pocked ground. Later, in November 1917, the first actual tank battle in the history of warfare was fought on the fields of northern France. It was at Cambrai, where some 400 British Mk IV tanks were sent forward en-masse in an attempt to break the German *Hindenburg Line*. That offensive was only partially successful, as the British tanks were able to break the line and send the German defenders fleeing in panic as the tanks lumbered across their trenches and crushed machine gun positions and wire obstacles.[2] Unfortunately, most if not all of those attacks were never properly followed up by reserve forces which could exploit the break-in of the tanks and fan out to attack the dug in infantry, supporting artillery and supply services. Secondly, many of the tanks were never able to break all the way through the defenses where they could roam at will behind the lines and raise havoc. But those early battles did show what could be achieved by this new tool of warfare.

The first German tank attack of the war came later in March 1918 near St. Quentin, where twenty German A7Vs and a number of captured British Mk IVs were sent in to attack the BEF positioned there.[3] The attack failed despite being supported by German airplanes, as the slow lumbering A7V behemoths stalled on the numerous trenches and were unable to cross over them. After this poor showing the German army all but dropped the idea of armored warfare. However, for the Allies, the British, French, and even Americans continued the idea of tank attacks, and were even now using newer French designed tanks. The next notable Allied tank attack was launched in August 1918 near the town of Amiens; it was another attempt to finally break the *Hindenburg Line*. The attack was again partially successful, as the tanks were able to route a number of divisions and breach the line to a width of some ten miles. In this attack the Allies copied the previous German concept of supporting the ground attack with air support, and a number of bomber and fighter planes took part in supporting the offensive. Although it did not immediately end the war, this offensive did hasten its outcome, and in just three months the war was concluded. With the signing of the Armistice and the end the First World War, Germany was bound to the *Treaty of Versailles*, which limited it to an army of just 100,000, and the air force was to be disbanded altogether. The treaty also stipulated that the army possess no heavy artillery or tanks, and that all production and development of such items end immediately.[4] *General* Hans von Seeckt was at that time the head of the *Truppenamt*, or troop department, a position he held from 1919-26. Seeckt, in the previous war, had been a Chief of Staff to a German corps on the Western Front, albeit for only one year, while the remainder of his time had been spent in the east. Seeckt was fortunate, in that he had not developed a static warfare thinking, which was now plaguing many of the top generals in the army. In the 1920s, as Hitler slowly began his rise to power, so too did the *Reichswehr*, or German army, as it found ways to equip and train a new breed of fighting men. Despite the *Treaty of Versailles*, the *Reichswehr* found ways to cover up the reforming of the various services and departments. Many of Germany's senior leaders at the time still believed that they were threatened by their neighbors to the west and east, namely France and Poland, and hoped and petitioned *The League of Nations* that they should be allowed to raise an army of some 300,000. They were, however, denied, and it was Seeckt who was now faced with the problem of how to defend Germany with an army of just 100,000. He therefore directed that the army select from only volunteers, and that each one be closely examined on his previous experience and personal qualities and traits. Furthermore, in an attempt to instill pride and morale in its soldiers, the army would safeguard the traditions and values of the old *Imperial Army*, but it was to do away with the social class barriers and build a closer comradeship between the officers and men based on mutual confidence in one another. Based on these principles, Seeckt was to create a *führer armee*, or leaders army, which trained its soldiers to be capable of performing and acting as noncommissioned officers, while its NCOs were trained to assume the role of junior grade officers, while those junior officers were trained for field grade positions and the field grades to general officer positions. Of the 100,000 men authorized, 5,000 were officer positions and 40,000 NCO positions. With this type of organization a solid cadre was formed in which a larger army could be built upon if it were to be called up in time of emergency.

In the 1920s, encouraged by Seeckt and motivated by the writings of such men like J.F.C. Fuller and Basil Liddell-Hart, a young German captain who was at the time assigned to the *Truppenamt* office of the *Inspectorate of Transport Troops* was quickly becoming an acknowledged expert on tank tactics. This young man was Heinz Guderian, a former infantryman who served as a communications and staff officer in WWI, and who had early in the war witnessed the slaughter of Verdun and been appalled by what he had seen there. Then, in 1918, he was witness to a

Chapter 1: The Early Years, 1936-1939

French tank attack near the town of Soissons. Having previously witnessed the outdated form of warfare and its terrible cost and the new age of the machine gun and tank, he was impressed by these new aged weapons and their potential value in the conflicts to come. Throughout the mid-1920s, Guderian was assigned to a number of positions with motorized units and the *Transport Department*, and it was in these positions that he began to examine and explore the previous studies concerning the workings of motorized troops in combat. Based on these works and his own experiences he began to write of the concept of a panzer division; his base of knowledge was founded on his work in the *Truppenamt* and as an instructor of military history, a job which allowed him to visit and tour many foreign army locations. In his book *Panzer Leader*, Guderian wrote that:

"In this year, 1929, I became convinced that tanks working on their own or in conjunction with infantry could never achieve decisive importance. My historical studies, the exercises carried out in England and our experiences with mock-ups had persuaded me that tanks would never be able to produce their full effect until other weapons on whose support they must inevitably rely were brought up to their standard of speed and of cross-country performance. In such a formation of all arms, the tanks must play the primary role, the other weapons being subordinated to the requirements of the armor. It would be wrong to include tanks in infantry divisions: what was needed were armored divisions which would include all the supporting arms needed to allow the tanks to fight with full effect."[5]

By 1930 Guderian, who was now a *Major*, and the commander of the *3rd (Prussian) Motor Transport Battalion*, was able to put into practice some of his theories and ideas on combined arms tactics. His battalion was composed of motorcycles, armored cars, dummy tanks, and anti-tank guns, and by having these items of equipment readily on hand gave him the insight to see how each individual section contributed to the overall theory of mobile warfare. Even though the battalion was considered a logistics unit, it was forbidden to cooperate with other units in combined exercises. At this time there were many officers critical of the theory of mobile warfare, and some of them even went out of their way to make this point known. Guderian, however, did not suffer as a result of these men, and in February 1931, he was promoted to the rank of *Oberstleutnant*. By late 1931, *General* Oswald Lutz assumed command of the *Inspectorate of Motorized Troops*, and he chose Guderian as his Chief of Staff. Guderian had been kept abreast of tank developments and experiments, especially those taking place in England and France, and he even hired a private translator, which allowed him to collect and translate much of what was being written and documented in the area of armored warfare. It was the direct result of this command and the research done in the 1920s and early 1930s that allowed him to publish in 1937 his famous book *"Achtung Panzer."* More than any other German soldier, it is Heinz Guderian who is known as the father of the German panzers. In 1930, the first panzer had been secretly produced at the *Gasonwerk* factory, and by the following spring, the *Reichswehr* was in possession of four light and six medium panzers, or tractors, as they were publicly referred to. When Hitler ascended to power in 1933, he came in with the determination of having a highly mobile army capable of performing a lightning strike and quickly devastating his enemy. Previously, in the late 1920s, the *Truppenamt* had planned on a standing army of some seventeen divisions, but that was quickly changed to twenty-one divisions by cutting the term of service from twelve years to just one, thereby creating a larger reserve of trained men. Throughout the 1920s and 30s, the Germans had been able to create an army and air force from almost nothing. By cleverly disguising and masking formations with civilian titles, and by using dummy companies abroad, the foundation was being laid for the new German *Wehrmacht*. In 1933, at a demonstration in Kummersdorf of new army and air force equipment, including the panzer Mk I, Hitler remarked when he saw the panzers for the first time *"That is what I want—and that is what I shall have,"* and by August of that year the famed *Krupp* factory had produced the first five panzers. A year later, in 1934, another one hundred Mk I panzers were produced, they were soon followed by the establishment of the first army panzer battalion later that same year. That panzer battalion was established under the guise of *"Motor Transport Training Unit,"* and soon after the *Armored/Motorized Troops Command* was established with Heinz Guderian as its Chief of Staff. That command staff would have the responsibility of commanding and coordinating the development of the panzer arm as it now began to grow in leaps and bounds. By October 1935, the first of three panzer divisions had already been raised and put through its tests. Even though the idea of modern motorized formations had begun to grow, there were still numerous opponents to not only the panzers, but the mobilization in general. Many felt that mobilization was necessary for Germany's survival, but saw the panzers as a direct threat to the future of horse cavalry, and that the main role of the panzers should be as a type of infantry support and tied directly to them. This opposition view was not just shared in Germany, but all through the world, including America, France, and England. But one thing was clear, German industry had to grow in order for a modern motorized army to be created and maintained. Unless there was a sound industrial base with sufficient amounts of raw materials and a skilled workforce there could be no mobile modern army which could even hope to win a large scale war. Still fairly fresh in Hitler's mind were the horrors of the *Western Front* of the *First World War* and its long, drawn out style of static trench warfare. Hitler felt that if he could avoid such a war and possibly launch a lightning campaign to quickly subdue his enemies it would bring him certain success.

By the mid-1930s, France and Poland had recently completed a number of fortifications along their mutual borders with Germany, and these fixed positions did not bode well for the type of lightning war Hitler felt was a necessity to conduct. So for men like Guderian, Rommel, and a host of others like them that had embraced the concept of combined arms tactics utilizing tanks, mobile troops, and aircraft, and linking them all together by modern communications and operations staffs especially designed and trained to follow the speed and tactics of this *Blitzkrieg*, Hitler showed great interest towards those individuals and embraced their ideas. In March 1935, the first panzer division was formed, and with the subsequent formation of an additional two panzer divisions by October of the same year, the *Panzertruppe* became the newest arm of the armed forces. *General* Lutz was appointed as the commander of this *Panzer Korps*, while Guderian was appointed to command the *2nd Panzer Division*. The men who would command and crew these new machines at that time were selected into the new arm based primarily on their intellect and physical fitness. Kurt Kathe explains how some men at that time were selected:

"We had in school a 1,000 people of which only thirty-five were selected for the cavalry when I started as a professional soldier. Of that number only five were taken out of them along with me, they had either bad teeth, or broken legs. The Reichswehr was only so big, 100,000 men. I had been selected because I had always been the best in whatever I did; sports, reading, essay writing and dictation, everything. Boxing was the same, I was unbeatable."[6]

The year 1935 was a big one for the budding panzer arm of the army, in which many decisions, both good and bad, were to be made. In January,

General Lutz called for the formation of three panzer divisions (the 1st, 2nd, and 3rd) and an additional three separate panzer brigades. All three divisions were to be activated by the beginning of October 1935, and the first two combat ready by April 1936, with the third six months later. These divisions would include *Panzer Brigades 1-3* and *Panzer Regiments 1-6*. During this time, many of the major powers of the world were catching the "tank bug," and so it was decided that a further expansion and acceleration in the panzer force was necessary to keep pace with those armies. At that time it was decided upon to expand the number of brigades being activated. The plan initially called for those three brigades to be activated one at a time in each year beginning in 1937 and ending in 1939. The plan was now altered, so that two brigades would be activated in both 1937 and 1938, and thus by 1939 there would be six brigades and twelve panzer regiments formed. Each panzer unit was to be raised in various locations throughout Germany where it was believed Germany was most threatened by its neighbors. For this reason it was believed that should the *French Army* launch any attacks on Germany, they would do so along the Neckar River, in Baden Württemberg. And so it was suggested that the next brigade, the *4th*, should be located in the region of Ludwigsburg-Tübingen-Reutlingen. Knowing that panzer divisions would be no good by themselves unless supported by additional infantry and reconnaissance forces, the high command made the decision that in addition to panzer divisions, there should also be motorized infantry and light divisions. The infantry, which at that time was foot borne, could never possibly hope to keep pace with the panzers and be able and available to exploit any breakthrough operations, and so it was deemed necessary to form a number of motorized divisions. The formation of these divisions required little in-house fighting by those in favor of panzer forces; however, the same could not be said about those of the light divisions. Since the staunchly traditional cavalry branch was already losing men to the panzer arm there was little support for these newcomers, and many heated paper battles took place to prevent the expansion of the panzer divisions. To assume the traditional role of cavalry, that of providing reconnaissance, security, and screening, the light divisions were formed from a number of different branches, and would be composed of panzers, motorized infantry, artillery, and reconnaissance elements. Although many opinions were presented as to the organization of the panzer division, by 1935 a rough *Table of Organization and Equipment*, or TO&E, was laid down which would see each panzer division being comprised of: one panzer brigade, consisting of two panzer *abteilung* (battalions) with light and medium panzer companies; one motorized infantry brigade consisting of one infantry regiment with two infantry battalions; one artillery regiment with two light artillery battalions; a motorcycle battalion; reconnaissance battalion; signal *abteilung*; and engineer company. This table of organization would continue to undergo many changes, and from time to time would see various formations added and taken away. On 3 March 1936 *General Lutz*, as *Kommando der Panzertruppen*, wrote to the *General stab des Herr* with respect to the planned increase in panzer units, and suggested that *Panzer Regiment 7* and *8* be immediately created in the Fall 1936 with six instead of eight companies in order to create a wider base for expansion during the following year.[7] In conjunction with the *National Defense Regulation* dated on 21 May 1935, and under the direction of the *Kommando des Panzertruppen*, the OKH, or *Oberkommando des Heeres* (Army High Command), was ordered in June 1936 to form two additional panzer regiments to take effective by autumn 1936. This would be the third phase of the panzer expansion program and would see the creation of the *7th* and *8th Panzer Regiments*. *Panzer Regiment 7* would be assigned to the *1st Panzer Division*, which already had the *1st* and *2nd Panzer Regiments* under the command of the *1st Panzer Brigade*. The *8th Panzer Regiment* would be assigned to the *3rd Panzer Division* and its *3rd Panzer Brigade*, along with its *5th* and *6th Panzer Regiments*. All plans to incorporate the *7th* and *8th Regiments* fell short, as the creation of the *4th Panzer Brigade* was placed on hold. And so the Regiment was officially recognized as a panzer regiment on 6 October 1936.[8]

Activation

The Regiment was activated near Berlin at the Zossen training camp with a table of organization and equipment, or TO&E in modern military jargon, that called for one regimental headquarters (*stabs*) and two panzer battalions, which within the panzer arm were more commonly titled as *abteilung* or detachments. The regimental headquarters was to be complete with the following: a regimental headquarters with one *stabs*, or headquarters company, which incorporated the following sections: a *nachrichten*, or signals/communications section; *artz* or medical; *musik* or band; *ingeneer* or mechanical engineering; *aufklärungs* or reconnaissance; and the *kradmelder*, or messenger sections. Later, the *kradmelder* and *aufklärungs* sections would be incorporated into the *leiche kolone*, or light column (*le Kol* for short). The strength of the Regiment would of course revolve around the two panzer *abteilung*; each *abteilung* was comprised of a headquarters company, whose structure resembled that of the regimental *stabs* company minus the band, and the presence of a workshop company and support company also known as the *workshop* and *stoss* companies, each consisting of military and civilian technicians. Four light panzer companies would constitute the primary component of the panzer *abteilung*. Each of these companies was to be equipped with twenty-two Mk I panzers. In addition to the normal compliment of the *abteilung's* panzers there were to be three larger Mk Is known as command, or *befehlswagens*, and five Mk I within the *stabs* section. The same number was also allotted to the regimental *stabs* for a total of exactly two hundred panzers and two thousand officers, NCOs, men, and technicians.[9] It would, in fact, be some time before the Regiment was brought up to strength in men and machines because, although the numbers appear correct, the fact is that the German armaments factories had a ways to go before they could even produce the number of panzers required for the existing panzer regiments. In most cases there were truly only a handful of panzers available for training purposes. The Regiment was formed from a cadre of troops from *Panzer Regiments 3* and *5* (*Kraftfahrlehr-Kommando Zossen*) and *Panzer Regiment 6*. From these pre-existing Regiments were pulled out the respective consistent company. The *6th Company* from *Panzer Regiment 5* now formed the *5th Company*; the *3rd Company* from *Panzer Regiment 6* (Heydebreck) became the *6th Company*, with its *6th Company* (Gersdorf) becoming the *7th Company* of *Panzer Regiment 8*.[10]

Oberst Johann "Hans" Haarde, an experienced officer in army motorization and the development of panzer troops, became the Regiment's first commander. Haarde was born on 21 June 1889 in Wilhelmshaven; he saw service in WWI, and later in the *Reichswehr*. Haarde was commissioned in November 1907 and later fought with *Infantry Regiment 78*, and in April 1917 had been promoted to *Hauptmann*. After the war he rose in rank, being promoted to Major in 1930, *Oberstleutnant* in 1934, and finally to *Oberst* in 1936. Since 1934, he had been the commander of the Army's motor vehicle school in Wünsdorf, near Berlin. Haarde assembled and formed the Regiment from men who were then influencing the development of motorized troops. *Oberstleutnant* Irmish, who, since 1932 had been assigned to the *Inspector of Motorized Troops* office, was given the I./*Abteilung*, and Major Wilhelm Conze, a highly decorated WWI officer and former commander of the *1st Lehr Troop* in the *1st Panzer Regiment* at the *Kraftfarhlehrkommando* in Zossen was given command of the II./Abteilung.[11]

Chapter 1: The Early Years, 1936-1939

Panzer Regiment 8 Chain of Command as of 6 October 1936[12]

Regimental Commander	Oberst Haarde, H
Adjutant	Hptm Bruns
Ord Offz	Olt Bernau
Regt Arzt	Dr Feller
StKp	Olt von Stunzner
I./Abteilung Commander	Oberstlt Irmisch
Adjutant	Olt von Arentschildt
1st Company	Olt Frhr von Bodenhausen
Zug Commander	Lt Plinzner
2nd Company	Hptm von Frankenberg and Proschlitz
Zug Commander	Lt Baron von Holtey
3rd Company	Hptm Aster
4th Company	Hptm Linke
Zug Commander	Lt Wahl
Workshop	HBmstr Stelzer
II./Abteilung Commander	Major Conze
Adj	Olt Kaufmann
5th Company	Hptm Frhr von Bulow
Zug Commander	Lt Jahns
6th Company	Hptm von Heydebreck
Zug Commander	Lt Von Stulpnagel
7th Company	Major von Gersdorff
Zug Commander	Lt Sahmel
8th Company	Hptm Kentel
Zug Commander	Lt. Von Portatius
Workshop	HBmstr Hauska

The Regiment's time in the *3rd Panzer Division* was to be short lived, when in November 1936 the fourth phase of the army expansion program was ordered. In this phase of expansion the fledgling Regiment was shifted to the operational control of the *4th Panzer Brigade*, along with the *7th Panzer Regiment* to the *Heerestruppen*, or Army troops of the *Fifth Armee Korps*. The effective date was given as 12 October 1936.[13] Just a short time later, in November 1936, a fifth expansion phase was ordered for early on in 1937; however, this did not affect the Regiment, and it would continue to serve under the *4th Panzer Brigade* for the next few years; even though at times its higher echelon formation would be changed the brigade would not. Intensive individual training in the classrooms and local training grounds filled the first couple of months. It was directed that each crew member was to cross train and learn the jobs of the others in his panzer crew, and prior to the end of the training it was fairly common that each man knew at least the job of one of his crewmembers. There was plenty of time reserved for driving instruction, which at the time was fairly brand new, and the wonder of many young men who found the new area of mechanical and technical instruction fascinating. Many, if not all the men who first went to the *panzertruppen* were selected by merit, and were second only to the *Luftwaffe* in general aptitude. In early 1937, each company received twenty-two Mk I Ausf A (Krupp) panzers. Kurt Kathe remembered:

"When we first got the Panzer I, it was small and had 2 machine guns, we had only pistols. At the training grounds in Berlin at Zossen we got issued cardboard and we took it to make a panzer. Later came the Panzer II with 2cm cannon, but these didn't last. The panzer was quick, but its penetration power with the 2cm gun was nothing."[14]

There were exercises conducted in section, platoon, and company sized formations at the training areas of Zossen, Döberitz, and Wünsdorf. For the first gunnery exercises the Regiment was relocated to the gunnery range located near Putlos, on the Baltic Sea, and there in the summer of 1937 tested the new panzer Mk II with its 20mm main gun; additionally at this time the re-armament of the Mk I Ausf B was undertaken. On 18 June 1937, in accordance to the directive from *Generalkommando Fifth Armee Korps* dated 3 October 1936, the Regiment assumed the traditions and honorary title of the *3rd Badischen Dragoner Regiment Prinz Karl Nr. 22/3rd Baden Dragoon Regiment*. This was the first indication that the Regiment would find its posting in the region of Baden-Württemberg, and was confirmed through the increased number of recruits from Baden-Württemberg.[15] The Regiment would not be completely filled with personnel until its final posting to Böblingen, near Stuttgart. *Oberstlt* Irmish handed over command of the I./*Abteilung* to *Major* Friedrich Haarde, the brother of *Oberst* Hans Haarde, and in turn assumed command of the newly formed *25th Panzer Regiment* of the *7th Panzer Division*. *Hptm* Kentel departed Zossen with him and became the commander of the *4th Company, Panzer Regiment 25*. The relocation of the Regiment from the Zossen training camp to Böblingen was ordered on 1 April 1938. The advance party, which consisted of some thirty-three men, was led by *Hptm* Otto and arrived in Böblingen on 23 February 1938, in order to prepare the Kaserne for its new garrison. Previously, in May 1936 the *Bürgermeister*, or mayor, of Böblingen, Mr. Rohm, received official notification by Reich officials that some 620 hectares of city forest had been selected by military officials as the planned site to garrison a new panzer regiment. At the price of only nine Reich's pfennigs per square meter including the wood, the Schönbuch town forest was purchased for the construction of the *Ludendorff and Hindenburg Kaserne*. The forest bordered the town of Böblingen to the south and east, and until 1936 had been an endless forested area with tall pine trees and impenetrable thickets of briars and berry patches. The area had once been the hunting area for the local gentry and was filled with deer and wild boar. The tranquility of the forest was greatly appreciated by the Stuttgart citizens, who sought peace and relaxation there from the noise, dirt, and smog of the big industrial city. In the spring of 1936, the peace and solitude all came to an end when lumberjacks began their work cutting down the large pines with chain saws. The town of Böblingen was no stranger to military activity; it was a garrison town during the *First World War*, housing *Luftwaffe* units on its airfield. Everything progressed rapidly, and in May 1936 the military construction agency in Stuttgart was ordered to begin simultaneous construction on two kaserne, each of which was to house a panzer regiment, one in Böblingen and the other in nearby Vaihingen. Initially Mr. Blind, a government employed civil engineer, was assigned both projects, but was soon overwhelmed, and in October 1936 Mr. Korsch, a Böblingen graduate engineer, assumed the Böblingen project, while Blind remained with the Vaihingen project. The first step in construction was making the site accessible, as at the time there were very few access roads, water lines, or electricity there; there were not even any maps of the area, and those that eventually turned up were from the preceding century. On 28 August 1936, ground was broken for the access road leading from the *Reich Strasse*, a road which connected Stuttgart to Böblingen to the actual kaserne site, the present day *Panzer Strasse*. By 10 July the surveyors were able to complete their work for construction of Section I by working day and night. In spite of the neverending rain the 1.5km road was completed by the end of September. Later this stretch of road was extended to a range complex. In the interim, plans for the kaserne were actively progressing so that the actual construction could begin on 1 October 1936. *Forestmeister* Spoerr, the chief of forest administration, had the forest cleared in no time, and once the land was cleared the construction began, with the buildings quickly shooting out of the ground like mushrooms. Every five minutes a truck loaded with material rolled down the newly built road, which was not surfaced, and was stacked with wood and tree stumps that hindered traffic, but nothing seemed to hold up the progress, not even the steady rain that caused drivers and vehicles almost to drown in the mud. Soon after beginning construction other problems began to arise, as the construction firms now encountered a lack of construction material. At that time the *West Wall*, or *Siegfried Line*, was also under construction, not to mention the numerous barracks springing up all over Germany to house the huge army that Hitler envisioned. Despite the shortage of iron and concrete, enough materials were found and most deadlines were generally met on time. By January 1937, with most of the rough work completed on the first section, construction also began on *Project B*, or the second section of the kaserne. Again the lack of construction materials was felt, but enough material was gathered and work progressed in record time. As an example of the speed in which the construction firms were working, one of the nearby construction firms was able to finish one of the large troop buildings in only forty-six working days, while another firm completed some of the troop billets and another of the large buildings just a few days later. Mr. Günter, the engineer in charge of underground construction, reported that, despite the rocky ground, in some places seven meters deep, the underground works and sewer lines were progressing on schedule. Much of the exterior work had been completed by July, and with this accomplishment there was a call for a celebration. In addition to the lack of building materials there was also an insufficient work force, and those that were available came from many locations only to discover that any available housing could not be found anywhere in Böblingen. One of the problems was that in addition to the *Ludendorff and Hindenburg Kaserne,* there was another kaserne being built in Böblingen to house a *Luftwaffe* squadron. To make up for the labor shortage and lack of housing, some of the workers from surrounding areas were transported to the construction sites, some from as far away as 100km. With the lack of manpower and scarcity of skilled laborers working hours had to be extended, and beginning Christmas 1937 all leaves were cancelled and work continued throughout the weekends. In late February, an advance party of approximately twenty-five men moved into the billets; a few days later a larger group of approximately 180 men were able to occupy their newly furnished billets. Also completed by the end of February were many of the larger buildings, like the officer casinos, clubs, and headquarters, along with the water tower, rifle range, and heating plant. When the troops moved in on 1 April 1938, the headquarters building and troop billets presented a neat look, as did the street and formation areas, and the water and electricity were connected and running, along with the sewer system. Much of the landscaping had yet to be completed because of the severe winter weather, but this hardly affected the troops moving in. Kurt Liestmann, at the time a young recruit, noted in his diary about his arrival to Böblingen and the new kaserne:

"Tuesday 29.3.38. Labor service and packing, departure mood. Hectic party. Wednesday 30.3.38. Received the black uniform in Wünsdorf. 1817hrs departure. During the way tested some of the vehicles, everything in order. 31.3.38 slept the whole night, wonderful weather and a nice trip through Thüringen, Schweinfurt, Würzburg (wonderful location) along the Nekar [River]. Already before Böblingen all villages and towns rejoicing welcome us. A fantastic mood and clean impression from "Schwobeländle" [Swabian country]. Triumphant welcome in Sindelfingen, the reloading train station, the Daimler Benz Kapelle plays the Panzer marching song. I am lucky, I am a rifleman in the combat vehicle and thus by the entrance a participant in a prominent place. We are adorned in our "schwartzen" or black uniforms. On the airfield are pilot candidates and we go into the barracks. Fantastic buildings in the middle of the beech-tree forest. Here we will feel well. Still much work in the evening, off-loading etc. Late to bed. 1.4.38. Labor service, cleaning, many things not yet finished but it is already very nice."[16]

The city of Böblingen had agreed to take care of the sewage coming from the kaserne, and this prompted the construction of a sewage purification plant by both the towns of Böblingen and Sindelfingen. The *Luftwaffe Kaserne* also placed a demand on the local water supply, and an additional water line had to be constructed from nearby Aidlingen. April 9th was a most memorable day for the town of Böblingen and marked a special chapter in the city's history. Representatives from the *Wehrmacht*, various city offices, and local citizens greeted the panzer troops in Böblingen as the entire town donned a festive look with garlands of flowers and flags hanging from houses and lining the streets. The *Bismarck Platz*, and especially the *Postplatz* were the sites selected for this special reception. At the intersection of *Stuttgart Strasse, Hermann-Göring Strasse,* and *Landhaus Strasse* the town *Bürgermeister,* Mr. Rohm, cordially welcomed the leading elements of the panzer convoy. Rohm told them that the home they would find in Böblingen could not be any better, and that the location of the kaserne in the Schonbuch forest and the friendly attitudes of the local citizens would contribute to their welcome. *Oberst* Hans Haarde, standing in the turret of his Mk I panzer, thanked the *Bürgermeister* for his welcoming words and assured the citizens that his Regiment would do all in their power to cement lasting ties of friendship in Böblingen, and with that he gave the command to move out. The panzers entered the town via *Panzer Strasse* and *Stuttgart Strasse* and wound their way through the various streets towards the town train station. Rows of local townsfolk were lining the roads and waving flags, as many of the local factories had been closed for the day. Members of the *National Socialist Workers Party* (*NSDAP*) and *SA*, and members of the Regiment lined *Adolf-Hitler Strasse* up to the *Postplatz*, which was to be the center of the celebrations. On the reviewing stand, in front of the *Dinkelacker Restaurant* were dignitaries of the city administration, *Nazi Party*, and the armed forces supreme command of the *Fifth Armee Korps*. Not only was the reviewing stand crowded to maximum capacity, but people were standing shoulder to shoulder along the streets and sidewalks trying to hear the various speakers. The celebrations were such that not even the falling snow could distract them from this festive occasion. At 0930hrs, the Regiment's band arrived at the *Postplatz* and the leading panzer, with *Oberst* Haarde perched atop, stopped in front of the reviewing stand, where he gave his speech. The crowd was jubilant, and during the speech an airplane performed acrobatics high above the troops and crowd. Mr. Meditsch, in his speech, addressed *Oberst* Haarde:

"Not only Böblingen but the entire county and many regions of the Württemberg State share an eager anticipation for the arrival of your Regiment at their home station in Böblingen. Hundreds and thousands have come from far and near to witness this special event. Böblingen is the home station of one the most modern combat branches of the Wehrmacht. It is with great pleasure that I welcome you, Oberst, your officers and your soldiers on behalf of the state and the county to our Swabian State and our City." *Oberst* Haarde thanked the speakers for their welcome and said, *"I believe this day is not only unforgettable for the Regiment but also for the city and entire county of Böblingen."*[17]

One of the local leaders of the *National Socialist Party* (*NSDAP*) expressed in his speech how pleased he was that the town of Böblingen, which had been a garrison town during WWI, was again serving in that capacity. Following the ceremony, the regimental band, conducted by SFw Ernst Isensee, a local music director and former *Hussar* in the First World War, began to lead the long convoy of vehicles and marching soldiers past the reviewing stand and then on towards the kaserne. On their way, they halted briefly when a little boy reached out to present a bouquet of flowers to *Oberst* Haarde. The little boy needed a hoist from his father to

Chapter 1: The Early Years, 1936-1939

reach up to the panzer, and Haarde accepted the flowers and then held the little boy up while spectators laughed and applauded the act of kindness. When the convoy arrived at the kaserne there was a white ribbon across the gate, and two high pylons and an arch of flags were erected there for the welcome. The band and companies of the Regiment then took up positions on both sides of the vehicles. In front of the gate, Mr. Blind delivered his welcoming speech where he stated how happy he was that in spite of all the hardships, the kaserne had been finished on time, and that the soldiers would be satisfied with the results of all the hard work. Haarde was presented a huge ornamental key to the front gate which ironically had yet to be installed; he then went on to thank the construction firms and workers for their hard work while the national flag was hoisted to full mast to the tunes of the *National Anthem* and *Horst Wesel Leid*. The Regiment had officially taken possession of the kaserne, and now it was time for them to show their appreciation to the locals as they sponsored an open house of the kaserne. The regimental field kitchen was open, and for the price of half a Reichsmark, visitors could sample the rations eaten by the soldiers. The main attractions that afternoon were the sporting events, which commenced at 1500hrs. The main square in the kaserne was filled with large crowds, which some estimated to be nearly 12,000. A *Quadrille* from the *18th Cavalry Regiment* from nearby Bad Cannstadt began to perform as an officer and twenty-four riders entertained the crowd with an exciting and spectacular show of which many in the crowd had never seen before. Following the show were some motorcycle stunts and an artillery demonstration in which the vehicles raced into the square and fired off a salvo. By 1700hrs, the heavy snow had begun to fall, which tested much of the crowd as they began to make their way home through the snow-covered forest. But for many of those in attendance, the chance to experience the celebration kept them there, as they chose to ignore the snow in favor of the music and dancing, which by now had been moved to the cover of the motor pool bays.

And so after the festivities were concluded the officers and men began to settle down to the mission at hand. The first order of business was to plan and organize a training regimen that would take the soldiers through the various skills needed to become an effective fighting force. The local training area around Böblingen was limited due to the large tracks of forest, and so the panzer and gunnery training was conducted in other training camps located within an hour or two from the garrison's home; locations such as Bergen-Hohne, Heuberg, and Münsingen were frequently visited, and the spacious training grounds provided the environment necessary for teaching the theories of mobile armored warfare. One of the largest training grounds was located near the Czech border at the Grafenwöhr training lager. This training complex is still utilized by the U.S. and its NATO allies today. The summer and autumn of 1938 were all devoted to basic training. The *ersatz*, or reserve forces, and newly transferred officers and *unteroffiziers* were subordinated. The panzer *Kampfwagenbuch* of *Olt* Kauffmann, the commander of the 4th Company, was followed according to the training guidelines prescribed by higher authority. Based on this, the company leadership and section and junior leaders were all thoroughly trained, and in later operations this intense training would show dividends. There was also time to visit the local small towns and big city of Stuttgart, located only a few kilometers away. Young Kurt Liestmann remembers the first time he visited Böblingen and Stuttgart:

"Visited Stuttgart, walked through Böblingen. We eat lunch in the 'Bären'[Bear Restaurant]. Walked through old Böblingen up the hill, and down through the lanes, which are very narrow and romantic and went back to the barracks. The balance: Böblingen is much nicer and more beautiful than Zossen, and Stuttgart is the crown!"[18]

For Karl Halverscheidt, also a young man at the time, who recalled in a speech to U.S. Army Forces stationed in Böblingen in the 1970s of how it was for some of the younger officers in those early days:

"The early years in Böblingen as a young officer were difficult, young Leutnants were always in good spirits but when they looked into their billfolds they had enough reason to be sad. Financially they were poor dogs with the exception of a few who received monthly checks from their parents. At the time a soldier earned .50 pfennig a day and officers DM 2.40 in addition the Leutnant received an additional tax deductable DM 170.00. The strict code of an officer forbid the wife to work and marrying a young officer limited her in many ways. The first proviso was officers had to be at least 27 years of age to get married, the second proviso they had to have permission of their commander, the third proviso was the background of the young lady and the fourth proviso was how rich were her parents. This was very important and for sure the commander's wife had her say so when a young officer with a future in the military intended to get married. In the Regiment three young officers married three sisters in one afternoon and evening."[19]

Despite the many hardships faced by these new recruits in having to deal with unfamiliar persons and locations, many of the new recruits soon found the experience exhilarating. Kurt Liestmann remembered these early days in his diary:

"There are exercises, sports, runs through the forest. 1.6.38., promotion to the rank of Unteroffizier and introduction to Uffz-Korps. From now on I eat in the Kasino and am introduced at the meal. There are terrain discussions by officers and the Uffz-Korps of the I./Abt. A visit to Burg Hohenzollern, excursions, lectures. I familiarized myself with the Nekar, bridges, river crossings, very interesting. From 1800hrs I have private accommodations in Daigerloch. I got a good one and in the evening a maneuver ball. Lots of music and at 0200hrs went to bed. From 0800hrs on there are terrain inquiries in the areas around Mötzingen, Hechingen and we have interesting discussions there. At 1800hrs we go back to Böblingen. Two very nice days full of real work and rich new knowledge, full of camaraderie and enthusiasm."[20]

For some who longed for new adventures and excitement, the idea of embracing modern technological achievements was even more stimulating. Many of the young recruits were from rural areas, and the idea of being part of something new and exciting was what drew them to the newest branch of the armed forces. Wilhelm Ludwig described his thoughts on driving the new panzers and motorcycles for the first time:

"I had never driven any car before and so I was immediately fascinated by the thought of this. I was a good soldier and attempted to learn the subjects very well. I was given a book by my commander for being the best student and attaining my drivers permit [license]."[21]

Unternehmen "Zauber Feuer," or *"Operation Magic Fire"* was the code name given for a program that was to aid and assist the Spanish Nationalists in the *Spanish Civil War*, which had broken out in the summer of 1936. The *Condor Legion* was a formation built around a number of volunteers from the *Luftwaffe*, which was sent originally to serve in Spain under the command of *Generalmajor* Hugo Sperrle. The mission did exclude direct military participation in combat operations, and so these volunteers were released from there parent units in order to train Spanish volunteers to support the *Spanish Nationalists* under *General* Francisco

Franco. Initially Hitler hoped this would not be necessary, as Franco claimed he was on the verge of victory, but there can be no doubt that many of Hitler's true reasons for intervening had little to do with the Spanish need for assistance. It was a simple desire to test and develop military equipment and tactics for Hitler's grandiose plans. From a strategic point of view the presence of a Nationalist controlled Spain would present a threat to France, as well as the possibility of placing U-boat bases on Spain's Atlantic coast, which would present a threat to British shipping routes through the Straits of Gibraltar to the Suez Canal. In mid-July 1936, Hitler approved the Spanish Nationalist request for military assistance in its civil war and within ten days, a number of Ju-52 transport planes were sent to Spain, flown by pilots from Lufthansa and the *Luftwaffe*. The initial force of about a hundred volunteers were sent in with explicit instructions to not participate in direct military operations. The *Freiwillige*, or Volunteers, were released from their parent units and were under orders only to train Spanish men. In September 1936, *Oberstlt* Walther Warlimont of the *OKW General Staff* arrived as the German commander and military adviser to *General* Franco. In October, he suggested that a *German Condor Legion* should be formed to fight in the civil war. The initial international reaction to Germany's intervention in Spain was immediate and hostile in its tone. The British lodged a formal protest against the German volunteers and began to support the *Spanish Republicans*. The Soviet Union initially backed the non-intervention plan and demanded that Germany should cease its program, but then it too began to aid the Republicans, and in November 1936 an International Brigade of aircraft and tanks from the Soviet Union began arriving in Madrid. The *Spanish Civil War* provided Hitler with an excellent opportunity to distract many of the European nations from observing his mobilization and rearmament activity, while allowing his forces, especially the *Luftwaffe*, to field and test much of their equipment and doctrine. The *Condor Legion* was primarily a *Luftwaffe* show, but it also included a number of non-*Luftwaffe* units. There were panzer crews with *Panzerkampfwagen* Mk Is and Flak gunners with the dual role 88mm gun, along with *Kriegsmarine* sailors who trained members of the National naval forces. Kurt Kathe remembers when he was asked to go to Spain;

> "He [Haarde] didn't order me directly 'you should go'. I was in Germany and got a letter from Herzog [in Spain], he said 'Herr Kathe, go to Spain and teach people in the panzers'. I said no and didn't go to Spain. No one fell [died] there; it was just the education of German soldiers to teach Spanish soldiers."[22]

In October 1938, the Regiment was again ordered to give up a substantial portion of its experienced officers to the various formations now being formed. In the Regiment, the following officers were transferred to *Panzer Abteilung 67* (later it would serve with the *2nd Light Division*) located at Gross Glienecke: *Hptm* Schmidt, Lt von Holtey, Lt Kracker von Schwarzenfeld, *Hptm* Motsch, Lt Nacke, Lt Sommer, and Lt Stephan. Lt Rother was transferred to *Panzer Abteilung 66* (later to serve with *3rd Light Division*) at Eisenach. *Hptm* Bruns and *Hptm* Mittermaier were ordered to the *Kreigs Academy* for further training, and *Olt* Wahl was transferred to the *4th Panzer Brigade* (*10th Panzer Division*). The greatest loss, however, was that of its commander, *Oberst* Hans Haarde, who was promoted and transferred to take command of the *8th Panzer Brigade* in Sagan. Haarde took with him *Hptm* von Frankenberg and *Olt* Proschlitz, who accompanied him as his adjutant.[23]

The new regimental commander was *Oberstlt* Botho Elster, a decorated *First World War* veteran and long serving professional soldier. It would fall on Elster to effectively and quickly expand the Regiment from its present state into a combat ready and highly effective panzer formation. In late 1938, Heinz Guderian was appointed to *Chief of Mobile Troops*, which included all panzer, cavalry, and motorized infantry, and would mark the beginning of a pro-armored doctrine, which would rely on the speed of "*Blitzkrieg*," or Lightning War, and thereby avoid the casualties associated with the static trench warfare of the *First World War*. Guderian had an immediate priority in reorganizing the *Panzerwaffe* (Panzer Arm) prior to any commencement of hostilities. The plans called for the upgrading of the light divisions, which had previously been marked for the traditional cavalry duties and included a number of panzer, cavalry, and reconnaissance sub-units to panzer divisions. The standard panzer division of 1939 was a well-trained and highly mobile force. The *1st, 2nd,* and *3rd Panzer Divisions* had been in existence since 1935, and one of the most recent additions, the *10th*, had been formed in 1938. Each panzer division was made up of a panzer brigade consisting of two panzer regiments each with two *abteilung*, or battalions. The *abteilungs* were further broken down to include three light panzer companies and, with the introduction of the panzer Mk IV, a fourth heavy company. Prior to the Polish campaign the *1st Panzer Division* had the largest compliment of the larger Mk IIIs and Mk IVs of any panzer division, and the *10th Panzer Division's 4th Panzer Brigade* with the *7th* and *8th Panzer Regiments* was not far behind them.[24] During its existence the Regiment would find itself using almost every model and type of German panzer, from the early panzer Mk Is to the late model Mk IVFs, and even later when the Regiment was resurrected as a panzer *abteilung* in 1944 and went on to serve in Russia with the *Sturmgeschütze* III and IV variants. It therefore is a good time to give brief overview of those various models of panzers, keeping in mind that there were many different types and with each type there were changes to the overall dimensions.

Panzer Mark I series A/B (Sdkfz 101)
Origin and Date: Germany, 1934
Crew: 2 Commander / Gunner and Driver
Weight: 5.4 tons
Armor thickness Max: 13mm Min: 6mm
Speed: 35kmh / 23mph
Range: 145km / 90miles
Armament: 2xMG 13s 7.92
Employment: early model panzer that saw uses as a trainer, reconnaissance, command and gun carriage.

Panzer Mark II series A-F (Sdkfz 121)
Origin and Date: Germany, 1935
Crew: 3 Commander / Gunner, Radio Operator and Driver
Weight: 9.5 tons
Armor thickness Max: 30mm Min: 5mm
Speed: 55kmh / 34mph
Range: 200km / 125miles
Armament: 1x20mm KwK L/55 main gun and 1xMG 34 7.92
Employment: early model panzer that saw uses as a trainer, reconnaissance, command, gun carriage and flame.

Panzer Mark III series A-N (Sdkfz 141)
Origin and Date: Germany, 1937
Crew: 5 Commander, Gunner, Loader, Radio Operator and Driver
Weight: 22.3 tons
Armor thickness Max: 50mm Min: 10mm
Speed: 40kmh / 25mph
Range: 155km / 96miles
Armament: early models A-D; 1x37mm KwK L/45, mid models F-H; 1x50mm (short) KwK L/42 and late models J-Ls; 1x50mm (long) KwK

39 L/60 main guns and 2xMG 34s 7.92
Employment: mid model panzer that saw uses primarily as a main battle tank and command later used as flame and assault gun.

Panzer Mark IV series A-J (Sdkfz 161)
Origin and Date: Germany, 1937
Crew: 5 Commander, Gunner, Loader, Radio Operator and Driver
Weight: 25 tons
Armor thickness Max: 80mm Min: 10mm
Speed: 38kmh / 24mph
Range: 210km / 130miles
Armament: early models A-F1s 1x75mm (short) KwK 37 L/24, later models F2-J 1x75mm (long) KwK 40 L/43 main guns and 2xMG 34s 7.92
Employment: early and later model panzer that saw initial uses as an infantry support vehicle later as a main battle tank and command tank. Later uses included mobile AA and assault gun carriage.[25]

In general, the panzer Mk I, II, and III were to be found in the three light companies, and the Mk IVs assigned to the heavy companies which, under the two *abteilung* four company table of organization were the 4th and 8th heavy companies. Even though it was quickly phased out, the Mk I was to be seen for many years throughout the Regiment serving in a variety of functions. According to Thomas Jentz, the exact number of panzers assigned to the Regiment amounted to: eighty-four Mk Is, eighty-one Mk IIs, three Mk IIIs, eight Mk IVs, and eleven command panzers.[26] The Regiment did not participate in the occupations of Austria and the Sudetenland, as it was employed for the time being in numerous field-training exercises through the remaining months of 1938 and early 1939. Most of the training was conducted at the Münsingen and Heuberg training facilities in Baden Württemberg. The large training grounds in Grafenwöhr were utilized by the men, and thanks to the diary notes of Kurt Liestmann we have a good indication of what training took place during that time:

"Wednesday 22.6.38 preparation for Grafenwöhr, from mid-day we move to Böblingen for an uncomfortable night trip through Nürnberg in the animal trucks. 0500hrs in the morning we arrive to Grafenwöhr. On the way to the camp we drive by artillery positions stretched for kilometers. 60 batteries sharply shoot in the morning. The troops in and around Grafenwöhr are estimated to be 40,000. In the afternoon I twice saw the 'Führer' who is also in the camp. Saturday, cleaning of weapons and technical services. The camp is big and the layout is generous. The terrain is similar to our Brandenburg homeland. Tuesday, a readiness alert. Afternoon we begin the march. The march route of 40km through a very nice landscape, similar to Brandenburg but more hills. One assembly position in the thick forest, rock, grass and blueberries. We built a very nice tent for our zug with lightning speed. Weber is the leader of our zug. At 0100hrs we begin the march. Blind-folded and sometimes without light. Cool roads and obstacles. Our crew drives well. Our panzers roll on all sides. The artillery still shoots. At 0300hrs went in the 2nd assembly position. About 1km from us fell the shells of artillery. The daylight comes. We are not deployed. The artillery must change position as a security precaution. A little disappointed and very tired we return along the artillery positions back to Grafenwöhr. Dust, heat, all dirty but in a good mood. Thursday at 0215hrs moving into the first assembly area. The artillery positions are around us in a wide semi-circle, they are shooting again. The slight noise shows that the shells go over us. On the horizon is a captive balloon. 66 batteries are involved in the exercise. One hour later we are deployed. The artillery fire shifted ahead and the woods screened with smoke shells. The panzer brigade attacks. Far from us explodes the shrapnel of artillery. We are 2nd to move, in front of us the II./Abt., to the left is Panzer Regiment 7. At the end we return back to the camp dirty, thirsty and sweating. Friday 1 July 38. The zug does combat shooting and our zug shoots well. 4.7.38 Two hours abteilung training. Almost 30 villages are cleaned on the 900 kilometer large training area, sometimes it feels eerie when one enters such a village. Fields and meadows were left behind and everywhere there are red poppy, chamomile and cornflowers. Our panzers easily leave their traces through these colorful fields, sometimes we sink over our knees in there."[27]

In mid-July, the Regiment departed Grafenwöhr and moved back to Baden Württemberg to the training grounds in Münsingen, where the panzers conducted a week's worth of training and combat exercises with the infantry. After the training event concluded the panzers conducted a night march back to Böblingen along the Reich autobahn (highway). Most of the panzers were found to hold up well during this trip. For the next month the men and machines remained in and around Böblingen, conducting night marches and assembly exercises until early September, when they again were loaded on trains for a trip north. The Regiment arrived in rainy Bergen for another week of gunnery exercises before heading back to Böblingen. In November, new recruits arrived to fill the ranks of those whose mandatory two years of Reich service was about to expire. For Kurt Liestmann the time was bittersweet, as he recorded in his diary:

"Friday 28.10.38 my two years service time are over. Hurray! Promoted to Feldwebel.
Friday 4.11.38 The Regiment orders that I stay with the new 2.Pz.Rgt.8. In the afternoon is the promotion celebration. Funny drunkenness."

Over the next few months the new recruits were taken in and given the basics of military life and service within the panzer arm. They would be schooled and lectured on many of the same topics which those instructing them had, until only recently, just learned themselves. By March 1939, the Regiment was again ready to move off to its training grounds and put the recruits through their initial field exercises. Those exercises were conducted at the nearby Heuberg, Munsingen, and Stettin training areas. Kurt Liestmann noted that the weather was having its effects on the men and machines:

"Thursday 16.3.39 Break-up to Heuberg. I lead the panzers to the train station. The road is completely icy, fantastic winter weather and a lot of snow, the trip through the winter to Stetten a.k.M. in 50cm of snow. Offloading and a 7km march through Stetten to the camp.
Overnight it snows continuously, 15cm of new snow. We conduct our exercises in the snow. The start of spring according to the calendar, this morning there is the perfect snow storm. We drive to the shooting ranges again, visibility is less than 50m. We return back to camp, the panzers are all covered with snow. In the afternoon we reload and in the evening go back to Böblingen."[28]

As the Regiment made its way back towards Böblingen on 28 March 1939 the *General Stab des Heer* ordered the following:

"The 10th Panzer Division is to be created as an occupational force in the Protectorate Boehmen-Maehren. The units under the command are to be exchanged every four months. The first units that are to be assigned to the 10th Panzer Division are one infantry regiment (Mot) and an Aufklärung abteilung (Mot) from the 20th Infantry Division, Panzer

Regiment 8 from the 4th Panzer Brigade, I./Aufklärung Regiment 8 from the 3rd Light Brigade and Pioneer Battalion 43 from the III Armee Korps."[29]

A short time later, the Regiment would begin its training in and around the Milowitz training grounds in Czechoslovakia. Only a few days later, on 1 April 1939, the sixth phase of the army's panzer expansion program was ordered; this phase was to be completed by 19 September 1939, and called for the Regiment, along with the *4th Panzer Brigade*, to be placed under the command of the *XV Armee Korps*. On 15 April, *Major* Wilhelm Conze turned over command of the II./Abteilung to *Major* Ramsauer. On the 20th, after having spent one year in Böblingen, the Regiment was officially assigned to the *10th Panzer Division* and transferred to Czechoslovakia to the Milowitz training area, which was located just north of the city of Prague. Kurt Liestmann recorded the departure from Böblingen and the arrival in Milowitz:

"Wednesday 19.4.39. On 22.4 we should be in Milowitz near Prague. Today is our promotion here. In the evening is a farewell party with girls. We have a festive promotion to Leutnant. Thursday 20.3.39. We move in the afternoon. In my new position I lead the company to the train station in Böblingen. All of Böblingen mourns about us. An immense number of people are at the train station and the soldier's brides have an emotional farewell. 21-22.4.39 Transportation by train with fine weather, from Eger over the border Sudetengau then along the border mountains over Karlsbadnach Lissa. The rejoicing in Sudetenland is great. During the night we are over the border of the Protektorat, and early morning in Lissa. We unload. The population behaves reserved. The answers are coming with eagerness. From Lissa its 5km to Milowitz, the smallest Czech training area. The camp is in a nice location. Milowitz is a small, nice, dirty village. We officers are accommodated very nicely in the new building, which was once an infantry school. In the camp are still many Czech military especially many officers, who will stay until the handover of all equipment. Our guards must watch carefully as the stealing is a common matter."[30]

While in the Milowitz area, the Regiment would continue to focus on its driving and gunnery skills in addition to the standard daily sports and training regimens. During their time in Milowitz, *Uffz* Fritz Haustein, a clerk with *Stabs I./Abteilung*, remembered a close call for one of the NCOs:

"Feldwebel Kümmel was beginning his duty as sergeant of the guard and didn't bother to check everything when he signed for materials from the Feldwebel he was relieving. Later on, when the officer of the day made his inspection, it was discovered that one round of ammunition was missing after which the officer informed Kümmel that it would be a court marshal offense for him. Fortunately for Kümmel he knew an officer who could help him out and gave him a clip of six rounds to make up for the loss. After getting the rounds Kümmel announced to the Leutnant that they had found the missing round of ammunition and that it must have fallen in the straw."[31]

Believing that it was in for a long stay at Milowitz, the Regiment quickly dove into an intense training cycle in and around the Brdy Wald; much of that training involved driver training and marches and compass and navigational exercises, along with tactics and drills in many of the surrounding villages in both day and night conditions. The training lasted through the summer of 1939 and, although very few in Germany could know exactly what was to come, many of the men realized that something was brewing on the horizon. The radio broadcasts and ever present camp talk spread rumors of impending war and reserve call ups. Kurt Liestmann noted in mid-August:

"The Polish crisis sharpens, the situation is intense. We [Germany] conclude the economic agreement with Soviets. Soldiers will be called up. Everywhere there are talks about the war. The Regiment is relocated to the north from Letky to Dolany and I have a private accommodation with Frau Inrczek. The non-aggression pact between Germany and Russia. Our observation sector is located in very nice landscape area here the Moldau River flows here with many turns through some steep and green rocky valleys."[32]

On 17 August, the Regiment was alerted to prepare itself for a possible early return to Böblingen, and a few days later on 25 August, the Regiment received the order to conduct a secretive movement back to Böblingen. On the 29th, an advanced party departed Milowitz in order to prepare the kaserne for the Regiment's early return. It was also during this time that a wartime mobilization was initiated which directly affected the Regiment and kaserne in Böblingen. For the mobilization there would be the expected influx of reservists and other wartime essential personnel. In addition to the outfitting of those new reservists there would be the receiving and issuing of ammunition, fuel, and provisions. Liestmann recorded:

"Thursday 24.8.39. The departure march order came during the night we break-up in the middle of the night, and country march to Milowitz. Friday 25.8.39. From today at 2400hrs is the first mobilization day of Pz.Rgt.8 in Böblingen. Saturday 26.8.39. Preparations, news and rumors collide. Sunday 27.8.39. Mobile reloading and accoutrements, ammunition is compiled in the transport. Return to Böblingen. Tuesday 29.8.39. Arrival in Böblingen during the night and immediately offloading, from Böblingen the citizens offer us the warm welcome. There is a war mood and in our barracks are pilots and reservists."[33]

It was during this time that the Regiment's table of organization changed to include two mobile workshop companies and light columns. The workshop companies came from the organic on-site workshops and would provide the maintenance teams necessary to repair the panzers while on the go. Those staffs and civilian workers were now augmented by some of the new reservists. The addition of the light column would guarantee that the *abteilung* received the necessary logistics for men and machines. As for the panzer companies, they were drawn down to three light companies per *abteilung*, as the 3rd and 6th Companies were detached from the Regiment proper and formed into *Panzer Ersatz Abteilung 7*, which was to be located in Böblingen with the 2nd and 7th Companies of *Panzer Regiment 7*. Additionally a bit of re-numbering took place, as the 4th Company was re-designated as the 3rd, the 7th was re-designated as the 6th, and the 8th Company now became the 7th.[34] There was very little time in which to carry out this reorganization, but within forty-eight hours the Regiment's reorganization would be completed, and on the evening of 30 August the Regiment was equipped and ready for action. The panzer strength report of the Regiment on 1 September 1939 included 162 operational panzers. The number included nine Befehls, fifty-seven Mk Is, seventy-four Mk IIs, three MK IIIs, and seven Mk IVs.[35]

Panzer Regiment 8 Chain of Command as of September 1939[36]

Regiment Commander	Oberst Elster	3rd Company	Olt Kauffmann
Regiment Adjutant	Olt Jahns	Zug Commander	Lt Bauer
Nachrichten Officer	Olt Sahmel	Zug Commander	Lt Kertscher
Ordonanz Officer	Olt Plinzner	Zug Commander	Lt Liestmann, K
Regiment Arzt	Dr Feller	II./Abteilung Commander	Major Ramsauer
StKp	Olt von Stunzner	Abtl Adj	Olt Schefold
I./Abteilung Commander	Major Haarde, F	Nachr Offz	Olt von Stulpnagel
Abtl Adj	Lt Knorr	Ord Offz	Lt von Hake
Nachr Offz	Lt Matthias, J	Abt Arzt	Dr Witzky
Ordonanz Offz	Lt von Bitter	Zahl Mstr	Zmstr Gisy
Abteilung Arzt	Dr Port	Ing Offz	HBmstr Hauska
Zahlmeister	StZmstr Tischner	StKp	Hptm Klien, Lt Uhlenhaut
Engineer Offz	Major Schnell	LeKol	Olt Weinert
StKp	Hptm Ehrbeck, Lt Stiefelmayer	5th Company	Olt Korner
LeKol	Olt Lindner	Zug Commander	Lt Eichberg
1st Company	Olt Bernau	Zug Commander	Lt Schwarzhaupt
Zug Commander	Lt Neumann	Zug Commander	Lt Jattkowski
Zug Commander	Lt Weber	6th Company	Olt Semerak
Zug Commander	Lt Springorum	Zug Commander	Lt Foellmer
2nd Company	Hptm von Heydebreck	7th Company	Hptm Ottens
Zug Commander	Lt Zeuke	Zug Commander	Lt Wuth
Zug Commander	Lt Groth	Zug Commander	Lt Wohrmann
		Zug Commander	Lt Seidler

2

The Polish Campaign
September 1939-May 1940

The Panzer Lied
Ob's sturmt oder scheit
Ob die sonne uns lacht
Der tag gluhend heiss
Oder finster die nacht
Bestaubt sind die gesichter
Doch froh ist unser sinn
Es braust unser Panzer
Im sturme dahin
Mit donnerndem Motor
So schellwie der blitz
Dam feinde entgegen
Im panzer geschitzt
Voraus dam kameraden
Im kampfe genz allein
So stossen wir tief
In die feindlichen reih'n
Und lasst uns im stich einst
Das treuloss Gluck
Und kehren wir nicht mehr
Zur heimat zuruck
Trifft uns die todeskugel
Ruft uns das schicksal ab
Dann ist unser panzer
Ein ehrenes grab[1]

After the annexation of the Rhineland, Austria, the Sudetenland, and Czechoslovakia, Hitler turned his attention to his neighbor to the northeast, Poland, which shared over 1,200 miles of border with Germany, and now, with the addition of Czechoslovakia, that distance was lengthened another 500 miles. For most Germans they resented the humiliation of defeat in the *First World War* and the harsh conditions placed on them by the *Treaty of Versailles*, as well as the loss of German territory to the new states of Poland and Czechoslovakia, and it was in these areas that Hitler saw the chance to regain those lost lands of Pomerania, Prussia, and Silesia. Another of the irritants to the German people was the subject of the Pomeranian corridor and the Polish control over the territories of Pomerania and Silesia which, although they had a majority of Poles living there, also had a large minority of ethnic Germans too. In this corridor lay the city of Danzig, which at the time had been declared a *"Free City,"* and was open to both Germans and Poles alike. There had been an idea of creating an extra access road through the territory to link this city to Germany. The Poles, fearing a repeat performance of what had just taken place in Czechoslovakia, responded negatively to all the German moves. The Polish situation was, however, a bit different, in that, although the Allies had begun to lose interest in Poland, they had come to the conclusion that Hitler must be stopped, and would therefore band together to halt any further German aggression. Many of the German military leaders feared an attack on Poland, for it would bring France and Britain into the conflict, but Hitler saw the Western Allies as weak, and led by timid men who could be easily bullied and bluffed into getting what he wanted out of them, as was the case of the Sudetenland and Czechoslovakia. In late August 1939, the *Ribbentrop-Molotov Pact* was signed, which gave Hitler his green light to ending the Polish problem. The pact ensured that there would be no Russian interference in Poland, and that Russia would be free to grab up territory in eastern Poland and the Baltic states, which had at one time been partitions of the Soviet Union.[2] The planning for *"Fall Weiss"* (Plan White) began in March 1939 and continued for the next six months. The initial date of attack was set for 26 August, but was postponed after the British announced on the 23rd that if Poland were invaded they would come to her assistance. The French had announced back in May that if Poland were invaded they would launch an offensive against the Germans within two weeks of that invasion. There were last minute diplomatic negations and attempts to discredit the Polish government and give credence to the German claims. But as this all was taking place, German forces were secretly moving forward until, by 31 August, it became all too difficult to hide their growing presence and keep the element of surprise. The plan for *Fall Weiss* called for a double inner and outer enveloping attack from both the north and south to trap and destroy the Polish Forces on the Narev and Vistula rivers. It would fall on the new and untried arm of the German *Wehrmacht*, the *Panzerwaffe*, to spearhead this assault and tear through the Polish defenses. The southern and largest pincer would be formed by *Armeegruppe Sud* (South)—886,000 personnel under the command of *General* Gerd von Rundstedt—and would see the *Eighth Armee* (Blaskowitz) protecting the left flank, while making for Lodz, while the *Fourteenth Armee* (List) was tasked with turning the Polish left flank, driving on Krakow, and advancing through Galicia to the San River. The *Tenth Armee* (Reichenau) would form the main thrust heading towards Warsaw and central Poland. It was in the south that the strongest forces were assembled and the largest percentage of German armor was concentrated. In the north, *General* Fedor von Bock's *Armeegruppe Nord* (North)—630,000 personnel—were organized into fourteen infantry divisions, two motorized divisions, a panzer division, a panzer brigade, and a cavalry brigade, along with various other *Armee* troops. The

Chapter 2: The Polish Campaign, September 1939-May 1940

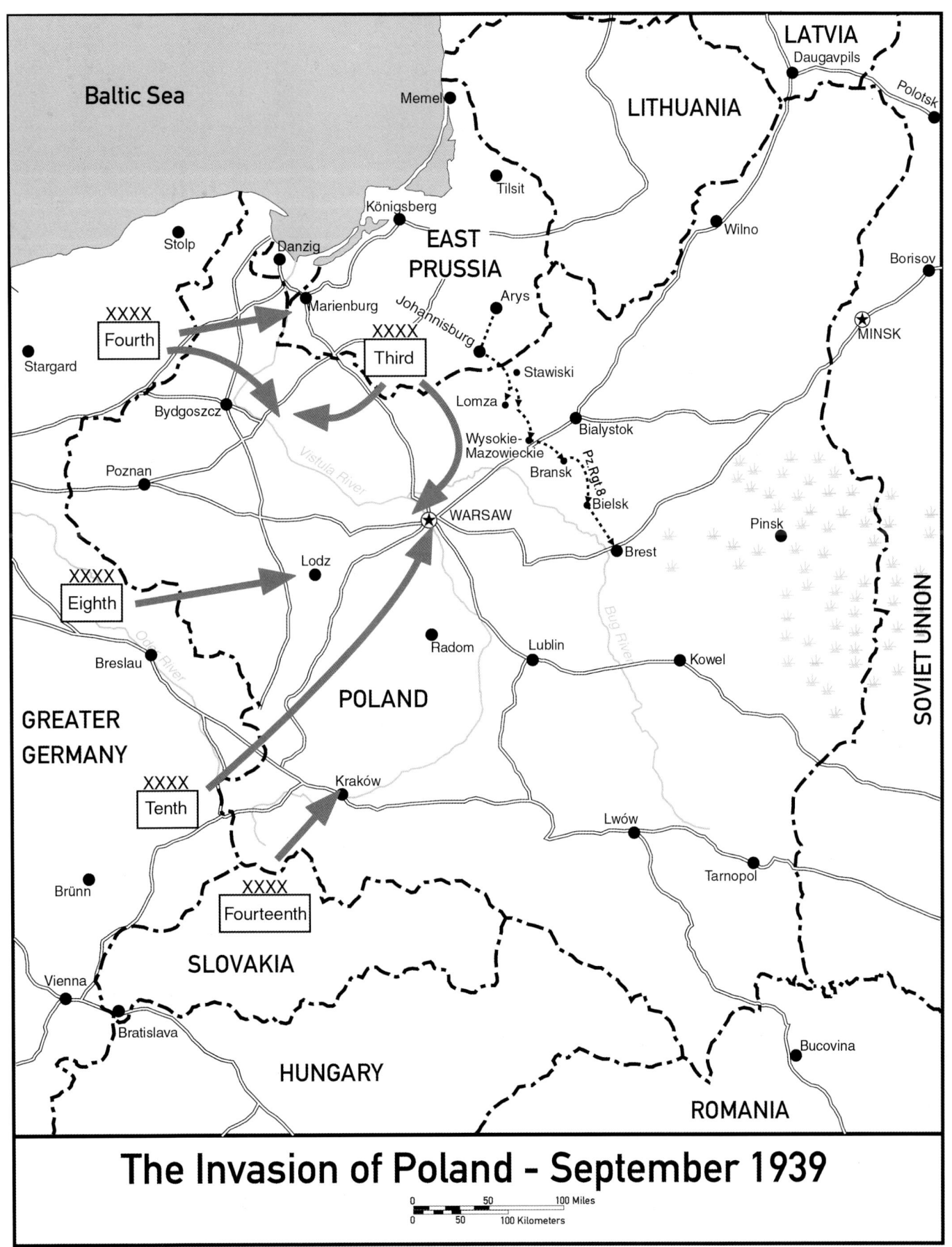

23

Armeegruppe had the *Third Armee* (Küchler) with eight infantry divisions, a panzer brigade, and a cavalry brigade, and the *Fourth Armee* (Kluge) had four infantry, two motorized, and a panzer division. The *Third Armee* would attack in the direction of Warsaw, while *Fourth Armee* would attack east and south, cutting off the Polish forces in the northern corridor. The Germans would employ a variety of formations, including thirty-seven infantry, one mountain, four motorized, four light, and six panzer divisions with a total of 2,511 panzers in the attack.[3]

The Poles had employed twenty-six infantry divisions, not all of which were fully mobilized, eight cavalry brigades, three mountain brigades, and one motorized brigade. There were few tanks, roughly some 600, of which many were worn out WWI French *FT-17s* and light tankettes. All told there were what amounted to approximately two battalions' worth, and almost all of them were scattered about the country.[4] The Germans had been building up their forces, and the Polish High Command knew those forces were forming for an attack; despite the build up, the attack still came as a tactical surprise to the Polish Army. On 30 August, the Polish government ordered a general mobilization of its reserve forces, but by the time the Germans commenced their attack many of the reservists were easily rounded up while still attempting to reach their mobilization locations, and those units that had formed were captured while attempting to organize themselves and move into their assigned sector. As the *British-Polish* pact threatened to undo Hitler's plans, he devised a plan that would make the outbreak of hostilities look as if they were the work of the Poles themselves. *SS* troops under the codename "*Operation Himmler*" seized a radio station located in the border town of Gleiwitz and began broadcasting inflammatory messages, urging the Polish people in eastern Germany to rise up against Hitler. To add a bit of reality to the ruse, a number of bodies of concentration camp inmates were dressed in Polish army uniforms and left on the site. The operation was hardly successful, in that it fooled few people, let alone the journalists brought to the town in the hopes that they would report on the "*Polish Incursion*."[5]

On 31 August 1939, the Regiment was loaded aboard trains at the train station in Böblingen, where it would embark on a journey that would take it through Thüringen, Berlin, and Pomerania. The panzers were marked with the white Balkan cross, and on the back side of the turrets there was the regimental emblem "*The Wolfs Angel*," or "*Wolf's Hook*." *Feldwebel* Kurt Kathe, a professional soldier in the 5th Company, remembers:

"When we started from Böblingen after we came from Czechoslovakia we loaded our panzers here at the train station. We didn't sit in the carriage we were in the panzers on the freight train; we were saying that we were going to the Bock Beer fest in Poland. It was a joke, as some people who had some fear. I honestly had no fear, I let destiny decide as some people did."[6]

The *Second World War* officially began in the northern city of Danzig, as the German battleship *Schleswig-Holstein* sailed from its moorings at Danzig and began its bombarded of the Polish transit port base and naval forces on the Westerplatte, which lay just across the canal that connected the port to the Baltic Sea. Shortly after the *Schleswig-Holstein* began its bombardment at 0448hrs on 1 September 1939, the German *Luftwaffe* commenced its attacks, as its *Messerschmitt*, *Stuka*, and *Heinkel* aircraft took off from their airfields in Germany and attacked Polish airfields in an attempt to destroy the *Polish Air Force* on the ground. While some planes strafed and bombed the Polish airfields from above, most went after preplanned targets, such as the vital bridges and communication centers. On the ground, the German offensive began rolling forward on schedule despite initial clashes with Polish Army patrols and border police that caused some initial problems and delays. Despite the initial confusion, this resistance was quickly overcome and the army proceeded forward. The German *Third Armee* drove south out of East Prussia heading for Warsaw, while the *Fourth Armee* attacked east across the Danzig Corridor from Pomerania. In the Eulenburg, an area of Neustettin (Szczecinek), the Regiment was off-loaded. The stations were located in Damerkow, Lupow, Rummelsburg (Miastko), and Bütow (Bytów), and the readiness of the Regiment was checked; it was also the last place for those members of the Regiment who had been on leave or the incoming reservists to catch up with the Regiment prior to entering combat. *Leutnants* Wuth and Wöhrmann had to use a *Luftwaffe* courier flight to get from their vacation spot in East Prussia via the Ostsee.[7] They reached the Regiment just in time before the panzers departed on their march. Liestmann again noted in his diary:

"Wednesday 30.8.39. At 2200hrs there is reloading and I am the reloading officer. 0130hrs departure with the target area Neu-Stettin, not far from the border. The civil population greets us heartily. Friday 1.9.39. We offload in Eulenburg not far from Neu-Stettin and go 9km further to Lubew for accommodations. The vehicles are made completely mobilized. It looks real. We are 70km away from the border. Heavy bombers fly over the white clouds towards the east. Polish military installations are bombarded. England mobilizes. Saturday 2.9.39. We march off at 1700hrs towards Neustettin, Bütow, and the border. A delighted welcome by [the citizens] marching through the villages and towns, receiving flowers, cigarettes, chocolates, sweets, sandwiches and fruits by the handful. Reserve units are located in all the villages. 10km away from the border we go into our accommodations. During the night the vehicles are fuelled and prepared for movement."[8]

The Regiment again found itself under the command of the *10th Panzer Division* (Schaal) which, along with the *207th Infantry Division* formed the reserve of *Fourth Armee*. Although it had been placed in reserve, there was never any doubt that a fully capable and highly trained panzer division would not take part in the campaign. In previous wars it had been the infantry and artillery which gave battle, but this was a new kind of war, one of speed and power, and it would not be long before the Regiment entered combat to prove that.

Crossing the Danzig Corridor

On 3 September, the *10th Panzer Division* was ordered to Dirschau and placed under the command of *Armeegruppe Nord*. It was planned to affect a crossing of the corridor with a strong panzer force as soon as possible. The Regiment crossed the border between Germany and Poland through the Danzig Corridor at 1130hrs, in conjunction with the *Second Armee Korps* (Strauss) of the *Fourth Armee*. Moving east to what would be the first taste of combat for almost all its members, the Regiment moved in the fine late summer weather, occasionally passing ethnic Germans and Polish citizens who were attempting to escape the battlefield. The march, which was without incident and almost casual, led them via the Tucheler Heide, Berent (Koscierzyna), Schöneck, and Stieblau. The Regiment reached the Danzig area north of Dirschau (Grudziadz) without any enemy contact. Kurt Liestmann again noted in his diary:

"Sunday 3.9.39. At 1000hrs we go further; we go through the corridor border in the occupied territory from time to time we see cleared road blocks and small obstacles. In the north there should be one more Polish division, which was cut off through the connection Pomerania-East Prussia on the line Danzig. Would we today have an encounter with them? The picture has changed; the population is closed in, afraid and shy. Now at 1600hrs we stop on the road, take provisioning and fuel. Near

the evening we continue over Berent, Schöneck, Turzo, and Dirschau to Stüblau in the city of Danzig."[9]

On 4 September, the Regiment passed the remains of a Polish barracks at Dirschau (Tczew) and witnessed the handy work of the Stukas, which had blasted the kaserne to rubble. It then crossed the Vistula (Wista) via the combat bridge at Käsemark and proceeded towards the area of Osterode and Allenstein. The Liestmann diary entry continues:

"Initially we wanted to go to Gross Lichtenau but all bridges over Weichsel are destroyed. We drive in the night through the Danzig plain. In front of Dirschau are Polish barracks, which were bombarded in the first hours of the Polish war by our Luftwaffe. Smoking, burning wreckage and shell-hole after shell-hole. Finally we get accommodations in Stüblau, our accommodation people on the property take care of us."

On the 5th, the men continued to see much of the same, as their panzers continued to roll ever forward and deeper to the east, as Liestmann noted in the follow account:

"Tuesday 5.9.39. A country march to Elbing a rejoicing reception in Danzig country. We cross the Weichsel on the pontoon bridge a beautiful picture. During the fine morning of early autumn our company thunders over the planks to an extraordinary welcome in Elbing. We were literally covered with the comforts. We reload at the train station of Rosswiesen; the people wish us all the best before departure. Our trip goes evenly through East Prussia in the direction of Almstein. Where is the target? In the farm gardens blossom flowers, cows are on the meadows. The picture is so peaceful and we drive to the war. Over Gutsstadt, Johannisburg, Arys to the camp south. Finally some sleep again."[10]

On 6 September, the *10th Panzer Division* was ordered to join *Gruppe Falkenhorst* at the training camp in Arys (Orzysz), located in East Prussia. The trip found the Regiment moving by road and rail until it finally off-loaded at the train stations of Johannisburg and Gehlenburg (Biala Piska). Liestmann noted:

"Wednesday 6.9.39. We compile the new Korps, of which belonged the 10th Panzer Division, at 1700hrs the Regiment is on parade and the Oberst gives us the overall view of the situation and the mission. We head to the south in Poland, in order to hit the troops in the flank when they flee from the corridor."

On the 7th, *Gruppe Falkenhorst*, with the *10th Panzer* in the lead, was put into action when it moved south on Lomza. After a short preparation period in the Johannisburger Heide, the Regiment crossed the border of Poland near Schwiddern (Swidry) in conjunction with the *10th Panzer Division* and marched towards Lomza with only the Polish *18th Division* (Kossecki) standing in its way. In a swift attack through the town of Stawiski the Regiment, with the I./*Abteilung* in the lead, attacked the ex-Russian fortress of Lomzader, and the Polish forces located there were quickly overpowered as the offensive continued to steam forward. Liestmann's account continues:

"Thursday 7.9.39. We break up in the morning dusk, now we stay on the road in front of the border and wait. My zug now has the codename 'Hilde'. We cross the Polish border close to the evening and the march gets into motion, when we drive through the first large village it gets darker. All the bridges over the streams are destroyed."[11]

On the 8th, the *10th Panzer* reached Wizna, on the Narew River, only about 10km northeast of the city of Lomza. Polish resistance along the Vistula River was finally broken, forcing the Poles to withdraw. As the panzers and motorized infantry kept nipping at their heels the *Luftwaffe* screamed in from above. The unusually warm and dry summer had carried on into September, thereby allowing those mobile forces the dry roads they needed to rapidly maneuver and outflank the Polish Army, and the *Luftwaffe* the clear skies to attack it at will. It was here that the Regiment suffered its first losses, which were caused by snipers and infantry concealed in trees, and by the Polish anti-tank rifles. The Poles had been especially keen on the development of anti-tank rifles between the two world wars, and the twenty pound 7.92mm *Marosczek* anti-tank rifle was capable of penetrating 20mm (3/4inch) of armor plating at 300yards, and could easily penetrate the 13mm armor of the Mk I and 15mm of the Mk II. Lt Neumann of the 1st Company was wounded when his panzer was hit by one of these anti-tank rifles. Also on the 8th, the *10th Panzer Division* was once again reassigned, this time to the *XIX Armee Korps*, which was commanded by *General der Panzer Truppen* Heinz Guderian and consisted of the *3rd* and *10th Panzer* and *20th Motorized Infantry Divisions*; it was a true panzer corps, in the sense that it consisted of two panzer and one motorized infantry divisions. On the night of 8/9 September, as so often happened in the Polish Campaign, there was a clash of horsed cavalry and armor when the Polish "*Suwalska*" (Podhorski) and "*Podlaska*" (Kmicic-Skrzynski) *Cavalry Brigades* attacked the Regiment near the village of Grobowa. The attack was repulsed with heavy losses. The Regiment reported attacks by partisans on some of its rear service columns, but these attacks were more than likely carried out by separated Polish Army forces that had been trapped behind the fast moving lines. Kurt Liestmann recorded:

"Friday 8.9.39. We halt on the road for the night and sleep in the panzers until the morning dusk. Lomscha [Lomza] is in front of us, the old former Russian fortress on the Marew is heavily occupied by the enemy. Our 1st Company has attacked, but had to turn close to the main bunker, because it got dark. Lomscha is under the artillery fire and covered by bombers. The air activities are quite lively. During the night as ghosts glow blood-red reflections of burning villages on the horizon. Today the crows circle over our dirty village, where we take the rest. I haven't seen anything such primitive, dirty and neglected. The men are called up [from cellars], the women and children live shred bare and bug-ridden in the holes in the ground and in half destroyed hay shelters. We go there for the rest. Around 2130hrs I am woken up by shots and loud alert cries. We leave our place in a hurry, and behind us the village is already in flames. Complete chaos in the head. The shooting was nonsense. The Polish cavalry reconnaissance troops wanted to assault us. Our posts noticed and alerted us."[12]

On 9 September, the Regiment's II/*Abteilung* stood at the north side of the Narew River; the corps' plan of attack was to pursue the enemy with the *10th Panzer* and *20th Motorized* (Wiktorin) and cut off those Polish forces attempting to form a defense east of Vistula. The *10th Panzer* was to head strait south to the Bug River in the direction of Siedlce and Mordy. But before it could achieve that objective it first had to get across the Narew. The infantry had crossed from the north side of the river, but had not yet reached the far sided entrenchments. Significant difficulties plagued the crossing, as the pontoon bridges were not yet ready, and a backlog quickly accumulated on the northern bank. Lt Kurt Liestmann recorded in his diary for 9 September:

"We stand on the road to Stawiski and want to go around the heavily entrenched Lomscha on the left side, and to cross the Marew by the temporary bridge in order to come to the town on the flank and on the back side. Yesterday evening the infantry attacked with no result. We are on the march. At Wizna we are set on the pontoon bridge over Narew. The heavy panzers unfortunately have to stay back, because the heavy bridge is just about to be built. The artillery shoots non-stop left and right around us. The commander arrives. Beyond Wizna are still located some middle bunkers. I take my Zug on the right of the street and drive downwards in the terrain covered with meadow bushes, terribly difficult. My vehicle gets damaged and I change vehicles. The first Polish MG cones whistle above us. The flanking fire comes from bunkers. 200m in front of us suddenly appears middle bunker. The 37mm shoots from the cupola to the right. The 7th Company with 20mm vehicles [Mk IIs] and my Zug surround it. The 20mm cannons and our KH crack in the slit. The Polish defend stubbornly. The pioneers lie flat on our panzers, they drive [with us] until very close, in the thunder of the hand grenades the Polish come out of the bunker."[13]

On the morning of the 10th, to the dismay of the corps commander, those bridges that were to be crossed by the panzers had been dismantled and taken down river by the *20th Infantry Division*, thereby delaying the crossing by the armor for 24hrs. It was during this period that the *Wehrmacht* found itself susceptible to attacks by the *Polish Air Force* and suffered some significant losses. But soon enough the skies were swept clear by the aircraft of the *Luftwaffe*, and soon afterwards the only planes to be seen were those flying German crosses. While the bridges were not ready, the heavier Mk IIIs and Mk IVs were ordered to move across on ferries, while some of the lighter Mk Is and IIs were able to find a suitable crossing site and reached the south bank of the Narew. Again at 1800hrs, there were continued attacks on the large bunker line on the southern bank. The bunkers were large concrete structures bristling with machine guns and small caliber artillery pieces. They were defeated by engineers and panzers, which used direct fire at the numerous embrasures to silence the guns. Near the village of Kal-Basie, which sat out in an open plain, there was a short fight, which resulted in a number of the homes catching fire. Around Zambrów the resistance of the Polish *Narew Army* grew, and they threw everything they had at the German panzers: a few tanks, artillery, and anti-tank guns and rifles. The Polish infantry dug in and stubbornly defended its positions with the support of their artillery in both the indirect and direct fire roles. But for the Poles it was a hopeless situation, and soon hundreds of prisoners began to surrender to the Regiment. At one point the 3rd Company went chasing after some of the retreating artillery, but ended up getting stuck in the marshy ground near a swamp and lost precious time. Liestmann noted on that Sunday, 10.9.39:

"Advance march to the Polish hinterland, to Wysokie. At one of the villages we receive heavy fire. Riflemen in trees, basement bunkers, tank cannons. The vehicle is shot through. One group leader and driver are lost due to wounds. Everywhere appear Polish soldiers in small groups and the refugees from the west. Soldiers and civilians are much more cunning, and have assassination on their mind. In the afternoon the 4th Company got stuck in a swamp. A super human effort [to get out]. No water, for many days no provisioning. Through the burning Wysokie further to the southeast, in the main direction of Brest-Litovsk. During the night on the road it is quiet, it's secured. For sleep there are just a couple of hours, [we are] all dirty, oiled as the devil, and suddenly again water and coffee and something to eat."[14]

Polish cavalry renewed their counter-attacks, which caused them considerable losses, but these all-out attacks were never really able to slow the German *Blitzkrieg* and the progress of the Regiment. That evening, as the Regiment reached the town of Wysokie-Mazowieckie, the panzers broke through the Polish lines there and a fierce battle developed, in which the town was burned to the ground. As the panzers rolled through they were engaged by the older model Polish 75mm gun wz 02/26, which was being used in the antitank role, along with the 37mm wz 36 anti-tank guns. Both weapons could easily knock out any of the panzers the Regiment had at the time. During the battle the tracer and larger cannons fire caused numerous house fires to break out, and by the morning the mostly wooden town was a pile of smoldering ash except for the stone and brick chimneys. That day, the *20th Motorized Division* was able to cross the Narew at Wizna and proceeded toward Zambrów and Sokołów Podlaski. The *3rd Panzer Division*, which had been resting near Arys, received its marching orders, and by midnight the first elements were moving south to reinforce its sister divisions. Also that evening the II./*Abteilung* reached Bransk. On the 11th, the Regimental *Stabs* and II./*Abteilung* reached Bielsk, encountering strong resistance by elements of the *33rd Infantry Division (Reserve)* (Kalian-Zieleniewski) and the "*Suwalska*" and "*Podlaska*" *Cavalry Brigades*. On the right flank, the *20th Motorized* ran into significant trouble on the 11th as it encountered elements of the Polish *18th Division*, which had broken through at Lomza. Those forces were able to cause significant problems and severed all connections with the *20th Motorized* and *XIX Korps*. It was at that time that the commanding general ordered the I./*Abteilung* to launch an attack against those forces.[15] The I./*Abteilung* had managed to stop the Poles at Nova-Wies and knocked out numerous artillery and anti-tank guns, many of which were sited right next to the road to fire point blank into the panzers. The *abteilung* now found itself without any supporting infantry, artillery, or air forces with which to halt or pursue the Poles, who were now able to break contact and melt away into thick surrounding forests. Over the preceding days the panzers and motorized infantry had been able to quickly break most of the organized resistance and then, as they raced on towards their next objective, they left a large number of scattered and disorganized Polish forces in the rear areas. But despite the courage and determination being shown by the Poles in the face of this overwhelming onslaught the end was now nearing for them. Kurt Liestmann noted:

"Monday 11.9.39 on the advance march road to Bransk. The Polish want to hold. Here inside Poland there are many Russians already, one can see from the prisoners. In addition to kidnapped Germans. The artillery shoots at Bransk. The II./Abteilung already combs the forest in front of us with the infantry. We stop in one village near Bransk. The infantry is here as well. Together we search through some houses and barns. New orders arrive. The II./Abteilung goes marching towards Brest-Litovsk. We, the I./Abteilung go back to Wysokie-Mazowieckie in order to watch over the surrounding villages and forests, which are crowded with unorganized Polish soldiers."[16]

On 12 September, *Major* Haarde formed a *kampfgruppe* from those still serviceable panzers of the I./*Abteilung* and led them back west to the town of Andrzejewo to engage those Polish forces of the *Narew Army* that had gathered in the area southwest of Lomza. Together with the I./*Schützen Regiment 86*, the *kampfgruppe* attempted to encircle those Polish forces south of the Narew. *Olt* Kauffmann, the commander of the 3rd Company, and Lt K. Liestmann, a Zug commander in the *3rd Company*, attacked with three Mk IVs and eight smaller Mk IIs. The Polish forces, which were equipped with 13mm anti-tank rifles, 47mm anti-tank guns, and 75mm cannons, put up considerable resistance and exacted a toll on the attacking panzers and infantry. It was during this fighting that Lt Weber, a Zug commander in the 1st Company, was killed after his panzer received numerous hits. The panzer of *Olt* Kauffmann also received numerous hits, but unlike Weber he was able to escape with only minor wounds. Lt Kurt Liestmann was also wounded in the action this day, and he was evacuated a few days later aboard the hospital ship "*Berlin.*" He wrote of the day:

"In the morning the long-awaited washing water finally arrived. Here comes the order to march. A new combat detachment is organized by order of the commander of the Abteilung. My light Zug will be reinforced, now it consists of eight vehicles plus three heavy panzers. We proceed to the next village. It is already on fire. I receive the order from the commander to attack the village located in front of us. Great resistance, but we did it. The commander has been shot through, so I as commander must now change to the heavy panzer. I receive the order to advance with my panzer. At that very moment when I thought I saw something moving on the side of the forest 300m in front of us, we receive a direct hit, then a second and third. I am wounded in many places, my driver is dead, the loader is seriously wounded. The week passes by with impossible transportation difficulties and severe pain over bumpy roads to the hospital located in the direction of East Prussia near Königsberg and then to Insterburg."[17]

As the I./*Abteilung* was fighting to the west, the II./*Abteilung* was pushing south and was able to reach Wysokie-Litowski on the 12th. *Major Ramsauer* then received a personal order from *General* Schaal, the division commander, to advance towards Brest-Litovsk (Brzesc) with all possible speed.[18] On the 13th, Polish forces at Andrzejewo finally capitulated, thus freeing the I./*Abteilung* for further service. The I./*Abteilung* had suffered the following losses and battle damage: five panzer crews lost, and only twenty of the *abteilung*'s panzers were ready for action. The I./*Abteilung* remained in the area southwest of Lomza for a couple more days until they began to search for its parent formation, all the while having to be wary of remaining Polish forces of the *Modlin* and *Narew Armies*, which still were attempting to break through to the east. It was while in the city of Ostroleka that some members of the Regiment witnessed Jewish families being rounded up and collected by *SS* and *SD Einsatztruppen*; these were some of the first such actions in Poland by Nazi forces.[19] Also on the 13th, the Regimental *Stabs* and II./*Abteilung* departed from Wysokie-Litowski and proceeded towards Brest. That same day, the *10th Panzer Division* received orders from the corps headquarters to attack the fortress.

The Battle for Brest-Litovsk
During the night 13/14 September, the II./*Abteilung* found itself approximately 25km from the city of Brest (Brzesc). The *XIX Korps* had previously engaged Polish armored forces near Zabinka, some 25km to the northeast of Brest. Guderian now assembled his divisions around Brest with the *2nd Motorized Infantry Division* (Bader), tasked with protecting the flank near the Bialowieser Forest, the *3rd Panzer Division* covering the corps' left flank by pushing out its *aufklärungs* forces, and the *20th Infantry Division* was rushed up to give *10th Panzer* additional infantry forces. An officer led recon party commanded by no less than *Oberst* Elster and *Major* Ramsauer soon discovered that the entire position was weakly occupied. *Olt* Schefold, the II./*Abteilung* Adjutant, and *Olt* Jahns, the Regimental Adjutant, pressed on and surveyed a bit further in the direction of the *citadel*, and recognized that the entrenchments and positions to the front of *Fort II* had not yet been occupied. *Oberst* Elster was quoted as saying:

"Gentlemen, the opportunity to acquaint ourselves with the Fort will never come! I will drive there, who wants to go with me? Please join me. Let's go!"[20]

Botho Elster, the commander of the Regiment, in a significantly shortened report, wrote of his own experience in the capture of the fort at Brest Litovsk, and it is through his report that we follow the actions there:

"We were supposed to attack the fortress with five divisions and for this [attack] we advanced closer with the divisions in the deep hours of darkness. I myself drove ahead together with the commander of the Second Abteilung of Panzer Regiment 8 and continued to move towards Fort II, which we were to attack. I gathered myself and drove in a jeep to the fort. I saw that the fort itself and the surrounding entrenchments had already been cleared in the past couple of minutes. When I myself went further into the town, we received heavy fire, so that we had to find shelter in a ditch and withdrew with some effort. When I returned at a speed of a hundred kilometers [per hour] back to division and reported that we took the fort and found it empty, it passed on immediately to General Guderian."[21]

Equipped with only small arms, the recon group made its way to the back gates, where it soon discovered that the fort was not occupied. Elster immediately informed the division that the fort was not occupied, and that the Regiment could immediately attack the fortress. At the division headquarters there was concern over the fact that if allowed to proceed the Regiment would be attacking without any artillery and air support, thereby making itself vulnerable to the Polish gunners. After a short time the Regiment received permission to move forward with its attack and the following order was issued:

"Panzer Regiment 8 will attack over the fort line in a file from the north, break into the town near the train station and airfield, move by the rail line and street bridges over the river Bug, and secure the way for follow on infantry forces to charge the citadel."[22]

At 1430hrs the panzers began to roll through the forward defensive lines and over the cobbled pavement, quickly picking up speed and engaging any likely enemy lair which could house a deadly antitank or artillery gun. The route took them past *Fort II*, and further on by the main fort, where they proceeded to the top of the airfield. Upon reaching the airfield the panzer surprised a number of Polish aircraft attempting to flee the city. These remaining aircraft were then quickly engaged and destroyed, ending any chance of an escape. The panzer companies then moved on towards the train station in wedge formation and once again thwarted a last minute attempt by some of the Polish troops to flee the German juggernaut. One train which was attempting to make its way east was quickly put out of action by eight 20mm rounds from the Mk IIs, which zeroed in on the locomotive engine and boiler. After crossing the railway at around 1530hrs, the Regiment then ran into a strong Polish defensive position manned by tanks and supported by artillery and heavy machine guns. Elster then wrote:

"We, the 10th Panzer Division, started the attack one hour later; we pushed through the town until the Bug and destroyed fourteen enemy cannons and five combat vehicles of the Polish. Unfortunately the attack caused us losses. The citadel of the fortress was held by the enemy, who was shooting directly at us from sapper trenches and rampart loopholes with machine-guns, anti-tank guns and field cannons. During this attack,

Oberleutnant Semerak (a direct hit on the turret) and many Unteroffizer fell."[23]

The Polish position was supported by a strong concentration of artillery that was located in and around the *citadel*. Those guns had plenty of ammunition and were able to be reinforced and re-supplied as necessary, but despite the strong stand made by the Polish forces those guns not in or under covered positions were quickly placed under machine gun fire by the supporting infantry, and the tanks supporting the defense were the outdated *Renault FT-17* tank, mounting a low velocity 37mm gun. Those *FT-17s* were no match for the German Mk IIIs and IVs, which were quickly able to destroy the slow moving tanks. In the gardens north of the *citadel* the battle between panzers, anti-tank guns, artillery, machine guns, and infantry raged for some time, as various groups and guns defended and attacked one another. In the end twelve tanks were put out of action, with the 5th Company reporting the destruction of three tanks and five cannons and the 6th Company destroying three tanks and four cannons, while the 7th Company destroyed four tanks.[24] The Polish artillery, in conjunction with machine guns and anti tank guns firing from the cover of trenches and embankments, was able to lay down a curtain of fire on the advancing panzers. One of the leading panzers in a 5th Company column moving on the fortress received a couple of 105mm rounds which destroyed the drive mechanism and the left side of the turret. Gefr Weber, the radio operator, was the only member of the crew to survive this encounter, and we have his detailed report:

"When our Regiment crossed the Polish border at Schwiddern on 7 September, I had no inkling that 7 days later we would attack Brest-Litowsk, whose fortress was known to us from the history of World War I. After one week of non-stop marching the enemy resistance appearing here and there was overcome in shortest time. When the enemy thought to stop us by demolishing their bridges, our constant advancement taught him a good lesson. The pioneers, who quickly appeared on the spot, cleared many of these obstacles. On the morning of 14 September we were in a forest 30km away from Brest, after a whole night of advancement. Here in the forest, we assumed we would have a rest for maybe one or two days. Our vehicles were excellently camouflaged and in order to get ourselves a bit more comfortable, we got out the tents. The weather was flawless, the sun was smiling in the sky, as overall the god of weather was good to us during the Poland campaign. But things went differently, as we thought. Suddenly, just before midday, after we had already gotten into our 'lazy mood' and prepared to take a short nap, there came the march order. According to it we should attack Brest on this same day, because it was confirmed that the enemy had either abandoned the forward defensive line or had it weakly occupied. Around 1500hrs we reached the forward positions of our own infantry. In order to provide us with a greater impact in our attack, we were supported by many batteries of artillery, which opened the fire at 1515hrs in order to not endanger us. Just when the first panzers of our company's wedge attacked and had reached the rails of the train station, we had already begun to receive heavy enemy artillery and anti-tank fire, but it was not able to stop us. On the contrary, these detonations raised our fighting spirit. I was deployed as the radio-operator of the leading vehicle for the 3rd Zug. I hardly noticed anything of the combat events and only from time to time heard the impact of enemy rounds in front and behind our vehicle. Our attack had happened so surprisingly, that different cannons were not even moved into their firing position and never fired. We were not able to get to all the cannons some of which were located in the cover of the citadel. It was one of these Polish cannons that was to become the fate of our vehicle. We drove along the street parallel to the citadel for the second time in order to combat against enemy artillery and machine gun resistance nests, which fired at us madly. Suddenly our vehicle received a terrible hit, the driver cried. The vehicle burst in the front, leaving many holes in the driver's boarding hatch, through which came the fumes. As the drive mechanism was completely destroyed, it was impossible to think about forward movement with the vehicle. My Zug-leader OFw Böckel therefore sent to the company: "leading vehicle 'Helene' heavily hit, we're getting out". At this time a second heavy hit shook our vehicle. The artillery shot completely destroyed the turret of our panzer on the left side and hit Böckel so that he immediately died. At that moment I was dumbstruck and suddenly a bright light. I then immediately realized my position; to get immediately out of the burning vehicle and search for cover were my first thoughts. Cover, even the smallest bit, I found in the roadside ditch and it was here that I first realized where I actually was. 75 meters in front of me was an enemy trench and on the right, behind it was the rampart and wall, from which the Polish artillery fired, as if obsessed, above me and there were riflemen in the trees. It was a great cannonade and it was only now that I saw that my left arm was bleeding heavily, quickly I put on a compression bandage with the help of the bandage package, and then I had to see how to get out of this bad situation. I had just got the bandage done, when I saw two Polish soldiers, who felt themselves very secure and they moved towards my panzer from out of their trench, as they did not know I was there. They only watched my destroyed vehicle and that was my luck. I got myself together very quickly with my pistol, which I carried as usual in my breast pocket and would now be my savior. The first shot was fired precisely, the second I probably missed, but with the third I was able to render the second enemy as combat ineffective and he had already covered himself by then. In order to be at least protected from the riflemen in the trees, I worked my way in the ditch seeking shelter in a water pipe. Here I spent about one and a half hours, which seemed to me to be forever. I found out that the fire was also coming from the top floors of some high buildings on the street, what a mean trick! But I would have to find the way out of this witch's cauldron, as I didn't want to loose the connection with my troops. But where was I to go? As the radio-operator, I had hardly seen anything from inside the panzer and didn't know from which direction we had come. I had to try to orientate myself somehow but everywhere I looked I spotted the enemy resistance nests, which cut off my escape path. Finally I noticed a sheltered position, which was hardly seen by the enemy, and where I didn't assume any Polish soldiers to be. My next task was to get there. When the fire ceased a bit, I jumped over the street and worked my way up approximately 100m until this position, from where I was picked up by a panzer from the 6th Company. After half an hour, as we fought the enemy resistance nests, which I now knew precisely where they were, we fired off all our ammunition. With nothing left for us to do except to return to the initial positions. From there I was led to the hospital to take care about my light arm-wound and it was here on that same night I met my heavily wounded driver, who I thought was dead. We were so happy to see each other, obviously and I discovered that with his last bit of power he had made his way out of the panzer after the explosion from the second round had shot through the driver's hatch and had found shelter on the other side in the bushes, from where he was later picked up after several hours by our infantry. Unfortunately, my brave comrade died from his wounds 12 days later. On 17 September, when I returned to the company after three days absence, I discovered that the citadel had given up that morning around 0400hrs."[25]

As the II./*Abteilung* reached the *Bug River* it found the bridges spanning it still intact, despite the strong enemy resistance. Olt Schefold, the Adjutant of the II./*Abteilung*, quickly decided to attempt and secure the far side, but as he ordered his Mk II forward and began to roll out onto the bridge it was blown up directly underneath his panzer. The bridge, which had been remotely detonated, caved in, and the panzer slid forward, trapping the panzer and its crew there. Schefold was slightly wounded in the incident, but was still able to get out with his crew and swim to the far side riverbank, where they were later rescued by an infantry patrol that evening. Wolf Schefold had this to say about the crossing:

"We had the orders to capture the bridge across the Bug. The parts of the regiment were in immediate proximity from one of the bridges, and the infantry was visible as well. Thus I decided to drive onto the bridge. When I was about two-thirds through the bridge, it was detonated from the citadel. The collapsed support columns prevented my panzer from falling into the water. We disembarked and waited on the other (enemy) side of the river until dusk fell in order to reach back to our shore. So the bridge was detonated not before but during the crossing over."[26]

Later in the battle, after the fighting had ended, members of the *abteilung* returned to the site and extricated the panzer, which was found almost damage free. Elster's account continues:

"Oberleutnant Schefold with his vehicle broke through to the south over the railroad bridge, in order to pull the infantry forward from there and to build the bridgehead on the south bank. At this moment the railroad bridge was detonated with an electric remote [firing] device from the fortress, he fell into the Bug with his vehicle and in the middle of the bridge there was only wreckage has he reached the bank under enemy fire with a head wound but alive."[27]

As the II./*Abteilung*, followed by the Regimental *Stabs*, moved further into the city they began to receive an ever increasing volume of fire from rifles and machine guns located in houses and on rooftops; this fire continued to cause further losses for the Regiment. One example of the type of defense put up by the Poles was the loss of the panzer of *Olt* Semerak, the commander of the 6th Company, which received a direct hit by a field artillery piece that ripped off the turret, killing Semerak and wounding his driver. *Uffz* Thust was then killed by a Polish sniper sitting atop a nearby rooftop as he attempted to escape the burning panzer. *Fw* Ladendorff, also from the 6th Company, was mortally wounded during these street actions.[28] Also during this assault the command panzer of *Oberst* Elster was rendered inoperable when an artillery shell hit it, which caused the panzer to throw its track. Unlike Semerak, Elster and his crew were lucky and escaped the incident unhurt. Elster then quickly spotted a nearby panzer and, while under heavy fire by snipers and infantry firing from trees and rooftops, ran towards the other panzer. Along the way Elster was forced to defend himself from the nearby Polish infantry by using his pistol to keep their heads down, but he was fortunate that Lt Eichberg from the 5th Company spotted his regimental commander's small dilemma and was able to cover Elster by maneuvering his panzer between the Poles and the other panzer. Despite being hit by a number of rounds, neither Eichberg nor any of his crew was wounded in the affair, and Elster was able to gain the safety of the other panzer without getting hit himself. Elster relates this in his account:

"I myself was hit with the cannon shot, one meter in front of the vehicle, where I sat with Oberleutnant Sahmel and directed the attack. The track broke, so that the vehicle was motionless under the enemy fire. I got out and caught another vehicle, on which I jumped on and lay along the side of the turret. Driving this way, I received a direct shot on the other side of the vehicle but it remained operable and we reached the nearest cover. When Leutnant Eichberg, who attacked next to me, saw my situation, he moved in front of me and covered me, but he [in turn] received a direct shot in the turret, which tore the corner of the panzer but inside no one was hurt. The darkness covered the burning town, where the firing came out of all corners and houses as if it was mad. Here we took our combat detachments [II./Abteilung] backwards, and sank exhausted in the straw behind the barn."[29]

That evening the Poles were able to move back into the citadel from the city, which was casting a glow over the fort from the many fires that had been ignited during the battle. The attempts to enter the citadel were halted when the Polish forces placed one of the vintage *Renault FT-17* tanks across the gates, thereby blocking access to the fort. Also that same day, Elster reported the following on Haarde and his I./*Abteilung*:

"The First Abteilung was engaged in combat with the 18th Polish Division which broke through from Lomza to the south, and tried doubtfully to escape to the east. Major Haarde had accomplished a great night march. He drove all by himself, disconnected from the group, through the enemy forest, where right and left stood Polish soldiers on the horses. He drove with his lights full on and was considered to be a Polish combat vehicle, and the Polish cleared the road in front of him. During the next attack Leutnant Weber unfortunately was completely worn down by the enemy tank defense. Weber was dead and the crews of five vehicles. Oberleutnant Kauffmann took five shots in his vehicle and was wounded in the knee; Leutnant Liestmann was also very heavily wounded by a direct shot. Hauptmann Ehrbeck was back again with grenade fragments. Leutnant Neumann, who was wounded on 09.09 at the capture of the bunker, was now in the hospital in Johannisburg [Prussia]. The losses until this point were two officers dead and six wounded, four unteroffiziers dead and three wounded and seven men dead with nine wounded. The losses were really high but the cause is in the essence of the combat. There was heavy damage to the panzers, so that at the moment only twenty panzers per Abteilung were ready for combat."[30]

By 15 September, the city of Brest was finally secured, but its citadel was still being strongly defended by Polish forces who were stubbornly holding out and refused to give up. At approximately 1430hrs, the *20th Infantry Division* launched its first attack on the *citadel*, which ended in failure. A short time later, the III./*Battalion Schützen Regiment 86*, along with *Pioneer Battalion 39* attempted to breech the eastern side of the fortress, but that attack also met with little success. A third assault, this time by elements of *Schützen Regiment 69*, attacked the *citadel*, but they too failed to dislodge the defenders. As darkness fell on the night of 15/16 September, the Regiment broke off its attack and returned to the assembly area on the northern side of the airfield. A few of the broken and partially damaged panzers where brought back into operation again by their crews. For the Regiment, it suffered the following losses: thirteen killed and eighteen wounded, and many of the wounds sustained were to the head and hands.[31] Fortunately for the Germans the *3rd Panzer Division* had been moving forward, and by that afternoon was nearing Brest. That division was ordered to attack the citadel early the following morning, and so it formed a *kampfgruppe* from elements of *Panzer Regiment 6*, *Pioneer Battalion 39*, and the 4th and 6th Batteries of *Artillery Regiment 75*. The *kampfgruppe* commenced its attack at 0345hrs on the 16th with the aim of making for and taking *Fort III*. As the *kampfgruppe* made its way into the city it did so without making any enemy contact and was able to secure *Fort III*, which was not being defended by Polish forces. After securing *Fort III* with a company the remainder of the *kampfgruppe* proceeded towards the central railway station, which they did without encountering any enemy forces, although the *kampfgruppe* did receive heavy fire from the *citadel*. Before long contact was established with the *III./Battalion Schützen Regiment 86*, and once contact was established and the area partially secured all of the artillery elements from both divisions were formed together under the command of *Oberst* Weidling of the *20th Infantry Division*, and they began to shell the *citadel*. Under this heavy artillery bombardment the *2nd* and *4th Companies* from *Panzer Regiment 6* were able to reach the fortress from the southeast, but towards the evening those units were ordered to break contact and fall back; however, some elements of the *kampfgruppe* remained to secure the southern suburbs, while other elements secured the prison where captured Polish soldiers where being held. At 2200hrs, the division received the order to halt any further attacks on the *citadel* and city; its *kampfgruppe* was to break off its attacks and begin following the main body of the division, which had already begun its march towards Wlodawa. The *10th Panzer and 20th Infantry* would again take up the assault on the *citadel*, and by the early morning of the 17th, the huge *citadel* was finally taken by elements from the *76th Schützen Regiment* of the *20th Division*, and the powerful fortress of Brest-Litovsk was firmly in German hands. Fortunately for the Germans, and the Regiment in particular, much of the Polish armor was destroyed, captured, or retreated before it could be properly employed against them. Polish Reserve forces were still assembling in rear areas when they were surprised and overwhelmed before they could offer any type of defense. In one documented action an entire battalion of French made *R-35* tanks which had escaped to nearby Romania, rather than give battle, were interned there having never fired a shot. In another action near Zabinka, just east of Brest, the *XIX Korps* surprised and destroyed an entire Polish armored unit that had been unloading its tanks from railcars before it could engage in combat. Overall, there were few armored encounters, and those that did occur were considered mere skirmishes. Elster finishes his report by stating:

"Yesterday General Guderian visited us personally and expressed his praise for the whole Regiment. The Regiment was brave in fighting through the masses. I am now sitting in a farm house with all officers; my sleeping bag accompanies me all the time. Many times we slept sitting in jeeps or in panzers, eating only from the field kitchen, sometimes we capture a chicken and eggs. When we come back from the attack, completely dirty, smeared, black uniforms unrecognized and three days un-shaved, we look dangerous."[32]

The panzer strength report of the Regiment on 17 Sept 1939 included seven Befehls panzers, sixteen Mk Is, forty-five Mk IIs, three Mk IIIs, and four Mk IVs, for a total of seventy-five operational panzers.[33] By the 18th, almost all organized resistance throughout Poland had ceased. Warsaw would continue to hold out until the 27th, and a final surrender would not be negotiated and signed until 6 October. The *10th Panzer* and *20th Motorized* would remain in the Brest area, while the *2nd Motorized* and *3rd Panzer Divisions* were ordered east and south toward Kobryn and Wlodawa, where they would continue actions against small pockets of Polish forces attempting to flee east. In ten days the *XIX Korps* had covered some two hundred miles, demonstrating the rapid and overwhelming success of the German *Panzertruppen*. Also on this day, *Oberst* Elster, *Major* Haarde, and *Hptm* von Heydebreck were decorated with the *Iron Cross First Class* (EK I) by the division commander for their leadership and actions. More decorations were awarded a few days later to the men of the Regiment for their actions and achievements during the campaign. Most notably was *OFw* Kümmel from the 1st Company, who received an EK I for the destruction of five tanks. *Fw* Kathe from 5th Company was decorated with the EK II for his actions at the *Bug River* Bridge, in which he was able to rescue an officer from his company. *Uffz* Gerdes from the 7th Company was also among those decorated with the EK II.[34] *Armeegruppe Nord* was informed on 17 September about the Russian Army's movement into eastern Poland, and it was therefore ordered to remain behind or on the west side of the Bug River from Brest to Bialystok. Despite the order there was some air and ground reconnaissance undertaken on the eastern side of the river for security purposes. *Armeegruppe Nord* and *Sud* linked up between Warsaw and Brest. There were a few setbacks with the Russians, especially in the northern sector, where in a number of minor incidents Russian aircraft attacked German troops and Labor Force workers on the east side of the Bug. On 22 September, *XIX Korps* turned over Brest to the Russians in a formal ceremony complete with a parade by both nations' forces; also on that day orders were received to evacuate the area around Brest, and indeed the *Fourth Armee* was already moving its headquarters north to Arys. The scheduled withdrawal was to be an orderly affair that would take place over a series of phase lines. It was planned where possible that an approximately 15 mile buffer would exist between the German and Russian forces. The withdrawal called for most of the wounded to be left behind with medical personnel for later evacuation, and the same was true for German materiel that could not be immediately evacuated; all capture stocks would be taken back as practicable. The *XIX Korps* rear guard was securing the line Wysokie – Litowski – Bielsk. The *3rd Panzer Division* was moving via Widomla – Ciechanowiec – Zambrow to Lomza, which was reached that day. Near Johannesburg the division crossed the border to Germany for the third time in September. The *20th Motorized* was near Siemiatycze, and *10th Panzer* was near Wysokie-Litowski. On the return march back through to East Prussia there were some minor fire fights with scattered Polish units, but fortunately for the Regiment it sustained no losses. On 24 September, the Regiment reached the area of Johnnisburg – Sensburg, from where they had departed some seventeen days earlier, but now there were a few open spaces in the ranks; some comrades had been lost forever, but for others their return from hospital was greatly anticipated by those comrades remaining. That day the *XIX Korps* reported its divisions at the following locations: *3rd Panzer* had reached the area Landsberg, Bartenstein, Heilsberg; the *20th Motorized* was near Schippenbeil barten, Rastenburg, and Rössel; and the *10th Panzer* near Lomza, Zambrów, and Ostrów Mazowiecka.

On an interesting note, many of the Polish campaign veterans interviewed for this book mentioned that on its return march, the Regiment took along with them some German and Polish refugees from the eastern regions of Poland, which was now being occupied by the Russians. Of these Polish refugees, there were some among them that belonged to the Polish aristocracy which Lt Knorr had picked up in Brest-Litovsk. As those refugees sought to return to Germany, they encountered difficulties when they reached the border at Sensburg. When they arrived there, some of the regional and local party officials (*Gauleiters*) wanted to arrest those refugees. It was at this time that Knorr again stepped forward to assist them, but not after crossing the *Gauleiter* of Sensburg, who petitioned the Reich's leadership and local *Gauleiters* for punishment. These leaders demanded from the *Oberkommando des Heeres* (OKH) a punishment for those responsible; however, both the regimental and division commander stood by Lt Knorr, and he received no punishment or repercussions from the event. Forty-four years later, in a letter to Knorr, the ex-princess and former refugee thanked her "rescuers" for their actions. Since its activation the commander and the officers of the Regiment had tried not to show any influence to the party. After the incident a few regional party leaders attempted to persuade the officers to join the *National Socialist Party*, but in most cases the officers refused, feeling instead that the war should first be concluded.[35]

The Regiment, after its brief stop-over in Sendburg, headed south towards the Thüringen area for a period of rest and recovery at the kaserne at Ohrdruf. The Regiment would spend almost two weeks here before returning to Böblingen. Finally, in late October, the Regiment then made its way back to Böblingen, where it re-entered its home station in early November. In their previous operations, the Regiment had taken on the spirit and tradition of the cavalry, and had now adopted that spirit to the panzer and lived by the age old creed once expressed by *Field Marshal Blücher* of *"Towards and through!"*[36] Indeed, the success at Brest-Litowsk exemplified the old and new cavalry spirit of "towards and through," and of quick thinking and seizing any opportunity, and that the enemy presented to the attacker in this new style of combined arms warfare called *"Blitzkrieg."* The Germans lost the following casualties, suffering 16,000 killed and 32,000 wounded. In addition, 674 panzers were knocked out, with 217 of these being complete write-offs. There was also the loss of 195 guns, 319 armored cars, and the loss of over 11,000 assorted vehicles and motorcycles. The Poles suffered the loss of 66,300 killed, 133,700 wounded, and 587,000 prisoners. An additional 100,000 were captured by Russian forces, of which only a few were ever returned or heard of again.[37] There were many lessons to be learned from this campaign, and the German Army had been fortunate in its opponent and his ability to wage war. Taking nothing away from the gallant Polish Army and Air force, who despite the lack of modern equipment had shown great determination, not to mention courage and élan, but in the end they found themselves totally outclassed and maneuvered by the Germans. The Regiment had learned and taken away many hard lessons; through an after action report filed by the Regiment at the end of the campaign the officers and men reported the following tactical problems encountered during the course of the campaign. The first and foremost was that the panzer provided speed and shock to the battlefield, and that hard realistic training had certainly helped to keep casualties to a minimum. It was clearly noticeable that the Regiment's personnel were of a higher caliber than their opponents, and their concept of teamwork and high level of training far exceeded what opposed them in other European armies of the time. The years of preparations and training had indeed paid off in something that in the latter years of the war could only be dreamed of. One of the first lessons learned in Poland was that the panzers could contribute greatly to offensive actions, but only if in cooperation with other supporting arms, such as the infantry and artillery, which was noted as being vital in accompanying and supporting any panzer attack. An example of this occurred when, during the advance from the Wizna to Brest-Litovsk, a panzer *abteilung* was in the lead without any motorized infantry, and when the panzers ran into the main body of the division's *aufklärungs abteilung* that was pinned down near Wysockie-Masowiecke a panzer attack was launched directly from the route of march. The attack was eventually successful in driving through the town and overrunning the few Polish forces defending there, but this success was credited due to the fact that the Poles were not able to repulse the attack because they did not have a sufficient number of troops on hand to launch a counterattack. The recommendation was that the tactical doctrine should not be altered, but instead reinforce the fact that motorized infantry must be in the advance elements of the division so that they could immediately follow the panzer breakthrough and occupy the surrounding area. The same was true when attacking or clearing forested areas; this was seen when the panzers were used to clear out the numerous woods that often flanked the route of advance. The employment of panzers in the woods was totally ineffective because the Poles were able to pull back along the trails, reappear after the panzers had passed by, and engage them with their anti-tank and artillery guns. Again it was recommended that there be accompanying infantry that could push through the wooded terrain on a wide front, thereby keeping those enemy infantry and anti-tank gun forces off guard and unable to reestablish themselves along the lines of communications. Another recommendation dealt with the clearing of bunker positions; this was seen during the attack on Wizna on 9 September, when the infantry became pinned down in front of the bunker line. Here the Regiment was committed in order to push the infantry forward. Because no intelligence was available concerning the layout of the bunker position the attack was not well coordinated between the infantry and panzers. Additionally, there was the problem of the wet marshy area in front of the bunkers which was not properly surveyed or reported back to the panzer forces in order to determine whether it was negotiable by panzers.[38] In this attack the heavy panzers did not participate because the bridge had not yet been completed before the attack was launched. The lighter Mk Is and IIs were, however, able to cross the river and take part in the battle, which was in the end successful. Much of the success was also due to the fact that there was little in the way of enemy minefields and artillery fire, which allowed the light panzers to get in among the bunker line and place concentrated fire into the apertures and firing slits while depositing the accompanying infantry and pioneers. When the battle moved into Brest-Litovsk the next area of concern dealt with fighting in urban and built up areas. To this extent the panzers attacked across the sprawling rail yard and into the city without any previous reconnaissance and without any accurate maps. In spite of attacking with the element of surprise, the Poles were able to put up a stout defense utilizing numerous guns and older model tanks. The breakthrough again succeeded, and the objective, the bridge over the Bug River, was reached, although it was blown up as the panzers began to cross. Again the lack of artillery, minefields, and proper anti-tank obstacles allowed the panzers to reach the bridge, and only the courage and determination of the Polish sappers brought the bridge crashing down. Polish anti-tank guns had been employed, but most of these guns were overrun during the run up to the bridge. In spite of this, combat in built up areas required proper reconnaissance by infantry and reconnaissance elements. The point was also made clear that panzers should not fight alone where they could be defeated by lone infantrymen armed with grenades and *Molotov cocktails*, and were susceptible to enemy close in direct fire and attacks from above. Other recommendations that were made for attacks in urban areas concerned the lack of detailed city maps, and it was recommended that each panzer have one with it, and that it was strongly recommended that the panzers be pulled back out of the city before sundown, or they were prone to getting lost within the city blocks. Also seen during the attack was the need for strong artillery that could protect and seal off the flanks during the attack. It was also mentioned that the covering smoke screens laid down on the citadel at Brest-Litovsk were too short in duration and at the wrong time. It was evident that many of the panzer casualties resulted from direct and indirect artillery fire that was able to penetrate the thin top side armor plating on many of the panzers, and so it was recommended that whenever possible the panzers should not be employed against these high-angle fire weapons, under whose barrages and concentrations they were unable to defend themselves against. When it came to organization and equipment it was strongly recommended that there was the need for an increase in the number of armored personnel carriers and self propelled guns which could accompany and support the panzers in the attack. During the campaign it did not matter whether those forces were motorized or horse drawn, as they all had a difficult time in keeping pace with panzers, and therefore had the need for armored carriers that could bring the infantry forward without sustaining casualties from various types of direct and indirect artillery and rocket fire. At that time the *Krupp* six wheeled truck constituted the primary means of transportation for the motorized infantry, and there was a great need for more of the *Hanomag* armored half tracks. Not all of the problems of mobility were seen with the infantry, as even within the Regiment it was noted that the *abteilung* and regimental commanders and their staffs had a very difficult time keeping pace with their own panzers, and would often halt their panzers until they themselves and the other supporting arms caught up. It was therefore recommend that those controlling elements and staffs be located well forward, where they could better direct the battle, and that they should be restricted to just a few armored vehicles that were all well equipped with radio communications. When it came to signals equipment, the current models of radios for communications between the panzer regiment and *abteilung* were seen as being not very useful, as they were too large and complicated to work under battlefield conditions.[39] Additionally, the commander of the panzer regiment had to be able to speak directly to the commanders of his two *abteilung*. This was a difficult task given the noisy insides of a panzer on the march, and it was noted that often the regimental commander had to shout to make himself understood to his signals officer, as that officer transmits various orders over the radio to the *abteilung* signals officer, which process then had to be repeated in reverse, as the *abteilung* signals officer had to shout the orders to the *abteilung* commander. Technologically speaking, the panzers were found to be mechanically reliable, although by the end of the campaign most were in serious need of servicing and complete overhauls. The sustained operations over poor roads and rough terrain would require extensive repairs to be undertaken. The greatest weakness, however, was found in the armor thickness, especially the Mk I and II, which proved to be totally inadequate. Of the 217 panzer casualties suffered during the campaign—eighty-nine Mk Is, eighty-three Mk IIs, twenty-six Mk IIIs, and nineteen Mk IVs—most were destroyed by anti-tank and artillery gun fire.[40] It was obvious that the Mk I was totally outdated and under-gunned as a combat panzer, but had some usefulness as a command panzer; the Mk II, despite its lack of armor, was still useful, as it was easily able to cross soft ground and pontoon bridges that the heavier MK IIIs and IVs could not. Other recommendations for the Mk II mentioned the need for improved vision devices so that while buttoned up the crew could effectively observe and detect enemy forces. The MG-34s, it was noted, must be flexibly mounted, or the gun was prone to numerous stoppages and jams. The 20mm KwK 30 gun was noted as being very good, but that the issue of high explosive ammunition was urgently needed. Despite being acceptable for the early campaigns and battles the MK I and IIs were soon to be found too light for combat operations, and only the Mk IIs were found capable and useful for reconnaissance operations. In the later battles to come both chassis types would find some success as artillery and Pak gun platforms. The Mk II and IV were good panzers, but they too were in need of heavier armor. The 37mm and 75mm KwK guns had proven to be successful, and it was not until later that those too would have to be up-gunned in order to deal with the Russian *T-34s* and British *Matildas*. For the crew armament it was recommended that the panzer crews should be equipped with modern sub-machine guns or machine pistols, and that hand grenades and explosives were needed to be issued to the panzer crews for close in panzer defense.

Between Campaigns
The Regiment had not even spent three full weeks in Böblingen before it found itself again departing its home station. The Germans had just pulled off a major coup by attacking Poland while their *West Wall* defenses lay bare. But the French and British had no intension of launching any counteroffensives, and most of the French forces fell back behind the *Maginot Line*. For the Germans, they immediately began the transfer of forces from Poland to the west, for it had been Hitler's wish to launch his attack in mid-November, but the weather and numerous staff postponements forced a postponement until May 1940. But what would soon be dubbed the *Phony War*, or *Sitzkrieg*, it was necessary that as many forces as possible be sent westwards toward the border so that if there was to be an attack there would be sufficient forces there to meet it. On 29 November, in conjunction with the overall move of *10th Panzer Division*, the Regiment was transferred to its new post in the area of Limburg-Hadamar, near the Westerwald. After the campaign in Poland, *Panzer Division "Kempf"* was disbanded and its headquarters reverted back to the *4th Panzer Brigade*, which was then assigned to the *10th Panzer Division* with *Panzer Regiments 7* and *8* under its command. The Regiment had fifty-eight Mk Is, fifty-five Mk IIs, six Mk IIIs, and nine Mk IVs.[41] The training was continued as much as possible at the eastern posts, and the experience of the Polish campaign was incorporated in the training. Even the panzers themselves underwent cosmetic changes, as the previous brownish colors of the panzer, which had not proven its worth in operations, was repainted using a light grey, or *anthrazit* color. Even the markings, such as the all white Balkan *Kreuz*, which had been very visible in the field, was modified and changed to display a black cross with a white border, and which from here on would be synonymous with the *Wehrmacht*. The Mk Is, which had served the Regiment so well over the previous three years, but were found seriously deficient in the rough conditions of combat, were almost entirely replaced with the Mk II. A few of the Mk Is were converted to command tanks and still found a place with the Regimental and *Abteilung* headquarters. At that time the Regiment was stationed at Milheim, with the remainder spread out in the villages of Windrich, Filzen, Braunberg, Andel, and Gonzerath. By the end of January 1940 the *10th Panzer Division* had been relocated back across the Rhine, and on 30 January 1940 the Regiment departed the *Westerwald* and moved into its new home in the Mosel region near the towns of Mülheim-Brauneberg and Wintrich. On 21 February 1940, the Regiment was authorized to reorganize in accordance with the *Sonder K.St.N.* originally dated 1 September 1939. However, an insufficient number had been, or would in the near future be produced to fill each light panzer company with seventeen Mk IIIs, and each medium panzer company with fourteen Mk IVs. The Regiment was ordered to adopt a *gliederung* (position) with seven Mk IIIs in each light panzer company and eight Mk IVs in each medium panzer company. All told, a light panzer company was to consist of a company headquarters and four *zugs* or platoons, and the headquarters would have with it one Mk I, two Mk IIs, and one small command panzer. The 1st and 2nd *Zugs* would each be outfitted with three Mk IIIs and two Mk Is. The 3rd and 4th *Zugs* would each have three Mk IIIs. For the medium company there would be a headquarters *Zug* with one each Mk I, Mk II, and Mk III, a light *Zug* with five Mk IIs, the 1st *Zug* with four Mk IVs, and the 2nd *Zug* with three Mk IVs.[42] The movement at this particular time of year and to this region adversely affected the training of the Regiment due to the cold winter weather and freezing temperatures that were often below zero. In fact, the temperature that winter of 1939/40 was so cold that much of the Mosel River froze and was covered by ice.

The day-to-day training and garrison duties continued throughout the winter, but in April those monotonous duties were finally broken by practice alerts and visits to the training grounds near Baumholder. Also in that month the first panzer Mk IIIs with the 37mm KwK gun became available, and most of the light companies in the Regiment were re-equipped with this new panzer. There was no time wasted in establishing new driver and gunnery training for these new panzers and their crews, and the Regiment would continue to train and remain in the Mosel region until the beginning of spring. The winds of war also began to blow again, as fighting in Finland, East Africa, Norway, the Atlantic, and the Far East continued to heighten. To the men of the Regiment there were no immediate and clear signs of the impending war with France and England, and only through the frequent alerts were they reminded of the serious situation that was soon to confront them. The final alert came on the afternoon of 9 May 1940. *"Y-yellow –0535hrs 10.5"* read the alert text message, but this time it was for real, and the Regiment was to be ready to march into action. For many of the men this would be there first taste of combat against a far better equipped and proven enemy who outnumbered them in men and machines. Many of them had mixed feelings as they prepared to go against the French and British. The Regiment's operational strength in panzers included twenty-two Mk Is, fifty-eight Mk IIs, twenty-nine Mk IIIs, and sixteen Mk IVs with a total panzer strength of 134 on 5 May 1940.[43]

Panzer Regiment 8 Chain of Command as of 09 May 1940[44]

Regiment Commander	Oberst Elster
Regt Adj	Olt Jahns
Nachr Offz	Olt Sahmel
Ord Offz	Lt Wöhrmann
Regt Arzt	Dr Becker
StKp	Olt Plinzner, Lt Prion
I./Abteilung Commander	Oberstlt Haarde, F
Abtl Adj	Olt Knorr
Nachr Offz	Lt Matthias, J
Ord Offz	Lt von Bitter
Abt Arzt	Dr Port
Zahl Mstr	StZmstr Tischner
Ing Offz	Major Schnell
StKp	Hptm Bach, Lt Stiefelmayer
leKol	Olt Weinert
1st Company	Olt Bernau
Zug Commander	Lt Neumann
Zug Commander	Lt Springorum
2nd Company	Olt von Merkatz
Zug Commander	Lt Hahn
Zug Commander	Lt Hess
3rd Company	Hptm Ehrbeck
Zug Commander	Olt Bauer
Zug Commander	Olt Kertscher
Zug Commander	Lt Liestmann, K
Zug Commander	Lt von Treuenfels
II./Abteilung Commander	Major Ramsauer
Abtl Adj	Olt Schefold
Nachr Offz	Olt von Stülpnagel
Ord Offz	Lt von Hake
Abt Arzt	Dr Witzky
Zahl Mstr	OZmstr Gisy
Ing Offz	HBmstr Hauska
StKp	Hptm Klein
Kradmelder Zug	Olt Ohlenhaut
leKol	Hptm Bartenschlager
5th Company	Olt Körner
Zug Commander	Olt Eichberg
Zug Commander	Lt Schwarzhaupt
Zug Commander	Lt H. Liestmann
6th Company	Hptm Ehrbeck
Zug Commander	Lt Foellmer
Zug Commander	Lt Sontowski
Zug Commander	Lt Jattkowski
7th Company	Hptm Ottens
Zug Commander	Lt Wuth
Zug Commander	Lt Risch
Zug Commander	Lt Seidler

3

The French Campaign
May-July 1940

In late September 1939, as the campaign in Poland was drawing to its end and German forces were already departing Poland and making their way quickly back into Germany and the border region of France and Belgium, Hitler immediately began to turn his attention towards France and Great Britain. It was these two nations that posed the greatest military threat to him, and he and his generals were eager to get the troops back in case those nations attacked the lightly manned and vulnerable western flank. As the German army moved back that threat began to decrease, so Hitler then began to turn his attention on his old nemesis. He then announced his desire to attack France and the Low Countries in November, a move that shocked many of his commanders. In October, Hitler issued orders to the *German General Staff* ordering them to devise a plan of attack. The German plan was given the code name "*Fall Gelb*" (*Case Yellow*), and this plan called for a large offensive by three army groups that would drive towards the North Sea through Holland and central Belgium. The main effort was to be undertaken by *Armeegruppe B* in the north with a massive forty-three division force that included most of the panzer and mobile divisions in the army. To support the main effort of *Armeegruppe B*, *Armeegruppe A* was to cover the southern flank by launching an attack into Luxembourg with twenty-two divisions, most of which were infantry. The third army group, *Armeegruppe C*, had the two fold mission of securing both the southern flank of *Armeegruppe B* and defending the *West Wall*, or *Siegfried Line*, with its eighteen divisions. *Fall Gelb* would for the next seven months undergo numerous modifications until, in December 1939, a base foundation was laid by *Generaloberst* Gerd von Rundstedt and his chief of staff, *Generalleutnant* Erich von Manstein, both of whom would later rise to great notoriety in the battles and campaigns in Europe and Russia. Manstein's plan was a variation of the famous von *Schlieffen Plan* of 1914 that had envisioned a large German Army moving in a great arch through Belgium and Northern France in order to capture Paris and destroy the French Army as it retreated south to the Swiss border. Whereas the *Schlieffen Plan* called for a larger northern push, the *Manstein Plan* envisioned a more central push in the Ardennes region of Belgium, where it was thought that the Allied forces could be drawn in and their lines then broken and forces finally encircled. During a war game exercise in February 1940, Manstein was able to present his plan directly to Hitler, who was impressed enough with the plan to direct the *OKW* to further study the feasibility of the plan.[1] In late February, the *OKH* issued a modified version of Manstein's plan that called for *Armeegruppe B*, with twenty-nine divisions, to strike against the Allied northern flank and hold those forces there, while *Armeegruppe A*, with forty-five divisions, which now included the bulk of the panzer and mobile units, struck in the central

sector along the Meuse River between Namur and Sedan. *Armeegruppe C*, with its nineteen divisions, was to hold the southern flank and demonstrate along the *Maginot Line*, as well as hold those French forces positioned in the Alsace and Lorraine regions in place. The plan was approved by Hitler in the early spring of 1940 and took on the following shape: *Armeegruppe A* contained some forty-five divisions, including seven of the ten panzer divisions, assigned to three armies; on the right flank was the *Fourth Armee* (von Kluge) with fourteen divisions; in the center was the *Twelfth Armee* (List) with nineteen divisions; and on the left flank was the *Sixteenth Armee* (Busch) with twelve divisions. *Armeegruppe B* contained some twenty-nine divisions, including three panzer divisions, and was composed of the *Sixth Armee* (Reichenau) and *Eighteenth Armee* (Küchler). *Armeegruppe C* (Leeb) had nineteen divisions and was composed of the *First Armee* (Witzleben) and *Seventh Armee* (Dollmann); additionally, there were forty-five divisions in reserve. The bulk of the German armor was attached to the *Twelfth Armee* under the control of a newly created panzer group commanded by *Generalleutnant* Ewald von Kleist. *Panzergruppe Kleist* had control over the *XLI Panzer Korps* (Reinhardt), the *XIX Panzer Korps* (Guderian), and the *XIV Motorized Korps* (Wietersheim). On the night of 9/10 May 1940 the Regiment began its march through the Mosel region through Bernkastel, Hetzerath, Ehrang, and Welschbillig in the direction of Luxembourg. The Regiment was once again a part of the *10th Panzer Division* (Schaal), and together with the *1st* (Kirchner) and *2nd* (Veiel) *Panzer Divisions* comprised the *XIX Panzer Korps* under the command of *General der Panzer Truppen* Heinz Guderian.[2] The *XIX Panzer Korps* was to lead the advance through the Belgian Ardennes Forest to Sedan and force a crossing of the Meuse River. Like the German *Schlieffen* and *Manstein Plans*, the Allies too developed a number of strategic plans for countering any German offensive moves. It was felt that in the south, the *Maginot Line* was sufficient for holding back any German attacks there, while in the center there was the Meuse River and Ardennes Forest, which provided a natural barrier against any mechanized attacks. It was also felt that sufficient fortifications had been built in that area to hold against any attacks. It was therefore in the north and Low Countries that the most vulnerable sector lay.

The Allied plan, better known as the "*D*" or "*Dyle*" Plan, was given its name after the river that flowed near the Belgian town of Namur. This plan, like that of the German plans, underwent a number of changes and added variants which were used to modify the overall plan as seen necessary or determined by the various Allied commanders. The plan was the brainchild of *General* Maurice Gamelin, and its first variant, the "*Escaut Plan*," called for a somewhat risky advance into the Low Countries

34

Chapter 3: The French Campaign, May-July 1940

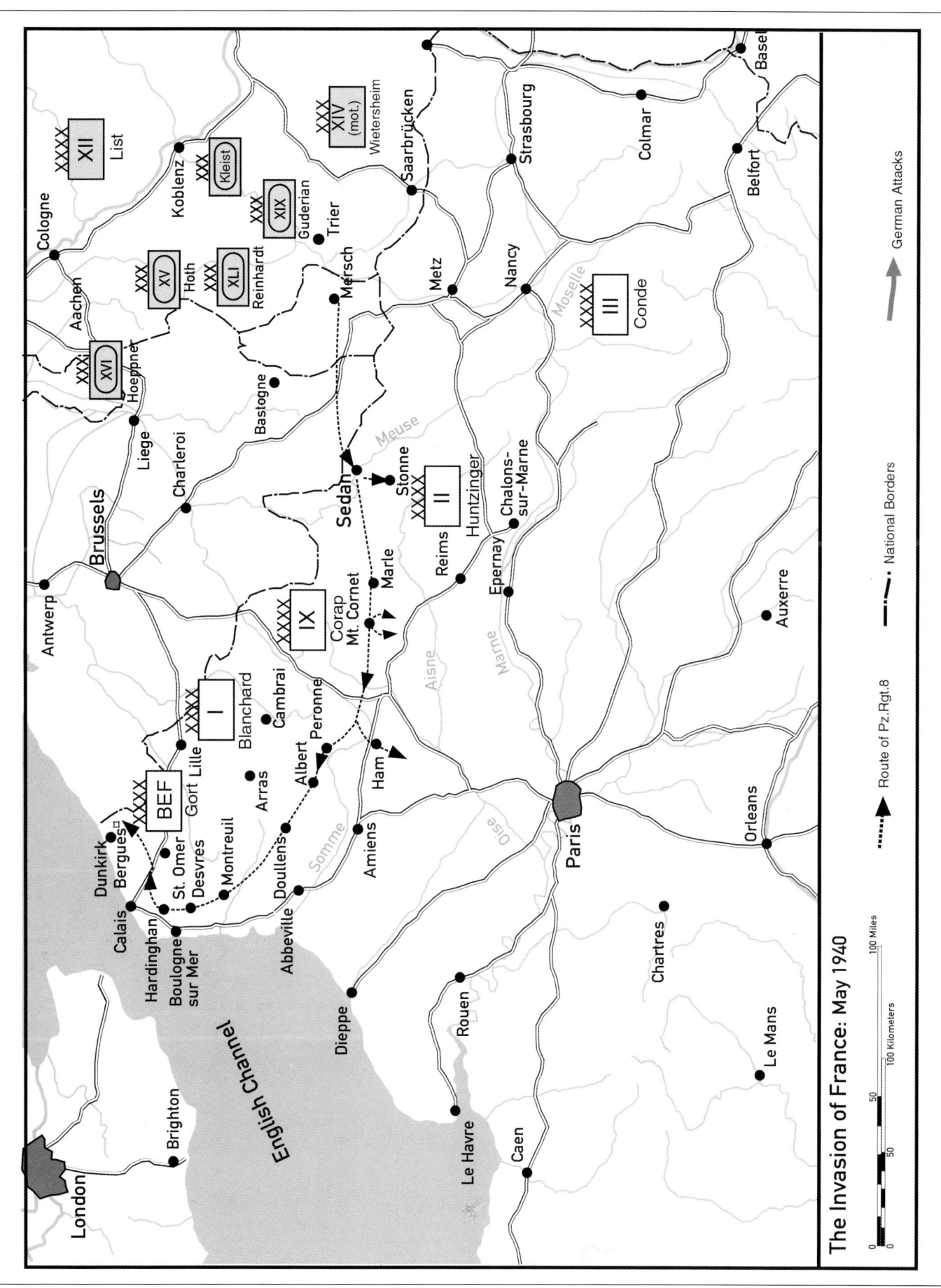

The Invasion of France: May 1940

in addition to requiring the Allied Armies to man a much longer and more vulnerable line, and in which there were a number of exposed areas that could be easily exploited.[3] That initial plan was met by strong opposition, as it was felt that Gamelin was playing directly into German hands, and so another variant was called for. This new plan, known as the "*Breda Plan*," called for some thirty-two French divisions of the French *First Army Group* to wheel into Belgium and the Netherlands at the beginning of any German hostilities. In addition to meeting the Germans and holding them there, the Allies felt that this plan also protected northern France, where much of France's industrial power was located. As winter of 1939/40 turned into spring, the Allies began to make a number of adjustments to the overall troop disposition, namely the shifting of the French *Seventh Army* north to Holland on the Allied left flank. One may view that this shift in forces was done in response to a number of signs picked up by Allied intelligence sources, but it was not; it was done purely on Allied initiative. In fact, a number of clear signs and signals were given, some by the German diplomatic corps, of which a number viewed Hitler's plans to start a war with France and England as madness.

In reality, the Allies were to be caught off guard with a host of defensive tasks left incomplete, a product of the many months of the *Phony War*, as many were to title it. Opposing the German Army were over 156 French, British, Belgian, and Dutch divisions that were under the command of the French Supreme Commander, *General* Gamelin, and were arrayed from the channel coast on the northern flank to the Swiss border on the southern flank. The French and British were grouped into three army groups: the *First Army Group* (Billotte) with the *Seventh Army* (Giraud), seven divisions, and 174 tanks; the *British Expeditionary Force*, or B.E.F. (Gort), with nine divisions; the *First Army* (Blanchard) with 10 divisions; the *Ninth Army* (Corap) with cavalry and three corps; and the *Second Army* (Huntziger), also with cavalry and two corps. The *Second Army Group* (Pretelat) had the *Third Army* (Conde), *Fourth Army* (Requin), and *Fifth Army* (Bourret) with thirty-five divisions, and in the south was the *Third Army Group* (Besson) with the *Eighth Army* (Garchery) with eight divisions. In addition to these formations, there were ten Dutch and twenty Belgian divisions and eighteen reserve divisions, including three armored divisions each of 150 tanks.[4] Unknown to the Allies at this time, a number of key mistakes and judgments had just been implemented that were to spell disaster for them, namely the movement of the French *Seventh Army* north and the belief that the Ardennes Forest and *Maginot Line* could prevent the Germans from pushing west.

The *Battle of France* and *Case Yellow* began on the evening 9/10 May 1940, when *Armeegruppe A* moved into Luxembourg; that same evening *Armeegruppe B* launched its diversionary attacks into the Netherlands and Belgium. In the early morning hours of the 10th, *Fallschirmjägers* from the *7th Flieger* and *22nd Luftlande Divisions* began airborne operations ahead of *Armeegruppe B*'s advance near The Hague, Rotterdam, Fort Eben-Emael, and a number of bridges on the German, Dutch, and Belgian border area. It seemed to many that the Allied forces were being attacked everywhere, both on the ground and in the air, as airfields, lines of communications, and troop concentrations were subjected to air and ground attack. None of those attacks came off as well as the one launched against *Fort Eben-Emael* when a small group of *Fallschirmjäger Pioneers* landed atop the fortress by small gliders and within hours had secured the previously thought impregnable fort. By the evening of the 10th, many of the Dutch and Belgian army and air force units were in total disarray and close to being put to the route, despite a handful of delaying actions that were costing the Germans dearly. The French high command reacted immediately and took the bait, as the *First Army Group* was sent north in accordance with the *Dyle Plan*. As those units were committed and sped northward, the Allies were losing any chance of halting a German push in the south. By that evening large areas of Holland, Belgium, and Luxembourg had been overrun, the governments of Holland and Belgium were desperately pleading for assistance, and the English parliament was in turmoil, as the major parties would not agree to follow *Prime Minister* Neville Chamberlain, who was soon forced to resign and give way to Winston Churchill. During this time in the higher headquarters of the divisions, corps, and *panzergruppe*, there was the conflict of the varying differences in opinions and tactics on how and where the powerful panzer elements would and should be employed as the advance reached France.

The goal of the German attack was the English Channel, and the *10th Panzer Division* had the vital mission of covering the *XIX Korps'* southern flank and that of the entire *Armeegruppe A*, protecting it from any French attacks. For its mission, the division was given an additional infantry regiment, the *Grossdeutschland*, which at that time was able to supply two additional infantry battalions, thereby making the *10th Panzer* the most potent division in the corps. As the offensive began rolling westward, and in accordance to orders, the *8th Panzer Regiment* jumped off on 10 May at 1000hrs and quickly crossed into Luxembourg just south of Bitburg, at the town of Echternach. Through the maze of roads and traffic congestion, the Regiment proceeded west in the direction of Redingen - Reuland-Mersch-Säul to the area Habay-La-Neuve and Etalle. So great was this undertaking that it has been said that the roads and towns on the German side of the border were full of formations that stretched as far back as the city of Frankfurt. As the division's motorcyclists and armored scout cars of the *kradmelder* and *aufklärungs* elements moved forward to screen the division advance, the infantry and panzers broke into two march columns and followed them. The right hand column, which entered Belgium near Attert, consisted mainly of the *86th Schützen Regiment* and the infantry from *Grossdeutschland* with an attached panzer company. The left hand column, which consisted of the *69th Schützen Regiment* and *4th Panzer Brigade*, moved through the area between Arlon and Florenville. Since the march routes had been preceded by the division's infantry and *1st* and *2nd Panzer Divisions*, there was little in the way of engagements that first day for the panzers. Lt Kurt Liestmann wrote in his diary:

"*Friday 10.5.40. Night march to Mosel, the good-bye in Brauneberg was short. Our troops should have crossed the border since the evening of 9 May. Now we are 15km before it. The radio reports we get from the locals of the villages, through which we drive. Brauneberg, Bernkastel, Osann, Ehrang, Kordel, Ralingen, Rosport, Echternach, Consdorf, Scheidchen, Mersch, Saeul. We march into the Belgium, the Netherlands and Luxembourg. Which direction will be next? One speaks about Arlon or Sedan. At 1135hrs we cross the Luxembourg border, shortly afterwards there is a heavy roadblock. The weather is fantastic and Luxembourg is beautiful. The population is indifferent or friendly. We were surprised with the speed. Saeul is reached by 1620hrs and we are protected strongly by Flak, after this we reach the assembly area. Busy aircraft activity. The Flak, which protects our area, has been attacked many times but with no success. Exactly at the time when we were waiting on the road, it shoots down one French plane. Two men jumped out with parachutes. In just a half hour it [the march] will go on, the sprint to the Maas [Meuse]. Will we reach it ahead of French? Infantry Regiment Gross Deutschland is within 6km and has won in combat against a bunker. We get fuel. The [first] panzer which will reach the other side of Maas will be introduced to Führer.*"[5]

As the Regiment moved forward all that was encountered were a roadblock or two, and those roadblocks presented little problem, and were either cleared away or simply by-passed. The same cannot be said about the infantry, which was still meeting strong resistance as it pushed towards

Chapter 3: The French Campaign, May-July 1940

the Meuse accompanied by only a few panzers. The Regiment established its panzer workshop at Habay prior to continuing the march into Belgium. On the night of 10/11 May, the Regiment crossed the Belgian border north of Arlon and headed west towards Etalle as the majority of the division's infantry began to swing north towards Neufchâteau. The Regiment then received orders to halt its advance and be prepared to deploy against possible French attacks from the south. The Regiment remained in place until it received new orders to move. At 1900hrs the division's advance was continued, and it was able to report its progress to the Semois River with the advanced elements at Cugnon-Mortehan, Thibesart-Leglise, and Assenois. Opposing the *XIX Korps* advance was the French *X Corps* (Grandsard), consisting of the *55th* (Lafontaine) and *71st* (Baudet) *Infantry Divisions* and the *3rd North African Division*, whose formations laid numerous mines and demolished bridges in an attempt to slow the German advance. Many of the demolished bridges had to be detoured around; however, some of the partially destroyed ones were able to be used. The progress was slow but steady, with the infantry now hours ahead of the panzers, which had been forced to negotiate the difficult terrain and road networks. Liestmann noted in his diary:

"*Sunday 11.5.40. I met on the road soldiers from Poland in the scout vehicle. One was with me in a Polish hospital for six days. We both were very happy. About 1900hrs we go on further through Alier, Leglise, south of Neufchateau. There a night rest at Assenois. It is cold. From one castle comes a little bit of provisioning. At Etalle there is minor combat with the French, who retreat. Now 2km north Herbeumont, in the primary direction of Bouillon to the Belgian-French border. In the evening comes the message that Lüttich [Liege] has fallen with all their forts. The 2nd Motorized Division of the French is destroyed by the Luftwaffe. What is with Sedan? In the evening the march goes in the direction of Bouillon. In the night we came under fire from French scouts.*"[6]

On the morning of the 12th, the "*Pfingstsonntag*" (Palm Sunday), the head of the *10th Panzer Division*, captured a segment of Semois between Cugnon and Herbemont as the Regiment closely followed through the forests of Herbemont and Bouillon. During the march the column was repeatedly attacked by French fighter aircraft, but luckily suffered no losses in these attacks, and by that evening the division had reached the Meuse just south of Sedan. The terrain of southern Belgium and Luxembourg was quite difficult for motorized formations with its steep inclines and declines, narrow roads, and steep curves, which no doubt caused numerous problems for the panzers and resulted in the first casualties, as one Mk II was lost when it skidded off the road and overturned, injuring the entire crew. By the end of the day all the French units withdrew west behind the Meuse. At 0700hrs on the 13th, German infantry began to cross the Meuse in rubber boats and quickly gained a number of small footholds. The infantry of *I./Schützen Regiment 86* crossed near Pont du Bouillonais, while the *II./Schützen Regiment 69* crossed near Wadelincourt. In this second crossing the infantry encountered stiff resistance near the town of Noyers and the cemetery there. These footholds would soon turn into tiny bridgeheads from which the panzers could surge forward. The crossings were supported by Do-17 bombers, which had begun to prepare the area for the assault by the division. Following the bombers, the divisional artillery, although without the use of the guns of the heavy battalion, began its bombardment which, over the next few hours, caused much of the French artillery fire to slacken. As the Germans built up their bridgeheads the French attempted to contain the build up until sufficient forces could be brought to bear and destroy the Germans on the banks of the Meuse. The *X Corps* had the French *4th* and *7th Tank Battalions* and *205th* and *213th Infantry Regiments* in reserve, and these formations were placed at Lafontaine's disposal for the attack. Lafontaine ordered a two-pronged attack on the German bridgehead to commence at 0400hrs on the 14th.[7] Liestmann noted:

"*Monday 13.5.40. Above us bombers; echelon after echelon [head] in the direction of Sedan. The Luftwaffe controls the air. The march goes through St. Medard, Cugnon and in the forests of Boullon. At the castle Amervix there is a groomed park, beautiful clean buildings. We spend two hours fuelling and getting provisioning, above us continuously flying bombers. All of a sudden there are four bombs dropped precisely in the proximity of our company. Two comrades are heavily wounded by fragments. These were our own bombers.*"[8]

As for the Regiment, it was still in Belgium near Bouillon and Amerois where for the first time it came under attack by French fighters and bombers, causing the *I./Abteilung* to suffer its first losses. In the meantime, the main body of the division remained on the northern bank of the Meuse at Balan and Bazeilles. The French, as was to be the norm throughout the entire campaign, were slow to act and to react to the quickly changing situation the German Blitzkrieg presented them. Their command and control lacked the mobility, communications, and presence of mind to control this new fast paced battle. The attack was delayed by some three hours as the *4th Tank Battalion*, hearing that the panzers had already passed them by, decided to halt for the evening; the *205th Infantry* was halted by a courier, the *7th Tank Battalion* reported they never received word of the attack; and finally, the commander of the *213th* would not risk bringing his men forward in the face of all the refugees flooding back.[9] In the end, the *7th Tank Battalion* and *213th Infantry* had to undertake the entire attack plan by dividing into two battle groups, where they were soon thwarted by the German panzers, which, due to the French delay, had already crossed the Meuse to support the infantry. Soon elements of *1st Panzer* attacked those French elements near Connage and Bulson, and were able to destroy half of the French tanks and maul the supporting infantry.[10] It was at this time that fears of French counterattacks from the south against the Germans grew, so von Kleist, the commander of the *Panzergruppe*, ordered the *10th Panzer* from its original route to counter any French moves. Guderian, the corps commander, later wrote in his book *Panzer Leader*:

"*I asked for cancellation of these orders; the detachment of one third my force to meet the hypothetical threat of enemy cavalry would endanger the success of the Meuse crossing and therefore of the whole operation. In order to anticipate any difficulties, I ordered the 10th Panzer Division to move along a parallel road north of its previous line. The advance went on. The immediate danger of a halt and a change of direction were passed. The Panzer Group finally agreed to this. The cavalry did not in fact appear.*"[11]

In preparation for the attack across the Meuse, *10th Panzer* had formed two *kampfgruppen*: the first *kampfgruppe* with *Schützen Regiment 86* on the right flank would attack from the south of Sedan, and from Balan towards Wadelincourt. The second *kampfgruppe* was formed from *Schützen Regiment 69* and would attack from Bazeilles across the Meuse at Pont Maugis. The ground over which the assault would take place was void of any built up areas, and most of the infantry and assault engineers would soon find themselves having to cross between 500-1000 meters of open terrain before they could reach any substantial cover. By that evening, the division had captured the bridge at Wadelincourt. Additionally fire from nearby *Maginot Line* fortifications interdicted and harassed many of the divisional elements as they attempted to rest and replenish, and prepare themselves for the next assault. The attempt of the *Schützen Regiment 69* to cross the Meuse at Bazeilles was halted by heavy French artillery fire, which sunk most of the rubber boats. A small group of engineers from *Pioneer Battalion 49* under the command of Fw Rubarth made it across the river under heavy fire, and soon the first bunker line was taken. Rubarth and his assault engineers had opened a gap for the division by destroying some seven bunkers in an action that would win him the *Ritterkreuz*.[12] Later that night the division was able to push small forces forward in order to expand the bridgeheads, but the French were still holding firm.

On 14 May, the Regiment crossed the French border near la Chapelle and quickly sped southwest towards Sedan, arriving there by mid-day. The bridge across the Meuse at Wadelincourt had been completed by German pioneers earlier that morning at 0545hrs, but was reported as being closed due to technical problems; this may have been caused by the numerous Allied air attacks that morning which were aimed at striking the German forces and preventing them from getting across the river. After pushing through the Ardennes the terrain now began to open into flat rolling hills, which continued until the Meuse. Upon arrival near Sedan the Regiment received the order that it was to attack just south of Sedan in the direction of Bulson together with its sister regiment, the *7th Panzer*, with the aim of securing the high ground and flank there. However, this attack was to be slow in coming, as the panzers encountered problems moving across the bridge. The Regiment was the first to cross, but it would not be until early morning on the 15th that the *7th Panzer Regiment* was finally able to get its panzers across. As the infantry from *II./Schützen Regiment 69* and *I./Schützen Regiment 86* encountered tough fighting as they attempted to secure the high ground overlooking the Meuse, they were soon supported by a panzer company from the Regiment. After securing this high ground the infantry battalions then attacked south towards the objectives located east of Bulson around the Beau Ménil farm at Hill 257, which stood three kilometers south of Noyers and two kilometers northeast of Bulson. Later in the afternoon of the 14th, the *10th Panzer Division's* formations were able to secure these positions as well. After the town of Chémery was taken Guderian had gambled and decided to turn his *1st* and *2nd Panzer Divisions* to the west and north, leaving his flank wide open with just the *10th Panzer* and *Grossdeutschland* Infantry Regiment to secure the bridgehead at Sedan until Wietersheim's *XIV Motorized Korps* could move up the *29th Infantry Division (Motorized)* and reinforce *10th Panzer*. During the crossing of the Meuse there were continued attacks by French aircraft, which again and again attempted to destroy the bridge over the Meuse and slow the Germans. Even though the attacks caused minor casualties, they were not successful in destroying the crossing site and halting the attack. These attacks represented one of the few concerted attempts by the French air force to support ground formations. All through the afternoon the leading elements of the Regiment were able to move forward and reach positions as far south as Hill 320, which lay just southeast of Bulson. By this time, *General* Schaal was himself able to move forward and quickly order those leading elements to attack towards the southeast of Maisoncelle. No orders had yet arrived from the corps concerning any movements to the west or south towards Stonne. By that afternoon the Regiment, with its I./*Abteilung*, stood on a north-south axis from Maisoncelle-Chaumont-Bulson. During this drive the Regiment encountered its first ground resistance by the remaining elements of the French *55th* and *71st Divisions*. There were numerous French tanks knocked out, and great quantities of weapons and materiel were taken, as well as hundreds of prisoners. In the 2nd Company Lt Hess, *Fw* Rathsack, and *Uffz* Rummler alone brought in more than two hundred French prisoners.[13] Kurt Liestmann again recorded in his diary:

"Tuesday 14.5.40. In the morning it goes further on to Chapolle through Givoene to Sedan. In Sedan a lot is going on. English and French bombers continuously attack the bridge over the Maas, a pontoon and are being shot in lines by our brave 2cm Flak. They fall down in flames and explode. At one time, shortly before opens two parachutes. We cross over the Maas Bridge, under the strong protection of Flak. Behind Sedan over Wadelincourt through the heavily fortified Maas position. Wadelincourt is a ruin, no stone on top of the other, done by Stuka and artillery. From Wadelincourt is the attack on the yards in the direction Chaumont, Bulson. From Bois de Haye we rush 40 French. We make them signs to return and to wave the white cloths. I converse with them shortly. There are some good soldiers. But they are finished mentally. We break through until La Blanche Maison southwest of Bulson. That night we rest in the woods. In Villers we are again attacked by light bombers of the French. One bomb sailed behind my vehicle. Air pressure and nothing else. Both were shot down afterwards. Our looks are like they were in Poland; dirty, burned, with beards! In the afternoon I chat with one Irishman, who was shot. A likeable guy, he jumped out alone. A dog-cold night."[14]

During the night of the 14th, orders were finally issued by *XIX Korps* for the capture of Stonne by the *10th Panzer*. In those orders it stated that the attack should strike southeast towards La Besace, which was located some 6km south of Maisoncelle, and then attack southwest towards Stonne. It is believed that the order to move south towards Stonne instead of west came about because both the *2nd* and *10th Panzer Divisions* had failed to get enough of their panzer forces across the Meuse in time to support a further drive west. For the advance south, the *10th Panzer Division* had once again assigned to it the *Grossdeutschland Infantry Regiment*. The "*Grossdeutschland*," or "Greater Germany" Regiment was a separate infantry regiment commanded by *Oberst* Graf von Schwerin. The regiment had been stationed in Berlin as the "*Wacht*" (guard) regiment, and its duties included escort and palace guard and, like many of those honor or bodyguard "*Corps d Elite*" formations, were seeing combat for the first time.[15] It would not take long before these small elite formations of the *Heer* and *Waffen SS* would soon prove themselves in combat and grow in size and gain much notoriety and prominence in the campaigns and battles to come. Since the night of the 14/15th, *General* Schaal had been attempting to contact that regiment in order to obtain a better picture of the situation and the unit's location, since it was last known to be fighting somewhere south of Maisoncelle. All attempts to contact the regiment failed, and so Schaal ordered the *4th Panzer Brigade* to move forward that night with only a small element towards La Besece and Stonne.

The Battle for Stonne

The town of Stonne stands just 15km south of Sedan; the town itself sits atop the heights of Mont Dieu and was locally know as "*Pain de Sucre*," and was surrounded by the forests of the Bois de Mont Dieu. The terrain and surrounding hills rose from the Meuse River to a height of 326m at Mt Damion, which was, located some 10km to the southeast of the town. The area around Stonne had numerous forests, villages, and farms that were connected by many streets and paths; in fact, some seven well paved and all weather roads were located near the town which could facilitate any counter-attacks launched by motorized forces. The terrain also offered the defender numerous positions that could provide good cover and concealment, as well as observation and, for the French, the ability to call in fires from their gun emplacements on the *Maginot Line*, which lay only some 12-14km away from the town and could cover the area with their heavy artillery. The town and its heights were critical for covering the

Chapter 3: The French Campaign, May-July 1940

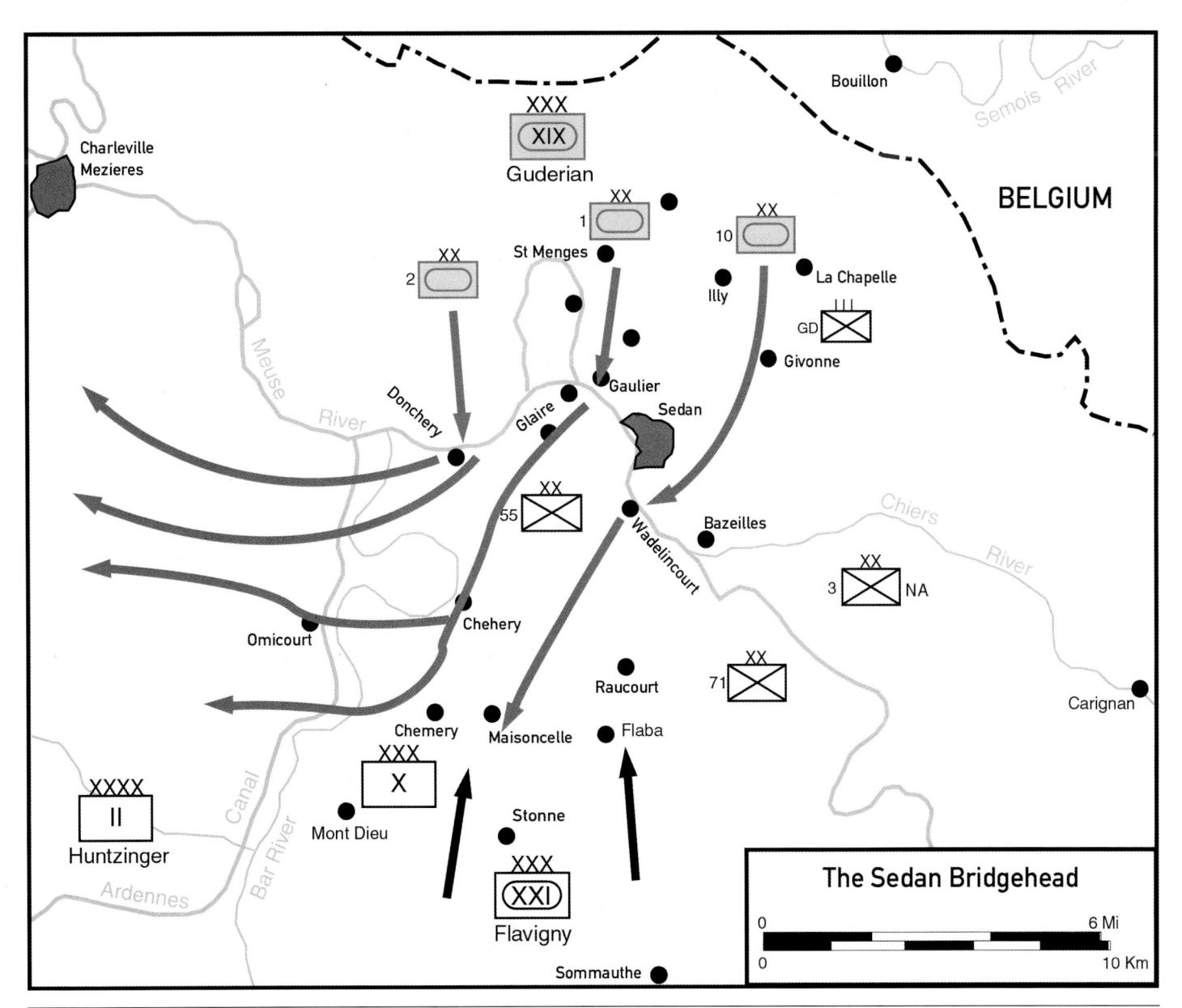

left flank of the *XIX Korps* and that of the entire *Armeegruppe A*. It was here that the German advance could be halted, and from where French counter-attacks could eventually be launched into the flank of the German columns, and was therefore seen as important to both the German and the French armies. On the 14th, there were only scattered French forces in the area and the Germans were still to the north of the town. The night of the 14/15th, the II./*Abteilung* was tasked with supporting the drive towards the south. Also that same day the French *XXI Corps* (Flavigny) ordered the *3rd Division de Cuirassier de Reserve*, or *DCR* (Brocard), and *3rd Motorized Infantry Division*, or *DIM* (Bertin-Boussu), which was located near Reims, to move forward towards Sedan. At that time the *3rd DCR* consisted of two battalions of *H-39s* and one battalion of *Char-B* tanks.[16] The French tanks of the time outclassed most of the German panzer in firepower and armor protection; the *Hotchkiss H-39* mounted a 37mm gun and 40mm of armor, and the *Char-B1* heavy tank was armed with a 75mm gun mounted forward in the hull and a 47mm mounted in a revolving turret with an armor thickness of some 60mm.[17] As the *3rd DCR* and *DIM* were moving forward during the night of the 14/15th, the *10th Panzer* had also moved up, and had begun turning west after getting through the Meuse at Wadelincourt. The *1st* and *2nd Panzer Divisions* had already swung westwards, and since the *Grossdeutschland* was already fighting in the area and the *10th Panzer* had been slowed in crossing the Meuse, it was logical that they were the only formations capable of covering the southern flank of the *XIX Korps* until the *XIV Korps* could move forward. At approximately 0400hrs, written orders arrived at the *Stabs* of the *10th Panzer Division* which outlined the mission and forces assigned to the task of taking Stonne. For the attack the division had assigned to it, in addition to the *Grossdeutschland*, the *I./Artillery Regiment 37* and *Aufklärungs Abteilung 4*, the mission was to seize the line running from the Ardennes Canal in the west across the heights of Mont Dieu and Stonne to a bend in the Meuse south of Villemontry. Upon completion of that mission the division was to defend that line and protect the bridgehead at Sedan and the flank of *XIX Korps*. Luckily, later that morning contact was made with the *Grossdeutschland*, and it was ordered to attack and secure the heights around the town. While the *Grossdeutschland* executed its mission the division was to launch two additional attacks: the first was a continuation of the attack that had begun the night before by the II./*Abteilung* through La Besece towards Stonne. The second was by the remainder of the *4th Panzer Brigade* with attached infantry, pioneers, and Flak and Pak companies. This attack had the aim of securing the heights that lay just southeast of the village of Yoncq. The battle that would rage around Stonne from 15-17 May 1940 is often referred to as the "Verdun of the Second World War." The actions that would take place here would see the small town change hands on numerous occasions, as the town was taken, lost, and recaptured a number of times. It is almost impossible to accurately describe the events that took place there, but through a number of different reports, photos, and eyewitness accounts it is possible to at least gain an understanding of the costly actions that were fought there. In the early morning hours of the 15th, the Regiment was preparing for the day's attacks: the I./Abteilung was positioned northeast of Flaba, moving south in preparation for the attack around Yoncq, while the II./Abteilung was located near Raucourt-et-Flaba, where it was locked in a difficult fight with French forces. While it neared Flaba, the II./Abteilung suffered casualties as heavy artillery fire mortally wounded the leader of the Kradmelder Zug, Olt Uhlenhaut. Another round hit just under the Mk II of Olt Wolf Schefold, the Abteilung Adjutant, and ripped the hull and turret off his panzer, but amazingly did not injure any of the crew, since they had not yet boarded the panzer.[18] Liestmann noted:

"Wednesday 15.5.40 during the first part of the day comes the message that the withdrawing French Division will be deployed for a counter-attack. We are ready. The French artillery shoots the harassing fire in our proximity. French fighters hunt one of our scouts and attack us as well. We move ahead, direction La Besace. There is almost no fuel and thirst as well. But it goes on, the French artillery doesn't stop shooting. The German artillery replies. Near us is a march road. A light French bomber hunts at a low altitude flight near us. Will he notice us? Heinz [the brother of Kurt] has passed his first attack as well, during which he had losses of vehicles caused by anti-tank guns. Also some wounded. Finally comes the panzer vehicle. In the area around Sedan and around us there were many captured PoWs. Now we are bothered many times by the French artillery. They shoot very precisely. Olt Uhlenhaut and two Uffz fell. A very great pity. One round hit my crupper. One man is heavily wounded."[19]

Early on the morning of the 15th, the German attack commenced against the heights around Stonne and Mt. Damion as the Grossdeutschland infantry succeeded in capturing the town and throwing out a small French reconnaissance group and a battalion of the 67th Infantry Regiment, both formations belonging to the 3rd DIM. As the infantry was making its assault the II./Abteilung was moving up to support them, advancing via La Besace and reaching Stonne at around 0700hrs. During its preparations and initial assault, the Regiment again received heavy artillery fire from the heights south of Stonne and from the Maginot Line fortifications. According to the records of the 3rd DIM artillery there is the report of Fw Karl Koch, a panzer commander in the 7th Company, who wrote this account on how the attack took place:

"Five Mk IVs and five Mk IIs are moving towards Stonne; suddenly three Mk IVs are knocked out by an ambushed French 25mm anti-tank gun. In my panzer IV the driver is hit but manages nonetheless to move the panzer a little bit more. The crew bails out except the driver which is heavily wounded and the radio operator who is still in shock. As we abandon the panzer, the crew comes under French infantry fire. I am able to see the French anti-tank gun very close to the three German panzers and one of them is burning. Behind those three destroyed panzers the two remaining Mk IVs and five Mk IIs are waiting."[20]

Looking at photos taken after the battle, it can be assumed that one of those panzers was number 711 from the 7th Company, which sustained damage and hits from a 25mm anti-tank gun. After firing off their rounds the crew from the anti-tank gun quickly ceased fire and relocated to another position. While they did so Koch, with his gunner and loader, returned to their panzer with the intent of using it as a pillbox. The driver was retrieved and brought to the rear, but the radio operator was found dead in the panzer with a bullet in his head. As Koch and his crew waited in the turret ready to engage any French tanks, the five lightly armored Mk IIs retreated out of town. Thankfully Koch was not alone, as the town was then occupied by the Grossdeutschland's I./Battalion, with its 14th Panzerjäger Company, equipped with nine 37mm Pak guns and the 1st and 2nd Companies from Pioneer Battalion 43. The II./Battalion of Grossdeutschland was positioned to the northeast, and the III./Battalion was to the northwest, facing the French 2nd Battalion, 67th Infantry Regiment. Fortunately for those German troops defending Stonne, three of the Pak guns had just been re-positioned to cover the southwestern exit of Stonne, and this is where the French launched their counter-attack. At around 0600hrs, the first tank element from the 3rd DCR, a company of Char-B tanks,[21] had reached the area near Stonne after conducting a 30km road march. Upon reaching the town, the commander was ordered to attack the town at 1100hrs in conjunction with units from the 3rd DIM. However, there was a delay in executing this attack because the division commander wanted to take the time to refuel and rest his tank crews, since they had been up all night. Additionally, he was waiting for the rest of the 3rd DIM to come up and support the attack, which he then planned to launch at around 1600hrs. By taking his time and issuing his orders, which could not be construed as either defensive or offensive in nature, he was able to achieve his desired pause. What is even more concerning was that later that morning he interpreted his orders as defensive in nature, and ordered that the tanks be organized into forming roadblocks, and thus scattered them to all the road junctions within a twelve mile radius. These "corks" were to consist of at least one Char-B and two H-39 tanks. As the French commander continued to stall and waste precious time, there is evidence that at least some of his tanks attempted to take the town as described in the account given by Fw Karl Koch. Koch and his remaining two crewmembers were now waiting for the expected French tanks to appear out of the town. The first French tank did so and was immediately knocked out after receiving just two rounds. Ten minutes later a second tank arrived beside the first one and some time later a third one. All of them were either immobilized or destroyed by the 75mm gun of Koch's immobilized Mk IV.[22] These French tanks were most probably Hotchkiss H-39s from the 45th Tank Battalion. There are also accounts that these tanks were being supported by some French infantry, most probably from the 51st Infantry Regiment. Unfortunately, these forces were forced to pull back in the face of such heavy fire from the German panzers and Grossdeutschland infantry. The first round in the battle had concluded with the town changing hands at least twice by 0900hrs, and it would continue this way for the next two days. Already in the battle there had been serious losses on both sides, and unfortunately, since no clear reports of what was taking place in Stonne were being relayed to the XIX Korps, the corps in turn did not see the need to send any additional forces there to assist in taking the town. The only report that was received at corps headquarters was a short note from the 4th Panzer Brigade that informed the staff there that the town had been taken at 0700hrs. What is interesting here is that French infantry and armor forces were now arriving on the scene in some strength while the XIX Korps, which was to hand over responsibility of the Sedan bridgehead to the XIV Korps, had the forces necessary to take and hold the town, but had not been informed that additional forces were needed.

Chapter 3: The French Campaign, May-July 1940

During the midmorning hours, the *H-39s* of the *45th Tank Battalion* (Petit) and *Char-Bs* of *3rd Company, 49th Tank Battalion* (Caravea) conducted piecemeal attacks which were poorly coordinated. The heavy *Char-Bs* initiating these attacks soon found themselves alone without infantry support, and they suffered heavy losses in their attempts to take the town. There were numerous rounds exchanged between German Pak guns and French tanks which soon got the best of the encounter when they were able to destroy one of the Pak guns at about 100m range. This loss caused some panic in the ranks of the German infantry, but the *Panzerjägers* held their ground, and before long one of the Pak gunners, who had had no previous luck with their small 37mm guns, were able to identify a small area on the side of the *Char-B* which looked like an air cooling-intake and began firing at that point. This discovery soon led to the destruction of one of the *Char-Bs*, when the tank "Chinon" was hit and knocked out at close range by a 37mm Pak gun. The next tank, another *Char-B* nicknamed "Gaillac," was hit and immobilized when it was hit on its track by Koch's 75mm gun, a third *Char-B* "Hauvillers" was also rendered useless when a round succeeded in damaging the turret. Koch also claims to have knocked out between two to three light *H-39s*, but with all the rounds being fired about, it is difficult to determine who exactly can claim the destruction of these *H-39* tanks. With the loss of these tanks the French, like the Germans before them, chose to withdraw from the town. While they did so Koch and his crew gathered more ammunition from the two disabled Mk IVs. Throughout the day, the *FCMs* of the *2nd Company, 4th Tank Battalion* and infantry from *1st Company, 51st Infantry Regiment* (Martin), and *1st Battalion, 67th Infantry Regiment* fumbled in their attempts to dislodge the Germans. Finally, near midday orders were clarified, and *General* Flavigny ordered the *3rd DCR* and *3rd DIM* to attack at 1500hrs, with two *Char-B* battalions and two infantry battalions each to be supported by a company of *H-39s*. The attack would take the shape of a conventional French infantry assault, with three bounds supported by tanks. The objective of the attack was to gain three lines: the first was the line running from Chemery-Maisoncelle-Raucourt; the second bound to the high ground south of Bulson; and the third bound to Marfee-Pont Maugis. The overall command of this attack would go to General Bertin-Boussu, but unfortunately by that time *General* Brocard's tank "corks" that had been sent to establish various road blocks had been so scattered that they could not be recalled in time, thereby forcing a postponement of the attack until 1730hrs. Later in the day *10th Panzer* ordered the *I./Schützen Regiment 69* to reinforce and support the *Grossdeutschland* infantry in a counter attack which was able to re-take Stonne. Later that night, the situation saw the *10th Panzer Division* with its infantry positioned forward, while the panzers were recalled to the rear and placed in reserve. The division now had all three of the *Grossdeutschland* infantry battalions and the *I./Schützen Regiment 69* in positions southwest of the village and the southern edge of the Bois de Raucourt. The *II./Schützen Regiment 69* was east of them from the Bois de Raucourt to Bois de Yoncq, while the *II./Schützen Regiment 71* was in the woods itself. The panzers were all located to the northwest and northeast of Stonne, just south of Maisoncelle. While all this had been taking place the *4th Panzer Brigade's* attack around Yoncq was busy parrying a thrust by the *1st Colonial Division* and the *2nd Light Cavalry Division (2 DLC)* which was supported by heavy artillery. The French attack failed when it ran head long into the panzers from almost three complete panzer *abteilungs*. Unfortunately for the Germans, the panzers did not pursue the French, as the follow-on German *VII Korps* was moving up and the decision to pursue the French was left to them. That evening, the panzers pulled back towards the Bois de Raucourt, leaving the sector near Yoncq to the *II./Schützen Regiment 71*. During the day's fighting at least five Mk IVs, twelve vehicles, and six Pak guns had been knocked out. The Germans claimed the destruction of some thirty-three French tanks, but the actual figure stands at about ten.[23] For the II./ *Abteilung*, it suffered nine dead and a number wounded; those killed were: *Olt* Horst Uhlenhaut, Lt Dieter Risch, *Fw* Heimberger, *Uffz* Gross, *Uffz* Koschig, *Uffz* Michelt, *Uffz* Schwede, *Uffz* Götz, and *Ogfr* Ott. Most of these men came from the *7th* and *8th Companies*.[24] Liestmann recorded in his diary that night:

"There is an alarm in the evening. Here comes the French tank attack. We wait for them in a good position. But in vain. We attack. Nothing to see. Here comes the darkness and in the night we take up the rest position a bit to the north in the beautiful forest of the Ardennes."

The morning of the 16th saw another French attack hit Stonne; this attack was launched by twelve heavy tanks and supported by artillery, which forced the German infantry back to the northern side of town. Like the day before the battle swayed back and forth, with both sides claiming to hold the town. Reinforcements came in to help throughout the day as the lines were reestablished, and even the town of La Besace was finally taken. Even though the French attack that was launched that morning was considerably better organized and supported, there had been no time in which to conduct a proper reconnaissance of the area, and the actual intelligence of the situation was very limited, in that even the French were unaware of who had control of the town. The attack involved the *Char-Bs* from the *1st* and *3rd Companies* of the *41st Tank Battalion*, the *3rd Battalion*, the *51st Infantry Regiment*, and the *H-39s* from the *45th Tank Battalion*. The plan of attack called for a heavy shelling of the area by the French artillery for 45 minutes, followed by the heavy *Char-Bs*, which were to open a breech for the infantry, which was to be directly supported by the *H-39s*. At 0430hrs the artillery began its bombardment of the town from the *"Pain de Sucre"* hill to the southern edges of the Grande Côte woods. At 0515hrs, the *3rd Company* of the *41st Tank Battalion*, lead by *Major* Malaguti, the battalion commander, began moving up on the western side of the town in an inverted "V" formation. This force drove in towards the center of town, where within minutes it encountered German infantry that was being supported by two Mk IVs from the *7th Company* undamaged from the previous day's fighting and a number of Pak guns. In the fighting that followed two panzers were quickly destroyed in intense combat. The company also succeeded in destroying the town's water tower, which had been occupied by German forces. To the left flank of the *3rd Company*, the *1st Company* under the command of *Captain* Billotte in the *Char-B* "Eure" moved north, but quickly became hampered by rough terrain that forced it to veer east, where it reached the northern edge of town. Upon reaching the town Billotte began to swing down through some houses, and as he did so came face to face with a column of German panzers.[25] This column was composed of thirteen panzers from the *7th Company* under the command of *Hptm* Ottens, and which was attempting to get through the town. The panzers had been driving up the slope past the Pain du Sucre hill when they began to receive fire. The first panzer was within about 100m of Billotte who, without hesitation, ordered his 75mm hull gunner to engage the last panzer in the column while he took aim with the 47mm turret cannon and targeted the first panzer in the column. Within seconds these panzers were immobilized and blocked any route of escape of the other eleven panzers, which could not maneuver out of the column. Billotte was then able to drive down the same road that the panzers were using, force his way through the German fire, and move through the town. Billotte's tank was able to move all the way down to the *Pain de Sucre* and along the way knock out an additional two 37mm Pak guns before turning around and making his way back to French lines. After successfully reaching his lines he and the crew were able to inspect the tank, which they discovered had taken over one hundred hits from

41

20 and 37mm guns. Billotte could also claim the destruction of seven panzers and two 37mm Pak guns. The attack was not, however, totally successful, as the German infantry and Pak gunners were still able to retain possession of a small portion of the northern half of the town and knock out a number of *Char-Bs* and *H-39s*. By this time the *10th Panzer Division* had ordered all its remaining infantry forward in order to defend Stonne, while the *I./Abteilung's* panzers were ordered off to meet a French tank thrust coming from the direction of Raucourt. In that encounter the French lost thirteen tanks for the loss of only one German panzer. At around 1000hrs, the town was heavily bombed by German dive bombers, which kept up the pressure on the French forces until German artillery could be brought to bear at around midday. By 1500hrs, the remaining French tanks were ordered back in order to be better utilized in other parts of town. By late afternoon, French infantry was forced back to the edge of town in the face of the heavy German artillery fire. The French were able to gain some small successes as more reinforcements arrived from the east of town. In another attempt to retake the remainder of the town, another assault was scheduled to commence at around 1700hrs, but only one battalion of *Char-Bs* and a few *H-39s* could be assembled for the attack.[26] Then, before they could be informed of the cancellation of the attack, the *Char-B* "*Riquewihr*" under the command of Lt Doumecq attacked toward Stonne, where he again encountered German infantry attempting to halt his advance with nothing more than a few infantry weapons. Doumecq's tank rolled forward, crushing both weapons and men beneath its tracks; it was said that once the Germans saw these bloody tracks they fled in panic. Nothing successful could be achieved in this feeble attempt, and about an hour later, at 1745hrs, the town was retaken by the Germans, but they found no time to rest, as another attack was launched on the village of Chémery, just to the northwest; fortunately for the Germans this attack was halted by *General* Flavigny after no gains could successfully be achieved. The remaining tank battalions of *3rd DCR* never moved from their positions, and *General* Flavigny later relieved General Brocard of command, replacing him with *General* Bertin-Boussu. By the end of the afternoon, the infantry of the German *XIV Korps* had begun to move up in some strength so that they could assume responsibility of the sector. A portion of the town was again secured that evening around 1800hrs by the *I./Schützen Regiment 69*. The town, however, remained neither in French nor German hands, as during the night both sides withdrew from the town proper and into the surrounding areas to lick their wounds and reorganize their forces, and were content to trade artillery fire with each other. Later that night the troops of the *XIX Korps* were withdrawn and relieved by the *16th Infantry Division*.

Those troops were ordered to move back and assembled near the town of Bulson, where after a day of rest they pushed to the west and joined up with the advance of the *1st* and *2nd Panzer Divisions*. The following day saw further action, as both sides attempted to wrest the town from one another, but without the use of tanks and in the face of fresh infantry forces the town was finally called secure by German forces that evening. Over the next few days the French in this sector continued to commit their armor in piecemeal and costly actions, which slowly wore down the number of operational tanks remaining. The Regiment suffered a number of dead and wounded; unfortunately, we only have the name of *Gefr* Peter Hartschen, who was killed near Stonne on the 16th. During a visit later in November, Kurt Liestmann recorded his thoughts following a short visit to the battlefield:

"*Sunday, 17.11.40. In the afternoon [I went] with a chief and Olt Kertscher to our combat places [battlefields] at Sedan and Stonne. On the road to Maisoncelles we see again the old Renaults, which still are there. Next to combat vehicles are the simple graves of French tank soldiers, most buried as unknown, because the vehicles had burned down. Old memories wake up: here the French bombers tried to get us, here crashed the burning English machines, etc. The heights of Stonne are ahead of us under black clouds. The mood of the day is filled with thoughts of the dead, who found their graves on these heights. We drive upwards. On the road and farm paths, on the banks and [tank] hatches stand the crosses with steel helmets. German soldiers next to the French. French tank soldiers next to our panzer gunners, whose black protective hats hang on the crosses. Shortly before Stonne is a combat vehicle of the 7th Company, ripped by an explosion of its own ammunition, the turret thrown 10 meters away. On the slope under the light wood cross are buried the crew who met their death together. Here was the tragedy, which happens frequently, and is not perceived as such by the soldiers anymore. They fought facing the French tank defense and light artillery cannons and French combat vehicles, who they were shooting at the gardens beforehand, and they fell. We stand in the rain, which drops from their cross, trickles over the faded protective hats and we may think but nobody speaks aloud: "here should be someone of the 'service crossed', ... who won the war only through their personality, who now, after the battle is over raise their nose and speak about the front, which they never saw up close and drove by when they were certain that the main action was over. And if such a person would not take off his hat in front of each of these graves, he should be slapped in the face in front of this silent heroism." I believe our brave dead would turn satisfied in their ground-sheets and sleep quietly. Behind the village lay the last ones, who had advanced further than the others. Their vehicles are torn as well. Further behind in webbing lays Dietrich Risch alone, quiet and contented as if he was alive, near to his panzer. His crew was not found, only the Leutnant. Now by the graves of the jäger regiment, Grossdeutschland. We come to the grave of Olt Horst Uhlenhaut in the German soldier cemetery, when the dusk colors everything more gray, unrealistic and solemn to appear. Near him lay one Unteroffizer and one Gefreiter, who were shot by French artillery. On the grave is a faded flag and welke laurel-wreath. In the darkness we drive through destroyed villages where no one lives, along the over flooded Maas to Sedan. It's quiet in the vehicle. Everybody sticks to their own thoughts. It's too dark to visit the grave of our panzer keeper Götz, who lays at the war memorial. Through Rethel and Reims we drive back to the camp.*"[27]

West towards Calais
By the evening of 15 May, the Dutch had capitulated, and French President Paul Reynaud had spoken with Churchill, informing him that to date the counterattacks had failed, and that the road to Paris was wide open. On the 16th, the units of *4th Panzer Brigade* were allowed to pull back to the area of Maisoncelle-Raucourt-Flaba, where they were able to reorganize, rest, and refit, and pull the necessary mechanical repairs on the panzers. The dead were buried as best they could—a simple hole in the ground with a simple cross and garland of flowers or a steel helmet. For many of the wounded they were able to receive better care once off the line, and for those with serious wounds evacuation back across the border to Germany. On this day the *4th DCR* had its first brush with the lead elements of the *XIX Korps*. The *4th DCR* had been in the process of being formed in Laon under the command of Charles de Gaulle. The *4th DCR* had at time two battalions of *R-35s*, one battalion of *Char Bs*, one company of Renault D-2s, and one infantry battalion.[28] At present the division was scheduled to take part in the *Ninth Army's* attack on the *XIX Korps'* flank, but as the situation moved faster than the French high command could keep up with, the *Ninth Army* was even now hard pressed to hold its present positions. Typically, the division was not notified of the cancellation and moved off with the town of Montcornet as its objective. Montcornet, which lay some 30km north, was to be the link up point with other forces, namely the *3rd*

DCR. As the advance kicked off it found itself having to make its way through a flood of retreating soldiers and refugees, which caused a slow rate of march and broke up the organization. There were minor contacts along the way which were limited to minor engagements that did nothing more than spook and shoot up a few supply elements. In the end many of the *4th DCR* tanks were chased off by elements of *2nd Panzer Division*. However, the attack did have its effects on the overall situation, as it was to reinforce fears that the left flank was far too extended and exposed to attack. Kleist, who had cautioned Guderian over the past couple of days, was now forced to rein him in and halt his advance until enough infantry could be brought up over the next couple of days to cover the flank. Guderian, who had no love of Kleist, was furious with the order, and immediately handed in his resignation. When Rundstedt discovered what had taken place, he sided with Guderian and granted permission to continue the drive. In the meantime, the *4th DCR* had received its artillery regiment and another battalion of infantry, as well as two more squadrons of *Somua* tanks. The *4th DCR* now had an overall tank strength of some thirty *Char-Bs*, twenty-six *Somua*, fourteen *D-2s*, and eighty *R-35s*. At Crécy, the opportunity again arose to attack the German armor head on. In the battle that took place, the supporting French air cover never appeared because of another confusing time change! In the brief battle that was fought, the *4th DCR* lost many of its *R-35s* and eight of the *D-2s*, and when air support showed up, it was in the form of German *Stukas*, which appeared overhead and quickly drove off the remaining *4th DCR* elements. After this attack, the *4th DCR* would not see service again until the end of May. Kurt Liestmann recorded in his diary:

"Thursday 16.5.40. We remain in the forest. After three days finally there is water, washing-up, shaving and a little sleep. Only a few warm meals. The vehicles arrive, which were broken before. The Company relaxes. Also the nervousness and irritation after the heavy artillery fire is settled down. The quiet, but cold, night follows. The troops [German] now come en masse to Sedan over the Maas. Our task to build the important bridgehead over the Maas at Sedan is now finished and tomorrow we will catch up with the others."[29]

The advance commenced again on the 17th, when the *XIX Korps* continued pushing eastward in the direction of Péronne with the *1st* and *2nd Panzer Divisions* up front arrayed to the right and left. The *XIV Korps' 29th Infantry Division* came up to relieve elements of *10th Panzer*, which soon departed in the wake of the rest of the *XIX Korps*.[30] The *10th Panzer*, along with the *XIV Korps*, still had the responsibility of blocking any interference from the southern flank. At 0700hrs, the Regiment started off with the I./*Abteilung* up front heading to the west of St. Just, north of the Aisne, and crossing through Bulson, Cheveuges, Fraillicourt, and Renneville, in the area around Montcornet; it was a march of about 150km. The II./*Abteilung*, still smarting from the losses at Stonne, followed the route which took it through Attigny, Chaumont, Porcien, and Fraillicourt. By that evening, the French were withdrawing their forces from Belgium, and the Germans had captured Brussels and were almost to St. Quentin and Cambrai. Instead of heading to Paris, like many thought they would, the German advance was turning to the northwest in an attempt to bag the remainder of the entire Allied force still in Belgium and block their reaching the channel coast. Liestmann again noted:

"Friday 17.5.40. Around mid-day it goes further to Buson. From there further to the west over St. Aignan, Elan, Baalons to Ligny. That's the start of the day with march directions [that] no one heard before and it's an effort especially for our drivers. Their achievement is unbelievable. From 1000hrs in the morning, until the following afternoon we are on the march with just one hour interruption. We hardly eat and drink, it's only forwards. Since Belgium, hunting castle Amervis, now we are deep in the country. The columns of PoWs get longer from day to day, they walk towards us. They trot with no guards rearwards. When one would converse with them, they are nice and swear about Tommy. The road Attigny-Mezieres compares to the wild refugee road. At the resistance points are dead Poilus, burned-down Renault tank vehicles and ammunition parts of all kinds. At night we go through burned-down villages and towns. The locals went away and left everything behind. Signich is partially destroyed, partially survived. Masses of captured French."[31]

On 18 May, after passing through Montcornet the Regiment reached the town of Marle, located some 18 kilometers to the west, and engaged in fighting between units of the *4th DCR*. In the short fight that ensued Lt Hahn from the *2nd Company* was seriously wounded in the action, as Kurt Liestmann noted in his diary:

"Saturday, 18.5.40 – from Signich the main direction to Chaumnot. Protection of the left flank. Alert. French super heavy tanks are reported. They don't come. Besides on the road are abandoned tanks, vehicles of all kinds. PoWs in big and small groups move rearwards. We are tired as dogs. Yesterday the leading panzer rolled over a mine. The blast was enormous, the track got broken and lead balls went through the track cover. The pressure was enormous. Nothing happened. Further on we come close to the border between the Departments of the Maas to the Department of the Aisne [regions/county]. Through the bread basket of France on frequently very straight roads surrounded by high trees, over slightly welling terrain to the west. Main direction St. Quentin. Cockchafer in huge masses. The weather remains very nice. The large crowd of French PoWs sits in the ditch and collects their strength for the long march rearwards. The lunch at 1225hrs at Marle. Short break. 15km before St. Quentin. The rest on the road. Also in the rest position comes many French fighters and English bombers. But strong Flak defense force them away. Finally a warm meal and coffee. Lt Hahn was wounded by a puzzled French scout vehicle. Hopefully Lt Risch is only wounded and captured as a PoW. When he got out he was hit by MG fire. It was not nice. I will try again to sleep this night and not to freeze. Until now it hasn't happened. Today there were some hot Renaults and one heavy R-35 on the road. Shot down and abandoned. The R-35 looked very impressive."[32]

Along the lengthy left flank of *XIX Korps* there were often engagements by French armored units in counter-attacks, which were originating from the north in the Laon area. Until now the corps' flanks had been generally left under limited cover, and only until recently had the *10th Panzer* and *29th Infantry* paid much attention to them by building up a defensive line against attack. During the previous attacks that struck the division at Sedan on the 15th by *3rd DCR* and here at Laon on the 19th by *4th DCR* they, like many undertaken by the French in the battle, were often ill planned, not well controlled, and the armor was often committed in a piecemeal fashion, allowing it to be destroyed in detail. The French possessed good tanks, but lacked the communication and means to control them in addition to never allowing the assembly of sufficient forces and bringing them to bear on the enemy. On the 19th, the Regiment reached the old Somme battlefield between Moy and Vendeuil, on the Oise River. A number of French tanks and, for the first time, British tanks, made repeated attacks from the direction of Cugny and Ham. Those attacks were beaten off at Montescourt, Lizerolleas, and Seranucourt le Grand with no losses suffered by the Regiment. Lt Kurt Liestmann wrote on that day:

"Finally slept well in the straw, again a nice May day. We break the eggs, eat, and the gramophone plays French popular music, people chat and are happy until suddenly comes the seriousness of the war. Bombers and French fighters, one is very high, so that no one can shoot at him. He saw everything. We lay in the proximity of the estate. At 1100hrs is the break-up. Alert. French tanks should be coming over the Aisne canal. From Marle we went further past La Fère, Cheresis until Ferroise-Freme, where we break up due to the tank alarm. The 3rd Company takes the point further over to Fay Le Noyon, Renausart, Brissay, Hamegicourt, Moy de l'Aisne to Cerizy. At Hamegicourt we go over the important canal, which runs near the Oise. South of Mag de L'Aisne and Vendeuil all the bridges are partially destroyed and our pioneers have mined the roads. Despite this there are French tanks R35s and mediums, which crossed over and continuously harass from the south continuously. We secure against them. Other troops are obsessed by the tank illusion and quite nervous. At Vendeuil the 88mm Flak shoots at three medium French tanks, and hits them directly. Also at Moy de l'Aisne there was one standing at the channel. We go with the 3rd Company ahead till Benay. In the evening I take over the night watch at Cerizy against south. In the evening we should be with pioneers for the detonation of the bridge at La Fère, where it seems that French tanks have crossed over and are deployed. But it's too dark. Already when we are in Vendeuil, one WL car drives over our own mines. It blows with the pioneer post. Hardly anything is to be found. Heinz [his brother] drives with us until Vendeuil and we connect with the Pioneers. At 2300hrs we went back to protection. The night spent without sleep."[33]

Near the town of Jussy, Lt Seidler and the *7th Company* engaged the French as they attempted to support the crossing. In a report written in August, Seidler wrote the following after action report:

"On 19.5.40 around 1400hrs on the crossroads Vendeuil – St. Quentin in Gainguette Fme. the Regimental Commander gave to me, together with the company the order to support the pioneers (of Olt Witkowski) with the demolition of the bridge. We were supposed to connect [link-up] with them at Gibercourt and to support the pioneers with our cannon fire their advancement on the road Montescourt – Jussy on the heights west of the Jussy- St.Quentin road. By no means was it permitted to get involved [become engaged] in combat as there was a danger of heavy tanks. During the advancement to Jussy we met with Olt W just behind the town of Cerizy, who reported to us that the enemy was on this side of Jussy forming a bridgehead and that the towns Montescourt, Clastres, Gibercourt, Remigny were in enemy's hands. As the continuation of the task was therefore impossible, me and Olt W went to the Regimental Commander to receive a new order and the company, in the meantime took up a secure position at Cericy. At the regiment [stabs] we met two infantry officers, one of whom gave the order to Olt W to immediately take his old position on the south border of Montescourt and from there to conduct the ordered demolition with the support of 7./Pz.Rgt.8. For this purpose the Pioneer Zug of the Regiment was also subordinated to 7./Pz.Rgt.8 under direction of Lt Loetz. The company went in continuous bounds under fire though Ninacourt until the crossroad 500m west of Gibercourt. As the advancement of the Pioneers toward Montescourt-Lizerolles continued too long, I gave an order to Lt Loetz with two zug vehicles to conduct surveillance of the level crossing approximately 1km north of Lizerolles and if it was possible to drive with panzers and cleared of enemy, and if positive, to report back to me. The surveillance was also to include the terrain around Clastres and the securing it. When the report came, the pioneers had already entered Montescourt. The 7th Company followed, securing it on all sides and reached the level crossing between Lizerolle and Montescourt, which was not possible to cross by heavy panzers due to our own tank barriers. Here I saw that some of the zug vehicles had crossed in the meantime the northern level crossing. I agreed with the commander of the pioneers that they remain in their combat position in Gibercourt and about the further advancement of the Pioneer Zug on the road Montescourt-Jussy with the direct support of the first Zug of the 7th Company, whereas the heavy half-zug would drive over the northern level crossing and advance to Jussy along the west side of this road. To the two zug vehicles which got stuck on the crossroad west of Gibercourt, the order was sent via the messenger, to immediately follow in the direction of the northern crossing after the heavy panzers. The agreement was immediately reached by both sides. After the crossing of the northern crossing there was spotted the movement of unrecognized soldiers on north and east side of Clastres, moreover the Pak guns were put into the position on the eastern side. I left the Pioneer Zug as protection against Clastres and crossed with two panzer Mk IVs over the Clastres – Lizerolles road as well as the highlighted road leading from Lizerolles to Le Burgenet on the southern side and reached the ordered position about 800m east of Point 82. Here I discovered that the factory and the forest blocked my vision to the bridge that was to be destroyed. The attempt to get gain the western view and field of fire to the southwest failed due to the ditches and swampy torn down forest, whereas the crossing of the terrain between Point 82 and Jussy was again not possible due to the swamps. The group of pioneers had in the meantime discovered that Clastres was taken by our own troops in order to secure the crossing and on the Jussy-Montescourt road, movement was discovered but it was hard to identify if that was our own or enemy forces. I decided to go back to Lizerolles through a recently discovered farm road, in order to reach the road to Jussy on the western site of the crossing but it was impossible to cross. Lt Loetz went first as protection for this move. The southwest exit of Montescourt was gained and we found out that some of the pioneers were unable to advance due to the strong fire and the light zug was also unable to advance as it was under anti-tank and machine gun fire. Due to this both heavy vehicles went into position to the left and right of Jussy and were systematically shooting at one house after the other on the border of the town. Suddenly the shout came from behind: enemy tank! It was already dusk, and the houses and the forest blocked the view along the left and right. I went therefore to the southwest entrance of Montescourt, in order to see for myself the enemy tanks which the pioneers had referred to. I met there with the Regimental Commander, who gave the order to interrupt the hopeless combat as soon as possible due to the coming darkness. So there was a shot fired without the observed impact in the direction shown by the two pioneers of the supposedly identified positions of the tanks and in order to observe better. One panzer went on the road again, whereas in the meantime another panzer left the road to the southwest to go around the patch of woods, in order to better hit the town border of Jussy. This renewed advancement brought the pioneers almost up to the burning houses of Jussy. During the next movement, the Mk IV received a strong and well placed fire from the forest located to the very north of the crossing. Also under fire was the Light Zug which was moving partially on the road and partially west of the road. In this circumstance Uffz Vogt was wounded by grenade fragment because his turret hatch was open. As the darkness seriously prohibited the continuation of combat and the sighting of our own fire, but our panzers were clearly visible to the enemy with the background of the burning houses. I soon gave the order to retreat. Along the road I met the pioneer Major, who reported to me, that the assault by the remaining pioneers was put on hold until the two infantry companies arrived in Montescourt. My Regimental Commander had given the order before his departure to halt

Chapter 3: The French Campaign, May-July 1940

the combat by the company. The company afterwards drove to the initial position at Gainguette Fme., which they reached without further losses to panzers and men at around 0100hrs."[34]

Gefr Reich, also of the *7th Company*, had these observations of the fighting near Jussy that he wrote of in August 1940:

"*I conducted the combat on 19.5.40 in Jussy as the radio operator in panzer Mk II, the commander was Uffz Vogt, the driver Uffz Koppe. Two 75mm panzers [Mk IVs] remained a little further back providing security. The task of the panzer Mk II was to find out where the enemy was located and which weapons they had available. Accompanied by pioneers we slowly approached the village. The sun was already down, and the dusk spread quickly. The enemy fire was enticed by several shots from the Mk IVs, which in the meantime drove close to us. We drove a little bit further and suddenly saw ahead of us enemy tanks. We had a big misfortune because our gun had stopped. Due to this we were forced to drive into the cover, in order to fix this problem, which we managed after a short while. Here the enemy artillery had begun to report [registered]. In order to better see the strikes, my commander strived with short intervals to the entry hatch. He had paid a high price for that. The grenade hit a few meters from our vehicle and the splitters flew to the vehicle. Also Uffz Vogt, who also had his head up at the time received some of these. Afterwards he left the vehicle to search for the Sanitäter echelon [medical echelon]. I moved into the commander's place. After a short while the return march was ordered.*"[35]

Gefr Harcher, also of the same company, had this view of the combat that day:

"*At lunchtime on 19.5.40, the company received the task to support a group of pioneers the size of about twenty-five men, who had to detonate the bridge in Jussy. Three panzer Mk IIs and two panzer Mk IVs drove before Essigny north of Lizerolles. Here I received the tasks from company leader, to discover [recon] with my Mk II, if the train underpass in Montescourt and the road to Jussy were free of enemy. At the approach drive through Lizerolles to Montescourt I bumped into the six remaining pioneers, who wanted to look at a enemy tank. I drove until the heavily blocked underpass, without seeing the enemy. In the meantime other panzers of our company had come as well. A panzer Mk IV made the break-through. I had to stay back with my panzer in order to take over the protection [security]. In the evening the commander of the Regiment allowed us to drive forward to the panzers who already were in combat. Unfortunately we were not allowed to take part in the combat. In the deep dusk the combat was interrupted for the day.*"[36]

In a rather smooth advance to Péronne, the lead panzer elements crossed the Somme River on the 20th, at Feuillaucourt and Clery sur Somme, and passed through the old battlefields and large British cemeteries located there. Later that day, elements of the *XIX Korps' 2nd Panzer Division* reached Abbeville and the English Channel, which effectively split the Allied armies in two. However, for the German *OKW* and *OKH*, no one yet knew what to do now that the English Channel had been reached. For the Regiment, the march continued through Maricourt, Carnoy, Fricourt, and Meaulte to Ancre. Elements of I./*Abteilung* secured the southern flank at Morlancourt and Ville sur Ancre. Two of the *abteilung's* panzers struck mines and were slightly damaged with the crews escaping unharmed. Later in the day, French *Morane 406* fighters appeared in an attempt to halt and destroy the column, but were driven off by *Luftwaffe Me-109s*. Kurt Liestmann had this description of the day's events:

"*In the morning we catch some sleep. Stukas arrive en masse and proceed in a nose-dive to the Oise channel bridge. Through the binoculars one can see the bombs fall down. Once appears a modern English bomber. Two Messerschmitt hunt him. He lets his bombs fall and turns around. He really manages to get away from Messerschmitt. Through the night was a great fireworks of flak. Once and again there is an enemy aircraft in the searchlight. In the night they arrive more often than during the day. Then we go further through Cerizy, Benay, Essigny le Grand, Serancourt, Le Hamel, Roupy, Vanx, Beauvois, and Péronne. Wide productive countryside, opposite the Somme. Again the traces of French retreat. Burned-down vehicles, pieces of accoutrements, now and again one shot-through and burned-down tanks and prisoners, who retreated in groups about the size of one tank regiment with officers and a few Tommies. French wounded are sent back. During the stop near Péronne there come four Morane fighters who bother us. And here appear four Messerschmitt. The Morane attempt to escape. After one hangs our 'Me' and in three minutes the Morane is shot down. It goes down in a belly landing. The winner accompanies it until it is close to the earth. It lands on the right of us near the woods. We left St. Quentin 6km to the north. Amiens on the Somme. The march goes through Danight, Flamicourt, Mont St. Quentin, Clery, Maricourt, Carnoy, Fricourt, and Meaulte. The Somme is ahead. Where our soldiers of WWI have fought. Even today one can see the flattened grenade trenches. The memorial cemeteries are everywhere, German, French, and English. Still 75km to the sea. Guderian, 'Schnelle Heinz', will reach the sea today with the 1st Panzer Division. At dusk we go with the 3rd Company behind Malaucart to the heights, which dominate the south of the Somme. Only the Flak remains here. When we go onto the heights, we encounter four Tommies, who were attacked in the field position and without weapons and lost come out shivering and scared. On the Somme heights we go along the large British memorial cemetery, to Morlancourt to have rest.*"[37]

On the morning of 21 May, *10th Panzer* relieved the *1st* and *2nd Panzer Divisions* at the bridgeheads of Amiens, Picquigny, Abbeville, and St. Valery sur Somme as the *1st* and *2nd Panzer Divisions* moved northward. Now that orders from *OKH* had finally arrived, Guderian and his staff quickly drew up plans that called for the capture of the channel ports of the Boulogne, Calais, and Dunkirk, but before these orders could be issued, the *Panzergruppe* ordered the *10th Panzer Division* to be placed in *OKH* reserve, which halted, at least temporarily, its attack on Dunkirk.[38] The reason for the halt was that further to the south there was the perceived threat to the open southern flank along the line of the towns of Contay, Vadencourt, Warloy, Baillon Hénencourt, Millencourt, Meaulte, and Morlancourt. But more important was the attack by British armored units that were attempting to break through to Paris with an attack near Arras. The German defense was thus shifted towards Beaucourt sur l'Ancre, and the defenses at Warloy-Baillon were reinforced. But there was to be no fighting for the *10th Panzer*, and the day was actually a quiet one for the men of the Regiment, as they were able to grab some much needed rest and perform much needed maintenance on their panzers, which had been on the go since the 10th and had covered more than 500km. On 22 May, the *10th Panzer* was released back to the *XIX Korps* and was relieved by elements of the *XIV Korps*. The division was therefore ordered to make its way in the direction of Calais behind the *1st Panzer*, which was now beginning its attack on Dunkirk. Since the original attack by the *XIX* had been disrupted by the temporary loss of *10th Panzer*, Guderian now ordered that *1st Panzer* attack Dunkirk while the *10th Panzer* attacked Calais. The Regiment marched through Doullens, Frevent, Hesdin, and the Pas de Calais. The obstacles of the Regiment now encountered consisted of refugees and broken down and demolished French and British vehicles and weapons. *1st Panzer* was still fighting over Desvres, but could only

45

move forward in certain areas, as British bombers had bombed and strafed the primary roads. What is interesting here is that at this time, there was little activity overhead by the German *Luftwaffe*. The link up of *1st Panzer* behind Canche on the morning of the 23rd was only possible because of the fast paced advance of the combat formations from Calais. Over good all-weather roads through Montreuil, and over Hucqueliers and Desvres, the panzers reached the section of Canche. The *Royal Air Force* (RAF) attacked more often and directed their attacks on the advance elements, and some crew members were wounded in these attacks. During the advance, there were large groups of prisoners—French, English, Belgian, and even some Dutch—who were encountered; to the panzer crews, they looked thoroughly beaten and in disarray. The leading elements had no time for these groups, which were constantly passed off to the follow on forces. That evening the first elements reached the small river of Slack at Rety – Hardinghen and Mont Cornet (Hill 120), some 15km from Calais. The elements of *1st Panzer*, which had been fighting near Calais, were able to depart on the 24th, and on the 25th the *10th Panzer* assembled all its available forces in preparation for an attack there. In addition, there were elements of the heavy artillery from the *1st* and *2nd Panzer Divisions* in support. With the noose tightening around the port city of Calais, weak and disorganized Allied units attempted to break through from the east to reach the Channel coast and the hope of rescue by sea. Many of these units never succeeded in their attempts, and the troops were disarmed and taken prisoner by the combat elements of the Regiment. Then, on Friday the 24th, there occurred one of the strangest events of the war, and to this day one that cannot be thoroughly explained. Hitler, to the intense frustration of many of his generals and senior commanders, not to mention the fighting troops on the ground, ordered the panzer divisions to halt at Gravelines, just southwest of Dunkirk. Apparently after the *B.E.F.'s* attack at Arras, Hitler had become a bit worried that the panzers and his offensive plans were too exposed and could be easily foiled by those Allied forces still located to the south. Guderian wrote of the order:

"*On this day (24th), the Supreme Command intervened in the operations in progress, with results which were to have a most disastrous influence o the whole future course of the war. Hitler ordered the left wing to stop on the Aa [River]. It was forbidden to cross that stream. We were not informed of the reasons for this. The order contained the words, 'Dunkirk is to be left to the Luftwaffe. Should the capture of Calais prove difficult, this port too is to be left to the Luftwaffe.' (I quote here from memory.) We were utterly speechless. But since we were not informed of the reasons for this order, it was difficult to argue against it. The panzer divisions were therefore instructed: 'Hold the line of the canal. Make use of period of rest for general recuperation.' Fierce enemy air activity met little opposition from our air force.*"[39]

On that day, *Panzergruppe Kleist* attacked towards the Aa sector from east of Lillers to the coast to establish a number of bridgeheads. The situation along the coast at Calais and Boulogne had to be settled, and as the preparations for the attack began in earnest that order to halt was received. Von Kluge was also upset about the order to halt, and he felt that he could have achieved a major breakthrough with an attack, but even though the attack of the *XIX Korps* toward Dunkirk was halted, the action against Calais was later approved. Later in the day several bridgeheads across the Aa Canal at St. Omer were secured, but the bridges at La Bassee and Bethune were destroyed. On the afternoon of the 25th, the British garrison in Calais rejected a call for surrender and continued to hold out and repulse German attacks there. Shortly thereafter the *10th Schützen* Brigade was ordered to attack and capture Calais. With *Schützen Regiment 86* on the left and *Schützen Regiment 69* and elements of *Artillery Regiment 90*, *Pioneer Battalion 49*, and some *Panzerjäger* and Flak batteries on the right the attack commenced when the artillery began its preparatory fire at 1830hrs. An hour later at 1930hrs the brigade attacked, with the infantry advancing house to house against heavy enemy resistance indeed, as some of the supporting fires came from the *Royal Navy* destroyers firing from offshore in support of the hard pressed defenders. The *I./Battalion* came as close as 800m to the Bassin des Chasses, but was stopped there by heavy fire around 2000hrs. Around 2200hrs, a small bridge in the middle of Calais was taken and a small bridgehead established there. Both sides held their positions until later on the afternoon of the 26th, when artillery guns again began to fire in preparation for a renewed attack. The attack was supported a half an hour later when approximately 100 *Ju-87 Stukas* from *Sturmgeschwader 2* and *77* and twenty *Me-109s* from *I./JG 1* attacked enemy positions. The *I./Battalion* of *Schützen Regiment 69* advanced up to the south of Bassin des Chasses, which was reached at around 1000hrs. The *3rd Company*, in its movement forward, was able to move through a weakly defended gap in the lines and advance to the west up until the railroad station and east quay. It was here that the attack was again halted by heavy fire. Around midday, French resistance weakened as the panzers of the *6th* and *7th Companies* and vehicles of *Schützen Regiment 69* advanced across the bridge into the city center, causing many of the defenders to surrender or retreat. The *3./Schützen Regiment 69* was able to take the eastern docks and capture some 1600 men. For the remaining bunkers and forts still holding out, a number of 88mm guns were brought up to engage them with direct fire. The Germans were very quickly learning about the numerous jobs the 88mm gun was suited for. At around 1700hrs, *Schützen Regiment 69* finally reached the ruins of the destroyed citadel, where *Brigadier General* Nicholson surrendered his troops.[40] After the battle, some 20,000 prisoners, 4,000 of them British, were counted and made their way into the POW cages.[41] Also on that day elements of the *XIX Korps* advanced across the Aa Canal and captured Wormhoudt and Bourbourgville. It was at this time that the Regiment formed an improvised or provisional unit within the ranks of the regiment in order to deal with the many rear area problems encountered; due to the structure of the panzer regiment, and the manner in which the panzers had moved so far ahead of their supporting infantry formations, the idea of a *Schützen* or Infantry company was then ordered. It is through this company and the excellent after action report written later on that summer that allows us to follow the trail end of the Regiment's progress and its actions during the *Battle of France*. Additionally, it offers a view of what some of those troops who served in the supporting elements encountered during the campaign. On 26 May, *Hptm* Betz received the order to compile a *Schützenkomp*, or S-Company as it was to be known; the purpose of this company was to be available for any and all possible purposes, such as supporting infantry during panzer attacks, security police after the capture of enemy settlements and towns, collection of panzer crews who could not be deployed due to the loss of their vehicles in combat or through mechanical breakdowns, and supporting and maintaining the vital supply lines which kept the panzers rolling forward. As with most provisional units, the Regiment on a whole could not provide the company with the vehicles, spare parts, provisions, and technical service, because it was expected that the company was to be utilized on multiple missions and separated or detached from the Regiment.

Despite these known obstacles and setbacks, *Oberst* Elster was informed the following day that the company had been organized and was ready to undertake its various missions. In the coming pages we will refer back to this company as it attempts to keep pace with the panzers and the encounters it has along the way. On the 26th, when Hitler and von Rundstedt realized what was going on in Dunkirk they released the panzer divisions and ordered them to attack. Fortunately for the Allies, the pause had given them the opportunity to mount a ring of artillery around their army, and the panzers were unable to penetrate to the beaches and prevent the evacuation. The *XIX Korps* departed on the 27th at 1600hrs to renew the attack and assist in reducing the Dunkirk perimeter. The attack by elements of *4th Panzer Brigade, 2nd Panzer Division*, and *Grossdeutschland* Regiment was aimed at the high ground between Pitgam and Crochte. For the Regiment it began its deployment north, just south from Ardres, in small detachments and crossed over the Aa River at Watten, where the lead elements were engaged by British anti-tank guns and one Mk IV was damaged in the encounter. On the 27th, the combat units stood together with *Grossdeutschland* at Pitgam, Crochte, and Socx, some eight kilometers from the center of Dunkirk. On the 28th, the II./*Abteilung* reached the town of Wormhout, just south of the Yser, and prepared for an immediate action on the town of Herzeele, but late that afternoon there was a thunderstorm with heavy rains that quickly transformed the fields and open areas into a morass and restricted all movement to the streets and reinforced roads. Here the Regiment got the order for the closed attack, to the north on Bergues. Again the Regiment should attack the fortress. At Bergues the British *3rd Division* (Montgomery) defended the outer belt of Dunkirk. Shortly before the start of the attack there came another order to halt the attack on Bergues; the regiment was pulling out to a staging area south of Guines via the villages of Fiennes, Hardinghen, Bousin, and Rety. Most people know the story of the "*Miracle of Dunkirk*," the great escape by the *B.E.F.* before the German panzers could roll in for the kill. Many have argued that by allowing the Allies to get away the Germans squandered their chances to win the war. But, one thing is for sure, the panzers would have had a very difficult time in wiping out the *B.E.F.* in its positions around Dunkirk. The terrain was not open, and had numerous man made and natural obstacles. So the Allies escaped, and as they did so the relationship between the French and British deteriorated even further. Some saw the British withdrawal as saving what they could for the eventual "*Battle of Britain*," while others saw it as the British saving themselves. Of the 338,526 troops that were evacuated, more than 200,000 were British and 125,000 French.[42] The losses in the battle for Dunkirk amounted to some 240 vessels, some 106 aircraft, 2,500 guns, 80,000 vehicles, and great quantities of abandoned British and French equipment and stores.[43] *General* Weygand demanded the return of the *B.E.F.*, as he felt that France should continue to resist, but that she needed every soldier and all the support she could get to do so. This was apparent when in some cases those men plucked from Dunkirk soon found themselves back in France, dropped off along the Normandy coast between Caen and the Seine. At the time, most military minds felt that there were only two options left for the French: the first was to pull back all remaining forces and evacuate them all to fight another day at another place; the second option was to establish a strong defensive bridgehead within France and along the coast which could maintain contact and be re-supplied by Britain. In the end Weygand, who was more preoccupied with his own reputation, failed to act on any of the options. Now the Germans turned their attention to the capture of the remainder of France. The S-Company Diary recorded:

"*On the 27th, after which the necessary means of transport for the company were procured in Boulogne by Hptm Betz, namely twelve trucks for the embarkation of teams and five trucks for the transportation of tires, provisions, spare parts, field kitchen and petrol. All this at the same time as the heavy combat for the cathedral and citadel were being conducted. The teams, which were organized for this purpose, were happy to follow the orders of the leader Hptm Betz, to search in the burning and shaken from the storm of combat, the town for the suitable vehicles and to bring them in motion and convert them to a useable condition, despite the recurring attacks from enemy aircraft. With the tension of all powers it was achieved to compile during one day quite an assortment and variety of vehicles in the vehicle park, this mostly consisted of the enemy vehicles. Already on the following morning at 0600hrs the company was deployed for the first time in Calais as an S-Company in order to maintain order in this captured town, in which there was still a huge storm of fire. It was not quite simple, because the remaining population came [to us] complaining in small assembles to demand food, clothes and water. Everywhere on the streets were dead and wounded, because many times a day the town was strafed by English aircraft, which carried their fire ambushes without selection on everything that shown signs of movement. Right at the entrance to the town the company became the target of such an attack and one vehicle caught fire, which stood in an open area near the city hall and was not able to be hidden or camouflaged in a suitable location. The company was now divided into eight single patrols and directed to all sides of the town. This task was not quite innocent, because ever one or two hours there appeared English aircraft, which had no obstacles to shoot through the streets and it was easy for them because there were not yet any actions taken to defend against them. Nowhere around the town was there any flak deployed. In the meantime the number of collected wounded grew and available military field aid stations were no longer large enough, so that many new military aid stations had to be open. The French and English military doctors and medics had to take over the care of the sick and wounded. The lightly wounded who were transportable, were transferred by the teams and vehicles of the S-Company to the military aid stations in the neighborhoods of Guines, Marqise etc. On the other hand, the enemy soldiers, who loitered everywhere around the town and neighborhoods, were attacked in houses and yards by the patrols of the S-Company and captured. At the same time the whole area was searched for food supplies, in order to feed the almost 400 prisoners and population. For this purpose a guard of four men was set on the south train station, in order to secure the provisions and the military supplies found in one of the train carriages of an English transport train. There were as well bombing attacks from English airplanes, which endangered the Belgian military hospital which was near the guard post. In the further course of work, which was continued under constant attacks by English aircraft and therefore various separated by firebrands, the main thought was about the accommodation of the heavily wounded who had been assembled in the city hall. The majority were the locals of the town, who were victims of the multiple strafing attacks by English aircraft. Often the relatives gathered around those wounded and contributed to the multiple confusion and obstacles. These wounded were also transported by the vehicles of the S-Company to the neighboring medical hospitals, where it was possible to accommodate them, so that by late in the afternoon the city hall was back in order. Only the refugees assembled there, mostly Belgians, who were asking about the opportunities to return to their motherland. Hptm Betz, who is personally familiar with Belgium and the situation there, quickly and without friction managed this storm and it more or less dissolved, whereas the conversation was conducted in French and Flemish. During the day there were many hundreds of prisoners from all possible nations, collected in the church, city hall and at the S-Company. They had to be accommodated, which took place in such a way so that the officers of the teams were separated in the church. During this time the leader of the company prepared the accommodation of the prisoners in the completely destroyed citadel. In the evening at 2200hrs the prisoners were transported there. For the provisioning of them, there were suitable cooks selected from the prisoners and two English field kitchens were brought in. The accommodation of the 800 prisoners was in the barracks located near the citadel and still covered with a roof. One part of the company was immediately deployed to secure the prisoners. This was connected with significant difficulties, because the French and*

Belgians tried to attack the British at every opportunity. The separated guard teams had a difficult situation during the watch as they had to oversee the cleaning details which were undertaken during the same night in the citadel. After the successful organization of these proceedings, the company was accommodated in a village. The vehicles stood covered under the huge hall of glass, which curved above the railroad tracks. It was likely that this position was reported to the enemy, who made a strafing attack at the train station during the night. Four bombs hit around and between the vehicles, the crews saved themselves by running away. Thus must be stressed the conscious dedication of Fw Heintz, Gefr Esser, Gefr Gauss and Gefr Eger, who supported the leader actively despite the machine gun fire from the aircraft, to rescue the drivers of the burning vehicles from the basements of the houses surrounding the burning train station located in the middle of the flames. Fw Heintz had saved many vehicles from the fire with the support of the company drivers, despite the danger that the vehicles could explode at any moment. Also they managed, uninterrupted the detonation of the English ammunition stored in the train station. The British continued their attacks from the air and lit up the whole area as if was day with the parachute flares. The whole thing was an extremely dangerous action and demanded the cold-blooded and enduring influence of the company leader and the readiness of the deployed teams who saved the vehicles, so that the enemy attacks would not turn into chaotic confusion. Immediately after the vehicles were brought under the trees of the nearby park at the train station, the company was assembled again and was accommodated in Zugs in the surrounding air defense dugouts. The company leader and one guard remained awake for the rest of the night with the vehicles parked outside, in order to address any further aircraft attacks quickly and effectively. Especially necessary to mention, that after the detonation of the enemy bombs, the whole area was covered in flames and also on such objects and construction material that did not contain flammable materials, for example metal and stone walls. The reason that there were no larger losses could be attributed to the fact that the largest part of the company was located in basements and closed premises of the area and only a small part was deployed under the machine gun fire during the rescue work. One civilian was found dead in the square in front of the train station and was discovered in the early morning. In the morning after this night the details in the prisoner of war camp were continued. Mainly these details were about the dispatch of the dead and numerous horse carcasses, which were sometimes totally carbonized. The works ordered by the company leader were conducted by prisoners under the supervision of the teams of the S-Company. At the same time many smaller food storage locations were discovered and those were secured, in order to protect them from the prisoners and local population. Despite the disturbances by enemy aircraft and the occasional shooting from the sea, the S-Company had taken advantage to increase their vehicle situation, had fueled their vehicles and acquired fourteen new Kräder, which were taken from the English army effectives and converted into a drivable condition. The company pulled away from Calais in complete deployment ready condition despite the disturbance of enemy attacks."

The report continued on the 29th:

"At 0600hrs the company marched away to Hardinghen with its own accommodation in the small castle, the park and industrial buildings which belonged to castle. The teams of the company were distributed to their company's, including the drivers with their vehicles, writers and watch personnel. A large number of vehicles, almost the half, were taken to the companies of the Regiment. The [panzer] companies demanded everything of what is usually supplied by the workshops and J-Staffel, which almost constantly were without equipment, while in the S-Company which had existed for only a few days and was not being supported by the Regiment but in contrary was facing its own limitations, this company equipment was provided to the Regiment. The so called rest stop in Hardingen has transformed into a unpleasant stay, during these three days the company was so cut down and pumped out in their vehicles, tires, spare parts etc. so that during the continuation of the march it was only partially ready for combat. On 30.5 in the morning at 0600hrs the company was released in Calais and again subordinated to the Regiment."[44]

Breaking of the Weygand Line and Amiens

By the time the bulk of the panzers reached the coast they had long since been worn out by the fighting and distance covered. Now on the eve of "*Fall Rot*" (*Plan Red*) they would have little time before they turned to the south and prepared to meet the remainder of the Anglo-French Army, which lay just to the south of the Somme River and ran roughly from the channel coast to the Rhine River. French *General* Maxime Weygand, who had replaced *General* Gamelin as Commander in Chief, had some sixty-six divisions at his disposal; unfortunately, these divisions were not of the type nor caliber which had initially faced the German offensive back in May. These divisions were battered second line divisions that suffered from poor leadership and morale and were equipped with old, worn out, and totally inadequate equipment. Thirteen of these were static divisions and three were cavalry; the remains of the surviving armored divisions were totally worn out, and had been almost decimated in the previous battles. There were still some 140,000 British troops in the southern regions of France, although most were of the rear echelon type. There were some seasoned formations remaining, such as elements of the *1st Armored* and *51st Highland Divisions*, along with a few infantry remnants, which all together amounted to approximately the size of a light mechanized division. For the German Army, it had been, over a short period of time, actually been reinforced by a number of fresh divisions, and had been now brought up to a total of some 163 divisions, with 140 of these taking their place in the fighting, while another twenty-three remained in reserve. Hitler and the *OKW* staff, sensing that a quick victory was at hand, had actually moved to a temporary headquarters in the Belgian village of Bruly-de-Pesche. Now a new plan was devised which saw a predominantly armored *Armeegruppe* conduct another mass assault, only this time across the plains of Picardy. With a quick reorganization the German order of battle looked something like this: *Armeegruppe A* (Rundstedt) consisting of the *Second* (Weichs), *Twelfth* (List), *Sixteenth* (Busch), and *Eighteenth* (Küchler) Armies now faced the French *Fourth Army Group* (Huntziger) with the *Second* and *Fourth* French Armies. While the first three German armies moved off to begin offensive operations, the *Eighteenth Armee* was to continue operations in the north around Dunkirk. The second of the German army groups, *Armeegruppe B* (Bock), consisted of the *Fourth* (Kluge), *Sixth* (Reichenau), and *Ninth* (Strauss) armies, and was broken down into ten army corps, of which six of the ten available panzer divisions were assigned.[45] They were facing the French *Third Army Group* (Besson) with the *Sixth* (Touchon), *Seventh* (Frere), and *Tenth* (Altmayer) French Armies. The third army group, *Armeegruppe C* (Leeb), was composed of the *First* (Witzleben) and *Seventh* (Dollman) Armees, and was to drive south towards Epinal in order to bag the French *Second Army Group* (Pretelat), which consisted of the *Third*, *Fifth*, and *Eighth* French Armies, most of which had been manning the *Maginot Line* fortifications.[46] In addition to the armies there were also two panzer groups formed: the first *panzergruppe* was commanded by *Generalleutnant* Ewald von Kleist and would be composed of three panzer corps. The first corps was the *XIV Panzer Korps* (Wietersheim), with the *9th* and *10th Panzer Divisions* and the *Grossdeutschland Motorized Regiment*. The second corps was the *XVI Panzer Korps* (Höppner), and consisted of the *3rd* and *4th Panzer* and

Above: Early panzer Mk Is on parade near Berlin in 1937 (Kathe)

Left: The panzers form up for the parade through the streets of Böblingen in April 1938 (BBN)

Below: A Mk I Befehls panzer drives down the streets of Böblingen (BBN)

The first panzer enters the Ludendorff-Hindenburg Kaserne in Böblingen as the Regiment formally takes possession of the kaserne in 1938 (BBN)

Below: The Regiment conducts its first official ceremony on its new kaserne (BBN)

The early panzer Mk I on maneuvers at the Munsingen training area in 1938 (K Liestmann)

The snow does not affect the troops as they continue to train with the newest Mk IIs (H Liestmann)

The panzers are used for ski touring while at Munsingen during the winter of 1938/39 (K Liestmann)

Above: A view of one of the motor pool bays on the kaserne in Böblingen (BBN)

Left: Loading a Mk II in Böblingen for shipment to Czechoslovakia and the Milowitz training area, April 1939 (BBN)

A heavy Mk IV is loaded onto a flatcar at the rail yard in Böblingen (K Liestmann)

The panzers are ready for their journey to the Milowitz training area (Kuch)

The panzers arrive in Czechoslovakia (Kuch)

Back in Böblingen the Regiment prepares for its next mission, combat in Poland (Kuch)

A lightly armored Mk I was fitted with only two machine guns (BBN)

Above: Moving through the Danzig Corridor, an Mk II takes the time to halt for a brief photo Below: A Mk I has a slight collision with a telephone pole while moving through the corridor (both H Liestmann)

The crew of a Mk I halts for a short break in order to get some warm food during the approach march towards Brest-Litovsk (H Liestmann)

The crew of a Mk II takes time out for a quick snap-shot. Note the early white Balkan Cross painted in the turret (Kuch)

A knocked out Polish 75mm artillery piece that had been used as an anti-tank weapon (Kathe)

Enroute towards Brest-Litovsk, Mk IIs cross a newly erected assault bridge over one of the many rivers in Poland (Kathe)

Some of the first Polish prisoners taken as the panzers approached the city of Brest (Kathe)

A Polish bunker, one of many encountered during the drive to Brest (Kathe)

A knocked out Mk II that was hit by a Polish field gun (Kathe)

A WW I vintage French FT-17 tank being towed away by a German panzer. These tanks were used by the Polish Army but were no match for the German panzers (H Liestmann)

A Mk IV Ausf A mounting a 75mm cannon. This was the heaviest tank the Regiment possessed at that time, however, there were but a handful of these panzers in the entire Regiment. (Hess)

A captured Czech T-35 tank, now seeing service with the German Army in Poland (BBN)

A knocked out Polish 25mm anti-tank gun (Kathe)

Mk Is of the II./*Abteilung* crossing a pontoon bridge in Poland (Kuch)

Oberst Elster (with map and black uniform) confers with the corps commander, General Heinz Guderian, just before reaching the city of Brest (BBN)

The mobile field kitchen serves hot food to the crew of an Mk IV during the advance (H Liestmann)

One of the bridges near the citadel of Brest, blown up as the Mk II of Olt Schefold crossed over it (BBN)

The bridge at Brest (Hess)

The Citadel at Brest after Polish forces had surrendered, troops of the 10th Panzer Division take time to inspect the fort (BBN)

Above: German and Russian soldiers meet as friends in Brest Litovsk Below: Members of the Regiment take time to inspect Russian T-26 tanks in Brest (both BBN)

Mk IIs from the Regiment moving through the French border (Kuch)

A Mk III crossing the Meuse River near Sedan (Hess)

A light Mk I negotiates the Meuse River (H Liestmann)

A Mk II crossed a destroyed bridge near Sedan (K Liestmann)

A destroyed river bridge is negotiated in France; these obstacles presented the greatest challenge to the panzers on the drive west (H Liestmann)

French prisoners assist in clearing a path for a II./*Abteilung* Mk III panzer as aircraft patrol overhead (H Liestmann)

An Mk II that has hit a mine (H Liestmann)

One of the heavy Mk IVs that was knocked out at Stonne. The graves of three crewmembers lay to the rear. (K Liestmann)

The Char B "Gaillac," which was destroyed near Stonne, photographed in November 1940 (H Liestmann)

Traffic jams and mines caused numerous detours (K Liestmann)

A line of Mk IIIs rolling west through one of the many French towns (H Liestmann)

The tired crew of a Mk III in France (K Liestmann)

A Mk III passing by a knocked out French Char-B tank (H Liestmann)

One of the French R-35 tanks knocked out near Stonne (H Liestmann)

A captured French Somua S-35 tank that has broken a track and is now in the service of the SS Totenkopf Regiment (K Liestmann)

Bringing in French prisoners, weapons were not needed (H Liestmann)

French refugees that have packed up their belongings and are attempting to escape out of the path of the advancing Germans (K Liestmann)

A French FCM-36 tank being inspected by members of the Regiment in the Fall of 1940 (H Liestmann)

Smoke rises from the harbor at Calais as the Regiment approaches (BBN)

Surveying the damage on the approach to Calais (BBN)

A Mk II in need of repair is worked on by its crew and the men of the *Werkshop Company* (Kuch)

A Mk IV which has thrown a track (BBN)

Long lines of French prisoners stream to the rear and the POW cages (H Liestmann)

A group of French prisoners moving to the rear; stop and assist in the removal of a German casualty from a field (H Liestmann)

A large group of French prisoners. Note the mixed collections of service uniforms (K Liestmann)

Moving forward to take up new positions for the drive into Southern France (K Liestmann)

A hasty road block of military vehicles and civilian cars did little to halt the panzers (BBN)

A member of the Regiment and a French Colonial soldier pose next to a knocked out French Char-B tank (H Liestmann)

A knocked out British A-10 Mk IIA Crusier tank belonging to the 1st Armored Division (BBN)

A knocked out British Mk VI light tank (H Liestmann)

A Mk III passes a long column of French Prisoners (K Liestmann)

A panzer company holds up in the drive south (BBN)

A French 155mm artillery piece that has been caught on the road is bypassed by a column of Mk IIs (BBN)

A French heavy artillery piece, now in the anti-tank role on the Weygand Line (Matthias)

A group of Mk IIs has pulled off the road to rest and camouflaged (Matthias)

Olt Wahl (left) and Hptm Ottens (third from left) pause for a map check during the fighting in France (Matthias)

Moving forward, a Mk III moves cautiously across a field (K Liestmann)

A Mk III moves through a French field on the drive south (BBN)

Olt Wahl scans the route ahead from the turret of his Mk III (Matthias)

Back in Germany in the Spring 1940, Hans Cramer (third from the right) takes command of the Regiment from *Oberst* Botho Elster (right) (Matthias)

Chapter 3: The French Campaign, May-July 1940

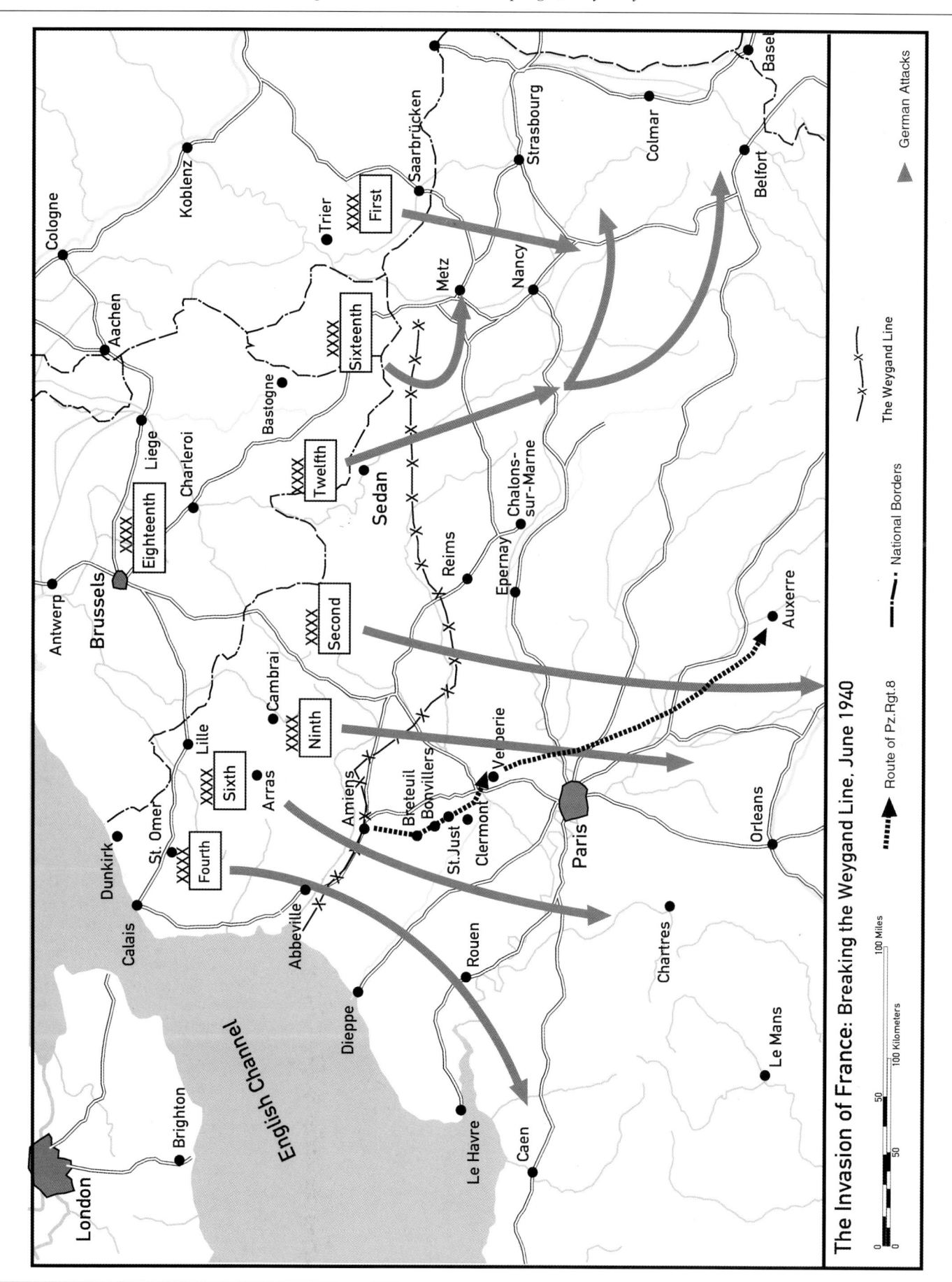

The Invasion of France: Breaking the Weygand Line, June 1940

13th *Motorized Divisions*. The third corps, the *XV Panzer Korps* (Hoth), was composed of the *5th* and *7th Panzer* and *2nd Motorized Divisions*. The second *panzergruppe* was commanded by *Generalleutnant* Heinz Guderian, the former commander of the *XIX Panzer Korps* in Poland, and whose actions there and in France had recently won him a promotion and command of the second panzer *gruppe*. This panzer *gruppe* was composed of *XXXIX Panzer Korps* (Schmidt), and would consist of the *1st* and *2nd Panzer* and *29th Motorized Divisions* and the *XLI Panzer Korps* (Reinhardt), consisting of *6th* and *8th Panzer* and *20th Motorized Divisions*.[47] The overall plan for breaking the *Weygand Line* called for a quick reorientation to the south by almost the entire German Army, where it would then proceed south and capture Paris, along with the channel ports and the remainder of France. The majority and most difficult task fell to Bock's *Armeegruppe B*, which was stretched from the English Channel to Amiens. At the time the Germans possessed three bridgeheads over the Somme at Abbeville, Amiens, and Péronne. The plan would be to launch two panzer divisions across each bridgehead. On 1 June, the *10th Panzer Division* was reassigned to the *XIV Korps* under *Panzergruppe Kleist*, and on the evening of the *2nd* the final preparations were made in readiness for the final push through these small bridgeheads.[48] On 2 June, the Regiment was deployed to an area south of Guines 150km from Amiens. The Regiment departed that night via Samer, Montreuil, Hesdin, Fevent, and Doullens, reaching an area near Contay by the morning of the *3rd*. Even though the 150 kilometers covered that evening were done to avoid the heat of the day, the distance and speed at which the panzers moved took its toll on many of those already worn out crews and panzers. By this point, the crews used every bit of free time to work on their panzers, but unfortunately by this time many of the panzers had reached a state where basic crew maintenance was not adequate enough to keep them rolling. To illustrate just how few replacement panzers were getting forward to the divisions and regiments, the *10th Panzer Division* was only provided with the following number of replacement panzers, which included: eight Mk Is, nineteen Mk IIIs, two Mk IVs, and two command panzers.[49] Once again the S-Company report for 2.6.40:

"The teams returned to company and divided in Zug and sections. The armament is still sufficient. The company still possesses temporarily the pistols and three light machine guns, out of which only two are ready for combat. The good vehicles of the company were taken and in their place came back the worn out vehicles which had to be abandoned even at the departure because they were absolutely useless. 1700hrs pull away to Contay. Almost at the very start the march was halted due to the aircraft danger. Following that was the long night drive, which continued until the middle of the 3rd, and finished at Courtenay. The company moved into bivouac on the pasture lands. We are located immediately in front of Amiens, which is heavily worn out due to attacks by aircraft and artillery but is still the key position for the enemy defensive area which stretches to the south."

On 4 June, the S-Company had this to report:

"Strong aircraft squadrons fly over the area. The company is located in the pasturage [farm land] at Courtenay and is repeatedly bombed by enemy aircraft which do not cause any damage. The Regiment receives a number of new panzers, which will enhance the essence of the panzer companies. The change in the company is very large. The panzers march in the direction of Amiens, where they will begin the new offensive in the morning."[50]

The Regiment's mission was to attack on the morning of the 5th from out of the bridgehead at Amiens and attempt to breakthrough the French *9th Infantry Division*. The *9th Division* was a fortress division made up of second-class troops that had been defending the area around Amiens. In order to prepare themselves for the attack the panzer divisions were provided a short thirty-six hour break in which they used every available minute to perform long overdue maintenance and replenishment, and if possible get some rest for the worn out panzer crews. Additionally, this short pause allowed for those panzers that had already fallen out on the earlier movement west to be repaired and catch up to their parent formation. Shortly before midnight on the evening of 4/5 June, the combat units departed for their assembly areas, which they reached at approximately 0230hrs. The Regiment was at approximately seventy percent strength for the attack. The attack commenced at 0500hrs, with the point of attack in the middle between Dury and St. Fuscien, located just south of Amiens across the Somme, with its aim set some 15km south on the high ground just short of Flers-sur-Noye. After a softening up by the artillery and *Luftwaffe*, the leading elements jumped off at 0515hrs. The panzers advanced, following the road south from Amiens towards Ailly-sur-Noye, and in the process left the accompanying infantry far behind them. Strong anti-tank and artillery fire quickly hit the lead elements of the I./*Abteilung*. Despite the pounding they were receiving the Mk IIIs and IVs advanced and had soon forged deep gaps in the French defenses. The Regiment was fighting against units of the French *16th Infantry Division*, which were putting up a hard fight. There are these reports which briefly describe the events leading up to the attack. The first report is from the S-Company diary, which stated:

"5.6.40 many hundreds of Stukas appear on the horizon in the morning dawn. The attack on the enemy's entrenchment line on the Somme has begun with brunt not to overhear. By 1000hrs already the first reports of losses had arrived. The wounded return, the spare teams must be provided by the company and are taken to the front with the vehicles of the combat detachment or by the company itself. The number of wounded in the Regiment were transferred by the vehicles of the S-Company in order to secure the further transport."

Serving in panzer number 100, the Mk IV command panzer of the I./*Abteilung* commander, *Uffz* Spathelf had this description:

"Our crew consisted of the following; the Abteilung Commander; Oberstlt Haarde, the Abteilung Adjutant; Olt Knorr, radio-operators; Oberfunkmeister Strack and Uffz Beer and the driver Gefr Kolbe. On 4 June at 2330hrs we left Contay in our factory new Befehlswagen, which we took over two hours ago, and we went in the lead of I./Abteilung in the direction of Amiens. About 0300hrs we reached the ordered assembly area, the allotment on the south border of Amien. Behind our panzer was located the light Zug stretched one from another, to the left of us was the 1st Company, about 50m ahead of us was a battery of 2cm Flak. About 0400hrs strong enemy artillery fire began over our area. The bomb craters lie closely behind or near our panzer. After approximately three quarters of an hour the enemy relocated his fire more towards the town itself, shortly after it was possible to hear our own artillery. Exactly at 0500hrs the commander transmitted the order via radio: 'Abteilung to march' and the Abteilung rolled forward with the 1st Company in the first echelon. After about thirty minutes the three heavy panzers of 1st Company, which were a row ahead of us, received anti-tank gunfire from the woods on the left from us, and caught flame immediately. We halted our panzer in order

not to get in the shooting range of the guns, and fired to the position from where the fire came on the border of the woods from our machine gun. In order not to get out of the attack lines of the Regiment, we had to keep more eastwards."[51]

Uffz Schöppler of the *7th Company* describes his day:

"I picked up the new panzer Mk IV in Mons in Belgium, and came with it to the workshop in Kontainan on 4.6. in the evening where it was already dark. The crew for the vehicle was already waiting for me in the night. I changed the oil, loaded the ammunition, and prepared the whole vehicle for combat. All was finished at 0300hrs and we drove in the direction of Amiens. As we arrived at Amiens at 0430hrs, heavy artillery fire was aimed at the road. The Regiment was already on the second hill when we reached them. We established radio connection with our company and went on. We went through to the village which was the point of our attack. We took care of different anti-tank guns and shot onto small enemy machine gun emplacements. Enemy artillery had several times already reached us. At 0800hrs a shell tore off the return roller rack on the left side, but despite this we went on. During the montage of the track, I received the fragment of a 4.7cm anti-tank round in my back, the gun was 1500m away from us and shot at us from far away. It was answered back by our cannon and with immediate impact. With the 2nd shot the shreds flew into the air. Despite my damaged return roller rack, which made the return drive impossible and with the fragment in my back, I drove further. Unfortunately we were not able to hold the terrain we won, because the infantry didn't come up and the enemy artillery became stronger. In the evening we had to retreat in our initial positions."[52]

OGefr Kaulbars, also of the *7th Company*, wrote in his report on the situation the morning of 5 June:

"In the morning at about 0300hrs we took the position in the allotment garden of Amiens. As the loader of our panzer Mk IV, I oiled once again the locks of my weapon, put aside enough ammunition and freed up the field of traverse. At 0500hrs our attack started. After we overtook our own infantry, we received fire from some wooded areas and from direction of St. Fuscien. We shot at the forest with the machine gun and we opened fire on the village with the cannon. During the further approach the right brake failed to pull anymore. The driver stopped the vehicle, climbed outside and fixed the brakes. With the further approach we again received damage in transmission. We were on a hill and received heavy fire from the artillery, because we were only able to move at the caterpillar speed. As the transmission continued to be further damaged and we were almost halted, we were unable to maintain the speed of the attack. After a long consideration we decided to turn back, because the [German] infantry had overtaken us already. We drove the panzer to the workshop in Amiens."[53]

OGefr Zängle, in another *7th Company* report, wrote about his day and the loss of his gunner and panzer:

"On the night from 4.6 to 5.6.40 we drove into the assembly area south of Amiens. In the time before attack we were under the heavy artillery fire. Sharply at 0500hrs the attack started direction south. I as a driver of a panzer Mk II of the light zug of the 7th Company, drove with the II./Abteilung. The first two hills were taken with the support of the infantry. Afterwards we made a short technical stop; I tightened the track which was loose. During our further march we attacked the enemy artillery position, which was protected by anti-tank guns. By driving around we received the anti-tank fire. A direct hit brushed against the track cover. My schütze [gunner], Fw Lüders, fought back immediately with the cannon and the anti-tank guns [were] shut down. Therefore I came to the rear of the Abteilung with my vehicle. When I passed the road Amiens – Paris as the last vehicle, I saw the enemy gunners in the terrain. These were Negros, who went under cover immediately. As I made it to one of them with the heaviness of my panzer, I came under the anti-tank fire and my track went in the air. My radio operator, Gefr Fluhrer, saw through the radio-man hatch as two other Negros approached the vehicle on their stomach. Fw Lüders fought back with an MPi and hand grenades, as the turret didn't rotate anymore. At this moment I took a direct hit in the engine, and cried: 'get out due to fire danger'. When I attempted to get out of the vehicle, I got the M.G. fire. I was hardly 5m away from the vehicle, when the turret was shifted to the side due to direct hit. Shortly after the radio operator went out of the drivers hatch, all covered with tatters of meat. This shot was the fatal bullet of brave Fw Lüders. When we looked around there was no panzer to see anywhere. The radio operator and me crawled into a pile of hay, in the distance of 1500m. All this took place under the enemy M.G. fire. Here we spent four hours and didn't know what to do. But suddenly around 0400hrs we heard the noise of engines. When we looked out, it was a German panzer. We got up immediately and went to them. Therefore we found traces of our panzers which I recognized on the ground and followed them. After the run all sweaty we end up at our company leader, Lt Seidler. We delivered the report where our vehicle was located but immediately afterwards the strong artillery fire interrupted our stay and we had to change assembly area again. So in the evening I returned to Amiens in the vehicle of Fw Geres."[54]

Finally, there is the report written by *Gefr* von Brunn, also of the *7th Company*:

"As part of the large attack on Weygand line, we crossed on 5.6 in the morning 0500hrs the front infantry line by moving from the assembly position south of Amiens. After the crossing the first hill we got strong fire, which we returned. After we went around the steep slope, we shot the hay pile from which the anti-tank gun fired and it caught fire. When we drove up towards the slope to change our position the panzer suddenly catapulted ahead. We drove onto the mine, which the driver was not able to see through the high grass. The commander noticed the smoke and ordered 'Get out, the vehicle burns!' On the outside we discovered that only the fog candles were torn away by the hit, but the panzer was still able to fire. However it was unable to move on the slope visible to the enemy, opposite the town St. Fuscien. We went inside immediately and conducted the combat against the machine gun nest which were set in the woods and on the border of the village of St. Fuscien and which prohibited the advancement of our infantry. The enemy artillery started to aim at our panzer and we shot at the observer position from about 1600m, which was located in the church tower of the village and from which came the fire. After two hours we had shot a large amount of splinter grenades [high explosive] and decided to retreat together with the crew of an Mk III from the 2nd Company, who had also drove onto a mine and Olt Wahl was wounded. One machine gun in which the position was not recognized and fought against us, had shot us without hitting anyone. During the slow retreat due to the wounded driver, we came under fire from the woods which were not cleared yet, it was a heavy machine gun fire forcing us to go around. After we took with us the prisoners captured by the infantry, we reached Amiens at 1030hrs. I drove as the loader in the Mk IV panzer during this attack."[55]

It did not take long before the Germans discovered that, despite their numerical superiority, they had made little progress and suffered considerable losses in attempting to open up the way south. Over the next couple of days, although some progress would be made, the French forces holding the line managed to contain the German advance and inflict numerous losses upon them. Weygand's army was well dug-in using a new tactic of the *Herissons*, or *Hedgehog* defense. Instead of a continuous linear defense the French forces now established strong points, or hedgehogs, that were arranged in a checker board fashion.[56] The hedgehogs were established in houses, barns, villages, towns, woods, and anywhere a variety of weapons from machine guns to 75mm artillery pieces employed as anti-tank guns could be hidden and camouflaged. Unlike the previous attacks, the French were able to hold firm in these positions and not break and run as before. Initially, as many of these hedgehog positions stubbornly held out, the German forces, now at a slight disadvantage, would have been in even more trouble if only some French tanks had been available to counterattack. Like most static defense, there is always the problem that the defense can be by-passed when not anchored on a strong natural or man-made obstacle, and this was especially true in this case, when considering the mobile *Blitzkrieg* tactics now being utilized by the Germans. So despite the fighting spirit and tenacity now being shown by Allied forces, the panzers, when appropriate, simply by-passed the stronger defenses and made their way around them by sticking to the more open and less defended terrain. By 0600hrs, the panzers had already penetrated the initial defensive line and were some five kilometers south of the river near the heights of Sains-en-Amiénois. The less mobile infantry formations had a more difficult time and had only made it to St. Fuscien, where they were still engaged in combat operations. A combat report from the I./*Abteilung* describes the situation:

"*At 0700hrs two Mk IIs ran into mines in front of us and became disabled. In the flow of the further advancement we lost radio contact with the 2nd and 3rd Companies and only received calls from the 1st and 7th Companies. At the corner of the woods we stopped for orientation. With that some destroyed panzerspähwagens of Regiment, which were keeping close up, were subordinated to both companies. In steady high speed we went ahead southwest until St. Fuscien, Grattepanche and Oresmaux, where we began exchanging fire with anti-tank and artillery in direct fire. Close to the cemetery of Oresmaux we assembled again. The rest stop was short, because to the west appeared six to seven enemy tanks. Part of these tanks were engaged by our heavy panzer, the rest went off in the distance. In the remaining time the enemy artillery were hunting us, wherever we took position it was less than five minutes until the arrival of the fumigating Dinger. This hunting continued till late in the evening.*"[57]

All morning long, as elements of the Regiment ran into the French minefields, they soon discovered that per doctrine these obstacles were covered by indirect fire, and as previously stated it did not take long before French 155mm began to shower the panzers with deadly fire. Following these initial delays and setbacks, the Regiment went through a brief reorganization and was soon assisted by its sister regiment, *Panzer Regiment 7*, as it battled its way through Sains-en-Amiénois and launched a new attack on Rumigny, now near the positions of the *7th Regiment*, through St. Sauflieu and Grattepanche, on the Oresmaux road. By the middle of the day, the combat units had penetrated some eight kilometers into the rear of the French positions and were near the town of Oresmaux. There were counter-attacks by *Type S-40 Souma* tanks, but those French heavies were successfully beaten off; however, because the infantry had still not yet come up to link up with the panzers the flanking fire coming from the many small villages was not easily suppressed. In one of the small attacks undertaken by the Regiment that day, *Olt* Neumann of the *1st Company* was mortally wounded while leading his company. Another panzer in the *1st Company* was a Mk II commanded by Wilhelm Ludwig, who remembered this attack:

"*It was on 5 June 1940 in France at Amiens during the attack on the Weygand line. In the morning gray, around 0500hrs the Regiment attacked in formation of the 10th Panzer Division. I drove in the formation of 1./Pz.8 with my crew, a driver and the radio operator, with a panzer Mk II to the enemy lines. From the forest on the left we started receiving the fire from an anti-tank defense battery. Many panzers were shot. We also received a hit in the engine and were almost totally unable to maneuver, but there was no fire in the panzer. The radio operator was mortally wounded with the fragment of the grenade in the stomach and the driver was wounded with the fragment in the left calf. I got out of this with no damage. It was luck that our panzer was not on fire unlike many other panzers of our company and we didn't have to get out. It was dreadful to sit in the vehicle in the burning heat with dead and wounded comrades, and to wait for more things, which could happen to us. The time wouldn't simply fly. I was able to see enemy soldiers through the visor, which were about 20 meters away, standing with their weapons at the edge of the forest, they watched and I had to look uninterrupted into the barrel of that very pipe [cannon], which had shot us. Each swiveling movement of the pipe caused the fear which was hard to describe, as one has to think it is aiming at you. Then after approximately 14 hours we were free from our dangerous situation by our Sturmpioneers. These were not only the saddest hours of my time in the war, but in my whole life.*"[58]

The panzers were under constant artillery and anti-tank gunfire from Oresmaux and Grattepanche, and the overall situation was worsening, as there was a shortage of fuel and ammunition in addition to a number of panzers being immobilized. The Regiment was then informed by wireless that it was to receive re-supply by air, but the day came and went, and still there was no sight of the promised transport aircraft. That evening there was another counter-attack by the *12th French Tank Battalion* which required some effort before it was beaten back. Later that day the *10th Panzer Division* made the decision to pull back the *4th Panzer Brigade* from its positions near Sains-en-Amiénois. Around 2100hrs, the combat units again came under continued artillery fire originating from Sains-en-Amiénois, and then began to receive even stronger anti-tank gun fire, but as the day ended the Regiment could be proud that it had overcome a difficult if somewhat successful day. That evening, at 2100hrs the panzers moved back in the direction of Amiens and reached their old assembly area shortly before midnight. The Regiment had accounted for some thirty-four tanks destroyed, one artillery battery eliminated, and approximately one hundred prisoners taken. The Regiment also suffered losses from the fourteen hours of uninterrupted artillery fire; heavy Pak-fire, minefields, and counter-attacks by French tanks caused a significant loss. June 5, 1940, had been one of the worst and bloodiest days for the Regiment, as it lost some nineteen men, including *Olt* Neumann of the *1st Company* and eighteen others: *OGefr* Bielmeyer, *Uffz* Breiter, *Gefr* Flöss, *Gefr* Hettich, *Gefr* Koch, *OGefr* Kussmaul, *Fw* Kraus, *Uffz* Laux, *Fw* Lüders, *Gefr* Meiser, *OGefr* Merz, *Gefr* Metze, *Uffz* Prüfer, *Uffz* Sobirei, *Gefr* Sonn, *Gefr* von Stackelberg, *Gefr* Steingraber, and *Gefr* Voges.[59] In addition to the nineteen men killed there were also a large number of wounded, including Hans Kümmel and Wilhelm Ludwig.

On the 6th, the Regiment was able to report only fourteen operational panzers ready for action, and the division made arrangements for the Regiment to be amalgamated with *Panzer Regiment 7*, which still had some seventy-six operational panzers. *Oberst* Elster raised significant objections to the division's proposed move, and in doing so succeeded in keeping the Regiment intact. At that time the Regiment's workshop

Chapter 3: The French Campaign, May-July 1940

companies, technical services, and panzer companies were putting forth a tremendous effort to increase the overall readiness and panzer strength of the Regiment. They soon were improving the overall maintenance situation and increasing the number of panzers ready for service; in fact, that morning four panzers had even been retrieved from a minefield and were moving forward to the Regimental assembly area. The I./*Abteilung* report continues:

"On the 6th at lunchtime our panzers moved forward again to the south at the head of the regiment were the remaining panzers of the 2nd Company of the Regiment. As Abteilung Commander we had this time Major Ramsauer in the panzer. The whole day we served with our panzer for the cooperation with the infantry. With the dusk of the night the commander collected the remaining panzers in Grattepanche, where we spent the night."

As the Regiment reorganized itself, the attacks were continued by the 10th *Schützen Brigade* towards the town of Essertaux. At the same time, the *Grossdeutschland* infantry regiment and the 10th *Panzer Division's aufklärungs* and *panzerjäger Abteilung* were ordered to reinforce the 4th *Panzer Brigade* in its attack. That attack went forward at around 1000hrs in a thin wedge towards Oresmaux, and was able to gain a small toehold in the village by 1100hrs. Unfortunately, the force that entered was not able to secure the village, as a good portion of the follow-on infantry was once again slowed as it attempted to move up and secure the terrain already captured. The division was again forced to reorganize its attacking forces, and so it ordered that the remaining elements of the Regiment be subordinated to the *Grossdeutschland Infantry Regiment*, while one *abteilung* from *Panzer Regiment 7* was sent to the 10th *Schützen Brigade*.[60] What had begun as a panzer attack supported by infantry now became an infantry attack supported by panzers. While those formations continued to keep pressure on the French defenses, some critical time was won for the Regiment in order for it to care for its wounded, and to improve the overall panzer readiness for continued operations. Many of those who had been only slightly wounded chose to remain with their comrades in their own companies. By that evening, the leading elements of the division stood at Essertaux and 5km south of Estrées-sur-Noye. For the Regiment, it continued its attempts to improve its overall operational readiness and reorganize the leading elements. Over on the Allied side, the French were able to strengthen the Essertaux defensive line with the addition of the French 24th *Infantry Division*, which was infused into the center of the French position. The addition of these forces would now seriously hamper and delay the German attacks scheduled to commence the following day. The only progress that could be made against the stiff resistance was very slow and short. Continuing his report, *Uffz* Spathelf recalls how tired the troops were:

"At about midnight on June 6th, after two hot days that had not been without loss we retreated to the outskirts of the village of Grattepanche where we were to spend the night. Dead tired, we lay down near our panzers determined not to be disturbed by any artillery while we were enjoying our well-deserved rest. Suddenly our slumber was disturbed by the gas alert; an airplane had dropped a few bombs not far off. We fell asleep again, despite the gas masks that we had to put on. The fuel tanker and the lorry with ammunition arrived a little later. The panzers were soon refueled and the ammunition restocked."[61]

Gefr Schlipf of the 7th *Company* wrote of the attack on Oresmaux on 6.6.40:

"At 1100hrs we left our assembly area in Amiens, and soon we entered the new assembly area in the beech [tree] forest. At 2000hrs via radio finally we got the order to attack. We advanced over Grattepanche – Oresmaux – Essertaux and fiercely fought [against] enemy infantry and some artillery positions with cannons and both M.G.s. Also we opened fire on the fleeing French troops. The infantry followed closely after us in order to clear the suspicious woods and occupy the obtained terrain. Around 2200hrs came the order to march back, as the darkness complicated further advancement. We drove back until Grattepanche, in order to spend the night there."[62]

The S-Company diary recorded the following:

"6.6.40. The combat continues. The Regiment operates now only 28 panzers, which are now organized into one company. The company remains in the rest area ready for operation. Again a number of crew members were exchanged. On midday Lt Bönisch was sent to Mons, to get the newly arrived panzers. The mail arrived again, which is this day's special event."

With the Regiment still subordinate to the *Grossdeutschland* and 10th *Schützen Brigade*, the panzers of the I./*Abteilung* were now ordered to support these infantry formations in new attacks beginning on the 7th. The S-Company diary recorded:

"7.6.40. The day started sunny; with it our Stukas appeared on the pink horizon and opened the way to the sun. During the night there was heavy artillery firing to the southwest of our position and it demonstrated that the enemy still defends. At midday suddenly came the order to march away. At 1230hrs march to Amiens. The company enters the accommodations in a large infantry barracks on the road to Paris. In the heavily destroyed town there was no water, no food, absolutely nothing to find. The company receives multiple expansions from panzer companies, which are now shrunk into the small unit of fifteen panzers. The S-Company is transformed in the Abteilung under the lead of Oberstlt Haarde."[63]

Uffz Koppe, of the 7th *Company*, wrote of the day's actions:

"The attack started on 7.6.40 in the morning. We were allocated to the vehicle of company Körner [which number]. The village on our right hand side was heavily occupied. We drove approximately 300m left from the village. And immediately were under anti-tank and artillery fire. The rounds fell ahead and around us. Four infantry men came with our panzer. And no one could answer the question from where was the fire coming from. Then came the order to march back and here I saw the firing cannon approximately 500m in front of us on the border of the village. The cannon was then taken care of. Now we went full speed on the road 1km backwards, where there was the assembly. One vehicle ahead of us was shot. Three vehicles which were ready for combat, drove back to the damaged vehicle. But there was no sight of the crew. Here we received the anti-tank fire from the village border. We quickly aimed our fire at the village. We returned and drove to the initial position. Numerous vehicles were shot by the gun. After close observation it was discovered that only two were ready for combat. We got the task to collect the wounded, which were left during the first attack on the village. During the advancement the anti-tank fire killed one infantryman, who drove with us sitting on the backside of the panzer. Those wounded who we were able to find, were placed on the backside of the panzer and driving backwards we returned.

I also reported to our own panzers, which were driving to the village, what was going on there. In the meantime it was afternoon time. We went back to the company on the same road."[64]

At around 1500hrs, the *Stukas* and artillery began a preparatory bombardment of the French positions south of Pappelalle, and by 1700hrs the panzers and infantry began moving forward again. During the attack the commander of the infantry regiment accompanied the I00 command panzer. That evening the panzers returned back toward Grattepanche to refuel and rearm. As these actions were taking place, additional elements of the Regiment were fighting near Essertaux and to the east of Flers, where both villages were taken by the early evening despite the stout defense put up by French troops. *Uffz* Spathelf continues his story on how his panzer was detailed to perform a special mission:

"About 1900hrs the Company Commander awaked us. Two Mk IIs, the remainders of the 1st Zug, I./Abteilung together with an Mk IV were assigned to Lt von Bitter's Zug. A little later our Zug was ordered to proceed to the infantry's command post. Once we reached the sentry posts of the German infantry, my vehicle received the order to go and secure the battalion commander's vehicle, which still held some secret files in it. It had been fired upon by French anti-tank gun and was now located in front of the French positions. In order to reach the vehicle we had to drive through an open poplar alley that was in full view of the French and constantly under fire. Therefore, we had to drive at top speed. The enemy forces were just 100meters away on our right. We came under violent fire and when we reached the vehicle there were shells exploding damn close. And now off the panzer, the towrope had to be fastened. Furious machine gun fire broke out. A very short whistle followed by an explosion; wasn't it the anti-tank gun? Again and again it fired at us. This won't do. We drove back about 10m and took cover and tried to neutralize the gun from our new position. After a few machine gun bursts in the direction of the muzzle fire of the anti-tank gun we resumed our attempts to carry out the order and take the vehicle in tow. As soon as we approached the vehicle, the anti-tank gun began firing again. After a few seconds a few more bullets hit us; it was high time we drove back. We couldn't do anything alone. With the driving wheel damaged in the firing, with shot up caterpillar tracks and a smashed guide-wheel we made our way back. The panzer was still moving, although with difficulty. Like a lame duck, we crawled back along the same road in our good old panzer. We must have looked like a target card to the French. On our return we couldn't find our Zug commander at the former position and so we drove back to Gradepanche where we reported to the Company Commander. From there we were sent to the repair shop and after several days our panzer was ready for battle again and so we set out in search of the forward echelons with renewed courage."[65]

And so the 7th passed; by 0930hrs on the 8th, with the I00 still subordinated to the *4th Panzer Brigade*, the commander's panzer had become non-expendable because there were only about a company's worth of operational panzers remaining in the entire Regiment. The I00 was then subordinated to *Panzer Regiment 7*, but by late afternoon it was released from its assignment with the *4th Panzer Brigade* and made its way towards Oresmaux, where its commander and crew met up with *Oberst* Elster, who was found at the head of the B Combat *Abteilung*. The Regiment, followed by the *10th Schützen Brigade*, proceeded along the route Beonneuil-les-Eaux – Breteuil towards St. Just-en-Chaussée. It arrived in Breteuil late that evening and remained there the following day. That evening, at 2035hrs, the Regiment reported only twenty operational panzers remaining; however, the attack of the division was halted during the night of 7/8 June, and those elements that had been detached from the Regiment were released back to it, which then brought the total panzer strength of the Regiment to some thirty-eight operational panzers. The S-Company, now taking the shape of an entire *Abteilung*, recorded in its diary for the 8th:

"8.6.40 1430hrs march of S-Abteilung to Breteuil, with the task to free up the road and to collect the multiple prisoners loitering around the multiple roads and to collect them in a large camp in cooperation with the military police."

As part of the reinforced *4th Panzer Brigade*, the Regiment was sent on the 9th towards Verberie; its orders were to undertake a crossing of the Oise River and form and secure a bridgehead for the follow-on infantry forces. At St. Just-en-Chaussée there was contact between the Regiment and elements of the French *1st Armored Division*, which was attacking to the west and south. In the action that followed, *Fw* Heinz of the *7th Company* was killed and Lt Kurt Liestmann of the *3rd Company* was severely wounded—this was his second wound, having been previously wounded in Poland.[66] In continuing his written account *Gefreiter* Schlipf wrote of the attack south of St. Just on the 9th:

"We left our assembly area south of St. Just at 0430hrs and after a short while encountered the enemy. We were shooting at the village border [outskirts] occupied by enemy, when suddenly enemy tanks appeared in a distance of 600m. These were nevertheless received by the heavy fire of our cannons, which destroyed many armored vehicles which were noticed in the village in front of us. We attacked by revolving to the side. They flee, but we caught up with them by driving fast in our vehicle and some of them were destroyed. 12 destroyed enemy tanks were the result of the whole fight, five of them were shot down by my vehicle, led by Olt von Bitter. In the afternoon the attack continued. We took one hill and pursued further on the other side towards the woods occupied by enemy. We had hardly reached the woods, when suddenly French anti-tank guns shoot and we as the first vehicle took four direct hits on the right side. Unfortunately the Richtschütze, Uffz Prüfer, was dead immediately, the Ladeschütze received fragments in the neck and hip. The panzer commander, driver and myself were only slightly wounded. The forest was under heavy fire from the panzers following ours. Many French surrendered. After we put the bandage on the Ladeschütze and buried Uffz Prüfer, the medical vehicle brought us back to the field hospital in Amiens."[67]

The S-Company diary reported the following details for them on this day:

"9.6.40 0300hrs The company enters the night accommodations during the short rest at the fruit orchard in front of the town. During this time one Zug was ordered to the protection of the Abteilung Stabs and to manage the lively vehicle traffic towards Breteuil, in the Chateau de Breteuil. The aircraft appeared over the rest area and were unable to discover anything despite the multiple light sources, because all the vehicles were well camouflaged and the engines were immediately turned off upon appearance of the enemy aircraft. The bombing by the enemy was thus prevented. At 0600hrs the Company was advanced to Farivillers on the order of the division to provide cover over Breteuil. Here it was assigned by the division to secure the advance march road from St. Just until Breteuil, to keep it open and to remove the multiple prisoners from it. The proposal of the company leader was to deploy one Zug to protect the road St. Just – Vadanvillers, two Zugs to protect the road Farivillers – Breteuil and the division. The division agrees with the proposal.

The company is immediately deployed respectively and the company commander, Hptm Betz approaches the Abteilung Commander Oberstlt Haarde, in order to report about the arrangements. In the meantime Fw Heintz, Gefr Raash with U.A. Dr. Zoeller and one Gefr of the 1st Zug of the company were driving ahead. When they arrive in St. Just, they receive the machine gun fire from houses and from the enemy tank. During this Fw Heintz is killed, other passengers of the vehicle were partially wounded some heavy and some lightly wounded excluding U.A. Dr. Zoeller. In the meantime there appeared a Sankawagen, which was used as return transportation. At 1700hrs the Company receives the order to advance to St. Just which is again assumed to be free of enemy after the personal reconnaissance of the company commander. For the searching of the houses and the neighborhoods of St. Just, Hptm Betz has deployed one Zug and two groups of infantry, which are combined from the straggler soldiers of other units, and ordered the clearance of the road from the prisoners in order to enable the advance march of the troops with no disturbance. Already at 1900hrs the whole advance march can be led via St. Just. In the meantime there are about 500 prisoners gathered in St. Just."[68]

Uffz Bauer, a panzer commander of the *7th Company*, reported on the day's combat:

"On 9.6.40 we as a reserve company of Pz.Rgt.8 were subordinated to Pz.Rgt.7. We entered into a temporary position on the northeast of the village of Valescourt. In the morning hours of 9.6. the Regiment started the attack. We were almost through the village Valescourt, when we got the task to secure the heights east of the village. After crossing the road we received the message from the Flak guns located ahead, that enemy tanks were approaching. We already saw the enemy tanks in the distance at about 200m. There were four vehicles, which were rendered unserviceable in the shortest time. The same destiny was also for the other six vehicles following. We got the order through the radio, to attack Erguinvillers. Our company drove around the village to the south. Our panzers almost reached the new direction of attack, when they faced three enemy tanks driving towards them. Three enemy combat vehicles drove north past us, as they didn't recognize us. I considered this as a very lucky chance and drove behind these tanks at full speed. From the distance of 40m we were able to demolish all three of them. On the heights of Erguinvillers the Regiment stopped for a short rest. Our vehicles were sent forward as a protection. We received fire from an enemy machine gun on the heights 150m southwest of Noroy. The recognized machine gun nests were destroyed. Suddenly we were under anti-tank fire from the close distance. My panzer received four direct impacts and our Richtschütze, Uffz Prüfer, as well as Gefreiters Koch and Schlip were wounded by fragments. Both Gefreiters were able to get out of the destroyed vehicle with the extreme force of their strength. I got out from the driver hatch. As I didn't possess any weapon, I crawled about 30m in the clover field. Despite my guess that there should not be any enemy, five French soldiers stood up with the raised hands. After short consideration, I took one of the enemy's weapons and captured them as prisoners. I positioned them in the proximity of my vehicle, so that I could watch them well. The wounded were first noticed by other comrades and were bandaged during the pause in the fire. They were brought back in the Sanitäter vehicle which had arrived in the meantime. At the end we buried our fallen comrade Uffz Heinz Prüfer in the presence of Doctor Witzky and eight other comrades. As my panzer was not able to drive anymore, I drove back in the direction of Amiens in a car and reported myself at the company in the evening. I handed over the prisoners to a Feldwebel of the infantry."[69]

In another report, *Gefr* Degner of the *7th Company* reported on the fighting around the village of Lienvillers on 9.6.40:

"On 9 June we were subordinated to Company Ehrbeck in Amiens. Our march route led from Amiens to the brigade [4th Panzer], which we were supposed to reach in the evening. On the march we were stopped by Major Ottens and deployed on the village Lienvillers. It was heavily occupied by the enemy. We immediately prepared our vehicles for combat. We saw there in front of us approximately 20 Flak-soldiers, who were advancing as infantry. When the Flak came over the hill, it was immediately hit by M.G. fire. Immediately afterwards began our attack. The 2cm zug drove ahead at the head. A panzer Mk IV drove until the hill and went there in the assembly position. The 2cm zug drove in the village. My driver called back: "hold on!" and immediately the level of the slope went down and up again. Suddenly I heard the hits of rounds [to the] left and right around the vehicle. On this the driver shouted 'half-right, enemy fire!' The schütze, Uffz Wald, rotated the turret in this direction. After this our cannon made a shot and hammered the M.G. The fire stopped after a short while, thus we assumed that the enemy was eliminated. Suddenly the vehicle on the left, our zug leader, stopped and turned in circles some many times. My driver therefore went with higher speed and we were the first vehicle entering the village. During the entry my schütze was shooting from the machine gun and cannon. We noticed the road block which the schütze took under fire as well. So this was shut down too. At the end of the village, on the cross-road, we drove half-left, other vehicles half-right. There was a hail and thunder of anti-tank guns and M.G. The 2nd vehicle took a direct hit from an anti-tank gun, but without much impact. The vehicle was able to drive back by itself. We together with the Flak eliminated the cannon. The French and Colonial troops came out of houses with raised hands and white cloth. Together with the Flak we took many prisoners, and took from them ammunition and weapons. It was around 300 prisoners, two anti-tank and three 75mm cannons, which was our booty. We continued our march to the final destination."[70]

On 10 June, Mussolini, thinking the war already won and afraid that he would miss out on the fruits of a conquered Europe, officially declared war on France. Also that day the *XIV Korps* was pulled out of the line in its drive south and reset farther to the east to Château-Thierry where it was placed together with the *XVI Korps*. Over the past six days the Regiment had battled hard against the strong and determined French forces that cost the Regiment and other German forces in this sector numerous casualties. Despite battering itself against strong and well prepared defense positions, and with a reduced combat strength, the Regiment was able to claim a degree of success and contributed significantly to the overall success of the corps and *10th Panzer Division*. Many of the previous attacks had begun without the proper support of the pioneers and artillery, but nevertheless, the panzers were able to break through the numerous defensive positions; however, the infantry continued to be slowed when tasked with moving up to support the breakthroughs. As much of the *Wehrmacht* was still foot borne at this time, it was the panzers on many occasions that had to attempt to breakthrough the many villages and forests. The urban and heavily forested areas usually dispersed the panzer formations and broke them up in smaller elements, where they could be more easily attacked and defeated. The reason for the lack of infantry support normally lay in the fact that the infantry still lacked the proper transport to keep up with the panzers; this was a lesson first taught in Poland, but had yet to be properly corrected. Another problem was that the panzers were also not able to attack the French artillery, which was skillfully positioned under cover and on reverse slope positions, where the infantry was needed to get in and put them out of action. This lack of supporting arms led to many unnecessary losses, and the lack of friendly forward observers did not allow for the timely and accurate fire to be called in time to suppress the French positions and to open up gaps through the numerous minefields. As with many actions fought in the early days of the *Blitzkrieg*, many of the senior officers were still new to this combined arms approach, and those that could think outside the box and embrace this new concept were to see their stars rise, as many of those from the old school would soon be pushed aside while the brash and daring of the new thinkers were placed to the forefront of command. The lack of success around Amiens and Péronne, and the shift of forces to the east left the Regiment little time for rest and replenishment, not to mention a chance to perform desperately needed maintenance. After pulling out of the forward positions the panzers began a road march that continued south and then east parallel to the Oise River towards Chauny. On 10 June, the S-Company diary recorded its actions:

"10.6.40 Transportation of the prisoners and management of the multiple traffic along the road of the advance march. The lead of the S-Abteilung is handed over from Oberstlt Haarde to Major Ramsauer. 2000hrs, forty-four replacements arrive from the replacement Abteilung. The company is structured anew and further vehicles are acquired to transport the increased company, because it can't be expected to get the subordinated vehicles from the Regiment. A number of French light machine guns were acquired, so that each group of the company can compose one machine gun troop. The company now possesses fourteen machine guns with ammunition, which were with one exception acquired by the company itself."

Once reaching the area of Chauny the Regiment then swung south towards Soissons, where it crossed the Aisne River on the 11th. The S-Company recorded:

"11.6.40. 0445hrs marched away to Chauny. The company is accommodated in two school buildings together with the S-Company of Panzer Regiment 7 and it is the first time that Panzerschützen abteilung 8 is gathered under the command of Major Ramsauer. The equipment is repaired, clothes, Pussdienst [visit to local brothel], sports, training in driving disciplines etc."[71]

On the 12th, as the Regiment reached the Marne River at Château-Thierry, *General* Weygand ordered a general retreat of Allied forces, which in turn gave up northern France to the Germans. A new defensive line was then called for, and was to be established along the line from Caen-Tours-Loire-Clamecy-Dijon-Dôle-Geneva. This line was actually a longer line to defend, and with all of the losses sustained over the past month was even more difficult to hold. In the meantime, the Regiment continued to push south against weak Allied forces attempting to fall back onto the new line. The S-Company recorded:

"12.6.40, The S-'Abteilung' is transformed into the company again under the previous commander, Hptm Betz. 0900hrs marched away to Villers-Cotterêts. The company is now again subordinated to the division at this time. The stop-over takes place in Viels-Maison, where the company leader has organized and conducted a undisturbed march through by the many troops."

On the 14th, the Germans reached the Seine River and a crossing conducted at Nogent-sur-Seine. *Uffz* Schöppler of the 7th *Company* continues his account, and wrote about the combat on the 14th at Nogent and locating a bridge on which the panzers could cross over:

"After a 36 hour drive from the workshop, in the early afternoon we entered the assembly area in the woods. After a short rest came the order to prepare for the attack on the bridge over the Seine by forming a bridgehead. After the short drive in the Seine valley, the first task was to search for the bridge. After a little back and forth, the bridge was found. On the same shore we came under fire. From the advanced vehicles came the message that enemy tanks are approaching. We were advanced with our panzer. We went into the position at the border of the village. We shot down all the enemy tanks. After this came the order to attack the woods in the distance of about 1000m. The woods were captured. We were able to shoot down the fleeing enemy anti-tank guns."[72]

In the meantime, the French government, which had previously moved to Tours, was now on the move again, this time to Bordeaux. The following day the French Army headquarters was again moved, this time to the Vichy region of France. Also on that day, the Germans entered Paris and found the city almost empty, with roughly one million of the population of five million choosing to remain in the city. The remainder had taken to the roads in an attempt to flee the oncoming German Army. Recognizing the seriousness of the situation and the need to conserve what forces he could for the *Battle of Britain*, Churchill ordered the immediate evacuation of all remaining British troops in France. The S-Company diary noted:

"14.6.40 – The division is already far ahead. The company follows after the tasks are completed. 0500hrs marched away towards Sourdin. Upon arrival the division is already in motion. The company is subordinated to the 4th Panzer Brigade and makes contacts with the brigade during the march. During the march the company is pushed forward, it moves away from the brigade and is subordinated to the division for the conduct of special tasks. With that the company is speedily thrown towards Clamecy, where the roads are totally blocked with prisoners, refugees, destroyed vehicles, garbage etc. The company takes care of opening the roads, collecting of the prisoners and clearing the passage ways. After a short while the marching columns come to the river and proceed across with no obstacles due to well organized traffic management, which is conducted by the company commander all over the town. The task is completed with excellence. 3000 prisoners were identified. As well the company had acquired eight new vehicles to replace the broken ones."[73]

Uffz Rebscher, of the 7th *Company*, describes his situation on 14.6.40:

"After the combat at Amiens, which finished on 9 June, we had three days of rest. Afterwards we went to the south over the Noyon, Oise, Aisne, Marne [all rivers]. On the second day, [14 June], we took up the assembly position at 1600hrs. We were in front of the Seine and it was reported [to us] about the enemy on retreat. The stay in the assembly position was very short, and then the attack began. I drove in a panzer Mk I as gunner for the commander Hptm Bernau. This company was the lead company. We went through the first village without any encounters with the enemy. In the second village we stopped at the crossroads. Suddenly an enemy motorcycle messenger appeared between the panzers. First four panzers, among them mine; shot with the machine guns and in a moment the messenger was taken care of. The same way we dealt with the vehicle which also appeared on the road. One Mk IV and my vehicle drove along the road to the right. We then took care about the cannon on the road. The Mk IV took aim at the truck and I did on the car. Then the enemy tanks were reported and the light panzers had to return, when the Mk IV took care of about five enemy tanks. Then the attack continued, not on the road

Chapter 3: The French Campaign, May-July 1940

as previously, but on the open terrain. Here and there, there appeared French soldiers in the fields, who raised their hands immediately when they saw our panzer approaching. By crossing the road were destroyed seven enemy trucks. The attack finished in the evening and we returned back to village and the security watch was set for the night."[74]

Uffz Baumann from the *7th Company* also made this report on the situation that day near Nogent:

"After the long drive we entered the assembly position in the early afternoon, in the small forest north of the Seine. After the short rest there was an order to begin preparations for an attack on a bridge over the Seine and for the composition of the bridgehead. After a short drive in the valley of the Seine, the first task was to find the bridge. After some back and forth, the bridge was found and now it was all about the quick crossing to the other side. On the other riverbank we first received fire from the 28cm battery which was on the retreat and was quickly taken care of. Then the message came from the advanced vehicles, that there were enemy tanks approaching. We were advanced with our panzer and additionally one Mk III. There were in total six enemy tanks of the small format. After the short combat they were all shot and caught the fire. Afterwards came the order to attack the small forest in the distance of 1000m. We reached the woods without much shooting. From behind we shot the fleeing anti-tank guns etc. Then the security was set up and we went back to the village for a nights rest."[75]

Uffz Himmelreich, also of the *7th Company*, reported this action near Provins on the 14th:

"Company Seidler [7th Company] was composed at the workshop after the combat south of Amiens. From there the march went to Provins. We caught up with the regiment and combined us with them. After the march of 31 hours we had covered 310km. The regiment was supposed to pull under the forest at Provins. Here came the order to attack the enemy troops which had retreated to the south. We drove into the town. Here the cannons were already made safe. The light companies, who drove first from the town, came back with the report about enemy tanks in attack. I drove with my panzer Mk IV out of the town and received the order from commander to stop. The enemy tank located 200m away we took immediately under fire and it burned. Afterwards I drove on the side of the road in the position. We were under fire from five enemy tanks and also fire from the forest. I got the attention of the gunner of the tank who tried to make a turn in front of us and was attempting to reach the forest. In our well aimed fire he stopped 1200m away and burned. After 1900hrs the regiment attacked. Many artillery cannons were destroyed and prisoners were taken. After the attack we drove back and took the security watch at the edge of the town for the night. More prisoners were brought in during the night."[76]

Finally of the *7th Company* reports there is *Gefr* Landthaler's account of the action at the village of Les Armes:

"On 14.6.40 we drove into the combat at Les-Armes after the very long march.

This village seemed to be occupied by enemy forces. We got the order to capture the village. The Pz.Rgt.7 and we were deployed together. We approached the village on a wide front. After searching through the area it was discovered, that it was free of enemy. We drove until the border of the village, and noticed that the enemy was approaching from the west. The panzers immediately searched for a good firing position. Before the enemy tanks were able to recognize us, we had already opened fire on them. After the long fire duel we gained the superiority. The vehicles were destroyed. Approaching artillery cannons were shot down. After the short stop we threw a rain of high-explosive shells on the woods in the background, in order to destroy M.G.-nests supposedly located there. We drove further until the hill in the background, in order to watch over the valley located in front of us. We shot the passing truck column with high-explosive shells and as a result some of the vehicles got stuck. From the village in the background we recognized the enemy tank units and retreating infantry troops. As the distance was too great, we were not able to shoot at them. We moved back to the next village and overnight we went in the hedgehog position. Some other vehicles took over the firing positions. On the next day both Regiments went back."[77]

Also on that day, the Regiment crossed the Yonne channel at Villeneuve-l'Archevêque, and the panzers were able to continue rolling south non-stop through Auxerre and on towards Chamecy, where they were able to break through some of the last organized defenses and reached Autun on the afternoon of the 16th. By that time, French *Premier* Paul Reynaud had resigned and *Marshal* Petain, the hero of Verdun, was tasked with the formation of a new government. The following day Petain asked the Germans for armistice terms. As the Regiment continued to push south, securing villages and capturing large numbers of Allied prisoners, the British began to evacuate some thirty thousand troops from the port of Cherbourg. The S-Company noted that during the day:

"Two Zugs of the company led by Olt Plinzner were advanced to Lormes, in order to secure there the advance march without obstacles and to remove the prisoners from the roads. Those prisoners were kept in the collection camp in the church." On the following day the diary went on to record the following: *"17.6.40 the division follows up in a forced march to the south and the S-Company goes with them. The marches of the S-Company are especially strenuous, because the company has to limp along behind in a jumping way. It is necessary as well to advance the column of the company frequently along the whole division or on narrow nearby roads again to the head of the division. The damage to vehicles was therefore very high. These difficulties didn't mean any restraints in fulfilling the assigned tasks. Many times the damaged vehicles were immediately replaced with booty vehicles. The company was almost continuously counting only on itself and thus had to provision itself, get fuel, spare parts, tires oil and motor grease, tools of all kinds, underwear, socks, working outfits, smoke material and so on. All this was arranged by the company itself without any support by the Regiment for a number of weeks. On the contrary, some of the companies of the Regiment came to the S-Company with their requests, while they knew that here it was more likely to get a battery, the acid for it, tools or spare tires, whereas the Werkshop Company was located almost a hundred or more kilometers behind the Regiment. It became a habit to expect the S-Company to be in a position to fulfill the requests of the other companies. At 1400hrs La Celle was reached. The company receives a task to secure the march for the division trough Autun. In Autun many roads were blocked at that time. The market square was crowded with refugees, scattered beds, clothes, broken vehicles etc. The refugees had camped on the plaster in the middle of the square. It was impossible for the company to enter the town therefore the leader of the company Hptm Betz drove to the town alone and cleared the cluster, which caused the blockage. The military police were here helpless and in a half-hour it was achieved that the march through for some columns was organized on certain march routes and so the march through went so well, that even before dark the division had considered this task as completed. Other divisions were kept away*

from the march route of the 10th Panzer Division and were redirected. About 1600hrs the company was moved behind one of the columns in the town and found a very good accommodation in a military school. The stripes were immediately organized to capture the prisoners and remove them together with thousands of refugees from the roads. The prisoners were collected in a camp. Due to the masses of refugees and soldiers there began to emerge the growing shortage of food in the town. The town's leaders watched it all with no action. The news about the decision of the French government to lay down its weapons reached us at 0200hrs in the middle of the turmoil of military and refugee vehicles, the roar of the engines, the cries of women for their children, the barking of homeless dogs and neigh of the abandoned horses. All looked towards each other. The civilians hugged the soldiers, women cried of joy, men starred in the blankness deeply moving. The German soldier didn't care about the news. They moved without hurry further to the south, vehicle after vehicle, panzer after panzer, as if nothing happened. The leader of the company was still Hauptmann Betz. At 2300hrs came the order from XIV Armeekorp that the leader of the S-Company was to take over the commandant's [mayor's] office."[78]

On the 18th, as the Germans captured the cities of Cherbourg and Brest, all towns and cities with populations of more than twenty thousand were to be declared "open," and were ordered to immediately surrender without further resistance. The S-Company diary follows up on its previous report and gives a good account on the new type of missions it was now tasked with conducting:

"18.6 as commandant of Autun, the company commander appeared in the city hall. To there were called the mayor and deputy mayor, secretary, directors of the town electric and water supply, some owners of large food enterprises etc. In the meantime two rooms were arranged as the commandant's office. The mayor of the city was first asked to provide knowledge about the situation with population in the town. The announcements were issued about immediate provisioning with electricity and water while short-term food shortages are being taken care of. Orders that the population should behave quietly and follow the guidelines as in previous announcements were issued. The acts of sabotage would be the case for a military court and punished by death. The municipal government receives the task to call for a continuation of work for city workers. A number of enterprises received a passport to go to the countryside in order to buy food. The town is obliged, to provide the necessary material for the supply of the prisoners which has grown to 5000 in the meantime. The prisoners were relocated to the barracks of the military school, where there was set up a kitchen and necessary personnel selected amongst the prisoners to assume duties. A number of prisoners had to clean up the market square and the streets under supervision of the S-Company, to remove all abandoned vehicles, to collect the clothes laying around and to deliver this to the city hall. After a few hours the town and the streets were clean and in order. The citizens' life began to slowly return to its normal form. In the commandant's office loitered from morning to evening the refugees, petitioners, soldiers etc., it was quite a job to settle all these wishes and applications and in parallel to take actions in order to bring the dumb municipal government into action and power. Everything that was not ordered by the commandant remained undone, because the mayor so far was very passive, until the commandant threatened him with the promise of rigorous measures in case the actions of the commandant's office would not be actively supported. The hostages were taken from the circle of citizens and kept in the barracks and the announcement was made that any attempt to destroy order will be radically punished and endanger the life of the hostages."[79]

As the men of the Regiment began the task of reestablishing local governments and gaining control over events in their area, events elsewhere began to unfold which would later affect the Regiment in the course of the war, and certainly be a tell tale sign of things to come. Since declaring war on the French over a week ago, Benito Mussolini now ordered the Italian *First* and *Fourth Armies*, consisting of some 450,000 troops, to attack the 185,000 strong *French Fourteenth* and *Fifteenth Corps* composing the *French Army of the Alps* (Olry).[80] The Italian attack was launched on the 20th in the Alpine region between Mont Blanc and the Mediterranean, despite numerous protests from his generals, including *Marshal* Badoglio. During the next five days, before the government of *Marshal* Petain signed an armistice with the Italians near Rome, the Italians made little progress against this highly trained and motivated French Army formation. The Italian *First Army* was only able to reach the city of Menton, and did so only by its vast superiority in numbers, but once in Menton, the Italian offensive quickly became bogged down. At St. Bernard, the Italian *Alpini Corps* failed to even take the French advanced positions in the Maurienne Valley. The *Italian First Corps* ground to a halt before French artillery and Italian tanks even managed to get into action in this short campaign. It was undisputedly a French victory, and despite the Armistice and capitulation, the stand by the French saved southeastern France from Axis occupation. In the five day campaign the French suffered just thirty-seven killed, forty-two wounded, and one hundred and fifty missing. The Italians lost over six hundred killed and almost three thousand wounded and missing.[81] Even as the panzers were closely nipping at the heals of the weakened and retreating French forces, the French Army and Air Forces could at times make life a bit difficult on the men, and on several occasions they would sally out and do battle. There is one instance during the advance to Le Creusot that the Regiment was attacked by a flight of *Morane-Saulnier MS- 406* fighters; two panzer crewmembers were slightly wounded in the attack. Despite these infrequent and ill-coordinated attacks, there was no doubt about the eventual outcome of the battle, and the advance continued forward towards Lyon. It was at this time that the Regiment was relieved of its position in the van and pulled out of the line in order to refit and reorganize itself while still on the march following the leading formations of the division as they continued south. By the 19th the leading elements of the Regiment found themselves at the edge of Lyon where, after a short halt, the Regiment made its way through the city on the 20th and then proceeded to move another 30km to the south, where it halted at the town of Vienne. The French Army was now almost completely incapable of doing battle for fear of getting the hundreds of thousands of refugees caught up in the mix; those refugees, in large numbers, clogged the roads and swamped the few remaining services still left intact, and hindered the French army as it attempted to defend itself. On the march through Lyon the panzers made their way through the streets, which were covered by locals and refugees; to many of the men it gave them the impression that at times the whole population of France was on the move. The S-Company diary records the actions taken during this time:

"19.6.40, the work continues. The apparatus organized by the commandant works seamlessly. The electricity is on, in the meantime some stores have received food, the bakeries work day and night after the [previously] issued admonition. Everywhere to see there are groups of people in front of the food stores. It's a feeling of satisfaction for the commandant, who brought everything back to its feet in this short time. Authoritative men appeared officially to thank the commandant and to express their adoration to these organizational skills. They were all united it that such tasks were quick and work oriented in France. The commandant's office and camp were taken over by the SS. The company is therefore free for new tasks and has taken on some already. By 18.6.,

Chapter 3: The French Campaign, May-July 1940

two Zugs of the company were sent to Le Creusot to the Schneider armor factory, in order to watch over this place.

"20.6.40 the remainder of the company follows on to Le Creusot to provide for the security of the large weapon plant Schneider – Creusot. Already in the afternoon the company is released and follows the division, who had hurried far away. The march of over 200km follows to Lyon. Here was an accommodation in an ideal park and the country house over the Sâone. 2200hrs the company commander reports to the division. The company is again subordinated to the 4th Panzer Brigade."[82]

Gefr Landthaler's report continues with the following on the combat action in Lyon on the 20th:

"We received the order to join the attack on Lyon. One part of Pz.Rgt.7 had already entered Lyon, when we arrived in the evening at 2200hrs there was nothing to see of the fight and resistance but small fires. We drove through the town and took over the defense at approximately 5km distance from the town on the south and west. We were positioned on the hill, and thus had a good field of observation. We recognized a fort approximately 1800m away from us, where French soldiers were occupied. On the right at the woods we recognized some French aircraft. By observing we found out that the aircraft were not been looked after. We asked the civilians who had come from that direction and we found out that there were 66 enemy aircraft, but no one from the fortress was there. We reported this to the chief that the scouting echelon should reconnoiter it, but shortly before our scouting echelon had come under heavy fire and three panzer Mk IIs [had] drove immediately to the fort and fired from all their guns. We were then called to one Oberleutnant and had to take up the defense in east and thus we were not able to complete the task."[83]

Lt Bönisch, of the *7th Company*, wrote this report on the actions near Chasselay that he was involved in. The report documents that not all French soldiers were ready to just surrender and give up, and the terrible work ahead that still remained:

"The advisory board of our division asked me to support them on the march from Mâcon to Lyon. Their workshop company entered the accommodations in Chasselay and was shot at by the anti-tank guns and some of their people were shot. With one wounded man, I advanced and wanted to clarify the situation, I then drove forward with one Mk III and two Mk IVs. I ordered the Mk IV to take up position and to place fire onto the directed position. I drove in the direction of Chasselay. The enemy recognized us and began to fire on us and the company showed itself. Some people of the workshop herded 40 to 50 Negro's [French Colonial Troops] ahead of them, about 200m behind followed 20 more French with one officer. Shortly before our panzer the Negro's tried to escape into the wine fields. We opened fire and killed them all except for the French, who we brought to Cheres. We searched the fields afterwards and eliminated the rest. The village was free of enemy and I continued my way to Lyon."[84]

In Vienne, the Regiment now received the order to halt and return back to the north, so after a journey of some six hundred kilometers the Regiment turned about and headed back. By midday on the 21st, the return march had begun as it retraced its steps back through Mâcon to Autun, along with a growing number of refugees and prisoners of war. *Uffz* Baumann of the *7th Company* continued in his account about the security that he was providing south of Lyon on 21.6.40:

"With my panzer Mk IV and two panzer Mk IIs we got the task to protect the road south of Lyon. We searched through the terrain and discovered a French aircraft at about 1000m distance. We searched everything very precisely and saw some bunkers with large patches of soil thrown up and some soldiers. First we wanted to walk over there, but this was forbidden by Lt Schnaidt. Lt Schnaidt sent back a message and a little later came the Kradmeldung echelon of I./Abteilung with the task of reconnaissance the village. We took over the fire protection [over watch] during the advancement of two Mk IIs with the Kradmeldung echelon. Already after the first hundred meters the machine gun fire began from a house. We shot the fragment grenades, but found out that there was a bunker ahead of us. Machine gun fire forced us to go inside. The Mk II attacked further and we took several positions on the road Lyon-Nice."[85]

Although some minor actions took place, the Regiment wasted little time as it continued to retrace its steps on the 22nd, reaching Saulieu-Avallon, in the area of the Sens. The march continued from here as the Regiment marched towards the east past Courtenay-Montargis-Bellegarde in the direction of Orléans. Short rest breaks were dedicated to catching a quick nap or performing the needed technical maintenance. That evening, as the Regiment made its way north, there was an eventful ceremony taking place in an old railway car in the Forest of Compiègne. The ceremony taking place was the signing of the *Armistice*, which took place at 1850hrs in the original railway carriage that was used for the 1918 *Armistice* signing. The carriage had been brought from a museum in Paris to the same exact spot of the 1918 signing just for this specific purpose, and once the signing had taken place the carriage was to be blown up.[86] With the signing of the *Armistice*, which would officially take place at 0035hrs on Tuesday, 25 June, the forty-six day campaign came to a close. Back in the S-Company, those men too had also begun to retrace their steps and had returned almost 200km to their old accommodations when, as the diary noted:

"22.6.40. The company is sent forward by the Brigade in order to gather the crews and occupy the vehicles and to acquire the spare parts. The roads today are still free and the column moves forward very quickly. At 1800hrs the Sens is reached. Here was a town bivouac in a school. 2100hrs, the leader of company is called to receive orders from the Brigade which is 75km away. The loudspeaker broadcasts about the signing of the armistice. The glass of sparkling champagne signs this portion of our war life. The return to the company is in the dark of the night during pouring rain, which can be called a masterpiece of driving without lights."[87]

The *Armistice* that was signed provided that two-thirds of the country, north and west of a line running through Geneva, Tours, and the Spanish border, would become occupied by German military forces. Additionally, the *Armistice* also provided the *Kriegsmarine* access to all French Channel and Atlantic ports. A minimal French army was permitted, and the navy was to be disarmed, although it had not yet surrendered. On Sunday the 23rd, the men used the lull before the official *Armistice* took place to clean and overhaul themselves and their vehicles. By the 24th, the majority of the panzers and crews had reached Orléans, where they first learned of the signing of the *Armistice* on the 23rd, and that it was soon to take effect. The Regiment's march continued on the 25th along the north bank of the Loire River towards Blois and Tours. From Blois the panzers rolled west, where they reached the area of Château-Renault, located on the north side of Tours. Also on the 25th, the 220,000 French troops still holding down the *Maginot Line* surrendered; most of those troops found themselves as never having engaged the enemy. The rain had subsided, and the fine French summer greeted the men on the 25th as they continued the march to Orléans, Tours, and Les Oeufs. The S-Company's diary has the following notes concerning the end of the French Campaign and the integration of the men back into the Regiment:

"25.6. Even though a strenuous march through sun-lit France. The company enters into the bivouac in Château la Roche d'Ambille and the surrounding area. The castle is inhabited and the refugee's families from Paris are there as well. The people are friendly and welcome towards the soldiers. They provided food as much as they were able to.

"26.6. Technical service and reparation of the clothes, acquired spare parts from Tours. A number of vehicles were newly fueled, for which the company has acquired three fueling heads, which were possible to connect to the unit's truck.

"27.6. 0800hrs Fussdienst [foot checks] and sport in the park of the Château la Roche d'Ambille. 1400hrs Fussdienst and bathing in the lake near the castle.

"28.6. 0445hrs. March to the west through the Loire Valley along the old castles and their rich historical past. The town and the castle of Amboise are the special landmarks. The wonderful old stone bridges were destroyed by the French. The destruction did not achieve any visible results. We had accommodation in Les Chapelles north of the Orléans.

"29.6. the company is again released from the brigade command and subordinated to the Regiment. In connection with them the company moves to Lion en Beauce at 1800hrs and enters the town bivouac in the rest area of the regiment.

"30.6. 1000hrs visit of the Regimental Commander and commanders of the Abteilung. The company is disbanded. The teams are again assigned to their old units. The spare teams which were with the company are distributed to the Regiment.

"3.7.40. the company is finally disbanded and the paperwork completed. 1700hrs the report of the company commander, Hauptmann Betz to the Regiment Commander Oberst Elster. S-Company is disbanded."[88]

4

Between Campaigns
August 1940-April 1941

As the Regiment ended its participation in southern France and began its return to the north in late June, it was halted near Chinon, and it was here that it would remain until early July. By this point in the campaign the cost to the Germans had amounted to some 27,074 dead and more than 111,034 wounded and 18,384 missing. The French had lost some 90,000 killed, more than 200,000 wounded, and 1.9 million taken prisoner or missing.[1] All remaining French forces were ordered to surrender, although some 38,000 assorted French and Polish troops, all from the *45th Army Corps*, ignored the order and crossed over into Switzerland, where they were interned. In Thomas Jentz's book he reports that 35 percent of the gun armed panzers were lost during the entire campaign; these numbers also include the Czech built Mk-35t and 38t models. The totals he gives are: Mk Is, 182; Mk IIs, 240; Mk 35t, 62; Mk 38t, 54; Mk IIIs, 135; Mk IVs, 97; and Befehls panzers 69.[2] On 3 July, the order was received to relocate the Regiment to Arpajon, south of Paris. The march started on the 4th and wound through the suburbs of Paris to Montlhéry, to Lagny sur Marne and Thorigny. The vehicles were provided with a new coat of paint and tactical signs in preparation to the planned victory parade in Paris. A pass in review diagram was drawn up for the *4th Panzer Brigade*, which was to align itself at the end of the *10th Panzer Division* column with the brigade commander, *Oberst* Landgraf, leading the brigade, which in turn was to be followed by *Oberst* Elster and *Oberstlt* Haarde with the panzers of the *I./Abteilung*, and those of *Panzer Regiment 7* bringing up the rear of the division column. The parade, however, was later canceled because of the threat posed by the still potent *Royal Air Force*. Despite certain difficulties, the men enjoyed their short time in Paris, and even some of the family members managed to take advantage of the situation and visit the "City of Lights." At the holdover facility near Paris the organization of the *Ersatz* (Reserve) began, as well as the replacement of company level leaders and non-commissioned officers, and the further maintenance of the panzers, vehicles, and equipment. New panzers models and improvements were also implemented. The experience in combat against tanks, anti-tank, and artillery guns were validated and included in the training of the companies. In a short time the Regiment was again completely ready for combat operations. Besides the standard training regimens there was also the preparation for the invasion of England, codename *Operation "See Loew,"* or *"Sea Lion."* The panzers were to be landed via Marne River barges that had to be modified to accommodate the various panzer models, and therefore the crews were required to practice on loading and off loading procedures. During one of these training events one panzer actually slid off one of those barges while attempting to drive off and fell into the Marne. On 17 July, *Generalleutnant* Guderian visited the Regiment, where he praised the leadership and recognized the achievements of the entire Regiment. Two days later, he himself was promoted to the rank of *Generaloberst*.[3] The *10th Panzer Division* departed the Paris area in August 1940 and began to reorganize at the troop training area located near Neuhammer (Schlesien). At this time, Hitler was very pleased about the performance of his *panzerwaffe*, and he ordered that the OKH double the number of existing panzer divisions within the army. The creation of additional panzer divisions did nothing in regards of increasing the total number of panzer that were presently on hand. The current panzer division had roughly four hundred panzers placed under the command of a panzer brigade headquarters with operational control over two panzer regiments. The new reorganization now called for just one panzer regiment with two battalions to be equipped with roughly two hundred panzers. It was at this time that the Regiment was selected to form the foundation of a new panzer division, but in the meantime, it was to remain in France and continue its occupation duties and training. That November, the Regiment trained near Suippes at the training area at Mourmelon le Grand. This training was conducted within the framework of companies and platoons (*zugs*). There were training courses for the company and battalion leadership as well, with much of the training focusing on combat exercises as well as gunnery practice. Shortly thereafter, the Regiment received the order to relocate to Dijon. The winter of 1940/41 was a harsh one, which made the Regiment's march south even more difficult. From the Marne region, the march route went through the Champagne region and on to the Plateau of Langres, where many of the streets were covered in snow and ice. The experienced drivers, many of whom had already logged thousands of kilometers, and who had been behind the wheel ever since the invasion began in May, were able to negotiate these difficult road conditions without any major accidents. The Christmas of 1940 and New Year of 1941 found the Regiment situated in winter quarters near Dijon. The New Year was brought in with a bang, as Fritz Haustein of the *4th Company* remembers:

> "*We had the idea to have some real fireworks, so our company commander Hptm Ehrbeck decided to load the main gun of a Mk IV with some training munitions which didn't fire anything they just made the sound. At 2400hrs sharp we fired the gun and it made quite a noise so much so we received a lot of complaints the most important one was from the Regiment HQ. Ehrbeck denied it was us and we made blame on the others.*"[4]

61

Despite the festivities and overall lack of activity, the leadership, hearing rumors of impending further movements, kept focused and held the men ready to transfer again when the order arrived. That order did indeed soon follow, and once again the Regiment departed Dijon for Toulon, in unoccupied Vichy France. If the men thought that their stay in southern France was to be their last for a while they were all soon disappointed, as events in far away locations began to alter many of their lives forever. Originally, Hitler had decided to leave Italian dictator Benito Mussolini an entirely free hand in conducting operations in the Mediterranean theater. Hitler and his General Staff had shown little interest in that theater of operations, which to them offered nothing of overall importance to Germany. Although it was not widely publicized, Hitler still had his mind on Britain, the Balkans, and his ultimate goal of invading the Soviet Union. This view changed somewhat in the summer of 1940 when it became evident that Italy was apparently avoiding any decisive action in the Mediterranean theater. The British, on the other hand, were continually reinforcing their forces in the Middle East without the Italian Navy taking even the slightest interest in closing down or interdicting the sea lanes to Egypt. In October 1940, a meeting took place between Hitler and Mussolini at the Brenner Pass, where the subject of possibly dispatching some German *Luftwaffe* and *Heer* formations to assist the Italians in North Africa was discussed. However, during this meeting, the offer of German forces was initially dismissed by Mussolini, even though the possibility of German forces under Italian command allowed for the offer to remain open, and so no final decisions were made. Shortly following this meeting, *Generalmajor* Wilhelm von Thoma returned from Africa, where he had been sent by the *OKH* on a feasibility assessment, and to observe and report on the *Italian Army's* offensive towards Egypt. *General* von Thoma outlined to Hitler what it would take to defeat the British in North Africa, and that not one, but two panzer divisions would be required to see the campaign through to a successful conclusion. Thoma was also scathing of his opinion of the Italians and their ability to supply their army as it moved towards Egypt. Shortly after von Thoma's report was presented to Mussolini, the Italian offensive began to slow between Sidi Barrani and Mersa Matruh. British Desert Forces under the command of *General* Wavell were beginning to halt the Italians, and would soon be forcing them back with staggering losses.

By early 1940, the information available to the *German General Staff* regarding North Africa was limited to the few reports furnished to it by the German military attaché in Rome, and from reports by German agents of the counterintelligence service. From the autumn of 1940, *Special Detachment Dora*, a detachment of the German counterintelligence branch, was working in Tripolitania (Libya). Its primary mission was to keep those French territories in Africa under constant observation. However, most of the data on which the *General Staff* based its decisions came from the military attaché in Rome, who used either his own personal impressions, gained while travelling throughout North Africa, or those from an Italian liaison officer assigned to the *Governor General*, who also doubled as the Commander in Chief of all forces in Italian North Africa. Furthermore, all positive information of a military nature on North Africa was taken from the files of the *Foreign Armies Intelligence Branch (West)* concerning the British, French, and Italian armed forces. With the exception of the experiences gained by *General* Graziani's army during its advance into Egypt during the second half of 1940, and those of the German East Africa Campaign during WWI, no further information was being gathered by the Germans, who showed little interest. One lesson that was pointed out was that the desert was like a sea, and operations in it required a commander to think and act like a naval strategist, and understand that troops that are not mobile are utterly useless, and can achieve little against a motorized enemy. This was dramatically pointed out when Graziani's army, which had consisted of primarily infantry forces, was pinned down, enveloped, and routed near Sidi Barrani beginning in December 1940, then pursued and destroyed by the more mobile British forces near Bardia, Tobruk, and Derna less than a month later.

As a precautionary measure, the *3rd Panzer Division*, which in peacetime had been garrisoned in the Berlin area, became the first German formation to be alerted for possible deployment to North Africa. The *3rd Panzer* was ordered to begin organizing various elements for immediate employment to a tropical climate. As far as the ground forces were concerned, the original thought of sending only a small, heavily armed brigade to bolster the Italians was eventually scrapped. Although the brigade was to be employed in a mobile defense, it soon became evident that such a small force could not possibly provide the Italians with any real effective support. As von Thoma had stated earlier, it would require two divisions to be effective against the British in North Africa. However, as the Italian offensive made surprisingly good progress in November, the *3rd Panzer Division* was ordered to stand down from its deployment. Hitler ordered this move out of respect for Mussolini, who was a loyal and faithful ally, and who was confident that the Italians would defeat the much smaller British forces. But, no sooner had the order to stand down been received than the situation began to change once again, as the Italians lost Sidi Barrani and began to retreat towards Sollum and Bardia. The route continued into early January 1941 with the loss of Bardia and Sollum on the 5th, and which now finally forced Mussolini to ask Hitler for those German reinforcements that he had previously offered to him.

On 11 January, the *Oberkommando der Wehrmacht* published *Order Number 22 (Führer Directive No. 22)*, which stated that events in the Mediterranean Theater demanded the strategic, political, and psychological support of the Italians. The *Oberkommando der Heer* was ordered to form a "Special Blocking Detachment" strong in armor, anti-tank, and anti-aircraft guns in order to assist the Italians in defending Tripolitania[5] from British armored forces. In addition to the blocking detachment, the *Luftwaffe*, under the operation codenamed "Mittelmeer," was to provide support through *Fliegerkorps X*, which was even now assembling its forces in Sicily. The Italians were also sending reinforcements in the form of the *Ariete Armored Division* and *Trento Mechanized Division*. However, reports from German generals assigned as liaison officers to the Italian *Commando Supremo* and recently back from North Africa advised Hitler and the *OKW* that a larger force than what had been initially envisioned was needed in order to halt the British before they reached Tripoli. The problem now was that the *3rd Panzer Division*, having been stood down, was now earmarked to support future operations in Russia, and that any formations sent to Africa would have to come from those forces assembling for the invasion of Greece. The *OKW* proposed the following: a new division, the *5th Light Division*, be formed from those *3rd Panzer Division* elements previously alerted for Africa. They included *Aufklärungs Abteilung 3*, *Panzerjäger Abteilung 39*, a light field artillery battalion, a panzer company, and a medical company, which would in turn be followed by *Panzer Regiment 5* and *Schützen Regiment zbV 200*. The *5th Light* began its journey to Africa in mid-February; the codename for the operation was "*Sonnenblume*," or "Sunflower," and on 18 February the division was activated in Tripoli. They had been preceded only days before by hastily formed teams of German researchers and medical and supply specialists which were to lay the framework for the logistical system that was to support those incoming German units. The second division scheduled to be employed in Africa was the former *33rd Infantry Division*, which, since October 1940, had been redesignated in France as the *15th Panzer Division*, and was under the command of *Generalmajor* Heinrich von Prittwitz and Gaffron. With its activation, the division now rushed to prepare itself for its new mission in Africa. During the

Chapter 4: Between Campaigns, August 1940-April 1941

first week in February, the newly appointed German corps commander, *Generalleutnant* Erwin Rommel, former commander of Hitler's own escort guard and the *7th Panzer Division*, was briefed personally by Hitler as to his mission and responsibilities. Hitler made it clear to Rommel that his mission was defensive in nature, and that he must prevent the fall of Tripolitania at all cost. Rommel was to depart immediately for Tripoli in order to take charge of all German and Italian mobile forces there and evaluate the Italian situation. After sizing up the current situation, Rommel was to return to Berlin and brief Hitler on what type of strategy he could impose, and recommend a course of action to clear up the situation there.

The British had been busy since mid-January, as they pushed past Derna and headed towards Benghazi. Then, in early February, they achieved a smashing victory at Beda Fomm that threatened to develop into an all out catastrophe and rout of Italian forces in all of Northern Africa. Luckily for the Italians and Germans, British ground forces were now being worn down by the harsh desert conditions and over-extended supply lines, while the *Luftwaffe*, flying out of bases in Sicily, was making its presence felt on British sea lanes and on the ground. There was also a significant loss of fighting forces to support those troops now fighting in Greece.

Since there had been so little time to make thorough preparations in getting those troops and equipment ready, only the most important and least time consuming actions were focused on. In his report written after the war, Alfred Toppe wrote of those preparations:

"Meanwhile, a special staff for tropical warfare (Sonderstab Tropen) had been formed at the headquarters of the commander of the Replacement Training Army in Berlin. It was composed of officers who had fought in the German colonies in World War I and was to assemble as speedily as possible all experience that could be helpful in the training, organization, equipment, and employment of troops in desert warfare. However, the march of events was too fast so that the first units of the German Africa Corps landed in Africa when the staff had just commenced its work in Libya. What has been said above goes to show that the German Army High Command was taken almost completely by surprise when the necessity arose to dispatch troops for warfare in the desert. In any event, the command had no time to make thorough preparations for this type of combat employment. For this reason, all preparatory work that was possible in the short space of time available had to be restricted mainly to the following measures:
(1) Medical examinations of all troops to determine their fitness for service in the tropics, with the application of very severe standards.
(2) Equipment of all soldiers with tropical clothing.
(3) Adaptation of a training program for combat in open terrain.
(4) Camouflage of all vehicles with a coat of desert-colored paint.
(5) Organization of special units to handle water-supply problems.
(6) Familiarization of the troops with the hygienic measures necessary in tropical climates.
(7) Orientation of the troops on the military-geographical conditions of the new theater of war. It was not possible within Germany to accustom the troops to the intense heat to which they would be exposed, particularly at that time of the year, the winter of 1940. To a certain extent, the troops that had to wait any length of time in Italy for transportation to North Africa adapted themselves automatically to the heat."[6]

With its activation the previous October, the *15th Panzer Division* now rushed to ready itself for its new mission to Africa before events there outpaced their arrival. In January 1941, the *8th Panzer Regiment* was transferred to the town of Schwetzingen, located near Heidelberg, and the move was completed by early February. The Regiment would remain in this location until the beginning of March, when it was then transferred to the troop training center at Baumholder. Wilhelm Hagios, a former medical attendant with the reserve forces who was then stationed in Poland, had this to say about his soon to be new posting:

"The end of January [1940] my relocation took place, service with the Luftwaffe was not possible due to my reserve position, and the relocation was to Panzer Regiment 7 in Vaihingen, although it was not there at that time. I prepared my vehicle for handover, and then came Oberartz Berik the abteilung commander at that time and told me he can reverse the decision about my relocation, and I said to him what is decided is decided. From Poland I came to Vaihingen, in the evening and from there to Böblingen. So I came to Ersatz [Reserve] Abteilung 7 or 8 if you want to call it that and so I ended up with Panzer Regiment 8. I was in the 2nd Company. In the meantime I was a Gefreiter and there was an instructional unit, the recruits were not obliged to service in it. I had some free time and then I went to the panzer school, it was very important to me to know how the panzer drives, even though it was a simple panzer Mk I."[7]

Another soldier who was soon to join the Regiment was Horst Sonnenkalb, who has written a three part story of his time in the German Army. That story was originally published by *"Die Oase,"* the official magazine of the *German Afrika Korps*. In the following, Sonnenkalb describes his early training:

"After a three year apprenticeship I was attached to a cavalry regiment in Bad Cannstadt, close to Stuttgart. There I received my basic training as an infantryman and cavalier. Shortly after my time as a recruit I was sent to retraining with the 1st Company of the Panzer Lehr Battalion 18 in Vaihingen, close to Stuttgart. How does a cavalier come to the panzer? Don't ask, as I said, being a soldier you have to follow orders and not think. In Vaihingen I received exhaustive training as a panzer driver on a Panzer I, then on a Panzer II and finally on the Panzer III. Of course that was quite different from the infantry training or sitting in the saddle as a cavalier. That was quite the grind. After my training time, which brought me to troop training spots in Münsingen, Heuberg and Stetten, I was then placed with the Panzer Lehr Battalion 18 and to my future Stammregiment 8 in Böblingen/Stuttgart. There we received our final training and then went with the regiment to the newly designated German Africa-Corps."[8]

While in Schwetzingen, the Regiment received four Mk IV Ausf E equipped with the 75mm KwK 37 L/24 (Kurz) and three command panzers in early February; these panzers were quickly disseminated to the heavy company and Regimental *Stabs* respectively. These were not the only new panzers that the Regiment was to receive; between the 16th and 22nd, the Regiment turned in thirty-one of its Mk III Ausf Es mounting the 37mm KwK L/46.5, and in turn received thirty-one brand new Mk III Ausf G equipped with the up gunned 50mm KwK L/42 (Kurz). The older model Mk II Ausf B and C were also upgraded with the Ausf D model, but unlike the Mk IIIs, the Mk IIs continued to mount the 20mm KwK L/30 or L/55 gun, which unfortunately was not up to the task of tank versus tank combat. The panzer companies were restructured and received new equipment: for example, the Light Companies were equipped as follows:[9]

1 Headquarters *Zug* with two Mk IIIs
1 Light *Zug* with five Mk IIs
3 *Zugs* with five Mk IIIs per *Zug*

Heavy Company was equipped with:

1 Headquarters *Zug* with two Mk IVs
1 Light *Zug* with five Mk IIs
3 *Zugs* with five Mk IVs per *Zug*

In Baumholder, the Regiment was together with other units also training for deployment to North Africa; these units, along with the Regiment, began their indoctrination for living and working in tropical climates. The men were issued a complete desert uniform that in part consisted of sun helmets and caps, tropical shirts, pants, and shoes made from khaki-colored linen. In Alfred Toppe's paper he wrote of the uniforms that would be supplied to the troops:

"Clothing and uniforms were entirely different from the clothing and uniforms worn in Europe. The German army uniform was made from a water-tight linen, cut in a style approximating the traditional uniforms of the former German colonial defense forces. These uniforms proved unsuitable both in style and material. The material was too stiff and did not give adequate protection against heat or cold. In the early mornings, the material absorbed moisture from the dew so that it became intolerable to wear the uniforms. The British tropical uniforms, in contrast, were made of pure wool and were excellent. Large quantities of the British uniforms were captured and worn by the troops of the German Africa Corps (with the addition of German insignias). The Germans especially liked the British trousers. The tropical uniforms of the German Air Force, however, were good. Their color, a yellowish-brown, was more appropriate than other German uniforms, and they were made from a material that was of a lighter and better quality which was cut in a more appropriate style. Uniforms of olive-drab color proved unfavorable. In view of that, normal camouflage difficulties in the desert, a yellowish-brown, which would have been a protective color, would have been best. High boots were unsuitable in every respect, since in hot climates, everything must be done to prevent soldiers wearing any apparel on the legs that restricts the circulation of the blood. In this matter, the troops helped themselves by wearing only slacks, most of which came from captured British depots and which the troops wore over their boots. The German shoe with laces and a cloth tongue proved suitable. The shorts issued to the troops could not be worn during combat, since they left bare legs exposed to injury by thorns and stones, and these injuries healed very slowly. The olive-drab caps with wide visors were excellent; the visor, in particular, was indispensable for the infantryman and for the gunner as protection against the intense glare of the sun. The tropical helmets that were issued could be used only in the rear areas and were entirely useless in combat. The German troops wore no steel helmets, in contrast to the British troops, whose steel helmets were more appropriate both in shape and weight, being lighter than the German helmets. The tropical coats issued, which were made from a thick woolen material, were good, but the English ones, which were fur-lined and reached only to the knees, were better. Owing to the stiff material from which it was made, the German tropical shirts were inferior to the British ones, which were made of so-called 'Tropic' material. To protect the abdominal area of the body against the cold, the wearing of bellybands was obligatory, which proved a wise measure. Tropical helmets and mosquito nets proved an unnecessary expenditure. The majority of the troops got rid of them immediately after debarking from the ships, since they were not able to take them along owing to insufficient transportation space. The troops were also furnished wall tents, which had a special sun apron. With the exception of footwear, no leather was used in any article of apparel; it was replaced by thick linen."[10]

Over time and experience much of what was issued would be deemed unfit or totally worthless, and before long the men would learn to adapt to their surroundings and outfit themselves with a number of Italian and British items. It was quite obvious that in March 1941 the means to acclimatize the troops to the intense temperatures they would face in North Africa would not be possible within Germany. Luckily for some of the troops, they would have a short bit of time in the warmer climate of Southern Italy to accustom themselves with the heat they would soon be facing. Along with the personnel preparation measures being undertaken by the men, so too were the collective training tasks that needed to be completed, since many of those troops deploying would be rushed strait off to the front. Some of the priority training objectives that were focused on usually revolved around day and night operations conducted in wide-open sandy terrain. Some of those exercises consisted of: driving and movement operations, desert cover and camouflage, gunnery and marksmanship drills of all weapons systems from panzers to pistols, recognition and designation of targets without instruments, exercises conducted without billeting and construction of shelters, compass orientation, celestial navigation, vehicle recovery, and mine laying operations. Beginning on 11 April 1941, the I./*Abteilung* was transported back to Schwetzingen, where it began the process of loading the rail cars that would take them and their panzers on a journey south through the Alps and Brenner Pass down through the Italian Alps, Florence, Rome, and finally stopping in Naples. Upon arrival in Naples the railcars were to be quickly off loaded and the preparations for embarking the transport ships were to begin immediately. Lt Kurt Liestmann recorded in his diary:

"13.4.41 Easter Sunday in Naples, during the night there is the offloading. We stay in the Hotel Terine in Agnono near Naples. The full moon and stars are in the sky, when we get there in the night the air is quite cold, not at all tepid Napolitano, how did we freeze in Italy, during the drive, as it wasn't so long ago."[11]

Preparing for Africa
On 15 March 1941, the Regiment was officially reassigned from the *10th Panzer Division*, the final transfers were completed, and the Regiment was now assigned to the *15th Panzer Division*. *Oberst* Botho Elster, who had led the Regiment so successfully in Poland and France, passed command of the Regiment to *Oberstleutnant* Hans Cramer on 25 March 1941. Cramer, who had been until now the commander of the *Panzer Aufklärung* training battalion, was paid the following compliment by Hans Haarde, now a *Generalmajor* and reviewing the event:

"Hans Cramer would be the Sauerteig [Yeast] that added to the bread will make it rise and for this new generation everything will bend in front of you and we will overcome everything and you can do everything."[12]

Later that evening the change of command ceremony was christened with a big midnight tattoo [evening military ceremony] in Heidelberg.

Panzer Regiment 8 Chain of Command as of April 1941[13]

Regiment Commander	Oberstlt Cramer
Regt Adj	Hptm Jahns
Nachr Offz	Olt von Stülpnagel
Ord Offz	Olt Jattkowski
Regt Arzt	StabsArtz. Dr Becker
Ing Ofz/Workshop Company	Major Schnell
StKp	Olt Prion, Lt Friedrich, OFumstr Strack

I./Abteilung Commander	Oberstlt Haarde, F
Abtl Adj	Lt Liestmann, K.
Nachr Offz	Olt Matthias, J.
Ord Offz	Lt Bock
Abt Arzt	OArtz. Dr Port
Zahl Mstr	StZmstr Tischner
Ing Offz	OInsp Lampe
StKp	Olt Sontowski, Olt Stiefelmayer
leKol	Olt Lindner
1st Company	Olt Kümmel
Zug Commander	Olt Heinrich
Zug Commander	Lt Springorum
Zug Commander	Lt Peters
2nd Company	Hptm Ehrbeck
Zug Commander	Olt Knorr
Zug Commander	Lt Hess
Zug Commander	Lt von Treuenfels
3rd Company	Olt Schubert
Zug Commander	Olt Kertscher
Zug Commander	Lt Keil
II./Abteilung Commander	Oberstlt Ramsauer
Abtl Adj	Olt Wuth
Nachr Offz	OFumstr Bulla
Ord Offz	Lt Schnaidt
Abt Arzt	OArtz Dr Witzky
Zahl Mstr	OZmstr Gisy
Ing Offz	HBmstr Hauska, Tech Insp Hering
StKp	Hptm Klein, Lt Pickel, Lt Matthias, Lt Eberspächer
leKol	Hptm Dr Kücklich
5th Company	Olt Körner
Zug Commander	Lt Bönisch
Zug Commander	Lt Weiss
6th Company	Olt Wahl
Zug Commander	Lt Adam
Zug Commander	Fw/OA Becker
7th Company	Olt Seidler
Zug Commander	Lt Danz
Zug Commander	Lt Liestmann, H
Zug Commander	Fw/OA Pierath

The panzer strength report of the Regiment on 10 April 1941 was 153 panzers, which were further broken down into nine Befehls panzers, forty-five Mk IIs, seventy-one Mk IIIs, and twenty-eight Mk IVs.[14] From 12 until 20 April, the various staffs and soldiers would prepare their panzers and equipment for passage to Africa. For the quartering parties and drivers that had accompanied the panzers on the freight cars, there was to be little free time. Whenever a military formation finds itself without much time and rushed into preparations mistakes are bound to happen, and the Regiment was no exception to this rule. This time the mistake was quite obvious, and appeared right before the men when they realized that the panzers were still painted in their light gray color when they should have been re-painted in a dark yellow/brown desert color. The *1st Company's* panzers, which had already been loaded on the 14th into the ship holds, were discovered to have been loaded without receiving the prescribed painting. Soon after the mistake was discovered the panzers were off loaded and painted in the regulation dark yellow. Wilhelm Bühler of the *1st Company* remembers:

"On 14.4.41 we boarded the ship and then had to disembark it, as luck would have it that ship was later sunk during the crossing. The following day we went on a sightseeing tour to Vesuvius."[15]

Liestmann continues in his diary account:

"14.4.41 Monday, the second Easter day begins the reloading on the quay installation. Loading of the 1st Company, plenty of operations. Oberstlt Haarde and I visited all four transports; the Alicante, Procida, Maritza and Santa Fe. The vehicles disappear in the bowels of the ship. The heaviest panzer hangs in the harness of the derrick, an imposing picture. In-between are German and Italian soldiers and sailors. Our men are in trophy uniforms and excited with the task. The previous day two barges were sunk, hit by English torpedoes. 900 men fell into the water, only 60 missing. Some of them sang in the water: 'We drive against the land of angels'. More evil tidings [bad news], our new Division Commander General Prittwitz fell near Tobruk, shot by an anti-tank [Gun]."[16]

Since Italy was at that time an ally to Germany, the men were allowed to tour around the city and catch a few of the sites, such as a visit to nearby Mount Vesuvius or a relaxing meal or coffee at a café, or just a stroll through the ancient city to see the sites and do a bit of shopping. Some even managed to find the local brothel, to satisfy their cravings or curiosity. On the 18th Liestmann recorded;

"A concert at the quay, performed by the regimental orchestra, there is big attention, especially by the crews of the surrounding Italian support cruisers and military ships. During the first part of the day there is boarding on the ship with giving away the identity card. In the afternoon onboard arrives another small contingent of Italian troops with some vehicles. Now we are very full, almost ready to burst, a fat piece [target] for submarines. In the evening again there is a harbor concert."[17]

Just prior to the second departure there was a large parade held on the 20th at the harbor in Naples; the I./*Abteilung* was formed along with some Italian soldiers and were reviewed by *Oberstlt* Haarde and some fellow Italian Army and Naval officers as a crowd of Italian dock workers and citizens observed from the nearby docks. The Regimental band, directed by *SFw* Ernst Isensee, played various national anthems and marching tunes as the small reviewing group inspected the *Abteilung* and gave it a few words of encouragement, and finally wishing it good luck in Africa. Kurt Kathe remembers a most interesting story just prior to departure:

"When we were loading in Naples, on our way to Afrika, there once came Emmanuel, the King, with his daughter. My panzer was ready to be buckled on to the ship, and he asked if his daughter could look inside. I said 'yes', my driver was down there and was sleeping and so she went down through the turret and didn't notice that someone was down there. And he looked above and had 'toten hosen.'"[18]

Across the Mediterranean in Africa, Rommel had wasted little time in attacking the British, and he had been quick to send his *5th Light Division* in pursuit—even as other arriving formations, many from the *15th Panzer Division*, became available—and keep the pressure on the British, who had been totally surprised and had been steadily falling back to their position in Egypt. Since the I./*Abteilung Stabs* and *1st Company* had been the first to arrive in Naples and were prepared to sail for Africa they were sent on ahead of the remaining companies of the Regiment.

Rommel needed the panzers more than anything else if he was to keep up the pressure and be able to strike hard at the British. On the 21st, the first men, equipment, and panzers were loaded aboard their transport ships which would take them to Africa. The journey the Regiment would undertake lasted roughly three days, and for this movement the following ships were to be used: the *Leverkusen, Rialto, Ankara, Birmania, Gritti, Kybfels, Poscarini, Reichenfeld,* and *Venerio*.[19] The route in which they would pass came out of Naples and down the western side of Sicily with a stop over in Palermo, then beginning again toward the eastern side of Pantelleria and finally into the harbor at Tripoli. The route, which at the time was patrolled by British submarines and naval vessels, along with *Royal Air Force* and *Royal Navy* planes, was at the time no sure bet for any convoy hoping to make its way through to Africa, and in the years to come would see numerous ships sunk along this exact route. For the journey to Africa there would be three separate convoys protected and screened by a hodge-podge combined sea and air surveillance package. Despite the obvious hazards lurking for them out in the Mediterranean, for which a few of the men were used to reinforce the ship's watch and pull air guard, most of them found time to catch up on their sleep in the fine Mediterranean sun, but for most there was the endless talk about what the future held for them in this far away place. In reading the following events and experiences the reader must please keep in mind that memories and events fade with time, and even though many of the men kept diaries, many did not have the luxury of a watch with day and date, and so the notes and memories are not always accurate. I hope that the following pages will give the reader just a small idea of how the men traveled and what they experienced along the way, even though the more avid military history buff may dispute some of the times and facts. I apologize that even after numerous interviews and research I must admit defeat at defining the exact times and routes of the Regiment as it made its way to Africa.

Crossing the Mediterranean
The first convoy (convoy number 22) departed at midnight 20/21 April with the *Stabs* and *Stabs* Company of the *I./Abteilung* and the *1st Company*.[20] During the journey, which normally took some eighty hours, the "*Rialto*" and two other transports were sent back to the port of Messina due to the danger from British submarine patrols in the area. Those three transport ships would finally arrive in North Africa after an eight-day delay. The remaining ships that had continued on reached the harbor at Tripoli at approximately 1700hrs on 24 April, so *Oberstlt* Friedrich Haarde and the I./*Abteilung* became the first regimental contingent to safely step foot on the African continent. The following diary entries by Kurt Liestmann give a good description of how their journey went:

"21.4.41 Monday. This night we take off at 0115hrs and cut into the sea. Accompanied by four destroyers, the convoy of three German and one Italian ship takes off. This night we still sleep in the quay. The weather is nice in the morning, the sea is clear. All wear the swim vests. There are set air warning and surveillance duty. The emergency places and floating bags are distributed to the units. In the zigzag course the destroyers hunt in front and near us. Our transports change direction of course each single moment for 50 degrees. At 1600hrs we reach the height of Sicily on the west coast of Palermo. Two ships appear on the horizon, one destroyer and one transporter join us. People sleep, write, read and sing. The sea is flat like a mirror. Still there is nothing yet too dangerous. Since the early morning we are protected by aircraft of our air forces; one Me-110, two Ju-88s and one Dornier. They provide protection against submarines from air, and search the horizon. They often fly by close to the water near us. The bombs under the belly shine in the sun. Near evening it gets even more clear, the sea more quiet. At 2200hrs we suddenly turn around and take the return course. All are stunned. No one knows the reason. The order came from destroyer. When we wake up in the morning, we enter the harbor of Palermo [Sicily]. Yesterday afternoon the German Stuka units attacked the English convoy on the road from Sicily, five transports sunk, two heavily damaged. 22.4.41 Tuesday We lay near Palermo and wait. Near us is the 'Ruhr' from a previous commando which received the torpedo in the belly but managed to be towed. As one hears, the English combat forces bombed Tripoli yesterday during the night. Maybe this is the reason which holds us back. There are recommendations issued to people: quiet, no panic. Already at 1500hrs we take off and go into the sea again in the direction of Pantelleria. About 2200hrs we are pulled to the quay. 23.4.41 Wednesday Early morning we pass by Pantelleria, German and Italian aircraft fly for protection. The destroyers are with us. From time to time the destroyer launches the depth charge. The dull quivering [concussions] we still feel. In the afternoon we reach the height of Lampedusa islands, in the same position where on the 20th the transporter with two of ours were attacked in the night by English cruisers and sunk. The wreck floats on the sand bank on the starboard from us. Near it lays an Italian destroyer, who fought till the last moment shooting from all its guns. Nearby one could see the tops of the mast of two transporters. Some comrades swam 15 hours, until they were fished out. The English shoot among them without attention, for the most part the crews were able to be saved. In the late afternoon we encounter many returning empty transporters, watched over by Italian destroyers and the German Luftwaffe. Later we get increased protection, two Italian cruisers and two torpedo boats who take over the protection against Malta. All are feeling better since our air protection increases. Different Me-110s come as well. Under their bellies are additional petrol canisters in the form of bombs. At 2200hrs it seems that far away to the rear is the sea combat. We see muzzle fire. If it's our cruisers, they combat with the British; we therefore make a big curve almost backwards in the direction of Djerba. Thursday 24.4.41 In the morning we remain starboard/right of the African shore, a narrow strip of sand with few trees. Around 1000hrs we are near the heights of Suara. Soon we will see Tripolis. Around 1600hrs we slowly run, due to the danger of mines, into the harbor. At the entry single wreckages and large/whole amount of ships with half-seas over. The aftermath of bomb damage and heavy shelling by the English who fired without regard into the town with 38cm shells, there are approximately 200 dead. One shell went through the tower of the lighthouse. The torpedoed Duisburg is here as well. The crews and us leave the ship, drive to the camp 5km away of Tripolis. The vehicles will be offloaded in the morning. During the evening is the usual bomber attack on Tripolis. No ships are hit. Friday 25.4.41 Offloading in 42 degrees [Celsius] heat and a sand storm. As we learn now, we were within an ace breadth that our convoy was torpedoed or shelled."[21]

The second convoy (convoy number 23) departed on Wednesday, 23 April, and sailed with the regimental *Stabs, 2nd, 3rd,* and *5th Companies*, and the *Light Column* (leKol).[22] Many in the *3rd Company* would sail aboard the *Reichenfeld*. Unlike the previous convoys, this one would experience a much longer journey, but in the end they were offloaded in Tripoli on the night of 1/2 May. Wilhelm Hagios recalls his journey:

"In early April 41, I was relocated to Schwetzingen, where the Regiment was located. From there in April we were relocated to Naples, there we were located in a school. The vehicles were fueled there, and then loaded in the harbor of Naples. The Kybfels had the regimental stabs, the Wachefels and Reichenfeld were there as well, these were ships of the Müller Würmer line, which usually cruised to Asia. We were departing from Naples to Palermo, where we arrived that evening and from there went into the city. Then we went from there via the Straits of Messina down to Augusta and Katania. The next night we tried to mix up the British, who thought that we were coming back to Palermo, and go by them. But we went that night backwards, and the next morning we were west of Sicily and heading in the direction of Tunisia. We did not hear of the U.K. submarines which lay on the bottom and we had only once an alarm. There was an Italian destroyer and our ships were not sunk, but those before us were sunk and many were in the water swimming."[23]

On 6 May, the third and final convoy carrying the Regiment to Africa departed on convoy number 24 and sailed with the *Stabs* II./*Abteilung*, 6th and 7th *Companies*, and the Regimental Workshop company.[24] The ships entered the harbor in Tripoli three days after departing on 9 May, and thereby completed the arrival of the Regiment to North Africa. We have a number of accounts of the journey across the Mediterranean, beginning with Fritz Haustein, a clerk in the I./*Abteilung Stabs* who later served in the 4th *Company* and recalled his journey:

"We loaded the ship in Naples I sailed aboard the Leverkusen it was a big ship I think maybe some 20,000 tons. We departed Naples for Sicily and the Port of Messina, which was the starting point of the most direct route to Tripoli. Soon after we departed the U-boat alarm was sounded and we returned to Messina. The Italians only provided 2 motor torpedo boats to escort us and there were larger ships in the harbor of Naples Lt von Drohenfels from the 4th Company was skeptical of our arrival but I did have a lot of respect for the captain of the ship and I saw with my own eyes how fast a transport can turn as we came under attack from a British U-boat. The captain turned the boat so that the first torpedo went ahead of the front and the second one missed the tail. Later we attempted to sail and different route from Messina to Palermo but we again had the U-boat alarm sound and returned again to Messina. On the third attempt we got through to Tripolis but we still had many problems the RAF even followed us to the harbor at Tripolis where they bombed the convoy [Division HQ]."[25]

Hermann Eckardt from the 3rd *Company* was also on the *Reichenfeld* and remembers his journey like this:

"In Napoli we boarded the ships, 6 transports, I was on the Reichenfeld. The transport was 12,010 registered tons when we boarded. We were on the second Geleiter[Convoy], the first one was attacked by submarines and torpedoed. We were six days on the way [under way], we were on the harbor Augusta, on the east cost of Sicily. We were there two days, then we went back through the Straits of Messina, then we went to Palermo. There we stopped again, we were brought by a row-boat to the harbor but then we were called back, and when we asked why, we heard that there was British surveillance. We went north of Sicily, from Palermo, to the west of Sicily in the direction of Partermeria then there was a storm on sea. A very stormy sea, with eight meter high waves and we were hanging on and throwing up. This was my first time being on the ship and I was mostly peeling potatoes, apart from being sick, there was not much else to do. When we reached Afrika, we went along the Tunisian coast, where the sea was so flat it would be easy to torpedo us. Near Tripoli there was an alarm, probably a torpedo, and later we saw how they had shot up the harbor there. When we finally reached Afrika, we were happy, especially after we had seen the first convoy torpedoed, we were so happy just to have firm soil under our feet."[26]

Olt Schubert, commander of the 3rd *Company*, wrote:

"Thursday 1 May, in the night we have passed Pantelleria. In the water swim Medusa's light [photo-plankton]. The bizarre rumors buzz around. That afternoon the escort torpedo boats throw water bombs [torpedoes] because presumably the English U-Boats were seen. The convoy makes bizarre zigzag maneuvers. Midday we pass by the Kerkemos Islands and come close to the African coast. That evening we arrive to Tripoli."[27]

Kurt Kathe from the 5th *Company*:

"In Naples we loaded the ship, all the tanks and crews were on the same boat, I was on the Reichenfeld a really beautiful ship I was not under the deck but on top and I slept in a room where there was materials and I remember there was a storm I was behind a door for 3 days and couldn't get out but I had plenty of food. We had airplane alarms but they were exaggerated [practice]. I remember one leutnant, I think his name was something like Weissenfels and he was the son of an aristocrat, he was on a different ship where he stood on deck in a life jacket. When the Brits attacked and bombed the ship he jumped down and a big box hit him on the head. So it happens but our group made it good [safely] over the Mediterranean and had no losses."[28]

Horst Sonnenkalb of the 7th *Company* made the journey in the third convoy:

"In the spring of 1941 my Company and parts of the Panzer Regiment 8 of Southern Germany were being loaded onto the military transport toward Italy. The long train ride took us across the Brenner Pass at Innsbruck, then via Rome toward Naples. From there our trip continued on to the Italian war port Augusta [Sicily] and during the night, with the accompaniment of an Italian war ship, we went across the Mediterranean Sea. We reached the harbor of Tripoli/Libya in the early morning hours. There we stepped on North African ground. I was restless during our trip from Sicily to Tripolis. For the first time I started thinking about what would wait for us on this African Continent. We had been vaccinated for dysentery and typhoid before we left Germany, after we had been tested if we were fit enough for the tropical climate. What other possible tropical diseases, like Malaria, were waiting here for us?"[29]

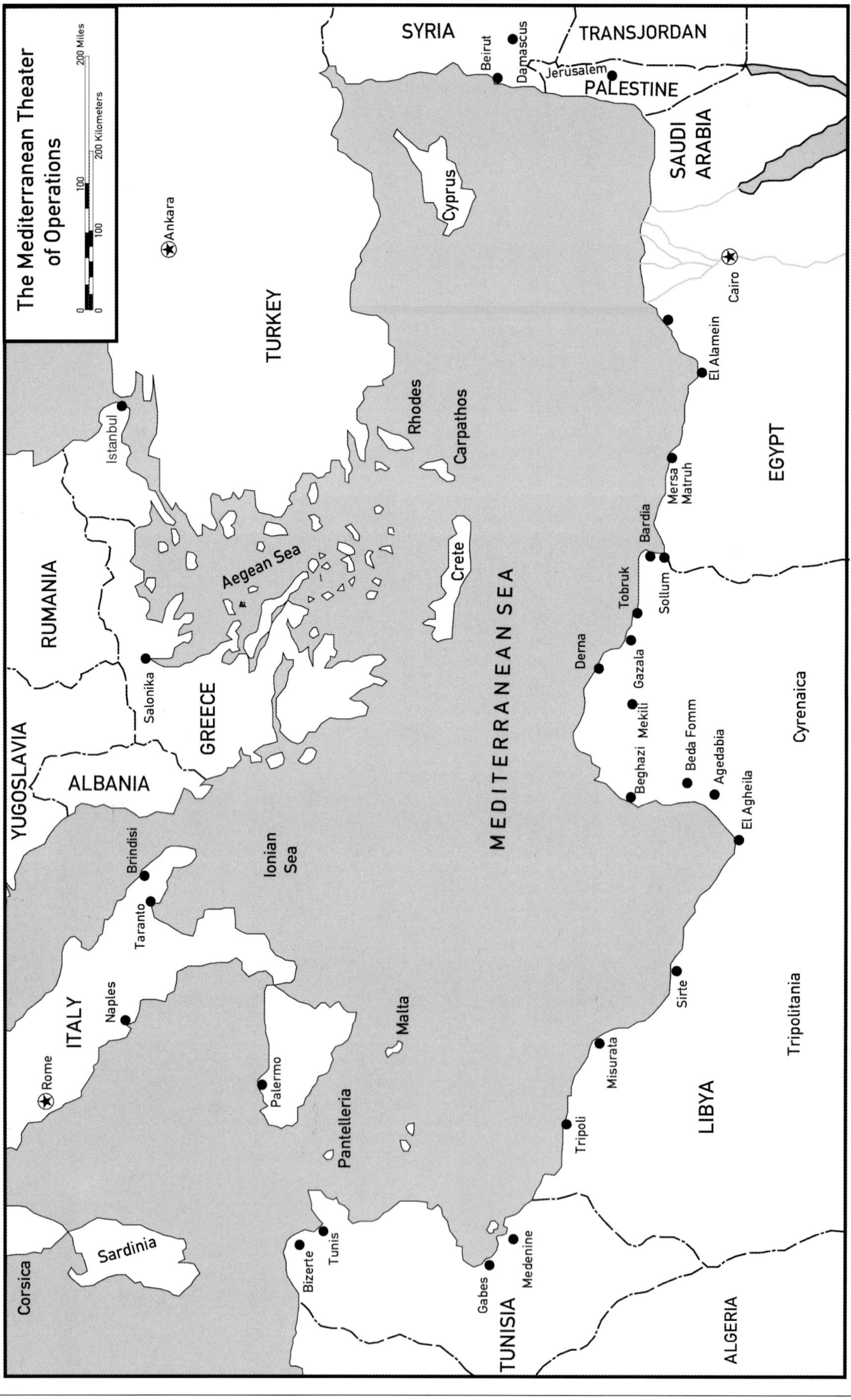
The Mediterranean Theater of Operations
0 100 200 Miles
0 100 200 Kilometers
SYRIA
TRANSJORDAN
Beirut
Damascus
Jerusalem
PALESTINE
SAUDI ARABIA
Cyprus
Ankara
TURKEY
Cairo
El Alamein
Rhodes
Carpathos
Istanbul
EGYPT
Mersa Matruh
Bardia
Aegean Sea
Crete
RUMANIA
Tobruk
Sollum
MEDITERRANEAN SEA
Derna
Gazala
Salonika
GREECE
Mekili
Beda Fomm
Cyrenaica
YUGOSLAVIA
ALBANIA
Beghazi
Agedabia
El Agheila
Brindisi
Ionian Sea
Taranto
Naples
ITALY
Sirte
Malta
Tripolitania
Rome
Palermo
Misurata
Pantelleria
LIBYA
Tripoli
Sardinia
Tunis
Bizerte
Medenine
Gabes
Corsica
TUNISIA
ALGERIA

Part II

5

North Africa
May 1941

Panzer Roll on into Africa
Over the Scheldt, the Meuse and the Rhine
The tanks thrust on towards France
Hussars of the Führer dressed in black
Thus they overrun France by force.
The tracks clank......the engines roar.......
Panzer Roll on into Africa!
Panzer Roll on into Africa!
Hot above the African sands the sun burns down
Our tanks engines sing their song
German tanks in the sunshine
Stand ready to fight against England
The tracks clank.......
The engines roar!
Panzer Roll on into Africa!
Tanks of the Führer, you Britons beware!
They are intended for your destruction!
They fear neither death nor the devil!
On them British pride will shatter!
The tracks clank.............the engines roar...........
Panzer Roll on into Africa! [1]

In the early months of 1941, as the planned five-day limited offensive begun by *General* Richard O'Connor's *Western Desert Force* in December 1940 entered its second month, the rout of the Italian Army in Cyrenaica continued. The British had achieved a spectacular victory over the Italians at Beda Fomm, and some 130,000 prisoners, 400 tanks, and over 1,000 guns were captured or destroyed, with the stragglers forced back towards Tripoli. But then events elsewhere in the Mediterranean forced a halt to the offensive, and the British troops held firm and began to take up positions at El Agheila, on the Gulf of Sirte. Because of the threats poised against Greece and Crete, the British began pulling out divisions for service in those locations, as the Germans began to strengthen their commitment to the Italians and built up their air, sea, and ground forces in the Mediterranean theater. On 19 February 1941, *General der Panzer Truppen* Erwin Rommel was appointed as commander of the *Deutsches Afrika Korps* (*D.A.K.*). Rommel was an energetic and aggressive commander who yearned again for action, and he wasted little time in laying down his own rules and judgments. Rommel had been briefed by both Hitler and officers of the *Oberkommando der Wehrmacht (OKW)* in early March that no large scale offensive operations could be undertaken until the fall of 1941; this order was based on the planned offensive against Soviet Russia scheduled to take place in the summer of 1941. Rommel would, however, be allowed to launch limited attacks when the *15th Panzer Division* (the second German division to be sent) arrived in theater, but that was not scheduled to be completed by late May. Rommel was not one to sit and wait, and as he grew impatient he sensed that the British were less prepared for a fight than their success against the Italians had previously suggested, and he resolved to test that theory. Rommel wrote of his orders:

> "I had already decided, in view of the tenseness of the situation and the sluggishness of the Italian command, to depart from my instructions to confine myself to a reconnaissance and to take the command at the front into my hands as soon as possible, at the latest after the arrival of the first German troops. General von Rintelen, to whom I had given a hint of my intension in Rome, had advised me against it, for, as he put it, that was the way to lose both honor and reputation." [2]

Rommel had established his headquarters near Sirte, with the advanced elements of the *5th Light* (Streich) having already advanced some 800kms east of Tripoli, where they had taken up good jump off positions near Mugtaa. At dawn on 24 March, *Aufklärung Abteilung 3* (Wechmar) went forward to recon and probe the strength of the British positions at El Agheila. This limited action soon discovered that the British were not in strength at El Agheila, but were beginning to dig in at Marsa el Brega. Equipped with the information he needed, Rommel ordered the *5th Light* to attack Marsa el Brega beginning on the evening of 31 March. That attack was able to push through El Agheila, and the surprised elements of the British *2nd Armored Division* fell back, surrendering their advantageous positions there without much of a fight and falling back to the stronger positions at Marsa el Brega. [3] By the evening of 1 April, that town also fell as the British fled in panic. Rommel's orders now required that he wait for the remainder of the *15th Panzer Division* to arrive before attacking Agedabia, but he was unwilling to allow the British time to regroup and bring up their armor, much of which had been pulled off the line for maintenance. By 2 April, the leading elements of *5th Light*, now exceeding their orders, had reached Agedabia and attacked the town, which fell that same afternoon. At this early point in the fighting the fledgling *D.A.K.* was showing a remarkable grasp of the situation, tactical maneuvering, and combined arms cooperation, something that the British just did not seem to possess; indeed, they failed to appreciate these traits for some many months to come. By the use of numerous schemes and ruses, the British were tricked into thinking they were being attacked by far superior forces;

by the bold use of concentrated *Stuka* dive bombers, panzers, 88mm Flak guns, and aggressive reconnaissance moves, the *D.A.K.* was able to push the British back. Rommel and his small German force, backed by two Italian divisions, had occupied the Agedabia area almost two months sooner than those at *OKW* had envisaged. The legend of the "Desert Fox" was beginning to take shape, as well as the endless circle of trouble Rommel would soon have with numerous officers in both the German and Italian High Commands. Not only did nobody know what Rommel was up to, nobody was able to answer Mussolini's questions as to what he would do next. On the night of 3/4 April, Gariboldi, the Italian Commander in Chief, chased after Rommel, sending him messages and ordering him to halt his advance until he himself could come up. These orders did not, however, meet Rommel's view of the situation, and he disobeyed them, and in turn ordered *Aufklärung Abteilung 3* towards Benghazi. At this time some in Berlin, including Hitler, recognized that success was at hand, and whether intended or not, they applauded Rommel's offensive spirit, even though they failed to support it by putting more men and materiel into the campaign.

As the British command and control system and unit organization began to break down, the Germans proved the opposite, with absolute organizational skills that seemed to take advantage of every situation that presented itself. The rout was now on, but in reverse, as Rommel pushed on from Benghazi, Mechili, Derna, and the Gulf of Bomba. Recognizing the British tactic of Beda Fomm was being performed in reverse, the British escaped the German net and retreated to their stronghold at Tobruk, where the decision was made to garrison the vital town, its harbor, and vast amount of stores. The Tobruk garrison consisted of some 36,000 troops, most of them from the *9th Australian Division* (Morshead), and an attached brigade from the *7th Australian Division*. There was also an armored regiment equipped with armored cars and an anti-aircraft brigade.[4] The initial German attacks on Tobruk began on 10 April and continued unsuccessfully until the 14th, when they were finally halted. By early April, the lead elements of the *15th Panzer Division* had begun to arrive in Tripoli, and Rommel wasted little time in bringing them forward. It was on the 10th that *Generalmajor* von Prittwitz, who was doubtful of the attack about to be launched, was chewed out by Rommel for not being forward with his units when the attack went forward, and for letting the British escape. Prittwitz was so upset by the reprimand that he borrowed a car and went forward to reconnoiter for himself the planned attack area. While forward conducting that reconnaissance, Prittwitz was killed by an exploding shell, the first in a long list of senior commanders who would be lost during the North African campaign.[5] *Generalmajor* Hans Karl von Esebeck replaced Prittwitz as commander of the *15th Panzer Division*. It was at this point in the campaign against Tobruk that Rommel began to lose some of his earlier magic, and back in Berlin certain circles began to view him as a man out of control. By late April, the *OKH* was quite concerned with Rommel, who they felt had gone completely mad in his dash across Cyrenaica and Tripolitania; they therefore ordered *General* Friedrich von Paulus, the *OKH* Deputy Chief of Staff, to assess the situation in Africa. When von Paulus arrived, he found Rommel preparing for his assault on Tobruk. The plan of attack called for the *D.A.K.* to bust through the western side of the Tobruk perimeter on the night 30/01 May. Once the breach had been made, the Italians would move in to widen and hold the shoulders, while the panzers from *Panzer Regiment 5* drove on Fort Pilastrino and Tobruk harbor. Rommel felt that the Australians were growing stronger, and that the time was right for an attack despite the condition of the *5th Light* and the recent arrival of the *15th Panzer Division*. To assist in the attack, the infantry and pioneers of the *15th Panzer Division* were ferried in by the *Luftwaffe* to bolster the attack on the Australian defenses. Also by this time there were numerous clashes between superior and subordinate commanders, none more visible than that with the *5th Light* Division's commander, Hans Streich, whose division had suffered terrible losses, and who now refused to blindly attack the Tobruk defenses without proper planning and coordination. The loss of men and materiel against the Australian's stubborn and well sited defenses had caused much concern in many circles, and so it was decided to halt any further offensive actions until the *5th Light* could be reinforced by the Italians, which had previously attacked and been repulsed, and the newly arrived *15th Panzer Division*. Despite the battle raging around Tobruk, Rommel ordered some of his formations to break off the Tobruk fighting and move on further to the east, where they were to begin assaulting the British positions on the Egyptian border. Fort Capuzzo was taken that Easter Sunday, but the British defenses were stiffening, and Bardia, Sollum, and Halfaya Pass would take a bit more time to overcome. On 2 May, the attack on Tobruk ground to a halt in the face of stiff Australian defenses and British artillery fire. The Italians were slow and reluctant to press home their attacks, and the German elements, which had been held up on the minefields, were systematically shot to pieces from well constructed defensive positions. As the attack ended in the face of sandstorms, both sides scrambled to secure the best defensive positions possible, and finally settled down to siege warfare. It was obvious that even with the Italians the *5th Light* lacked the punch and manpower to hold the British, as many of those forces were able to fall back further to the east. Rommel tried to quickly reinforce the units investing Tobruk and attempted to reduce the one thorn in the side of his *D.A.K.*

Moving to the Front
The journey for the Regiment across the Mediterranean was fortunate, in that almost all of its personnel and transport made the crossing successfully. This was, however, not the case for many of the *German Merchant Marine* vessels, which between January and May 1941 lost some eleven ships to the *RAF* and *Navy*. Some of the worse losses came on 16 April, when four British destroyers attacked the Axis convoy near Kerkinnah Island. In the half hour action the following transport ships were sunk: *Adana, Arta, Aegina,* and *Iserlohn,* and on the following day the *Samos* was lost. On 1 May, there was the loss of the *Arcturus, Larissa,* and *Leverkusen*. Lost with those ships were some of the vital equipment and sections of the *15th Panzer Division*. Kurt Liestmann wrote a few days later when he heard of the losses:

"Sunday 27.4.41. After the clear cool night full of stars in the morning at 0900hrs we are in Misurata, where we enter the tent accommodation under a few palm trees. Postscript: the 20th sea convoy was sunk by English cruisers. Large loss of men and material. Unbelievably cynical behavior by the English, who shoot everything moving on the waters with cannons and MG, rafts and survivors, and nothing fished out. The remaining [German] soldiers were fished out 20 hours later. Many wounded by cannon fire. Saturday, 3.5.41. We march further over Torra, Barce, Maraua to Derna. From one of our aircraft we hear that our beautiful 'Leverkusen', which brought us to Tripolis, and another ship were sunk on the return trip. The crew should have been saved."[6]

As the various formations landed in Tripoli, they were immediately put into march formation and sent off in the direction of Tobruk. Some units had been promised eight days off in order to get familiar with Africa and its hot climate, but Rommel would have none of it—all elements were to be sent at the fastest possible speed eastwards. These are now a couple of accounts by some of the men on their arrival and first impressions on landing in Africa. For Lt Schubert of the *3rd Company*:

"Friday 2 May all is off loaded nicely. We ourselves receive the report in the German quarters from the Hauptmann, who wears a white Africa uniform. Probably it's his fantasy outfit. The following day in the harbor there was an explosion of a munitions ship, the other one burned out. The steam-engine ship, Reichenfelds, with which came our company, was damaged. The ship's captain was killed. That afternoon at 1700hrs there was the big parade through Tripoli, after which happens the departure march. The first kilometers after Tripoli the terrain were still o.k. but afterwards it was miserable. We are marching the whole night."[7]

Kurt Liestmann remembered:

"Thursday 1.5.41. In the morning to Benghazi. The company arrives punctually with five Mk IIIs. Large losses, bogies and no spare parts in Benghazi. Almost every house in Benghazi is scared, the harbor destroyed. We organize bogies and spare parts. Rumors from ahead. Much military in Benghazi. What do that many Italian officers do in Benghazi? The impression is getting worse, also fed by the rumors from the front."[8]

Hermann Eckardt remembers:

"The Afrika we had imagined was different, it was a poor country with ninety percent desert, and it was very hot. In front of Garibaldi and Rommel we went on parade. We went to the camp 5km away from Tripoli and there we got fresh water, filled canisters and boiled water, then we went off in the direction of the desert without any maps and headed towards Misurata. Before us had come the 21st Panzer Division [5th Light], and the British were on the retreat, we didn't see any enemy until we reached Sollum and Capuzzo."[9]

Horst Sonnenkalb;

"After we reached the Tripolis harbor we unloaded immediately. We started preparations for making our panzers combat-ready. Then we rushed along the coast line on the asphalt street Via Balbia toward Homs, Misurata, Buerat, Sirte, En Nufilia, Arco del Fileni, the swampy terrain at El Agheila all the way to the defensive position at Marsa El Brega."[10]

Because of Rommel's order to move all incoming combat formations forward to the front at once, the units that arrived and departed Tripoli were in a piecemeal fashion, and lacked unit cohesiveness as they began their movement east. Alfred Toppe wrote of the intelligence planning, and in most cases, the lack of it for units arriving in Africa:

"When the first German units were shipped to Africa in February 1941, the officers responsible for the operational planning had no data of any kind on the nature of the terrain and circumstances in the desert. The intelligence data furnished by the Italians was extremely meager, and the Italian maps were so inaccurate and so incomplete that they were used only for lack of something better. The pamphlets Military Geographical Descriptions for Libya, Northeast Africa, and Egypt were published by the Military Geographical Branch of the German Army High Command. Since they contained only information on cities, roads, oases, and a general survey of the entire region, they could serve the command only as a source of general orientation, for which purpose they proved valuable. They contained very few important tactical details. They were put out in such large numbers that they could be made available down to regimental staff level. At these lower levels, their value was naturally restricted. In Libya, the German Army was initially solely dependent on the hastily reprinted Italian maps (scale 1:200,000), since at first, good German maps were available only on the scales of 1:1,000,000 and 1:500,000 which were mainly destined for use by the Luftwaffe. The Italian maps were poor and often showed points of interest more than twenty kilometers from the coast as several kilometers off. In compensation, there were captured British maps that included Libya and Egypt. They were excellent and as a result much prized. Later, they were reprinted. The French maps, used for the first time in Tunisia, were serviceable but were later replaced by German maps. The lack of good maps made itself felt, especially in defensive operations. New photographs were accordingly taken of the area of the Marsa el Brega position and of the Buerat position in cooperation with the Luftwaffe, the cartographic detachment of the Africa observation battery, the cartographic section of the German Army High Command and the Military Geologic Office."[11]

In most cases, it was usually left to each unit commander to organize his unit for movement as best he could, and get them to the front as rapidly as possible. The route forward to catch up to those German and Italian forces already in the east would take the men and their panzers primarily along the northern coast of Africa. There was, at the time in Northern Africa, only one hard paved road, the Via Balbia. The road had been constructed many years earlier by the Italians in an attempt to connect the numerous Italian settlements that dotted the northern coast of Africa. Kurt Liestmann recorded about meeting many of these people for the first time:

"Sunday 4.5.41. Morning at 0400hrs in Derna. We wait until the whole unit is there and enter our camp. We live in an Italian colony. The colony inhabitant tells the horror stories about corruption and the high treason of Italian officers (also Balbo should have been a betrayal!). The betrayal of the whole Italian front, 375,000 lost, endless materials was lost. They have a lot of trust in us. According the information from Lt Bock it is tough in front of Tobruk. Moroccans and Australians fight tough. Tobruk is a powerful hedgehog position and Rommel is a biting terrier."[12]

One of the first problems encountered by the Regiment, and for that matter the entire *D.A.K.*, was the total lack of navigable maps of Libya. The *D.A.K.* was initially dependent on reprinted Italian maps on a 1:200,000 scale. Those maps had been quickly reprinted, but were of poor quality and had a tendency to be, at times, over 20 miles from the actual location, and focused on mainly tourist points of interests. The first quality maps available to the *D.A.K.* were only available in a larger scale, as they had been printed for use by *Luftwaffe* flight crews. Luckily for the Germans, there were captured British maps that included Libya and Egypt, and they were of excellent quality, and as a result were much prized by German commanders. Later on in the African campaign, many of those captured maps, along with some maps of French origin, would be reprinted until they could be replaced by quality German maps. The route to the front, once out of Tripoli, would pass through the Tripolitania Region of Libya and pass to the southeast through the towns of Homs, Misurata, Buerat, Sirte, En Nofilia, Merduma, the Arco Fileni, and El Agheila. Beginning on 26 April, the *Stabs* of the I./*Abteilung* with its *1st Company* moved off to the east from Tripoli along the Via Balbia; even as the first elements began to make their way east, the other convoys were slowly making their way to Africa to unload their cargo in Tripoli. The town of Misurata, located some 200km east of Tripoli, was initially reached on the 27th; by now the initial impressions of this far away land had begun to quickly fade as the crews soon discovered the terrible heat, sand, dust, and mud. They were also introduced to the sandstorm, which was normally referred to as either a Ghibli or Chamsin, and blew so that it got into everything: the eyes, ears, and every nook and cranny—it even defeated the issued dust goggles, which could not keep the eyes free of dust and sand. Kurt Liestmann's diary has this note about the sand and dust:

"Friday 9.5.41. On the way to Tobruk. Behind Acroma is erected the tent camp. Bare stone desert, with that miserable sand storm. We are completely dusted over. The faces are brown-yellow covered with sand. The sweat streams down. In the vehicle is a yellow fog. Huge dust clouds behind the vehicles. In the evening the wind turns into a storm. Artillery impacts are not far away in front of Tobruk. The whole night it grudges on."[13]

Horst Sonnenkalb:

"The usually silent desert was filled with the noise of engines and the clanging of our panzer tracks. We drove in a zug in a tight formation next to and behind each other. The raised sand covered our view, entered our vehicles, glued eyes shut and got them infected, got stuck in the corners of our mouths and grated between our teeth. First we were busy with trying to feel at home in our panzers and getting to know the other crewmembers. Our equipment, packed up in a rucksack, weighed almost 110 lbs. They included our tropical garments, long and short pants and 'Stiefelhosen', tunic and shirts with neck ties (Panzer soldiers with the Wehrmacht were called 'Schlipssoldaten – Neck tie soldiers'), a pair of lace-up shoes and a pair of boots whose shafts were made out of linen, then underwear, consisting of undershirt and underpants, a coat, a tarpaulin and we also had mosquito tents with poles, mosquito nets which were mostly used as head and face protection from the big swarms of flies. Swarms of flies were our constant, annoying companions in the desert. Our sun and steel helmets were fastened on top of the rucksack. Our body bandages [Sleeping Bags] were the funniest things, which we had to wear especially at night. Even though soon they were ridden by lice, we didn't want to be without them during the cold North African nights. The differences of temperature between the heat of the day and the cold nights were extremely high. It was real easy, while lying on."[14]

Hermann Eckardt remembers his journey and some of the troubles the heat caused for the panzers:

"We marched only during the nights, during the day we rested. The rubber on the bogies had to be replaced on the running gear. Gas was given to us all in 20 liter canisters, from our own supply lines. It was the I-Staffel, they supplied us with gas and repaired some small damages, as well as replace ammunition. Each company had its own supply and fuel vehicles and there were all kinds of light vehicles; Opels and Fords but there were no diesel vehicles. There was a good paved road until Tobruk [Via Balbia], then we went through the desert and many of the panzers fell out of order, especially the Mk III which broke down because they took air from outside and the [intake] pipe was just above the tracks, the air filters quickly filled and became unserviceable. The Mk IVs had different system, thus they had no damage, and the air was taken not directly from outside but from the work area inside. The construction of Mk IIIs had to be changed for this reason in order to take air from within the panzer."[15]

In the meantime, the Regimental *Stabs* and Support Company, along with the *2nd*, *3rd*, and *5th Companies* were being off loaded in Tripoli, the panzers, which obviously took more time to unload, prepare for movement, and traveled much slower than the wheeled vehicles, were placed under *Hptm* Ehrbeck and would follow later. The wheeled vehicles were sent on ahead in order to become more familiar with the area until the panzers arrived. The *3rd Company*, which sailed on the second convoy, passed through the same towns a week later, as the company's war diary recorded:

"Sunday 4 May, by 1100hrs it is already damn hot. We arrive in Misurata. All quiet until 2000hrs. The Arabs sell us eggs, each for two Lire. On Monday in the morning we reach Buerat, one miserable nest. There was swimming in the Mediterranean. In the evening we march at 2000hrs towards Brega. On Wednesday 6 May we reached in the evening El Agheila. The fortress is like in the fairy-tale, but not when looking closely. A strange fortress of walls and towers. The fortress is occupied by Italians. On Tuesday, 7 May in the morning we are in Marsa el Brega. During the march to here, we passed a small but nice oasis. There were many white-stem and green palms. At 1730hrs we continue to march."[16]

Now the Regiment's panzers were entering the Cyrenaica Region of Libya and moved north, passing the towns of Marsa el Brega, Agedabia, Msus, and Benghazi. It was there at Agedabia that some of the sections and panzers left the Via Balbia and cut across the desert towards Tobruk. The road march to Tobruk through the rough open desert covered approximately 180km each day, and that distance was only possible due to the skilled performance of the crews, especially the drivers. During the march, when combat was least likely, the crews rode on the outside the panzers in the open air in order to escape the oppressive heat of the panzer and catch what breeze there was. This barren, rocky, sandy land represented a significant change for the men and machines of the Regiment, who were used to the good roads and deep green color of Germany and France. For many of the crews this was their first experience abroad, and at first many of them were in awe of their new surroundings. Horst Sonnenkalb:

"Shortly before Agedabia we went through the desert and then toward the Cyrenaica plateau via Antelat and Msus, this was our first close encounter with the enemy, the 'Feuerprobe' as the German soldiers called it. During this panzer battle, which was my first, the turret on our panzer Mk III was hit which luckily didn't have a big impact. The sheer power of the strike of the enemy's round caused me to have such a great amount of respect, it gave me the creeps. I was so blissfully ignorant then, not knowing that this was only the beginning and that I would experience much worse later on. We continued our way toward El Mechili. It got more serious there. Our supply package [storage bin] got blown away and a few other things also. We regretted the loss of the turret that was attached to the supply package, because it consisted of clothes and other paraphernalia. Everything inside the panzer stayed unharmed. We had to get to the panzer repair depot anyhow which was close to Martuba. After Derna had fallen we continued on towards El Adem and passed by Gazala and Tmimi. There we had an intense exchange of fire with the Brits. We got some damage on our panzer, but we were able to fix it ourselves."[17]

Again the *3rd Company* diary recorded:

"Thursday 8 May, yesterday evening marched out of El Agheila. In the night had two hours rest and arrived via Agedabia. On the further march we hear heavy explosions noise in the direction of Benghazi. We arrive on Thursday in the morning at 0900hrs Benghazi. We stay in the cover of the undergrowth lines, and experience our first heavy sandstorm in the middle of the day. In the evening we take a bath near the harbor of Benghazi. The harbor is full of sunken ships and boats, in Benghazi there are ruins caused from aerial bombs. We eat in the only open restaurant that evening and have three eggs sunny-side-up, bread and wine.

Friday 9 May During midday we take a bath in the Mediterranean again. At 1700hrs we march away through the city. In the city borders is an Italian restaurant, where sit Italians and want to serve us. They offer us tea. Now I am leading the regimental column as all the other officers went ahead. The chief of the 2nd Company hurries to the front and grumbles that we should allow the panzer crews to get tea."

After departing the Benghazi area, the panzers began climbing the Djebel Akhdar (*Green Mountains*) on to the high desert plateau to Barce, Mechili, Giovanni Berta, Derna, Gazala, Tobruk, El Adem, and Acroma. For the group which included the *3rd Company*, they recorded:

"*Saturday 10 May in the early morning around 1000hrs our panzer column arrives into Maraua. It is overwhelmingly hot and we are all fatigued. At 1700hrs we resume the march and on Sunday morning 11 May we arrive at 0800hrs in Giovanni Berta. After the miserable desert march, Cyrenaica is good for a change. Giovanni Berta is already green and beautiful. The Regimental Stabs was first spotted here again. Hptm Jahns cruises along with an Italian Sahara uniform, with which he appears everywhere. We get water from the spring, it would be the last spring for many for a long time, and for some the last one in their lives.*"[18]

At El Gubba and the Martuba Oasis, the *Stabs* I./*Abteilung* paused the first week of May to wait until the remainder of the Regiment had caught up with it. On the 9th, all units were ordered to assemble 20km southwest of Tobruk. By the 6th, the *Stabs* II./*Abteilung* with the 6th and 7th *Companies* finished offloading in Tripoli, and at once made preparations for the march east, where they would link up with the rest of the Regiment in Cyrenaica. With the final arrival of the *15th Panzer Division* and a few other subordinate units, the "*Deutsches Afrika Korps*" (D.A.K.) would be officially operational. The diary of the *3rd Company* recorded:

"*Monday 12 May, yesterday on Sunday evening we left Giovanni Berta at around 1900hrs. We go to Tobruk. The usual suspects wished us luck as we march through the deserts and not through Derna. In the morning at around 0400hrs there is an RAF air-force attack. The bombs fall near the march column. No damage. It [march column] goes through Ain el Gazala to the Via Balbia and onto Tobruk in the white [desert] on and through. There is the hospital. Some graves left on the road. In the evening we advanced until Acroma.*"[19]

On 13 May, the Regiment was located in an assembly area southwest of Tobruk near Acroma. After a tough 1,350km road march in the scorching sun and over the Via Balbia and other dusty desert tracks, such as the Trigh Capuzzo and Trigh el Abd, the panzers were finally able to link up with their infantry brothers. Kurt Liestmann wrote of that day:

"*Tuesday 13.5.41. The Regiment arrives, the abteilung are now together. We get the news that Rudolf Hess has jumped with the parachute in Scotland. He is great! The Führer is concerned about his surrounding. It will be a heavy hit for him personally.*"

And once again the *3rd Company* diary reported:

"*Tuesday 13 May we stay at Acroma, there is a visit from Hptm Voigt of Schützen Regiment 115, who are in position and based in the area.*"

The Regiment was able to cover the enormous distance because of the new condition of the panzers, but still the engines suffered serious damage and would complicate the operational readiness of the Regiment for combat operations. The additional space and weight taken up by the addition of water, fuel, spare track links, and bogies, which were normally carried on the tanks themselves, increased the weight and caused numerous failures to the brakes and steering. At each of the halts, the air filters had to be cleaned from the accumulated dust and sand which caused many of the engine breakdowns. Worst still, was the amount of rest that the already sun baked crewmembers were able to catch. The panzer and all its moving parts required an enormous amount of servicing along with the grease, oil, and other fluids which required constant changing, in addition to the brakes and bogies, which were also subject to breaking and required constant changing. To give a clear example of the type of wear this road march had on the vehicles, we look to the I./*Abteilung* and *5th Company's* road march, which had, as of 12 May, used over one hundred and thirty bogies, of which over thirty went to just the *5th Company*. The increase in miles and dirty dusty days increased the number of mechanical breakdowns, which soon began to test the Regiment's maintenance, recovery, and workshop services. The effect of the dust on weapons and equipment, including motor vehicles, was considerable in the desert. Dust was probably the greatest enemy of the panzers, because the dusty air was sucked into the engine and attacked the cylinders and pistons, which caused these moving parts to wear out very quickly. In his after action report, Alfred Toppe wrote of the problems with the desert sand and dust:

"*Special air filters were later designed to reduce the wear on the engines but could not prevent it altogether. Being in the desert effectively cut in half the life of an engine, for the average panzer this resulted in a service life of between 3-4,000km and between 12-14,000km for other types of motor vehicles. There were other factors, such as driving long distances in low gear, a greater need for special lubricants and the general lack of such items all-further subtracted from a vehicle's service life. The effects of dust on weapons and equipment, including motor vehicles, were considerable in the desert. Dust had the greatest effect on motor vehicles, because the dusty air that was sucked into the cylinders attacked the cylinders and pistons and caused these parts to wear out quickly. Special air filters reduced the wear but could not prevent it altogether. In general-purpose cars (Volkswagens), the air intake openings were installed in the interior of the cars to give the engines purer air. In tanks, the air was sucked out of the battle compartment. In spite of this, the average lifetime of a Volkswagen engine in the desert was only 12,000-14,000 kilometers in comparison with 50,000-70,000 kilometers in other theaters of war. In the desert, it was necessary to change tank engines after about 3,500 kilometers, while they would last for 7,000-8,000 kilometers in Europe. To be sure, this was due not only to the effects of dust but also, to a considerable degree, to the necessity of driving long distances cross-country in low gears. The other parts of motor vehicles (such as brakes, chassis, and all parts that could be penetrated by dust) also suffered considerably more wear and tear than under normal conditions. It is not possible to give any figures on this point. What is certain is that motor vehicles in the desert need substantially more lubrication than in other theaters of war. No special greases and lubricants were used.*"[20]

And to make matters worse, as Kurt Liestmann noted:

"*The order from division to march off to Tobruk is received. Individual ventures on bunkers in front of Tobruk should be started. In Tripolis the first ship with spare parts and ammunition have been sunk. The Italians again allowed the English bombers to come through in the light of the day, a great obscenity. The opinion about Italian soldiers, as we know them until now, becomes even worse.*"

Kurt Kathe remembers:

"Usually we drove during the evenings as it was too hot during the day, but at first we also drove during the day to advance to the enemy. When we drove in the day the rubber [wheels/bogies] wore quickly from the panzer and then many of our panzers became broken due to the dust, which went in the engine, in the cylinders, and the grease was no longer there and then the panzer broke down. Afterwards one must get much airing [hi-pressure air] to get it out which took time because the desert rubs and makes things break it's not good for the engine."[21]

Gotthilf Haidt of the *Werkshop* Company adds to this:

"I remember the problem of the water and the sand storms; this was the main problem, the sand storms. In Tripolis we landed and went from there to Egypt thousands of kilometers, we were not the first in Africa and the panzers were under pressure, under the sand and heavy marches. The air filters were always dirty and there was always dust there, there were paved streets in Africa that were built by Mussolini, but despite it there was always sand storms and if you work in the desert there is no one to come help you. In the night we were in the tent and partially slept together where it was possible to sleep, sometimes under vehicles, if possible."[22]

The panzer strength report of the Regiment at the beginning of May 1941 stood at 146 panzers: ten Befehls panzers, forty-five Mk IIs, seventy-one Mk IIIs, and twenty Mk IVs.[23] The wear on weapons, especially the moving parts and gun barrels, was also considerably higher, and those weapons used by the infantry were more prone to damage because they were close to the ground and in more contact with the dirt and dust. For the panzer main gun, it was necessary to protect all the moving parts, especially the breechblock, when not in use with tarps and covers, and to ensure that all gun barrels had muzzle caps. The hard, rocky, and dusty desert certainly took its toll on vehicles and equipment in the North African campaign, but the panzers were not the only thing that suffered from these hardships; the crews also suffered. Horst Sonnenkalb offers this description of the heart of every panzer, its crew:

"The panzer crew consisted of five men. The commandant had his place in the tower, on the left in front of him sat the gunner (Zielschütze) behind his Zieloptik, to the right of him sat the Ladeschütze who was often thrown back and forth during the drive. That resulted in a lot of bruises. Up front down on the left was the driver's seat, and to the right next to him the radio operator (Funker). All of the crewmembers were connected by radio and listened to the commandant's orders through the rubber sealed earphones. They were also able to talk to each other with their throat microphone. During the first years of war the Panzer men were being trained over months, which was of great effect among the individual Panzer crews during front assignments. Later on however, when the front was weakened by a big loss of men and materials, the training time of the panzer crew was shortened. That resulted in adverse effects of the deployment strength and power of impact of the Panzerwaffe. But in Africa the panzer formations possessed well-trained panzer soldiers, which were a pledge to the attained successes in the North African theatre of war."[24]

Klaus Hubbuch gives an excellent description:

"The days were always very long, starting with the dawn and from about 4am one attack followed by another attack, until the darkness asked for a 'stop' and in the far desert the star-shells [flares] allowed us to see where our friends and enemies were. The vehicle was [made] combat ready for the next day and so it was possible to sleep a little from about midnight, [if you] must not take a watch. But even half-an-hour was enough to feel again fresh, as the excitement of the evening subsided. As soon as the first sunlight appeared on the horizon, the hatches were locked and so it went on. Around midday we had heat of between 70 and 80 degrees C [158-176F] inside of the panzer. At last we were not bothered by artillery fire and we let our hatch open until we again went panzer against panzer."[25]

Operation Brevity

In the first part of May, a small *Fieseler Storch* flew over the I./Abteilung, dropping a small case that contained the message for the recall of *Oberstlt* Friedrich Haarde. Haarde had received a number of wounds in the *First World War*, and the desert condition was not good for a man of his age and health. So on 15 May, Haarde handed over command of his beloved I./Abteilung, a unit which he had commanded and led in the battles of Poland and France over the past three and a half years, to *Major* Crohn, who had just arrived from Germany. Haarde was recalled to Berlin, where he went on to become an *Oberst* and commander of the *Unteroffizer Academy*; later in the war he would move to a position in the *Heerswaffenampt*.[26]

Also taking place those first weeks of May was the passage of the British "*Tiger*" convoy that made its way through the Straits of Gibraltar and the Mediterranean, heading for port in Egypt with tanks and aircraft reinforcements for the *Western Desert Force*. The five ship "fast" convoy was sent along the shorter, but more dangerous Mediterranean route, instead of going around the longer, but safer *Cape of Good Hope* route. The reason for this was so that the tanks and their crews would be ready for the new offensive planned for the end of the month. The ships docked on the 12th in Alexandria, having suffered the loss of just one ship that hit a mine and sank with all fifty-seven tanks it was transporting. Despite the loss of this ship, some forty *Hurricane* fighters and 238 *Matilda* and *Crusader* tanks were unloaded.[27] The British Mk II infantry tank, or more commonly known as the "Matilda," was equipped with a 2-Pounder or 40mm gun, which at the time was thought to be a match for the German 37mm and 50mm main tank guns. Even though it was an infantry tank, the *Matilda* possessed no high explosive ammunition, only the tank busting solid shot round. Soon it would be revealed that, in fact, the 2-Pounder was no match for the German Mk III and IV panzers with their short 50mm and 75mm guns. The 2-Pounder gun had too low a velocity, and lacked the punch necessary to defeat those models face to face. The one distinct advantage that the Matilda did have was its armor protection, which ranged from between 14-78mm and was thick enough to deflect most anti-tank gun rounds now being employed by German and Italian gunners. The Matilda's greatest fault, however, lay in its overall speed, for it had a relatively slow speed of just 27mph/43kph on good roads and 8mph/12kph over broken terrain. Also in the convoy were eighty-two of the new *Crusader* Mk VIs and twenty-one older model cruiser light tanks. By mid-May, the *Western Desert Force* was down to its last hundred tanks; some reports differ, and list that number at approximately fifty operational tanks located in the border area, while the other half, between 50-100, were reported as being in various states of repair in maintenance facilities all throughout Egypt.

The British realized that with each passing day the *D.A.K.* was growing stronger, as more and more ships arrived in Tripoli to disgorge the men, weapons, equipment, and panzers of the *15th Panzer Division*, which was now almost operational, and at full strength. British Intelligence services knew that the ill-supplied German forces were still widely scattered, with most of the panzer forces being located around Tobruk, and a slim garrison in the Bardia-Sollum-Halfaya Pass area. The time to launch a spoiling attack and gain favorable jumping off positions for a larger offensive was now. British Intelligence had placed the majority of German-Italian forces around Tobruk, with only a weak, unarmored force covering the frontier area near Bardia and Sollum. The British plan called for an attack on those Axis forces scattered around Sollum-Bardia-Capuzzo and Halfaya Pass; if this attack was successful, there might be the off chance that once those Axis forces were defeated, the advance could drive for Tobruk, and possibly even relieve the surrounded garrison there. For the attack, the British, under the command of *Brigadier General* W.H.E. *"Strafer"* Gott, had two weak infantry brigades: the *22nd Guards Brigade* and *7th Armored Brigade Group*, which were supported by the *7th Support Group*. Twenty-nine cruiser tanks from the *2nd RTR* and twenty-six Matildas from the *4th RTR* supported the infantry. The plan of attack called for a battalion of the *2nd Rifle Brigade*, supported by an artillery regiment, to advance along the Via Balbia and seize the coastal road and the lower portion of the Halfaya Pass. The middle column, consisting of the *22nd Guards Brigade*, and supported by the *4th RTR* was to strike across the upper escarpment and make for Halfaya Pass and Fort Capuzzo. The left hand column, composed of the *2nd RTR* and *7th Support Group*, was to move around the open left flank towards Sidi Azeiz. The British had based their plan of attack on intercepted signals transmissions that indicated that the *D.A.K.* was in dire need of resupply and reinforcement if it was to hold the British along the border area; unfortunately, these signals gave a false impression of just how weak the *D.A.K.* was. The Germans, on the other hand, were also intercepting poorly coded British signals traffic, which tipped them off that an offensive was coming soon. Based on these intercepts, Rommel had correctly predicted that an attack was in the making, and therefore, he placed all those units along the frontier on alert, including the I./*Abteilung*. On the 14th, orders were issued by division headquarters in preparation for Operation *"Landau"*; the I./*Abteilung* was visited by a number of generals that same afternoon as it began to prepare itself for a rapid movement eastward once it was discovered that the British attack had commenced. Kurt Liestmann remembered:

"Wednesday 14.5.41 Orders about operation 'Landau' arrive. In the afternoon the general visits us. Tomorrow evening begins operation 'Landau'. At 0900hrs suddenly an alert. March off to the east, around Tobruk. Forced march until the night 0100hrs to Sidi Azeiz. On the way we get disturbing messages via radio about the situation at Sollum. The English must have broken through. Via Me-110 in the middle of the desert a message was thrown down. The English seem to be making an attempt to break through to Tobruk."[28]

Presently the *5th Light* and its panzer regiment, the *5th*, held the border area, with the *15th Panzer* moving into and reinforcing the positions around Tobruk. Despite the growing concerns, those Germans located on the frontier did not have the proper amount of time and material to properly reinforce their positions. On 15 May, the British attacked; the infantry and artillery moving in the coastal column were temporarily held up on the lower Halfaya defenses, but they were finally able to overcome the resistance and make their way forward later in the day. The *22nd Guards Brigade* came forward and attacked Halfaya, where it was quickly able to take the upper defenses and then roll forward to capture the garrisons of Sollum and Capuzzo. The far left column was able to push back the German reconnaissance screen and make its way toward Sidi Azeiz. Those early gains were about all that would be achieved by the British, as the offensive soon became overstretched. The *Guards* infantry column quickly became too dispersed around Halfaya, Capuzzo, and Sollum to press on towards Bardia, and there had been poor cooperation between the infantry and tanks of the *4th RTR* resulting in the loss of nine Matildas.

The *5th Light* had also been busy with the *5th Panzer Regiment* launching a counter-attack towards Capuzzo. Wilhelm Hagios of the *2nd Company* recalls his arrival and move to the front:

"On the 1st May we landed. From there we went to the east, 1-2-3 days later we were in Tripoli, we went with the wheeled vehicles and the panzers were not able to drive in the afternoon. A maximum of 20km we were able to drive as it became too hot and we couldn't drive due to the damage to the laufrolle. We drove at 8pm and overtook them [the panzers] and built tents and rested there. So it continued in the direction of Benghazi, Sirte was the first location, then towards Nofilia. Our commander had his coolant [system] broken, all his stuff was with him for decision making, and so one of us had to go back with this coolant. When I came to Barce they [the regiment] were away from there, they were in Acroma. There we were until the 14th. On the 15th, the British attacked Halfaya [Pass] and we went to the east in the morning. The British fighters had almost completely destroyed our supply lines. I was at the Regiment along with the long range construction troops, I had two vehicles and four men and we helped install cables. I had evaded this work quick enough and left them and did not stop again. On the following evening we arrived in Bardia, on the Capuzzo to Bardia road, there was a repair station set up there and the senior mechanic, who no longer had a vehicle, commandeered my vehicle. I also had to take the wounded which had been shot that morning back. I had this one man with an open stomach wound with me the entire day, he was in the back seat, and I knew the wound should not be touched and kept sterile so I put a bandage on him and brought him to the medical attendant. When I brought him to the medics he was already dead, and we noticed that he had one more wound in the head. It was on 15 May."[29]

The Regimental *Stabs* and the I./*Abteilung* were at that time in *D.A.K.* reserve, and they were ordered that morning to proceed to El Duda and take up positions there, and await elements of a reinforcing Flak battery that would accompany them. Later that afternoon, orders were again received that ordered the combined *kampfgruppe* of panzers and Flak guns to move forward to Sidi Azeiz by the fastest possible route. Rommel, in his book, wrote about those orders:

"I accordingly sent a Panzer battalion reinforced by A.A. guns, under the command of Oberstlt Kramer to Herff's assistance. The two forces, Herff's and Kramer's were to join up during the night 15-16 May west of Sidi Azeiz. Our air reconnaissance and the units holding the Sollum-Bardia line had formed the impression that the British intended to concentrate their troops south of Sidi Azeiz, in order to sweep aside Herff's force on the morning of the 16th and then completely unhinge our Sollum-Bardia front by a further thrust to the north. My intension, therefore, in uniting Herff's and Cramer's forces, was to prevent this British move being driven home."[30]

By 1800hrs, the panzers were moving through El Adem, and by midnight had received instructions to link up with *Kampfgruppe Herff* west of Sidi Azeiz. The Regiment continued all through the night, moving along the Trigh Capuzzo and eventually arriving at Sidi Azeiz around midnight. Rommel went on to record:

"Herff's force drove towards Kramer's during the night in order to ensure that the enemy had no opportunity of tackling the two forces separately in the morning. But the two formations missed each other and, on the morning of the 16th, Kramer arrived in the Sidi Azeiz area alone. Contrary to expectations, however, the enemy had meanwhile withdrawn to the south and obviously broken off his attack."[31]

After a short halt in the early morning hours, the march south continued until 0300hrs on the morning of the 16th, when the I./*Abteilung* reached a position just north of Fort Capuzzo. Unfortunately, the *Abteilung* was not ready to fight once it arrived; the fuel tanks were all but empty, and the fast paced march, which had covered over 130km of rugged desert terrain, coupled with an average march speed of between 18-22mph/30-35kph, had caused many of the panzers to fall out of the march with mechanical breakdowns. The Regimental *Stabs* and I./*Abteilung* together were only able to report some thirty-one operational panzers at Capuzzo. Horst Sonnenkalb describes some of the terrain that the panzer fought over:

"Our panzer attacks in the desert took place on hills, fields covered with debris, from depressed areas downward through a wadi, then upward again, but mostly across wide areas abundantly covered with knee high camel horn bushes."[32]

The brand new panzers, which had been designed for operations in Central Europe, not the hot dry dust climate of North Africa, continued to suffer from mechanical breakdowns. Oddly enough, many of these breakdowns could have been easily avoided if there had been any forethought by some of the senior commanders. Like many new vehicles, the manufacturer's service manual called for travel speeds of 12mph/20kph on good streets and roads, but by sending the panzers pell-mell across the desert, the commanders violated the book and never allowed the panzers the recommended break-in period, which most likely would have reduced the number of breakdowns and repairs. The German workshop commanders supporting the panzer regiments were pleasantly surprised by the performance of the panzers on the march east from Tripoli. Most panzers had suffered few mechanical troubles, provided they moved at night or in cooler temperatures, and at fairly low travel speeds. Later, once the panzers were properly broken in, they found even these measures to be unnecessary. Kurt Kathe comments on the Werkshop Company:

"We had a werkshop group, about 20 men, who repaired our panzers when they were broken; they were either in the panzer or Stabs Company. It was the workshop company zug, who had such cranes and tow-cars, there were people with them who repaired engines and also installed them."[33]

But it was Rommel's impatience and the current situation that forced him to order the Regiment forward without the proper break-in period and time for proper halts to allow for services and repairs. This lack of knowledge would continue to haunt Rommel for his entire time in Africa, as his panzer forces never came close to being equal to his enemy, and it was only the back breaking and thankless work by the workshop companies that did a brilliant job of keeping the Regiment supplied with those panzers that could be recovered and repaired. The damage caused by this forced march was so serious that the Regiment never fully recovered a large number of its panzers, and consequently a large number of them were constantly in the workshop for maintenance. The fallout, of course, meant that the Regiment would never be able to reach its full table of organization and operate at full regimental strength. As the sun came up that morning of the 16th, the British, sensing the table was about to turn on them, had already begun to withdraw their forces back towards Halfaya Pass. The Regiment, in turn, sent out three Mk IIs with orders to conduct a reconnaissance of Fort Capuzzo, and to determine if the British were still in the immediate area. Fritz Haustein remembered:

"I was in the Mk II and we had been receiving fire from unknown locations, we proceeded to locate the enemy who was using a hunter's cover. Hptm Ehrbeck was in charge and our panzer threw a track, in the confusion the other panzer drove off and didn't know our situation. We jumped out and repaired it but it wasn't exactly correct but we made do and held until we could get behind cover. In this action I was wounded in the lower jaw when my panzer was hit in the turret. I was taken back to Bardia and then flown out on a Ju-52 to a dentist in Athens who was without work and was happy to fix me up. From Athens it was to Salonika and then back to Böblingen and that was it for my time with Regiment 8 in the desert. When I returned to Böblingen I was promoted to Feldwebel."[34]

The British forces Haustein speaks of positioned around the fort surely must have been a covering force, and as battlefield reports differ, some stating that the British had already evacuated Capuzzo and others that state that earlier that morning a German unit had already recaptured it, it can be assumed that as so often happened in the desert war, where one force quickly moved on others moved in. Regardless of that fact, reports then state that those British tanks were then attacked by three of the heavier Mk IIIs and were pushed back. At around 0630hrs, the Light *Zug* from the I./*Abteilung* quickly moved in and secured the fort, where it was later reinforced by a number of Mk IIIs from the 5th Company. According to other German reports, by 0730hrs, Sidi Azeiz and Fort Capuzzo had been taken and were back in German hands. Despite the encounters that took place that morning, the British had already decided the previous evening against any further attacks to the west, and so a general order to withdraw was issued. The attack by *Panzer Regiment 5* the day before had made the British commander realize just how extended and unprotected his slim force was to attacks by the *D.A.K.* There was some discussion, but in the end Gott, who had requested a general withdraw order from Bereford-Peirse, was delayed due to poor communications, and so he ordered his forces back across the frontier wire early on the morning of the 16th. By 0800hrs that morning, elements of *Kampfgruppe Herff* and the Regimental *Stabs* had made a link-up near the fort, where Cramer was then ordered to proceed toward Point 208, located just to the west of Capuzzo. All that morning reports began arriving at *D.A.K.* headquarters that many of the British elements had disappeared from the battle field and repositioned themselves further to the south and east. As the British pulled back they did so with little contact, and suffered more from mechanical loss than actual combat loss. As the morning passed and reports came in informing him of the British situation, *Oberst* Herff decided that he would order an attack on Halfaya Pass that afternoon, but he was frustrated in this effort by the lack of fuel, which all but immobilized the panzers and mobile forces.[35] By mid-afternoon, the seventeen panzers of the I./*Abteilung* had been sufficiently refueled and re-supplied, and began the advance in a southeasterly direction towards Point 206 and the Egyptian border, where they were to attack the British forces assembling there. Before long the combat elements came under attack from British artillery located around Point 206 and by *RAF Hurricanes*. Kurt Liestmann's diary had the following concerning the day's action:

"Friday 16.5.41. In Sidi Azeiz only traces of English tanks. They went back to the desert in the south. In the midday Oberst von Herff with his units comes to us. Our zug reports that Capuzzo is free of enemy. English scout cars search in the area. One falls into our hands. The radio still works. We attack south in the of point 208 west of Capuzzo. After a few kilometer a heavy artillery fire, which seem to be directed by the quick armored scout cars. After few kilometers the Abteilung turns around and disconnects itself. No fuel anymore. After few hours the vehicles are here. We fuel. Until now are five partially and heavily wounded of the crew from a wheeled vehicle. The 5th Company has one dead, two wounded. We attack further on point 206 eastwards. Again artillery fire, which follows

us during the whole attack. Shortly behind 206 we drive over the barbed wire through the Libyan border and are in the attack on the Egyptian terrain in the direction of Sidi Suleiman, which we reach in the evening. About 15 enemy tanks on the horizon, the fire is commenced from 1200m and till the dusk there is great fire mystery. One small armored car is shot and catches fire in front of us. The crew can get out. When it gets dark, we disconnect and go south of Capuzzo for the rest. One English truck and three prisoners, one panzer Mk II destroyed. We have one dead and two wounded in the Regiment Stab. At the rest area we bury Fw Benecke."[36]

Sonnenkalb remembers those first tank encounters:

"I started feeling anxious when the enemy tanks got closer and closer. But later on I got used to it and there were worse things that could happen. One time I had to get out of my shot up panzer, because some barbed wire got twisted around our track. With the help from the radio operator and ladeschütze and lot of exertion on our part we were able to free the panzer from the iron shackles while grenades exploded next to us and machine gun salvos were whistling around our ears."[37]

The *RAF* was also busy over other parts of the battlefield, as the Regiment's supply column was attacked during its drive from El Adem to Sidi Azeiz. In addition to a number of vehicles being lost, *Uffz* Eckert was killed in the attack, along with the loss of five panzer mechanics and a driver, all of which were wounded. Earlier in the day, the Mk III of Lt Bönisch, which had broken down due to engine trouble, was spotted by the British tanks as they made their way north, but they were forced to ignore the lone panzer until later when they made their way back south. As the British returned past the panzer, fourteen tanks began firing at the broken down panzer, finally succeeding in setting it alight. The crew, however, had to bail out of the stricken machine, but was able to make good their escape without suffering any injuries. At approximately 1700hrs, the Regiment crossed over the Egyptian border for the first time just south of Fort Capuzzo, where British tanks from the *2nd RTR* engaged it.[38] The panzer crews easily recognized the distinct shape of the British tanks as they entered Egypt for the first time. An engagement took place in the latter part of the day with both sides unable to claim much, as the fading light often distorted optics and blurred the gunners' vision. At dusk, both sides retired to their respective assemble areas, with the British pulling back to a night lager position, and the Regiment relocated some 2km behind the border wire. As the two sides withdrew that evening, the battle effectively came to an end, and the following losses were reported by the *D.A.K.*: 12 killed, 61 wounded, and 185 missing, in addition to the loss of one Mk II and two Mk IIIs. The British lost a reported 100 men captured, four Matildas destroyed, and an unknown number of tanks, trucks, and various pieces of equipment left on the battlefield—many of the vehicles were left there due to mechanical breakdown.[39] On the 17th, it became clear that the British had withdrawn the majority of their forces back towards Sidi Barrani, although they maintained forces near Point 206, Sollum, Halfaya, and the coastal plain. The German forces were able to maintain contact through reconnaissance elements, but were ordered to hold their present defensive positions until a revision of plans could be made. For the Regiment, its light column, regimental headquarters, and *I./Abteilung* were able to secure Capuzzo, while a few of the British entrenchments located near the border wire were taken by elements from the *5th Company* with four Mk IIIs. In that action, the panzers engaged some of the British tanks and armored cars, forcing them to turn away to the south, but both sides reported no serious losses in the engagement. On the 18th, with new directions from Rommel, attacks were launched at Halfaya and to the south towards Sidi Suleiman. The attack launched against Halfaya by the *Aufklärung Gruppe* met with little success, despite the British gunners being low on ammunition. In the south, the attack met with a bit more success, as the British were pushed out of Point 206 and sent south. After forcing out the British, the Regiment *Stabs* and *I./Abteilung*, low on fuel, were forced to pull back in the late afternoon to Point 206, where they established an assembly area. The break in the action allowed the crews to catch up on a bit of rest and perform some much needed technical maintenance and services in an attempt to keep those panzers that were still operational up and running. Two Mk IIs and two Mk IIIs, which had previously suffered mechanical troubles and broke down en-route, were also returned. Later in the afternoon, a flight of *RAF* bombers attacked Capuzzo and the nearby assembly area, causing four casualties, all of whom were wounded by flying fragments and splinters. On the morning of 19 May, the *I./Abteilung* was transferred to a new assembly area five kilometers north of Fort Capuzzo, in close proximity to the Via Balbia, where it was to link up and establish a large hedgehog position with *Panzer Regiment 5*. The *abteilung* was to remain in this area until the 25th. A small detachment was left behind to secure Point 206. Also during this time we have a diary entry from *Olt* Schubert of the *3rd Company* who recorded:

"Monday 19 May, Major Kriebel [the Divisional Ia] comes to our defensive [positions] and orders, that some of my panzers should undertake an attack against the village in order to shoot the towers. We go with three panzers and one vehicle against the village. 500 meter from there suddenly arrive English tanks from the ruins of the house and fire on us. Besides the English artillery shoots as well. We retreat without losses."[40]

The diary entry of Hermann Danner describes in a bit more detail the action as the *"Assault Detachment"* moved on Quala:

"The barbed wire is in front of us, the border between Libya and Egypt and beyond nothing, except the desert again and again. The sand and camel thorns are everywhere. On the left is the vehicle cemetery. Shot through and burned out English and Italian tanks and trucks. Far away is the village, Quala [Qalala]. The white walls are unclear and floating in the view. The hot air shimmers and complicates the surveillance. The wind fell asleep. The heat pressures like the goblin over the yellow sand. We try to do as little as possible, as each movement costs a bucket of sweat. We sit here already for two days as a protection. 4-5km away is an English defensive position. We can recognize light surveillance vehicles (Spähwagen) and fat Mark II tanks through the field-glasses. Then it becomes too stupid. Our panzer Mk IV starts shooting at the English. Already the first shots are well laid and Tommy hurries up as if a fire brigade, leaving just a fat dust cloud behind. Our happiness is immense but doesn't last long. We immediately hear the shooting of the artillery battery in the distance and soon it's playing hell over us here. We stick our heads down unwillingly. The round lands 200m behind us. Now to get back in the crate and close the hatch tight. The next round is already on the way. The British must have an excellent B-position [observer position or OP]. As a flash among us comes the realization, the towers of Quala and simultaneously the towers must be destroyed. The Regiments commander visits us around mid-day. He supports our opinion. This evening the assault detachment should depart to put down the towers. 'Quala is free of enemy' he calls back to us, while he drives away in his vehicle. Two Mk IVs and two Mk IIs are prepared. We start around 1700hrs. The crew sits on the turret. Behind on the rear are boxes with hand grenades. One more short halt about 800m away from our destination. The Chief (Hptm Ehrbeck) stands in front of his vehicle, the field-glasses in front of his eyes. Suddenly his panzer shoots

and it looks like this shot was a signal for English, everything is lit up around us and Tommies conduct the fire mystery around us which I haven't seen before. Anti-tank guns shoot towards us and in between the hisses of artillery. At the village entrance appear 6-8 Mark IIs. We disappear in our turrets immediately after the first blessing. One Mk IV turns back, in a few seconds one can only see a dust cloud. During our turn-around something cracks in our vehicle. No one pays attention to this in the heat of combat. When August (Wangler) tries to pull the joystick, he notices the loss of the track. Damned, this one as well and the Tommies are shooting like crazy. Our track is far behind us. The second Mk II drives back. We trot along. The track is fixed and again we go. The Richtschütze and Ladeschützen deliver a truly masterpiece performance. Shot after shot leaves the pipe. We haven't fixed the track as quickly as today and the streams and rivers of sweat run but the track is on. We reach our departure position out of breath. The property of the Reich is not damaged and the Tommies have stopped their shooting."[41]

On the 20th, there was no movement by either side, except for a few reconnaissance elements that ventured a sortie in for a quick peak at the other side of the defenses. The British artillery, however, was very active, and was able to keep many of the German positions under harassing fire throughout the day and night. The *RAF* also ventured over the battlefield on the occasional strafing mission but caused little damage to the Regiment's panzers and crews. The 3rd Company Diary entry recorded that day:

"Tuesday 20 May In the first hours of the morning our defense company comes suddenly under the English ambush fire. The rounds explode in the middle between two panzers. We were just having breakfast. We immediately leave the hilltop and go to the slope. It was bad for Lt Wöhrmann. He was sent forward from the Regiment, in order to reconnoiter [investigate] on the reasons for the artillery fire. He did not see us in the slope position and drove into the English and he was captured. Some hours later came [Oberstlt] Haarde with the whole I./Abteilung to defend us. [Hptm] Jahns [Regimental Adjutant] implies to me that I went against the village [on the day prior]. He doesn't want to believe that this operation was ordered by Major Kriebel. The first mail arrived."[42]

From Kurt Liestmann's diary we have the following which adds to the account:

"The alarm at 0127hrs in the morning. The English should attack, the [Point] 206 seems to be occupied. Ehrbeck turned [back] due to heavy artillery fire. The Abteilung attacks and takes possession of 206. Now it is found out that Olt Wöhrmann is missing. Due to insufficient orientation he drove further on until Point 207 and 205 (observation towers) which were taken again by Tommy and ran into their hands. The English radio report confirmed this: 'Two Germans in a small vehicle of Pz.Rgt. 8 were captured.' We send the surveillance troops but it was all in vain. Strong heat and no fluids. One imagines the picture with trees and a water view, women come as 3rd in this sequence. We sit tired in the vehicles near the panzers and listen to the occasional English reports in German language: 'At the moment there are no German soldiers on the Egyptian territory'. We cry of joy, because we stand on this territory. In the evening [the] English are surprisingly quiet and leave back to their camp behind the defense. Finally there is food and drink."[43]

On the morning of the 21st, the Regiment's security detachment occupying Point 206 came under attack by a British force supported by tanks, including several Matildas. The security detachment, along with the accompanying infantrymen, was able to halt the attack and suffered no losses. The main body of the I./Abteilung also came under repeated attacks, this time by *RAF* Bombers. The 5th Company, which was temporarily subordinated to the I./Abteilung of Panzer Regiment 5, and was defending near Sollum, was also attacked by the *RAF*; no losses were reported in either location. Later in the day, both of the security detachments occupying Points 196 and 206 came under constant artillery fire and were forced to remain inside their panzers for almost the entire day. The only movement that could be undertaken came only at night. Kurt Liestmann continues his account:

"Wednesday 21.5.41. In the morning comes 'Operation Bock'. [We] conducted a violent reconnaissance and are in a good position. Bock's panzer IV has received a direct hit from a tank, presumably a Mark II. Two lightly wounded. [The] Flak dislodged the tanks by direct impacts. Our Flak which moves with us, behaves extremely good. In the afternoon the scouting group with panzers and pioneers pushes forward to Point 207 and 205 and detonates the observation towers."

On the 22nd, there was again an attempt to retake Point 206 by the British, but this attack also failed with the loss of two Matildas. Later in the day, as Liestmann reports, parts of the Regiment had a special visitor:

"Thursday 22.5.41. In the afternoon General Rommel visits us. He drives to our bases, A and B and expresses his special recognition to the Regiment for the achievements on 16, 17, and 19 May."[44]

On the 23rd, as the crews continued to enjoy this short break in the action, Rommel issued his orders for the seizure of the Halfaya Pass. The 24th and 25th passed with little activity by both sides, except for an increase in aerial reconnaissance. The panzer crews had now had their first experiences in desert combat, and they soon discovered that the shimmering hot air complicated and hindered their observation. Objects which stood a meter in height now became very hard to discern, and objects which appeared above a meter in height appeared to be much higher and larger than they actually were. It was also discovered that contours and shapes became blurry until the eyes had become accustomed to the sun, and then they could recognize and pick up certain movements. During the sandstorms, which were very frequent, a man's vision would darken and be limited to only a few meters distance by the blowing dust and sand. Kathe remembers just how bad the weather was, and especially the sandstorms:

"The sand storm was bad, when the wind blows the sand was all over, we closed our tent and removed everything [from outside]. It was impossible to cook with sand all over everything. Thankfully they only happened from time to time."[45]

Horst Sonnenkalb remembers one of the many problems encountered by the panzer crews:

"With the great heat you'd see mirages like a Fata Morgana. Rolling vehicles, even tanks, were only recognizable in the heat when they were only 800 – 1000 meters away. First you'd see a small or big dust cloud, then a vertical line that looked like a telephone pole that changed into a horizontal line across an apparent water level, until finally you could recognize them as vehicles or tanks. The D.A.K. took advantage of that. Or so to say: let's disperse a lot of dust and sand. Big sand dust simulated panzers. The greatest ideas were born. We attached panzer tracks to VW's and attached tank mock-ups."[46]

Operation Skorpion

The Halfaya Pass or, as it was soon to be christened by the British, *"Hellfire Pass,"* was one of two points, the other being Sollum, which one could rise from the coastal plain and the low-lying eastern area of Egypt to the great plateau of Cyrenaica. The Halfaya Pass, still held by the British *22nd Guards Brigade* after Operation "Brevity," afforded them the opportunity to threaten and harass German forces in the Sollum area, as well as those Axis formations investing Tobruk with their armored cars and tanks. By mid-May, it was decided that the British presence at Halfaya must come to an end. In order to take the Pass, the *D.A.K.* assembled the following forces and placed them under the command of *Oberst* Maximilian von Herff, the commander of *Schützen Regiment 115*. Herff was given command of the operation, with the following forces organized into the following *kampfgruppen*: *Kampfgruppe Cramer*; *I.* and *II./Abteilung* of *Panzer Regiment 5* and the *I./Abteilung Panzer Regiment 8*; *Kampfgruppe Bach* with the *I./Battalion Schützen Regiment 104*; *Kampfgruppe Knabe* with *Kradschützen Battalion 15* and *I./Abteilung Artillery Regiment 33*; and *Kampfgruppe Wechmar* with *Aufklärungs Abteilung 3*.[47] The attack on Halfaya began early on the morning of the 26th as the infantry of *I./104 Schützen Regiment* had the night before dismounted their trucks and begun moving from their assembly area near Sollum towards the Wadi Agrab. Cramer led his *kampfgruppe* on a parallel route through Bardia and Fort Capuzzo, crossing the frontier wire near Point 206 and then on to the south in the direction of Sidi Suleiman. The panzers were spread out, with two panzer *abteilung* abreast and one echeloned off to the right rear. From the very beginning, two British patrols were encountered, both of which were made up of infantry and armored cars supported by Mk II Matilda infantry tanks. It was assumed that the British patrols were on a mission to attack German security forces arrayed near Point 206 and Qalala. The attack at Point 206 was repulsed, but German forces defending that position did suffer some losses in addition to the loss of one Mk III. The advance by *Kampfgruppe Bach* as it made its way towards Wadi Agrab was also attacked, but it too was able to beat off the attack, which came in broken terrain that offered little advantage to attacking armored forces. By mid-afternoon, *Kampfgruppe Cramer* and the headquarters *15th Panzer Division* crossed the border; these forces soon encountered a group of British armored cars which withdrew in the face of overwhelming numbers. At 1540hrs, from an area north of Sidi Suleiman the *panzergruppe* came under attack by tanks and artillery that hit the left flank of the *kampfgruppe*; on orders from the division, Cramer turned to the east with the *II./Abteilung* of *Panzer Regiment 5* in order to take out an enemy artillery battery from the rear as the *I./Abteilung of Panzer Regiment 5* was sent after a weak enemy tank patrol that also withdrew to the southeast. In the brief engagement, six enemy tanks were knocked out, with the remainder withdrawing to the east. At 1700hrs, the first objectives were reached—Points 203 and 204, which were located 4km southeast of Sidi Suleiman. At 1715hrs, *Kampfgruppe Knabe* began moving southeast towards Abar Abu Talaq, while Cramer ordered the *panzergruppe* to turn northeast to edge of the escarpment and hit the British that were fighting there against *Kampfgruppe Bach*. Cramer had also been ordered to cooperate with both infantry *kampfgruppen*, and so he then ordered the *I and II./Abteilung of Panzer Regiment 5* to move back and support his move to the northeast. The panzers began moving forward with one *abteilung* up front supported by the second panzer *abteilung* echeloned to the rear and along both flanks. The move north began at 1845hrs, as *Kampfgruppe Bach* again reported coming under attack by strong armored forces in a renewed attempt to dislodge his *kampfgruppe*. As the remaining daylight began to fade, the *panzergruppe* was ordered to launch a high-speed attack directly at Halfaya Pass in order to destroy those British forces attacking *Kampfgruppe Bach*. Near Point 206, *Oberstlt*

Cramer allowed the *kampfgruppe* to advance to the north and attacked Halfaya Pass from the rear. *Artillery Regiment 33* supported the attack. The fires from the guns were able to detonate mines and created breaches for the panzers to roll through, closely followed by the motorcycle and troops of *Kradschützen Battalion 15*. The panzers drove to the Pass along camel trails and open fire on the move. As the panzer *kampfgruppe* moved northeast of Sidi Suleiman it encountered a large sandy area that slowed down the *panzergruppe's* advance. As the last light began to fade, the panzers became disorientated, and by 2030hrs were forced to halt for the night just 7km from Halfaya Pass. The panzers then organized a hedgehog defensive position and prepared the panzers and themselves for the attack the next morning. For most combat forces fighting in the desert, the nights were a chance to catch up on their rest and maintenance, and this was no exception for the panzer crews, which also had a long list of tasks to perform. However, caring for a panzer and completing these tasks usually left little time for the crewmembers to catch any sleep. Kurt Liestmann recorded the following in his diary:

"Monday 26.5.41. Three days of a strong sand storm. Today are in preparation for the undertaking 'Scorpion'. At 1030hrs we march towards the Egyptian border at Bir Ghirba. At 1500hrs the attack follows in the desert with three abteilung. Only later they notice Tommy. After 28km the enemy is encountered with scout vehicles and enemy tanks. A couple of times the 4cm rounds whistle above us and away. The [British] scout vehicles pull away in high gear chased by our 5cm and 8,8 Flak rounds. Then we begin the large curve to the left. We, the I/8, lead forward. In the dusk of the desert, through the sand dunes overgrown by camel briars, our panzers pull up with the high yellow dust clouds, but the wheeled vehicles struggle and often get stuck. With impossible speed we go to the south on to Halfaya Passage, a strong English position. Soon it gets cooler and darker. Star-shells [flares] show the direction and the leader. Only the compass and course gyroscope are appropriate here. Everything stops! The old 'desert hedgehog' is built. A couple of hours for sleep. Our comrades at Halfaya Passage are in combat, 'are in distress' according to the last radio report. Our old report foxes [kradschützen], those splendid reliable guys meet in the middle of the night striking from all directions. It's amazing."[48]

Wilhelm Hagios remembers the day and had this to add:

"The Regiment was based between Bardia and Capuzzo; I don't know where the other lines were. Again the British attacked on 26-27 May, and we had panzers at Halfaya Pass and resisted them that morning, at night we drove into the position, I was on the left side behind, the kradmelder [Messenger Section] which were in front of me. On the following morning we saw that no one was visible, no one paid attention that all the [abandoned] vehicles left at that same time. I was alone, there was no one else around and there were no tracks because of the rocky ground. What to do? I knew approximately where we were so I decided to drive north and see how it goes there. It could be that the British could be on the move too. I had shot down a Matilda tank and also captured an officer with the driver, their reconnaissance tanks were quicker than our Mk II and had a 4cm cannon, and our Mk IIs had only a 2cm gun. I found a German 3.7cm Pak (the first Pak gun which we had) and saw two German comrades dead. I saw a gun a bit further on and did not know if it was German or British. There came a sand storm and no further traces were possible to see. I tried to drive through it and we drove step by step and were ready to jump out if something crashed into us. However nothing happened, as it was an abandoned British road wheel. I just let it lay and didn't do anything to it as I was cautious that they may have left something inside it.

Chapter 5: North Africa, May 1941

I was on a djebel and tried to search for any traces and attempted to see if they had gone up or down on the djebel, at any moment I was ready to fall down on the gravel. I was at lower Sollum and went east, and finally found them a bit further on, they said to me 'we knew you would find us'. I also saved the life of a British soldier when I noticed one in a ditch on the road and thought he was dead, then I noticed that he was still breathing and his whole shoulder blade was missing. I saw up front the German medic and told him about the location of the wounded British and asked him to take care of him. Then I went back to Sollum, on the road up, and then to Capuzzo and then to our spearhead point and so for me the Halfaya Pass was a done deal."[49]

Later on 26 May, the II./*Abteilung* with the 6th and 7th Companies moved into the area just south of Bardia near Sidi Azeiz, and although still not completely consolidated, the Regiment was moving closer towards an eventual link up. During the night of the 26/27th, the crews did get some sleep as they awaited the arrival of the fuel trucks, which unfortunately never arrived. The lack of fuel would seriously affect the battle on the following day, as the high-speed movement had consumed a large amount of fuel, and the fuel gauges were now showing just enough fuel remaining in the tanks to undertake a few short movements. By midnight, the German forces were arrayed as so: *Kampfgruppe Cramer* was located just south of Halfaya; *Kampfgruppe Bach* was still defending near Wadi Agrb; *Kampfgruppe Knabe* was located near Abar El Silgiya; and *Kampfgruppe Wechmar* was located west of the frontier wire near El Hamra performing its reconnaissance mission. In the early morning hours of the 27th orders were issued for all three *kampfgruppen* to attack those British forces located in front of *Kampfgruppe Bach*. The attack would commence at 0430hrs on the 27th with *Kampfgruppe Cramer* attacking towards the escarpment near Mingar el Shaba, where it would engage those British elements along the coastal plain. *Kampfgruppe Knabe* was to move to an area near Abar Abu Talaq, and *Kampfgruppe Bach* was to attack along the escarpment along the base of the Pass.

It was hoped that the combined attacks by three separate *kampfgruppen* would push the British from the Pass. As the *panzergruppe* moved out at 0430hrs it left behind one *Abteilung*, which was to be prepared to repulse any British advance from out of the southeast. Back near Halfaya, the British anti-tank and artillery gunners, which had been expecting an attack to come from the west, had emplaced their guns in a screen facing that direction. The same was done with those guns expecting any attack to come from the east. During the fighting, those gun positions were overrun by a combination of fire and movement. As was to be very common in the desert war, the British 25-Pounders were employed in the anti-tank role and fired over open sites, but unfortunately for the British, in this encounter those guns had to be re-positioned in order to meet the German panzers that were soon upon them. During the attack that evening, the strong defense being put up by British Guardsmen and tanks held the panzers at bay and forced them to remain out of effective firing range. After this attempt, the panzers were halted and forced to establish a secure hedgehog for the remainder of the evening. At 0500hrs, heavy artillery began to rain down upon the *panzergruppe*, but despite the fire, the panzers were able to make it to the escarpment, and by 0530hrs had begun putting down suppressive fire on those British forces along the coast. After a short time, the left flank *abteilung* began receiving extremely heavy fire from artillery pieces in the direct fire role and anti-tank guns all located near Halfaya Pass. It was then that Cramer ordered that *abteilung* to turn west while the main body of the II./*Abteilung* continued to secure the escarpment to the southeast. It was at this time that *Kampfgruppe Knabe's* attack on Halfaya went in with the support from the panzers of II./*Abteilung*; also at this time *Kampfgruppe Bach*, which had been coming forward on foot, hit the British in the face of heavy fire, but they were finally able to overcome it as the German infantry and motorcycle troops stormed the positions with only small arms and forced the last defenders, which were from the 3rd Coldstream Guards Regiment, from their positions. The Pass was now in German hands. The I./*Schützen Regiment 104* and the 3./*Kradschützen Battalion 15* immediately began to set up their defense in the vacated positions and round up the remaining prisoners and vast quantities of supplies left behind. By 0630hrs, it was reported that the Halfaya Pass was in German hands.[50] The British forces along the coast also fled, leaving behind stockpiles of equipment. *Kampfgruppe Knabe* took up the pursuit of the British forces; since many of the panzers were now out of fuel, that pursuit was conducted by unarmored wheeled vehicles, since they used less fuel, but this element was kept at bay by the well armed British armored cars which covered the British withdrawal. The armored cars would continue to hold off the pursuing forces until orders were received that halted the pursuit. *Kampfgruppe Bach* was immediately ordered to occupy the positions at Halfaya while the other *kampfgruppen* moved back to their previous locations. As the battle ended the fuel trucks arrived, and the panzers were finally able to refuel three kilometers northwest of the Pass, by 0800hrs Cramer could report his forces ready for further action. There was to be no further action, as the *kampfgruppen* were to return to their initial assembly areas. For the Regiment, the I./*Abteilung* was assigned to the Sollum front to await the remainder of the Regiment, which was at that time moving towards it. With the large quantities of captured British goods and vehicles the Regiment was able to resupply itself, as many of the goods and vehicles were taken back and used to reinforce and supply the "I" *Staffel* and maintenance units within the Regiment. For the panzer crews, they were able to get their hands on a number of Matilda tanks that at the time were considered a great prize due to their heavy armor protection. Kurt Liestmann recorded the following actions that day:

"Tuesday 27.5.41. Wake up 0300hrs, 0400hrs attack direction Mingar el Scia'ba [Shaba], south of Halfaya Passage. Soon artillery fire begins. We drive until the steep slope, which dominates on the shore level of Halfaya Passage. The Tommy are surprised. A violent flanking fire from our combined weapons catches them, Paks [anti-tank guns], battery [artillery], two KW and panzers, the terrible Mark IIs are destroyed. The artillery covers us from time to time pretty nicely. But when it is spotted, it shuts down. The British retreat head over heels. Some jump in the sea. The Halfaya Passage is captured. Cars, trucks, tanks, one [artillery] battery and anti-tank guns and other weapons are taken as a booty. Our in destructible kradschützen have captured three BMW engines from the British. They come from 2.Kradschützen Kompanie, which was some time ago [itself] captured by the English. In the middle of the day we move through the desert and back to the old camp."[51]

Hermann Eckardt remembered some of those early encounters with the British Matildas:

"When we took Halfaya Pass, the British fell back quickly, there was no chance for us to break through with our cannons as they were the short barreled 7.5cm, which were not able to shoot through the thick armor, only from close distances of 300 meters was this possible."[52]

The Matildas were given to those crews who had either lost their panzer to mechanical breakdown or combat damage, and soon the Matildas were decorated with the black and white *Balkan Cross*. The captured tanks and equipment weren't all that the men were eager to get at. Kurt Kathe explains:

"I remember the first time when we hit back at the Brits, our provisioning was bad; bad vegetables, old meat, and salt water to cook with. Then we threw the Brits back and our provisioning became better. There were many tents of theirs loaded with bread, potatoes, vegetables it was all possible [there]. They had good provisioning; in one can was such a nice bunch of potatoes, all cleaned. We drank the water, as we had nothing; we had only salted water until the equipment to desalinate the water arrived. We took this all for ourselves and it helped us until our additional supplies from Germany could arrive. We took much food and clothes from the Brits, they were well equipped, it was all worthwhile."[53]

On Wednesday the 28th, those elements of the II./*Abteilung* were finally able to affect a link up with the Regiment and those elements of *Panzer Regiment 5* that had been working in conjunction with the Regiment. New orders were then issued which directed them to process west, back towards Tobruk. The following day, Halfaya Pass was firmly secured and new belts of mines laid to strengthen the positions there. That evening, the Regiment was sited in the *Wehrmacht Daily Report* and praised for its actions in the attack on Halfaya Pass. On the 31st, Hans Cramer was specifically recognized in the *Wehrmacht Daily Report* and was proposed for the award of the *Ritterkreuz* for his leadership during the capture and subsequent defense of Fort Capuzzo, and for the Regiment's role in the capturing of Halfaya Pass.[54] With the situation now somewhat stabilized, the time now came for the men to enjoy a brief rest after their long journey to the Egyptian border and initial contacts with the British and Commonwealth forces. It was now that the men were able to discover that the vast Libyan Desert that they had been sent to consisted mainly of flat, rocky terrain that was almost completely flat, with only a slight elevation change between heights. The flat terrain was separated by many ridges or *djebels*, which were further broken up by deep, dry valleys, or *wadis*, that stretched between 30-100km wide and were composed of flat sandy surfaces. There were few markings to be found in this desert, and those that did exist normally consisted of only a pile of rocks or empty fuel drums. On the issued maps, the towns and villages like Bardia, Sollum, Fort Capuzzo, and Sidi Azeiz were all well marked, as they normally consisted of between 15-20 buildings, but there were only small signs on the map for the rocky heights in the great vastness of this desert. Sonnenkalb describes how the crews navigated:

"For orientation the panzers used a gyrocompass, which was operated by the radio operator. He had to keep a blotter, in which he would record the distance they had covered, according to the driver. The compass direction was being recorded on it also, so we could then figure out our position on a map. That usually didn't work out too well. There was no straight road out in the real terrain and a lot of times the driver messed up the recording of the exact distance we had covered. Understandably so, because he was too busy concentrating on the driving, the shifting, the steering, and finding the best path."[55]

Panzer Regiment 8 Chain of Command as of 1 June 1941[56]

Regiment Commander	Oberstlt Cramer
Regt Adj	Hptm Jahns
Nachr Offz	Olt Stülpnagel
Ord Offz	Olt Jattkowski
Regt Arzt	StabsArtz. Dr Becker
Ing Ofz	Maj Schnell
StKp	Olt Prion, Lt Friedrich, OFumstr Strack
Werkshop Company	Olt Blidschuhn
I./Abteilung Commander	Major Crohn
Abtl Adj	Lt Liestmann, K.
Nachr Offz	Olt Matthias, J.
Ord Offz	Lt Bock
Abt Arzt	OArtz Dr Port
Zahl Mstr	StZmstr Tischner
Ing Offz	OInsp Lampe
StKp	Olt Sontowski, Olt Stiefelmayer
leKol	Olt Lindner
1st Company	Olt Kümmel
Zug Commander	Olt Heinrich
Zug Commander	Lt Springorum
Zug Commander	Lt Peters
2nd Company	Hptm Ehrbeck
Zug Commander	Olt Knorr
Zug Commander	Lt Hess
Zug Commander	Lt von Treuenfels
3rd Company	Olt Schubert
Zug Commander	Olt Kertscher
Zug Commander	Lt Keil
II./Abteilung Commander	Oberstlt Ramsauer
Abtl Adj	Olt Wuth
Nachr Offz	OFumstr Bulla
Ord Offz	Lt Schnaidt
Abt Arzt	OArtz. Dr Witzky
Zahl Mstr	OZmstr Gisy
Ing Offz	HBmstr Hauska, Tech Insp Hering
StKp	Hptm Klein
Pioneer Zug	Lt Pickel
Nach Off	Lt Matthias, J, Lt Eberspächer
Kradmelder Zug	Fw Brill
leKol	Hptm Dr Kücklich
5th Company	Olt Körner
Zug Commander	Lt Bönisch
Zug Commander	Lt Weiss
6th Company	Olt Wahl
Zug Commander	Lt Adam
Zug Commander	Lt Heuscher
Zug Commander	Fw/O.A. Becker
7th Company	Olt Seidler
Zug Commander	Lt Danz
Zug Commander	Lt Liestmann, H.
Zug Commander	Fw/O.A. Pierath

6

The Summer Battles
June-September 1941

By 27 May, a strong defense was established based on a number of strong points that stretched from Halfaya in a wide arc to Strong points 206 and 208 on the Hafid Ridge and to Sidi Azeiz. The Germans wasted little time in constructing these fortified positions that were built around the 88mm Flak gun and other anti-tank guns. Those guns were dug in so that only the barrels were above the ground, allowing the gunners a clear field of fire while denying the British the opportunity to easily locate and spot them and place direct fire on them. On the following day, the Regiment returned to its assembly area north of Fort Capuzzo, between the Trigh Capuzzo and Via Balbia. The *15th Panzer Division* was at that time in the *D.A.K.* reserve; all of the divisional elements had gathered in the Capuzzo, Bardia, and Sollum area. *Generalmajor* Walter Neumann-Silkow, who had previously been the commander of the *8th Panzer Division*, had replaced *Generalmajor* Esebeck, who had been wounded near Tobruk in May. In addition to commanding the *15th Panzer Division*, Neumann-Silkow also had responsibility for all of the German and Italian formations on the frontier border area.[1] The first days of June 1941 offered the Regiment time to improve its operational ability by making repairs on the various vehicles that had been worn out on the trip east. During this time the *RAF* made numerous appearances, but other than disrupting the daily activities caused no losses. By now the panzer crews had learned to dig themselves in at every opportunity. The normal protection for panzer crews was to dig out a trench large enough to accommodate the entire crew to sleep in, and then roll the panzer over the position, thereby making the panzer a type of retractable roof. The panzers were dug in, and either sand bags or stone sangers were built up around the bogies and tracks in order to ward off the damaging rays of the sun. The sangers also protected the panzers from stray rounds and flying shrapnel in the event of air attack. Tarps or tents were then strung up on the sides of the panzers in which the men slept—the tarps and tents help ward off the cold nights which were not uncommon even in the summer months in Africa, as Kurt Kathe remembers:

"When the sun was down we had to wear underwear, coat, shawl, we had sleeping bags in the tent to cover ourselves. It had gone from 40 degrees, [104F] to 10 [50F] degrees. It was bad if you did not have a good blanket, but we had everything. The panzers were in place where there was no combat; we put them so the cannons were turned to the left or to right, and from the left around come the watch [guard]. I had always a dog, a jackal that always warned me by barking. The guards always told me I should shoot the dog but that was stupid."[2]

In early June, the panzer strength report stood at eighty-two operational panzers, with approximately forty panzers per *abteilung*.[3] As both sides took the time to lick their wounds and prepare for the next engagement, which would not be long in coming, the men set up small camps throughout the desert, with each crew showing that the desert did not detract from overall discipline and organization. When it was possible the men could go for a swim in the ocean and get the chance to wash away the sweat and grime of the desert. Even though this time was spent in relative quiet, it was also still dangerous, as Kurt Liestmann recorded in his diary:

"Saturday 7.6.41. At 0330hrs suddenly an alarm, prepare immediately. I must go to the regimental adjutant meeting. I overheard reports informing us to count on a possible attack by the British, but the order to march doesn't follow and we are awake until the sun rises, which breaks through the wet haze. Increased alarm readiness for the night. Around 2100 hrs [there] arrive two aircraft, clearly visible in the moonlight. Some of the bombs fall far behind us. The second is captured by the beam light and turns around in the violent 2cm Flak fire, without dropping anything. After a quarter of an hour we receive the disturbing message from von Stülpnagel 'Due to aircraft attack Hauptfeldwebel Hellstern was killed.' Only him, how tragic, he was a Hauptfeldwebel as if from the book and a loss for the whole Stabskompanie. A good friend has left us."[4]

Another account comes from the unknown diary of the *3rd Company* recorded on Saturday, 14 June:

"We have to build the bed stands because it's too cold on the plain ground. In the morning at 0500hrs Fw Gerlach drives with one truck to Tripoli in order to get the not ordinary provision and water from the well. We all still suffer from dysentery. In the evening 2300hrs comes the alarm. We are all ready by early 0400hrs."[5]

Operation Battleaxe
During the break in the fighting between the end of May and the first weeks of June, both sides took the opportunity to refit and reorganize themselves for the fighting that was yet to come that first summer. The British commander, *General* Wavell, had been devising his new plan of attack, which he had hoped to launch in late May or early June once the new tanks of the "*Tiger*" Convoy were ready for combat. Wavell's plan was to attack and retake the border positions at Sollum, Capuzzo, and Halfaya Pass.

Panzer Regiment 8 in World War II - Poland • France • North Africa

OPERATION BATTLEAXE: 15 - 17 JUNE 1941

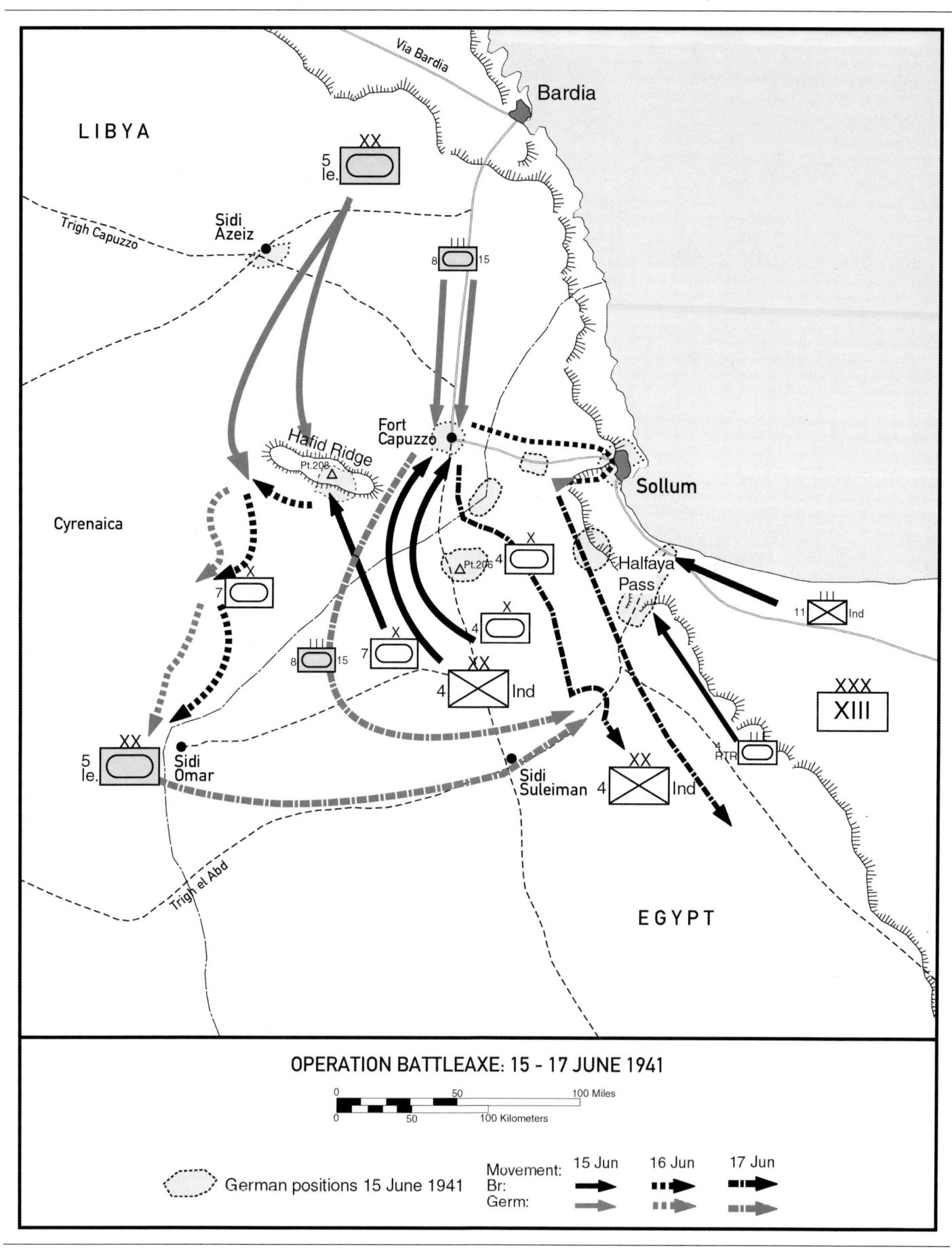

Chapter 6: The Summer Battles, June-September 1941

Once the Axis defensive line had been breached and those key positions captured the advance would then make for Tobruk and relieve the garrison there. It was thought that once Tobruk had been relieved its garrison, together with the *XIII Corps* (Beresford-Peirse), would push on to secure a line between Derna and Mechili. The British and Wavell estimated the German/Italian strength to be around 13,000 men and a hundred panzers located in the near proximity of the frontier wire, with a further 27,000 men and two hundred panzers located in and around Tobruk.[6] It was thought that for the plan to succeed those Axis forces located on the border had to be defeated before reinforcements could arrive from the Tobruk area. To assist Wavell in this new offensive he had been sent the "*Tiger*" convoy, which had docked on the 12 May in Alexandria with over two hundred tanks. Of those newly arrived tanks, 135 of them were Mk II *Matilda* infantry tanks and eighty-two of them the new Cruiser Mk VI *Crusader* tank. The *Crusader* was a quick and agile tank that had a top speed of 37mph/60kph, but its handicap was that it too was under armed with the 2-Pounder gun. There were also a small number of light cruiser tanks sent with that convoy. Those tanks were distributed as follows: the *Crusader* and light tanks were sent to the *7th Armored Division's* (O'Moore-Creagh), *7th Armored Brigade* to equip the *2nd* and *6th Royal Tank Regiments (RTR)*. The *4th Indian Division's* (Messervy) *4th Armored Brigade* was given the *Matilda* infantry tanks to equip its *4th* and *7th RTRs*, in order to support that division's infantry force. Unfortunately for the British, many of the tanks that arrived were in varied states of disrepair and had suffered from water damage during the voyage to Egypt.[7] It appeared that some extra time would be required to conduct the proper repairs in order to make them serviceable for combat operations. Additionally, time was needed to train and familiarize the crews, especially those taking possession of the new *Crusaders*. All these delays took up valuable time and further postponed the jump off date, but still the time allotted for training never afforded the British with the proper training period that was needed. So after a brief but intensive training period the attack date was set for 15 June 1941. The objective of the attack was to break through the German defensive positions with the infantry and then send the armor racing on towards Capuzzo and Sidi Azeiz. Once those positions had been taken the tanks were to roll forward towards El Adem and Tobruk and link up with the garrison, which would then break out; when the infantry and tanks had joined up they would then destroy the *D.A.K.* The *XIII Corps* plan was based on three lines of advance: the first or right hand column consisting of infantry from the *11th Indian Brigade* and supported by two troops of *Matildas* from the *4th RTR* would attack Sollum and the lower defenses of Halfaya Pass. The center, or second column, was composed of the infantry from the *22nd Guards Brigade* and the remaining *Matilda* tanks from the *4th RTR*, and was to swing south around the escarpment, then drive north to Musaid and Capuzzo, coming up on the rear of the defenses at Halfaya. The third, or left hand column, consisting of the *7th Armored Division's 7th Armored Brigade* and *7th Support Group*, which held the majority of the armor, was to make an even wider sweep south and come up in the rear of the *D.A.K.*'s frontier forces and cut them off near Sidi Azeiz. If all went according to plan, once the initial objectives were met and these Axis forces destroyed, the armor, after linking up with the *4th Indian Division*, would proceed towards Tobruk, while the infantry would head north and capture Bardia. During the first weeks of June there was little doubt that once either side had sufficiently rested and reorganized itself it would go over to the offensive: Rommel to continue his drive to the Suez, and Wavell to destroy the Axis forces in Africa. *Olt* Hans Kümmel, commander of the *1st Company*, wrote the following of the prelude to the offensive:

"The first days of June went by quietly. In May we reached the Sollum front, after we had forced the English out of Fort Capuzzo. We did not think [that in] those days the heated fighting would again play around this Fort Capuzzo. During the large two-day deployment we captured the strategically important Halfaya Pass from the English, which was serving them as the gate to invasions into the desert. Since then an unusual quietness had spread over the front. We spent most of our time in defense halts and it became almost as a recreation for us. A few separate artillery rounds bothered the quietness of the lonely and single-colored desert landscape. Individual scout groups were on the way, in order to spread their sensors towards the invisible enemy. Individual Mark II made ghost appearance in this flickering desert land. To us, the panzer troops, we didn't like the quietness and we constantly hoped to be deployed. We wanted to browse further as we didn't believe it possible, that the English would so easily get over the loss of the Halfaya Pass. Suddenly the rumors spread, that the English high command had experienced the regrouping. Soon it was whispered that there were preparations for an attack by the English and as the English aviation activity had increased in the days and nights up to the 15th we were able to guess at the upcoming events. But we had not guessed that ahead of us was to be a large tank battle which would have to be fought. Only 12-15 of these monsters (Mk II Matildas) wrapped in thick armor were mentioned in our conversations, the majority of them having been destroyed at Halfaya-Pass. What would happen to us? The light cavalierly of the English, as we guessed it, was not able to avoid its destiny. Oh, us poor fools, that was just a dream."[8]

For the Germans forces, the lack of fuel and supplies made any offensive plans unlikely at this time, but this was not the case for the British, whose supplies continued to flow into Egypt. In order to conserve what fuel there was and be prepared for any British offensive actions, the *D.A.K.* was positioned in areas where they could respond to either situation, and so the *5th Light Division* (Ravenstein) was located between Tobruk and Gambut for rest, refitting, and training, while the *15th Panzer Division* continued to arrive in the border area. Its panzers were stationed near Bardia, and its mobile elements in and around the frontier defenses. Unfortunately for the British, the total lack of communications security and the reusing of previous codes allowed the *D.A.K.* to detect the preparations for the attack via its radio intercept unit. During the evening of the 14th, Rommel ordered all *D.A.K.* elements located along the frontier to be placed on alert, and told them to expect British attacks anytime the following day. *Olt* Kümmel went on to write:

"The African nights had an unreal light, when the moon came into the sky the night became day, much to our disappointment. Despite that, the moon was a bit forfeited on the night of the 15th, the silhouettes of our panzers and our tent village was lifted from the ground and appeared enormous in size. The quietness spread over the camp. Only the heavy steps of the night guards were to be heard. Then a fine tone spread over [the camp] from the sea to our position here, with the sounds coming closer and closer. This was the English, who rendered us a visit. Soon the familiar shooting stars that were to be seen, became shining stars hanging in the sky, but thanks to God it was not [meant] for us. The visit seemed to be for Bardia, as there everything was lit brightly. At this very moment a light Flak gun went off and the great fireworks appeared. The sounds of the bomb attack were muffled, attack after the attack, it seemed that the English had gone crazy. We started worrying about our supply lines which had entered their rest area near Bardia. Slowly the time reached 0400hrs and the new day began. The British bombers had gone on their return flight, after they had dropped their eggs. Now we could finally enjoy the quietness again. But there was none for us. Already the messenger arrived out of breath: 'The Company must immediately get ready for combat'. Alert! Alert! Sounds through the tent camp as life begins to wake up.

During the first few minutes the panzers were made ready for combat; the motors sing their songs and get warm. Finally the moment came, which we had waited for so long. The order for combat was still expected, and we had enough time to start our quiz about the upcoming fighting. The time goes by and our tension grows from one minute to the other. Where would we encounter the enemy this time? On the Halfaya-Pass or further into the desert? Is this a small attack or a big action? We don't know, but we know that wherever it will appear we will beat them."[9]

At Halfaya Pass, which had been converted into a strong defensive position and under the able leadership of a former pastor from Mannheim, *Hauptmann* Wilhelm Bach, the commander of the *I./Battalion Schützen Regiment 104*, held this position. The Italian *Trento* Division under the operational command of *15th Panzer* was scattered about the area of Sollum, Capuzzo, and Bardia. At 0430hrs on Sunday, 15 June, the *XIII Corps* attacked out of the rising sun along a roughly 15km front in three attack columns. A sound, mutual supporting offensive plan much like that seen during *Operation Brevity*, only this time the attack lacked the vital principal of surprise, which had been lost some days before thanks to quality German intercept capabilities and poor British communications discipline. As a result of these intercepts the *5th Light* was ordered to push forward one of the panzer *abteilung* from *Panzer Regiment 5* in addition to an artillery battery; this reaction force was to be in position near Gambut, some fifty miles distant from the frontier, and prepare itself for action. The British launched their attack with three columns coming across the Egyptian border, or frontier wire, as it was more commonly known, with some three hundred tanks. Waiting for them was the *15th Panzer Division* and *Panzer Regiment 8*, which had approximately one hundred panzers, of which eighty-two were actually fit for combat. The *I./Abteilung* had thirteen Mk IIs, eighteen Mk IIIs, and eight Mk IVs.[10]

Halfaya Pass and Strongpoint 206
The British right hand column's infantry brigade (the *11th Indian*) and supporting troops of *Matilda* tanks advanced along the thin coastal plain, and as they did so, they became entangled in a recently laid minefield placed down along the Via Balbia. Six *Matilda* tanks rumbled forward in the lead, but four of the tanks were quickly destroyed or disabled, the victims of German "Teller mines," which blew off tracks and running gear. The remaining two tanks attempted to support the infantry as that force attempted to make its way forward to the base of Halfaya Pass. In the end the infantry was halted short of its objective, and as the tanks began to receive fire from the defenders on the heights above, the remaining *Matilda* crews became confused and began to withdraw back along the coast, leaving the infantry to go it alone under a hail of artillery and machine gun fire. By midday, the *11th Indian* column had beat a hasty retreat to the rear, and the situation along the coast came to a quick end.[11] In the middle, or Halfaya, sector, along the upper escarpment, the *22nd Guards Brigade*'s right flank column, consisting of the *2nd Cameron Highlanders* and *C Squadron* of the *4th RTR* began their attack on Halfaya. This column was to be supported by artillery, which was scheduled to begin the attack by firing a heavy concentration into the German and Italian defenders. However, those guns became stuck in the deep sand while moving forward to their pre-designated firing positions, and this delay forced the supporting tanks to go in alone with the infantry close behind them. The British tanks that came forward against Halfaya expected an easy time, but were soon met by a hail of 37mm and 50mm Pak guns, 88mm Flak, and 105mm artillery guns firing from protective stone sangers and well-concealed positions that gave little indication of where they were actually located. The supporting tank squadron was literally shot to pieces with the loss of eleven of its twelve *Matilda* tanks.[12] The attacks against Halfaya had stalled, and the British were forced to pull back to regroup their forces and re-look their plan of attack for the 16th. The second element from this middle column, consisting of the remaining *Matilda* tanks from *A Squadron, 4th RTR*, were detailed to provide security for the main column as it attacked Halfaya Pass. This element came forward with armored cars and tanks, and initially had some success when it overran an Italian artillery unit and captured two hundred men and eight guns. This was to be the only success it would have as it made its way towards Strongpoint 206 and the dug in guns located there.[13] Fortunately for the British, Strongpoint 206 was only manned by a handful of 20mm Flak and 50mm Pak guns, and had not yet been outfitted with the 88mm Flak gun. As the British column trundled forward it was quickly engaged by the German Pak gunners, who were able to focus on certain sections of the march column and quickly shot them to pieces. The Pak gunners were able to claim a number of *Matilda* tanks in the initial action. The sudden loss of at least three of its tanks caused some confusion within the *4th RTR's A Squadron*, and while it attempted to find and locate the source of these losses a number of other tanks were hit as well. The remaining tanks quickly withdrew to the south, where they were to regroup for another attack against the strongpoint. In the meantime, the *4th RTR*'s B Squadron, with sixteen tanks, was in reserve a few miles away, but was held up from assisting *A Squadron* for the renewed attempt on Point 206 by the division commander. Later in the day, despite the lack of reinforcement, *A Squadron* re-grouped and renewed its attack on Point 206 with its four remaining tanks. Those four *Matildas* rumbled forward and, despite the fire against them, actually managed to capture the strongpoint, but lost three of the remaining four tanks in doing so. Unfortunately this attack was all for naught, as the Germans were able to launch a counter-attack and drive off the one lone tank with artillery fire. The attacks by *A Squadron* on Point 206 had not been in vain, as the attacks had significantly weakened the German defenses there. Later that evening, *B Squadron* was finally released for the attack on Point 206 and, behind an effective artillery barrage, went forward with massed Matildas and infantry, and finally succeeded in overrunning the strongpoint once and for all.[14] The fall of Strongpoint 206 resulted in the loss of 500 men and a number of Pak and artillery pieces. While the assault on Strongpoint 206 was taking place another element of the center column, led by the tanks of the *7th RTR*, managed to push on towards Fort Capuzzo.

Fort Capuzzo
This left flank column had also been delayed a number of hours as it attempted to move forward, and by mid-morning was finally able to advance along the upper escarpment between Halfaya Pass and Sidi Suleiman. This column was under the direction of the *22nd Guards Brigade Group*, and was composed of the *1st Buffs, 2nd Scots Guards*, and *3rd Coldstream Guards*. *Matilda* tanks from the *4th Armored Brigade's 7th RTR* supported the column's attacks towards Fort Capuzzo, which was being defended by Italian infantry and artillery forces, with some elements from the *15th Panzer Division* located in mobile reserve nearby. As the British tanks approached the fort from the south, the Germans and Italians attempted to engage them with machine gun and light Flak guns, but could only watch in nervous frustration as their rounds bounce harmlessly off the thick skinned *Matildas*. An infantry company from *Kradschützen Battalion 15*, which had been moving south in an attempt to relieve Strongpoint 206, came upon the British column. When the company had been released for its mission at Point 206 the fort's defenses had been unknowingly weakened, and now the company was struggling to retrace its steps back to Capuzzo, but could not successfully return to its previous positions, as the tanks from the *7th RTR* were hard on their heels. When the *kradschützen* and their attached 20mm Flak guns passed through Capuzzo they were fortunate to be covered by one lone 88mm Flak gun that had

been previously detached from the defenses at Halfaya Pass and was in position off to the east of Fort Capuzzo. This lone 88mm gun provided just enough cover for the *kradschützen* as they fell back to the north, and the fire from the Flak gun had effectively halted the British attack with the loss of four or five tanks, but not before the British had captured a portion of the fort.[15] That day a couple of counter-attacks were launched by the Germans in an attempt to recapture Capuzzo, but they did not succeed, and the southern portion of the fort remained in British hands. Earlier that morning the Regiment, which had been in position between Bardia and Fort Capuzzo, had been picking up situational reports which had been flowing into the Regimental *Stabs* and informed Cramer and his staff of the British attacks against Halfaya and Capuzzo. It was here in the center of the battle, around Fort Capuzzo, that the Regiment was to find itself initially engaged. By mid morning, the Regiment had already been alerted and ordered south, where it was hoped it would arrive in time to rescue the remaining infantry and Pak gunners now under siege by British tanks around Capuzzo. Hans Kümmel's report continues:

"At 1015hrs the orders arrived. *1st Company* was to attack over Height 206 (4km southwest of Capuzzo), to ensure the connection with Italian and German artillery and attack weak enemy tank forces and destroy them. In a short time the Zug leaders received their positions and soon they brought their thundering colossus in motion. We drove along the road to the south and stopped at a distance from the nearly invisible Fort Capuzzo, which we had obtained with difficulty during the previous fighting. It is a proud feeling, to see the fierce and combined power rolling towards the enemy. On my order we leave the road and turn into the desert. A long dust flag spans behind us and it seems that it wants to stay in the air. Now the fort is on the left side. Ahead of us all is quiet. Have they guessed about this havoc? The melting sun shines, it's damned hot in our boxes. Now we see the remains of the fortress wall of Fort Capuzzo in the distance, it is marvelously broken. Crazy country!"[16]

At Capuzzo, the British axis of advance had run roughly on a line just to the northeast of Strongpoint 208 towards Capuzzo and Strongpoint 206. Because of this alignment the Regiment was sent in east of Point 208 in order to strike the British armor located on the western side of Capuzzo. Responding to the reports of massed tanks, the Regimental *Stabs* dispatched panzer companies south once they reported that they were ready for combat operations. The *1st Company* arrived near Capuzzo at around 1130hrs, where it was quickly engaged by British tanks. The company itself was not strong enough to handle all of the British armor that had appeared at Capuzzo and was forced to pull back. At that time there seemed to be so many British tanks and armored cars moving around Capuzzo that in the "fog of war" the number of tanks was now being reported at 300, when actually there were no more than about thirty British tanks actually at Fort Capuzzo.

Indeed, the tanks of the *4th Armored Brigade*, some of which had gone around the Pak gun screen further south and had come up around the western flank and taken Capuzzo, gave the appearance of vast numbers of enemy tank formations in and around Capuzzo. A second panzer company arrived to reinforce the *1st Company* already in contact, but it too had suffered from some mechanical breakdowns along the way and could not provide the necessary force needed to help halt the British thrust. Kümmel, in his after action battle report, wrote of the opening round:

"Suddenly, artillery explosions are seen ahead of us. Ah, the first greeting from Tommy. The company immediately developed into a wide wedge on my order, the light Zug clears out in the direction of Height 206. In a sharp motion we breeze through the artillery fire. Soon the border fence was visible, left and right from it surface are single dark spots. There must be our battery position we were looking for. But why is the artillery is not shooting? The answer comes from the message of the leader of light Zug: '12 o'clock 15-16 enemy tanks, Mark IIs spotted'. Here comes the moment that we are German panzer men. My voice was quiet on the radio: '12 o'clock, enemy tanks, attack them with the highest [possible] speed, light Zug move into position'. The Tommy already sends us [his] first metal greetings. Soon we recognize them better, they are our dangerous, thickly clad enemies, and they are Mark IIs. We know that we can hardly impact them with our weapons. Only in few places can they be wounded. Despite this, we move towards them in the wide attack form and open fire from all our cannons. Our beautiful fighting begins tank against tank. The heavy Zug had moved by me on the left side, in order to attack the visible tanks on the flank. Suddenly the guns of the battery we were looking for appeared ahead. In the middle [of them] is a Mark II. But what is this; the German artillerymen are climbing in their foxholes and are held in check by this Mark II. Two Mark IIs are on the lookout behind him and provide covering fire to the Mark II, which had, broke in the German positions. So there is no waiting for this [heavy] Zug. At the highest speed it comes forward, the moves are met by dangerous fire from our enemy brothers. The panzer sends grenade after grenade from its cannon. This firefight is short and strong. The sweat pours, but we all know it's about one thing: you or me. We managed to halt the Tommy through our combined fire; his destiny was defined by a shot to the wheels. His crew stops their fire, but made no signs to leave the vehicle and give up. Still our brave comrades the artillerists do not dare to get out of their holes. They look on stealthy. The Zug leader decides to drive forward. One Tommy gets out doubtfully and raises his hands. His intention to gather booty was defeated. Shining [faces] of happiness as the artillerists captured him, in order to take him as a PoW. In the meantime a second panzer of the Zug draws close to another enemy tank. The Feldwebel jumped from his panzer onto the Mark II, and energetically knocks at the turret until the hatch opened. The dismayed crew surrenders. But the rest of the enemy tanks are not beaten from the battlefield. Constantly firing, they yield behind the border fence. German panzers quickly follow them, as fire, passes through openings under the protection of the wire entanglement; the [panzer] spreads itself and set the second Mark II on the fire. The crew got out under fire as another enemy tank drove by to takes them in and drives away. Satisfied and happy of their success, the Zug can now return to the company position. The artillerists' surround the liberators then hurry to their weapons to hunt for the escaping Tommies."[17]

This initial battle for Capuzzo was confusing, with German and British tanks tangling with each other in a number of small actions. Also during that time a third panzer company had arrived in the vicinity of the battle and, along with other mobile elements of the Regiment, took up positions to the northeast of Point 208. This company was to attack and halt the British tanks reported to be gathering there. Throughout the day the Regiment would use Point 208 as a rallying point, where it could regroup itself after its attacks. By this stage in the fighting the panzers had begun to expend a large amount of their ammunition on the thick skinned *Matildas*, and after roughly an hour of fighting were forced to break off the fight with near empty ammunition racks. With the withdrawal of the initial two panzer companies the door was open for the British at Capuzzo. At 1330hrs it was reported that Capuzzo had been finally lost to the British, and that the tanks from the *4th Armored Brigade* had pushed through and advanced to a position roughly four kilometers north of the fort. Two Mk IIIs had been reported knocked out in the morning's encounters, and a number of other panzers had gone down suffering from a variety of damage, most commonly to the gun and drive mechanisms. The remaining panzers rolled to the north and northwest of Capuzzo, where they would quickly regroup and plan their next move. By attacking in company strength the I./*Abteilung* had violated a major rule of armored warfare and doctrine which preached that panzer forces should always attack in well concentrated and overwhelming force, and not in separate uncoordinated elements.[18] By rushing up to engage the British, those three companies were severely dealt with and forced to retreat from the field. At 1400hrs, a second attack was launched against Capuzzo by both the Regiment's panzer *abteilung* with between twenty and twenty-five panzers. During this attack the Regiment attacked with each of its *abteilung* in succession, where again British *Matilda* tanks, which had by now been identified as those belonging to the *7th RTR*, met them. Once again the panzers failed to break the British defenses, as the main guns of the Mk IIs and Mk IIIs proved to be no match for the thick armor of the *Matildas*, and many of the 20mm, 37mm, and 50mm high explosive rounds were seen to just ricochet off. The 20mm gun of the Mk II was far inferior to the thick armor of the *Matilda*, and from only about 500m were the 50mm guns of the Mk III able to pierce that armor plating. During the second encounter of the day three more panzers were reported as knocked out by the British tanks, which suffered the loss of just two *Matildas*, and those tanks were knocked out only at close range. As an added reinforcement to its attacks, the Regiment was given four 88mm Flak guns from the I./*Abteilung Flak Regiment 33*. Those guns were quickly brought forward from Bardia, where they were quickly put to good use northeast of Capuzzo when they were able to temporarily halt the next British attack, when the *7th RTR* was ordered to move up towards Musaid. As the Matildas made their way up they were engaged by the 88s, which were able to knock out the first three tanks. The sudden loss of its leading tanks caused the attacking tank squadron to halt its attack, regroup, and attack again, this time under the cover of a smoke screen. The Flak guns would eventually claim twelve tanks and force them to withdraw back to Capuzzo, but they themselves were subjected to artillery fire that forced them to withdraw back north along the Bardia road. Wilhelm Hagios:

"We had relatively quiet time until the next British attack, 15 June it was. Around mid-day came the Italians who were saying 'Mamma Mia', they were ambushed by British artillery. We stayed in our position until mid-day. Then came the alarm, the same British artillery ambushed us. Oberst Cramer was wounded in the attack. Panzers were deployed to Points 208 and 206, I was upfront, I had a ZbV vehicle and if somebody needed a vehicle (the adjutant, etc) I was in service with some others and ordered by Rommel himself, we went until Height 208 and identified that the British tanks had broken through and we took a Flak gun and took it to the place where we saw tanks, where they opened fire. 4cm shells were coming at us but the distance was too great to hit what they were aiming at. In the evening we were searching for the rest area, we had no further tasks and the day was over for us."[19]

The delays caused by the 88s allowed the I./*Abteilung* to reach an area just west of Capuzzo and renew its attack against the *4th Armored Brigade*. There were some minor engagements that took place over the late afternoon hours, and at around 1700hrs a small panzer attack against the western section of the fort made it in, forcing the defenders out. This small success was short lived, however, when they themselves were counterattacked from the southwest and pushed out. Kümmel's account goes on:

"Soon a quick fire came against the company, after we had attacked those Tommies who had drove on and away from the barbed wire. The outcome [of this fire] was hard on the panzer of Feldwebel Kruck. One round went through the panzer, through the radioman's body and wounded the crew, some lightly and some heavily. Immediately after the round hit, the panzer went up in flames. Only the wounded were recovered alive, the radioman was killed and found his grave in the flames. The destiny of the panzer soldiers who are hit by enemy fire is terrible. But someone has to die in tank combat. If we were to achieve complete success, there was no time for delays. We were pushing the remaining tanks backwards with the heavy fire from our weapons, the enemy attack collapsed, until it turned into an escape with no rules. One tank remained, hit by our fire, I ordered the Company to go back into position, because the pursuit in the far desert was a push into nothing. The first success was achieved but it was bitter with the loss of a good comrade. Still, when we assembled, distant dark points become visible again and they soon got bigger and bigger, behind them was a large dust cloud. 'Damn! It seems to be enemy tanks', I thought and watched my small and brave group with concern. Still we were happy in the hope that on our right flank must be the [remainder] of the Regiment. What can happen to us? The light Zug moved off towards the enemy, in order to find out what was happening there. The number of dark spots was growing quickly and many more appeared from the dust curtain. They were swinging in a wide curve. I saw the mass approaching us with concern, these were not German. Soon we were able to hear the roar of the English diesel engines. At this point a message arrived from my Zug leader, Lieutenant Stiefelmayer: '40-50 Mark IIs recognized, attack developing on the right'. I thought at this moment about this morning, when the situation was explained to me I thought the light panzer forces would be sufficient [to halt them]. At this moment my vehicle stopped. 'The panzer has engine damage' reported my driver with a sad voice. There is no time to reflect about it. I quickly signaled to another vehicle to come over and change vehicles together with my Oberfunkmeister. The radios were re-installed quickly, a company without its leader, it's hard to think about. My nerves were tense to the limit, the thoughts roamed through my brain. What were the consequences, if the English should break through? It's clear to me, that this would be beyond comprehension. So I came to the difficult decision, to attack the overwhelming enemy forces and hold them at any price. '1000 o'clock enemy tanks, free fire'. I heard my orders in the radio clearly and hard. Each nerve and muscle was tense at this moment, when we search for the enemy through the optics. We all know that the enemy was far exceeding us in numbers, combat power and especially in the armor clad skin. Each of us feels the moment of the crash test and it's clear to all that it is more than a local attack. It demanded a relentless, sacrificing deployment, if this would come to success to stop this thundering herd, which makes the earth shutter. They believe they are safe in their fortresses of thick steel and concrete, deployed for the first time en masse. They firmly believe in the victory, but the German soldiers are against them, that was a mistake in their calculations. Now they came in to shooting distance. Short and clear came the orders of the commanders. The first round leaves the cannon with a loud noise, M.G.s start to clatter, steel knocks on steel. The tough and hard fighting, tank against tank begins to roll out. The noise of the engines, detonating rounds, banging of the cannons, whistle of shooting and the irregular hammering of the M.G. mix up in the devil's noise. The dust and the gunpowder whirl up high, partially blocking the sight. Now and again there are flashes to the front. The shot comes whistling, and dives into the soil or hits the side of the panzer. It seems that there is a fighting of steel giants going on in full power, and it endeavors to destroy us. Only nerves made of steel allow us to hold on through this chaos of mutual elimination. The heated tank combat continues for many minutes. The enemy was overwhelming in numbers and endangers to outflank us, to hit us in the flank or in the rear. Only through a slow backwards evasion we get out of the pincer movement. So I give the order to my brave men:

Chapter 6: The Summer Battles, June-September 1941

'evade slowly and keep firing, in front of the Capuzzo position, the fort must be held by all means'! We slowly get away from the enemy, which pushes hard. [We] drive a little backwards, go in the position, fire and go further backwards. It's not an escape, but an organized decoupling from the enemy, which we conduct with difficulty. There were many shots at the enemy. The amount of enemy tanks is so large that individual losses have no meaning. We force them to shoot their valuable ammunition, which later on will have bad consequences for them. On the right flank are our brave comrades of 2nd Company fighting in this almost hopeless tough combat. This Company too has shrunk due to losses. Soon the walls of the Italian border fortress flicker in the sun heavily shot through. We take shelter behind stonewalls and the remains of the [fortress] walls. Here we prepare a hot welcome to the oncoming enemy. By no means will we let the English get to the fort easily. But for how long will our ammunition hold? But we don't have time to think about it. The group of Mark IIs already goes around us under the cover of the dust, even before we take up our position. We have no other choice but to take the fight to this overwhelming enemy with our few remaining rounds. We were attacked from three sides, we defend ourselves bitterly, allowing the Mark IIs to roll as close as 300m and burn their hides with our rounds. The radioman shot doubtfully with his M.G. into the sides. The enemy fires from all his cannons. It is luck that the English aim so poorly. Despite it, direct hits are unavoidable the steel death knocks many times on the panzer walls. And we exhale every time the armor holds. And time goes by, there is no decision yet. My soldiers fire light rounds in the thick clusters of the approaching tanks. The English shoot from all their cannons, they combine their fire on the opposite German panzers. Here one panzer fights until it boils over, there one shoots its last round and rolls backwards when an enemy tank causes him life damage. And yet again one is followed by many of the Mark IIs, firing at them from 300m, a couple of rounds, it slides in the turn and hits with it's last round the track of the other. With a broken ventilator and without ammunition, it later had to be towed away. The fourth vehicle got shot, starts to smell, drives backwards, extinguishes the fire and drives forward again. One other is shot through; the crew is wounded but gets out and is able to reach a safe place. Unfortunately this vehicle burns out completely. The Zug leader of the 1st Zug receives the charge of enemy chienon block. The crew is mysteriously unwounded, only the leader is lightly wounded by fragments in his hand. The vehicle stays in combat and first drives backwards, when a hit destroys the leading wheel. The examples of sacrificing fulfillment of the duty are countless."[20]

After pushing out German forces and retaking Fort Capuzzo, the British were finally able to get their remaining infantry forward in order to properly secure the fort. At around 1830hrs a strong counter-attack, the second of the day, was launched from the north and west. Olt Kümmel, commander of the *1st Company*, went forward in a drive to the fort with his remaining Mk IIIs and a couple of heavy Mk IVs. The panzers drove through the British tank fire utilizing the cover of the fort's old ruins in order to screen their movement, where a deadly game of cat and mouse was played. In the following attack, Kümmel and his crew were able to destroy eight British tanks at close range. With this action he forced those *7th RTR* elements to break off the engagement and withdraw to regroup and reorganize themselves. The Italian soldiers who were present and witnessed this extreme act of bravery and reckless disregard for one's own safety gave him the nickname *"The Lion of Capuzzo."* Kümmel recounts in his after action report:

"My vehicle stands behind the corner of the wall. Only one will inspires us, to force the English to halt. The English attack us from all sides, but my Richtschütze aims calmly and renews his fire. Death knocks against the walls of our panzer loudly but we still fight. 300 meters ahead of us is one Mark II, a couple other Mark IIs are on the right, and they come as close as 50 meters. The rounds leave the cannon with a hissing sound. Thank God, they are stuck in the fire and do not respond. At such a short distance for them as well there is no mercy. Others hesitate to come closer. The rounds audibly whistle all around us. Suddenly we hear a crash; there is nothing left of the provisioning box. We consider it a lucky outcome. But the happiness was short lived, the English hit us again. The ventilator is shot through; the vehicle is showing 100 degrees. Is there any rescue for us? With the last power from our trusted and shot up panzer we manage to drive back into the fortress. We renew the fight at the gates. Our ammunition shrinks. The Ladeschütze hesitantly reports to me that there are only five grenades left. So we position our panzer in such a way, that every Mark II which dares to enter the fortress, gets the lights shot out of it from a distance of 20 meters. We manage to prepare for close defense. The radios were dismantled and buried. We didn't want to leave anything to the English, if we didn't manage to break through to our comrades. With a heavy heart we said good-bye to our trusted panzer and set it on fire. We were equipped with a machine gun, machine pistol and pistols. The egg hand grenades disappear in our pockets. That is a bitter feeling, to be encircled, but I saw it in the eyes of others and I myself had just one wish: with our without our vehicle, we must get out. Now I was no longer the leader of a proud panzer company, but still a leader of this brave band. The rounds audibly crackle into the wall, the fragments rain down on us. When we looked around in the fortress, we surprisingly discovered some other wounded and medics, who were completely surprised by the recent English attack. Later they were rescued to a safe place in the medical vehicle protected by my panzer. We quickly split into all four sides of the fortress, in order to keep our enemy constantly in sight. Now we had to witness how the English tow their broken tanks and bring them to safety. Only now we were able to see the great success, which we had achieved. But for a portion of their tanks there is no rescue. Some of the Mark IIs disappear on the horizon, probably to fuel and get ammunition. We spot the dark spots on the horizon, with the binoculars, which move up and down and we guess that they are trucks. 2-3 Mark IIs constantly circle around the fortress, because they believe they have already secured their booty. But I would not suggest to them to dare to get into the fortress. The gun flashes are seldom to see, they seem to be saving their ammunition as well. That is for me the sign of break-up. We quickly assembled and prepared ourselves. Will this be successful? Our panzer limps through the gates like a wounded animal, we save our last five grenades as a good-bye for a Mark II. 80 meters ahead is one of them, probably covering the gates. The first grenade quickly leaves the cannon. It hit, but the tank rolls on further. Ahead of us is a flash, thank God it's just the column which got hit. Fragments and stones fly around us. Quickly firing the remaining four rounds the colossus is hit and remains halted. You were a knightly enemy. We slowly win back the territory. But they can't let us go so easily. Machine gun fire knock on the walls of the panzer, the rounds whistle by us, some hit us, but luck is with us. 800 meters north of Capuzzo I met both of my remaining panzers, who were still trying to get me out of the fortress. Happy of my undefined lucky destiny, I was able to report back to my commander. The English breakthrough was stopped by the will of German soldiers. Often left on his own, the German panzer soldier proved, that the concrete and steel alone can not guarantee the victory."[21]

Hermann Eckardt also remembered the attacks this day:

"On 15 June we started the attack; in the dawn German fighter aircraft had combat with the British, as they went towards Tobruk. We had combat with the British in desert and they attacked with the Mk II

Matildas, a very slow, only 15km/h infantry tank. They went only as fast as the infantry. Our tactic was to drive like crazy and as quick as possible and sometimes we were too close to the enemy, and due to this speed were many collisions and damages. We were overwhelming in the attack, our panzers drove on at 40km/h and we went quickly towards them, they shot at us and we quickly fired back shooting Mk IIs and then there were two of them hit with a splinter grenade [HE]. The English were crying 'help us', we so we stopped and helped them. The hatch on one tank was stuck and they could not get out. Later on, when I was a commander I never closed the hatch, just in situations when it was really dangerous. Only artillery could get inside the panzer, because we moved so quickly."[22]

Unfortunately as the light began to fade, the attack was checked and finally called off, having been successfully repulsed and leaving the British in possession of the fort. Other elements of the Regiment were ordered north along the Bardia road in order to prevent any further attacks or breakthroughs there. Under the cover of a watchful Mk IV the remaining panzers formed a blocking position on the road to Bardia and held that position during the night against the probes of the *4th Armored Brigade*, which had succeeded in moving back through Capuzzo and rallying its armor that evening just south of the fort.

Hafid Ridge
Over on the far left flank the *7th Armored Division*, which had the task of covering the *4th Indian Division's* attacks at Halfaya and Capuzzo, rolled across the frontier wire and made its way towards Hafid Ridge and Strongpoint 208. The column was led by the *2nd RTR* of the *7th Armored Brigade*. The *2nd RTR* was equipped and led by thirty-eight older model A-9, A-10, and A-13 cruiser tanks which allowed the fifty new Crusaders of the *6th RTR* to be kept in reserve in order to exploit the situation at just the right moment.[23] The going was a bit easier, as the speedy light tanks and Crusaders hooked around towards Hafid ridge, the column's first objective. As the speedy cruiser tanks quickly closed the distance to the ridge, which was in fact a series of three ridges, the *7th Armored Brigade* quickly lost the means to identify terrain features in the dust and extreme heat of the day. Initially there was no opposition spotted or encountered, except by a couple of light reconnaissance parties that had been sent forward to observe and report that morning. As the tanks approached the ridge orders were issued for the Pak gunners to hold their fire in order for the tanks to come within effective killing range. In the meantime, orders had been sent to the *5th Light* ordering it to send its panzers and Pak guns down from Tobruk in order to reinforce the forces now defending Hafid. The strongpoint was bristling with a good number of 37mm and 50mm Pak guns, and like Halfaya it had been reinforced with four 88mm Flak guns from *Flak Regiment 33*. Like the center column that went in without its artillery support, so too here on the left and the vital support necessary for keeping the German Pak gunners' heads down was lost. Along the first ridge the garrison there had been successfully holding off the initial British advances, as only the small caliber 37mm Pak guns were used to drive off the pesky armored cars. The initial attack came at 1000hrs by just one squadron of cruiser tanks which, as they neared the crest, came under fire by the numerous Pak guns defending the ridge; the volume of fire was so great that it forced the squadron to immediately withdraw. It was at this point that the commander of the strongpoint ordered every available gun to open fire, including the four 88mm Flak guns. It was the 88s that halted the attack, claiming eleven British tanks. Horst Sonnenkalb wrote of the 88s:

"The 88mm was the wonder weapon of the North-African campaign. During the direct ground assault they were used against pressing tanks and the battlefield was littered with burning or disabled battle vehicles. You could say: Each shot a hit! At the same time the gunners were protected by only a real thin shield against enemy hits and machine gun fire. The 88mm played [the role of] fire brigade a lot, and yes, they determined the outcome of a lot of battles."[24]

After the first attack the British reformed and went in again at 1145hrs, this time with two tank squadrons properly supported by artillery. The German gunners estimated that the attacking force consisted of approximately forty tanks. The attack this time was a bit more successful, and the first ridge and its gun positions were overrun with the loss of just one tank. Then, as the tanks rolled further on, they spotted a large number of Pak guns concealed on the reverse slope of the second ridge. After spotting the guns the commander ordered the tanks to turn back and head south away from the guns, but five of the tanks were lost when they either failed to hear or disregarded the order. Farther to the west, at Strongpoint 208, which was located near the end of the Hafid ridge line, the defenders continued to come under attack by British tanks from the south and east. The strongpoint, aided by the 88mm Flak guns, continued to resist, and during the day's attacks claimed eight of the fourteen tanks sent against it. After a delay lasting roughly four hours a third attack was launched against the ridge beginning at 1730hrs. The attack went in with an estimated seventy tanks from both the *2nd RTR* and two squadrons of the *6th RTR*. The attack was launched after a number of reports stated that the Germans were withdrawing from Hafid Ridge. The attack went in and ran right into a well laid ambush, baited by a number of dummy supply vehicles.[25] In the ensuing fight eleven *Crusader* tanks were lost and six damaged. Before the day ended the *6th RTR* had lost seventeen of its tanks that were either destroyed outright or put out of action by mechanical damage. Late that evening the *5th Light* arrived in the battle area and was spotted off to the northwest, where it was immediately engaged by British armor. The German panzers counter-attacked, and this thrust was met by a squadron of the *2nd RTR*, which by this time had only twenty operational tanks left, but with orders to hold this force at all cost. The battle became a long-range duel; with the British 2-Pounder guns hopelessly outclassed by the German 50mm and 75mm guns, by nightfall only fifteen tanks remained ready for combat. After this short fire fight in the waning light of the day both sides finally disengaged for the evening, with the panzers from the *5th Light* pulling back to Sidi Azeiz and the two RTRs, now reduced to just thirty-seven operational tanks, back across the wire to resupply with fuel and ammunition. By the end of the first day of battle the situation did not look all too promising for the Germans forces on the frontier: they had taken a serious beating with the loss of Fort Capuzzo and Strongpoint 206, in addition to the loss of some 500 men and over half the panzers. Halfaya Pass was holding, but it was virtually surrounded, and Hafid Ridge was on the verge of collapse; to make matters worse, the *RAF* had been quite active, attacking the supply convoys attempting to make their way forward to the *15th Panzer*. Olt Schubert of the *3rd Company* recorded:

"Sunday 15 June at 0400hrs the early alarm. Heavy fire along the front. At 0500hrs the Regiment is ready. At 1000hrs follows the deployment in the direction of Capuzzo. The whole day there is heavy combat. In the evening we managed to win back the rest place of the Regiment. The panzer of Schneider is destroyed. Uffz Schmidt falls."[26]

However, all was not lost as Rommel saw it; the *5th Light* was arriving on the battlefield, and he felt that the British would soon be ripe for a major counter-attack. For the British commanders, the losses they suffered on this first day of battle caused no immediate need to panic or modify their plans of attack on the following day. British attacks would continue on

Halfaya Pass and Hafid Ridge while consolidating the area around Fort Capuzzo and Strongpoint 206. It was also planned that once those British forces at Capuzzo had consolidated their gains they could possibly strike north towards Bardia. It was also planned to send the *Matildas* from the *4th Armored Brigade* over to reinforce the *7th Armored Brigade* at Hafid in order to finally capture those positions. The *7th Armored Brigade's* main task would be to check the advance of the *5th Light* as it worked its way around the open flank. For the British, the *22nd Guards Brigade* still remained at Fort Capuzzo, and was entrenching itself there and attempting to strengthen its position. On the night of 15/16 June the Regiment's combat units received a re-supply and were able to begin the retrieval and repair process on some of the damaged panzers. Rommel had been carefully studying the British moves, and now as night came on personally took charge of the battle and issued his orders for the morning.

16 June 1941
The plan for the 16th was to begin at sunrise, and called for the relief of Halfaya Pass by advancing the panzers of the *5th* and *8th Panzer Regiments* into that area. Both regiments would advance on parallel arcs, with the *5th Light* on a wide arc via Sidi Omar and then on towards Sidi Suleiman. Once *Panzer Regiment 5* had reached that position near Sidi Suleiman it would strike east towards Halfaya Pass. *Panzer Regiment 8* was ordered to undertake a shorter wheel around Fort Capuzzo in the hopes of pinning down the main British force located there, and once those forces had been dealt with the Regiment was to move towards Halfaya. As dawn broke, the battle was still raging at Sollum and Hafid Ridge as the *D.A.K.* advanced under the observation of the ever-present British armored cars. The 16th would be a day of rapid movement and hard fighting which would initially favor the British in the morning, but then turn to favor the Germans in the afternoon.[27] The Regiment jumped off at 0555hrs as it launched its counter-attack south towards Capuzzo, again supported by the 88mm guns of *Flak Abteilung 33*. Kurt Liestmann describes the previous evening and early morning prior to the attack:

"In the dawn of this day we attacked again. During the night our short sleep was disturbed by some night surveillance from Tommy. In Bardia they dropped bombs. The early morning fog, never so thick as today, finds us in the northeast in an attack towards Capuzzo."[28]

During the movement towards Capuzzo the I./*Abteilung* went through a long gorge where it encountered tanks from the *7th RTR*, which had begun its attack at 0745hrs. The encounter between the I./*Abteilung's* nineteen panzers (nine Mk IIs, four Mk IIIs, six Mk IVs, and thirty-four Matildas) resulted in immediate troubles for the panzers.[29] Indeed, the entire Regiment was headed towards trouble that had arrived during the night in the form of British anti-tank and artillery guns, that after being held up earlier on the previous day had come into the area that evening and were now poised along the flanks of the Regiment's axis of advance. The *5th Light* also had run afoul of the *7th Armored Brigade* near Sidi Omar, as it ran into the British gunners who had finally gotten their act together. The British would continue to hang on the flanks and tail of the *5th Light* column as it passed through Sidi Omar and attempted to make its way towards Sidi Suleiman. However, the British situation was far from satisfactory, as they had again failed in their attempts to take Halfaya Pass in spite of having captured Sollum, Musaid, and Strongpoint 206, as well as holding off a counter-attack by elements of the *15th Panzer Division*.[30] Kurt Liestmann continues his description of the actions around Fort Capuzzo:

"The II./Abteilung attacks from the north and northwest. In the meantime there is nothing to see. So our vehicles slowly creep up towards Capuzzo. At 1 kilometer distance the ruins appear from the haze, and already it begins to sparkle and thunder around us. The greetings are of 4cm size. Mark IIs and anti-tank guns are already located and well dug in on the perimeter of Capuzzo behind the stone walls. Today the shelling is dangerously close and it hisses over the turret. The heavy haze is an obstacle. Our 7.5s answer, and soon explosions are all around. Involuntary one has an impression and the situation of sea combat in the desert. One shoots, changes position and attempts to break through the iron-clad. Whoever has the thickest, like the Tommy, has an advantage at longer distances. We slowly roll closer. I regret [that I have] to sit with the commander in the command vehicle. Without the cannon one can only wait helplessly at the first impact. The commander [Maj Crohn] could hardly lead. There is not much to see in the haze. On our sides and behind us creep other vehicles. They disconnect a little. One 7.5 near us is hit, but it didn't do much. Light wounds. In front of us something bursts and hisses above us, but I pull my head into the hatch."[31]

That morning the *15th Panzer Division* had reported less than fifty operational panzers fit for combat operations, but after running into the British gunners that number had shrunk to just thirty by 1030hrs.[32] As the Regiment's panzers slugged it out it was obvious that they were not in a good attack position, and many of the panzer commanders attempted to break contact with the British armor and move off at a high speed until they could begin to engage at the more favorable distance of about 300m. By late that morning the temperatures had already reached 140F/60C, which did aid the Germans as they attempted to maneuver and break contact with the British tanks. The attack of the *3rd Company* under *Olt* Schubert experienced significant losses: the panzer of *Uffz* Olsberg was hit and exploded into flames, trapping the crew inside, and there were no survivors. Lt Peters, a *Zug* commander in the *1st Company*, witnessed the hit and attempted to rescue the crew, but as he ordered the driver forward towards the burning panzer his panzer also took a direct hit which disabled the running gear, leaving the panzer immobile and forcing the crew to bail out. Peters then called Kümmel to ask for covering fire before attempting to flee the stricken panzer. Kümmel moved forward and soon found himself engaging two British tanks which were attempting to finish off Peters' panzer. Again Kümmel was successful, and Peters and his crew were able to make it safely to cover.[33] The command panzer of *Major* Crohn, the I./*Abteilung* commander, was also hit by two 40mm rounds that entered the turret directly behind Lt Liestmann, the *Abteilung* Adjutant. Liestmann suffered only a singed shirt and he, Crohn, and the radio operator were able to bail out and find cover behind a nearby berm. While the panzer was burning, Liestmann and the radio operator attempted to search for shelter on the other side of the panzer, but were both wounded by a machine gun burst. Later in the attack, *Major* Crohn would have a second panzer shot out from underneath him. Kurt Liestmann describes the encounter:

"On the order of the Regiment we break up to the right rear, in order to attack the main weapons but unfortunately by doing so we display our flank and come between two lines of fire. We increase the speed but despite this, fire hammers on the turret at every moment. It is [either] small caliber or too far away. The commander and I make checks and wait for another impact. I look into the stereo telescope to figure out were the enemy is that is holding us under the fire. On the left side across the direction of travel there are three Mark IIs at 200m distance behind a low piles of stones. At the same moment we receive a terrible hit. The fighting

compartment is bright red, behind my back moves the scorching heat wave, it's so hot as if I am burning. A direct impact. Something glows at the floor. The vehicle stops. The right side hatch is opened and we get out like paratroopers. The tropical helmet rumbles behind me. At this moment we are in the shadow of the panzer and as we begin to run into the flat desert in order to find the next hole, here comes the fierce MG fire of the three enemy vehicles. It whistles, sings and buzzes in all tones around our legs, arms, head and other limbs. The commander on my left side finds the only hole on this damned yellow tabletop. He is an older soldier compared to us, so I think comically at that moment and jump up again in my attempt to flee. It sings around me again. Now my trust in the tropical suitcase on my back fulfilled its role. I receive a hard hit on my right hand. I fall down automatically and roll along the long axis with my head towards the enemy, who I now clearly recognize. The MG fire stops. From the bend of my elbow sprays the red blood in regular intervals. Right through the elbow! I press a finger onto the exit hole but it doesn't help. When I look to the side, 30m left of me lies the radio operator. He is alive. When I wave and shout, he crawls and jumps awkwardly to me and lies down next to me. I point to my arm. He looks and quickly tears my compass strap from the shoulder and bandages my arm while lying down. I nod to him and tell him; 'well done, old man.'"

Liestmann continues the story:

"Now we lie flat. The Tommy do not stir. Behind us roars the engine. Behind us comes the 2cm [Mk II] with high yellow dust flag. Olt Stiefelmayer looks from the turret as if he is on the training ground. An elegant turn and he covers us against the enemy. Someone packs us on the front part of the bow (nose) between the cannon and MG and soon the panzer moves back, now followed by some shelling, which explodes near us. After a few hundred meters backwards there is an 8.8cm Flak and the doctor. The emergency bandage place is behind a vehicle. Only now I notice that the radio operator is bleeding from his leg. His toe is shot away."[34]

The Mk II panzer of *Olt* Stiefelmayer also came under heavy fire; Stiefelmayer was wounded, but fortunately the panzer was able to disengage itself and retire to a more secure location. In the II./*Abteilung* sector *Oberstlt* Cramer had placed himself in the lead and attacked the British tanks along the left flank. Staying with the German panzer tactic of quickly closing the distance between the enemy tanks in order to take advantage of the main gun, the panzers rolled forward at a high rate of speed and into the British armor. But on this day the distance to the British was too great, and the British gunners' aim was true, resulting in the loss of a number of panzers before they were able to get within favorable engagement range. When the panzers finally did manage to close the distance they were able to claim three enemy tanks destroyed. During the engagement with the *7th RTR*, the II./*Abteilung* was then hit on its left flank by some twenty-three *Matildas* from the *4th RTR*. Cramer was able to immediately deal with this threat, and he issued clear and concise orders to the *1st Company*:

"Kümmel, attack and hold the twenty Mark IIs on the flank!"[35]

Kümmel immediately collected his remaining panzers, which amounted to just three Mk IIIs and two Mk IVs, and counter-attacked the British newcomers. It was the Mk IVs with their heavy 75mm guns that brought the situation to a close, as the *4th RTR* was forced to halt its attack after losing eight of its tanks. This successful maneuver by Kümmel gave the II./*Abteilung* the breathing space it desperately needed, but instead of withdrawing to regroup and reorganize itself, Cramer gathered together all the remaining operational panzers and went after those Crusaders of the *7th RTR*. As the remaining panzers moved off to the east the Mk IV command panzer was taken under fire by two enemy tanks. *OFw* Kruck of the *3rd Company* destroyed one of the British tanks, and the other enemy tank was engaged by Cramer's command panzer. In this engagement the British tank crew proved to be faster on the mark, and another hit was scored on Cramer's panzer, wounding him in the head and hand. Kruck brought his panzer over to Cramer's and picked up his regimental commander and the driver, who had also been wounded in the encounter. They were both brought back to the combat supply trains by an Mk II. Kurt Liestmann's account continues:

"We are quickly packed into a Sanka [medical vehicle] and down to Bardia. During the ligation my arm hurts badly. After the seemingly endless drive there is a quick check-up at the H.V.P. It seems that no bones are damaged, but the artery is torn and the pulse is again set. I lie near the open door of the bandage room, and watch the coming and going. Every moment there are new wounded, many from the regiment and some English. The boys have terrible wounds and burns. But everybody holds themselves perfectly. One sits next to me, his chest and face all burnt and thickly bandaged. During the afternoon almost the entire stabs is brought in; commander, adjutant, radio officer and ordnance officer, all as a result of an explosive round. In the afternoon during a break in the combat with the exhausted enemy my commander, hauptfeldwebel and my comrade visit me. They explain the situation. A new counter-attack should be started soon. In the late afternoon the regimental commander and myself were transported in the vehicle to Derna. In the desert we had to get out twice from the vehicle and hide in the sand due to the attacks by low-flying aircraft, every time totally exhausted. During the night we lose our way in the area of Tobruk and as a precaution we overnight in the desert. We are all covered over with a yellow crust and are as dirty as the Arabs. In the morning dawn further to Acroma. The cemetery at the 'White House' grows larger. [Later] a new bandage and short reinforcement and then further on towards Derna and finally on the good road [Via Balbia]. In Derna I receive a splint bandage and at around 1500hrs we leave with the Ju-52 to Benghazi and the airfield at Benina. Here in the hospital I receive a plaster bandage [cast]."[36]

Oberstlt Ramsauer, the commander of II./*Abteilung*, assumed command of the Regiment as the battle continued to rage. After dropping his regimental commander off with the medical personnel, Kruck returned to the action, where his panzer quickly drew the attention of three British tanks. These tanks, which had been covering the retreat of the *7th RTR*, were in excellent position to engage Kruck, and they quickly did so, setting the panzer alight. Hearing the distress call over the radio, Kümmel, who was again right in the thick of the fighting, rolled forward and attacked the enemy tanks with his two remaining panzers; in the action that followed Kümmel and his wing man were able to knock out the British tanks and rescue the panzer crew of *OFw* Kruck. Klaus Hubbuch, a loader in a Mk IV from the *8th Company*, wrote of the details the day his panzer was hit:

"I was wounded as the Ladeschütze (gun-loader), the 40mm solid shot at that time went through between my body and my right arm, when I was about to pull a panzergranate (round) from the mounting, the round was later lying in the engine compartment but the fine fragments from the big hole in our own plating went into my face and chest and I was bleeding like a pig. I didn't even notice it in the heat of the battle, a second Pak (anti-tank) hit penetrated our fog gadgets (fire extinguishers) and infantry explosives loosened our 4 return rollers our vehicle was only good for limited use!"[37]

Also near Capuzzo that day, the four 88mm Flak guns that were still attached to the Regiment were able to knock out a further eight Matildas, but were later engaged by British artillery, which forced them to withdraw. Later on British tanks that had reappeared engaged the Flak guns; the tanks were able to get within 500m and place effective fire on the guns, causing damage to three of the four. The one remaining gun was able to pull back, where it continued to engage targets and claimed a further three tanks. Hermann Eckardt remembered this incident from the battle:

"We were there with our own company and went inside the fortress; all around us were the British. There was an English commander who had been caught and he said to us I want to see the cannon with which you destroyed the Mark II [Matilda], we showed him the 8.8cm and he said it's not fair to shoot from such cannons."[38]

By 1100hrs, the attack by the *4th Armored Brigade* had been effectively halted, and the potential break-through to Bardia warded off, but the attempt to recapture Capuzzo had been lost. Schubert recorded the losses his company suffered that day:

"Monday 16 June, Heavy attack against Capuzzo from 0400hrs. At first we do not advance at all. The company attacks from the east of Capuzzo. The Company commander's vehicle is destroyed. Irmisch is wounded. The panzer of Kertscher has the cannon is broken. The panzer of Göb is on fire. The panzer of Treuenfels destroyed. Danner is burnt out. The remains of the company were brought back in the Regiment formation."[39]

Thomas Jentz gives the following report concerning the Regiment's panzer losses:

"The I./Abteilung had now only six Mk IVs, four Mk IIIs and nine Mk IIs of the nine Mk IVs, eighteen Mk IIIs and thirteen Mk IIs panzers with which it had started the battle. The British tanks struck out of the morning mist and once more there were heavy casualties in the 3rd Company. The commander of the I./Abteilung had his panzer shot through twice by fire from infantry tanks [Matildas] at a range of 300 meters. The I./Abteilung had to withdraw with only three operational Mk IIIs and one Mk II. It is clear that if the British tanks had been able to take Bardia, Panzer Regiment 8 would have been finished. By the evening of the second day two Mk IIs, nine Mk IIIs and two Mk IVs had been repaired (the damage had been mostly to guns), and stood ready to defend Bardia."[40]

That afternoon the Regiment was ordered by the division to break contact with the British armor and pull back to an assembly area near Sidi Azeiz, which lay just six kilometers north of Capuzzo. The *15th Panzer Division* had been ordered by *D.A.K.* to throw all its mobile reserves, which at the time consisted of panzers, infantry, artillery, and reconnaissance troops, to the east of Point 208 heading towards Sidi Suleiman. It was hoped the *15th Panzer* could hit the British flank and relieve Halfaya Pass while the *5th Light* continued to engage British forces around Sidi Omar and Capuzzo. The previous day's action and mechanical breakdowns had caused significant damage to the Regiment, which was now down to roughly thirty-five operational panzers. Even though the British armor and *4th Indian Division* had been badly shot up they still remained in positions around Musaid and Point 208, and posed a serious threat to the *15th Panzer* and Bardia. That is when Rommel decided to attack in the south and trap those British forces by cutting off Sidi Omar and Sidi Suleiman from the south. Indeed, already the situation was turning, as the German counter-attacks had forced the *4th Armored Brigade* to remain with the *4th Indian Division*, and the attack on Hafid ridge was called off. By nightfall the *7th Armored Brigade* was down to just twenty-one operational tanks, having lost twenty-five of its tanks to mechanical breakdown. The *2nd* and *6th RTRs* had been forced to fight separate engagements all day before they were finally driven back to the east, where they could refuel and rearm. That night the *6th RTR* reported that it was down to only nine operational *Crusaders*.[41] That evening the Regiment's workshop company, working feverishly throughout the day, was able to return two Mk IIs, nine Mk IIIs, and two Mk IVs. Those panzers were ordered to position themselves on the road to Bardia in order to keep that vital town secure. Again that evening the British commanders were not swayed from their original plan, and they again looked at securing the gains at Capuzzo and Sollum so that the *4th Armored Brigade* could be dispatched to reinforce the attack at Hafid Ridge. Rommel, for one, was not overly concerned about the losses suffered by the *15th Panzer*, nor the fact that it had been dispersed and scattered in the day's fighting. Halfaya was still holding out despite the fact that the garrison was desperately short of ammunition. Nothing was immediately known of *5th Light*'s situation, and there had been repeated air attacks on the supply columns. Rommel still suspected that the British would advance toward the north from the Capuzzo area, and he planned to launch a spoiling attack on the morning of the 17th to disrupt the British and finally get to Halfaya. He ordered the *5th Light* to turn east and make for Sidi Suleiman; the *15th Panzer* was ordered to skirt the western flank of the British middle column and link up with the *5th Light*, where it was planned that both formations would make for Halfaya, and once that position was relieved the *D.A.K.* would drive north and strike the *4th Indian Division* in the rear. After a short rest, the remaining panzers of the Regiment went forward during the night 16/17 June between Capuzzo and Point 208, heading south towards Sidi Omar. *Kradschützen Battalion 15*, units of *Schützen Regiment 115*, two batteries of *Artillery Regiment 33*, and units of *Aufklärungs Abteilung 33* followed the panzers. Rommel had looked at the withdrawal of the *2nd* and *6th RTRs* and various radio intercepts as a sign that the British left flank was crumbling on the night of the 16th, and he was determined to concentrate both the *15th Panzer* and *5th Light* and strike hard at the left flank of the *7th Armored Division*, smashing straight through the British lines to a show down near Halfaya Pass.

17 June 1941

At around 0430hrs, as the Regiment prepared to move out for another day's combat, they did so thanks in large part to the repair and recovery teams of the division and Regiment, which had worked feverishly throughout the night to get the Regiment's panzer strength back up to forty-five operational panzers. Additional firepower was allotted to the Regiment in the form of four 88mm Flak guns.[42] At Ghot Ahediba, the II./*Abteilung* came upon an element from the *7th RTR* with fourteen tanks, and in the ensuing fight it destroyed nine Matildas, of which four were claimed by the Flak gunners. That previous evening the *5th Light* had continued its battle with British forces east of Sidi Omar, and by 0600hrs had reached a point near Sidi Suleiman where it was then to swing northwards; the division had beaten the British to the open flank and were about to drive on those forces vacating the Capuzzo-Sollum sector. Unknown to the *D.A.K.* was that the *7th Armored Division*'s cruiser tanks had pulled back across the border wire to refuel and rearm, leaving just the Matildas of the *4th Indian Division* near Capuzzo and Halfaya to cover the withdrawal. *15th*

Panzer had begun its attack on schedule, and by 0830hrs the Regiment was in combat near Ghot Adhidiba. By 0900hrs it was quite clear that the British were in trouble, as *D.A.K.* radio intercepts noted that the British ammunition supply was beginning to run low. The *D.A.K.* then ordered its divisions to again strike for Halfaya Pass with the hope of capturing those British forces still around Capuzzo and Sollum. By 1000hrs, the panzers had concluded their brief engagement with the British rearguard, which in the process had suffered heavy losses. Heinz Liestmann's Combat Report dated 17 June gives us an idea of how the day progressed for some of the men in the II./*Abteilung*:

"At approximately 0630hrs we start marching in the old direction, and reach near by point 206, Neznet Kihirb, the border fence of the Egyptian border. On both sides of the border in about 2000m distance appears a number of Mark IIs. We take them under heavy impact fire in cooperation with 88mm Flak, which panzer rounds arrive from a height on the left and together with our panzer rounds take from some of the Mark IIs the light of life [destroyed them]. The enemy retreats, we continue to attack. Five enemy Mark IIs are destroyed. Despite this the enemy decides to attack, from 1000m my vehicle receives concentrated fire. I order my Zug to change their position. The company chief gives by radio [the command] for the Zug's clear direction of fire, in which he allows one zug to unite the fire on a certain vehicle. The Flak hunts, one shot after the other, to get two further Mark IIs destroyed. Others shoot now all that they can, the fire is placed very well. I get shot with the jingle [bang], the impact takes both tracks from the frontal wall and almost gets through the wall itself. And then jingles again, my driver cries and sinks with a short glance. We pull him out; he is bleeding from his head. Now the Lade is the Richtschütze and I load myself and play a commander. We continue to shoot, the driver relaxes, and he takes over as the Ladeschützen clenching his teeth. After some struggle my Richtschütze drives the vehicle about 200m backwards, we boot out the driver. Via the Kradschützen I get Ogefr Komorowski from the I-squadron to sit down as my driver, we drive forwards and get into the attack after the radio message is received. The British bombing squadron appears and covers us and the following supply column with bombs, but without impact. We attack again, the English defend themselves stubbornly, the Mark IIs retreat step by step, and shoot from their wide side forward [90 degrees]. I and my Zug receive the task, to attack the enemy covering on the right, in order to force the English to change their front and advance some of their tanks. The enemy reacts on this, turns some of his tanks towards me, so that I receive a concentrated fire. I continue to attack with success, so that the English go back slowly, firing fiercely. I get the order via radio from my chief, not to advance any further, because I am now located 2000m by waving to the left in front of the fire line of our own panzers and so there was a danger to get under our own fire. After rejoining our own fire line, I get the order to attack the stonework of Sabr el Aahab on the right completely. While two of the Zug vehicles were quite faded, I attacked with one vehicle alone and advanced to the walls at about 1000m, there were behind them seven to eight Mark IIs in fire position, only the towers [turrets] visible. I had permission, in case of absence of prospects, to shoot white light balls and return. Under concentrated fire of Mark IIs, which got me twice, I returned to our own panzers. The additional joint attack pushed the enemy tanks slowly backwards. Then the attack was turned north for the whole Abteilung, the company secured to the east. Further in the east I discovered after exact observation a large number of German panzers, which came close from the direction southeast. I reported my observations further, and the panzers looked like they belonged to Panzer Regiment 5. The Abteilung was joined the Panzer Regiment 5 and occupied the rest area to the northwest of Qalala. With that the main combat activity was finished."[43]

By 1045hrs, those British forces at Sollum and Musaid were ordered to withdraw and cross back over the frontier wire. Throughout the late morning and into midday the *D.A.K.* continued to engage the rearguards until they had reached a position within a few kilometers of Halfaya. Other *D.A.K.* elements were sent back to clear up Sollum and Capuzzo. As the Germans swung south those British forces in and around Capuzzo soon discovered that the *D.A.K.* had slipped past them and would soon be in a position to cut them off, and so, without corps approval, the commanders of the *4th Indian* and *7th Armored Division* ordered a general withdrawal back across the frontier. The remaining Matildas were sent off to hold open the escape routes and cover the retreat, a job they would do quite effectively. After undertaking the maneuver south the I./*Abteilung* then re-formed itself for the drive to Halfaya Pass and a link up with the II./*Abteilung*, which had been attached to *Panzer Regiment 5* for the attack there. As the I./*Abteilung* advanced it caught a column of retreating British trucks, which it made short work of. Before long, dust clouds were spotted on the horizon as British tanks and vehicles continued to make their way toward the east. *Olt* Kümmel, again at the forefront of his company, attempted to follow with the few remaining panzers and pursue the retreating enemy in the extreme midday heat. At 1230hrs, the I./*Abteilung* had halted near Gabr el Qalala, some six kilometers short of the Halfaya Pass, with its fuel tanks dry and ammunition racks empty. Horst Sonnenkalb:

"Of course fuel was very important to us, because with an empty gas tank you can't move an inch, even in the desert. Our 12 cylinder Maybach engines with their 230 horsepower were very thirsty and in that terrain used up about 350 liters of gas per 100 km and the street the same amount of gas per 200 km. The 21 tons overall weight had to be moved. There were no streets in the desert, only rutty slopes in the sand. And the battles themselves were fought in the desert."[44]

Fortunately, an element of the light column (*le Kol*) managed to work its way forward and re-supplied the panzers with fuel and ammunition, but it was already becoming too late to catch the British. At 1600hrs the I./*Abteilung* continued its movement to attack those British forces around Halfaya, but while en-route it came under attack by six *RAF Hurricanes* and three bombers. In the attack one Mk IV was destroyed, five soldiers were killed, and sixteen wounded. That aerial attack halted the I./*Abteilung's* drive to Halfaya, and the *Abteilung* returned back to the west. *Olt* Schubert recorded:

"Tuesday 17 June The new company is constructed from repaired vehicles from the whole Regiment. The company commander is Ehrbeck and as the leader of the whole Abteilung is nominated Major Crohn. To this belong one flak gun, two guns, some Sankas [medical ambulances] and ten panzers. At 1100hrs we march in the direction of Hill 208. At 208 came an air force attack. English dive bombers fly un-shot under the march column. There are heavy losses, especially in the open transport vehicles where the infantrymen sit. That evening we take Igel [hedgehog] position near hill 206."[45]

By 1650hrs, the two panzer regiments had linked up near Halfaya, where they attacked off to the north, but unfortunately the main body of the British *4th Armored Brigade* had already pushed past the *5th Light* in its previous drive north. That evening a link-up was made between the panzers and the defenders of Halfaya Pass. By 1945hrs, the *D.A.K.* had begun to signal its divisions that the battle had been won, and that complete success had been achieved. The remaining panzers were ordered to halt in their present positions, while some *D.A.K.* elements were ordered to prepare themselves for a pursuit the following day, but for the panzer crews that had been in constant action without a break for over seventy-two hours, it meant a chance to get some desperately needed sleep. Not all of them though had that chance, as Heinz Liestmann explains:

"In the evening there took place the advancement to the southeast direction with the task, to sweep clean the steep wadi from the enemy. We attacked under the light of enemy artillery fire, hunting several escaping Mark IIs, which were stopped by the concentrated fire of our own panzers. Already in the coming darkness we reached the wadi occupied by the enemy. We took the escaping enemy under the fire of high explosive rounds and machine gun fire. In complete darkness the Abteilung assembled in the rest area at Qalala, which we secured during the night to the northeast."[46]

By the evening of 17 June, the remaining British forces had slipped back down the escarpment heading east; with the Matildas covering them, those forces withdrew back through Halfaya to the defensive line at Sidi Barrani and Sofafi, where they had started from three days ago, but now having lost some 1000 men, almost a hundred tanks destroyed, twenty-seven cruisers, and sixty-four infantry. Total German losses were listed as between 5-700 men with an unrecorded number of Italians taken prisoner or fallen (that number is estimated at roughly five hundred men). German panzer losses were listed as between twelve and fifty, but it must be assumed that a large number of these were caused by mechanical breakdown and were later recovered. It appears that twelve panzer seems to be a more correct number when looking at the total number of losses or complete write offs. The German recovery teams and services were kept quite busy after the battle, but were able to bring the panzer regiments back up to operational strength quite quickly. One of the prizes afforded the Germans was the fact that they held the ground and could undertake recovery operations and salvage a number of previously disabled panzers. There were also twelve Matildas that were recovered and later pressed into German service.[47] Heinz Liestmann's Combat Report for 18 June mentions this:

"On 18 June the advancement was continued in the direction southeast, where our company got the order, to accompany the advancement of the light companies on the south and west with 88mm Flak cannons and secure it, and without enemy encounters we went back together with the Abteilung until Qalala."[48]

Schubert's diary recorded:

"March back towards Capuzzo there is no combat with the English back to bivouac. The panzers of Fw Döweling and Göb stay on the frontline."

The Battle of Sollum was the first big tank battle for the Regiment against British armored units. The Regiment, despite being under-gunned and under-equipped, was able to hold its own against the speedy *Crusaders* and heavily armored *Matildas*. The initiative and timely actions taken by those commanders and junior leaders led to the success. Hermann Eckardt explains:

"During the day the British tanks were easily recognizable, the Mark IVs, their Valentines, the Matildas and so on since they had recognition flags on their radio antennas. On that we built our combat strategy. First we tried to disable the tanks with the most flags, because we knew troop commanders were sitting in those tanks. That's how we took down the British command during battle. And that happened numerous times with great success."[49]

The total number of losses sustained in *Battleaxe* by the Regiment during the period 15-17 June consisted of seventeen killed and twenty wounded, amongst them: *Oberstlt* Hans Cramer, his adjutant *Hptm* Jahns, and communications and ordnance officers *Olts* Stülpnagel and Jattkowski. Also wounded were Major Crohn of the I./*Abteilung* and his adjutant, Lt Kurt Liestmann, and crew. On 18 June, the Regiment reported the following panzer losses: twenty two panzers damaged, of which three Mk IIs, four Mk IIIs, and one Mk IV were listed as complete write-offs. The operational panzer strength of the regiment on 18 June consisted of seventy-one panzers.[50]

The battle had shown that the British tanks, even the heavily armored Matilda, were no match for the dreaded 88mm and the long barreled 50mm anti-tank guns (*Pak-38*), which were now beginning to arrive in greater quantities and were almost as effective as the 88mm. Looking back, there can be little doubt that the battle was won because of the 88mm gun, which once again effectively halted each British armored thrust, and in the end claimed almost eighty tanks, compared to the sixty-four claimed by the panzers themselves. For the British, they would have to begin a serious review of their tank tactics presently in use by their armored forces, as the German Flak and Pak gunners now became masters of the desert battlefield. On the morning of the 19th, the Regiment moved back towards its old rest area 5km north of Capuzzo, where it formed a large panzer lager with some of the panzers from *Panzer Regiment 5*. With Cramer temporarily in the hospital, the first priority for *Oberstlt* Ramsauer, now the acting regimental commander, was to ensure that all the wounded had been collected from the battlefield and evacuated to the regimental and division medical aid stations. Whenever possible the men preferred to remain with their friends and comrades, but in some cases those who had received more serious wounds and were unable to remain in the battle area with their companies were transported farther to the rear to the much larger hospitals located further to the rear in Derna, Benghazi, or Tripoli. The companies and *zugs* were reorganized, personnel changes were made, and preparations were made for a continuation of combat operations. At the Regimental *Stabs*, *Hptm* Bernau was assigned the duties as Regimental Adjutant, and in the II./*Abteilung*, *Hptm* Wahl was appointed the new commander, with Lt Bock becoming the *Abteilung* Adjutant. Lt Heuscher was named the *Abteilung* Ordnance Officer, and Lt Adam assumed command of the 6th Company. In addition, the Regiment possessed almost fifty percent of its organizational equipment.[51] Beginning on 20 June, the Regiment assumed positions between Halfaya Pass and Sidi Suleiman, where it was tasked with securing the border. In the meantime, brief formations were held where awards and decorations were handed out to the men. Many of those serving as a panzer crewmember received the *Iron Cross Second Class* and panzer assault badge, in addition to the wound badge for those who had been wounded in the fighting. The workshops and "I" Services wasted little time in the retrieval and repairing of many of the broken down and lightly damaged panzers. In the aftermath of the battle nine of the twelve captured *Matildas* were given to the Regiment, and from those nine, seven were found suitable for continued service and were quickly made available. There was plenty of ammunition available for the guns, and once the crews were properly trained the tanks were added to the ranks of the I./*Abteilung*. On the 20th, the Regiment reported the following panzer strength: three large and two small befehls panzers, twenty-eight Mk IIs, twenty-six Mk IIIs, and thirteen Mk IVs.[52] In the aftermath of the battle *Prime Minister* Winston Churchill was extremely disappointed with the failure of "*Battleaxe*" and the performance of

Wavell as Commander in Chief, *Middle East Command*. Churchill wasted little time in replacing Wavell on 21 June 1941 with *General* Sir Claude Auchinleck, the Commander in Chief India. *Lt General* Alan Cunningham, newly arrived in North Africa from a successful command in East Africa, was placed in command of the newly formed *British Eighth Army*, formerly known as the *Western Desert Force*. Churchill would insist on conducting another offensive action soon, but Auchinleck would have none of it until he was properly prepared and strong enough to do so. It was to be five months before the British attacked again. On 22 June 1941, while recuperating in the hospital as a result of the wounds suffered during Battleaxe, *Oberstleutnant* Hans Cramer was decorated with the *Ritterkreuz* (Knight's Cross) for his conduct and leadership of the Regiment in the combat actions at Fort Capuzzo and Halfaya Pass. Hans Cramer was a veteran soldier of WWI; he had been born on 13 July 1896 in Minden, and had entered the German army in September 1914. By the end of the year he had already been promoted to the rank of *Leutnant*. Cramer was assigned to the *15th Infantry Regiment*, where he was decorated with both the Iron Cross First and Second Class in addition to the Wound Badge. After the war he served in the *Reichswehr* in the *18th Infantry Regiment*, and was later appointed to command the *13th Cavalry Regiment*. In early 1939 he was promoted to the rank of *Oberstleutnant* and command of the *Panzer Aufklärungs Lehr Battalion*. From that position he was assigned as the commander of *Panzer Regiment 8*. After his wounds he was sent back to Germany, and while recovering from his wounds was posted to the position of *Chief of Staff, General Mobile Forces*. He rejoined the Regiment in time for the "Crusader Battles," and was wounded again in November 1941; on 5 March 1942 he was awarded the *Deutsches Kreuz in Gold* for his actions during "*Crusader*," and he later served as the commander of the German Mobile Forces and served a brief tour in Russia. In November 1942 Cramer was promoted to the rank of *Generalmajor*, and on 1 March 1943 was named the commander of the *D.A.K.*, and was destined to be its last commander. On 1 May 1943, he was promoted to the rank of *General der Panzertruppe*, and within two weeks was forced to surrender the *D.A.K.* on 12 May 1943. Cramer, along with *General* von Arnim, were taken prisoner by the British and were taken to England, and in an almost unbelievable act Cramer was exchanged on 15 May 1944 due to his chronic asthma condition. He was later to retire from active service and passed away in 1968. Cramer would be the first, but certainly not the last *Ritterkreuzträger* of the Regiment.[53]

A Break in the Action
As the summer heat of the North African desert beat down upon the men and tanks on both sides of the fighting, the two sides took the time to review the battles that had just been fought. It was during this time that both sides slowly attempted to build up their respective forces, as events all over the world and thousands of miles away influenced the battle for North Africa. There was the continued fighting by British forces in Syria and Iraq, which even though small and all but forgotten by many, drained British troop strength in the Western desert that May and June 1941. Those Commonwealth Forces battled and defeated the French Vichy forces and claimed a small victory in July. Also ongoing that summer was the drafting of the *Atlantic Charter* between the United States and England, which began to provide England with the much needed Lend-Lease materials for the British war effort. However, the largest event that took place that summer was Operation "*Barbarossa*," the invasion of the Soviet Union by the Axis Armies. This event more than any other that year was to have the greatest amount of impact on what decisions and actions were to be taken in the North African Theater. It was during that summer of 1941 that Rommel was nominated for promotion to the rank of *General der Panzer Truppen*; in July he was officially promoted, and on 5 August he was named the commander of *Panzergruppe Afrika*.[54] *Generalleutnant* Ludwig Crüwell arrived to take command of the *D.A.K.* In May another general had already arrived with his staff in Africa; *Generalleutnant* Alfred Gause was initially sent to Africa to act as liaison with the Italian African Command and to assist the *D.A.K.* in its command and logistical problems. Gause and his staff were not well received by the Italians, who felt as if the Germans were beginning to take over the entire North African campaign from them. Rommel himself felt threatened by the addition of another German general in Africa, and soon complaints were lodged in Berlin and Rome. Since Gause had never really begun to do what it was he was sent to do, he and his staff were incorporated into the new headquarters of *Panzergruppe Afrika*. Gause would assume the position of *Panzergruppe Chief of Staff*, with *Oberstlt* Siegfried Westphal as the *Ia*, while *Oberstlt* Fritz Bayerlein was sent to the *D.A.K.* as the Chief of Staff for Crüwell. Unbeknownst to Rommel at that time, he would later get on well with all of them, and the addition of these key staff officers was to become a major factor in the successes gained by Axis forces in North Africa. The greatest concern that summer for Rommel was to build up his striking power in order to defeat any British offensive attempts that were suspected of commencing in possibly October or November, and finish the business of driving the British from Africa. At the time there were rumors the Italian High Command realized the necessity of considerably reinforcing the Axis forces in North Africa. The German element was to be brought up to four mechanized divisions, and the Italians to an armored corps of three divisions.[55] Although this sounded like an excellent idea, in reality the campaign in Russia was at the forefront for receiving men and materiel, and for the near future the *Panzergruppe* would have to make do with what it had on hand. But for the men of the Regiment, they were thankful just to be alive that summer after the battles of May and June had passed, and they were once again able to take advantage of the extended break in the action. In the diary notes of the *3rd Company* it was recorded that on 26 June:

"*From the defense position at Qusllalla [Qalala] we should conduct the reconnaissance attack up until Bir Nub. Maier digs around in the old graves of derwish and he takes the skull of the dead as a memory. We set a Hurricane on fire, which had had an emergency landing. In the evening the 2nd Company relives us.*"[56]

Through the letters of *Gefr* Klaus Hubbuch we are able to gain a view of what it was like those early summer days of 1941:

"*The first difficult days are over, the Brits are not to be heard and felt, and they are forced to swallow a big defeat after their big attack. Over 200 of their panzers remain on the battlefield. They believed with their weapons and their thick hide [armor] "invulnerable" panzers to be superior to us, but we were holding tough and were not evading, instead we pushed on them until their steel colossus remained stationary and on fire. The most beautiful picture was always in the evening, when on the far horizon the burning tanks and crashed aircraft lit the night for a long way. My small fragment wound on jaw is almost healed. Here it goes very quickly, as long as it doesn't suppurate [get infected]. And we are again in our old place, we drive again to take a bath and continue with our usual desert lake, until the Brits will feel themselves strong again to attack us or the other way around. I have no idea anyway, and it doesn't matter to me. I was anew and struggled with every attack in this combat, when one can miss on this British enemy, who doesn't want to evade [retreat]. Finally we felt ourselves in our panzer secure only until we got one [destroyed one] ourselves. And even this had not influenced our crew. Now there is again smoke in the East [Russia] from the North Cap [Pole] until the Black Sea.*

Chapter 6: The Summer Battles, June-September 1941

Therefore it's so important for us here below [in Africa] to stay against main enemy, England. I got a lot of post in the meanwhile. Best regards to all who want to hear from me."

Later he wrote:

"I look out of the panzer. Around are sand and stones, then buried tents and again panzers, then nothing for a while, until the brier and again sand and again stones, destroyed Italian vehicle, and 1 km away a cistern with 'salted water' here to wash, then the sand hill, where from time to time pass the supply columns and SPWs, then again sand and stones, which go beyond the horizon flickering in the midday sun up to the blue sky. And so weeks long! In many letters [you write me] 'what can't you see and experience in the other part of the world' or 'how beautiful it must be to be able to take bath in the Mediterranean almost every day'. I have to laugh and think about how beautiful it must be for you who write such letters. But I am still delighted, that I am with the Deutsches Afrika Korps because here we have an important task, at the moment we are at the most important outpost for the motherland. And all of you at home are in our good feelings with us. Imagine, yesterday I received assorted magazines from the leaders of old troop 12, and similarly also often. Then I got a package from Aunt Wanda and grandmother, and with that many nice letters from you, all, which helps me for the short time to forget the above described surroundings. Especially evenings, we talk here often about the home. Recently we made a wonderful imagination walk through the Black Forest and took with us the great weather from our surroundings. And you at home hear the special reports, which are all about the soldiers in Russia, which successes are of course more visible as ours here [in Africa]. But yet don't forget us. Please continue to tell me in great detail and remain with my best wishes."[57]

In the first week of July, the men were off in pursuit of various training events; there was hand grenade practice on the 3rd, while on the 5th a sand storm blew up that caused very little activity on both sides. Since taking up positions near Sidi Suleiman, the Regiment was slightly harassed by daily British artillery fire until it too finally slacked off by the 10th. There were no casualties reported by the Regiment in these attacks, although on the 7th there was an attack by some Crusader tanks in approximately company strength; the attack was easily beaten off with the claim of one Cruiser tank that was destroyed by the *3rd Company*. By the second week the Regiment was out conducting a few minor reconnaissance missions, seeking information about deployment possibilities along the Via Balbia to the south, southwest, and southeast, as well as the area to the west of Capuzzo. Some of the Regiment's panzers were also moved in the area of El Ranla and along the coast. Wilhelm Hagios:

"During July we were in our old position and we had a shooting probe, Rommel was there with his adjutant, the press and some Italians. We were shooting at a Mark VI; it was sort of advertising itself. Since that time nothing else happened."[58]

On the 9th, *Olt* Johannes Kümmel, the commander of the *1st Company*, was ordered to report to the divisional headquarters, where he was decorated with the *Ritterkreuz* by the division's commander, *Generalmajor* Neumann-Silkow. In his speech the commander stated that:

"The attacks of Olt Kümmel on 15 June 1941 on the enemy west and east side of Capuzzo originated from his own initiative. With the coolness of this decision and its performance with no compromises he stopped any enemy penetrations to the north, where it would have broken into the sensitive combat supply lines and reaps Major destruction. Without these supply lines, which supported the Panzer Regiment 8 during the 3-day combat in the desert on the go with immediately needed ammunition and fuel, the successful fight against the enemy would not be possible. The hardness and dedication to his own decisions is to thank for the avoidance of the massive break-through in that point."[59]

Hans Kümmel was born in Coswig on 21 July 1909, and joined the *Reichswehr* in 1928, where he quickly obtained a rank of *Unteroffizer*. Kümmel remained in the military as the *Reichswehr* became the new *Wehrmacht*, and in 1938 he was transferred to *Panzer Regiment 8* and stationed in the town of Böblingen. In 1939, Kümmel was promoted to the rank of *Oberfeldwebel* and *Zug* Commander in the *1st Company*, a unit which he commanded all through the campaign in Poland. On 27 September Kümmel was awarded the *Iron Cross Second Class* in recognition for his leadership and the destruction of three light tanks. These three tanks would be the first in a series of destroyed tanks for this rising panzer ace. On 20 October, after the conclusion of the Polish campaign, Kümmel was awarded the *Iron Cross First Class*, this time for the destruction of four additional tanks, and soon after he was promoted to the rank of *Oberleutnant*. On 1 April 1940, just prior to the beginning of the French Campaign, Kümmel assumed command of the *1st Company*. During that campaign Kummel was always up front where the fighting was thickest, and took part in the break through at Sedan and the race to the Channel coast. On 5 June, Kümmel's panzer was destroyed when it rolled over a mine in the attempt to break through the *Weygand Line*. Kümmel was slightly wounded in the incident and was subsequently awarded the wound badge in black. After the victory over France in June 1940, the Regiment was then assigned light occupation duties in Southern France. Kümmel's *1st Company* was one of the first to arrive in Africa, and it was soon ordered east, in the Bardia area. It was during the attacks of *Operation Battleaxe* that June and the fighting that took place in and around Halfaya Pass, Sollum, Bardia, and Fort Capuzzo that Kümmel was seen by many Germans and Italians alike, who were amazed at his personal courage and daring in which he destroyed numerous British tanks despite being outnumbered. It was during this battle that Kümmel was given the name he would be forever known as, *"The Lion of Capuzzo."* On 9 July 1941, Johannes Kümmel was awarded the Knight's Cross.[60] He would continue to serve in the I./*Abteilung*, and within months he would reach the rank of *Hauptmann* and become the *abteilung* commander, where he would take part in all of the Regiment's battles through 1941 and 1942.

On the 11th, the Regiment was ordered to pull back to an area east of Sidi Azeiz and Bardia, and it was here that the Regiment would remain until the end of September. Kathe tells of a story during that time off:

"Once in Bardia, where there was also a sport festival organized, there were also Italians in the harbor. We were sitting there, so nice, and all of a sudden 'boom-boom-boom'. What did the Italians do? They went fishing with hand-grenades, they came with ammunition! They went over the cliffs and threw them from above. I went there with some of my soldiers and saw the wounded; one was with no leg the other was with no head. Over an hour later the Italians came and took them back, they were so reckless. To go fishing with hand grenades and now 10 soldiers dead. There was no combat at that time; we just had a rest there. So with my 3 soldiers we put bandages on the wounded."[61]

On 13 July, the officers and men of the Regiment were inoculated against Cholera; throughout the North African campaign many of the men would be victims of what the British termed *"Gympy Tummy,"* or as the Americans later termed the *"Trots."* In his report written in 1952 for the U.S. Army Historical Division, *General* Alfred Toppe wrote of the medical problems faced by the men of the *D.A.K.* in Africa:

> "In 1941, there were a great number of jaundice and dysentery cases. The reason was bowel irritations provoked by the drinking of bad water. Quick treatment with sulfa drugs afforded relief. (The tales that the health of some people was gravely damaged by sand fleas and scorpions are pure fiction.) The health of the troops requires constant control, which should go hand in hand with thorough instruction. The battalion and other medical officers do not suffice for this purpose. It is, accordingly, advisable to assign a sanitation officer to every company and battery to do this work in close cooperation with a competent medical officer. The sanitation officer should give special attention to a number of protective measures. He will have to see that the soldiers wear warm clothes after sundown and that they do not drink un-boiled water. Excretory matter should be buried after each movement of the bowels (the 'spade system' is preferable to the latrine system). Whenever the situation permits, the soldiers should observe a siesta. Control of flies should be organized (mosquito nets were used only in the latrines). Vitamin C should be taken regularly. In specified districts, Atabrine tablets should be taken to prevent malaria. If necessary, the water supply should be controlled (but only in the case of detached units). There should be a hygienic consultant for every two divisions, and he should be provided with a mobile bacteriological laboratory. In respect to insects, there are flies wherever there are people. At first, the troops had no effective means to combat them. It was only during the final phase of the African campaign that the newly developed means (for instance, a preparation called DDT) could be issued. There was no way of preventing infectious diseases, such as dysentery and contagious jaundice, from spreading. The only preventive measure that could be taken was the order for the men to bury all fecal matters immediately. Infringements were severely punished. In contrast to flies, which were everywhere, mosquitoes (anopheles) were present only in the oases and their immediate vicinity. Since these insects fly only at night, use of mosquito nets is an absolute necessity in these areas. Atabrine tablets were used to prevent the malaria transmitted by mosquitoes. Orders specified that one Atabrine tablet a day was to be taken. Since the units did not often stay at the oases for long, malaria cases were few."[62]

Men like *Uffz* Max Lebold would agree with some of *General* Toppe's comments, as even to this day Lebold, like a host of others, are forced to go for regular visits to tropical medicine clinics, and even in 2005 the doctors still do not know what the cause of his problems are, other than his service in Africa. During this relatively quiet period we again hear from *Gefr.* Hubbuch, who reflects in his letters:

> "*My Dearest!* Forty days since the tank combat, the quiet lies over the wide desert, where we stay looking forward somewhere through stereo telescopes [large bino], to recognize if anything moves behind the many destroyed vehicles in nobody's land outside or behind the horizon. The desert is like the sea, one can't find a shelter anywhere and stands as if on the presenter's table [stage], but can yield anywhere, from any distance change the fire discharge of guns. But one day we will again be able to take a bath in the sea and have more water as momentarily, I have to use some of the cologne sent to me by grandmother to wash myself and freshen up. We don't drink for a long time much of the liquid, which seemed to be unbearable a month ago. But when the evening comes, with you at home comes a corresponding 'breeze' and where you go for a walk in summer evenings with short sleeves, here we already wear the pullovers and overcoats with the collars high like those Africans ... on Rhine, whom I watched on our trip from Kehl and was not able to comprehend how can one wear the shawl, pullover and coat in the warm summer. But everybody is at the moment at its appropriate place and has to hold out. The single one is never happy, therefore his opinion is not counted in present times, and he should be given orders and with this badly disposed. That's how it is now and from this depends the success of the activity ruled from above, of every single one in the war, when they are gathered together come to impact in the victory. Now I have it enough for such a hot day as today, and for such a disconsolate surrounding. Where should I find the stimulation for further words? With all my heart felt wishes."[63]

While both sides were mainly content to refit during the brutal summer months, some moves and repositioning were made for Rommel's ultimate goal of capturing Tobruk. One such move even caused a bit of confusion when, on the morning of the 17th, an order meant for the Italian *8th Tank Battalion* (Rizzi) was intercepted by some of the divisional elements, and in particular the *8th Panzer Regiment*. The order stated that the *Rizzi Battalion* was to move that morning from its present position towards El Adem, located near Tobruk. The result was later reported to *D.A.K.* when it was discovered that the panzers covering the area around Sidi Suleiman had begun to pick up and move out. It was a simple error that was caused by an errant transmission, and fortunately was caught in time; the panzers were able to return to their positions that day. Even though the division was not on the move as a whole, orders did arrive detailing various elements of the division to form various *kampfgruppen* in the wake of any British probes or ventures to the west.[64] On the 27th at 0915hrs, the Regiment and some elements of *Artillery Regiment 33* received a telephonic order to prepare for a deployment to the south of Halfaya Pass and Sidi Omar. The order called for one panzer *zug* and one or two of the artillery batteries to take up positions there.[65] Once again reports indicate that nothing significant took place during this time, but still orders were issued to form a *kampfgruppen* or attach various elements to one another in order to meet any unexpected threats. Indeed, on the 4th the *D.A.K.* ordered the attached *3./Flak 33*, which until now had been subordinated to the Regiment as a supporting battery, should be ready for fire on the 5th at 0900hrs into the area near Bardia; as nothing ever came of the firing that evening, the Regiment was ordered to release the battery. However, some firing was taking place when, a week or so later on the 18th, the division pleaded in its evening report to the *D.A.K.* that it do something about the meaningless firing by some of the Italian elements that were hitting the assembly areas of the Regiment. On 21 August, as the men continued to relax and enjoy the break in action, there was an attack by *RAF* bombers on numerous targets to the west and southwest of Bardia. At the division's ammunition depot, located at the "*Brown House*" (6km west of Bardia), there was one soldier killed; this man, who is unknown to us, belonged to the supply service of the Regiment. A few days later on the 25th there was another *RAF* bomber attack, again on the "Brown House." Seven ammunition staples caught fire, and again the supply column lost another man killed.[66] As the summer passed, the men found themselves without too many defensive tasks to perform; there was little moving around and constructing fighting positions for the panzers every time one halted. Horst Sonnenkalb describes the summer and life on the frontlines:

> "*The front, that during the desert war wasn't a real front so to speak because the troops were so spread out. There were big distances between them. When there was no battle, when everything was silent, then there were about 8 – 10 kilometers between friend and enemy, called no-mans-land. That was the area for tank reconnaissance. Usually 8 wheeled*

vehicles drove their doing the reconnaissance. They got close to the enemy there, because Tommy was driving through there also, but no battles erupted."[67]

To make matters even more enjoyable, attacks by the *Royal Air Force* (*RAF*) against the divisional assembly areas were few and far between. The time off was, however, not wasted, and was put to good use, as the crews underwent extensive training in new battle tactics and gunnery drills, in addition to conducting mock exercises. One especially important item of instruction that was included was how to defeat the British *Matilda* tank; at the time that tank was the panzer crews' primary nemesis. Every tank commander and gunner was trained in identifying the weak points in the armor and where to best hit those heavily clad monsters. The primary principles of tank combat were especially valid in the desert: fire and movement, the quick advancement to close with the enemy while driving forward while holding fire, moving in the wedge formation with each panzer maintaining a certain distance between the panzers on the left and right, while maintaining a large enough distance to allow each panzer to be uncovered so that they could engage the enemy with individual and concentrated fire. It was still important to concentrate the combat power of the panzer wedge while not presenting the British tank and anti-tank gunners with too large of a target that would require only minor adjustments in traversing their guns. On 1 September 1941, the Regiment again added to its table of organization the heavy panzer companies. With the addition of the 4th and 8th *Companies*, which had been missing since the Polish Campaign, the 3rd and 7th *Companies* were reformed and given the designation as a heavy company. Wilhelm Hagios:

"On 1 September we were relocated to Gambut, east of Tobruk, there was an airfield there and we were down from there on the sea. Directly on the sea, at that time it was possible to swim in the sea. Olt Liestmann was our chief. Also on 1 Sept I moved from the Kfz to a panzer, I was there as a ladeschützen in a Mk III that was the accompanied panzer for the commander, we had at that time two of these. Olt Stiefelmayer was the commander and Beyer was the richtschütze."[68]

The Regiment had now been in North Africa for almost six months, but the constant changes in their operational environment and in weather conditions were still extremely difficult for the men to acclimate themselves. The Western or Libyan Desert, as it was known, was a broiling, desolate place that covered some two million square miles; it stretched from the Nile Delta to the frontiers of Tripolitania. This desert was dry, and considered one of the most uninhabitable places on earth. Vegetation in the desert was sparse; it was only along the coast or at a distant oasis that any green vegetation could be found, and only the small patches of scrub brush better known as "camel thorn bush" afforded the men a means of camouflage and fuel for cooking and warming fires. The extreme daytime temperatures could reach as high as 120F/50C in the shade, while the nighttime and early morning temperatures could drop to as low as 32F/0C. The cold was further aided by a cold biting wind that came up in the early morning hours. The extreme difference in temperatures caused the men to become quickly cold when the sun dropped below the horizon. This harsh environment allowed for few living things to exist, and those that could survive this country included the occasional gray fox, gazelle, jackal, and desert rats, in addition to a few types of small birds. But unlike those animals, there was a vast array of scorpions, chameleons, and beetles, and of course the ever-present fly and gnat. The fly was no doubt the scourge of the Western Desert; it pestered both friend and foe alike, it was present almost all day long, and not until the cool evening temperatures fell did they finally disappear for the night. There was little rain, and the fresh water sources were few and far between. With water hard to come by, and only a few times a year in which it rained, the occasional oasis and strips of vegetation near the coast were considered to be priceless. To collect water for the troops positioned further inland required either drilling or transporting it from elsewhere. For both the Germans and the British they were forced to de-salinate or chlorinate much of their water. Needless to say, water was a precious commodity, and it was rationed and reused whenever necessary—every drop was precious, and even shaving and bath water was later used in the radiators of the vehicles as coolant. There are few arguments that the Germans were nowhere near as prepared to fight a desert war as the British, who had been in the desert for many years. There will always be comparison to who had it worst or suffered the most, or who ate the better food, but there can be no doubt that the German soldier had it far worse than his British or Australian counterpart. The German rations were terrible; they were lacking in basic nutritional value and consisted primarily of whatever was at hand or could be scrounged from the Italian or Commonwealth forces. Much of what the German soldier survived on indeed came from British sources, and was a much anticipated prize after the fighting had ceased. Horst Sonnenkalb had this:

"Every once in a while we managed to capture a British tank truck. And we soon realized that the British food supplies were nothing to be sneezed at. The meal plan for the German Africa-Corps was put together by the kitchen chef 'Schmalhans' or Slim Hans. We neither had fruit nor fresh vegetables, only food in cans: rice with beef, noodle or pea stew, also white beans. When you got some bread once in a while you were lucky, usually we got crisp bread. Yes, and then there was cheese in tubes, sardines, Italian cans of donkey meat, imprinted with the initials AM, which we called Alter Mann [old man] and some called it sarcastically: Armer Mussolini [Poor Mussolini], in blocks chopped marmalade, which we disrespectfully called Adolf Hitler bacon. Every once in a while we'd get a bottle of beer, usually Paulaner or Münchner Hofbräu. Interesting who all made money because of the money. But in North Africa the rule was: No drinking alcohol from 10 am until 6 pm. If you drank one bottle during the heat of the day it could get a whole tank crew of 5 people feeling dizzy. During the heat of the Libyan Desert just one cup of alcohol was enough. Oh, before I forget, we also received aviation chocolate in flat tin cans with the inscription: Scho-Ka-Cola. I guess us panzer men had a privileged position compared to the rest of the formation. But the pilots stepped into their airplanes and chased the enemy, shot at the platoons with their aircraft weapons and dropped bombs on them. When they returned, the mechanics took over the planes while the pilot took a shower and then went to the casino. However, being a panzer crewmember you were a driver, gunner, loader, radio operator and a flight mechanic all together. You weren't able to return from a deployment and walk right into the casino, no, you had to get busy and make sure your panzer was ready for the next deployment. Even though, we didn't envy the pilots. We saw some of their planes crash to the ground while burning. So we at least enjoyed their chocolate. We did have a ration of last resort on board. But that was off limits to us, even though, if the meal crate would fly off, our ration of last resort would fly off with it. So we looked for kitchen cars with the Brits also. They had lots of delicious food in them. Argentinean corned beef, peeled potatoes in jars, cans with peaches, apricots, and big tin cans filled with cookies, also pudding powder, bitter orange marmalade, which we had to get used to, thick sweet canned milk, American cigarettes, sugar, flour, rice and all kinds of yummy things that our troops didn't have. In shot down British tanks we would find chocolate in tin cans, probably their ration of last resort. Rarely did we find water canisters. That was a tough one for the Brits too. I am sure the list of looted food wasn't complete either. You have to know though, that the British soldiers prepared their

food themselves. They had their stuck into one another square cookware and their cookers. That wouldn't have been good for us. It was better to get the warm food from the field kitchen or brought to the front lines in food canisters."[69]

Another means of acquiring foodstuffs was by trade, and here Kathe explains:

"*We normally did not have much contact with Bedouins, when the saw us, they were always very friendly. Only it was not allowed to touch and take pictures of the women. They made an emphasis on this. Only the men and children were brought to us for the wounds, which were caused by the Brits, by their bombs fragments. They never brought women. One time they brought me a radish; I planted the radish and onions at the oasis. There was the sickness, this diarrhea, and I had in the desert many canned food cans, there were letters 'AM' we use to say 'Armee Mussolini'. I collected it, I had sickness for 2 days also. I said to my cook, who was from near Altdorf, Ziegler you must make me a soup now with these 2 cans, with onions and leeks, and I ate that and it was good. I went to the Stabs doctor and told him about it. He then wrote to every company about it. None of us soldiers had anymore of the sickness; the meat had made it stiffer.*"[70]

Water at this point in time was still a great problem, one that had plagued the *D.A.K.* like the swarms of flies; the water still had to be brought from the de-salination and treatment facilities over a distance of 1,000km, and naturally when it arrived was still foul tasting, as it still contained a lot of salt. The re-supply for such items was the overall responsibility of the Italian forces; there were no fresh fruits and vegetables available. The men subsisted on mostly canned meat and legume or bean soup, which soon came to be the standard meal ration. The Germans have always been criticized for their lack of imagination and variety of combat rations for the fighting troops, as Kurt Kathe recalled:

"*First, it was normal for the German soldier to eat tube cheese and sardines which came from Norway, in the can there were two of them, thick and with scales, bleeeeeh, it was not possible to eat them. The first half-year for the German soldier was very very bad, until they understood what we needed and it was only through the Brits, who left us tents full of provisions that we survived.*"

Another veteran panzer man remembers:

"*It was horrible for the fighting formations, they use to whisper: Why don't you go and get it from Tommy? We took advantage of that numerous times in our awkward circumstances.*"[71]

The intense climate and lack of proper nutrition caused, first of all, jaundice and amoebic dysentery to set in; the number of sick men was always high, and detracted from the Regiment's overall fighting strength. Some of the sick were so bad off that doctors, when possible, prescribed a period of treatment back in Germany. During this time one such man was *Olt* Seidler, the commander of the *8th Company*. The sand flea and flies were also a constant menace, as Klaus Hubbuch remembers:

"*We are bothered by dreadful plague, the gnat. In there thousands there is no escape and with that they reach the critical mass that until now never presented such insolence. They don't bother to fly away in dozen to be spread like marmalade on the bread and throw themselves into the sweet coffee, so that the whole pot swarms, something dreadful. They sit on the face, around the mouth in bright patches and once it opens, they are already inside, in between the teeth, without [the need of] any additional meat ration to wish to oneself. Apart from this, there is nothing missing, we can satisfy our stomach with additional Corn beef from Argentina, Australia and England. So you hanker probably for the Mediterranean seashore with its hinterland and we the same way but later to home.*"

Klaus Hubbuch continues in letter excerpts from 17-23 July 1941:

"*My dearest! Yesterday and already once on Sunday we and our leutnant made real climbing party over the steep Wadis to the sea. This is a huge, eroded ravine, on which sides appear limestone layers and especially edged rocks. Sometimes one must jump down on 2 ½ meters in the places where vertical wall makes the climbing impossible, then again one must creep on all four on precipice under overhanging stones. From time to time there is some greenery, some hart leafage greenery, crickets chirp; how would it be here in the rainy season, where some places will gather water? Here are even sweet water sources, and we drank till all our bodies sparkled in water drops. We were like water carriers, with flasks hanging on the left and on the right, a little bit difficult, but we brought sweet water back and were able to brew tea with the help of the package from our comrades. The day before yesterday my comrades and I received the EK II [Iron Cross II] fixed to the stone [Medal], within the scope of the short writing from Abteilung Commander. One should wear it for three days, according to the soldier's tradition and later only the ribbon ornament. I was the youngest, not only by age, but also as a soldier here in Africa and for the first time in combat during the three days of Sollum combat, whereas other comrades were already in Poland and France in combat. At first I could not believe this. The official [Ceremony] concluded with the vow to further pursue our soldier's duty, and in the evening we had a comfortable meal together in company commander's tent together with our leutnant. I got it because after I received the bandage on my wound, I went back to the panzer and continued the assault at my post till the end of the combat. For me it was self-evident [obvious] as in the combat detachment every person counts during the panzer assault. I enclose to this letter five small nice mussels, which I found during my bathing on a light sand beach under the blue clear seawater. We frisked about as salamanders in the wonderful sea after a tiresome walk through the Wadi. The salt water holds you almost without moving. So we have here in Africa also pleasant hours. Today on 23.7.41 I also received the wound badge.*"[72]

In North Africa, life was hard for both officers and the troops alike, and there was very little difference between life on the front line and life in the rear areas. There were a few service and supply centers that could give one a temporary illusion of relief from the desert wastes. A few soldiers' centers, or *Manschaftheims*, were established, but they were a weak imitation of what lay elsewhere for resting troops. Because of the close contact of the troops with each other it was important that the officers set the example in bearing and living. Any extravagance on the part of an officer was immediately noticed by his men and scrutinized with a magnifying glass. On the other hand, life in the desert fostered the unique opportunity to create a high level of comradeship and *esprit de corps*, which in battle would bring out the best in both officers and men alike and prompt them to do the most extraordinary of feats. The desert offered few distractions for the troops, and it was the responsibility of the leaders to ensure and monitor the welfare of their personnel when possible. The German soldier endured far worse than his opponents, and in some cases his allies. The fact that there were few outside distractions made it easier for leaders to provide attention for their men. The desert offered an immense feeling of loneliness, which would overcome soldiers and leaders alike, and was more frequent in the desert when one felt himself totally isolated from his world and all that he held dear. The mood swings and bouts of depression had to be closely monitored, and leaders had to offer encouragement so that such moods would disappear. Even more important than rations for the well being of soldiers in the desert was the maintenance of regular communications with home. The word "mail" occupied a place of high priority in desert warfare as with all soldiers in every army, and every man and section concerned themselves with the rapid distribution of mail to the front lines. Newspapers also brought up-to-the-minute news from home and helped occupy a small bit of time, along with movies and theatrical performances—although few and far between—that brought a pleasant distraction and helped relieve the monotony of the soldiers' lives. During the weeks of training and waiting before the attack on Tobruk the men of the Regiment were fortunate that their Regimental band, under the able leadership of *StFw* Ernst Isensee, provided them with many hours of music. It was recognized early on that service in the desert took an enormous toll on the health and well being of the individual soldier, and it was recommended that each soldier be given a home leave if at all possible after six months of service. It was recommended that each man assigned to the *D.A.K.* be granted at least three weeks home leave in order to avoid any possible long-term damage to his health. In the very beginning of the North African Campaign, the normal service time for a German soldier was to be six months with regular rotations home. This plan, however, was quite impracticable, and between the years 1941-1943 was often never fully instituted. The result was that many soldiers found themselves having to serve without a break for anywhere from twelve to eighteen months, and it took its toll. It was well documented that even the hard-core leader Rommel himself incurred bouts of depression and disease that required treatment back in Germany.

A Reconnaissance in Force

The summer and autumn of 1941 was used by both sides to rest and reorganize. The British tactic for monitoring German intensions consisted of harassing fires by the long range guns of the Royal Artillery and constant surveillance carried out by reconnaissance groups equipped with *Marmon-Harrington* and *Humber* scout cars. Also during this time David Sterling's *Long Range Desert Group (LRDG)* carried out numerous reconnaissance and lightning fast attacks against Axis targets. The Germans, however, were less inclined to keep eyes on their opponent, and during those months of inactivity carried out only one reconnaissance in force. In mid-September 1941, led by Rommel himself, Ravenstein's *21st Panzer Division* was ordered to conduct a raid across the frontier wire into Egypt. The main objective would be the British supply dump at Bir Khireigat, about fifteen miles on the other side of the wire near Sofafi. Having subsisted on British rations over the past year, it was not hard to entice his men into another round of British supplies. "*Unternehmen Sommernachstraum*," or Operation "*Midsummer Night's Dream*" was also meant to help disrupt British offensive preparations and solidify the front before Rommel's intended attack on Tobruk. The raiding force would consist of panzers, armored cars, guns, and infantry. On 14 September, the *21st Panzer Division*, formerly the *5th Light* and recently re-designated as such, slipped out of its assembly area and moved southeast. The division split into two battle groups, the panzer heavy *Kampfgruppe Stephan* and *Kampfgruppe Schutte*. The plan called for *Kampfgruppe Schutte* to steal the booty while *Kampfgruppe Stephan* fought off any opposition.[73] To screen the operation, *Aufklärungs Abteilung 3* was ordered to move along the frontier at high speed in order to raise large clouds of dust and then begin transmitting confusing radio messages. Ravenstein's panzers, with Rommel at the head, swung deep into the British positions, but captured very little, as the *7th Support Group* under Brigadier "*Jock*" Campbell had already pulled back from the frontier and left Rommel empty handed before the forts of Sofafi. At this time the British *Ultra* intercepts were playing havoc with Rommel's plans; the British had secretly broken the German code system and were quietly spying on every directive that Rommel sent out. It is very possible that the British had been given ample warning of this impending attack, and had thwarted it by making a withdrawal from the area. There was one good bit of luck for the *D.A.K.* that came from the raid; it was the capture of a South African staff vehicle that had broken down and was captured with important documents and cipher material on board. However, there was speculation that even the documents were planted in an effort to mislead Rommel into believing that no major offensive was planned for the near future. To make things even worse, the *21st Panzer Division* ran out of fuel and was then bombed mercilessly by two squadrons of the *South African Air Force*. Rommel's *Mammoth* was hit; he had the heel of his boot blown away, and his driver was badly injured in one of the attacks.[74] This enterprising little raid had netted nothing, and Rommel was forced to retrace his steps back into Libya with little to show for his efforts. On 15 September, *Oberst* Hans Cramer returned from the hospital and led the Regiment on the 18th to an assembly area just north of Gambut, along the Trigh Capuzzo and Via Balbia, where the final preparations were made for the attack on the Tobruk garrison. The operational ability of the Regiment was significantly improved with the introduction of new personnel from the *Ersatz Company* in Böblingen and the addition of ten Mk IIIs and one Mk IV, which had arrived in Tripoli on 12 August. The Regiment did, however, suffer the loss of one of its members when *Olt* Springorum was killed when his transport plane was shot down on his return flight from Italy. The panzer strength report on 17 September totaled 134 operational panzers with forty-one Mk IIs, seventy-five Mk IIIs, fourteen Mk IVs, and four captured Matildas. The 134 panzers corresponded to approximately 90 percent of the Regiment's authorized combat strength.[75] On 15 September *Major* Crohn, commander of I./*Abteilung*, was reassigned to the *Heereswaffenamt* in order to validate the experiences of the panzer formations in Africa and implement new changes to panzer doctrine. Crohn was replaced by *Major* Günther Fenski, an experienced panzer man who came in from the *I./Abteilung Panzer Regiment 10*.[76]

7

The Crusader Battles October-November 1941

The months of September and October passed without much of anything taking place to affect the Regiment's situation. The men passed the time building small camp settings where they attempted to regain a sense of normalcy. On occasion the crews could get down to the coastal areas and take a swim in the cool waters of the Mediterranean. With the war in Russia going extremely well for the *Wehrmacht*, it was the plan of the *Oberkommando der Wehrmacht (OKW)* to support the assault on Tobruk, which was estimated to begin in early 1942. However, Rommel's attention had been totally focused on the taking of Tobruk, and though he was firmly committed with the plans of the *OKW* he had his own timetable for this attack, and set the date for 23 November. Rommel had now been promoted to the rank *General der Panzer Truppen* and placed in command of the *Panzergruppe Afrika*, and he was now determined that it was time for a move against Tobruk. The *Panzergruppe* had been steadily growing in strength, and Rommel's timetable demanded the fall of Tobruk by November and the neutralizing of any British attacks that winter, so that he could begin his final drive towards the Nile Delta by spring. It was thought that after Egypt was taken the *Panzergruppe* could be reinforced for a push towards Iraq and link up with German forces pushing south through southern Russia. These were grandiose plans to be sure, considering that the war in Russia was going well for now, but Hitler was totally focused on this theater, which would continue to garner the priority of men and materials, and the campaign in Africa would continue to be just a sideshow. For British *Prime Minister* Winston Churchill, the German attack on the Soviet Union made it clear that Hitler's armies would not be undertaking any invasion of the British Isles anytime in the near future. However, the British High Command did envision the potential danger that German forces presented to British positions in Africa and the Middle East, especially if they were able to push down through the Caucasus and link up with those forces pushing eastward from Africa. For Churchill, the North African campaign represented the primary means in which the British could still influence the conduct of the war and defeat Germany on the ground. Churchill was pushing his generals hard to defeat those Axis forces in Africa before they could endanger British positions in the Middle East. With the threat of a German invasion passing, large quantities of men and materiel that had been held in England were now freed up and allocated to the *Western Desert Force*. However, there was still the problem of getting these reinforcements and supplies past the German and Italian Navies and safely to Egypt. On occasion, like that of the "*Tiger Convoy*," British transports could make a voyage through the Mediterranean, but in most cases those transports were forced to make their way from Britain along a route that stretched along the coast of Western Africa down to the Cape of Good Hope and up along East Africa through the Suez Canal to the ports in Egypt.[1]

On 26 September, the British and Commonwealth forces comprising the *Western Desert Force* were re-designated as the *Eighth Army*, and since 10 August had been under the command of *Lt General* Alan Cunningham, an artillery officer who had just completed a successful campaign in East Africa. *General* Auchinleck, who was in command of the *Western Desert Force*, despite immense pressure from Churchill resisted all the latter's attempts to begin an offensive earlier than he was prepared for. And so throughout the summer and early months of fall the British re-equipped and reinforced those forces in North Africa. According to the British official history, by the end of October 1941 a total of 600 Cruiser tanks, 300 *Crusaders*, 300 *Honeys*, 170 Infantry tanks (*Matildas* and *Valentines*), 34,000 trucks, 600 field guns, 200 anti-tank guns, and 900 mortars had reached Egypt. The *Eighth Army* had just over 750 tanks, with another 259 in reserve.[2] At that time the *Eighth Army* was deployed in the following manner: the Tobruk Garrison, which consisted of the *70th Infantry Division* (Scobie)—the *9th Australian Division* having been replaced that summer—the Polish *1st Carpathian Infantry Brigade Group* (Kopanski), and the *32nd Army Tank Brigade* (Willison). The garrison was well dug in behind numerous obstacles, and was equipped with a fare share of the heavy Matilda II infantry tanks. The *XIII Corps* was commanded by *Lt General* A.R. Godwin-Austin, and consisted of the *2nd New Zealand Division* (Freyberg) and *4th Indian Division* (Messervy), and was supported by the *1st Army Tank Brigade* (Watkins). The *XXX Corps*, under the command of *Lt General* Willoughby Norrie, consisted of the *7th Armored Division* (Gott), *1st South African Division* (Pienaar), and *22nd Guards Brigade* (Marriott), and was supported by the tanks of the *4th Armored Brigade* (Gatehouse) and *22nd Armored Brigade* (Scott-Cockburn); those brigades were equipped with some 469 tanks (210 *Crusaders* and 165 *Honeys*).[3] By the autumn of 1941 enough men and materiel had arrived for a major reorganization within the *D.A.K.*, which since September 1941 was under the able leadership of *Generalleutnant* Ludwig Crüwell, the former commander of the *2nd (Motorized) Division* in France, and more importantly a person known to Rommel. The *D.A.K.* was now comprised of the *15th Panzer* (Neumann-Silkow) and *21st Panzer* (Ravenstein) Divisions. In an attempt to shape the *D.A.K.* into a true panzer corps, each division within the corps was reshaped along the standard table of organization for a panzer division. The *15th Panzer* transferred one of its two infantry regiments (*Schützen Regiment 104*) to the *21st Panzer*

102

Chapter 7: The Crusader Battles, October-November 1941

Division, and in return received the *Stabs* of *Sonderverband zbV 200* [for special use] and *Machine Gun Battalion 2*. With those two elements, and by absorbing *Kradschützen Battalion 15*, the division was able to form a second infantry regiment, *Schützen Regiment 200*. Each infantry regiment within the division was composed of four infantry battalions. In the 21st *Panzer*, there remained *Panzer Regiment 5*, and *Schützen Regiments 104* and *155*, each with three battalions. Even though the 5th *Light* had been upgraded and reorganized into the 21st *Panzer Division*, it still had not received any additional panzers. Additionally, there was the newly designated *"Afrika" Division zbV* (Summermann). This division was formed from a number of independent battalions and smaller, more specialized units. The principle formation of the division was the 361st *"Afrika" Regiment*, which was composed of a number of Germans who were former members of the *French Foreign Legion*.[4] Later in November this division would be re-designated as the 90th *Light Division*, and would become a highly mobile infantry division equipped with plenty of firepower in the form of artillery and anti-tank guns, but it would never have any panzers assigned to it. Although this division was technically not a part of the *D.A.K.*, it was there fighting right alongside both panzer divisions. Over the late summer and early fall no new panzer formations had arrived in Africa, but there was a substantial replacement of many of the medium panzers. *Panzergruppe Afrika* at this time was theoretically under the command of Italian Field Marshal Ettore Bastico, and was organized in the following manner. The Italian *XX Corpo d'Armati di Manovra*, a mobile corps under the command of *General* Gambara, consisted of the 132nd *"Ariete"* Armored Division (Balotta), 101st *"Trieste"* Motorized Division (Piazzoni), and the 55th *"Savona"* Infantry Division (de Giorgis). The corps was equipped with the improved *M-13* tanks, artillery, and a large number of 47mm anti-tank guns. The second Italian Corps, the *XXI Corps*, was under the command of *General* Navarini. In this corps were the 27th *"Brescia"* (Zambon), 102nd *"Trento"* (de Stefanis), 25th *"Bologna"* (Gloria), and 17th *"Pavia"* (Franceschini) Infantry Divisions. Those infantry divisions were considered non-mobile and mostly second-class, as they were equipped with some supporting artillery but totally lacked the most modern equipment. Those units were deployed from west to east as follows: Brescia, Trento, Bologna, and the 90th *Light* around the Tobruk perimeter, with the *Pavia* Division just a bit south of El Adem. The *Trieste* Division was deployed just north of Bir Hacheim, and the *Ariete* was just to the east at Bir el Gubi. The 21st *Panzer* was in lagers south of Gambut on and around the Trigh Capuzzo, and the 15th *Panzer* was scattered in camps along the coast north of Gambut. Out in front of the *D.A.K.* there were the 3rd and 33rd *Aufklärung Abteilungs*, which were screening from just south of Gabr Saleh to the Trigh Capuzzo. Finally, around Halfaya Pass, Sollum, and Sidi Omar were the *Savona Division* and the *Panzergruppe* pioneers with the *I./Battalion Schützen Regiment 104*, in addition to various other smaller detachments. The *Panzerarmee's* primary striking power, however, lay in the 249 German panzers, of which there were 139 Mk IIIs and 35 Mk IVs, with the remainder being the lighter Mk Is and IIs. The Italians had some 146 *M-13s* that brought the total to some 320 Axis panzers.[5] There were no reserves, and some fifty odd panzers could be found in various states of repair in the workshop companies. The Regiment reported 144 operational panzers at this time.[6]

Panzer Regiment 8 Chain of Command as of 01 November 1941[7]

Regiment Commander	Oberst Cramer
Regt Adj	Hptm Schefold
Nachr Offz	Olt Lehn
Ord Offz	Olt Jattkowski
Regt Arzt	StabsArtz Dr Becker
Ing Ofz/Werkshop Company	Major Schnell, Olt Blidschuhn
StKp	Olt Prion
Nach Zug	OFumstr Strack
I./Abteilung Commander	Major Fenski
Abtl Adj	Olt Bock
Nachr Offz	Olt Matthias, J.
Ord Offz	Olt Sontowski
Abt Arzt	OArtz Dr Port
Zahl Mstr	StZmstr Tischner
Ing Offz	OInsp Lampe
StKp	Hptm Ehrbeck, Lt Staengel, Lt Streibel
leKol	Olt Lindner, Lt Haag
1st Company	Hptm Kümmel
Zug Commander	Olt Heinrich
Zug Commander	Lt Peters
Zug Commander	Lt Thurow
2nd Company	Olt Kertscher
Zug Commander	Olt Knorr
Zug Commander	Lt Lüttich
4th Company	Olt Stiefelmayer
Zug Commander	Olt Schary
Zug Commander	Lt Bauer
Zug Commander	Lt Ihde
II./Abteilung Commander	Hptm Wahl
Abtl Adj	Olt Hess
Nachr Offz	OFumstr Bulla
Ord Offz	Lt Schnaidt
Abt Arzt	OArtz Dr Estor
Zahl Mstr	OZmstr Gisy
Ing Offz	Hptm Hauska
StKp	Hptm Klein, Lt Bastigkeit, Lt Bohland
leKol	Olt Weinert
5th Company	Olt Körner
Zug Commander	Lt Bönisch
Zug Commander	Lt Weiss
Zug Commander	Lt Friedrich
6th Company	Lt Adam
Zug Commander	Lt Becker
Zug Commander	Lt Lahusen
8th Company	Olt Wuth
Zug Commander	Lt Danz
Zug Commander	Lt Liestmann, H.
Zug Commander	Lt Pirath
Zug Commander	Lt Voigt

The Attack

The primary objectives of *"Operation Crusader"* were to first trap and destroy the Axis formations in Eastern Cyrenaica, and secondly to occupy Tripolitania, thereby pushing Axis forces from Africa entirely. The *Eighth Army* plan of attack called for the infantry heavy *XIII Corps* to attack, pin down, and isolate the garrisons of Bardia, Sollum, and Halfaya as the armor heavy *XXX Corps* advanced across the frontier wire on a wide front between Sidi Omar and Fort Maddalena, and then swung up south of Gabr Saleh and the Trigh el Abd, eventually moving off to the northwest and Tobruk. It was hoped that by these actions and movements the *D.A.K.* would then be forced to come out and do battle with them. The *XXX Corps* offensive was designed to challenge Rommel's armor and destroy it in a battle of attrition. Once the *XXX Corps* had successfully penetrated into the Axis' rear areas, the *XIII Corps* would then attempt to swing just south of Axis forces and take the Halfaya-Sollum-Capuzzo Bardia area. Once the *D.A.K.* had been destroyed the *XXX Corps* would link up near

El Duda with the Tobruk garrison, which would be ordered to break out of its perimeter at the appropriate time. Once linked up, together they would then defeat the remainder of *Panzergruppe Afrika* and force the remaining Italian and German troops investing Tobruk to give up their positions there and in Cyrenaica. The British operation was anticipated by many on the *Panzergruppe* and *D.A.K.* staffs, but Rommel himself seemed to be about the only one who could not convince himself that it was indeed coming, and therefore went forward with his plans to reduce the Tobruk garrison. So sure was Rommel that the *Eighth Army* would not attack, that a couple of days prior to the British attack he flew to Rome to present his own plan of attack and attempted to gain further forces. Rommel had only just returned to his headquarters the day before the British attacks began. One reason for Rommel's judgment was probably due to the fact that German intelligence and reconnaissance units had failed to pick up any substantial indicators of an impending offensive. On 26 October, Rommel had alerted his forces to prepare themselves for an attack on Tobruk anytime between 15-20 November. In response to this warning order, on the 13th the *15th Panzer Division* began to organize itself into three *kampfgruppen*; each of these *kampfgruppen* were to be formed around the primary combat formation in the group and bore the name of its commander. The first *kampfgruppe* was commanded by Hans Cramer and consisted of: *Panzer Regiment 8*; *Pioneer Battalion* 33 (minus the 3rd Company); *I./Artillery Regiment 33*; an infantry group of two companies from *Schützen Regiment 115*; the 3rd Company; and half of the 5th Company of *Flak Battalion 33*. The second *kampfgruppe* was formed around the *Stabs* of *Schützen Regiment 115*; it was commanded by *Oberst* Erwin Menny and consisted of: *Schützen Regiment 115* (minus two companies); *II* and *III./Artillery Regiment 33*; the 1st Company of *Panzerjäger Abteilung 33*; and the second half of 5./*Flak 33*. The third *kampfgruppe* was formed around *Regiment 200* and commanded by *Oberst* Erich Geissler; it consisted of: *Machine Gun Battalion 2*; the 3rd Company of *Pioneer Battalion 33*; *Panzerjäger Abteilung 33* (minus one company); and one heavy battery from *I./Flak 18*.[8] For weeks, the Regiment had been laying up in assembly areas along the coast north of Gambut, where various maintenance and training tasks were performed. But for many of the men it was a time to just relax and enjoy the relative comforts of this coastal position. One of those soldiers who was busy writing his thoughts was *Uffz* Klaus Hubbuch, a gun layer, or *richtschütze*, on a heavy Mk IV in the 8th Company, who thanks to his diary notes gives us a graphic and in-depth description of the battle to come:

"I was participating in a war officer application training seminar (KOB) but was lying for days in the sick bay tent of the company with my left arm tied upwards the wounds terribly discharging pus that wouldn't heal anymore. Our bodies were not used to the climate, the sun, the heat; the losses through the amoebic dysentery and pus wounds were heavy. Also the rationing was bad, no vitamins; for our provisions, [and] also for the D.A.K., the Italians were responsible. The bread often was moldy; the beef was tough and fatty in small cans with the inscription 'AM' and we often said 'Alter Mann' [Old Man], 'Alter Müll' [Old Garbage] or 'Ave Maria'; only very rarely a piece of melon; the normal ration, pea and lentil stew which went undigested into the shits; the tea was often salty when the water truck had waited too long in line, the drinking water was pumped dry and underground sea water had pushed into the well."[9]

The British attack commenced early on the 18th, under the protection of the *RAF* as the New Zealanders moved to just south of Bir Sheferzen before they began turning to the north. The *XXX Corps* crossed the frontier wire just north of Fort Maddalena to begin its march to the northwest. The *XXX Corps* advanced with the *4th Armored Brigade* on the right, the *7th Armored Brigade* in the center, and the *22nd Armored Brigade* on the left. Axis resistance was light in these areas, and most of the mobile reconnaissance elements simply fell back in the wake of such overpowering force. The advance was slower than expected due to the rains that had fallen the night prior and caused a number of delays, but by nightfall the British armor had reached the Trigh el Abd. Initially the German reaction to the offensive was slow, mainly due to the lack of ground and aerial reconnaissance, which had been grounded due to the mud and rains. Many of the German commanders felt that this attack was a major move by the *Eighth Army*, and wanted to move out immediately in order to meet it, but Rommel, who was still focused on Tobruk, was hesitant to give up most of his striking power to quell the attack. Both panzer divisions were alerted, however, and finally on the 19th ordered to assembly areas: south of Gambut for the *15th Panzer Division*, and Gabr Saleh for the *21st Panzer*. The Italian *Ariete* Division located at Bir el Gubi was ordered to be vigilant for enemy forces coming from the east. The Regiment had been alerted for possible action on 18 November, but little was known of the British attack and its objective, although it was widely guessed that the attack had the aim of relieving the Tobruk garrison. In his account Fw Gliese of the *Light Zug* of the *Stabs* Company I./*Abteilung* gives this account from his report written in February 1942:

"After the Tommy offensive in June 1941 had completely failed due to the defense of the German and Italian Africa Korps, it was clear to all of us that Tommy will make another attempt to destroy the small combat forces of the Africa Korps in order to get to the French border (Tunis). But when and how will they execute this intention? Our assumption didn't let us wait for long. On 18.11.41 in the evening at 1900hrs suddenly came the order to prepare for the departure march, something heavy was in the air. The zug leader was Olt Foders, nicknamed 'The Eye of the Abteilung'. I myself was leading the 2nd Gruppe with the driver OGefr Ade and the radio operator OGefr Krieg. The zug consisted of 5cm and five 2cm vehicles. The short question about what's going on was answered with a quick answer. The enemy broke through with strong forces at Sidi Omar. Sidi Omar was enough for us, as we knew the area well from the [previous] battles of June."[10]

The Regiment's vehicles were quickly prepared for combat, with only the most necessary of equipment being taken along, since most of the crews expected to return soon enough to their small encampments. Shortly after 2400hrs, the *abteilung* were pulled out of their positions and took up a line formation heading south into the desert. Since the 16th the weather had been poor, with numerous rain storms that transformed the desert floor into a sticky morass; the water pooled and was not absorbed quickly by the desert. Because of the poor weather conditions and the desert's inability to absorb the water, few, if any, perceived a real threat by friend or foe alike. Horst Sonnenkalb describes one such storm:

"On one November evening between Tobruk and the Halfaya Pass it was raining cats and dogs. Rain, finally rain! In the middle of the desert! It was a downpour, water in great quantities. The dried up 'Wadis' became torrential rivers. Anything that was in the way got torn away: guns, tents, even trucks and VW jeeps. All that drowned in the flood. Soldiers drowned in the desert."[11]

During the reorganization over the past months, it had been difficult to compile enough panzer crews in the combat units, as the number of sick within the Regiment was still very high. Many of the sick had reported themselves as "ready for operations" in order to remain with their own panzer crew. Klaus Hubbuch wrote:

"The Kampfstaffel was organized. I was asked whether I feel ready for action. Of course, the notification of sickness was forgotten! It was because of my success at the [gunnery] exercises that the 2nd or at least the 3rd shot of the Panzerkanone hit the target at a distance 600 -1200m, (my own estimation) that I was allocated as the gun-layer by Oberleutnant (Olt) Wuth. Long lines were standing in front of the ambulance tent - everyday life. My left index finger was cut open into my hand, the skin was partially removed, also there was much pus; a red ointment spread on it and bandaged. So that the first day I was sitting with splinted hand at the gun-layer seat until because of the good and fresh rations, which we fetched from the Toring-Trofs, the wound was healed."[12]

On 19 November, at 0800hrs the companies were informed that numerically superior British armored forces had been attacking in a westerly direction since the 18th, and that like the Sollum battle this attack was expected to be much the same, only longer in duration. The men were also informed that they would still be allowed the use of their tents during this phase. At 1500hrs a new alarm was received, and the combat units began their movement from their assembly areas south of Gambut. The entire *15th Panzer Division* was on the move towards Capuzzo and Sollum to do battle with the British troops who had infiltrated into the area west of those locations. The march route took them due south across the Via Balbia, where *RAF* bombers were interdicting the movements of the *D.A.K.* After crossing the Via Balbia the Regiment proceeded west along the Via Balbia, and eventually turned to the south once again, heading to its new assembly area located 30-40km into the desert south of the Trigh Capuzzo. According to Fw Gliese:

"The Light Zug moved to the single small palm tree south of Gambut on 19.11 and stood there for security protection during the night."[13]

At around 0030hrs, the order was given to halt, and as the crews peered out into the desert night they could see English flares popping overhead in the evening sky. That evening, as the crew of Klaus Hubbuch's panzer bedded down, their conversation turned to other thoughts:

"Around our panzer, the mood is good, finally after the long desert summer and fall, again combat in sight. Many are also thoughtful, what will happen to us? Lt. Heinz Liestmann is suspecting it, he thinks he won't survive the battle! Others are cheerful the ladeschützen [loader] Gefr Hans M. who just after his basic training flew in over the Mediterranean, telling about his last night in Naples before moving to the desert, he just wanted to know how it goes with the women, so he went to the whorehouse."

That evening, the situation at the headquarters of both the *Panzergruppe* and *D.A.K.* began to clear some, despite the fact that the overall situation and enemy intensions still remained unknown, although it was assumed that the attack was aimed at Tobruk. The company commanders passed down what little information they had to their men, and this much was clear; the enemy had attacked the Sollum front between Capuzzo and Sidi Omar. Sollum was still under attack, and a number of British armored groups had attacked the day before from the border region between Bir Sheferzen and Fort Maddalena; they were driving towards Tobruk from the southeast, and had already tangled with some elements of the *D.A.K.* But unknown to the Germans at this time this was the British offensive, and the armored forces sweeping up from the border region constituted the three armored brigades of the *XXX Corps*. Of these three brigades, the *22nd Armored Brigade* in the south was pushing on the 18th and 19th towards Bir el Gubi, where it would soon become engaged with units of the *Ariete Division*. In the fighting that took place there the Italians put up a much stronger than expected defense, and before long forty British tanks were lost compared to the loss of thirty-four Italian tanks. The middle element from the *7th Armored Brigade* was moving up towards Sidi Rezegh, and the brigade's journey had been almost uneventful, as it halted on the night of the 18th north of the Trigh el Abd and approximately 20 miles south of Sidi Rezegh. On the 19th, the brigade moved up and temporarily occupied the airfield at El Adem, which at that time was located to the rear of the *D.A.K.* While they were at the airfield the brigade destroyed a number of grounded aircraft, but after doing so withdrew a few miles south of the airfield. The brigade had also attacked some of the Axis forces tasked with investing the Tobruk garrison, and those troops were able to report the presence of British armor. A mixed group of infantry and Pak guns were moved to hold the ridge on top of the escarpment at Sidi Rezegh. The third armored element, from the *4th Armored Brigade*, was operating near Gabr Saleh and securing the left flank of the *XIII Corps*. This brigade had been in contact with German units since the 18th, and was now strung out for some distance while being engaged by *Kampfgruppe Stephan* (*Panzer Regiment 5*) of the *21st Panzer Division* near Gabr Saleh. One of the brigade's armored regiments, the *3rd RTR*, had advanced towards the airfield at Sidi Azeiz as it chased after elements of *Aufklärungs Abteilung 3*.[14] Early on the afternoon of the 19th, Crüwell had ordered that *Kampfgruppe Stephan* move to the southwest towards Gabr Saleh, where *Aufklärungs Abteilung 3* had reported a large British armored force. The *21st Panzer Division* moved off to the south towards Gabr Saleh, and in the late afternoon, after a long march, *Kampfgruppe Stephan* met with and engaged a strong enemy force consisting of tanks, artillery, and anti-tank guns. These forces were located about 10km northeast of Gabr Saleh. *Kampfgruppe Stephan* had formed for its attack in broad panzer wedges in order to meet the *4th Armored Brigade*, which had just been reorganized and now included the *3rd* (Ewin) and *5th* (Drew) *Royal Tank Regiments (RTR)* and *8th Kings Royal Irish Hussars*, and was outfitted with eighty tanks, including the American built M-3 *Stuart*, or *Honey* tank.[15] The M-3 was a technically reliable tank and had a cross-country speed of some 20mph/32kph; it weighted just 20 tons, and was armed with a 37mm main gun and up to four machine guns. *Kampfgruppe Stephan* struck the *8th Hussars* and was able to inflict a number of casualties on it until the *3rd* and *5th RTRs* could retrace their steps and come back to the fight. The battle was confusing, but died down as the sun began to set, and the *4th Armored Brigade* withdrew towards the south, while some elements of Stephan's *kampfgruppe* withdrew towards the north. In the meantime, the first elements of the Regiment were arriving in the area at around 1800hrs; however, they were too late to influence the battle. The British gunners claimed that day of having destroyed a large number of panzers, in some cases over twenty-five, but in reality only a handful of panzers were reported destroyed. That night, as the panzer crews finish preparing their panzers and began to settle down for a short rest, the *D.A.K.* issued orders for the following morning. The orders were for the *15th Panzer Division* to continue its advance towards Capuzzo at 0700hrs in the hope of catching one of these armored formations and defeating it. The *21st Panzer Division* was to break off the engagement at Gabr Saleh and concentrate all its forces for a drive on Sidi Omar. The *D.A.K.* Headquarters would accompany the *21st Panzer*, while *Aufklärungs Abteilung 33* continued patrolling the Trigh el Abd.

On the morning of the 20th, the entire *D.A.K.*, except *Kampfgruppe Stephan*, which remained behind near Gabr Saleh, was on the move east to do battle with the British forces there. Later in the morning *Kampfgruppe Stephan* broke off contact with its opponent and came up to support the attack on Sidi Omar. In the meantime, another *kampfgruppe* from *21st Panzer* sited a British force of approximately thirty tanks and called for help from the *15th Panzer*, which was operating just off to the left of it.

The sighting turned out to be nothing more than a group of armored cars, but it had temporarily halted the advance of the *D.A.K.*, and more time and, most importantly, valuable fuel was wasted before the advance could get going again. By this point, the panzers of *Kampfgruppe Stephan* had run out of fuel and ammunition, and an emergency resupply had to be called for.[16] As the *21st Panzer* was forced to halt and await its resupply, the *15th Panzer* had, after a 40km march, reached the airfield at Sidi Azeiz by 0930hrs, but nothing except for a few armored cars had been seen during the entire movement. At 1030hrs, the division discontinued its advance to Capuzzo and turned south towards Sidi Omar to assist the *21st Panzer*. At midday the division halted to conduct a resupply, and as the division took on new supplies reports came in to the *D.A.K.* Headquarters that the armored groups back at Gabr Saleh and along the Trigh el Abd were moving on Tobruk. At 1430hrs, Crüwell issued orders for the *15th Panzer* to turn south and west and move unsupported towards Gabr Saleh in order to cut off the Trigh el Abd and interdict British supply columns as they attempted to move forward and re-supply their armored columns. By the afternoon of the 20th, the situation was as follows: from the frontier wire to Tobruk, the *D.A.K.* was surrounded in the desert by strong British forces, as it sat immobile and out of fuel. The British *XIII Corps* was still attacking along the frontier around Bardia and Sollum, and the *7th Armored Brigade* stood well to the rear of the *D.A.K.* near the airfield at Sidi Rezegh. At 1500hrs, the *15th Panzer Division* was ordered to turn back to the southwest towards Gabr Saleh. The division advance was to be led by the Regiment, with *Oberst* Cramer taking the lead in his panzer. Throughout the 19th and 20th, through various ground actions and radio intercepts, clues were finally given as to the British positions. Most of the radio message traffic had been significantly hampered by British radio interference and jamming techniques, which had kept the *D.A.K.* mostly in the dark as to British intensions and movements. In the late afternoon hours, at approximately 1630hrs, after a nearly 60km march, the Regiment met with and engaged the flank of the *4th Armored Brigade*. With the sun behind them the Regiment formed and attacked in broad panzer wedges and met its previous foe from the Sollum battle. A violent attack followed, with the Regiment getting the better of the engagement, as it pushed the smaller and lighter British *Honeys* back to the south. The Regiment claimed a total of twenty-two tanks destroyed, but it is more likely to have been about half that number; the Regiment reported no losses in the encounter.[17] Fw Gliese wrote of the day's activities:

"We started the drive early on the morning of 20.11 at 0630hrs in the direction of Sidi Azeiz to the east. The Light Zug was deployed as reconnaissance in front of the Regiment, along the Trigh Capuzzo. After a speedy drive through 150km of desert, at 1600hrs in the afternoon we began the battle with the enemy for the first time. Shortly after the combat started the first Tommy tanks caught fire, the enemy preferred to retreat. Due to darkness the combat stopped for this day, as the enemy was defeated today."[18]

With the coming of night, the *4th Armored Brigade* withdrew a few kilometers over the Trigh el Abd to the south, where contact was finally lost with it. The Regiment, after its long march and subsequent battle, settled down for the night in a hedgehog position. The supply trains, after a bit of searching, moved up to re-supply the panzers with fuel and ammunition. The consumption of ammunition during the day's short combat action was extremely high. Some of the panzer crews reported shooting up to sixty main gun rounds. Hubbuch remembers:

"As the gun-layer on this day I shot sixty-two Granaten [rounds]. After a longer night drive we went into a hedgehog, the 2nd Zug [platoon] takes over the security."

However, there was still work to be accomplished on the panzers until 0130hrs, such as refilling fuel tanks and ammunition racks with high explosive rounds for the main gun and belts of ammunition for the machine guns. Radio operators, in addition to cleaning the bow machine gun, had to fix their communications equipment and antennas that during the day took a tremendous beating. Horst Sonnenkalb describes how the panzers and equipment were beginning to take a beating:

"At that point we still initiated battle repeatedly with the British tanks that were pressing forward. Because of the preceding arduous tank battles our combat strength had suffered tremendously. We had had too many casualties. We started to have engine and transmission damage. In a few panzers the very high frequency radio wouldn't work anymore. Troops that had to disembark got hurt or killed. I had to disembark numerous times also. I had to do small repairs outside the panzer, so our 21 ton vehicle would stay ready for operation. Luckily nothing happened to us."[19]

That evening, the Regiment received a better overall picture on the developing battle and the dire need for the panzers, which were needed to halt the British attacks near Sidi Mufta and Sidi Rezegh. At 0230hrs, the men were roused from whatever sleep they had been able to catch and readied for departure, which was scheduled for around 0300hrs. The 20th had been an almost fruitless day for the *D.A.K.*; except for the losses it inflicted on the *4th Armored Brigade* most of the day had been wasted, along with valuable fuel chasing after an enemy who was nowhere to be found. As the *D.A.K.* searched in vain and finally ran out of fuel, the situation at Tobruk was becoming increasingly serious. The tanks and infantry of the British *7th Armored Division* had captured Sidi Rezegh and were threatening to break in to Tobruk and relieve the garrison there. Therefore, orders were issued during the night calling for the *15th Panzer* and *21st Panzer*, once it had been re-supplied, to move northwest and attack the British in the rear. The plan was to send the *D.A.K.* northwest with *15th Panzer* on the left and *21st Panzer* on the right. It was the first time that the *D.A.K.* was operating as an entity.[20] The situation was now critical, and it was important to get a good start on things before the British resumed their attacks on Tobruk. At 0300hrs, the Regiment began to slowly break contact with the British as it disengaged itself and took up its march positions at the head of the division. After forming into two separate columns, the division began the march northward at approximately 0600hrs. The Regiment took the lead position in two columns, followed by the majority of the artillery and Flak guns,[21] while they in turn were followed by *Schützen Brigade 15* as the division headed off in the direction of Sidi Mufta. The division moved out quickly through the desert with the *5th Panzer Regiment* moving along its right flank; the Regiment had been realigned off to the left, where the *22nd Armored Brigade*, attempting to reach the *4th Armored Brigade*, presented the greatest danger to the left flank of the division. As the *D.A.K.* broke contact south of the Trigh el Abd the British attempted to follow them, but a screen of Flak and Pak guns from *Regiment 200* were able to halt them. It was a cool, slightly overcast and rainy morning as the panzers rolled northwards; however, the cool weather and time of day allowed the panzer crews an unlimited view of up to ten kilometers. During the march there were some British tanks spotted off to the left, and a short time later another group of German panzers were observed securing the area behind the Regiment. The British tanks that were spotted were most likely those of the *22nd Armored Brigade*, which had moved from Bir el Gubi to help support the *4th Armored Brigade*. Along the way some of the panzer crews actually took time out to quickly halt between burning British tanks and help themselves to a breakfast of leftovers—items like canned fruits and vegetables, chocolate, bread, and even canned beer were easy to come by. After a brisk and uneventful movement that was free of enemy contact, except for the occasional sighting of armored cars, the division continued its march northward. Near Abiar Edeidat the division encountered a motorized column from the *1st South African Division*, which was advancing northward from the south. A small detachment was sent off from the main column to attack them, and after a brief action was able to disperse the South Africans. At around 0900hrs, after covering approximately 25km, the Regiment found itself approximately 10km northwest of Sidi Mufta. At this point the first elements of the division began to receive strong artillery fire as they attempted to close up on the Regiment. Earlier that morning the British had been alerted to the movement of the *D.A.K.* and had turned two of the *7th Armored Brigade*'s tank regiments south to meet the panzers. While the *6th RTR* (Lister) remained at Sidi Rezegh, the *2nd RTR* (Chute) and the *7th Hussars* were ordered to move south in an attempt to halt the drive. Those two armored regiments came on with over a hundred Crusader and Cruiser tanks, and as they did so they were hit by the *21st Panzer Division*, which came on striking the *7th Hussars* in the flank as the *15th Panzer Division* drove forward between the two regiments and split the them in half. The British attack was fully supported by artillery, but it was overcome, as the panzers rolled forward and began laying down a deadly fire that halted the attack and eventually forced the British to break off their assault and withdraw. After another advance the first elements of the Regiment rolled upon a line of tanks from the *2nd RTR* supported by a number of anti-tank guns. It was here that the Regiment suffered its first losses of the battle, which initially did not go well for the Regiment, according to British after action accounts; the German panzer gunners initiated the engagement by opening fire on the move, and were quick to turn about and withdraw before they could be engaged. The account goes on to mention that much of the fire was extremely inaccurate, which was most likely due to the inability of the gunners to fire on the move.[22] The Regiment suffered two dead and many wounded. The wounded were taken care of by the supply trains, but there was no possibility of evacuation because of the threat posed by the *22nd Armored Brigade* located further back to the southwest. *Olt* Wuth, commander of the *8th Company*, and another crew member were wounded when their position came under sudden artillery and machine gun fire and they attempted to re-enter the hull of their panzer. Wuth was hit between the abdomen and thigh, but his crew wasted little time in notifying the *Oberarzt* by radio for a pick up. However, there was no way the doctor could be brought forward, and the crew was instructed to bandage him as best they could and bring him to the closest aid post for treatment. Wuth was in horrible pain, but the panzer was still surrounded and unable to move out of the immediate area. *Olt* Wuth was adamant that he did not want to be taken captive! And so, he remained with his company and continued to lead it until the situation finally presented a chance for evacuation. The *2nd RTR* was to claim fifteen panzers destroyed in the engagement, and the Regiment claimed an equal number before turning away to the north.[23] This number seems to a bit exaggerated, as the British only reported one tank being destroyed. After this initial attack there was a lull in the battle as the panzers withdrew to refuel and rearm before continuing their attack later that afternoon. Even though the British tanks did not attempt to follow them, the Regiment moved off slowly and encountered a number of anti-tank guns, forcing some elements to halt.

Only through the high expenditure of ammunition was it possible to silence these anti-tank guns. Early in the day, after the *D.A.K.* had departed the Gabr Saleh area, the British advanced northward and struck *Regiment 200* and *Schützen Regiment 115* in the rear and along the flanks, but those formations fought off their pursuers and were able to successfully link up with the division a short time later. After a short halt to reorganize and resupply itself, the battle continued as the *15th Panzer Division* struck to the southwest and hit the *7th Armored Brigade* and the *7th Support Group*. As the panzers rolled forward to do battle with the British armor, the infantry elements from *15th Schützen Brigade* advanced on Sidi Rezegh, but were held up by well entrenched infantry forces; they eventually overcame this resistance by the late afternoon. For the second attack, the panzers were now supported by a number of Pak and Flak guns, which were able to secure the flanks and hem in the British tanks with their direct fire. As the panzers rolled forward they were successful in knocking out twelve of the remaining twenty-six tanks of the *2nd RTR*, which was then forced to withdraw from the battle area. The Regiment also reported that several British tanks, as they withdrew, attempted for the first time a direct attack on the accompanying 88mm Flak guns located on the flank. The attack against the 88s soon proved fruitless, as a number of smoke pillars soon appeared and some fifty prisoners were brought in. Only the arrival of the *22nd Armored Brigade*, which arrived on the scene a short time later, and the coming of darkness saved the British tanks from certain annihilation. At approximately 1630hrs, the attack on Sidi Rezegh had progressed towards the airfield some eight kilometers to the north. Also at this time the Regimental *Stabs* issued an order for panzer commanders and gunners to conserve their ammunition! The weather was again turning a bit worse; it had begun to rain again, and to complicate matters that day, *RAF* fighters had attacked the division and Regiment throughout the afternoon in groups of about forty aircraft. During those attacks a number of panzer commanders and crewmembers were wounded by flying shrapnel, but luckily none of the panzers were immobilized in these attacks.[24] Up to this point the Regiment had claimed twenty-eight enemy tanks and six armored cars in the day's fighting. *Fw* Gliese wrote in his report of the day's fighting:

"But already on 21.11 there were further tasks for our proud Panzer Regiment, which had proved itself in the Poland and France campaigns. The names of the battlefields of Nova Weiss, Stonne and Amiens were enhanced in Africa by Capuzzo in June and more would be added soon. So the speedy advance went on 21.11 in the direction of Sidi Rezegh, so that the enemy's intention to destroy the ring around Tobruk would not come true. Up until that time the Light Zug remained with all its vehicles despite that a small part of them have damage after the long and speedy drive. Around mid-day 21.11 the Regiment had to break contact from the enemy, in order to rearm with ammunition and fuel. Due to the quick withdrawal from the enemy three panzer Mk IIs had not regained the Regiment and so came the first losses. From now on we were only three vehicles available for our not exactly simple tasks. In the afternoon the Regiment was to be deployed against the enemy's overwhelming numerical strength. Already by the morning the enemy had caused us some heavy and bloody losses and had retreated behind a hill. The Light Zug got the mission to find the enemy and force it out of its position which was not good for us. We had hardly reached the hill as the shooting of English cannons and anti-tank guns started whistling in our ears. When the zug leader's vehicle shot its first 5cm round, the enemy tanks went into the fire position with the main aim on our three panzers. We were able to achieve the better attack position for the I./Abteilung and therefore the task of the Light Zug was completed and the enemy was under attack from the flank by the 2nd [Company] and in front by the 1st Company and lost in this fight over 30

tanks. This was another big win for the history of the Regiment. But the battle was not over yet, and there was no silence. On the same evening we went further, in order to hit and destroy the enemy wherever it was possible to fight. We drove distances up to 100km, the thoughts and hopes that our three panzers will get through well did not materialize."[25]

Towards sunset the attack began to bog down in the fog and twilight, but the *7th Armored Division* was still in action with over two hundred tanks, and when one of its brigades pushed in between *Kradschützen Battalion 15* and *Schützen Brigade 15* the Regiment was once again called on to plug the gap and check the British attack. As the sun set that evening and a low fog swept the battlefield contact with the enemy was lost, and 8km south of Sidi Rezegh the Regiment moved into a hedgehog position for the evening. Earlier in the afternoon the pressing enemy situation and the day's events around Tobruk influenced Crüwell in his decision to pull the *D.A.K.* out of the area around Sidi Rezegh in order to gain more freedom of movement and avoid being encircled. His plan was to move the *D.A.K.* out to the east, and so he issued orders for the *21st Panzer Division* to strike at Belhamed, near the axis bypass road, while *15th Panzer* held its positions and assisted in supporting the move of *21st Panzer*. The attack by the *21st Panzer* came off quite easily, as the area had already been secured, and the British had withdrawn from that location. Late in the afternoon, reconnaissance parties were sent out along the Trigh Capuzzo towards Gasr el Arid in order to determine British positions. The withdrawal was scheduled to begin the following morning, with rearguard elements holding their positions until 0300hrs. The *15th Panzer Division* departed at around 2000hrs and found the going very difficult as it attempted to locate and negotiate the steep escarpment in the rain and fog, but in the end the division was able to make a successful, undetected move. Later that night the Regimental supply trains were able to move up to deliver ammunition and fuel to the panzers, and by midnight the re-supply operation was in full swing. Because so many high explosive rounds had been expended throughout the day by the panzer crews the number of high-explosive rounds was insufficient, and the crews had to make do with only half full ammunition racks. Klaus Hubbuch of the *8th Company* wrote:

"*I still have to report fuel and ammunition; then a short nap until 2200hrs when the ammunition arrives, our panzer has fired fifty-nine rounds; 2230hrs watery soup arrives but the water for drinking is not sufficient; 2400hrs fuel for refilling.*"[26]

Later that night, the Regimental *Stabs* with the I./*Abteilung* moved off to an assembly area north of Gambut, having to again undertake a night march of about 30km. Needless to say there was no time for the crews to rest.

Battle of Sidi Rezegh
At around 0500hrs on the morning of the 22nd, the II./*Abteilung* received its wake up call and began its day. It had remained in position just north of Sidi Mufta, and had spent a rather easy night, but with the coming of dawn began to receive strong artillery fire from distances of about 2,000m—these artillery positions had not been discovered during the night. There also appeared a number of armored cars in the valley in front of the *Abteilung*. It did not take the panzer gunners long before they were returning fire, mostly with the 75mm cannons from the Mk IVs, which caused the British guns to fall silent, and four enemy armored cars which ventured in too close were hit and destroyed as well. The situation that morning found the British *7th Support Group* still in possession of the airfield at Sidi Rezegh, while the *22nd Armored Brigade* with seventy-nine tanks lay 3km to the south on a ridgeline, and the *4th Armored Brigade* lay 4km to the southeast with 108 tanks.[27] Unknown to both sides was that the II./*Abteilung* had spent the night located in the middle of these two tank formations. Further in the north the *21st Panzer* was still operating around Belhamed, while *Aufklärungs Abteilung 3* covered the ascent to the southwest of Gambut, on the Trigh Capuzzo. The *4th* and *22nd Armored Brigades*, after re-organizing and re-supplying themselves, went searching for the main body of the *7th Armored Division*, and along the way made contact with the II./*Abteilung*. The British tanks opened fire from distances of over 2,000m with the II./*Abteilung* returning fire, but at that great a distance was unable to determine the impact of their rounds. Under the protection of a fog bank, the II./*Abteilung* withdrew from the enemy at 0930hrs to the northeast over the Trigh Capuzzo into the assembly area of I./*Abteilung*. During the withdrawal elements of *7th Armored Division*, possibly the *2nd RTR*, attacked the II./*Abteilung* from the left flank; a lively fire fight broke out as both sides exchanged fire, but with little success, because of the distance and visibility. After that fire fight the British tanks broke off the contact and melted away into the desert, where they were lost in the growing dust and fog. After the II./*Abteilung* had departed the high ground it was again forced to halt, this time because all of the available fuel had been expended, but by mid-day the *Abteilung* was able to replenish its fuel and ammunition racks and resume the march towards Gambut. Accompanying the panzers was a section of *Panzerjäger Abteilung 33*, which was echeloned to the left as flank security. The II./*Abteilung* reached the regimental assembly area located 10km from Sciaf Sciuf at around 1530hrs.[28] In the meantime, *General* Crüwell ordered *21st Panzer* to move and secure the high ground south of the Trigh Capuzzo, and not allow the British possession of that high ground, which dominated the valley through which the track ran. By securing the escarpment the plan was to hold the British while *15th Panzer* moved into a favorable position in which it could attack the British flank. While *Panzer Regiment 5* was sent on a wide counterclockwise sweep around to the west, *Schützen Regiment 104* swept clockwise and then drove south to the northern escarpment. Those formations were able to inflict serious losses on the *7th Armored Division*, and it was forced to give way to the east of the airfield and take up positions on the southern escarpment. At around midday, *Aufklärungs Abteilung 33* reported a strong enemy force of up to three hundred vehicles advancing from the south on Sciaf Sciuf, and therefore it was decided that the *15th Panzer* move to attack the flank of this formation. The terrain did not permit driving due west, so instead the division swung to the southeast, where it hoped to use the steep terrain to its advantage by pushing up from the rear of this formation and pin them against the escarpment. After suffering a number of delays, the advance, which was scheduled to begin at 1400hrs, was postponed until 1430hrs, as the division departed in battle formation, with the Regiment taking the lead, followed by the remaining battle groups. *Panzerjäger Abteilung 33* was aligned to the left of the division in order to provide a flank security. As the division reached a point roughly 10km southeast of Sciaf Sciuf it sighted two large tanks formations, which were observed southwest and northwest of the division. As the southwestern group—most likely that of the *5th South African Brigade*—was approaching the division it was assessed as the greater threat, so it was attacked first. For the panzer crews the situation looked grim; with hundreds of armored vehicles located on both its flanks it looked to be just a matter of time before they would be overwhelmed and taken prisoner, so many of the men began to prepare themselves for the inevitable. *Fw* Gliese of the I./*Abteilung Light Zug* gives his account of the day's fighting:

"*Already on the afternoon of 22.11 the vehicle of Fw Kynast fell out of combat due to transmission damage and could not make the fast speed. Thus we had to fulfill the mission of the Light Zug [with] only with one panzer Mk III and one panzer Mk II, whereas normally it should be six panzers to conduct it. When we were driving on the reconnaissance for the Regiment, we found one of our own Panzerspähwagens which had already made a reconnaissance in the necessary direction and thus simplified our mission. It located around 150 vehicles at 15km distance, among them a large number of tanks, which should not escape their elimination. We [had] hardly passed by the burned out tanks from yesterday, when we saw the gun flashes of English tanks, which seemed to be in the fight with another unit and thus hadn't noticed our advancement. They discovered us only at 1000m distance. With six tanks they approached us at a high speed in order to prevent our advancement. But at the same time our cannons spoke their word of elimination. Already after two minutes four tanks [had] caught fire whereas the others were leaving the field in a rush. But Olt Foders with his vehicle in high speed hit the right flank of the enemy and I was not able to follow this speed in my panzer Mk II which already had two [drive] springs damaged."*[29]

But unknown to the panzer crews, the battle was going very much in their favor, and it was the British forces who found themselves in a bad situation—a situation in which things would only get much worse. The attack went in as the division threw in the weight of its panzers, flak, and artillery guns, and struck a serious blow to the British column, which after leaving a number of its tanks on the battlefield fled in panic. The division did not pursue this force, but instead it turned about to attack the northwestern group, which consisted of the *4th Armored Brigade*. However, as the panzers turned and approached the group it failed to give battle and quickly withdrew to the north. The time was now 1700hrs, and as night began to fall over the battlefield the division continued to pursue this enemy towards Hill 175 in the failing light. As darkness began to fall the division ordered the Regiment towards the northwest, where it was to strike the eastern flank of the *7th Armored Division*. While en-route, the panzers unexpectedly stumbled across a British truck column that was making its way forward to conduct re-supply operations. The lightly armed column was taken by surprise and was engaged by the panzers, which had little trouble in destroying a large number of those vehicles and scattering the rest. After making short work of the column the advance continued, where the Regiment again came upon another force, this one composed of British tanks, but before they could engage those tanks the British tankers wisely chose to withdraw rather than fight it out with the panzers, who were now smelling blood and in hot pursuit. Wilhelm Hagios explains:

"Stiefelmayer was at that time our commander in the panzer, he was the adjutant. On 22nd November in the evening (this date many also get it wrong, so it was really on the 22nd when the regiment stab had its first encounter with Stuart tanks), they were driving to the west parallel to us, in the same direction as we did the entire night. We mostly drove at night but for the Brit's [their] evenings were mostly free, as they couldn't orient themselves and so they disturbed our radio with stupid la-la-la music so that we couldn't communicate by radio. During the evening there was a short combat with one or two tanks, British Stuarts."[30]

Hans Cramer decided to pursue those forces in the darkness towards Hill 175 with just his I./Abteilung. At the head of the *abteilung* was Major Fenski, in his command panzer, with the rest of his companies following slowly behind. Gliese's account goes on:

"The darkness came already and the distance to Olt Foders at the head of the 1st Company was already 1000m. The amount of enemy tanks in the meantime [had] increased to twelve and they were already of the altitude of the standalone. Olt Foders only observed forward and so I reported by [radio] call to the Abteilung that at the distance of 300m there are located a large number of English tanks. He [Folders] hunted them successfully with several rounds, so that one enemy tank was put on the curb [damaged]. With deepening darkness there was a danger that Olt Foders could be interpreted as an enemy tank. In order to avoid this I drove with high speed towards the head of our panzers. The Abteilung gathered and the 1st Zug received the task to continue reconnaissance until the position where the steep slope would prohibit the advancement of panzers. What will happen now? because we were to reconnoiter in the direction of Tommy's retreat. We hardly drove 5km when the zug leader stopped suddenly, 'I am 5m left of him.' At the same moment the light beams of the zug leader flashed and I recognized two Tommies, who ran to their vehicle. But it was not enough. He stands in front of the Tommy tank! What happens now? Would we drive forward, or return or stay put, because the Abteilung is 50m behind us. Due to our halt and our report, the Abteilung already took measures to prevent any opportunity for the enemy to escape. The enemy was surprised as they had not counted on our arrival in such darkness. But the ammunition car caught the fire and lit the night as if it was a day."[31]

Before long Fenski's panzer ran into a cluster of tanks, and only from about ten meters did he recognize the outline of a Stuart tank. Fenski quickly decided to drive into the assembly area with just his command panzer and one Mk III while he ordered the remainder of his *Abteilung* to deploy as follows: the *1st Company* to move around to the left with the *4th Company* to follow it, while the *2nd Company* was ordered to the right with the *Le Kol* following. The order to march was given with the additional order to *"free fire"* into any tanks attempting to escape. Olt Bock, the Abteilung Adjutant, quickly began sending up white flares, which illuminated the lager area, and then Fenski ordered the panzer commanders to switch on their headlights, and in no time the encirclement was complete. With the British tanks illuminated in the glow of headlamps and Bock's flares, *Uffz* Sauter and his *Kradmelders* were ordered to drive forward into the lager and begin rounding up prisoners with their *MP-40* submachine guns. One of the British tanks attempted to make its escape, but Sauter was able to quickly jump up and force the hatch open, spraying the inside of the tank with his submachine gun.[32] As the surprised and shocked British tanks crews began to give themselves up a couple of tanks attempted to break out of the encirclement, but all three were quickly knocked out, sending the message that there was going to be no escape here. The situation was extremely tense, and in order to speed up the removal of the crews from their tanks, Fenski ordered that the panzer commanders were to dismount with their *MP-40s* and assist the *kradmelders* in rounding up prisoners while the gunners and loaders were to be ready to open fire at the slightest attempt to escape. As the Germans moved in some of the British tank crews took their personal weapons and shot three of the panzer commanders. Despite warnings to the contrary, one of the British officers did manage to set fire to three of the Honeys before he was killed. In the headlights of his own panzer, Fenski now began to realize just what he had stumbled into. He and his *abteilung* had just captured and taken prisoner almost the entire headquarters of the *4th Armored Brigade* and *8th Hussars* Regiment. The account by Hagios continues:

"Then around 2300hrs, or earlier, Major Fenski who led the I./Abteilung captured a brigade headquarters of the British tanks we had encountered during the night. Shortly after we said [to them] 'Everyone get out peacefully', the richtschütze and ladeschütze stayed inside [the panzer]. We captured the whole quarter of a British, triangle of vehicles, only three tanks escaped out of thirty-five tanks, and a general of the tank headquarters also got away. We were able to provision ourselves, as they

all had brand new clothes, [there were] mostly Stuart tanks in which they had thrown there items into the tanks, everything was good and we took it."[33]

Gliese's account goes on:

"I couldn't believe my eyes when I recognized about 30 English tanks. By the order of the commander, the leaders got out of the vehicles with machine pistols and took the English as prisoners. Some of them tried to escape with weak resistance or were afraid to be taken prisoners but one could see the hopelessness of this intention. During this night's coup de main were taken about 200 prisoners, among them a Brigade general, 25 tanks and one battery of artillery and supply vehicles. With that the successful 2nd day of combat has finished and one more honorable page was written in the annals, where more was still to come."[34]

Horst Sonnenkalb wrote of the event:

"At 1430hrs we were standing in the area of Sidi Muftah with the front-line to the north with the following formation ready for the attack: on the left the Panzer Regiment 8, to the right of it Panzer Regiment 5 from the 21st Panzer Division with 40 panzers which was directly attached to Panzer Regiment 8 during this attack. After nightfall our regiment centered close to the airfield at Rezegh for the attack. We achieved a duly noted success. The English 4th Armored Brigade was destroyed. During the night hours our regiment lost contact with its enemy who was losing ground. Totally unexpected our 1st Battalion came across a clustered crowd of tanks during the dark night. They weren't able to tell that they were Brits until they were really close to them. Both sides were totally surprised. No shot was fired. Within seconds the battalion commander Major Fenski took the initiative. His adjutant Leutnant Beck had to shoot white flares nonstop. Then the following order came through the radio: "All panzers turn on your headlights!" Now the adverse cluster of tanks was being illuminated as if it were daytime and they still didn't move. The enemy seemed to be paralyzed. Major Fenski drove through the hedgehog position with his command panzer. We received more orders via voice radio. He [Fenski] ordered his companies around the hostile crowd of tanks. A few Tommy tanks tried to escape at the north end. Again via a voice [from the] radio: 'Fire!' The tanks that tried to escape were captured and the iron ring around the enemy tightened. In order to avoid panic and to not shoot ourselves the next order came: 'Cease Fire!' And the next: 'Panzer commanders dismount! Take machine guns with you!' Was Fenksi insane? Again via voice radio: 'Take prisoners! gunners and loaders stay in your panzer!' The Brits surrendered. Among the prisoners were a general, 17 officers, 150 NCO's and troops. We captured 35 tanks, numerous scout cars and other war machines. That was one of the greatest adventures I experienced in Africa."[35]

Amongst the prisoners taken were some 250 Officers, NCOs, and men, thirty-five *Honey* tanks, eight armored cars, a loudspeaker vehicle, and eleven trucks.[36] With this action the *4th Armored Brigade* was virtually destroyed, and the *7th Armored Division* seriously weakened. On the night of the 22nd, the Regiment reformed again in the assembly area south of Sciaf Sciuf, where there was warm and cold food waiting for the tired panzer crews, but first there was weapons cleaning, rearming, and refueling to be done. According to its daily report the Regiment suffered the following losses: seven dead, amongst them Lt Lüttich and *Fw* Harmgarth of the *2nd Company*; ten wounded; and three missing. Six Mk IIs, eight Mk IIIs, five Mk IVs, and one large and two small command panzers were destroyed, of which one Mk II, the Mk III, and one Mk IV were complete write offs.

Since the offensive had begun the Regiment claimed the destruction of the following: seventy-four main battle tanks and ten armored cars, as well as the capture of some thirty-five tanks.[37]

The Battle of Totensonntag

The situation had been more or less peaceful from about 0100hrs onward, but there was a wake-up call and orders issued at 0230hrs to prepare for movement. The *II./Abteilung* was ordered to relocate again downhill from the escarpment and move to the northeast approximately four kilometers to link up with the remainder of the Regiment. In the *8th Company* Olt Wuth returned to assume command of his company, but was only able to do so by following his panzer in a wheeled vehicle. *Uffz* Hubbuch, the gunner in Wuth's panzer, moved up to assume the position of panzer commander. From 0300hrs on there was quiet again, and the crews took the time to lounge around and catch a few additional minutes of sleep before the order came at 0630hrs to begin departure. The *II./Abteilung* was ordered to move to and link up with the Regiment, which was still located at the spot of the previous evening's capture of the *4th Armored Brigade's* headquarters. It was Sunday, 23 November; the German *"Totensonntag,"* or "Sunday of the Dead," where back in Germany the date was used as a day of remembrance to remember the fallen soldiers from the *First World War*. Before this day was over there would be many more young soldiers joining their fallen fathers and uncles. During the night and early morning both sides made a number of moves, and developed plans so that the overall situation looked something like this: the British *XXX Corps* was to reform south of the southern escarpment, while the *5th South African Brigade* and *22nd Armored Brigade* were to hold their positions along this escarpment. The *1st South African Brigade*, which had been previously located further in the south near the Trigh el Abd, was ordered to move up and assist them in that task. The German plan, after a slight modification by Crüwell, was to move the *D.A.K.* southwest across the rear of those British forces defending the southern escarpment and link up with the Italian *Ariete* and *Trieste* Divisions of the *XX Motorized Corps*, which would strike out from Bir el Gubi and link up with the *D.A.K.* The non-motorized elements of the *21st Panzer Division*, consisting mainly of infantry, were to hold their positions near Sidi Rezegh and along the northern escarpment. For the attack *Panzer Regiment 5* was to be detached from its division and subordinated to *15th Panzer Division*. After the link up had been achieved the combined German-Italian force was to then strike north and pin the British against the escarpment and destroy them. The morning had dawned with a thick layer of surface fog, and by 0700hrs it had barely lifted as the Regiment began to move out. The divisional commander, *Generalmajor* Neumann-Silkow, issued a statement that morning to all divisional elements stating that today the British forces would be finally destroyed. The planned attack formation called for *Panzer Regiment 5* to comprise the second echelon, but due to lack of communications it was not possible, because that regiment failed to appear in time to launch the attack.[38] As the Regiment moved off its order of march was the *I./Abteilung* up front, followed by the *II./Abteilung*, and when it showed up, *Panzer Regiment 5* would form a second echelon behind them. All formations were ordered to move southward in the standard panzer formation of a broad panzer wedge. Within a half a hour of beginning its movement, a number of stalled British formations were spotted heading northwest directly in the Regiment's line of march. *Uffz* Paul Etzel of the *Stabs* Company *I./Abteilung* now provides a glimpse of what he saw that day in a report written on or about 22 February 1942:

"We started driving early in the morning, and could not guess how memorable this day would be. The previous evening we captured an English brigade, and were proud and in a good mood. I drove as the 5th Z.b.V.

vehicle close after the commander, Major Fenski, when from the small hill ahead of us descended two German panzer Spähwagens and approached us at high speed. Our commander stopped, the same as Spähwagens, and I saw how the officer from one of the vehicles had greeted our commander and chatted with him. At that time I realized that there would probably be something to shoot at and said to my radio-operator, who just awakened and asked what was going on, that something will start really soon. Right after speaking the words, there was an appearance of the group of three English armored scout cars from behind the small hill, with their typical small flags on the antennas. So our [panzer] commander Uffz Bohmann roared: 'scout cars, turret 12 o'clock, distance 1000m, HE grenade, free fire!' Our little Ladeschützen Gefr Oster, had already prepared the round and our Richtschütze, who was snoozing with his head buried into his aiming apparatus, was awake in the same moment and already launched the round from the pipe. Our round hit the soft ground 1-2 meters behind one of the vehicles! We wanted to shoot again, but the Tommies escaped from our view at high speed."[39]

The Regiment rolled forward and took these British formations completely by surprise; the appearance of such a strong force behind them confused the British, who had thought that the various elements of the D.A.K., namely the panzer formations, were still located in the vicinity of where they had been the previous night, north of Sidi Rezegh, but now they suddenly appeared to the rear of the British, striking the 7th Armored Division and 5th South African Brigade as it was moving up to Sidi Rezegh. The order was quickly given, and the panzers rolled west into the British columns to begin the destruction of these unlucky strays. At the same time, a small number of approximately twenty British tanks and armored cars were spotted moving in from the east. Both of these elements had neither the desire nor the force to begin tangling with such a heavy concentration of German panzers, and so they quickly attempted to move out of the path and kept away at a safe distance. Etzel continues:

"In the meantime we stopped on the small hill and saw in front of us a huge formation of the supply line vehicles, in the distance about 2-3000m. I thought: splendid, here will be a funny battle, and already we went into the racing drive with our commander ahead [of us]. I had to take everything from my vehicle, sixth gear and pedal to the metal, often even pulled the starter, so quickly we rushed. I shouted to my Richtschütze 'Man, shoot, will-ya!' but apparently there was a ban on shooting, so only a few shots went [over] from our side. Only our radio-man, who probably had itchy fingers, got his MG and gave it a full go. The Tommies remained totally puzzled standing next to their vehicles. They probably had frozen in place. Some still had coffee mugs and breakfast rolls in their hands. The kettles were still above the fire, and we were already very close. The surprise disappeared and some Tommies made attempts to escape in their trucks. Some were lucky, but many stopped, burning in front of our tank rounds and MG-bursts of fire, immediately everything we had was shooting. Our comrades ahead of us were now in panic. They threw themselves into protective trenches and I as a driver did everything possible to drive along the trench with my tracks."[40]

Reports soon came in that the lead panzer elements were encountering and rampaging through many of the disorganized and separated British units that consisted of mainly soft skinned vehicles. Seeing the destruction that was about to befall the helpless column the twenty odd tanks, stragglers from an unidentified armored unit, now attempted to distract the panzers away from their main task. Fortunately for the British that unidentified unit was the 3rd RTR, which was at the same time moving southeast when it ran into the panzer column. With the arrival of the 3rd RTR and some additional anti-tank and artillery guns they were able to save some of the light skinned motorized columns from total destruction. The bothersome tanks were kept at bay by the guns of *Panzerjäger Abteilung 33* while the I./*Abteilung* struck the large gathering of vehicles. The fighting was not all one sided, and while *Major* Fenski, who was being closely followed by *Oberst* Cramer, attempted to reach an over watch position he drove on with his panzer only to find himself directly in the middle of a British artillery park. Soon a hail of machine gun and tank rounds were fired at his panzer and he was mortally wounded in the head. Etzel's report goes on:

"Suddenly I noticed the common dust fountains ahead of me and soon the air starts singing above. Aha, I think, we are getting fire and here I close my driving hatch. As the driver I can't identify where this fire comes from, but it must be tanks and anti-tank guns, which open up a fierce fire on us. In between here are some shots from the damned gipsy artillery. Here it goes off the entrance hatch and the vehicle becomes lit as a day. What is going on, I think and turn around to see the puzzled faces. Little Oster is so frightened that he is not yet even thinking about closing the hatch. The 4cm shot has broken through, torn the hatch and went in front of Oster's face ripping the ceiling lights. But here we are already through the formation. The fire ceases, the smoke is everywhere and in the distance one can see the English supply line vehicles disappearing at a high speed. Here is time to collect things, we get out as the fire has ceased completely, and we smoke and fix our broken tracks. The hole of the round shot through the hatch and looks like it has been drilled through and is observed with mixed feelings. And now what is this? It whistles and pipes in the air and soon the first rounds hit near our panzer. We set ourselves aside a little more but remain in place. It's here when we hear that our commander Major Fenski and the driver of our light Zug, Olt Foders, have fallen. Thus the mood is somewhat lower, but when I saw that Hauptmann Kümmel took over the Abteilung, I was in a good mood again."[41]

The 3rd RTR was doing a good job of keeping the division occupied while allowing many of their own vehicles to scatter and escape. The panzer wedges now began to lose their formation and become intermingled while burning up precious fuel and ammunition.

Oberst Cramer in his command panzer, along with one other Mk III, re-entered the killing zone, where his panzer was soon hit by anti-tank guns and was damaged and unable to move. Under the covering fire of the accompanying Mk III the command panzer was finally able to extricate itself and fall back to the I./*Abteilung*, which was now under the command of Hans Kümmel. As the panzers continued their advance the I./*Abteilung* came in direct contact with the 3rd RTR, which attempted to hit the flank of the *abteilung* from the south. A violent firefight then ensued in which three Honeys were destroyed before the remaining twelve broke off and withdrew at high speed. During this attack, the panzer companies were constantly being harassed and followed by strong artillery fire. Time and time again the Regiment came across British transport columns, which it was able to make short work of and easily break any defensive stand. A number of prisoners were taken and sent back to the rear while their vehicles were given to the supply trains. The engagement would continue for the next couple of hours until, at around 1130hrs, the D.A.K. finally ordered its formations to go around these supply columns and continue on its mission to link up with the *Ariete*. The division continued to the south, where it was forced to halt to replenish fuel and ammunition. Etzel's final notes of the day:

"The artillery blessings have stopped finally and after some time we drove again and arrived to the 21st Panzer Division and Ariete Division, *and here we learn that soon the attack will begin. I think for myself that when the 21st and Ariete attack together, nothing can go wrong. We drive immediately into the attack position. Next to my vehicle the artillery battery takes the position and sends some packages towards Tommy, who doesn't take long to respond and lay some well aimed shots discovering our battery, so that we must get into diving position as soon as possible. Here begins our attack. In the distance at approximately 2000m is located again a huge formation of light yellow colored English vehicles. From there I notice a wild fire from the muzzles. But from the left and right must come the [artillery] blessings, because some smack on my vehicle. It must be Pak, I think for myself. Our attack progresses quickly. Kurt shoots, halts, 2-3 shots, and quickly drives ahead; soon we are located amid the torches of burning supply line vehicles. Here it's only valid to be careful, and browse around with Karacho, because we get nice anti-tank fire from everywhere. Some more bursts from our MG into the vehicles, and now through at high speed, and again get together. We get out and see how the following infantry and Pak complete the picture and closes up so that no Tommies can escape. Shortly afterwards arrives General Rommel, and our commander Hauptmann Kümmel reports to him. He seems to be happy about this attack, so that, like in other days, we captured a lot of prisoners; many vehicles were destroyed and captured. The vehicles of Tommy burned like torches all night. This is a Totensonntag which no one who participated will forget, as far as I can see it from my driver's seat."*[42]

The appearance and subsequent scattering of these British forces had made the division commander want to swing north immediately and continue the destruction of these formations, but the plan was adhered to, and so the panzers continued their movement south to concentrate their forces. The advance towards Bir el Gubi was continued with the panzers continuing to receive strong flanking fire, but at around midday the Regiment had finally established contact with the *Ariete* Division 8km north of Bir el Gubi. As seemed to be the norm for the Italians, they were very cautious in their advance to the link up with the *D.A.K.*, and that delay, coupled with the action against the many supply columns, allowed the disorganized British forces to escape eastwards. At 1235hrs, the Regiment was ordered to halt in order to prepare for its attack to the north. In the meantime *Panzer Regiment 5*, which had been engaging British tanks in the east, finally appeared, taking up positions behind the Regiment.[43] The *D.A.K.* now issued orders for an attack northward lead by the *15th Panzer Division* and the attached *Panzer Regiment 5*, with the *Ariete* Division invited to take part since it did not fall under the command of the *D.A.K.* The plan called for an attack to be launched on a wide front instead of the single concentrated punch normally favored in order to prevent the encircled enemy from escaping destruction. After the number of delays suffered during the morning hours the *5th South African Brigade* had been allowed enough time to construct a defensive zone some 10km in depth with a screen of anti-tank guns pushed out to cover the rear. The *22nd Armored Brigade* had also been able to move up to support this plan. By 1430hrs the Regiment had reached an area near Sidi Mufta with its front facing to the north, with the remainder of the division organized further back in successive lines. The first line was composed of both panzer regiments: the *8th*, with nearly one hundred panzers, was on the left where the heaviest contact was expected, and the *5th* was aligned to the right with its forty panzers. The second line was composed of two infantry regiments: *Schützen Regiment 115*, located closely behind the II./Abteilung, and *Schützen Regiment 200* located on the right with *Panzer Regiment 5*. For this attack the infantry had been ordered to follow closely behind the panzers and remain seated in their vehicles until they had breached the initial defensive positions. This was an unusual order,

because it was the standard tactic for the infantry to dismount just prior to its objective and advance on foot. This new tactic was ordered because of the depth of the enemy positions and the time it would take the infantry to move in and take the various positions. As the division's formations began to take up their attack positions they were subjected to a number of problems: there was a steady pounding by British artillery, which was in action with over one hundred guns and had a serious effect on the preparations. The other was that the division was unable to gain the proper amount of space to form for its attack due to a large swampy area located further to the rear. In an attempt to halt the British guns, German artillery opened up with counter battery fire, but were foiled in their attempts to do so because the British guns were located in strong, well concealed defensive positions, and the German guns were too weak to cause them much damage. At 1445hrs, the division ordered the advance to begin, and the panzers rolled forward, with the infantry following in the second line. Artillery fire, which was already disrupting the preparations, now increased, and especially began to target the German panzer and infantry regiments. Under the cover of the guns of *Artillery Regiment 33* the division began its attack. Hans Cramer was quick to recognize early in the attack that success could only be made possible if the Regiment could keep its given direction of attack, which was aimed at the center of the British position, and without paying any attention to the flanks, which had now begun to become very disruptive due to the absence of the *Ariete* along the left flank. The South Africans had deployed numerous anti-tank guns, all cleverly concealed among the many destroyed vehicles already littering the battlefield. It was these guns which began to inflict heavy losses on the supporting infantry. Despite the firepower arrayed against him, Cramer led the Regiment on their assigned azimuth and controlled it via short radio commands. By 1530hrs, the I./Abteilung had broken into the enemy positions and destroyed a number of the 2-Pounder anti-tank guns. The break-through paralyzed the South African gunners, who let up the amount of fire directed against the Regiment, and for a few minutes the frontal and flanking fire ceased, but further to the rear the British artillery fire hitting the II./Abteilung and follow on units remained very heavy. *Hptm* Kümmel now made an urgent call for additional infantry forces, which were needed to move forward through the battlefield and begin scouring and routing out the numerous gun emplacements and to round up prisoners. Finally, from the left rear came *Schützen Regiment 115* moving through the openings created by the panzers. The *115th* was able to quickly overrun the positions, and it captured over one thousand prisoners and numerous guns.[44] The excitement, however, was short lived, as the infantry again came under concentrated artillery fire from the left flank and suffered extremely heavy casualties in the process. With a number of breaches now created in the defense and the infantry forces now closed up, the Regiment moved off to the north, and in stiff fighting broke through into some of the British artillery positions. As the panzers began rolling up some of those positions the Regiment again came under attack from direct fire from 25-Pounder guns, but instead of waiting for the infantry to move up Cramer decided that the attack must continue without waiting. At 1600hrs, the Regiment was located deep behind the South African positions, with the I./Abteilung attacking to the north through 10km of defensive zone manned by the South Africans. The II./Abteilung was driving to the northwest, in order to gain some maneuver area and free up elements of *Schützen Regiment 115*, which were then located behind the *abteilung*, and push back a counter-attack which had begun by a force of some twenty British tanks belonging to the *8th Hussars*. After knocking out seven enemy tanks the British force withdrew. As the battle remained stable on the left the same could not be said about the present situation to the east, where *Panzer Regiment 5* was located. That regiment, along with their accompanying infantry, had drifted too far to

Chapter 7: The Crusader Battles, October-November 1941

the right and was taking heavy fire from the north and east, which caused it to give ground. The result was that only a handful of panzers were able to link up with the I./*Abteilung*. The failure of *Panzer Regiment 5* to move forward seriously hampered the entire assault, and caused the attack to lose its strength and momentum. To make matters worse, radio contact with *Panzer Regiment 5* was lost after its withdrawal and valuable time was lost in re-establishing contact. Neumann-Silkow continued to call on the *D.A.K.* to speed up the arrival of the *Ariete* Division and help relieve some of the pressure on the left flank. The Regiment was now faced with having to continue its attack with just the I./*Abteilung* because the II./*Abteilung* was unable to move up quickly enough, as they were still fighting off the attacks by the *8th Hussars* and waiting for the infantry to move up and secure the area. These actions caused a lull in the attack, and by failing to concentrate all the available panzers the British defenses again became quite active. The II./*Abteilung* was still attempting to fight its way north and link up with its sister *abteilung*, but the going was agonizingly slow, as calls came in from the infantry, who continued to ask for panzer support in order to help deal with the British along the left flank. A section from the II./*Abteilung* was ordered to turn around and move back to the south and link up with the infantry. At 1620hrs Cramer, who was located in the middle of II./*Abteilung*, was able to report the following: Kümmel and his I./*Abteilung* had been successful in breaking through the positions in the north and destroying the enemy artillery in the rear areas. The II./*Abteilung* was still situated on the left flank, where it had moved into the enemy positions and was defending itself until the infantry could get through to it. The II./*Abteilung* was able to suppress most of the fire against it, and had been able to destroy a further nine tanks. Also at around this time *Panzer Regiment 5* had finally been able to close up on the right flank, but there was still no contact with it. With the situation improving on the right flank and fearing continued delays on the left, Cramer quickly ordered the II./*Abteilung* to attack and force the enemy back while bringing the infantry forward under any circumstances.[45] Under a hail of accurate fire these orders were carried out and conducted without regard of casualties, which in the end resulted in the loss of all the company commanders and a great many of the panzers. The Regiment was fortunate that *3./Flak Regiment 33*, which had been subordinated to the Regiment and led by its I./*Abteilung* commander *Hptm* Fromm, was able to provide strong supporting fire with its guns and secure the release of the panzers that had been attacking. Klaus Hubbuch remembered:

"*Enemy tanks are fleeing from our attack, a large group of them are captured and many prisoners taken, a swampy area makes the pursuit harder; British artillery fire hits exactly between us with fragments hitting the panzer, the 88mm Flak arrives to help, but the distance to the forty enemy tanks is to great and therefore nobody attacks and a fire fight cannot develop. In the south we assume there are one hundred British tanks, to the east our supply column is being chased by the enemy and in the north there is strong English support and artillery that are moving into position. A Radio call comes in: Moving direction south-southwest there a meeting takes place with the Italians and together we break out of the English surrounding.*"[46]

By the sacrifice of the II./*Abteilung*, it was now possible for the infantry to move forward another 100m, but before long the II./*Abteilung* was again on its own and under fire. The II./*Abteilung* had run across the broad front of artillery and anti-tank guns manned by the resolute South Africans and had paid a high price. The *8th Company* had suffered heavy losses, and even *Olt* Wuth, who had been previously wounded and was weak from his wounds, continued to take part in the attack by climbing back into his command panzer. Hubbuch has this vivid description of the attack:

"*The attack is rolling, it was in the second phase, but soon I had to pull ahead to the left, because the Italians couldn't follow our attacking speed. First of all, cannon towards left nine o'clock position aiming at the fleeing English supply vehicles. Olt Wuth demands that I shoot during movement and towards the left also on faster moving vehicles at long distance, I am aiming and hitting at this speed and wavy underground is practically impossible. Olt Wuth was shouting; 'Boy, you've never shot that bad before', what a wonder? Then breaking into the heaviest enemy formations of artillery, Pak and Panzerbüchsen, there are infantry throwing grenades in the open cannon barrels and with carbines shooting at our observation slits. Our panzer rolls over the vehemently fighting English who just refuse to surrender. Distorted faces in front of my optic, I shoot with the machine gun, which often has to jam exactly when I need it, in a thick enemy formation at very short distance, the English tip over like nothing. We are all rabid, the radio makes the head sets spin. Olt Wuth is in ecstasy and is throwing hand grenades from the turret towards Tommies who are too close to the panzer to be reached by the machine gun. Suddenly streams of blood are running over my right shoulder. Through my optic I have seen the guy, the marksman aiming before my machine gun took him out. Olt Wuth is pulled in with a headshot, he is still breathing. Immediately I bandage him and lift up his head, the panzer driver Felitzer races back to the first aid place as the radio operator is in the meantime trying to pass on command of the company to Lt. Liestmann, which does not answer anymore, because his panzer is shot to pieces and standing right beside us. The crew has also left the panzer of OFw Rad.... by a thorough English hit on the Rohrvorholer the smashed panzerkanone including the turret platform and the bodies have flown out through the back. Many of the others have also fallen out.*"[47]

Next, we have the report dated 13 January 1942 by Klaus Hubbuch, which vividly describes the loss of the panzer and death of Lt Heinz Liestmann. This report gives us a good idea of the terrible fighting that took place that day. Heinz Liestmann was one of the bright young officers in the Regiment and the brother of Lt Kurt Liestmann, who was also with the Regiment, and who had been wounded early in the summer of 1941. *Uffz* Konz, the only surviving member of the crew, told the story to Hubbuch:

"*Lt Heinz Liestmann died as the Zug leader of 2nd Zug, [8th Company, II./Abteilung] on Totensonntag, 23.11.1941, in the evening at 1700hrs during the crucial attack on enemy positions south of El Adem. We stood in the enemy positions after we broke through with a quick attack, in heavy combat against Infantry, Pak [Anti-Tank], Artillery, 4cm SP gun-carriages and enemy tanks. I drove as the Richtschütze [gunner] in the commander's panzer. Olt Wuth was mortally wounded by a head wound, next to me. Our radio operator communicated this fact and regarding the further leading of the company to Lt Liestmann, who was in front of me about 50m to the right on the same height breaking through to the enforced enemy position. The acknowledgment of this report was no more received.*

It was already dark, the panzers on the right and the left were pushed forward. We went back to the 1st field dressing station, in order to hand over Olt Wuth to the doctor. Here I later met the radio operator, Uffz Konz, from the panzer of Lt Liestmann and he reported following details: In the middle of the position their panzer received several simultaneous pak hits and shots from a 4cm SP gun-carriage. The tank stand, the driver was mortally wounded and Lt. Liestmann gave the order to bail out. Our radio message was not heard anymore. Lt Liestmann, his Richtschütze Uffz Packeisen and Uffz Konz found each other again in the cover of a disabled panzer from the 5th or 6th Company. Lt Liestmann bleeding from a head wound and was immediately bandaged. They lay in the middle of the enemy position under heavy infantry fire. Lt Liestmann and Packeisen jumped up and headed to the rear. During this escape Lt Liestmann stretched out high, tottered and fell forward. His Richtschütze fell next to him. The British machine gun fired and Uffz Konz was able to fallback a little later back to the dressing station. Uffz Konz later that night came to the hospital. The next morning we went at dawn with our panzer and drove to combat detachment and had to pass through yesterday's positions. Here in the middle of the position and surrounded by a number of destroyed panzers stood the panzer of our abteilung. The 8th Company panzer of Lt Liestmann was still burning and had numerous 4cm gunshot holes through it. The driver sat in his place in the burning down panzer. In front, over the driver's hatch was the dead Ladeschützen, Gefr Ohr, with head and chest wounds. He probably wanted to help the severely wounded driver to bail out. Further to the right was Lt Liestmann near a 5cm vehicle [panzer Mk III], dead laying face down, hands left and right along the body, legs slightly crossed. I turned Lt Liestmann to his back. The head shot was bandaged and the uniform bloody. He still had on his webbing with pistol, binoculars and larynx microphone. The face was without distortion, eyes open, the mouth shut. His face characters were clear and fresh as he always was. A little bit on the side was his Richtschütze dead with head and chest wounds. Shortly after the position we pushed to the combat detachment. I immediately reported to the Oberartz Dr Estor about the many dead German panzer crews, amongst them Lt Liestmann, who still lie on yesterdays battlefield. Oberarzt Dr. Estor drove there. I don't know where the grave of Lt Liestmann is. I learned later, that also the Brits made sketches of the grave positions and transferred it to the German officials via the Red Cross."[48]

At approximately 1700hrs, the action in the north had finally drawn to a close, as the *5th South African Brigade* had been wiped out and the *22nd Armored Brigade* had lost ten of its thirty tanks. The terrible fighting in the west was also accompanied by the savage fight raging in the north. The strongly held enemy defense line was still holding out in certain locations despite the attacks on it. The British artillery fire continued to hit the Regiment and supporting infantry with undiminished intensity. Oberst Cramer was then forced to order the Regimental Pioneers in their armored personnel carriers and all available escort panzers from the Regimental *Stabs* in order to help achieve the decisive breakthrough. Displaying great courage and initiative, the pioneers were able to make their way forward and take over the task assigned to the infantry, and they were able to secure the anti-tank and artillery guns that had been overrun by the panzers. But on this day every success seemed to be followed by failure or frustration, as in the meantime the radio connection between the Regiment and the I./*Abteilung* was lost when the radio antenna mast was shot away and radio damaged when the command panzer of Kümmel was hit by flying lead and anti-tank gun rounds. Not to be discouraged, Kümmel, ignoring the danger to himself, stood upright in the cupola of his panzer and, with a signal flag in his right hand, began to direct the movements of his *abteilung*. Finally, at 1655hrs Kümmel was able to report that the I./*Abteilung* had broken through to the airfield at Sidi Rezegh and established contact with elements of the *21st Panzer Division*'s *Schützen Regiment 104*.[49] As the battle had been raging in the north, various elements of the *XXX Corps* had been able to slip past the *D.A.K.* along the right flank and make good their escape to the south. The depleted *3rd RTR* was able make for the north, where it was able to link up with the *6th New Zealand Brigade*, which had come up from the east and had taken up positions near Hill 175 after fighting with the German *361st "Afrika" Regiment*. The remaining tanks from the *7th Armored Division* had been able to head for Gabr Saleh, where they were needed to cover the two enormous maintenance centers that had been established south of the Trigh el Abd. The tanks of the *4th Armored Brigade*, low on fuel, had been mostly stationary that day and remained near the southern escarpment. Wilhelm Hagios was one of those who remembers that day and had this account:

"In the morning we went towards the south, we really went along the British border, they [the British] sat there with their weapons and trucks, they were South Africans. We received the order to halt and we thought what to do as we waited on the order to begin again. We had with us two panzers sent to conduct a reconnaissance, we had seen ten to twelve Matilda tanks and when we came back we had to report that we had not found the British. Where had they gone? We noticed the tracks of two tanks, then we saw the British positions and destroyed German panzers and British vehicles, I saw from the 'schlitze' [observation slit] that they were running around with their carbines and thought that this could not be true. Then we had contact with a tank at 800m distance, 'John 11' a Stuart, we shot into this tank and in the meantime an antitank gun had hit us. The first impact hit on the front and I received fragment hits to my face and burns, the richtschütze was dead, and Stiefelmayer was above crying out; 'shoot, shoot', I had to do it all and I had to move around in order to shoot and tried to aim by myself as the richtschütze wasn't moving at the sighting mechanism. I was not able to aim the cannon, probably due to damage in the electric firing device and so I couldn't shoot. I turned the turret to 12, as the panzer drove away and then we received another impact next to me. I received a fragment in the arm as the next one [round] went into the engine area and we caught fire. We escaped, 'booted out' Erdman, and Gesser were there, Olt Stiefelmayer and me as the ladeschütze, everyone except Beyer the richtschütze. I had luckily, I don't know why, a hatch on the right side [which was] not open, as we booted out on the left side and the British didn't see us as they were shooting from right and they were not able to recognize us behind the panzer. In the meantime I knew that the British had clear written instructions to kill the crews from the panzers, as they liked to say, 'Panzers could be built every day, but one needs twenty years to become a soldier'. So we were four and found a rain washed trench and we hid ourselves there so that they wouldn't see us. We were there for a while. We saw some people with a 'flitzer' and thought that if we moved in such a direction there must be Germans. We started moving and found some Germans who had carbines. Then we were surprised by English tanks, two were on the way towards us and I saw for the first time how the 21cm grenade flies through the air at a short distance. One tank had turned to the left towards the unit; I can't remember which, but they were the one composed of the French Legionnaires who went to Africa to be allied with the Germans. [361st African Regiment]. We were with this unit but we had no panzer, so we built the tent and the stone walls for fragment protection around it. Then here comes one of the tanks, we shot at it with the MGs and cannon as the tank drove by over the tent. As I was wounded and I didn't know what had happened with the others who hid there but this tank went up to the left as Rammke in the other panzer [a Mk II] shot at it with a 2cm cannon from above. With hand weapons we couldn't do much to it."[50]

The Italians were also able to make an appearance, finally driving up on the left flank. Klaus Hubbuch had this praise for the Italians:

"The elite troops of the Italians, had saved the D.A.K. since the English were standing wide in our back [rear] in front of Tobruk, and wanted to attempt to encircle us, but they were attacked by the Italians

in heavy combat that forced them to retreat on this horrible battle on the Sunday when the dead were commemorated [Totensonntag]."

With a breakthrough achieved in the north and the battle there beginning to wind down, Hans Cramer starting thinking about sending his I./*Abteilung* back to the south to assist the II./*Abteilung*, but that movement was no longer necessary, since from about 1700hrs the British had begun to pull out and attempt a break through to the southeast with those remaining forces. Of these shattered formations, only a few small elements managed to slip past the panzers and wind their way through to the south aided by the coming of darkness. It was only with the coming of night that contact was finally broken with the British, and the Regiment was ordered to assemble at the airfield near Sidi Rezegh, where it reassembled its scattered elements and began to take stock of the damage it had sustained. After the battle had ended and darkness began to envelope both sides, Klaus Hubbuch was able to take a bit of time and wrote this short description of the aftermath:

"The front is illuminated in flames, the battle seems to slowly come to an end, it is getting dark and us? We follow the supply column which is driving ahead to the re-supply point meeting the second panzer of our company and we stay there for the rest of the night. Scattered soldiers, also from our Kampfstaffel, are coming in, many are told to be dead or wounded, exploded panzers everywhere, the screams of the wounded and the detonations of ammunition in flames. I am completely worn out and have a fit of the shivers and take a seat in the panzer, the whole night through I am sitting and freezing, half dozing, barely sleeping."[51]

As the Regiment began the task of reorganizing itself, the supply trains were called forward to rearm and refuel the panzers, and of course the most urgently needed field ambulances were hurried forward to transport the critically wounded. Because of the destruction wrought on those enemy formations the Regiment had the opportunity to appropriate huge amounts of destroyed and abandoned materiel and equipment. That evening many of the survivors, or at least those who found the stomach to do so, dined on captured British rations. In the darkness *Oberst* Cramer was only now able to begin to take stock of the losses suffered by his Regiment; it had been a tough day for the Regiment, and the losses sustained that terrible bloody Sunday were very high, especially among the key leaders. In the I./*Abteilung* the commander, Günther Fenski, was killed, and every company commander in the II./*Abteilung* was also killed, amongst them: *Olt* Körner from the *5th Company*, Lt Adam of the *6th Company*, and *Olt* Wuth of the *8th Company*. There was also the loss of the following officers: *Olt* Sontowski, Lt H. Liestmann, Lt W. Matthias, and Lt Pirath. Overall the Regiment suffered the following losses: sixteen killed, fifty-one wounded, and six missing in action. The losses in panzers consisted of: fourteen Mk IIs, thirty Mk IIIs, nine Mk IVs, and one large and one small command panzer. Of the panzer losses six Mk IIs, ten Mk IIIs, and three Mk IVs were listed as complete write-offs.[52] As mentioned previously, Wilhelm Hagios was one of those wounded that bloody day; he survived his wounds and the close call with a British tank, and was soon on his way by medical evacuation. He had this description of his experience:

"I went to the Truppenverbands area, to the station at Derna and from there to Benghazi to Crete and from there to Athens and from there to a lazaretto. But as there was a second front open and so all the wounded were sent to Greece or Italy. I was supposed to fly with the aircraft from Benghazi to Italy but had to get out of this [plane] as it was only for the seriously wounded, the whole lower part of the aircraft was full with empty gas canisters. From Athens I went to Böblingen to the Reserve Abteilung and received a convalescence leave, two days before Christmas I came home and was on vacation until January."[53]

Overall the *D.A.K.* lost some seventy panzers, thereby cutting in half the number of panzers that had begun the attack in the *D.A.K.* The British lost a large number of men, tanks, and equipment, and a countless number of vehicles, many of which found further use in the formations of the *D.A.K.* For the *D.A.K.* one of the greatest losses in the entire campaign occurred that day when elements from the *2nd New Zealand Division* attacked and captured a good portion of the *D.A.K.* battle staff near Bir Chleta, along with numerous pieces of vital radio equipment and code books. *General* Crüwell and *Oberst* Bayerlein were almost captured with it, and if not for the luck of a few minutes would have been taken prisoner.[54] The *15th Panzer Division* also lost some of its communications vehicles, which in the end hampered communications and delayed further offensive plans, as new codebooks and radio procedures had to be sorted out. The *D.A.K.* had, however, achieved a great victory, and the success and contributions by the Regiment succeeded in weakening the British *XXX Corps*, which was so weakened and disorganized after the battle that it was unable to continue the attack to relieve Tobruk. That night, as Hubbuch was moved to the aid station for treatment of his wounds, he remembered:

"Over night, they set up a new sick bay, beside me, many heavily wounded were dying and many dead are lying around. Crowds of wounded and prisoners were brought back in long lines, English, Indians, Blacks, Australians, and New Zealanders a lot of tall, slim guys."

The panzer strength report of the Regiment on the night of 23 November stood at eighty-nine operational panzers, of which twenty-four were Mk IIs, forty-six Mk IIIs, and twelve Mk IVs.[55]

Battle for the Trigh Capuzzo (24-28 Nov 1941)

After returning that night to his headquarters located near El Adem, Rommel, who had spent the day in the east where the New Zealanders were attacking Hill 175, was extremely upbeat about the overall situation. Even though Rommel was not up-to-date with the current status of the *D.A.K.* and the serious losses it had sustained in the previous day's fighting, he had already begun to formulate new plans for the continuation of the battle. It was his intension to strike immediately and destroy the remainder of the *7th Armored Division*, and then continue the drive towards Sidi Omar and launch an attack on the Sollum front. Rommel issued his first orders the night of 23/24 November, in which he informed *Oberst* Westphal, the *Ia* of the *Panzergruppe*, who had been left in charge of both the *Panzergruppe* headquarters and the Tobruk front, that he himself would lead the *D.A.K.* to the frontier wire at Sidi Omar. Rommel's plan, whether through negligence or ignorance, did not take into consideration the *2nd New Zealand Division*, which was coming up along the Trigh Capuzzo and could still threaten the German lines of communications and the Tobruk perimeter, which still poised a respectable threat. At that time the *7th Armored* and *1st South African Division*s had been almost totally destroyed during the previous days' action; however, there were still plenty of remnants from both divisions scattered about in the desert that could possibly cause serious problems for the *Panzergruppe*. At this point Rommel had declared that the battle had been decided, and now he looked to pursue his adversary into the desert. At 0600hrs Rommel, accompanied by his chief of staff, Alfred Gause, met with Crüwell at the headquarters of the *21st Panzer Division* to discuss events. At that time Crüwell proposed his plan, which outlined the pursuit of those scattered Allied remnants and the clearing of the area between the Trigh Capuzzo and Trigh el Abd to salvage and recover the enormous amounts of equipment and stores left behind by the Allied forces on the Sidi Rezegh battleground. Rommel instead vetoed the proposed plan, and at 1000hrs ordered *D.A.K.* with the attached *Ariete* Armored Division to the southeast to relieve the Sollum front. At 1030hrs, with Rommel at the head of the *21st Panzer Division*, the *D.A.K.* moved off on the Trigh el Abd in what would become one of Rommel's greatest adventures and one of his most erratic moves while in the desert. The *15th Panzer Division*, along with the Regiment, had a few hours that morning in which to finish re-supply operations and make good its losses from the abandoned British stocks. That morning the division received orders to prepare for movement to the southeast against the forces of *XIII Corps*, which had surrounded the German garrisons at Halfaya, Sidi Omar, and Bardia. For the men of the Regiment they began to rise and take stock of what had transpired the day before. There was the major task of reorganizing the command structure within the Regiment.[56]

Panzer Regiment 8 Chain of Command as of 24 November 1941

Regiment Commander	Oberst Cramer
I./Abteilung Commander	Hptm Kümmel
1st Company	Lt Arnold
2nd Company	Olt Knorr
4th Company	Olt Stiefelmayer
II./Abteilung Commander	Hptm Wahl
5th Company	Lt Bönisch
6th Company	Lt Becker
8th Company	Lt Voigt

Klaus Hubbuch again vividly describes how the men woke up and carried out the business that morning:

"At dawn we begin to move on back in the direction through the battlefield along our attack route we hear only light artillery fire from a distance. We came upon the destroyed and burnt out panzers of our company and here was Lt Liestmann lying dead in the desert, next to him Uffz Packeisen shot in the lungs but still breathing, Uffz Ring burnt on his seat in the panzer (he had just shortly had a long-distance marriage ceremony), the small Gefreiter Ohr dead on the panzer, also the vehicles of the 5th and 6th Companies with many dead. Ahead the English front line in a deeply echelon formation, all dead, Pak and Panzerbüchsen destroyed including the crew and here is the place where we turned around because of Olt Wuth and here the row of dead English with machine guns marks, mowed down by my bursts. I am shattered by the picture now! But we have to keep going so we load up Uffz Packeisen and bring him back. We barely find the rest of the Abteilung and Company but Olt Körner, Lt Adam, and many other Unteroffizier and crewmen are dead. Some men had nervous breakdowns after they were hit. Unteroffizier Fass, Reichert and Mohr were all dead. We returned and began refilling fuel, reloading ammunition and we receive our rations, we found English preserves, cookies etc. and began reorganizing the fighting compartment. Soon the discouraged mood lightens up, we meet such and such; I meet Peter, so he is still alive; earlier he barely could look at all the dead as it could have been himself! There are many English trucks captured and taken by our supply troops and driven by prisoners of all races, only with German co-drivers under weapon. Our panzer took many shots from infantry weapons; on the panzer, on cannon, in the engine compartment, in the observation slits etc... A Pak hit right in front of me as Richtschütze (gun-layer) but didn't penetrate through the armor plating."[57]

To the German troops, the situation seemed better than expected; the remainder of the British forces were sitting without re-supply, safely locked up in a kessel (cauldron), and they only had to be tracked down and finished off, or so they thought. The truth of the matter was that the *XXX Corps* was still a very dangerous foe, and as the *Panzergruppe* rolled toward Halfaya Pass and the *XIII Corps*, the *XXX Corps* took the time to regroup and resupply itself. The *Eighth Army*, unlike the *Panzergruppe*, had a vast materiel strength in men and equipment, and it would be able to make good its losses, especially in the number of tanks it could bring to the battlefield. Hubbuch continues to describe the day:

"We are getting some rest, the day is sunny and warm and we can recover; only in the distance near Tobruk, the canon thunder is rolling in the northwest. We ask ourselves 'Why did the attack bring so much loss to our Regiment?' Was the attack too sudden and without artillery preparation against such a powerful front line? With this attacking speed, it was impossible to knock down and hit all the many targets. But probably the decision had to be made before the night. Also Germans, originally English prisoners, came back; some of them have achieved great pieces as some of them had received already boat tickets for Australia, they were treated well and were kept at a distance from the Negroes. The Tommies seems to be very pious, everywhere on the battlefield are bibles and prayer books."[58]

At 1200hrs, the Regiment was finally ready to begin its march in the wake of *21st Panzer*. Rolling eastward with eighteen Mk IIs, thirty-six Mk IIIs, and seven Mk IVs, the Regiment sped towards Sidi Omar and the frontier wire. The march was conducted quickly, and with a total disregard for the flanks. Along the way the Regiment received artillery and other direct fire from scattered British units along the flank, and even the *RAF* made repeated attacks on the huge column, which by 1600hrs had seen the *Panzergruppe* strung out some 60 miles. Rommel, Gause, and Ravenstein were up front with *21st Panzer*, while Crüwell, with his *D.A.K.* headquarters, were co-located with *15th Panzer*. The Italian *Ariete* Division, now under the command of the *Panzergruppe*, was bringing up the right rear of the column, but was still lagging far behind the German panzers. The Allied formations were scattered about, with most of the service and supply elements heading east towards Matruh, away from the onslaught—the British were to refer to this as the "*Matruh Stakes.*" However, the same was not true of the combat formations, which hung on to the flanks and monitored and harassed their pursuers. A number of British airfields were overrun, which forced the *RAF* to also withdraw, limiting them to only minor attacks against the *Panzergruppe*. But for all its success in driving to the wire and scattering the British columns, the most precious prize of all was missed. The vital areas which the *Panzergruppe* missed in its drive towards Sidi Omar were the two British *Field Maintenance Centers FMC 62* and *FMC 65*, which had been established just south of the Trigh el Abd; if they had been discovered and captured it would have inflicted a serious loss upon the *XXX Corps*, which was heavily dependant on them for re-supplying those forces in the west. The vast quantity of supplies and equipment located in these centers would have provided enough supplies to keep the *Panzergruppe* rolling for months. Unfortunately, as the *D.A.K.* neared the frontier wire it found itself alone, as the *Ariete* had been halted by the *4th Armored Brigade* near Taieb el Esem. By early evening, the Regiment had reached an area some 20km south of Sidi Omar on the Trigh el Abd, and shortly before darkness German artillery and Pak guns engaged British reconnaissance forces that appeared along the left flank. As darkness descended the panzer crews were able to conduct about two hours of technical work, refueling, reloading ammunition, rations, and eating a warm meal. Then the march continued in darkness, with all of the crews at full combat alert. By 0200hrs on the 25th, the Regiment's panzers were securing the front of the division's sector until about

Chapter 7: The Crusader Battles, October-November 1941

0500hrs, when the crews were ordered to wake up and prepare themselves to move out. At this point the Regiment had approximately fifty-three operational panzers, with the remainder being left behind for repairs or because they were unserviceable.[59] The mission of the division on this day was to advance at once to the north with the right flank even with the border, and upon reaching that point the division was to deploy over a wide front stretching northwards to Sidi Azeiz in order to hem in the enemy in the Sollum area. In the *8th Company*, Hubbuch reported the loss of his panzer when it dropped out because of mechanical break down and transmission damage, leaving the company with only three Mk IIs and three Mk IVs with which to continue. Farther to the east of Hubbuch's broken down panzer, the 25th dawned with a very lucky Rommel returning to the safety of his own lines. The previous afternoon Rommel's *Mammoth* had broken down, and Crüwell and his *Mammoth* eventually rescued him and his party. The two men and their assistants then drove off in the one vehicle, but before they could locate the gap in the frontier wire darkness descended over the group, which then decided to spend the night on the eastern side of the wire. There were some anxious times that night, as Allied patrols passed by but paid little attention to the vehicle or its occupants. Upon his return Rommel paid a visit to the *15th Panzer*, which had halted some twelve miles short of the wire the previous night and had only now just arrived there. Rommel, having misread the British situation along the Sollum front and thinking the numerous service and support columns fleeing eastward included the majority of the British *XXX Corps*, issued the following orders to the *D.A.K.* The *15th Panzer* was to move north and destroy the *XIII Corps* elements north of Sollum passing around Sidi Omar and taking up positions between that location and Sidi Azeiz. That division was also to secure the lines of communication for the *21st Panzer*, which was to attack the enemy groups southeast of the Sollum position and drive them back into the minefields. These plans were bold but wholly impractical given the size, strength, and state of logistic support of the *D.A.K.*, which had its elements scattered all over the Sollum front. Unfortunately, the *15th Panzer* was late to arrive and the *21st Panzer* began the march north without it. *Panzer Regiment 5* was now under the command of *Major* Mildebrath, who had taken over when *Oberst* Stephan was mortally wounded. The *5th Regiment* was equipped with approximately twenty panzers. When the *15th Panzer* arrived it was ordered north, where it was to form a cordon west of Sollum. As the Regiment moved off to the north, at 0800hrs the I./*Abteilung* was struck by a number of *Crusader* tanks which had rolled up from the west, and in the short firefight that followed three *Crusader* tanks were knocked out, which forced the remainder to break contact and withdraw to the northeast, remaining out of engagement range. It was later discovered, through a captured prisoner, that these tanks belonged to the *7th Armored Brigade*. As the Regiment moved north toward Sidi Omar its sister regiment, the *5th Panzer*, having received a number of confused signals and last minute verbal orders from Rommel himself, broke from its parent division, and instead of supporting the movement to Halfaya broke away to attack Sidi Omar from the east. The attack went in unsupported, and the *5th Panzer* lost almost half its panzers to the Indian gunners, who fired their 25-Pounders over open sites. After this fiasco Rommel became impatient and directly involved in the positioning of troops and units. The *15th Panzer* was then ordered to break off its drive towards Sollum and move over to support *Panzer Regiment 5*. The Regiment moved off to the north, but still came under artillery fire from the east, and it was even attacked from the west by some twenty Matilda tanks from the *6th RTR*. Acting swiftly, *Hptm* Kümmel met the attack with his I./*Abteilung* and quickly closed the distance between the panzers and the thick skinned Matildas, opening fire from only 300m. Within fifteen minutes sixteen British tanks had been destroyed. The II./*Abteilung*, under *Hptm* Wahl, was able to destroy three tanks with one tank escaping. It was later determined that two *Valentine* tanks were among the destroyed tanks. In a depression close to Bir Ghirba the Regiment encountered a British supply column and the light recovery section and mobile repair shop of the *1st Army Tank Brigade* working on a number of *Matildas* damaged in the attack on Sidi Omar on the 22nd. There were some eighteen tanks in various stages of serviceability spread about, and despite the attempt to maneuver some of the tanks into fighting positions the panzers had already closed in and brought them under fire.[60] After a short time, a number of Flak and artillery guns joined the panzer attack, and the column was totally destroyed; its workshop was taken in addition to many prisoners. Even as the Allied supply columns were being shot up and taken prisoner the same fate was almost surely about to befall some of the German forces. Hubbuch's letter reflects the situation:

"At the end of the huge column are all the vehicles, which cannot move anymore and many want to be towed by us but we have no time, we have to get ahead again! Who will now come to help these drivers in the midst of the African desert? They most probably will helplessly fall behind and will be captured; you can see it in their begging faces. But now we must be hard towards our companions and remain tough because our location after repair is at the head of the Division."[61]

By 1230hrs, with the panzers short of fuel, ammunition, and provisions, the Regiment was forced to halt. The supply trains, which for the previous twelve hours had taken a beating from a number of *XXX Corps* combat elements and the *RAF*, had been able to locate some cached British fuel dumps, and were able to move up at around 1600hrs and begin re-supply operations. During the day the *D.A.K.*, and especially the unprotected armored columns, had been the focal point for a number of *RAF* fighter attacks, which had returned to the battlefield and would, over the next couple of days, take a toll on the *D.A.K.* Indeed, for the next couple of days the *RAF* would inflict on the Germans a number of irreplaceable losses, as the *D.A.K.* made a series of uncoordinated moves. As Hubbuch's panzer attempted to make its way forward and link up with the rest of the company he had these reflections:

"Artillery fire from the flanks is answered by our artillery but RAF Bomber squadrons of up to forty aircraft, so called 'Parteitagsgeschwader' [Party conference squadrons] which are unloading their loads, there is heavy Flak-fire but mainly for morale effect although there are a few losses through the bombs, Uffz Hahnen was wounded. But where are our planes? They are supposed to be in action against an English Armored Division, which is pushing through the desert towards Benghazi. After a long stop near Sidi Omar we are turning towards the northeast along the Egyptian border, which is often visible on our right in the form of a barbwire fence. We eat our liver sausage from New Zealand and again push through to the very front of our Kampfstaffel and continue the drive towards Sollum. The whole day we have to endure artillery and dive bomber attacks. We hear that a new English Armored Division has broken through the Sollum front with Mk II Matilda tanks and already heavily putting pressure on the Italians in their Bardia position. We are coming! Suddenly, already there are Matildas ahead of us, we swiftly attack with our panzers, a great fight, and we rely on our gunnery experiences from the Sollum battle, we attack at very short distance because at a longer distance the Matilda is too heavily plated and un-destroyable! In the fight, I shot one Matilda for sure and got a probable hit on another one all by myself. We were then chasing after some trucks with machine guns fire but unfortunately one of our own towing vehicles from an 88mm Flak gun was burning but there were no other losses. The combat continues towards us, so we continue to be the lead panzer. A 20mm Mk II panzer comes back to our Abteilung and two

117

75mm Mk IVs slowly followed our 'sick panzer' with sick other panzers, the rest of the proud 8th Company!"[62]

By 2000hrs that evening, the spearhead of the division was on the Trigh Capuzzo west of Sidi Azeiz, with the tail end just north of the Trigh el-Abd. It was along this thirty kilometer line that the division formed a series of hedgehog positions and settled down for the night. The panzer strength report of the Regiment on 25 November was fifty operational panzers.[63] Despite the series of uncoordinated moves and the lack of success the *D.A.K.* achieved that day against the *Eighth Army*, they were influential in removing its commander, which at the point of nervous breakdown was prepared to issue the order for a general retreat back into Egypt. Cunningham was overruled in his decision and ordered to continue the attack by the overall commander General Auchinleck, who removed Cunningham on the 25th and replaced him with his *Deputy Chief of Staff*, Major General Neil Ritchie.[64] By the evening of the 25/26th, the situation was becoming a bit sticky; there were wounded that could not be evacuated and resupply which could not be affected. To help alleviate the supply situation the Regiment was ordered to attack the area around Bardia, in order to capture a supply of ammunition, fuel, water, and provisions. Early on the 26th, the Regiment marched from Bardia to the south, in order to secure the right flank of the *21st Panzer Division*. While en-route to the south the *II./Abteilung* was engaged by some 2-Pounder anti-tank guns, which managed to hit the panzer of Lt Voigt, the company commander. Flying shell fragments wounded Voigt and his radio operator, *Uffz* Baumann. Klaus Hubbuch was the gun layer on the panzer and has this description:

"Early in the morning we begin driving again but this time towards the south, a deception? Our lead panzer is at the very front on the right and he reports: 'enemy from the right', but we are not noticed until heavy anti-tank fire is coming at us from there. Immediately we attack after changing direction. Before we can fire our first shot we are already hit twice; flashing and twitching in the panzer after the horrible bang. Uffz Baumann, the radio operator, is shouting, and then a second bang above the cupola, Lt Voigt is suddenly thrown out and his radio transmission is interrupted. While driving backwards, we bandage Uffz Baumann, who was injured on his chin and bring him to the Doctor at the supply trains. Uffz Zechiel, whose panzer was also hit, becomes our new radio operator and Uffz Fluher becomes our panzer commander again. We have taken two 40mm solid shot rounds from a self-propelled anti-tank gun during right turn at night. It was three English carriages and all are burning now after the attack. The first hit penetrated to the lower on the right, where the radio operator is sitting, reflected at the machine gun mounting and was lying as Vollgeschoß between the feet of Uffz B. What luck! Fragments were lying around the whole fighting compartment. The second hit ripped the lid off the top and a fragment injured Lt Voigt on his head. Voigt was driven back in an automobile and we return to the Kampfstaffel and continue the desert ride again towards the northeast."[65]

The Regiment had already gone some distance before it received an order to return to Bardia. With a turn to the northeast it reached the Bardia-Sollum road, and here it was placed in reserve for the attack on Fort Capuzzo. Hubbuch again describes what took place:

"We position along the road, I./Abteilung on the left, II./Abteilung on the right, attacking direction Fort Capuzzo. Finally we leave the open desert behind us, in which not even camel thistle bushes and flies are present and are back near the coast. The Division takes up security positions behind a hill. English infantry and vehicles are visible through

binocular at the Fort. We do technical service on the panzer, weapons cleaning and belting machine gun ammunition, eating English booty of sausages, ham, cookies etc which the old Frank with his booty truck gave to us and the rest of the Kampfstaffel; there is a warm meal served for the third time it was green beans."[66]

The attack was ordered for 1700hrs, and was to be conducted by *Schützen Regiment 115*, with *Artillery Regiment 33* in support and *Panzer Regiment 8* in standby. During the preparation many of the crews used the time to conduct much needed maintenance and catch up on some sleep. There were four Mk IIIs broken down, along with twelve men wounded. Hubbuch reflects:

"It is 1700hrs, we are in the panzer ready for the attack, which is supposed to come. Our own artillery is bombarding Capuzzo and upper Sollum. Rommel and other Generals are visible on the battlefield. Will it go well? Hopefully, it is the last attack of this battle series.

Infantry, Pak, Artillery are moving forward along the road. A wild night combat develops as we ate standing on our panzers, on call for attack. Towards 2300hrs everything from the front is returning. They say that the 21st Panzer Division has broken through Capuzzo. I wonder if it is back in German hands?"[67]

That evening, just west of Sidi Azeiz, under the protection of the hedgehog the crews were able to get a bit of rest before continuing the battle in the morning. The morning of the 27th dawned cool with a bit of haze over the battlefield. Rommel, who had been present the night prior to witness the attack on Fort Capuzzo, was nearby in Bardia. Rommel issued his orders for the day to the division, and especially to the Regiment, which were to attack and destroy the enemy around Sidi Azeiz. The *21st Panzer*, which was refueling at Bardia, was to continue its movement westward towards Tobruk. The *Kampfstaffel* began their movement from the hedgehog position west of Sidi Azeiz with the *I./Abteilung* upfront, followed by the remainder of the *II./Abteilung*. Thanks to its early morning start the Regiment was able to surprise and capture the headquarters and support elements of the *5th New Zealand Brigade*, which after a short fight near Fort Capuzzo surrendered. The bag of men and equipment included the brigade commander and five hundred of his men, along with a number of vehicles, six cannons, four anti-tank guns, and a large quantity of supplies.[68] Kurt Kathe remembered speaking with some of those prisoners that had been captured:

"The Brits had many soldiers from New Zealand, when we captured their rations these people went to the prisoner camp, but behaved well, one commander said when he became a POW 'why do you Germans shoot such big guns at small tanks?' we laughed as we had the 88mm to fire on their small tanks."[69]

After the morning's success, the *15th Panzer* was ordered to proceed west along the Trigh Capuzzo towards Tobruk, where a number of developments over the past few days had threatened to bring about a collapse of the entire *Panzergruppe*. Since the 24th, the day that Rommel left his headquarters in order to launch the *D.A.K.* in their attacks along the Sollum front, the situation around Tobruk and Sidi Rezegh had become very serious. Just following the *Totensonntag* battle, *General* Crüwell had wanted to take the time to police and recover the vast amounts of equipment left behind after the battle and to sweep clear all the remaining *XXX Corps* elements that had either been immobile or escaped destruction on the 23rd. Rommel of course vetoed this idea and, thinking the battle all but finished, headed off pell-mell to the frontier to finish off the *XIII Corps* and block the escape of any *XXX Corps* elements attempting to regain the Egyptian border. During his absence *Oberst* Siegfried Westphal, the *Panzergruppe Ia*, was left behind at El Adem to deal with a number of problems both internal and external. Since the departure of the *D.A.K.*, the *XXX Corps* had been left unattended and was able to recover a large number of its tanks and equipment and, along with fresh reinforcements that were arriving from Egypt, was able to reform many of its broken and scattered formations. The Tobruk garrison had also become very active, and was now attempting to break out of its perimeter and link up with the *2nd New Zealand Division*, which had come up along the Trigh Capuzzo from Bardia and gone unmolested until it had reached a point east of Hill 175. Westphal also had a number of internal problems to deal with, one of which was with the Italian commanders manning the Tobruk perimeter. Westphal was time and time again forced to deal with these senior officers, many of which had become unnerved by the amount of activity coming from Tobruk. Another, and probably the single most important problem, was the lack of clear and concise orders, and the means to transmit such orders and situation updates. At this point in the battle the *Panzergruppe*, and especially the *D.A.K.* and its panzer divisions, had lost an enormous amount of their communications equipment, and had almost no means in which to communicate with one another. There were no organized communications plans drawn up, and about the only way in which to communicate was to send messengers and radio signals in the hope that they would reach their intended recipient. To make matters worse Rommel, Crüwell, Gause, and Bayerlein were all missing. Rommel and Gause had broken down in their vehicle in the late afternoon as they attempted to return towards Sidi Omar and the *Panzergruppe* headquarters. They were stranded in the open desert along the Egyptian border as British units passed them by, paying little attention to their car in the fading light. Later that night Crüwell and Bayerlein, out and about in their captured British *Mammoth*, happened by the broken down staff car and picked them up. However, the episode did not end there, as the group quickly became disorientated and lost in the open desert. For the remainder of the night, the group huddled in the *Mammoth* amid the passing vehicles of the *4th Indian Division* as they sweated out a very uncomfortable situation. As the sun rose that morning, the group was finally able to make their way safely to the *21st Panzer Division*.[70]

By the 25th, the *4th New Zealand Brigade* had reached Zaafran and the *6th Brigade* had retaken the airfield at Sidi Rezegh in a series of night attacks. Despite failing to reach El Duda and link up with the Tobruk garrison, Belhamed was retaken from the "*Afrika*" Division (*90th Light*). That night the attacks continued, this time supported by the tanks from the *4th RTR* which, despite getting held up on minefields, had succeeded by the morning of the 26th in capturing a number of strong points covering the El Duda escarpment. During the afternoon of the 26th, the attacks again continued, with the entire *32nd Tank Brigade* launched toward El Duda, where it succeeded in making it to the top of the escarpment and overrunning the positions there. Another attack was launched by elements of the *4th Brigade* and *44th RTR* (*Yeomanry*) from the direction of Belhamed; the two forced worked in close conjunction with one another, and within an hour had linked up with the *70th Division*, which had taken El Duda.[71] The unhindered westward movement by the remainder of the New Zealand Division had endangered the combined Axis forces, the majority of which were still investing Tobruk. Westphal was greatly disturbed that at this critical time in the battle, while Rommel was away from his headquarters he was in charge of the situation, which continued to grow more bothersome. For Westphal there was only one thing to do, and that was to get elements from the *D.A.K.* back to the west near Tobruk and to help restore the situation there. Westphal had then sent an order to *21st Panzer* directing it to break off its attacks in the Bardia-Sollum area and return at once back towards Sidi Rezegh.

"*From: Panzergruppe Afrika Ia, 27.11.41, to: Befehlshaber 0430 Kampfgruppe Böttcher under heavy loss back on both sides 158 left Please send D.A.K. immediately only then will the situation be saved.*"[72]

By the morning of the 27th, the bulk of the *21st Panzer Division* was making its way westward along the Via Balbia with the *15th Panzer* soon to follow on the Trigh Capuzzo. The situation was now changed somewhat, as the division, which was to attack toward Bardia and Sollum, was ordered by the divisional commander to now reverse direction and make its way west once again towards Sidi Azeiz. After receiving its orders, the Regiment took up positions on both sides of the Trigh Capuzzo and began its journey west towards Gambut. The division commander had ordered the Regiment and the majority of the artillery forward, where they were to be followed by the infantry and pioneers a short time later.[73] The panzers had not gone more than 10km before a wall of British supply trains and positions were spotted in the open desert near Sidi Azeiz. Unbeknownst to the Regiment, they had just stumbled across the headquarters of the *5th New Zealand Brigade*. Cramer quickly ordered the Regiment forward and the attack began; it was an unfair fight, as the panzers were easily able to overrun the positions of the lightly armed New Zealanders and captured six guns and 800 prisoners.[74] In his book *Rommel in the Desert* Volkmar Kühn writes:

"'*All of a sudden the division came upon the headquarters of the Fifth New Zealand Brigade near Sidi Azeiz. Oberst Hans Cramer immediately led PR 8 at high speed to Sidi Azeiz. The regiment overran enemy anti-tank guns and artillery and shot up the enemy positions. The fast-moving panzers overran the infantry trenches and machine gun positions and smashed the brigade. About 700 New Zealanders were captured.*' The story continues with a report by Hans Cramer who reported; '*After we broke into the New Zealanders' lines a large number of unarmed prisoners streamed toward us. What were we to do with prisoners when our infantry had no vehicles? We couldn't just send them to the rear, because in the desert war the 'rear' was an uncertain concept. If we left them to themselves they would have picked up their weapons again as soon as we left and found transport somewhere. While the first prisoners assembled I stood with my adjutant in the open on my command tank and received the enemy commanders who were brought over by several panzer crewmen. More and more New Zealanders gathered around my command tank. As was usual in Africa when someone had suffered a misfortune, I spoke a few friendly words to the officers and emphasized that their people had fought bravely. At that moment my lookout shouted: 'Two enemy tanks, Matilda type, coming toward us!' I turned quickly. Through my field glasses I saw the two tanks were wearing German markings and just then I remembered that our Panzer pioneer-Company 33 was to have employed these tanks at Capuzzo. It was the Pioneer, and subsequently our infantry from the 115th arrived and led the prisoners to the rear.*"[75]

Klaus Hubbuch had this description of the fight:

"*The divisional artillery and flak guns, which had already been warming up, were joined in the attack by our panzer cannons and machine guns. The attack succeeds and the English camp is burning and while we are driving through with the panzers, hundreds of captured soldiers are surrendering, among them, one Brigadier General. A beautiful episode because our infantry stayed back during the attack and of all people it* was the panzer crews, who took the surrendering troops captive. Then it happens, Indians, first with their hands up, then they disappear behind the burning vehicles then the shots are fired and we have losses. The English defend themselves with artillery in direct fire, many self propelled carriages and Panzerbüchsen. His fuel and ammunition trucks exploding under great detonations, which cause clouds of smoke, a powerful battlefield and picture but most of all much booty! The 'Old Frank' [supply sergeant], who filled his booty truck, brings it to us during the break after the battle when we are driving towards the west, cans with sausage, cheese, tobacco, milk, chocolate and cookies etc. Tommy has everything! We are cleaning our tracks from the barbwire, which has gotten stuck during the attack, its terrible work."

After cleaning up the battlefield the Regiment continued its movement west, where it came under numerous air attacks by RAF *Kitty Hawk* and *Hurricane* fighters that caused serious loss to the *Kradmelder Zug*, of which four were killed and eight wounded. Hubbuch again describes the attacks:

"Suddenly, English fighter planes in low flight, first from the left and then after a turn from the right, we are jumping from one side of the panzer to the other in order to protect ourselves against the heavy machine guns; but they also drop bombs and again the shouts 'medical aid'. Some are dead, others wounded."[76]

The British had been alerted of the oncoming *D.A.K.* and had rushed up forces to engage them along the Trigh Capuzzo. The 4th and 22nd Armored Brigades were ordered north, with the 4th ordered to hit the flank and tail portions of the column near Gasr el Arid, while the 22nd was ordered to hit and block the path of the lead elements near Bir el Chleta. That British blocking force was able to halt the forward movement of the division with a combined attack by tanks and artillery as flanking elements harassed the division's lighter transport columns. Beginning at 1300hrs that afternoon and lasting until the evening, the division, minus its *Schützen Regiment 115* and *Pioneer Battalion 33*, was involved in heavy fighting east of Sciaf Sciuf as British tanks and artillery attempted to engage the head of the division where the Regiment was located, but those forces were too far away to score any direct hits on the panzers. From out of the vast waste of the desert Crusader tanks of the 3rd RTR appeared and attacked the left flank of the column, and after a short firefight three of the tanks were left burning. The remaining tanks quickly pulled back to about 3-4,000m. On the west side of Gasr el Arid the combat elements began to receive heavy artillery fire, which lasted until that evening. During the afternoon the division was faced with a deteriorating situation, as it was outgunned and facing numerically superior forces that threatened to destroy the division, but the arrival of fifteen panzers from the repair depot near Gambut and the arrival of *Schützen Regiment 115* at 1730hrs helped turn the tide. As darkness began to descend upon the battlefield the British called off their attacks and pulled back to their lagers for the night. As the British withdrew the division took full advantage of the departure, as it continued to roll towards the west until they had reached an area south of Sciaf Sciuf, where a halt was finally ordered. A hedgehog position was formed south of Sciaf Sciuf with the panzers facing south into the open desert. The crews then began to perform their standard technical services on weapons systems and equipment before food and sleep could be had, and then there was always a turn on guard duty; with all these technical services to be performed the panzers crews got very little sleep that night. As the combat elements conducted their services, so too were the unsung heroes of the *Werkshop* and "I" services under OZmstr Gizy. That evening they returned two broken down panzers to duty, and *Uffz* Persekowsky

was scheduled to return shortly with another three. It was around this time frame that Gotthilf Haidt had a particularly, if not amusing run in with some Commonwealth troops, and what could occasionally happen on the battlefield in these very confusing times:

"I had the experience of being there with the British and Canadians, in November near Tobruk and how they saw us with our vehicle. We had no connection [separated from] with the Regiment, we went to the assembly area in the darkness. When morning came, we saw on the horizon some troops but we didn't know which. The zug vehicle [panzer recover vehicle, 8-12 ton tractor] makes a lot of noise when they drive at full steam through the desert terrain and the morning it is quite cold in Africa and young soldiers are not familiar with which side we were, we saw them doing breakfast, when they saw us coming. They quickly got on their pants and coats and ran away, [as] we were driving in the direction of the sea we did not halt; I believe other vehicles behind us took advantage of this place, but not us."[77]

In the meantime, the British attacks from the south had so worried Crüwell that he ordered the 21st Panzer to move down from the Via Balbia to assist the 15th Panzer along the Trigh Capuzzo. That division had had a difficult time west of Bardia when it ran into a strong defensive position there, and was unable to push past it. By the 27th, the division was ordered to break off its attack and link-up with the 15th Panzer, which it was able to do after going around Sidi Azeiz. The *Ariete* Division too was finally able to move up from the east, where it had been lagging behind. A cloudy, rainy morning greeted the exhausted panzer crews that had been looking forward to a day of rest, but instead all they got was the order to advance. Thanks to the workshops, the Regiment went forward with a total of forty-three panzers: twelve Mk IIs, twenty six Mk IIIs, and five Mk IVs.[78] The day began with the sighting of swarms of *RAF* fighters, which were quite active in scouting out the desert and reporting the German positions. The previous night, when the British had departed the area, they had failed to keep any type of blocking force in position along the Trigh Capuzzo to halt the *D.A.K.* advance. As the *D.A.K.* moved off that morning it did so behind a screen of well-sited Pak guns that were able to easily keep the British armored forces at bay. At 1430hrs, the division continued its advance west; it did so with the *Ariete* aligned to the left flank. The march route took the Regiment west along the escarpment south of Sidi Rezegh, and as the Regiment neared this location it came under an immense artillery bombardment from British guns. The barrage was the strongest yet encountered by the Regiment, and to make matters worse, British tanks were sited on the horizon. Klaus Hubbuch describes the bombardment:

"Never before was the artillery fire that heavy between us. Fragments upon fragments were twitching and banging on our turret. The waiting for a fatal hit was testing our nerves! The panzer of Lt Voigt began to burn; did he have fuel containers for reserve on the outside? But fire can be extinguished. Uffz Fold falls at the supply truck, another one! The mood inside the panzer for the first time is miserable. The Rot! Uffz Fluher does not want it anymore! First I try it as the Richtschütze but I need a favorable distance and view order, then I try to bring up a positive attitude but the old warriors are finished and are offended by my attempts, they are completely fed up! But I must be able to shoot! I need the order from the commander to march not to halt in order to get closer to the enemy tanks. There even comes a cigar to our commander over the radio from the Abteilung commander, who at the moment is ahead of us; that helps!"[79]

The division was forced to halt and deal with the armored threat with its Pak and artillery guns while *Schützen Regiment 200* was sent to the north to attack the British positions there. Both situations were successful, as the infantry was able to overrun a British camp and twenty tanks were claimed along the southern flank.[80] In a lengthy report written in February 1942, *Uffz* Fritz Lang of the *Stabs* Company I./*Abteilung* gives a good description of his activities as a transport / ambulance driver from 22-29 November and the encounters he had during this period of time:

"On 22.11.41 I drove over the slope [escarpment] Gambut – Trigh Capuzzo with a co-driver OGefr Richter, returning from the hospital at km 42 to the I./Abteilung after [conducting] the medical transportation. As I drove on approximately the same route the previous night, I believed that it would bring me back to the Regiment. Due to the seldom contact with other vehicles, we were not able to find the exact location of the Regiment and as we came close to the Trigh Capuzzo, we saw the column of German supply vehicles driving eastwards. Despite the accelerated drive we were unable to reach them. We also discovered on this route a different group of vehicles such as Kfz 15 and some English tank chassis. Firmly believing and happy about such booty I drove immediately away with the intention to collect the discovery. However we were hardly 50m ahead, when the machine gun fired at Kühler, simultaneously the English came towards us with raised hands to signal us to stop. I made a quick decision to turn around and drove as quick as the car allowed, despite the immediate fire from several machine guns the vehicle wasn't damaged significantly. After a half kilometer drive we encountered three German surveillance vehicles. I reported the accident to the leader of these vehicles, whereas the Leutnant took his course towards the column of supply vehicles. With one more experience, we then drove to the divisional communications leader from where we went with the reserve column and reached the Regiment south of Tobruk in the middle of the night. The wounded from the previous day's combat were waiting for us. In the dawn of the morning of 23 November we brought them to the hospital at El Adèm, which was again under artillery fire from Tobruk. On the return trip by the mosque we encountered endless columns of prisoners, some on captured trucks, others walking. As the advanced continued an enemy bomber tried to trigger panic by dropping several bombs, the attempt failed. From the panzer crews of Regiment 5 we learned that our Regiment would transfer to the eastward direction of attack. After many hours of rash driving we reached the combat supply trains of the Regiment. Shortly before the supply lines had to withstand the attack by a deep flight of aircraft. As we noticed this attack in time, we were able to stop and seek the cover under the vehicle. One burst [of fire] struck along the instrument panel of my car; the other one from the same machine ignited the fire in a captured vehicle near to us. After the quick transportation of the wounded we had to seek the doctor in order to provide the wounded with the necessary care. A further 100m away the Hurricanes attacked a second time. The shots hit my car while it was still driving and the bombs fell between the vehicles. The wounded were reloaded and taken care of thanks to the help from a medical Feldwebel. We were warned just before our departure with these wounded, that the enemy forces were spread by pieces. We tried to catch up with the Regiment while on its tail. Shortly afterwards enemy tanks attacked from the left. Despite the defense of Panzerjäger and combat vehicle of the Regiment, one part of the supply turned off from the unit and was wandering in the desert, until an officer put himself in charge and took connection again. After an endless drive through the night we reached the Regiment on the morning of 24 November, by then the Regiment had swung to the north. The units were constantly under the attacks from bombs and long range aircraft attacks. Due to our fully loaded vehicles we were unable to drive into combat and therefore made connection with the newly arrived Zug from the medical company. The vehicles filled up momentarily and more were needed. Heavily wounded comrades died and we had to bury them while on the way, because the space in the vehicle had to be kept free for the newly wounded. On 25 November we tried to conduct a transport to Bardia which was led by Stabsartzt Dr. Nolde. By crossing the Trigh Capuzzo we came under artillery fire and as we tried to turn to the east, we encountered the enemy forces again, who shot at us with machine guns. Then we quickly drove in the westerly direction. After we drove in the direction of El Adèm until the middle of the night, we stopped in order to continue our march in the early darkness on 26 November. But in the dusk of the dawn we [found ourselves] standing directly in front of the lines of a division from New Zealand. Due to the lack of the fuel supply and the long transportation of the heavy wounded, our leadership decided to go to prison instead of attempting a free drive. After the enemy searched through our vehicles, they led the transports further through their supply vehicles and we came to the end of a wadi southeast of Tobruk. Here was the tent of the hospital and the prisoner of war camp. Knowing our destiny, they allowed the drivers and co-drivers to place only a few things under their armpit. So we went after some searching behind the barbed wire. The hospital took over the care of the wounded, with help of our doctors and some of our medical services. We were able to watch from the prisoner of war camp, how the tents were arranged and our vehicles were parked nearby. Here we spent the time from 26 to the evening of 27 November, among several hundred of our own comrades, mostly infantry men and legionnaires. As we knew that our panzer combat forces were on the east, we had a strong hope to be set free. On 27 November the surrounding enemy forces and vehicles grew less and already the first German rounds fell around the camp, from one to another we passed around 'they are coming'. It didn't take long when the jeep appeared on the hill about 100m from us, there was an officer conducting surveillance with his binoculars on us. At the same moment appeared a wave of infantrymen and the barbed wire was destroyed. There was a shout of joy as a greeting to our liberators, who took weapons from the guards and drove them away. Me and my co-driver returned to our vehicle and prepared to drive on. Stabsartzt Dr. Nold ordered us to stay, until the wounded would be able to be transported further. On 28 and 29 November in this area went in an attack by Ariete and 21st Division. The enemy was not able to hold the battery positions behind and in front of the hospital. A direct shot hit the tent with the heavily wounded, new wounds and victims resulted from it. After digging the fragment (protection) caves we brought them in there. Further doctors arrived and made constant operations in the O.P. vehicle. On the evening of 29 November the way was clear and we were able to take many German wounded with the transport to the hospital at km 42. From there we returned to the divisional communications officer detachment and shortly afterwards the combat was over, and we returned to the rest area together our Abteilung."[81]

Elsewhere, attacks by the "*Afrika*" Division and *Kampfgruppe Böttcher*, defending near Tobruk, were successful in reaching Sidi Rezegh. North of Sidi Mufta and Bir el Halad, British tanks repeatedly conducted hit and run attacks as they attacked from out of the open desert and began engaging the panzers at long distance, then quickly sped off, frustrating the German gunners, who could not get an accurate sight picture and return fire. But as soon as the panzers made the attempt to challenge those tanks they quickly stopped firing and withdrew to a safe distance. This cat and mouse game was normally just a waste of ammunition, but on occasion a gunner could score a lucky hit, and that happened when one of the British tanks was too slow off the mark and received a hit that left it a smoking hull in the desert. That evening the Regiment was located along the high ground 15km southwest of Sidi Rezegh, close to the *Kampfgruppe Böttcher*, but was unable to break through to it, mostly due to a lack of fuel and ammunition. Fortunately the supply trains were able to locate the panzers and replenish them with fuel, ammunition, and provisions, but for the weary panzer crews there was little time to rest after the standard services had been performed. As the 28th ended, the Regiment reported its losses for the day, which included five dead and ten wounded, in addition to the loss of one Mk II and two Mk IIIs.[82] Hubbuch continues in his letter:

"Finally it is getting night again. We have much to do like cleaning weapons, restocking ammunition; our panzer can take 135 rounds, oil change, refueling, cleaning the filters, and getting some food at last! While I am on guard, a panzer with Uffz Wurster is returning from repair; the panzers of Uffz. Bauch and Persekowsky are still missing; but we are again six panzer combat vehicles strong. Mine or our Mk IV is the only one which so far was there all the time and never had to go in for repairs. It does have lots of scratches but it is still moving and shooting and the crew of course is not the original one anymore two crewmembers dead or injured and a radio operator heavily wounded."[83]

During the night of 28/29th, orders were issued by the *D.A.K.* headquarters that called for the continued attack on the *2nd New Zealand Division* with the aim of pushing it into the Tobruk perimeter. The attacks were to begin at 1000hrs on the 29th, with the *21st Panzer Division* ordered to attack along the central escarpment and retake Belhamed. The *"Afrika"* Division, which was not under direct control of the *D.A.K.*, was asked to support the *21st Panzer's* attack on Belhamed. The *15th Panzer Division* was ordered to attack along the southern escarpment past Sidi Rezegh toward El Duda, where it was to take the high ground. *Kampfgruppe Böttcher*, also not under *D.A.K.* command, was asked to support that attack with its artillery. The Italian *Ariete* Division was ordered to secure the area around Sidi Muftah in order to block any advances by the British *7th Armored Division*.[84] The orders issued by the *D.A.K.* did not sync with what the *Panzergruppe* had in mind, as it insisted that all attacks launched against the *New Zealand Division* had the aim of cutting it off and preventing it from gaining the Tobruk perimeter. The *Panzergruppe* also wanted the entire *D.A.K.* to retake Belhamed and defend to the south; only artillery was to be used in striking at the area west of Sidi Mufta. The reason for this conflict was that the *D.A.K.* had not received any orders on the evening of the 28th, and so by 2030hrs it had sent its orders to *Panzergruppe*, which did not reply until 2130hrs with its own set of orders. For unknown reasons, other than feeling the plan too difficult to execute, the *Panzergruppe* orders were never carried out, and at 0800hrs on the 29th Crüwell verbally reissued his attack orders to his commanders. As the dawn broke over the desert, Klaus Hubbuch remembered that morning:

"On the morning of 29th Uffz Greif brought us some ham, six boiled eggs and oranges for our satisfaction; unfortunately no real bread, always Knäckebrot [cracker bread].
Kesselring's Luftflotte is supposed to be in full action in Northern Africa, coming from Crete where are they are stationed? We drive towards the west through German and Italian defensive positions until El Adem."[85]

That day the Regiment reported its panzer strength as eleven Mk IIs, twenty-five Mk IIIs, and three Mk IVs. The combat report on the attack at El Duda on November 29, 1941, states that the Regiment had received the order to attack on the night of the 28th with the specific mission of taking the El Duda position.[86] The entire *15th Panzer Division* began rolling westward at 0950hrs. The initial movement of the division was aided by the fact that the British forces previously located there the night prior had moved off to the south. As the division neared Sidi Rezegh is came under strong artillery fire from several artillery batteries located nearby. Despite receiving strong flanking fire from these artillery positions, the attack moved ahead at a brisk pace, but at 1030hrs the supporting Italian infantry and artillery positions were un-expectantly hit hard by coordinated fires that caused the Italians to falter, and in some cases break and run. Realizing that the difficult terrain around Sidi Rezegh hindered ideal panzer movements, the division was ordered to swing further to the southeast in an attempt to descend the escarpment further to the west. At 1230hrs, the Regiment moved against those positions in the north and, despite strong enemy artillery fire, difficult terrain, and soft sandy ground, was able to descend the escarpment near Bu Creimisa and cross it without loss. The division commander, *Generalmajor* Neumann-Silkow, had decided that by pushing his forces further out to the west he would be able to come up and attack El Duda from the western flank. *Machine Gun Battalion 2* was ordered to drop out of the division's order of march near Sidi Rezegh in order to keep the British forces located there occupied and prevent them from moving south and getting behind the division. Near Bir Creimisa the panzers made contact with elements of *Kampfgruppe Böttcher*, which it passed through as it continued east before turning north and making for El Duda. As the division descended the escarpment, making its way toward Bir Salem, it began to receive artillery fire, which inflicted only minor losses. Near Bir Salem the division linked up with its supporting artillery and coordinated the attack on El Duda. As the situation in the south was progressing according to plan the same could not be said of the attacks by the *21st Panzer* farther to the east. That division had had another difficult time as; it began its attack on Belhamed it realized that it was out of position for the attack, and it took additional time to form the forces for the attack. While forming up, the division was unexpectedly hit by British armor coming from the west, then more British armored forces were seen moving up from the south and the rear as artillery firing from the Trigh Capuzzo began to totally disrupt the division's movements. These attacks further delayed the division as, it was forced to move enough forces back to cover the division's rear. The *Ariete* was also being attacked from the south, and it too was delayed, as it was forced to turn its tanks around to meet the new threat. And finally, to make matters worse, a large British force of tanks and guns was seen moving from El Duda southeast towards Sidi Rezegh. All these attacks and movements by the British led the *D.A.K.* to believe that the New Zealanders were attempting to escape the net being thrown out by the *D.A.K.* Additionally, the *D.A.K.* was in such a position that it looked as if the entire plan was falling apart, and the corps would be eliminated piece by piece. After meeting with Rommel at around midday, the *D.A.K.* issued new orders, which called for the *21st Panzer* to attack Zaafran, while the *Ariete* was to hold the escarpment east of Sidi Rezegh and block any attempts by the British to move south and east. The *15th Panzer* was ordered to continue its attack on El Duda, but once that attack was completed it was to move east towards Belhamed instead of driving west on Tobruk. As the Regiment rolled west around midday Rommel's *Fieseler-Storch* was spotted overhead before coming in to land close to *Oberst* Cramer's command panzer, where they briefly spoke, and Rommel personally issued orders for the next phase of the battle.[87] By 1300hrs, the Regiment had crossed the Trigh Capuzzo and was driving forward under heavy artillery fire as it attempted to reach Bir Salem, which it finally did at approximately 1310hrs. Upon reaching that position, the Regiment was able to make contact with some of the Italian artillery positions located nearby. The volume of British artillery fire was still heavy, as numerous heavy batteries continued firing from the Tobruk perimeter and were able to inflict some damage on the Regiment as it reached the Axis by-pass road and began turning to the east towards El Duda. In order to accomplish this final maneuver for the attack, the regimental commander drove at the head of his Regiment's panzers, and with his signal flag issued the order to *"follow the leader"* in the direction of El Duda. With Cramer leading the way in a display of true leadership the Regiment immediately moved off to the east. Due to the many deep wadis that were located on both the left and right sides of the Axis by-pass road, the panzers were forced to spread out their panzer wedges. Realizing that the terrain would seriously hinder the panzers and break up their formations as they attempted to overrun the El Duda defenses, Cramer decided to employ the Regiment into two pincers for the attack. The first, or northern pincer, consisting of the I./*Abteilung* under *Hptm* Kümmel, would move to the north of El Duda, while the II./*Abteilung* under *Hptm* Wahl would drive directly towards the center of the British positions.[88] A short halt was called to allow both *abteilungs* to take up their battle configuration, and when this was completed the panzers began their movement, with the Regimental *Stabs* following in the wake of the I./*Abteilung*. As the panzers rolled forward and began to leave the Axis by-pass road they began to encounter numerous machine gun and infantry positions arrayed along the western slope of the escarpment; these positions offered little resistance, and the panzers were able to quickly overrun them, leaving the scattered remnants behind for the follow on infantry forces. Shortly before reaching the heights at El Duda, Cramer ordered the I./*Abteilung* to commence its attack to the north, while the II./*Abteilung* attacked towards the small transport road on the hill south of the I./*Abteilung*. As the attack began to develop the I./*Abteilung* quickly struck against the northeastern defenses, and was then attacked by some twenty Mark IIs. What the *D.A.K.* did not realize, and had been unable to detect, was that the British had moved in forces from the Tobruk perimeter into the El Duda sector, and had strengthened their positions there with a number of artillery batteries and twenty *Matilda* infantry tanks. Almost immediately tank rounds began to fill the air as British and German gunners attempted to zero in on one another. In the meantime, the II./*Abteilung* attack came up against numerous British positions, which included anti-tank gun and machine gun pits protected by wire obstacles stretched along the hill. At 1415hrs, Hans Kümmel reported that the British tanks he was engaged with had begun to withdraw to the northeast behind the small hills there, and that any further advance by his *Abteilung's* panzers was not possible because of a wadi that stretched for some distance across the axis of advance. Finally, at around 1500hrs Cramer pushed forward his attack on the El Duda feature. The combat elements again came under heavy artillery fire as they turned to the north and ran into some heavily defended positions, which forced the panzers to swing to the east and then left and right on the axis road. The heavy defensive fire put up by the *Matildas*, artillery, and anti-tank guns halted the German advance that now had to wait until enough of their own artillery could be brought to bear on the British defenses. As the afternoon began to fade the attack was again resumed, this time with the infantry attacking with the panzers and supported by the artillery from *Kampfgruppe Böttcher*.[89] Cramer now ordered Kümmel to shift his panzers off to support the right flank as the Regiment now attacked in force on the right. The main point of attack now had the II./*Abteilung* slightly ahead and echeloned to the left with the I./*Abteilung* echeloned to the right. It was here that Wahl displayed his fine leadership, a trait that was all too common in the Regiment, as he led his *Abteilung* forward, setting the example to his men and showing little concern for his own safety despite the danger of thick belts of landmines and rolls and strands of barbed and concertina wire, as well as an abundant number of anti-tank guns and flying artillery fragments. The I./*Abteilung* was also driving forward under the command of its own superb commander, and it began to successfully engage a number of enemy infantry positions in addition to a number of *Matildas* that had reappeared from the northeast. Kümmel himself was able to knock out a number of the Mark IIs. Despite the strong artillery fire directed against them, by 1715hrs the Regiment was finally able to consolidate its gains, with all its elements more or less intact on the hotly contested positions at El Duda. The Regiment was able to reach the heights, where it was able to collect numerous prisoners and equipment, along with the destruction of six *Matildas*. But even though the panzer attack had gone reasonably well and they were in possession of the El Duda feature, they had expended up to twenty percent of their ammunition throughout the afternoon's battles getting there. The same could not be said of the supporting attacks undertaken by the infantry battalions, which had become quickly bogged down under the heavy fire from artillery, infantry, and anti-tank guns. As was to be expected, the infantry in their carriers were slowed by the amount of artillery falling around them; they finally reached the heights a short time later. However, the panzers did not wait while the infantry was moving up; instead, they drove off to the northeast towards the axis bypass road in an attempt to link up with elements of the *"Afrika"* Division. That link up was never affected, and the infantry following the panzers remained pinned down at El Duda. In order to be able to continue the attack and to protect itself from any counterattacks Cramer, despite the strong fire still falling on the Regiment's positions, ordered the combat field trains to move forward and conduct a re-supply. As done so many times before, *Olt* Lindner and his men performed the task in an extraordinary and very precise manner, getting the all important fuel and ammunition to the panzer crews. Thanks again to the letters of Klaus Hubbuch we get a sense of how the attack progressed for the Mk IVs of the *8th Company*. In that company the panzer of *Fw* Bastigheit took a direct hit to its running gear and was rendered inoperable; the panzer of *Fw* Gerder took a direct hit on the gun mantle and was placed out of commission, while the panzer of Lt Voigt, the company commander, was hit and Voigt was wounded again. Despite the combined attack little headway was made and the attack was called off. Hubbuch had this description of the battle:

"The English Trommelfeuer [drumfire] begins the heaviest ever so far! Dirt is flying through upper gap in the fighting compartment, through the side gaps flashes of the fragments are twitching. Hissing and clattering, a test of nerves, but we already don't care anymore. Outside, infantry is shouting everywhere; wounded and then begins the coming of the night, it is scary. The English tank attack by Matildas from the right and the left of the axis road come to within 300m of us. The machine gun fire with red and green tracers is terrible, the 40mm solid shot of the Matildas is hitting our few remaining panzers; we are getting hit at the hull, thank God not at the panzer turret."[90]

As darkness began to descend, the British artillery increased the amount of fire it was throwing at El Duda, until finally it began to let up, a sure indication of an impending attack. That counter attack was not long in coming, when at 2000hrs infantry forces supported by *Matilda* tanks came on with great intensity. As the *Matildas* and infantry came forward, the panzer gunners, having dealt with these armored pillboxes before, held their fire until the tanks came to within 250-300m. The British tanks paid a price for their counter-attack in the darkness with the loss of two of their tanks. It was thanks to the light panzer Mk IIs, with their high rate of fire and their 20mm tracer ammunition, that played a special part in halting the attack. The British attack was held, but only by an extremely high consumption of ammunition. In many cases the panzer gunners found themselves having to expend on average three rounds per *Matilda* in order to destroy it or render it inoperable; therefore, it took some time before the British tanks finally broke off their attack. Hubbuch was one of those gunners:

"Our order was that it was forbidden to fire; no moving back, shooting but through 'ear shells' a code for saving ammunition; letting the target get really close. Our front is holding, the British are retreating from our defensive fire, the rattling of the Matildas are moving away; it is pitch dark the whole time only once in a while a light flare somewhere.

We are inspecting the battlefield, there is whimpering and screaming everywhere, many wounded and dead, here a leg still sticking in its boot, there another one, a head, there an arm, it was a solid hit. One of our Mk IVs is burning, Uffz Rink is dead and Rosshaderer and Fringskarte are heavily wounded. Our panzer is pickled with artillery fragments, ration boxes and many containers; mountings and covering steels have all been penetrated several times. At around midnight we move back towards the west, the English are following under a murderous fire and are taking hold of his former positions. We are making a defense front, refueling, reloading ammunition and standing guard and staying the whole night on alert, 'ready for combat'. The field kitchen this night is not getting through to us so we don't get any warm meal, tea or coffee."[91]

After the last counter attack had been dealt with, the division was finally able to reorganize itself on the heights near El Duda. The division also put in a request for the *D.A.K.* to move up a strong relieving force of infantry and Pak guns, which could allow the division to continue its attacks on the following day. As the panzers rolled off to the low ground southeast of Bir Salem to take on a fresh supply of ammunition and fuel, another British attack was launched at 2330hrs by forces coming from the Tobruk perimeter. That attack, again supported by tanks, was successful in throwing the infantry of *Schützen Regiment 115* off of the El Duda heights. A counter attack by *15th Panzer* was scheduled to take place later that morning, but it was called off when the division misinterpreted an order assigning it to the *Panzergruppe* and mistakenly began moving off for an attack near El Adem. By 0300hrs, the division was finally able to clarify the mistake and ordered a halt for the night near Bir Salem. The battle had been raging for days now, and the *D.A.K.* was exhausted both in manpower and machines; there had been no new panzers sent to Africa, and the Regiment had only a quarter of its original panzer strength from when the battle had begun. But even more important were the men, who had taken a beating and were just about at the end of their physical endurance; the lack of sleep, poor hygiene, and constant fighting was wearing even the toughest of them down. As the 29th finally ended, the *D.A.K.* found itself a spent force, having suffered serious losses and having almost nothing to show for it. The *Ariete* had been able to hold its positions near Sidi Rezegh, while the *21st Panzer*'s attacks had ground to a halt, and to make matters worse, the division commander, *Generalmajor* Ravenstein, was captured when he became disorientated and stumbled into the middle of a New Zealand position.[92] For the Regiment, it was able to report the following claims and losses, including the destruction of numerous Matildas, along with multiple anti-tank guns and infantry-guns, as well as the capture of approximately 150 prisoners. In addition to suffering numerous losses, they also suffered some four killed, including Lt Voigt, and sixteen wounded. The number of panzer losses amounted to one Mk II, one Mk III, and two Mk IVs—most of those losses had been caused by British anti-tank guns. Additionally, there were three panzers that were damaged due to mines, and the *Werkshop Company* later repaired all of these panzers. The vast majority of the panzers all suffered various damage caused by anti-tank guns and artillery fragments which fouled running gear, jammed turret and gun mechanisms, and shredded almost everything located on the outside of the panzers.[93] As the morning of 30 November dawned, the men were able to take in the scene before them; the Regiment had sustained a number of key losses, and those vacancies were keenly felt. Klaus Hubbuch:

"It is sunrise on Sunday, the First Advents; English bombers in large number are trashing our supply column. Uffz Greif becomes our panzer commander, he is telling jokes and finally the miserable mood of Uffz Fluhrer, with all his sudden 'stop-commands' during the attack, is over. Our engine is loosing water, the I-Staffel is able to repair the water pump but with considerable interruption; again a bomber attack, you can see the eggs [bombs] dropping. After the horrible detonations there are many vehicles are burning. Again, we have no water the containers are empty, punctured or are used up as coolant. For two weeks we have neglected body washing and we are covered with 10-day-old dirt."[94]

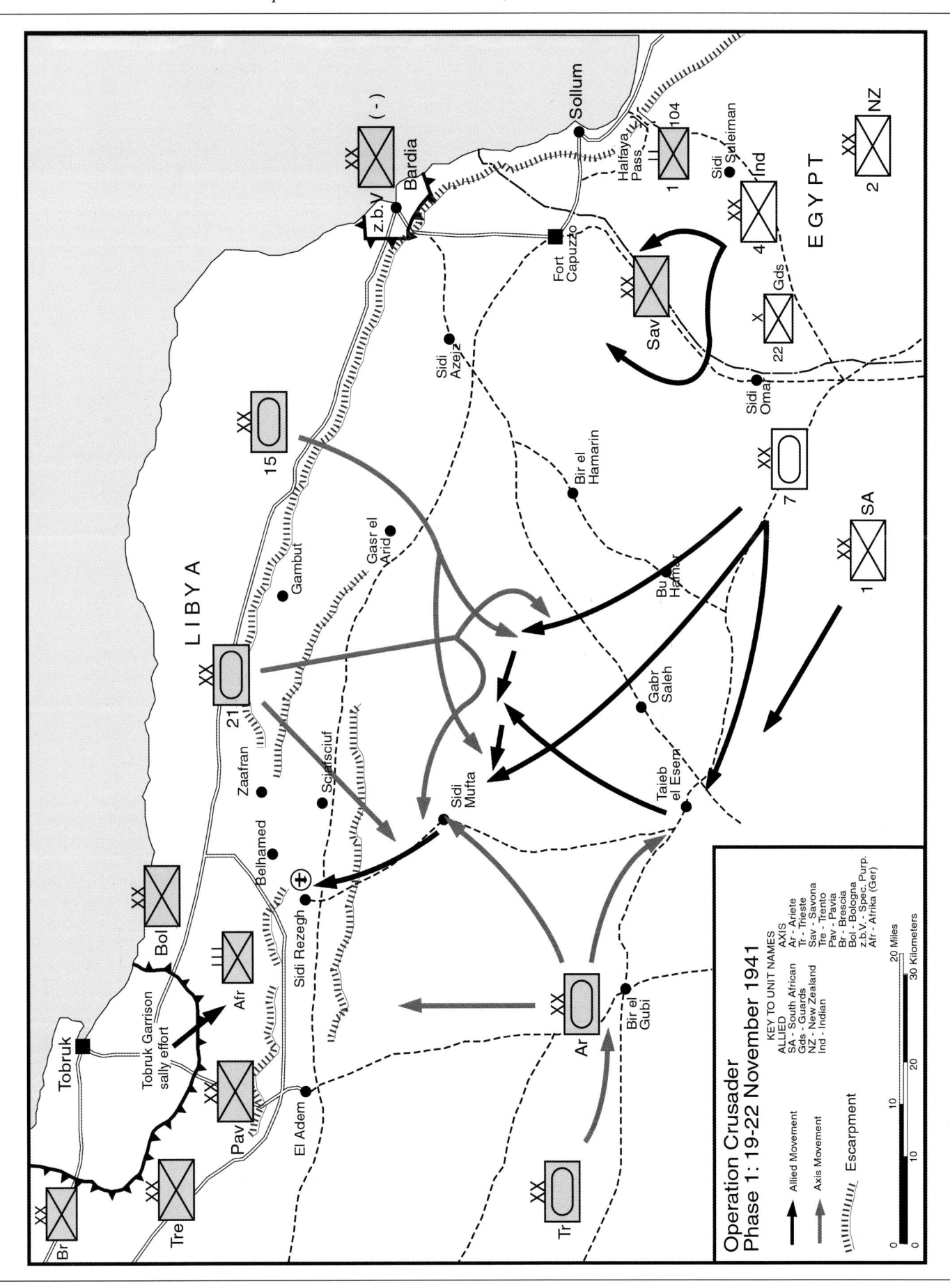

Chapter 7: The Crusader Battles, October-November 1941

125

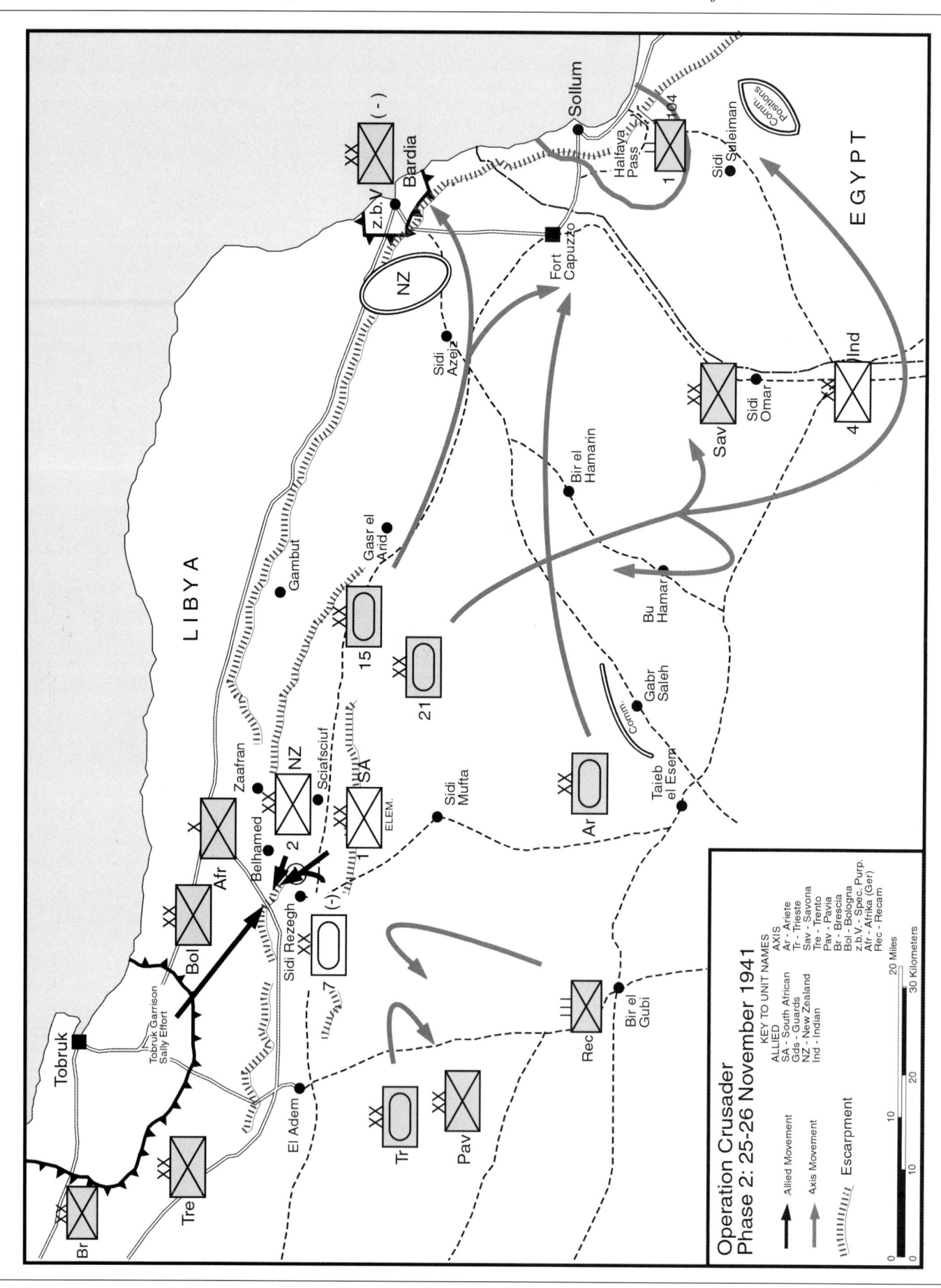

Panzer Regiment 8 in World War II - Poland • France • North Africa

**Operation Crusader
Phase 2: 25-26 November 1941**

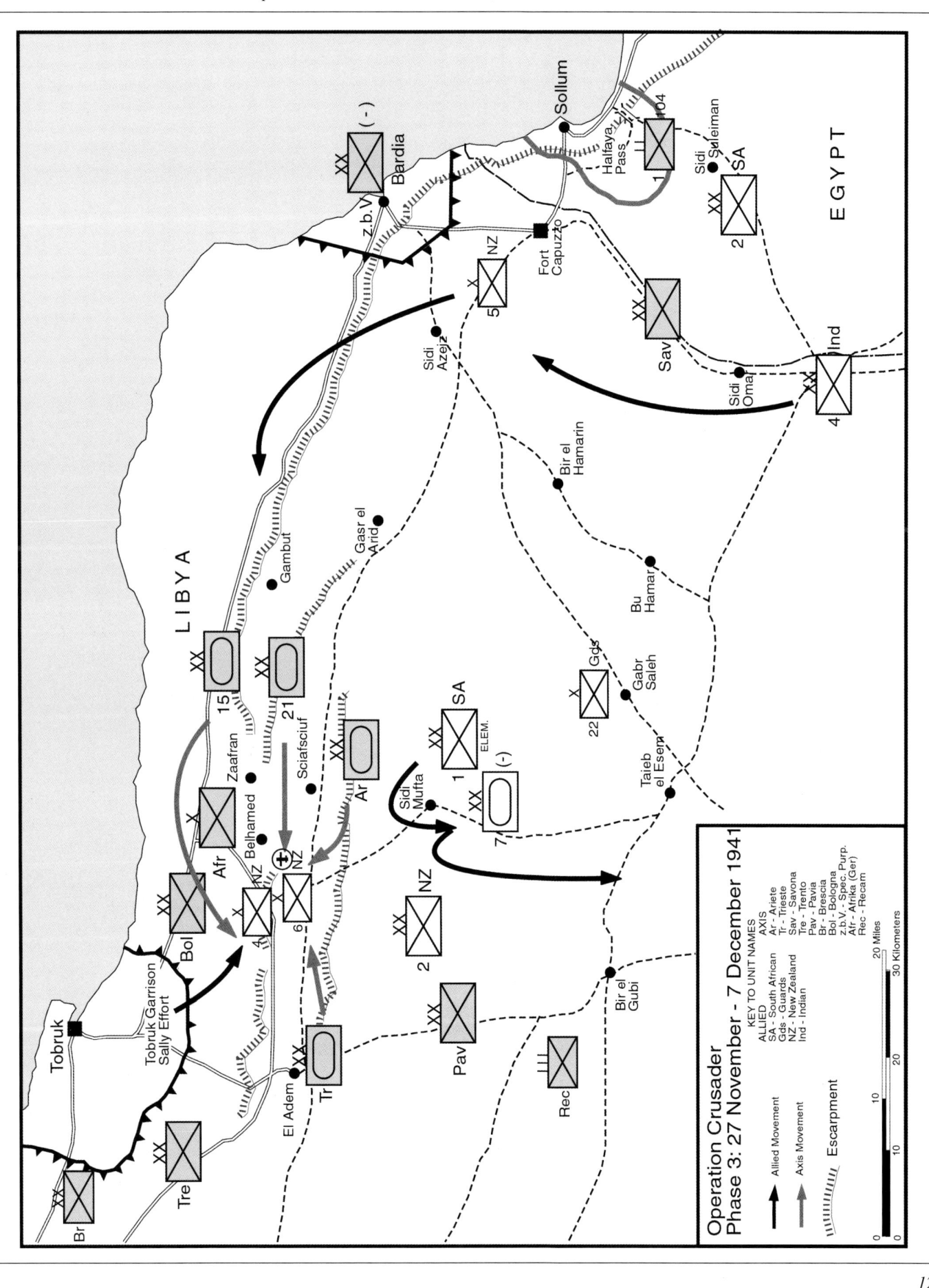

Chapter 7: The Crusader Battles, October-November 1941

8

Withdrawal from Cyrenaica December 1941

The situation that greeted the *D.A.K.* the morning of the 30th was not a good one; El Duda had been lost to the New Zealanders, who still maintained contact with the Tobruk perimeter, and had even sent elements to Sidi Rezegh. The *Ariete* was still holding the *7th Armored Division*, which was still attempting to break through from the south and link up with those forces at Sidi Rezegh. Strong British forces from the *4th Indian Division* were moving towards Bir el Gubi in an attempt to outflank the *Panzergruppe*. The *21st Panzer* was still located near Zaafran, but at this point the division's striking power was seriously diminished. The same was to be said for the entire *D.A.K.*, which was now given the "*Afrika*" Division and the artillery of *Kampfgruppe Böttcher* to assist it in its attacks to destroy the *2nd New Zealand Division*. The *Panzergruppe* artillery was now under the command of *Oberst* Johann Mickl, the former commander of zbV "*Afrika*," after Karl Böttcher had been sent to take over command of the *21st Panzer Division*.[1] The one element that could be used for striking back was the *15th Panzer Division*, which although down to approximately half its strength had been able to reform around Bir Salem, and was that morning ready for continued operations. Orders were then issued that called for attacks by the *Ariete* and *Kampfgruppe Mickl* on Sidi Rezegh, while the *21st Panzer* was to continue holding its positions in order to block any escape attempts by the New Zealanders. The *15th Panzer Division* that morning was released from its present task, and was all set to march to the west, but it was then halted and issued a new set of orders to attack Sidi Rezegh. The *Ariete*, which had been initially assigned this task, was completely engaged to the south with British forces there, and so the division moved its formations via Sidi Veimum into the low ground northwest of Bir Creimisa, making use of the depressions there to cover its movement. *Schützen Regiment 115* was to be left south of Bir Salem to reorganize its forces there. The division was to position itself so that it could undertake either an attack to the southeast to assist the *Ariete* or northeast to assist *Kampfgruppe Mickl*. Forming up for the attack proved difficult, owing to the need to avoid a minefield in the sector of the assault. Just after midday, the plan was altered somewhat by Crüwell, who suggested to Rommel that the attack should be launched at 1500hrs with *15th Panzer* aligned to the left of *Kampfgruppe Mickl* with the objective being the saddle west of Belhamed. To support the attack Rommel ordered that the "*Afrika*" Division strike at the same time from the north. The march route took the Regiment back to the east, where the Regiment began to turn to the north and approached Sidi Rezegh from the west. Neumann-Silkow then decided to modify the plan and send the Regiment across into the area occupied by *Kampfgruppe Mickl* to attack Sidi Rezegh first, so as not to expose the right flank. *RAF* bomber attacks that afternoon had delayed the start time, as the *15th Panzer* had moved forward from Bir Creimisa with the Regiment in the lead closely supported by a number of 88mm Flak guns. The I./Abteilung descended at once, finding the steep slope and going rough as it made straight for the Sidi Rezegh escarpment to a point one kilometer east of Abiar el-Amar. The I./Abteilung carried on eastwards along the foot of the escarpment towards the Mosque, meeting little opposition along the way. The II./Abteilung, with the Pak and artillery echeloned to the right rear, was not as fortunate, as it came under heavy fire from the *6th New Zealand Brigade*, and the *abteilung* was forced to halt in the face of such fierce resistance and face it. *Oberst* Cramer then ordered Kümmel to send reinforcements back to the top of the escarpment to assist the II./Abteilung in overcoming this resistance.[2] As the first panzers broke through in the low ground along the Trigh Capuzzo they encountered strong resistance from a number of machine gun, anti-tank, and artillery positions. The attack soon developed into bitter close quarters fighting between the panzers and the hardened New Zealanders, who attempted to pick off the panzer commanders with hand grenades and rifle fire. The panzers replied in turn using their coaxial machine guns and firing high explosive rounds from short range. It was this effective fire that forced the infantry to keep their heads down and allowed the panzers to roll over those positions, thus breaking the New Zealander defenses and capturing some six hundred prisoners and twelve guns. Hubbuch wrote about the fight:

"*Again the attack on Sidi Rezegh against strong English positions; murderous machine gun and Pak fire is hitting us, but the Matildas are not getting close to us and finally are moving back. We overrun English infantry positions and our machine gun is hampering again the gun-layer Gefr Stein must work he is cursing and sweating, so continuing with rounds from 100m distance into trenches, shreds are flying around, we are rolling over anti-tank, vehicles are shot and burning, Uffz Greif is shooting out of the turret opening from above with the pistol and is throwing hand grenades; it is a real short range combat. It is getting dark. Then numbers of Tommies are surrendering, by the hundreds, right among our panzers; our own infantry pulls ahead and takes up position. It was a hard and successful fight; the other company had significant losses through artillery fragments and gunshots on the commandants who participated [in the attack] from the panzer turret to keep the English from attaching a sticky bomb. That evening, we go through the abandoned English positions with loaded pistols searching for booty; English walkie-talkies still turned on*

Chapter 8: Withdrawal from Cyrenaica, December 1941

and weapons of the Tommy we find in large numbers along with many English, German and Italian dead bodies!"[3]

Horst Sonnenkalb wrote of the previous two days:

"We weren't able to rest. On November 29th there was another tank fight near Sidi Rezegh, this time with soldiers from New Zealand. We weren't able to take the town, but we managed a victory at the mountain crest of El Duda. The daily report included the number of panzers that were still ready for action. That number became smaller each day. Panzer Regiment 5 was in the most critical position. However, Rommel didn't let up. On November 30th we advanced once again toward Sidi Rezegh, where we'd received a bloody nose the day before. This time we were successful. We didn't just capture the small area, but also 1500 Brits became German prisoners. The positions that had been held by Brits were cleaned up and taken by infantrymen. The number of panzers that were ready for use was getting smaller by the day. On December 3rd the whole DAK only had 34 operational panzers left. During the fierce battles of the last week of November, the Brits had managed to destroy 167 German and Italian battle vehicles."[4]

As the remaining New Zealanders retreated towards Belhamed, a number of British tanks were seen just to the north, but they were weary of the German panzers, and so they remained at a safe distance, not wanting to cross the Trigh Capuzzo and do battle. Those tanks finally departed alltogether, leaving their positions and Sidi Rezegh to the German infantry. At 1715hrs, the panzers drove in among the abandoned positions and began assisting in rounding up prisoners, but this process lasted until dusk, and made Neumann-Silkow postpone the Belhamed operation until the next day.[5] Elsewhere that day the *21st Panzer* had again suffered a number of losses, as its attack on Zaafran met with no success, and the division was pressed from both the south and southeast by British and New Zealand forces; at one point the division even asked for the *Ariete* to attack to help relieve some of the pressure on it. As the division finished up consolidating and policing the battlefield, Crüwell, who had watched the battle from his headquarters, appeared at the division command post to issue his orders for the continued attack on Belhamed. Crüwell wanted the attack to go in that night before the New Zealanders had time to reorganize their defense. Neumann-Silkow, however, disagreed with him, because he felt that only a well-coordinated attack that was well supported would have any chance at success. Crüwell agreed with the assessment and issued the necessary changes to his orders. The *15th Panzer* would not have to take Belhamed that night; however, by first light on the 1st it was to secure a position northwest of that location on the axis bypass road in order to be in a position to both support and cover any attacks from the south. The evening of 30/1 December 1941 there was to be no rest for the combat and service and support elements, as they prepared for the next phase of the battle. There was also the harassing fire from British artillery that struck the assembly areas from the east of El Adem to the west of Sidi Rezegh. The Regiment had to send two of its Mk IIIs into the workshops, but received three Mk IIIs in return. As the preparations continued and battle plans were drawn up a number of reconnaissance patrols were sent forward to see what awaited the division at Belhamed. The patrols returned and informed the headquarters that Belhamed and the dominate saddle to the east of it were strongly held by infantry forces, and studded with a large number of artillery and anti-tank gun positions. The plan that was drawn up called for the division to cross the low area around the Trigh Capuzzo and have *Schützen Regiment 200* and *Kradschützen Battalion 15*, along with *Machine Gun Battalion 2* to lead off by moving up the low slope towards the town. Once in position, the infantry would signal the panzers, which would then move up, and both forces would go in together. The attack was to be supported by both the division artillery and *Panzergruppe* artillery firing from the south of the Trigh Capuzzo.[6] As the morning hours slowly passed the Regiment found itself in an assembly area surrounded by thick fog. After moving closer to the start line, the Regiment, with its I./*Abteilung* up front and in close cooperation with the infantry and artillery began its attack at dawn. Klaus Hubbuch was with one of the II./*Abteilung* panzers that day and gives a good description of what it was like:

"That night, we receive an order to attack Belhamed (Height 154m), there the Tommy is still sitting, he is dug in and without connection to Tobruk, and only the Matildas are once in a while able to break through the surrounding [perimeter]. We are sitting in the panzer, it is dawning; our alert position is east of El Adem near a mosque and a spring. Artillery is preparing the battlefield, how will it go? The I./Abteilung is already rolling, we follow, a swift attack; vehicles shot and on fire and English anti-tank guns eliminated; but nothing else to see in the dust of the detonations caused by the murderous defense fire of the English artillery, the ground here is very fine sand, just like dust."[7]

At 0637hrs on the morning of 12 December, the Regiment began one of its most difficult battles. The morning fog was heavy and covered the ground, which provided limited visibility of nearby British forces. Ascending from the mosque at Sidi Rezegh, the previous day's attack was continued to the north. The objective of the attack was the heights of Belhamed. The Regiment was formed up with the I./*Abteilung* in the lead, followed by the Regimental *Stabs*, and finally the II./*Abteilung*, which was echeloned to the rear. Each panzer *abteilung* had an attached Flak battery from I./*Flak Regiment 35*, which had the mission of directly supporting the attack. The division's infantry were to follow closely once the Regiment attacked. After an artillery barrage to soften things up, the I./*Abteilung* moved off at a high rate of speed, anxious to close the distance to the enemy. At 0630hrs, the Trigh Capuzzo was crossed, along with German infantry positions, which had been advanced forward during the night. The Regiment moved forward quickly, and when the morning fog began to burn off at around 0700hrs, the I./*Abteilung* reported strong enemy infantry forces directly to the front arrayed along the southern slope near Belhamed. The infantry, as so often happened in these high-speed attacks, was unable to keep up with the panzers, which needed speed to close the distance between them and the anti-tank and artillery guns. As the panzers emerged from the covering mist they began to receive heavy fire as the attack rolled uphill. Simultaneously, *Hptm* Kümmel recognized a large number of enemy tanks and trucks also located on the heights, but was unable to engage them because of the extreme range. Shortly thereafter, the right flank of I./*Abteilung* was engaged by heavy artillery fire from a ravine on the east side of Belhamed. A large volume of heavy machine gun fire and anti-tank gun fire was also being thrown against the flanks. *Hptm* Kümmel ordered his *1st Company*, led by Lt Arnold, to form a firing line on the right flank in order to suppress those guns while he continued the attack to the north. At 0830hrs, the initial line of resistance in the south was overcome, and the panzers then began to head for the northern slope, while the infantry was sent over to the right in order to deal with that threat. At 1040hrs, *Hptm* Kümmel led his *abteilung* through a wall of dust and fire towards Belhamed and the center of the resistance. The Regimental commander, Hans Cramer, immediately recognized the danger that this fire, coming from Zaafran, could have against the right flank, and could possibly disrupt the entire attack. Cramer quickly ordered that the II./*Abteilung* take up positions to the front of the I./*Abteilung*, in order to begin engaging the British threat coming from the right. As that *abteilung* began taking up positions facing east, the I./*Abteilung* was ordered to keep up the attack towards the northwest. Arnold's *1st Company*, which had been the subject of the British fire, was relieved, and quickly sped up to rejoin the remainder of the *abteilung* as it pushed on. With little regard to the situation, the I./*Abteilung* continued towards Belhamed, the objective of the day's attack, without paying attention to the clearly visible enemy artillery, which was firing directly at the panzers. The New Zealand forces' defense of the area was tough and obstinate, but the flanking fire coming from the left and right could not halt the I./*Abteilung*. Kümmel led his panzers forward without paying attention to the numerous losses, until he managed to break through the enemy artillery park and capture it. The weight of the supporting German artillery bombardment began to cause some panic and unnerve the tough New Zealanders, some of which began to surrender. Hundreds of prisoners were soon rounded up by the I./*Abteilung*, along with a couple of batteries of 25-Pounder guns and sixteen of the new 57mm (6-Pounder) anti-tank guns. Despite the losses he had suffered in the attack, Kümmel decided to take advantage of the situation and continue the attack towards the west. At this time, the division received reports about a strong enemy tank attack coming up from the south; this force consisted of approximately eighty vehicles. The divisional commander, Neumann-Silkow, personally asked Cramer as to whether he would be in a position to respond to this attack and support those friendly forces now being engaged. A redeployment of the II./*Abteilung* against this attack was not possible, as it was too heavily engaged with enemy forces in the east, as the enemy was now pushing towards the east and the southeast of Belhamed with a large number of vehicles and self-propelled gun carriages. With a continued threat to the division's flank, Cramer struggled to make the decision to halt the I./*Abteilung* in its successful advance towards the west and turn it around to the south. Cramer ordered that the II./*Abteilung* continue its attack along the eastern slope of Belhamed, with parts of the *abteilung* positioned to the north and others to the east. The current task of I./*Abteilung* was then transferred to the accompanying panzers of the Regimental *Stabs* and the Pioneer *Zug*, which succeeded in taking a large number of prisoners and preventing further escape towards Tobruk, until additional infantry forces could move up and take over the defense in the north. The divisional commander approved of Cramer's orders as he transmitted them by radio. Communications within the Regiment and to the division were working extremely well, thanks to the efforts of *Olt* Lehn and his communications section, which had been well prepared and trained for such events. In the meantime, *Hptm* Wahl, commander of the II./*Abteilung*, which was covering the right flank, became involved in heavy combat. Against him and his panzers there appeared more and more enemy forces. Multiple anti-tank, artillery, and self-propelled gun carriages were seen moving forward and firing from all their guns and inflicted losses to the *abteilung*, which by now had only a few Mk II and IIIs remaining. However, at around 1030hrs *Olt* Prion managed to break through an enemy artillery park with his company and quickly captured twelve guns. Despite this the enemy continued his uninterrupted fire, and there was still some very heavy combat for the panzers in order to drive the enemy from their positions. Losses even came against the divisional headquarters, which was closely following the Regiment. *Major* Kriebel, the divisional operations officer (Ia), had to bail out of his damaged panzer under heavy enemy fire. Klaus Hubbuch, of the *8th Company*, recorded the following description of events taking place around the II./*Abteilung*:[8]

"*Everywhere in the combat area; a change of position succeeds, it smells like fuel, after pulling back a pool remains in front of us, our panzer is riddled with bullet holes and leaking and we didn't explode – a miracle?! New Pak hits and the panzer stands still...*

Commander: 'get ready to get out!' but English machine gun fire is concentrating on us while we grab machine pistols and important documents, maps etc. to be burned. Yes, the driver is able to start the engine backwards, it knocks and sputters terribly, and the drive gear seems heavily damaged. Sparks from the grinding steel; if the fuel gets inflated, we are finished. But we have to save the vehicle and us; getting out during this machine gun fire would be fatal. Where is backwards? We are driving aimlessly, very slowly, outside salvos are hitting against the panzer, machine gun fire, and the panzer turret is like in a cheese cover. Suddenly, the vehicle moves forwards again, we are getting out of the battle field, far away, we can see the mosque in the mist, our starting point of the day; the slope of the area is slightly going up, the transmission breaks, the vehicle stands still, what next? Wounded are everywhere; Flak operators are returning they have no more guns; next to us they are burying dead bodies; in long lines prisoners of all races, huge guys, often wounded, barely bearded; that is the other side of the battlefield. Every body is asking us about the outcome? How should we know? It is horrible for us, we cannot move, the supply trains are not visible and we couldn't leave our panzer now and in front of us, the flaming, raging front; we are turning the turret towards the enemy and remain halted; hopefully the front will hold. Now some [soldiers] are shouting tanks, Matildas appear at the right flank of the front; everything that has an engine is moving back in haste, our driver and radio operator are loosing their nerve, a dead vehicle, but still able to fire with a turret crew of three men and watch artillery fire around us. But the enemy tanks are returning again, on the right, the English Troß is retreating, we are firing on them in 3-5000m distance, the shots are going well in the low fields southeast of Belhamed. Our own artillery on the left, fires towards El Duda. We are alone! - We try to get in radio contact but it doesn't work, the radio documents [codes] are already burned. The machine pistol, bread bag and coats are packed for getting out, if it has to be, we will shoot, then we'll detonate the dead vehicle and if possible run away. The front is getting quieter, the German attack was again successful; supply vehicles of the Troß are moving forward, Fw Himmelreich – our driver – comes back with the I-Staffel repair vehicles. Our panzer has among others a 40mm bull's eye on the left side that penetrated the panzer and the drive shaft, a second hit on the right destroyed a roller, a third hit again on the left penetrated into the engine compartment, but was deflected from there, also there are many artillery fragments that penetrated the steel plates. Machine gun salvos are loud inside, but outside, they leave no marks except on containers and such."[9]

In the south, the I./*Abteilung* quickly came in contact with elements of the *4th Armored Brigade*, and together with German artillery, managed to quickly destroy six British tanks and drive the remainder off to the southeast. At around 1130hrs, enemy resistance in the south began to visibly weaken, and Kümmel reported that the enemy were beginning to get up in front of his panzers and surrender everywhere. Unfortunately, the I./*Abteilung* was unable to pursue the beaten enemy due to the shortage of ammunition and fuel. After receiving these reports, Cramer decided to halt the I./*Abteilung* and turn it back towards the northeast, with the task of rolling onto the enemy position along the ridge between El Duda and Belhamed.

After the I./*Abteilung* had arrived back near Belhamed, it again encountered British armor, this time from the northwest. A large group of approximately twenty "Matildas" had been attacking in the north from the direction of El Duda, and were causing some concern to those forces fighting there. Those British tanks quickly retreated as the remaining guns of the heavy Flak battery of *Olt* Zurmar drove forward, without loss, through the heavy artillery fire and continued to participate in the attack of the I./*Abteilung*. Shortly after this took place, a number of German infantry arrived to occupy the heights and take control of the prisoners. At around 1330hrs, the Regiment's supply vehicles arrived on scene, and the panzers had the opportunity to replenish ammunition and fuel. *Olt* Lindner and his supply detachment were always in the right place and where they were needed the most; here again they were able to refit a significant portion of the Regiment and make it ready for action. At around 1420hrs, the British became active once again in the east around Zaafran. There was also a bombing attack on Belhamed by the *RAF*, but no losses were suffered.

By midday, the "*Afrika*" Division, which had not yet appeared to the north, and the *21st Panzer*, which was busy defending itself from attacks further to the south, were now ordered to move forward and link-up with the *15th Panzer Division*. The "*Afrika*" Division was ordered to move south and take up positions on the north side of Belhamed, while the *21st Panzer* was ordered to move west and link up with *15th Panzer* as it continued east towards Zaafran. Because of the interference caused by British radio jamming units, Kümmel, having been partially re-supplied with ammunition, decided to continue the attack with his few remaining panzers on towards Zaafran, which was also being held by *2nd New Zealand Division*. Kümmel was followed at 1500hrs by the remainder of the division. At 1637hrs, the Regiment began its new attack from Belhamed towards Zaafran. With a speedy advance the panzers covered some 6km and quickly captured a British artillery battery with a long range gun. As the panzers rolled on towards Zaafran they encountered very little resistance, as the New Zealand defenses began to come apart, and the panzers were able to make their way to Hill 143, located just east of Zaafran. Along the way the I./*Abteilung* had overrun a couple of artillery batteries and captured over two hundred prisoners, which were sent back towards Belhamed. Enemy anti-tank guns which attempted to resist the movement were rolled over and destroyed. Late in the afternoon, a mix up in radio signals caused the division to halt its pursuit of the enemy, and the drive eastward came to an end 3km from Zaafran. Because of this mix up, a great chance was lost to finish off the *2nd New Zealand Division*, which managed to escape the net thrown out by the *D.A.K*. Even though the New Zealanders were able to escape total destruction, it would be months before they were ready for even the slightest bit of action, and their attempts at breaking the Tobruk perimeter came to naught, as that evening the *Panzergruppe* forces began to hem in the garrison there once again. The prize for the *D.A.K.* was a rich one, as over a thousand prisoners were taken, along with twenty-five guns and numerous anti-tank guns and vehicles. The Regiment had had a very successful day, mission wise, but when it reported its losses that evening the success of the day was tarnished by the losses suffered. Six panzer commanders were mortally wounded (most suffered head wounds), twenty-one others were wounded, and four soldiers were listed as missing. Lt Arnold, commanding the *1st Company*, was one of those wounded, and he was replaced by Lt Thurow. Seven Mk IIs, twelve Mk IIIs, and one Mk IV were damaged in the course of the battle, with three Mk IIs and one Mk IV listed as complete write offs.[10] By this time, though, the panzers were truly on their last leg, as a combination of fluctuating temperatures, daily wear and tear, and combat damage began to take its toll. A lot of the materiel was covered in rust brought on by the heat and dust, which covered the panzers with every movement. The dust was so fine that it entered the vital engine spaces and caused abrasions on the metal parts. The crews found that the air filters constantly became blocked with this dust, and they had to be carefully watched and emptied often. Oil and water consumption was extremely high, but it could not be replaced often enough, which caused the engines to overheat and the pistons to seize up. The clutch and transmissions were all worn out through overuse, and almost every panzer in the Regiment either slipped or stuck in gear. Hubbuch then describes the beating some of these machines could take:

"*The panzer is a wreck; transmission locked up; machine guns jammed, radio system out of order, codes and procedures destroyed. We are quickly moving back, still the panzer is visible in the sunset, the cannon is threatening, pointing towards the enemy; since November18th it [the panzer] was my home day and night, of all the panzers from the 8th Company it endured the most, participated in every attack and now finally the last out of order, heavily hit!*"[11]

With the New Zealanders out of the battle and their link with Tobruk cut, the situation facing Norrie and his subordinate commanders was grim, and they were now even contemplating breaking off the attacks and pulling back. However, they were stopped when *General* Auchinleck arrived at the headquarters of the *Eighth Army* to reassure and help steady nerves. He informed them that reinforcements were now on the way, and that they should continue the attack. Unfortunately for Rommel, he wasn't counting on this type of thinking, and knew that if he was to launch a counter-attack on an enemy who was still determined to destroy him instead of retreating, he would be wasting men and machines that he could ill afford. For almost twelve days now the men and machines had been in constant combat with only short rest breaks, and were both exhausted and worn out. That first evening of December some men did receive some rest, as Hubbuch relates:

"*I find shelter at the supply trains at the I-Staffel and fall asleep immediately on the back of the panzer until the next arrival at the Abteilung; the 8th Company is still represented by three 20mm Mk IIs, two of them have just come out of the repair shop; there are no more 75mm Mk IVs which use to be in large numbers and the backbone of this heavy company.*"

That night Hubbuch had these observations:

"*The Situation is this: Outside the Tobruk perimeter the enemy is hopefully and completely beaten, with the exception of some parts scattered in the desert and with the exception of El Duda, which actually could be counted as part of the Tobruk perimeter and where our night attack, two days ago, wasn't successful. Different then in the beginning – Sollum battle or Totensonntag battle – a panzer attack with all its battle noise, hits etc. doesn't bother me any more, I stay completely calm, only I always need something to chew.*"[12]

After the morning report was issued to the division, *Oberst* Cramer informed his Regiment that combat operations were temporarily over. The Regiment now was the only unit in *Panzergruppe Afrika* suitable enough for mobile combat operations, and because of that fact had to remain prepared to undertake any missions at any time. The operational ability of the Regiment was able to improve slightly on the 2nd with the Regiment reporting the following numbers: eleven Mk IIs, twenty-four Mk IIIs, and three Mk IVs, for a total of thirty-eight panzers.[13] Even though it could count the number of serviceable, the Regimental *Stabs* still did not have an exact number of its killed, wounded, or missing troops. The pause after the battle did allow the division the opportunity to replenish its losses, as shortly after concluding elements began to pick through the remains and restock themselves with vehicles, uniforms, and most of all provisions. Even though the battle seemed to be over and won, there was still some unfinished business to attend to; the *D.A.K.* was ordered to mop up around Zaafran, and a couple of *kampfgruppen* were sent towards the Sollum front in an attempt to deliver supplies to the garrisons still holding out there. These two *kampfgruppen*, each about the size of a battalion, were sent down the Via Balbia and Trigh Capuzzo. The *21st Panzer's kampfgruppe*, under the command of *Oberstlt* Knabe, was ordered to proceed along the Trigh Capuzzo, and was able to reach as far as Bir el Giaser (Sidi Azeiz) before it was halted by the *4th Indian Division*, which was now moving up into the battle area. The British reported that four of the eight panzers in the *kampfgruppe* were knocked out by 25-Pounders.[14] The *15th Panzer kampfgruppe*, under the command of *Oberstlt* Geissler, was able to progress along the Via Balbia, and was only able to advance as far as Gambut before it too was halted, this time by elements of the *5th New Zealand Brigade*. While those forces were engaged to the east, the "*Afrika*" Division, along with the Italian *XXI Corps*, was ordered to regain their previous positions along the east side of the Tobruk perimeter. Both advances failed to gain any ground, and both formations were forced to return back to where they had started. That morning the Regiment found itself in the assembly area just northeast of El Duda with the supply trains nearby on the Via Balbia. The panzer crews used the break in action to conduct limited repairs, and hopefully improve their overall operational ability. As the crews performed what limited maintenance they could, the retrieval section went forward into the desert and located those recoverable panzers and brought them back to the *Werkshop* Companies and "I" Services, who worked around the clock attempting to salvage what panzers they could. The severe shortage of spare parts normally meant that some panzers had to be cannibalized, or stripped of their parts, which were put to use on other less damaged panzers. Also that morning Neumann-Silkow informed *Oberst* Cramer that the Regiment would be relocated to its previous assembly area just north of Gambut, where it would be in position if it were needed in the battles near Sollum. As the Regiment continued its repairs, the remainder of the *15th Panzer* would move off towards Gambut. Hubbuch remembered:

"*The supply column stands not far away on the Via Balbia just southeast of Tobruk, I kip [nap] and nurse myself back with three meals in 24 hours for three days, there is also beer and chocolate; all collected by Uffz Greif and myself. The war seems to be finished!*"

The situation on the 3rd saw the panzer regiments of the *D.A.K.* still attempting to rest and recover their strength while *Kampfgruppen Knabe* and *Geissler* were attacked as they attempted to move up to the Sollum front by elements of the *2nd New Zealand* and *4th Indian Divisions*. Both of those *kampfgruppen* were nearly destroyed in their attempts to reach Bardia and Sollum. However, those attempts did succeed in making the *Eighth Army* think that the entire *D.A.K.* was again on the move towards the border. For the men of the Regiment their rest and recovery in the assembly area was disturbed by heavy artillery fire coming from the area around El Duda; that artillery was soon joined by sixteen *RAF* bombers that attacked the assembly area, killing three soldiers and wounding another seven. One Mk III was also damaged in the attack.[15] The Regimental supply trains were also severely hit in the attack, and twelve vehicles were destroyed and fourteen soldiers were wounded. Hubbuch's diary recorded the following:

"*Situation: If no support is needed for the Sollum battle, where they are still fighting, we will move back to the resting place at the sea near Gambut, from where we had left on November 18/19. The trucks are towing the abandoned panzers from the battlefield in the desert; will we get to use ours again? First, it came differently. Around noon, very heavy artillery fire came from the west near El Duda, our supply column escapes towards the east; a bad bomber attack follows sixteen English bombers with fighter protection. These bombardments and low-flight attacks with illumination [tracer] ammunition are becoming repetitive, a scary feeling in the trench beside the vehicle, you can see the guys flying over you in the mist of the bomb attacks, several vehicles are burning.*"[16]

On 4 December, the German attempt to recapture the El Duda position also broke down under the weight of heavy British artillery fire. Crüwell was objecting vigorously to these moves by Rommel, but he was overruled by him. The *D.A.K.* was now only a skeleton of its former self, and Crüwell wanted to rebuild his units before any more of his men and machines were lost in these minor objectives. The *D.A.K.* report for 3 December had stated that more than 167 of its panzers and armored cars were a total loss. The Italians had lost more than 90 percent of their armored fighting vehicles, but the British had suffered the destruction of over 800 machines. In personnel the German casualties were 600 killed, 1,900 wounded, and 2,200 missing. The Italians suffered less, as the bulk of their forces were not deeply involved. The British and Commonwealth forces had lost heavily, and more than 9,000 of the *Eighth Army* had been taken prisoner.[17] Crüwell was now proven correct in his assessments, when through radio intercepts and air reconnaissance the movement of the *4th Indian* and *7th Armored Divisions* was detected moving around to the south towards Bir el Gubi. These moves were a clear signal that the *Eighth Army* was attempting to cut off and destroy the *D.A.K.* Rommel now chose to abandon his Tobruk attack, and ordered Crüwell to gather all his troops on the eastern flank of the Tobruk perimeter, while his panzer divisions and mobile elements were to prepare to meet the British near Bir el Gubi and prevent them from commencing offensive operations there. The *D.A.K.* moved west that evening to assembly areas southwest of El Adem. Earlier that morning, the Regiment was alerted and received the mission to advance towards Sidi Azeiz, where a strong British force was again attacking between Sidi Omar and Sollum. Moving east along the Trigh Capuzzo past Gambut, the Regiment arrived in the late afternoon just west of Sidi Azeiz, which was again under British control. Before it could launch its attack on the British at Sidi Azeiz another order was received that ordered the Regiment to break off its attack and march immediately back before it could be encircled by British forces moving along the Via Balbia and Trigh Capuzzo. While the Regiment was moving to and fro, the leading brigade of the *4th Indian Division* was moving against the Italians northwest of Bir el Gubi. The Indians were screened to the north by elements of the *4th Armored Brigade*, which had at that time 136 tanks.[18] Fortunately for the *D.A.K.*, the Italians were putting up a stubborn defense and were able to hold off the Indians and elements of the *5th RTR* which were providing support. The *5th RTR* lost a number of its tanks in the attack. As the Regiment turned and executed an about face in order to move back to the west beyond El Adem, Hubbuch remembered:

"*A ride towards the east on a wide strip, old walls in the desert along the Gambut airfield, continuing towards the southeast into the desert. Already the day before, we, the people of the old Kampfstaffel, received the order to return with the trucks to the old resting place. Uffz Greif went there too but he forgot to take me along while I was sleeping. So I am still riding with the supply column through the desert but I have to see that I get back soon to the resting place and there to the repair and maybe back to our old repaired panzer? Late in the afternoon, far in the desert, we reach an old battlefield; there are many destroyed friendly and enemy panzers. But then for reason why, the desert ride went back the same way we came, and even 150km further until behind El Adem, where we arrive upon dawn after a long night ride. I have never experienced such a night ride, as a co-driver: Curving around holes, pitch dark, unbelievable sand*

Chapter 8: Withdrawal from Cyrenaica, December 1941

and dust caused by the column, it was terrible! Everything was swarming around, we couldn't find our group, Supply train of II./Abteilung until the next morning. During the night, English illuminating parachutes [flares] were in the sky, bombs fell from the sky, crashed with a thud, also low-level planes attacked; we throw ourselves in the sand beside the vehicle, then quickly got back and continued the ride until the next fire storm. Around morning, the driver was about to fall asleep at the wheel."

On 5 December, Rommel received word from Rome that no further reinforcements would be forthcoming before January 1942. This startling news obviously struck home, and Rommel finally acknowledged the fact that he could no longer remain where he was, and that he would have to withdraw from Cyrenaica until he could rebuild his depleted forces.[19] The *D.A.K.* was now down to between forty and fifty panzers between the two panzer divisions, and the *Ariete* could only muster some thirty machines; these numbers, coupled with the loss of some 8,000 men, were troubling to a commander whose adversary like the *Eighth Army*, could steadily replace and make good its losses from the vast pool of reserves. At 0700hrs on the 5th, the combat sections (*Kampfstaffel*) halted for a rest 16km west of El Adem and south of the Trigh Capuzzo—they had moved over 190km in the last sixteen hours! The leading British elements were also moving west over the Via Balbia, and that morning stood just short of the assembly area where the supply trains and workshops were located. The sudden arrival of the British forced those units to flee west, leaving behind their baggage and immobile machines to the enemy. The greatest loss, however, was the thirty immobile panzers in various states of repair, which had to be destroyed by their crews at the last minute; the loss of ten Mk IIs, fifteen Mk IIIs, and five Mk IVs was a severe blow to the Regiment. Luckily, four recently repaired Mk IVs from the *8th Company* were returned that day to the *II./Abteilung*, but now there was the problem of finding enough men to serve in those panzers. Since the battle had begun the Regiment's total number of casualties amounted to ninety-two men listed as killed in action, one hundred and four listed as wounded in action, and twelve listed as missing in action.[20] That afternoon the Regiment reported the following operational panzer strength: twelve Mk IIs, twenty-four Mk IIIs, and seven Mk IVs.[21] Klaus Hubbuch recalls the day spent with the supply troops moving westward:

"At 1500hrs we stopped, time to sleep and eat but again there is no water for washing; for weeks I am still wearing my old clothes, we look and smell like pigs. The three Panzerkampfwagen IVs are coming from the repair and Lt. Kanz is leading the Company.

In an old mail bag I find some mail, also some for me, from home that calms me down.

Situation: Last night – probably for the same reason as we returned – in a sudden movement the old resting place at the sea had to be left and the supply [troops] there had to retreat towards the west until behind Tobruk, leaving much behind, because of danger along the Via Balbia? Stukas returned from the front, for the first time, a large German flight unit. Then, a ride into the desert towards south begins, our Kampfstaffel [Abteilung] is in the front and getting involved in combat with English self propelled gun carriages. Artillery is firing and panzer cannons are barking. From our supply column we cannot see anything."

Just south of the Regiment's position that morning, more elements of the *4th Indian* and *7th Armored Divisions* continued to move into the area around Bir el Gubi. Further attacks were launched against the Italians, and again were met by heavy resistance that ended in even worse fashion than the day before. Sensing the threat to its southern flank, the *Panzergruppe* ordered the *D.A.K.* to launch the *15th* and *21st Panzer Divisions* against the threat and push those British and Indian forces back towards Gabr Saleh. By 1430hrs, with *Aufklärungs Abteilung 3* and *33* in the lead, the two panzer divisions rolled south, pushing the British forces there back towards the southeast. Late that afternoon, at around 1630hrs, the *4th Armored Brigade*, which had been covering the northern flank, pulled back into an assembly area near Bir Berraneb. It was at that time in the day that the Indian brigade reported seeing two panzer columns of approximately twenty panzers each moving south towards Bir el Gubi. It was the attack here that Hubbuch makes mention of in his diary. The Regiment's combat report dated a month later described the engagement that took place that afternoon northwest of Bir el Gubi. The Regiment had been given the order to enter into the march of the division in the third line, behind the *aufklärungs*, infantry, and artillery forces. From this position the Regiment had the responsibility to cover the right rear and the other elements of the division, and keep the pesky British tanks and scout cars at bay. But at 1700hrs, Cramer recognized in the fading light that the infantry from *Gruppe Geissler (Aufklärungs Abteilung 33)* were working their way towards a large British tent encampment, some marked with the Red Cross. Cramer was able to observe the fire between the tents and made the decision to use the speed of his panzers and launch an immediate attack in support of the infantry. He made this decision in spite of the constant danger to his flanks by British tanks, which had been already reported by the Regiment's *Leiche Zug* (reconnaissance element) at 1600hrs. Cramer knew that launching such an attack would allow the bogged down infantry the chance to move forward, as they had become stuck under violent machine gun and artillery fire coming at them from nearby the British camp.[22] With his accustomed gut feeling, *Hptm* Kümmel moved out at the head of the *I./Abteilung* and rushed headlong through the German infantry against the encampment. In the meantime *Hptm* Wahl, with his *II./Abteilung*, was tasked with the heavy burden of silencing the guns and holding the dangerous situation that was poised against the flanks. The Regiment *Stabs* drove through the battle area, protected by the accompanying panzers of *Olt* Stiefelmayer. A short action followed, and when darkness settled over the area the attack had succeeded in seizing the encampment and scattered infantry positions; they also captured about 150 prisoners from the *4th Indian Division*. After the panzers consolidated near the position they began questioning some of the prisoners, and from those prisoners the Regiment was able to further report that the enemy was making plans for a large offensive that was of great importance. This information made a lot of sense, because also during that time, the division had encountered a new and unidentified motorized group operating against it. At 1803hrs, there was an order issued by the division that ordered the Regiment to hold the line, which was now being occupied, and to remain in position there for as long as it took to bring the infantry forward to the heights and the panzers' position. As usual Cramer, Kümmel, and Wahl managed to collect their scattered elements, assemble them in the darkness, and begin to position them in the defense. At 1930hrs, after Wahl's *II./Abteilung* had entered the hedgehog and taken up positions behind the right flank of the *I./Abteilung*, the entire Regiment was able to begin rearming and refueling the panzers. During the attack, in addition to the capturing of 150 men, the Regiment was able to claim the destruction of a number of anti-tank guns and self-propelled guns without suffering any friendly losses. As the Regiment began to consolidate the position, it could do so knowing that the remaining elements of the Indian Brigade were moving back to the south to their divisional assembly area. It was this attack that prompted *General* Norrie to postpone his flank attack towards Acroma, and with it he lost his chance to bag Rommel and the *D.A.K.* During the night of 5/6 December, the *15th Panzer Division* informed the Regiment that the area east of Tobruk, as far as Bardia and Sollum, was being abandoned by the *D.A.K.* The *D.A.K.* then proposed plans for a move further to the west of the British advance by moving its elements west of Bir el Gubi on the road to Bir Hacheim. The division, as well as the Regiment, was ordered to begin moving forces west while launching small scale advances against the British forces in order to hold the frontline and allow time for those German and Italian elements located around Tobruk to disengage themselves and move westward. Shortly after midday on the 6th, the Regiment, along with the remnants of the *D.A.K.*, was ordered to attack eastward towards the heights located some ten kilometers west of Bir el Gubi. The *D.A.K.*'s attack went forward in the face of heavy artillery fire; despite suffering a number of casualties, the attack succeeded in pushing the British from the heights and forcing them off to the east. By 1500hrs, the division had reached its first objective, where it halted. This halt was called in order to allow additional time for elements of the *21st Panzer Division* and supporting *Luftwaffe* formations to move up to support the attack and attempt an envelopment of the British there. Both air and ground support failed to materialize, and at 1645hrs, as the sun began to fade and evening darkness began to settle in, the attack was continued under a hail of British artillery fire. The attack met with little success in the face of the overwhelming artillery fire arrayed against it, and so it was called off to avoid further losses. That night, as the infantry from *Schützen Regiment 115* went forward of the panzers to throw out a screen, the Regiment's remaining panzers were withdrawn to a hedgehog position in the rear. In the attack the Regiment had suffered a number of casualties and the loss of two Mk IIs, two Mk IIIs, and two Mk IVs. One of the Mk IIs and both of the Mk IIIs were completely destroyed.[23] That evening *Oberst* Cramer was informed of the loss of *Generalmajor* Neumann-Silkow, the divisional commander, who had been mortally wounded by the heavy artillery fire and would die from his wounds three days later at the hospital in Derna. *Oberst* Erwin Menny from *Schützen Brigade 15* was named the acting division commander. Again, there was no rest for the Regiment, as that night the vital maintenance work that had to be constantly performed on the panzers was often interrupted by the constant shelling. In Franz Kurowski's book *Panzer Aces II* he gives the following account on the loss of Neumann-Silkow:

"*Generalmajor Neumann-Silkow drove to the front to see Cramer. 'Cramer', he said laconically, 'We are going to attack and destroy the enemy.' 'I believe that we can do it sir!' The attack began. Kümmel saw tanks hit and knocked out to his left and right and behind him. It was an almost unbearable scene. 'Tanks from the right!' reported Stiefelmayer, who was leading his 4th Company on the near flank. Seconds later Kümmel heard that the enemy had arrived on the right. He immediately ordered I Battalion to turn towards the right flank. Kümmel's crew knocked out the leading enemy tank, and the rest pulled back into the desert. Suddenly there was gunfire on the right flank. The division commander's tank appeared. 'Kümmel, follow me with four vehicles.' They drove towards the enemy tanks, which kept up a steady fire. Oberfeldwebel Kruck's panzer was hit in the tracks. 'We're fighting on!' reported the Oberfeldwebel. Then he heard a warning call from Oberleutnant Prion: 'Watch out Kruck, tanks from behind!' There were several shattering blows, then a call from Kruck: 'Sir I...' The transmission ended abruptly. Kümmel had heard the voice of his old comrade in arms for the last time. He drove on, halting and firing. All of the tanks of the 1st and 2nd Companies pressed towards the enemy. Suddenly enemy tanks appeared from clouds of dust and smoke. There were shots, shattering impacts. Through his vision port Kümmel saw Generalmajor Neumann-Silkow. He was standing in the open turret hatch, apparently in order to be in better command of the attack. Suddenly Kümmel saw him jerk backwards then collapse into the hatch. Anxious seconds passed. Then suddenly an anguished call: 'The division commander has been killed!' An armor piercing shell had struck the commanding officer in the chest killing him instantly.*"[24]

That evening, as the Regiment began to move south, Hubbuch had this to write:

"*0200hrs I am beginning to drive towards the south deeper and deeper into the desert, even passing swampland, enemy artillery is shooting from the front, right and left, has brought terrible confusion to the supply columns which went in all kinds of directions. Around noon we stop, calming down and gathering. For the first time I am able to wash and shave, with a bottle of Italian mineral water I could get a hold off. My old wounds, left index finger and palm, left knee and right calf, look shocking, deep, pus covered holes. When the alarm came, on the evening of November 18th at the resting place near the sea, I actually was laying in the sick bay with my left arm tied upwards. But I was ordered as the gun-layer in the company commander's panzer at a nightly gunnery exercise on flashing pitching barrels I scored the best. So I had the doctor splint and bandage my finger, and joined the Kampfstaffel and even shot already on Totensonntag with the splinted hand. Then, Uffz Weidelener comes from the Kampfstaffel with the Kübelwagen and takes me to the front. The panzer of Uffz Gross came from the repair and Uffz Koch came from the sick bay. Koch became the commander and I was the gun-layer but the radio operator was still missing. [Uffz Gross was the driver]*"

As he rejoined the attack Hubbuch remembered:

"*A towing vehicle [8 ton tractor] of an 88mm Flak exploded, a bull's eye. On the left of us, the 21st Panzer Division attacked, also the korps headquarters, including the general are there, there must be something in the air, but what? In the evening, the usual technical work with the panzer 2400-0100hrs standing guard, I can't believe how cold it is!*"[25]

On Sunday, December 7th—the second Advent of Christmas—as dawn broke over the battlefield, the tired crews began to wake and shake off the early morning cold. The evening prior the *Panzergruppe* had ordered the *D.A.K.* to discontinue any further attacks eastward and to maintain their present defensive positions.[26] The plan was to withdraw the entire force towards the Gazala position, which was located between Tobruk and Derna and just west of Acroma. It was hoped that from this position the *D.A.K.* could cover the retreat of the Axis troops investing Tobruk. The positions in the east at Halfaya Pass, Bardia, and Sollum were to be left to their own fate, despite the rumors that those German forces would be withdrawn to Bardia, from where they would be evacuated by ship. Also taking place that evening was the build up of British forces facing the *15th Panzer Division*; those forces had received considerable reinforcements during the night, and by dawn were already attempting to push westward. At approximately 0830hrs eighty British tanks moved forward against the German positions, but the Regiment quickly checked their advance. That slight setback did not cause the British to break off their attempts, and throughout the day attacks came from the northeast and south against the *15th Panzer*. In the day's fighting the Regiment's panzers had fought off a number of attacks and claimed ten tanks destroyed that day. Artillery and tank rounds damaged two Mk IIIs during the attacks.[27] Hubbuch continued:

"*Again and again, we are attacking; we are always the same, the Tommy always with fresh forces; this time again, an English Panzer brigade is standing ahead of us. Despite my apathy to take and endure*

Chapter 8: Withdrawal from Cyrenaica, December 1941

everything, I often think of a Heimatschuß [home shot or million dollar wound]: wounding, sick bay, airplane, home!" I am now radio operator in the panzer because Uffz Persekowsky became the commander and Uffz Koch became the gun-layer. The panzer of Persekowsky was taken over by Lt. Stängel who came from the supply column. Many of our own trucks are burning, because the English artillery fire from the front, left and right is horrible. Then, enemy tanks appear and already we are hit. A straight 40mm penetration above me in the turret but is deflected before it hits the gun loader. Similar to the hit that wounded me when I was gun loader in the Sollum battle. It is hissing and spraying in the combat compartment and Persekowsky is wounded by fragments in his neck. We are driving back, Persekowsky is being bandaged. We are checking our engine and carburetor during the English artillery fire; the vehicle doesn't want to move anymore. By now, the panzers have been in the desert for more than three weeks, day and night, the demand is too heavy. That's our internal situation. We use to say: 'serious but not hopeless as long as we still have bullets for our pistols.' We return to the Kampfstaffel which managed to pull out of the artillery and 40mm tank fire; two of our 50mm Mk IIIs panzers are burning. This turn on the evening of 4.12.41 was necessary because the English could start a second, new offensive with strong, new forces and further in the south of Egypt, he pushed towards Derna. We have to prevent the new danger of a left closing. Therefore, the supply vehicles had to flee suddenly from the old resting place at the sea, north of Gambut, because English troops broke out at the Tobruk east front. Also all our baggage was left at that place, so we only have left what we are wearing on our bodies! 2100hrs, the night march begins; during a three hour break, I have to stand guard for one hour; sleeping is a luxury in the past three weeks; towards morning, we have made 30km. On the morning, I have some time to write Christmas greetings to home; they go with the vehicle of Uffz Gerdes to the repair shop and from there, hopefully further on. 1400 – 1700hrs I am standing as a melder [Signaler] at the Abteilung headquarters leaders meeting, this is necessary because we have to maintain radio silence. Through changing our position, we escape new artillery fire. At the Melder service, I meet Uffz Boser and Kant from the KOB /ROA training seminar but Uffz Behr fell at Sidi Azeiz. In the evening, Lt. Stängel explains the situation: Since 0300hrs, Japan is at war with America and England. We are building a new front at the heights of Gazala, there are already newly arrived Gebirgsjäger. The superiority of the English became too strong after his 2nd offensive and our troops were too scattered."[28]

During the day, the *D.A.K.* received a bit of help in shoring up its tattered lines when the *Ariete* Division returned and chased off some of the British *XXX Corps* forces poised along the northern flank of the *15th Panzer Division*.[29] The pressure was still greatest on the southern front, with tank, and especially artillery fire, inflicting serious casualties. Word also came in that the divisional baggage trains and service units had made good their withdrawal towards Gazala, and so, despite being able to hold their positions, the *D.A.K.* units slowly began to pull back. That evening the Regiment marched off without being harassed by enemy artillery or tanks and covered some 30km before it settled in for a rest. December 8th dawned crisp and clear, and with it news that Japanese Naval Forces had bombed *Pearl Harbor* and attacked the United States. By midday, strong artillery fire once again forced the Regiment to change its positions. At 2330hrs, the Regiment moved off again on a night march towards the west - northwest covering another 40-50km. Horst Sonnenkalb wrote of the withdrawal:

"Finally, during the night of Dec. 8th 1941 it happened. The exhausted alliances had to give up the siege of Tobruk. Most of the remaining German and Italian troops poured through an opening of three kilometers located close to El Duda toward the west to the city of Mara el Brega. Our motto was: don't engage in battles, gain ground. Easier said than done. During our retraction and our backing up the North African frontline, we had to oftentimes stop to shoot and to slow down units of the 8th British Army that were pressing after us. Then we had to quickly separate from the insistent enemy so that we wouldn't receive a hit from the enemy. Our ammunition supply was almost depleted. During our fully battle ready deployment we had 99 rounds in the ammunition racks, usually about 75% of that were high explosive (HE) rounds and 25% armor piercing rounds and a few thousand rounds for gunner [bow] and turret machine guns. Even though, our inventory showed big gaps. That's all we needed on top of the constant scarceness of gasoline. During the conditions of the North African campaign men and material were exposed to enormous pressure. How many times did I have to hear: time check, stoppage of gun or failure of the radio equipment? At the same time the panzer repair platoon, the radio mechanics, the panzer repair shop were doing all that was humanly possible to sustain the unit's fighting power. During this altogether orderly retreat, where no German formation succumbed to a panicky flight, we had to also fear bypassing attempts by our adversary, which tried to cut off our path by coming from the south and heading toward the north."[30]

On the morning of the 9th, the Regiment was positioned south - southwest in the desert just in front of Acroma, where it formed a hedgehog and secured the immediate area. Its main task was still that of screening the retreat. That evening there was another night march that was continued until the following morning. The crews had continuous radio watch, and were on constant standby for any gaps to plug. Hubbuch gives a description of what it was like inside the panzers at this time:

"We have continuous radio alert; always lollop [3rd gear without full gas], together with the terrible heat next to the engine down on the drivers seat, with nothing to see, not a moments sleep, my legs pulled up and the painful wounds at the knee, the next morning after a 30km ride I am completely fed up!"

The Regiment spent a fairly quiet day on the 10th performing technical maintenance, guarding, and sleep. The night was icy cold with a biting wind, and was all that more rough with the loss of the baggage trains. Most of the troops spent the night in the panzers, which provided a bit more warmth than out in the open air. December 11th began with a short march at 0830hrs, and by noon the Regiment found itself along the southern wing of the new positions at Gazala, where it again was facing and securing eastwards. Hubbuch wrote:

"We are planning to stay here for three days to eat, sleep, write etc. I am about to clean my suit in the fuel but there we are leaving again but only 5km, then securing again.
Situation: Germany and Italy declared war on the USA."[31]

By December 12th, after a masterful withdrawal well protected by disciplined rearguards, Rommel and his forces finally reached the *Gazala Line*, where it immediately took up defensive positions on the southern flank; it did so with just eight Mk IIs, twenty-two Mk IIIs, and three Mk IVs. That morning the *Luftwaffe*, which had been visibly absent during the previous weeks, even put in an appearance. Klaus Hubbuch recalls:

"In the morning, three German Messerschmitt were attacking the enemy artillery position in low flight. Unfortunately, two were forced to an emergency landing, one was tilting to the side, the other is standing on its head, both catch fire. We moved ahead a few kilometers and secured again towards the east."

Rommel's thoughts of holding this position were dashed, though, when the British broke through the Italian *XX Motorized Corps* and now enveloped him on both flanks. The Axis forces streamed westward until they reached Agedabia, and here they made a short stand.

Although Crüwell was all for setting up defenses at Agedabia, Rommel was afraid that a wide sweep through the desert could outflank this position, and chose to move back to Marsa Brega. Indeed, such an attempt to outflank them was underway, as elements of the *22nd Armored Brigade* rushed forward, but fortunately for the Axis forces it was met and halted, as the *D.A.K.* was able to meet that thrust, and in the fighting that followed the *D.A.K.* lost seven of its panzers compared to the thirty-seven lost by the British. Hubbuch wrote of the situation:

"*The enemy was blocked by our new defensive front to the east and was forced to move towards the southeast with his thirty-eight tanks and supply trains that would soon come in front of our pipes [guns].*"

As the *D.A.K.* made its way back and the threats began to diminish, the mood and morale of the officers and men seemed to grow strong again. Hubbuch describes some of the officers:

"*I am watching a joyful command vehicle: harmonica, singing, jokes; Hauptmann Wahl and Oberleutnant Hess in perfect mood, that's exactly right! Finally they are arguing whether tomorrow we should move another 5km forward or back?*"

On 12 December, the *15th Panzer Division* began to march in the direction north-northeast, about parallel to the line El Hasqiad-Agedabia. Nothing was seen of the enemy, except for three scout cars moving towards the north. After a drive of almost an hour, a larger troop unit became visible in a depression along the march route of the Regiment. On the left flank, about two kilometers to the west, appeared another group of vehicles either belonging to British or Italians troops. Upon further observation it was determined that the group located to the west was clearly identified as Italians, but the group along the march route was not yet determined. The panzers moved slowly closer on a wide front, and after a few hundred meters they were clearly able to identify them as British. Immediately the group was taken under fire, and the surprised group of British withdrew in haste towards the northeast to take up positions in the hilly terrain near Belaudah. It was there that the British began to put up fierce resistance. The Regiment attacked with *Company Prion* on the right and *Companies Schubert* and *Rochol* on the left. Despite occupying the more defensible position, the British were forced to retreat to the north while being pursued by the panzers. With the panzers pushing forward over the hilly terrain, the divisional *panzerjäger*, now alerted by the division, quickly moved forward and took up firing positions along the right front flank of the panzer formation. This was a classic movement operation, as the British were driven into the guns of the *panzerjägers* laying in wait; the tactic almost always guaranteed success, and did so here, as the results of the attack amounted to some thirty armored combat vehicles, six anti-tank guns, and some other wheeled vehicles, as well as one armored car captured. For its part in the attack, the Regiment suffered only seven wounded. On the 13th, the provisioning situation improved, with enough supplies being delivered to the combat units so that the panzers could be refueled and restocked with ammunition. Even though fuel and ammunition were the life blood for the panzers, the crews too had to eat, and as those rations arrived Hubbuch happily noted in his diary:

"*New rations arrive. Bread, butter, jam, two bars of chocolate per person, five eggs, brandy, schmaltz (fat), candies, fruit and canned pears and cigarettes, we are having a wonderful life now.*"

Despite the local successes achieved by the *D.A.K.*, the Allied forces still came forward and were aligned along the entire front waiting to attack. There was plenty of ground to cover and not enough troops for the task, which inevitably led to gaps between some of the units. One of these gaps was northwest of Bir el Temrad between the Italian *Trieste* and *Ariete* Divisions, where the nearby Hill 204 had been lost by the *Trieste* Division.[32] At this time, the *D.A.K. Assault Gruppe* (consisting of *Panzer Regiment 8* and the remaining tanks of the *Ariete* Division, and the infantry of *Machine Gun Battalion 2* along with supporting artillery) were ordered to launch an attack to reestablish communications with *Trieste* and shore up the main battle line. At 1300hrs, the Regiment was ordered out of its rest area and to relocate 7km to the north in the area of the *Gambarra Corps* combat positions. The Regiment moved to the concentration area at 1330hrs, and at 1400hrs the Regiment received further orders for an attack to the east with the goal of reestablishing contact with *Trieste* and eliminating those enemy forces that had pushed into the gap between the Italian Corps and the *Trieste* Division, and were now endangering the backside of the Gazala position. At this time the Regiment had approximately forty panzers distributed into its two *abteilung*. As the situation was still fluid and the promised coordinated attack by the *Ariete* Division failed to materialize, the regimental commander aligned the Regiment and the attached panzers of *Panzer Regiment 5* into three prongs of attack. After covering just 2km the panzer group began to receive such strong artillery fire from the right flank that he decided to give up the large abyss, which was advantageous for the flanking fire, and to place the II./*Abteilung*, led by *Hptm* Wahl, to the right next to I./*Abteilung*. *Hptm* Kümmel, who led the I./*Abteilung*, then received an order to throw caution to the wind and speed up his rate of march in order to escape the deadly flanking fire hitting the panzers and advance his *Abteilung* without further consideration. The initial attack was being met by a large number of British tanks and self-propelled anti-tank guns. As the two sides spotted each other, British artillery support was called in to cover those forces and place concentrated fire on the panzers in the hope of breaking up the attack. In these circumstances the drill was to move forward quickly under the bombardment and close the distance to the British forces before they could react and cause serious damage to the attacking panzers. The first British force (a battalion and ten tanks) quickly moved off, leaving the battle in the artillery's hands. After driving just 3km it was now possible for the panzer crews to recognize two British artillery batteries with anti-tank and rifle positions in plain sight along the right flank. These were overlapped British gun positions on the djebel borders. Soon after another armored force was spotted and battle was again given; in the ensuing firefight that followed some twelve tanks out of the twenty that showed themselves were destroyed by the assaulting panzer group. As the assault continued to run into heavy fire it was now ordered to halt before the heavy anti-tank gun screen sited along a shallow depression on the right. The British gunners had now forced the German forces to turn south. Now the regimental commander ordered the right rear alignment of *Panzer Regiment 5* to advance energetically and run through the British fire in order to reach and destroy the enemy batteries with the II./*Abteilung*, which was to push on towards the south. The advance of *Panzer Regiment 5* was complicated by small salt marsh lakes. And so the pressure on the enemy developed slowly. Immediately recognizing the situation, the Regimental commander ordered the subordinated heavy flak battery of I./*Flak Regiment 18* to pin down the enemy artillery by direct fire until *Panzer Regiment 5* had overcome the difficult terrain and begun moving quicker. In the meantime the I./*Abteilung*, under Kümmel,

Chapter 8: Withdrawal from Cyrenaica, December 1941

who was following the Regimental *Stabs* very closely, was ordered to continue to run through the artillery fire and gain the terrain by moving forward, despite the artillery batteries and driving uphill. The British launched a tank attack from an easterly direction, which first hit the II./*Abteilung* and the right flank of the I./*Abteilung*. During this attack, which was covered by the fog and therefore was hard to recognize, eleven enemy tanks were destroyed, while the other six withdrew to the southeast at high speed. As there was no renewal of fire, one could conclude that they were also heavily hit. After recognizing the British tank attack, the heavy flak battery of the *3./Flak 33* led by *Olt* Zurmahr was moved forward to a point where it could immediately engage the British armor, and soon it had announced the clearly recognizable destruction of two tanks. It was now possible to continue the attack after the successful defense against the British tank attack, and after the removal of both artillery batteries, as well as the elimination of the anti-tank and rifle positions on the foot of the djebels. In the meantime, while still under the heavy flanking fire from some self propelled anti-tank guns that had recently arrived on the djebels, the Regiment was able to link up with the scattered elements of the *Ariete* Division, which were now subordinate to Kümmel. Any further attacks were then put on hold by the order of the *Ia* of the General Staff, which had accompanied the attack on one of the panzers. As the British escaped to their position at Dscherba they left behind numerous weapons and equipment. The Regiment was then turned around to take up positions on the left flank. The success of the attack was only possible due to the reckless advancement of the German panzers, which had advanced without consideration of their own losses, and had fought with difficulty under a constant barrage of British artillery and anti-tank guns. The German artillery too had played its part in the action, and *Hptm* Maier was noted in the after action reports for his support and cooperation with his guns in support of the panzers this day. The afternoon's fighting saw five panzers destroyed in action, with the crews being lucky enough to escape and hitch a ride to safety. The command panzer of *Hptm* Wahl received two anti-tank and one artillery round which severely wounded Wahl. *Olt* Prion then assumed temporary command of the II./*Abteilung*. Klaus Hubbuch remembered:

"1200hrs the order: march and radio alert, soon after marching, also a combat alert and here we are in attack again. Our three companies or panzers are pushing forward on the left flank and are chasing the English tanks towards the right in front of the Abteilung. We capture some bearded Indians. Right of us in the east a battle is storming against enemy tanks, artillery and Selbstfahrlafetten in large numbers. We also receive flank fire from there. A Pak hit sticks in our tub. The panzer of Lt. Stängel stops functioning, tracks off, engine kaput. Hptm Wahl is heavily wounded and Olt. Prion takes over the Abteilung the whole radio contact goes now on Abteilung frequency. The attack stands still, it is getting dark, we withdraw to our starting position, but before that, upon order, we shoot the panzer of Lt. Stängel with panzergranaten and we took the crew with us."[33]

As dusk settled over the battlefield the British continued to rain down artillery fire, which succeeded in halting the attack and forcing the Regiment to withdraw back to its starting line; as it withdrew it did so with some forty-eight prisoners, mostly Indian soldiers. All told, the engagement cost the Regiment a command panzer and ten other panzers that were hit and suffered some type of damage. Two Mk IIs, three Mk IIIs, and one Mk IV were completely destroyed in the fighting. The Germans claimed the destruction of eleven Mk IV tanks, six field guns, a large number of anti-tank guns, and 10-15 trucks. It was impossible to calculate the large amount of infantry weapons and equipment taken from the British that day.[34] Unfortunately, by this point in the battle the Regiment had shrunk down to the size of a company, and the companies to the size of a *zug* or section. The panzer strength report of the Regiment on 14 December 1941 listed a total of just twenty-three operational panzers, of which five were Mk IIs, sixteen Mk IIIs, and two Mk IVs, while *Panzer Regiment 5* had just six operational panzers.[35] On the 13th and 14th, the *D.A.K.* was given a large portion of the *Panzergruppe* defensive sector; the *D.A.K. Assault Gruppe* was still located behind the Italians to shore up their sector. *Eighth Army* and *XXX Corps* units probed and attacked all along the line that day, but achieved limited success. Towards noon on the 14th, the *Ariete* again lost Hill 204, and the *Assault Gruppe* was again alerted for offensive operations. Hubbuch spent the day:

"The rest of the Abteilung is added to the 1st Company. We do maintenance, changing the rollers and cleaning weapons. In the afternoon, there is radio and combat alert, but no attack. At night, it is raining; I am staying in the narrow radio operator seat, and have stomach pain and a tooth ache."

That third Advents Sunday was without combat, and was dedicated to maintenance and weapons cleaning. Also on that day the Regiment was reorganized; due to the extremely high losses suffered over the previous week's battles, the remaining panzers of *Panzer Regiments 5* and *8* were combined into one panzer *abteilung*, which came under the command of *Hptm* Kümmel. Those remaining panzers of *Panzer Regiment 5* were formed into the *1st Company* under the command of Lt Rompel; the remaining panzers of I./*Abteilung* were formed into the *2nd Company* under *Olt* Schubert, and the II./*Abteilung's* panzers were formed into a *3rd Company* under *Olt* Prion. Additionally, two Flak Batteries of 88mm guns and the I./*Abteilung Artillery Regiment 33* rounded out the *Assault Gruppe*, which was now to become the fire brigade of *Panzergruppe Afrika*. The *Assault Gruppe* was set to counter-attack against the advancing XXX forces, but a message was received that stated that the Italians had retaken the lost heights. A crisis again arose on the 15th, when the Italians once again lost Hill 204, and the *Assault Gruppe* was again called on to restore the situation around Bir el Temrad once and for all. The *Assault Gruppe* departed Alam Hamza and reached Bir el Temrad around 1000hrs, where a reconnaissance was quickly sent forward to size up the situation. After meeting with the Italians, it was discovered that between two to three infantry battalions with supporting artillery and approximately ten tanks were presently located 8km east of Bir Temrad on Hills 190 and 189.[36] Under the cover of a sandstorm and the guns of I./*Abteilung Artillery Regiment 33* the infantry of *Machine Gun Battalion 2* went forward and secured a spot just 2km from Hill 190. At 1600hrs, as the Flak guns laid down covering fire on the left flank, the panzers and infantry came up on the right of Hill 190 and overwhelmed the defenders located there. The panzers then spread out into a wide wedge, wheeled to the left, and broke the remaining strong points. The rout was complete, and eight *Matildas* were hit by the panzers; the Flak guns claimed another six. Additionally, eight hundred prisoners were taken, along with three batteries of 25-Pounder guns, seven cannons, and thirty anti-tank guns. The battlefield was littered with all kinds of vehicles and equipment. *Kampfgruppe Kümmel* had won valuable time for *Panzergruppe Afrika* with this operation in order to withdraw the troops, which still were at Derna-Benghazi-Agedabia. At the same time the enemy forces were significantly wasted. The Regiment suffered the following losses: two Mk IIs, eight Mk IIIs, and two Mk IVs—it must be noted that most of these losses were the result more of mechanical breakdown than enemy fire. The *1st Company* lost two of its panzers.[37] Hubbuch remembers:

137

"Are these our own vehicles or Italians or Tommy? Then the attack on the identified enemy begins: tanks, vehicles, artillery much supply vehicles and radio vehicles. We attack swift and far spread out, our 88mm Flak is present; despite the radio being furious, as radio operator, I am shooting with the lower [bow] machine gun, according to own observation on recognized gunman, I am shooting to the maximum. The front is burning; we are pushing right into it. Large groups surrender. Here, directly in front of our panzer is a stubborn one [British soldier] who doesn't want to surrender, lying in the hole shooting at us, 10m distance, and then, a hand grenade, thrown by Uffz Persekowsky from the turret is shredding him right in front of my optic, disgusting war! Only few enemy vehicles escape in a hasty retreat and then, we get the booty: beside a lot of food, we also have very important items like new socks, two large wool blankets and even writing paper. This was a great Attacking day!! While pursuing, we only meet Italians."[38]

On 15 December 1941 *General* Rommel reported to OKW:

"After four weeks of combat with no breaks and many losses, it is visible the decrease of the troop's war power despite excellent individual performance, especially the supply of weapons and ammunition. The army is planning therefore to hold the area around Gazala on 16 December. The retreat over El Mechili – Derna latest in the night 16-17 December is unavoidable in order to get out from the encircling of the dominating enemy and from the destroy."[39]

On the night of the 16th, *Kampfgruppe Kümmel* returned to Alam Hanza, where it took on fresh fuel, ammunition, and supplies. Around midday, after the re-provisioning was complete, the *kampfgruppe* was sent towards the west in the direction of Fort Mechili, which was located just to the southwest of Derna. British armored cars were seen here in the distance and small engagements took place, with the British losing two of their Humber scout cars and the remainder scattered into the desert. Despite the terrain becoming more difficult, the desert here was mostly a stone desert crossed with numerous wadis, with some flat terrain covered with lakes and swampy areas, which had now become much larger due to the recent rains and caused fewer breakdowns on the withdrawal. *Kampfgruppe Kümmel* withdrew from El Abiaar and Er Regina in the direction of Benghazi. On the 17th, it was more of the same, and by early that morning the Regiment was once again on the move west. Hubbuch describes the march:

"At 0400hrs we continue marching to the west through sandy, later rocky terrain with Wadis, lake and swamp areas, it was the rainy season and we spotted rabbits, camels and even fresh green areas, a very unusual picture and for most of us the first time since May and June. In the afternoon, we reach Fort Mechili southwest of Derna, deep in the desert. We moved in a single column through a mine barrier. We continued our withdrawal in the south; we had to force ourselves to continuously keep marching towards the west to escape from being surrounded. In the distance an English ammunition dump is burning, it was discovered and set on fire by our reconnaissance units. The English had prepared themselves for months in the south behind our rear for their next offensive. During a break in the march, we receive food; worked on the rollers, air filter, weapons etc, in the evening, the company is assembling, Olt Prion makes it clear: 'despite our withdrawal we still must continue and even all the more fulfill our duties.' At 2100hrs again another night march towards the west."[40]

The morning of the 18th, the panzer crews were greeted by an air alert as the *RAF* began to strafe the column. There were no losses to the panzers, but a number of light skinned supply vehicles were set alight. At that time the Regiment could count only twenty-two operational panzers, of which six were Mk IIs, fifteen Mk IIIs, and one Mk IV.[41] The panzers continued to withdraw all day long. The men were beat, and vehicles were quickly wearing out. The desert south of the Via Balbia was a swarm of vehicles al fleeing east, some along the coast road, others through the open desert; despite the organized and controlled withdrawal units became stranded and mixed up. Klaus Hubbuch describes the scene:

"Our panzer is forced to remain in the rear waiting for a low-loader trailer [Tieflader], which must be towed. But the low-loader is broken and so we have to hasten back to our division alone and during darkness. We follow the red, green and white flares. In the desert often there are flashlights shining when we come by, stranded vehicles, but they have to be destroyed in place. Then we are in hilly terrain. On the pitch-dark night, we are driving up steep slopes, through gorges, over rocks and suddenly we are stuck crossways in a wadi, the panzer seems to tilt but after long shunting we manage to drive on; we are getting closer to the flares. Suddenly, in the weak glimmer of one we recognize some vehicles and halt, there in front of us are two unidentified tents, two meters in front of us, what luck! Or otherwise we would have run over four men. It is 2200hrs but on this night and in this darkness, we cannot move further to the other panzers because between them and us is the whole Division in resting positions so we are napping for a long night."[42]

On 19 December, the town of Derna was evacuated by the Germans, while farther to the southwest the transport ship *Ankara* had already docked in Benghazi harbor and unloaded twenty-two new panzers, much to the delight of Rommel and Crüwell.[43] These new panzers were the first reinforcements to reach the *D.A.K.* since early November. The panzers were not the only reinforcements to arrive; there was also the arrival of personnel for two new panzer companies under the command of *Hptm* Schefold, which had been training just south of Stuttgart at the Heuberg training camp. Hans Killermann was one of those who arrived that December and has this account:

"When we came to Böblingen [from Heuberg] two companies were established, one for the I./Abteilung it was the 3rd Company, I was there. The other was for the II./Abteilung which got one for the 7th Company. We sailed aboard the 'Ankara' it was not a war ship it was a civilian ship about 22,000 tons and arrived after a three-day journey, which was our third attempt to get through. Only the drivers were with the panzers the others came later with the airplane. I was driver and it was not very comfortable on the ship, there were big bombs for the Stuka down at the very bottom then covered with wood stocks then came the panzers, they were also covered and on top of them was the ammunition but we didn't know what kind of ammunition, they were in boxes and brought with the tracks. We had all our stuff; all clothes we kept it on the panzer at the rear deck were there was a container."[44]

The *Ankara* off loaded five Mk IIs and seventeen Mk IIIs in Benghazi, but unfortunately the arrival of the *3rd Company* personnel to Tripoli forced the supply and logistics personnel to move the panzers forward. In most cases those crews would have married up with their panzers upon arrival and moved them forward. Regardless of the situation, the *Ankara* was indeed fortunate to have disembarked its cargo, because by Christmas

Chapter 8: Withdrawal from Cyrenaica, December 1941

Eve the town of Benghazi had fallen to the British. On the 22nd, Rommel proposed a further withdrawal to the El Agheila and *Arco de Fileni*, where the *Panzergruppe* could set its defenses on the salt marshes and Marada Oasis and establish a much shorter line of resistance. But time was short for the Germans, as British armored formations were constantly advancing on them in the hope of bagging the remaining heavy combat power now forced to defend the weakened infantry, artillery, and supporting formation. On 23 December, Benghazi was cleared, and *Kampfgruppe Kümmel* conducted a further withdrawal south through Solluch and Agedabia. From Antelat, where the djebel (ridge) descends to the coastline, a British armored force attempted to block the coastal road, and Kümmel's panzers were immediately ordered to attack that British force, which then forced the British armor to withdraw; they did so, but not until leaving six of their Crusaders and five armored cars behind claimed by the panzer gunners. The Regiment lost just two Mk IIIs, which had broken down and had to be destroyed in place.[45] In a report written in February 1942, *Uffz* Willi Scheib of the *Stabs* Company I./*Abteilung* reported on his experience during the days leading up to Christmass 1941, and the situation he faced being alone in the vast wastes of the North African desert:

"Report about 22 December 1941. After five weeks of heavy combat, the Regiment had completed the planned return march through the desert over El Adèm – Mechili – Benghazi in front of Agedabia, and in order to initially hold here the pursuing enemy. Due to the fatigue and previous battles the available panzer combat vehicles were very worn and engines were not able to perform. This destiny was also for my panzer Befehlswagen, [command panzer] in which our brave Major Fenski had died on the famous Totensonntag [battle] which will remain a special day for the Regimental history. The new Abteilung commander, Hauptmann Kümmel as well as adjutant and first radio operator changed the vehicle when my engine broke down. At the caterpillars speed we, the second radio operator as a leader and me as a driver, tried to follow the traces of the panzer vehicles. This was possible until the heights 40-50km southeast of Agedabia, where the Regiment had a rest stop for one day and positioned itself towards Tommy in the direction southwest of Benghazi. We tried to reach the Werkshop Company which was located 40km away from this rest area, but we didn't succeed without obstacles. On the road broke down the heavily shelled track and the vehicle sat in the sand up until the transmission ring. Any movement forward was no longer possible. It was hopeless to try to fix the broken track ourselves. There was nothing else to do but to wait for any sort of help to come. The 22.12 went by and we reported our situation to an infantry radio vehicle which passed by. The 23rd it started with the rain. No people to see, except Arabs sneaking around. Something should happen to establish the connection with the Regiment. The leader decided to walk towards the Via Balbia. It was about midday. Now I was waiting alone at the vehicle. About 1400hrs I was discovered by three English scout cars because they took position at about 1200m distance and watched. I did the same, because that's all I could do as my panzer was unable to maneuver and my cannon was replaced with the dummy one. The sun disappeared behind the horizon. The scout cars were still in the same spot! I spent the night in the immediate proximity of the vehicle, and during the daylight I discovered that the gaze of the Tommies on me had shifted. Now it was Christmas Eve. Great presents! And only about 0900hrs the scout cars turned around. Now I would prefer to give the radio devices from the vehicle to a passing by Leutnant from the infantry so that in the worst case these would be safe but the situation was not yet clear for me. My leader was not yet back with the zug vehicle. Similar vehicles, which could pull us out with chains, also didn't come by. But around 1000hrs I discovered a trace of dust on the horizon. I used the binoculars and could guess these must be our panzers. The happiness was appropriate, but not for very long, as the Regiment had passed by at a great distance from me, so that it was impossible to signal them. So it was worse than I thought. The fire started around me and I was protected only by the diving compartment, after I tore down the pennant [that] hung on the antenna it was clear to me, that our own heavy Pak had mistaken me with the pennant as the English scout cars. After the vehicle didn't move and the pennant disappeared, the Flak realized the situation and the fire ceased. The approaching reconnaissance troop, three pieces of 2cm vehicles could prove the mistake. I welcomed the Späh troops and they were helpful to fix the broken track. Now I was able to proceed by myself. I quickly asked for directions and drove without the leader in a general northwest direction in order to arrive on the Via Balbia at approximately 4-5km distance. The direction gyroscope, without compass, served me poorly, besides as a driver it was difficult for me to navigate. So 6km, 8km and still no main road to see."[46]

Unfortunately, the remaining page of the report was lost, but it is safe to assume since he was able to write the report some months later the he did indeed succeed in returning to the Regiment. On Christmas Day 1941, the Regiment with *Kampfgruppe Kümmel* was released from its service, and ordered to take up positions on the right flank near Agedabia at Giof el Matar, which lay approximately 50km away from the coast. The panzer strength report of the Regiment on 26 December 1941 included fourteen Mk IIs, forty-two Mk IIIs, and two Mk IVs for a total of fifty-eight panzers.[47] On the morning of the 27th, the British *XXX Corps* attacked the Agedabia positions with the aim of outflanking the *Panzergruppe* and breaking through toward Tripoli. The *22nd Armored Brigade* again attacked the Regiment's position supported by strong artillery fire. German Pak, Flak, and artillery gunners were able to lay a concentrated barrage of counter battery fire that was able to slow down the British attack; this barrage was quickly followed up by a counter-attack by the Regiment's panzers. In the short but violent firefight that followed the British lost some thirty-eight cruiser and *Crusader* tanks, with most of those tanks being engaged and destroyed at close range. The total number of British tanks lost that day at Agedabia amounted to a staggering seventy-two. For the Regiment, its losses amounted to only three panzers knocked out: a Mk II, Mk III, and Mk IV, in addition to three soldiers being killed and eight more wounded.[48] Amongst the wounded was *Olt* Schubert. That night, as the Regiment formed its hedgehog position along the right flank of the division, the temperature dropped to below freezing, to 20F/-6C. The combat report of 28 December 1941 describes the attack and pursuit of the British *22nd Armored Brigade* at Wadi Faregh. On the 28th, at approximately 1200hrs, the Division began moving out of its hedgehog positions in order to attack the enemy, located on good high ground positions. On a wide front, the panzers began to roll through enemy artillery fire. The Regiment was organized with the *3rd Company* (Prion) on the left, *2nd Company* (Schubert) in the center, and the *1st Company* (Rompel) on the right. Despite the heaviest of defensive fire, the Regiment was able to quickly gain ground. On the left flank the enemy was thrown out of his defensive positions on the high ground, but this only came about after a hard fought battle. The *2nd Company* commander, *Olt* Schubert, was wounded and forced to drop out of the battle, but the company maintained its positions on the high ground for some time against a superior enemy before it slowly began moving back. As the attack ground to a halt and finally ceased, the companies were reformed and arranged with the right flank being strengthened by the *2nd Company*; as this reorganization began, Prion's *3rd Company* began closing up on the right flank units. The void left by the shift of the *3rd Company* was filled by the six self propelled guns of *Panzerjäger Abteilung 33*, which took over securing the left flank. The British had had enough, and as they

139

began to disengage to the nearest height, they revealed their strength of about seventy-eighty tanks and armored cars. The division ordered the attack to continue despite the lack of ammunition, and so the panzers immediately renewed their attack and, after a brief encounter, threw the British out of their positions and drove them off to the east. As the British began their withdrawal, some two kilometers to the east they attempted to turn southeast; this maneuver placed heavy pressure on the left flank that was being held by the *3rd Company*. Each attempt by the British to gain a foothold and establish a hasty defensive line to hold back the German forces was frustrated and met with failure, as they came under the effective fire of the Regiments panzers. The pursuit continued for over ten kilometers, but because of the greater speed of the British tanks they were able to succeed in placing some distance between themselves and the German panzers. Soon the appearance along the right flank of some new panzers joining the fight caused this small British group to flee quickly towards the southeast. The bulk of that force, while attempting to conduct a fighting withdrawal, tried to move off towards the northeast; at this moment, the panzers on the left flank, moving a bit slower than the British, hit the British on their flank and forced them to turn towards the east in a wild attempt to escape. The regimental commander, *Oberst* Cramer, spoke with the divisional *Ia*, *Major* Kriebel, who had been driving with his panzer along the front line, about whether a continued pursuit of the British should be undertaken. After a short conversation with the division commander a pursuit was ordered. However, it was quickly interrupted as it neared Wadi el Faregh, because of an imminent Stuka attack that had been called in on the enemy. After crossing the Wadi el Faregh, the panzers on the right flank pushed the British forces towards the northeast in an attempt to achieve a more favorable firing position for the panzers moving on the left flank. Because of the growing darkness the pursuit was halted, and a hedgehog position was formed. During the evening hours a separated enemy formation coming from the southeast passed near the right wing of that hedgehog position. The engagement distance, well over 2,000m, was too great for the panzers to effectively engage the force, but a *Pak Zug* from *Machine Gun Battalion 2* approached quickly from the right, also passing the panzers' flank, where it set up its guns and began to engage the enemy group. The attacks, as well as the pursuit, were superbly supported by the *I./Battalion Artillery Regiment 33* (Maier). The Regiment claimed some twenty-eight tanks and four self-propelled anti-tank guns. Only the midday heat, which had caused a mirage effect on the gunners' optics, halted the further destruction of even more British armor. The Regiment suffered the following losses: Lt Becker from the old *6th Company* was killed, along with three other panzer commanders. Fourteen soldiers were also wounded, and two Mk IIs, four Mk IIIs, and one Mk IV were lost.[49] Although the date is unclear, *Uffz* Göb of the *4th Company* filed this report of the battle that was written a few months later in March 1942; although there is no exact date on the report, it can be likely assumed that it was during this same timeframe and action that Göb's report details:

"*It's end of December 1941. The retreat is well advanced and we are hardly pushed by the enemy. In the area where the combat is now there are high sand hills, so it is the real desert. For vehicles on wheels it's almost not possible to cross the terrain. The enemy assaulted and destroyed the base; destroyed parts are lost in the desert all around. On the following day, much earlier than the dawn, we get the task to push back the strong enemy and to cover the retreat of destroyed elements. We stick to our course with ten panzers and shortly we should arrive at the assigned location. Around us are high sand hills, which block the vision substantially. The position is verified once again. Now we drive further. My engine gives only half of its power, so I have trouble to stay within the formation. As usual, when it rains it pours. Suddenly we come under the well-placed artillery fire from the direction unknown to us. As we don't know where the enemy is located, we first have to detach from them and so we drive in the monkey-drive to the east. My engine coughs and can't do any more. In the rush we are unnoticed by other comrades as each on his own has to deal with the mystery of the fire. It didn't last long and so we are all alone. I am tickled to be smashed to smithereens. The commander slowly drives me mad with his constant tempo, 'hurry up'. The other crew members also become impatient and can't understand that I can not drive any quicker. I am soon at the point once reached by the Schwabian Knight. But the outcome is different, as the fine sand starts to spray around us. One can clearly hear the whistle of 4cm cannons. Now I have to even take a zigzag course, when I should be happy to be able to drive forward at all. Luckily our Zug leader noticed our absence and drives with the zug towards us. He holds the enemy, who is behind us in the strength of approximately 40 fast tanks, for a short while and then covers our retreat. Our position now is so bad that we can only save ourselves by sullen fighting. The retreat could be our destruction. With that we come on the hill which allows us to see far. Here we receive the order to hold under all circumstances. The shots are authorized only by order due to the lack of ammunition and the unclear position. So we stay and watch how the enemy comes closer. They drive behind the sand hills and have good cover, whereas we are clearly visible from 10km. The enemy soon opens up with the stormy fire, we still have to wait. Apparently Tommy stops shooting and watches us, then we see how they come closer step by step. Our cannon has been loaded long ago, the sight set on 1000m. The Richtschütze follows 'his' selected enemy. Only from 1000m are we allowed to shoot. The commander gives the distances to the Richtschütze: '1,200 – 1,150 – 1,100 – 1,050 – attention – free fire!' The light flashes through the vehicle as the next round is already in the tube. We already think 'missed', but here the flames come from the turret of the enemy tank. One man jumps out, and nothing else moves. A man stands next to the vehicle and seems not to know where to go. We let him run, as we remember well our own destiny. The other Tommies were also well received and pull back quickly. Then it's quiet again. We let the hours pass and each movement is stiff. We sit seven hours in the closed vehicle and watch, we are not allowed to speak as we have to hear any engine noise. Far behind the enemy one could see the cloud of the dust coming closer. It could be only reinforcements. Against us were already 40 tanks and we are 10. The reinforcements are building up on the left and right wing. We can see how the wings are moving to form a semi-circle around us. With binoculars one can now clearly recognize one anti-tank gun which is being installed in front of us. Shortly after 1400hrs the Tommies becomes noisy, their tanks constantly change positions, quickly drive towards us, stand up and then quickly drive back. They want to make us crazy, but they don't succeed. Nothing moves around us. It seems we have fallen asleep. So that they can't move us this way, now they try with their 15cm Gypsy artillery. It shoots on our left flank where we stand with our zug. The shots are placed well. They must have a good observation team and then heavy fire is set against us. We still don't move. The fragments hit the wall of the panzers. We actually feel the heat, the pressure builds in the throat, the palms of the hands get wet and so we sit down on our seats and tense when explosions comes close. We hear the muffled discharge, light whistle, then short and loud roar, the air shakes and the ears and brain hurt from the violent detonation. A short breathing out as it goes well for us this time. But so we are not moving, and Tommy tries another method. It seems that they brought their artillery closer and aim now at every single vehicle. It starts on the left side. We see our comrades and hold our breath every time the panzer becomes hidden by the cloud of smoke and dust and breathe out if it still there undamaged. But even now nothing moves. No one withdraws even one meter without the order to do* so. Then comes permission for a short change of position. The vehicle in danger drives two lengths backwards, but is again thereafter covered in the cloud of smoke and dust. Now it changes its position so quickly, so that the enemy observer is unable to report it back quick enough, and so discharges are badly placed. Tommy finds it stupid and takes aim on the next one. This one first allows them to shoot at it and then repeats the same maneuver. So it goes from one vehicle to another. We are on the line near the evening. The first explosion is closely behind us, the next is spread around the vehicle. We wait a moment, and move a few meters back, get into cover and prepare ourselves for the next day. My first task is to repair the engine; the night is quiet as usual. About 0400hrs we are woken up, 'Prepare yourself!' With the daylight come the Stukas and start preparing for the attack. Soon begins our artillery and in the meantime we reach our assembly area and from there we are already able to see Tommy. They don't move. Sharply at 0900hrs we attack and soon come to the proper distance for engaging the enemy, but no shots come at us yet. From yesterday we know where the anti-tank gun is installed and watch it closely. No cannon is to be seen and the enemy tanks go backwards slowly. We drive quicker to stay [in contact] with the enemy, but don't forget about the anti-tank gun which should have already shot. Yesterday, right in our sector, were so many cannons and that is why we can't forget this thought of why is it so quiet now. But who of us can trust the Tommies? From the right one of the vehicles from our zug moves forward and carefully drives up the small sand hill. He had not yet reached the top of the hill when we see the small whirl of dust at the nose of the panzer. The vehicle stops. He must have received direct shots one after the other, because suddenly he caught fire. 'That must be the anti-tank gun though!' quickly comes to our mind. The danger is forgotten, now it is realized that we must find the enemy, who camouflages so well that we can't see the gun flash. The turret swings continuously from 11 o'clock back and forth. The commander swears. Finally the dangerous gun is recognized as for a short moment we saw the small dust cloud. The shot is for us. Shortly ahead of us it bursts. But before our first round leaves the pipe, the massive hit occurs. My seat comes high. I hit heavily on the panzer wall with my head. Fire, dust and gunpowder fumes! I can't see anymore. Ducked down on my seat I am waiting for the pain, which should come now, because the shot went near me. In this position I sit and watch my feet. I can't recognize anything there. Everywhere are think fumes, which slowly settle down. What is it? Why is it so bright at the bottom? The beam falls askew on my right foot. Now I can see the hole through which the sun shines. That's what has destroyed my seat. The shot went between my feet under the seat. There is no time for me to think, as there is another strong hit and brutal blue flames. 'Backwards – march!' My nerves are about to break. I can't immediately find the backwards transmission. A further shot forces me to move quicker. The engine roars, but the vehicle goes only slowly backwards. I want to put it askew in order to possibly provide a bad angle for the enemy shots. The vehicle squeaks and with some effort goes into position. All my attempts are in vain. The vehicle doesn't obey me anymore. 'The direct hit on the right driving gear!' Unfortunately we are now positioned diagonal to the enemy. Thoughts haunt me and everyone shouting at once. Once again we receive a hit in the combat area. Now only one thing left: to get out! As if on a single command the turret hatches are thrown back, then we lay flat on the ground next to the panzer and we see how the rest of the zug vehicles go back. From our panzer rises the black flag of smoke. It has caught fire. Now we cannot miss the connection. One after the other we jump up and run back. We just started to rise when behind us began a machine gun and the hell is behind us. It's impossible to even raise our head. The whistling above us doesn't stop. We can't stay here and we crawl behind the nearest hill. Here are wounded comrades, who ask for our help. We attracted the attention of the panzer by waving, and it picks us up and brings backwards."[50]

As dusk fell, the remaining British forces fell back towards the east. The night grew cold, and a small amount of snow fell that night. The Regiment formed a hedgehog position in the desert north of Giof el Matar despite the harassing fire from British artillery. On the 29th, after a preparatory barrage by British artillery, elements of the *7th Armored Division* attacked towards the Agedabia defensive line. *Oberst* Cramer ordered a counter-attack aimed to the northeast, which pushed the enemy from his positions and into the waiting guns of *Flak Regiments 18, 33,* and *35*. Here the British tanks and self-propelled anti-tank guns were halted, and in a heavy firefight with *Crusader* and *Matilda* tanks the Regiment claimed nine tanks and five anti-tank guns.[51] The 88mm flak guns of the various Flak *Abteilung* claimed a further nineteen tanks. Shortly after midday the British units retreated to the northeast, and as darkness began to envelope the battlefield much of the artillery fire died away, and for the remainder of the night the Agedabia positions remained quiet. The Regiment suffered the following losses: seven wounded, one Mk III destroyed, and two Mk IIIs lost to mechanical breakdowns.[52] That night the division ordered the Regiment to return and take up positions behind the right flank on the defensive line. The Regiment would remain in this area until 9 January, while the *Werkshop* and "I" Services were relocated further to the west near El Agheila. While it remained in the assembly area the Regiment continued to perform such tasks as digging in and reinforcing positions and entrenchments, as well as technical service and maintenance of the panzers. On the 31st, a posthumous *Knights Cross* was awarded to *Major* Günther Fenski for his action on 23 November 1941 during the Totensonntag battle. Fenski was the third member of the Regiment to receive this high decoration and the first one posthumously.[53] The loss of one its most experienced panzer commanders was felt throughout the entire Regiment. That same cold, dark evening the sky soon gave way to a number of green, red, yellow, and white lights, as from out of a number of positions a small celebration began. It began with a rifle shot or a flare, and was soon joined by a series of tracer bullets from a machine gun that might soon be followed by a tank gun round, or artillery, and even a Flak gun. And so, for a few minutes that night the men fired in celebration that was only to last a few minutes, as ammunition was something not to be wasted. Shortly afterwards a few individuals began to sing, and the tune drifted from position to position, from panzer to panzer—it was the German national anthem. To many of those who were there it was one of the most memorable times in their lives. As 1941 ended and 1942 began, the average German soldier could feel good about his situation; despite the recent setbacks to the D.A.K. in Africa, all the men felt sure that Rommel would soon set the matter right again. The overall situation facing the *Wehrmacht*, which had seen almost nothing but victory after victory since 1939, lead most Germans to believe the current situation would not reverse itself. But already ominous signs were presenting themselves, as the *Russian Red Army* and winter halted the drive on Moscow, the *Luftwaffe* had been defeated in the *Battle of Britain*, and soon America and its *"Arsenal of Democracy"* would be felt throughout the world. On 1 January 1942, the *Panzergruppe "Afrika"* was redesignated as the *Panzerarmee Afrika*; unfortunately, unlike most German army formations, it was not provided with the necessary reinforcement, nor with the respective reserves to be officially labeled and meet the manpower standards of a *Panzerarmee*. By the beginning of January 1942 the D.A.K. could report 111 operational panzers,[54] but the previous fourteen days of combat had exhausted the Regiment's overall fighting strength in men and machines, and the constant movement had taken a toll, as panzer after panzer succumbed to mechanical breakdown and ate up precious fuel. It was only due to the timely arrival of fuel and ammunition, which quite often tilted the fighting in the Regiment's favor, but regardless of what was able to get through to the panzers, the long supply routes were seriously hampered by the British, and the lack of supplies grew larger each day. At the same time the endangered supply lines forced the drivers to undertake long drives often under enemy air attack, and the dispatching of combat forces from the front line to the rear areas in search of more food, fuel, and ammunition hindered the overall defensive schemes and counterattacks. It always seemed to the men that the British forces were able to recover more quickly from their losses, and were able to re-supply their units from well sited and vast supply points, some of them located south of the Trigh el Abd. The surprisingly quick recovery of the 4th Armored Brigade at the end of November clearly outlined this fact to the panzer men, as a once beaten and demoralized enemy force in just a matter of days again reappeared to do battle. Thankfully for the D.A.K. and Panzergruppe, on the 5th another convoy arrived at the harbor in Tripoli carrying an additional load of panzers, armored cars, and a number of Pak-38, 50mm anti-tank guns.[55] With the arrival of the convoys in late December and early January the D.A.K. was ensured of its survival for the time being. It was also discovered during the previous weeks of fighting that despite the successes achieved, no single unit or arm could conduct the fighting and win the battle on its own. Doctrine was being changed or modified to include Pak guns and Flak cannons, which it was found should accompany panzer units because of the ever-present open flank and wide-open terrain that made it almost impossible to hide from the RAF. Other lessons too were being learned, including the ever-important logistics operations, which almost always dictated the outcome of the battle. It was noted that every commander at all levels must know the performance level of both his men and machines, and the limit with which each was capable of performing. A commander who failed to take these qualities into account would surely over use or extend them and find himself in a very unpleasant situation. It was also noted that the commander without proper reconnaissance was blind, and a commander who lacked the means of conducting a proper reconnaissance should balance that deficiency with hidden combat reconnaissance. In one commander's letters home he wrote that:

"boldness without reconnaissance is left to its own luck, which in most cases ultimately fails as opposed to boldness with reconnaissance that has the promise of greater success".

The commanders and men of the Regiment knew and practiced much of this on a daily basis; they knew that they were opposed by a brave and skillful enemy who always seemed to have superiority in tanks, guns, and manpower reserves, and that they were able to act with great courage and gallantry. The Swabians too could show great courage and élan in the attack; they were known by other Germans as hard heads, but it was this trait that endeared them to their commander Rommel, a Swabian himself, for they were surely the iron fist of the entire D.A.K. Horst Sonnenkalb had the opportunity to serve alongside Rommel as an escort and wrote the following about him and his influence over the men:

"When Rommel, coming from the desert, arrived at a battlefield, which he liked to do, he always had the perfect overview. He informed us of the situation, plotted, and feigned big attack formations. He irritated the enemy and made them lose their head. Often I experienced General Rommel early in the morning driving up and down the front in his jeep. During bad weather no noteworthy act of war happened. That provided us with a breather every once in a while during those weeks. On the other hand no strong positions were obtained or held. The pressure by Tommy was too great. Two times during that time I drove as Rommel's escort and also supported the Italian Infantry. During those days that was normally the job of the war volunteers. Erwin Rommel, our commander-in-chief, didn't know fear, never avoided dangerous situations if it meant stopping the enemy, cheering up the exhausted troops. Then again he flew across the desert in the 'Fieseler-Storch', also across enemy territory. His attitude, the close connection he kept with the troops, his battle tactics, to control the troops from the front, was his foundation stone for all his victories. His ingenious tactical intellectual power, his farsightedness, his personal bravery and also his stratagem compelled even his enemy to have big regard and respect for this German military leader. With us it carried forward to the troops and their morale. The German soldier appreciated that. There couldn't have been any other commander-in-chief, no matter at which front, who got more trust and respect from his troops than General Field Marshal Rommel. Even from captured Brits we received praise of the fighting power of the German troops, crediting the German command. The name Rommel was a definite term for them. A name they respected, and even caused fear. They called him 'Wuestenfuchs' (Desert Fox). You fight like the devil, they said. They, who thought the German Africa-Corps was bleeding were being disabused. Then they put their hand up, while forcing apart two fingers to a V, their sign for Victoria, the sign of victory."[56]

As the New Year began so did the retreat, as the Agedabia position, which was in constant danger of being outflanked both in the north and south by the much stronger British forces, had to be abandoned. Ever since the 6th British and Commonwealth armored car elements were often seen in the distance, and on occasion would move in close enough to engage in minor skirmishes with the Germans. These contacts were normally brief, with the German troops engaging the light skinned armored vehicles, which usually forced them to withdraw back to the safety of their own lines. Over time more and more reconnaissance forces made their appearance on the battlefield; these forces were soon joined by a number of light armored forces, and they usually could be seen gathering in front of the Regiment's assembly area, but were cautious, wary to venture in too close, and instead opting to remain at a safe distance. Armored cars and light tanks were not the only worries, as the British artillery soon began to increase in its intensity, but fortunately many of the rounds were either too long or short, and the rounds that did land within the perimeter usually hit between the panzers, causing only minor damage. The RAF was also able to put in an appearance, as fighter-bombers swooped in to deposit their loads on the assembly area, but like the artillery they failed to cause anything other than minor damage; there were no reported casualties during these attacks. On 1 January, Hptm Wolfgang Wahl became the fourth member of the Regiment to be nominated for the Knights Cross for his actions as the II./Abteilung commander during the Crusader Battles. He was presented the award on the 6th.[57] The actions of men like Kümmel, Fenski, and Wahl, and a host of others gave the impression that combat was something easy, just jump into a panzer and charge off to glory. In some circumstances that was almost true when you look at how Kümmel seemed to defy the odds by charging ahead of his panzers. But all combat soldiers know differently, and most leaders ended up dead or horribly maimed. In the following excerpt, Kurt Kathe describes how some of those men that thought themselves immortal and wanted to make a name for themselves ended up:

"When the commander wanted to know where the Australians and British were hiding in the desert, he usually sent one or two panzers. My colleague, Hans Pusse, he was always crazy to become an officer. The commander said 'Pusse, you define [locate] where are the Englanders'.

Chapter 8: Withdrawal from Cyrenaica, December 1941

He went ahead with one panzer and reported to the commander the situation. Then the commander said 'drive further, I want to know exactly where they are'. Then he got shot and that was it. He could have become an officer after one year in a combat school and could have been sent to Russia. And what would have happen? He would have got a kick in the ass! We had people, soldiers, who wanted to have the Knights Cross, one leutnant in the 3rd Section, I don't remember his name, and he decided to drive forwards with no orders. The commander called me and said 'one of yours drove off by himself'. Kümmel calls, who is that? He was 14 days in Africa; he had no experience and had just come from the school and wanted to have a Knights Cross right away. That was it for him, these type of people were reckless, they thought if you sit in the panzer then nothing happens. I lost over two years 11 company chiefs [commanders]. One looked out of the panzer, down there said the driver to him, 'Herr Oberleutnant, don't get that far out as there is British fire, and bop he gets his head shot off. Many of the people were under the impression that if they come to Africa and drive with the panzer that they can just right away get a Ritterkreuz. I never thought and believed this."[58]

In this first week of January, after nearly two months of near continuous combat, the depleted and worn out Regiment began to consolidate and reorganize itself, with the remaining panzers being consolidated into one panzer *abteilung* under the command of *Hptm* Kümmel. The Regiment's reorganization looked as follows: half of the *1st Company* and *2nd Company* came under the command of Lt Hahn, while the other half of the *1st Company* and *3rd Company* were under *Olt* Prion; half of the *5th Company* and *6th Company* under *Olt* Rompel, and the second half of the *5th Company* and *7th Company* came under the command of *Hptm* Klein. The heavy *4th* and *8th Companies* under *Olt* Stiefelmayer came directly under the command of the Regiment.[59] On the 7th sand storms again began, and continued over the next couple of days, making the march westward more difficult. On the 9th, the Regiment was ordered by division to begin its withdrawal from its positions near El Hasselat. The route westward passed back north of Wadi Faregh towards Marsa el Brega, and the Regiment continued west until it had reached the *El Agheila-Marada Line*. On the 10th, the Regiment was able to join the rest of the *Panzergruppe* on this line, where it was hoped a series of strong defense positions along the broad band of salt lakes, sand dunes, and cliffs would offer the *Panzergruppe* protection, especially in the south, if they could be established in time to hold off the oncoming British. The Regiment finally reached a position south of El Agheila during the night of the 12/13th, where it was finally allowed some time to rest and reorganize. As the *Panzergruppe* settled into its positions the arrival of fresh reinforcements and supplies were able to make their way forward unhindered. For the Regiment it meant the arrival of its missing companies, and with the addition of the *3rd* and *7th Companies*, which were now led by *Olt* Prion and Lt Rompel, the Regiment was able to bring itself back up to a respectable number of panzers and equipment. Over the next couple of days there were only a small number of limited actions and skirmishes, mostly in the south around Wadi Faregh, where the *15th Panzer Division* was sent to bolster the line. It was during one of these actions that a small group under the command of Lt Mahr was attacked during a sand storm and taken prisoner by the British. After the attack, as additional forces arrived in the area they were able to recover and identify the body of Mahr, and determine that he had fallen mortally wounded in the action. As the *Panzergruppe* attempted to reconsolidate itself it faced one giant problem; most Axis formations, especially the Italian troops, had been so far reduced in numbers during the previous month's fighting that they could hardly be expected to hold the line against any major attack for more than twenty-four hours. Luckily, the garrisons left back in the east slowed the assembly of those pursuing British forces. As the Regiment had been conducting its final series of moves, back in the east the garrisons around Bardia, Halfaya, and Sollum began to end their long holdouts. On the 2nd the Bardia garrison surrendered. Bardia had been a good sized supply base for the earlier attacks along the frontier wire, but on 30 December the British had made a concerted attack on the garrison, making use of land, sea, and air bombardment. By the 2nd those attacks, supported by armored units, had finally managed to penetrate the defenses, and as the situation became quite hopeless, the city was surrendered later in the day. Sollum, occupied since 21 November, was now being defended by the *10th Oasis Company*, the *Stabs* of the *300th Special Purpose Oasis Battalion*, and the remnants of *12th Oasis Company*. That garrison, now down to approximately seventy German soldiers, had managed to hold off several vigorous attacks on the 11th and 12th but, having used up the last of the food and ammunition stocks, finally surrendered on the 12th.[60] At Halfaya the defenders, consisting mainly of the *I./Battalion, Schützen Regiment 104*, were well dug in and, except for the lack of water, had plenty of food and ammunition. In an attempt to secure some water a company was chosen to undertake an assault on a nearby well. The infantry was to secure the well only long enough for water trucks to move in and fill up. The attack failed to achieve its stated purpose, and so the garrison was unable to resupply itself, and now had to rely on other means. Several attempts were made to resupply the beleaguered force by air, with night flights of *Ju-52* transport aircraft flying out of airbases on the island of Crete. However, this too proved to be unsuccessful when most of these flights were discovered by the British and intercepted and shot down by British night fighters. A short time later the remnants of the Italian Savona Division, which had been holding out further to the west, were driven back towards the pass, as their situation became more and more hopeless. Eventually preliminary surrender negotiations were begun with the South Africans, and on the morning of the 17th the last defenders of Halfaya Pass, under Rommel's permission, surrendered the garrison and were marched off into captivity. The surrender of these important garrison posts were, however, not in vain, because the longer that they had been able to hold out, the more British troops they kept from reaching the forward positions around Agedabia and El Agheila. Indeed, those garrisons had tied up a number of troops and prevented others from rushing up to the front along the Via Balbia. It was at this time that Rommel decided to launch a limited attack in order to regain the offensive and destroy as many of the British formations immediately facing him as possible before they were ready to do the same to him. Along the *Marada Line* it was determined that the German and Italian forces arrayed there were actually superior in numbers to the British, which were still scattered hundreds of miles from the main battle line. This superiority, however, would not last long, and it was determined that the longer it took those British forces to assemble and coordinate their actions the better the chances for the *Panzergruppe* to take a number of preventive measures and actions to interrupt the anticipated continuation of offensive action by the British. At the time Rommel was not sure such an offensive was possible, but after hearing from his staff, and especially his Ia *Oberst* Westphal, he quickly became enthusiastic, and ordered that preparations be made for a counterattack. As planning began in earnest under a veil of secrecy, Rommel personally undertook a number of air reconnaissance missions and determined that the attack must fall on those British formations on the northern portion of the *Marada Line*, where it was thought the majority of the British *1st Armored Division* (Messervy) was assembling. German intelligence had placed the remaining *Eighth Army* (Ritchie) elements as follows: *XIII Corps* (Godwin-Austen), *4th Indian Division* (Tuker) was near Benghazi and Agedabia; *1st South African Division* (Pienaar) near Msus; *2nd New Zealand Division* (Freyberg) was farther back in Cyrenaica;

and the ineffective British *7th Armored* (Gott) and *9th Australian* (Morshead) Divisions were still at Tobruk refitting.[61] The attack, which was scheduled for the morning of the 21st, called for a strong force to advance northwest along the Via Balbia. This northern force would be led by an ad hoc *kampfgruppe* under the command of *Oberstlt* Werner Marcks of *Schützen Regiment 155* from the *90th Light*, and would be known as *Kampfgruppe* Marcks; it was to be supported by the panzers of *Panzer Regiment 5*. Following *Kampfgruppe* Marcks would be the remaining mobile elements of the *90th Light Division* (Veith), in turn followed by the Italian *XXI Corps* and *XX Motorized Corps* (Zinghales). Once Marcks had broken through the initial British positions, it was to advance up the Via Balbia with the follow on forces advancing on both sides of the Via Balbia, and head towards the town of Agedabia. The Italians were to follow immediately behind the *90th Light* and advance south along the Via Balbia. The southern force would be composed of the *D.A.K.* (Crüwell) and consist of the *15th* (Vaerst) and *21st* (Böttcher) *Panzer* Divisions. Those divisions were to start out from an assembly area thirty kilometers south of the Via Balbia and, in an enveloping pursuit that was designed to prevent the retreat of the British *1st Armored Division*, bag as many troops as possible. In order to keep the attack as secret as possible and to ensure success, the *Commando Supremo*, in addition to the divisional commanders, were only told of the operation the night before. The Italians approved an advance as far as Agedabia, but feared any movements beyond that position would endanger their non-mobile infantry divisions to British counterattacks. They further stressed that employment of the *X* and *XXI Corps* forward of the *Marada Line* was not permitted, and demanded that the *XX Corps* advance no further than Marsa Brega. The Regiment reported a total of eighty operational panzers on 20 January 1942. Another twenty-eight panzers—five Mk IIs, twenty-one Mk IIIs, and two Mk IVs—were in the workshop.[62]

9

Back from Tripolitania
January-April 1942

On the evening of 20/21 January, the Regiment received the following order of the day from the headquarters of *Panzergruppe Afrika*:

"The Supreme Commander of Panzergruppe Afrika; Armee order of the day. German and Italian soldiers! Behind you lie heavy battles with a vastly superior enemy. Your morale remains unimpaired. At this moment we are considerably stronger than the enemy facing us in the front line. Therefore we shall proceed today to attack and destroy the enemy. I expect every man to give his utmost in these decisive days. Long live Italy! Long live the great German Reich! Long live our Führer!
The Supreme Commander
Rommel
General der Panzertruppen"[1]

At 0830hrs on the cold, gray morning of 21 January, *Panzergruppe Afrika* began to move forward to once again engage the forces of the *Eighth Army*. The *D.A.K.* was poised with the *15th Panzer Division* taking up positions along the right flank of Wadi Faregh, while the *21st Panzer Division* was arrayed along the left flank. The panzers began to roll forward in a blowing sandstorm against little resistance, as British patrols quickly withdrew to the east without putting up any kind of a fight. But as the panzers rolled forward they were quickly halted by sand dunes around Bir Bettafel, and only the panzers and tracked vehicles were able to advance, while the wheeled vehicles quickly became bogged down in the soft sand and had to be pulled free. At approximately 1000hrs, after having moved approximately 30km, the first contact was made with British tanks, which were barely visible in the early morning gray, and which could only be recognized by their shapes. The panzers were quick to react, as the Mk IVs from the *4th* and *8th Companies*, led by *Olt* Stiefelmayer, opened fire with their powerful 75mm guns at just over 700m. Three British tanks were soon hit and began to burn, and as the engagement continued eight more tanks, belonging to the *2nd Hussars Regiment*, were quickly destroyed. In the blowing sand storm contact was finally lost with the British, who withdrew to the east, leaving behind five *Crusaders*, eight cannons, two anti-tank guns, and some fifty vehicles.[2] After the initial encounter the panzers turned to the northeast, leaving the slower wheeled vehicle columns behind them. At around 1430hrs, the first panzer elements reached Gefera, but did so without any of their supporting elements. Regardless of the sand and the slowness of the supply columns, the *D.A.K.* headquarters ordered the panzers to continue their march towards Bir Bilal, which was reached at approximately 1700hrs. Unfortunately, at this point the panzers were now without any fuel to continue the pursuit, and were forced to halt until a resupply could be affected. Further to the north, the initial breakthrough by the *90th Light Division* had succeeded as planned, but British resistance, and especially the swampy ground along both sides of the Via Balbia, later slowed the advance. *Kampfgruppe Marcks*, in the van, was finally able to reach En Nogra at 1430hrs, but halted and went over to the defensive until the *D.A.K.* could come and close the trap. But the anticipated arrival of the *D.A.K.* was not to be seen nor heard of for some time, since there had been no progress reports from them during the entire day. Because of the failure to close the trap in time many of the British forces were able to make good their escape to the north and east, despite leaving behind numerous vehicles and pieces of equipment, which were quickly seized by German units. That evening it became clear to Rommel that the British forces were far too weak and scattered to be capable of halting his offensive, but now the only way to destroy those British forces, now believed to be reconsolidating around Agedabia, was to push up the Via Balbia with a strong force and block any further withdrawal by taking Antelat and Saunnu. Orders were now issued for the 22nd that called for *Kampfgruppe Marcks* to advance before first light towards Agedabia, while the *D.A.K.* and Italian *XX Corps* were to move north to the Via Balbia and then advance behind Marcks.[3] Marcks would then move through Agedabia and deploy a blocking force to cover the northern approaches while the *D.A.K.* moved through Agedabia and headed east towards Saunnu. At 0530hrs, the advance began with *Kampfgruppe Marcks* encountering little resistance as it moved up the Via Balbia towards Agedabia. By 1000hrs the town was captured, and the weak forces defending it either thrown back or taken prisoner. Rommel, who had been traveling with the lead elements, now believed that the British were located east of Agedabia, and so he ordered Marcks at around midday to continue his pursuit to the northeast towards Antelat, and once that town was secure turn to the southeast and drive towards Saunnu. As *Kampfgruppe Marcks* made its way north, further in the south the *D.A.K.* was still not able to move out of the desert and up to the Via Balbia, again mainly due to the lack of fuel and soft sand. Further delays were encountered when at 1400hrs the *D.A.K.* was ordered up the Via Balbia, but now it was faced with numerous mix ups and traffic congestion as units attempted to jockey for position near the road, which was still sown with mines leftover from the previous December. As the *D.A.K.* struggled north, *Kampfgruppe Marcks* was able to take Antelat, which fell at 1530hrs. The *kampfgruppe* was able to capture a great deal of war material when it suddenly appeared and surprised a number of British formations located near that town. Not wasting any time, Marcks then ordered his *kampfgruppe* to keep up the pressure and drive on Saunnu, which despite the growing darkness fell at 1930hrs. By late morning, the lead elements from the *15th Panzer Division*, specifically *Machine Gun Battalion 2*, were finally able to break free of the traffic congestion and reached Agedabia at around 1300hrs, where they were ordered by Rommel himself to move up and secure Antelat, which they were able to do by 2000hrs. The *21st Panzer Division* was also able to get its re-supply forward that morning, and it quickly moved north to Agedabia, and by late afternoon was driving along the track north towards Antelat. Once those elements reached a position just south of Antelat they were instructed to turn east and move in and help surround those British forces deployed around Saunnu. The remaining mobile elements from the *90th Light* were also able to move north through Agedabia, where they were placed into defense positions covering the northern side of that town. The Italian *XX Corps* also moved up to Agedabia that day and was placed to the east of the town, forming the western side of the bag. By mid-afternoon on the 22nd, after covering approximately 120km, the Regiment was finally able to reach the Via Balbia, where it was ordered north accompanied by various infantry, artillery, pioneers, and *panzerjäger* elements. This collection of combat elements was placed under the command of *Oberst* Hans Cramer, and was given the temporary title of *Kampfgruppe Cramer*.[4] The *kampfgruppe* was able to reach Agedabia by 2400hrs, and it continued to drive through the night, reaching a point twenty kilometers southwest of Antelat. After conducting a series of short halts in which the panzers took on fresh supplies of food and fuel, Cramer received the order to make contact with British armored formations in the vicinity of Saunnu and destroy them. As happened so often, the I./*Abteilung* was ordered to lead the advance and quickly moved off towards Giof el Matar. In the gathering darkness the *2nd* and *3rd Companies* made contact with British tanks and began to engage them from distances of 600 meters. Even in the fading light the panzers were able to successfully engage and destroy seven tanks while losing just one Mk III of the *2nd Company*. In his book *Panzer Aces II*, Franz Kurowski describes a portion of the attack:

"While south of Antelat elements of the Africa Corps veered east, the 8th Panzer Regiment drove towards Saunnu in a wide arc. Black forms appeared far ahead. Kümmel looked through his binoculars. Those weren't boulders or bushes, they were British tanks! The enemy vehicles were still at least four kilometers away. 'Enemy tanks in front of us!' reported the battalion commander. '4th Company attack frontally. All others turn toward Giof el Mater!' 'Commander to 4th Company: attack and tie down the enemy.' Kümmel saw Stiefelmayer's company press ahead while he rolled toward Giof el Mater with the main body and the regimental commander. The vehicles raised towering dust clouds as they raced across the desert. The 4th Company was able to carry out its assigned task. The main body of the 8th Panzer Regiment was now behind the British 1st Armored Division. The panzer companies attacked. Kümmel led the battalion in the direction of the airfield. They came upon two British antitank guns and knocked them out. One panzer was hit and disabled by a third gun firing from the airfield boundary. Now it became a target. 'Range six-hundred! Twelve o'clock! Armor-piercing shell!' The routine work of destruction began to function again. The shots

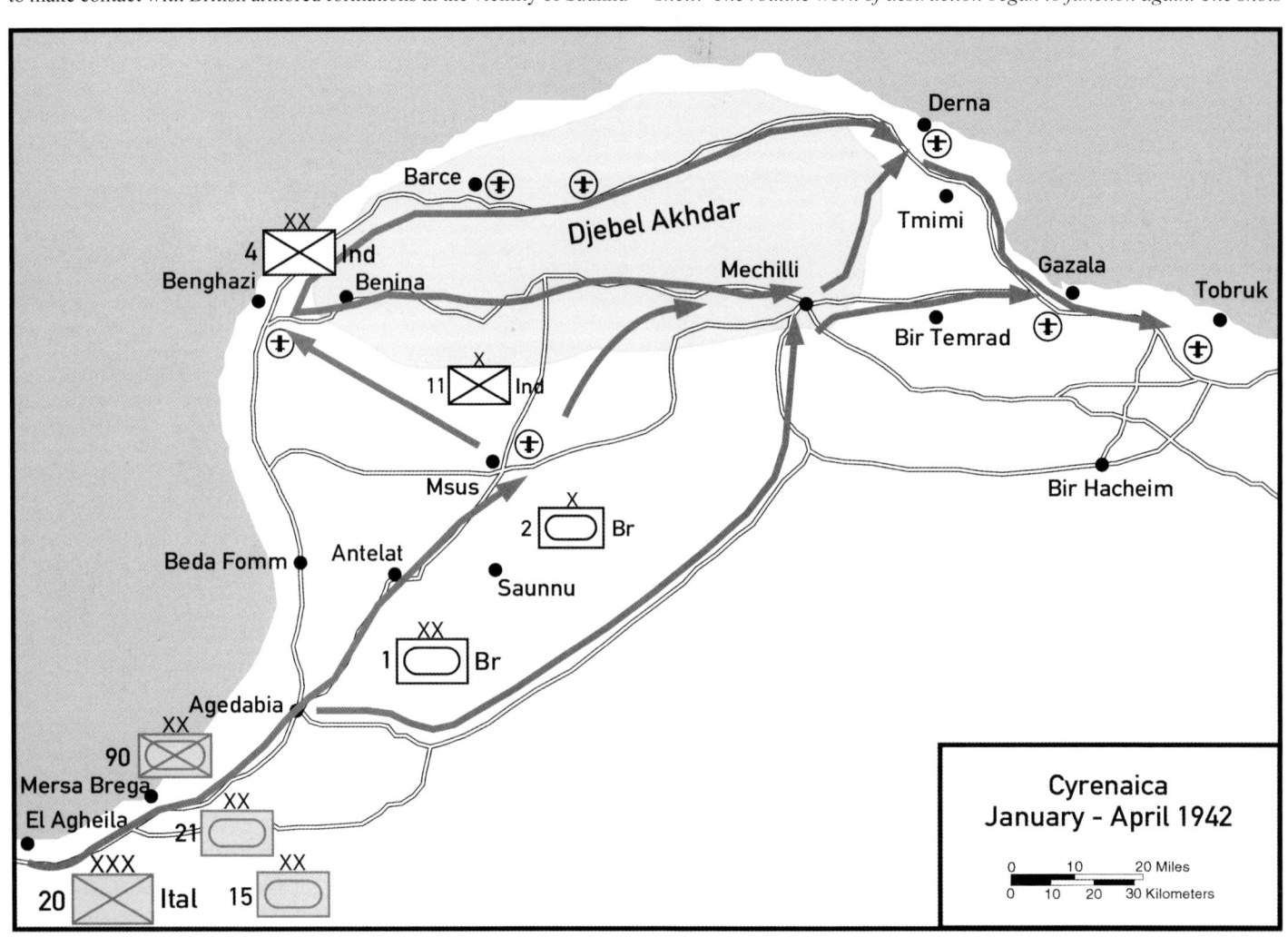

came in rapid succession, followed by flashes as the shells struck home. One fundamental rule in armored warfare states: shoot first! The crews of the 8th Panzer Regiment knew this all too well. Kümmel directed the companies as the situation required. Surrounded, under fire from three sides, elements of the 1st Armored Division surrendered."[5]

As dawn broke over the battlefield on the 23rd, British forces were finally able to begin their attacks against *Panzergruppe Afrika*, which only the day before had been redesignated as *Panzerarmee Afrika*.[6] The *21st Panzer Division* was in heavy contact as British armored forces came up from the south and engaged the German panzers. That division was successful in its defense, but failed to contain many of the British forces, which were able to escape to the northeast, past Saunnu. While the *21st Panzer* continued to fight hard all day, the *15th Panzer Division* had it a bit easier; during the day the *21st Panzer* had requested additional support, but the *D.A.K.* overruled them because of reports that the *4th Indian Division* was moving south from Beda Fomm.[7] It was not until 1500hrs that the *D.A.K.* finally released the Regiment and ordered it and its accompanying infantry and artillery to take up positions near the *21st Panzer*. Oberst Cramer sent the *I./Abteilung* to engage those British forces that were attempting to drive north to break through the German defenses. The Regiment soon came into contact with approximately ninety British tanks, and in the difficult fight that followed the *I./Abteilung* was able to engage the British and pushed them up against a screen created by the *7th* and *8th Companies*. This excerpt from Paul Carell's book *The Foxes of the Desert* gives us an idea of what it was like during one of the tank engagements:

"Ahead of the 8th Panzer Regiment they were not camel thorn bushes, which loomed on the horizon. Oberstlt Cramer led the regiment, on the march. Far on the far flank were the 4 panzers of the left column of 4th Company. 'Attention! Orange 2. Attack enemy tanks on the left!' echoed in the tank commander's headphones. Orange was the code word for the 2 flank panzers of the column and the commander of Orange 2 understood. 'Eleven o'clock engage enemy armor,' he called into his intercom. Inside the panzer the driver, gunner, commander and radio operator heard the order. Eleven o'clock meant a slight turn to the left '800yds armored piercing shells fire!' Inside the stifling metal box in a temp of 120 degrees the commander and gunner work like clockwork. The turret gun was aimed; the driver had stopped, for firing could only take place when the tank was stationary. Now the gunner pressed the electronic-firing button. 'Up fifty!' came the commander's order. The shot had been fifty yards short. 'Reload. New Range. Aim. Fire! On the target cried the commander.'"[8]

The British quickly withdrew from the engagement to the northeast and southeast. Fourteen tanks were claimed by the I./*Abteilung*, and seventeen tanks were destroyed by the *7th* and *8th Companies*. After the action, as the men combed over the battlefield, they could not help notice that almost every one of the destroyed tanks bore the markings of the *9th Lancer Regiment* and the White Rhino markings of the British *1st Armored Division*. The Regiment suffered losses that amounted to two soldiers killed and eight wounded. Five Mk IIs and thirteen Mk IIIs suffered from either engine or mechanical breakdowns.[9] Also during the 23rd, the *90th Light* and Italian *XX Corps*, aligned to the north and east of Agedabia, respectively, saw little action, and were to remain in those positions throughout the day. *Kampfgruppe Marcks*, which had been located at Saunnu the night before but was not present when the *21st Panzer* had attempted to link up that morning, had apparently withdrawn when it realized that it was surrounded by superior British forces. What the *21st Panzer* did find was that Saunnu was still occupied by those British forces, which had apparently moved back in on the evening of the 22/23rd. As the bulk of the *Panzerarmee*

fought and defended around Agedabia, Antelat, and Saunnu, another force (*Aufklärungs Abteilung 33*) was ordered to conduct a reconnaissance in force towards Benghazi. As dawn broke over the battlefield on the morning of the 24th, the *D.A.K.* could now begin to take stock of the damage they had inflicted on the British, and especially the *1st Armored Division*, which had suffered the loss of over a thousand prisoners, ninety-six tanks, thirty guns, and over six hundred trucks either destroyed or captured. Much of that success was directly attributed to the courage and daring of the many *D.A.K.* elements. As the day ended the *Panzerarmee* was still sure that it had the bulk of the *1st Armored Division* trapped in a large pocket to the southwest of Saunnu, and so that night orders were issued for a continuation of the offensive and the final destruction of those British forces trapped in the bag. *Kampfgruppe Marcks*, now located near El Grara, was to be relieved by the *21st Panzer* that night, then prepare itself and stand by for a continued drive to the east in pursuit of the British. The *90th Light* was to maintain its present positions around Agedabia, while the *15th Panzer* and Italian *XX Corps* were to drive into the bag from the north and west, respectively, and destroy the remaining forces still there. In the early dawn of the 24th, British patrols were encountered at numerous points around the perimeter of the bag attempting to break out, but unfortunately almost all of these attempts ended in failure. Unbeknownst to Rommel and the *Panzerarmee*, most of the British forces had been able to escape, and the resistance that was encountered that day came mostly from those units separated and attempting to flee, or those covering the withdrawal. Towards midday the *15th Panzer Division* was ordered to move north past Saunnu towards Msus, and with the I./*Abteilung* in the lead the Regiment set off in its battle formation. As it neared Saunnu it ran into scattered elements of the *1st Armored Division*, which were quickly engaged. The panzers traded fire with British tanks and anti-tank guns, losing just one Mk III that was hit and lost its track. Other panzer elements from the *2nd* and *3rd Companies* began to engage British anti-tank gunners, and were able to destroy nine anti-tank guns without sustaining any losses of their own. By 1500hrs, the Regiment, along with other *15th Panzer Division* elements, was able to reach El Grara. During the night of the 24/25th, the combat formations formed a hedgehog position north of Saunnu and waited on the supply trains for reprovisioning with fuel and ammunition. Since the start of offensive operations on 21 January the Regiment had covered more than 300km. Towards the end of the day the *Panzerarmee* came to the realization that the bulk of British forces had escaped the trap and had withdrawn towards Msus. Orders were issued for the 25th with the plan of engaging those forces and destroying them. *Kampfgruppe Marcks* was to return to Agedabia and await further developments, while the *D.A.K.* would plan on striking towards Msus the following day. On the 25th, Rommel sent *Kampfgruppe Marcks* west to cut the road north to Benghazi, while the *D.A.K.* feigned an attack towards Mechili. The *90th Light* and Italian *XX Corps* were released from their positions near Beda Fomm and advanced north to cover the area south of Benghazi. On the morning of the 25th the *D.A.K.* began its drive east with *21st Panzer* taking up positions on the right with an axis of advance from Saunnu to Bir Melezz, and the *15th Panzer* on the left, with an axis from Saunnu to Msus. At 0745hrs, after moving roughly 10km northwest of Saunnu, the *15th Panzer Division* ran into a heavily armored British force supported by artillery, but these thirty odd tanks were soon dealt with by the Regiment, which was closely supported by artillery and *panzerjäger* units.[10] The British units (elements of the *1st Armored Division*, *22nd Armored Brigade*, and *1st Support Group*) had very little desert experience, having just been called up from England and placed in the line, while the *7th Armored Division* was refitting back in Tobruk. The British armor was routed and retreated east, and if it had not been for a lapse in staff work at the *D.A.K.* headquarters the remnants of those formations would have been unable to escape and would have been destroyed in detail. Regardless of the errors made, the advance the *21st Panzer*, encountering only weak resistance, was able to reach Bir Melezz by that evening. The Regiment, which was at the head of the *15th Panzer Division* columns, conducted a forced march of some 80km, and by 1100hrs had reached the airfield at Msus, where it was able to throw the *11th Indian Brigade* out and captured large quantities of war materiel and provisions from the many supply depots located there. Most of these supplies had been pre-positioned there in anticipation for the planned British assault on Tripoli. The score was enormous, and would go a long way in sustaining the future advances of the *D.A.K.* Hundreds of vehicles, guns, and even tanks, including *Crusaders*, *Valentines*, and *Stuarts* were captured; additionally, there was also a tank workshop with thirty serviceable *Valentines*. But the situation was far from rosy, as much of the captured material was destroyed, and the precious fuel to keep the drive moving forward was slow in making its way forward to the panzers, which were now sitting, immobile. The Regiment alone was able to claim numerous tanks, guns, vehicles, and the capture of over one hundred prisoners. The haul might have been even more if the supporting infantry was able to make its way forward to halt and round up many of the stragglers. The abundance of captured British rations proved to be a quite satisfying and welcomed change for the men, and went far in improving diet and morale. Also that day, the *2nd Company* was able to claim the capture of twelve *RAF* aircraft, which were ready and awaiting take off instructions before the panzers arrived. In two reports written a month later, two *gefreiters* from the *2nd Company*, Karl Gaiser and Gefr Kneck, wrote of the day's fighting. The first report is by Gefr Kneck:

"After the hard but successful day the following morning of 25 January 1942 started early as usual. After short time the enemy artillery reported itself, and immediately afterwards one could recognize on the horizon the large amount of cannons. I was therefore involved in the hard combat. The Tommies seem to be however very surprised about our attack, because instead of shooting the English artillery stopped and drove away at high speed, but they could not escape from us! The order came via radio to follow the artillery at the highest speed and to destroy it, and immediately afterwards began the speedy hunting. Our panzers didn't want at first to come close to the Tommies, so actually we came to within the firing distance and we had the English cannons within several hundred meters of us. Immediately we shoot from all pipes [guns]. That was a meal for my Bug MG! After a few seconds we were able to find out that our cones of fire were set well, because the vehicles with the cannons stood still. The fragment grenade [H.E.] was launched on the halted vehicle during our drive, and the flames immediately started there! The attack still moved ahead with the same speed. Our other panzers had made a good achievement, as many more enemy cannons were demolished and left behind. Suddenly we received fire from 11 o'clock! Immediately afterwards we got hit on the screen on the cylinder, thankfully it didn't get through. The English tank was shooting at us. This one was immediately in the sights of our Richtschütze, and after our third shot the crew left the tank. The Mark IV caught fire after the fourth shot! Shortly after this episode the airplanes on the ground were reported in the middle of the vehicle formation. It was of course a case for us because we had to seize these airplanes. With full speed we went to this formation. Some of the vehicles were able to escape but it seemed that there was an order no to start for the airplanes and not less than 12 ready-to-start airplanes fell into our hands! During the short stop we fuelled and quickly cleaned the weapons. Then it went further, with only a few vehicles that were able to escape, and with demolished cannons. After this happening, we finally stopped for the evening and went into the hedgehog position. With pride and happiness we heard over the radio the special report about 12 captured airplanes that will not make any more trouble for us!"[11]

Karl Gaiser's report goes on to state:

"After some obstacles I finally came to Africa on 13 January 1942. I had the luck to immediately come to the combat detachment. The drive to Derna, from Tripolis, was not exactly the best one. We sat in the truck fully loaded with petrol canisters. The drive continued for 3 days. When we left from the Via Balbia we got another truck also fully loaded. One of my friends said "Thank God when this drive is over". But there was still some more to come! The desert as it went was over the rocks and stones and supplies had to be thrown from the vehicle when we got stuck in the sand. Then we came to the supply lines. On 18 January we came to the combat detachment where we were distributed to the various companies of the I./Abteilung. I went to the 2nd Company and was very proud, that I was assigned to this company as I heard that this company was one of the bravest in the Pz.Rgt.8. I had spent four days getting to know things before I drove into my first combat. On 25 January as we began the drive in the morning at 0800hrs. After a short while one could see the vehicles on the horizon. We drove happily on them with the thoughts to hit the Tommies as it happened over the last four days. We sat in the panzer; the Ladeschütze prepared the weapons, I helped with the telescope at my feet. It was the tank reconnaissance [scout car] which was closest to us. My commander told me the distance and I positioned it and went to shoot. The shot went a little bit high and I made corrections and again shot and I saw through the telescope as there was another English tank reconnaissance car. In this fight there were two tank reconnaissance vehicles, SP vehicles and two tanks. In contrary to other combats, it went immediately further and after the quick drive we were ready for to combat. I went though my numbers and was not able to see anything, because the terrain was very wavy. But suddenly I was not able to believe my eyes, when ahead of us were standing aircraft; I thought it was probably an airfield, which Tommy had left in a hurry. I heard the order over the radio from my commander and afterwards the 3-engines vehicle burned. My neighbor vehicle did the same so that many airplanes quickly went up in the flames. We took some prisoners on this airfield as well. We drove on this day many kilometers so we had to stop and fuel. Afterwards it went on further and after a few hours we were again given the readiness order for combat and again I saw Tommy ahead of me before he noticed me. We took prisoners before we halted and the day ended, and we hit the Tommies again. I will not forget this day, I am grateful to my destiny that I had the luck to experience such a day and hope to have many more such days to experience."[12]

The Regiment sustained only a few minor casualties and reported the following losses: Lt Hahn, three *unteroffiziers*, and five crewmembers were reported as wounded. Four Mk IIIs suffered mechanical breakdowns and three Mk IIs were returned from the workshop.[13] After refueling, the advance was again continued to the north of Msus, and along the way the battle staff of the *1st Armored Division* was captured in addition to more vehicles and supplies.[14] By the end of the day the British *XXX Corps* had been torn to pieces and was unable to conduct further combat operations. On the 26th, as the British continued their retreat to the north and east, the *D.A.K.* remained immobile around Msus and Bir Melezz, cleaning up the battlefield and refitting with the haul of British rations, vehicles, fuel, ammunition, and other large amounts of war materiel. After that short break the Regiment prepared itself for a continuation of the pursuit. Rommel and his *Panzerarmee* were now secure, with Marsa Brega, Agedabia, and Antelat firmly in Axis hands; now it was time to focus on

Chapter 9: Back from Tripolitania, January-April 1942

Benghazi and Mechili. The next act would be to secure these positions by destroying the enemy located there and finish off the remaining *Eighth Army* formations before they could escape to the east. The lure of driving east was appealing, but the *Panzerarmee* was hamstrung by the lack of supplies, especially fuel, to undertake such a long march. Instead, the city of Benghazi and its harbor seemed a better, more strategic option. At the time there were still brigade-sized elements from the *4th Indian* and *1st South African Divisions* located in Benghazi and occupying and defending the outlaying towns of Er Regima, Solluch, and Ghemines. It was determined that an attack from the south would have little chance of success, and so Rommel's plan was to move in from the east over the rough mountainous and sandy terrain of the Djebel Akhdar and secure Benghazi. In order to achieve this objective the highly mobile *Kampfgruppe Marcks* was ordered to prepare itself for action. The *kampfgruppe*, which had already been augmented with elements from the *21st Panzer Division*, was now given parts of *Aufklärungs Abteilung 3* and *33* and an Italian artillery battery. As the *kampfgruppe* gathered itself 20km west of Msus on the afternoon of the 27th the weather began to turn, with rain beginning to fall and turn the ground into a sticky morass. The *D.A.K.* had the task of creating a diversion in the east by making it look as if the *D.A.K.* was underway from Bir Melezz to attack Mechili. The British were fooled by this maneuver and moved their armor up to meet the threat. That day the Regiment's combat elements went without making any contact with the British, and since the division was unable to provide much fuel for the Regiment it remained idle. In the south, the *90th Light* and Italian *XX Corps*, which were ordered to demonstrate in the south, advanced towards Solluch and Ghemines. That evening, at 1700hrs *Kampfgruppe Marcks* began the march westward towards Er Regima, which was to be taken by first light on the 28th. The terrain and weather, of course, would have something to do with that plan, as the advance soon became bogged down in the rough terrain and wadis, and then, to make matters worse, a sandstorm and heavy rainstorm, lasting two hours, broke over the *kampfgruppe*. Twice that night there were heavy rainstorms and hail, which had not previously been experienced in this strength and intensity. The rain turned the ground into a sticky morass that brought a halt to much of the logistics support, and re-supply operations were discontinued until daylight. The main force's advance was halted in the early morning hours when it too became bogged down and found it impossible to proceed, but this did not deter the *kampfgruppe* from its primary objectives. As the column continued to push forward under the supervision of Rommel himself the going became a bit easier, and by 1100hrs the column had advanced to within 10km of Er Regima, and by 1600hrs the town was finally captured. The appearance of a German *kampfgruppe* popping up from the east and taking Er Regima took the British by complete surprise. The *kampfgruppe* was not content to sit still, as it wasted little time making for the airfield nearby at Benina, and almost succeeded in capturing the airfield intact. Rommel then ordered that a small strike group be sent towards Benghazi in an attempt to take that town by a *coup de main*. The strike group was forced to halt short of the town when it ran into British forces attempting to escape the Axis force pushing up from the south. The *kampfgruppe* was then placed into a series of strongpoints strung across the line Goefia-Benina-Er Regima in an attempt to halt the fleeing British. Throughout the evening and early morning of the 28/29th, elements of the *7th Indian Brigade* and the support group of the *4th Indian Division* succeeded in escaping the German trap when they were able to slip past the *kampfgruppe* and the spread out *D.A.K.* to the east. The same weather that had aided *Kampfgruppe Marcks* in moving up and taking Er Regima by surprise now worked against them, as the British forces were able to make good their escape to the southeast. Not all of the British formations were successful in their escape attempts; one infantry battalion was caught,

and a number of other, smaller detachments were picked up throughout the 29th. By midday, Benghazi had fallen, and although it did not yield the prize envisioned, it did give the *Panzerarmee* a harbor in which it could bring in more forces and huge stocks of supplies, which would go a long way in easing some of the Axis' logistics shortfalls. Some of the stores capture in Benghazi turned out to be German; these stores had been stockpiled and then left to the British the year prior when the fortunes of war had been reversed; most of the booty had remained intact since the retreat the previous year. When news of the triumph and capture of Benghazi reached Berlin, Hitler promoted Rommel to *Generaloberst*.[15] As *Kampfgruppe Marcks* was moving on Benghazi, the majority of the *D.A.K.* was still located around Msus, where it was demonstrating towards Mechili; however, the lack of supplies, especially fuel, was thwarting most of these movements. The division was not able to provide any fuel to the Regiment, thereby halting all further attempts at catching the British as they flew the trap at Benghazi. It was here that the Regiment formed a hedgehog position and remained there until 31 January. On the 31st, the *Panzerarmee* was able to send two *Kampfgruppen* (*Marcks* and *Geissler*) eastwards across the Djebel Akhdar towards Mechili. The Regiment received the mission to continue the attack towards Mechili, which began at 1100hrs and continued in the rain, which made the march over the wadis and slippery rocky ground very difficult. Towards the afternoon the Regiment reached the djebel that dropped off towards Mechili, but was forced to halt at 1500hrs because of the lack of fuel. The heavy rains and hail returned, with hail being reported as big as grapes. At 1800hrs, the first fuel trucks arrived and began refuelling the panzers before they continued their march east, and that evening the Regiment halted again, this time just west of Mechili. On 1 February, the weather began to improve some and the advance continued. As the *D.A.K.* advanced it came under attack by *RAF* fighter-bombers, and the Regiment sustained a couple of casualties: two commanders and one loader were wounded, with an Mk II suffering a mechanical breakdown.[16] It was at this point in the battle that the *Eighth Army* finally withdrew its forces to the *Gazala Line*, accepting that it had been beaten, and its forces, now scattered, disorganized, and demoralized, stood little chance of succeeding with any type of counterattack. In the meantime, the Regiment received the order to conduct an attack between Derna and Mechili towards Gazala. West of Mechili the panzers came under fire from a battery of 25-Pounder artillery. The *2nd Company* was sent in to attack this battery and succeeded in destroying it and capturing twenty-five of the gunners, most of which were Indians. At this point in the attack the panzers again were forced to halt because of the lack of fuel. Over the past couple of days many of the panzers had had to make do with only half a tank full of fuel in which to conduct operations. That evening, the supply trains were able to make their way forward and conduct a resupply. With its fuel replenished the I./*Abteilung* proceeded once again, heading east on the morning of the 2nd. Approximately 50km southwest of Derna the *abteilung* ran into a battle group from the *4th Indian Division*, with about fifteen *Valentines*, eight anti-tank guns, and a large group of Bren gun carriers. As the *abteilung* began to deploy its panzers into fighting formation it came under well-placed British artillery. The *6th Company*, which was aligned to the right of the formation, soon became engaged with a number of tanks, and in the action that followed was able to claim three tanks and nine carriers destroyed. The remainder of this small group quickly broke off the engagement and withdrew to the north.[17] As the *6th Company* continued to hold their attention and drive into the position the remaining panzers had deployed into a wide wedge and, as the remaining elements fled, ran into the awaiting panzers. Another seven tanks, five anti-tank guns, and eight carriers were destroyed. After the engagement ended the *abteilung* proceeded towards Derna before its fuel tanks once again ran dry and forced it to halt 20km from that city. In the last two weeks the Regiment had covered over six hundred kilometers, and was now back in Cyrenaica, but like all the mobile elements of the *Panzerarmee* it was hamstrung by the lack of fuel. On the bitterly cold night of the 2/3rd, the supply trains and *Light Column* managed to make their way forward and locate the stranded panzers, which were resupplied with food, fuel, and ammunition. Another bonus for the Regiment was the return of three Mk IIs and four Mk IIIs from the workshops that accompanied the supply trains forward and were able to rejoin the Regiment. The Regiment reported a panzer strength of sixty-eight on 3 February 1942.[18] The Regiment continued its attack on the 3rd north of the Trigh el Abd towards Gazala. In its customary formation of wide panzer wedged the panzers rolled forward, encountering numerous small groups of the *Eighth Army* that were attempting to delay the pursuit and get back to their own lines. The delaying elements usually consisted of a small number of speedy Crusader tanks and armored cars, allowing them to race up at high speed, fire a few rounds, and then quickly withdraw to a safe distance. In one of these encounters on the 3rd the panzer gunners proved to be quicker on the trigger and were able to destroy two armored cars. Another car was taken when it suffered a mechanical break down and was captured. Another threat to the panzers was *RAF* fighters, which attacked the panzer columns shortly after midday and repeated their attacks until the evening. Ten soldiers were wounded in the attacks by flying fragments and ricocheting bullets, and two Mk IIs and three Mk IIIs suffered mechanical breakdowns.[19] That night the supply trains moved forward and were able to undertake a resupply, which came off without any difficulties, but once again there was not enough fuel available, and many of the panzers had to make do with only enough fuel to fill about two-thirds of their petrol tanks. On the 5th the weather again turned bad, as a cold north wind brought in rain and ice which began to pelt the cold, hungry, and exhausted panzer crews, forcing them to huddle together and await the morning sun. The advance east continued albeit slowly, and again columns of British vehicles were again seen from time to time; one of these columns was spotted as it ran across the line of march, presenting the panzer gunners with a prime target. The *I./Abteilung* under the command of Johannes Kümmel allowed his panzers to take the column under fire, and in no time a number of the vehicles were burning. The situation was well under control until a British artillery unit arrived on the scene and began engaging the panzers in the direct fire mode. The 25-Pounder artillery gun was a feared opponent for the panzers, but they had encountered them in the past. The best tactic for dealing with close range artillery was to drive directly at them at a high rate of speed and spray the area with the bow and coaxial machine guns in an attempt to panic and keep the crews off balance. Utilizing this tactic the panzers were able to move in and overrun the guns, in the process destroying four of them. By the evening of the 5/6th, the *Panzerarmee* was halted in linear defensive position centered on the towns of Mechili and Tmimi. The Regiment itself was halted only 20km west of Gazala, where it was awaiting a resupply of fuel and provisions. The supplies were finally able to be brought forward later that day, and after taking on fuel and provisions the panzers were then ordered to remain in place and await further orders. On the 10th, *Hptm* Zügener came forward with fifteen brand new Mk IIIs that had been recently delivered to North Africa; in addition to the new panzers a number of other recently repaired panzers were brought up. On the 15th, the *Panzerarmee Afrika* ordered the formation of a booty detachment; this detachment, primarily designed to reconstitute English and American tanks and vehicles that had been captured or abandoned on the battlefield, was to be the responsibility of *Oberstlt* Ramsauer, and was to be formed at Benghazi. Ramsauer was to form a headquarters with various officers and men from other regiments from within the *15th Panzer Division*. His *Stabs* was to consist of Ramsauer, one *Ordinance Officer*, two weapons specialists, one English translator, one clerk, one driver, and one *unteroffizer* and five men for headquarters details. The men were ordered by radio to pull back from their front line positions, consolidate at a designated place and time, and move off to Benghazi to link up with Ramsauer, which would then form a replacement training company. Since some of the men who would eventually be called upon to man these captured tanks had little to no experience in panzer warfare and tactics, a number of experienced panzer men from the Regiment were called on also. These included: one company grade officer; three panzer drivers, all of which had to be instructor qualified; three panzer commanders; and three panzer lookouts or identification specialists—again, all these men had to possess instructor or trainer credentials.[20] The company would be short lived, but would eventually be responsible for the refitting and reinforcing of some of the *15th Panzer's* panzer *zugs*, which because of supply shortages were under strength. By 18 February the *15th Panzer Division* had taken up a series of large horseshoe positions southeast of Derna on a line laying south on the Via Balbia between Martuba and Umm er-Rzem. The Regiment was in position along markers 43-47, with I./*Abteilung* forward and centered with the Regiment *Stabs* further to the rear on the right, or western flank, while the II./*Abteilung* was situated along the left, or eastern, flank, also in the rear. The Regiment was flanked by *Aufklärungs Abteilung 33* to the east and the divisional *Stabs* to the west. That afternoon a British column of approximately eighty vehicles, among them tanks and armored cars, was reported to be advancing towards the northwest. Taking into account the *D.A.K.*'s precarious state of fuel and the overall Axis troop disposition, the movement caused some concern, and so *Oberst* Erich Geissler, the commander of *Schützen Brigade 15*, who had just been in charge of Rommel's second major *kampfgruppe* that had chased the British forces from Marmarica and cleared much of the area from Barce, Mechili, and Tmimi was ordered to reform his *kampfgruppe*. The *kampfgruppe* was to prepare for an undertaking on 19 February in the area south of Ras Chechiban, which was located just to the southwest of Tmimi on the Mechili Track. At 1230hrs the *D.A.K.* Chief of Staff ordered the Regiment to prepare one panzer company itself for future deployment with *Kampfgruppe Geissler*, and also alerted all other elements to increase their combat alert status and readiness. Shortly thereafter, at 1300hrs there followed another radio transmission to the Regiment that the previously mentioned panzer company was to be prepared immediately for deployment. At 1500hrs, the Regiment radioed back to the division confirming that the panzer company had been alerted and was prepared to link up with *Kampfgruppe Geissler* the following morning, and that it would be commanded by *Olt* Prion and would consist of the following: two Mk IIs, twelve Mk IIIs, and two Mk IVs.

Later in the evening, at 1930hrs, a reconnaissance element from *Aufklärungs Abteilung 33* had reconnoitered towards Hill 125 and found it free of enemy forces, and that the British had pushed off to the south. Despite this movement, at 2000hrs the *D.A.K.* ordered that the panzer company be subordinated to *Kampfgruppe Geissler*, and to effect link up and report to the *kampfgruppe* no later than the 19th.[21] By 0630hrs the following morning, the *D.A.K.* was informed that the *3rd Company* had departed to the link up. Fuel was also a problem at this time, and the DAK was concerned about the limitations it would have on any further combat actions, and thereby ordered all units to conserve fuel whenever possible, which in most cases meant that only during an attack were units to move about to engage the enemy. The panzers made good time moving down from their positions near Umm er Rzem, and by early morning Prion had affected his link up with the *kampfgruppe*. Also that same morning a reconnaissance element departed from Chechiban and moved forward towards Gabr el Aleima, where it was able to identify that the British still remained in the area and that Gabr el Aleima was occupied. The reconnaissance also revealed that the British forces on Gabr el Aleima itself had approximately forty to fifty vehicles, and among them were seen numerous artillery pieces. This was no easy feat, in that the British around Gabr el Aleima were using a strong smoke-screen in a radius of approximately 6km to hinder the Germans from identifying their forces located there. Towards mid-morning seven panzers were sent out to test the British defenses around Chechiban, but this small panzer force was quickly forced back by British artillery fire. Following this failed attempt to breach the defenses an attack was ordered which was to be executed in the form of a pincer movement beginning from Chechiban by the *3rd Company* and supported by an artillery battery. At 1300hrs the panzers began their assault, while one company from *I./Schützen Regiment 115* and an additional artillery *zug* began their assault from Point 63/65, which was located just to the southeast of Chechiban. As the panzers began rolling towards Gabr el Aleima they were followed at 1330hrs by the infantrymen. The arrival of panzers and infantry caused the British to begin withdrawing en masse their forces off to the south and southwest. The smoke-screen which had been obscuring the German view now began to dissipate, and as the panzers emerged from the smoke they spotted a total of twenty-seven armored cars moving off to the south. These vehicles were engaged by the panzers, but unfortunately there is no record of their success. By 1440hrs, a radio message was sent back to the division reporting that Gabr el Aleima had been simultaneously occupied by both the panzers and infantry without further fighting. With the area now secure, the infantry and attached Pak gunners began constructing their defensive positions without delay. The *Stabs I./Schützen Regiment 115* ordered up the *1./Schützen Regiment 115* and one Pak-*zug*, and relocated the *8./Schützen Regiment 115* up towards Chechiban and the H.K.L. to positions at the airfield, which had been given the title *Stützpunkt* (Strongpoint) "Ehle." With the area now secured and the British threat to the division and *D.A.K.* greatly diminished, Prion and his company were released at 1700hrs back to the Regiment. The British response to their losing Gabr el Aleima was to continue firing artillery from further in the south towards Point 63/65 and on the other strong points nearby, but this fire was weak and caused few casualties. The ever present scout cars, ever fearful of the German panzers, could be seen off in the distance, but they seldom ventured in closer than about eight kilometers. The *3rd Company* had done a good job in its support of the *kampfgruppe*, but unfortunately there are no figures present as to what damage they inflicted or had suffered. On Friday the 20th, with the weather warm and sunny the panzers of the *3rd Company* were able to rejoin their comrades by 1900hrs that evening.[22] Also on this date, *Olt* Heinz Hess, the Adjutant of the *II./Abteilung*, was awarded the *DKiG* for his actions during the *Crusader Battles*.[23] Unknown to the men of the *D.A.K.*, the British XIII Corps had thrown in all its available forces and reserves, including the *1st Army Tank Brigade*, to form a defensive zone some 65km in width. While these minor skirmishes were taking place Rommel ordered the *15th Panzer Division* to remain halted, and allowed only parts of the *90th Light* to advance toward the east. At 1100hrs on 23 February, the *RAF* paid a visit to the division in the form of a dive bombing attack; in the attack the Regiment and division's *stabs* were the focus of the planes, but they inflicted no casualties or damage on them. On 26 February the division commander, his Ia, and Adjutant drove to the Regiment's location to present the Iron Cross to a number of the men for their actions over the previous three months.[24] Also during this quiet time a number of the officers and men were tasked with writing after action reports and their accounts of the battles fought in November and December 1941. The Regiment was ordered back to an assembly area some 30km east of Derna near Tmimi, and from here it moved to the area of Um er Rzem-Martuba, where it would remain for the next month for a well-earned rest. During this time the desert was in bloom, which cast a very unusual picture for those of the Regiment. On 1 March 1942, *Oberst* Hans Cramer was reassigned to Germany as the Chief of Staff to the Commanding General of *Schnell (Mobile) Truppen*. Cramer, perhaps the most successful of all the regimental commanders, handed over command of the Regiment to *Oberstleutnant* Willi Teege, an experienced panzer man who came from the *Panzer Lehr Abteilung* at the *Panzer Truppen School*. On the 5th, Cramer was awarded the *Deutsches Kreuz in Gold* for his actions in leading the Regiment during the battles of January and February 1942.[25] He was one of the first soldiers in Africa to receive this award, and as he departed he spoke with Hans Kümmel:

"I know that it was you and the other comrades who led our regiment to victory. And I ask that you maintain your attitude and aggressiveness, which I have always admired, even under a new commanding officer."[26]

Panzer Regiment 8 Chain of Command as of 01 March 1942[27]

Regiment Commander	Oberstlt Teege
I./Abteilung Commander	Hptm Kümmel
1st Company	Olt Knorr
2nd Company	Olt Heinrich
3rd Company	Olt Prion
4th Company	Olt Stiefelmayer
II./Abteilung Commander	Hptm Zügener
5th Company	Olt Lehn
6th Company	Lt Friedrich
7th Company	Hptm Klein
8th Company	Olt Danz

The panzer strength report of the Regiment on 1 March 1942 was 134 operational panzers, with almost one hundred of those being Mk IIIs, and a further forty-six panzers (ten Mk IIs, thirty Mk IIIs, and six Mk IVs) were still in the workshops.[28] With the break in action, both sides began to plan their next moves. In his after action report, Alfred Toppe wrote the following concerning German plans for the Summer 1942:

"Since it was now to be expected that the exhaustion of the troops on both sides would lead to a period of comparative quiet, Rommel flew to Rome and Germany to learn the intentions of the Italian Supreme Command and Wehrmacht High Command with regard to the conduct of the war in the Mediterranean in 1943. He found that practically no plans existed and that the Italians were even very averse to any offensive operations before autumn. In April, Rommel therefore again took the initiative on his own responsibility. His opinion was that it was necessary to take preemptive action against a new offensive by the enemy, which he expected in June, with probably even stronger enemy forces than before. It was vitally important to the Germans to capture both Tobruk and Malta, the latter of which, as a naval and air base, interfered to an intolerable extent with German seaborne supply traffic. Since the German Air Force could support only one of these operations at a time, however, it would be necessary for them to take place in succession. Rommel considered it desirable to attack Malta first and then Tobruk. However, if the preparations for the capture of Malta required too much time, he thought it best to attack Tobruk first so that after that town had been taken and the border line from Sidi Omar-Bardia reached, all air force strength could be concentrated against Malta. Rommel's suggestion was that the attack on Tobruk should open in the second half of May."[29]

The month of March was a relatively quiet time for the men on both sides; the *Panzerarmee* came under occasional aerial attacks by the *RAF*, but because their positions had been well dug in and camouflaged, the number of casualties and damage incurred was minor. The British were able to keep close tabs on the *D.A.K.* with their vast numbers of armored scout cars, which skirted around the lines of the *Panzerarmee* in order to maintain contact and look for weak points in the lines. During this time the *15th Panzer Division*, because of the large area it was forced to cover and the many gaps between its forces to the north and south, formed two strong mobile *kampfgruppen*. The first of these was *Kampfgruppe Geissler*, which consisted of elements of *I./Schützen Regiment 115*, *1./Artillery Regiment 33* (two guns), *1./Panzerjäger Abteilung 33*, and elements of *Nachrichten Abteilung 78*. This *kampfgruppe* was supported by the panzers of *I./Abteilung*. The second *kampfgruppe* was *Kampfgruppe Baade*, which consisted of *III./Schützen Regiment 115* and *I./Artillery Regiment 33*, and was supported by the panzers from *II./Abteilung*. According to the divisional *KTB*, on 21 March at 1600hrs, *Sdf* (special translator) Kruehler, who was returning from his duties with *Panzer Regiment 8*, reported that there had been an alarm in the Regiment, and that a request to the *D.A.K. Ic* about the developing situation was needed. *Olt* Klinghammer of the *Stabs Ic* reported that air reconnaissance conducted at between 13-1400hrs southeast of Bir Bu Giadalla had observed the presence of approximately eighty vehicles. Further air reconnaissance was still to be provided. As reports continued to come into the *Stabs*, the *Ia*, *Hptm* Knoblauch, informed the staff that the enemy had placed the Martuba airfield under artillery fire and was moving against it with a fast moving column, amongst which were supposedly tanks, but they had been forced back to the northwest by *D.A.K.* Flak guns.[30] A German *kampfgruppe* consisting of one panzer *abteilung*, one *schützen* battalion, one *panzerjäger* company, and one artillery battery working together under *Oberstleutnant* Geissler were ordered to move in the direction of Wadi Maalegh, south of Martuba, and eventually deploy against the British forces seen there. Later the *D.A.K.* reported that air reconnaissance had reported that in the area of Martuba-Mechili-Tmimi there were 600 enemy vehicles, including tanks and artillery. *Kampfgruppe Geissler* moved to its new area of assignment as the British quickly broke off their attack and moved off to a safe distance in order to avoid any serious engagements with the *D.A.K.* This engagement was typical of those actions that took place that spring, with moves being made by the British to test the *Panzerarmee* defenses and find out what Rommel was planning next. In early April, the *15th Panzer Division* was again on the move, relocating to new positions located to the northwest of Bir Temrad, while other divisional groups were scattered around the Tmimi-Mechili Piste and to the northeast of Bir es Sferi. The division was split into four separate but self-supporting elements that consisted of: 1st *Gruppe* with the *Stabs* of *Schützen Regiment 115*, *III./Schützen Regiment 115*, and *I./Artillery Regiment 33*. The 2nd *Gruppe* consisted of *I./Schützen Regiment 115*, *II./Artillery Regiment 33*, and *2./Panzerjäger Abteilung 33*. The 3rd *Gruppe* was made up of *Panzer Regiment 8*, the *Stabs* of *Artillery Regiment 33*, *III./Artillery Regiment 33*, and *Nachrichten Abteilung 78*. The final group consisted of *II./ Schützen Regiment 115*, Pioneer Battalion 33, and *Aufklärungs Abteilung 33*. On the afternoon of 9 April, "*Panzer Company Prion*," which had been active with *Kampfgruppe Geissler*, along with elements of *Aufklärungs Abteilung 33*, engaged two British field artillery batteries. The panzers and armored cars quickly overran the positions, and in the process captured seven officers and thirty-seven men, along with four guns and one truck. In addition to the booty, the force claimed the destruction of five scout cars, four jeeps, six self-propelled vehicles, three munitions trailers, one truck, and one gun. The company also reported the following losses: *Olt* Prion was wounded, and Lt Boland from one of the transport sections was killed; one *unteroffizer* and man were killed in action, while three *unteroffiziers* and five men were wounded. In addition to the men, one Mk III was reported as totally destroyed and three Mk III were temporarily damaged.[31] Throughout the month of April the Regiment continued to receive replacement personnel from *Panzer Ersatz Abteilung 7* in Böblingen, while a number of those previously wounded returned to carry on their service with the Regiment, which once again began to attain its authorized strength. One of those returning was Wilhelm Hagios, who had been wounded the previous November during the fighting on *Totensonntag*. Unknown to him, his friend Giesser had been killed in action with Prion's company. He remembers:

"I came back to Böblingen from leave to the reserve company until my return in April. Then I went by Naples, Brindisi, Crete, and Martuba and there was the regiment, they told me 'you came back, so stay with us'. Then I was at the regiment stab, and went immediately to the panzer, Fw Beckers was my commander and Mainkel-Schmitt was the driver. Giesser, my friend, had gone to the 1st or 2nd Company and I had promised [him] that I would return after recovering from my wounds. But in early April he [Giesser] was killed, they had attacked with the 1st or 2nd Company at the positions near Signal Esyd [Segnali] and were shot down. The British had for the first time the full rounds in the artillery cannons similar to what the Germans already had and so we buried him, my friend. We were near Martuba then, on 10 April we were relocated to the south from the position near Signal Esyd, [Rotunda Segnali] there was our assembly area for the attack on 26 May."[32]

On the 22nd, the *2nd Company* and one *Zug* of Mk IVs from the *4th Company* under the command of *Olt* Stiefelmayer were detached from the Regiment and ordered to augment *Kampfgruppe Menny*, which was commanded by Knights Cross recipient *Oberst* Erwin Menny, the commander of *Schützen Brigade 15*. The panzers departed on the 25th for their tour of duty with the infantry. The entire force consisted of three Mk IIs, fourteen Mk IIIs, and four Mk IVs. The purpose behind the move was to allow the infantry and panzers to conduct joint training together while developing better cooperation and relationships prior to the inevitable attack on Tobruk. The panzers would not return to the Regiment until 14 May. Also that May, Hans Kümmel, the tried and true commander of the *1st Company*, and one of the Regiment's ablest panzer commanders, was officially given command of the *I./Abteilung*. For the past months Kümmel had been leading his company and other panzer elements, setting a new standard that others could only hope to emulate. The appointment would come just in time for Rommel's great offensive in Cyrenaica and the subsequent pursuit into Egypt. The number of operational panzers also rose at this time, with a total of 139 panzers being reported by the *15th Panzer Division*.[33] A welcomed addition to the Regiment at this time were a number of 88mm guns from the *5th Battery*, *Flak Regiment 18*, minus two of its *Zugs* (5 Guns); these guns would provide good long range fire and security for the upcoming attack. Another addition to the Regiment was the arrival on the 25th of the first Mk III "Specials," which were known as Ausf or model Ms, and they were equipped with the long barrel 50mm KwK L/60 main gun. There were also two Mk IV model F2s which would also come to be known as "Specials," and like the Mk III Specials these too sported a new long barrel, the 75mm KwK L/43 gun. Unfortunately, the ammunition for the 75mm guns had not yet been delivered, but the men were still able to begin a series of crew and gunnery drills with them. Horst Sonnenkalb wrote of the newest panzers:

"Operational again, I was assigned to the 7th Company of the II./Abteilung of our regiment. There I became the driver of the panzer Mk III of the chief of the company. We were located in the rest area. Now the urgently required weapons arrived as well. The first panzer Mk IIIs with the 5cm-long cannon were there. Each one of companies from both

Chapter 9: Back from Tripolitania, January-April 1942

Abteilungs received panzers with these cannons. We were looked at as a little bit envious, because here was the panzer weapon for which the British had nothing comparable. Each Abteilung also possessed two companies with the medium 5cm L42 tank cannon and each Abteilung had one company with the Panzer Mk IV with 7.5cm L24 short cannons, which were later, equipped with 7.5cm long cannon."[34]

By 30 April, the *15th Panzer Division* was able to report an operational panzer strength of 196 gun armed panzers. The months of April and May were a time for the Regiment, as well as the entire *Panzerarmee*, to reorganize and refit; the priority was the integration of new men and materiel that was now successfully making the journey to Africa, for the time being unimpeded by the *Royal Navy* and *RAF*. Horst Sonnenkalb wrote of the supply situation and the problems that the *D.A.K.* faced:

"Already we had discovered that we had serious supply problems. What we lacked most was fuel and ammunition. The supplies that were supposed to reach us in Libya via the sea from Italy were being destroyed by bomber planes leaving from Malta or by torpedo strikes. Pretty soon a question arose that kept us occupied the whole rest of the African campaign: Why did the Italian and German Army command put up with the dangerous supply routes? Why don't you get rid of the enemy in Malta? When would you destroy Malta, the thorn in the flesh of the Africa Corps? It was a riddle that was never solved."[35]

It was vitally important that new recruits and returning veterans alike were reintegrated into those positions that had been vacated by men who had succumbed to wounds or sickness. The young drivers and gunners of a year ago now found themselves in command of their own panzer. Hans Killermann remembered:

"It was important that new recruits be placed as a loader, the experienced soldier was given the service as a panzer driver because he had to know very fast how to get out of trouble and must be able to know what the commander wants."[36]

The Regiment's training program focused on gunnery drills and marksmanship, both with the main gun and co-axial machine guns—even pistol and rifle marksmanship was conducted. The men continued to push themselves hard, believing in the old axiom that tough training makes for less combat casualties, and even their leader, Rommel, could often be seen inspecting and even participating in some of the training events. And so the month of April and the first weeks of May passed under the blazing sun which scorched the desert, with the daytime temperatures reaching almost 122F/50C. On 4 May, the *D.A.K.* ordered the construction of a new airfield in the area of Gabr el Aleim. The *21st Panzer Division* was overall responsible for its construction with assistance from various *15th Panzer* units. For this detail the Regiment had to furnish one *unteroffizer* with thirty men, while other divisional units had similar taskings. Another of those who returned at this time was Kurt Liestmann, who had been wounded the previous summer on 16 June 1941. During his time recuperating in Germany he was given the terrible news of the loss of his brother Heinz, who had been killed during the *Crusader* Battle while serving in the II./ *Abteilung*. Despite the loss, Kurt returned to the front in May; his diary does not record the loss of Heinz, but it does record in detail his trip back to Africa and the Regiment:

"4.5.42 An evening trip with 2 soldiers heading towards Afrika, in the early morning we pass München [Munich], Brenner [Pass], to Rome. From Wednesday to Thursday we spend in Rome and Thursday afternoon have the luck of flying to Brindisi on a four motor Condor [Fw-200]. In the evening I make my last purchases with the last of my Lire. On Friday morning I fly with a Savoia [Savoia SM-79] transport to Heraklion on Crete, it was a beautiful flight along the Albanian Coast and Peloponnese to Crete (4 Hours). I transfer to a Ju-52 for a 40 minute flight to Maleme the combat airport of the Fallschirmjägers. There is the Stuka camp located in the wooded barracks. Saturday evening 9.5.42 in the morning with nine transports [Ju-52s] in flight towards Derna. Over the sea comes the first motor damage and painfully we reach the airfield. At midday we go in 15 machines escorted by 2 destroyers [Me-110s] over the water to Derna. Afrika comes in sight, we land in Derna it is extremely hot and with a LKW to the Regiment. A reunion near Urn er Szem in a southerly direction in the desert and in the evening we come to the Tross of the regiment and I meet with Hptm Jäger."[37]

Towards the middle of May, the Regiment was on the move in preparation for the attack on Gazala. As the Regiment began to depart from its assembly area Kurt Liestmann described the night that his II./ *Abteilung* moved off:

"Sunday 16.5.42, during the night at 0300hrs we marched away to the northwest. One can sense the cool weather. The panzers move through the desert like ghosts, suddenly the desert is full of movement. The shadows are like ghosts everywhere, the division moves. In the morning dawn we reach the new area, it is located in the slight hollow, a bit better and a bit more overgrown than the previous one. There are the old positions of the Italians, we settle between them. The storm starts again in the middle of the day; there is a meeting with the commander. According to the latest intelligence report the enemy has against us two tank divisions [1st and 7th]), 1 Spahi regiment [de Gaulle group], 1 Polish battalion, 1 Czech battalion, 1 South African and 1 New Zealand infantry division, and two army tank regiments, Mark II and our old enemy, the Lancers (scouts) and Hussars. Our Luftwaffe is superior and would achieve superiority in the air in case of eventual attack in 2-3 days over Tommy, who now have about 300 fighters and 60 bombers. In the evening the storm continues. Since this morning I have a light diarrhea, fever and pain in the head and belly. I take brandy and grape sugar. Probably it's common acclimatization and common cold symptoms. One can hear the artillery thunder far away. It's getting colder."[38]

10

Gazala and Tobruk
May-August 1942

Based on existing knowledge, Rommel and his *Panzerarmee* had calculated that they must attack the British near the end of May before the British could launch their own summer offensive, which was anticipated sometime in the middle of June. It was hoped that an offensive launched along the *Gazala Line* as British forces were preparing themselves would not only disrupt the anticipated offensive, but also allow the seizure of the long awaited prize of Tobruk. There were other German strategic aims as well during this time, with the attacks in Russia and a new air campaign against Malta, but for Rommel it was his chance to finally defeat the British, capture Tobruk, and move towards the Nile Delta. In the far grander of schemes it was envisioned that eventually the *D.A.K.* would move towards Persia and link up with Germans forces coming south from the Caucasus region. The *Gazala Line* stretched roughly 100km from Gazala on the coast to Bir Hacheim in the desert. The British *Eighth Army* (Ritchie), with its *XIII Corps* (Gott) and *XXX Corps* (Norrie), held a front that was well defended and protected by huge interlaced minefields on a scale never seen before—over half a million were sowed there. Behind the minefields were heavily defended and well-equipped brigade sized elements grouped together into "Boxes." A "Box" was a strong point, and the backbone of the Gazala position. The most heavily defended of these positions were surrounded by thick minefields, and manned and equipped with infantry and artillery. The *Eighth Army* had the equivalent of six divisions and a number of separate brigades deployed on or behind the *Gazala Line*. On the right flank of the line, the *XIII Corps* had the responsibility of covering from the coast to Sidi Muftah. The *XXX Corps* also had formations forward, but most of its armored striking power lay behind the line, ready to strike out in either offensive or defensive operations. The "Boxes" were manned by brigades from three infantry divisions, with elements of the *1st South African* (Pienaar), *5th Indian*, and *50th British Divisions* (Ramsden), along with a separate French brigade providing the majority of forces manning these boxes. The boxes were arranged from north to south, with the *3rd South African Brigade* south of the Via Balbia, followed by the *2nd South African*, *1st South African*, and British *151st*, *69th*, and *150th* near Sidi Muftah. Further to the south, the *1st Free French Brigade* (Köning) was located at Bir Hacheim, with the *3rd Indian Motorized Brigade* (Filose) southeast of that box. The *Gazala Line* was bolstered by a number of armored brigades: in the northern half of the line there was the *32nd Army Tank Brigade* (Willison), followed by the *1st Army Tank Brigade* (Watkins/O'Carroll). In the south, the *XXX Corps*' *1st* (Lumsden) and *7th Armored Divisions* (Messervy) deployed the *22nd Armored Brigade* (Carr) in the middle of the line, while the *4th Armored Brigade* (Richards) was located in the south, to the rear of Bir Hacheim. The *2nd Armored Brigade* (Briggs) was also deployed, being located further east of the *Knightsbridge Box*. Further to the rear at Tobruk, which was being strongly defended by the newly arrived *2nd South African Division* (Klopper), there were the *4th* and *6th South African Brigades* and the *9th Indian Brigade* (Fletcher). There were also five separate brigade boxes located at Acroma, Knightsbridge, El Adem, Retma, and Bir el Gubi. The *Knightsbridge Box*, located along the Trigh Capuzzo, was being defended by the *201st Guards Brigade* (Marriot); El Adem was the center for the *XIII Corps*, and Bir el Gubi was defended by the *29th Indian Brigade* (Reid). Lastly, there was the *Retima Box*, which was only partially occupied by elements of the *7th Motor Brigade*. Those brigades were arrayed to the south and west of Tobruk to protect that city from attack. Thanks to their superiority in armored cars, which were able to screen the *Eighth Army* from probing *D.A.K.* reconnaissance elements, and good communications security, the British were able to conceal many of their positions, including the *150th Brigade Box* from the Germans, which had no idea how many boxes there were and where those British positions were located.[1] Rommel had already dictated that 26 May 1942 would be his start date for "*Case Venezia*" (Theseus). The intention was to attack and hold in the north and conduct a wide sweep to the south. To do this, the *Panzerarmee* was to be split into two separate formations: *Gruppe Crüwell*, made up of the German *Schützen Brigade 15* (*15th Panzer*), the Italian *X Corps* (*Sabratha* and *Trento* Divisions), and the *XXI Corps* with the *Brecia* and *Pavia* Divisions. They would attack the *1st South African* and British *50th Divisions* head on. The main striking force would be led by Rommel himself, and would consist of the Italian *XX Motorized Corps* (*Ariete* and *Trieste*) divisions, the *D.A.K.* (Nehring) with *15th* (Vaerst) and *21st* (Bismarck) *Panzer Divisions*, and the *90th Light Division* (Kleemann). It was hoped that by moving rapidly by night, this group would advance through the minefields, move south of Bir Hacheim, and then sweep northward towards Acroma. The *Ariete* Armored Division would be tasked with capturing the *Free French* Garrison of Bir Hacheim as the *90th Light* made for the supply bases between El Adem and Belhamed. The *Panzerarmee* had been considerably beefed up during the winter of 1942; between the winter and spring, a total of 20 Mk IIs, 211 Mk IIIs, 49 Mk IVs, and 4 Befehls panzers were sent as replacements. Additionally, the *21st Panzer Division* received an additional ten Mk IIs and thirty-four Mk IIIs.[2] The *D.A.K.* entered this battle with 363 panzers, 238 of which were Mk IIIs and 18 of which were the 50mm long barreled "Specials." There were also some 228 Italian tanks, many of which were ill equipped

Chapter 10: Gazala and Tobruk, May-August 1942

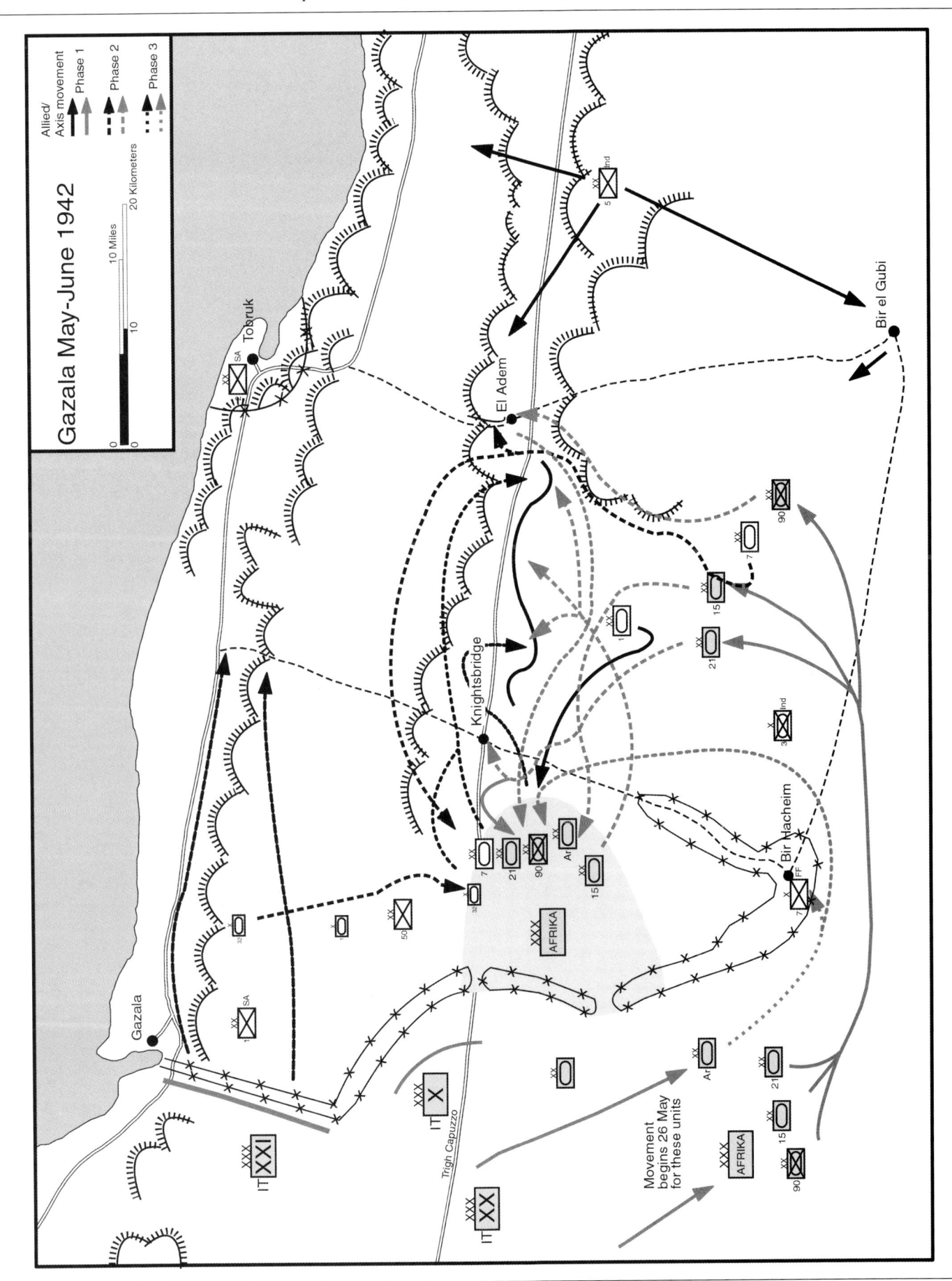

155

for tank versus tank engagements, but solid enough to be employed in supporting actions and missions against light armored forces. The *D.A.K.* also was fielding a number of captured Russian 76.2mm anti-tank guns, which had been mounted on older panzer and halftrack chassis. Nine of these guns were given to *Panzerjäger Abteilung 605*.[3] On the 25th, the Regiment was busy finishing up its last minute checks and services as it readied itself in preparation for the move on the 26th. The commencement order would be the key word "*Venezia*." The panzer strength report of the Regiment on 25 May listed the following: four Befehls panzers, twenty-nine Mk IIs, one hundred and thirty-one MK IIIs, three Mk III Specials, and twenty-two Mk IVs, for a total of 189 operational panzers.[4]

Panzer Regiment 8 Chain of Command as of May 1942[5]

Regiment Commander	Oberstlt Teege
Regt Adj	Hptm Schefold
Nachr Offz	Olt Baumann
Ord Offz	Lt Blidschuhn
Regt Arzt	OArtz Dr Krupar
Ing Ofz/*Werkshop* Company	Major Schnell
StKp	Lt von Brunn
I./Abteilung Commander	Hptm Kümmel
Abtl Adj	Olt Thurow
Nachr Offz	Ofumstr Strack
Ord Offz	Lt Paschy
Abt Arzt	OArtz Dr Hochstetter
Zahl Mstr	OZmstr Hadler
Ing Offz	OInsp Lampe
StKp	Olt Bock
leKol	Hptm Lindner
1st Company	Hptm Knorr
Zug Commander	Olt Jattkowski
Zug Commander	Lt Keil
2nd Company	Olt Heinrich
Zug Commander	Lt Hoffman
3rd Company	Olt Prion
Zug Commander	Lt Eberspächer
Zug Commander	Lt Probst
4th Company	Olt Stiefelmayer
Zug Commander	Olt Staengel
Zug Commander	Lt Chrestin
II./Abteilung Commander	Hptm Wahl
Abtl Adj	Olt Hess
Nachr Offz	OFumstr Bulla
Ord Offz	Olt Ritter
Abt Arzt	OArtz Dr Estor
Zahl Mstr	OZmstr Gisy
Ing Offz	Hptm Hauska
StKp	Hptm Klein
	Lt Bastigkeit
leKol	Olt Weimann
5th Company	Olt Lehn
Zug Commander	Lt Betzel
6th Company	Hptm Siemens
7th Company	Olt Liestmann, K
8th Company[8]	Olt Seidler
Zug Commander	Olt Danz

Throughout the 26th, the *D.A.K.* formed up in columns east of the *Rotonda Segnali* aided by numerous sand and dust storms that helped to conceal the assembly of units and hide them from British air and ground reconnaissance. Each march column, carrying enough sustenance to last it four days, was to be headed by panzers and pioneers who would be ready to open gaps through the minefields. At 1600hrs, the Regiment began its march towards its designated assembly area and departure point; by early that evening it had reached an area just south of the Trigh Capuzzo, near El Cherima, where it continued to ready itself until the attack order was given. Horst Sonnenkalb wrote of the events that took place just prior to moving out on the attack:

"Around midnight came the order to halt. The provisioning was distributed, the panzers were fuelled, equipment was checked, Split pins on track bolts were replaced where they have been loose. The track bolts which moved due to loose split pins, were hammered into the right position again. When these track bolts moved, they hit with a strong metallic sound into the hull of panzer. These checks belonged to the constant ritual during halts by the panzers. Then the cleaning of the air filters, This was required after each 50km drive in the desert. Because of the fine sand, which was raised by the columns and settled into the air filter. The engine covers where opened, the driver stood in the engine area and dismantled the filter. The sand was washed out by petrol from the fine filter made of brass wickerwork, fresh oil was filled in the air filter. Afterwards the air filter was installed back in place. This process had got into the blood and bones of each panzer crewman. For us it was normal to get rid of the old oil with sand and petrol from cleaned air filters right into the desert sand. At that time there was no ecology minister in the desert."[6]

The *15th Panzer Division* was organized into two march groups: the first was located just southwest of El Cherima, and was formed into two kilometer boxes that were lead by elements of *Aufklärungs Abteilung 33* and followed by the panzers of the I./*Abteilung* and the various artillery, pioneer, and *panzergrenadiers* of III./*Schützen Regiment 115*. The second group was formed in a similar manner, but was located further back and northwest of El Cherima. This group contained the Regiment's *Stabs* and II./*Abteilung*, along with the remainder of the division's artillery, *aufklärungs*, and *panzergrenadiers* from I./*Schützen Regiment 115*. At 2100hrs, Rommel placed himself at the head of the highly motivated, battle ready, and well equipped *D.A.K.*, which began to move out under a bright moonlight. These advancing German columns numbered over 10,000 vehicles of all types. They were about to move nearly 75km in the dark on compass and speed bearing that had been carefully calculated in order to hold down the dust and keep the formation in good order. Dust created the greatest problem, especially at night, and so each commander was instructed to move at a slow rate of speed in order to avoid crashing into other vehicles on the right and left. In order to assist the commanders and drivers in navigation, the pioneers had placed lights concealed in empty gasoline drums along the march route to act as reference points. At 2030hrs the Regiment received the codeword "*Venezia*" and immediately began to move out in its march formation; *Oberstlt* Teege had placed his light companies up front with the heavies to the rear. The I./*Abteilung* was again in the lead, and it spread out on a large front some two kilometers wide and a kilometer deep, and was followed closely by the II./*Abteilung* and various regimental groups. The entire division headed to the southeast in the moonlight navigated by compass and distance bearings. Horst Sonnenkalb, a panzer driver in the *7th Company*, wrote of his experiences driving that night:

"We returned back on the night from 26 to 27 May, and the following day. After the halt the troops started the movement again. For us the drivers that meant the fullest concentration, because there was no night vision devices. Due to the sand [and] dust from the tracks of the leading

Chapter 10: Gazala and Tobruk, May-August 1942

machine it was hard to see the one preceding us. At that time we referred to commands and advices of the panzer commanders. We had luck during the night drives. There were no collisions. After almost 3 hours driving we stopped again. Again fueling, cleaning of air filters, checking split pins and track bolts. The provisioning and hot coffee were distributed. During the fueling we got the order to empty the petrol canisters and to stack them on the supply vehicles. The weapons were cleaned, as well as panzer cannons and automatic weapons. The halt duration was may be 70, 80 or 90 minutes. During this night drive one had no feeling for time, location and orientation. We knew we were moving south. It was not possible to work with the gyro-compass. All was concentrated to stay in the column, not to loose the connection and not to drive in the preceding vehicle. Who can identify the location in the night, when your eyes are burning and there is no marked points in the desert, but only camel briars. Each stop has its end."[7]

At approximately 0230hrs, the Regiment was located some 15km south of Bir Hacheim, and as they rolled to their refueling points southeast of Bir Hacheim, everything was moving along and according to plan. As dawn broke on the morning of the 27th, the wide sweep around the southern flank at Bir Hacheim had been successful, and now the advance began turning to the north. Even though at this point things were going well, the situation was far from acceptable. The *4th South African Armored Car Regiment* shadowed the Axis movement with its scout vehicles and kept up a constant reporting of the situation and progress being made. The Italian *Ariete* Division, having overtaken the *3rd Indian Motor Brigade*, made its way toward Bir Hacheim but never attacked, and its sister division, the *Trieste*, despite making its way through the British minefields, never affected link up, as it got lost and bogged down in soft sand. Horst Sonnenkalb continued his story, and describes how the day began for him:

"So it was in these early morning hours of 27 May 1942. The day started in the east, first sun beams launched the new morning. Before that we had an absolute radio ban, and now we got the order for radio readiness. 'Panzers, March!' We rolled further, now one can recognize the preceding vehicle in the morning dusk. The new day wakes up, the sun rose over horizon. It may have been 0900hrs. Our PzRgt 8 swung to 90 degrees to the left, crossed the vehicle column which drove near us through the night like an endless worm. Soon our Regiment had formed itself in full drive into broad frontal attack formation from panzer to panzer around 40m side distance. The hatches were closed. For me as driver it was only possible to view upfront through the width of the hatch. If this was closed during combat, my view forward was only enhanced with the triangular optic. I struggled to recognize anything in the distance, while I was driving the panzer and switching the gears. The terrain was luckily the even sand desert. The order came by radio: 'Clear for combat!' The barking of tank cannons was audible already. In the distance I noticed the sparkles of the cannons from English defense front, sand fountains marked the impacts. In headset I hear the voice of commander: 'Driver, stop! Panzer granaten, 2 o'clock, 600 meters enemy tank, Fire!' The discharge was muffled by rubber shells of the headset. 'Driver, march!'" came the next order. We rolled further. As frequently trained, there came the halt orders and fire commands. Then march again! This tank combat was like nothing we experienced in North Africa before. The collisions of steel with one another, tank against tank. First shots of enemy tanks were reported by radio, and also our own losses. And we had quite a few losses during this first encounter. The enemy had shot down 32 of our own panzers, out of them 10 caught fire. Their crews died because of that. How awful is the war! But we had no time for consideration, thoughts and reflection. Drive, stop, shoot and drive again. Since my first deployment in North Africa in middle May 1941 I had so much experience that nothing could shake me, but despite this I was fully concentrated."[8]

On the far right, the *90th Light* and the *Aufklärungs Gruppe* comprising elements of *Aufklärungs Abteilungs 3, 33*, and *580* overran the *Retma Box*. In the middle, the *15th* and *21st Panzer Divisions* continued to push northeasterly towards the Via Balbia between El Adem and Tobruk. The Regiment was moving forward with I./*Abteilung* forming a front about two to three kilometers wide and about a kilometer in depth. The II./*Abteilung* was now following closely about a kilometer to the rear and echeloned a bit farther to the right. Later that morning, just after sunrise, the Regiment halted for about an hour to take on supplies, and a short time later at 0700hrs it crossed the Trigh el Abd just south of Bir el Harmat. In his book, Volkmar Kühn has this excerpt that describes the first hours of combat:

"Looking back, Hptm Kümmel could see the tremendous armada of his regiment's 180 panzers, which were led by Oberstlt Teege who was driving in the lead group. When the specified frontal width of his battalion threatened to increase Kümmel had the companies close up, as the existing width of 3 kilometers was already difficult to oversee. The depth of the battalion wedge was 1.5 kilometers. Close behind Kümmel's I./Abteilung and to the right was second battalion. Kümmel called the regiment and asked about enemy reconnaissance aircraft. Oberstlt Teege replied that none had been seen so far. Somewhere in the desert was the enemy; but where? Suddenly British tanks were sighted, emerging from a shallow depression 3 kilometers away. The crews were ordered to battle readiness. A short time later they recognized the turrets of the new American Grant tanks, camouflaged behind camel thorn bushes in the depression. They belonged to units of the British 4th Armored Brigade which had apparently been waiting for the DAK. It was equipped with 65 Grant tanks and had also set up several anti-tank barricades. Kümmel gave the order to attack and drove off at the head of his battalion. His panzers followed close behind ready to fire. Orders crackled through the commanders' headsets. 'Firing halt by platoons!' The first shots were exchanged. Then the panzers, which had fired raced on at full speed. All of a sudden from ahead came a dozen harsh flashes. Shells struck the ground to the left and right of the approaching panzers. The scene was shrouded in smoke fire and dust. The enemy tanks discarded their camouflage. The German commanders could see that the new enemy tanks had at least 75mm guns. Their guns could not penetrate the frontal armor of the Grant. 'Get closer!' shouted Kümmel's gunner. He had already hit one of the enemy tanks without effect."[9]

By this time of the morning the intense heat of the day was causing mirages, which had begun to affect the eyes of the commanders and gunners, but there was no mistaking the line of tanks that lay in front of the Regiment. At that point the panzers, most still armed with the short KwK 50mm gun, had to use the proven tactic of quickly closing the engagement distance between themselves and the British tanks, where their guns could defeat the British armor. As the two sides began to open fire on each other the first panzers began taking hits. At this point and distance it was clear that the 50mm fire was not effective in knocking out any of the British tanks, and some of the gunners later reported that it took between three and four rounds just to be able to knock out a tank!

"'We need artillery!' called Kümmel. The radio message was sent. Oberstlt Teege called the artillery to support PR 8's attack."[10]

157

For the attack, the Regiment was supported by the *II./Artillery Regiment 33*, which at the time was lagging far to the rear, and its guns were not able to help out in the attack. With the *I./Abteilung* hung up and unable to move forward, Teege began making attempts to get his *II./Abteilung* around to the right and attack the British flank:

"'Hang on Kümmel!' Teege called to his friend, who was drawing most of the enemy fire, 'I'm coming with second battalion!' Oberstlt Teege led II./Abteilung in an arc around the center. While Kümmel constantly changed positions to present a moving target while trying to get close enough for a lethal shot, II./Abteilung arrived on the enemy's flank. The arrival of Teege's panzers took the British completely by surprise. The Germans poured armor-piercing rounds into the vulnerable flanks of the Grants. Soon the first one was burning, then more. At that point Kümmel drove forward with the heavy company. He raced toward the enemy tanks and reached a favorable firing position. From such close ranges the crash of the guns and the impact of the shells were nearly simultaneous. Soon the battlefield was a scene of blazing tanks and explosions. The pall of dust became thicker and thicker."[11]

There were two Mk IV "Specials" armed with the long 75mm KwK 40 L/48 gun in the Regiment, but they could not effectively participate in the engagement, because they lacked the armor piercing (AP) and high explosive (HE) ammunition that could have knocked out the British tanks at greater distances. With the *I./Abteilung* keeping the attention of the British, the *II./Abteilung* was able to skirt around and hit them on their flank. Finally, the success that had eluded the *I./Abteilung* in its headlong charge was there for the *II./Abteilung*, as the first British tanks began to burn. Led by *Olt* Seidler, the *8th Company* was soon able to destroy twelve enemy tanks and, with the pressure against it relieved, the *I./Abteilung* was able to gain a bit of breathing room:

"All of a sudden the British began to pull back. The 8th Hussars, the core formation of the 4th Armored Brigade pulled out and the 3rd RTR lost 16 Grants in this phase of the German attack alone."[12]

After a brief reorganization, and with Kümmel again in the lead, the *I./Abteilung* quickly moved forward, closely followed by the *4th Company* under *Olt* Stiefelmayer and the *1st Company* under Lt Keil. They wasted little time in mixing it up, and before long the first successes were finally achieved. During the fighting that took place some thirty-five enemy tanks were destroyed, many of them at close range, and the *II./Abteilung* was able to claim a further twelve tanks knocked out:

"Just then the division commander's command panzer appeared on the scene. Generalmajor von Vaerst assumed the lead. 'Where to Herr General?' asked Lt Max Keil who was temporarily in command of 1./PR 8. But before von Vaerst could answer his adjutant shouted: 'There men! There's Rommel!' It was Rommel and moments later Kümmel heard the voice of the Generaloberst ordering him to close up and follow."[13]

By 0850hrs, the *4th Armored Brigade* (Richards) had lost over half its tank strength and was forced to break contact and evade eastwards towards Bir el Gubi. It was here that the Regiment discovered from the wounded British soldiers that they had been up against elements of the *8th Hussars Regiment* and *3rd RTR* from the *4th Armored Brigade*; however, the worst discovery was that this brigade had been equipped with the American made *Grant* tank which, despite its high silhouette, mounted a 37mm gun in a rotating turret and 75mm gun mounted in a right handed sponson. The *Grant* had armor protection of some 47mm and could obtain speeds of 25mph/42kph. With the appearance of the *Grant*, the German panzer crews now found themselves at a disadvantage, for now they faced an opponent that outclassed them in too many ways. At that time there were some 167 *Grants* deployed with the *Eighth Army* at Gazala and another 250 in Egypt.[14] Of interest is the fact that there were six American tank crews that had come over to gain battlefield experience, and they were dispersed throughout the brigade. These Americans would be the first to fight in North Africa.[15] Horst Sonnenkalb of the *7th Company* wrote about the new Grants and that first day:

"This tank combat of 27 May 1942 is forever in my memories; our regiment was on the right flank of the Gazala front in the area south of the desert fort of Bir Hacheim at the start of the summer offensive. First against us were tanks which we didn't know of previously and which possessed a high rate of fire. They were equipped with two guns; one gun was on the turret rotating 360 degrees, and another 7.62cm [75mm] tank cannon in a vertically attached bay on the right side. This one had a limited traverse area, but a very respectable fire power. This tank was made in America, a 'General Grant' type M with a British crew, it was 28 tons heavy, and whose existence we didn't know of until this day. They were the one's who caused the most heavy losses to our regiment. But we were able to break through this steel front. The combat field was covered with tanks of enemies and friends, out of order or on fire, giant smoke pillars from burning tanks of both sides. These days in the summer offensive of 1942 the German Afrika-Korps lost in the Gazala front about a third of the deployed panzers. Later with our panzer we evacuated the crew of a Mk III from our 7th Company as well, amongst them were three heavily wounded and our slightly wounded comrade, with only a scratch on the right hand, Günter John, who I met again decades later at a veterans meeting of PzRgt 8 in Böblingen."[16]

Kümmel then wasted little time before quickly reorganizing his *abteilung* and leading them north in hot pursuit of the remaining British tanks in an attempt to finish them off. The *abteilung* was able to follow those tanks, but shortly before 1100hrs the leading element began receiving artillery and long-range anti-tank gunfire. Two Mk IIIs from *2nd Company* were lost in this short engagement. On the eastern side of Bir el Harmat the *I./Abteilung* came upon and broke through a defensive position, and for the second time that day experienced another bad surprise, the new 6-Pounder anti-tank gun. Later that morning, around 0900hrs, the *22nd Armored Brigade* was ordered south from its positions near the Trigh Capuzzo to intercept those *D.A.K.* elements moving north. Unfortunately for that brigade, it was hit by elements of the *15th* and *21st Panzer* while attempting to move into position. The brigade suffered numerous losses in the encounter; however, it was able to disrupt the logistics tail of the *D.A.K.* At that point things looked pretty good for the *D.A.K.*, as it had overrun a number of British units and caused serious casualties. Around mid-day the situation began to deteriorate, as the midday heat took its toll on men and machine alike, and the glaring sun caused some strong mirages that hampered the panzer crews' ability to identify and recognize friend and foe alike. To make matters worse, and unbeknownst to the Regiment, it was just to the south of the *Knightsbridge Box*, a highly fortified box defended by the *201st Guards Brigade*, and in position were two more armored brigades; the *1st Army Tank* and *2nd Armored* were about to pounce on it. In the glaring heat the tanks looked like trucks with their large squat shape and silhouette, but before long these "trucks" were unleashing a flurry of 75mm rounds. They turned out to be more of the *Grants*, and they were now attacking the Regiment in earnest. In the engagement, one Mk III from the *3rd Company* took a round in the engine compartment and went up in flames, but not before the crew was able to escape. Within minutes the panzers of the *4th Company* were able to regain their senses and quickly shot three tanks and set them alight. By 1230hrs, the panzers were desperately short of fuel, and to make matters worse, British armor was advancing from the east and southeast. Fortunately for the Regiment, the British never realized what a predicament the Regiment was in and never forced the issue with their own attacks, which were ill-planned and executed, and all too prone to failure. By 1500hrs the fuel and ammunition had arrived and the panzers were topped off and rearmed, and thus able to react to any new developments. Throughout that afternoon Rommel had urged his panzer commanders on in the hopes of reaching Acroma by nightfall. The commanders obeyed him, and they suffered because of it. That afternoon there were multiple encounters between German and British tanks, with various size groups engaging one another all the way from Bir el Harmat to the *Knightsbridge Box*. At around 1700hrs, as the I./*Abteilung* neared the Trigh Capuzzo it was attacked by *Stuarts* and *Crusaders* coming out of the northeast; these tanks were from the *2nd Armored Brigade*, which was attempting to cut the panzers off from their line of supply. A short firefight broke out in which nine tanks were claimed without the I./*Abteilung* suffering any losses. With the coming of darkness the I./*Abteilung* found itself just north of the *Knightsbridge Box* and approximately 10km southwest from Acroma with the II./*Abteilung* attempting to close up. The Regiment was out of contact with the division, and was again in dire need of replenishment; it spent the night in a hedgehog position between Rigel Ridge and Bir Lefa without any enemy interference. Wilhelm Hagios remembered this day:

"That morning Beckers asked me 'Do you smell fuel?' and I smelled the exhaust, we had been losing [fuel], then we met with the British Pilots [M-3 Grants]. They appeared suddenly through the 1st, 2nd and 3rd Companies and fought with us bitterly. But we quickly managed them and remained close to them in the same proximity. After a short encounter with the enemy everything calmed down and then, we moved into positions south of the Trigh Capuzzo. In the afternoon we went by the Trigh Capuzzo then we went further up towards the east and then came upon more British tanks. We got out of there quite well and I shot four tanks on that day, two with driving antennas [command tanks], A Mark VI from 600m came along our flank and made a reconnaissance, and we stood on his flank approximately 500-600m and I heard [over the radio] 'Beckers shoot, Beckers shoot'. One unit of the British were in front of us and they broke away from our I./Abteilung and a Pilot from about 200 meters came directly at us firing with the cannon, we had to turn the panzer in order to engage it and we shot them down from the [same] distance. I shot the Pilot at the last moment. Many of them [British tanks] were there, and they made the day a boiling hell for us. In the evening we broke contact from the enemy and stayed there almost without moving until 28/29 May."[17]

The supporting *panzergrenadiers* from *Schützen Regiment 115* had been unable to follow up the rapid advance by the panzers, and by 1600hrs were being hit on their flanks by elements of the *7th Motor Brigade*. Rommel, his staff, and most of the supply vehicles lay not far away near Bir el Harmat, cut off from the panzer divisions by British armored units that had successfully severed the supply lines late on the 27th. As the *32nd Army Tank Brigade* sat out this first day, the *2nd* and *22nd Armored Brigades* and *1st Tank Brigade* were busy cutting supply lines in the north and east, and attacking isolated elements of the *21st* and *15th Panzer* and *Ariete* Divisions. The *4th Armored Brigade* continued to harass the *90th Light*, and the *7th Motor Brigade* continued to hit the long strung out supply columns in the south. The *D.A.K.* was fortunate that its artillery, flak, and antitank guns were able to keep the British at bay and protect the main concentrations near Bir el Harmat. During the night orders were issued to bring in the forces to consolidate and protect the rear area and supply line. In an attempt to shorten the supply lines, the Italian *Pavia* and *Trieste* Divisions were ordered to clear routes eastward through the minefields along the Trigh Capuzzo and Trigh el Abd. The 27th had been a very long, tiring, and difficult day for the Regiment: it had lost a total of 148 panzers through combat action or mechanical difficulties; from that overall total, 23 panzers were listed as complete write-offs. The Regiment's operational strength stood at two befehls panzers, thirteen Mk IIs, twenty-two Mk IIIs, one Mk III Sp, and three Mk IVs.[18] The personnel losses amounted to sixteen killed and twenty-five wounded. During the afternoon of the 27th, twenty-five of the damaged panzers were transported from the Bir el Harmat area southward, where they were placed into a hedgehog position to await the field recovery teams that would attempt to get some of them back into operation. Hermann Eckardt remembered those two days:

"Gazala was very bad. Here we met for the first time the U.S. 'Grant' tank; with the cannon on the side. The 'Sherman' we first saw later at Alamein. The English tanks; Mark II as well as the Mark IV and Mark VI were no problem for us, we were able to shoot them excellently. At first we thought we would get through quickly and would get to drink coffee there but at the Gazala fortress were the first 'Grants' and for over three hours the combat there was terrible. The entire mass of the Afrika Korps against the British, we drove south and then headed to the north. In two to three hours we lost eighty-six German panzers and our company had lost almost all of our commanders during the 27th and 28th of May. Later on we had to replace parts from the damaged panzers, the I-company helped us, the Germans were known to quickly repair their panzers, we even had dismantled engines in the desert!"[19]

Despite the beating it took that day, the Regiment had inflicted serious losses on the *3rd RTR* and *8th Hussars* Regiments, both of which belonged to the *4th Armored Brigade*. Unfortunately, later that day and night, as it was moving east, that brigade ran into elements of the *90th Light* and forced them to withdraw south from El Adem. The 28th saw the Regiment, along with a few other elements from *15th Panzer*, stranded in place near the Rigel Ridge and the *Knightsbridge Box* due to a lack of fuel. The *22nd Armored Brigade* kept the division under observation, but never attempted to attack it. Also on that day the division commander, von Vaerst, was wounded and temporarily replaced by *Oberst* Crasemann from *Artillery Regiment 33*. The *21st Panzer* was able to push another 10-15km north, where it took the *Commonwealth Keep*, and where it was able to engage targets on the Via Balbia coastal road. The *Ariete* was ordered up from the south and placed along the Bir el Harmat to form an anti-tank screen and protect the supply trains, while the *Pavia* and *Trieste* Divisions were successful in clearing "passable" lanes through the minefields. Later that evening the Regiment organized a search party with three Mk IIs and two Mk IIIs that were sent south in an attempt to locate the supply trains. The small group was fortunate, and was able to locate the trains that evening and make it back in the early morning hours of the 29th. Unfortunately, what those supply trains brought in was only a fraction of the fuel, water, and ammunition that was required by the panzers and their crews. The partial issue did allow the panzers to receive a half tank of fuel, which would allow the panzers to at least protect themselves, but was not enough for a continuation of offensive operations. Since beginning the offensive, the Regiment had lost ninety-six of its panzers: four Mk IIs, seventy-six Mk IIIs, and sixteen Mk IVs. Twenty-five of these panzers were listed as total write-offs. The panzer strength report of the Regiment on 28 May stood at just fifty-eight operational panzers.[20] During the 29th, as the Regiment attempted to hold its positions, it came under a heavy artillery bombardment and armor attack by elements of the *9th Lancer*

Regiment of the *22nd Armored Brigade*. As the British tanks approached from the east, *Oberstlt* Teege quickly ordered the Regiment to form a strong defensive front facing those tanks. In the early stages of the attack the British tanks were reluctant to charge strait ahead into the German guns, but after keeping back at a safe distance the tanks then came on at high speed. After a short firefight, in which the *9th Lancers* lost nine of their *Crusader IIs*, the remaining tanks turned tail, leaving a number of tanks in front of the German lines. The Regiment lost two panzers and a number of wounded in the attack that achieved little, other than draining some of the fuel tanks. Also that day, *Olt* Weiss with two panzer *zugs* was sent on a limited reconnaissance in force towards Acroma with the aim of moving against the box located there once enough supplies had reached the Regiment to allow it to continue its advance. This small force was able to break through the British defense, but was unable to breach the anti-tank gun screen and artillery positions. Hans Killermann, a panzer driver who participated in this operation, remembers this story:

"We were shot and we had our extra vehicle and extra loader a man named Paulus, his uncle was Paulus, the one who was in Russia and his father was an Oberst in Stuttgart. He had to make 3 deployment days and he came from the school as an Unteroffizer. He was sent to us and we had to take care of him so he gets his days as a soldier. In the evening we brought in the evening provisions and ammunition and he came with us as a loader. It was already dark when he arrived and we didn't look at exactly on what he had on. Normally you had you your 'Solbuch' [soldier's book] and dog tags etc. – it was for us self explanatory that one has this and takes it with him. He apparently didn't have his. On one of the deployment days, it was difficult deployment, the Italian Division and infantry were locked up by the Brits, there was a Hauptmann Weiss who was called in by Rommel to lead the command, Lt Mayerding got up and we drove to the deployment. We had von Paulus with us as a loader. When we drove towards the railroad station at El Duda where we would attack, we thought it's crazy to drive down and then up again, we thought we can't drive our vehicles because it was so steep. The grade crossing over the rails was too high and the panzer can only get over when it can have the gear wheel in the middle. When it is too high, the tracks couldn't catch. And we were sent down there, in two Zugs – 8 vehicles of which none of them got out. We were also hit and we told Paulus to open the hatch, and to get out. He was so scared that he didn't know his way around anymore. He thought the hatch lever was defective and turned. He was sitting kind of below us, near the commander. There is the Richtschütze (gunner) sits near me (driver) near the cannon, and near the loader is the radio-operator who also operated the MG-34, he was back and told Paulus to get out. The radio operator opened the hatch and told Paulus to get out. But the time was delayed and he looked out and didn't want to go out so we pushed and threw him out but he blocked the hatch for us too. When the panzer burns and the hatch is open, the flame naturally comes up as the oxygen gets it. [Usually] the commander gets out, Richtschütze (gunner), radio man and Ladeschütze (loader) then, and I am the last to get out as I am at the very bottom. There is also an emergency exit, but in this case it was almost impossible to get out. We had very bad burns from the foot to upper parts of the body. All of us were burned. Hermann [Eckardt] had his right leg very badly burned and fragmented, and was laying there. I told him 'get out with me'. We were under artillery fire and Leutnant Leule was up there with his radio and he saw us down there fighting and not able to get out. He called down and the artillery was shooting over the Brits and New Zealanders over there, so we were able to get out with the artillery fire. Paulus was not there and we asked where he is? He was just standing there and now we didn't see him anymore! He was never to be found and he didn't have his dog-tags and Soldiers book. He was listed as 'unknown soldier' missing in action. His wife was probably told that he had been shot. The father came searching for him afterwards and made awful reproaches, asking 'Why did you do this?' 'I had wounded comrades, I was wounded myself.'"[21]

During the evening *RAF* bombers attacked the assembly areas, and as a result, two panzers were damaged and fourteen soldiers wounded by bomb fragments. The transportation of wounded was causing some concern, as the transport route south of Bir Hacheim was too long and dangerous; therefore, it was decided to send them off to a dressing station near the Trigh Capuzzo, where they could be cared for. There was a bit of reorganization necessary, as the commanders of the *5th* and *8th Companies*, *Olt* Lehn and *Olt* Seidler, were mortally wounded, along with *Olt* Staengel of the *4th Company*. Lt Heckel assumed command of the *5th Company*, with *Olt* Danz taking command of the *8th Company*.[22] The 29th marked the end of Operation "*Venezia*," and on that day the *D.A.K.* found itself in a serious situation. There had been very little progress by the *Pavia* and *Trieste* Divisions as they continued to work their way through the minefields, and then, to everyone's surprise, discovered the *150th Brigade Box* which had, until this point, gone undiscovered by the Axis forces. To make matters worse Crüwell, in an attempt to help relieve the pressure on *D.A.K.*, had launched an attack in the north which met with little success, and later, as he was flying in his small *Storch* airplane to a coordination meeting with Rommel, he was shot down over the *150th Brigade Box* and captured. There were also fierce clashes that day near Knightsbridge, as the *2nd* and *22nd Armored Brigades* from *1st Armored Division* continued to hammer at the *D.A.K.*, where they were able to inflict a number of losses and force the *15th Panzer* and *Ariete* Divisions back between the Aslag and Sidra Ridges. In the north the *21st Panzer Division* was also forced back to the south from its attack near the *Commonwealth Keep Box* by the threat of being cut off by the attacks of the *1st Army Tank Brigade*. That afternoon the *90th Light*, returning from its mission in the east, was able to link up with the *Ariete* on Aslag Ridge. As the day began to end and the fuel and ammunition supplies dwindled, Rommel ordered the remainder of the *D.A.K.* to fall back and take up defensive positions on the western side of Bir el Harmat, near Sidi Muftah, between the Trigh Capuzzo and Trigh el Abd, a position that would soon be dubbed "The Cauldron."[23] Fortunately, during the night of 29/30 May the supply trains were able to locate the panzers after an incredible nineteen hour drive south around Bir Hacheim. The supplies that were brought in were in sufficient quantity to allow the Regiment unrestricted movement. But instead of attacking, the Regiment found itself moving to the southwest and joining the rest of the *D.A.K.* in the perimeter. On the 30th, Rommel decided to build his force for further operations. His plans included the opening of supply routes through the minefields, but first he needed to destroy the *150th Box*, whose presence and artillery kept the routes through the minefields covered. Once the box was destroyed and the supply lanes were opened, Rommel proposed to strike south and destroy the Bir Hacheim Box, thereby clearing the entire southern flank. Once that was accomplished he would again attack, this time focusing on the *XIII Corps* and Tobruk. But before any of that could be attempted the first issue would be to dig in as quickly as possible and fortify the perimeter before the inevitable British attack came at him. The *D.A.K.* was arrayed as follows: *Ariete* still held the Aslag Ridge; the *90th Light* had moved to the west to face and hold the *150th Brigade Box*; the *21st Panzer* held the western half of Sidra Ridge; and *15th Panzer* was ordered to take up positions in the southwestern portion of the perimeter. The British attack came on that day, with the *2nd* and *22nd Armored Brigades* impaling themselves with heavy losses on the *D.A.K.* Pak gun screens. That morning there was an attack by some sixty tanks that came in from the northeast. *Oberstlt* Teege was able to form a hasty defensive line using

Chapter 10: Gazala and Tobruk, May-August 1942

various elements from the *1ˢᵗ*, *2ⁿᵈ*, *4ᵗʰ*, *6ᵗʰ*, and *7ᵗʰ Companies*, while the remaining companies (*3ʳᵈ*, *5ᵗʰ*, and *8ᵗʰ Companies*) moved out to attack the British from the south. The defensive fire caught the British tanks off guard as they rolled in at a high rate of speed. Twelve tanks were soon hit and put out of action, but these losses did little to discourage the attackers, and they continued their headlong attacks on the *15ᵗʰ Panzers'* positions. As the British tankers continued this futile charge they lost a further twelve tanks before a small flanking attack forced them to halt and then withdraw from the area. Kümmel, in his courageous style, charged forward with the *2ⁿᵈ* and *4ᵗʰ Companies* and attacked the British head on, which caused them to withdraw to the east. The remaining tanks retreated so fast that the *abteilung* could not keep pace with them, and finally had to break off its pursuit. Twenty-eight *Crusader* and *Stuart* tanks, all bearing the white Rhino of *1ˢᵗ Armored Division*, remained in front of the defensive positions without having achieved a thing, other than causing the loss of three panzers and forcing the rest to burn up precious fuel and ammunition. It was now important that all unnecessary movements and firing be avoided due to the limited supply of ammunition and fuel. On that day, the Regiment lost three more soldiers killed and eleven wounded, which brought the total number of casualties between 27-30 May to twenty-two killed and fifty-five wounded.[24] Once again the British commanders had fumbled their handling of the battle, and now they desperately tried to reorganize their forces for an infantry attack that they felt would dislodge the anti-tank gun screen and open the way for the armor. However, it would take them until 1 June to get the necessary forces assembled, and in the meantime the *D.A.K.* was left alone. For two days (30ᵗʰ and 31ˢᵗ) the regiments of the *150ᵗʰ Brigade* had been holding firm in their strong positions against the determined attacks by the Italians and Germans, whose constant artillery fire and air attacks pummeled the box. With the help of the *1ˢᵗ Army Tank Brigade* the brigade's defenses were holding, but no matter how strong the brigade held out it could not hold out forever. Unfortunately for those men, the British commanders misread the situation by thinking that the *D.A.K.* was ready to succumb from a lack of supplies, and thereby failed to exert enough pressure on the *D.A.K.* In fact, no attempt to relieve or reinforce the *150ᵗʰ Box* was undertaken until it was already too late. By the evening of the 31ˢᵗ the last infantry reserves had finally been used up, the artillery was down to its last 100 rounds, and there were only about ten serviceable *Matilda* tanks remaining from the *44ᵗʰ RTR*. For the Regiment fortune again smiled on it, for during the night of the 30/31ˢᵗ two Mk IIs from the Regimental *Stabs* that had been detailed to search out lost and separated supply vehicles returned with three lost fuel trucks belonging to *Flak Regiment 135*. These fuel trucks were able to top off many of the panzers, and allowed the Regiment the ability to maneuver, which it soon would against the *150ᵗʰ Brigade Box*. The final attack commenced on 1 June, with Rommel personally directing the infantry and panzer regiments of the *21ˢᵗ Panzer Division* in the attack. Shortly after the attack began it was held up on a minefield, and as the minefield was being cleared, *Luftwaffe Stukas* were called in to support and bring some momentum to the attack. So desperate was the state of the *Panzerarmee* in the Cauldron that the infantry from *II./Schützen Regiment 104* at one time were personally being lead by Rommel himself.[25] That morning the Regiment reported forty-four operational panzers of all types. In an attempt to add weight to the attack by *21ˢᵗ Panzer*, the Regiment's I./Abteilung was sent to assist with its nineteen panzers. To further strengthen and protect the I./Abteilung attack, the *panzerjägers* from the *2ⁿᵈ Company*, *Panzerjäger Abteilung 33*, and the guns of the *II./Abteilung Artillery Regiment 33* were tasked to directly support the panzers. At the time there were still very few secure lanes that had been cleared through the British minefields. Never one to shy from the attack or a challenge, Hans Kümmel took the initiative, and with *III./Schützen Regiment 104* on

board his panzers moved through the lanes, all the while taking fire from the *Matildas* of the *1ˢᵗ Army Tank Brigade*. Despite the stubborn defense and a few panzer losses, the *abteilung* rolled forward closely supported by the fire from the artillery. By midday the I./Abteilung found itself on the western side of the box, and later that afternoon the commander of the *150ᵗʰ Brigade*, Brigadier Haydon, surrendered his three thousand men and hundred guns. Over the previous two days the I./Abteilung was able to claim the destruction of thirty *Matildas*, eleven anti-tank guns, two anti-aircraft guns, sixteen artillery pieces, and forty squad machine guns.[26] With the destruction of the *150ᵗʰ Brigade Box* the supply routes through the minefield were open, allowing a flow of supplies to the *D.A.K.* and saving it from destruction. In addition to the supplies, the wounded could now be evacuated back to the field hospitals. Now that the British armor had been successfully held off, the *150ᵗʰ Box* eliminated, and a secure supply route cleared through the minefields, it was time to settle the problem of Bir Hacheim. Wilhelm Hagios:

"We were set to march to the west, 10-12km, and reached the base near Got el Ualeb and Box 150, there was an attack there in June, our attack from the east. What bothers me is that in no report is it stated that Pz8 was involved there, we were actually attacking there from the east. We had there a scout driver (Aufklärungfahrer), it was an artillery position, we had destroyed the guns and ammunition. We got three tanks from the front and the [150 Box] base fell on that day. We saw their table and the cards, they were playing cards. This base was in our way and now we had a free way."[27]

For the next couple of days (2/3ʳᵈ) the Regiment, along with the *D.A.K.*, remained in its assembly areas north of the Trigh el Abd awaiting the expected British counterattack, but sandstorms blew up on the 3ʳᵈ and 4ᵗʰ which made any movement extremely difficult. Recovery operations were the priority at this time, with the companies being a mixed match of crews from disabled and abandoned panzers and those soldiers previously wounded who had recovered enough to return to duty and continue fighting. Due to the reopening of the new supply lane through the minefields the Regiment was able to bring forward six new Mk III Specials and three Mk IV Specials, bringing the total of operational panzers to some sixty-nine. On the 4ᵗʰ, Rommel ordered a recovery operation to be launched in the hope of salvaging some of those abandoned panzers and guns lying out in the desert south of Bir el Harmat. The *15ᵗʰ Panzer Division* was ordered to open up gaps in the minefields southwest of Bir el Harmat on the night 4/5 June.

On the 5ᵗʰ, the *Eighth Army* finally launched its anticipated offensive on the "Cauldron," which was given the codename "Aberdeen." The two phased plan of attack called for *General* Briggs and the *HQ*, *5ᵗʰ Indian Division*, to launch a night attack with the *10ᵗʰ Indian Brigade* to clear the *Ariete* anti-tank gun screen from Aslagh Ridge. *General* Messervy with his *HQ*, *7ᵗʰ Armored Division* would follow at daylight with the *22ⁿᵈ Armored Brigade Group* and *9ᵗʰ Indian Brigade* into the center of the *"Cauldron."* As these attacks were moving forward the *32ⁿᵈ Tank Brigade* was ordered to strike against the western end of Sidra Ridge in order to tie down the *21ˢᵗ Panzer* and prevent it from interfering.[28] At 0250hrs the British artillery opened up in advance of the infantry that would soon follow; however, the barrage that went in on the Italian *Ariete* Division holding Aslag Ridge hit too far forward of their position in empty desert and caused no damage, other than to alert the Italians of the attack about to come their way. At dawn a determined attack by the *Indian 10ᵗʰ Brigade* went in and forced the *Ariete* to give way; the ridge was soon cleared, and a path created for the *9ᵗʰ Indian* (Fletcher) and *22ⁿᵈ Armored Brigades*. As the *22ⁿᵈ Armored* drove forward it was met by well coordinated and a high volume of anti-tank and artillery gun fire, which soon caused severe casualties and drove the remaining tanks back to cover behind the Bir et Tamar. At that time the German and Italian panzers rolled forward and hit the unprotected infantry in its flank, again causing considerable casualties. In the ensuing battle the British tanks failed to protect the infantry, and the eastern attack was beaten back without serious loss to the *D.A.K.* The situation in the north was no better for the British, where the *32nd Tank Brigade* attacked at daylight. The tanks rolled forward without any infantry support and just the supporting fire of two batteries of artillery. The tanks immediately became hung up on the minefields and were easy targets for the Pak and panzer gunners, which destroyed approximately fifty of the seventy tanks involved.[29] The German forces on Sidra Ridge were such that had the British attempted a coordinated night assault by infantry and tanks, supported by enough artillery they most certainly would have taken the ridge. By midday, Rommel was convinced that the British attack had failed, and so he then decided to launch the *D.A.K.* on a counterattack. The *21st Panzer* rolled out from Sidra Ridge southeastwards towards the Bir el Tamar, while the *15th Panzer* rolled out of the gaps cleared during the panzer recovery effort south of Bir el Harmat in order to strike those forces holding Aslag Ridge in their flank and rear. Gerhard Kienzle, who was a loader in one of the Mk IVs, recalls that day when his panzer was hit:

"5.6.1942, British artillery shelling blew the armor plate away, so that the sun shines inside. The MG of the radio operator flew towards his body from its mounting but no one was wounded. During the night the [armor] plate was again welded by the fitters of the maintenance squadron, and the new MG was installed. We loaded sandbags underneath the turret for reinforcement. We found the company again in the morning."[30]

By that evening the *D.A.K.* had thrown a bag around the *10th Indian Brigade*, *22nd Armored Support Group* and four regiments of artillery. The only hope to save these troops lay with the British armored formations, which unfortunately never made an appearance on the battlefield, having been off in the east attempting to regroup themselves and moving back and forth on orders which were quickly countermanded by new ones. Wilhelm Hagios remembers the day with this account:

"On the 5th we had contact with tanks, in the evening we drove through positions where I saw for the first time the American 5.7cm, [actually the British 6-Pounder] before we had seen only the British 4cm. The 5.7cm was a sharp weapon! In the morning we went to another position, near the top [of the escarpment] was a mine field, where we saw the Me-109 landing in an emergency and right on top of the mine field and exploded. We shot the whole morning against English, Bofors were there 4cm Flak-Pak, trucks, and everything was there. I said the Lords prayer as lives were blown away, there was a position which was covered by artillery, there was the cannon 21cm with a crew which flew through the air. We went in the position and saw the traces and went through the barbed wire, I saw that one of the remaining crew was aiming the cannon against us and I had the last bullet in my MG and I was able to stop him with that. If he had hit us from that distance we would not be able to drive back. We went in this position and this unit was from the 10th Army from Basra. I got the notebook from one of them, who wrote 'Alexandra, we had beer' and their passports were from Basra, from Irak. Then the operation was over. In the afternoon came ammunition, we loaded ammunition, and we went to the base. In the afternoon there was the attack on our other Abteilung from the right, Kampfgruppe Baade. There was fighting against a larger base, not a fixed one, the mobile one. The commander Teege said 'Beckers, attack the artillery in the ground, they are shooting Kampfgruppe Baade' We drove through the area and exchanged shots with them and we were hit by a missile and it didn't take a long time. They hit us in the front and that was it for us. If that missile would have come any deeper, then I wouldn't be sitting here. The missile went right where the cannon was over the mantlet overflow and broke the cannon. When there was an inspection by the weapons foreman who spoke about the shot we had there I saw that the cannon had a gouge which drilled it out."[31]

On the 6th, the *15th Panzer Division* was ordered to counterattack those enemy forces that were located north of Bir el Harmat. The I./*Abteilung* was on the eastern flank of the division as it moved forward and through the minefields and into the flank of those elements from the *9th* and *10th Indian Brigades*. By afternoon the defense was broken, and in addition to the capture of the *10th Indian Brigade* commander, another 4,000 troops and hundred guns went into the prisoner of war cages.[32] During the attack there were a few tank scuffles which broke out among stray tanks and the Regiment as it was moving forward. The *Matilda* and *Valentine* Infantry tanks, with their thick hides, stood little chance now that the Regiment was equipped with the new Mk III and IV Specials, which had finally been supplied with the proper ammunition, and the few Mk IVs were able to knock out those British tanks at a longer distance. During these attacks the British tanks were quick to break contact with the I./*Abteilung*, which was by this time down to its last five operational panzers, driving them off with effective long range fire. The I./*Abteilung*, under the strong leadership of Hans Kümmel, continued to pursue these scattered remnants, but in the growing darkness they were forced to break off their pursuit, as the British continued moving farther east towards their supply bases. Gerhard Kienzle remembered the day well, and continues his account for 6 June with this:

"The fire and shelling started early in the morning. During the first re-ammunition [resupply] we found out that a British anti-tank gun shot away the external canisters and the cover. We haven't yet been 10 minutes at the front, and here comes a bang and powder fumes. The sound of metal fragments flying around and a hit in my right hand, which was on the handle of the firing mechanism. A shell from the quick moving English 'Gypsy Artillery' hit right on the plate above the driver and pushed it in. As Richtschütze my position was slightly elevated above and behind the driver. My wounds were caused by fragments from the smashed equipment from the driver compartment. The firing mechanism was located in front of my stomach and part of the chest. It was a cast-iron block with wheels for easy movement of the turret and the cannon. This was my protection from larger internal wounds. Four men took to the crew exit over the commander's hatch as we saw the light there. It was the most dangerous, because we had to jump down over the tracks to the ground, completely visible to the enemy. Whatever, just to get out of the shot panzer. I didn't feel the pain at all, despite the broken ankle. Our Feldwebel put the bandage on me in the nearest hole. The chase went on in the shelled terrain from one low area to the next hole in the ground 100 meters away, supported by two comrades. When we got together we noticed the absence of the driver, he was killed immediately. The commander found a VW jeep from the Flak, which brought me to the regimental doctor. The company chef, Stiefelmayer, came by during a break in the combat. The long drive from the collection point of wounded to the main dressing area is to report about. I lie as well as the others on the carrying-frame in the truck. About ten captured Tommy's (not wounded) were transported back on the same truck. They took care of us and gave us water from here and there. So we drove through the desert, and also through the mine fields, where we were under fire from the Tommy's. When the truck was bouncing too much as it drove over the camel thorn, we were held by a couple of black soldiers.

Chapter 10: Gazala and Tobruk, May-August 1942

We were flown, presumably, from the airfield at El Adem by Ju-52 to the hospital in Derna. I don't know how long I was there. In the twilight of consciousness I recall the Italian doctor on the hospital ship, who poked around in the wound. He flirted at the same time with the female doctor or the nurse. In Naples the wounds were more seriously taken care of and the foot was put in plaster casting."[33]

First light on the 7th brought the arrival of the supply trains in addition to the spectacle of the previous days' combat, in which some seventy *Matilda*, *Valentine*, and *Crusader* tank hulks lay smoking or abandoned. Of these, the I./*Abteilung* alone could claim forty-one of the hundred tanks lost in addition to the hundreds of cannons and guns left on the battlefield. The 8th and 9th brought a bit of rest and relaxation to the Regiment, which had performed well over the last few days, but was in dire need of reorganization. While the Regiment was able to catch a bit of a rest, in the meantime the remaining elements of the *15th Panzer* were ordered to send strong detachments south to support the attack on Bir Hacheim. Rommel was still regrouping his forces in the "*Caldron*," and would not attempt any further movement east until the box at Bir Hacheim was taken and the southern flank secured. Wilhelm Hagios remembers:

"We drove for three days until the evening of the 9th with the combat detachment, then we were sent to the workshop and on the way we drove into a minefield and over the mine with the right side mechanism [track], we had to shorten it and couldn't assemble the bogie and couldn't fix it. The next day on the 10th we were out of water and around the Trigh Capuzzo there were many [German] trucks around and they came under fire from [British] scout vehicles, and from others. They (the trucks) now had two panzers with them, and were happy to see our panzer with them. But one of the panzers had a round lodged in the firing mechanism and the other, our panzer, had a broken cannon."[34]

On the 9th, some elements of the *15th Panzer Division* were sent to bolster the attack on Bir Hacheim and quickly captured Hill 186, which overlooked the desert fortress, and which gave the Germans a vital piece of ground that allowed them to look down on the defenders. The seizure of this high ground would eventually lead to the French evacuation of the box the following night. For over a week the French had put up a stubborn defense that caused the *D.A.K.* considerable troubles along its supply lines. Only after the battle did German commanders comment on the fighting spirit of the garrison and give them credit. By the 10th it was clear that Bir Hacheim would fall within the next few hours, but before that took place, the remnants of the *French Brigade* escaped to the east in an attempt to link up with other *Eighth Army* formations. Even before the capture of Bir Hacheim was accomplished, Rommel began ordering the *D.A.K.* to begin marshaling itself for the upcoming attack and push east, which would commence the following day. The *Eighth Army* was still a powerful force, and it still possessed about three hundred tanks and was still holding a number of key positions, such as the *Knightsbridge* and *El Adem Boxes*. The northern portion of the *Gazala Line*, with the *1st South African* and *50th Northumbrian Divisions*, were still strong formations, and were well protected by the Gazala defenses. As for the *Panzerarmee*, it had less than 150 panzers, and most of the divisions had been pretty well shot up. As for the Regiment, it reported sixty-seven serviceable panzers ready for action, and so it was ordered to reposition itself from its present assembly area near Bir el Harmat to another assembly area just south of the Trigh Capuzzo.[35] On the afternoon of 11 June, Rommel again launched his divisions forward; his plan called for *21st Panzer* to demonstrate against British forces on the northern sector of the "*Cauldron*" while *15th Panzer* was to make the main effort moving northeast towards El Adem,

with *Trieste* on the left and *90th Light* and the *Aufklärungs Gruppe* on the right. The Regiment led the push north, and during its advance encountered nothing more than a sandstorm to slow it down. By that evening the division reported its position as southeast of the *Knightsbridge Box* at Naduret el Ghesceuasc. The *90th Light* had made it to a point just south of El Adem, and *21st Panzer* was positioned to the west of the *Knightsbridge Box*. Opposing the *15th Panzer* to the southeast of its drive were the *2nd* and *4th Armored Brigades*, which had taken up a defensive line there. During the night German radio intercept units picked up British radio conversations which indicated that the *4th Armored Brigade* had refused to carry out any further attacks. Knowing that the British commanders wanted an attack carried out by *4th Armored* in the southeast, Rommel then ordered the *15th Panzer Division* to form a defensive front for the 12th and hold its positions as he sent the *21st Panzer Division* over from the west and hit the two British armored brigades in the rear. As the morning of the 12th dawned, the expected battle was slow to develop, as both adversaries faced one another, with the *15th Panzer* expecting an attack and the *2nd* and *4th Armored Brigades* still awaiting orders. Finally Nehring, the *D.A.K.* commander, ordered the *15th Panzer Division* to attack, and the Regiment began its attack, leading off with the three Mk IV Specials from the *4th Company*, which quickly began to lay down a flurry of well-aimed shots. Within no time six British *Honey/Stuart* tanks were knocked out, and the remainder of the squadron withdrew back to the north, beating a hasty retreat. By this time German panzer and Pak gunners began to exact a toll on the British armor using the sandy haze being kicked up by the wind to their advantage. Although the weather conditions were favorable they soon began to worsen, along with the enemy situation, when around mid-day the sun appeared to break through the dust clouds and a regiment of British *Valentine* tanks were seen bearing down on the division. It was at this point that Rommel decided to loose *21st Panzer* to take the open British flank. As roughly seventy *Valentine* tanks came on towards the Regiment, the regimental commander, Willi Teege, quickly ordered the formation of a hasty defensive line with the attached *panzerjägers* of *Panzerjäger Abteilung 33* taking up positions to the right of the Regiment. Within no time the gunners began scoring hits, and by the day's end they would account for some forty tanks. The *2nd* and *4th Armored Brigades* were now in serious trouble, and as the *22nd Armored Brigade* was coming to their assistance it was hit by the *21st Panzer* and *Trieste*. With no chance of receiving help from their sister brigade, the *2nd* and *4th Brigades* were forced to break off their attacks and withdraw north towards the Raml escarpment. By that evening the British had lost over 120 tanks which littered the battlefield. The Regiment received some artillery fire that night, but not enough to disrupt the arrival of the supply trains and the replenishment of food, water, fuel, and ammunition. The wounded, of which there were sixteen, were bandaged up as best they could and then taken by the supply vehicles back to the main dressing stations and field hospitals. During the day the regiment had lost six panzers: three Mk IIIs and two Mk III "Specials."[36] The morning of the 13th began with a sand storm, as both the *15th* and *21st Panzer Divisions* advanced north against Rigel Ridge. The ridge was now defended by the *Scots Guards* and supported by anti-tank guns and artillery from the *1st South African Division*. The I./*Abteilung* advanced forward, and no sooner had it begun its movement than it ran into a minefield. Once again *Hptm* Kümmel placed himself in the lead, and without paying much attention to the mines rolled forward with the remainder of the panzers, which followed in his tracks. *Panzerjäger Abteilung 33* covered the movement through the minefield, and the II./*Abteilung* followed in a two echelon formation. At 1100hrs, the I./*Abteilung* started to receive incoming artillery fire which was firing in support of the infantry and anti-tank guns still stubbornly clinging to their defense of Rigel Ridge. As the panzers continued to roll

163

forward, they soon began receiving accurate fire from the main defensive line, and a number of hits were scored on the panzers. In the ensuing attack the *4th Company* took up positions and began to lay down a heavy base of fire as the *1st*, *2nd*, and *3rd Companies* formed a wide wedge and attacked. By using the technique of laying down a good base of fire, and by spreading the formation out as much as possible, the *abteilung* was able to reduce the amount of fire concentrating in any one location. Additionally, a larger attack formation usually required the British anti-tank gunners to take a longer amount of time in acquiring their targets, and at times, the relaying of the gun itself. These precious few seconds could mean the difference between life or death to the panzer crews. In the attack on the ridge, two Mk IIIs from the *3rd Company* were knocked out, and as the panzers rolled forward to the ridge the British launched another armored attack in an attempt to relieve pressure on the ridge defenses. The Regiment now turned its attention on the British armor, and before long discovered that there were some more *Grant* tanks in the fight. As the battle ensued between the Regiment and the British armor, the I./*Abteilung* quickly got the best of the encounter, as its panzers were able to knock out twelve *Grants* and sixteen *Crusaders* by using quick fire and maneuver tactics. The II./*Abteilung* followed suit over on the right flank as it shot up fourteen *Crusaders* and *Stuarts*. Later in the afternoon another sandstorm blew up that affected the further conduct of the battle. As the II./*Abteilung* remained in place securing the area, Kümmel, with his I./*Abteilung*, charged off in pursuit, despite the limited visibility and growing darkness. The I./*Abteilung* continued to fight, showing no mercy as it rolled into the remaining British armor and destroyed another eight tanks from extremely short range. Despite the coming of darkness and the complete exhaustion of the panzer crews, Kümmel still continued his attack, causing further loss to the disheartened British tankers, some of whom threw open their hatches and surrendered. Because of the daylong battle that stretched into the night, it was not known how many casualties the Regiment suffered that day. Those figures would have to wait until the following day. That night of 13/14 June, with the British armored attacks having failed and the defense along Rigel Ridge broken, the commander of the *Knightsbridge Box* and *201st Guards Brigade* suddenly found his force isolated and cut off, and so he ordered the remaining force to break out to the east. As the morning of the 14th dawned and the supply trains worked their way forward to the I./*Abteilung* positions, the first rays of sun soon revealed to the tired panzer crews that they were between a large number of *Crusader* and *Stuart* tanks. Thankfully these tanks had all been either knocked out or abandoned by their crews during the previous evening. A *Crusader* and six *Stuarts* were found to still be operational, and so they were taken back and put to use by the supply trains. All of these tanks had the markings of the *5th RTR* and *7th Hussars Regiment*.[37] That morning, as the Regiment counted the cost of the previous day's fighting, it discovered that losses amounted to two men killed and nine men wounded, along with twelve panzers lost. The Regiment, along with the rest of the *D.A.K.*, was then ordered north to the Via Balbia, where Rommel intended to cut off the remainder of those British forces covering the *Gazala Line*. The Regiment began its movement in a blowing sandstorm, which caused problems, as the Regiment had to slowly make its way through a number of minefields. As the *D.A.K.* neared the Via Balbia, a battle quickly broke out near Eluet et Tamar with those *XIII Corps* forces attempting to make their way east and those forces attempting to hold up the advance by the *D.A.K.*. There were also a large number of tanks present, the remnants of those that had escaped the earlier battles. As the Regiment finally arrived along the coastal road in the late afternoon, it was greeted by a hail of tank and anti-tank gunfire. After returning fire, the I./*Abteilung* was able to claim the destruction of three tanks and one anti-tank gun. Horst Sonnenkalb wrote about what had taken place over the preceding two days:

"With that combat continued. The British were well camouflaged at Knightsbridge. The Italian tank division 'Ariete' was not able to hold the overwhelming push anymore. So our regiment had to drive to Bir el Tamar for the relief attack. Afterwards we got the new order to march to the road crossing Sidi Mahmud, where we shot down about 50 enemy tanks. The desert fortress Gebr Casem appeared, and we captured it towards the evening. In the course of time our enemies showed a lot of weakness. They were able to match it only with their superiority in people and materials. In the desert near Acroma as well there were conducted sullen tank fights, which had a special meaning for me. Seven impacts by anti-tank guns on the wide side of my panzer signed its destiny. My four other comrades were killed, I myself was lightly wounded. So is the war. But I had no time to think about it."[38]

By early evening the Regiment was positioned just south of the Via Balbia near Bu Amaia, on the Solaro Escarpment. Over the previous couple of days the I./*Abteilung* had sustained numerous losses, and by this point had only three operational panzers remaining. By this point in time the Regiment, along with the rest of the *D.A.K.*, was a tired and spent force in dire need of rest and refitting. Despite the limited effectiveness of the Regiment at this point in time, it was soon ordered by the division to continue moving forward in order to halt the further escape by those elements of the *XIII Corps*. By the morning of the 15th, the remaining elements of the *XIII Corps*, primarily the *1st South African Division*, were quickly escaping to the east, prompting Rommel to order all remaining *D.A.K.* assets forward down the Solaro Escarpment in an attempt to cut them off. The Regiment continued its advance to the Via Balbia, where it was constantly coming under attack by scattered groups of British tanks attempting to move east, and the panzers were often forced to shoot their way out. These chance contacts resulted in the further destruction of some sixteen *Crusader* and *Stuart* tanks. Kümmel was relentless in his pursuit of the enemy, and demanded that his panzers keep pace with him, despite the high rate of speed, which was causing numerous mechanical breakdowns. Already the *abteilung* had left twelve panzers scattered over the last 20km of desert, all with some sort of mechanical damage. At around 1500hrs Kümmel radioed to Teege the following message:

"The I./Abteilung has reached the sea with six panzers!"[39]

Rommel now hoped to keep the *Eighth Army* off balance by attacking it before it had time to regroup its scattered forces and reorganize them. For Rommel, his plans now focused on a continued drive towards Gambut that would allow him to isolate the Tobruk garrison and then finally capture it. Along the way the *D.A.K.* would also knock out the remaining boxes around Tobruk, like the ones located at Acroma, El Adem, El Duda, and Sidi Rezegh. Already the *90th Light* had moved towards El Adem with orders to attack it right away; the *21st Panzer Division* had already moved on Acroma, and was now making its way to El Adem with orders for it to proceed towards Sidi Rezegh and Belhamed. The *Aufklärungs Gruppe*, along with *Ariete* was to protect the southern flank against possible attack. On the 16th, the Regiment was finally able to link up near El Duda, which at the time was still occupied by the British. The I./*Abteilung* was the last to get to the assembly area after its long trip from interdicting along the Via Balbia. Once the Regiment had regrouped the supply trains arrived and were able to replenish the Regiment and get it back up to fighting form. In the meantime, the workshop companies and "I" services had been working overtime to get many of the broken down and abandoned panzers back into the fight. Their services paid off, as they were able to get the number of operational panzers up to fifty-three. The Regiment lost little time as it rolled east along the Axis By-Pass road towards Belhamed,

Chapter 10: Gazala and Tobruk, May-August 1942

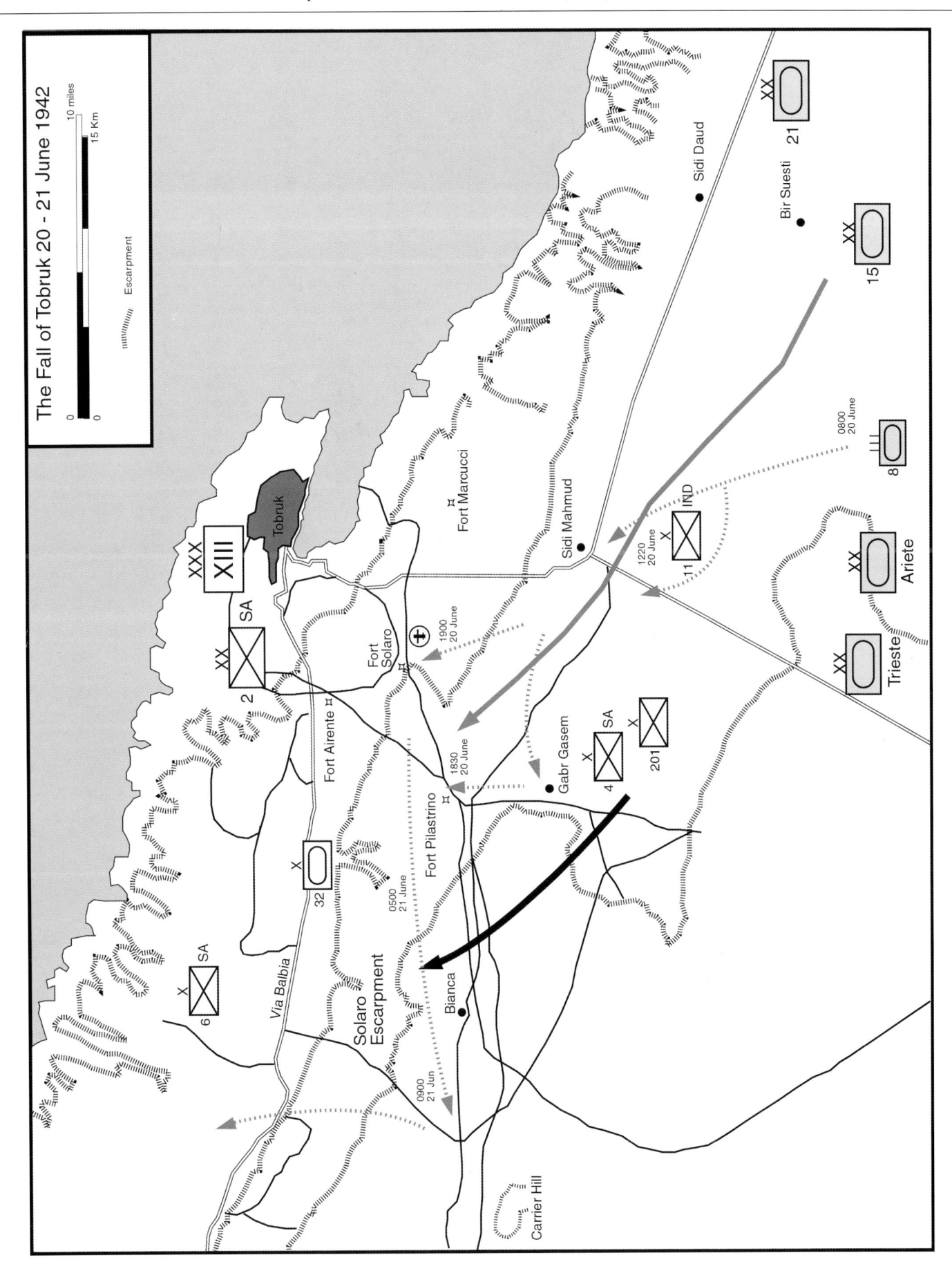

arriving just north of the town during the afternoon, where it soon ran into a column of *Bren* gun carriers, artillery, and anti-tank guns. In the fighting that erupted, the Regiment opened fire and quickly destroyed some twenty vehicles and seven self-propelled anti-tank gun carriers. One Mk II was hit by anti-tank gun fire, killing the radio operator; the commander and driver were able to escape unharmed. As darkness began to fall, *Oberstlt* Teege allowed his *abteilungs* to halt for the night, as many of the panzers were now low on fuel, and the Regiment was in unfamiliar territory and uncertain of what enemy forces were around. Ammunition and fuel were brought up, and the panzer crews quickly went to work taking care of their panzers. Hans Killermann describes how as the driver he was responsible for refueling his panzer:

"*Afterwards, in the evening we got ammunition and fuel, re-fuelling was my job along with cleaning of the air filters, it was all my job. There were always the filters full with dust. I did it every day two to four times a day; there were six of them to clean. The loader handled the ammunition. My job was to fuel, and to have petrol available. It was 300-320 liters of petrol all in canisters [jerry cans], in the fuel vehicle that would come, they would throw down the canisters and we had to carry them back in both hands.*"[40]

The *Sidi Rezegh Box* fell that night to the *21st Panzer Division* despite an armored attack by the newly reorganized *4th Armored Brigade*, which charged the division, but was severely shot up on the division's Pak gun screen. The *El Adem Box*, being held by the *29th Indian Brigade* (Reid), was still holding out against the *90th Light*, which at the time was down to approximately regimental strength. That night its garrison also broke out and headed east. As the sun came up on the 17th, the Regiment prepared itself for the renewed advance and was soon rolling towards Gambut, where it took up positions just south of its old workshop area used in the previous year, and awaited Rommel's new orders. Also on this day *21st Panzer* was involved in another armored battle with *4th Armored Brigade*; in the ensuing fight, the British brigade lost almost half its tank strength before retreating east. Later that day the *21st Panzer* cut the Via Balbia east of Gambut. The following morning the *20th Indian Brigade*, which had been holding out at Belhamed, finally attempted to break out and was almost totally destroyed in the process. With the loss of these final boxes, the entire *Eighth Army* was now in full retreat toward Egypt.

The Attack on Tobruk
Since the 15th Rommel had only one thing on his mind, the Fortress of Tobruk. He wasted little time and gave the British no rest before his *Panzerarmee* quickly had Tobruk invested on the 18th. There would be no need to draw up long deliberate plans, because many of them already existed from the previous November and only required a dusting off. The *90th Light* and the *Aufklärungs Gruppe* were ordered to move east towards Bardia and Sollum along the Egyptian border in order to provide a screen for the *Panzerarmee* as it began to reposition those forces assigned to attack Tobruk. As those forces began to move into position, they soon discovered that in many places the original German stockpiles of supplies and ammunition, previously emplaced for the previous years' attack, were still there and had gone untouched by the British. Over the past few days, Rommel had been husbanding his armored formations for the attack on Tobruk. Now they were ordered to turn about and begin gathering to the southeast in preparation for the assault. That same day, the Regiment was ordered to an area northwest of Belhamed at Bir Bu Asaten, where it was to begin its preparations for the attack on Tobruk. Willi Teege and his commanders wasted little time in their preparations and conducted limited reconnaissance of the attack area. As the leadership prepared its battle plan, the panzer crews were busy performing the necessary checks and services, making sure that their panzers were ready for the battle to come. Having smashed the Gazala Line and driven the British from the field, it was now time to enjoy some of the captured war booty that was left behind in the supply dumps and abandoned camps that were not either burned or destroyed in the retreat. Over the previous year, the German soldier had made his existence off the spoils of war and been living off the captured stocks of British food and clothing; after a year in Africa many German soldiers had been completely outfitted in British clothing, and had even grown accustomed to many British items, as *OFw* Kurt Kathe explains:

"*In the beginning we had our German uniforms and when we went on further and there was no further supply of uniforms, we usually only got trousers, we were allowed to wear the British clothes.*"[41]

The 19th saw orders being issued and passed down from *Panzerarmee* to the *D.A.K.*, and then on to the divisions and regiments; the staff officers had to quickly coordinate and check the specific responsibilities of each section, targets, times, and boundaries with adjacent units. For the attack there was to be only limited reconnaissance, and none of the *Panzerarmee* formations were to enter their assembly areas prior to the afternoon of the 19th. There was to be no artillery to soften up the defenders prior to the attack; that would come in the form of aerial artillery provided by the *Luftwaffe*, which would be quickly followed by the infantry and pioneers that were to open the breaches that the panzers would be free to exploit. The attack alignment from east (right) to west (left) was as follows: *21st Panzer*, *Kampfgruppe Menny*, *15th Panzer*, *Brescia*, *Ariete*, *Trieste*, *Pavia*, *Trento*, and *Sabratha* Divisions. Opposing those Axis formations were the *2nd South African Division* with its *4th* and *6th South African Brigades*, in addition to *11th Indian Brigade* in position along the outer perimeter. Additionally, there was the *201st Guards Brigade* and the *4th* and *7th RTRs* manning the inner perimeter.[42] The Regiment received its orders assigning it to a position just north of the east-west running ridgeline from Sidi Rezegh, to a point just south of the Axis bypass road between El Duda and Belhamed. The axis of attack was to move north from Bir Bu Asaten towards the crossroads at Sidi Mahmad, then continue north across the djebels to Fort Solaro, and then turn to the west and Fort Pilastrino, where it would continue towards Giaida, then north again to the Via Balbia and Ras Belgamel. The remainder of the 19th was spent moving into the jumping off points and performing last minute checks, a quick meal, and what rest one could get. The *21st Panzer*, which had been farther to the east on the previous day, was able to make it back and into its assigned position by 0330hrs. During the early morning hours of Sunday, 20 June, the infantry and pioneers crept forward into their final assault positions. The breaching plan of attack called for the clearing and breaching of the minefields, wire, and other obstacles by the pioneers, who would be closely followed by the *panzergrenadiers* of *Schützen Regiment 115* to assist in securing and exploiting the gaps as they moved through. Once the initial gaps were breached the pioneers would move on to tackle the anti-tank ditches and begin filling them in. With Rommel observing from a nearby ridge the attack began at 0520hrs, as the first wave of *Luftwaffe Ju-87* Stuka dive-bombers came in exactly as promised. They were soon followed by a second wave of *He-111* bombers and *Me-110* fighters, which bombed and strafed the forward positions. At that same time the *D.A.K.* artillery began to lay down its barrage, which, coupled with the air attacks, covered the battlefield in smoke and flames. Most of the bombardment landed on the one lone Indian battalion that was defending the proposed breach sector, the *2/5th Mahratta Battalion*, which was quickly overcome by the *D.A.K.* With the artillery barrage and aerial bombardment covering them, the pioneers moved forward and began filling in the anti-tank ditch. At

Chapter 10: Gazala and Tobruk, May-August 1942

0630hrs the wire was reported cut, and the *panzergrenadiers* were moving forward covered by the terrific amount of smoke and dust. The Regiment then began its movement forward in its standard order of march: the I./*Abteilung* and Regimental *Stabs* followed by the II./*Abteilung*. As the pioneers were busy filling in the ditch, *Schützen Regiment 115* had already begun moving over the ditch and attacking the bunker system supporting it. At 0745hrs reports came in that stated that the required gaps and lanes had been opened for the panzers, and at 0800hrs the panzers began to roll forward through the wire. Within a half hour the *15th Panzer* had breeched the outer perimeter and the anti-tank ditch.[43] Horst Sonnenkalb wrote of the attack on Tobruk and what he saw that day in this account:

"*I took part in the attack on Tobruk with the new [panzer] crew. On 20 June 1942 we went on towards the rock fortress of Tobruk with its war harbor. The British defenders numbered 30,000 men. The terrain front around Tobruk stretched over 40km. A wide tank trench, deeply echeloned mine fields and barbed wire obstacles up above the limit were set up by British in front of their defense positions. The pioneers cleared the mine alleys during the night, arranged free driving paths through the obstacles. Artillery shot the drum fire [intense bombardment], Stukas dove with howling Jericho sirens, throwing their bombs. They flew already at 0530hrs from Crete in their uninterrupted attacks. At 0830hrs our first panzers from the regiment rolled over the alleys cleared by the pioneers, twelve dozen followed. We threw orange smoke signs so that our flying squadrons could distinguish friend from foe. On the rear of the panzer we fixed the swastika flag in order to clearly identify ourselves to the airplanes so that they wouldn't aim at us. But their bombs were offloaded a few meters from us. In close cooperation between all weapons branches of service we forced ourselves into the fortress kettle, and turned off the defending positions by well placed fire.*"[44]

Hptm Kümmel, as usual, was driving at the head of his *abteilung* in his command vehicle, and crossed the ditch at 0830hrs; as he did so he quickly began motioning his panzers forward over the crossing point. It was about this time that the panzers began receiving British artillery and anti-tank gunfire from the heights opposite the breach point. Fortunately for the Germans, the volume and effectiveness of that fire was extremely poor, especially compared to the 1941 attacks; most of the artillery fire went astray due to the improper coordination and use of fire control. The panzers paid little attention to this fire and continued to cross the ditch and move forward. Over on the right flank the Regiment had not yet crossed the anti-tank ditch, and over on the left the Italian *Ariete* was hung up at the ditch and was slow to follow up. The German artillery continued to fire in support of the panzers, which now began to fan out inside the perimeter. The attack against the fixed defensive positions moved ahead rather slowly; the original Italian built bunkers offered good protection to the defending troops, but unfortunately the minefields surrounding many of the bunkers had fallen into disrepair, thereby creating gaps that the panzers soon exploited with the assistance of the infantry and engineers. The attacking assault troops were supported by direct fire as they attempted to knockout the bunkers. In the meantime it had gotten rather hot, and through the smoky, glittering air, the bunkers became only shadowy figures barely recognizable by the panzer crews. At 1000hrs, the *Stukas* came in again for another attack, and the I./*Abteilung* was quickly forced to mark its position with purple flares, as their bombs landed so close that many of the panzers were covered in the dust kicked up from the explosions. Around this time the amount of enemy fire began to noticeably decrease, and the first defenders from the *11th Indian Brigade* began to surrender their positions. Around mid-morning, as the Regiment was nearing Sidi Mahmad, or Kings Cross, it was engaged by better coordinated artillery fire that was soon followed by the appearance of a number of tanks from the *32nd Tank Brigade*, which came on in an uncoordinated attack. The *Matilda*, *Valentine*, and *Crusader* tanks lumbered forward, and as they did, Kümmel ordered his *abteilung* to form a wide wedge and begin to open fire. The heavily armored infantry tanks caused the expenditure of a high volume of ammunition before they were halted. As the I./*Abteilung* continued to lay down its base of fire, the II./*Abteilung* quickly swung around to the left, came up on the right flank, and drove the British tanks off to the east, where they were hit by *Panzer Regiment 5*, which had been moving up. In the hour-long battle, seventy-six enemy tanks were claimed destroyed; fifty-three of those tanks were claimed by the Regiment. By 1220hrs, the leading elements of the I./*Abteilung* had reached the Kings Cross road junction, where they were engaged by a few remaining tanks and artillery guns that had begun to lay down a better concentration of fire. The panzers were able to deal with the artillery with their machine guns and HE shells, which left numerous vehicles and guns burning. That afternoon, prior to its attacks on the Pilastrino Ridge, the *15th Panzer Division* divided into two *kampfgruppen* for the remainder of the attack. The first *kampfgruppe*, led by *Oberst* Crasemann—then the acting divisional commander—was composed of the II./*Abteilung*, III./*Schützen Regiment 115*, and *I.* and *III./Artillery Regiment 33*. This *kampfgruppe* was to move against the positions at Fort Solaro. The second *kampfgruppe* was formed from the I./*Abteilung* with various combat groups from *Schützen Regiment 115 (-)*, the *II./Artillery Regiment 33*, and *Panzerjäger Abteilung 33*; this *kampfgruppe* was to attack Fort Pilastrino. Due to the delays with getting the supporting infantry forward, the *II./Schützen Regiment 200* was stranded far to the rear with no motor transport, while the *III./Schützen Regiment 115* was still lagging behind attempting to get forward.[45] Hans Kümmel began to organize his *abteilung* into battle formation as they awaited the infantry and artillery to arrive. The attack on Fort Pilastrino would come from the south, as the *kampfgruppen* followed the attack that led it near Gabr Gàsem. The I./*Abteilung* rolled west towards Gabr el Gàsem with the *2nd Company* in the lead. As the company neared the strong point it came under fire by some anti-tanks guns, which were able to quickly knock out two Mk IIIs. The *abteilung* reacted at once, as the *4th Company* maneuvered to take up positions that quickly put the anti-tank guns in a deadly crossfire. That move allowed for the destruction of a number of those guns, and forced the remaining gun crews to surrender after realizing that their situation was hopeless. By 1400hrs, the *21st Panzer* had reached the escarpment north of Kings Cross that overlooked Tobruk, and they wasted little time as they descended the escarpment, and by early evening the division had reached positions on the outskirts of Tobruk. The II./*Abteilung* moved along the same escarpment, and with the Regimental *Stabs* in tow attacked Fort Solaro, which it secured by 1900hrs. After the fighting at Gabr Gàsem ended, the I./*Abteilung* turned north toward Fort Pilastrino, and by 1830hrs the *abteilung* had made it to a spot just south of the fort near some bunkers. The panzer crews wasted little time, and rolled forward using their machine guns and high explosive rounds to clear out the remaining bunkers. The panzer fire was too much for many of the Guardsmen from the *201st Guards Brigade*, which began surrendering their positions soon after the attack. Finally, at 1900hrs the fort's garrison flew the white flag of surrender. Once again the panzers had moved far ahead of their supporting infantry, and so when Fort Pilastrino surrendered there was no infantry available to finish mopping up the positions. Knowing how vulnerable they were, the I./*Abteilung* remained outside of the fort until the *panzergrenadiers* finally arrived. By last light, the I./*Abteilung*, along with the infantry, had secured the fort and area around it. The Regimental *Stabs* which had been with the II./*Abteilung* at Fort Solaro linked up with that *abteilung* three kilometers east of Fort Solaro, where it spent a rather quiet night. The supply trains would not

167

arrive until the following day, so the crews settled down, performing their after action checks and services in the light of burning and destroyed vehicles. Hermann Eckardt recalled:

"After the battle we took whatever we found in the English tanks, we were happy we were in Tobruk and we got an extreme amount of English provisions. It was enough for several months. It was forbidden to take their uniforms, but whatever else we got, as provisioning was no problem. In the German supply we had just cookies [hard tack], not normal bread. It was not good at all. We also had 'donkey meat' in cans."[46]

Wilhelm Hagios was a member of one of those crews that had their panzer damaged in the fighting before Tobruk, and he describes his experience as the attack on Tobruk commenced:

"On the morning we [the Regiment] went around Tobruk, on the evening of the 10th at about 1800hrs we arrived in the werkshop and stayed there awhile. We stayed with the [I./Abteilung] Werkshop Zug as they fixed everything on the panzer except the petrol tank as they had nothing to fix it with. They had no electric welding equipment and so they sent us to another unit. And it was in the proximity of Tobruk, we were there until everything was all fixed. So on the day when Tobruk was attacked we were still at the werkshop and unfortunately missed it all. Our comrades had captured plenty of cigarettes and food there."[47]

The most notable loss of the day was that of *Hptm* Klein, the commander of the *7th Company*, who was killed in action near Fort Solaro; he was replaced by *Olt* Ritter. There were other losses in men and vehicles, in addition to the previously mentioned Mk IIIs, but incomplete records of the attack do not mention their names or numbers. At 1000hrs on the 21st, the Regiment was rolling toward Giaida when it received word that the Tobruk garrison had surrendered earlier that morning to elements of the *21st Panzer Division*. After receiving word that Tobruk had fallen, the Regiment continued north to where the Via Balbia ran into the western side of the Tobruk perimeter. During its march north the panzers continued to come across disorganized and separated groups of British, Indian, and South African soldiers. These soldiers were quickly passed off to the *panzergrenadiers* of the *II./Schützen Regiment 200*. Shortly before mid-day the Regiment neared its objective north of the Via Balbia at Ras Belgamél. The panzer crews were exhausted and worn out from the previous day's fighting and drive north. The Regiment had achieved a lot over the last day and a half: they claimed eighty-two tanks either destroyed or captured; forty-eight cannons, fifty-six anti-tank guns, and some thirty vehicles. The number of prisoners taken could not be accurately determined since the advance had been so rapid.[48] *Uffz* Max Lebold reflected on some of those prisoners that were taken:

"The British officers appeared as being so superior and above everyone else, there was this time [at a PoW collection point] when a wounded British officer with a bandage around his arm refused to sit he would only stand and pace back and forth while the enlisted men sat down in the sand. Then when Rommel passed by the British soldiers would all jump up to [the position of] attention while the British officer sat down but we took care of that with a number of boot kicks to his backside!"[49]

With the capture of Tobruk, Rommel next turned his attention toward Egypt, and a final showdown for North Africa with the *Eighth Army*. To his victorious *panzerarmee* he issued the following order of the day, which read in part:

"Now for the complete destruction of the enemy. We will not rest until we have shattered the last remains of the British Eighth Army. During the days to come, I shall call on you for one more great effort to bring us to this final goal".[50]

Field Marshal Kesselring, who had flown in to discuss future events with Rommel, pointed out to him that he was forbidden to move on Egypt unless Mussolini had given his authority to do so. The two also discussed the issue concerning Malta, and the serious problem that island presented if it was not quickly settled. Furthermore, Kesselring stated that the *Luftwaffe* could not support the attack on Malta and an advance to Egypt, which he knew did not stand a chance of success unless there was proper air support to cover it. The supply lines were also stretched to the limit from Tripoli and Benghazi, and the *Panzerarmee* itself was nearing its operational end in both men and machines, despite the large quantities of materiel captured in Tobruk. But Rommel, soon to be a *Field Marshal* himself, had the support of Hitler and Mussolini, and so he was allowed to proceed towards the border and leave Malta to its fate. He wrote:

"I requested the Duce, immediately after the capture of Tobruk, to lift the restrictions on the Panzerarmee's freedom of operation and allow us to advance into Egypt. Permission was granted, whereupon orders went out immediately to all formations concerned to prepare for the march."[51]

That afternoon the Regiment was resupplied by its logistical trains, which had brought up large quantities of captured war booty that had come from the enormous stocks captured when Tobruk fell. The Regiment was counting on a long break, but shortly before midnight it received orders to move east toward the Egyptian border. The departure time was set for sunrise the following morning. With forty-three panzers the Regiment began its march east, rolling along the Via Balbia undisturbed by any *Eighth Army* elements. By the evening of the 22nd, the Regiment had reached an area near Fort Maddalena, located some 50km south of Sollum, on the Egyptian border. That night the supply trains came up and resupplied the Regiment as it formed a hedgehog and settled down for the night. As the *Panzerarmee* rolled towards Egypt, British commanders discussed how to halt it. There were a few different thoughts on how it should best be attempted. Auchinleck knew that Sollum and Halfaya Pass could not be effectively held, but agreed with Ritchie that a stand at Mersa Matruh was possible, even though he planned to establish a defensive line at El Alamein.[52] In the end the decision to give ground in order to gain more time offered the best course for the *Eighth Army* as it attempted to right itself. The *X Corps* (Holmes) was brought forward out of Syria and placed in the Mersa Matruh area in order to establish a defense there with the *2nd New Zealand* (Freyberg) and *5th Indian* (Briggs) Divisions. The *XIII Corps* (Gott) was still reeling from the previous months' battles, and was still arriving in the area further to the south of Mersa Matruh, where it was ordered to hold the frontier line with the *1st South African*, *1st Armored*, *4th Indian* (Tuker), and *50th Northumbrian* (Nichols) *Divisions*. Once the XIII Corps reached the *Matruh Line* they were to then assist in its defense, except for the South Africans, who were to fall back and assist the *XXX Corps*, which was moving into another defensive line being established at El Alamein. The *Panzerarmee* rolled forward, with the Italian infantry divisions of the *X* and *XXI Corps* investing the Sollum and Sidi Omar positions. The *D.A.K.* and Italian *XX Motorized Corps* were to drive south and cross the frontier near Fort Maddalena. For the Regiment, it crossed the frontier and began the march east on the morning of the 23rd. The *Panzerarmee* was aligned from north to south, with the *90th Light*, the newly arrived Italian *Littorio* Armored Division, *21st Panzer* in the middle with *15th Panzer*, and finally *Ariete* and *Trieste*. The plan here was to swing out to the south and then move north, thereby avoiding the minefields and occupied defensive boxes established there by the *Eighth Army*, and attempt to cut off their route of escape. The chance of catching those *XIII Corps* elements was not possible, however, as those forces had already withdrawn into the *Matruh Line*. The advance for the next few days was swift, and moved forward without any interference from the *Eighth Army*. The Regiment moved forward with a number of its light Mk IIs positioned out in front and along the flanks in order to provide reconnaissance and early warning. By this time there were only forty-four panzers remaining operational in the Regiment.[53] The only appearance by the *Eighth Army* was the usual armored car, which kept close tabs on the division and then quickly sprinted away before they could be engaged. On the night of 23/24 June, the Regiment was forced to halt its progress due to the lack of fuel and formed a hedgehog position deep in the desert. It was a quiet night and passed without problem. The supply trains caught up with the panzers the following day, but they had only brought with them a small amount of fuel, which at best would only allow the Regiment to move forward about 15-20km. The division had promised more fuel and supplies for the Regiment's panzers, but it was taking time before the supply services could make their way forward, gather the necessary supplies from captured British supply dumps, and then transport them forward. During the 24th and 25th, the Regiment was repeatedly attacked by the *RAF* which, now closer to its airfields, had the range to be an effective deterrent and play an important role in the battles to come. The *RAF* had been overhead ever since the *Panzerarmee* had crossed the frontier wire, but in comparison, the *Luftwaffe*, farther from its own airfields, had almost disappeared from the skies. During these aerial attacks the Regiment suffered twenty-eight men wounded.[54] By the evening of the 24/25th, substantial quantities of fuel and provisions had finally made it forward, but there had been almost an entire day lost in waiting for them. That same evening the first German forces reached the *Matruh Line*, and Rommel immediately decided to attack the following day. Wilhelm Hagios, with his panzer repaired, was finally able to move out and rejoin the Regiment:

"We went away [from Tobruk] 1-2 days later, we were set to march to Bardia, then down Halfaya Pass into Sollum, from there we went to Mersa Matruh. On that evening when the British broke out of Mersa Matruh we were 3-4km away, otherwise we would have fully participate in that [attack]. They all went with their vehicles to the south. We heard shooting but didn't know what was going on. On the next day we met with our Regiment. From there we went to El Alamein. On 1 July in the morning we arrived near El Alamein. We went during the night with not enough speed, the vehicles got stuck in the sand and had to tow out other vehicles. When we arrived to El Alamein the Light Zug was already there and we remained there for awhile."[55]

In order to do this, the *D.A.K.* first had to drive off the British *1st Armored Division*, which was positioned farther to the south and poised a direct threat to the flanks of the *D.A.K.* The plan of attack called for the Italian *X and XXI Corps* to invest Matruh from the west, while the *90th Light Division* moved to the south, between the two escarpments, and turned north to cut the Via Balbia from the east. The *21st Panzer* was also to drive between the escarpments and pivot to the north, assisting the *90th Light*. The *15th Panzer Division* would advance east, south of the Sidi Hamza escarpment, in order to tackle those *1st Armored Division* positions. The Italian *XX Corps*, when it arrived, would be south of *15th Panzer* and support its attack. The British were in position with two strong flanks: the northern flank consisted of the *10th Indian* and *50th Northumbrian Divisions*, while the southern flank was held by the *1st Armored* and *2nd New Zealand Divisions*. The center position of the line was the weakest section, and had the least amount of protective minefields; it was only defended by the *Glee Column* and *Leather Column*.[56] The 25th saw the Regiment begin its movement east as it crossed Siwa track, which ran from Matruh to the Siwa Oasis; it again came under attack by the RAF, which began to bomb and strafe the column. In an attempt to avoid the falling bombs the panzers increased their speed in an attempt to drive under the bombs. The Regiment continued east along the Sidi Hamza escarpment, where it eventually ran into a small minefield and had some difficulty in locating a passage through it. As the panzers halted, the crews used the break to catch a short nap, and the division's pioneers came through to locate and clear a lane through. It took until that evening of the 25/26th to complete the task, and the Regiment found itself forming a hedgehog position at Alam el Agali, where the supply trains caught up with it and conducted a resupply. In the early morning hours of the 26th, with the lanes finally cleared, the Regiment continued its advance eastward. At approximately 1000hrs, the I./Abteilung was again halted by another minefield, which caused another two hour delay before a passage could be finally cleared through it. Not long after resuming the march at mid-day a third minefield was encountered, which caused a great deal of frustration for commanders and crews alike. Also at this time one of the leading Mk IIs then began to receive a bit of artillery fire near its position; the fire did not succeed in hitting the panzer, and actually helped with the clearing of the minefield obstacle. In other sectors the *D.A.K.* was having its way again with the *Eighth Army*, as the *90th Light* was able to destroy "Leathercol" and the *21st Panzer* was able to do the same to "Gleecol." The thin belt of minefields and lack of substantial forces coupled with the failure of communications led the weaker *D.A.K.* to be able to destroy the heavier *Eighth Army* formations. As the sun began to set, the Regiment was able to continue its advance through the minefield, but as the I./Abteilung began to exit the minefield it quickly came under artillery and anti-tank gun fire. Kümmel ordered his panzers to lay down a base of heavy concentrated fire which soon left many of the British guns destroyed, and once the British fire slackened, the panzers rushed forward and were able to capture those gun positions. As the panzers rolled into those gun positions the crews were able to ascertain that the troops belonged to the *2nd New Zealand Division*. The prisoners were quickly rounded up, where they were soon handed over to the division's pioneers, who were moving forward and relieved the panzer crews so that they could continue the advance. A quick count soon revealed that almost a hundred prisoners had been taken, along with the destruction of ten artillery and anti-tank guns. In the growing darkness the Regiment was forced to halt and formed a hedgehog position until the morning came and a reconnaissance screen could again be placed out to the front. The morning of the 27th saw the *90th Light* continue its rapid advance eastward, where it captured a 300 man battalion left stranded in the desert. That division then continued its advance until it was finally forced to halt due to heavy artillery fire. The *21st Panzer* was also advancing, but it did so with only twenty-three panzers and about one battalion's worth of infantry as it began to encounter the main body of the *2nd New Zealand Division* on the northern edge of the Sidi Hamza escarpment, near Minqa Qaim. The *21st Panzer Division*, under the cover of an artillery barrage, was then able to roll eastward and come down and attack the eastern flank of the New Zealanders. Those *1st Armored Division* elements to the south of the Sidi Hamza escarpment were still blocking and holding up the *15th Panzer*, but they never attempted to counterattack the *21st Panzer* and disrupt the attack. That evening, the headquarters of the *15th Panzer* and *D.A.K.* were quite surprised by a message they received from the Regiment *Stabs* that stated that they had come across an organized and well-defended position.[57] The message was shocking for those commanders, in that it showed them that the *Eighth Army* had not just simply melted away to the east, but were organized and defending well sited defensive positions. What was unknown to those

German staffs was that the *D.A.K.* was right in the middle of a corps worth of armor and infantry. The Regiment was now ordered to continue its advance in a northeasterly direction, where it would be able to assist the *21st Panzer* attacks. During the drive forward the Regiment came under attack by a large number of British tanks that attacked from the northeast. This attack was being carried out by the *22nd Armored Brigade*, which since its last action at Gazala had been reorganized and, along with the *4th Armored Brigade*, now possessed some 159 tanks, of which sixty were *Grants*.[58] In the ensuing battle the British armor was able to destroy five Mk IIIs, but lost thirty-one of its *Grants* and *Crusaders* in the process. During the attack *Panzerjäger Abteilung 33* had come up to support the Regiment by sealing off the northern flank. At 1100hrs, the Regiment again advanced in wide wedges towards the *2nd New Zealand Division*, but again came under attack by British armored forces from the *1st Armored Division*, this time from the south. This time it was the II./*Abteilung* which was engaged, and it moved forward to establish a base firing position. In the ensuing fire fight one Mk IV from the *8th Company* was hit and put out of commission, but again the British armor was routed, with the loss of some thirty-eight *Crusader* and *Stuart* tanks. As the II./*Abteilung* was busy fighting off those tank forces in the south, the I./*Abteilung* came under fire from British artillery and anti-tank guns positioned in sturdy defensive positions. In the fierce battle that ensued, the *Maori* soldiers of the *2nd New Zealand Division* attacked the panzers with only hand grenades and infantry weapons. *Hptm* Hans Kümmel wasted little time, and knew that the best chance for his panzers to succeed was to charge forward into the guns and get under their fire before they could shoot the *abteilung* to pieces. So with the *4th Company* providing covering fire, Kümmel led the remnants of the remaining companies (the *1st*, *2nd*, and *3rd*) into the British line and routed them from their positions. After the II./*Abteilung* concluded its fight in the south, it attempted to move back to the north and link back up with the main body of the Regiment, where it was again counterattacked by eight British tanks and six self-propelled guns. In the fighting that followed the *abteilung* destroyed five tanks and two of the self-propelled guns. By that evening, the *4th* and *22nd Armored Regiments* had been seriously depleted, and the *4th New Zealand Brigade* had been totally smashed, losing some 800 men, which were quickly handed over to the *panzergrenadiers* of *Schützen Regiment 115*. Sixteen 25-Pounder, eighteen anti-tank guns, and four heavy mortars were either destroyed or captured during the battle. But for the Regiment and the rest of the *15th Panzer Division* the fighting had exhausted the supply of fuel and ammunition, and sapped its strength, which prevented it from pushing forward and linking up with the *21st Panzer Division*.[59] That division was now in serious trouble itself, also being far too weak to adequately protect itself and almost completely surrounded by the British forces around Minqa Qaim. To the north of the *D.A.K.*, the *90th Light Division*, with Rommel accompanying it, had succeeded in cutting the Via Balbia between Mersa Matruh and Fuka and trapped the British *X Corps*, but with only some 1500 troops that division stood little chance of holding the line and sealing off those forces still south of Mersa Matruh. But Rommel, unlike his opponents, saw things differently, and actually sent orders to the *21st Panzer Division* ordering it to be ready to move against those *Eighth Army* positions located near Fuka. British commanders, on the other hand, were very uncertain of their own situation, being so out of touch with other units in the *X* and *XIII Corps*. That evening, after the attacks that day by the Regiment against the New Zealanders, *General* Gott, the commander of *XIII Corps*, ordered his forces and the *1st Armored Division* to fall back towards the Fuka position. No rest came to the Regiment that evening, as those *X* and *XIII Corps* forces attempted to retrieve what they could from the battlefield before they withdrew, and they laid down plenty of artillery fire in order to cover the withdrawal. During that withdrawal, the *1st Armored Division* went south around the *21st Panzer*, but the *2nd New Zealand Division* went straight through their positions and a violent battle erupted; despite the tough fighting the British and New Zealanders succeeded in getting through to the east. During the night enough supplies made it forward to allow the Regiment to continue its advance to the east the following day. Again that morning the Regiment was attacked by the *RAF*, which caused damage to one Mk II, two Mk IIIs, and one Mk IV, along with six wounded.[60] At around 1500hrs, the Regiment again came under attack from the south by some forty British tanks and was hit by artillery fire from the east. The II./*Abteilung* commander, *Hptm* Wahl, formed a defensive line in the south with his *7th* and *8th Companies* and attacked the British right flank with his *5th* and *6th Companies*. In the battle which followed the Regimental *Stabs* ordered the I./*Abteilung* to attack along the left flank. After a short fight twenty-eight British tanks were put out of action, and the remainder broke contact and beat a hasty retreat to the southeast. It was again discovered that the attack had been carried out by elements of the *4th Armored Brigade*, and many of the destroyed tanks belonged to the *5th RTR*. *Hptm* Knorr, a long serving member of the I./*Abteilung* in Poland and France, and presently the commander of the *1st Company*, was severely wounded in the fighting when he was hit in the right forearm. Command of the company was passed to Lt Max Keil. The wound Knorr suffered was quite serious, and he was to spend the next eight weeks in the *lazarett*, where his forearm was removed. Knorr would later return to duty as the personal adjutant to the German military commander of Amsterdam, and later he became the first commander of *Panzer Abteilung 8* in July 1943, where he would see further action on the Eastern Front.

The *Panzerarmee*, spurred by Rommel, pushed on to attack the *Eighth Army* as it began to withdraw once again to the east. The panzer strength report of the Regiment on 28 June totaled just twenty-six operational panzers.[61] On 29 June, Mersa Matruh fell as the *90th Light* entered the town that morning and wasted little time in renewing its drive to the east. The battle of Mersa Matruh was over, and again the *Panzerarmee* was victorious; they had achieved much, including the capture of over 6,000 troops along with numerous vehicles, guns, and supplies.[62] They had achieved this with a bit of luck and a commander who never gave his opponent a chance to breathe. This was more than evident when, on the afternoon of the 29th, Rommel ordered the *90th Light* forward again along the Via Balbia to El Daba. For the Regiment and *15th Panzer Division* they were ordered east along the northern rim of the Sidi Hamza escarpment, where it was to eventually swing north and come up behind Ruweisat Ridge, which stood some 20km south of El Alamein in the hopes of capturing those remaining *Eighth Army* elements moving back towards Alamein. Horst Sonnenkalb remembered a funny incident that took place at about this time:

"It was around July/August of the year 1942 southeast of Mersa Matruh. Our field kitchen had gotten lost and had landed by the Brits. We were pushing ahead when we saw at the Dschebel border in a 'Wadi' our field kitchen among a British platoon. The Tommies were already standing in line to get food with their canteens in hand. They were looking forward to their German lunch. We threw two panzer grenades into the middle of them, pushed the Panzers forward and the Tommies went Hands up! We had our field kitchen back, and also a whole company of prisoners with long faces, because we stole the food away from them. They must have been so excited about their German lunch that they had forgotten to put guards up. I guess you can't call this theft of food, can you?"[63]

Shortly after the Regiment began this movement it was engaged by British artillery fire, and in the barrage Hans Kümmel was wounded in the right forearm. After dressing the wound Kümmel returned to continue leading his I./*Abteilung* eastwards. As the Regiment drove on it encountered a number of smaller British elements also moving east, and often the two sides would make minor chance contact with each other. Rommel wasted little time before he made known his plans for the attack on El Alamein, which he proposed for the 30th. Those plans called for a feint towards the Qattara Depression and then a strike north on the night of 30/1 July to a position just southwest of El Alamein. The plan was designed as one of maneuver, and getting the *D.A.K.* behind the *Eighth Army* lines, where it was assumed that once the *D.A.K.* was behind it, the *Eighth Army* would retreat all the way back to the Suez Canal. On the 30th, as the Regiment was now moving east through some very rugged stone desert, it again hit a minefield and was caught by the *RAF* as it attempted to negotiate its way through. The panzers were attacked by *RAF Blenheim* bombers, which actually assisted them in getting through when the bombs landed wide of their mark within the minefield and detonated many of the mines. After the attack and towards late afternoon the panzers rolled slowly ahead, where they again encountered another minefield; the minefield was not under direct observation, but two Mk IIs were lost when they hit mines. At that point a halt was called for the night, and the panzers awaited the resupply trains to arrive. That night a dispatch rider brought in a message from *Panzerarmee* that ordered all elements forward at all possible speed. The attack that was to begin on 1 July saw the *Panzerarmee* arrayed from north to south as such: the Italian *XXI Corps* was facing the British *50th Infantry Division* in the *Alamein Box*; the *90th Light Division* was next in line, and was to swing south between the *Alamein Box* and Ruweisat Ridge. The *D.A.K.*, with the *21st Panzer* on the left and *15th Panzer* on the right, was to push through the middle of the line between Deir el Shein; and the *90th Light* formations were to fan out and make their way towards Ruweisat Ridge, while the Italian *X* and *XX Corps* covered to the south of Deir el Shein and El Mireir.[64] On 1 July, the Regiment possessed only seventeen operational panzers that were now consolidated and placed under the command of *Hptm* Kümmel. The previous couple of days and the many rough miles had taken their toll on the panzers, which had begun to break down much more frequently. The Regiment, now the size of a small *kampfgruppe*, advanced at approximately 0300hrs towards the east and Ruweisat Ridge. A number of problems arose that night when the *D.A.K.* became mixed up near its assembly area near the Tel el Aqqaqir, and then was bombed by the *RAF*. A few hours later, as the sun began to rise the Regiment encountered another minefield, this time under observation by British elements dug in behind a strong defensive barrier. Wilhelm Hagios remembers the situation at this time:

"During our time there the bearer of a flag of truce was sent to the British to ask them to give up. A German Hauptmann went with them. I thought to myself 'if this guy will tell them what stands in front of them, they will laugh until they get sick'. On 1 July, the whole day we saw British tanks moving here and there, but had no contact with them or any other vehicles. We would head to the east but it didn't matter how far we could go as there ahead of us were the British and they had New Zealand troops deployed there also."[65]

The division and regimental pioneers were ordered forward in order to clear lanes through the minefields; as the pioneers went in to begin their dangerous task the dangers were increased, as they became targets for the British, who kept them under a constant artillery barrage. As the pioneers were busy with the mines, a new threat emerged in the form of anti-tank guns, which began to engage the panzers from another defensive position. *Olt* Stiefelmayer of the *4th Company*, and riding in the last remaining Mk IV, moved out against those guns and was able to knock out three of them. Hermann Eckardt remembered Stiefelmayer as being a good officer who looked after his men, but when in battle paid little attention to the losses suffered in attacks; in fact, during one of the battles Eckardt saw him change panzers sixteen times. The British defensive line that the Regiment was now being held on was occupied by an Indian infantry battalion that continued to delay the panzers. Knowing how important it was to keep moving, Kümmel ordered the panzers to quickly break through those Indian positions and to leave their mopping up to the *panzergrenadiers* which were soon to arrive. The *kampfgruppe* continued to push forward, but again the *RAF* appeared overhead throughout the afternoon and slowed the advance to a crawl. In the attacks that followed more time was lost, and two panzer commanders and three *Kradmelders* were wounded. Further losses were suffered, but this time they were mechanical, as one Mk II and three Mk IIIs fell out of the advance. The attacks that day never came off as planned by the *Panzerarmee* because the *Eighth Army* was not positioned as Rommel and his staff had thought. The line of British defensive boxes was not in the exact alignment as German intelligence had them, and when the *D.A.K.* went north or south to come in from behind a box, they actually found themselves coming up in front of the actual location. This was evident in the north, when the *21st Panzer* captured the Deir el Shein Box despite being held up by the *18th Indian Brigade* in a severe fight. Despite the fierce resistance the box was taken, but it cost the *21st Panzer* eighteen of their thirty-five panzers. The *90th Light* advanced south of the Alamein position, but strayed from the designated route and ran into three South African brigades and their artillery defending the *Alamein Box*. The South Africans sent the division reeling back to the rear in complete confusion; even Rommel himself could not sway the attack, and was soon pinned down by artillery fire.[66] Kümmel kept up the pressure and drove hard for Ruweisat Ridge, but late in the day he received reports that an unidentified British tank unit was moving to the south against him. The *22nd Armored Brigade*, coming from the east of Ruweisat Ridge, was moving south along the ridge in the hopes of catching the *15th Panzer Division* in its flank. Kümmel wasted little time, as he placed his remaining fourteen panzers to the south some 15km from Bab el Qattara. As soon as the British tanks came within range Kümmel noticed there were approximately forty of them, and that there was a wide depression between him and his opponents. Quickly making a decision Kümmel, despite the enemy fire, drove forward into the depression with ten of his panzers, all of which made it to the opposite slope. As Kümmel was keeping the British busy with his charge, *Olt* Stiefelmayer, with the remaining four panzers, came at them from the flank. In the short battle that followed, twelve *Grants* were soon hit and left burning, while the remainder withdrew back towards the southeast. One Mk III was lost when it took a direct hit that mortally wounded the commander, but the remaining crew members, despite being a bit shaken, were able to escape unharmed. That night Kümmel drove north with the remaining thirteen panzers to a position near Ruweisat Ridge, where he was able to link up with elements of *Schützen Regiment 115*. Wilhelm Hagios remembers:

"On the 1st we stood there as the British drove up with approximately thirty tanks. We had shot some of them but they didn't completely burn. I realized later in the night that they had good vehicles and recovery platform vehicles and that they had taken them away. With us it was a complicated thing to load the panzers, and especially to tow them away. We also recognized that the Pilots [Grants] were there as well."[67]

During the night 1/2 July, the *RAF* again attacked the *kampfgruppe's* assembly area, but the bombs failed to cause any damage other than preventing the crews the time to rest, which they were in desperate need of. On 2 July, Rommel personally briefed the *15th Panzer Division* for the

171

day's attack, which called for a renewed effort against Ruweisat Ridge. The plan now called for the *panzergrenadiers* to move forward under the cover of supporting artillery fire and seize the enemy positions. As the attack kicked off, the *panzergrenadiers* struggled to make it forward against the New Zealanders manning the box to the southwest of Ruweisat Ridge. At 1150hrs the order came down for the *kampfgruppe* to be ready to move forward. Finally, at 1400hrs the thirteen remaining panzers led the attack on the ridge ahead of the *panzergrenadiers* of *Schützen Regiment 115*. As they moved forward they received heavy anti-tank gun and artillery fire from dug in enemy positions. Despite the concentrated fire by all of the panzers, the *kampfgruppe* could not muscle its way through the position. During the attack the *kampfgruppe* was able to destroy four anti-tank guns and three artillery pieces, but were soon counterattacked by nine Matildas, and only through the high volume of fire were they able to destroy four of them. By this time the *kampfgruppe*, which had begun the attack with only thirteen panzers, was down to seven operational panzers. One Mk II, four Mk IIIs, and one Mk IV were put out of action.[68] Shortly afterwards two additional panzers were disabled and left on the ridge, and their crews captured. One of the disabled panzers, however, was later retrieved and brought back with the remaining five panzers. The day ended with the *RAF* again returning overhead on the night of 2/3 July and hitting the assembly areas; fortunately, the *kampfgruppe* suffered no casualties. The *Panzerarmee* had achieved nothing in its attacks that day. Wilhelm Hagios continues his account from 1 July:

"On the next day at mid-day I scanned the flank area as I was set on the side of the 1st or 2nd Company as I had the richtschütze duty. I saw at 2700m an anti-tank gun and shot at it, and he pursued us for awhile as I heard the rounds pass by but he didn't hit us. I went to the south towards the attack, and hadn't seen anything there. The commander said to halt, then all hell became hot and I first shot with the high-explosive shell and missed it, and with the second shot I heard that it had started burning. We had no radio to report to the company chef but he told us to 'Aufschliessen' or close ranks. But we had quieted the anti-tank gun and had no further enemy encounters. One of our guys had even seen the English tanks and division radio station had cleaned up [moved out], but no one shot towards them. I even saw that there was a radio station and then here comes a Pilot and cleans everything up and departs. We were not able to report as we had no radio. In the afternoon there was an attack which we hadn't seen and so in the night we went further east."

On the 3rd, Rommel abandoned the plan of getting around the British lines, and instead concentrated his forces on the *Alamein Box*. There was also to be an attack that afternoon on Ruweisat Ridge with the remaining panzers of the *21st Panzer*. That same morning saw the *kampfgruppe*, which was by this time the size of a panzer *zug*, receive its supplies as the crews attempted to get the remaining six panzers ready for action. Shortly after 1000hrs, the New Zealanders came out of their box at Qaret el Abd with *Matildas*, *Bren* carriers, and anti-tank guns, and hit the right flank of the *15th Panzer* and *Ariete* Division. In the *15th Panzer Division* sector, *Panzerjäger Abteilung 33* and *I./Schützen Regiment 115* were able to seal off the attack, and Kümmel, with his six panzers, came up to throw back the New Zealanders, costing them five tanks and eight *Bren* carriers.[69] However, the real damage was done to the Italians, as the *Ariete* lost its entire divisional artillery element to the New Zealanders. That afternoon another attack was launched against Ruweisat Ridge; the attack initially managed to gain some ground with the assistance of the artillery, but in the end, the panzers failed to break through, as Wilhelm Hagios remembered:

"On the evening of the 2nd July we defended against the attack, and on the 3rd I was on watch and I had my eyes on the other side of a dzerba and noticed that something was moving up there, it was two British soldiers and a jeep. It was a VB or Vorgezogene Beobachtung [Forward Observer] of the artillery. I didn't trust myself to shoot, and had no orders and didn't know that if I fired that this could give away our position. They got out and talked with each other, and we watched. We didn't know if this was permitted or not. They went up and up, and stayed there, it would be easy for me to shoot them, as it was only 800m. In the middle of the day the crew came back to us, the richtschütze and ladeschütze. Then I came out of the panzer, but our friends had already gone away, at midday they were at our flank during the counter-attack. And we went into a rear position, and the artillery was shooting like mad, [the terrain] was bad and I thought that if went down on this steep slope that we could get into a dangerous area, but nothing happened to us. I was back in the panzer, when Becker said "there is stale air" and I put the round on that direction and then there was a shot from the 5.7cm anti-tank gun which made a hole [in the panzer], but didn't damage the engine. So that was it. We went on further on the 6th and 7th but not much happened to us."[70]

The *RAF* again attacked the *Panzerarmee* and divisional rear areas; in multiple waves the *RAF* came overhead to pound the German and Italians troops attempting to move forward. The Regiment was fortunate that no losses came to its service and supply troops. Occasionally a few *Luftwaffe* fighters appeared overhead in an attempt to interdict the *RAF*, or the various Flak units were able to claim a lone victim from the ground, as Kurt Kathe explains:

"Once on a nice morning, over my position was this cruising airplane, we were near an airport. There was one single Brit, maybe he lost his way and then he was shot down in front of my place about 100m. I went there and saw the pilot, who had got shot from behind, and had crashed. We buried him, and the airplane was all broken."[71]

By the evening of 3 July, Rommel had to face the facts that the *Eighth Army* was not as beaten as he had previously thought, and the British were not retreating any further, but were now dug in behind well prepared defensive positions. The *D.A.K.* was a completely spent force, totally worn out from the previous month's fighting. The *RAF* had complete air superiority, and controlled and restricted all freedom of movement, and to make matters worse, the supply routes of the *Eighth Army* had become shorter and shorter, while those of the *D.A.K.* now stretched for over 2,000km. Orders were now issued for all units to halt where they were and dig in. On the 4th, the workshop was able to return seven Mk IIIs to the *kampfgruppe*, which brought the total strength to twelve operational panzers. Oberstlt von Mellenthin, the *Panzerarmee Ic*, wrote that at this time the *D.A.K.* had just thirty-six panzers, compared to the British *1st Armored Division*, which had just over 100, and a few hundred German *panzergrenadiers* that were now totally exhausted.[72] German artillery, as in the case of the *15th Panzer Division*, was now down to just two rounds per gun, but luckily in the last month a large number of British 25-Pounder guns had been captured along with huge stocks of ammunition. There was no doubt that the *Panzerarmee* could have withstood a determined attack by the British, and General Auchinleck had actually ordered an attack to commence on 4 July. The attack by elements of the *5th New Zealand Brigade* attacked the infantry positions of the Italian *Brescia* Division near El Mireir, while another attack by British armored forces struck near *Schützen Regiments 104* and *115*, positioned near Ruweisat Ridge. The *panzergrenadiers* were barely able to hold their positions against the tough New Zealanders, who had been supported by a number of tank. At around midday the Regiment's small *kampfgruppe* was called on to assist the grenadiers, and was able to throw back those New Zealand elements in a counterattack, which caused them the loss of three *Crusader* tanks. During the night 4/5 July, six more operational panzers were brought forward with the supply trains, bringing the total number of operational panzers to sixteen. The *Panzerarmee* was ripe for the picking, but the *Eighth Army* could not move itself forward and attack. On 5 July, the *4th New Zealand Brigade* attacked the positions of the *15th Panzer*, and just as Kümmel was preparing to counterattack them, nine Ju-87 Stukas appeared overhead and dove on the New Zealanders, wiping out their headquarters and forcing them to cease their attacks towards El Mireir.[73]

On the following day the *15th Panzer Division* began to reinforce its positions with mines and captured *Eighth Army* equipment, like the 25-Pounder artillery piece, since many of the *D.A.K.* guns had already run out of ammunition. These guns, captured in the preceding weeks of fighting, were a welcome addition to the normally robust German and Italian artillery formations. The Regiment was not deployed forward at this time in order to allow the panzer crews the time to rest and repair their machines. Also on this day the *D.A.K.* reported forty-four operational panzers. The chances for the *Eighth Army* to overrun the *Panzerarmee* were beginning to slip away. On the morning of the 7th, the Regiment received a report that approximately twenty enemy tanks were driving on the right flank of the *Ariete* Division, and also endangering the flank of the *15th Panzer*. A panzer *kampfgruppe* was ordered to deploy to meet them, and within a short time Kümmel was swinging his panzers to the east, where he and his *kampfgruppe* were able to catch the British tanks in the rear. After a fierce firefight twelve *Crusaders* were put out of action, but during its return to the assembly area the *kampfgruppe* was hit by *RAF* bombers that caused damage to one Mk III. Also on this day *Olt* Danz, the commander of the *8th Company*, was reported as missing, along with his entire panzer crew. In the following statement by Wilhelm Hagios, it sounds as if Danz was not the only one to be captured at that time:

"*On the 8th we were sent to the workshop for the new engine and we got it, after so many kilometers the engine was worn out. We were at the workshop on the 7th and 8th and then I got sick with diarrhea with blood, and just wanted to lay down, I was in sick-bay and couldn't eat and only received tea and crackers. Hausmann, the medical man said to me that if this condition would remain this way then they would send me back to Germany, but I got better and went back to my combat squadron. There was not much going on during the summer, [Oberst] Teege was for a short while in the PoW cage, I don't know if it was the New Zealanders who surprised and captured them, but I was not there.*"[74]

The Regiment continued to recover itself, and was not deployed forward over the next couple of days. The time was put to good use for resting and improving the readiness of the panzers. On the 9th, the New Zealanders, in an attempt to reconsolidate their forces, abandoned the brigade box that was located at Qaret el Abd, and from which some of the most recent attacks had originated from. The *21st Panzer* and *Littorio* Divisions were ordered to occupy the abandoned positions that commanded much of the surrounding area. The *90th Light* was also brought forward to the south in support of the next move on the *Kaponga Box*. On the morning of 10 July, the *9th Australian* (Morshead) and *1st South African* (Pienaar) *Divisions* launched an attack out of the *Alamein Box* along the Via Balbia against the Italian *Sabratha* and *Trento* Divisions, which broke and ran under the weight of a terrific bombardment. The *9th Australian Division* was a fresh division that had just arrived and was eager to get into the fight after easy duty in Syria. The division made

its way towards Tel el Eisa, while the South Africans drove towards Tel el Makh Khad. Both units succeeded in not only capturing the positions and shattering the *Sabratha* Division, but they also disrupted Rommel's planned assault against the New Zealanders in the south and captured his very best radio intercept unit, the *621st Radio Intercept Company*. If it had not been for the *Panzerarmee* staff and some elements of the *164th Light Division*, just then making its way forward, the entire *Panzerarmee* headquarters would have been overrun and captured, not to mention that the Via Balbia would have been opened, but the entire northern sector of the *Panzerarmee* was in jeopardy.[75] Rommel, who had just sent the *D.A.K. Aufklärungs Gruppe* eastward in an attempt to look for a way around the *Eighth Army* lines, heard the bombardment going in and immediately moved north to investigate. He also alerted the *15th Panzer Division* for a move to the north in order to help seal off the breakthrough. After this attack, the Italian *X Corps* was assigned the mission of occupying this sector. On the 11th, six Mk IIIs and one Mk IV came forward with the supply trains and brought the number of operational panzers to nineteen. The Australians renewed their attacks along the Via Balbia and caused numerous problems for the *Trieste* Division before the *D.A.K.* artillery finally halted them. It was now apparent that the Italians could no longer be relied on to hold their positions in the line. On the 12th, the Australians seemed to be consolidating their positions in the north around Tel el Eisa, and so Rommel ordered the *21st Panzer* be brought forward to bolster the line. Also on that day, *Olt* Otto Stiefelmayer became the fifth member of the Regiment to be awarded the Knight's Cross for his leadership and bravery while commander of the *4th Company* during the previous months' combat.[76] Looking back on the intense combat that had taken place at this point, Gotthilf Haidt had this reflection:

"*My memories are sometimes about those dead soldiers, I had not always seen how they were killed but we saw many of those killed in the panzers which we towed back. I didn't know much of what [had] happened around them and did not like to think about it.*"[77]

Over the next couple of days, the Regiment was able to catch its breath; as it rested just to the west of Ruweisat Ridge, the Regiment had the responsibility of holding the line and being prepared to parry any thrusts by the *Eighth Army*. The Regiment would not be deployed again until the 14th. In the meantime, the number of operational panzers were consolidated and divided up into two combat groups. One group was lead by *Hptm* Kümmel and the other by *Hptm* Wahl. Those two combat groups were subordinated to the Italian *Brecia* and *Pavia* Divisions to act as "corsets," and reinforce and stiffen the Italians, who always seemed to fight better when German units were close at hand. That statement, however, was to be quickly put to the test. On the night of the 14/15th, the *4th* and *5th New Zealand Infantry Brigades* and *5th Indian Brigade*, which had been reorganizing to the rear of Ruweisat Ridge, attacked those two Italian divisions. The aim of the attack was to secure the western end of the ridge and make their way to Deir el Shein, where they could hit those *Panzerarmee* forces assembled and ease the pressure on the battle taking place to the north at Tel el Eisa. The New Zealanders and Indians pushed forward and were able to quickly overwhelm the *Pavia* and *Brescia* Divisions. Unfortunately, in the darkness the attacking forces bypassed a lager of twenty panzers belonging to *Panzer Regiment 8* and failed to clear a number of German infantry positions that suddenly came to life at daybreak.[78] The combat groups were able to quickly deploy and counterattack the New Zealanders and Indians and push them back. The fighting that took place was done so in the swirling sands at close range, which made it almost impossible to recognize friend from foe. During the attack the panzer of *Hptm* Wahl received a number of direct hits, and one round struck the turret, which wounded Wahl—his fifth—while a second round hit the running gear and damaged the track. While attempting to escape from the stricken panzer, Wahl, *Olt* Hess, the *richtschütze*, and radio operator were taken prisoner by the accompanying infantry. The only member of the crew that was able to make good an escape was the driver, who was able to slip away in the growing darkness. Another notable loss was that of Lt Bühler, who was mortally wounded in the fighting.[79] The capture of Wahl was a great loss to the Regiment, and especially the II./*Abteilung*; in recognition of his long and successful service Wahl was later promoted to the rank of *Major* while in a prisoner of war camp in the U.S. *Oberstlt* Teege had also been wounded the day prior during an air attack by *Hurricane* fighters and was brought to the main dressing station with a high fever. The *RAF Hurricanes*, equipped with 40mm cannons, went after single panzers and scored hits on numerous panzers, and even managed to destroy the last remaining Mk II, killing or mortally wounding the entire three-man crew. A counterattack was launched later that afternoon by additional elements of the *D.A.K.* and struck the left flank *4th New Zealand Brigade* and overran it. What is most remarkable is that throughout the day British armored forces from the British *1st Armored Division* were in the vicinity of the ridge, but they either failed to support the infantry or arrived far too late to influence events taking place. The New Zealanders lost between 12-1500 men, many of which became prisoners, while the *D.A.K.* lost a few hundred men, and the Italians suffered losses estimated to be at 2,000.[80]

On the morning of 16 July, as the Italian units again took up their positions supported by the *D.A.K.*, Hans Kümmel reformed his *kampfgruppe*, which now consisted of some fourteen panzers. No major actions took place that day, as each side was busy digging in and reinforcing their positions. The *kampfgruppe*, however, found not a moment's peace, as on the 17th Australian forces struck the Italian *Trieste* and *Trento Divisions* in the north, piercing their lines and requiring the assistance of the few remaining panzers to seal off the penetration. The panzers were ordered north, where they launched a counterattack on the armored forces that were supporting the Australians in their attack. In the fighting that soon followed the panzer crews claimed nine *Crusaders* and twelve *Bren* gun carriers destroyed, but sustained a number of casualties themselves, one of which was *Uffz* Hermann Eckardt, a gunner in the *4th Company*. His panzer was hit by a high explosive round that virtually destroyed the panzer, but since the crew had not expected heavy resistance, Eckardt had left his gunner's hatch partially open, and was able to escape the burning panzer along with the rest of the crew. Eckardt suffered minor burns to his face, but the others were not as fortunate, as the loader and driver were severely burned. Some time later in the *Soldatenheim*, he remembered meeting up with the driver, whose burns no longer allowed him to turn his head to the side. With the assistance of *Panzerjäger Abteilung 33* and *I./Schützen Regiment 115* the breakthrough was finally contained, but not before the Italians had fled further to the west; they did not return until the morning of the 19th. After the fighting had ended, *Oberstlt* Teege was transferred from the main dressing station to the Lazarett, where he would remain for the next couple of months recuperating from his wounds.

Over the next three days the Regiment's *kampfgruppe* remained idle in an assembly area located just to the rear of some of the defending Italian units between Miteiriya Ridge and Deir el Shein. By placing the Regiment in this position it was able to support *Panzerarmee* forces in both the north and center. During the night of 21/22 July, the forward lines of the *D.A.K.* began to receive heavy concentrations of artillery fire; in the past the firing of heavy artillery bombardments normally signaled the beginning of some type of offensive maneuver. This was again the case, as the Regiment soon received an order to immediately relocate itself behind the forward positions of the *15th Panzer Division*, which were south of the *21st Panzer* and Ruweisat Ridge. By 0300hrs, the entire *D.A.K.* front was under attack by the *161st Indian Motor Brigade* on the northern side of Ruweisat Ridge and the *6th New Zealand Brigade* coming up from the south of the ridge. Those infantry forces were supported by the newly arrived *23rd Armored Brigade*.[81] Like the previous battle of the 15/16th, the *Eighth Army* attack went well in the early morning darkness, but then went bad as the sun began to rise. New Zealand and Indian infantry made good progress through the various minefields, but the supporting anti-tank guns and tanks failed to reach them. During the Regiment's march to the south, the small *kampfgruppe* under Hans Kümmel stumbled across one of these unidentified formations, which it was just able to spot in the early morning light. This formation was equipped with an estimated thirty tanks, twelve self-propelled guns, and numerous Bren gun carriers, and was most likely a portion of the *6th New Zealand Brigade* and *23rd Armored Brigade*, which was moving forward to support the infantry that had progressed to the El Mireir Depression. As the two sides began to size each other up the *kampfgruppe* began receiving harassing fire from British guns. Kümmel, steady as ever, ordered his panzer commanders to hold their fire and allow the British tanks to drive towards them until they came into range at about 300m. Once the British tanks reached that position the panzers opened up on them. The British tank commander initially reacted to the German fire by sending some ten *Valentine* tanks towards the *kampfgruppe*, while the remaining tanks in the formation continued to advance further to the west. With the *Valentines* holding the German panzers in place, the second element swung around the *kampfgruppe* in an attempt to outflank it. Kümmel quickly moved with two of his Mk III Specials forward to interdict the second group, while the remaining fifteen panzers remained in position in order to deal with the main body. The panzer crews fought with maximum effort, and by mid-day had scored hits on some twenty-three tanks, nine self-propelled guns, and twenty-one *Bren* gun carriers. The Regiment itself lost two Mk IIIs, three *unteroffiziers* killed, and eight *unteroffiziers* and six men wounded.[82] After the fighting, Kümmel ordered his *kampfgruppe* into the depression and began to secure the position for the night. In most of the panzers the ammunition racks were down to their last few rounds, and the gas tanks were down to less than half full, so the supply trains were called for. The panzer crews were totally exhausted, and were in urgent need of some rest and relaxation. However, there was to be no time for rest, because the British were not through with the panzers, and again began attacking just to the north of the depression on 22 July. The panzers were unable to launch a counterattack because of the shortage of ammunition. The depression came under artillery fire that caused some unrest, but fortunately caused no damage to the panzers and crews. After some fifteen hours the enemy artillery fire was finally silenced when elements of *Panzerjäger Abteilung 33*, *Kradschützen Battalion 15*, and four captured 25-Pounder guns came up on the left near the *kampfgruppe's* position and forced the British to withdraw. The situation was similar in the north, where the *21st Panzer Division* was able to handle the Indian infantry and tanks. That evening the *XIII* and *XXX Corps*, having totally exhausted themselves, halted all movement west, broke off their attacks, and began moving back to the east behind Ruweisat Ridge. The *23rd Armored Brigade* lost a total of eighty-seven tanks in the day's fighting. For the *D.A.K.*, it also was totally exhausted and had stretched itself to the end of its endurance, and only through an all out effort had it been able to deflect the British stroke. For the Regiment, it returned during the night of 23/24 July to its assembly area, located some twelve kilometers southwest of El Alamein, near the Rahman Track. The battlefield remained quiet for the next few days until the Australians launched another attack in the north on Miteiriya Ridge. Those attacks were again poorly coordinated, and did little to threaten the northern sector before the *D.A.K.* was able to halt them.

With the absence of a regimental commander, *Oberstlt* Werner Mildebrath from *Panzer Regiment 5* was assigned to the Regiment as its temporary commander until Willi Teege was well enough to return to duty. Hans Kümmel, despite his wounds, remained in command of the I./*Abteilung*, and *Hptm* Zügener had command of the II./*Abteilung*, with the heavy 8th Company being reformed under the command of *Olt* Heinrich. On 27 July, the Regiment received nineteen of the new long barreled Mk III Ausf Ls and seven of the new Mk IVF2, or "Specials," as they were more commonly referred to.[83] This brought the operational panzer strength of the Regiment to sixty-eight panzers. On 31 July, the Regiment received a few more replacement panzers from the workshop and from Tripoli; however, many of the new Mk IIIs and IVs which were available at that time in Germany and Italy remained on the docks. The original panzer Mk IIIs and Mk IVs that had arrived with the Regiment and had spent the past fifteen months in constant combat were totally worn out, and in dire need of replacement. The combination of time, mileage, combat operations, and the harsh desert conditions had severely worn out and caused more damage to the panzers than the enemy ever hoped to. But until those new panzers reached the Regiment, they would have to make do with those panzers that already had over 2,000km of hard desert behind them. The *Royal Navy* and *RAF*, which were based out of Malta, Alexandria, and Cairo, dominated the Mediterranean, and were causing serious losses to Axis ship convoys attempting to reach Africa. The Italian navy, which was constantly getting hammered, was not in a position to ship and protect the large convoys crossing the Mediterranean, although during the summer of 1942 an odd convoy or two was able to reach Tripoli or Benghazi unscathed and deposit what supplies it could. The failure to knockout *Royal Navy* and *RAF* forces on Malta was to become a serious problem now and in the months ahead. During July and August, meetings and conferences were held, and promises were made, but in the end almost nothing got through to the men in Africa, and those that did were not arriving in sufficient quantities to sustain them. In spite of the fact that few ships were getting through, Hitler ordered that preparations continue for an attack towards Alexandria, Cairo, and the Suez Canal. In comparison, the *Eighth Army* was receiving a steady flow of men and equipment through large convoys that sailed a forty-five day journey around the Cape of Good Hope to Alexandria and Cairo. During the summer of 1942, the *Eighth Army* was augmented with the 44th (Home Counties) and 51st (Highland) Infantry Divisions in addition to the 8th and 10th Armored Divisions.[84] For Rommel, the problem of logistics once again caused him significant grief, and weighed heavily on his mind for the conduct of this offensive. His staff drew up plans that called for the landing of some 30,000 tons, but by late August the *Panzerarmee* had received only about 6,000 tons. To make matters worse, the vast amount of supplies captured during the summer battles and in the warehouses in Tobruk were now almost gone. The *D.A.K.*, which for months now had been driving and living on about eighty percent captured British goods and equipment, were now finding themselves without replacement trucks, ammunition, food, and weapons, and to make matters worse still, the supplies had to be brought up from great distances from Tobruk, Benghazi, and Tripoli. These trips caused the further consumption of fuel and supplies, and were constantly hampered by the *RAF*, which subjected the ports and convoys to attack and disrupted the flow of supplies to Rommel's troops. Haidt remembers those attacks:

"Air attacks were plentiful, a lot there was. I myself was [normally] with a vehicle and personally I was not involved [never attacked], either I was too quick or too slow. But on average there were many air attacks. Our team, we were in the harbor of Tobruk, in there we visited harbor, in the evening came aircraft attack, but we were out of this [bombing] area, *the panzers were marched away. One of our drivers got the car, got the bag in the car and went away and it was our luck and destiny as we drove away before the attack."*[85]

The *Panzerarmee* reported its panzer losses for the period 26 May to 20 July as twenty-five Mk IIs, 161 Mk IIIs, fourteen Mk III Sp, twenty-nine Mk IVs, two Mk IV Sp, and two Befehls panzers. Of these 233 panzers, all of them were so burned out and destroyed that none of them could be repaired. The *D.A.K.* claimed the following: 1388 tanks, 249 armored cars, and 269 carriers destroyed.[86] But the *Afrika Korps* veterans suffered and made due with what they had on hand, and occasionally they were treated to a special load of supplies, or just had a bit of good luck, as the next account describes:

"We cooked pancakes in the desert, first we had only salt water until those on top [higher up] sent us the right provisioning. The support from Luftwaffe was of course very good, we had the famous fighter pilot, Marseille; he became the sponsor or godfather of our company. I baked a lot of pancakes and he always got us flour from the bakery. He was once stuck in the desert with his car in the sand, and we came along with our panzer and helped him and so began our friendship."[87]

Horst Sonnenkalb describes how life in the desert was at this time in this humorous account;

"On the following day was the morning parade, arrival in the full uniform. Then took place technical service. The Schirrmeister [Motor Sergeant] asked me as the driver of the Chief's panzer, if I need anyone to help me out. Spontaneously I answered: 'The Fähnrich [officer cadet] can help me'. This one was subordinated to me, and didn't dare to argue. In the meantime he recognized that he had to do things for me, an Unteroffizier. In retrospect he must have recognized, that the day before had he found the wrong man to carry his luggage. The technical service began, I explained to him what and how things needed to be done. He appeared to be not so bad at all. But during the exchange of oil and relief of the transmission oil his face mainly got dirty with old oil. The good advice was the value of gold here. We had almost no water. Not enough even to drink, needless to say for washing. I wiped him as good as it went with the cleaning wool, than cleaned his face with a cleaning cloth soaked in gasoline. Finally as not all of it came off his face, I took an old cleaning cloth, and soaked it in a little water and tried to clean his face. Now he looked like an Indian, but he had no African tan on his pale face because he had just come from Germany. The officer cadet was taken care of. He probably would never forget this. He drove in our 2nd Company in two or three panzer attacks, but soon reported himself from the company because of sickness with diarrhea, and went to the field hospital. That was a good timing [on his part]. The hospital needed to free up space, and as I learned later he was sent in a hurry with the hospital ship to Greece. That happened quite seldom, but was possible."[88]

On 13 August, Winston Churchill and his Chief of the General Staff, *General* Sir Alan Brooke, flew to Egypt to once again clean house of the Middle East Command. *General* Sir Harold Alexander was named the new *Commander in Chief Middle East Forces*, replacing *General* Auchinleck, and *Lieutenant General* W.H.E. "Strafer" Gott was named as the new *Eighth Army* commander, but before he could assume command he was shot down in an unescorted aircraft, and *Lieutenant General* Bernard L. Montgomery was named to the *Eighth Army* post.[89] On the 15th, this new command team took over operations and began to issue its first orders.

One of Alexander's first orders to Montgomery was plain and simple; he and his *Eighth Army* were to destroy the Axis forces in Africa. In turn Montgomery issued his uncompromising first message, stating;

"Here we will stand and fight; there will be no further withdrawal. I have ordered that all plans and dealing with further withdrawal are to be burnt, and at once. We will stand and fight here. If we can't stay here alive, then let us stay here dead."[90]

Almost immediately Montgomery made his presence felt throughout the *Eighth Army*, which over the previous years had seemed to favor and admire Rommel more than many of its own commanders. One major undertaking was the co-locating of the *Eighth Army* headquarters with that of the newly designated *Desert Air Force* (DAF), so as to foster closer cooperation between the two forces, something that had definitely been lacking in the past. Another move was the forming of an armored corps behind the line from various uncommitted formations. Both moves would eventually have severe consequences on the *Panzerarmee*. Also at that time the *Eighth Army* now had in its possession over 900 tanks, an increase of over one hundred and twenty-five from the previous year. At that time, the best tank the British possessed was the American made Grant, which had just recently appeared on the battlefield during the Gazala and Tobruk battles. The *Eighth Army* was equipped with more than 160 of these tanks, which in addition to coaxial machine guns had a revolving turret that housed a 37mm gun and a side mounted 75mm gun. With this 75mm gun the British had a tank that was truly able to match the German Mk IIIs and IVs. The other tanks that the British possessed consisted of *Valentine*, *Stuart* or *Honey*, and *Crusader* tanks, but most of these tanks had only the 2-Pounder main gun, which could not effectively deal with the Mk IIIs and IVs, at least until the Valentines and Crusaders could be up-gunned with the 6-Pounder gun. In a short time the *Eighth Army* would soon have the first American made Sherman tanks that also mounted a 75mm gun, but housed in a revolving turret; unfortunately, none of the Shermans would be present during the battle. By the middle of August there were approximately 200 gun-armed panzers with the *D.A.K.*'s *15th* and *21st Panzer Divisions*. Approximately one half of these belonged to *Panzer Regiment 5*, while the other half belonged to *Panzer Regiment 8*.[91] It is important to point out that the number of operational panzers versus those actually capable of tank on tank engagements in the *D.A.K.* amounted to only about two-hundred. The reason for this was that at least thirty-five of these panzers were Mk IIs and command panzers that were armed with only the 20mm gun or machine guns, and which, like the Italian tanks, were no longer suitable for tank on tank actions. The main striking power came from the 160-170 Panzer Mk IIIs, of which seventy-four were later model Ausf Js and Ls with the long barreled 50mm gun. There were also thirty-five Mk IVs, of which twenty-six were the newer model F-2s armed with the long 75mm gun. Troop reinforcements, however, did arrive to the *Panzerarmee* in the form of the *164th Light Division* (Lungerhausen), a division which had been scheduled to take part in the capture of Malta. Another unit, a *Fallschirmjäger Brigade*, under the command of *Generalmajor* Bernhard Ramcke, also arrived after having assisted in the formation of the Italian *185th Folgore Parachute Division*. These light formations were, however, flown into Africa aboard *Ju-52* transports, while their equipment, heavy weapons, and vehicles were loaded onto ships for the sea voyage. In the end most of those ships were lost at sea, and the units became more of a burden than help, as other units were stripped of their vehicles in order to outfit these newcomers. The one element missing and most desperately needed was the addition of new panzer formations. The Regiment's former division, the *10th Panzer*, having just finished fighting in Russia, had been promised to Rommel,

but it would be hard to count on that division, since it was scheduled to arrive much too late to influence the campaign now ongoing in Africa. Rommel and his commanders had known of the British build-up, and knew it was just a matter of time before they had the men and equipment, trained and ready, to launch an offensive that would crush their weakened enemy. Rommel knew that it was now or never for his next move before his enemy was too strong to defeat, and so he prepared to launch his attack before the British could do the same to him. Alfred Toppe wrote of the situation facing the *Panzerarmee* that August:

"At the beginning of August, the strengths on both sides were about equal. Neither the British Eighth Army nor the German forces had any appreciable measure of superiority. Nonetheless, it was clear to Rommel that time was working against him and that as soon as the enemy had brought forward sufficient reinforcements, he would launch a powerful counteroffensive. Rommel, therefore, did everything possible to improve the German positions, with particular stress on the use of mines, including air bombs that were buried and prepared for electrical detonation. He even had what he called "mine gardens" laid in the outpost area and had all battalion command posts surrounded by minefields. In distributing the forces in the northern half of the defense line, which he considered the most endangered and which were in the zone of the Italian XXI Corps, he placed Italian battalions and battalions of the 164th Light African Division alternately. As soon as the supply situation permitted, Rommel intended to make another effort from the other end of the line to break through to Alexandria. However, for the moment, this was not possible, especially because of the fuel situation. Toward the end of the month, sufficient supplies of fuel would at last be available, if a large tanker that had left Europe managed to reach Tobruk, It was on this hope that Rommel-on the night of 30-31 August, supported by the Italian Supreme Command and by Kesselring-based his plan to break through the southern part of the front (which was held by weaker forces than the rest of the British line) and advance by way of Alam el Halfa to Alexandria."[92]

In early August the Regiment began to receive an influx of replacement personnel from Böblingen, which were flown into the airfields at Tobruk and Derna aboard *Ju-52* transports. Amongst those replacements were the following: *Leutnants* Förster, Golinski, Halverscheidt, Hubbuch, Marquardt, Wiegels, and Woldsen. Lt Hubbuch was again assigned to the *8th Company*, which he had previously belonged to as an *Unteroffizer* before leaving for officers training. Despite the difficulties, supplies continued to trickle forward, and with them were a few items to help improve morale. Items like cigarettes, newspapers, journals, and the occasional board or card game were passed out to the men. Horst Sonnenkalb was allowed time out for a short break as he explains:

"After so many actions and the many times under the enemy fire, my company commander sent me for a few days to the supply lines, so that I could really relax. But what did our company Spiess, [1st SGT] Hauptfeldwebel Weidlich do? He organized me to be on guard duty. That was the top, so much for a good thing. With grinding teeth I followed his order. After few days I returned to my panzer crew, my commander asked me if I had a good rest. I reported what happened to me. Two weeks later Hauptfeldwebel Weidlich came to the company combat section. On his way he also lost the much desired postal bag with letters from Germany. Now the fat's in the fire! I had not ever seen my company commander and for that matter my panzer commander that mad before."[93]

During the first weeks of August, the Regiment participated in a number of radio and combat exercises; the heat was almost unbearable,

Chapter 10: Gazala and Tobruk, May-August 1942

and the crews sweated in temperatures that reached 130F/56C, but it was important that the training be conducted to properly integrate the replacements that came in over the summer to make good the losses of the *Gazala Battles*. Supplies, unlike personnel that could be flown in, were again beginning to go down as the *Royal Navy* and *RAF* began to take a toll on the *Panzerarmee* lifeline. The fuel situation that always seemed to plague Rommel was not present in enough quantity to allow the *Panzerarmee* to train and be operationally ready to meet any *Eighth Army* attacks. On the 25th, the Regiment was relocated to an area south of Wadi Kalakh, which lay just north of the Qattara Depression about 50km from the coast.

Panzer Regiment 8 Chain of Command as of 31 August 1942[94]

Regiment Commander	Oberstlt Mildebrath
Regt Adj	Hptm Schefold
Nachr Offz	Olt Baumann
Ord Offz	Lt Blidschuhn
StKp	Lt von Brunn
I./Abteilung Commander	Hptm Kümmel
Abtl Adj	Olt Thurow
Nachr Offz	Ofumstr Strack
Ord Offz	Lt Paschy
Zahl Mstr	OZmstr Hadler
StKp	Olt Bock
1st Company	Lt Keil
2nd Company	Olt Schellhaus
3rd Company	Olt Prion
4th Company	Olt Stiefelmayer
II./Abteilung Commander	Hptm Zügener
Abtl Adj	Lt Bastigkeit
Nachr Offz	OFumstr Bulla
Ord Offz	Lt Hubbuch
Zahl Mstr	OZmstr Gisy
StKp	Lt Bastigkeit
5th Company	Hptm Siemens
Zug Cdr	Lt Heckel
6th Company	Olt Decker
Zug Cdr	Olt Euen
7th Company	Olt Ritter
Zug Cdr	Olt Schulz
8th Company	Olt Heinrich

The Regimental had the following officers in various technical positions: Surgeons—*StArzt* Becker, *StArzt* Hochstetter, *OArzt* Estor, *OArzt* Krüger, and *UArzt* Maisch. Engineering: Major Schnell, *Hptm* Hauska, and *OInsp* Lampe.

11

The Battle of Alam Halfa
August-September 1942

During the month of August, Rommel was now feeling the pressure from Hitler, Mussolini, and their various commanders and staffs into continuing the drive to the Nile Delta, and finally defeating the British in North Africa. There is no doubt Rommel also wanted to keep the drive going, but he knew his men and machines were too worn out to do so. The British were also in a similar state, but unlike the Germans, they were receiving fresh reinforcements and materiel, which Rommel was now in desperate need of. Rommel's *Ic* (Intelligence officer), *Oberstlt* F.W. von Mellenthin, wrote:

"The general staff of the Panzerarmee did not believe that we could break through to the Nile, and before the attack was launched we pointed out to Rommel that in armored strength the British had a superiority of 3:1, and in air power of 5:1. .....and there could be no disputing our argument that we had insufficient gasoline for a major battle."[1]

Rommel had wanted to begin his attack against the *Eighth Army* in and around the El Alamein position near the end of August, where he hoped to take advantage of the full moon and lull in battle before the British could launch their own attack, which was expected soon. The greatest concern for Rommel was once again that of logistics; this problem had plagued the Germans since they had first set foot in Africa, and was the catalyst of all offensive and defensive operations. Of those supplies, fuel was the most critical item needed to survive in the desert, for without it there could be no movement, and it was a battle of movement that Rommel excelled at. For launching the attack, the *Panzerarmee* was promised an abundance of material from fuel and food to panzers and guns, but as the date of attack approached, very few of those items had arrived, and what little fuel that did arrive was quickly consumed during the movement to the front. *Oberst* Fritz Bayerlein, at that time the *D.A.K.* Chief of Staff, wrote in his CGSC report:

"He [Rommel] made this contingent upon his receiving several thousand cubic meters of gasoline by water or by air. Now or never, it was Rommel's belief that he could once more attempt the drive to the Delta. In conversations on 27 August, Marshals Kesselring and Cavallero guaranteed him that he would receive 6,000 tons of gasoline, of which 1,000 would come by air. Rommel stated, 'The battle is dependent upon the prompt delivery of this gasoline.' Cavallero answered, 'You can begin the battle now, Herr Field Marshall, the gasoline is already under way.'"[2]

Rommel's plan of attack called for the Italian *X* and *XXI Infantry Corps*, augmented by the newly arrived *164th Light Division* and *Ramcke Brigade* to launch a series of diversionary attacks from the area around Tel el Eisa, in the north, to the Bab el Qattara. It was hoped that those attacks would hold the bulk of the *Eighth Army* in their positions as an armored thrust by the *D.A.K.* and Italian *XX Motorized Corps* struck to the south between the Deir el Munassib and Qaret el Himeimat, along the northern edge of the Qattara Depression. After the breakthrough by the panzer elements had been achieved, the *D.A.K.* would strike east, past the eastern side of Alam Halfa Ridge (located about 10 miles from the coast), and then drive north, bagging or scattering the *Eighth Army's XXX* and *XIII Corps*, where they could then be defeated in turn. Once the *Eighth Army* had been defeated at Alam Halfa, troops from the *21st Panzer Division* were to be sent directly on towards Alexandria, while the *15th Panzer* and *90th Light Divisions* moved on towards Cairo and the Suez Canal.[3] Trusting in the promises made by the Italian *Commando Supremo* to deliver him enough fuel and supplies to support this operation, Rommel set a tentative start date for 30 August, but unknown to him, the British, through "Ultra" intercepts, had been alerted to his plans and requests, and the *Royal Navy* and *RAF* were able to interdict many of the convoys being sent to Africa. In fact, of the thirty ships, fourteen barges, and six supply submarines that left Italy in August, the *Royal Navy* and *RAF* sunk seven of the largest ships, with the loss of 1,660 tons of ammunition, 2,120 tons of general supplies, 43 guns, 367 assorted vehicles, and most critical 2,700 tons of fuel and oil; although 12,800 tons of fuel did arrive, it was hardly enough to sustain the *Panzerarmee*.[4] Additionally, Allied bombers began attacking the assembly areas of the combat formations every night during the last week of August. The Regiment suffered no losses in these attacks, because most of the men and panzers were well dispersed and dug in. By the end of August the promised supplies of munitions and fuel had not yet arrived, and the period of full moon, which was absolutely necessary for the execution of the operation, was already waning, and further delays would have meant the complete abandonment of the offensive plans. On the eve of the attack, Axis forces were arranged as follows: the Italian *XXI Corps* was positioned in the north from the Tel el Eisa south with the *Trento*, *Bologna*, and *Brescia* Divisions. The *164th Light Division* and the *Ramcke Brigade* were then split up and moved between the Italians, in order to help secure key pieces of terrain and provide support and strengthen the Italian lines. The Italian *X Corps* was positioned further south, and was to remain ready for defensive operations. The *90th Light*

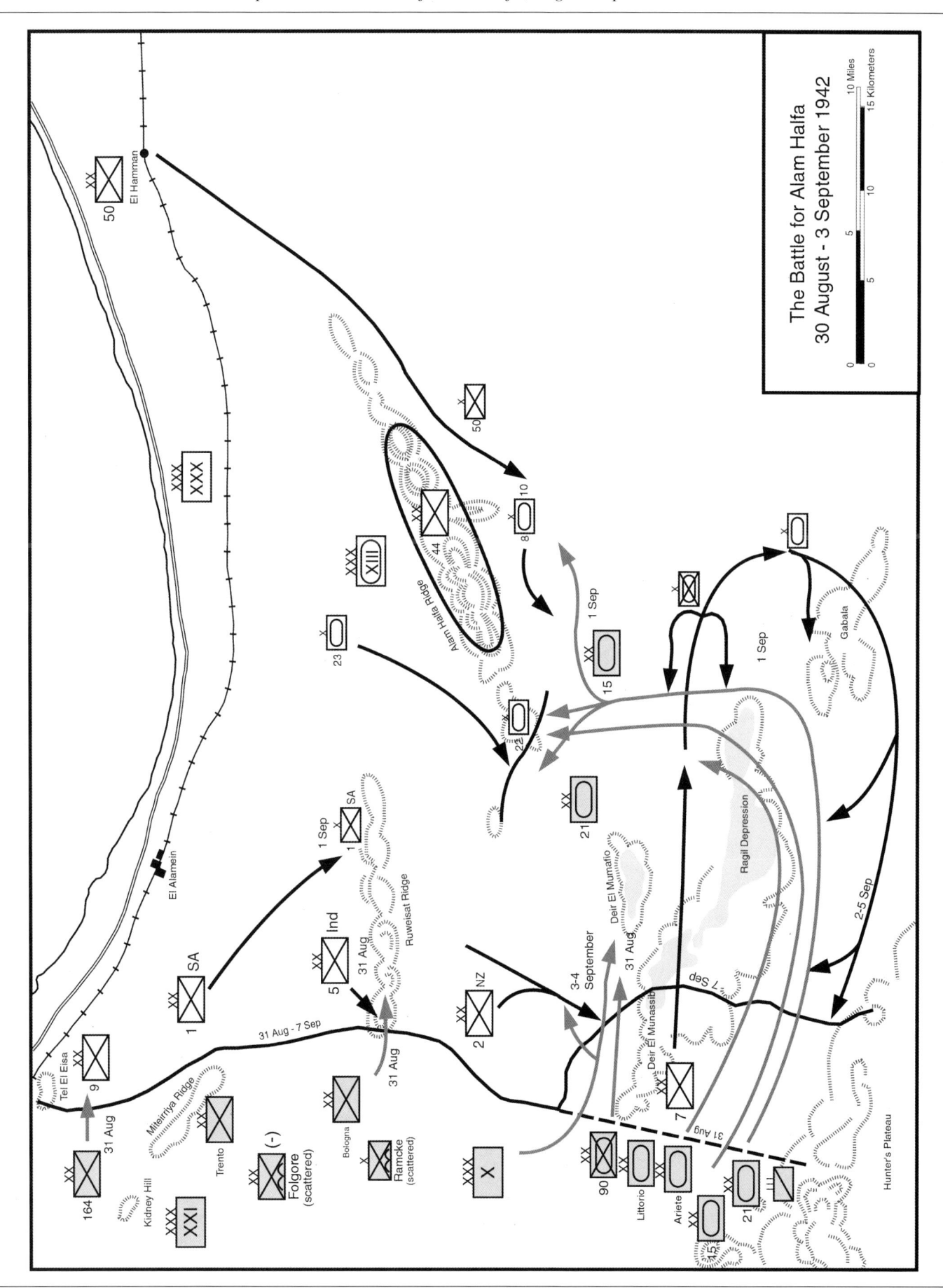

Chapter 11: The Battle of Alam Halfa, August-September 1942

Division (Kleemann) was located north of the Djebel Kalakh, and was responsible for holding the line there and securing the left flank of the offensive groups in order to secure against any British counterattacks. The *90th Light* was followed by the Italian *XX Motorized Corps* (de Stefanis), consisting of the *Ariete*, *Littorio*, and *Trieste* Divisions. The main striking power of the *Panzerarmee* lay in the *D.A.K.*, with the *21st* (Bismarck) and *15th* (Vaerst) *Panzer Divisions*. Finally, there was the newly arrived Italian *Folgore* Parachute Division and the *D.A.K. Aufklärungs Gruppe*, consisting of the *3rd* and *33rd Aufklärungs Abteilung*. These last formations skirted on the El Taqa plateau, which bordered the Qattara Depression.[5] Looking at the British situation, from the north to south along the defensive line were the divisions of the *XXX Corps* (Leese), with the *9th Australian* (Morshead), *1st South African* (Pienaar), and elements of the *5th Indian* and *2nd New Zealand* (Freyberg) Divisions with the *7th Armored Division* (Renton) in the very south. Montgomery appreciated that Alam Halfa Ridge was the cornerstone of the defensive position, and because of this he ordered forward the newly arrived *44th (Home Counties) Division* (Hughes) to occupy the high ground itself.[6] Within the perimeter of the division's defenses there would be the divisional artillery and other corps artillery units. Also, there was every effort being made to get forward the *10th Armored Division* (Gatehouse), but the division's two armored brigades had been badly mauled during the summer battles, and only the *8th Armored Brigade* (Custance) had been re-equipped. The headquarters of the *10th Armored* did manage to arrive in the Alam Halfa area on the 27th, and the *22nd Armored Brigade* (Roberts) was put under its command.[7] At that time each armored regiment consisted of two squadrons of twelve *Grant* tanks, and one light squadron of either *Crusader* or *Stuart* tanks, with the exception of the *County of London Yeomanry* (CLY), which had only one *Grant* squadron of fifteen tanks.[8]

Advance parties from the *8th Armored Brigade* arrived on the 29th, but the main body did not arrive until the 30th. The *22nd Armored Brigade* was at that time an independent armored brigade that operated directly under *XIII Corps* (Horrocks) command, and therefore it was ordered to select and to prepare static defensive positions on the southern and eastern slopes of Alam Halfa Ridge. The other armored formations left in the *Eighth Army* were the *23rd Armored Brigade* (Richards), which consisted of a weak brigade of *Valentine* tanks, and the *4th Light Armored Brigade* (Roddick), which was outfitted with a regiment of *Stuart* or *Honey* tanks, two regiments of armored cars, a motorized infantry battalion, and one artillery regiment. At the very southern end of the line, the *7th Armored Division*, which consisted of the *7th Motorized Brigade* and *4th Armored Brigade*, held the line behind the minefields from the left flank of the *2nd New Zealand Division* to the southern edge of Deir el Munassib, with the *7th Motorized Brigade* securing the remainder of the minefield and the open flank as far back as Qaret el Himeimat. Rommel's plan called for strict security measures to be maintained by all panzer and motorized elements as they moved into their assembly areas north and south of the Djebel Kalakh. It was hoped that by swapping out the service and supply echelons with those of the combat echelons that the British would not become keen to the movement of the offensive elements of the *Panzerarmee*. Of the combat echelons, the panzer elements were to be moved by a series of night marches to their respective line of departure over a period of four days and nights. The panzers were under strict orders to move only at night, and with the coming of daylight they were to move into well camouflaged positions in order to avoid detection by the *DAF*. The panzers were to be followed by the motorized elements on the final night of preparation. By the morning of the 30th, the Regimental *Stabs* was a flurry of activity, as various Regiment, *Abteilung*, and Company staff officers hurried about in an attempt to finalize the orders and plans. Shortly before midday the company adjutants were able to return to their companies carrying those orders and instructions to issue to their respective company. The instruction of the mission, enemy situation, boundary lines, movement timetables, fire plans, code words, and frequencies were given to the company and *zug* leaders. There was the announcement of the line of departure, which was to be occupied after conducting one final night march that was scheduled to begin that evening of 30/31 August. The plans had been drawn up in the hope that this new offensive would lead the *Panzerarmee* east on a 50km deep penetration into the rear of the British positions. Just prior to the battle all of the men in each company were read the following order from Rommel:

"Panzerarmee Afrika
A.-Gef.-Stand, 30.8.1942
Der Oberbefehlshaber
Army Day Order
Soldiers! Today the Army reinforced with new divisions newly begins the attack for ultimate elimination of the enemy. I expect that each soldier of my Army will give the very last in these deciding days!
Der Oberbefehlshaber
gez. Rommel, Generalfeldmarschall"[9]

At 1930hrs the crews were ordered to begin removing their camouflage nets that covered each of the panzers, and to drive their panzers out of the protective dug-outs from where they would begin to move towards their respective company and *abteilung* assembly areas. Once having assembled, the companies were to then begin moving into the line of departure, where the panzers companies would begin to line up in rows of two. The Regiment reported a panzer strength of 110 on 30 August 1942; this number included two Befehls, fifteen Mk IIs, forty-three Mk IIIs, thirty-four Mk III Sp, three Mk IVs, and thirteen Mk IV Sp.[10] At 2145hrs the Regiment began to form itself for the attack. In the lead was the I./*Abteilung* and Regimental *Stabs*, closely followed by II./*Abteilung*. As the Regiment began to move off it did so as the last element of the *15th Panzer Division*. This was a reversal of normal operating procedures, in which usually the panzer led the attack, but this time it was those other divisional elements that would clear the minefield lanes and open gaps, through which the Regiment would then charge through. The route was posted with light canisters—empty canisters filled with a gas and sand mixture—to assist the formations with finding their way forward to their jump off positions. A combat report from the II./*Abteilung* dated 31 Aug 42 reads:

"After the short assembly of the Regiment in the area of Wadi Kalakh the night march progresses constantly to the east but slows down due to the extraordinary darkness of the night and extremely strong dust development. The course of the march is slightly marked by the light canisters. The Regiment drives at the end of the division. After a march stop in the departure point of the 164th Light Division in the area Quaret el Khadim the march was continued shortly before midnight and continues without significant disturbance by the enemy. The only active aircraft action is in the sector of the units positioned further north for the breakthrough. The friendly march starts to be bothered in the morning dawn by the bombing attacks and partially heavy artillery fire. By 0300hrs the night march of 20km is finished at the 164th, the panzers drive away from each other, air-filters are being cleaned. The division is restrained in front because of deep echelons of enemy minefields."[11]

During the march on the night of the 30/31st, the II./*Abteilung* suffered the following losses due to mechanical breakdown: two Mk IIIs, two Mk III Sp, one Mk IV, and one Mk IV Sp.[12] In the early gray dawn of 31 August, the bombers of the *DAF* attacked the Axis forward areas and began a bombing run on those formations positioned and assembling there. Wave after wave of heavy bomber formations dropped their loads of high explosives and added to the already brilliant display of lights, as the sky was intermittently filled with the glow of parachute flares and pyrotechnics as they began to rise up either to provide illumination or send a signal. In the bombing attack *General* Nehring, the *D.A.K.* commander, was severely wounded in the arm by a bomb fragment; Bismarck, the commanding general of the *21st Panzer*, was killed by a direct hit, and Kleemann, from the *90th Light*, was also wounded. Things did not look good for the German offensive, as Rommel, due to illness, was not immediately present, and now three of his key commanders had already been killed and wounded, and just as the battle was beginning! *Oberst* Fritz Bayerlein, the *D.A.K.* Chief of Staff, quickly assumed command of the *D.A.K.* and lead it forward. He wrote of the attack:

"During the night of 30/31 August we jumped off in the attack against the southern bastions of the British Alamein Front. Shortly after our troops had crossed the eastern limits of their own minefields and traversed No-Man's-Land, they ran into heretofore unknown British mine obstacles which were tenaciously defended. Under cover of heavy artillery fire and after several assaults, our pioneers and infantrymen succeeded partially in driving narrow passages through the British barricades. As a result of this, our losses were considerable and we lost much time since the mine fields were of considerable depth and had been additionally planted with a great number of booby traps."[13]

The *Luftwaffe* made an appearance over the battlefield in support of the ground forces; unfortunately, many of the bases that the *Stukas* and *Me-109s* were flying from were located a good distance from the actual frontlines, and therefore could not provide the proper amount of support required by the forces on the ground. By that time the British, who knew that the offensive was coming, had properly dug in, and had prepared both primary and alternate fighting positions, so that in the end the *Luftwaffe* air support that was provided turned out to be not that effective. As the leading elements moved off it did not take long before they were halted as a result of previously undiscovered minefields. By daybreak the most forward elements of the *D.A.K.* had only reached a point some 15-20km east of their own minefields. It had been Rommel's intention to drive some 50km to the east with his panzers during the first moonlit night, and to further press the attack northward at first light. The element of surprise upon which the entire plan was built had consequently been lost, and now the *D.A.K.* and its panzers were immobile, stuck in the minefields. At 0500hrs, the Regiment formed for the attack, with the I./*Abteilung* in the lead, followed by the Regimental *Stabs*, and finally the II./*Abteilung*. The plan at this point was to drive as the lead element of the division as it moved from the area north of Deir el Risw through the minefield alleys cleared by the division's pioneers and proceed east. At 0530hrs the Regiment moved to the head of the division, but as it attempted to do so it was quickly engaged by anti-tank guns in positions along the flanks. These guns more than likely belonged to those elements from the *4th Light* and *7th Motorized Brigades*, which were able to fire off a number of volleys before they made their way to the rear. As the II./*Abteilung* pulled into the line it was able to report that it had suffered no losses. Shortly after 0600hrs the Regiment began to fan out in its wedges as it began to move against the anti-tank guns, some of which were over 2,000m away. The British anti-tank guns, most of which were mobile, were able to keep their distance as the panzers attempted to close the distance and engage them. After driving through the minefields the II./*Abteilung* came up on the left next to I./*Abteilung*, which was facing towards the northeast, in order to slowly push forward in order to gain maneuver room for enlargement of the bridgehead and keep the British anti-tank guns and tanks at a safe distance. By 0730hrs the deployment to the east had begun, with the double files of the II./*Abteilung* behind the I./*Abteilung* to the place close to Samaket Gaballa. At 0830hrs the II./*Abteilung*, which had now assumed the lead, strayed into another minefield and was forced to swing more to the northeast because there were no other lanes cleared at that time.[14] The Regiment was now spread out from the northwest to the southeast. Orders were quickly issued by the Regiment that the attack to the east must be executed, and that the II./*Abteilung* was to move back to the left rear of the formation in order to provide protection along the flanks of the minefields. There were also reports of enemy tanks, which had been spotted off at a distance of 3,000 to 4,000m. By this time the *D.A.K.* was far behind the timetables set for it, and worse, the British commanders had clearly been able to determine by mid-morning that the Axis attacks launched in the north were just feints aimed at gaining nothing more than their attention. These attacks were not well executed, and the *XXX Corps'* infantry were able to absorb each of them with ease. Only the attacks near Ruweisat Ridge, located to the north, had been successful, but soon those too were halted, as the earlier gains were soon lost after the ridge was recaptured. In the south, where the panzer columns had penetrated along the southern minefields, there was little doubt that this was the main effort. The *4th Armored Brigade* had withdrawn east to Samaket Gaballa, but it was immediately unclear what the *7th Motor Brigade* was doing. Both of these brigades would continue to harass and report on the activities and progress of the *D.A.K.* by tagging along its flanks throughout the day and into the next. By 1030hrs, the soft sand and constant maneuvering had almost drained the fuel tanks, and the Regiment had to halt while the fuel trucks were brought forward; unfortunately, what they brought up was not enough to fill the gas tanks and keep the drive moving east. At around midday, the panzers had finally received enough fuel and ammunition to allow them to continue their drive, which they did at approximately 1245hrs. The panzers began their movement, first to the northwest, then north, and then to the northeast; all these changes in directions and detours were caused by the numerous minefields sown by the British. Shortly after moving though a large wadi, most likely the Rigel Depression, a short, long distance fight developed against British tanks, armored cars, and self propelled gun-carriages. *OFw* Spohn of the *5th Company*, commanding a Mk III Special, made a remarkable shot when he fired and was able to score a direct hit on a *Crusader* tank from a distance of approximately 2,000m.[15] After the loss of this *Crusader* the remaining tanks began to lose a bit of their nerve and withdrew off to the east and northeast. By 1300hrs, as the *abteilung* had begun to reassemble for their push east, a sandstorm began to develop that blew dust and sand towards the east and directly into the face of the British. With the aid of this sandstorm the attack by the *15th* and the *21st Panzer Divisions* recommenced, but because of the morning's delays the focus of the attack now shifted towards the western side of the Alam el Halfa ridge. Fritz Bayerlein wrote:

"After the Deutsches Afrika Korps had refueled and rearmed, which took considerable time, it assembled at 1300 hours. During an intense sandstorm, which was blowing from our backs into the face of the enemy, the attack of the 15th and the 21st Pz Divs got underway well in the beginning. Unfortunately, at this time the Italian armored divisions Ariete and Trieste were still held up by clearing lanes through mine fields and by the serial movement of their The units through the captured British defense system. For this reason they could only begin their attack by evening."[16]

With precious time having been lost that morning as the panzers attempted to pass through the minefields, and while the *DAF* kept those forces under heavy bombardment, the British gained precious time in which to deploy the *23rd Armored Brigade* southward in support of the *22nd Armored Brigade*. The latter brigade was now in position just to the southwest of Alam Halfa Ridge, and with these two armored formations poised along the left flank, the *D.A.K.* could ill afford to continue its drive eastward, and so it was ordered to turn northward to engage the British armor and destroy them prior to continuing the drive further north. The added delay in bringing forward fuel and ammunition now allowed the British the time necessary to concentrate and make ready their tanks for immediate combat actions. The *22nd Armored Brigade* had been deployed with its *1st RTR* on the right, the *CLY* in the center, and the *5th RTR* on the left; in reserve were the *Scots Greys*, which were kept about three kilometers to the rear. There were also a large number of anti-tank guns from the *133rd Rifle Brigade* in support near the *5th RTR*.17 The objectives for the *Panzerarmee* were as follows: Hill 132 (Alam Halfa Ridge) for the *D.A.K.* and Deir el Munassib for the *XX* Italian Corps and *90th Light*. By 1430hrs, the Regiment continued its advance in a fluid motion to the north while continuing the pursuit of British motorized units. The Regiment now had the mission to skirt around to the east of the heights and attempt to move towards the coast. After driving through the Wadi Deir el Râgil the leading panzers made contact with British tanks, armored cars, and self-propelled gun carriages, which engaged the panzers, but also kept well out of range. As the panzers rolled towards the ridgeline, the British were about to be treated to a nasty surprise by the new Mk IV Specials with their long 75mm guns. The *4th CLY* and *5th RTR* were preparing to move out of their defensive positions, but held firm, as the leading panzers suddenly came to a halt and began turning to the left, where they slowly advanced. The greatest concentration of German panzers appeared to be opposite the *4th CLY* and the anti-tank guns of the *Rifle Brigade*. The II./*Abteilung* was on the left, adjacent to the I./*Abteilung*. The *5th Company* was scattered in a wide wedge forward to the left of the *Abteilung's* center, and the *7th Company* was similarly echeloned to the right. Behind them was the *8th Company* in a double file, echeloned to the right, and in the depth with the task of providing flank protection towards the east. The *6th Company* was in reserve behind the other companies.18

The light *Zug* of the II./*Abteilung* was forward in a screen on the open right flank to the east, and was able to report the presence of multiple enemy armored reconnaissance groups in the distance. The British were able to count some eighty-seven panzers along this part of the front. As the panzers came on, the British gunners were told to hold their fire until the panzers were within 1,000 meters. As the *4th CLY* opened its fire the new Mk IVs quickly began exacting a toll, and within a few minutes nearly all the tanks of the *Grant* squadron were on fire. Some of the panzers had halted, as they too were being hit, but in the meantime another group of panzers began working around the eastern flank to engage some of the tanks that had moved east. The *5th RTR* was now being engaged, and again in the center the panzers began edging forward, and once again artillery was the only thing available to halt them. As other panzers began edging forward, this time towards the *Rifle Brigade's* anti-tank guns, the 6-Pounders opened up and started to inflict heavy casualties on the attacking panzers. The drive, however, could not be halted, and soon some of the guns were quickly overrun. At that time artillery fire began to fall, and most of it came down right on top of the panzers. The Regiment then took up the pursuit and chased after the British tanks in a wide wedge, with I./*Abteilung* on the left and II./*Abteilung* off to the east. As the Regiment continued its pursuit, it again began to receive strong and well-placed artillery fire from the east. During this action, as the two sides continued to exchange rounds, the *8th Company* was ordered to detach itself from the pursuit and work its way around the *5th RTR* positions and make for the artillery gun line in order to silence these guns. The company was then able to locate the guns and begin engaging them, which caused the gunners to disengage themselves, but not before the company was able to claim six vehicles destroyed. By 1730hrs, after a movement of about 12km, the pursuit continued to the north and northeast. By 1815hrs, the Regiment had reached the lower ridge area, which was still heavily occupied by the British. The II./*Abteilung* maneuvered itself on the right flank of the I./*Abteilung* for the next attack. The *5th Company* was swung over to the left flank on a wide front, and pushed through a large wadi lying in front of the ridge to the north, where it was able to end its advance facing to the west and northwest. To the right of the *5th Company* was the *8th*, which had taken up positions there with the *7th* on its right flank and the *6th Company* all the way over on the far right flank and echeloned to protect that flank. British artillery and anti-tank gun fire again forced the panzers to halt their attacks. Some British tanks were seen to be moving to the rear under the protection of a smoke screen. At around 1900hrs, the steep terrain in front of the Regiment was being sprayed by all kinds of automatic fire from the panzers, whose commanders soon noticed that their fire was not being returned, leading them to believe that the British had retreated.19 As daylight began to fade, the panzers had been able to reach the edge of the ridge, but without infantry to protect them, they were forced to withdraw in order to take up a *hinterhangstellung* (reverse-slope) position. At 1930hrs, with night beginning to fall, the companies of the II./*Abteilung* received the order to leave their reverse-slope positions and move south 3-4km through a wadi in order to establish connection with the I./*Abteilung*. The II./*Abteilung* departed its positions with the *5th Company* taking the lead, followed in turn by the *7th*, *8th*, and *6th Companies*. This change of position proved to be an appropriate choice, because during the night there was a heavy artillery bombardment of the former positions along the ridge. That night, after a tiring morning and day that saw a slow movement through the minefields and a quick pursuit, followed up with an attack on a strongly fortified position that had not fallen in the initial assault, the panzer crews dropped down in complete exhaustion. As the last evening light faded and the center of the British line began to stabilize, reinforcements from the *4th CLY* (what remained of them) moved around to the eastern flank to cover the gap between the *5th RTR* and the *44th Division* defenses. Some flashes and tracer fire could be seen off to the east, but the panzers had been halted, and had withdrawn in the growing darkness. By 2100hrs, the Regiment was again reunited with all its panzers, and had formed a hedgehog position in the area south of Deir el Agram, which was located some 8 to 10km south-southwest of Hill 132. Because the Regiment had strayed too far from the main division battle area, the supply trains, which during the day had been unable to keep up with the panzers, found it difficult to locate them during the night, and so the Regiment spent the night of 31/1 without any resupply of food, fuel, and ammunition. For the tired panzer crews, the night passed by almost uneventfully, even though the *DAF* appeared overhead and attempted to bomb the *D.A.K.* formations below as *DAF Pathfinder* planes passed overhead dropping their "Christmas Trees" (multi colored flares) in order to illuminate, for the follow-on bombers, the large concentration of vehicles below. With the battlefield being void of cover and concealment it made it difficult for the *D.A.K.* to find cover, as throughout the night *DAF* bombers passed overhead in an unending stream in attempts to keep up a steady and relentless bombardment of the *D.A.K.* It must be noted that the day and night bombing campaign conducted by the *DAF* was a very important factor in halting the German offensive. Because the Regiment's panzers had pulled away from the main battlefield areas, the bombs dropped that night caused little damage to the panzer crews. As the *DAF* passed overhead throughout the night, there were clashes between British demolition parties and German tank recovery parties attempting to recover a few of the lightly damaged panzers and vehicles. During the

Chapter 11: The Battle of Alam Halfa, August-September 1942

entire campaign in Africa, German recovery operations continued to be more successful than Allied efforts, and the Germans placed greater value in undertaking this vital service. But on this night a great many more panzers were finished off by British demolition parties, as the British were finally learning. At 0300hrs, British tanks were able to launch a night attack that morning from the west-northwest of the Regiment's hedgehog. This attack was repulsed with minimal effort when the panzers, firing from within the hedgehog, opened fire and sent a violent volley of high explosive rounds crashing into the British tanks. However, that attack was successful, in that it forced the Regimental supply trains, which had been located some distance outside the hedgehog, to quickly pick up and move off in an attempt to evade capture or destruction.[20] As dawn broke over the battlefield on 1 September the British strained their eyes to discover how the *D.A.K.* dispositions had changed during the night. For the Regiment and others in the *D.A.K.*, the lack of supplies meant that many of their formations weren't going anywhere. The Regiment was spread out in various hedgehog positions, and were scattered about in a rather wide area in order to avoid bombardment from British artillery and bombers. A short time later, at 0500hrs the British attacked again with between forty to forty-five "Pilot" (Grant) tanks from the north and northwest, and advanced until the line of telegraph poles that stretched from west to east through the wide Wadi Deir el Agram. The Regiment quickly responded to the threat, as it was able to immediately deploy from its hedgehog position and position itself in order to launch a counterattack to the north heading towards Hill 132. The panzers were able to do this despite coming under fire from very strong artillery, tank, and anti-tank gun fire. II./*Abteilung* moved to the east of I./*Abteilung* with the *6th Company* on the left, the *5th* taking up positions in the middle, and the *8th Company* aligned to the right. The *7th Company* was to the right rear behind the *8th Company* in order to provide flank protection. The light *Zug* of the II./*Abteilung* was also deployed forward for reconnaissance purposes. The British armor attack was halted and forced backwards towards a deep djebel to the north. The British lost five tanks that were destroyed in the attack. The *Abteilung* attack was then halted when it accidentally stumbled into a heavily laid minefield. After hitting the minefield, the *6th Company* was ordered to swing west, while the *5th Company* was ordered to occupy a reverse slope position facing to the northwest in order to provide covering fire. The *8th Company* remained in the immediate proximity in order to cover north and northeast. The *7th Company* was still facing to the east and covering the large wadi located to the rear of the II./*Abteilung*. From these positions, the panzers were able to target individual artillery and anti-tank guns, as well as groups of British infantry that were moving about the base of the hill. At long range distances the panzers of the *6th* and *8th Companies* were able to claim the destruction of sixteen trucks and two anti-tank guns.[21] The panzer commanders and gunners were clearly able to observe an intense flow of vehicular traffic on the enemy side of the hill along the road between the minefields, and along the slope to the base of the hill to the east, which bordered a minefield there to the north. These vehicles were neutralized by well placed machine gun fire and high-explosive rounds that were fired from distances of between 1,500 to 2,000 meters. The panzers were constantly forced to change their positions due to the heavy amount of artillery fire that was coming against them from the west, northwest, and north. At 0700hrs the *8th Company* reported to the II./*Abteilung* commander, *Hptm* Zügner, a large concentration of enemy tanks advancing from the east and northeast in the area around Hill 111 (Alam el Khadim). The company reported that the formation consisted of approximately 110 British tanks, predominantly *Grants*, along with follow-on elements and multiple logistical vehicles.[22] These tanks were from the *8th Armored Brigade*, which was beginning to launch its attack. In order to fight back against this attack, at 0715hrs the *8th Company* was forced to reposition itself into a reverse slope position facing east, in a wadi that stretched from the north to the south across a minefield. The company did so while under constant fire from the base of Hill 132 and the threat of attack from its flanks. In the meantime, *Hptm* Zügner ordered the *5th Company* to fall back from their old position in the northwest and fill in the gap between the *8th* and *7th Companies* in order to also help contain the attack. With that move, the II./*Abteilung* suffered its first losses, when during the change of position two panzers from the *5th Company* were knocked out at long range by the 75mm guns of about twenty *Grants* that were moving in from the east. There were also two British tanks that were knocked out from a long range distance of about 1500m. The loss of these two tanks caused the remaining tanks to halt their attack and withdraw to the northeast, where they were soon swallowed up by the dust from the slower moving formation. The II./*Abteilung* suffered further losses when some of its panzers were hit by well aimed British artillery fire coming from the northwest. Despite this artillery fire, the *6th Company* was able to hold its position facing to the west and northwest, but its commander, *Olt* Decker, was wounded during one of the barrages when a round scored a direct hit on his panzer. *Olt* Euen assumed command of the company in his place.[23] By 1045hrs, the British were observed in the distance, at about 2,000 to 3,000m, and had begun to deploy for their attack on the east. Some of the *Grants* were seen deploying to over watch positions in order to act as mobile artillery against the panzers, and shortly thereafter, the high-explosive rounds from their 75mm guns washed over the positions of the *5th* and *8th Companies*. By 1100hrs, the attack was progressing from the east, in parallel to the minefield there. As the *Grants* and *Crusaders* attacked, they were beaten back by the fire of the *5th* and *8th Companies*, which fought from their reverse slope positions. Some of the British tanks were reported to close within 200 to 300m distance before they were destroyed or forced to withdraw. In this attack nineteen British tanks were knocked out, either catching fire or destroyed under the impact of 50mm and 75mm rounds. After the loss of so many tanks, the British immediately retreated to a position 6km away in order to replenish ammunition. Unfortunately the panzers were unable to pursue them, as they were by in large stranded and without a drop of fuel. *Hptm* Zügener, in an attempt to resupply his *abteilung* with fuel, sent some of his lighter Mk IIs to the rear in an attempt to locate the supply columns and carry the fuel forward in jerry cans. In a report written by Lt Klaus Hubbuch he wrote of the aftermath of this action:

> "*After the attack, the disembarked British crews were not shot at by us, as well there was no shooting at the rescue attempts by the English wounded by their doctor who stood in the distance at only 200m. As opposed to this, the enemy shoots on our disembarked crews with MG and artillery.*"[24]

During the attack the II./*Abteilung* suffered the following losses: losses due to enemy tank fire amounted to two Mk IIIs, one Mk III Sp, and one Mk IV Sp. Losses due to enemy artillery fire amounted to three Mk IIIs and two Mk III Sp. The heavy fire also caused a number of casualties that day, as the following leaders were hit: in the *5th Company*, *Olt* Russow was wounded, along with Lt Mittelmeier, who was mortally wounded by artillery fragments. The panzer of *Olt* Heinrich, commander of the *8th Company*, also received a direct hit, wounding him and destroying his panzer. Lt Hubbuch was then forced to assume command of the company. Even the II./*Abteilung* commander, *Hptm* Zügner, and his Adjutant, Lt Bastigkeit, were wounded when their panzer was knocked out, and they had to be rescued by a passing panzer. Josef Zugner would later be decorated with the *DKiG* for his leadership and actions during the battle.[25] *Hptm* Siemens, the commander of the *5th Company*, assumed command of the II./*Abteilung*.²⁶ The I./*Abteilung*, which was located in the immediate proximity of the base of Hill 132, was under constant pressure and fire from numerous 6 and 25-Pounder guns. In an attempt to ease this fire, *Hptm* Kümmel, the *Abteilung* commander, wanted to launch an attack under the cover of supporting artillery fire, in order to break through those gun positions. He was interrupted in his attempts to do so when his panzers were attacked from the northwest by elements of the *1ˢᵗ RTR*. As the *1ˢᵗ RTR* came in from the northwest, one of its squadrons was ordered to move and take up positions west of the main *1ˢᵗ RTR* attack. Both those moves were an attempt to delay the panzer attacks for as long as possible. In the engagement that followed nine *Crusaders* were destroyed, and a number of panzers from the *1ˢᵗ Company* were hit as well. Despite the losses suffered, the I./*Abteilung* attempted to maneuver towards the northeast in an attempt to get into the rear of the Alam Halfa position, but the attack was never able to develop and remained as just another attempt because of the lack of the fuel, which allowed the panzers to move no further. It was here, 15km from the coast and deep in the rear of the El Alamein position, that Rommel's attack ground to a halt. The Regiment was unable to move any farther in the wake of such concentrated artillery and anti-tank gunfire. It was at this point that the *D.A.K.* achieved its farthest easterly progress in the entire campaign in Africa. The Regiment and a few smaller, lightly armed formations now found themselves opposed by a number of British armored units; luckily those units remained a safe distance away from the Regiment. On the western flank *Panzer Regiment 5* had not yet come up to secure that open flank. That afternoon the British launched a large bombing attack in the south which soon developed into a violent air battle. During the aerial combat the panzer crews were forced to throw smoke markers in order to mark their front. The *DAF* had by this time almost complete control of the air space above the battlefield, but there were times when a few *Me-109s* appeared overhead and attempted to disrupt these bombing attacks. In most cases the *Luftwaffe* was easily chased away by *DAF* fighters. However, that day in the skies overhead there was one special event that needs to be mentioned when the young *Staffelkapitain* of 3./*JG-27*, Hans Marseille, shot down seventeen *DAF* planes in just three sorties.²⁷ *OFw* Kurt Kathe, who was with the *5ᵗʰ Company*, remembered that Marseille always had a soft spot for the panzer crews of the Regiment, and he recalled what happened when the young ace flew overhead:

"When Marseille was flying, the Brits were broadcasting 'careful, careful, Marseille is in the air'. I was watching all [of it] on that day when he shot down so many airplanes, how he hit all these airplanes. There was also one German Leutnant shot down on that day, he had to parachute, and I went there and wanted to take his parachute but he took it with him and so nothing happened to him. Small things."²⁸

A second attempt to push the Germans from the foot of Hill 132 came that afternoon as the British launched another attack, this time attempting to swing towards the southwest, where they came upon the remaining panzers of the *5ᵗʰ* and *7ᵗʰ Companies*. This attack had been launched by approximately eighty tanks that had advanced only after multiple bombardments by the supporting Grants. In the face of the effective fire being laid down by the panzers, the British were forced further south, where they came up against the *7./Panzerjäger Abteilung 33*. One of those who participated in the battle that day was *Uffz* Gerhard Weidelener, a long serving veteran of the Regiment who had just moved over from the *Kradmelder* section to command an Mk III Special in the *8ᵗʰ Company*. He had this account:

"On 1 September, we were already without the fuel the whole first half of the day, and had [taken up] positions in a hinterhangstellung in the small hollow. Sometimes we came under the strong anti-tank fire from the flank. Due to lack of fuel, changing of positions was impossible. At 1300hrs came eleven 'Pilots' from the front towards us. We allowed them to come at 300m distance and then in five minutes they were all in flames, four of them were on my account, a perfect start of my richtschütze's work. In the meantime, on our side there was a change of Pak positions. [A short time later] the first impacts of shelling hit against the sand bags, we used sandbags as protection, those bags were exactly at my level, and if those bags had not been there, the shells would have gone right through. The second [round] hit against Kuschka, that was my driver, and he was wounded. Koch who was richtschütze and Knobelspiess who was the ladeschütze, were both dead in the vehicle. The vehicle of Hauptmann Zügner, he was our abteilung commander, came and took those of us left, back but after five minutes he received a direct hit and [began to] burn. After this, it was not fun anymore and it took us five hours to get back to the supply lines in the morning hours. Around us on the left, there were mountains, and there were the British and they shot [at us] with everything they had. We were crawling 4-5km and it took us five hours to get to the 'tross' (supply lines). We were crawling the entire time and we took breaks under the cover of abandoned vehicles."²⁹

That evening the British again withdrew under the cover of a smoke screen to positions located 4-5km in the distance. With the loss of *Olt* Heinrich that afternoon, young Lt Klaus Hubbuch assumed the duties as the commander of the *8ᵗʰ Company*. After taking command that afternoon, he and his company were tasked with holding the flank in front of the base of Hill 132 with just five panzers. During the afternoon, two of those panzers were knocked out by anti-tank gun fire from some 6-Pounder guns that had been firing from the left flank (north, northwest) during the second attempt that had come against the II./*Abteilung* that day. As the afternoon wore on the situation did not look good for the Regiment, as British armored forces were able to regroup; the *23ʳᵈ Armored Brigade* had reached their new positions, and as the day gradually drew to a close were observed taking up positions along the flanks of the Regiment. The growing presence of British armor on both flanks placed the Regiment in serious jeopardy, and so it was decided that the Regiment should be ordered further to the south in order to escape this potentially disastrous situation. In fact, that evening, along the entire Alam Halfa front the *D.A.K.* had withdrawn out of effective tank gun range, and the only fire they received came from British artillery. By that evening the fuel situation throughout the entire *Panzerarmee* was at a critical level, and there was only enough gasoline left to keep the supply columns going in order to conduct their resupply of the forward elements. By this point there was little thought for any tactical movements, and only the most necessary movements were undertaken at this time. The Regiment had received just enough fuel to allow it about 8-10km of movement, and that amount would only last through the most conservative of maneuvers. That afternoon Lt Halverscheidt, who was just returning from the Regimental *Stabs*, was able to surprise a group of British tanks, and succeeded in knocking out two *Valentines* with his Mk IV.³⁰ Later that afternoon, Lt Förster and his section from the *7ᵗʰ Company*, which had been augmenting the *8ᵗʰ Company*, were able to bring forward some desperately needed fuel, which allowed the *Abteilung* some freedom of movement. Even as the British tanks were moving away from the battlefield the British artillery fire still kept harassing the panzer crews; then through this fire a lone vehicle was observed moving from panzer to panzer as it slowly made its way to the Regimental *Stabs*. It was soon discovered that the vehicle belonged to *StZmstr* Gisy, who was bringing forward some *Löwenbräu* beer for the panzer crews. The crews accepted it with extreme gratitude, but right now was not the time to sit back and relax, as the need for refueling the panzers took priority. The night of 1/2

September was extremely dark, as the companies gathered near Hill 79, located about 5km south of the Alam Halfa Ridge. The Regiment moved into a hedgehog position, and those panzers that had broken down during the day were recovered and brought back into the hedgehog, where they underwent what maintenance and repair the *Werkshop* (I-squadron) could manage. Those panzers that had suffered heavy damage were transported to the southwest. *Uffz* Gotthilf Haidt was a member of the Regimental *Werkshop Company* and describes his job:

"I was with the workshop leader, Major Schnell was his name, we were at the workshop and not bothered on too many things, we were driving around a lot, towing broken panzers to the workshop, the workshop was not deployed in combat areas, and we were on the backward sides [rear areas]. In principle we were not in combat areas, our tasks were to repair broken panzers. I was not directly involved in combat myself, that I can remember. I was there when the combat was over, to get the broken things. We were not wearing weapons, no weapons; there was carbine in the vehicle, but apart from this nothing."[31]

The losses to the Regiment were significant: the day had cost them twelve killed and twenty wounded in action, with four reported as missing. That whole night of 1/2 September and into the following morning the *D.A.K.* came under continuous aerial bombardment by the *DAF*. After a night of unrelenting bombing attacks and a catastrophic supply situation Rommel decided at 0825hrs to discontinue the attack and pull his forces back, step by step, to positions extending from the El Taqua plateau to Bab el Qattara. Thankfully, that morning at around 0400hrs the supply trains were finally able to get forward with fuel and begin refueling operations. The other commodity needed was ammunition, which they were not able to bring forward. The panzers would just have to make do with what they had onboard. During the refueling operations the hedgehogs began receiving artillery fire. At 0530hrs, the Regiment reported sixty-one panzers operational and moved off in their wide panzer wedges, headed north towards Alam Halfa. With the I./*Abteilung* aligned to the right and the II./*Abteilung* aligned to the left the Regiment moved forward. The *8th Company* was aligned even further out on the left flank in an attempt to maintain contact with *Panzer Regiment 5*, which had not yet closed up. The *Leichte Zug* was sent forward in order to clear the area in front of the II./*Abteilung* from the northeast to northwest of enemy forces. During the advance the Regiment continued to receive heavy artillery fire, and enemy tank formations were spotted marshalling in the distance at approximately 5km, but with very little ammunition there were not any thoughts of engaging them. *Oberstlt* Mildebrath then allowed his *Abteilung* to spread out, making the wedge into a battle line. Near 1100hrs, the ammunition trains finally arrived, although the continuous artillery fire prevented them from conducting an effective resupply operation. Obviously these trucks, laden with cases of main gun rounds, had to be careful when conducting this type of operation, as it was not only dangerous for the supply column, but for the panzers too. The section found the situation a bit tricky, and it was decided that each panzer *zug* would come back to pick up the issue and bring it back to their *zugs* and companies. Just after the resupply concluded, the I./*Abteilung* found itself under attack by some sixty tanks from the *8th Armored Brigade*. The *Abteilung* moved forward in a counterattack and was able to destroy twenty-eight *Grants* and *Crusaders* in a tough firefight before the British broke off the engagement. The *Abteilung* lost only five panzers that were destroyed in the engagement.[32]

After the losses sustained on the 1st there were a few changes that needed to be made immediately. Within the II./*Abteilung*, Lt Golinski was to take on the job as *abteilung* adjutant, and he reported to the Regiment *Stabs* and *Hptm* Siemens for further orders. At 1230hrs the *8th Company* received an order to send six of its panzers to the combat positions of *Panzergrenadier Regiment 115*. The panzers were to form up with elements of that regiment and other units from *Kampfgruppe Weichsel*, which were then to be deploy to protect the resupply routes that were built during the advance march in an area of minefields to the southwest.[33] For the first half of the day the *DAF*, with bombers and fighters, attacked the Regiment and *Panzerjäger Abteilung 33*, causing a few losses to some of the crews; however, the unarmored supply trains got the worst of the attack, as nine trucks were lost in addition to four soldiers killed and fourteen wounded. Towards evening the Regiment moved back towards Hill 78, where it again formed a hedgehog position. On the night of 2/3 September the Regiment received plenty of harassing fire that fell on the hedgehog positions; to make matters worse, British armored cars would quickly move forward towards the hedgehogs and fire into the positions, then quickly depart before any effective fire could be brought to bear on them. In an attempt to halt these attacks, the *Leichte Zug* of the II./*Abteilung* sent one *unteroffizier* and two men out on foot in an attempt to locate the source of the attacks, but they returned without success. On the morning of the 3rd, the division ordered the Regiment to fall back through Wadi Deir el Râgil, and once it had completed the move through the wadi it was to take up a blocking position facing to the east. As the Regiment departed the area south of Alam Halfa they left in their wake numerous vehicles, some of them smoking wrecks, others just sitting idle with empty gas tanks. In order to salvage as much as they could, a few of the panzers were able to attach tow cables to a number of serviceable panzers that had either suffered minor damage or had just run out of gas and tow them off to the west. With the failed attack on Alam Halfa, the possibility of eliminating those British forces in the El Alamein salient had failed. The lack of supplies coupled with the extensive minefields and the enemy's air superiority were mostly to blame for the failed attack. On the tactical level, the panzers and their crews performed well, but the enemy, given the advantage of terrain, large quantities of well armed tanks and powerful anti-tank guns, and well supported by plenty of artillery left no doubt as to the outcome. Later on the 3rd, the Regiment was assigned one company from *Panzerjäger Abteilung 33* to help secure its northern flank against attack.[34] Also on this day, the *6th Company* of *Olt* Euen, with its ten panzers, was subordinated to *Kampfgruppe Ebert*, where they were to move north in support of the *Ramcke Fallschirmjäger Brigade*, but because of illness, Euen was forced to hand over temporary command of the company to Lt Karl Halverscheidt. At 1500hrs, Halverscheidt's ten panzers, in addition to the panzer of Lt Förster of the *7th Company*, departed on their mission.[35] As this small group departed they did so with very little fuel remaining in the gas tanks of a number of the panzers, some of which were already reporting fuel tanks on empty. Regardless of the lack of fuel, the mission had to be accomplished, and as the company drove north it only managed to cover some 10km before the lack of fuel forced it to halt. Lt Halverscheidt then departed the main body of the company in an attempt to locate the Regiment's resupply column, and only by a stroke of luck was he able to find the column moving up from the rear area. The supply trains were able to replenish the panzer's fuel tanks, which were topped off and allowed them to continue on their mission.

As the fighting around the Alam Halfa Ridge was coming to an end and those German forces began to pull back to the south, *General* Montgomery had ordered his staff to begin planning for a counterattack operation on 1 September that was to begin early on 3 September. The plan that Montgomery had in mind was to close the gaps created in the minefields by sending two forces—one from the south, the other from the north—to move up to seal off the corridors, and thereby trap and destroy those Axis forces east of the minefield gaps. The operation was given the codename "*Beresford*," and was the first such operation undertaken by

Montgomery himself. The attack was scheduled to begin on the 3rd by elements of the *2nd New Zealand* and *7th Armored Divisions*. The operation was given to the *XIII Corps*, under *General* Brian Horrocks, whose corps had been in the north along the coast and had not been too involved in the battle since the first day. That corps was ordered to thin out some of its formations and provide the reserves for an operation to be conducted in the south from the New Zealand sector. Operation "*Beresford*" was planned as a set piece battle, and was to be conducted by the *5th New Zealand Brigade* with the *50th RTR* providing support. Additionally, there was the *132nd Brigade* of the *44th Division*. The attack was launched from the middle of the Alamein sector, and it moved southward toward the Deir el Munassib and the *90th Light*. The attack lasted only a short time before *General* Freyberg of the *2nd New Zealand Division* called it off after losing almost a thousand casualties and twelve *Valentine* tanks.[36] The *21st Panzer* had been ordered forward, and the *15th Panzer* was placed on standby for this attack. During the day and night the *D.A.K.* came under numerous air attacks, again by the bombers of the RAF; the complete air superiority over the battlefield allowed the *DAF* to continually attack the German and Italian troops as they attempted to disengage from the battlefield. Vehicles that were not stuck in the soft sand were slowed or halted due to the lack of petrol that never arrived as planned, and now those forces were trapped between the Alam Halfa Ridge and the Qattara Depression, and the *DAF* was able to attack these formations on six different occasions within a two hour period on 3 September without interference. It was thanks to the well-dispersed positions that no losses were suffered in the aerial attacks. Harassing attacks were continually stepped up by both the *DAF* and *7th Armored Division* in the south, and by the afternoon of the 3rd columns of the British formations were reported moving west from the gaps in the minefields. The fighting would continue for the next two days between the two minefield belts, and it was clear that the British were prepared to fight hard for this area. On 4 September, the day began with the all too frequent bombing and artillery attacks against Axis positions. The British put out feelers, but as tanks appeared in front of the *I./Abteilung* it wasted little time in launching a counterattack and forcing the British to retreat from the area. In this brief encounter, nine British tanks were destroyed for the loss of two Mk IIIs. With the loss, the total panzer strength of the Regiment was down to thirty-two operational panzers.[37] The Regiment remained on the defensive to await further enemy attacks from armored formations located approximately six kilometers further back in a wadi and out of immediate observation. The remaining panzers of the *5th Company* under the command of *OFw* Spohn were grouped together, and launched an attack on a number of advancing self-propelled guns and their accompanying artillery spotters. One self-propelled gun was destroyed, and the anti-tank position was closed. By this time, with the loss of a large number of its panzers and with others being detached to other formations, the Regiment was forced to reorganize its meager numbers into a consolidated group. Fortunately, *OInsp* Lampe and his workshop personnel were soon able to send forward twenty-seven operational panzers, and when Lt Halverscheidt, with his detached *6th Company*, returned with eleven panzers, the Regiment was now able to report forty-two operational panzers.[38] The lone panzer of Lt Förster from the *7th Company* was attached to the Regimental *Stabs*, while *Oberstlt* Mildebrath was now able to reorganize the Regiment and re-fit his panzer companies. The night remained quiet, despite some harassing fire by British artillery, but it was bothersome enough to interfere with the resupply operation. Fuel continued to remain scarce, with many of the panzers unable to be completely refueled. The following morning the Regiment was ordered to withdraw to the west, where it took up defensive positions behind the protection of a minefield. The *I./Abteilung* fanned out and took up positions on the left flank while the *II./Abteilung* spread out along the right flank. The panzer of *OFw* Thamphald from the *7th Company* was ordered to secure the gap through the minefield. From behind the protective minefield the Regiment was able to form a strong defensive line with the panzers facing back to the east. After a reconnaissance of the new deployment area in Quattaret el Diyura, the Regiment marched under cover of a small security screen to the east, and without further incident reached its new assembly area. Once in the assembly area the men wasted little time in digging in and camouflaging their panzers. The commander of the *7th Company*, *Olt* Schulz, who had been quite sick for some time, relinquished command of the company to Lt Krüger before being evacuated out. Schulz was not the only member of the company to be replaced, as the company had suffered a number of losses due to wounds and sickness, and was now forced to reshuffle its remaining crews and panzers. The Alam Halfa operation was over; it had failed in its objective to destroy the *Eighth Army* in the field and the capture of Alexandria and Cairo. It had failed for a number of reasons, and in a report written by Fritz Bayerlein after the war he listed his reasons why the German attack had failed:

"The offensive failed for the following reasons: (1) we were too weak for such an extended enveloping operation. (2) The British positions in the south were, in fact, exceptionally heavily mined as compared to the information we had from reconnaissance; and the British knew our intentions. (3) Devastating attacks by the RAF, which had complete command of the air and which literally nailed us to the ground, made any orderly advance and any effective movement impossible. (4) The fuel, a necessary requirement for the completion of our plan, did not arrive. The ships, which Cavallero had promised us were either sunk, delayed or never sent. Kesselring, unfortunately, was not able to keep his promise—if necessary, to fly 500 tons per day to the front."[39]

After the operation the losses suffered by the *Panzerarmee* were crippling, not only in men and machines, but in the amount of precious supplies used up and lost, some never to be replaced. There is no doubt about the role the RAF played in defeating the attack, but one must also look at the British artillery, which for the Regiment caused them the majority of their casualties. Another factor is that the British armor never came out to openly attack the *D.A.K.* panzers, and so the opportunity to destroy the armored formations was never achieved. It would be these formations that were soon to play a major role in Montgomery's next move against Rommel. The losses suffered by the Axis forces amounted to almost 3,000 killed, wounded, and captured (570 KIAs, 1,800 WIAs, and 570 PoWs); these numbers included the Italians, who lost some 1,000 men killed, wounded, or missing. There was also the loss of over four hundred vehicles, which the *Panzerarmee* desperately needed, and fifteen field guns, thirty-five Pak guns, and most importantly 113 German panzers had been damaged, with thirty-eight being complete write-offs; these included in the *15th Panzer Division* two Mk IIs, five Mk IIIs, four Mk III Sp, one Mk IV, and two Mk IV Sp.[40] This number of 113 amounted to almost a quarter of the total number the *D.A.K.* had begun the battle with. The Italians lost eleven tanks and fifty guns. According to the KTB, the *15th Panzer Division* listed the following losses: 3 officers and 73 men killed, 16 officers and 258 men wounded, and 3 men missing in action. In addition, *Panzer Regiment 8* listed the following vehicular losses (totally destroyed/partially destroyed): 16/77 trucks, 6/18 motorcycles, 4/0 staff cars, 0/5 Zgkw tractors, 0/3 low-boy loaders, 2/4 Mk II, 8/25 Mk III, 4/14 Mk III Sp, 1/0 Mk IV, 2/7 Mk IV Sp, and 1/0 large *befehlswagen*.[41] According to British and Axis reports, the British suffered some 2,000 killed, wounded, and taken prisoner, along with 150 tanks and armored vehicles that were either destroyed or captured, of which sixty-seven were tanks, along with ten pieces of artillery and twenty anti-tank guns. But most importantly, Rommel's forces had been halted and beaten back, and the initiative in North Africa now began to shift to the British and her Commonwealth forces. The shift in momentum also came as preparations began in earnest towards the largest Allied offensive of the war to date, the battle of El Alamein.

Calm before the Storm Sep/Oct 1942
On 6 September, the *Panzerarmee* began to dig itself in along the 60km of desert from the small village of El Alamein on the coast and ran south southwest across Ruweisat Ridge until reaching the northeastern tip of the Qattara Depression. The *Alamein Line* was a rocky, waterless, barren desert, unmistakable because of the debris littering the battlefield: burned out tanks, abandoned guns, bloated corpses, spent ammunition cases, and makeshift crosses topped with helmets all lay testament to the battles which had been fought here in the previous months. Some men were allowed leave, while others were destined to remain in Africa with the only entertainment provided in the *Manschaftheims* or *Soldatenheims*. Gotthilf Haidt remembers:

"The leave was approved, for those who were married and for those who were long at the military service. For us [young, single soldiers] there was a vacation ban. There was a danger to go down from U-Boats over the sea, or to be shot down. In Alamein we had some days for vacation and we decided to take it, some went to the heim [soldatenheim or soldier rest center]. As for me, I went into the military and [not until] October of '45 was I back home."[42]

Kurt Kathe gives a story of how life was at this time:

"The people who lived there, Bedouins, they were decent people. One time me and my adjutant drove with a car and without uniform, in our car we had a box with a red cross, for bandages, there was a nice oasis. We went there and there were women in there. Immediately the men said 'you can't go there, there are women'. They saw my box with the Red Cross, and I was wearing shorts and a light shirt. They told me 'la docteur' in French, the doctor. They brought me children and wounded people. With Haerte, we first cleaned the people, they were dirty, and we applied iodine for healing the cuts, and also ointment. We had one with 5-6 cuts. And we left them the whole box. One was so old, I told him, don't take the bandage off we returned in few days and removed the bandage and all was well healed. I put on another bandage just with ointment then. So grateful they were and they gave us eggs. They were very happy, and applauded then gave me eggs. We had good contacts with them. I gave sugar to the children, as they had not much food for the children. When we drove over and made a stop, the children came to eat and I said to my adjutant, take the food from field kitchen and give it to the children. They all got a full spoon and they were so happy they danced. And so on each of our stops, when the children came they got food from us."[43]

Horst Sonnenkalb wrote of the days:

"We conducted our fighting mostly in the southern and middle parts of the front in the desert. We saw the Mediterranean Sea on our north when we captured Tobruk. But when we entered the position at El Alamein, the repair company of our regiment was located directly on the shore. The crews, which moved forward with the repaired panzers told us about the swimming in the Mediterranean Sea and swarmed about it. They were fishing with hand grenades, and grilled them over an open fire. But one day they had a war adventure. The floating mine came close to the flat sandy beach. It was possible to see its horns. There was an alarm and everyone went under cover. Two panzers opened MG-fire. They hit the mine, it detonated and with a big water pillar the mud and seaweed flew in the air. Water was the most valued and most limited [quantity]. When we had an extra canister, we allowed ourselves a 'full tub'. 10 liters of valuable wetness were put into the ammunition box and covered with a zinc sheet, and the bath was ready. But these 10 liters should have been enough for all 5 crew members. What a rare luxury in the North-Africa desert!"[44]

As the late summer heat bore down relentlessly on the men of all sides, the troops made do as best they could. The constant change in temperatures during the day meant that temperatures could change by as much as forty-five degrees from daytime to nighttime. The ever-present swarms of flies invaded every crevice of the body in search of moisture, and it was nearly impossible to eat without swallowing a number of them. The night brought some form of relief, as the flies disappeared, the strong desert winds subsided, and the temperature began to fall. It was at this time when both sides would begin their work on the front line positions and continue sowing mines. For the men of the Regiment, and indeed much of the *D.A.K.*, they had been partnered up with various Italian units in order to add more combat power to their allies, but more importantly to bolster their confidence and staying power. This technique had been attempted and used somewhat successfully in the past, and it was thought to be a good idea, especially when faced with the overwhelming superiority in men and machine that the British and her Commonwealths possessed. For the Regiment, it meant being near the Italian *Littorio* Division. Kurt Kathe remembers some of the Italians he was located near:

"The Italian soldiers were not exactly good; they were poor soldiers they had no cigarettes and nothing really to eat. They looked at us when we parked and they picked up our cigarette butts, they came to us and asked for food. They were so grateful to get cigarettes from us. They were badly disciplined and organized."

Also taking place at this time were the arrival of new replacements that had come in to replace many of those who had either been wounded in the fighting or were due home leave after surviving 18 months in the desert without a break. One of those replacements was a young man from Stuttgart named Adolf Lamm, who described his arrival in Africa:

"During the last days of August 1942 we departed from the Böblingen panzer kaserne to Bitsch in Alsace as replacements. On the 7th of September 1942 we loaded onto trains for the journey to Greece through Serbia. I arrived in Athens after two to three days then proceeded on foot to the camp by the airfield at Tatoi at the beginning of October 1942. Everyone with a Wehrmacht driver's license was flown out of Tatoi. Those remaining troops marched on foot to the Peloponnese and loaded onto ships. I later learned from comrades that a few of them were supposedly sunk. I reported with my driver's license and was flown out in a Ju-52 at 0700 in the morning with some other soldiers who were total strangers to me. Everything went fine up to Crete, but later we had to fend off an attack with machine gun fire, after which we were left alone to land in Tobruk around midday. Once there, the air-raid siren started immediately under heavy fire. In a large, designated tent set up for processing us, I received my marching orders for El Daba. Nobody asked about my driver's license either there or later. The marching orders were; Jump into a truck, any truck! but the drivers swear at us and don't want to take anyone. I caught a ride with a few others by sitting on top of the barrels on a fuel transport truck. I had evidently suppressed the danger of flying sky-high. [Being blown up]. As I didn't have a map and never even saw one on the entire

trip to El Alamein and back to Tunisia, I couldn't orientate myself. During this drive, there was a heavy sandstorm that even lasted a few days in El Daba. After abating, a truck took me to 'my unit', where I didn't know a single person. I was directed to a tent whose occupants didn't want to take anyone in. The atmosphere was similar. This was around the October 7th, 1942. The company I was assigned to trained in the mornings; calisthenics, drill, field exercises, cleaning weapons, etc. We were in the 15th Panzer Division."[45]

In addition to the replacements, there was also the departure of some of the old hands, men who had fought over the previous year and a half, and due to persisting illnesses and diseases, in addition to a number of wounds received in battle, were given their ticket home. Men like *Uffz* Max Lebold, who had been wounded and suffered countless bouts with dysentery, were sent off to schools and courses back in Germany to pass off their knowledge to the younger recruits now coming through the system to replace the losses suffered in Africa and Russia. The most celebrated member of the Regiment to leave that autumn was the "*Lion of Capuzzo*" himself, Hans Kümmel. On 11 October 1942, just prior to the great British offensive at El Alamein, Kümmel was awarded the *Oak leaves to his Knight's Cross* for his actions during the summer battles. He was posted back to Böblingen, where he was given the command of *Reserve and Training Battalion 7* in Böblingen, and on 1 December 1942 Kümmel received a promotion to the rank of *Major*. Following the defeat in Africa Kümmel was transferred back into action, this time to Southern Italy. He was promoted to the rank of *Oberstleutnant* and was assigned to the Headquarters of *XIV Panzer Corps* under *General* Hans Hube. In October 1943 Kümmel received command of *Panzer Regiment 26* and saw action near Salerno and Cassino. On 30 January 1944, Kümmel's regiment was part of the attacking force attempting to destroy the Allied landings at Anzio. The initial counterattack failed and a second attempt was called for. That second attack was scheduled for 27 February, but before Kümmel's panzers could again charge ahead he was accidentally killed that evening while visiting his panzer crews when a panzer turret was swung around, striking Kümmel in the head and killing him. A freak accident, and an unbecoming end for the man hailed as the "*Lion of Capuzzo*." On 20 May 1944, Johannes Kümmel was posthumously promoted to the rank of *Oberst*.[46] In his memory there is a plate erected in his hometown of Böblingen honoring him. Kurt Kathe remembers him:

"*It is all very important for the history and history is not officers, it's all about people.*
The officers were imaginary and Kümmel began the war as a Feldwebel, in Africa he was an Abteilung Commander. One knew who Kümmel was but who else was in the first company or like me in the fifth, nobody knew their names. That's how it was, only the officers, when officers came to Casino, they did not know where their crew was, but Kümmel was also there in civil clothes without his Ritterkreuz. Why? Later he was detached from Africa and then detached [sent off] from Böblingen to Italy. One evening there he drove his car, a normal car; he had parked next to the panzer. When you parked the panzer you turn the cannon to the back. So his driver did and so he died, he was good soldier. He fought in Poland and was in his 11th year of service. He lived near me in Böblingen. He died because his driver was stupid, but its just destiny."[47]

The logistical situation for all armies fighting in the North African desert was one of great fortune, and in some cases misfortune, where even victory in battle could lead to defeat in keeping one's troops properly supplied. In preparation for the upcoming battle, the Allies received a continuous stream of supplies, ammunition, and weapons that were constantly arriving from Great Britain and America. These supplies were quickly transported to the front from their bases in Cairo and Alexandria. Some of those items arriving at the front included the new American built *Sherman* tank, self-propelled artillery, and the 6-Pounder anti-tank gun. Many of these items arrived in great quantities and replaced those items that were lost in the summer battles at Gazala and Tobruk. It was not only the new machines that arrived, as fresh troops and units arrived to replace those that had been serving and were in need of rest. Even though many of those arriving had limited combat and desert experience, they were eager to get at the Germans, as they began a vigorous training cycle that would prepare them to confront an experienced enemy now digging in behind a thick defensive belt. Allied manpower was now twice as much as the Axis forces, and there was a tank strength ratio of 3:1, a 2:1 ratio in artillery, and a 5:1 in aircraft, all in favor of the Allies. Vast administrative arrangements had been prepared also, and the supplies to sustain the offensive for 10-15 days had been carefully stockpiled and concealed. As the build up of troops, equipment, and supplies continued unabated, everything possible was being done to hinder and interdict the *Panzerarmee's* reinforcements and resupply. The *Royal Navy* and *DAF* were continually attacking the ports, sea routes, and land transport routes. The supply situation had been pressing for some time now, as units of *DAF* had gained air superiority some months before over the *Luftwaffe*, and now those aircraft were constantly deployed in bombing and interdiction missions against supply installations, airfields, harbors, and on patrol over the Mediterranean, wreaking havoc on Axis supply ships and sending a number of vital fuel tankers to the bottom. Indeed, the ground forces spent their downtime watching flights of *DAF* aircraft heading out towards the Axis lines, and then counting them on their return. Sometimes a fighter was missing, but seldom a bomber. Aerial dogfights provided an exciting spectacle for troops on the front line. After the *Panzerarmee* finished digging itself in and anchoring on the Mediterranean coast and Qattara Depression, it soon began to reinforce its positions, as there was little doubt that as soon as the British had amassed the huge quantities of men and materiel necessary they would move to overwhelm them. There was little chance of withdrawing the *Panzerarmee*, as almost all of it consisted of non-mobile infantry, and once a withdrawal was detected it could expect to be attacked by Allied Forces. Accepting that fact, the *Panzerarmee* knew it had to reinforce its present positions until more troops and supplies could be brought forward and it would be able to launch its own offensive operations. Before Rommel departed for his rest treatment, he held a meeting with his Chief Engineer, *Major* Hecker, and the respective divisional engineering officers, and explained to them what he wanted; a defensive belt in which the attacker couldn't pass and detectors couldn't clear. The answer was the standard minefield augmented with what was termed "Devil Gardens." The construction of those Devil Gardens were to be left up to the imagination of each individual pioneer unit, and would be based on the tricks of the trade that they had learned during their time in the North African Desert. The Gardens consisted of a series of standard and improvised booby trapped devices and mines, which were designed to spread confusion and panic along the attacking formations. The Axis forces laid 249,849 anti-tank mines and 14,507 anti-personnel mines; along with the already existing British minefields the total number of mines was some 460,000.[48] These mines were laid in two major fields running north and south across the entire front about two miles apart, and interconnected by lateral belts, making a honeycomb effect, and within the cells of the honeycomb were located the gardens. The first Box "H" was located in the coastal sector just south of the Via Balbia, followed by the "I" Box just west of the Tell el Eisa, the "L" Box opposite the Tell el Makh Khan, and the "K" Box located at Bir Qusur el Tash. The supplies to construct these Gardens were promised by Rommel himself and came from a variety of sources. Mines of German, Italian, French, and Egyptian origin were brought forward from the various depots from Benghazi to Marsa Matruh and pulled from existing fields in the rear, especially the Cyrenaica Egyptian border area. The old frontier border provided mines, wire, pickets, and other elements necessary to construct the barriers. However, there was still not enough wire, mines, and other materials to cover the amount of ground necessary and construct the defensive belt as impregnable as Rommel would have liked. The Devil Gardens measured some three to five kilometers in length with a depth of between three and six kilometers, and they were open in the front to allow the attacker to penetrate into the Garden. To the front and sides there was wire surrounding the Garden, then mines laid in a horseshoe pattern just a few meters from the wire. Once past the initial line came the "T" mines laid in layers of twos and threes, or just a simple "T" mine with a grenade underneath it. There were also aerial bombs from between 50-250lbs, which were laid in a checkerboard pattern and had numerous trip wires spread out just waiting for some unlucky soldier to stumble upon. Once the Gardens had been completed the troops, which had been forward of them, fell back to prepared positions and activated the mines. Gaps between the Devil's Gardens were closed off with a barrier of "T" and "S" mines and covered with direct fire from within the Gardens themselves, or fighting positions just to the rear. To aid in the deployment of the mobile forces like panzers, artillery, and *panzerjägers*, the defensive line was set on with three distinct north south tracks, or pistes. All three tracks ran generally north to south, and allowed the mobile elements to move quickly to any threatened sector of the front. The first, or eastern most road was called the "Alarm Piste," and it was located directly behind the minefields and initial line of Axis infantry; the road was given its name because panzer and mobile forces could be quickly moved along it to support non-mobile forces. The second road, or "Otto Piste," began at a point south of Rahman at the point it branched off of the Rahman Piste and ran down the middle of the Axis sector—many of the Axis headquarters and panzer units were centered on this track. The third road was known to the Axis forces by a number of different names, the most common of these were the "Rahman Piste" or "Telephone Piste," so named for the line of telephone poles that ran alongside it. The road ran from Sidi Abd el Rahman in the north all the way to the Qattara Depression in the south. To the *Eighth Army* this road was known as the "Qattara Track." Additionally, there were a number of smaller roads or tracks that criss-crossed with the first three, and they too also went by a host of names, in most cases by the units that operated along them. One of those small tracks was known as the "Stone Course" or "Stein Piste," which is mentioned by a number of veterans and in some of the German divisional war diaries.

Within the Regiment there was a regimental pioneer section; unfortunately, there is very little mentioned about these men in combat reports, and I have been unable to locate any living members of this section. Nonetheless, their service to the Regiment was important, as *Uffz* Gotthilf Haidt of the *Werkshop Company* had this reflection on the tasks they were usually assigned to perform:

"The pioneers with us were not with us, there was a Zug in the Regiment. Their tasks were to clear the minefields and if there were obstacles, they were to remove them, if there was a panzer to be removed from the obstacles that was the work of the pioneers."[49]

As the Germans prepared their Devil's Gardens, the *Eighth Army* was busy too with its preparations. Many of the British tactical preparations were concealed under a heavy cloud of secrecy, and very few if any indications were given as to the start date of the offensive. The Germans had lost one of their best agents earlier in the year, and the *Aufklärungs*

Abteilung were hardly equipped and prepared for deep reconnaissance, and if indeed they had been there was little fuel to spare for them. The *Luftwaffe* was able to conduct some aerial reconnaissance, but the close proximity to the airfields of the *DAF* facilitated the amount of fighter cover over the British battle lines and kept the German recon flights to a minimum. For the British, Montgomery was a stickler for his assaulting troops to be well trained prior to undertaking any offensive operations, and so ordered that many of the units slated for the attack were to be withdrawn from their positions for a period of rest, immediately followed by intensive training in conditions as similar as possible to the actual attack. For example, practice minefields were laid out exactly as they were expected to be found, and infantry assaults were conducted with support from artillery and tanks firing live ammunition. Weapons and guns were painstakingly checked and calibrated. Special attention was paid to the clearing and breeching of wire obstacles and minefields, as both sides had vast areas defended by these means. Patrols would go out almost every night in an attempt to gather intelligence, salvage materiel, bury the dead, and conduct raids. The Germans grew wary of these raids, and would spray the ground with machine gun fire and launch flares at the slightest movement. When dawn came both sides would remain in contact by lobbing shells at one another until the sunshine and dust began to create mirage effects and targets became blurred. Horst Sonnenkalb wrote about another interesting way the British attempted to gather intelligence:

"It was slowly getting very unquiet at the front. Sufficiently known as the 'Stubborn 18' [RAF Bombers] dragged their flags [dropped bombs] as always, but also other formations. From our side there were almost no Jagfliegers [fighter aircraft]. The Tommy's increased their activity. The German Italian troops have placed deeply staged mine fields and hedges of barbed wire in front of their positions, and dug themselves in the prepared defense positions. In order to learn of their locations the English reached again into their bag of tricks, the awful trick. They guided the camel herds into German and Italian positions and when the camels stepped on mines, they were torn apart by the explosion. This way the Tommy's got rid of our mine fields. The pictures of dead animals were in my memory for the long time."[50]

Rommel left Africa on 23 September for his rest and treatment in Germany and Austria. Like many of his men, he fell victim to the harsh desert life and strains of command. He was to hand over temporary command of the *Panzerarmee* to *General der Cavalrie* Georg Stumme, who was coming in from Russia. Stumme, the one time commander of Rommel's old *7th Panzer Division*, was a rather fat, bald, and red faced man who failed to instill much confidence in Rommel, despite having achieved some notoriety in France and Russia. Stumme was not necessarily the first man the *OKW* had thought of when replacement candidates were screened for. One of those whose name had been brought up as a temporary replacement was none other than *General* Heinz Guderian, the master of mobile warfare, and a man whose talents might have taken him as far as Rommel in Africa. However, Guderian had fallen out of favor with Hitler and his cronies back in Berlin, and he was being kept far away from any combat commands, so when his name appeared in a message the kurt reply was a simple "Guderian unacceptable."[51]

The German dispositions from north to south and defensive plan were entirely Rommel's, and were still based on the first line corseting of the predominately non-motorized Italian infantry units with German elements to stiffen their resolve and bolster the line. The four German and eight Italian divisions in the line at Alamein consisted of 108,000 men, of which 54,000 were German and the remainder Italians. They were equipped with 548 tanks, of which 249 were German panzers, in addition to 552 artillery pieces and 1,063 Pak guns.[52] The panzer elements were grouped together, with one German panzer division partnered with one Italian armored division and held in reserve as the second line of defense. The panzer divisions were further broken down into three mobile *kampfgruppen*, which contradicted the armored doctrine that called for massed formations. The Axis forces were well-sited and dug in behind the protective Devil's Garden minefields. From north to south the first line of defense consisted of the Italian *XXI Corps* (Navarini) with the German *164th Infantry Division* (Lungershausen), the Italian *Trento* (Nuvoloni) and *Bologna* (Gloria) Divisions, and one battalion of the *Ramcke Fallschirmjäger Brigade*. To the south were the Italian *X Corps* (Nebbia) with the Italian *Brescia* (Brunetti), *Folgore* Airborne (Frattini), and *Pavia* (Scattaglia) Divisions, while two battalions from the *Ramcke Brigade* and *Aufklärung Abteilung 33* held the line to the Qattara Depression. In the south, just to the north of the Qattara Depression, behind the *X Corps* was the *21st Panzer* (von Randow) with the Italian *Ariete* Armored Division (Arena). In the northern sector, behind the *XXI Corps*, was the *15th Panzer Division* (von Vaerst) with the Italian *Littorio* Armored Division (Mayneri). The *15th Panzer Division*'s *kampfgruppen* consisted of *Kampfgruppe Nord* (North), which was under the command of *Oberst* Crasemann, the commander of *Artillery Regiment 33*, and consisted of the *I./Battalion Panzergrenadier Regiment 115, II./Abteilung Artillery Regiment 33, 3rd Company Flak Battalion 617*, and the Italian *51st Battalion Tank Regiment 133*. *Kampfgruppe Mitte* (Middle) was under the command of *Major* Schemmel, the commander of *Panzergrenadier Regiment 115*,[53] and consisted of units from *II./Abteilung Panzer Regiment 8, III./Battalion Panzergrenadier Regiment 115, III./Abteilung Artillery Regiment 33*, and the Italian *6th Battalion Tank Regiment 133, 23rd Infantry Battalion Bersaglieri Regiment 12, 24th Battalion Artillery Regiment 3*, and *Semovette* (Tank Destroyer) *Battalion 556*. *Kampfgruppe Sud* (South) was under the command of *Oberst* Willi Teege, and it consisted of the following units: *I./Abteilung Panzer Regiment 8, II./Battalion Panzergrenadier Regiment 115, I./Abteilung Artillery Regiment 33*, the Italian *12th Battalion Tank Regiment 133, 36th Infantry Battalion Bersaglieri Regiment 12, II./Battalion Artillery Regiment 3*, and *Tank Destroyer Battalion 554*. The Divisional Reserve was under the command of *Hptm* Hinrichs, commander of *Pioneer Battalion 33*, and consisted of his battalion with *Panzerjäger Abteilung 33* and the *10./Abteilung Artillery Regiment 33*. The following formations were held back behind the front in reserve positions to guard against amphibious attack from the sea near El Daba: the *90th Light Division* (von Sponeck) with the Italian *Trieste Motorized Division* (La Perla). There were also the *300th Oasis Battalion, Panzerjäger Abteilung 605* (Fischer), and a *Combat Escort Gruppe* under direct command of the Headquarters *D.A.K.* The *288th Special Gruppe* and *Aufklärung Abteilung 580* were located at Mersa Matruh, and the Italian *Pistoia* Division was guarding the rear areas near Bardia and Sollum.[54] For *Panzer Regiment 8*, it reported the following combat strength: forty-three officers, no civilian technicians, 230 *unteroffizer*, and 698 men from an obliged strength of forty-nine, eight, 505, and 1,298 respectively. There were also 102 panzers reported as operational.[55] For the remainder of September and into the first weeks of October the Regiment split into its respective *kampfgruppen* and dug in its panzers. There was little fuel, so only necessary movements were allowed. The panzers were concealed as best they could from the *DAF*, and this normally meant in a wadi or depression, or near some camel thorn bushes. Each panzer was made into a bunker, with a hole dug for the crew beneath the panzer and rocks piled up around the sides. The companies received replacement personnel and quickly brought them up to speed in the necessary crew drills. Although replacement personnel could be brought over, most of them aboard *Ju-52s*, new panzers and other heavy equipment could only be brought over aboard ships. The failure to go after Malta earlier in the summer was now causing havoc to the *Panzerarmee*, as urgently needed equipment and fuel sank to the bottom of the ocean. The workshop companies and "I" services were constantly busy in order to put the broken panzers back into operation. On 30 September 1942, while the men went about their daily duties, a strange episode took place, and it was witnessed by Kurt Kathe, who remembered:

"*Once when we at El Alamein came 3 planes 150 meters from my location it was Marseille who always brought us mail and such,…he had connections, he flew over our place and made it so we knew [it was him] The Brits always use to broadcast to their comrades 'Careful Marseille is in the air' By the time Marseille had crashed, he had shot over 100 airplanes, he shot 17 in a day [1 Sep 42]. We were in a position, we had halted there and set up tents, we made it so, then he flies in the middle, on both sides of him were 'kettenhunde' [escorts] and he went over the British positions without shooting and comes back. He had to test the engine in the fighter aircraft and suddenly we heard one plane was shot and heard over the radio 'I have smoke in my cabin' then again 'I get out' we saw a parachute and off we went. His aircraft with the colors [smoke] going down, shit! A couple of meters further, he leaves [jumps out] of his aircraft, he crashed 500m in front of my tent, we went there and Marseille was there, he had with him a imitation of the Ritterkreuz and papers. Then came the Geschwader (Group) Neumann from Derna, and they landed there, I was with my 'Waffenmeister'. At that time we did not call it a 'propeller' but a 'latte'. We screwed it out, and engraved on it. We wrote the death day and the name 'Marseille' and 'From the 5th Company Pzr Rgt 8' and then we gave it to Geschwader Neumann, who was the chief of the group. Later the Brits made a wreath and dropped it out for him. The other two planes went back and reported [what happened]. They buried him at Capuzzo it was where we buried people. It was a graveyard, bad soil, only stones. Wild dogs use to get them out [dig them up] and eat them.*"[56]

It is almost impossible to track the specific company and troop movements during these final days of summer, as most of the companies and *zugs* ceased to exist due to panzer losses and reorganization. It is, however, possible to track some of the major officer assignments within the Regiment. Since the beginning of the Gazala attack, the various leadership positions within the Regiment and the subsequent replacements changed on an average of every week to two weeks. With the loss of experienced *abteilung* commanders like Kümmel, Wahl, and Zügner, the Regiment was now beginning to suffer from a lack of senior leadership. In many cases throughout the war, the Germans, time and time again, were able to bring up excellent junior level officers and NCOs and place them into more senior positions of leadership and responsibility. This was also the case for the Regiment, as junior and senior *unteroffizers* were promoted and given command over platoons and companies. Fortunately, the regiment had a good corps of young officers who had expert tutelage under those officers that had been either replaced, killed, wounded, or captured. One of those was young *Hptm* Otto Stiefelmayer, who had followed in Kümmel's steps and was promoted to commander of the *I./Abteilung*.

Panzer Regiment 8 chain of command as of 23 October 1942:

Regiment Commander	Oberst Teege
I./Abteilung Commander	Hptm Stiefelmayer
1st Company	Lt Keil
2nd Company	Olt Baumann
3rd Company	Hptm Hirschfeld
4th Company	Olt Schulz
II./Abteilung Commander	Hptm Siemens
5th Company	Olt Schellhaus
6th Company	Olt Decker
7th Company	Olt Lindner
8th Company	Olt Bänger

The following officers, listed alphabetically, served in various positions within the Regiment; most commanded or led what remained of the Companies, *Zugs*, and Sections:

Hauptmann Heinrich, Hirschfeld (KIA), and Schefold.

Oberleutnants Baumann, Bänger, Blidschuhn, Chrestin, Danz, Decker, Eichberg, Halverscheidt, Keil (KIA), Lindner, Marquardt, Nürnberger, Russow, Schellhaas, Schultz, Thurow, Tschech, Voigt, and Weiss

Leutnants Aich, Baeck, Bahnert, Ballhaus, Baudert, Bastigkeit, Bischoff, Bohr, Bohland (KIA), Boser, Bösebeck, von Brunn, Erb, Förster, Golinski, Gottfried, Haag, Hohnecker, von Houwald, Hubbuch, Ihde, Kehrer, Keil, Keller, Krüger, Kuhlhoff, Langenbach, Mayländer, Melber, Mittelmayer (KIA), Paschy, Rösch, Rummler, Schuberski, Steinel, Streibel, Thamphald, Toffert, Tomaszewski, Wickenhäuser, Wiegels, and Woldsen.

Regimental Engineering officers: Major Schnell, *Hptm* Hauska, and *OInsp* Lampe.

Regimental Doctors: *StArzt* Becker, *StArzt* Hochstetter, *OArzt* Estor, *OArzt* Krüger, and *UArzt* Maisch.

The Regiment reported a total panzer strength of 105 for 23 October 1942. The I./*Abteilung* had forty-six of these, while the II./*Abteilung* had fifty-eight. This total number was made up of seventy-nine Mk IIIs and seventeen Mk IVs.[57]

12

The Battle of El Alamein October-December 1942

In the weeks prior to Montgomery launching "*Operation Lightfoot,*" the great battle of El Alamein, or "*Second Alamein,*" as many in the *Eighth Army* had termed the battle, the days went on as usual for the *Panzerarmee* and *D.A.K.* It was a time for rest and refitting, but also of preparing for the next round, which many desert veterans knew was not long in coming. It was clear to Rommel and his troops that the critical time had arrived for either victory or defeat. Despite all the losses the Regiment had endured in its 18 months of fighting, morale was still extremely high, and the men still believed that victory could be achieved. The day preceding the great offensive had been no different than any other that October; sporadic shelling had taken place, and troop and transport movement had been normal. In other words, there was nothing to indicate to the Germans that an attack was imminent. In fact, intelligence reports from *OKW* stated that no British attacks were possible for at least a month.[1] Wilhelm Hagios remembers:

"For us then there was not much going on, we were upfront with the Italians as corsets, they buried their Lire [money] and the British kept them under heavy cannon fire, we made a bunker under the panzer just in case of emergency."[2]

At 2045hrs on Friday, 23 October 1942, the first artillery spotting rounds were fired into the battlefield area in the offensive's opening moments; these rounds were used to judge the meteorological data necessary to provide the most accurate of fires. In the previous months the guns and howitzers had been calibrated and registered to ensure accuracy without giving away their positions and hinting that an attack was in the making. Although unknown at that time, the great battle had begun along the El Alamein line. Gerhard Weidelener remembered:

"On 23 October at 2045hrs, all the British artillery batteries were engaged, and there was tremendous noise and non-stop lightning all over the horizon. Now we understood what was going on and [wondered] how we had ended up in this mess."[3]

Quickly the reports from various units began to stream in to the *panzerarmee*, corps, and divisional headquarters informing them that they were under heavy attack. At 2110hrs, *Kampfgruppe Sud* reported that enemy infantry attacks were observed between mine boxes K and L. At about 2115hrs, the *Stabs* of the *15th Panzer Division* had reported to the *D.A.K.* that they had been under fire for approximately three minutes. This bombardment was a part of the *24th Australian Brigade's* pre-planned deception firing.[4] At 2130hrs reports from the liaison officer to the *Littorio Division*, *Olt* Wandruszka, informed the division that at 2045hrs enemy artillery fire had begun, and by 2105hrs the division's artillery positions were coming under attack. At 2115hrs *Kampfgruppe Mitte* reported that enemy bombers were overhead and hitting the *kampfgruppe's* units.[5] A short time later, at 2140hrs, the largest artillery barrage ever seen in the desert war began, when over eight hundred *Eighth Army* artillery pieces opened fire on Axis positions. The whole of the Alamein line was set alight by this tremendous fire, and a thunderous roar could be heard from great distance. For the German and Italian troops of *D.A.K.* and *Panzerarmee* they could only cower in their foxholes and endure this deliverance from hell. For the next fifteen minutes those guns belched fire and roared in earnest as the barrage rolled forward on that full moonlit desert night. At 2200hrs the guns fell silent, as that initial bombardment had taken a short pause before it again continued in unimaginable intensity. It was under this second barrage that the British infantry and engineers began to move forward under the protection of a creeping barrage. At this point the guns of the *Panzerarmee's* artillery batteries were visibly silent, and might have inflicted considerable damage had the British assembly areas been targeted. However, *General* Stumme refused to allow Axis artillery batteries to open fire, and denied all their requests to do so in an attempt to husband the precious stock of artillery ammunition.[6] With the absence of any counter-battery fire and the confusion created by the *Eighth Army* artillery barrage, the British and Australians in the north were able to move forward in this initial phase. The Commonwealth artillery batteries would go on to fire various pre-planned fire programs all throughout the night and for the week to come, almost without pause. According to some *D.A.K.* reports, British artillery was not as effective on many of the Axis positions and equipment, since those positions had been well dug in and widely dispersed. However, there was considerable confusion and disruption in communications within the entire *D.A.K.*[7]

Montgomery had opened his offensive with the fire from over a thousand guns; this offensive had come not in the south, where the Germans had thought to expect it, but in the north along the coastal road, against the infantry formations of *Panzerarmee*. With the artillery designed to blast gaps through the Axis line of defense, in particular the extensive minefields, it was up to the engineers and infantry to begin breaching operations and clearing lanes through the minefields in which the infantry and armor would move through. For the battle, *GHQ Middle East* (Alexander) and *Eighth Army* (Montgomery) had assembled 200,476 troops, 939 tanks, 892 artillery guns, 1,452 anti-tank guns, and 530 aircraft.[8] In addition to these numbers, additional men and equipment

192

Wearing their new desert uniforms, member of the 3rd Company prepare for their journey to North Africa. Hans Killermann is second from the right. (Killermann)

A new Mk III, belonging to the 2nd Company, and mounting the short 50mm cannon is ready for shipment to Africa (Hess)

Oberstlt Friedrich Haarde (with the white arm band), Hans Killerman (second from the right), and some Italian officers review the I./*Abteilung* as it prepares to depart from Italy. Hans Kummel is the officer on the far left. (Weber)

Loading a Mk III for the journey to Africa (BBN)

One of the ships that carried the Regiment to Italy (H Liestmann)

An Italian escort ship pulling alongside one of the transports during the journey to Africa (H Liestmann)

Arrival in Tripoli (H Liestmann)

The panzers of the *2nd Company* forming up for the march to the east (H Liestmann)

Taking a short nap before the long drive to the Egyptian border (BBN)

Mk IIIs of the 7th *Company* during an inspection prior to the journey east. These panzers are all equipped with the short 50mm gun (BBN)

A previously damaged Mk II of the 3rd *Company* loaded down for the journey ahead. Note the Regimental and *15th Panzer Division* symbols on the storage box. (BBN)

Hptm Hans Kümmel (bare chest) speaks with Italian officers during the journey (BBN)

A break during the journey east, sampling the Italian wine (H Liestmann)

A Mk IV being repaired, the harsh desert sand begins to take effect (BBN)

A panzer lager in the middle of the desert. The fuel cans with white crosses denoted water containers. (BBN)

The coast at Sollum (H Liestmann)

The command panzer of *Oberstlt* Hans Cramer halts to issue orders (Hagios)

88mm Flak guns in stone sangers at Halfaya Pass (H Liestmann)

Members of the I./*Abteilung* survey the ground ahead as Gerhard Kienzle pokes his head out from inside the turret; his friend, Hermann Eckardt, stands along side. (Kienzle)

A Mk II overlooking the coast near Bardia and Sollum (BBN)

Mk IIs and IIIs moving up towards the front (Bühler)

A pair of British Mk II Matildas destroyed near Sollum and Bardia (BBN)

The new owners of a captured Matilda (H Liestmann)

The Matildas are pressed into service by the Regiment near Halfaya Pass (H Liestmann)

A British Mk VI Crusader II tank is also pressed into German service (Hess)

A captured Matilda ready to be towed off, in the rear are Mk IVs that have set up camp (H Liestmann)

A captured British tank transporter is used to transport a captured Matilda (K Liestmann)

A destroyed Mk IV from the *8th Company* and early British Mk VI Crusier tank (Hess)

A knocked out British A-13 Mk IVA Crusier tank (BBN)

A knocked out British A-10 Mk IIA Crusier light tank (Hess)

A knocked out American M-3 Stuart light tank, known as the Honey by British troops (Killermann)

A German soldier takes the time to cover the face of a dead British soldier as a Crusader burns. (Huttenlocher)

An 8 wheeled Sdkfz 263 communications vehicle (BBN)

A German Sdkfz 251 command halftrack (BBN)

Rommel inspects a captured British A-13 Mk IIA tank (Hess)

The stone sangers near Halfaya, they are now occupied by a captured Matilda tank and Mk IV (Kienzle)

A Sdkf-8 tank transporter in bivouac (BBN)

The crew of a 2nd *Company* Mk III sets up camp in the desert (H Liestmann)

A Mk-IV destroyed in the early fighting (Boger)

A Mk IV moving towards the front and kicking up a lot of dust (H Liestmann)

The crew of a Mk IV conduct daily services (BBN)

A Mk III moves up along the Egyptian border wire (BBN)

Panzers forming up for the attack in the Summer of 1941 (BBN)

The Hotel Capuzzo where a number of the early actions in the desert war took place (Hess)

A Mk III belonging to the *1st Company* moves up (BBN)

A British artillery park overrun during the Crusader battles of November 1941 (H Liestmann)

A destroyed British 25-Pounder artillery gun near Sidi Rezegh (Huttenlocher)

A large group of British prisoners being directed to the rear during the Crusader battles of November and December 1941 (Kienzle)

The crew of a Mk IV has loaded down their panzer with captured booty (H Liestmann)

During the summer of 1941, the men line up to receive inoculations (BBN)

With the Regimental band providing entertainment, the men take time to relax in the African sun (H Liestmann)

The Arco Filini, where some members of the Regiment found their final resting place (Hess)

A captured British 2-Pounder anti-tank gun finds a place in the Regiment's lager (H Liestmann)

A Mk III is used as a protective bunker for its crew (Hess)

A 2nd Company Mk III in a desert camp (Kienzle)

A Mk IV is partially dug in as the crew begins the daily services (Huttenlocher)

Oberst Hans Cramer and his crew after he was awarded the Knights Cross (Boger)

Olt Jahn (left), Hans Cramer (center), and Wolfgang Wahl (right) pose for a picture together (Boger)

A Mk IIs has its engine removed for repairs by the *Werkshop Company* (BBN)

Reinforcements arrive in Derna aboard a Ju-52 transport (Hess)

A small donkey is enlisted to transport water; the white cross was used to designate water from fuel (H Liestmann)

The crew of a damaged Mk IV can only take a break until repairs are made (Killermann)

The crew of this Mk IV sets up house keeping in the desert (BBN)

The crew of an Italian AB-41 armored car poses with members of the 3rd Company (Killermann)

Preparing for the attack, a Mk IV moves up pass a group of officers who are busy scanning the battleground ahead (Hess)

The driver of a Mk III poses with his panzer (Huttenlocher)

The attack begins, Hans Kümmel (standing) issues orders as his I./Abteilung advances (BBN)

Max Lebold (right), the gunner of a Mk III, loads belts of machine gun ammunition (Lebold)

A Mk III Special and its commander, *HFw* Thamphald (Boger)

Oberst Fritz Bayerlein spends some time with the Regiment and takes the time to snap a quick photo (Huttenlocher)

One of the new 75mm Mk IV "Special" arrives at the front in May 1942 (BBN)

A new Mk IV is broken in for the tough desert conditions (Weidelener)

Above left: A new Mk IVF2 "Special" of the *4th Company*, under going some minor repairs. Center: One of the first Grant tanks destroyed during the Gazala battles in May 1942 (Both Killermann)
Above right: A quick bite to eat during a break in the fighting during the summer of 1942 (Lebold)

A Grant or "Pilot" that has fallen victim to the Regiment's guns during the Gazala battle (BBN)

A new British 6-pounder AT gun and its transport that were captured in the fighting around Gazala and Tobruk (Huttenlocher)

OFw Spohn and a German *panzergrenadier* watch over a line of Commonwealth prisoners being escorted to the rear (BBN)

Olt Otto Stiefelmayer, recently decorated with Knights Cross, checks out a BMW motorcycle used by the *kradmelder* section (Mayer)

A *1st Company* Mk III "Special" during the drive towards El Alamein, the tank in the background is an Mk IV "Special" (Boger)

A Mk III damaged by British artillery fire near El Alamein (Hagios)

A *5th Company* Mk III Special, during a pause in the action September 1942 (BBN)

Hptm Hans Kümmel poses with the crew of a Ju-52 as he prepares to depart Africa for home (BBN)

A dug in Mk III faces forward in the area near El Alamein (BBN)

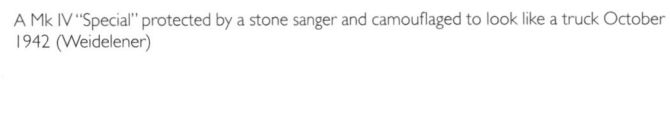

With *Olt* Karl Halverscheidt looking on, the cooks are preparing to serve a special treat (Halverscheidt)

A Mk IV "Special" protected by a stone sanger and camouflaged to look like a truck October 1942 (Weidelener)

A Mk III "Special" is dug in near El Alamein, its barrel used to dry laundry (Weidelener)

A Mk IV being transported to the rear for repairs (Haidt)

Panzers and supply trucks moving over hilly terrain towards Tunisia in December 1942 (Haidt)

A Mk III Ausf N, of the I./*Abteilung*, moving through a Tunisian village. *Hptm* Stotten is in the commander's hatch. (Mayer)

A Mk III in a camouflaged position near the Tunisian border (Mayer)

Oberst Irkens (seated) issues orders to his *Abteilung* commanders, *Hptm* Siemens (second from the right) and *Hptm* Stotten third from the right. His driver, *Uffz* Wilhelm Hagios, stands to the left (Hagios)

Hans Mayer, a dispatch rider, awaits his orders in early 1943 (Mayer)

The Regimental band photographed in Tunisia, February 1943 (BBN)

Hptm Stotten (facing) and Hptm Siemens in the turret of the
I./Abteilung command panzer (Mayer)

A captured American M-3 halftrack is used by the Regiment
after the Kasserine battles (Maisch)

March 1943, Oberst Irkens addresses his soldier in one of the
last formal gatherings of the Regiment in Tunisia. (Hagios)

The Regimental *Stabs*, dug into the side of a wadi in Tunisia, April 1943, *Oberst* Josef Irkens stands to the far left (Hagios)

Wilhelm Hagios (middle) and the crew members of the Mk III regimental command panzer pause for a quick meal in Tunisia (Hagios)

The remains of the *Oberst* Irkens' staff car after being struck by Allied fighter-bombers in Tunisia (Hagios)

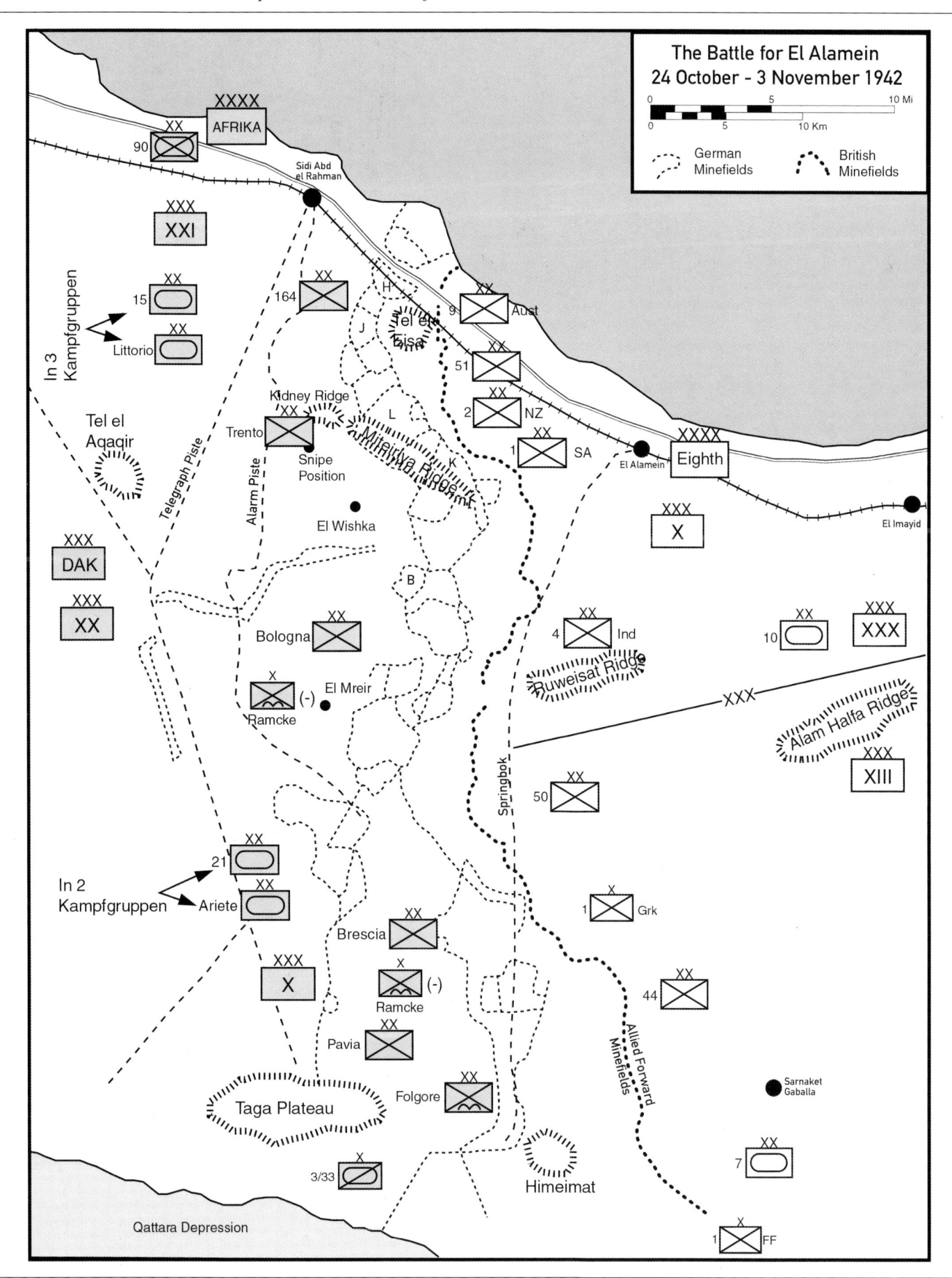

Chapter 12: The Battle of El Alamein, October–December 1942

were further to the rear in Egypt. The *Eighth Army* was arrayed from the north to south with the infantry heavy *XXX Corps* (Leese) forward in the line. This corps consisted of the *9th Australian Division* (Morshead), *51st (Highland) Division* (Wimberley), *2nd New Zealand Division* (Freyberg), and *1st South African Division* (Pienaar). Behind the infantry were the armored divisions of the *X Corps* (Lumsden), which consisted of the *1st Armored Division* (Briggs) and *10th Armored Division* (Gatehouse). Finally, there was the *XIII Corps* (Horrocks) with the *4th Indian Division* (Tuker), a *Greek Brigade* (Katsotas), the *50th (Northumbrian) Division* (Nichols), *44th (Home Counties) Division* (Hughes), and the *1st Free French Brigade*.[9] The first phase of the operation was to last from 23-25 October; the *Eighth Army* plan was to launch a diversionary attack with its *XIII Corps* in the south, while the main push would come in the north by the *X* and *XXX Corps*. After the gaps were created the sappers were to lead the way, clearing lanes, detonating explosives in the enemy wire, and placing colored electric lights to indicate the cleared paths. As the young replacement Adolf Lamm remembers:

"Around 23 October, we heard a continuous roar of heavy shelling in the distance and knew this was serious."[10]

The artillery fires had only a limited effect, and as the engineers moved forward they were met by some rather heavy resistance in the form of mortar and machine gun fire from those positions intermingled within the minefields. However, most of the initial tasks were accomplished, and the follow on infantry moved forward towards their initial objectives.

The Regiment and its *abteilung* were alerted and prepared for immediate deployment; most of the panzer companies were centered on the Otto Piste, which allowed them to move quickly to the decisive points of attack. The Regimental *Stabs* was located south on the Otto Piste near Alam Burt Sabai el Sharb, behind the command post of the I./*Abteilung*. That *abteilung* was further split into two groups: the forward group, consisting of the *1st* and *4th Companies*, was situated along the Alarm Piste further forward than the headquarters, but behind those German and Italian formations arrayed in front of minefield "K." The *2nd* and *3rd Companies* were located further west, behind the regimental *stabs* and the Otto Piste, and grouped just south of Alam Burt Sabai Gharbi. The command post of the II./*Abteilung* was located further north with *Kampfgruppe Mitte*, and just north of Kidney Ridge, centered on minefield "J" east of the Otto Piste.[11] The *abteilung* had three of its companies positioned forward (the *5th*, *7th*, and *8th*), while the *6th Company* was placed in reserve to the rear of the *abteilung* headquarters. As in most modern defensive alignments, the Axis positions were aligned in depth, which allowed each different service to be able to mutually support one another while avoiding enemy artillery and bombing attacks. The heavier and valuable panzer forces remained behind the forward infantry and anti-tank positions, allowing them the ability to maneuver and reinforce the lighter forces and seal off any attempted enemy breakthroughs. The massive artillery barrage that had preceded the infantry attacks had effectively targeted the minefields and the dug in grenadiers and Pak gunners supporting that line. In addition, the barrage had managed to knock out much of the wire communications. The loss of the secure communications and the heavy amount of radio traffic flooding the airwaves was enough to effectively keep the *Panzerarmee* in the dark as to what was taking place. On the morning of the 24th, *General* Stumme, shedding his normal escort, went forward with only his operations officer and driver in an attempt to make contact with his forces. The small trio set off in search of the headquarters of the *90th Light Division*, which at that time was located just to the north of Stumme's command post. That would be the last time that anyone from Stumme's headquarters would see him alive. It is strongly believed that while en-route forward, the driver of the command car became lost or disoriented, and accidently strayed into an area occupied by Australian forces. The remainder of the story and the events that transpired that morning differ slightly. Many experts believe that the most plausible cause of Stumme's death was as a result of enemy fire, while others believe that Stumme suffered a fatal heart attack. What is known is that the command car strayed into a forward area where it was struck by enemy fire, which either killed or mortally wounded the operations officer. The driver, who it is believed became so frightened by the sudden encounter with enemy forces, is thought to have sped off just as Stumme was getting out of the car in search of cover. As the car was making this maneuver, it is believed that Stumme continued to hold on and attempted to run with the car as he struggled to remount the vehicle. Stumme, who had a history of heart problems, is believed to have then suffered his fatal heart attack and fell from the car. Although plausible, that assertion is complicated when the body was found a couple of days later, and there appeared to be traces of wounds.[12] Regardless of how it happened, it was some time before he was listed as missing, and it further aggravated the Axis command and control situation. After the disappearance of Stumme, von Thoma was summoned from the *D.A.K.* Headquarters that afternoon to take command of the *Panzerarmee*. Upon his arrival Thoma was aghast by what he found; a static line that had been breached in many places, and no mobile reserves to seal those breaches with. He immediately left the headquarters and drove to the *15th Panzer Division* in order to organize a push north by *Panzer Regiment 8*.[13] By the time Rommel, who was still on medical leave and recuperating in Austria, returned on the evening of the 25th, the situation had dramatically worsened, and almost every element of the *Panzerarmee* would be deployed into the battle.

It was in the northern sector that first day where the brunt of the battle was fought between Miteiriya Ridge and the coast. During the night of 23/24 October, the *XXX Corps'* infantry divisions had been able to gain some of their objectives on the *Oxalic Line*, and had pushed forward enough forces to gain a portion of the Miteiriya Ridge. The brunt of the *X Corps* armored attack was to also fall in this sector, as the *1st Armored Division* drove due west towards Miteiriya Ridge, while a follow-on attack by the *10th Armored Division* drove southwest to capture the ridge itself. The I./*Abteilung*, positioned along the right flank of the *15th Panzer Division's* defensive sector, was not hit on the 24th by the full force of the attack because this sector was situated along the left boundary of the attacking *XXX Corps*, and therefore was not fully covered by the overlapping artillery fires. However, the II./*Abteilung*, combined with *Kampfgruppe Schemmel* further in the north, did receive the full impact of the artillery barrage and later the ground attack. At 0200hrs the British attacked at various points along the northern portion of the line and were able to break through the defensive minefields in front of the III./*Panzergrenadier Regiment 115*. The II./*Abteilung* was then ordered to counterattack in order to throw back those *XXX Corps* infantry and armored forces. The counterattack was launched in the early morning hours of 24 October, with the *6th Company* taking the lead; the remaining companies followed them, while the *8th Company*, with its long barreled Mk IVs, had been left behind in an over-watch position in order to provide security and covering fire.[14] At 0645hrs *Olt* Wandruszka, the divisional LNO, reported that the Italian *IV/133 Tank battalion* was advancing along the right flank of the II./*Abteilung* in order to provide additional cover and flank security. At 0700hrs the *7th Company*, led by *Olt* Lindner, along with the *6th Company*, which was deployed to the right and led by *Olt* Decker, encountered large numbers of enemy tanks. *Hptm* Siemens ordered *Olt* Schellhaas, the commander of the *5th Company*, to remain in *abteilung* reserve a short distance to the rear. In the attack that followed, the II./*Abteilung* encountered a mixed group of *Matilda*, *Valentine*, and *Grant*

Chapter 12: The Battle of El Alamein, October-December 1942

tanks, most probably from the *2nd Armored Brigade*, which were met head on and quickly forced back. The attack was supported by the guns of *Artillery Regiment 33*, which were able to engage targets between the panzers and the minefields, but had a difficult time covering the exit gaps, which were obscured by the dust, fumes, and noise of the battle. Three British tanks were destroyed in the action before Siemens then ordered the *5th Company* to move forward in order to form a defensive line behind the *hinterhangstellung*, in order to hold the newly won position and defend it against further attacks. The divisional war diary recorded that at 0830hrs, the *II./Abteilung* was located near A.P. 407 in the southeast, while the Italian *IV/133rd* had returned to their old positions as the British armor withdrew back about four kilometers to the northeast.

Just before the *II./Abteilung's* attack had begun in the north, the *I./Abteilung* had been ordered to launch its own counterattack beginning at around 0630hrs. That attack had been ordered by *Kampfgruppe Sud*, and was launched in the direction of A.P. 489 with the *1st* and *4th Companies*, with the hope of gaining the HKL position in the area of Italian *II./Jäger Regiment 62*. The *I./Abteilung* was directly subordinated to *Kampfgruppe Sud* and under the command of *Oberst* Willi Teege.[15] It was in front of *Kampfgruppe Sud* where few Axis formations still remained, either having been destroyed in the initial attacks, or simply melted away to the west like many of the Italian infantry battalions had done after coming under a constant rain of artillery fire. The *XXX Corps' 2nd New Zealand Division* infantry, closely followed by the tanks of the *9th Armored Brigade*, began its attack through the newly created minefield gaps. The infantry had done fairly well in its advance, but it was the British armor that had the problem of getting through. The tanks were stalled in their attempts to get through by the confusion and lack of cleared lanes, not to mention the fire from German artillery and Pak gunners, which succeeded in making the trip through the gaps highly dangerous. Sensing an opportunity to catch those forces off balance, *Hptm* Stiefelmayer immediately launched a counterattack with his panzers and quickly rolled forward to close the gap between the two sides before they began to engage the British tanks. The decision proved to be the right one, as the first Grant tanks of the armored brigade began to burn in the sudden confusion. It was during this attack that the crews identified another new type of tank following just behind the *Grants*. The new tank had a large round turret and sported a large cannon.[16] These were the new American *M-4 "Shermans,"* which were armed with a 75mm main gun and two .30 caliber and one .50 caliber machine guns. The turret and hull were made from cast steel that had armor protection between 40-90mm thick, a top speed of some 40kmh, and a range of some 300km. But those *Shermans* were, for the time being, unable to break through because of the congestion caused by the leading *Grant* squadrons, which had attempted to maneuver through and exit the minefields. As the *Grants* made that attempt, they were met by accurate tank fire from the *I./Abteilung*, which succeeded in destroying and setting alight a number of them, forcing the remainder to scurry for cover further to the rear. With so much confusion going on a number of the new *Shermans* were forced to move off of the cleared mine lanes, where they inadvertently wandered into the minefields. In those minefields and Devil's Gardens there were all types of mines and nasty surprises waiting just under the sand. As in the case of minefield "L" there were aerial bombs, which had been planted like mines and were set to detonate like a land mine whenever an enemy vehicle drove over them. These nasty surprises caused all kinds of confusion in the attacking columns, and panicked the tanks crews so much that they lost all sense of order in their haste to disengage from these places. Within a short time the advance was halted, as the fire from the *I./Abteilung* coupled with the artillery, Pak guns, and minefields allowed only a few survivors to escape. With the loss of just two of its panzers, the *I./Abteilung* was able to claim the destruction of twenty-seven British

tanks, and noted that an additional thirty-five of them had been abandoned in the minefield.[17] As if the situation was perfectly under control Teege sent out his analysis of the action as of mid-morning on the *24th*:

"The enemy has failed again to captured terrain within the main combat field due to the counter-attacks of I./PzRgt 8 and II./Pz.Rgt.8. It [the enemy] is located in Kasten 'L' with about 100 tanks. The HKL is by [in] large won back. Now it's all about forcing the enemy out of the minefields, while it is in position to take as many mines as it's necessary to get free movement. Also in the area of the break-through by the Italian III/ J.R. 62 the situation within the main combat field is cleaned. The enemy, with infantry and tanks is still located here in the blocking zone between the combat outposts and HKL. Also here it's all about forcing the enemy out of their positions. In this situation the division commander drives forward, in order to talk with commander of 164th Light Afrika Division and commander of the kampfgruppen about further actions."[18]

At 1130hrs, in an attempt to close the gaps between minefields "J" and "L," *Kampfgruppe Mitte* was ordered by the *D.A.K.* to counterattack those *XXX Corps* forces in that area. The *kampfgruppe* was given the following reinforcements in order to accomplish its mission: *II./Abteilung Artillery Regiment 33*, *I./Panzergrenadier Regiment 115*, and the Italian *51/133 Tank battalion*. With the bulk of the *15th Panzer Division* already involved in heavy combat and presently stuck in its attempts to drive out those British forces from its area of responsibility, the *II./Abteilung* was ordered to fall back to its old positions as soon as it became dark in order to provide a mobile reserve. At 1445hrs the *II./Abteilung* reported that so far it had suffered the loss of fourteen panzers that had been put out of action in the day's fighting. From its current position the panzer crews could clearly see that British tanks were only about three kilometers in the distance, with infantry forces gathering behind them. *Hptm* Siemens reported at 1620hrs that his *abteilung* was again under heavy tank attack, estimated to be at some two hundred tanks, and that urgent support was needed. The *abteilung* was being hit by elements of the *9th Armored Brigade*, which was equipped with over one hundred and sixty tanks.[19] The British armor flooded in, and the *abteilung* was attacked simultaneously to its front and on its flanks. The fighting was brutal, as both sides gave their all and gained little for it. Siemens led the *abteilung* with an unflappable determination as he ordered his panzers to stand fast, remain quiet, and continue to engage the enemy. As the battle continued, the *abteilung* was able to thwart many of the supporting infantry attacks and knock out many of the supporting tanks, but it continued to suffer losses from the ever-pressing British armored formations. In order to provide assistance to the *II./Abteilung*, the division quickly ordered the tank destroyers of *Panzerjäger Abteilung 33* to report to the *II./Abteilung*, where they would fall under the operational command of Siemens and render what assistance they could. Axis sound detector reports also were detecting large British tank movements in the direction of the previous breakthrough, and that heavy armored forces were in the "L" and "J" mine boxes. Once again *Kampfgruppe Mitte* was ordered to render support and make available all its heavy artillery, and direct the guns on the tanks now attacking the *II./Abteilung* position. During the attack Lt Hubbuch, now the *Abteilung* Ordnance Officer, was able to coordinate for some supporting fires, but it was not enough to halt the attack, and as the battle continued to rage the chance of getting further artillery support quickly dwindled, as the artillery was overwhelmed with calls for help; there were just too many targets and fire missions, and not enough guns and ammunition. As the pressure mounted on the *abteilung* it was forced to withdraw westward behind the Pak gun line and elements of the *III./Panzergrenadier Regiment 115*, which had arrived on the scene to help stabilize and plug gaps in the line. As dusk approached and the darkness slowly crept over the battlefield the seven remaining panzers (it had began the day with twenty-eight Mk IIIs and IVs) were able to disengage and fall back to the defensive lines that were presently being held by the Pak and Flak guns. The British attacks continued into the early evening, but with the assistance of the *panzerjäger* and artillery the II./*Abteilung* was finally able to be pulled off the front line at around 2000hrs, when it pulled back to its old assembly area. The II./*Abteilung* had suffered significant losses in the day's fighting, with eight killed, including *Olt* Decker, and twenty-two wounded, including *Olt* Schellhass. The only officers who remained with the II./*Abteilung* were *Hptm* Siemens, *Olt* Lindner, *OArzt* Dr. Hochstetter, Lt Golinski, and Lt Hubbuch. On this day the II./*Abteilung* claimed the destruction of the following: forty-five tanks, five trucks, one 25-Pounder, one self-propelled anti-tank gun, and one Bofors anti-aircraft gun.[20] Wilhelm Hagios remembered those first two days with this small story:

"On 23 October we went on again, the first day there was very heavy fire and we couldn't move. The next day [24th] we got provisioning, we were at the field kitchen in the evening and here comes [a tank] and fires the shot, we were next to the truck and the shot ricocheted from the metal bumper and buzzed by high above us and struck behind us in the house with the spare tires."[21]

Even though the British had made some progress across the entire front, many of the initial objectives had not been reached. Once again it was the numerous minefields and Devil's Gardens that had slowed their attacks and forced them to postpone further advances until darkness fell, so the mine detection and lifting parties could renew their dangerous assignments. During the previous night and day the infantry and engineer parties had paid a terrible price, and unfortunately still had not pushed out far enough to completely pierce the Axis defensive line and clear enough maneuver room for the armor. During the night a number of repositioning movements were made by the British armored brigades that unfortunately did nothing more than add to the confusion and congestion along the line, especially near Miteiriya Ridge. As the men from the II./*Abteilung* caught their breath behind the Pak gun screen, the commander of *Kampfgruppe Mitte* ordered that the *abteilung* once again relocate to a new position behind the *III./Battalion Panzergrenadier Regiment 115*. As it took up positions behind the grenadiers, the *panzerjägers* were again subordinated to the *abteilung*, which was still deployed as a mobile reserve. During the night of 24/25 October the Axis positions again came under a constant artillery bombardment, as the guns of the *Royal Artillery* continued to fire in support of the infantry and armor attempting to break through. In addition to the artillery, the *DAF* was constantly overhead; its bombers, escorted by fighters, had complete air superiority, and they continued to pound Axis positions at will. *Oberst* Willi Teege, who had only just returned from Germany a few days before the attack began, had gone to great lengths, and made an extreme effort to reconsolidate his Regiment. The companies had been thrown into the fight separately, and were already worn out from the endless fighting. There was, however, little relief to be had, as all along the front the *Eighth Army* continued to creep its forces forward under the cover provided by the artillery and the *DAF*. Far to the south in the sector assigned to the *21st Panzer Division*, the British *XXX Corps* launched a number of holding and diversionary attacks, and despite the fact that they gained little ground achieved the goal of tying down vital panzer elements that were desperately needed in the north. At 0600hrs on the 25th, the Regiment was positioned in the following manner: the Regimental *Stabs* was still situated near Alam Burt Sabai Sharqi, while the I./*Abteilung* had brought forward all of its companies, with three companies placed forward and one company held in reserve near the *abteilung's* headquarters. According to the divisional KTB and situational maps, the II./*Abteilung*, which had been severely battered and pushed south the previous day, was located in two separate positions. A part of the *abteilung* was located to the northwest of El Wishka, behind the Otto Piste, while the second was located further north and west of the northern portion of minefield "J."

Early on the morning of the 25th, Lt Klaus Hubbuch, acting as a forward observer, went forward to minefield "L" in order to conduct a reconnaissance of British forces there. As Hubbuch searched the area he was able to identify the British as they gathered their forces in preparation for their next attack. Tanks, artillery, and vehicles were all moving around, taking up various positions for the renewed effort. Hubbuch continued to monitor their preparations until a sandstorm blew up and concealed the British from further view. At 1200hrs, the II./*Abteilung* received orders to attack those enemy forces gathered around the minefield. The *abteilung* was given elements of *Panzerjäger Abteilung 33* and the Italian *133rd Tank Battalion* to assist it in its mission. Just prior to jumping off, Hubbuch again moved forward and began to direct artillery fire towards the British tank and artillery assembly areas. The II./*Abteilung* launched its attack at 1230hrs, but could not break through the heavy defenses. The supporting Italian tank battalion quickly lost its will to fight after its commander was wounded, and it withdrew back to its initial departure point. Another casualty in that attack was *Olt* Lindner, who was also wounded, and was fortunate to escape his burning panzer after it was hit. The II./*Abteilung*, which was now down to just six operational panzers, broke off its attack and pulled back to the *Hinterhangstellung*. The British had lost two tanks in the attack, and chose not to follow up the attack as the panzers broke contact and moved off to the rear. However, the panzers were subjected to an hour long artillery barrage by British heavy guns that laid down fire along the *abteilung's* positions. Later in the afternoon, British infantry, with supporting armor, attacked in the same sector, but were turned away, leaving behind another two tanks that were destroyed.[22] *Oberartzt* (Doctor) Hochstetter, along with his medical detachment, was busy until late in the evening, as they attempted to locate and treat the dead, dying, and wounded men, and evacuate them from the battlefield to medical treatment facilities in the rear. All of the doctors and medical staffs and services were constantly in action over these tireless days and nights, and their achievements are impossible to describe, as countless wounded were saved by their swift actions and courage under fire. Many of the panzer crews knew that if they were wounded the doctors and medical personnel would move forward from their positions close to the front. Horst Sonnenkalb shares this brief description of one such medical attendant in his company:

"To the benefit of Africans [A long serving members of the Rgt] I must say that they are extraordinary in their courage, bravery and huge ability to carry on to the end. Our medic Obergefreiter Volz was constantly on his feet. He sacrificed himself for the many sicknesses. There were many cases of jaundice, but mostly diarrhea and most spread by amoeba dysentery. Those sick with it were prescribed with Chinin. Many of us also had ulcers on the feet, caused by the thorns of the camel bushes, which were scratching us. And last but not least the changing of bandages for those wounded who remained with the troops. Most certainly the insufficient provisioning was the cause of many illnesses in these tropical conditions, and contributed also to the insufficient body hygiene. If one had dysentery and felt for the spade, he'd run a hundred meters away from our position in the desert, quickly dig the hole and squat over it with his pants down to do his business. Here shines the field spade we said jokingly, some became constant runners when blood and mucus were in the stool."[23]

The I./*Abteilung*, which was deployed with *Kampfgruppe Sud*, had fought off three separate armored attacks throughout the day of 25 October; these attacks were launched from just south of Miteiriya Ridge by the *1st* and *10th Armored Divisions*. Otto Stiefelmayer formed his defensive front with the *1st*, *2nd*, and *3rd Companies* while deploying the Mk IVF2s of the heavy *4th Company* to the right flank. Having possession of dug in and well sited firing positions, the *abteilung* was able to claim the destruction of some seventeen tanks, nine of which where the recently introduced American *Sherman* tank. The loss of this many tanks effectively halted any further attempts to breech this area of the line by British armor. The I./*Abteilung* lost two of its Mk IIIs in the engagement. As the British tanks reorganized, Stiefelmayer gathered his remaining panzers and launched another counterattack towards a small stony track, and in the process destroyed a further seven tanks. With this daring counterattack the I./*Abteilung* had actually trapped over one hundred tanks up against its defensive line and the mine belts, where it proceeded to destroy a further fourteen tanks for the loss of just three Mk IIIs.[24] The British armor fled in panic and disarray, and if not for the lack of fuel and ammunition the *Abteilung* would have hounded them back to the safety of their own lines. After the battle the *abteilung* reformed itself and settled down for a bit of hard earned rest; however, during the night the entire division sector came under harassing fire by British artillery gunners. That evening the entire *15th Panzer Division* could only field some thirty-one operational panzers.[25] Rommel was able to reach his headquarters on the evening of the 25th after receiving a phone call from Hitler and the *OKW* asking him if he felt well enough to resume command of the *Panzerarmee*. Rommel, not wanting to be known as a general who gained his laurels at his men's expense and then left them in their time of need, immediately boarded his plane and flew via Rome and Sicily to return to his beloved *Afrika Korps*. The situation when he reported late that evening was indeed grim, and von Thoma briefed him on the overall situation facing the *Panzerarmee*. In the north the German *164th Light Division* and Italian *Trento Division* had taken a severe mauling, and the latter had been almost completely wiped out. However upbeat the situation in the north might be, the *15th Panzer* and *Littorio Divisions*, having contained the British attacks there, had suffered heavy losses in the process of doing so. In the south, the formations located there were more or less intact, but were still engaged with the *XIII Corps* and of little use to the hard pressed forces in the north. The greatest problem he faced was in the area of logistics; since the battle had begun little if any fuel had made its way to North Africa, and the *Panzerarmee* was beginning to run critically low on it. Fuel was not only needed to move the mobile elements, but to replenish them with food and ammunition, which lay a good distance to the rear. Rommel wasted little time informing his men of his return, and despite being unable to directly influence the battle now taking place, he was able to bring a certain amount of determination and much needed lift in morale to the German and Italian units now fighting it out along the line. The news that Rommel had returned quickly spread along the line and bolstered those fighting formations with a sense that the situation would soon be reversing itself. Rommel now ordered that the all-important coastal sector be secure by regaining Point 29, and that the panzers be conserved and the 88mm guns moved up in order to deal with the British armor. By that evening the *90th Light* and *Trieste Divisions* were to move forward from their positions near El Daba to reinforce the coastal sector.[26] To the south, the *21st Panzer* and other Axis formations defending there had not, as of yet, been directly involved in the fighting, and were still in good shape to help influence the battle by launching counterattacks. So the *21st Panzer* was ordered to move north to reinforce Rommel's planned panzer assault. On the British side, Winston Churchill began to become concerned with the progress of the battle to date, and felt that it was becoming another no win situation. Montgomery, on the other hand, held no such feelings, believing his forces would continue to wear down the German and Italian forces in the battle of attrition. On the morning of 26 October the Italian fuel tanker *Proserpina* was torpedoed and sunk by *Royal Navy* planes near Tobruk harbor.[27] The loss of this large tanker carrying precious fuel, which was the lifeblood of the *Panzerarmee* and would allow the army to properly attack and defend itself, was a significant loss. The loss of this tanker would be one of the most significant losses suffered by the *Panzerarmee* in the entire battle, and as some historians have stated, the entire North African campaign; unfortunately, it would not be the last. For the Regiment, it continued to come under heavy artillery fires from the British guns, with several positions getting caught in the bombardments. These fires caused significant damage and losses in the Regiment, and it was forced to send some of the I./*Abteilung* panzer crews that were without their panzers forward to fill the gaps in the front line. It was at about this time that the panzer men observed a new and deadly development in British tactics, as the infantry was now accompanied by *Bren* gun carriers towing the 6-Pounder anti-tank gun in company strength. In general, many of the previous infantry attacks could be beaten off easily enough, but the introduction of numerous anti-tank guns supporting the infantry allowed for these attacks to succeed and then hold the ground, compared to past attacks when they had been forced to retreat in the face of the panzers.

Defense of Outpost Snipe 26/27 October 1942

One of the most interesting actions of the Battle of El Alamein was the defensive stand at an obscure low depression known as the "*Snipe*" position. The battle that took place there has, over the years, been well written about, and subsequently much lauded by the British Army, and especially the *Light Infantry Regiment*. In this action a small but potent British infantry force, supported by a number of anti-tank guns, played a vital role in the outcome of the Alamein battle. After the battle, the British Army would award one *Victoria Cross* (VC) and a number of *Distinguished Service Orders* (DSO), *Distinguished Conduct Medals* (DCM), and other gallantry in action awards to those defenders.[28] This action has a direct connection to the Regiment, because it was near this location that elements of the Regiment and I./*Abteilung* first engaged the British infantry and anti-tank guns, and attempted to overrun the position there. Since the battle had begun, Montgomery had wanted the *Oxalic Line* to be extended past the Kidney Ridge feature, and more space won around the divisional boundary between the *51st Highland* and *9th Australian Divisions*. To accomplish this task he instructed *General* Briggs of the *1st Armored Division* to devise a plan of attack. Since the *1st Armored Division* would not be withdrawn into a reserve position, Briggs decided that he must keep his forces pushing to the west. His plan called for his infantry, accompanied by anti-tank guns, to move forward and establish positions west of the *Oxalic Line* near Kidney Ridge, so named because of its contour line, which resembled the shape of a kidney bean. If his forces could push out and secure these positions they would be in position to sever the German supply lines running north to south. It was also thought that by enticing the Axis panzer forces to attack these positions they could be held in check by the anti-tank guns and then destroyed by the tanks of the *2nd* and *24th Armored Brigades* as they moved up and further west. On the 25th the *1st Armored Division's 7th Motor Brigade* (Bosvile) was ordered to attack with two of its infantry battalions on the afternoon of the 26th. The original plan had called for both battalions to attack and secure the position known as "*Woodcock*," north of Kidney Ridge, but now they called for a battalion to attack and secure not only *Woodcock*, but also a second objective south of Kidney Ridge known as "*Snipe*." Both objectives would be secured during the evening of the 26/27th. The infantry objectives at Kidney Ridge were to be secured by the *2nd Battalion, 60th Rifles* (Heathcoat-Amory)

Kings Royal Rifle Corps (KRRC), which was ordered to secure *Woodcock*, while the *2nd Battalion, The Rifle Brigade* (Turner), would secure *Snipe* in the south. Both infantry battalions were to be augmented by an anti-tank company, and because the Rifle Brigade battalion had been previously used on mine clearing and security details and had lost some of its strength, the battalion was to be augmented by *G and H Troops of 239th Battery, 76th Anti-tank Regiment*.[29] Turner now had a force of some three hundred men armed with nineteen 6-Pounder anti-tank guns. To lend support to the plan of attack, all available artillery from both the *X* and *XXX Corps* was called on to fire in support of the infantry. Once the objectives were secure the *1st Armored Division's 2nd Armored Brigade* was to move around to the north of *Woodcock*, while the *24th Armored Brigade* was to move around to the south of *Snipe* and expand and secure the boundary area. The armored brigades would then be followed by the *133rd Infantry Brigade* (Lee), which would move up to reinforce the *7th Motor Brigade* and assist the armor brigades in their tasks. Both battalion commanders had little time for reconnaissance, and orders were hastily issued early on the evening of the 26th. The attack was to commence at 2300hrs on the 26th, with artillery laying down a barrage ahead of the infantry, which kicked off its attack at 2310hrs through a large gap between minefields "J" and "L." *2nd/60th Rifles* moved forward towards *Woodcock* behind the artillery barrage, but soon found the going rough because of the large amounts of dust created by the barrage had churned up. The dust, darkness, and navigational errors, coupled with German and Italian resistance, caused the battalion just a few problems that night, but they were able to overcome these problems as they made their way forward, and in the process captured a number of prisoners and anti-tank guns. After settling into a location that was actually some distance short of *Woodcock* and none too defensible, the battalion gathered up its force and moved forward again into a position that it would remain in throughout the 27th. Since the actions at this position do not reflect any fighting with the Regiment, this ends the description of the fighting at *Woodcock*, which now shifts to *Snipe*. In the south, Turner's battalion was also caused many problems by the dust raised by the barrage, which was supposed to fire on a prescribed azimuth, but because of some communication errors fired on a different one. The artillery actually forced the battalion to deviate from its planned axis of advance, and forced it to move further south. The lead elements, which had to pass through elements of the *51st Highland Division*, ran into a Scottish column and dummy minefield, which caused further delays in the attack.[30] After overcoming these early delays, the column continued forward, where along the way, it was able to overrun a number of Axis infantry positions and capture a large number of prisoners. Those Axis personnel not taken captive were quick to make good their escape to the west. Just after midnight the battalion then came across a shallow depression previously occupied by elements of *Pioneer Battalion 33*; thinking this was the objective a marker round of smoke was called for, and after it landed about 250m from the depression the order was given to dig in. The position that was occupied measured roughly 700m in length by 350m in width, and was about a meter deep and covered with camel thorn bushes; ideal for sighting and camouflaging the 6-Pounder anti-tank guns. Unknown to Turner, his unit's actual location was some 700m southeast of the planned *Snipe* position. As the infantry and anti-tank gunners dug in and set up their guns, reconnaissance elements were sent forward to the northwest and southwest, and the latter group soon came upon a large group of German and Italian Pioneers, some of which were more than willing to surrender. However, before they could make good the capture of these pioneer troops, it was discovered that the battalion had accidentally strayed into an area also occupied by Axis forces. After making this discovery, and to cover their withdrawal, the small group opened fire with machine guns, which succeeded in setting a couple of vehicles on fire, but the fire created from these burning vehicles illuminated the small force, and they soon drew fire from some of the Axis forces there.[31] As this reconnaissance force withdrew back to the main body it was also discovered that there was another Axis position located almost a kilometer to the north. The battalion now found itself in the middle of a large Axis defensive position located just to the west of the Otto Piste. The Axis forces in that area came from a variety of units assigned to multiple German and Italian divisions. One of those units was that of *Kampfgruppe Stiefelmayer* from the *I./Abteilung*, which had roughly thirty-five panzers and self-propelled Pak guns[32] with it. The northern hedgehog position also belonged to the Regiment, and was most likely the positions of an element from the Regiment's *II./Abteilung* and *III./Panzergrenadier Regiment 115*. At around 0345hrs, panzers were heard moving out from the southern hedgehog that was located around Hill 37, and lay approximately a thousand meters to the southwest of *Snipe*. The panzers were seen deploying out of their hedgehog position behind Hill 37 in two groups, with one element being sent north to the German hedgehog position located there, while a second group of panzers and self-propelled guns was seen moving east towards *Snipe*. The British anti-tank gunners by this time were ready, and as the panzers came closer they were allowed to get well within range before they were fired on. In the opening salvo, one of the Mk IV Specials and a self-propelled *7.62 Pak* gun mounted on a MK II chassis were hit and knocked out.[33] The loss of these two panzers was enough for Stiefelmayer to order the assaulting *kampfgruppe* to break off its attack and await first light. As the panzers withdrew back to the west a number of them halted and took up positions in some broken terrain 500m west of *Snipe*. Only one member of the Mk IV crew was able to escape, and he moved to a small trench, where he sniped at the British gun crews until he was killed later in the day by a rifleman.[34] At approximately 0600hrs the panzers of both the northern and southwestern groups were heard moving about and breaking camp. With the sun just beginning to rise in the east, the British gunners observed the movements of these groups and were soon under a new effort to dislodge them. As both groups struggled and stumbled around in the early morning light they were engaged by the anti-tank guns. In the fighting that followed, eight panzers and self-propelled guns from the northern group were knocked out. In the south, the panzers that had gone hull down in the broken terrain only a few hours before suddenly appeared and were quickly engaged, as they showed their vulnerable rear and flanks to the British gunners. Of the panzers claimed destroyed in this area, the claims were later verified as all eight in the north, and the three in the south were found still remaining in position a month later. Not realizing that the British had emplaced a strong force in the vicinity of Kidney Ridge, Rommel had ordered that an offensive begin in which he hoped to push the British back to the east. This attack was to be Rommel's first offensive action since his return on the night of the 25th. After that fighting ceased, German artillery came into action and began to shell the *Snipe* position, and inflicted a number of casualties in addition to knocking out three of the 6-Pounder guns.

Even though the British at *Snipe* had so far exacted a good toll of Axis armor with their 6-Pounders, the men were becoming concerned about the late arrival of the tanks from the *24th Armored Brigade* (Kenchington). Elements of that brigade, specifically the *47th RTR*, finally appeared on a low hill just to the north at 0730hrs, but due to the navigational error in attempting to reach *Snipe* and the presence of so many knocked out panzers, that unit began to engage the *Rifle Brigade* battalion, thinking it was a German *kampfgruppe*. Over the next half an hour the infantry and anti-tank gunners had to endure over-enthusiastic friendly tank fire until they were finally informed of their mistake and ceased firing. Almost as soon as they had appeared the British tanks had caught the attention of the German and Italian panzer crews, which quickly

Chapter 12: The Battle of El Alamein, October-December 1942

began to move against them. As the sun had now risen to where the British gunners had a perfect site picture, they soon spotted a large number of German panzers and Italian tanks laying low in hull down positions less than a kilometer away near Hill 37. The 6-Pounders were quickly back in action, and the gunners were able to claim the destruction of another three panzers in the process. At 0830hrs the British tanks of the *41st* and *47th RTRs* finally arrived at *Snipe*, but when they arrived, they were not warmly received by the infantrymen, and now they drew the concentrated fire from both Axis artillery and panzer gunners. The *41st RTR* lost twelve of its tanks, and the *47th RTR* was reduced to just eleven Sherman and Crusaders before quickly withdrawing back to the east.[35] For the Regiment, it lost another of its Mk IV Specials during the encounter. For the British infantry and gunners at *Snipe*, they now found themselves stranded just over a kilometer from friendly lines and on their own once again. The British artillery continued to shell the area around *Snipe* until it was finally called off, but this did not take place until around midday. During these attacks the British noted that the German panzers employed the highly effective tactic of accurately firing a smoke round just in front of the British tanks and then firing into the smoke with armored piercing rounds.[36] As the remaining tanks of the *24th Armored Brigade* withdrew back to the *Oxalic Line*, the attacks against it continued when they were hit again by the northern panzer group. This attack was successful until those panzers presented gunners of the *239th* with long range targets, and they began to score hits on the panzers. For the Regiment, it lost another of its Mk IV Specials during this encounter when it was hit at over 1000 yards, but it was towed away by another panzer.[37] After the British tanks departed the area around *Snipe*, a force of Italian infantry was seen to be forming for the attack, which they began just after 0900hrs. The Italians were reluctant to push the attack, and as soon as the British realized this they sent out a number of *Bren* gun carriers to counterattack them and throw them back. The *Bren* gun carriers easily halted the attack and inflicted a number of losses on the hapless Italians, who had almost succeeded in capturing two of the 6-Pounder guns. After the Italian infantry failed in their attempt to secure the *Snipe* position, at 1000hrs two more attacks were ordered by *Oberst* Teege. In this two pronged attack *Hptm* Stiefelmayer was ordered by Teege to take his group of 25-30 panzers from Hill 37 and move to the south of *Snipe*, and continue the attack on the *24th Armored Brigade*. This movement, however, would bring Stiefelmayer's panzer under flanking fire from the gun positions at *Snipe*. In order to keep the British gunners' heads down Teege ordered the Italian *12th Battalion, 133rd Tank Regiment* (Preve) of the *Littorio* Division to move towards *Snipe* from Hill 37 and wipe out the positions there. Capitan Preve went forward with thirteen *M-13* tanks that came in from the southwest, where they were engaged by just two 6-Pounders. In this attack, the Italians again seemed slow to press forward with the attack, which was nothing more than a demonstration for the larger German panzer attack. After losing four of their *M-13* tanks in the attack, the remaining *M-13s* broke off their attack and withdrew back to the southwest. In the meantime, Stiefelmayer's panzers began their attack on the *24th Armored Brigade's* tanks still in the surrounding area east of *Snipe*. With the failed Italian tank and infantry attacks on *Snipe*, the British gunners began to engage this group. Under heavy fire, Stiefelmayer was now forced to detach a portion of his panzers to attack *Snipe* while he went after the British armor. The presence of those anti-tank guns at *Snipe* poised a serious concern to the overall attack plan, and it was important that the *Snipe* position be secured before other attacks could move forward. Now, as the panzers rolled forward, the British tank and anti-tank gunners had near perfect targets when the panzers exposed their thin sides to the gunners. The panzer group was now in a cross fire, as those panzers sent to attack *Snipe* came within range and began receiving fire from the British tanks, and the panzers sent to attack the tanks now began to receive fire

from the 6-Pounders located at *Snipe*. In this aborted attack, the *I./Abteilung* lost no less than eight of its panzers and was forced to break off the attack.[38] After the Germans and Italians withdrew, the positions at *Snipe* continued to receive a steady dose of indirect fire throughout the morning and midday. The German attack plans for the 27th were now in jeopardy because of the position of *Snipe*, which lay directly in the path of the planned assault that was scheduled for 1500hrs. The Italians came on again from the southwest at 1300hrs with infantry and supported by eight tanks and one or more *Semovente* assault guns, but again were beaten back, losing five of the eight tanks and the *Semovente* to a lone 6-Pounder gun that was very low on ammunition.[39] Despite the destruction of over half of the Italian tanks, the remaining three tanks continued to push forward to within 200 yards of *Snipe* before all three were knocked out. At 1500hrs, Rommel's attack against the British lines commenced as Stuka dive-bombers and artillery guns began to engage Allied targets in the northern sector of the battle area. Unfortunately for the *Luftwaffe*, many of their aircraft were intercepted by *DAF* fighters, which claimed a number of the Stukas and completely disrupted the beginning of the attack. At 1600hrs the British *1st Armored Division's 2nd Armored Brigade* (Fisher) appeared to the east of *Snipe*; this force made the previous mistake of thinking the positions at *Snipe* were German, and so they too began shelling the remaining infantry. At the same time Axis armored forces were seen forming up for their attack near Kidney Ridge; this force was from the *21st Panzer Division*, which had been brought forward by Rommel, who ordered it to push the British armor back. This panzer force consisted of some seventy German panzers and Italian panzers that were formed into two *kampfgruppen*. The first and largest of the groups was moving off to engage the *2nd Armored Brigade*, and was unaware of the anti-tank guns still operating from *Snipe*. Those groups began taking fire from the four remaining 6-Pounders from the *239th Battery*, and before very long the British gunners were able to immobilize twelve of the panzers, with six of those panzers seen clearly on fire. The remaining panzers broke off the attack and moved back towards Kidney Ridge to a shallow depression. A short time later, another attack was launched towards *Snipe* by fifteen panzers, which came on carefully, using the terrain to mask their movement. The panzers came to within 200m of the British positions before losing six panzers and retiring to a low depression 800m away, where they continued to engage the anti-tank gunners from a safe distance. The *Snipe* position would continue to receive direct and indirect fire until it was finally given permission to withdraw that evening at 2300hrs. After the battle the British, investigating the action at *Snipe*, determined the Axis panzer losses at twenty-one German panzers, eleven Italian tanks, and five self-propelled guns.[40] It was also determined that another fifteen to twenty panzers were destroyed, but had been recovered. This ended the action at *Snipe*, but not the battle, which continued to rage around it. With this action the *I./Abteilung* virtually ceased to exist as a viable fighting formation; the loss of men and machines at this point in the North African campaign was a severe blow to not only the Regiment, but also the entire *Panzerarmee*. Further to the north, in the *II./Abteilung's* sector, the few remaining panzers continued fighting, where they were able to destroy two forward observer vehicles and set fire to a Bren gun carrier. Even with the loss of some of these observers, the panzers were constantly forced to change position, as there was still plenty of well-directed artillery fire coming against them. At 1600hrs British armor attacked the *II./Abteilung* in force; the six panzers of the *abteilung* had been reinforced by the *panzerjägers*, with their deadly 7.62cm Russian Pak guns, and were able to halt this attack. It was not until later that night before the British, again supported by strong artillery support, attempted to break through the positions. The *II./Abteilung* was able to later report that all of the attacks had been successfully repulsed with the loss of only one panzer.[41] A short time later, in the *Kampfgruppe Sud* sector, a group of approximately forty British tanks were able to break through, and the remaining panzers of the I./*Abteilung* were ordered to launch a counterattack in order to seal off the penetration. The panzers moved in quickly, engaging the tanks from the closest possible distance; twelve tanks were reported destroyed in the fighting, and their burning hulks lit up the battlefield. The two sides remained in close contact with one another throughout the night; there was no other choice for the German panzers, as their fuel tanks had begun to run dry, and they were forced to remain in position throughout the night until more fuel could be brought up. Of the thirty-nine operational panzers that were reported by the I. and II./*Abteilung* on the morning of 26 October, only thirty-one of them remained operational by the morning of the 27th.[42] By midnight, the I./*Abteilung* was moved further north in order to take up position to the west of El Wishka. The II./*Abteilung* was still split into two smaller detachments, and remained north of Kidney Ridge. Gerhard Weidelener of the 8th Company had this short account:

"From 24-27 October, we were engaged in various combats with an enormous enemy and aviation attacks. We secured our position along the familiar telegraph line, and the 'sturen achtzehn' (the 'stubborn 18') came over on a regular basis. I wish we had as much ammunition as they had, but at that time we lacked everything: ammunition, and fuel."[43]

During the early hours of 26/27 October, the British armored brigades again continued their push, after first consolidating and reorganizing those battered regiments earlier in the morning. It was obvious to the Germans that the *Eighth Army* wanted to force a breakthrough on both sides of Miteiriya Ridge with the *10th Armored* and *51st Highland Divisions*, and at the same time in the north near Rahman with the *9th Australian Division*. The elements of the *15th Panzer Division* now found themselves in the middle of these attacks. While these attacks were taking place, other divisions in the British *XXX* and *XIII Corps* began to conduct a relief in place operation to place fresh troops at the decisive point of attack. By 0500hrs, the II./*Abteilung* was already under attack, so the five remaining panzers and the last 7.62cm Pak gun of the attached *panzerjäger abteilung* formed a small defensive front facing east to the west of minefield "J." In the action that followed two Mk IIIs were lost, while five *Bren* gun carriers and one anti-tank gun were destroyed. Just to the south of that fighting, a group of approximately fifty British tanks were spotted heading west.[44] *Hptm* Siemens deployed his remaining three panzers into well-covered positions and spaced them wide apart in order to extend his defensive line. As the British tanks approached the panzers let loose with well aimed fire, and soon seven of the tanks were hit and the rest forced to lay down smoke in order to screen their retreat back to the east. In the encounter, the panzer of Lt Hubbuch was hit twice by a 6-Pounder anti-tank gun and began to burn; Hubbuch escaped unharmed, but the remainder of his crew were all wounded, two of them severely. It would take over four hours before an older Mk II could come forward and rescue the crew under a hail of machine gun and artillery fire. Klaus Hubbuch later wrote of the experience:

"I think about my crew of the first deployment days, near the end of October. We were day and night in combat. There my panzer shot, one of the last. Just after mine was hit the commander's [panzer] was also hit. My panzer took two shots almost simultaneously, and immediately caught fire. We were in the middle of the enemy defense positions. We helped each other to boot out [escape] and lie nearby in the deep part of a trench. All my four men were wounded, two heavily, and I had received nothing. And how brave were these guys, one must express their courage. Our panzers were no longer here. We were bandaged, splinted and laced up. It had happened early in the morning. What to do? Once the head was up, there was a burst of fire from a machine gun nearby, always above the side of the trench. Then they fired the artillery on us. It was midday, very hot, and we had no water for these poor guys. Here in the midday the enemy evaded a little bit back under the counter-attack of our riflemen, and how we tried to be noticed! One small panzer picked up us. Then I was in a different panzer with different people. They were also very brave. Even worse hours followed with constant night attacks, after the dreadful combat days were over. But we stood and held and therefore made it possible for the powerful retreat."[45]

At sometime during the afternoon's actions, *Hptm* Siemens and his adjutant, Lt Golinski, were wounded in these same attacks, and fortunately both were able to escape with their crews back toward friendly lines. The British had made slow but determined progress to get past the *Oxalic Line*, which lay just east of Kidney Ridge, and now they too began jockeying troops and equipment for the continued assault. The New Zealand Division, *9th Armored Brigade*, and *10th Armored Division* were withdrawn from the *XIII Corps* sector in the south and moved north, while the *9th Australian Division* was to continue its attack along the coast. Fortunately for the Germans, they were able to move faster than the British and reinforce their forces in the north with elements of the *90th Light* and *15th Panzer Division*s, and were able to check the Australians in the north. Those forces would be further augmented by the arrival of additional units of the *21st Panzer* that were immediately ordered into the attack.

Back at the Regimental *Stabs*, *Oberst* Willi Teege organized and led an attack against those British forces south of Kidney Ridge at approximately 1500hrs. This attack was launched in conjunction with the remaining elements of the *15th Panzer Division* and the recently arrived *21st Panzer Division*, and was centered on the Kidney Ridge sector of the battlefield. The panzers of the I./*Abteilung* and a company of tank destroyers from *Panzerjäger Abteilung 33* participated in this attack. Teege led this small *kampfgruppe* through a wall of dust and smoke against the British armor. The Sherman tanks located in the distance began to open up a deadly fire on the panzers, and in a short time were able to knockout six Mk IIIs and a Mk IV before the panzers could reach their designated firing line.[46] The remaining Mk III and IV Specials did, however, begin to engage the British, and were able to claim the destruction of some thirty-two enemy tanks in this armored duel. The battle raged on, with neither side obtaining a distinct advantage until the guns from German and Italian artillery joined the battle and forced the British armor to break off the engagement and withdraw. However, the British armored units did not run for cover like they had done so many times in the past; this time those forces were quickly reformed and now, supported by strong artillery fire, turned around and once again moved forward. That attack turned the tide of battle in favor of the British, as the panzers attempted to evade the deadly fire that saturated the leading panzers attempting to move forward. Both *Panzer Regiment 5* and *Panzer Regiment 8* could not force the issue, and by this time *Panzer Regiment 5* had lost thirty of its panzers. As the sun began to set, the Regiment reported only eighteen operational panzers remaining, and was soon ordered to withdraw to locations in and around El Wishka. Willi Teege made an effort to reconstitute the Regiment during the night of the 27/28th and to get any and all operational panzers to the front lines. Thanks to the work of the recovery teams and workshop personnel, a number of damaged panzers were returned to their *abteilungs*. October 28th began with numerous air attacks by the *RAF* and *USAAF* on the Axis lines; these attacks caused some damage and inflicted losses, including two of the Regiment's panzers that had been moving up to the forward lines when the attacks came. However, it was the loss of the fuel tankers *Proserpina*

Chapter 12: The Battle of El Alamein, October-December 1942

and *Arca*, sunk off the coast of Crete on the 26th, and the replacement tanker *Luisiana* sunk that day off the coast of Greece that would have an even more devastating effect on the *Panzerarmee*, as thousands of tons of precious fuel went up in flames.[47] Later in the day the *I./Abteilung*, which had only seventeen combat ready panzers, was hit by some fifty British tanks in a surprise attack. Under the direction of Otto Stiefelmayer the *I./Abteilung* was ordered to quickly form a defensive line and return fire. The Mk IVs, with their longer range guns, were quickly able to lay down a base of fire while the Mk IIIs were able to maneuver in closer to get within range of their 50mm guns. The British tankers, knowing the gunnery skills of the German gunners, quickly changed their positions after firing, but as the action closed the Regiment was able to claim some seventeen tanks for the loss of five panzers. British artillery fire was able to claim a further two panzers. However skilled the German gunners were, they could ill afford to suffer losses on this ratio. The *9th Lancer Regiment*, which was now armed with the *Crusader II*, slowly pulled back and remained at a safe distance. With the ten remaining panzers Stiefelmayer reformed and took up reverse slope positions, which he held until that evening while the panzers of *Panzer Regiment 5* could come up on the left flank and push back the British armor. In the battle that followed *Panzer Regiment 5* suffered the crippling loss of another twenty-eight of its panzers; this amounted to almost half its total panzer strength.[48] The British plan to "crumble" the Axis forces was succeeding, and they were winning the battle of attrition. Karl Halversheidt, in a letter home, recalled:

"I am good and healthy, and since yesterday with the supply column. The worst is over, Tommy has suffered tremendous losses, but they didn't get through anymore despite their enormous superiority. Six hours of drum fire [artillery barrage], such that I have never experienced before, so it all started."[49]

The *15th Panzer Division* withdrew on the night 28/29 October, moving westward past El Wishka until it reached an area just to the east of the Telegraph, or *Rahman Track*, where the I./*Abteilung* was placed in division reserve. The *abteilung* would remain in that position until the 31st. Wilhelm Hagios remembers:

"On 28/29th we were in a combat position east from the Telegraph Piste, the British attacked Tel el Eisa during the night and for half the night had used artillery. Slowly I gave up hope of getting out of there. We had to change positions and drop down 3km to the west, Oberst Teege was still there as our commander, Lt Paschy as ordnance officer and translator was also there. We wanted to start the panzer but it didn't start and so in the stale air we had to get out with two men and try to turn the crank in the rear, then came shooting and luckily the panzer turned on and was able to drive for 3km. The next morning we were standing there, when a pioneer came and told us about broken British tanks. With four to five, maximum six, panzers we drove there, this was of course utter stupidity, what could we do against the Sherman with a 5cm gun. We were on the left flank as were approached and noticed that some of the tanks were partially destroyed and some were not occupied with their crews, as they were broken and stood in the middle of the mine field. Then one of them turned the turret towards me, we got out but nothing happened, then we shot five or six times and the last shot was the final one, 'Finito'. We had a cartridge jammed inside [the breach] and when this happens you get a warning and we couldn't shoot anymore. So we were not able to shoot anymore. Then we drove at walking speed backwards and at this moment there comes the message from Teege [telling us to] stay where we were. There was a small hill there and we stood a bit further east from it, we wanted to capture one of the Shermans and so we began to towed it and then attempted to drive away with it, but the British artillery chased us in such way that we had to give it up and let it remain there."[50]

As the Germans withdrew *Oberst* Teege had been able to gather what was left of his scattered and disorganized Regiment and other wandering *D.A.K.* elements, and form them into a mixed *kampfgruppe*. In the meantime the technical services, workshop, and repair columns had been busy day and night repairing a few of the broken down panzers; these services and their contribution to the battle cannot go without mention, as the panzer companies were able to again reform themselves, and by midnight those services had once again performed magic by restoring some thirty-eight panzers. At this time a number of soldiers were able to reflect back on the past few days, and it is here that we get an idea of their experiences. Karl Halversheidt wrote:

"I am out of the witch cauldron for two days now, and I can say that I never have experienced anything similar and will never experience again, and I don't demand for it.

On the night of 23.10 at 2340hrs began the drumfire, six hours it went on. During this time I had packed my things and put them safely away. Then the artillery fire was reinforced by air attacks and in the dawn of the morning the Tommies attacked. With a vast quantity of tanks, it seemed that they didn't expect to find any of us alive. But we taught them what's what. Like in a miracle, we had just one lightly wounded. Then we performed our counter-attack. I was not inside the panzer, that was the most painful I can say. But I was useful with one other lieutenant, when I got out some goods and tents, and over the next two days provided our vehicles with rations, ammunition, gas, water etc. Tommy had suffered unbelievable losses. Our losses were small against all expectations. Now one can say that the crisis is over. The Tommy weren't pushing more, and the artillery fire, which hasn't let up in its strength for the last seven days, began to get weaker. One can already say that the Tommies were much too hesitating, even timid. If we were them, we would have already been in Benghazi. With such superiority, it's hard to imagine, what an unspeakable heathenism of German soldiers was performed during these days with glowing heat and cold nights. Literally clutched in the soil they didn't leave a single width of the thumb [inch] without fight. Today we are staying in our old positions."[51]

The *15th Panzer Division* reported a panzer strength of forty-six panzers on 31 October. The number included thirty-five Mk IIIs of various calibers and only five Mk IVs.[52]

Operation *Supercharge*

The British plan for the continuation of the battle was known as *Operation Supercharge*; this operation was scheduled to take place on the night of the 31st once the Australians had undertaken their second attack along the coast. The intention was to penetrate into the area below the Australian sector and then out into the open desert beyond the Axis defenses, thereby dividing those forces in two. The plan was similar to the original attack plan of "Lightfoot," but this time it would include much heavier artillery support. Once the Australians were successful in the north, the main plan of attack called for the *XXX Corps* to breech the Axis defensive front, with the *2nd New Zealand Division*, reinforced by the *151st Durham Brigade* (Percy) from the *50th Division* and the *152nd Highland Brigade* (Murray) from the *51st Division* clearing the lanes through what minefields remained in this area. There would only be one New Zealand infantry battalion, the *Maori Battalion*, involved in the initial attack, as all the other New Zealand infantry formations were completely worn out; they would later move up behind the main assault and secure the ground won.

The infantry were to be supported in the attack by the heavy infantry tanks from the *23rd Armored Brigade* (Richards).[53] Once the initial minefield gaps were created, the *9th Armored Brigade* (Currie), equipped with seventy-two *Shermans* and *Grants* and forty-nine *Crusaders*, would pass through and widen the gaps as they rolled on to attack the anti-tank gun screens along the Rahman Track and secure the flank for the *X Corps*. The *X Corps* would follow those formations and pass through them in the morning with the *1st Armored Division* and the attached *8th Armored Brigade* (150 Shermans and Grants and 110 Crusaders).[54] That division, it was hoped, would break into the rear of the Axis positions and defeat the remaining Axis forces. As in all military plans there were to be changes, and they quickly appeared after reviewing the recent Axis dispositions. The *Panzerarmee* had positioned the *90th Light*, *15th Panzer*, and *Littorio* Divisions in the path of the proposed axis of advance, thereby making an attack in the northern sector less likely to succeed. In order to give his forces every chance of success, Montgomery was advised by his staff and commanders to postpone the offensive one day and move the axis of advance further south of Point 29, with its primary aim at the low heights of Tel el Aqqaqir. The first Australian attack had fallen short of its objectives, and now, with the second attack planned, *General* Freyberg had a difficult time gathering his forces and artillery support and issuing them their orders.[55] When the second attack went forward, even though it too failed to gain all its objectives, it did, however, make some headway, and more importantly continued to tie down those mobile Axis forces and lead the German commanders to believe that these attacks would be the main area of focus. With the approved delay, *Supercharge* was now scheduled to kick off on the evening of 1/2 November. With a new attack planned, the Australians attacked again for a third time, and again suffered heavy casualties, but they were able to succeed in pinning down those Axis forces along the coast.

Panzer Regiment 8 Chain of Command as of the evening 31/1 November 1942[56]

Regiment Commander	Oberst Teege
I./Abteilung Commander	Hptm Stiefelmayer
1st Company	Lt Ihde
2nd Company	Lt Baumann
3rd Company	Lt Schuberski
4th Company	Olt Schulz
II./Abteilung Commander	Hptm Siemens
5th Company	Olt Blidschuhn
6th Company	Lt Halverscheidt
7th Company	Lt Krüger
8th Company	Olt Bänger

On the evening of 31/1 November the Regiment had a total of forty-six operational panzers ready for action. The Regimental *Stabs* was located in the middle of its two panzer *abteilung* along the Rahman Track. The *I./Abteilung* was located a kilometer or so northeast of Tel el Aqqaqir, while the *II./Abteilung's* remnants were located near A.P. 505, about a kilometer southeast of Tel el Aqqaqir. *Olt* Wandruszka, the LNO to the Italian *Littorio* Division, had gathered the remnants of that tank battalion near the Regiment's positions.

Despite the overwhelming losses being suffered by the Regiment in men and machines, there was still a trickle of men returning to Africa. Adolf Lamm gives us a good description of the hardships the replacements faced when joining a new unit:

"*Replacements were called up around October 30th and so was I. After nightfall, we proceeded to the front by truck. Where to and what for were unknown. Nobody asked about it. We disembarked in front of a tent teeming with soldiers. I sat down by the others who were waiting to be called up. With me were a few comrades from the company. We were soon torn apart, everything being pretty well in a state of confusion, or at least it seemed so to me at the time. A Feldwebel came around and scrounged up a panzer crew; driver, radio operator, loader, gunner, and commander. He got hold of me for radio operator. We were looking at each other for the first time. The commander didn't make a confidence-winning impression. We arrived by Kübelwagen to a panzer in the assembly area, mount up and move out! But where to? I didn't have a radio manual, table, frequencies, or cipher. I was hopeless. Shells exploded in front of us. We oriented ourselves by following the other panzers. That was how the night was spent. The following morning, I got a radio table from someone; this was sufficient to at least maintain the connection to the left and right. I still didn't even know which unit I had wound up with! The commander got sick, I had been suffering from dysentery already and couldn't hold out any longer but he finally just caved into himself completely and the gunner had to assume command. We had in the meantime become aware that the battle was not going in our favor and we still hadn't seen to which extent. Things become continuously worse. The gunner didn't want to accept responsibility anymore and one night the ailing Feldwebel was evacuated and a Lieutenant took over our panzer. Avanti, Avanti! – I didn't have the slightest idea where we drove. I only knew we were going backwards, always in reverse. During the day, I sat in the panzer and saw through the small slit in front of my eyes-only desert and thorn bushes. In the pitch-black darkness of night, we threw ourselves down next to our panzer and tried to sleep as well as we could despite the cold. We often drove at night and took short breaks during the day. Enemy aircraft were incessantly over us.*"[57]

The evening of 1/2 November the *DAF* attacked the *Panzerarmee*, striking the rear areas and successfully severing all communications with those front line formations. Numerous ammunition and supply dumps were hit, and a number of huge explosions were seen and heard. At 0100hrs a tremendous artillery barrage began along a four-kilometer front. One hundred and fifty thousand rounds were fired over the next four and a half hours, creating a great red glow in the sky. To better detail the events of that morning we follow the *15th Panzer Division* diary, which reported that the Axis intention was for the *Panzerarmee* and *D.A.K.* to order all units to hold their present positions and not, under any circumstances, give up terrain without a heavy price paid by the enemy. At 0010hrs reports from *Panzergrenadier Regiment 115* noted that enemy artillery fire was hitting behind the first line of defense and along the entire front. The communications with the front had been partially destroyed, and radio communications in many cases were not yet available. At 0100hrs the British attacked the southern flank of the *90th Light Division*; this attack and the dimensions of it had yet to be determined. At 0200hrs, in the vicinity of the *164th Light Division*, there was also concentrated artillery fire. Fires were also hitting near the Regimental *Stabs*, and communications between the division and the Regiment were severed. Following this terrific barrage, the British and Australian infantry stepped off behind a curtain of steel and thunder; in certain sections they encountered dazed and bewildered German and Italian troops, but in others well-emplaced infantry and machine guns met them head on. But suffice to say that the initial attacks had come off well, and by 0400hrs a number of the initial infantry objectives had been taken. At 0220hrs messages received through sound locators and signal intelligence noted the British to be in good spirits, as their armor had been finally able to cross the minefields and were moving forward all along the front. By 0320hrs the British had broken through the first lines of defense, and had even reached the headquarters

Chapter 12: The Battle of El Alamein, October-December 1942

positions of *Panzer Regiment 8*, located in and around the Otto Piste.[58] Wilhelm Hagios explains a bit of what took place that night:

"We were on the hill above the terrain and we hid behind it so that the British couldn't see us anymore. At about mid-day I was in the panzer and we heard someone crying 'Beckers, go to the Regiment Stabs and clear away the tanks!' I cannot recall what exactly was said here but I recall that a person said 'You are the panzer crew and you must still have an MG!' We thought to ourselves, who is that? Soon I discovered that it was a general, von Thoma who had been arguing with Beckers in German, he said 'drive to your commander, he needs you'. We established radio contact with Regiment; we demanded a flare at about where we should go. We went into the march to the south and I sat on the top and heard the shooting and turned the turret to see what was there as I didn't have a richtschütze. I looked at the left and saw the whole row of British tanks, but they were not experienced in combat, they shot at us and we drove at high speed and didn't give them chance to hit us. If there were any experienced gunners with them then we would not have moved very far. We moved up and went in the light hinterhangstellung and the Befehls panzer of commander was there. We asked for the commander and the answer we got was that he was further ahead with the commander of the Schützen Regiment. We drove there with the panzer under the artillery fire. We came to the place and Beckers went from our panzer and Oberst Teege said to him; 'Beckers, what are you looking for here? You should drive back, here you can be destroyed'. He didn't join us on our drive back, maybe we should have persuaded him to drive back with us or maybe it was General von Thoma who slowed him down. We didn't have faith in ourselves to turn the panzer around and return as there was heavy artillery fire which was firing madly."[59]

At 0327hrs orders were issued to *Artillery Regiment 33* that with the beginning of daylight the artillery was to begin laying down blocking fires all along the left flank of the division sector from A.P. 410 southwards. With this new British offensive the entire Axis position was in serious jeopardy of being overwhelmed and outflanked. It now appeared that the Italian *Jäger Regiment 65* and German *I./Panzergrenadier Regiment 115* had been overrun; the British had reached the combat positions of *Panzergrenadier Regiment 115*, and had practically reached the *Telegraph Piste*. There was no connection with *Major* Schemmel at *Kampfgruppe Mitte*. The breakthrough was so great that the division was forced to report that it was unable to handle the current situation alone. The division commander reported to the *D.A.K.* headquarters that he was moving off to assist and orient the commander of the *21st Panzer Division*, whose units were moving up to reinforce and help contain the breakthrough. The *21st Panzer Division* had reported that it would be able to attack along the left flank of the *15th Panzer Division* in one hour. At 0410hrs the *15th Panzer Division* reported to the *D.A.K.* commanding general that strong enemy tank forces had overrun the left flank of the *15th Panzer Division*. The first tanks were now located along the *Telegraph Piste*, and fighting along the *Otto Piste* was also taking place, but details were not yet available due to the many breaks in the communications. At 0415hrs the *D.A.K.* headquarters issued orders to all its formations that beginning at dawn they must counterattack with all available forces in conjunction with the *21st Panzer Division*, and that it was imperative that they throw the enemy back. *Generalmajor* von Randow arrived at *15th Panzer Division* at 0420hrs to report that the *21st Panzer Division* was almost ready to begin its counterthrust, with the direction of the attack aimed at attacking over A.P. 509, then moving to the northeast before turning to the east. By 0445hrs the connection with *Panzer Regiment 8* had been once again established. It now appeared to the Germans that the British attack seemed to be in two separate attack groups: the northern group was moving along the right flank of *Panzergrenadier Regiment 200*, with a second thrust directed towards the center of the *15th Panzer Division*. The *XXXIII Bersaglieri* on the left flank was reported to be still holding out. At 0505hrs a broadcast from the *90th Light Division* reported that enemy infantry at 0115hrs were near *I./Panzergrenadier Regiment 200* and had broken through along map grid line 237.5.[60] The battlefield was now covered by great clouds of dust and smoke that had been churned up by the hundreds of vehicles moving along at high speed, and the air was thick with the smoke from many of the destroyed vehicles and positions. This smoke and dust caused a few problems, especially for the tanks of the *9th Armored Brigade*, which had begun their assault in the early morning hours and suffered many of the previous problems, as elements lost their way in the dark and dust filled corridor. As the hours of darkness quickly faded, the armor just barely had time to link up with the supporting infantry and artillery observers. As the sun came up over the battlefield the British tankers soon found themselves confronted by a number of 88mm Flak guns that soon began to take a toll on the advancing British. Some estimates place the number of tanks lost that day to the Flak guns at around sixty-seventy of the ninety-four tanks that took part in the advance.[61] At 0636hrs the *II./Artillery Regiment 33* reported that from their positions they could see British tanks along the Otto Piste from the southwest to the northeast. Also at that time the *21st Panzer Division* had begun to reach the Otto Piste in the area of A.P. 412. They intended to hit the British near A. P. 411 in their flank to the south. At 0705hrs orders were sent to *Artillery Regiment 33* to engage the enemy armored force—comprised of some eighty tanks—located near A.P. 411, while the *21st Panzer Division* had the order to take up positions immediately along the assault line to the south. Also at that time *Panzer Regiment 8* was ordered to attack to the east in order to close the gap that had opened in the Axis lines. *I./Abteilung* was still situated in its original sector, and *II./Abteilung* was near A.P. 507. Willi Teege was allowed a short respite before he had to attack, as the British attack was now becoming uncoordinated, as the infantry was slowed a bit as they picked their way through the minefields. Teege's orders called for the establishment of a hasty defensive line using his *II./Abteilung* and an Italian tank battalion from the *Littorio* Division with its twenty-seven light tanks. This defensive line ran eastward along the *Rahman Track*, with the *II./Abteilung* on the left, the Italians in the middle, and *I./Abteilung* on the right. The opening barrage that felled the Axis positions that morning had targeted the forward and rearward areas, and it was because of this that the Regiment's positions in the middle had suffered little damage. As the British tanks came forward they were greeted by a hail of fire from many of the well-sited positions, and the results were predictable. By 0600hrs some smaller groups of British infantry supported by a few tanks had managed to reach the Rahman Track, and some had even crossed over it. The *II./Abteilung* was able to destroy eight *Crusader IIs* in the opening round, but by 0700hrs both *abteilungs* were beginning to find themselves being engaged by more and more tanks. At 0730hrs the *II./Abteilung* was again attacked, this time by some eighty *Grants*, and an additional sixty tanks soon followed the first wave, striking between the *II./Abteilung* and *I./Abteilung*, where the *Littorio* tank battalion was positioned. At 0735hrs a message was received at the divisional and regimental *stabs* that *Hptm* Otto Stiefelmayer had fallen in the fighting that morning. By this time the *I./Abteilung* was down to just nine battle worthy panzers. Against this overwhelming numerical superiority, *Hptm* Siemens ordered his *II./Abteilung* panzers back to the *hinterhangstellung*. The dust and smoke that had impeded the British advance now caused those forces withdrawing the same problems, and it was impossible to recognize friend from foe in the dusty haze. But at 0803hrs on the 2nd, the *II./Abteilung* reported the presence of between 90-

100 enemy tanks that were gathering in the immediate area and looked to be preparing for an attack. A short time later, at 0810hrs *Oberst* Teege received orders that informed him that the panzer elements from the *21st Panzer* were to attack along the 236 grid line and continue the battle there. As the morning passed the tide of battle was still very confusing, and again German signal intelligence sources reported that the British were still stuck in no man's land and were unable to breakout. That morning the bombers of the *DAF* continued to make appearance after appearance over the battlefield in flights of eighteen, as they dropped their deadly loads on the rear area support facilities and suspected command and control sites. By 0915hrs the I./*Abteilung* had reported destroying twenty British tanks, the II./*Abteilung* claimed an additional thirty, and the guns of *Artillery Regiment 33* claimed another fifteen. As the morning passed the anticipated attack by the *1st Armored Division* was slowed as it attempted to follow up on the *9th Armored Brigade's* breaching attack. The *1st Armored* was also suffering from the same confusion and problems that had plagued the *9th Armored Brigade's* attack as its forces attempted to form up in the rear and get through the minefield gaps. *General* Freyberg now began to worry when the progress of the *1st Armored* was slowed, and there began to be a noticeable stiffening of German resistance, along with signs of a growing German counterattack. The British tanks came on at an even pace and did not rush blindly into the awaiting German Pak and Flak guns. The forward progress was actually aided by this tactic, and it would have been a costly mistake had they rushed forward. In the meantime, the German panzers were initially ordered to the north, where the Australian attack had succeeded in fooling the Germans into thinking that this was the main effort of *Operation Supercharge*. By 1000hrs *Panzer Regiment 8* reported the following situation: at 0940hrs, on the southeastern flank, in approximately the old position of I./*Abteilung*, there were only four vehicles ready for combat. *Hptm* Stiefelmayer had been killed leading his panzers. There was no connection with the grenadiers on the front line, and attempts to clarify the situation had failed, and the British had only been pushed back slightly. On the left flank, near the I./*Abteilung*, the Italian tanks had retreated a short distance, but had since then moved forward to take up those lost positions. Consequently, the left flank near II./*Abteilung*, which by now was down to just twelve operational panzers, had taken up positions one and a half kilometers north of A.P. 507 running over to the *Telegraph Piste*. The Regimental *Stabs* was situated behind the right flank of *Hptm* Siemens on the *Telegraph Piste*. At about 1040hrs, the *21st Panzer Division* had taken up positions near the hill at A.P. 411, and it had sent one company to the right in the hope of linking up with the left flank of the Regiment. It was not until mid-morning before the true aim and intensions of the *Supercharge* attack were identified, and the panzers were shifted north and south to meet it. At 1100hrs von Thoma ordered the two *D.A.K.* panzer regiments to deliver a counterattack along the flanks of the British attack. The Regiment was ordered to launch a counterattack from the south late that morning in order to secure the area up to the *Rahman Track*. As the British managed to push through the initial line of defenses, the II./*Abteilung* was soon hit by some sixty *Grants*. The *abteilung* counterattacked in a wide wedge formation, and was able to push back the British. The *abteilung* suffered the loss of five of its panzers and sixteen casualties in exchange for nine British tanks. The same was not so for the Italians, as the *Littorio* tank battalion suffered massive losses, and was effectively wiped out by British tanks and well directed artillery fires. A short while later approximately one hundred and fifty *Sherman* and *Crusader II* tanks were reported to be engaging the I./*Abteilung*. Locked in fierce combat, with each side continuing to resist the other, the panzers began the game of fire and maneuver. The I./*Abteilung* struck the British flank, and soon the panzers had claimed thirty-two tanks, with most of the fighting being done at close range. With the loss of so many tanks the British armor then attempted to move off well out of range of the German gunners. With the loss earlier in the morning of Otto Stiefelmayer command of the I./*Abteilung* was given to *Olt* Lindner, who had recovered enough from his earlier wounds to assume command. It is interesting to note that Stiefelmayer had been mortally wounded that morning and he had been carried to the rear for treatment, but it was to no avail, as he would die the following day. After the morning's fighting the I./*Abteilung* reported that seventeen of its panzers had been destroyed or severely damaged. Hermann Eckardt, who participated in the attack, recalls the battle:

"I was hit on the same day as Stiefelmayer and it was at that time when Stiefelmayer attacked the British position [defended by] many anti-tank guns, but Stiefelmayer was not driving in the attack, and he had planned what was not possible to perform, there were only 20 panzers, which was not too much to [perform the task with] and be overpowering. We all felt that the thing went wrong, we took anti-tank rounds and there was a terrible fire from the British, the morale was at its lowest point."[62]

At 1130hrs Teege was ordered to launch another attack in the direction of Hill 32, and once that was secure he was to move north, form a defensive front, and dig in. For the attack he was promised more artillery support. At around 1200hrs the *21st Panzer* neared A.P. 411; facing to the east, the Regiment was to affect a link up with them along the Otto Piste on 411, with its front also facing east. A supporting Flak battery was ordered to move up and help secure the flanks. The goal was to move east to the old positions and dig in. By 1215hrs the II./*Abteilung* had reached the link up position and established contact with *Panzer Regiment 5* on the Telegraph Piste. At 1240hrs the Regiment was ordered to increase the speed of its attack toward A.P. 411, while in addition to keeping in constant contact with the *21st Panzer*, and to drag the Italians along as well. About an hour later, at 1335hrs, reports came from the II./*Abteilung* that the enemy was attacking all along the front from the east to the southwest. There were also reports of over two hundred British tanks moving from minefield "J" and driving southwest, and that *Panzer Regiment 5* was noted as lagging behind. There was also concern over the situation with the Italian *Jäger Regiment 65*, which had not been heard from for some time; the *Trieste* Division had had no contact, and it was feared that the regiment had been wiped out. While those attacks against the line were taking place, *Oberst* Teege gathered all the available panzers of the Regiment, and at around 1500hrs led them in a counterattack against the renewed attempts by the British armor. It was in this last ditch attempt to halt the British and send them reeling back eastwards that Teege himself was mortally wounded when his panzer was hit by a 75mm round and destroyed. *Hptm* Siemens, who assumed command of the Regiment, replaced the brave *Oberst* Willi Teege. In the end the panzer attack failed, and the Regiment suffered further losses as the I./*Abteilung* was now down to ten operational panzers, and was now being commanded by Lt Ihde, who himself was soon wounded and had to be replaced by Lt Schuberski. The II./*Abteilung* was down to seven operational panzers, and was being led by *Olt* Lindner, who had come over from I./*Abteilung* to replace Siemens. A short time later Lindner was wounded for the second time in the battle and had to be replaced by Lt Marquardt. The Mk III Special of *Uffz* Weidelener, of the *8th Company*, was also destroyed that day, but he fared much better than most of the others that day:

"On the night of 1/2 November, it was the same as 23/24 October with uninterrupted artillery attacks. The alarm was given on the morning of 2 November, tank fighting against a giant and overpowering enemy, but

Chapter 12: The Battle of El Alamein, October-December 1942

this was a well known fact. At 1400hrs I was shot down again and all my clothes, pictures and belongings were gone."[63]

After the counterattack both sides paused to reorganize and recover their tanks and wounded, but the British artillery kept up a constant bombardment of the battlefield area and made this task quite hazardous for the Axis forces, which continued to lose men and equipment. The panzer counterattack that was launched that afternoon had been met by the *1st* and *10th Armored Divisions*; it had been repelled with heavy losses, and by the end of the day approximately fifty Axis tanks and ten 88mm Flak guns had been destroyed. With the loss of the few remaining panzers and the defensive line beginning to crack wide open the armored cars of the *Royal Dragoons Regiment* were able to sneak through the lines and begin wreaking havoc on the *D.A.K.*'s rear echelon facilities, while disrupting communications and destroying a number of supply dumps.[64] The *DAF* continued to attack the assembly areas and disrupt communications throughout the *Panzerarmee*; almost every thirty minutes a new squadron of eighteen bombers appeared overhead to drop their loads. Wilhelm Hagios continues his story from the previous day:

"We managed to move backwards to the hinterhangstellung and when we arrived there we received the message from Kaiser that Oberst Teege had fallen. That same day a short while later we heard that Stiefelmayer had also fallen near the same location. We were in any case back and were then sent to the workshop to repair our cannon and then on the morning of the 3rd, Beckers left our panzer, he told us that he was getting a leave but he couldn't explain why. I got my clothes from the panzer and anything else which was important and in good condition and brought them to the Zug, I threw away the optics and I never thought it could come to that. I didn't know."

With so much pressure coming against it, and the inability to properly protect the guns, the decision was made that all of the divisional artillery along the Telegraph Piste was to fall back for the night. On the order from the *D.A.K.* commanding general, *Artillery Regiment 33*, which had already taken up positions near A.P. 509, was ordered to fall back during the night to a safe daytime position 800m west of the *Rahman Track*, as it was in danger of being overrun by British armor. The division commander considered the order for *Artillery Regiment 33* as being too dangerous, and provided the *D.A.K.* with an alternative proposal to leave the *Abteilung* in its current position at A.P. 509, but that proposal was declined.[65] As the British tanks halted to recover men and machines they created a few gaps between Hill 28 and the *III./Panzergrenadier Regiment 115*; these gaps were then filled by the thin composite units of *Panzergrenadier Regiment 104*. By 1605hrs the Regiment reported that *Oberst* Teege had been killed in action while leading his panzers in the attack; it was a great loss to both the Regiment and division. With the failure of this last panzer attack, the *D.A.K.* and *15th Panzer* now had to rely on infantry to hold what remained of the crumbling defensive line. *II./Panzergrenadier Regiment 115*, which had been previously detached to help plug the lines elsewhere, was again back under the command of the division, and was deployed on the west side of the *Rahman Track* near the *III./Panzergrenadier Regiment 115* with its front facing to the north. The remaining guns from the divisional artillery were now being protected by various divisional units: *Aufklärung Abteilung 33* was to the front of the *I./Artillery Regiment 33*, while *Pioneer Battalion 33* was screening to the front of *II./Artillery Regiment 33*. At 1645hrs a report from the Regiment noted that the British had begun to lay down a heavy smoke screen in order to mask their movements. At 1715hrs the division once again had radio contact with *III./Panzergrenadier Regiment 115*, which it ordered to maintain its present position, while to the west of them, the *II./Panzergrenadier Regiment 115* was to take up positions. It was unknown what was taking place to the north of them.[66] At 1845hrs the *D.A.K.* Chief of Staff (Bayerlein) briefed the division commander about the new decisions and orders that had come from the *Panzerarmee*. Those topics included, in part: the *Panzerarmee* was to avoid the further shattering of its divisions from the overwhelming British tanks and artillery forces. The *Panzerarmee* had also made the decision to move back to the west in small bounds, with all units that were not presently engaged and the non-motorized elements of the *Panzerarmee*; these units were to begin to establish a new defensive front near Fuka. The *Panzerarmee* and *D.A.K.* also knew that there would be difficulty on the non-motorized divisions, and thereby the *15th Panzer* was ordered to provide some of its vehicles for elements of the *164th Light*. Sixty trucks from various sub-units and *15 Panzer's Supply Battalion 33* were sent on to march to A.P. 463. The time and place for disengaging the remainder of the division had not yet been determined. It was also determined that the British would continue to launch infantry attacks, and the division was to continue combat operations throughout the night.

The breakthroughs that had been achieved the night prior were to be contained that night by the infantry of *III./Panzergrenadier Regiment 115* on the right flank and *II./Panzergrenadier Regiment 115* (again subordinated to division and taken from the previous position) on the left flank. *Aufklärung Abteilung 33*, *Panzerjäger Abteilung 33*, and *Panzerjäger Abteilung 605* were to move consecutively along the *Rahman Track* through a battalion of the *21st Panzer Division*. The primary mission of these units was to provide security during the night for the panzers and artillery guns in such a way that prevented any breakthrough into their positions. To help correct the situation on the right flank, *Hptm* von Mayer, the division adjutant, drove to *Aufklärung Abteilung 33* and *II./Panzergrenadier Regiment 115*, where he was to establish a direct line of communication with the *Panzerarmee* in order to direct those units in the event of attack. In order to prepare for the planned withdrawal, the division sent a radio message to the *III./Panzergrenadier Regiment 115* explaining that it was to hold its position, but that it was to be prepared for a withdrawal with all its vehicles. The order had no sooner been received when at 2100hrs that unit notified the division headquarters that it was being hit by a heavy artillery barrage and was already conducting a fighting withdrawal to A.P. 506.[67] From 2130hrs until 2300hrs the area on both sides of the *Rahman Track* again came under the attention of the *DAF*, which conducted a number of low level bombing and strafing attacks. Heavy artillery fire rained down on every section of the divisional front, and it was not long before British tanks were spotted moving forward. At 2340hrs, as the artillery continued to fall around it, the divisional headquarters was forced to relocate to an area three kilometers to the west. November 2nd had been an extremely tough day for the division; it had paid a heavy price while putting up a stubborn defense. The division had lost numerous regimental and battalion sized headquarters elements: the *I./Panzergrenadier Regiment 115* was considered lost, as well as *Jäger Regiment 65* and two battalions of the *Bersaglieri Regiment 12*. There had also been a significant loss in the number of artillery, mobile tank destroyers, and Flak and Pak guns. The *panzergrenadier* and pioneer battalions had been reduced to the size of an under strength company, and many of them had lost all of their officers and senior NCOs. The fighting strength of *Panzer Regiment 8* was down to its last eight panzers, and it had lost its commander, Willi Teege, as well as Otto Stiefelmayer, its *I./Abteilung* commander. The backbone of the division was therefore virtually wiped out, and was at that time totally incapable of launching any kind of offensive operations. In fact, the small number of remaining men and machines were barely capable of handling the defensive roles that they were now forced to undertake. Indeed, the only real defensive power the *Panzerarmee* had at that time lay in the few remaining 50mm and 75mm Pak guns, which at the time were widely scattered and manned by whatever forces could be found at hand. The only divisional unit capable of holding up the British onslaught was *Artillery Regiment 33*, which had managed to salvage about seven of its guns.[68] Unfortunately, these guns were desperately short on ammunition, and the prime movers required to haul the guns had little fuel remaining in their tanks. If these remaining elements were to be salvaged then they would have to be withdrawn as soon as possible before they too were lost. Accordingly, and possibly on its own accord, the division issued an order that called for all divisional elements that were presently exposed to British fires to begin the withdrawal to the west that night. By the end of the day the Regiment's *Werkshop* and I services were able to recover a large number of panzers that had sustained various degrees of damage. The number of recovered panzers is documented at fifty-six, and if this number is to be believed those services had pulled off a major, if not unbelievable undertaking. But at this point did it really matter, for to get those panzers back into the fight they would need time, which was just about up, for the British were poised to engulf the *Panzerarmee*. By the end of the day's fighting the Regiment had withdrawn to a *hinterhangstellung* position located to the west of the *Rahman Track* between Points 43 and 44, just to the north of Tel el Aqqaqir. It also claimed the destruction of approximately sixty British tanks that day, but those sixty could be quickly replaced, unlike those of the Regiment.[69] By the evening of the 2nd, von Thoma reported to Rommel that he had held the British attacks, but he was now down to just thirty-five operational panzers; he was outnumbered and outgunned, and there were only a third of German troops remaining.[70] The British penetration of the Axis defensive line was now at a critical state, with the line not yet broken but severely cracked. It was at this point in the battle that it became clear to Rommel and Thoma that there was no other option but to withdraw those remaining *Panzerarmee* forces before the British succeeded in enveloping the entire Axis position. At 2015hrs Rommel and von Thoma decided jointly on a withdrawal to the *Fuka Position*, and the next morning, as Rommel visited positions near the coastal road, he was extremely pleased when he was informed that much of the pressure in that area had decreased. Rommel had been facing the dilemma of standing fast or withdrawing since he had received a note sent to him by Hitler, which read in part:

"In the situation in which you find yourself there can be no other thought but to stand fast, yield not a yard of ground and throw every gun and every man into battle...

It would not be the first time in history that a strong wills has triumphed over bigger battalions. As to your troops, you can show them no other road than that to victory or death."[71]

In the end Rommel chose the path in order to save as many of his beloved *Afrikaners* as he could; the plan was simply to order all non-mobile infantry forces back westward, while those mobile forces continued holding until they could disengage and move back. As the 2nd passed into the 3rd the British continued their bombardments by artillery and heavy bomber attacks. The British infantry came on again shortly after midnight, but they were halted and beaten back, but only at close range. Before dawn those combat formations that could continued to fortify and hold their defense positions, and fire back at the attacking infantry. However, there was little hope in holding the infantry ground assaults, which were being supported by *Bren* gun carriers and closely followed by armored units that now had little to fear from German panzers. There were a few operational Flak and Pak guns along the front that managed to destroy a small number of the small carriers and supporting tanks. By standing firm and holding out to the very last, the German Pak gunners were able to seed just enough doubt and hold back the far superior British armored elements throughout the day. A few counterattacks were ordered, but they came to nothing in the face of such overpowering odds. The Regiment—or for the use of a better word, now a *kampfgruppe*—had between ten to fourteen operational panzers; during the day it continued to engage British infantry and armor, and was able to claim the destruction of thirteen tanks and eight Bren carriers.[72] Despite being under the constant strain of air and artillery attack, the division's supply trains were actually able to make their way forward to the frontlines in the early evening and conducted a resupply operation. There can be no doubt that everyone in the Regiment did his part in this battle, whether it was in a direct combat role or that of service and support. Everyone who was there suffered from not only the grim realities of combat, but the endless days with little time for rest and a lack of food and water. The previous two days had proved to be some of the Regiment's most difficult days in Africa; by sacrificing itself against a numerically superior enemy force, the Regiment, which would never again approach anything comparable to its authorized strength, sacrificed itself in an attempt to allow those other Axis forces to make their way to the west. It had lost leaders, men, and equipment that could and would never be replaced again. Many military historians would agree that had the British been able to complete their breakthrough near Tel el Aqqaqir a bit sooner they would have been able to outflank and maneuver the *D.A.K.*, thereby surrounding it and finishing it off in detail. It was the selfless struggle here that was able to preserve the *Panzerarmee* and *D.A.K.*, and thereby give Rommel the chance to continue the war in North Africa.

In the early evening of the 3rd, after receiving the order to finally withdraw, the remaining panzers and men of the Regiment, withdrew to a new position six kilometers to the west in the area of Tel el Mmpsra, where the first defensive line was to be occupied by the remaining panzers.[73] On the evening of 3 November the remnants of the *15th Panzer Division* were formed into two *kampfgruppen*, the north and south. The first *kampfgruppe*, *Kampfgruppe Nord*, commanded by *Hptm* Siemens, had been formed from the remnants of *Panzer Regiment 8*, and subordinated to it were the remains of *Pioneer Battalion 33*, I./*Abteilung Artillery Regiment 33*, the first half of the 1st and 2nd Companies from *Flak Regiment 43*, and the remainder of an Italian tank battalion with twelve tanks. *Kampfgruppe Sud* was now under the command of *Hptm* Fischer of *Panzerjäger Abteilung 605*, and consisted of the remains of his *abteilung* and II./*Abteilung Artillery Regiment 33*, and the other halves of the 1st and 2nd Companies from *Flak Regiment 43*.[74] However terrible they had been, the losses suffered by the *Eighth Army* since the beginning of the battle were actually, in some cases, found to be totally acceptable. This is based, of course, on the number of men, machines, and equipment that were still waiting in reserve. Unlike the *Panzerarmee* and *D.A.K.*, which could no longer make good their losses in the battle, the *Eighth Army* still had the ability to introduce fresh formations and new equipment into its corps and divisions. At this time the *D.A.K.* was down to approximately regimental strength, with each of the divisions reporting the following: *90th Light* with 1,000 men, *164th Light* with 800 men, and the *Ramcke Brigade* about 700 men. The *15th* and *21st Panzer* combined only totaled about 2,200 men, with roughly eleven operational panzers between them.[75] At the same time, the *Eighth Army* possessed nearly six hundred tanks, and even the Italian contribution of less than one hundred inferior model tanks could not help hold the tide of armor moving into the battlefield. Even the Axis command structure had suffered considerable change since the beginning of the battle. Rommel was now back in command of the *Panzerarmee*, but he was without any of his senior commanders: Stumme was dead, and von Thoma had been captured, after declaring Hitler's order as "Madness and the death warrant of the army," then driving off to the front, where he

Chapter 12: The Battle of El Alamein, October-December 1942

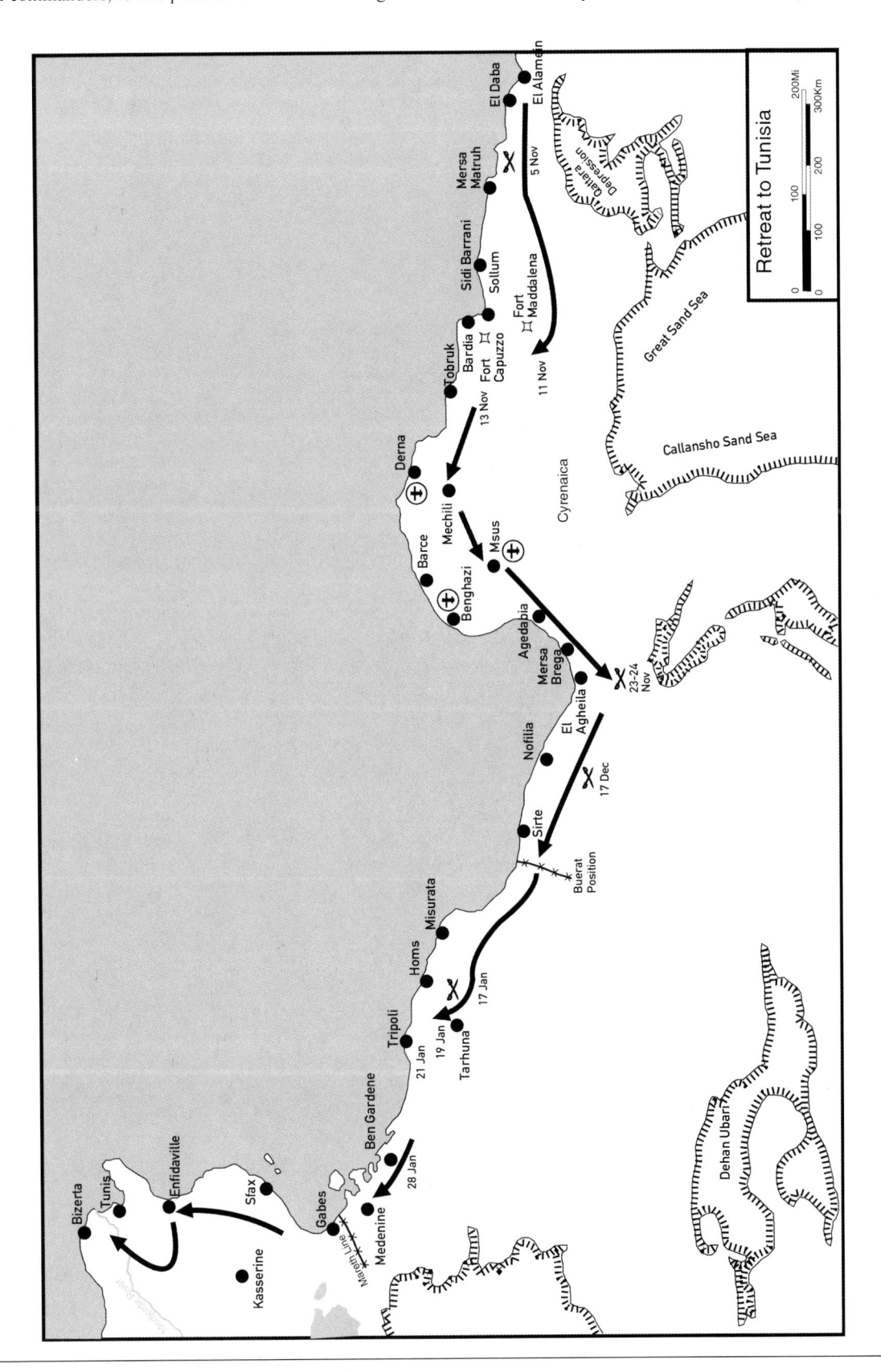

was taken prisoner.[76] Thankfully Rommel had the trusty Fritz Bayerlein, the *D.A.K.* Chief of Staff, who had himself narrowly escaped capture with von Thoma and now found himself again in charge of the *D.A.K.* For the divisional commanders, to this point all of them had managed to escape serious injury or death, but each one of them was totally engrossed with holding their respective division together and maintaining their own divisional front from being overrun. Over the past two days Rommel had been tormented by his oath as a soldier to obey Hitler's order and that of a realistic, caring commander who was attempting to salvage something of his *Panzerarmee* and men. He had juggled the options for some time, but once the retreat had begun there was no way that it could be halted; indeed, as all this was going on Axis rear echelon and combat elements were already streaming to the rear. Kathe remembers seeing some of the Italian soldiers fleeing towards Fuka:

"They were not really provisioned, they were very poor soldiers, when the Brits fired; they cried 'Mama Mia! Mama Mia! Odorio!' At the El-Alamein position, here was the sea, here we Germans were and here were the Italians. Here came the Brits, who broke through and immediately as soon as they started firing they threw their guns away. We tried to reach them but couldn't contact them."[77]

The order to stop all further retreats and continue to fight to the last bullet was nonsense and could not be undertaken by the troops, because even as it was issued, the British *1st*, *7th*, and *10th Armored Divisions* began bursting through the thin *Panzerarmee* defenses, and there would be no altering of the plan and no hope of holding out against the Allies. After much frustration by Rommel, he again agreed to the withdrawal; even Kesselring, who had just flown into Africa, and was all for the salvaging of the army, had attempted to persuade Rommel that there was no other option but to continue the retreat. Hitler a short time later withdrew his absurd order and agreed to the withdrawal; a signal was sent off on the evening of the 4th, but it arrived far too late on the 5th to do any good, because at 1730hrs Rommel finally ordered a general withdrawal to the *Fuka Position*, abandoning much of his non-mobile forces in order to save the vital mobile elements. But fortunately for the *D.A.K.* the British were slow to follow up their successes; very little foresight was given, and those plans that existed were wholly inadequate concerning the time period initially following the initial breakthrough, and if it had not been for the tired and worn out staffs, the confusion and mottling about on the battlefield may have been the end for the *D.A.K.* At this time the number of operational panzers is quite difficult to determine, with panzers constantly breaking down or running out of fuel. Coupled with the arrival of repaired panzers, the best determination is that the Regiment possessed on average ten operational panzers from the period of 3-8 November. The total number of panzers in both the panzer divisions totaled only about thirty-five,[78] compared to the hundreds of *Grant*, *Sherman*, *Crusader II*, and the newly arrived *Churchill* tank with its 6-Pounder main gun. All of these tanks were now superior to the Mk III, and it was the Mk IVF2 that possessed the comparable firepower to reach out and engage these Allied tanks.

The Retreat
At around 0800hrs on the 4th, enemy armored cars appeared in front of the defensive lines, followed shortly by a tank unit in approximately regimental strength. The tanks opened fire at a distance of 2,000m, but could not break through the Axis defensive positions. Loosely positioned from one point to the other, just fourteen panzers made up the entire firepower of the Regiment, which at the time could amount to nothing less than an under strength company. Even though it was a *kampfgruppe* and labeled such on divisional maps, the men continued to fight on, and were even able to knock out seven more enemy tanks while continuing to repulse more British attacks. Lt von Houwald was able to make his way forward from the workshop with three more operational panzers, raising the combat power to seventeen panzers by that evening.[79] In the following account Wilhelm Hagios describes his encounter with a *Leutnant* who might have been von Houwald:

"On the 4th in the morning our commander with some other unteroffiziers drove forward with 12 or 13 panzers that were there. One of the leutnants, I don't remember the name, as he was probably from the Regiment Stabs where as the others were from the [panzer] companies came to us and took away our 5cm panzer, he said that he needed a vehicle and I said to myself 'something is wrong here if he takes a 5cm from me', no one exchanges for a shorter one [cannon size], but I hadn't the right to say anything to him."

On orders from the *15th Panzer Division* the *kampfgruppe* was to disengage itself from the enemy under the cover of darkness and link-up with the remains of the division at Bir el Tamr, which lay approximately 25km southwest of El Daba. On the same day, the following message was sent from *Kampfgruppe Siemens* to the divisional headquarters:

"Panzer Regiment 8 and remaining Italian tanks have reached the assigned area. 1./Artillery Regiment 33 and Pioneer Battalion 33 were personally instructed by the leader of this kampfgruppe but until now have not yet arrived. The same exact order was transmitted five times to 1st and 2nd Companies Flak 43. An officer was sent to obtain a connection, but until now he has not yet returned. Until now in this new area there has been no encounter with the enemy."[80]

Hagios continues his description of the situation:

"In the mid afternoon we drove 3km south and stopped where some other panzers were. Not a single shot came from our side during the afternoon. In the evening about 1700hrs, it could have been earlier or later, two tank columns broke through to the south of us as there was no defense from us, nothing. It was two divisions who broke through. I watched the whole time, through some optics. They went tank to tank, oh well. I watched them until the evening. The British during the night highlighted the way where they drove and they drove until 20-2100hrs and then stopped for a break. At 2000hrs came the order to retreat. We drove a couple of kilometers until the vehicle became overheated, then the panzer where we were got stuck and couldn't pull well, the engine was finally broken. There was a 15cm assault gun that belonged to Pz8 and they towed us to the west. About 0400hrs in the morning it started to get cold and they said we should stay there and that the I-Staffel will come. I said to the Unteroffizer that I would remain in the vehicle and that certainly no I-Staffel was going to show up and that we should keep driving together as long as it would be possible. We drove with them and in the morning we had to stop and the driver, Karl Munz, argued that it was impossible to drive this way and that he will check the carburetor and fuel. The Uffz asked how long that we would remain and I said 'about an hour'. The driver took apart the carburetor, and I maintained a watch. I realized that during the night we had driven to the west about 20-25km. When there was some more daylight I looked through binoculars at the platoon of vehicles to the south of us in a slight hollow. I didn't know if these were German or British, so I watched them. The driver had been busy with tearing apart the carburetor and I noticed in the daylight that two tanks were approaching us and behind them some more. I recognized them as Shermans. I called the Unteroffizer and told him about the Shermans. He hadn't noticed them beforehand either. There was a short fire fight, and they withdrew. The new commander, the Uffz, asked me what to do now and I said 'that's easy, if they capture us we go into the prison, otherwise we stay with our last panzer."[81]

No doubt the reason for failing to contact the other elements came from the constant air and ground attacks that all but wiped out communications between units. The rearguard of the *kampfgruppe* was under the command of Lt Golinski, and had been formed from the few remaining panzers; that rearguard was successfully able to hold back any flanking or pursuit attempts by the British, and by 0300hrs on the 5th the *kampfgruppe* was able to link-up with the rest of the division and to resupply itself with fuel and ammunition. The divisional war diary noted the following:

"After the withdrawal during the night 4/5, which had succeeded without any enemy encounters, the enemy with 200 tanks, 200 vehicles and trucks had reached the rearguards of Panzer Regiment 8 at 0700hrs and destroyed some panzers. After the interval distance was again achieved at around midday there was observed enemy reconnaissance forces south and eastwards of the division and consisted of about a reinforced reconnaissance detachment. They attack shortly before darkness from the south and was beat back through artillery fire. In the view of the engagement of attacking enemy forces with 90th Light and 21st Panzer, the further evading movement of the division continues without enemy encounter until 6.11."[82]

Adolf Lamm remembers the retreat:

"The state of a defeated and retreating army is indescribable, fortunate were those who had a vehicle or who could jump aboard one. We drove through a place overflowing with Italian infantry. They stormed our panzers, trying to get a lift, however the Leutnant commanding our panzer prevented all attempts to board, sometimes violently. He was probably just acting under orders. I thought it was brutal. But what did we Landsers know about how the high command was dealing with our lives? Germans, Italians, and on the other side the English, all this just swarming ants, tearing each other to pieces, not knowing why, animals, following the instinct of the moment and the masses."

At the time of the retreat the *Panzerarmee* was aligned from north to south, with the *90th Light* in the north along the coast, followed by the *21st Panzer* and *15th Panzer*, with the remaining Italian mobile formations being located farther in the south. The division then formed three march groups for the continued withdrawal westward; these columns were now commanded by *Hauptmann*, as most senior divisional leaders had either been killed or wounded. The Regiment continued to secure the entire width of the division. With the first light of the morning the combat unit realized that strong armored units were following them, as a *Grant* tank suddenly opened fire and shot three panzers. After this short skirmish the *kampfgruppe* evaded further action in order to maintain connection with the division, but already in the south it was overtaken by *Crusader II* and *Sherman* tanks, with armored cars and light tanks following closely. In the short action that followed *Leutnants* Houwald and Marquardt were both wounded, and four more panzers were lost due to mechanical breakdowns, and had to be destroyed. It is most probable that one of those panzers belonged to Hagios, who now had no panzer, and so he decided to destroy it less it be captured by the British:

"I had two hand grenades and petrol canisters, so I jumped off and made my quickest 100m run and hid near the bogie on the right side of the turret, and ignited the petrol canisters through the hatch."

Adolf Lamm remembers his bad situation:

"Somewhere on our retreat through the desert, it might have been by Sidi Barrani, in the morning around 0900, our panzer stopped. It didn't want to go on. The desperate attempts of the capable driver were useless. Dismount. Rotate the cannon to the rear. Open the motor compartment. Guessing Game: when will Tommy catch up to us? Our Lieutenant abandoned us, he grabbed a Feldwebel from the accompanying company, turned over the panzer with a few 'operating instructions' for the event of the worse case, and away he went in the Feldwebel's intact panzer. I didn't have much luck with Feldwebels in the army and Africa wasn't any better. Neither was this time an exception. Presumably, our Lieutenant didn't get along well with him, either, and had therefore entrusted him with this suicide mission. He was an underhanded, sly type, well practiced in the art of making his subordinates' lives hell. The driver showed us the disassembled carburetor, a cast block, one half of which he was holding in his hand. Inside sparkled a few large drops of water. Wash it out, install it, get in, and fire it up. 'Come on!' someone called. The panzer started to move, the track rattling and gnashing. Move; let's get out of here! Strangely enough, there was no hostile fire."[83]

The *kampfgruppe* continued to evade and skirmish with British armor, in many cases estimated to be of over one hundred tanks, in this continuing fighting withdrawal. In one instance four British armored cars that unknowingly attempted to drive past the panzers to the west were quickly engaged and left burning on the battlefield. *Leutnants* Golinski and Hubbuch were sent to march with the II./*Abteilung*, in order to protect the combat supply trains. The seven operational panzers remaining with the Regiment were now under the command of Lt Kehrer and Lt Schuberski, which continued to form the rearguard of the division.[84] Under the cover of night the division marched westward until it reached the area southwest of Marsa Matruh, and here the Regiment assumed defensive positions facing eastwards on the road to Siwa. One more panzer was lost to mechanical breakdown, and another was destroyed. Wilhelm Hagios continues his story:

"On the morning of 5th Nov we were able to escape and we were the last Pz 8 panzer to get away. There were only eight panzers available, on the morning of the 5th that was all. I no longer had any vehicle and Munz, the driver, was with me. I didn't know where the other panzers were and so I said: 'We have just one thing left to do; go west'. There was a truck driving by and that was the first good fortune for us and I said 'let's go', and we drove with him. It was an ammunition vehicle bringing ammunition to the front lines and we drove with him in the direction Marsa Matruh."

The day went by without any contact with the enemy, and the crews found a bit of time for rest, but only after the mechanical checks and services had been performed. On 6 November the rains came to the aid of *D.A.K.*, as it rained heavily during the evening and night and was able to turn the ground into a muddy mess that slowed down and temporarily halted the pursuing British *Eighth Army* for about a day. Wilhelm Hagios concludes his story of the retreat:

"We were on the east side of Marsa Matruh, and I said: 'This night we have to go through Marsa Matruk no matter what, because the next morning the British will hit us from the other side'. The whole night we drove, the road was full with columns, truck after truck, Luftwaffe, Wehrmacht, all mixed up. I said 'If we get stuck, we have to run on foot'. During the night there was a bombing attack, and we really had to run and drive, and in the morning we reached the west side of Marsa Matruk and thus got out of the trap. We were lucky that the British were not quick enough to advance, as they were waiting for their fuel. So we escaped from Marsa Matruh and then we went towards Halfaya Pass, upwards, in the direction of Bardia and after Bardia we finally met a vehicle of the regiment which carried the symbol of the wolf's angle. We saw it on the

road, and drove with them backwards: Derna, Bardia, and Benghazi, until El Agheila."

The 7th passed without any significant contact with British forces, but towards evening a small probing attack was beaten off in the south as an advance force of British armored scout cars made contact with *Sonderverband 288*. In that encounter five armored cars were reported knocked out, but due to the unclear situation, which was reporting that British armor formations had been identified in both the north and south, there was little information as to who was where on the battlefield. This confusion led to the following incident, when later in the evening *Sonderverband 288*, which had been securing Marsa Matruh and was screening the *D.A.K.* retreat, engaged the lead element of the Regiment. In this friendly fire incident, three panzers were hit by friendly fire. There are no figures on personnel casualties in this incident.[85] On the 8th, there appeared a new threat to the *Panzerarmee* and *D.A.K.* in the form of the *Allied Expeditionary Forces* that landed in western North Africa. 80,000 U.S. and 20,000 British soldiers were landed near Casablanca, Oran, and Algiers. The operation, codenamed "Torch," was led by a then unknown American General, *Lieutenant General* Dwight D. Eisenhower. Those landings were initially successful, and met with little resistance. The landings were aimed at Tunis, where it was hoped that the Axis positions in Africa would be squeezed between two pinchers that would eventually come together, and with overwhelming force grind the weakened Axis formations between them. Also on the 8th, all non-operational panzers were ordered removed from the forward areas to the workshops in the rear, where it fell on those services to attempt to rebuild the combat formations. Despite the total confusion and disorganization that reined within the *Panzerarmee*, the *15th Panzer* made an all out effort to reconstitute its main combat formations and make them operational once again. The Regiment had been unable to form its combat detachments, and with just eight operational panzers the Regiment was no longer a cohesive combat formation, as those remaining panzers were employed in drips and drabs in an attempt to hold together the battle lines.

The task of slowing down the *Eighth Army* offensive was an almost impossible one, seeing that much of the *Eighth Army* was highly mobile with all its armored divisions, and many of the infantry divisions being fully equipped with wheeled and tracked vehicles. In contrast, many of the Axis formations, especially the Italian infantry in the south, had little in the way of mobile transportation. At this time it was necessary to preserve what vehicles, fuel, and other provisions that remained for those combat formations which had the greatest value of salvaging something out of the situation. It was an almost impossible task to slow down the advance of the British *X Corps* while under a constant carpet of bombs by the *DAF* and the formations of armored cars and light *Crusader II* and *Honey* tanks that constantly nipped at the heels of the rear guard. In an attempt to slow down the British pursuit, *Sprengkommandos* (demolitions squads) were responsible for destroying all abandoned equipment and leaving nasty little surprises for the British troops. It was Rommel's opinion, which often differed from his Italian bosses, that the most important thing was to get every soldier and as much materiel back to the west, where the *Panzerarmee* could make a final stand in Tunisia while it attempted to pull off its own Dunkirk. By 11 November the *D.A.K.* had passed through the Halfaya-Pass, which was unable to be properly defended like it had been in the past because of the small, ill-equipped force. By the 13th Sollum, Capuzzo, and Sidi Omar were evacuated as British forces pushed along the Trigh Capuzzo. Adolf Lamm continues his description of the retreat:

"Halfaya Pass – Sollum, The road was choked up with retreating infantry and vehicles and we drove right by them through the desert. Italian engineers built gun emplacements next to the road and there were Death Squads also there. A little bit later the air-raid siren wails. How many times is that, now? This time we were right in the middle of a column. Everyone jumps from the vehicles, runs into the field and tries to find cover. At the front of the panzer is a fixture that can be used to mount an anti-aircraft machine gun. The gunner and loader tried it out, and it sure banged away. Both of them were just able to jump to cover next to the panzer, fortunately on the right side, since the other side was strafed, as we later discovered by the machine gun tracks. The racket went on for five minutes before the fighter-bombers disappeared. The desert came alive again, the men returning. The screams of the wounded also animated the air. 'Take no wounded, we can't let them slow us down!' This time they were Germans. A truck was burning up front on the slope. We broke out of the convoy. While driving off I saw behind the vehicle a boy lying on the ground, he repeatedly heaved himself up, only to fall backwards weakened each time. Next to the truck lay the body of a man, motionless. Go on, move on! All just scraps of memories. In a narrow pass next to the slope was a man's cadaver stripped down to the underwear. It is said that he was a downed pilot, German, Englishman? Who knows? Robbing the dead? The naked feet in the long johns were twisted. Someone had first ripped off his shoes because good footwear is rare. Sometimes living depended on it. The wreck of a downed aircraft were nowhere to be seen. Somewhere we changed a bogie wheel. I was to direct the work, while the Feldwebel excused himself in order to go get instructions, supposedly. I was trained as a radio operator. I didn't know much about changing bogie wheels. The others were stubborn, so the work couldn't be completed. Obscene cussing followed the Feldwebel's return. I felt humiliated and degraded it was as if a clock maker had been instructed to shoe a horse."[86]

The previous month had been, needless to say, very exhausting on the men of the *D.A.K.*, and it was not only the young men and front line troops that suffered from the strains of combat. The commander of the *15th Panzer Division*s, *Generalmajor* von Vaerst, fell critically ill and had to be replaced on the 11th by *Oberst* Crasemann. Crasemann remained in command of the division until the 18th, when *Oberst* Borowietz replaced him. On the 13th Tobruk, which had cost so much blood since the spring of 1941, was abandoned. Alfred Toppe wrote about the possible plans concerning the holding of the city against the *Eighth Army*:

"The idea of defending Tobruk was weighed but rejected almost immediately, as it would have amounted to voluntarily accepting a siege. The retrograde movement continued, the Cyrenaica being abandoned up to the Marada-Marsa el Brega line, which was reached by the first combat units on 18 November. Here, at last, there was an opportunity to reorganize the units. Rommel expected a long stay at this point, since the enemy required time to close up his units from the rear and to move his supply bases forward."[87]

Later in the day the *D.A.K.* had been able to close up on Gazala, where it was forced to negotiate the thin passages through the old British minefields still located there. Indeed, the entire withdrawal continued to be slowed by a number of these old minefields, which despite having some of the mines removed for the Alamein position were still very dangerous. As the last elements made their way towards Benghazi, the situation once again became critical when the supply of fuel ran out, and for a time the *D.A.K.* remained stalled until fuel could be brought up to them. This, however, was not so simple a task, as the supply warehouses in Benghazi began to go up in smoke when many of the rear area supply and logistics personnel began to panic. On the 15th, the *D.A.K.* made its way towards Barce. The *15th Panzer*'s order of march continued to be the Regiment followed by the remaining *panzerjäger*, artillery, headquarters,

Chapter 12: The Battle of El Alamein, October-December 1942

signals, pioneers, and Flak guns. They slowly made their way towards the processing point at Maraua, where the division attempted to reform many of the stragglers and separated soldiers and formations. On the 17th, the Regiment reported its march position as eight kilometers west of the airfield at Benina near Benghazi. On the 18th, the *15th Panzer Division* was deployed around Magrun, with the Regiment proceeding to an area 20km north of Ghemines, where it was placed in divisional reserve. On the 20th Benghazi was also abandoned. According to the divisional war diary dated 21 November 1942, the *15th Panzer Division* suffered the following losses from the period 21 October to 20 November 1942: 183 men killed, 480 wounded, and 899 men missing in action. The Regiment suffered the following losses: six officers and thirty-five men killed, and ten officers and one hundred and fifteen men wounded, with twenty-six men missing.[88] The Regiment's reported combat strength was eleven officers, eight civilian contractors, thirty-three *unteroffiziers*, and seventy-six men. On an interesting note, at this time in the campaign there appears in the divisional war diary the mention of a number of panzer Mk III 7.5cm. This was not the more common *Sturmgeschütze III*; it was the Mk III Ausf N, which was equipped with a short-barreled KwK L24 7.5cm (Kurz) gun formerly mounted on the early Mk IVs. This type of panzer was only produced in the model "N," which according to most resources would not have arrived in North Africa until early 1943, but the first of these panzers were in place in November '42, as *Uffz* Wilhelm Hagios was the driver and later commander in one that doubled as the command, or Befehls panzer. Most of these models are known and pictured in service with the *501st Heavy (Schwere) Panzer Abteilung*, which later fought in Tunisia with its *Tiger* and Mk III "J" models. On 22 November, the Regiment was ordered to gather all its available panzers and combat vehicles and consolidate them into a single panzer *abteilung* of three companies. The first two companies would be formed around the remaining panzers and crews that still possessed some type of unit cohesion. It would be these two companies that would bear the brunt of rearguard duties. The third of these companies was to be formed around the Regimental *Werkshop Company*, and would consist of predominantly those panzers that required a minimal amount of maintenance, but as yet were still not ready for daily combat operations. Even with the loss of so many of the panzers and other motor vehicles, there were still about a hundred men and large quantities of equipment, fuel, ammunition, tools, and other provisions that needed to be transported west in order to keep what remained operational. The Regiment expressed the need for one hundred vehicles with which to transport these men and materials, since most of its supply vehicles had been lost in the fighting. There was one bright spot, in that the *Werkshop Company* was fully operational, and it would be this company that would allow the Regiment to maintain its fighting abilities. Also looking ahead, there was a request made for replacement panzers, signals equipment, and personnel. To many this request may seem quite humorous, considering the present state of the *Panzerarmee*, when every Axis formation in Africa was screaming for replacement men and equipment. But more importantly, the request demonstrates the determination, professionalism, fighting prowess, and *esprit de corps* that this Regiment showed time and time again, and it further demonstrates why this regiment was one, if not the best regiment in Africa. The Regiment, now worn down to the size of a weak *abteilung*, was able to report the following panzer strength for 22 November: twelve Mk III Sp, four Mk III (7.5), and ten Mk IV Sp.[89] On the night of 23/24 November the *15th Panzer Division* was able to reach the Marsa Brega / El Agheila position. Klaus Hubbuch's letters reflected back to the Alamein battle:

"Dear Parents! Look, I thought so much about you in the last weeks, but was unable to write you much, because my big task to serve others hasn't allowed this. You will definitely be able to understand, the days here were endlessly difficult. Now on the quiet evening I can write to you. And it is from the point, where I last year was allowed to take off home to you. The memories of these days over the past year don't allow us today to drop our spirit. We achieved so much and will continue here in far country to solve the tasks, which we are given. Everybody is with the whole soldier's heart for this. These were till now the most difficult hours of my life, which we experienced here in Alamein. And our boys, these soldiers, are so great, ready for combat and reliable, even though they have been here in Africa for almost 18 months and always in deployments. And if somebody at home speaks stupidly about it, then this one should spend just one day, no – just one hour, here in Africa with us! It's just not possible to explain, how it was. Dear parents, I told you about something which was long ago, almost one month ago, and why not? Continue to think about us, until we will be together again. The moment will come. Dear parents! Last year on this day it was Totensonntag in Africa. Can my father remember my report?, when all the officers including my company chief and commandant fell in the assault by our panzers. At that time the crews were tough, now they are even tougher, I think, never to surpass the material and ammunition deployment of the enemy. In Africa it is being fought for the sinking World Reich! And this year? Today is a rest day and for me one of the best days of my young life. I received today from the commander the EK I on my chest, which was awarded in the Abteilung for these deployments. We will celebrate a little bit this evening; I have such brilliant comrades amongst the officers here. They were so happy for me. And you, my dear parents, I hope you do too. As it is being said so nicely: 'The brave grasp the luck!' In the war one trusts such saying. I ask you to continue to trust to the greater luck, which is granted to this young soldier."[90]

On the 26th, the remainder of the Regiment was located to the west of the Marsa el Brega position. At this time the Regiment was still without a commander, after the loss of Willi Teege on 2 November. *Major* Schnell, the Regiment's Engineering officer, had assumed the duties as acting Regimental commander until a qualified panzer troop commander of appropriate rank and experience could be brought in to take command of the Regiment, even though there was little left of the Regiment. Also at that time the twenty-eight operational panzers were divided in half between the newly reformed I and II./*Abteilung*. Lt Wandruska, once again without a panzer to command and the *Littorio* Division destroyed, was sent back to the Divisional *Stabs* to assume duties as the *O-3*. Lt Halverscheidt again assumed command of the *6th Company*, and Lt Hubbuch assumed duties as *Stabs* Company commander in addition to his responsibilities as the Ordnance Officer of the II./*Abteilung*.[91] In a letter home Hubbuch wrote:

"My dearest! I will drop you a few lines quickly. There is not much time for this. In my previous letters as orderly officer of the Abteilung, which I completely fulfilled, I received a further task. Yesterday I got subordinated the Stabskompanie of the Abteilung with more than 200 men. This is very interesting and new big progress, but this is a lot. And so far it works! Hope also in the future, with this firm believe on the success, I wish you all the best."

The Regiment reported a panzer strength of twenty-eight operational panzers on 26 November 1942.[92] Wilhelm Hagios describes a few of the events that took place at that time:

"In El Agheila we had again no vehicle but what was good, I came down with jaundice, I hadn't received treatment for weeks and the Unterartz [Doctor] said that they have to send me to Germany. But

they needed every man, so I had to report to the hospital in the morning otherwise they would leave without me so I was not sent away. On 27/28 November I got another panzer again, the *Befehls panzer* of *Hauptmann Stotten*. *Hauptmann Stotten* was the chief of the I./*Abteilung* which didn't exist any longer."

With the arrival of *Hptm* Hans-Günther Stotten, a decorated and experienced panzer commander from *Panzer Regiment 3*, the Regiment now had a capable leader to see it through until a more senior man could be flown in. On 28 November Rommel flew to Hitler's headquarters, where he unsuccessfully suggested that the African theater of operations be abandoned, or at least a withdrawal to the *Mareth Line*. Hitler, Mussolini and the *OKW* staff, however, had other plans, and Rommel was ordered to hold the *El Agheila Position*. However, this was not practical as events were to show, and the next withdrawal began in mid-December towards the *Buerat Position*. Rommel had decided earlier to attempt and construct a new defensive line at Buerat, and by 8 December work on this position had begun. Those German units that were in desperate need of a period of rest and refitting, namely the *164th Light Division* and the *Ramcke Brigade*, were employed for this purpose, as well as other rear echelon elements of the *D.A.K.* and local native labor, all under the direction of the commander of the *164th Light Division*. One of the main features planned by Rommel in this line was an antitank ditch in front of his positions, but owing to the lack of time and the inadequate labor forces available, the ditch was only partially completed.[93] In mid-November Walter Nehring, the former *D.A.K.* commander, after recovering from the wounds he received at Alam Halfa, arrived back in Africa as the commander of "*Stabs Nehring*." Nehring had the mission to begin the establishment of the Tunisian bridgehead and covering the north. On 8 December, the *XC Korps* was redesignated as the *Fifth Panzerarmee*, but Nehring, who was known to be a quite outspoken critic, was quickly replaced the following day, and he turned over command to *Generaloberst* Hans-Jürgen von Arnim, a former panzer division and corps commander in Russia.[94] On 10 December Rommel abandoned the *El Agheila Position* as *Eighth Army* formations closed in. Alfred Toppe wrote:

"On 10 December, Rommel found himself compelled to abandon the Marada-Marsa el Brega line, since he feared that it would be bypassed. For the same reason, he abandoned the Buerat positions on 18 January 1943. At no point did he have sufficient armored reserves with an adequate supply of fuel to counter any attempts the enemy might make to outflank him. Altogether, fuel supplies had become the major problem of this retreat. As no ships at all arrived in African ports, with the exception of a few military transports with a gross tonnage of 400 tons, the army was entirely dependent on air transportation for fuel supplies. On one single day, 200 tons were delivered in this way, but on all other days, the performances were far lower, rarely being more than 80 tons, and on one day, only 2 tons arrived. At any rate, the promised performance of 300 to 400 tons daily to be delivered by air was never achieved because of weather conditions and enemy activity. The fuel shortage was so serious that it was not even possible to take advantage of the favorable opportunities that frequently presented themselves to damage the pursuing enemy forces, since every drop of fuel had to be hoarded. Things got so bad that, in order to conserve fuel supplies, one motor vehicle was used to tow several others. This could usually be done along the coastal road, which was fairly level in most parts."[95]

Between 10 and 11 December the *2nd Company* diary recorded the following;

"The British attacks, supported by armor, on [strongpoint] Ariosto (located roughly south of Marsa el Brega between the Wadi Faregh and the Via Balbia) other positions in the area are becoming more intense. Strongholds are temporarily falling into enemy hands. The company [is] on day and night alert at half-an-hour combat readiness but cannot be deployed as it lacks the necessary fuel."[96]

Adolf Lamm remembers:

"*We finally continued. Around Tmimi – beyond Tobruk – we met our fate. We had no more fuel even though a supply and fuel depot was right in the vicinity. Everything was coming apart at the seams and a section of the fuel dump was burning. Stacks of barrels were still left undamaged, however but the Feldwebel claimed it was aviation fuel and useless to us. An Mk III needs 300 – 400 liters of fuel for 100km and a panzer without fuel is nothing but scrap metal On the road, the Feldwebel had already surprised us with his piece of news; the Americans had landed in Algeria and were marching towards Tunisia. That sealed our fate, the African Campaign was finished. We no longer had a fighting chance, an entire German army was surrounded in Stalingrad and was being destroyed, and the whole war was lost already. It's all for shit! Whether it suited him that our fuel ran out? I met him again later in Camp Bowie in America as a POW. He was still the same old sick bastard and he didn't forget to remind me that he had been right about everything back then. Our panzer was driven a ways into a depression off to the side and everyone grabbed what few clothes he had. Blankets were most important. The gunner, loader and I were sent away as the Feldwebel performed the task alone with the driver. I can't remember hearing the explosion or seeing a cloud of smoke in the area where we left the panzer. It had been hot over the day and we were dying of thirst. God knows how we had been supplied up until then. Now everyone had to fight through on his own. The plundering Landsers surged over the supply depot and I had to think about our paymasters back in the garrison, about their order and accounting for every slice of bread. I don't remember what I took with me. A few cans of corned beef as large as fist and some tomato puree that I used as a spread until someone told me it was poisonous if not cooked. At the exit of the building I met the loader, who was trying to open a large can of pickles without a can opener. We accomplished this with our combined strength and we wolfed down the pickles in an attempt to still our thirst. Pickles have never tasted better to me than back then. I do not recall how I proceeded from there, by truck, on gun carriages? But the pickles had done their job and I caught African diarrhea. It had gotten me already gotten me the first time back in El Daba, before we had advanced. I hadn't found a place in any of the tents and lay outside under the awning. It was always very cold at night. There it happened, every ten minutes to the side. Our latrine was the desert and the spade with which one threw over a handful of sand, either that or stones or sagebrush. I was ready to die and I ate nothing for days. Later a serving of milk rice seemed like a gourmet feast to me. I didn't then know that this condition would repeat itself every six to eight weeks. I was unaware that this was the sickness of the African soldiers and at times it also provided some with a plane ticket home, the sickness was not entirely unwelcome. Now, 'on the run', it hit me hard. I recall one night sitting on a gun carriage I had jumped aboard. The truck pulling the carriage drove all night long, through sand, over stones, across pits. I clung onto some piece of iron, unable to think about my certain death if a slipped off and let my bare ass hang out in the wind so as not to continuously soil myself. I believe the gun crew was 'Ithacan'. The evening of the following day I could have a bit of their meal, goulash with tomato sauce. It tasted excellent. Dietary measures for diarrhea. I also don't remember thinking about the fact that we didn't take their comrades on our panzer back then.*

Chapter 12: The Battle of El Alamein, October-December 1942

But today, while I write this, I think about it. I do not know how and where I returned to my unit. An Oberfeldwebel asked me what I had been up to the last four weeks but he wasn't really all too much interested. This was probably around Agedabia."[97]

On 12 December the *2nd Company's* diary recorded:

"Alarm! After a quarter-of-an-hour, the company rolls southeast towards Ariosto.

Mission: relieve pressure on our positions by counterattacking and prevent strongholds from being taken. Around 1500hrs, the company is received by 'pilots', well-entrenched in a reverse slope position at a distance of 2 - 3 km. Lt Thamphald's 1st Zug moves into the Ariosto stronghold. Our own minefields make a planned attack impossible. After a brief firefight, the enemy disengages at twilight. The company reassembles at 1900hrs to return to the old stand-by [assembly area]. Friendly casualties: none."

That evening the diary again recorded:

"The code word was received indicating the planned further withdrawal of the enemy. By midday the company had reach El Agheila and its new assembly area located 40km east of Nofilia. After a night march, which was complicated and slowed by complete darkness the company strayed off course and blundered into a couple of unmarked mine fields. That evening the company vehicles of Uffz Peters and Fw Hanske succumbed to mechanical breakdown and a panzer nicknamed 'Friedrich' remained stalled on the road with engine failure as it and its crew awaiting a tow by the I-Staffel and Bergezug."

Since the withdrawal from the *Alamein Position*, the workshop companies and "I" services had worked round the clock, all the while under the constant strain of the retreat, in their attempt to get as many combat ready panzers forward as possible. Without interruption they used every opportunity to repair the broken panzers, and allowed those few remaining panzers the ability to operate from one day to the next. But no matter how hard they worked, it was still a question of fuel, and the eventual outcome of the withdrawal would be based on this one factor alone. Regardless of the tactical demands on the *D.A.K.*, each section had to calculate every move in relation to the amount of fuel on-hand, and halts were conditioned more by fuel shortages than by tactical necessity.[98] On the 13th the *D.A.K.* finally withdrew to the other side of Sirte Bay, where Rommel intended to move into the Buerat position and possibly link up with elements of the *Fifth Panzerarmee* (Nehring/von Arnim), which had been arriving in Tunis in order to join the fighting in North Africa. The Regiment once again had to form the rearguard, and deployed its units to screen and protect the *D.A.K.* from further attack. The panzers and crews assigned to this task took their role seriously, and vigorously attempted to slow down the tanks of the 7th Armored, 51st Highland, and 2nd *New Zealand Divisions*, which were again at the forefront of the *Eighth Army*. The British armored regiments again attempted to tangle with the panzers and hold up the *D.A.K.* retreat, but in most cases a well determined counterattack could blunt the British attempts. The diary of the *2nd Company* recorded:

"The panzer strength melts down; the supply section brings no new panzers. The Regiment moves back to Buerat-el-Hsun, past Sirte, approximately 300km eastwards of Tripoli. In this area they were to remain over the Christmas holiday."

The Regiment spent the majority of the 13th and 14th performing various technical and mechanical services that were bombed daily by the *DAF*, which often appeared overhead, conducting harassing and interdiction missions on the retreating *Panzerarmee*. The Allied flyers, which often appeared as many as ten times a day, were assisted in their tasks by the lack of fuel, which had left almost all of the panzers immobile and presented the flyers a perfect target for their strafing attacks, since the panzers were unable to maneuver into various hiding positions and conceal themselves from above. The crews attempted as best they could to camouflage their vehicles as they awaited the supply trains to show up and bring with them the vital petrol needed for maneuver. During the night of 14/15 December the panzers were finally able to be fueled, and once this task was accomplished the panzers set off in the early morning hours to a point some 30km to the southwest. The task of the Regiment at this time was to strike out at the *Eighth Army* whenever it attempted to maneuver around the *Panzerarmee*. Over the past few days *Luftwaffe* reconnaissance aircraft had detected the movements of just such an attempt. After receiving their orders the panzers rolled off, conducting an unmolested road march obstructed by neither ground nor air interference. The Regiment was aligned with the *2nd Company* leading, followed by the 7th *Company* in a double-row formation. The panzers were able to reach an area approximately 10km south of Merduma in the early morning hours of the 15th. For many it had been a while since such a movement had been conducted without enemy interference, and the success of the road march did much to lift the spirits of the men. Adolf Lamm remembers:

"In the morning hours the panzers reached the new assembly area, it had been a successful day, which made us proud and gave us all new lift, trust, confidence and hope, is was finally over."

It is also important to point out that at this time the Italian *Centauro* Armored Division had moved up to help support the *Panzerarmee's* withdrawal. In December the Italians had combined all of their tanks and armor into this armored division. Late on the morning of the 13th the *Ariete* combat group attached to the *Centauro* had been involved in repulsing an attack by *Eighth Army* forces. Despite the fact that they were equipped with the antiquated *M-13* and *M-14*, the Italian tanks provided a much needed reinforcement and fought well in the encounter. The Italians fought off eighty British tanks for the loss of twenty-two of their own before the battle ended some ten hours later.[99] That evening the alarm was once again sounded, as elements of the *Eighth Army* had once again been able to envelope some of the *Panzerarmee's* combat troops, and had reached the Via Balbia east of Nofilia. The cause of the alarm came about when the 7th *Armored Division* reached Merduma and began to put pressure on the *Panzerarmee*, while during the night of 15/16 December the *2nd New Zealand Division* was able to swing up from the south and seal off the Via Balbia in the hopes of cutting off the *Panzerarmee*.[100] With the primary escape route of the *Panzerarmee* now being blocked, the Regiment was ordered to open the way. The *2nd Company* went forward in the lead as the "*Spitzenkompanie*," and they moved north and reached Merduma shortly after midnight. The panzers were then fueled, and the crews prepared themselves and their panzers for combat operations. As dawn began to break over the desert that morning, the combat elements moved out and began their attempted breakthrough of the New Zealanders, once again lead by the *2nd Company*. The panzers were to create a gap in which to facilitate the breakout of the entire *D.A.K.* After moving only a couple of kilometers the *Spitzenzug*, or leading platoon, under the command of Lt Houwaldt, encountered a well extended New Zealander line located in ambush position. The diary of the *2nd Company* recorded:

"In dashing procedure the positions were improved forwards. The 2nd Company received the order to halt, because the 7th Company was to attack the enemy from the right was slowed. Without waiting for further orders, the Company attacks and throws the enemy back to the south in drafty and dashing procedure. The extension in this direction by the left flank of the Company consisting of the 1st and 3rd Zugs under Fw Honecker had to be halted and called back in accordance to the orders of the higher command, in order to march enclosed in the direction of the ordered attack. The enemy was confused by our own strike and by the quick advance and wants to give up partially, a new enemy position located on the heights, attempts to hold us up with their 'ratsch-boom' (Pak/anti-tank) but they fail to do it. Our long-cannons are hunting enemy tanks and scout vehicles until the new ones pick up positions 10km southeast of Nofilia, even some of the Italians were worried. At the discussion about the attack and breakthrough even the subordinated foreign 'weapons' have agreed, that for months there was no such dashing attack conducted in Africa."

Unfortunately, the Regiment and the *15th Panzer Division* lacked the combat power and fuel to follow up on the early successes of the attack. The Regiment was soon forced to halt the attack because its primary mission of opening an escape route had been achieved. The New Zealanders were not strong enough to hold the line and the breakthrough was achieved; however, the New Zealanders claimed eighteen panzers, twenty-five guns, and 450 prisoners captured.[101] The panzers were able to consolidate their gains, and spent the remainder of the day performing various tasks. The crews would continue the repairs and servicing, but the short break would only last through the 16th. Wilhelm Hagios:

"We left on 16 December and went towards the Buerat position. In that position we were there until the day before Christmas. The British made an attack and from our side came the counter-attack, on the same night, the entire night. From El Agheila I drove the whole night until the following afternoon and during the night I fell into the crater hole left after a bomb blew up and as it was dark I thought we had fallen into a wadi. I wanted to jump off the panzer and lay on the slope as it was very steep. But with the help of a second panzer we were able to get out, in addition we had a Kfz-15 with broken steering and we had to take it with us as well. On the following evening at 1700hrs we had it repaired and so it went."[102]

On the 17th, the Regiment was located just two kilometers from Nofilia, and at around midday it was hit by an unexpected artillery attack that began falling around the panzers as the men were performing their technical work and services. As in most attacks in Africa, a sudden artillery bombardment was usually the sign that an attack was in the making. Once again it was the *2nd New Zealand Division* that had moved around the rearguards and attempted to bag the *D.A.K.*, as it launched an attack straight from their transports on the *15th Panzer Division*.[103] In the fighting that took place on 17 December, it is fortunate that the notes of Adolf Lamm, a radio operator in the command panzer of the *2nd Company*, have survived to describe the attack as it took place:

"After the last few days no one expected that the enemy would have gone around us but they appeared already on the horizon just 4-5km to the southwest. Alarm! An after fifteen minutes the companies were ready to roll. Our task was to hit the enemy on the right and thus prevent any encirclement. Moreover, I had one extra task, Olt Schellhaas learned that I could take down shorthand and so ordered that I should take notes of certain radio conversations between the Abteilung and Company during the combat. These notes which were in shorthand were written down afterwards and they marked a precise time record of the battle and were enclosed in the Company diary. They made the reconstruction of the combat events significantly easier. Before the 7th Company had even begun to engage the enemy in combat, the Zug of Lt Houwaldt had rolled forward to engage the British tanks and did so by advancing smartly in a bold maneuver swinging out around the attacking British armor. The day's combat action began when the first British Mk IV which fell victim to the 75mm gun of Houwaldt's Mk IV as it appeared on a nearby hill. But instead of pushing forward the 1st Zug had to be ordered to halt and take up position on the right flank of the 2nd Company because at that time another ten British tanks had in the meantime moved into positions in the convenient folds in the terrain as they attempted to strike the right flank of the 2nd Company. But not all the British tanks were as fortunate as the panzers of Houwaldt and Uffz Peters were able to claim three of them as they attempted the maneuver in the covering folds. In the meantime the enemy armor had multiplied behind the known hill as the entire 2nd Company quickly succeeded into establishing its own position behind the hill despite the strong enemy fire directed against it. But the German panzers were quicker and as each new enemy attempt to destroy the surrounded company and each of the attacks ended in failure. The right flank of the 2nd Company was made up of the panzers of Fw Kalinski, Uffz Oppold and Uffz Honecker who began to engage targets as close as 50m. Many of the panzer crews later commented that in no time during the war in Africa were enemy tanks destroyed at such a close range. But the close combat continued and because of the distance and terrain the company was unable to disengage itself from the British armor. The panzer of Uffz Oppold remained like a rock against the sea as he and his crew stood by their guns paying little attention to the hail of fire and approaching enemy tanks. Despite the numerous hits his panzer sustained and even the final destruction of his Mk IV the crew was able to claim one tank, two anti-tank guns, a Zugmachine and three other vehicles. Oppold was later nominated by the company commander for promotion to Feldwebel for his bravery in the face of the enemy. According to the order, the company was taken back to a nearby hollow. The release was connected with big difficulties, because if the enemy assaulted we would loose. At this point Fw Honecker distinguished himself, because he was the last who stayed on the hill and destroyed two tanks and was finally able to make his way on foot with an important surveillance report. The 7th Company on the left back from us was already engaged in heavy defense combat. Panzer Regiment 5, which was ordered to relieve us, had still not arrived. The situation continuously worsened, because if we could not prevent the encirclement then we would be lost. The enemy was well supported by their own artillery and wouldn't give up its attempts. Around 1600hrs, Panzer Regiment 5 attacks on the right side from us with its four vehicles, however these four retreat behind the slope as soon as they are covered with the Pilot [Grant] fire. The company received the order, to disengage itself further and to turn away to the north-east. At 1700hrs both companies once again went into position in the area around Point 121. With the darkness we start in the direction of the division to the north. The engines start to stutter due to lack of fuel. At the division there is big excitement as parts of the enemy have broke through to the Via (Balbia). It's questionable, whether and if the dismissed divisions would be able to keep the street open. The 2nd Company as seemed to be the norm was the lead company and it received the order to break through as quick as possible and reach the assembly position of SV Menton [Sonderverband 288]. The fuel Zug led by Lt Thamphald. The assembly position was reached without difficulty and the broken down panzers were towed off by recovery vehicle. In the early morning hours the company reached the new (assembly) area at the Via Balbia, approximately 35km west of Nofilia. The commanding general, Vaerst, the leader of the division, reports to our Regimental leader, Hauptmann Stotten, his full

recognition and gratitude to both companies for the heroic deployments of yesterday. We, the locals who sat in the panzers, experienced these battles differently, as a company radio operator, I had to service both of the receiver and transmitting devices, which were set on the frequency of the Abteilung, and another which served to communicate with the companies besides also the board communication device [intercom], which would have been switched on immediately when the 'chef' wanted to give orders to the driver. Not only our lives depended on the error-free functioning of these devices but also the destiny of the company with all its vehicles. These [radio] boxes have never let me down."[104]

After fighting off the attacks against it on the 17th, the *Panzerarmee* pushed on through Nofilia and reached Sirte on 18 December, while the remaining German and Italian non-mobile units continued on foot towards the *Buerat Position*. Between 18-20 December another conference was called for by Hitler in which he insisted that the *Buerat Position* be held, and that the *Panzerarmee* was not authorized to retreat back to Tunisia. What is interesting is that both the Italian *Commando Supremo*, which was now finally realizing that the *Panzerarmee* could not continue to hold its positions, and the *Eighth Army*, which was constantly outflanking the army, had finally brought to life the need for the *Panzerarmee* to move into the *Mareth Line*. With the pressure on it continuing, the *D.A.K.* rearguards, in this case, the Regiment and *Sonderverband 288*, continued their mission of providing over-watch and protection for the remainder of the *Panzerarmee*. As the Regiment moved back towards Sirte in the week prior to Christmas it was able to report the following number of vehicles on hand; it had thirty-one panzers of various models, in addition to over sixty motorbikes, trucks, ambulances, recovery vehicles, and staff cars of all various makes and models.[105] As Christmas Day approached the overall situation was not a good one, even though it had improved slightly in the past few days after reaching Sirte and Buerat. In a letter written to the Regiment's veterans association sometime after the war, one of the veterans wrote of the lighthearted times that occurred around that Christmas 1942:

"*The orders to withdraw came. We landed in Zliten near Homs, about 50km from Tripolis. It was a small paradise in comparison to previous rest areas. There were palm trees and the water was not salty and drinkable cold. No abteilung or regiments commander lost his way in this direction and our circle was undisturbed. So one could guess how far behind we were. Nearby was an Italian barracks. Already by the first days we agreed with our Italian allies to play a game of soccer. Our team led fairly quickly and was strong and overwhelming. The Italians remembered that they had a couple of international players, they changed players and our situation changed to the worse. But from the loss we were saved by an unscheduled whistle of the Hauptfeldwebel (I think it was Kathe from the 5th Company). Shortly thereafter the oriental luxurious tent of this Hauptfeldwebel was burned out. May be it was the revenge of the disappointed Italian soccer hotheads. A few days before Christmas there appeared the provisioning officer of the II./Abt with several hundredweight of fresh potatoes, we quickly prepared the potatoes and bought some meat from the locals, initially live animals, and baked some cakes in an Italian bakery oven.*"[106]

Klaus Hubbuch, in a letter written on 1.12.42, reflected on the approaching Christmas holiday:

"*Dear parents! I don't know why, the thought just came to me. But I would like to write you my Christmas letter today. This is the third Christmas, which I cannot celebrate with you, first in France, then the last year in retreat in Afrika after heavy combat, and this year? One gets so distant from the beloved motherland. How often I stand in the quiet minutes under the wide sky full of stars and think back, convulsively attempt to transfer me home, to imagine one evening at home, how it always was, when all of us – parents and children – were together. At that time, when I said good-bye to you with my small suitcase in the early morning, I left behind the parent's house and my beautiful youth. Since then I was never long enough with you, in order to take the staying impression with me in the remote places. Father said at that time, I should become a decent soldier. And mother said 'be brave and honest'. I hold to my word. Or can I do more, than 20 years as company leader, with EK I, which I deserved in the hard combats? I have not allowed myself a single quiet day here since I got to Afrika; it's simply impossible. But I will think even more about you in the quiet hours in the evenings, will read your letters and look at your pictures. Then I will be able to stay in my thoughts at Christmas evening with you, and our wishes to happy holidays and healthy reunion will somehow cross.*"[107]

Wilhelm Hagios:

"*On Christmas Eve I saw for the first time Oberst Irkens, who was [our new] Regimental Commander. At first I didn't come close to this new 'shining', but then I was introduced to him. From there we went away into the Buerat position and kept moving across until Tunis. By the end January we were in the workshop in Tarhuna.*"

Adolf Lamm remembers that Christmas of 1942:

"*In the meantime I had rejoined 'my' company and had been assigned to a panzer. We spent the 'celebration' near El Agheila dug in somewhere in the desert the headlong retreat was over. Frozen geese were distributed, one goose for every 8 – 10 men. One can imagine the distribution process!*"

Hermann Eckardt, himself spending his second Christmas in Africa, could recall little about those special days in Africa:

"*I cannot recall anything special of these days maybe we would receive some special food or maybe a bottle of beer. I never had a celebration for a birthday or milestone, in fact even after I was awarded the gold cross [German Cross in Gold, in 1944] I was to have some leave but it never came to be.*"[108]

Even Rommel himself was moved by the morale and professionalism that his men still showed on that Christmas Eve as he wrote to his wife:

"*I'm going off very early this morning into the country and will be celebrating this evening among the men. They're in top spirits, thank God, and it takes great strength not to let them see how heavily the situation is pressing on us.*"[109]

However relaxing that Christmas of 1942 might have been, it was quickly interrupted when a column from the *7th Armored Division* was spotted that day moving up towards the rearguard positions, which forced the men to quickly pack up and beat a hasty retreat back to the Buerat Position. On 27 December, the *Eighth Army* continued the pursuit and advanced towards the *Panzerarmee* with the *2nd New Zealand Division* and British *44th* and *51st Infantry Divisions*, as well as the *7th Armored Division*, from the direction of Sirte. *Oberst* Josef Irkens, in the meantime, had unofficially assumed command of the Regiment from *Major* Schnell, and found his first task as commander to be that of preventing the hand-over of experienced panzer officers, *unteroffiziers*, and crews to the various *panzergrenadier* and *panzerjäger* units. The infantry ranks, having been depleted, and with little resupply of new panzers, the call went out that those crews without a panzer were to be mustered into the ranks and flesh them out. In addition to *Hptm* Stotten, commanding the I./*Abteilung*, *Hptm* Wolfgang Schnelle, a holder of the *DKiG* from *Panzer Regiment 7*, was brought over to take command of the II./*Abteilung*.[110] Stotten had little time to organize his himself before he was given command of a *kampfgruppe* consisting of the remaining panzers of the Regiment, along with a group of pioneers from *Pioneer Battalion 33*, one battery from I./*Abteilung Artillery Regiment 33*, and the *2nd Company, Flak Regiment 43*. At the time the *kampfgruppe*, which like all German *kampfgruppen* took its name from its commander, was located near A.P. 358.[111] The II./*Abteilung* was withdrawn from the regiment and sent towards Tarhuna and Ben Gardane, where they, along with the *21st Panzer Division*, would be reorganized and refitted with new equipment. *Abholkommandos* (retrieval details) were formed and sent to Tripoli and Tunis, in order to receive some new panzer Mk IIIs and IVs (Specials) that had been lucky enough to make the Mediterranean crossing and avoided being sunk; those small convoys were able to unload there in the last days of the December.[112] Also arriving at this time were elements of the *10th Panzer Division*, *Luftwaffe Fallschirmjägers*, additional *Luftwaffe* squadrons, *Nebelwerfer Regiment 71*, additional infantry and mountain troops, and the experimental *Heavy Panzer Abteilung 501*, equipped with the new *Tiger I* that mounted the 88mm gun. Italian formations had also arrived, including a revamped *Ariete* Armored Division that had been rebuilt around a cadre of surviving officers and NCOs from the Alamein battle, and the Italian *1st Superaga Division*, which was heavy in self propelled artillery. During this period in late December, an interesting event took place in which one of the former officers from the Regiment was captured. During the war in Africa fate and luck could be so fleeting, and there are numerous cases where a senior commander was captured or just barely escaped. One such event was documented by *Hptm* Kircher of the *15th Panzer Division's* headquarters element on 30 December. It is of interest because it mentions Lt Wandruszka, formerly of the Regiment, and who had been serving as a liaison officer to the Italian *Littorio* Division, and in November had actually assumed command of the II./*Abteilung* for a short period of time:

"*During the reconnaissance which I received the order to do, with O3 [Assistant Adjutant to the Division Ic] Lt Wandruszka accompanied me in the second vehicle Kfz 12 [a 4x4 command car]. As we reached the exit of wadi El Klef, about the height A.P. 492, I continued the reconnaissance in order to find out the practicability of the adjacent north-south-wadi, and to get the view of the road Bu Ngem. About 4km of east-southeast A.P. 492 my vehicle a Kfz.12 stopped due to the damage in the petrol supply. While my driver was cleaning the petrol filter and carburetor, Lt Wandruszka drove by me further 300m to the east. Until this point during the whole continuation of the reconnaissance there was no observation of the enemy. From my previous position the road was not yet possible to recognize, because it partially went on the mountain border and partially under the waves of the ground. The course of the road I was able to discover later when accompanied by the reconnaissance group. During the repair of my car I heard the machine gun fire behind the eastwards of mountain border, and I saw the cloud of smoke. Shortly thereafter Lt Wandruszka drove from the mountain border downhill in direction north-northwest and disappeared behind the chain of the hills. Shortly thereafter followed English scout cars, later recognized six vehicles total. Due to the changed course of Lt Wandruszka the look-out cars were distracted from me, and seem to not recognize me at first. In the meantime my vehicle was operational again. I drove to the west away from the fire distance of the scout cars, then to the north, in order to get the view behind the ground waves, behind which disappeared Lt Wandruszka. There were all six scout cars driving together. I saw how Lt Wandruszka approached the English scout cars which were about 100m away from him. I assumed that his vehicle was shot down and that he had to surrender in the view of the English scout cars. I drove back to own lines, reported the case and asked a look-out group to reconnoiter against the enemy vehicles and to find out what happened there. Accompanied by two 20mm and one 37mm Sfl. [self-propelled vehicles] led by two Oberleutnants I drove to the place of the ambush. The enemy vehicles were nowhere to see. The vehicle of Lt Wandruszka stood with the tank and motor shot through and on the beaten track, some hundred meters away we found the driver, who walked away from the shot and out-of-order vehicle to the lines of camel-brier in order to hide away. He reported that the vehicle was shot through, and Lt Wandruszka was captured prisoner. He was not able to watch the capture in details, because he left the vehicle in a different direction from Lt Wandruzska. Lt Wandruszka had no paper of secret nature either on him or in the vehicle. He had only the map 1:400.000 Beni Ulid which we got before the reconnaissance trip, with no marks on it. He left his Soldbuch behind. The personality and the service position of Lt Wandruszka as O-3 guarantee, that the enemy obtained any knowledge from the prisoner.*"[113]

As the Axis forces continued to fall back and blunt the British attempts to halt them the divisional commander, *Oberst* Borowietz, sent his division the following New Year message:

"*Division Order of the Day. 'My comrades! The Division is not broken by the enemy at the change from 1942/43. Each of us who belongs to the division should be conscious, that the spirit of the German Army and the soldier's attitude in each of us has mastered every difficult situation. Unshakeable belief in the final victory, rock-hard trust to our Führer and the good will to protect our motherhood are the sources of the power, which enable us in the New Year to fulfill our duty in fidelity. So I wish you all who belong to the division in the 1943 the true soldier's luck. Forward for the Führer and Great Germany!' m.d.F.b. Borowietz Oberst.*"[114]

Adolf Lamm remembers:

"*1 January 1943, New Year's Day marks the beginning of my cursory calendar notes. I started the New Year with a visit to the dentist. Somewhere in the desert, covered in a valley between dunes, a medical tent had been set up. The dentist had a pedal-driven drill, operated by a medic. I received a temporary filling. I was supposed to return later for them to pull a tooth. As I stepped from the tent, an African downpour was in process. I didn't care about anything but getting rid of the tooth pain. With some effort I crossed the sand dunes, which look the same in every direction, looking for stone markers on my way back to the company.*"

13

Fighting for Time in Tunisia
January-February 1943

At 0500hrs on 2 January, the division ordered the Regiment's *7th Company*, in addition to *Kampfgruppen Pätzold*, to keep ready their combat elements in order to support an attack by the combat group of the Italian *Centauro* Division. The *7th Company* was now known as *Kampfgruppe Lindner*, named so for its commander, *Olt* Lindner. Both of these small *kampfgruppen* were directly under the control of the *15th Panzer Division's* headquarters. It was all too common at this point in the retreat that the division would form various *kampfgruppen*, usually centered on the primary combat formation and taking the name of the unit commander. Many of these *kampfgruppen* were hastily organized and then quickly reformed or disbanded as the corps, division, and regimental commanders saw fit. These small units were usually formed to undertake a specific task or mission. On 3 January, the *15th Panzer Division* issued orders to all subordinate units that the primary mission of the division was to defend itself with all available elements along the entire front line position, as well as being available en masse for mobile use.[1] The first order of business was to fight off those *Eighth Army* formations then attempting to envelope the *Panzerarmee* in the Buerat Position. *Kampfgruppe Lindner* was to remain as a reserve in the sector behind the right flank of *III./Panzergrenadier Regiment 115*, and its deployment was to be authorized only by the division headquarters. For the planned counterattack by the mobile elements of the division it was intended to regain *Kampfgruppe Lindner* and one light artillery battery on the east side of Wadi Zemzem. By 4 January, the Regiment, minus the *II./Abteilung*, was again separated into two distinct *kampfgruppen*: *Kampfgruppe Lindner* with the *7th Company*, *2./Flak Regiment 43*, and one *Zug* of *4./Flak Regiment 43*. The second was *Kampfgruppe Stotten*, which consisted of the *I./Abteilung's* panzers, minus the *7th Company*, with one battery from *I./Artillery Regiment 33*, the *3./Flak Regiment 43*, and one section or group from *Pioneer Battalion 33*. Some of the other divisional *kampfgruppen* were *Kampfgruppe Lindemann*, which consisted of *II./Panzergrenadier 115* (minus one *Zug*), *Flak Battalion 617* (minus one *Zug*), *3./Panzerjäger Abteilung 33*, and *4./Flak Regiment 43* (minus one *Zug*). *Kampfgruppe Schneider-Eicke* had the *Stabs I./Flak Regiment 43*, one *Zug* from *II./Panzergrenadier Regiment 115*, *2./Panzerjäger 33*, *1./Flak Regiment 43*, and *5./Flak Regiment 43*.[2] At 1330hrs on 5 January 1943, *Oberst* Josef Irkens was officially appointed as the new commander of *Panzer Regiment 8*. Irkens would be the last commander of the Regiment, and would see it through some of the most trying of days. Irkens was soon faced with a number of tasks, as the *Panzerarmee* ordered that all holding detachments were to deploy from the southern flank of the *164th Light Division*, and to immediately begin installing dummy minefields forward of their present positions. The latter part of this order was done in order to deceive those *Eighth Army* reconnaissance units that were now observing the *Panzerarmee*. To assist those units establishing the defense, *Pioneergruppe Perser* was ordered to remain with the *15th Panzer* and the Regiment in order to provide direct engineer support. Later that evening, various officers from the division's subordinate regiments arrived at the divisional command post to receive orders for their future withdrawal. The following chain of command structure is the author's best estimate at placing those officers with their respective companies; in only a few cases was it exactly known who was commanding what at this time during the withdrawal:

The Regimental command structure as of 6 January:

Regiment Commander	Oberst Irkens
I./Abteilung Commander	Hptm Stotten
2nd Company	Olt Schellhaus
4th Company	Olt Schulz
7th Company	Olt Lindner
II./Abteilung Commander	Hptm Schnelle
5th Company	Olt Blidschuhn
6th Company	Lt Halverscheidt
8th Company	Olt Bänger

The *15th Panzer Division* reported a total of thirty-three panzers for 6 January, and this number included eight MK III Sp, nine Mk IIIs (7.5), and sixteen Mk IV Sp. The *I./Abteilung* had fifteen panzers: five Mk IIIs Sp, three Mk IIIs (7.5), and seven Mk IVs Sp.[3] On 7 January the *15th Panzer Division* formed into four branch oriented *kampfgruppen* for the withdrawal to the Sedada position; there was a panzer *kampfgruppe* under the command of Irkens, with *Panzer Regiment 8* (minus the *7th Company*), the *3./Panzerjäger Abteilung 33*, and *I./Artillery Regiment 33* (minus two companies). There was also a grenadier *kampfgruppe* under the command of *Major* Wissmann, an artillery *kampfgruppe* under *Oberst* Crasemann, and finally the Flak *kampfgruppe* under *Major* Schneider-Eicke.[4] At 1400hrs, before the start of the *Panzerarmee's* withdrawal, the *15th Panzer Division* was still without *Kampfgruppe Pätzold*, which had been relocated to an area 15km south of Sedada, where it established the division's new assembly area. The withdrawal was initiated by the codeword "*March West*," and the march route was via the slope of Gheddahia – Sedada as previously laid out by the *D.A.K.* headquarters. In the meantime the

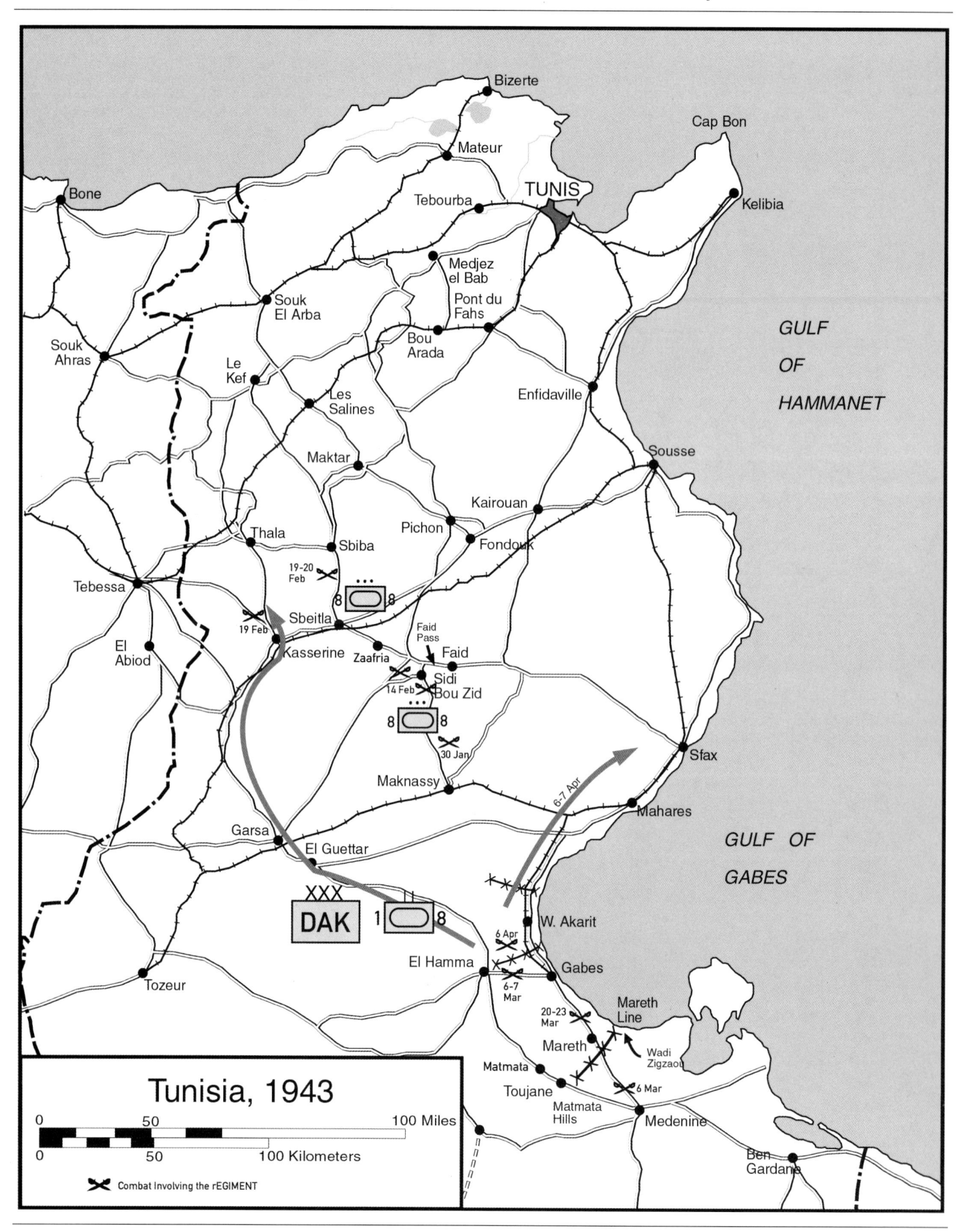

Panzer Regiment 8 in World War II - Poland • France • North Africa

Chapter 13: Fighting for Time in Tunisia, January-February 1943

Regiment, with the attached *panzerjägers* and artillery, were sent into a reserve position in the area 5km west of A.P. 492.[5] On the 8th at 1100hrs, the Regiment received orders to move forward and conduct a reconnaissance past Bir Garania [Bir Umm el Gharaniq] in the direction of Sedada. On the 9th at 1330hrs orders were received from division assigning the Regiment, along with the *3./Panzerjäger Abteilung 33* and one company from *III./Panzergrenadier Regiment 115*, to the divisional reserve. That evening at 1800hrs, the Regiment reported to the division that the reconnaissance of the track from Bir Garania to Sedada was overall passable to the division and was marked by stone pyramids. At 2130hrs, orders were received from the division headquarters that informed all the *kampfgruppen* to continue their withdrawal. On the following day, orders were received ordering the Regiment to launch a counterattack in the direction of A.P. 494, which was located along the Wadi el Chlef and on the left flank of *Blocking Gruppe Nord*. The panzers were to take up over-watch positions in order to secure the withdrawal of the blocking groups. There was also the additional task of exploring the reverse slope positions and rallying points located along the *HKL*.[6] Since, in many circumstances, it is extremely difficult to visualize just how the terrain looked, the actual report is included to offer the reader a glimpse of the terrain. Additionally, the report offers a glimpse of the situation facing *Oberst* Irkens and his men. In a report filed in the *15th Panzer Division's* KTB on 11.1.43 the report revealed the following reconnaissance of the terrain:

The main approach offers the enemy opportunities on both flanks from the east and south through the open terrain on both sides of Bir Recha and along the Wadi el Chlef on both sides of Bir Garania. In between these points is located the high ground from A.P. 523 (map 1:100,000) which continues to the south, southeast and in this direction it is generally descending until the area approximately 4km northeast of Bir Tueil el Ase. These heights ascend mildly from the east to the west and then fall steeply, especially in the northern area. The Wadi el Chlef and the deep levels on both sides of Bir Recha are sandy desert with multiple stony stretches. In the Wadi el Chlef between the visual position and Bir Garania are located separate flat mountain crests, which ease the combat cut outs. This is not present on the southern flank in the direction east and southeast of Bir Recha. Passage for panzers is through undulating terrain between Bir Tueil el Ase and the flat high ground 4 to 6km northeast of there. In front of Bir Garania on the south and west are located singular pronounced hills, which are suitable for consolidation or advanced position. The German *HKL* between Bir Recha and Bir Garania should be established along the line of hills as follows: heights on the north and north west of Bir Garania in a generally westwards direction, then jump over the high terrain and over A.P. 523 to the southeast until the undulating terrain 4km northeast of Bir Tueil el Ase and from there to the west detouring the Bir Recha. On both sides, especially east of Bir Recha the terrain is completely flat, well mobile terrain, which is challenging due to enveloping of the south flank by the enemy. Apart from that, the infantry and artillery defense hit mainly on the heights north, west and south of Bir Garania and on the high ground on both sides of Bir Tueil el Ase, during which time the mobile forces (panzers) can gain the open terrain to protect the south flank. Especially important is to pay attention to the flanking position on the heights north and southwest of Bir Garania with the open terrain both sides of Bir Garania. At the same time a shorter trace of the *HKL* is possible along the heights east of El Faschia in almost a precise northeast direction on the heights northwest of Bir Garania but a closer reconnaissance here was not possible. The choice of this *HKL* appeals also to the enemy due to the longer distance for a new departure march.[7]

On the 13th, *Kampfgruppe Irkens* continued to protect and secure the rallying points and the withdrawal of the division as far as Bir Garania; from there it was to assume the mission as the divisional rearguard. As Irkens and Stotten continued the fight in this area, the *II./Abteilung* under *Hptm* Schnelle was sent towards Ben Gardane and Gabès in order to refit and reorganize itself for the battles that lay ahead. Other elements too had tasks to perform, one of which was *Uffz* Haidt of the *Werkshop Company*, who describes his primary task at this time:

"Our company was at an airfield and a white house [mosque], there we assembled a sondercommando from the Regiment and we drove straight to Tunis and based near the harbor there. The task was driving to the harbor and securing the vehicles which were destined to our regiment. It was January 43, if we saw the vehicle coming to the Regiment, we secured it and drove it to the assembly area."[8]

The 14th was a warm day with a slight morning breeze that kicked up a light sandstorm. The Regiment was given another mission that day which it was to perform with *Pioneer Battalion 33*. The pioneers had the mission of laying a series of eighteen Hungarian teller mines along the evasion route in order to cover the remaining rearguard panzers. Once the mission was complete, the pioneers were to immediately march off to a point 4km south of Sedada and report to the leader of traffic regulation command that the mission had been accomplished, and then return back to the Regiment.[9] In the meantime, *Field Marshal* Rommel had made a decision that went against the wishes of the Italian *Commando Supremo* and even Hitler himself, for those fighting the war in Rome and Berlin did not approve of an evacuation of Tripolitania and Tripoli. Rommel, fighting the war in Africa, knew what folly it was to try and defend towns and areas for the sole purpose of prestige when those areas offered nothing constructive to holding back an enemy who was constantly nipping at his heels and attempting to outflank him. Rommel then ordered the *21st Panzer Division* to part with its remaining panzers and sent it towards Southern Tunisia, where it could assist in the defense there with the *Fifth Panzerarmee* and be more easily re-equipped with equipment flowing in from Tunis.[10] It was also during this time that a third panzer division, the *10th Panzer*, arrived in Tunisia to bolster Axis forces there. It is ironic that now that the campaign in Africa looked quite dim OKW was sending a veteran panzer division which only six months prior may have tipped the scales of the entire campaign. Those American and British forces that had landed in northwest Africa in November now posed a direct threat to Rommel's rear area and main artery of supplies flowing in from Italy; the growing Allied threat now forced the *Afrika Korps* to move back towards Tunis to meet that threat. The rain that had fallen over the previous weeks had both assisted and complicated the movement back; it had kept the *Eighth Army* from following up too quickly, but hindered the *Panzerarmee's* quick withdrawal towards Tunisia. On 15 January, the *Eighth Army* with the *2nd New Zealand Division*, *51st (Highland) Division*, and *7th Armored Division* began to once again attack the *D.A.K.* All three of the British divisions had made good their losses from the previous months of campaigning, and were close to full strength in men and equipment. Each infantry division had been freshly outfitted with three motorized battalions, equipped with numerous half-tracks and Bren gun carriers, and equipped with a full compliment of arms and equipment, including over a hundred 6-Pounder anti-tank guns, 40mm Bofors anti-aircraft guns, and about two-hundred pieces of artillery. The *7th Armored Division* was now equipped with one reconnaissance brigade armed with some 210 Stuart or Honey tanks, and one tank brigade with over 340 Sherman and

Grant tanks.[11] As the coast turned to the north from Buerat [Bu' ayrat al Hasun], the *Eighth Army* was now able to gain some deployment area for its armored and motorized formations to spread out to the south and west as they attempted to encircle the *Panzerarmee*. The first rush came against the *D.A.K.* between 16-19 January near the Tarhuna [Tarhunah]-Homs [Al Khums] position. The Regiment and the remaining elements of the *15th Panzer Division* continued to defend themselves in the Buerat position, in order to again slow down the advance of the *Eighth Army* as the rearguard of *D.A.K.* Hermann Eckardt remembered those days:

"After Alamein there was another battle in Buerat. There had been a combat pause in Buerat. We had gotten some new panzers that had been off loaded in Benghazi from the ship. There was a bit of mountainous terrain and we assembled there. The day was cold. In our company we had lost two panzers and we were able to recover one, it was all shot up and broken. Terrible! We had at least seven dead from there. Then we went for two nights, south of Tripoli in an area we finally had break to sleep. There was a 200km crater and we went there. It was a cold night, we had gone day and night, we cleaned the air filters and held the British, and then we went over the crater until our next stop. We had been able to bury our dead comrades."[12]

On 15 January, combat reports and diary notes mention that elements of the *I./Abteilung*, or *Kampfgruppe Stotten*, participated in the defense of Hill 489 (Fort Fortino). There was tough combat during the entire day against multiple British attacks all along the line. That morning at 1010hrs, as the situation began to develop, Irkens was ordered to report to the division command post for instructions. An hour later, at 1120hrs, the Regiment was ordered to immediately send one panzer company to a position behind the middle of *Kampfgruppe Lindemann* at the *hinterhangstellung* (reverse slope) position. By 1310hrs, Stotten was reporting that he was in heavy combat with British tanks. Again at 1400hrs, the Regiment was ordered to send an additional panzer company to *Hptm* Moest, as the British had begun to envelope his position from the right. At 1455hrs, Moest sent back a message to the Regiment that the panzers should go back to the new *hinterhangstellung*. At 1511hrs, orders were issued to *Company Feller* (a *panzergrenadier* company) from the Regiment to regain the heights that had been previously lost by *Hptm* Moest. At 1535hrs, the panzers from Lindner's *7th Company*, which was located on the left flank near *Kampfgruppe Lindemann*, reported that twenty British tanks with over ten guns were on the march to the south at a distance of 2500meters. Stotten then launched an attack on the previously lost heights south of A.P. 492 and attempted to outflank the British forces there from the right. By 1555hrs, Stotten was able to report that the lost heights were in his possession. At 1625hrs, Stotten reported that in the south he was engaged with some sixty enemy tanks. At the same time, recently promoted *Hptm* Lindner reported that he was southeast of the panzer attack. Even though the day's actions had been successful, the division ordered a withdrawal, and with the passing of the codeword "Nelke" the mission of the Regiment was to act as rearguard. Beginning at 1930hrs, the panzers were ordered to form the last portion of the divisional rearguard and begin their withdrawal. *Hptm* Lindner and *Olt* Schellhaas were both wounded in the day's fighting, and the division reported the loss of nine men killed, nineteen wounded, and eleven missing. The division also claimed thirty-two British tanks destroyed, a remarkable feat, since at that time the division reported only a total of twenty-eight combat ready panzers, with four additional panzers still under repair.[13] Adolf Lamm noted that day in his diary:

"I sat from 0800hrs in the morning until 0200hrs in the night non-stop at the radio and hold on attempting to understand through the smoke of this villager talk [dialect] the radio talk describing the combat situation. During the night of the 15/16 January there was a return march of approximately 80km through a large wadi [Wadi Zamzam]. After reaching it and halting for only a couple of hours we departed again with our cannons at 6 o'clock, this is when the guns are rotated backwards, a sign for the retreat. There was combat again this night but the division allowed us to remain and then orders us back."[14]

Thanks to the various combat reports from the divisional war diary (KTB) and a detailed report that was written on the 25th, it is possible to track the actions that took place from 16-18 January. On the 16th, *Oberst* Irkens reported to *Oberst* Borowietz at the divisional command post, where he was verbally given the following mission. The Regiment, with a subordinated Flak *kampfgruppe* under the command of *Major* Schneider-Eicke, was to join forces and form the divisional rearguard for the division's withdrawal from Sedada [As Saddadah] to Beni Ulid [Bani Walid]. The orders went on to state that the rearguard was to detach itself from the British after the departure of the mass of the *15th Panzer Division*. The rearguard was, at the beginning of the 17th, to reform the defensive line on the high ground four kilometers south of Point 102 on the long slope of Sedada-Beni Ulid, which had previously been reconnoitered by Irkens, and then fall back from the pursuing enemy towards Beni Ulid. The *Schneider-Eicke Flak Kampfgruppe* at this point was located north of Sedada, and consisted of the *1./43 Flak Regiment* with the attached *10./Panzergrenadier Regiment 115*, the *2./Artillery Regiment 33* (three guns), the *1st* and *3rd Companies* with two 88mm guns, and the *4th Company* with ten 20mm anti-aircraft guns. The orders went on to state that the *I./Abteilung* was to break contact from the enemy simultaneously with *Kampfgruppe Wissman*, which was located on the eastern flank of the division, so that the preceding withdrawal of *Kampfgruppe Wissman* would be possible to the north. On that same day, the 16th, Irkens pulled out the majority of the Regiment's combat supply trains and moved them immediately to the northern side of the Sedada airfield and the protective minefield located there. Secondly, he ordered that the supply trains be prepared to supply those elements of the Regiment that would be involved in combat. Likewise, the Regiment *Stabs* was to be pulled out of its positions in the Wadi Zurzur [Wadi Zerzer], south of Sedada, to the same location as the supply trains, because the *I./Abteilung* under *Hptm* Stotten had just been quickly deployed by the division. At this time the *I./Abteilung*, or *Kampfgruppe Stotten*, was composed of the *2nd*, *4th*, and *7th Companies*, and had a combined strength of fifteen panzers, which was further broken down with five Mk IIIs Sp, three Mk IIIs (7.5kz), and seven Mk IVs Sp.[15] During the day's actions, the division reported the loss of two killed and twelve wounded, including Lt Kehrer, and twenty-six missing. Simultaneous orders were then issued to *Kampfgruppe Schneider-Eicke*, and a *stabs* officer was to be sent immediately to the new command post of the Regiment, now located on the north side of the airfield, where that officer was to receive orders for that *kampfgruppe*. Previously there had been a personal conversation between Irkens and *Hptm* Endres at the division's command post regarding the planned laying of mines on the return road for the withdraw. Irkens had demanded at that time that the laying of mines take place only after the transfer of the last elements of the rearguard had passed through. *Hptm* Endres then went on to pass this same exact request on to the pioneer officer at *Kampfgruppe Schneider-Eicke*. At 1900hrs, the division headquarters had issued orders to *Hptm* Stotten that he immediately detach himself and his *I./Abteilung* from the enemy at 2015hrs, and to make their way towards the north end of the minefield located on the Sedada airfield. By this time Schneider-Eicke was able to report personally to the Regimental command post to inform the officers there that his *kampfgruppe* was already in action north of Sedada, just east of the road there on the Wadi Zurzur. Of interest here is that the previously mentioned Pioneer officer was not in fact subordinated to Schneider-Eicke, and was not even present to receive his orders, but that the orders had been conveyed to him that the laying of the mines on the slope should only take place after the withdrawal of the last elements of the rearguard. For at that moment the Pioneer officer was engaged in overseeing the demolition of the serpentine road south of Sedada that paralleled the Wadi Zurzur. According to the agreement with the Pioneer officer, his pioneer section, which was now busy closing the mine roadblock on the west of Sedada, would emplace a prepared mine plan as soon as the last parts of the rearguard began to move off to the north. Through a number of consultations and communications from the Regiment to Schneider-Eicke and his attached Pioneer/mine laying section, the emplacement of the mines was ordered to begin after the first departure of the last rearguard elements, and it was further agreed to provide mine laying to the very north of the positions of the Italian *XXI Corps*, which was located approximately 10km north northwest of Sedada. As all this talk about the mine laying detail was being sorted out there took place another communication with Stotten in which he was ordered to reach the north side of the minefield at the Sedada airfield after the planned withdrawal of the *I./Abteilung's* forces from the British. Once at this location, Stotten was to receive supplies and to leave behind one of his panzer companies, the *2nd Company* (Schellhaus), in order to secure the planned assembly area and the withdrawal of the rearguards along the northern side of Sedada. Due to the fact that at this time Stotten had received no radio reports from the division concerning his breaking contact with the enemy, he took the initiative and made the decision to begin withdrawing his forces from the British beginning at 2000hrs, and send them on towards the road junction at Sedada even as the last elements of the division had already begun moving off to the north. After negotiating the minefield and positioning the *2nd Company* just to the north of it, the minefield was closed by the pioneers on the basis of assuming the prepared mine plan. In all, the division's breaking contact with the British, the execution and withdrawal of the supply troops, and the preparation of resumption of the withdrawal came off well with no interference from those British forces located nearby. In the meantime, units of the Italian *Centauro* Division were identified in the area of the rearguard, and according to radio reports, there were still approximately fifty vehicles located on the high ground to the northeast of Sedada near a fork in the road. This information was then communicated to the Pioneer officer who had been tasked with laying the mines, in the hopes of having him halt the mine laying in order to allow the Italian vehicles time to negotiate the obstacles and move on towards Beni Ulid. The reason for the presence of these *Centauro* Division vehicles is that almost all of them had run out of fuel. The Italians asked those rearguard elements for fuel before moving on, but this was impossible to provide, since the motor ("Otto") fuel that the German vehicles used was not compatible with the Italian vehicles, which burned diesel fuels, and more importantly there was no diesel fuel available with the rearguard. Help was, however, provided by towing the Italian vehicles, and soon approximately eighteen Italian armored combat vehicles were being towed by the *zug* machines of the Flak *kampfgruppe* until they were able to reach an interim position south of Point 102. Unfortunately, the towing burned up further fuel in the prime movers, and now caused the German rearguards to end up having fuel problems of their own. It was also discovered, but not until the following morning, that as all this was taking place, the fuel trucks of the Regiment had accidentally departed the area during the night of the 16/17th by mistake with another Italian column, and were now lost and unable to render any assistance. Given all this, the Italian commander, an *Oberst* Ruffo, promised that by the morning there would be a resupply of diesel fuel. As a testament to this officer, the Italian vehicles later departed the rearguard positions sometime later that morning and moved off to the west—it is a sure bet that the fuel had actually arrived that morning.[16] At 2230hrs, *Kampfgruppe Schneider-Eicke* was finally able to return from the area north of Sedada and begin moving to its newly assigned area, the high ground area south of Point 102, in order to occupy the *HKL* along those heights. Its mission was to be in position by daylight on the 17th, where it was to begin engaging the approaching British from long range with its 88mm guns. A short time later, at 2315hrs, Stotten and the *I./Abteilung* were following the Regimental *Stabs* with the task of reaching the wadi on the west side of the *HKL* position, where it was to hold itself in preparation for operations to begin again as soon as the sun came up. Furthermore, the *I./Abteilung* was also ordered to send out a small reconnaissance element back towards the defensive positions on the high ground approximately eight kilometers east of the *HKL* position in order to monitor and report on any enemy activity. This reconnaissance element was further ordered to immediately break contact in a timely manner, and evade back to the *HKL* position if it came under any enemy attacks. For this task, it was determined that two panzers from the *2nd Company*, under Schellhaas, were to undertake this assignment under the direct supervision of Stotten himself. Throughout the evening and early morning of the 17th, the division sent out a number of orders via radio, in order to define the next set of positions for the continued withdraw of the division and its rearguards. The next location was to be on the western side of Beni Ulid, where the division would join forces with the *Centauro* division, which for the most part was now deployed on the north side of that location. During the early morning hours of the 17th this plan was again changed, when it was ordered that instead of the *15th Panzer Division* taking up positions near Beni Ulid, the plan was now modified, and those positions were now to be occupied by the *164th Light Division*, which was now ordered to remain in position south and southwest of Beni Ulid, while the majority of the *15th Panzer* was ordered to continue marching further in the direction of Tarhuna. The task for the rearguard, however, would remain unchanged. Early that morning, at around 0700hrs there took place another meeting between Irkens, Stotten, and Schneider-Eicke in which detailed instructions were provided concerning the mission, enemy situation, and terrain that lay ahead of them. By 0800hrs reports were again flooding into the regimental headquarters concerning the identification and movement of British vehicles on the hills to the northeast of Sedada; a short time after these initial reports came in, there followed others that identified British forces in the area of Sedada itself, as well as numerous dust clouds spotted off to the northwest of that village. By 0930hrs, the Flak *kampfgruppe* was engaged in extremely long range firing with some British tanks, which had arrived to the north and west of Point 80. The British were now increasing the length of their flanks by continuously side stepping to the north of those Axis rearguards. An hour later, at approximately 1030hrs, it was reported that approximately sixty British tanks were identified advancing west on the line from Bir Belezar to Ed el Agheila. The British armor was heavily engaged and delayed by the Flak *kampfgruppe*, but by about 1115hrs the British had been able to push forward as far as that of the *2nd Company*. The panzers of the *2nd Company* began a short exchange of gunfire with the tanks before finally being forced back to the defensive positions south of Point 102.[17] The extension of the British flank to the north was therefore able to continue unmolested. Dust clouds were again visible moving from Point 61 near Bir Belezar, as well as the Wadi el Merdum to the northwest, and on the slope in direction Bir Dufan. Luckily, at that time there were no enemy sightings to the south and southeast; however, the hills west of Sedada prevented any observation further to the south. Since those first sightings that morning, the division and Regiment had been attempting to get an aerial reconnaissance of the area, but unfortunately there were no *Luftwaffe* planes available for this task. Even without any aerial reconnaissance, the commanders on the ground were quickly able to determine the enemy intent. By midday the situation was all too clear; the British were attacking in ever increasing numbers. At present there were roughly sixty tanks pressing in on the fifteen that the I./*Abteilung* possessed, and there were clear indications that the British were attempting to envelope those Axis forces in the north. Since the initial tasks had been successfully completed by the rearguards and the British had been delayed for a number of hours, the decision was made at around 1230hrs that a continuation of the withdrawal should commence. In order to successfully disengage those rearguard forces without further loss and in a timely manner, Irkens ordered that the Flak *kampfgruppe* disengage first under the protection of the panzers of the I./*Abteilung*, since the panzers had been already deployed, and had been in position since 1000hrs that morning. After the Flak guns were clear of the immediate area the panzers would be able to pass through the minefield in the south and fall back to Beni Ulid in one bound. The only authorized halt would be near the small desert village of Cantira, where the panzers were to take on fuel and ammunition that had been brought up earlier by the division supply trains. Both formations were ordered to cover each other's preparations for the withdrawal, and that the time for executing the withdrawal commence at 1300hrs. Earlier that morning, even before the situation began to deteriorate under the ever increasing British pressure and the decision to pull out was made, a reconnaissance had been conducted in the area of the proposed minefield. By first light it had been quickly determined that all along the slope, over which the panzers and Flak guns were to traverse, had already been mined. Further proof that the area was now mined came later on when *Oberst* Ruffo, the commander of the armored elements of the *Centauro* Division, reported that shortly after daybreak he and some of his vehicles had driven over these mines.[18] By mid-morning, there had been an immediate request from Irkens to the division to clear the slope of mines. On top of this, the ordnance officer of the I./*Abteilung* was sent to the respective pioneer officer, informing him that he must clear away the mines, but he declined to perform the task of removing the mines, as they were far too difficult to disarm. However, the pioneer officer was able to explain that on the mined slope, only 20-30m on both sides of the positions had been mined in accordance with the divisional mine plan. Based on this information the Flak *kampfgruppe* was able to identify during the first part of day a route around this minefield. The withdrawal began according to plan, beginning with the Flak *kampfgruppe* and supported by the panzers, which began their pullout shortly after 1300hrs. During the return march, between Point 102 and Point 190 several vehicles fell out with damage when they rolled over mines that were located out of the areas identified on the mine plan. Stotten then issued orders that all vehicles keep a 50 meter interval when proceeding up the southern slope. The reason for moving along the southern end of the slope was that up in the north there had been sightings of enemy activity. As the German rearguard passed along this route, it encountered multiple Italian vehicles that had previously driven over mines. There were some abandoned Italian vehicles on both sides of the slope; some had fallen out due to mines, while others succumbed to the lack of fuel and others mechanical damage. Four German vehicles were also damaged by mines as they attempted to traverse the slope. By 1330hrs, the last panzers had cleared the minefield, and Irkens was able to link up with Stotten. At 1220hrs, a signal was received at the divisional headquarters informing it that elements of *Aufklärung Abteilung 33* were located, without fuel, on the eastern side of Saadat, and that it requested that the division halt elements in order for the *abteilung* to catch up and refuel. At 1415hrs a radio transmission was received at the Regimental *Stabs*, ordering it to halt its progress west and to render assistance to *Aufklärung Abteilung 33*. By this point *Kampfgruppe Schneider-Eicke* was located roughly 8km southeast of Point 190, while Irkens and the I./*Abteilung* were located a further 8km to the southeast of Schneider-Eicke. The Flak *kampfgruppe* then was ordered to return the flak elements of the *kampfgruppe* and move into position with the panzer elements, which were continuing their return march to a more suitable defensive position. This position could only be found on the heights where the flak elements were now located. But now this position was receiving enemy fire from the north by those advancing British formations, and the panzers too, coming from the north, were receiving fire, and for this reason began taking up defense positions there. With the arrival of German panzers the British tanks were halted, and in some cases forced back. In the meantime, at around 1500hrs the Regimental fuel trucks, which had mistakenly gone off with the Italians the previous night and gotten lost, had finally made their way to the location of the main body of the Flak *kampfgruppe*, which wasted little time in refueling its vehicles and making its way towards Beni Ulid. From the Regiment's position it was clearly visible that the British were continuing in their attempts to envelope them from the north and south, as dust clouds could be seen as far off as 20km. A quick analysis of the situation was determined and the following conclusions made: the arrival of the division with its main body to Beni Ulid should be completed before darkness, but the divisional rearguard, which still had to cross the difficult terrain and minefields east of Beni Ulid, could possibly be cut off by the British before they reached that town. Therefore, Irkens requested that the rearguard be allowed to return immediately, in order to reach the positions at Beni Ulid before darkness fell; thankfully, that request would be approved by division headquarters, even though it would come later in the day. Fortunately, before that permission was received, at 1600hrs *Aufklärung Abteilung 33* was able to break through the British lines in the south and affect a link up with the rearguard forces. With the Flak *kampfgruppe*, already set to immediately march off with all its mobile elements, the *Aufklärung Abteilung* was resupplied with fuel under the protection of the panzers. That *abteilung* had made its way to the rearguard on its last remaining drops of fuel, and there was no doubt that the *Aufklärung Abteilung* would have fallen into enemy hands if the British advance had not been delayed by the timely resistance of the rearguard company near Point 102. At 1700hrs, the march continued together with the *Aufklärung Abteilung* in the direction of Beni Ulid on a small desert trail south of the slope in order to avoid the numerous mines scattered about the area. The decision to march along the southern end of the slope was made despite the observation and radio reports that identified British tanks in the area south of Point 190, and there were reports of the presence of British armor on the northern end of the slope, where they had already begun to take up positions there. A deployed road reconnaissance group from Sedada reported that no enemy tanks were observed at this time on the southern end of the slope. There was no flank guard protection possible at this time due to the arriving darkness, but the open terrain provided sufficient observation to the south. As the rearguard continued on they were able to observe on both sides of the slope more and more abandoned Italian vehicles and tanks, many of which had driven over mines, simply succumbed to mechanical breakdown, or run out of fuel. As darkness fell, the leading motorized elements of the rearguard column were reported as being still 15km to the east of Beni Ulid, while the panzer elements followed at the tail end of the column.[19] The Regimental *Stabs*, in addition to several supply vehicles, was located between the motorized elements and panzer elements. At 2030hrs, the last portion of the motorized group was hit by a British ambush, which became more and more violent as the destroyed and burning vehicles lit up the night. Irkens and his subordinate commanders issued instructions that the motorized elements continue their advance despite the losses now being suffered. This decision to drive forward regardless of casualties was strictly obeyed by the men, and therefore losses were held to an acceptable level. The panzer elements, under the veteran leadership of men like Irkens and Stotten, answered the British fire even as they continued to roll forward. The panzer commanders and *richtschütze*, in an attempt to not waste their precious ammunition, engaged only those targets that were clearly visible to them. As the motorized and panzer elements were able to continue on their way towards the west, the most troublesome fighting occurred a short time later when the *2nd Company* under Schellhaas became engaged in one last fire fight with the British. The company, being at the trail end of the rearguard column, had been assigned to protect the trail end of the entire column in addition to providing over-watch for those vehicles that had fallen back and were struggling to catch up. The men of the company did not panic, and performed their task with extreme bravery, during which they caused the British significant losses. Adolf Lamm was the radio operator in one of those panzers and describes the situation that night:

"A tough combat retreat, some elements to which we belonged were encircled and had to break through. Then, approximately 8km from Beni Ulid, our panzer took a hit in the bogie. In total we were three operational panzers. This night belongs to my most exact and exciting memories. We were in combat and the Richtschütze [gunner] Rothländer was shooting with anything that would fit in the barrel. Suddenly here comes a hit, which shook the panzer. It [the panzer] turned to the right. Hold on! We are shot, everyone get out! We were trained to escape so many times. Outside on the left and right from us stood brightly blazing vehicles. I still can still see their red glowing on the completely dark night. The rounds continue to strike near us but the new bogie must be put on and the new track must be put on, otherwise we can write ourselves off. In order not to loose the radio connection with the Abteilung, I was ordered to get back to the panzer and radio, while the others installed [the bogie]. Finally there is an order 'Get in, march!' Luckily the bogie and track holds."[20]

Once making their way through the British ambush positions the rearguard pushed on unmolested to Beni Ulid, and once the column reached a position just 3km from that town they again came upon a minefield. Here the pioneers of *Aufklärung Abteilung 33* were able to clear a gap through the minefield so that the combat elements could continue their march after only a short halt. By 2200hrs the mass of the rearguard had crossed friendly lines at Beni Ulid, and an hour later the last elements were finally able to reach Beni Ulid. Adolf Lamm continues:

"In the middle of the night we re-connected with the Abteilung, which assembled in an old fortress, or what I thought was. I had to take over the radio guard despite that I was dead tired. There is continuous smoke held over the Dead Point. Then, what is this? There is giggling and conversation chatter on the frequency of the Regiment. I hear fragments of a beer-party, half-drunk voices, songs and yelling. The highlight: the International song! Then there is silence and then it started again and many times it switches on and off, this chaotic conversation chatter. I got the radioman from the company, whom I could trust and we guessed, that the unforeseen transmission came from 'Mitropa'. We called to the vehicle of the Abteilung, in which the officers met. Then there was the silence, the end. I did not report anything, because I was afraid that Olt Schellhaas, who slept near the panzer, would get upset by the unpleasant situation if he knew of this episode. It was forbidden with the fee, to switch on the transmitter except for the communication of orders or reports, because the enemy could quickly discover the location through knowledge of the bearing."

Shortly after crossing friendly lines an organized search group was sent out in search of any missing vehicles or stragglers in the area of the previous combat, but this search brought no results. In the day's actions the division reported the loss of just twenty-five men wounded. After crossing friendly lines that night on the 17/18th, the rearguard assembled at a point to the northwest of Beni Ulid, where they were able to take on fuel and ammunition for the continued withdrawal. With the *164th Light* and other Axis elements manning the defensive lines around Bani Ulid, the *15th Panzer* was ordered to immediately proceed towards the town of Tarhuna [Tarhunah]. By 0030hrs *Kampfgruppe Schneider-Eicke* departed to the northwest, followed at 0130hrs by the Regiment. In the darkness and steep wadis located to the west of Beni Ulid the two *kampfgruppen* soon came upon significant traffic jams caused by other Axis formations attempting to move northwest to Tarhuna. By 0630hrs there was radio traffic coming from the division asking the *kampfgruppen* to quicken their pace, as there was a growing threat of being cut off by the British. With this threat, and the danger of the British advancing from the east and cutting the road to Tarhuna, it fell once again to Stotten and his I./*Abteilung* to keep the road open for the retreating Axis forces still in Beni Ulid, and to attack the enemy wherever he threatened the road. By early morning the leading elements of the rearguard had reached the assembly areas of the *panzergrenadier* battalions from *Oberst* Menton's *Panzergrenadier Regiment Afrika*, which was located in the area of Tes Maamura and Point 408. Luckily, there was no contact with the British that day except for the observation of some British vehicles further to the east, and by the time the panzers reached a spot 30km from Tarhuna they were able to halt and take on more fuel. While halted at the resupply point the *kampfgruppen* were attacked twice by *DAF* fighters that missed their mark, and did not inflict any losses on the forces located there. Over the entire day there had been an active presence by the *DAF* over the route from Beni Ulid to Tarhuna, as the *DAF* attempted to block the road and block those Axis forces from escaping. Thankfully, shortly before darkness, the last elements of the rearguard were able to reach the new assembly area located just four and a half kilometers to the southwest of Tarhuna near Point 477. As the Regiment entered the relative safety of the Tarhuna area they were able to finally report the casualties suffered over the previous two days' fighting withdrawal. One contractor, *Obzlm* Hadler, had been killed due to aircraft machine gun fire; one officer (Lt Kehrer), eight *Uffz* and twelve men had been wounded due to tank and artillery fire, and three *Uffz* and nine men were reported as missing. The panzer losses amounted to one Mk III Sp, two Mk III (7.5 kurz), and two Mk IV Sp; in addition there were another twenty assorted vehicles (one Zgkw-18, Zgkw-1, twelve Lkw, and three assorted vehicles and bikes) lost to tank and artillery fire, mines, and mechanical damage. *Kampfgruppe Scheider-Eicke* suffered the following losses: I./43 Flak suffered ten vehicles, one 20mm gun, and one flak wagon, in addition to three killed, seventeen wounded, and seventeen missing. The *2./Artillery Regiment 33* suffered one killed and four wounded. The British losses that were claimed by the rearguard amounted to five tanks, four artillery guns, three trailers, five vehicles, seven self-propelled vehicles, two anti-tank guns, and one aircraft shot down by the gunners of I./Flak Regiment 43.[21] On the 18th, as the I./*Abteilung* had been fighting around Sedada and Beni Ulid, the II./*Abteilung*, which had been refitting, reported the following panzer strength: one Mk II, two Mk IIIs, ten Mk III Sp, six Mk III (7.5), and fifteen Mk IV Sp. On the 19th, in addition to roughly fifteen panzers, *Kampfgruppe Stotten* was reported as consisting of three 37mm Pak guns, three 75mm Pak guns, four 76.2mm self propelled Pak guns, one heavy field artillery battery, two 88mm Flak guns, and one 20mm Flak battery. The *2nd Company* diary went on to record the following locations and movements from 19-21 January:

"Tuesday, 19.1.43: Rest at Tarhuna. The radios were damaged in all the vehicles. Artillery fire. Departure during the night of the 19/20 Jan. at 0135hrs we depart in the direction of Tripolis. Via Benito and Azizia [Al Aziziyan]. From 1200hrs on the 20th we establish the camp and clear the combat area. On Thursday, the 21st the panzers found themselves located to the south of Tripoli near an old plantation with its many palm tress, the panzers remained until midday when they once again departed."[22]

Since its departure early in the month there is little mention of the *II./Abteilung*, and the only information that is available is that concerning the *8th Company*, which was ordered to augment the newly reformed *I./Abteilung, Panzer Regiment 5* on the 17th.[23] That company's actions are covered later in this chapter.

By mid-morning on the 22nd, radio reports were received by *Kampfgruppe Irkens* informing him that the British were attacking in the northwest across the Azizia – Garian road. Shortly after receiving those reports, Irkens was able to report back confirming this attack, and that the British were being reinforced, and that enemy pressure was building against his forces and attempting to push to the west on the northern side of the hills in an attempt to once again envelope his positions. At that time Irkens was without Stotten and the *I./Abteilung*, and was requesting that the division return those panzers, as they were the only force capable of halting the British attack. By 1600hrs, as the divisional headquarters attempted to get the needed artillery support for Irkens and his men, the lead panzers were asked to fire off flares in order to help direct the artillery fire. A short time later the division's ordnance officer arrived at Irken's command post to report that Stotten and his panzers would not be available to support him. Luckily for Irkens, the British armor assault was halted a short time later, and a large portion of the force coming against him began pulling off to the north, where it was attempting to follow the railway tracks there. At 1640hrs, the same ordnance officer returned from Irkens' command post with the following information and requests: located around his positions were between thirty to forty enemy tanks, on the high ground behind the armor was a large assembly of vehicles, and along the road to Garian were counted over three hundred vehicles all heading west. Despite the current situation, Irkens requested that Stotten and his panzers should arrive back to his position no later than darkness in order to supply that detachment. Sensing that no help was to be forthcoming from either the division or *D.A.K.*, Irkens ordered his meager forces to make preparations for disengaging from the British. At the time *Kampfgruppe Irkens* (now referred to by call sign 123) was located with the rearguard elements of call signs 121, 141, and 135; realizing that the riflemen of 135 were the slowest and most vulnerable to British attack, he ordered them out of their positions and to the rear under the protection of three panzers. At 2320hrs Irkens notified the division that at 2400hrs he would break contact with the enemy, and that after a short halt to resupply his elements, he would again be ready to resume the march at 0130hrs. Under strong and ever-increasing pressure by Allied forces, the city of Tripoli was evacuated on the 22nd, and the following day the *Eighth Army* marched triumphantly in, and actually took the time to hold a parade. At this time the Regiment was nowhere near its authorized strength in both men and machines, but fortunately in Tripoli a small number of Mk IVF2 "Specials" had been unloaded before the city fell, and those panzers were able to fill a few of the voids within the *I./Abteilung*.[24] The next week would be filled with more withdrawals and halts; it is again through Adolf Lamm that we are able to follow the progress of the Regiment through that of the *2nd Company*:

"On the 23rd (Saturday) we moved through Zavia [Az Zawiyah], Sabratha [Sabratah], and a Palm forest. We noted the following places in the calendar; Sunday the 24th the Harbor Zuara, and Regdalin. On Monday the 25th, we departed at 0500hrs in the morning and covered 10km during the course of the day. Tuesday the 26th, the distribution of EK II (Iron Crosses) at that time not yet the cookware decoration! On Wednesday the 27th, we passed Zelten [Zaltan], Pisida and reached the Tunisian border. On Thursday the 28th, we reached Ben Gardane [Ben Guerdane] where we rested in an area in the desert. On Saturday the 30th we drove south in the morning and had a further rest."[25]

According to an excerpt from the divisional KTB, at 1345hrs on 27 January *Panzer Abteilung Stotten* was sent to march over to Zuara [Zuwarah] to Aluet el Gounna. Its task was once again that of eliminating any *Eighth Army* probes and breakthroughs, which at the time were being reported by *Panzerarmee* as having taken place east of Ben Gardane. *Kampfgruppe Lindemann* was also deployed with the same task, and was ordered to establish contact with a *Luftwaffe Brigade (Fallschirmjäger)*.[26] By Sunday the 31st, Adolf Lamm noted in his diary:

"Our positions or terraces were built with sand and camouflaged with camel thorn bushes, a field table and chairs were taken from the chief's vehicle. Then it was a feast for the officers, the picture of it. We baked Berliner [bread]! Somebody got a hold of the white flour and may be even some egg powder. Gefreiter Rothländer operated two alcohol cookers and filled a wash basin with olive oil and mastered a sort of a coffee cake, which tasted excellent."

The respite was short lived, however, as the position soon came under artillery fire, and the combat began again at around 1300hrs. Lamm continues:

"At 1600hrs we launched a counter-attack to cover the retreat of the infantry and in the evening conducted a return march to the old position at Djebel Zebeus to further cover the retreat, there were heavy attacks by bombers and low-level flights us and Feldwebel Oppold was killed in one of these attacks."

The *Kriegsoffizerbewerber (KOB)*, which had not been in session since April 1942, was once again established by the division and assigned to the Regiment as a source of replacements. The *KOB* was an in-house program that was designed to take perspective officer candidates, most of which were decorated NCOs of long experience and highly capable junior soldiers that showed exceptional talent, and turn them into combat leaders. The title given to these candidates was *Fähnrich*, and in the past a number of soldiers from the Regiment, like Liestmann, Hubbuch, Thampald, Rummler, and Spohn, had passed through this training and become commissioned officers. *Oberst* Irkens was able to reorganize and make good some of the earlier losses with the arrival of some new replacements, and those slightly wounded personnel; especially welcomed was the return of those "Old Hares," the experienced panzer crewmen like *Leutnants* Ballhaus and Rummler.[27] Again, the Regiment was deployed by the division as the rearguard for the entire *D.A.K.*, which was constantly fighting off the probing reconnaissance and vanguard elements of the British. It was vital that the rearguard prevent any smooth advancement by the *Eighth Army* and gain the necessary time to allow the *D.A.K.* to reach the *Mareth Line*. As the *D.A.K.* made its way back

Chapter 13: Fighting for Time in Tunisia, January-February 1943

towards Mareth there continued to be many different situations which arose, and from time to time, as often happened in Africa, the panzers were rushed off to restore one situation after another. At that time during the retreat it was attempted to keep the I./*Abteilung* as close together as possible in order to keep one strong element, or "*Fire Brigade*," ready to meet any unexpected British breakthrough. This was not the case for the II./*Abteilung*, which continued to prepare for its re-entry into combat by receiving new or reconditioned panzers and reorganizing the panzer crews to outfit them. Time and time again a company would be dispatched for assignment with various *kampfgruppen* in order to provide the vital armored protection they lacked. Since the *8th Company* had already been dispatched to *Panzer Regiment 5*, it was now the turn of the *6th Company*, at the time led by Lt Halverscheidt, which was sent off to bolster one of these *kampfgruppe* that consisted of elements from *Aufklärung Abteilung 33*, *Panzerjäger Abteilung 33*, *Pioneer Battalion 33*, and a few guns from *Artillery Regiment 33*. It was the job of Lt Rummler to maintain contact with these far-flung units via the *Kradmelder* and the *ErkZug* (reconnaissance platoon). In the last days of January those remaining elements of the Regiment crossed the border of Tripolitania and entered Tunisia, where they entered the *Mareth Line* near the town of Médenine. Rommel had done a masterful job at bringing his army some two thousand miles from Alamein, all the while seemingly one step ahead of his *Eighth Army* pursuers. The *D.A.K.*, if it could still be called such, was able to enter the line of old French blockhouses that had been originally constructed to keep the Italians out of Tunisia, Algeria, and Morocco, but which had ever since been partially destroyed and left neglected. Situated on the Gulf of Gabès, the *Mareth Line* stretched some 50km along the coastal plane; the position was bordered in the west by the Matmata Hills, which ran almost north to south, and to the front was the Wadi Zigzaou, which provided a natural obstacle against armored attacks. The Mareth was just one of three designated positions in which those *Panzerarmee* forces could fall back on. Also on that day the *Panzerarmee* itself was redesignated as the *First German-Italian Army* under the command of Italian *General* Giovanni Messe, who had just been recalled from Russia, where he had been the commander of Italian expeditionary forces there. Messe was to take command of the *German Italian Panzerarmee* (*AOK 1*) from Rommel on a date of his choosing. The *AOK 1*, which manned the *Mareth Line*, was composed of the following formations: in the line were the Italian *XX Corps* with the *Pistoia*, *Trieste*, *Giovani Fascisti*, and *Spezia*, and the German *90th Light Division*, which was placed into positions to bolster the Italian divisions. The east-west running passages at Kieddache and Halouf were held by the *164th Light Division*. The *15th Panzer Division* and *Kampfgruppe Menton* were located in the rear as the army's mobile reserve. The line had sixty-five German and 340 Italian field guns, thirty-six batteries of anti-aircraft guns, and eighteen light and eighteen heavy, while among the twelve batteries of German 88mm flak guns were two batteries fitted out with guns of the new and improved 1941 pattern. Additionally, there was another defensive grouping made up of ten batteries from the *19th Flak Division*.[28]

In the north, the *Fifth Panzerarmee* under von Arnim was facing west against the Anglo-American Army front that had moved since November through Algeria and western Tunisia into the central portion of that country. The Allied forces had by January reached the eastern most dorsal, and were in position to cut off the line of communication between *AOK 1* and the *Fifth Panzerarmee*. The terrain in central Tunisia was mainly composed of high desert plateaus and mountainous terrain that formed two distinct dorsals known as the eastern and western. These dorsals formed an inverted "V," with the point facing to the north and the city of Tunis. The eastern dorsal, of which the Allied armies had just taken up positions, had a number of passes that opened up onto the coastal plain of eastern Tunisia. Possession of these passes would be vital for any further Allied advances in order to cut off and finally trap Rommel and his army, while possession by Axis forces would ensure that the Allies remained bottled up. The most prominent of these passes, and also of the most military value, were from north to south: the Karachoum Pass in the north down to the Kairouan and Fondouk Passes in the center, and finally the Faïd and Maknassy passes in the south.[29] In mid-January, the forces of the *Fifth Panzerarmee* consisted of the "*Von Broich*" *Division* in the Bizerta sector, the *334th Division* (Weber) opposite Medjez-el-Bab, the *Luftwaffe Hermann Göring Division* facing Bou Arada, the *10th Panzer Division* (Fischer), located south of Tunis in the vicinity of Kairouan, and the *21st Panzer Division* (Hildebrandt) in the Faïd and Maknassy area. In addition, there was the Italian *Centauro* Division, which was located northwest of Gabès. When the *21st Panzer* was sent ahead of the *D.A.K.* and attached to the *Fifth Panzerarmee* in early January, no one at that time considered that this move might prove to be the end of the original *D.A.K.*. But this was in fact to be the case, as both panzer divisions would never again fight side by side together as a single corps. Facing the *Fifth Panzerarmee* were the combined Allied armies of three nations: the Americans, British, and French, all under the command of *General* Eisenhower. From the north to the south there was the British *First Army* (Anderson) with the British *V Corps*, followed by the French *XIX Corps* (Koeltz), and in the south was the U.S. *II Corps* (Fredendall). It was the first time in the war that these three nations would have to all work together in order to achieve a single goal, and it was here in Africa where Eisenhower would prove to be the man who could handle the task of keeping all these nations on the same path. However, this was yet to be seen, and there were to be a number of major problems in Tunisia regarding Allied command and control, and the handling of operations there. By mid-January the British in the north were held up south of Bizerte, while in the center the French had moved to the eastern dorsal and were holding a number of passes there. In the south elements of the U.S. *II Corps* with a French division were still moving through the western dorsal, and had elements located between both dorsals, while a thin holding line was stretched along the eastern dorsal. The *II Corps* itself was back at Tébessa, prepared for its own operation, while other divisions within the corps were moving down to join them. On 18 January, von Thoma struck at these Allied forces in an operation known as "*Eilböte I*." The attack was not a resounding success for the Germans, as the weather and the quick reaction by British armored elements thwarted most attempts to gain the vital passes. By the 25th, the operation ground to a halt, but the outcome of the attack was that around Bou Arada the front had held, while the three northern passes were captured with heavy losses sustained by the French units guarding them. Fondouk Pass had been seized, but Faïd Pass and Maknassy Passes still remained in Allied hands, and were being held by lightly equipped elements.

Back at Mareth, the few panzers of the Regiment were sought out again and again to hold back the pursuit by the forces of the *Eighth Army*. At around this time plans were drawn up calling for limited counterattacks by the panzers, which in the desert was one of the best ways in which to halt a pursuing enemy. On the 29th, *Oberst* Irkens was able to conduct a reconnaissance and investigate the possibilities of such an attack. Upon his return, Irkens requested that the *HKL* be relocated 5km to the west, as that course or line would give the best possibilities for a successful panzer counterattack, since the terrain was better suited for his panzers. After a careful examination of the new *HKL* by *Oberst* Borowietz, the division commander, the regrouping was ordered for that same afternoon. By the end of the month the Regiment had claimed thirty-one *Stuarts* and nineteen *Sherman* tanks destroyed for the loss of seven panzers.[30] The lightly armored *Stuart* and *Cruiser* series tanks with their small 37mm and 2-pounder guns posed little danger to the Regiment's Mk IIIs and IVs, but it was the heavier *Grants, Shermans, Crusaders*, and even now the new *Churchill* tanks that worried most of the panzer crews, since each of these tanks possessed both the armor protection and killing power in the main gun. It was only with the Mk III and IV Specials that German panzer crews had an even chance of winning in most tank engagements. As it made its way along both sides of the coastal road from Tripoli to Gabès the Regiment withdrew to an area near Ben Gardane. The *15th Panzer Division* reported sixty-three panzers on 30 January. The number included two Befehls panzers, one Mk II, two Mk IIIs, fourteen Mk III Sp, nine Mk III (7.5), and twenty-four Mk IV Sp with an additional eleven panzer Mk IIIs and IVs in the workshops.[31] In the final days of January von Arnim launched the continuation of "*Eilböte I*" with "*Eilböte II*," the attempt to capture the southern passes at Faïd and Maknassy. With both Rommel and von Arnim planning and competing for panzers and resources, von Arnim did not want to waste the precious little time he had remaining in striking at the Anglo-Americans that were thinly arrayed along the southern sector of the eastern dorsal. The plan for *Eilböte II* called for the *21st Panzer Division*, now under the direct command of the *Fifth Panzerarmee*, and aided by the Italian *50th Special Brigade* (Imperiali), and army troops to strike at the southern passes. The mission was to control the pass, install Italian security detachments from north of Faïd Pass to Sened, and to reconnoiter halfway to Sbeïtla. At the conclusion of the operation, the attacking force was to withdraw all but the security detachments.[32] As most of the Regiment held positions along the *Mareth Line*, it should be remembered that one of the panzer companies, the *8th*, under the command of Lt Marquardt, had been sent to reinforce the *I./Abteilung, Panzer Regiment 5* (Grün). The plan of the *21st Panzer Division's* seizure of Faïd Pass called for two *kampfgruppen*: the first, *Kampfgruppe Pfeiffer*, was to strike west and take Faïd Pass, while the second *kampfgruppe*, *Kampfgruppe Grün*, was to swing around to the south and come up from behind the pass in order to capture the pass from the rear. At that time Faïd Pass, which sat directly astride the main Sfax to Sbeïtla road, was being held by roughly 1,000 French troops from the *Constantine Division*. The attack by *Kampfgruppe Grün* was to begin from a location just north of Maknassy near Meheri Zebbeus, where it was to move north along the Maknassy - Sidi Bou Zid road towards the Maïzila Pass. It is the actions in this area that are focused on, since they directly involve the participation of a panzer company from the Regiment. On 30 January, the attack commenced against Faïd Pass as *Kampfgruppe Pfeiffer*, now split into three smaller *kampfgruppen*, moved in towards the pass. To the south, *Kampfgruppe Grün* was preceded by elements of *Aufklärungs Abteilung 580*, which was to cover only the first half of the journey before being sent west, moved up the road. Before long, the *kampfgruppe* was halted by a stubborn French defense that succeeded in delaying the *kampfgruppe* for over five hours before withdrawing towards Sidi Bou Zid. As the *kampfgruppe* neared the village of Faïd, it was again delayed in fighting around the village, which eventually fell to the *kampfgruppe*. *Kampfgruppe Pfeiffer*, in the meantime, was pushing westward towards the pass, but was being held up by French troops that managed to put up stiff resistance throughout the day. In the afternoon *Kampfgruppe Grün* was attacked from the northwest by a small task force group of tanks, infantry, and artillery from the U.S. *1st Armored Division's Combat Command A (CCA)*. Eventually that task force was beaten back, but before long the *kampfgruppe* lost four of its panzers to mines as it attempted to move back to support the attacks at the pass.[33] By the evening of the 30/31st, the *21st Panzer's* two *kampfgruppen* had encircled Faïd Pass and were digging in around the pass, and they had succeeded in holding back the relief attempt to regain the pass. The French defenders were still in possession of some portions of the pass, but their situation did not look good, and if they were not reinforced or relieved they would be forced to abandon their positions. In the early morning hours of 31 January another attempt by the Americans to relieve the French had failed. The Americans lost a number of armored vehicles, and their artillery was being hit by counter-battery fire and *Luftwaffe* air attacks. By 1400hrs, the Faïd Pass finally fell to the *21st Panzer*, which by the evening was firmly entrenched there.[34] The next bit of trouble came at around midday on 1 February when *Task Force Stark* (CCC) of the *1st Armored Division* attacked the village of Faïd with infantry and tanks. The attack there did not go well for the Americans when the infantry, moving up behind an artillery barrage, was suddenly confronted by a number of panzers that had come from the village and attacked the infantrymen. The northern flank of the American attack fell back in confusion, and quickly called for the supporting armored force to move up. As the American tanks moved up they were hit by a flurry of Pak and artillery rounds that halted the attack and forced the entire force to withdraw back towards Sidi Bou Zid. There are no known losses for these days, and one can only assume that the *8th Company*, which was equipped with Mk IIIs and IVs, may have had a key hand in holding the positions at Faïd Pass. In his diary Gerhard Weidelener, of the *8th Company*, wrote a few lines describing the actions since the end of January:

"By 28-29 January, we had marched to the Atlas Mountains, on 30 January, we had combat for the [Maïzila] pass and opening of the bypass road, we suffered no losses, and our enemies were the French. From 31 January to 3 February, there was fighting to defend the pass against American tanks and infantry attacks, which suffered multiple losses of there own. Oh well, one could notice that they do not understand a lot about how to conduct the war From 4-11 February we secure positions behind the pass. Each vehicle here has certain amounts of booty, which served for improvement of our provisioning. At this time here in Africa, it was a great springtime, the blossoming almond trees were especially beautiful."[35]

On 2 February, as the grenadiers and Pak gunners dug in even deeper and selected more advantageous positions in and around Faïd Pass, the panzers were recalled towards positions in the pass. While this battle at Faïd had been ongoing, further to the south and west of Maknassy the forces of the *1st Armored Division's CCD* (Maraist) attacked from near Sened, towards Maknassy. The Americans were slowed in doing so by elements of the Italian *50th Special Brigade* force that had been moved up to support the attack at Faïd, and had taken up positions between those two towns. The American *1st Armored Division's CCD* continued its attempts to push on through towards Maknassy, but their assault was called off on the 3rd. Of considerable interest is that during these first days of February the German attacks were well supported by the heavy artillery, which only days beforehand was down to just a few rounds, and the *Luftwaffe*, which was able to make a strong showing during the entire battle. After the attack, the *8th Company* remained with the *I./Abteilung Panzer Regiment 5* until later in the month. The company assisted in holding the Faïd Pass against strong Allied counterattacks, and shortly after the battle had concluded Lt Marquardt was awarded the EK I for his actions during the battle.[36] After the recent battles of late January and early February the Allied commanders were anticipating even more German offensive actions, and so they kept an eye on central Tunisia, and especially the movement of Axis panzer formations, which were a good indicator on where the next round of attacks would fall. It was also at this time that various Allied units were pulled off of the line where they could be reconsolidated, while others were pulled back for refitting and retraining. This large movement of Allied troops did not go unnoticed by Axis intelligence planners, who

Chapter 13: Fighting for Time in Tunisia, January-February 1943

knew that the Allies were not retreated, and still controlled the passes of the western dorsal from the Gafsa Oasis to Tébessa, Sbeïtla, and Sidi Bou Zid.

Rommel and von Arnim, still not comfortable with each other, began to make ready their plans for further attacks. Rommel, having shaken off the illness, depression, and frustration that had plagued him the previous month, now gained his second wind and aimed to hit the Allied forces where they were weakest, and before Montgomery's *Eighth Army* was close enough to interfere. His plan was to hit both his opponents one at a time before they could coordinate their actions and launch their anticipated spring offensive, which would be sure to finish off *AOK 1* once and for all. Arnim's plans called for attacks by both the *10th* and *21st Panzer Divisions*, which he hoped to use against the Americans in and around the Gafsa area. Much like in the past, *Field Marshal* Kesselring and *Commando Supremo* intervened between the two and finally approved a plan that called for von Arnim to strike at Sidi Bou Zid, and Sbeïtla, with the *10th* and *21st Panzer Divisions*. After that attack had succeeded Rommel was to regain control over the *21st Panzer*, and together with his force from the *D.A.K.* attack Gafsa. The initial phase of the plan, Operation "*Frühlingswind*" (Spring Breeze), was to be commanded by von Arnim's chief of staff, *Generalleutnant* Heinz Ziegler. That force had a panzer strength of 200 Mk IIIs and IVs and 11 or 12 Mk VI Tigers. The *10th Panzer Division* had 110 panzers in four battalions, while the *21st Panzer* had ninety-one panzers in three battalions. The Italian *Superga* Division had an attached German company with several Tigers.[37] Ziegler was to launch a three pronged attack through the recently captured eastern dorsal passes and attack those American forces arrayed near Sidi Bou Zid, thereby drawing their attention away from Rommel, who would then join the battle the following day with Operation "*Morgenluft*" (Morning Air). For the operation, Ziegler had the *10th Panzer Division* further broken down into three *kampfgruppen*: Kampfgruppe Gerhardt, Kampfgruppe Reimann, and the reserve Kampfgruppe Lang. The *21st Panzer Division* was broken down into two separate *kampfgruppen*: Kampfgruppe Schuette and Kampfgruppe Stenkhoff. Rommel's forces consisted of the remainder of the *D.A.K.*, which had been consolidated and given the title *Afrika Korps Gruppe*; this force was commanded by *Generalmajor* Kurt von Liebenstein, formerly of the *164th Light Division*. The *D.A.K. Gruppe* included *Panzergrenadier Regiment "Afrika," 1st Luftwaffe Jäger Brigade, I./Abteilung of Panzer Regiment 8*, and *Aufklärungs Abteilung 33* from the *15th Panzer Division*, in addition to various artillery, pioneer, rocket, and Flak units. There was also the Italian *Centauro* Armored Division with two infantry, two artillery battalions, one assault gun battery, one motorized battalion, and one tank battalion.[38] These forces would strike in a northwesterly hook, which after capturing the American base at Gafsa and the airfields of Fériana and Thélepte would continue towards Kasserine and link up with von Arnim's two panzer divisions, then proceed towards the American administrative and logistics center located near the Algerian border at Tébessa.

Back in the south, along the *Mareth Line*, in the early morning hours of 6 February the alarm was again sounded, and by 0500hrs the panzers of the *I./Abteilung* were placed on alert and made ready for action. Later in the day a sandstorm blew in, causing some minor delays to these preparations. Since being virtually wiped out three months earlier in the battle at El Alamein, the Regiment had been able, through various measures, to begin reorganizing some of its sections and elements. Though still not up to even half of its authorized strength in men and machines, the Regiment was able to make a series of adjustments and modifications which would allow it to remain an effective combat formation. At this time the Regiment was able to report that the following sections could be considered combat operational, including: the Regimental *Stabs* and *Werkshop Company*, the *I./Abteilung Stabs* and *Stabs Company*, the *2nd*, *3rd*, and *4th Panzer Companies*. Additionally, there was the *II./Abteilung Stabs* and *Stabs Company* and the *5th*, *6th*, and *7th Panzer Companies*.[39] Also in that report it was noted that the *1st* and *8th Panzer Companies* required additional weapons and vehicles if they were to be reactivated within the Regiment. The final paragraph reported that with additional framework, *Stabs*, personnel, weapons, and vehicles the regimental *Light Zug* and two *staffels* of the *II./Abteilung* could once again be made operational. The *15th Panzer Division* reported fifty-nine operational panzers on 7 February with an additional three in the workshop.[40] At 0730hrs, the *II./Abteilung* was ordered, along with one field artillery battery, to proceed to a point southeast of Ben Gardane in order to secure the line and be ready for action. As that *abteilung* was used to scout out new positions, the division again ordered the formation of a *kampfgruppe* consisting of the *I./Abteilung*, *1./Panzerjäger Abteilung 33*, and *I./Flak Regiment 46* to ward off any enemy attacks against the division. On 9 February, the *II./Abteilung* was ordered to attack those British forces in their sector in order to keep the area secure and push the British back. It was also the aim of *AOK 1* to deploy another *kampfgruppe* in order to attack those Allied formations located to the west of Gafsa. The *15th Panzer Division* was tasked to provide the *I./Abteilung kampfgruppe* for this mission. The mission was carried out, but unfortunately there is no record of the outcome; however, late on the afternoon of the 10th, the *I./Abteilung* was set to begin its march back to its previous positions. As manpower levels actually began to rise a bit, the Regiment was tasked on the 11th to detach two company grade leaders and three platoon or *Zug* leaders to fill various leadership and staff positions within the division reserve. Friday, 12 February 1943 marked the second anniversary of Rommel's arrival in Africa, and so at 0800hrs that morning, the Regimental band under the able leadership of *SFw* Isensee struck up the *Panzer Lied* for its beloved commander.[41] Later that day, at 1730hrs the withdrawal began again with the *Luftwaffe Field Brigade*, which consisted of *Fallschirmjäger Battalions Hubner* and *von der Heydte*, *Panzergrenadier Regiment "Afrika," II./Artillery Regiment 33*, and the *1./Panzerjäger Abteilung 33*, which made their way to approximately twenty kilometers behind Médenine. Adolf Lamm wrote in his diary:

"On the 12th at 1730hrs finally the long hoped for departure. All hearts beat high when we retire marching past the division commander for the big offensive. At around 2400hrs the company reached an area 15km east of Mareth. On the 13th we had a rest day as we are waiting for further orders from the Kampfgruppe D.A.K., to which we are subordinated. One Mk IV (Sp) (Fw Geilenbraun and Kühn) has old bogie damage and is in the workshop."[42]

On the following day the division issued instructions for the Regiment, still minus one of its panzer *abteilung*, that the road from Ben Gardane to Médenine was restricted from use, and that the Regiment was to be deployed en-masse south of this road. On the 14th the panzers again departed, this time at around 1400hrs towards Mareth and the Gabès bypass, and the panzers halted that evening at around 0200hrs and spent the night in a palm forest. The march continued again the following morning at 0500hrs from Gabès. All of these movements undertaken during the previous week were the first in a series of moves to position and make ready those units designated to participate in the *Morgenluft* operation. *General* Eisenhower, who was now the commander of all Allied forces in North Africa, was unhappy with what he had seen during a recent inspection trip of American forces defending the numerous mountain passes along the eastern dorsal of Tunisia. Eisenhower had little confidence that the U.S. *II Corps* under Fredendall was ready to face the veteran German formations, as most of those U.S. forces were green and had never experienced combat before. Eisenhower also discovered that

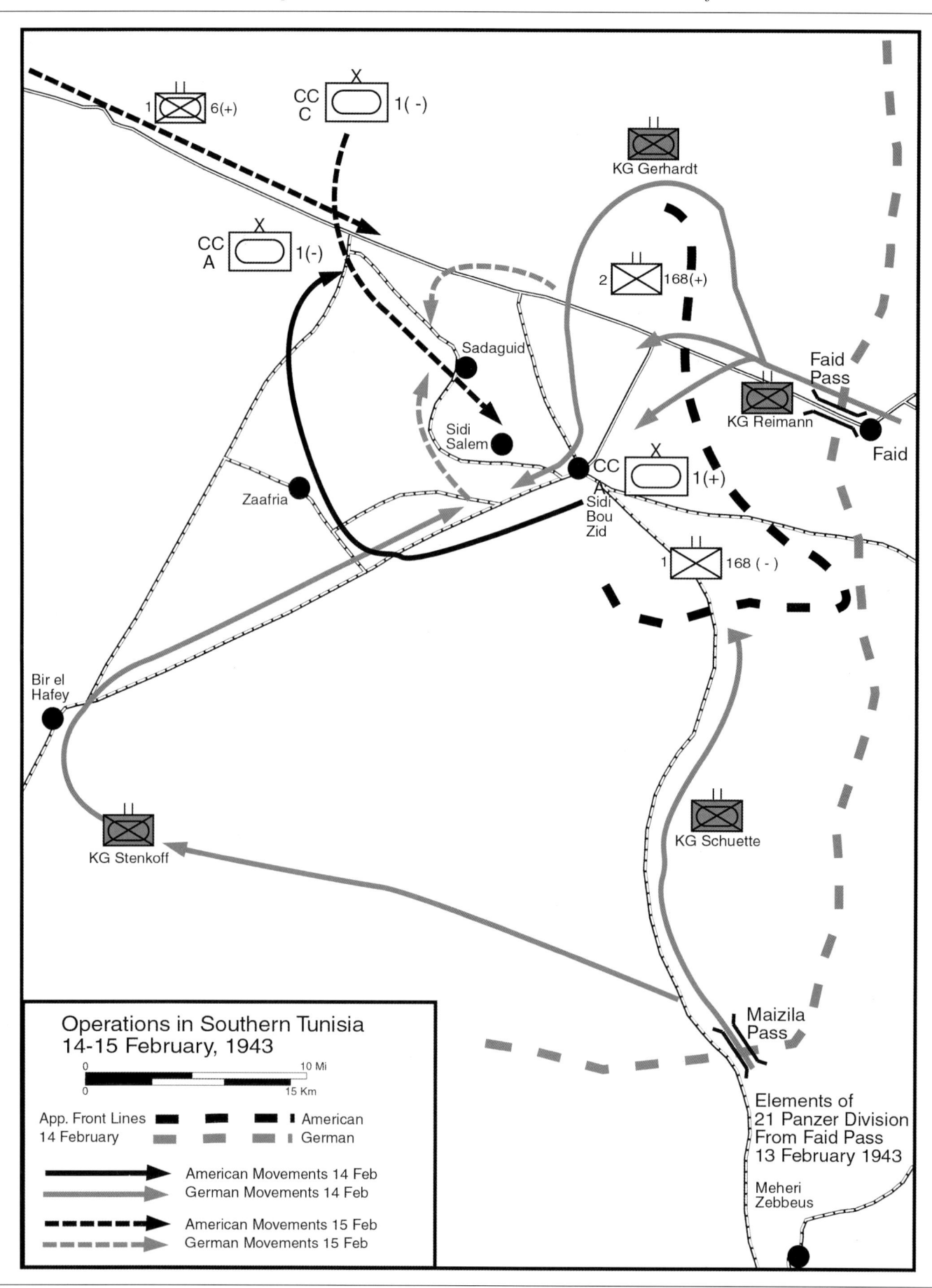

Panzer Regiment 8 in World War II - Poland • France • North Africa

Operations in Southern Tunisia
14-15 February, 1943

Map locations: Sadaguid, Sidi Salem, Zaafria, Sidi Bou Zid, Bir el Hafey, Faid Pass, Faid, Maizila Pass, Meheri Zebbeus

Units shown: CC C 1(-), CC A 1(-), CC A 1(+), 1/6(+), 2/168(+), 1/168(-), KG Gerhardt, KG Reimann, KG Stenkoff, KG Schuette

Elements of 21 Panzer Division From Faid Pass 13 February 1943

Legend:
- App. Front Lines 14 February — American / German
- American Movements 14 Feb
- German Movements 14 Feb
- American Movements 15 Feb
- German Movements 15 Feb

Scale: 0-10 Mi / 0-15 Km

many of the senior officers were complacent with their defensive positions and lacked a serious appreciation for the enemy. To the south of the Americans, Montgomery's *Eighth Army* was slowly building up its forces for a renewed attack against the *Mareth Line*. Rommel and von Arnim too were busy positioning their respective forces in order to launch the *Frühlingswind* and *Morgenluft* operations against the Anglo-Americans. The Italian *Commando Supremo*, which had initially favored the attack on Gafsa by Rommel, had since received creditable intelligence reports that discovered that many of the American formations around Gafsa were on the move north, and so the decision was made to order the attack against Sidi Bou Zid to commence first. Arnim's plan focused on those green Americans forces of the *II Corps* located between Faïd and Gafsa, and was aimed at destroying those forces in and around Tébessa and gaining more favorable defensive positions. Rommel, on the other hand, had wanted to do a concentrated spoiling attack launched by all three panzer divisions and aimed at Gafsa. The lack of a unified command in Africa and the two, strong willed commanders, resulted in no action being taken for over a week. It appeared that both commanders would have to rely on mutual cooperation instead of a direct set of orders. In the end, the Axis strategy called for attacks at both Gafsa and Sidi Bou Zid, which although they were offensive in nature, were defensive in concept.

Operation *Frühlingswind*

Operation *Frühlingswind* commenced in the early morning hours of 14 February, when Zeigler sent his forces in against the American *1st Armored Division* (Ward) and *34th Infantry Division*'s *168th Infantry Regiment* located around Faïd and Sbeïtla. The panzers and infantry of the *10th Panzer Division*'s *Kampfgruppe Reimann* advanced through the Faïd Pass down the Faïd-Sbeïtla road supported by the heavy Tigers of the *501st Heavy Tiger Abteilung*. The advance was lightly contested by U.S. armored forces, and those forces that were able to put up some sort of resistance were quickly dealt with by a combination of *Luftwaffe* air attacks and the long range 88mm guns of the *Tigers*. The second group, *Kampfgruppe Gerhardt*, advanced north around Hill 644 (Djebel Lessouda), and then moved south in order to block any reinforcements from coming down the Sbeïtla road; this *kampfgruppe* also encountered scattered and varied resistance by the *1st Armored Division*'s *CCA*. Farther to the south, the *21st Panzer Division* had moved up during the night of the 13/14th, and by 0600hrs had breeched a minefield and was rolling forward through Maïzila Pass. The division's *Kampfgruppe Schuette*, built around *Panzergrenadier Regiment 104*, was ordered to break through and open the Maïzila Pass for the main body of the division, and once this had been accomplished it was to head north towards Sidi Bou Zid. The second element, *Kampfgruppe Stenkhoff*, with two panzer battalions and built around *Panzer Regiment 5*, was to move through Maïzila Pass and then undertake a wide flanking maneuver and strike west cross-country to Bir el Hafey, then swing north to Sidi Bou Zid. Both elements were protected in the south by *Aufklärung Abteilung 580*, which was screening that flank. *Kampfgruppe Stenkhoff* met no resistance other than mechanical, and by midday was on the road leading to Sidi Bou Zid. *Kampfgruppe Schuette* encountered a company of the *81st Reconnaissance Battalion, 1st Armored Division* that was quickly cut off and captured. The *8th Company*, still attached to *Panzer Regiment 5* and part of *Kampfgruppe Stenkhoff*, entered the village of Zaafria at mid-afternoon and surprised elements of *CCA* attempting to regroup there. *OFw* Stohlmayer and *Uffz* Weidelener, at the head of their *8th Company*, captured a number of prisoners and destroyed or captured a number of guns and vehicles. Weidelener wrote these short notes in his diary detailing the actions during those days:

"12 February we had departed to the south, and on 13 February we were in preparation for [new] combat; the attack would be in the morning. We were still awaiting our mail, and there are nothing more to smoke, a quiet time. During the night, at 0200hrs, came the mail and for me 150 cigarettes, nothing can go wrong now. 14 February, the attack on Zaafria, [OFw] Stohlmeyer and myself came first to the village and captured 150 prisoners, one artillery battery, five half tracks, seven radio vehicles, and some other vehicles. We took them by surprise when we suddenly appeared there."[43]

By 1700hrs, elements of the two panzer divisions had linked up at a point just west of Sidi Bou Zid; there would be some mopping up operations still to conduct, and some of the American units stranded atop a few hills would have to be dealt with, but for the most part the initial objectives had been reached, and plans were quickly being drawn up to exploit them the following day. Zeigler then ordered the non-mobile elements to begin mopping up operations around Sidi Bou Zid, while the *10th Panzer* was ordered to recon north toward Hadjeb el Aioun. The *21st Panzer* was ordered to reassemble its forces for the drive on Gafsa expected to take place the following day. The threat of an American counterattack prevented the Axis commander from venturing out too far. That evening, the Americans began to pull out of Gafsa, feeling that that position was too extended, and that those forces would be better utilized to the north. The last unit to depart Gafsa was the U.S. *1st Ranger Battalion*, and the withdrawal to Fériana was covered by the British *Derbyshire Yeomanry*.[44] To make matters worse for the Allied commanders, they had no idea where the *10th Panzer Division* was at this time, since this division had not been identified at Faïd and Sidi Bou Zid, and was thought to be opposite the French *XIX Corps*. Because of this, American commanders were slow to pull their units out of the front or where they should send reinforcements, thinking that they were only facing one German panzer division near Sidi Bou Zid. The German attacks that were launched on the morning of 14 February were not as surprising as one may think, as Allied intelligence had previously picked up indicators of an attack, and most Allied units were in some state of readiness. The German attacks had initially gone well, and overall resistance was mixed, and in some cases nonexistent. As with all green troops, the American commanders began receiving a number of varied reports and did not recognize how dangerous the actual situation was for them. Because of this those commanders were slow to take appropriate action, whether it was withdrawal or reinforcement. Rommel wrote of this later in his book:

"No doubt the operation we were planning would have been fraught with great dangers for us if the Anglo-American command had made its correct operational move and launched the mass of its force against our long flank, with the object of taking our supply bases and leaving out striking force high and dry. But commanders whose battles have so far all been fought in theory tend as a rule to react directly rather than indirectly to the enemy's moves. Beginners generally lack the nerve to take decisions based on military expediency alone, without regard for what is weighing most heavily on their minds."[45]

While the men of the *8th Company* were busy engaging the enemy, those in the *2nd Company* were certainly having a better time of it, as Adolf Lamm described in his diary:

"14.2.43 There was an unexpected march forward but it doesn't work well after the consumption of alcohol. That's what happens when the Boss

is not here! We are still in the palm grove of Mdou. That evening the 2nd Company is 'very loud'. No wonder when the Oberfeldwebel of Stab I (OFw Spohn) celebrates his 'Deutsches Kreuz' at the company. We had the following break-downs; OFw Kalinski with one Mk IV Nr.83413 goes to the workshop due to damage of the left brake. The situation with the panzers is; two Mk IV (Sp), three Mk III (Sp) and five Mk III (Sp) of Kampfstaffel D.A.K. were subordinated to the commander of the company."[46]*

On the following day (the 15th), the U.S. *1st Armored Division's CCC* attempted a counterattack from the northwest of Sidi Bou Zid. The Americans were slow in developing their attack and gave plenty of warning to the Germans defending the area around the village. The *Luftwaffe* also came into play, as it strafed and bombed the columns of tanks, infantry, and artillery as they made their way south. Both sides traded artillery fire as the American tanks began to move across a series of wadis located northwest of Sidi Salam. The American tanks were engaged by well concealed Pak and Flak guns that destroyed a number of the tanks and halftracks. By late afternoon, *Kampfgruppe Stenkhoff* sent forward three of its companies to attack the southern flank of the advance, while *Kampfgruppe Gerhardt* sent elements to attack the northern flank. By now the American *CCC* was getting hit from the front and both flanks, and was in danger of being encircled. By approximately 1730hrs the attack was halted, and the withdrawal began back to the northwest and Sbeïtla and Kasserine. The *8th Company*, which had by chance found itself in a very advantageous position that day, was able to claim the destruction of thirty-five Sherman tanks.[47] This claim seems highly inflated for just one panzer company, but Gerhard Weidelener's statement adds some creditability to the claim, along with American losses reported by the *1st Armored Division*, which do add legitimacy to the report:

"15 February it was quiet, the alarm was given in the afternoon and a half hour later we were engaged in a perfect tank combat. We all had good shooting positions, and out of twenty-five attacking heavy tanks, Shermans, the abteilung shot down twenty-four of them. We didn't suffer any of our own losses. Our commander was asked afterwards why we let go one of those tanks. We had thirty-five vehicles, had suffered no losses in men and equipment, all the companies were well engaged as all the [American] tanks were burning and illuminating the darkness. An American lieutenant made a comment that [they, the Americans,] still had a lot to learn."[48]

The following day the *1st Armored Division* estimated its losses at forty-six medium, two light tanks, 130 vehicles, and nine self-propelled 105mm guns (*M-7 Priests*). The *10th Panzer Division* alone claimed thirty-nine tanks, seventeen halftracks, and one 105mm howitzer, in addition to various guns and vehicles. *CCC* itself claimed the destruction of thirteen Mk IVs, five 88mm, and ten artillery guns.[49] While the majority of the *1st Armored Division* and *II Corps* withdrew that night to begin taking up positions along the line Kasserine-Fériana-Sbeïtla, there remained a number of infantry units from the *168th Infantry Regiment* stranded atop Hill 644 (Lessouda), Hill 620 (Garet Hadid), and Hill 560 (Ksaira). These forces had been holding out since the 14th, and they were still a cause for concern, even though they did not possess any heavy weapons. Their presence still required German units to hold them in place while attempting to capture their positions. The force on Hill 644 attempted to escape the night of 15/16 February, while those units on Hills 620 and 560 were ordered to withdraw on the night of 16/17 February. A few hundred men managed to return to friendly lines, but almost 1,400 were taken prisoner as they attempted their escape.[50]

In the south that day, the *D.A.K. Gruppe* under von Liebenstein moved from Gabès towards Gafsa; the drive by the *D.A.K. Gruppe* was slow and deliberate, because Rommel was cautious, not knowing the disposition of Allied forces in front of him, and that his own force was not large or strong enough to handle a large attack on it. This operation was to begin once the *21st Panzer* had been released from its commitment in the north. The striking power of the *D.A.K. Gruppe* for this attack centered on the *I./Abteilung*, which was given the designation *Kampfgruppe Stotten*. The *kampfgruppe* was composed of some twenty-six Mk IIIs and IVs, and they were augmented by an additional twenty-three M-13s from the Italian *Centauro* Division.[51] The "*Morgenluft*" operation began on the 15th despite the absence of the *21st Panzer*, which was still being retained at Sidi Bou Zid by Ziegler. Early on the 15th, the forward *aufklärungs* elements of the group discovered that the Americans were evacuating El Guettar and Gafsa, which were occupied without fighting by that evening. The *I./Abteilung* followed up the main body as it marched through the hilly terrain approximately 40km to Gafsa. Adolf Lamm describes a bit of the journey:

"15.2.43, we marched until we could see the outlines of mountains and in complete darkness we reached them by 0530hrs. At 1135hrs a further march in groups of four vehicles for better camouflage and to cover up the troop movement was conducted. At 1730hrs we arrived at the assembly area approximately 25km south of Gafsa. At 2100hrs there was a warning order and orders to stand-by. There we bartered goods and the wine supply was constantly splendid, either the company can drink too little, or there is plenty to drink!"

The morning of the 16th saw the following dispositions: the *21st Panzer* was still being held in the north around Sidi Bou Zid to await further operational plans, and at 0745hrs von Arnim informed Liebenstein that he was not sending that division to him. Instead, the *10th Panzer* was ordered to recon towards Sbeïtla early that morning with the hope of attacking that town later in the day. Since the plans had now been altered by von Arnim, the *21st Panzer* was ordered to pass through those *10th Panzer* elements near Sbeïtla while that division moved north to strike a blow near Fondouk. In the south, the *Centauro* Division was placed to the north of Gafsa, while other elements of the *D.A.K.* were sent off on a reconnaissance towards Fériana. That probe was begun at 0200hrs when *Kampfgruppe Menton*, which had already taken Gafsa, moved off to the north. By 0900hrs the *I./Abteilung* had arrived in Lala, which was only a short distance to Gafsa. Lamm again recalled:

"16.2.43: The tension about the upcoming first attack against the Americans and the anticipation of wiping them out all at once has reached it's pike (pinnacle) at 0330hrs we again begin marching off. But Gafsa was taken without combat. We arrived at the olive grove of Lalla [Lala] at around 0800hrs. A further march was conducted at 2130hrs, which no one had counted on. We had beautiful weather and were in a great mood."

It was during this time that Wilhelm Hagios, who had been without a panzer, now found himself otherwise employed, as he describes:

"In February there were attacks on the Americans, the I./Abteilung was involved. They needed a supply man and so I did it. I drove over 100km to Gabès to gather provisions for 150 people of the combat units upfront. Three days back and forth. One day we almost drove with our provisions into the British: we had a captured British vehicle and were on the way back after we had picked up the provisions and we wanted

Chapter 13: Fighting for Time in Tunisia, January-February 1943

to stop near *Gafsa* and we thought it's no problem, then we saw two men jump from the right side of the road from the trench and asked us where we wanted to go, I saw at the last moment that they had the Balkenkreuz on their vehicle, so they were Germans. They asked us where we were going and we answered them and they said that the British had already taken the place, so we would have driven directly into British."[52]

The march kicked off again at 2000hrs, and when the panzers attempted to move north they found the road ahead of them blocked. In all the day passed without any major offensive action by the *D.A.K. Gruppe*. On the 17th, the following actions and movements were undertaken: the *10th Panzer Division's Kampfgruppe Gerhardt* was moving north to Fondouk, while the *21st Panzer Division's Kampfgruppen Stenkhoff* and *Pfeiffer* pushed northwest along the main road to Sbeïtla. *Kampfgruppe Pfeiffer* was essentially the same formation, as it was *Kampfgruppe Schuette*, but was only now under the command of a new commander, *Major* Pfeiffer of *III./ Panzergrenadier Regiment 104*. The *21st Panzer Division* was able to push up towards Sbeïtla, where it encountered mixed resistance from the *1st Armored Division's CCB* and other units tasked with holding back the German advance. *Kampfgruppe Stenkhoff* attacked from the southeast of Sbeïtla during the afternoon, and according to records, reported twenty-seven damaged or disabled American tanks.[53] Eventually, the Americans were ordered out of the town and to take up a new defensive line at Kasserine; by nightfall Sbeïtla was in German hands. In the south, Rommel ordered Liebenstein's *D.A.K. Gruppe* to continue the drive from Gafsa towards Fériana, a drive of approximately 40 miles. After a short stand by the American rearguards south of town the Americans pulled out, and at about midday the town was captured. After Fériana was taken, the *D.A.K. Gruppe* continued its advance to the northeast about three miles towards Thélepte. That town and its airfield were captured, along with some ammunition and fuel stocks later in the day. For the *I./Abteilung*, it had begun its march early that morning at about 0400hr. During the day the *abteilung* participated in some minor skirmishes with the American rearguard forces located near Fériana. Also on that day there was the notable loss of the *D.A.K. Gruppe* commander, *Generalleutnant* Kurt von Liebenstein, who was wounded by a mine and forced to relinquish command to *Generalmajor* Karl Bülowius, the former artillery commander of the *D.A.K*.[54] The panzers were supported in this attack by the Flak guns of *Flak Regiment 135*, and soon Fériana was taken, as the Americans continued to fall back towards the north. In the day's fighting the *I./Abteilung* claimed twelve tanks and eight halftracks. Adolf Lamm wrote about that day and the movements of the *2nd Company*:

"17.2.43: After the company was wrongly advised about the route of the Abteilung and got to the old road through the barriers and mines, it reached the rest area 40km north-eastwards of Gafsa at 0300hrs. Everyone was asleep. We were led to the black ice and got to sit down. At 0500hrs again we marched off. At 0700hrs SV Menton attacked the road in the direction of Fériana. The Abteilung, with the 7th Company in the lead diverts to the northwest. It reached the main road again around 1000hrs near Fériana, where the combat supply lines and [Lt] Tschech, the 'Conqueror of Fériana' were already waiting for the 'fighting panzers'. The weather had become terribly cold in the meantime and around 1100hrs the Abteilung secured the southern border of Fériana against the enemy troops cut off from the main body in the east and southwest. The company gets the order to advance a patrol, which will be done by Lt Thamphald's Zug. The enemy was discovered in the direction southeastwards. The company gets the order to push forward but it was not possible to catch up with the enemy who escapes with such high speed.

It reaches the favorable position of the Hinterhangstellung ahead of us, and it forced us to stop. The strength of the enemy is approximately five tanks, ten armored Selbstfahrlafetten 7.62 (Tank destroyers) and supply services in the strength of a regiment. The Flak was subordinated to us as reinforcement but the enemy managed to get himself settled down in this favorable position where they are well bombarded by the flak. At 1800hrs the company was brought back to the initial position. The Zug of Lt Thamphald remained 3km to the north-eastwards to safeguard the movement. The re-supply and repairs continue until the late evening. One truck was obtained and one Selbstfahrlafette was knocked out. The company Chef was shot."[55]

By the evening of the 17th, the situation was looking very favorable for the German offensive: Sbeïtla, Fériana, and Thélepte had all been captured, and the American and French troops in those sectors were quickly falling back. Those forces now all looked to be withdrawing back towards the north and west to Kasserine and Tébessa. It was at this time that Rommel understood that he had an opportunity to strike deep into the Allied rear areas at Tébessa, but only if he had control over the majority of panzer and mobile troops. He wrote:

"The Americans seemed to be pulling back to Tébessa. Their command appeared to be getting jittery and they were showing the lack of decision typical of men commanding for the first time in a difficult situation. Now that the operation had gone successfully for four days, I wanted to push forward with all our strength to Tébessa, take possession of this important airbase supply and transport center, and strike on deep into the Allied rear."[56]

That morning of the 18th, Rommel spoke with von Arnim to discuss his plan for the continuation of the offensive; Arnim was against his plan from the very beginning, and knew that it meant the end of his control over the majority of the panzer divisions now in Tunisia. That afternoon Rommel sent a message to the Italian *Commando Supremo* and *Field Marshal* Kesselring outlining his proposal for the offensive. Kesselring, who had just returned to Rome after a meeting with Hitler, approved of the plan, and later signaled both Rommel and Arnim that he supported the move towards Tébessa. The plan was then sent to Mussolini and the *Commando Supremo*, where it took until later in the evening before a message approving the plan was finally sent to Rommel, but with the modification that the offensive's initial objective be launched through Thala to Le Kef instead of Tébessa. Rommel later wrote about the decision made to go further north rather than farther to the south:

"This was an appalling and unbelievable piece of short sidedness, which did, in fact, ultimately cause the whole plan to go awry...At other times our higher authorities were so wildly over-optimistic that they hardly knew what to demand of us next; now, however, when a little boldness really was required, they lacked the guts to give a whole-hearted decision."[57]

Regardless of what decisions were made that day, the most critical item that transpired on the 18th was the complete lack of offensive movement by any of the German formations. At a time when the Americans were shaky and on the run, no movements were made against them. This delay would prove to be critical, in that it gave the Americans time to regain their senses and begin constructing a more deliberate line of defense. Adolf Lamm describes what transpired with his company and the I./*Abteilung*:

"At 1100hrs the Abteilung advanced on a broad front in order to eliminate or pressure the group of forces in Dschebel Zebeus to surrender. SV [KG] Menton attacked from the north. Instead of the American troops, which were cut off from their main body that is nowhere to see, the 7th Company is exchanging shots with SV Menton! The company drives the patrol in an easterly direction and gets the order to attack approximately 10km to the southeast, in order to eliminate another group of enemy forces at Bir Orm Debana. Due to a message error for the second time (that day) and bad road conditions (mountainous) the company returns around 1900hrs to Fériana after the useless deployment."[58]

Rommel wasted little time in ordering his division commanders to begin their movements in order to take up positions and concentrate for the initial phase of this operation, which would commence at first light on the 19th. The *D.A.K. Gruppe*, located near Fériana and Thélepte, was ordered to immediately begin movements north towards Kasserine, while the Italian *Centauro* Division was ordered north from Gafsa to strike towards Tébessa. The *21st Panzer Division* at Sbeïtla was ordered to move north to Sbiba; elements of the *10th Panzer Division* were ordered to move south towards Sbeïtla, where they were to follow in the wake of the *21st Panzer's* drive to Sbiba. Since beginning the offensive both German forces had made considerable gains, and had captured various Allied supply dumps in addition to vehicles and fuel stores. To the veterans, the situation reminded them of the good old days whenever they routed the British and subsisted off their supplies of fuel and rations. By that morning, the *21st Panzer* sent a reconnaissance element up from Sbeïtla to Sbiba, where it became stalled on minefields and was eventually halted by an Anglo-American force consisting of elements from the American *1st* and *34th Infantry Divisions* and British *6th Armored Division*. In the actions near Sbiba that day, the panzers of the *8th Company* claimed the destruction of twelve tanks and two tank destroyers. The company was then pulled back and assumed the role of providing support for the *I./Panzer Regiment 5*.[59] The Kasserine Pass lay just over 5 miles west of the village of Kasserine along Highway 13, where the pass itself was just over a mile wide, and protected by the Djebel Semmama to the north and the Djebel Chambi to the south. The pass was further dived by the Hatab River, which ran northwest to southeast, and further separated both the northern and southern portions of the pass. Once through the pass, Highway 13 continued to the west towards Tébessa, while Highway 17 wrapped around Djebel Semmama and curved north towards Thala. Between the two highways, in the west, the terrain opened up into the broad Bahiret Foussana valley. A reconnaissance element from the *D.A.K. Gruppe* was sent towards Kasserine Pass; according to Rommel, this was *Aufklärung Abteilung 3* (Luck), which was to move quickly during the night of 18/19 February and attack the pass the following morning. However, the Americans were waiting for them, as elements of the *1st* and *34th Infantry Divisions*, in addition to heavy artillery fire directed by forward observers on the high ground, forced the Germans to halt their attempt to capture the pass.[60] The initial attack on Kasserine Pass had failed, but it was too under strength for the mission at hand, and it was determined that a heavier attack would be needed to push the Americans from the high ground that they held. Later that morning *Kampfgruppe Menton* (*Panzergrenadier Regiment "Afrika"*) of the *90th Light Division*[61] was sent in to renew the attempt to capture the pass. Menton's *1st Battalion* was ordered to proceed left along the floor of the pass towards Bordj Chambi, overlooking the Tébessa Road, where it moved towards Wadi Zebbeus, but it was halted just short of the wadi by heavy artillery fire. The *2nd Battalion* went right onto the Djebel Semmama, overlooking the Thala road; the battalion was able to capture a prominent knoll, but when it attempted to move west it too was halted by heavy artillery fire. Unfortunately, due to a combination of bad weather and poor visibility, there was no *Luftwaffe* air support and counter-battery fire was ineffective. It was here that Bülowius made the decision to commit *Kampfgruppe Stotten* to reinforce the *panzergrenadier* attack. The *I./Abteilung* pushed off for the pass at about 1100hrs without encountering any American forces, but at around midday an exceptionally strong sand storm blew up, halting all movement until 1500hrs. The attack commenced at 1530hrs, as the panzers began their attack moving along the Tébessa Road, but like the grenadiers made only limited gains in the face of stubborn resistance from high atop the mountain pass. The cause of this resistance was due to the arrival of a battalion from the American *9th Infantry Division's 39th Infantry Regiment*, which reinforced those forces already fighting in the pass.[62] Rommel was later to write that although the Americans were new to combat, they knew the value of the high ground, and that his troops, long accustomed to fighting in open desert, were unused to fighting in high terrain. True to its long combat record, the I./Abteilung pushed on to the northwest along the Tébessa road, where a small group of panzers worked their way forward through the narrow gap at Djebel Zebbeus. Once past this gap the panzers and grenadiers moved on crossing the Hatab river bed and continuing until they hit another minefield. During its movement through the pass the panzers were subjected to intense machine gun, anti-tank gun, and artillery fire from Hill 712 and Zebbeus. Five panzers were knocked out by these guns, and an additional number of panzers succumbed to mechanical breakdowns, or were immobilized in the minefields. Adolf Lamm documented the day's fighting in this account:

"On the 19th OFw Kalinski was back from the workshop with his panzer. At 0430hrs came the warning order about the further march to Kasserine which takes place at 0915hrs. At 1500hrs there is an assembly at Chambi [Chanibi]. At 1520hrs there is the attack on the Pass of Chambi [Djebel Chanibi]. The attack along this unfriendly terrain is connected with drastic complications. The whole Abteilung in the attack had to twice get through obstacles to reach the position, one was over a railroad embankment and the second was through hollow ground (depression). The heights were captured, with the 2nd Company on the right wing but a mine field forced us to stop and the infantry had barely come forward in the heavy, rugged terrain. A Selbstfahrlafette was knocked out. One Mk III (Sp) belonging to Fw Dehnicke of (D.A.K.) had to be towed away due to a Pak-shot in the left transmission. Around 2300hrs we moved off to the old assembly area [southeast of Djebel Chambi]."[63]

As the panzer attack ground to a halt in the early evening hours, throughout that afternoon the German *panzergrenadiers* and American infantry continued to battle in the high ground on both sides of the pass. Although the Americans had been reinforced, they were still not in sufficient strength to cover the entire sector, and lacked the armored support to hold the pass and launch counterattacks. Late in the afternoon the Americans were seen to be moving back forces on the Tébessa road, and Bülowius ordered that patrols be kept in close contact with them as they withdrew. As dusk fell, patrols of *panzergrenadiers* began to infiltrate the American lines and work their way up onto the heights along the northern side of the pass; a number of positions were overrun and a few hundred prisoners were taken. That evening the I./Abteilung was withdrawn to Djebel Chambi, as Italian tanks and infantry from the *Centauro* Division were moved up to support the attack scheduled for the following morning.

To the north, the *21st Panzer Division* had begun its march towards Sbiba at 0900hrs, and had arrived some six miles short of that town when it ran into a hasty minefield. With the panzers held short of their objective, American heavy artillery fire forced them to pull back and attempt a

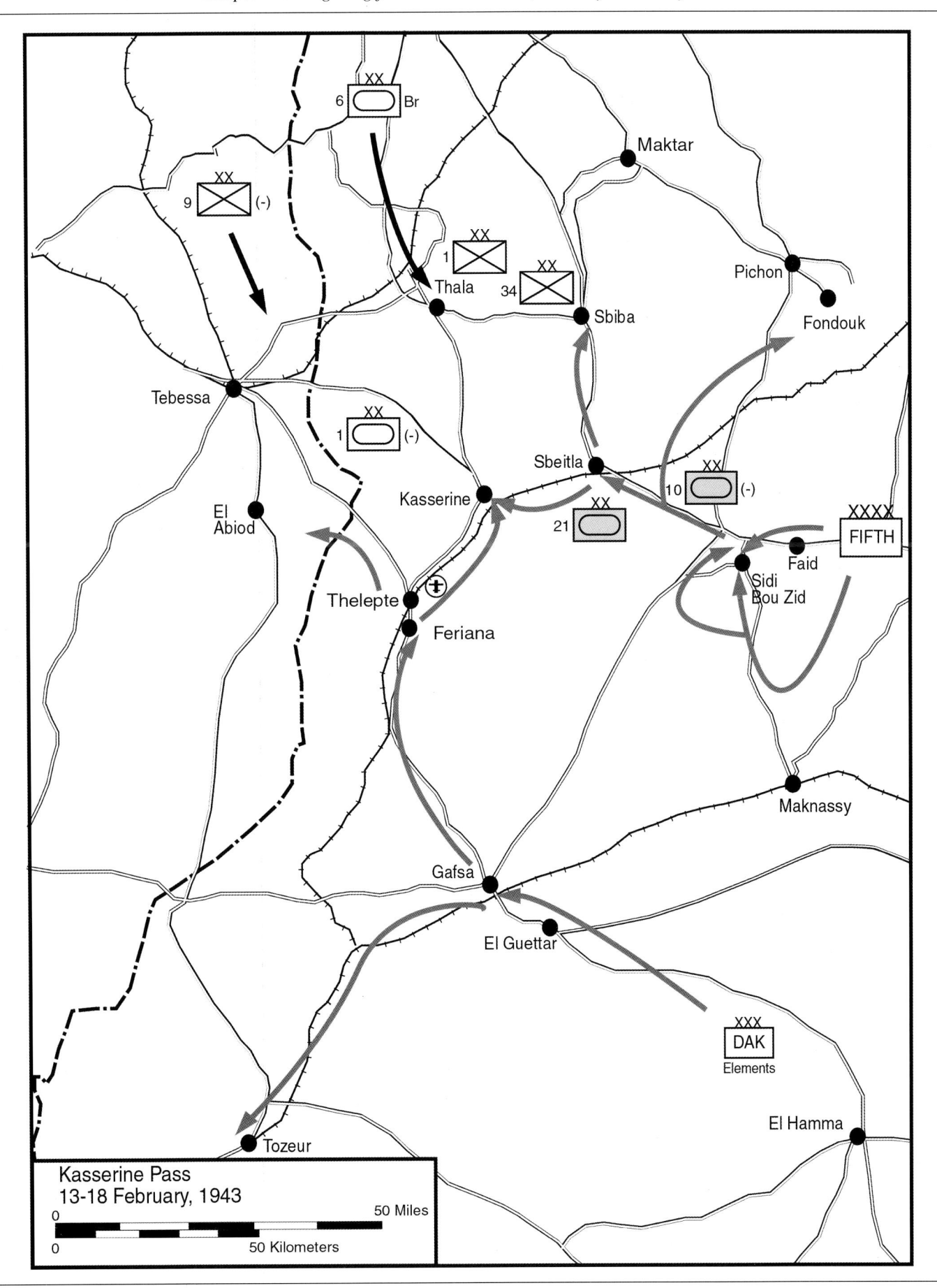

Chapter 13: Fighting for Time in Tunisia, January-February 1943

**Kasserine Pass
13-18 February, 1943**

flanking maneuver further to the right. Both moves met with little success, and the two sides continued to trade blows all day. Gerhard Weidelener describes a bit of what the *8th Company* was going through with that division:

"16-17 February, there were further successful tank fighting and we shot down tanks and took over Sbeïtla. 19-20 February, unfortunately on this day, we could no longer move forward, due to strong enemy superiority, and [our] vehicles were broken due to damage caused by artillery and anti-tank gun impacts. Koppe was killed, and that was sad [because] he was a happy and good comrade of mine."[64]

It was this stubborn defense that influenced Rommel's decision to continue the drive toward Le Kef through the Kasserine Pass. Rommel ordered the *21st Panzer* to continue its attacks south of Sbiba, while the *10th Panzer*, now reaching Sbeïtla after its journey south from Kairouan, was to continue its movement towards Kasserine Pass, where it was to augment and exploit the attack on Thala once the *D.A.K. Gruppe* had opened a way through it. That was easier said than done, since the weather did not permit such a quick maneuver, and the leading elements of the division only made it as far as Sbeïtla by the evening of the 19th. By the morning of the 20th, elements from the *10th*, *21st*, and *15th Panzer Divisions* were in front of Kasserine Pass with the Italian *Centauro* Division quickly closing up. The bad weather continued, and prevented the intervention of air forces from both sides from influencing the battle. Early that morning the Americans began a small counterattack with light tanks and infantry in order to recapture some high ground and be in a position to launch a counterattack in the event of a breakthrough. At 0830hrs elements of the *D.A.K. Gruppe*, *Centauro*, and *10th Panzer* began their attack into the pass. The attack was carried out by the grenadiers of *Kampfgruppe Menton* and the *5th Bersaglieri Battalion*, and supported by the fire from artillery, Flak, and *Nebelwerfers* from the *71st Werfer Regiment*.[65] The attack was slowed down considerably as it met the American force moving forward earlier that morning. The grenadiers pushed forward supported by the artillery, and for the first time by the multi-barreled *Nebelwerfers*, whose large caliber rockets, it was hoped, would help tear a gap in the Allied defensive positions. The panzers and tanks of *Kampfgruppe Stotten* and *Centauro* would only be committed to the fight when the Tébessa road was opened. All morning long the fight continued for the pass, with additional infantry and *Kradschützen* battalions being ordered forward at around midday. In the early afternoon the continuing pressure by the grenadiers allowed various groups to pick their way through the minefields covering the Tébessa road. As the first German and Italian units made their way through the minefields, American artillery began to displace to the rear, and thereby allowed a pause in its supporting fires. The panzer crews not yet in action were actually enjoying a brief rest before being committed. Adolf Lamm of the *2nd Company* remembers:

"There was a rest for our panzers, we fried a chicken, cooked a mutton leg, and ate pork ribs with mixed pickles. At 1630hrs there was very heavy combat with the leading vehicles attempting to break thorough."

It was now the second day of the battle for the Kasserine Pass; the Germans had to this point not been able to take the pass even though at least five infantry battalions had been deployed to capture it. Every delay was costly, not only in men and equipment, but to the overall success of Rommel's plan, as his forces grew weaker and the Allies grew stronger. On the morning of the 20th, in the Sbiba sector, the *21st Panzer Division* found itself still unable to press forward its attacks and make any headway in the face of the strong Allied defense. In an attempt to break through to Sbiba, a plan was constructed that attempted to push two *panzergrenadier* battalions forward to attack the Allied positions while a panzer force of thirty-three MK IIIs and six Mk IVs went on a wide sweep around the eastern flank to envelope the town and cut the road north. The attack was poorly conducted and hampered by bad weather and lack of air support. Despite these setbacks, the attacking force managed to close the distance to the Americans, and in one location four panzers were able to break into the positions held by the *34th Infantry Division*. However, these panzers were quickly knocked out by artillery and anti-tank guns. All throughout the day the Germans were pummeled by Allied artillery.[66] At around 1630hrs, all those German elements at Kasserine were ordered to reform themselves, and to undertake an online charge in the hope of finally clearing the pass once and for all. While those elements of the *10th Panzer* headed towards Hill 974, the *D.A.K. Gruppe* was ordered to make for Hill 812. This attack was to be supported by a large artillery concentration of at least five battalions of artillery. With the fire against it receding, this final attack succeeded in finally clearing the last defenders from the pass. German and Italian armored forces were quick to follow up on the success of the *panzergrenadiers*, which cleared the way forward. The *Centauro* tank battalion followed up their attack by making its way to the northwest along the Tébessa road, where they proceeded for five miles without finding any Allied troops. On the north side of the pass, *Kampfgruppe Stotten* moved north at around 1700hrs along the Thala road, where it engaged mixed elements of American infantry, armor, and tank destroyer units, and even a small detachment of the British *26th Armored Brigade's 10th Buffs Regiment*, which lost all eleven of its tanks.[67] *Hptm* Stotten, who was in the vanguard of the attack, was able to push his *abteilung* forward despite the pounding it was taking. Adolf Lamm describes the fighting as the *kampfgruppe* went forward that day:

"20.2.43: With the bad weather, the coldness was bitter; we wait for the further order. During this time we slaughtered three pigs of American origin and they were to come in handy. The 2nd Company got the mission at 1630hrs to push forward 12km to the north in the direction of Thala and as the lead company freed up the passage there. With <u>that</u> terrain it's was a true suicide task! The Spitzenzug or point platoon of Fw Honecker moved off. Together with us in the attack are the Kradschützen and after the most difficult and bitter fighting we finally got through with the support of the 4th and 7th Companies and caused large losses to the enemy. The acquired war booty was not possible to overlook in the darkness. Lt Thamphald was wounded at the head of his Zug after the exemplary and extraordinary deployment, he was only wounded but with him was his whole crew. Fw Oppold was shot as well but he won over the enemy infantry in close combat and brought his partially wounded crew back alive. The successes and who made them in the attack are not communicated in my short-hand notes."[68]

On the night of February 20th, the situation in the Allied camp looked gloomy; it appeared that German forces were everywhere, pressing forward, and still achieving success. However, the situation was far from desperate: there were the leadership failures and breakdowns in communications, but in many locations the Allies were holding strong positions, and vital reinforcements were making their way forward to support those units. At Sbiba, the *21st Panzer* was being effectively held up by units of the American *1st* and *34th Infantry Divisions* in addition to the British *1st Guards Brigade*. Along the road south of Thala the British *6th Armored Division* was establishing a provisional Allied force under the command of *Brigadier* Nicholson, the division's assistant commander. The force was given the name "*Nickforce*," and consisted primarily of units from the *26th Armored Brigade*, along with various scattered American

Chapter 13: Fighting for Time in Tunisia, January-February 1943

and French units. The force was holding positions just nine miles north of Kasserine Pass. Along the primary roads that led to Haïdra and Tébessa the American *1st Armored Division* and other *II Corps* units were beginning to establish strong blocking positions. Supporting each of these positions was the Allied artillery, which was firing in defensive support despite the bad weather that hampered observation. In addition to those forces previously mentioned there were elements of French *XIX Corps* and U.S. *9th Infantry Division*, not to mention the separate tank destroyer and engineer battalions. In one example of just how well reinforcements were moving into the battle area, the U.S. *9th Infantry Division's* DIVARTY (divisional artillery) had been alerted for movement to Tébessa when Sbeïtla was being evacuated. At that time it was in the vicinity of Tlemcen, in western Algeria, when it was ordered to move without delay and with all of its available artillery and field guns by a forced march to Tébessa. The *DIVARTY* commander, Brigadier General S. Leroy Irwin, would lead a four day, uninterrupted march of over 800 miles through mountainous roads and in terrible weather. This force arrived with its three *Field Artillery Battalions* (the *34th*, *60th*, and *84th*), consisting of twelve 155mm guns and twenty-four 105mm guns, and by the morning of the 22nd, those guns were in position west of Thala.[69]

With Allied blocking groups and reinforcements continuing to hold off the German attacks, the entire situation was beginning to change, as Rommel had feared might happen. Delays on the 18th, as well as having taken two days to get through Kasserine Pass, were beginning to be felt. To further complicate matters, almost all of the forces under his control were now being employed, and there was little in the way of mobile reserves. Part of this had been that von Arnim had withheld almost half of the *10th Panzer Division* in the north, and more importantly, he had withheld the panzers and small detachment of Tigers that were still under his control in the north. In an attempt to bring more mobile forces into the fighting at Kasserine, Rommel ordered the *21st Panzer* to detach *Aufklärungs Abteilung 580* to that sector. The division itself was to remain in contact with Allied forces and keep up the appearance of an active defense, so as to ensure that as many allied troops as possible were tied down there. The *8th Company*, still fighting with the *21st Panzer Division*, destroyed fourteen tanks, and *Uffz* Weidelener, in his Mk IV, was personally responsible for the destruction of five *Sherman* tanks, which he knocked out within an hour. The following day he was promoted to *Feldwebel* and awarded the EK I. Here he describes the situation he and his company were faced with:

"21 February, the alarm is given in the evening, [there is] heavy artillery fire, and we drove on to a steep slope into a hinterhangstellung position in which on the opposite side were American tanks. There was fighting from a distance of about 100m, five tanks were shot down, this hour [of fighting] cost us a lot of nerves. There was a bigger tank fight taking place at a longer distance from us. The next day, 22 February was quiet and I received the EKI."[70]

Back in the Mareth position, the II./*Abteilung* lost *Hptm* Hirschfeld, the commander of the *6th Company*, who was killed when attempting to defuse a U.S. made hand grenade. The company once again came under the leadership of Lt. Halverscheidt.[71] By 0200hrs on the 21st, *Aufklärungs Abteilung 33* was sent northwest along the Tébessa road with a few Italian tanks, light howitzers, and engineers. As that formation pushed northward it encountered only retreating American units, until at a location about eight miles from Djebel el Hamra it encountered a reconnaissance company from the *13th Armored Regiment* of CCB, *1st Armored Division* that blocked the way. A similar *aufklärungs gruppe* was also sent north, but this time along the Thala road, where in the early morning fog it encountered the blocking positions of "*Nickforce*." Based on the reports from these two reconnaissance groups, Rommel made the decision to keep moving on with the offensive; his plan was to send the weaker *D.A.K. Gruppe* west along the Tébessa road in order to secure the western flank, while the recently arrived and much fresher *Panzer Regiment 7* was to move north towards Thala, where stronger opposition was being encountered. The time was now mid-afternoon on the 21st, when *Aufklärungs Abteilung 33* was ordered forward again to attempt to capture the pass at the northern end of Djebel el Hamra. The attack began, but was quickly checked by American forces that had been moving into the area, and the increasing fire from American artillery. The attacking force was halted between the road and the Hatab River, where it waited on the follow up elements of the *Centauro* Division. A second recon battalion, *Aufklärungs Abteilung 580*, was directly along the Tébessa road, where it was to turn off to the west towards the Bou Chebka plateau in an attempt to outflank American positions there. That force too was checked by the rough terrain and American defenses.[72] For the remainder of the day the situation along the Tébessa road remained a stalemate, with both sides struggling to secure positions in the rough terrain. Neither side attempted to launch any strong counterattacks against the other. For *Kampfgruppe Stotten* the day passed along fairly quietly, as the unit was not called on to support any of the attacks now being executed by the *D.A.K. Gruppe*. Despite the battle beginning to turn against them, German propaganda teams were moving through the Kasserine Pass to document the early attacks there. The Germans were quick to follow up on their success, and began to film the battlefield for the people back home; the war footage films would be sent back to the *Third Reich* in an attempt to bolster the morale of the German people, as Adolf Lamm noted:

"It was Sunday 21.2.43 and we drove approximately 14km through the pass at Djebel Zebbeus in the direction of Tébessa, that evening there was battle stations on the fire plan and the Newsreel crews were here also. The first part of the day was quiet, which was excellent for us. The war trophies are filmed for the 'Wochenschau'. At 1530hrs we march forward approximately 20km in the direction of Tébessa. The company situation with vehicles was as follows; two Mk IVs (Sp), Five Mk IIIs (Sp)."[73]

To the north that same morning the situation was much the same, as *Panzer Regiment 7*, with supporting *panzergrenadiers*, pushed cautiously north toward Thala. That force continued to encounter elements of "*Nickforce*" as it put up a stubborn defense, despite taking a number of casualties and losing a large number of its tanks. The British tanks were older models, lightly armored and inferior in the gun they mounted. The panzers attempted to outflank the stronger positions in the hopes of getting around the weaker flanks. With the attack moving forward at such a slow pace, Rommel, who had arrived on scene, took command of the battle and got the attack moving again at approximately 1600hrs. For three hours the panzers moved forward, and were able to reach a point just in front of Thala. Finally, at 1900hrs, the German attack petered out in the face of stubborn Allied resistance and reinforcements that had been moved in during the afternoon. Rommel wrote about the attack that day:

"By 1300hrs the 10th Panzer Division was advancing in great strides towards Thala, 35 miles north of Kasserine. I had gone forward to the 10th Panzer Division at about midday. The division was not getting forward fast enough, and I had to be continually at them to keep the speed up; they did not seem to realize that they were in a race with the Allied reserves. To form my own judgment of the situation I drove forward to the leading scouts to see what was happening. I found them lying in a cactus grove close beside a Arab village. Heavy artillery fire was falling in the

village and confusion was complete. We now moved off to a hill about 500 yards away, from where we watched the course of our attack. Seventeen destroyed tanks lay in front of us, they were Mk VIs (Crusaders) so it was small wonder that they had come down so quickly from the north. Our artillery had joined the battle and shortly afterwards we ourselves came under the fire of the tank attack and had to make another getaway. Shortly afterwards I drove forward again to the infantry east of the road and called on them to speed up their advance. I gave General von Broich orders to have the Panzer Grenadiers follow up the tanks lorry-borne. At 1900hrs the 10th Panzer Division succeeded in penetrating into Thala, which was already held by the enemy. During our entry a British battalion allowed itself to be overrun by the panzer spearhead before opening fire. Our tanks wheeled about, attacked the enemy in the rear and drove them out of their positions, 700 prisoners falling into our hands. However we were soon forced to leave Thala again, after the enemy had brought up more units of the 6th British Armored division and other Allied formations."[74]

On the night of 21/22 February, the situation confronting the German and Italians was a stalemate; they had been unable to achieve any decisive results in their attacks launched over the previous two days, and were now beginning to suffer manpower and logistical shortages because of it. With each passing hour, Axis forces around Kasserine, Thala, and Sbiba grew weaker while the Allies grew stronger, as they continued to feed in reinforcements to all sectors. The time had passed for a chance at breaking through toward Le Kef, or even Tébessa. Although some ground had been taken on the 21st, it was not firmly in the hands of those German formations that had captured it. With very few uncommitted units remaining and no reserve forces to speak of, the *D.A.K. Gruppe* ordered *Kampfgruppe Stotten* to move forward with all possible speed towards the west through the Bahiret Foussana valley in the direction of Tébessa, where units of the *1st Armored Division's CCB*, equipped with tanks, tank destroyers, and 105mm howitzers were holding up the advances of the German *panzergrenadiers* and Italian *Centauro* Division. During the night and early morning hours, *Kampfgruppe Menton* and the Italian *5th Bersaglieri Battalion* had succeeded in moving to the west and northwest around Bou Chebka Pass, where despite capturing a few smaller elements and causing the Americans to pull back a short distance, became pinned down by American artillery. With a few assault guns from the *Centauro* Division, *Kampfgruppe Stotten* moved up the valley to help relieve the pressure on the *5th Bersaglieri Battalion*, which despite fighting extremely well over the past few days was now beginning to show signs of wavering. Between 1030hrs and midday, the *kampfgruppe* moved up and attacked, where it was successful in relieving the pressure on the Italians.[75] However, the panzers soon encountered fierce resistance by the American's guns, despite the panzer crews continuing to press home their hard nosed attacks. *Hptm* Stotten and his panzers were able to make some gains and destroyed a number of American tanks and guns. During this attack the panzers were reportedly strafed by Allied fighter-bombers that were making some of their first supporting over-flights since the battle had begun. During this fighting the panzer crews encountered for the first time the American made rocket launcher known as the "*Bazooka*." It was not long before the German panzers began to fall victim to this new weapon when later in the afternoon one of the Mk IIIs was reported being hit and destroyed by one. After the fighting died down the *kampfgruppe* was able to take stock of the losses it had inflicted on the Americans: nine tanks, three tank destroyers, and four self-propelled 105mm howitzers. In return the *kampfgruppe* had suffered the loss of seven panzers and sixteen soldiers wounded. After continuing to meet strong resistance, the *kampfgruppe* was forced to break off its attack and fall back. This final Axis attack marked the high water mark in the drive for Tébessa. Adolf Lamm wrote this description of the attack in his diary report for the 22nd:

"The road reconnaissance had to be done by the company Chef during the night; it seems that the Abteilung is no longer responsible for such things. At 0500hrs the panzers begin marching off to the new assembly area near Ben Mouldi [Metlaoui]. Already in assembly area we were greeted with heavy enemy artillery fire. At 0830hrs the Abteilung advanced on a broad front, the 2nd Company was on the right wing, up against strong enemy forces that defended the bottleneck. The task was to support our own troops who had deployed on the right wing and to push against the stronger enemy tank forces there. We got into position in the flat wadi/hollow on the height of the Pak-positions. Already during the entrance of the bottleneck as we rolled on we were heavily engaged from a long distance by thirty to fifty tanks with larger caliber guns. Houwaldt's Zug drove on and had to immediately withdraw due to the strong enemy fire. At 1150hrs we took-off to the initial position in the sequence of 4th, 2nd, and 7th Companies. Why should we take-off? As it rains the whole day and one can watch the strong enemy movements on the different sides. At 1800hrs the company received the order, to push forward again against the village at the base of the bottleneck in order to relieve the Italians and our own Pak-units from the up close danger of the strong enemy which are supported by a large amount of tanks. It gets dark during the attack by the 7th and 4th Companies, which have attacked on the right flank from us. Honecker's Zug puts out feelers as a patrol and after the withdrawal of KG Menton, the Pak-units and Italians were taken back by the 4th and 7th Companies. The 2nd Company again remained to safeguard the passage. After identifying that all our forces have moved off, the company drove back at around 2015hrs. It's pitch-black. By reaching the combat supply lines it was once more assigned to safeguarding the rear until they too march away. The withdrawal movements in three columns on bad roads offered the same shameful picture. We are very disappointed and shaken by this turn of events. Fw Oppold, commander of the Exchange team and Gefr Kühn from the I-Staffel died from the bomb fragments during multiple Tiefflieger and bombing attacks. At midnight we reached the assembly area of the day before."

On 22 February, the offensive nature of the Axis attack was now becoming one of a defensive nature, as the number of Allied reinforcements moving into the battle area gave the appearance of a major counterattack in the making. On the morning of the 22nd, after viewing for himself the fighting at Thala, Rommel ordered von Broich to halt any further offensive actions there and assume a defensive posture. Later that afternoon Rommel met with *Field Marshal* Kesselring and *General* Seidemann of the *Luftwaffe* to discuss the future of operations in the Kasserine sector. It was agreed that the prospects of achieving a breakthrough either towards Le Kef or Tébessa held little chance of success, and that the operation should be called off, and some of the troops returned to von Arnim in northern Tunisia. However, the majority of the mobile troops, panzers, and grenadiers were to be sent south to the *Mareth Line*, where there was a chance of striking a blow at Montgomery and the *Eighth Army* before it could launch its long anticipated offensive. Fortunately, the causalities so far sustained in the battle were not so costly as to prevent Rommel and Kesselring from further offensive actions. The Axis forces had lost roughly two thousand casualties (dead, wounded, and missing), twenty panzers, ten guns of various caliber, and approximately seventy other vehicles. The Allies in turn had lost roughly six thousand men, approximately two hundred tanks, and eighty guns of various caliber, along with hundreds of other vehicles to include armored and unarmored vehicles, in addition to a

Chapter 13: Fighting for Time in Tunisia, January-February 1943

large quantity of supplies and fuel.[76] At that time the *15th Panzer Division* reported thirty-four operational panzers with an additional two in the workshop. The numbers included ten Mk III Specials and fifteen Mk IV Specials.[77] But the battle was yet to be completed, and there was still the problem of withdrawing those Axis forces from the battlefield in the face of growing Allied formations. Adolf Lamm:

"During the night of the 22nd we are alerted to movement in the battle area and at 0500hrs we drove to the battle area. From 0900hrs there was heavy artillery fire and combat that lasted until 1300hrs. From 1600hrs there was a counter attack to cover the infantry withdrawal. During the evening we conducted a return march to our old position at Djebel Zebbeus to cover the retreat and again came under heavy bombing and low level fighter attacks."

The German rearguards, aided by the bad weather, had just enough time to emplace a few mines and booby traps before having to make their way back along the route that they had just advanced along only a few days prior. The Germans were skilled at this type of military operation, and the withdrawal went well. The following morning, as the Americans and British awoke they still believed that they were facing a strong enemy to their front. It would take them some time before they discovered just what they were facing—a few stragglers and ghosts. For the panzer crews, they of course attempted to salvage as much as they could in the short time remaining and little space available in their panzers. It was vital to get back as much damaged and captured equipment as possible, but the men had a tendency to focus on the smaller things. After the battle Hermann Eckardt recalled:

"After the combat at Kasserine Pass with the Americans, where we had shot up some tanks and vehicles we heard for the first time from Swiss radio that the Germans had in Afrika the Tiger panzers but it was a different unit, probably parts of the Hermann Göring Division, but not us. We were not supposed to get them, we could just dream about it. We returned with loads of American food of all types, this was the best thing we captured from the U.S. Army, and this was very important since many men did not have proper food and were underweight, we never had any fresh vegetables and our canned food was terrible and normally had worms in it, the Americans had many good things. Shortly after returning, Stotten presented me with the Iron Cross I."[78]

Horst Sonnenkalb saw that the Americans had learned much since those first attacks:

"The Americans hadn't expected our counter-attack. Their troops were in panic, at that time they were inexperienced in combat, but they gathered again, found time to [regain] consciousness and hit back. Armed to the teeth and with incessant low-level fighters and supported by bomber formations, they fought for their positions that they lost on the previous day. Finally we had to withdraw due to chronic inferiority versus triple superior forces."[79]

The withdrawal from Kasserine was covered by diversionary attacks launched by the *Fifth Panzerarmee* in the north along the Ousseltia valley. The *10th Panzer Division* was responsible for covering the withdrawal of the *D.A.K. Gruppe*, which was making its way to Thélepte and Fériana.[80] The withdrawal out of the Kasserine Pass was completed by noon on the 23rd, even though it did not mark the end of combat, as some of the formations came under attack by Allied fighter-bombers; it was the end of further attempts to push the Allied Army from central Tunisia. *Kampfgruppe Stotten* itself withdrew towards Gafsa at 1500hrs and arrived there at 2100hrs. *Oberst* Irkens and his men were extremely happy when the I./*Abteilung* returned to the Regiment following the battle at Kasserine. Not only was it comforting to have all his elements back under his control, but there were also the spoils of the battle, from which the Regiment was resupplied with captured vehicles and various items. Stotten was himself recommended for the Oak leaves to his Knights Cross for his leadership during the actions at Kasserine. He received the decoration on May 10, 1943.[81] However, the Regiment had little time to sit around and enjoy the American booty, as Adolf Lamm describes:

"Tuesday 23.2.43: At 0500hrs we marched forward to the old assembly area of Chambi. The arrival of mail helped us a little to cope with the situation, nevertheless, even with the wine ration, we by that time had a smaller number of friends. At 1300hrs there was again a further retreat back toward Thélepte. The alarm came when we arrive there at 1700hrs; therefore we were on constant readiness and had to march off. The enemy tanks had broken through at Djebel Serugaia approximately 15km northwest of Thélepte. During the night in the proximity of our assembly area there was artillery fire from only a short distance. That day I also had to take over the duties as the combat writer, because Gefr Rebel was wounded."

Also that same day the *OKH* ordered the formation of *Armeegruppe Afrika* under the command of *Field Marshal* Rommel; it was to consist of the *Fifth Panzerarmee* (Arnim) and the *AOK 1* (Messe).[82] Finally, but possibly a bit too late, Rommel was now in control of all Axis forces in Africa. Rommel wrote of the order:

"On the evening of the 23rd February, an order arrived from the Commando Supremo stating that to satisfy the urgent need for a united command in Tunisia, Armeegruppe 'Afrika' was to be formed under my command. I received the news with mixed feelings. I was glad that I would be able to have some wider influence over the fate of my men-General Messe having shortly before assumed command over the Mareth front; on the other hand I was very happy at the prospect of having to go on playing whipping-boy for the Führer's HQ, the Commando Supremo and the Luftwaffe."[83]

As the Kasserine battles came to an end and the I./*Abteilung* made its way back to the south to link-up with the Regiment, it should be remembered that the Regimental *Stabs* and II./*Abteilung* were still in the south awaiting their replacement panzers. On the 20th, the Regimental *Stabs* was involved in a small action that is worth mentioning here, as it gives an idea of what was taking place along the *Mareth Line*. On 20 February, the Regimental *Stabs* and the subordinated II./*Panzer Regiment 5*, commanded by *Major* von Senfft, were located with thirty-three panzers in the area 7km northwest of Metameur. This small panzer force was under the command of the *15th Panzer Division* as it attempted to hold the British *Eighth Army* along the *Mareth Line* near Médenine. During this time, the division was located in defensive positions on both sides of Metameur. Since 12 February, the I./*Panzer Regiment 8* had been attached to the *D.A.K. Gruppe* for *Operation Morgenluft*, and the II./*Panzer Regiment 8* was located in the area northwest of Gabès, still awaiting its replacement panzers. With that, the Regiment possessed only one tactically subordinated detachment. The combat echelon of the Regimental *Stabs* at the time consisted of only one staff car, one *Kübelwagen*, two motorcycle combos, one command panzer, one middle-wave radio detection van, and one *Fernsprechtrupp* (messaging group). As the fighting raged to the north, the Axis positions along the *Mareth Line* remained unusually quiet, but sure enough, the British would attack once they had enough men and equipment to do so. Limited reconnaissance was conducted in the surrounding area to determine possible routes to launch counterattacks from and isolate any *Eighth Army* breakthroughs along the H.K.L. The ability to move in this area was severely hampered by numerous German minefields, which had been laid along the wadis, especially between Metameur and the road leading north. Both air and ground reconnaissance had failed to detect any movements over the preceding days, which would have led to the discovery of an expected attack. On 20 February, the weather that morning was shrouded in a heavy mist when at around 0830hrs the division reported that forward outposts had sighted approximately ten British tanks crossing the Medenine–Bou Ghrara road, 8km northeast of Medenine. Shortly after this report was received, further reports indicated that these tanks were turning towards the west and seemed to be advancing against the left flank of the division. The division immediately sent forces to occupy a surveillance position along the northern flank of Hill 102, while a panzer company (the 6*th*) was ordered to move up and support them. A request by the company for an artillery observer was granted, and by 0910hrs the company departed with three Mk III Specials, two Mk III 75mm, and four Mk IV Specials to take up a *hinterhangstellung* position just north of Hill 102. By this time, five more British tanks were spotted near Point 84, driving to the southwest, with two Mk VI tanks screening the movement. At the same time another vehicle column, consisting of tanks (Mark VI and Grants), self-propelled gun-carriages, and artillery was spotted moving west in the same vicinity. The leading element of the column was taken under fire and immediately withdrew to the north. In the meantime, at 0900hrs the Regiment received a report that approximately twenty British tanks were moving north in the area of Sidi Rehila (7km north of Medenine). Soon after this report was received another followed, which placed the enemy tank movements as having already passed around the division's northern flank. Those tanks had been lost in the misty weather and had advanced into the saddle, southwest of Tadjera Srhir (6km northwest of Metameur) towards the Médenine-Gabès road. The Regiment was simultaneously given orders to deploy the remaining two panzer companies against this force. The Regiment ordered the panzer *abteilung* to advance from their assembly area and move north in order to pass around Djebel Rouiss from the west, and then strike to the east and southeast in order to destroy the enemy force on the road. At that time the Regimental *Stabs* was located with the II./*Abteilung*, while the 6*th Company* was directly subordinated to the Regiment. The panzers began their movement at 0945hrs, and at this exact moment the command of the *abteilung* was passed from *Major* von Senfft, who was ill, to *Hptm* Schnelle, the commander of *II./Panzer Regiment 8*. The *abteilung* continued north until it reached the road near Wadi Hallouf, where it merged with the wadi. From there the panzers turned to the southeast, and the 5*th Company* was deployed with its nine panzers to the west, while the 7*th Company*, also with nine panzers, was deployed facing east along the Metameur-Gabès road. The Regimental *Stabs* did not accompany the *abteilung* that far, but went towards the high ground on Djebel Rouiss, which offered a perfect over-watch position. At this point, the 6*th Company* reported that it had reached Hill 102 without encountering any British forces along the hill and in the saddle east of Djebel Rouiss. However, multiple British tanks were spotted 2km north of this position, and were firing towards the road at a German howitzer battery. According to a report received from the division, this battery was in danger of being overrun by British tanks. Irkens acted quickly and ordered the *abteilung* headquarters with its befehls panzer, one Mk II, two Mk IIIs, and one Mk III Special to move around the north side of the djebel and attack. Further reports were received that identified stronger enemy forces having captured the ridge of hills north of Djebel Rouiss, along the Metameur-Gabès road. As Schnelle and his panzers reached the heights to the north of the road, they received well placed fire from approximately ten tanks. It was quickly determined that to continue the attack in the north against this enemy force would result in heavy losses, and in order to succeed, the panzers would have to attack across country void of cover. An additional fear was that the panzers would be cut off from the division. So despite the wish to keep the Médenine–Gabès road free of British forces, the attack was abandoned, and the *abteilung* was ordered to halt and set up an overwatch position 2km northeast of Djebel Rouiss. Throughout midday, the British tanks in the east were placed under well aimed fire by the 5*th* and 7*th Companies* which forced the tanks to withdraw, but despite having a clear field of fire, the panzers were exposed to British tank fire from the north and had to frequently change position to avoid getting hit. The situation facing the 6*th Company* on Hill 102 continued to develop as the British began to occupy positions northwest of Point 84. The British combat power here consisted of approximately thirty tanks and at least two batteries of artillery. In the area to the northwest of Hassi Moussa there appeared a large truck column that was protected by tanks. German artillery fire was called for, and the column came under effective fire and was destroyed. Between 1100hrs and 1200hrs the situation developed to where there were three enemy groups of similar strength of about thirty tanks, with self-propelled gun-carriages and artillery. These groups were each located approximately 3-4km from the German front lines, and continued to move north under thick smokescreens. By 1200hrs several British tanks had successfully reached the Médenine–Gabès road, northeast of Point 154, and were able to link up with other forces there before attempting to move northwest along the road. *Oberst* Borowietz, the division commander, arrived at the Regimental command post and agreed with Irkens that the overall situation along the northern flank was worrisome. He then ordered the Regiment to protect the northern flank of the division, as well as preventing the enemy from entering Wadi Hallouf. A *kampfgruppe* was then formed under Irkens, which consisted of the *Regimental Stabs (Pz.Rgt.8)*, the 5*th* and 7*th Companies of II./ Panzer Regiment 5*, and further units consisting of one 2cm Flak battery from *5./ Flak Regiment 43*, four self-propelled 7.62 Pak guns from *4./Panzerjäger Abteilung 33, I./Artillery Regiment 1 (Afrika Artillery Regiment)*, and one 88mm Flak battery of three guns from *2./Flak Regiment 33*. Irkens then requested that the 6*th Company* be released from its current assignment at Hill 102, but the request was denied by the division. The Regimental *Stabs* relocated its combat position on Djebel Rouiss to the northwest, and Irkens personally instructed his subordinate commanders to conduct a timely repositioning along the western flank while being careful as to not tip the enemy off as to what was taking place. Irkens then formed a smaller *kampfgruppe, Kampfgruppe Thinkel*, which consisted of a 2cm Flak battery and the four 7.62 *Panzerjägers*. This *kampfgruppe* was deployed in Wadi Hallouf, between the heights of Djebel Rouiss and the eastern branch of Zemlet el Lebene. In the meantime, the artillery and Flak guns took up positions to the south and southeast, while the *kampfgruppe* received additional artillery support in the form of the recently arrived *Artillery Verbindungs Kommando of III./Iz. A.R. 33* (army heavy artillery). The commander of *I./Artillery Regiment 1* was given the mission of retrieving the howitzer battery from the road northeast of Djebel Rouiss. As the defensive line was being formed further to the west, the British continued again and again a series of disorganized attacks. During the afternoon the British attempted to advance against the 6*th Company*, but did so with only a single tank or self-propelled gun. These feeble attempts were disrupted by well placed fire, and in particular the short 75mm guns from the Mk III Ausf Ns. During the afternoon, Schnelle's force in the north was engaged with approximately thirty enemy tanks at a distance of about 3-4km. The panzers were able to successfully deflect this attack,

Chapter 13: Fighting for Time in Tunisia, January-February 1943

and reported the destruction of two Mk VI tanks, which had advanced to 800m and were now burning. To the northwest the *abteilung* had placed one *Zug* in this area, where it attracted fire from British tanks, but could not properly engage the tanks because of the distance and difficult terrain. In the west, British tanks were taken under well placed fire from *Kampfgruppe Thinkel*, as well as fire from howitzers of the *4./Artillery Regiment 33*, the 88mm Flak battery of *2./Flak Regiment 33*, and other cooperating artillery. Further activities by the British in the west across the Médenine–Gabès road, north of Zemlet el Lebene, were not expected, because Italian troops were dug in and manning the *Mareth Line* positions there. Regardless, the division ordered that a reconnaissance group from *Kampfgruppe Thinkel* move forward and take up position along the slopes in the north. To further protect that critical flank, the *Luftwaffe* was requested to launch a *Stuka* dive bombing attack there against the British beginning at 1600hrs. However, the *Stukas* did not appear until 1700hrs, and when they did arrive, they flew past in the direction of Médenine. Despite having marked the forward line with identification signals and markers, the *Stukas* dropped their loads on the 6th *Company's* positions in the south; fortunately no casualties were reported. A second Stuka attack took place an hour later, but as the *Stukas* appeared overhead searching for their targets, they missed their reference point and turned more to the southeast along the course of the road and dropped their bombs, which fell approximately 500m from the German positions. During their departure from the combat zone, the *Stukas* flew off to the northeast and directly into unusually strong British anti-aircraft fire coming from the north. At around 1730hrs and shortly before darkness, the British renewed their attacks against the 6th *Company* and *Abteilung Schnelle*; this time each attack consisted of between 6-10 tanks. The combined fire from the panzer companies forced the British to withdraw from these areas, and with darkness the battlefield fell silent once again. As darkness enveloped the German defenders engine noises could be heard from the British lines, and star-shells were being shot off in the far distance. At 1800hrs, the division ordered the defenders to break off contact with the enemy. The Germans began to pull out at approximately 1900hrs, and the withdrawal continued into the night without interference from the British. *Kampfgruppe Irkens*, minus *I./Artillery Regiment 1* and *Flak Battery 2./Flak Regiment 33*, then formed the night watch for the division. At 0045hrs a final withdrawal took place along the Matmata slope, as the route was sealed off by pioneer mine laying detachments. The last rearguard detachments of Flak and *Panzerjägers* withdrew at around 0400hrs, and the entire force was pulled back to a more secure position in the *Mareth Line*, approximately 18km west/northwest of Metameur.[84]

On 24 February, the Regiment reported the following panzer strength: the Regimental *Stabs* had two Befehl panzers and the *I./Abteilung* had thirty-three panzers, while the *II./Abteilung* was also equipped with the same number. On that same day Adolf Lamm recorded that for the past couple of days:

"The company had received many different orders, we are either here or counter-attacking, in reserve, or moving further backwards, or reporting to the Regiment."

At 1500hrs, the *I./Abteilung* was detached from the force of combat troops assigned to the *D.A.K.*, in order to allow them to return to their regiments and divisions. At 2200hrs, the *I./Abteilung* arrived to the assembly area in the olive grove of Lalla (Lala), located a short distance from Gafsa. On the 25th, with some of the Italian formations covering the withdrawal, the *Fifth Panzerarmee* launched a series of small attacks to keep Allied forces occupied; the Germans withdrew to the east and succeeded in disengaging from the area. Lamm's diary noted:

"At 0800hrs we began marching off in groups to El Mdou which lay about 10km south of Gabès. We continued to march, it was all heading backwards and it was enough to make you sick! In the middle of the road was a bristled [shot down] American airplane.

After the road march we arrived at 1700hrs to the palm forest at Mdou, the vehicles have suffered a lot due to the long marching efforts of last deployments the movements have been about 160km."

It was not only the Axis forces which underwent a variety of changes, and by late February the Allied forces were busy reorganizing, and the ground order of battle now looked something like this: Commander of all Allied Forces (Eisenhower) with the *Eighteenth Army Group* (Alexander) consisting of two armies, the *First Army* (Anderson) with the U.S. *II Corps* (Patton), British *V Corps* (Allfrey), and the French *XIX Corps* (Koeltz). The second army was the familiar *Eighth Army* (Montgomery) with its *X Corps* (Horrocks) and *XXX Corps* (Leese) and a *New Zealand Corps* (Freyberg), which was nothing more than the *2nd New Zealand Division* with an attached French infantry brigade. Additionally, there was the U.S. *Fifth Army* (Clark), which was forming with the U.S. *I Corps* (Keyes), *VI Corps* (Dawley), and the British *IX Corps* (Crocker),[85] which was now just arriving in Tunisia. In late February and early March, Allied units in Tunisia increased their combat power with the addition of two fresh British divisions. The British *6th Armored Division* was able to completely refit with American built *Sherman* tanks, and the French *XIX Corps* too was able to turn in much of its antiquated prewar equipment and draw more modern American weapons and equipment. The U.S. *II Corps* was able to regroup its combat formations, and now possessed real combat power instead of separated and scattered elements. The remaining components of the *1st*, *9th*, and *34th Infantry Division* arrived from Algeria, and lost equipment was quickly replaced as fast as the ships, trains, and trucks could bring it to the front. Engineer and other supporting arms specialists improved and expanded the ports, rail, and road networks, and finally, for the troops on the ground, Allied air support was vastly improved. The *I./Abteilung* spent the 26th at Mdou resting and recovering from the previous week's action. Adolf Lamm wrote the following:

"Finally a day for rest, the first since the 12th of February, and the day were filled in with technical services and hygiene. That evening all of the Officers, Commanders and Hauptfeldwebels were at a 'Comrades Evening' [Officers Call] at the Abteilung Stab. During the night and day there were repeated air attacks, which can not shake us in the heavenly palm grove. We have all taken a significant part in latest deployments, which involved first of all the concluding retreat and secondly the worsening weather conditions."

At 0800hrs on the 27th, the panzers from the *I./Abteilung* continued their march south towards Mareth, which they were able to bypass later in the day, and then proceeded to their assembly areas located just behind the German-Italian lines, where they began the technical and mechanical repairs and services. On the 27th, the *8th Company* was officially released from its service with the *I./Abteilung Panzer Regiment 5*, and it returned to the Regiment on the 28th, bringing the panzer strength to forty-eight operational panzers and allowing the reformation of two panzer *abteilung*. The panzers moved off that morning towards Mareth to positions located approximately 10km west of the town in the desert. Further technical services were performed as best they could, and many of the panzers were sent off to the workshop company for more detailed repairs. The *15th Panzer Division* reported a panzer strength of sixty-eight panzers for 27 February; the number included thirty-four Mk IIIs (Sp and 7.5) and twenty-nine Mk IVs (Sp).[86] The end of February 1943 found *Armeegruppe*

Afrika preparing for defense operations, as it no longer had the means and strength to attempt ambitious offensive operations. Along a front that stretched 625km, over a hundred thousand men began to dig themselves into the sand and stones. The *AOK 1* was still manning the *Mareth Line*, and had been holding that position while the *Fifth Panzerarmee* was making its attack against the British *Eighteenth Army*. For the panzer crews of the I./*Abteilung* they continued the march towards Mareth at 0800hrs, and moved to within approximately 10km of the main defensive line, where they began technical and mechanical repairs and services on the worn out panzers and equipment. For some time now the Germans had been expecting an attack by the *Eighth Army* against the *Mareth Line*. Friend and foe alike realized that Montgomery would not attack until, once again, all the pieces were in place to conduct a set piece battle. The *Eighth Army*'s attack was now dependant on a thousand mile long supply route, which because of the destruction left behind in the port cities by the retreating Germans on their withdrawal into Tunisia, forced the British to bring all their supplies overland, instead of into a harbor like Benghazi. Rommel once again looked forward to an encounter with the *Eighth Army*; it was clear to him that the *Mareth Line* could not be held for long, because the position was exposed to a flanking attack. Rommel had hoped to withdraw further into the mountainous heart of Tunisia, where his army would be better suited to defend against the Allied attacks from the west and south. On 1 March, *Generalmajor* Borowietz paid a visit to the candidates of the *KOB* that was still located with the Regiment. The Regiment reported a total strength of 429, with thirty officers, one hundred and eighteen *unteroffiziers*, and two hundred and eighty-one other ranks.[87] The Regiment's command structure from January through March '43 looked something like this:

Regiment Commander	Oberst Irkens
I./Abteilung Commander	Hptm Stotten
1st Company	Olt Keil
2nd Company	Olt Schellhaus, Olt Baumann
3rd Company	Lt Schuberski
4th Company	Lt. Ballhaus
II./Abteilung Commander	Hptm Schnelle
5th Company	Lt Blidschuhn
6th Company	Hptm Hirschfeld, Lt Halverscheidt
7th Company	Lt Krüger
8th Company	Lt Marquardt, Lt Hubbuch

14

The Final Battles of the Afrika Korps March-April 1943

Operation "CAPRI"

By the end of February 1943, the *AOK 1* and *Fifth Panzerarmee* were combined to form *Armeegruppe Afrika*, under the overall command of Rommel himself. Rommel had wanted a unified command under his direction for some time, but had been overruled by *OKW*. With the incomplete victory at Kasserine Pass still fresh in his thoughts, Rommel now turned back to dealing with the British *Eighth Army* before they could strike. Just before the beginning of March, the *Fifth Panzerarmee* had launched Operation "Ochsenkopf" (Ox Head), an offensive that had as its aim the capture of a line of hills south of Tunis and the entire Medjez el Bab basin. This offensive was one of the last German offensives in North Africa, and it was to end shortly after it began with a German defeat. To Rommel, many of the faults of this operation lay with von Arnim himself, but there is no doubt that the lack of manpower and equipment, not to mention the weather, terrain, and amount of resistance encountered led to its failure. What it did, however, was further reinforce Rommel's idea that he must strike at Montgomery before the rest of the *Eighth Army* was brought up and online before the *Mareth Line*. In order to undertake this offensive, Rommel directed his senior commanders, Messe and Ziegler, to develop a plan for striking at the *Eighth Army* before it arrived en-masse. Presently the forces under Rommel's command consisted of the *AOK 1* (Messe), the *D.A.K.* (Ziegler), *10th Panzer Division* (Broich), *15th Panzer* (Borowietz), *21st Panzer* (Hildebrandt), *90th Light* (Sponeck), and the *164th Light* (Liebenstein) with the Italian *Giovanni Fascist* (Sozzani), *Trieste* (La Ferla), *La Spezia*, and *Pistoia* (Falugi) Divisions. In addition, there was the *Armee* artillery (Krause) and various other formations.[1] The plan that was finally agreed upon was presented by *General* Messe, and called for the offensive to be launched on 4 March with a holding attack conducted by the infantry and motorized divisions south of the *Mareth Line*, while the *D.A.K.*, with the three panzer divisions drove south through the Matmata Hills [Djebel Matmatah], and then turned east to attack the British forces at Médenine [Madanin]. Rommel did not particularly like this plan, along with some of his commanders, since there was so much risk involved, but in the end they all favored this plan, as opposed to anything else that might have been conceived and executed in such a short period of time. The problem was just that—time—and Rommel knew that there was little remaining before Montgomery attacked. There were also the tactical problems of maneuver space and number of forces available to conduct this attack. At this time, despite his recent elevation to *Armeegruppe Afrika* commander, Rommel slipped back into despair, and as the battle plans went forward for the attack on the *Eighth Army* at Médenine, he began to wash his hands of it. Since many of the panzer elements within the three panzer divisions had to make the long and exposed journey south from the Kasserine area to the Matmata Hills the operation was postponed for two days, until the 6th. On 5 March, the former regimental commander, Hans Cramer, now a *Generalleutnant,* was appointed commander of the *D.A.K.*, but unfortunately for Cramer, the *D.A.K.* was only a shell of its former self since the days when he last commanded the Regiment in it, and now within a day he was to direct it in an attack which stood a good chance of failing. On the 4th, *Kampfgruppe Irkens* was ordered to begin positioning its panzers for the upcoming attack. Irkens' orders read that he was to move his panzers south through the Matmata Hills past the southern end of the escarpment with Metameur [Al Matamir] to the east. The panzers were to pay careful attention, and to avoid the numerous minefields placed along the Médenine-Matmata road. Then the panzers were to move forward between the minefields to the road junction 12km west of Metameur and Bir Bou Gaba to the northeast, and then finally reach Hir Ksar Koutine. The passages through the minefields had been reported by some of the messengers from *Pioneer Battalion 33*, and that the minefields from the Metameur slope were visible to the south through the border fence. The orders went on to state that it was anticipated that enemy resistance would be difficult to break, and it would be all about speed in reaching the point of attack. Should the panzers encounter slight enemy resistance once the attacks began the panzers were to move quickly along Wadi Hallouf and reach the high ground at Hir en Nraa.[2] For the men of the *2nd Company*, they began their movements to get into position on Friday; there was a half hour preparation for the march, which began at 1830hrs. The panzers began to arrive in an assembly area west of Médenine around 2300hrs. The Regiment formed its battle line with the II./*Abteilung* up front, followed by the Regimental *Stabs* in the middle, followed by the I./*Abteilung* in the rear. Adolf Lamm remembers the movement:

"I remember exactly about this night march with panzers in conjunction with the whole Regiment. We knew, that this upcoming action would dictate our future destiny in Tunisia. The dusk came quick, I can still remember the picture of endless snaking panzers and vehicles over the desert road, complete silence was ordered but the rattle of panzer chains and noise of vehicles were probably audible miles away. Suddenly it was complete darkness, so dark that from the tower [turret] of the panzer [you] were not able to see the end of the cannon. The Richtschütze Rothlaender and Ladeschütze had to walk from the left and from the right of the panzer therefore, in order to prevent the panzer from driving off

241

the road. I sat in the hatch, Olt. Schellhaas stood next to me in the turret. 'Lamm, what do you feel?' he asked me. It was not his style to ask like this. We had been together in several heavy deployments already. If I should be honest, I didn't feel that well. But I didn't want to say so. 'Why should it be different from elsewhere?' I said evadingly. 'So far it always turned out to good'. 'Look', he said, 'the war conduct and soldier are like a lottery game. Even if you're lucky a hundred times, once it will get you. It is only a question of time.' This conversation had impressed me so much, that I can remember it almost word for word after many years."[3]

The *15th Panzer Division* reported sixty-one operational panzers on 5 March. Also on that day the division reported—without *Observer Battery 33, Aufklärungs Abteilung 33*, and one artillery battalion of *Artillery Regiment 33*—a total manpower strength of only 8,470 from the normal compliment of 13,323, which was further broken down into 383 out of the authorized 525 officers and 8,087 of the authorized 12,798 non-commissioned officers, men, and other ranks. The division's panzer strength was a combined sixty-six panzers, of which not all of those were operational. Of the authorized nine command panzers there were only two, of the twenty-five Mk IIs there was only one, of the one hundred and eleven Mk IIIs there were none, of Mk IIIs Sp there were only twenty-four, of Mk III (7.5kz) there were twelve, of the thirty Mk IVs there were none, and of the Mk IVs Sp there were twenty-seven. Of the eight panzer companies authorized to the Regiment it now had only six, and every one of those was under strength.[4] As the *D.A.K.* panzer divisions began to align themselves for the attack, the *15th Panzer* took up positions along the northern flank, where it would drive slightly to the northeast towards Metameur with the Regiment in the lead, and the Zemlet el Lebene as its initial objective. The *21st Panzer* was in the center, and it was to drive towards the south of Metameur, while the *10th Panzer* on the southern flank was to drive towards Médenine. In the north, along the *Mareth Line*, the German and Italian infantry and motorized elements now grouped together into what was called Column Bari, and began their preparations for driving south, centered along the Gabès-Médenine road. Unknown to Rommel and his commanders was that all of the movement prior to the attack, in addition to aerial reconnaissance and radio intercepts, had alerted the *Eighth Army* of the presence of strong Axis forces now taking up positions against its formations south of Mareth. The two day postponement further allowed Montgomery time to rush up additional forces with which to blunt any Axis movements against him. Initially, the *AOK 1* was only opposed by the British *XXX Corps* (Leese), with the *51st Highland Division* (Whimberly) and *7th Armored Division* (Erskine), but with the two day postponement of the operation there was just enough time to allow reinforcements to be moved up from Tripoli. Those forces included the *2nd New Zealand Division, 8th Armored Brigade*, and *201st Guards Brigade*, in addition to the *4th Light Armored Brigade* at Médenine. The British positions, which were spread out along the 30 mile (48km) front, curved around the town of Médenine like a fishhook. In the north, the *51st Division* occupied positions from the Gulf of Gabès to the Gabès- Médenine road. Moving south between the Gabès-Médenine road and Matmata Hills, the *131st* and *201st Brigades* had taken up positions with the New Zealanders extending the line further south towards Médenine. The *8th Armored Brigade* was centered in the north behind the *51st Division*, and the *22nd Armored Brigade* was centered to the rear in the *7th Armored Division's* sector.[5] The Axis plan called for an attack to be launched simultaneously along the front using almost two hundred panzers, two hundred guns, and ten thousand infantry. They were faced by the British, who had roughly three hundred tanks, three hundred and fifty guns, a substantial number of 2 and 6-Pounder anti-tank guns, and almost four divisions of infantry and supporting troops.

During the night of 5/6 March, the elements of the *15th Panzer Division* began to arrive in the designated assembly area; the march there had been difficult, and many units had arrived piecemeal and separated, and to make matters worse, they found other *D.A.K.* units occupying their assigned areas. The last guns of *Artillery Regiment 33* arrived at 2300hrs. At 0515hrs a final briefing was called for by Irkens in order to brief his subordinate commanders for one last time. As *Kampfgruppe Irkens* began to form its line of attack at 0600hrs with some sixty operational panzers, *Kampfgruppen Schiffmann* and *Wissmann* also began to form their lines in order to follow them. The main objective for this attack was the area centered on Médenine and Metameur. Arriving from their assembly area south of the Djebel Tebega, these *kampfgruppen* formed the left flank element of the center attack group; *Panzer Regiment 5* would form the right flank element, with *Panzer Regiment 7* located further south near Ksar el Hallouf. The morning of the 6th dawned with a heavy, grey mist, which had been caused by the heavy rainfall the previous evening. As the attack commenced at 0600hrs that heavy mist initially assisted and masked the movements of the panzers as they began to roll forward. However, before it could get moving the advance was delayed, because the pioneers who were to clear the area south and east from the saddle at Point 208 could not find their way, and failed to effectively clear the area. Soon after, one of the panzers rolled forward and detonated several mines, in addition to rolling over some loose barb wire that wrapped itself around the driving gear and carried away the wire fence. Irkens then personally took charge of the situation and placed himself in the lead of the column in order to continue the march. The point elements reached a position 1 km northwest of Point 152, and after crossing Wadi Oued en Beugrm turned to the northeast. As *Kampfgruppe Irkens* advanced it did so without encountering any enemy. The division's heavy artillery was lined up behind *Kampfgruppe Wissmann*, but just before reaching the track to the northeast of Point 139 that lead to the intersection at Points 144 and 102, the first contact was made at around 0820hrs west of Metameur. The leading elements of the division came under fire from British artillery located near Zemlet el Lebene, and a short while later British tanks were spotted to the right and left flanks. The II./*Abteilung*, in the lead, was in position to attack towards Point 101, while the I./*Abteilung* was near Bir Kinit and poised to strike at Ksar. The initial attacks moved forward quickly, but were slowed by the strong defensive fires being laid down by the British gunners. In an attempt to quiet the British artillery the division called for additional fire support at 0900hrs, but this was not granted, and a planned *Stuka* strike that morning never materialized, so the infantry and panzer elements were forced to go at it alone until friendly artillery could come up to support their attack. In the meantime, the II./*Abteilung* was halted near Point 129, and the I./*Abteilung*, already fighting on unfavorable ground, was seeing its right flank being pushed back. Irkens himself was able to make personal contact with the division commander, and informed him that continuing the attack was only possible with more forces, and even then would only lead to greater losses. With that the division commander ordered a temporary postponement to offensive actions, and stated that the attack would continue at 1200hrs. Adolf Lamm remembered the attack, and had this vivid description of this day:

"It was the worst day, where I participated during the whole of the Africa Campaign, rich of dangers and the threat of falling [dying]. The pictures can't be erased from the memory. From the early morning hours we came under very heavy artillery fire of incomparable violence. We were shooting but I had the feeling that we never clearly had a recognized target. Suddenly, it was probably about 0730hrs, our vehicle was hit; the powerful stroke had shaken our panzer with unimaginable strength. I cried. The heavy radio equipment dropped from its holders on my feet, the panzer

Chapter 14: The Final Battles of the Afrika Korps, March-April 1943

turned a little bit to the side. In the silence that followed Olt Schellhaas cried 'Get Out!' The others whizzed from the hatches, as we had trained so often. I dragged my feet from the radio equipment, seized the hatch and pulled myself high and tried to get to my feet, but my knees failed and I fell down from the panzer. The larynx microphone was still around my neck, but the cable was torn. 'Are you wounded?' asked Schellhaas. At the first moment I was not able to speak. Then I yelled, 'I can't walk' When I took off the microphone, I noticed that I was bleeding. The fragment had cut my lower lip. On the left and right of the larynx there was also bleeding abrasions. Schellhaas yelled 'I'm changing the vehicle, and you should go to find some cover' I was lifted from left and right. The firing howled around us. We had to get out quickly. The terror was stronger than the pain as I tried to run. Others pulled and dragged me as we were just able to get out of there! We hoped to find some cover in the dry streambed, which was surrounded by low hills and therefore not visible. There were some others from different units, amongst them one Major. There was no recognition of ranks here as we threw ourselves on the ground. The following hours were the most terrible and dangerous in my life. It was so, as if the enemy artillery was shooting exactly on this small wadi where we were. Maybe it was really so, because shortly after our arrival a vehicle drove in our proximity and we thought it might be the artillery observer. We thought he might have taken the bearing of our position. We remained pinned down there from 0900-1800hrs. Non-stop and during the many hours there was hell all around us. The sounds were singing badly, whistling, howling in sharp, hissing tones, in dull, spraying impacts, and thunderous descents. I was pushing myself hard into the ground, and wished my nails were claws, with which I could scrape myself into the earth. The sky was light blue and the sun shined. During those moments when I was able to slightly lift my head, I saw in front of me a bush with pale pink flowers which rose on the horizon of a small hill. There a bird sat and sang. The approaching howling charge forced me to quickly look down and when I looked up again, the bird had gone away. In the late afternoon the fire eased. Three others, the Rothländer with the Ladeschütze and the driver, tried to get back to the panzer. They told me later that the artillery round had torn away the machine gun and radio and struck my Sichtluke[observation hatch]. The rounds impact thus had drilled into the panzer almost 20cm from my head. Around 1800hrs with the coming darkness we were able to leave the area where we had laid down in the wadi. I met the units, who advised me further on where to go. We, the separated panzer men and me were supposed to take some English prisoners with us. We marched with them in the suggested direction through the darkness. They could have been able to do us in and easily run away but luckily none of them dared. After approximately a half-hour of marching we turned them over to our forces. Here I met with Uffz Hagen, who took me with his panzer to the 7th Company. It was not possible to continue the journey due to the darkness. Hagen also told me that the whole thing had gone wrong and that all of our forces had to retreat. Lt Houwald from my company was killed. A shot panzer man is the most miserable creature in the field to look at and one soldier gave me his cover as it was pitch-black and very cold. I don't remember if I had eaten at all during the entire day."[6]

Later in the morning, after a softening up by the division artillery, the Regiment moved forward over open terrain at a high rate of speed. The *I./Abteilung* was deployed in a wide wedge on the far left of the axis of advance as it moved towards the positions of the *51st Highland Division*. As the panzers reached the junction of Wadi Negueb and Wadi Hallouf they were greeted by a heavy concentration of British artillery that effectively halted the forward elements and stalled the attack. Over on the right flank, the *21st Panzer* was online with the division, but was halted just two miles west of its objective (Hill 270); here too the British guns not previously under fire came to life and began to pummel the two panzer divisions. The German artillery and infantry forces had a difficult time locating and adjusting fire on the British gunners. Lt Ballhaus and Lt Hubbuch, at the head of the *4th* and *8th Companies*, were seen leading their respective companies forward into the teeth of the anti-tank barrier.[7] The heavy and very accurate artillery and anti-tank gunfire had already begun to take its toll, as four panzers were soon hit and set alight. The *II./Abteilung*, which was attacking towards Hill 138 in the ensuing action, was able to capture thirty-five prisoners during its run up to the hill. Due to the fact that the accompanying *panzergrenadiers* had to remain back in the wake of such strong artillery fire, *Oberst* Irkens then decided to move forward towards the British artillery positions and attempt to destroy them, a tactic which had proven successful in the past, but now as they attempted to do so many of the panzers began taking heavy anti-tank gun fire from well camouflage positions scattered along the ridgelines. At this point, with the momentum of the attack beginning to slow, Irkens now had to deal with both direct and indirect fire, and so he called for the forward observers to place counter-battery fire on the British guns in an attempt to silence them, but to his complete dismay the forward observers were nowhere to be found—they were hunkering to the rear with the grenadiers. However, by 1000hrs the attack in the center had been stopped cold, and the small breakthrough that had occurred near Zemlet el Lebene had been sealed off by the appearance of two troops of *Sherman* tanks from the *7th Armored Division*. Shortly before midday the *kampfgruppe* was then attacked by Allied fighter-bombers, which added their cannons and bombs to the hail of lead being thrown at the panzers. Seven panzers were hit and destroyed in these aerial attacks. The remaining crewmembers would continue to fight with their small arms to help secure the Regiment's remaining panzers from close in attacks. Volkmar Kühn's book mentions the tough fight Irkens had that day:

"Oberst Irkens managed to reach the Allied front line but his panzer was then hit hard. Rolling into cover the Oberst drove on. More and more of his panzers were knocked out and their crews advanced on foot."[8]

By noon Rommel's initial attack plan was a total wreck, but he went ahead with it in a renewed effort by the *15th* and *21st Panzer Divisions*, which continued up the Hallouf riverbed. The Regiment lost two additional panzers that had to be abandoned after rolling over anti-tank mines and throwing their tracks. At 1315hrs another discussion regarding the attack was held by the division commander with his regimental commanders and liaison officers. It was again decided to continue the attack, and they set 1430hrs as the new time for the attack to begin anew. At 1430hrs the attack kicked off, this time with the assistance of the *Stukas* and artillery, which went in against the Tadjera Hills. For the Regiment, I./*Abteilung* was ordered to move back and link up with the *I./Artillery Regiment 33*, while the II./*Abteilung* was sent to link up with the *III./Artillery Regiment 33*. The new direction of attack was to be north, with the I./*Abteilung* ordered to push towards Bir Koutine, while the II./*Abteilung* was ordered to push towards Chott Koutine. The supporting Flak guns were to cover them by firing into the area around Point 174. At this point in the battle Irkens, in an attempt to silence the British guns, requested friendly artillery fire from a nearby battery, which began to lay down a barrage on Point 174. The artillery was soon joined by the rocket launchers of *Werfer Regiment 71*. Unfortunately, most of the shells fell close, but failed to hit and silence any of the guns. The British, however, did not suffer from the same problems as the Germans, and shortly after beginning their fire the German battery was attacked by British fighter-bombers, which came in and destroyed them. The loss of this supporting battery of guns slowed the overall attack, which was now forced to plod step by step toward the British positions all the time coming under an ever-increasing barrage of British artillery and anti-tank guns and fighter aircraft. This constant barrage claimed another twelve panzers that afternoon. Kurt Kathe remembers how he was wounded during the battle:

"Here I was sitting on top of a Mk III and there was a shot on the left side of the panzer, it was not a tank [round], it was a anti-tank gun, I think it was a tank missile [armor piercing]. It ricocheted up and hit me like this, it was a minor wound and I placed a bandage on it and at the end of the battle I mentioned this to the doctor. I was on my way home and would be gone in 30 days anyway."[9]

The panzers were not the only targets of the British gunners that afternoon, as the *21st Panzer's* divisional headquarters became a target that initially kept it from directing its combat elements for over half an hour, and finally forced it to withdraw to the west in order to seek safe haven. That action effectively halted the *21st Panzer's* renewed effort for the afternoon, as it lost control over its combat formations. At 1430hrs the *Stukas* arrived, but were so far from the mark that they were observed by two panzers from the II./*Abteilung*. The attack went in, and again ran a gauntlet of fire from artillery and anti-tank guns. The II./*Abteilung* began its attack towards the chott with the I./*Abteilung* providing fire support, but progress was limited, and by 1720hrs was stalled on the wadi and protective minefield. The *D.A.K.* was now forced to rethink its plans, and so based on the report that the *10th Panzer* had captured Metameur, orders were issued to pull back all forces in the center of the line and attempt to renew the attack the following day with the *10th* and *15th Panzer* exploiting the gains made in the south, while the *21st Panzer* was to go over to the defense. Unfortunately, this plan was based on the false report that the *10th Panzer* had captured Metameur, which was found out not to be true. In the end the panzers were ordered to pull back towards the mountains, which they did, but only under a hail of fire, which cost them more casualties in men and machines, and there they awaited orders. At this point Rommel was forced to accept the fact that his forces were up against a superior and well dug in enemy, and so he called off the offensive. Despite the gains made by the *15th Panzer* that afternoon, they were all for naught when the British counterattacked at 2000hrs and retook the ground. During its return to the initial jump off positions, the *kampfgruppe* took almost one hundred and seventy prisoners from the *51st Highland Division*.[10] That night it was too dark to drive on any further; the division had ordered a withdrawal for 0200hrs. Resupply and recovery operations were not possible due to the heavy shelling and unfavorable terrain, and this became apparent when two *Sdkfz 18* recovery vehicles were lost as they attempted to recover six panzers from the II./*Abteilung* that had been immobilized in a minefield. With the panzers providing over-watch the division first attempted to pull out its remaining artillery and Flak guns of I./*Artillery Regiment 33* and 2./*Flak Regiment 43*. At 0200hrs the Regiment's panzers were in position near Bir bou Gaba, where they took on fuel and ammunition, and by 0510hrs were moving towards their previous assembly area. Later the Regiment moved back to an area about 20km north of Matmata, where it took up defensive positions behind the II./*Panzergrenadier Regiment 115*. Klaus Hubbuch described the combat in this letter excerpt written the following day:

"I have just had my most difficult combat day in a panzer behind me. The attack was against a most difficult enemy position. I drove with the lead company as the lead Zug leader, and first broke through to the position. I received this order. My men were unprecedented alert, and I was in my element, and lucky as usual. In the heaviest of enemy defensive fire, my panzer was damaged, others too due to mines, Pak and artillery fire. But we broke through and were in the middle. We fought the infantry with our weapons, and took many prisoners. I myself was behind the machine gun and thank god I was able to put down Tommies before they could hit us, to be more precise I cannot write of but the commander expressed the recognition to me for this success as the prisoners were important."[11]

During the battle the Regiment was able to claim nineteen 6-Pounder anti-tank guns destroyed, and the total number of British losses amounted to six tanks, sixteen scout cars, thirty-three vehicles, thirty-two anti-tank guns, and roughly fifty captured. These losses were acceptable when compared to the combined German and Italian losses, which amounted to ninety-four killed, over five hundred wounded and missing, and the loss of forty-one panzers. The *15th Panzer* suffered the loss of twenty-four of its panzers, including eleven Mk III Sp, nine Mk IVs, and four Mk III (7.5).[12] The Regiment lost twenty-one of those panzers, including twelve dead and forty-three wounded, in a matter of just twelve hours. Lt Freiherr von Houwaldt of the *2nd Company* was one of those killed, and *Uffz* Hagen from the *7th Company* was wounded.[13] This action marked the final battle for Rommel in his African Campaign; he was to depart in two days' time, having fallen out of favor and ending his illustrious career in the desert with a defeat. Many questioned the reasoning of this attack into a well-prepared enemy defensive line, and most agree that this was Rommel's worst action as a commander in the two years since he had arrived in Africa. One of the most interesting stories about this battle involves the possible betrayal of the plan to the British prior to its commencement. As the story goes there was a suspected Italian officer on the staff of the *AOK 1* who is thought to have betrayed the plan, and this is why it was thought that the British were well prepared and dug in awaiting the attack. On the 7th the Regiment formed the trailing element of the *kampfgruppe* as it took on fuel and ammunition, and continued the march north. *Oberst* Irkens was able to realign and reorganize the Regiment and replace some of the vacated positions. Lt Hubbuch, whose spirited attack the day before had gained him notice by the division commander, was selected to become the new Orderly Officer, or Aide de Camp, to *Generalmajor* Borowietz, and so he departed the Regiment for a position in the divisional headquarters. For Adolf Lamm, his wounds required that he be moved back to the rear, and on that Sunday he wrote:

"Retreat! Lt Keller takes me with his vehicle to the old rest area and in the afternoon to the Supply trains of the II./Abteilung near Mdou where there was a palm spring and heavenly accommodations."[14]

As Rommel departed the battlefield, so too for Klaus Hubbuch, as in a letter to his parents dated the 8th he wrote:

"Unfortunately I must say goodbye to my old combat regiment, my many friends of good and bad times. I came to the division stabs [headquarters] as the personal orderly officer to General Borowietz. Of course, it is for me a difficult and interesting task, but the departure from panzers was really difficult for me. But there will be a come back, the war is not over yet and I have had my most difficult combat days in a panzer behind me."[15]

Also on this day after the battle *Field Marshal* Rommel drove past the men and panzers of the Regiment with a bowed head; the years of strain and desert sickness had taken their toll on the man who was revered by them as a legend, and he spoke briefly to them on this his final visit, for unknown to the men he would depart Africa in two days. Karl Halverscheidt remembers the visit:

Chapter 14: The Final Battles of the Afrika Korps, March-April 1943

"Rommel came for a visit, he always preferred his Swabian Regiment and use to visit us a lot, and his words were short but never forgotten by those of us who were there. 'Keep on Boys'."[16]

Adolf Lamm, Monday, 8.3.43:

"On Monday 8.3.43, I rest and recovery from my wounds, a heavy bruise on the left knee and abrasion on the chin. Olt Schellhaas took care about me in a touching way and drove me in the bucket car [Kubelwagen] to the nearest medical aid station in order to make the x-rays of both knees. Luckily the bones were intact. The left knee was so swollen, that I was not able to walk the whole day. Schellhaas also took care about me and that I received all the necessary items; the covers, toiletry, dishes etc."[17]

On 9 March, as Rommel bid farewell to Africa for the last time, another familiar face to the men of the *D.A.K.* appeared; it was *General der Panzer Truppen* Gustav von Vaerst, the former commander of the 15th *Panzer Division*. Vaerst, who had been recently promoted and given command of the *Fifth Panzerarmee* when Arnim had been moved up to succeed Rommel as the *Armeegruppe* commander, had seen his fair share of action in Africa over the previous two years. Also that day, at 1400hrs, six panzers from the Regiment were sent off to the *Aufklärung Gruppe* to act as reinforcements. The *15th Panzer Division* reported a panzer strength of thirty-six panzers on 9 March 1943. The number included 22 Mk IIIs and 11 Mk IVs.[18] A day later, on 10 March, the *15th Panzer Division* reported a total manpower strength of only 8,813; this was further broken down into 288 officers, 89 technicians, 1,666 NCOs, and 6,770 men. The division's panzer strength was at forty-seven, with Mk IIs 1/24/0/1, Mk IIIs 0/85/0/0, Mk III Sp 17/0/9/6, Mk III 7.5 9/0/5/3, Mk IVs 0/12/0/0, Mk IV Sp 18/0/7/8, and Command panzers 2/7/1/1.[19] By mid-March the Allied forces in Tunisia were just about to go back over to the offensive, and in northern Tunisia the British *First Army* and German *Fifth Panzerarmee* continued to do battle on a lesser scale in an attempt to pin each other's forces down, so that both sides found it difficult to properly support any offensive actions. Also at this time additional forces from both sides were being brought into the area to bolster and reinforce any planned attacks. Montgomery's *Eighth Army* in the south was now preparing for its long awaited attack against the *Mareth Line*. By the 15th Montgomery was ready with a multi-division force to break through the old French positions and drive to the north into Tunis. Despite the rigors of combat and the overwhelming tide arrayed against them, the men still found time to celebrate, for it was important now in any case to help bolster the morale of the men now that the end loomed so near. On the 14th, *Hptm* Hans Stotten, commander of the I./*Abteilung*, was awarded the *Deutsches Kreuz in Gold* for his actions the previous month at Kasserine Pass.[20] In Adolf Lamm's 2nd *Company* the men took a short time out as medals were awarded on the 12th; Lamm was one of those who was awarded the wound badge for his wounds suffered on 6 March. The following day there was also a small celebration when the company took time to wish a happy birthday to their leader *Olt* Schellhaus. Later in the day heavy rains came that caused the ground to become a muddy mess, and even managed to cause some flooding in the wadis. On Wednesday the 17th, the first "vacationers," as Adolf Lamm put it, began departing Tunisia for bases back in Germany. It was apparent that Hitler intended to leave the *D.A.K.* to its inevitable fate, and it was now time for the generals and regimental commanders to get the tired and experienced men and commanders out to fight another day. Rommel had previously been all for the evacuation of the *Panzerarmee* in a Dunkirk style evacuation in order to save the one resource that was not limitless in Germany, and that resource was the experienced men of the *D.A.K.* In another letter written home ten days later and dated 18.3.43 young Lt Hubbuch gives us an idea of what he had gotten himself into at the divisional headquarters:

"So I arrived today to the Division. My new field post number is .... I haven't written to you for 10 days. But it was impossible. I have never thought that it's possible to be that drop-dead-tired and exhausted like I am now, and all we here. The deployment was terribly difficult and hard. Day and night there was no break, here at the division stab absolutely none. How and what is here to work on, is simply amazing. In addition, the general [Borowietz] is extremely smart, drives till the very first riflemen and panzer. He found in me his true companion. We understand each other flawlessly. With a small handful of men we brought armies to hold. But it goes, when the old spirit lives. And we carry for this, each soldier on the front. As for example recently, when after most difficult days the commander with his remaining 40 brave soldiers snatched the bunker height away from the enemy shortly after midnight. The guys assaulted with Hurrah and erected bayonet. Or when we with 7 panzers hit the enemy army in the flank and knocked down the whole plan of Tommy. Unprecedented heroic pieces were accomplished. And now we have combat time-out. I slept like dead almost the whole day under the palm-trees on the grass, now I am fresh again, here is a nice surroundings. And we hope for further things. The paper is a little bit bad, with the deep flight attack recently my car was sifted and everything is again more or less broken. But that's not to worry; just I was not able at this moment to get a different paper. Main thing is that I had again the whole day endlessly lazy. We have again very hot days; temperatures up to 35C and the sand storm are often. Yesterday I received an Italian decoration, I'll send it to you it with the same post and you can translate the document."[21]

Operation PUGILIST GALLOP

As the Axis forces licked their wounds after the aborted failure of Operation *Capri*, Montgomery was just about ready to launch the long anticipated *Eighth Army* offensive against the *Mareth Line*. For this offensive the *Eighth Army* had the *XXX Corps* (Leese), the *X Corps* (Horrocks), and the *New Zealand Corps* (Freyberg). Opposing this was the *First Italian Army* (*AOK 1*) (Messe) and the Italian *XX Corps* (Orlando), with the Italian *Young Fascists* (Sozzani) and *Trieste* (La Ferla) Divisions. In the center of the line was the *90th Light* (Sponeck), and in the west was the Italian *XXI Corps* (Berardi), with the *La Spezia* (Pizzolato) and *Pistoia* (Falugi) Divisions. The German *164th Light* (Liebenstein) was defending the critical sector along the Mareth-Médenine highway, while securing the far western flank was the Italian *Sahara Group* (Mannerini). Along the coastal sector, the *19th Flak Division* (Frantz) employed numerous guns, from the light 20mm to the dual role 88mm, in support of the defense. There were also numerous adhoc and smaller detachments scattered along the line. The *15th Panzer* had the mission of covering the gaps between the Mareth-Gabès highway and the Matmata Mountains. The *21st Panzer* was farther to the north, and would not be available until the 19th. The *AOK 1* had roughly fifty-six panzers under its control, with twenty-nine German and twenty-seven Italian; there were an additional one hundred in D.A.K. reserve with the *10th* and *21st Panzer Divisions*.[22] Montgomery's main attack would commence along a front roughly 1,200m in length and be lead by the *XXX Corps* with its *50th Northumbrian* (Nichols), *51st Highland* (Wimberley), and *4th Indian* (Tuker) Divisions, in addition to the *201st Guards Brigade*. That corps would concentrate and attack between the coast and the main highway in order to breech the Axis defenses. The *X Corp*, which was tasked with exploiting the *XXX Corps'* breeching success, was located behind that corps, and was scheduled to pass through the *XXX Corps* once they had cleared and widened a gap wide enough for the armor to roll through. *Lt. General* Freyberg was appointed to handle the attack through the Tebega Gap with a left hook by his *New Zealand Corps* (Provisional), a multinational force consisting of roughly 25,000 troops from New Zealand, Britain, Greece, France, and her colonies. He would have 120 tanks from the *8th Armored Brigade* and three hundred guns supporting this move.[23] The preliminary attacks commenced during the night 16/17 March, with attacks launched by *XXX Corps* reconnaissance patrols that had the mission of scouting the Axis defenses and gathering intelligence pushing back a number of observation outposts, and to hopefully mislead the defenders as to where the main attack would come. These minor probing attacks succeeded in a number of areas, but in others the Axis defenders were waiting for them, and sent the reconnaissance troops off with a severe beating. In the meantime, the Regiment still had the extremely strenuous work of repairing many of its broken down panzers, and on 18 March the Regiment was in an assembly area northwest of Zarat with forty-one operational panzers. On the 19th an order was sent from *AOK 1* that ordered all its subordinate formations on the *Mareth Line* to stall the enemy advance for as long as possible, so that the situation in Tunisia may be put back in order. The main British attack commenced the evening of the 20/21st with a huge artillery barrage by over 300 guns; the inclement weather prevented the *DAF* from conducting many of its planned bombing raids, however, a few smaller attacks were able to get in under the weather, but these attacks were very limited in size and effectiveness. While the *Eighth Army* moved forward, it was assisted in the north by the U.S. *II Corps*, which began an attack against elements of the *Fifth Panzerarmee*; the aim of this attack was to help pin down Axis forces and prevent them from moving south and reinforcing the *Mareth Line*. As the British *XXX Corps* went ahead, Freyberg's *New Zealand Corps* began its two hundred mile end run west of the Matmata Mountains and the *Mareth Line*, making its way for the Tebega Gap. The *XXX Corps* attack began that evening with the aim of attacking frontally and clearing a path through Wadi Zigzaou, and the establishment of three crossing points. The British attack was lead by the *50th Northumbrian Division*, with support provided by the *50th RTR* equipped with fifty-one Valentine tanks. The Axis defenses consisted of the wadi itself, which was mined on both sides; the banks were also steep, and the bottom of the wadi was soft with water and mud. Behind the wadi was an anti-tank ditch that had been previously dug out and laced with mines, wire, and covered by French blockhouses and anti-tank guns. The British knew of these problems, but it was thought that the wadi itself would be able to handle the crossing at a number of points. The anti-tank ditch was to be taken care of by the leading tank squadrons, with each tank carrying a wooden fascine to assist in crossing the ditch and broken terrain. *Scorpion* flail tanks were to deal with the minefields. The leading elements were able to reach the wadi and cross it, but not without encountering numerous problems. Only four tanks were able to make the actual crossing, with a fifth breaking down in the cleared gap and preventing the passage of any further tanks, even though the infantry were able to get across the wadi without many problems. The fascines that were to aid in the crossing succumbed to problems, and the replacement fascines, located far to the rear, had to be called forward. The *Scorpion* flail tanks, unable to cross the wadi, could only provide cover for engineers with mine detectors, which were now called up and tasked with clearing the openings in the minefields. The infantry was, however, able to move through and begin seizing their objectives.[24] By the morning of the 21st, the British formations were able to regroup themselves from the previous night's fighting, and by later in the day had gained some success by clearing a lane roughly one mile deep and two miles wide. Additionally, some of the Italian forces manning positions along the line took the opportunity to surrender themselves without much of a fight, much to the dismay of their German counterparts. During the day the British engineers had constructed a causeway over the wadi, which allowed the further deployment of the *50th RTR's Valentine* tanks across the wadi. Unfortunately, the tanks were sent ahead of the lighter support vehicles, and the armor, along with the returning rains, all but destroyed the causeway, and hampered efforts to cross forces over the wadi. Despite the rain the entire *50th RTR* was able to make it across the wadi, but was missing its anti-tank guns and artillery. That evening (the 21st) the Regiment was ordered to move from its assembly area towards the *HKL* in order to reinforce and bolster the line. As it moved forward towards Wadi Zigzaou, with the *I./Abteilung* in the lead, the panzer crews were briefed on the growing British situation developing there. Wilhelm Hagios remembered that night especially well:

"The commander's driver, Leidig, who I knew as a truck driver from the supply services (Versorgungstross), and had since then become the driver of Oberst Irkens, was looking for a replacement. He was told that if he could find a replacement, then he could go on leave. He knew that I had driven a kübelwagen in 1941 and at that time I had been at Regiment as ZdV where I was responsible for transporting. So I was called to the company Spiess and he told me to take over the vehicle from Leidig so he could depart on his leave. On 21 March I became the driver for our commander, Oberst Irkens. I drove the vehicle around a little, tested the brakes because before I didn't need any and made the vehicle ready. And then came the alarm on the 21st in the evening, the British had broke through on the Mareth position. We started the march in the evening, with the remaining panzers which were there. Oberst Irkens made sure that the very last panzer would go with us and then during the night I had to overtake the panzer column. There was no map, nothing, I went over open terrain and Irkens told me 'Drive! Otherwise I will put you in prison!' So I did, I overtook the last panzer, his Befehls panzer, where Johannsen his translator was on top. I wanted to drive good and wanted to drive up from behind on the right side and pass by on the right. Then as we began to pass, the panzer bounced up onto the left side skid and tore off the antenna mount. Oberst Irkens shouted at me 'I will put you in prison now!' and I replied 'Oberst, I cannot do anything if the panzer shifts to the right at the moment when I am passing by it'. It was the last time that Oberst Irkens threatened to put me in prison. Later I saw how lucky we actually were, as I had no previous knowledge of the road that dropped down into a wadi about the height of a room and into a very steep riverbed. I had recognized at the last moment that it went down and so we drove down through it and on to the other side. In the morning we arrived at the Mareth position, Oberst Irkens didn't stay with the combat units, but he was with the abteilung and company chiefs. The British were thrown back from the position and in the afternoon Oberst Irkens and I returned to our assembly area and in the daylight I saw what I had missed during the night, the hole in the ground, we really had some luck."[25]

On the morning of the 22nd, the weather permitted little movement on the ground and in the air, as low morning cloud cover and heavy rain showers kept both sides at bay. Later in the morning the Regiment was alerted again, because the British *50th Division* was able to again demonstrate and place effective attacks on the Italian *Giovanni Fascists* Division with engineer and tank support. At 0800hrs, the lead elements of the Regiment went up to assist in the repulse of this attack, which temporarily forced the British to halt their attacks and pull back with the loss of four Valentines. By 1300hrs, after organizing near Zarat, the *15th Panzer Division* was able to move forward with the Regiment and two battalions of supporting grenadiers, which were able to launch a counterattack with almost thirty panzers. As the Regiment went forward it engaged in a minor scuffle with some *Valentines*, which along with some effective artillery fire were able to temporarily halt this counterattack, with the British suffering the loss of only four *Valentines*. But these *Valentines*, of which only eight had been equipped with the 6-Pounder gun, were little match for the heavier gunned Mk III and IV specials with their 50 and 75mm guns. By 1700hrs, the attack had resumed and was in full gear, with the Germans soon getting the best of the situation thanks to the weather conditions, which allowed the panzers to attack the *50th Division* unmolested by the *DAF*. By the time the weather cleared the two sides were too close to give proper aerial support. The commander of the *50th RTR* led three of his *Valentines* forward, only to be killed when his and the two others accompanying him were knocked out. The remaining *Valentines* of the *50th RTR* were then ordered to form a perimeter around the wadi passage point. As the I./*Abteilung* moved in, it began engaging infantry forces that soon forced the remaining infantrymen back towards the wadi and under the cover of their own tanks. Elements of the *4th* and *8th Companies* formed a firing line and began engaging the British *Valentines*, of which there was estimated to be some forty-five on the northern side of wadi. In the firefight that followed the two sides engaged each other at distances of between 800-600m, but by not being equipped with the heavier 6-Pounder main gun the *Valentines* were no match for the German panzers, which were able to claim sixteen tanks for the loss of just six panzers. The *1st Company*, under the command of *Olt* Max Keil, alone claimed the destruction of more than fourteen of the British tanks.[26] As the day began to fade some of the men moved about the battlefield assisting the wounded and speaking with some of the survivors. It was then that they learned that the enemy was a part of the *50th RTR* assigned to the *23rd Armored Brigade*.

The British forces, now tired and low on fuel and ammunition, were ordered to hold out at all costs until darkness, when later on in the evening and following morning of the 22/23rd they were allowed to begin withdrawing back across the wadi, but not before they left almost thirty of their tanks and some 200 prisoners behind. With the failure of this *XXX Corps* attack and the heavy losses sustained to this point, it was now clear that the attack had failed in its task to gain a quick penetration. It was at this point that Montgomery chose to put his main effort in backing Freyberg and the *New Zealand Corps'* attack, which was moving up the west side of the Matmata Hills and the Tebega Gap. At this time that gap was being defended by the forces of the Italian *XXI Corps*, augmented by the German *21st Panzer* and *164th Light Divisions*. Unfortunately for the British, the movement of forces north, even though a majority of them moved behind the Matmata Hills, tipped off the Axis commanders that the next attack would come at the Tebega and El Hamma Gaps. With the situation now stabilized along the *Mareth Line* and the British forces pulling back, the *15th Panzer Division* was pulled back late on the 23rd to an area northwest of the village of Mareth. The move, which would continue during the night of the 23/24th, was made towards the area north of Matmata hills, from where the division could quickly react in order to support the actions at either Mareth or El Hamma. The Regiment was able to be pulled back behind the lines near Zarat in order to reorganize and replenish its fuel and ammunition. On the following day (23rd) the Regiment came under renewed attack by Allied fighter-bombers in its assembly area, and those aerial attacks caused the following losses: three panzers damaged, and four *unteroffiziers* and six crewmembers wounded. Adolf Lamm noted that on Tuesday:

"The boss [company commander] drives off to the Abteilung, which was again deployed. The English attacked at Médenine and are through as if greased. Fifty-five tanks were knocked out with only one loss to us. We continue to receive bombing attacks during the night."

By the morning of the 24th all of the British forces along the *Mareth Line* had withdrawn back to their initial jump off positions, and as the weather began clearing the *DAF* once again appeared overhead and began bombing attacks on Axis positions. Since the 21st the *New Zealand Corps*, which had been able to reach the Tebega Gap almost unopposed, was now probing forward in order to find weak points in the Axis defenses through which it could advance. The New Zealanders wasted little time, and pushed forward with light forces and succeeded in capturing Hill 201, a key piece of terrain on the south side of the Tebega Gap, as well as its Italian defenders. Plans by *General* Mannerini and *Oberst* Hildebrandt, the commander of the *21st Panzer*, to launch a counterattack by that unit in order to retake this key hill were cancelled. Also on that day *General* von Arnim spoke with *General* Messe and ordered him to pull out from his positions and move towards the *Chott Position* (Wadi Akarit). The *Chott Position* was thought by some, including Rommel, to be a better position that could be more easily defended and held. Surprisingly, Messe was not immediately in favor of this move, and instead favored launching a counterattack against Mareth with the *15th Panzer Division*, but the actions at Tebega cancelled these plans, and the following morning the Italian infantry began to pull back. During the night of 24/25 March, the *15th Panzer Division* was in positions southeast of Djebel Halouga. On the 25th, with pressure building at Tebega Gap and to the north at Maknassy, von Arnim was now faced with the decision of a mandatory withdrawal from the *Mareth Line* before those Axis elements manning it became hopelessly cut off and lost for good. It was an especially hard time for the men, as many of them had been through a great deal together since the first of the year, and even some of the older hares, or *"Alten Hasen,"* which had seen difficult times before, but always seemed to buoy up when it counted, soon became discouraged, and they seemed to know the end was near. Certain key leaders and experienced men were sent back to Germany on leave or detailed to some other position. As Adolf Lamm describes, this time it did not look as if many of them would be coming back, and so now many of the men began to feel as if they were being abandoned and sacrificed:

"Thursday 25.3.43 the combat squadron was back at Gafsa. Olt Schellhaas had gone on vacation and Lt Thamphald had taken over the company. I had diarrhea! The peculiar atmosphere began to establish itself, Schellhaas went away, and Stotten was gone to a 'vacation' as it was told to us. We knew and felt that there was nothing left to save in Tunis but quietly we hoped that we would be transported out. Lt Thamphald, until recently the tight, very brave and humanly extraordinary officer, had changed after the wounds he had received, something seemed to be broken in him and now he was leading the company!"

The facts were now becoming clear that the *Panzerarmee* and *D.A.K.* must do what it could in order to save what it could. The equipment and panzers could be replaced, albeit now an almost impossible feat due to the superior strength of the Allied forces in the Mediterranean, but those experienced gunners, drivers, and junior leaders had to be saved in order to train and raise a new crop of young inexperienced recruits. Utilizing the tricks that had made it famous, the company, battalion, and regimental commanders began to find excuses and ways to get their men out. Using such reasons as old wounds or previous illnesses, or the fact that a man had not been on home leave in some time, a few managed to find a plane or ship and returned back to Italy. The night of the 25th there was a repeat performance of the previous night's bombing, in which the *DAF* bombers hit the remaining German rearguard elements at Tebega and El Hamma.

247

The *21st Panzer* and *164th Light Divisions*, which had both been sent to the north in order to close the Tebega Gap before the New Zealanders could get through it, took up their positions along the eastern end of the gap, and were initially very successful in their defense, as the New Zealander attacks met with little success. However, back on the *Mareth Line*, the *XXX Corps* was not sitting idle, as Montgomery began to launch a new offensive aimed at finally breeching the *Mareth Line*. Since the sector and gaps created by the departure of the *164th* had not been filled in sufficiently, it was here that the British hoped to outflank the *Mareth Line* and get into the rear of the Axis position. In order to do so the *5th* and *7th Indian Brigades* from the *4th Indian Division* were sent west through the Matmata Hills and ordered to pursue the rearguards of the *164th Light*, and eventually link up with the New Zealanders coming out of Tebega near the town of Matmata. On 26 March the *2nd New Zealand Division*, followed by the attached *8th Armored Brigade* and the British *1st Armored Division*, moved forward behind a blowing sandstorm against the Tebega Gap. The fighting went on all day; the infantrymen and tankers were aided in their mission by the good weather and the *DAF*, which came in to pound the *21st Panzer* and *164th Light Divisions*, which at the time were defending the exits to the gap. The air attacks by the *DAF* were so devastating that they effectively cut off and destroyed many of the Italian and German elements, and while they attempted to recover they were greeted by a rolling barrage of artillery on which the tanks and infantry quickly followed up. The situation was such and the damage inflicted so great that the *164th* failed to exist as a cohesive unit, and the *21st Panzer* had but a few panzers left, and those that were intact were pushed back without a thought. The attack was able to push on for about four miles, where it was then forced to halt in the growing darkness. However, this halt did not last long, for as soon as the moon came up to light the surrounding landscape the attack continued. In the darkness the New Zealanders bypassed a number of smaller Axis units, and by the morning of the 27th had reached the southern edge of El Hamma. These armored attacks by the *1st Armored Division's 2nd Armored Brigade*, heavily supported by the *DAF*, were finally able to break the last remnants of resistance near the Tebega and El Hamma Gaps, and the allied armor was able to begin its advance toward El Hamma in strength. As the *1st Armored Division* was driving hard for that town it was halted just a few miles short of its objective when it ran into a scratch force consisting of a few panzers, artillery, Pak, and Flak guns that were able to halt the armor and allow the small, scattered groups from the *164th Light* to reach the town and assist in its defense. As the *New Zealand Corps* and *1st Armored Division* raced for the towns of Gabès and El Hamma, the *D.A.K.* and *AOK 1* ordered the *15th Panzer Division* to launch a counterattack towards El Hamma. However, since the majority of the division had been further south near Zarat providing support and over-watch for the *AOK 1* and was still manning the *Mareth Line*, and was only now beginning to fallback towards Gabès, it would take some time before the *15th Panzer* was able to move north and hopefully influence the situation there. As the Regiment once again prepared to meet the enemy Horst Sonnenkalb remembered how his panzer was still ready for action:

"So came the 26th of March. Our Regiment possessed about 18 to 20 panzers, about a company in force as well. Amongst them was my panzer. It already showed numerous wounds [scars] as it was heavily damaged. From the outside one would think it was a scrap collector. But it was still ready for operations! Many asked me, if the thing was still operational and able to drive. I answered: 'Faultless, just a honey'. They went away smiling and shaking their heads."[27]

On the evening of the 26/27th, the last defenders of the *Mareth Line* evacuated their positions as the *15th Panzer* made its way to the northwest in the hopes of cutting off the *New Zealand Corps*. Although some estimates have the Regiment possessing some fifty panzers, initially it was only able to commit a small panzer force in an attempt to halt the Allied breakthrough. By the morning of the 27th there was no hiding the fact that the Axis forces south of Gabès and El Hamma were in serious trouble. To the northwest, the U.S. *II Corps* was preparing to launch an attack from El Guettar against Fondouk; the *AOK 1* forces were still moving north and strung out from Mareth to Gabès, with the British hot on their heels, and to the west, the *4th Indian Division's* infantry brigades were secured in the Matmata Hills. The New Zealanders had now broken through at Tebega and were meeting scattered but determined resistance as they took aim at Gabès. As the Regiment neared its objective it was fortunate to cross just in front of the main New Zealand force that was attempting to get to Gabès, but it then bumped into the right rear flank of the *1st Armored Division* making its way towards El Hamma. The panzers began to engage the lead New Zealand elements and the tanks of *1st Armored Division*. In Volkmar Kühn's book he has the following quote from *Oberst* Irkens on the battle that took place; unfortunately, he has placed it in the wrong place in his book, as Irkens describes:

"Oberst Irkens describes the action in his terse style;
In the morning twilight we came upon an assembly of enemy trucks with munitions and fuel, obviously meant for the enemy tanks which had broken through. They were destroyed or captured, not a single truck escaped. We reached and secured the breach in the line, but a further advance was impossible, because at that moment 50 tanks which had broken through and then been cut off from their supplies came rolling back. They were engaged by the Ihde Company and then by the following tanks and anti-aircraft guns of the division. After suffering losses they turned away to the west. In the area of the breach in the line we found about twenty cut off and stranded tanks of PR5 and refueled them. The great success of the day was preventing of the British outflanking of the Mareth position. We were able to withdraw the units still holding out there to the Schott position north of El Hamma and Gabès."[28]

The Regiment had a difficult fight on its hands, as its panzers fought off over one hundred and twenty *Grant* and *Crusader II* tanks. The Mk IVs of the *4th* and *6th Companies* were able to account for some fifteen tanks destroyed this day, but were soon overwhelmed by Allied air and ground elements, which quickly forced them to withdraw towards Djebel Halouga. Some of the men who fought there that day remembered that the Grant tanks took up over-watch positions and formed a firing line at 2,000m distance, and with their 75mm guns began to lay down a base of fire in order to cover the deployment of their combat squadrons. After the battle Kurt Kathe remembers some of the New Zealanders he encountered:

"After the battle we took many prisoners, also some New Zealanders; we once took 20 people, officers amongst them. We didn't do anything to them, drove them to POW camp, they were well treated and fed, even as POWs. One nice evening close to the end, me and my adjutant Albert, came out of the tent and saw a half-black man running through the desert. I don't know exactly where they were from and I was wondering where they were from and it turned out they were from Johannesburg, South Africa. We spoke with them and found out that they were not even soldiers, one was the truck driver. One I let go and the other I made him my adjutant 'my number two', he washed himself and tried to be white, he tried to become white. I told him 'Comrade, you'll be never white'. I invited him to go to my tent to sleep, as I had such a big house tent. He said 'No', he didn't want as he was British and slept near my tent, later I built him a

Chapter 14: The Final Battles of the Afrika Korps, March-April 1943

small tent and had him as an orderly until the end, he was always with me. He found me the food and other soldiers asked where did we get him from? I told them we have him as a cook and cleaner, he was a nice guy, he told me he wanted to go to Berlin to sweep the streets. But in the end we had to give him up, as we were returning to Germany, and he went to POW camp at Tunis."[29]

Late in the afternoon the situation calmed some, and the Axis forces were able to halt the Allied attacks until the following day. As those scattered and worn out defenders continued to hold in front of Gabès and El Hamma they were able to buy a few precious hours for the slower elements of *AOK 1* as they made their way north. With the loss of both the Tebega Gap and the *Mareth Line*, there now began an all out retreat towards the *Chott Position* at Wadi Akarit, the next line of defense for Axis forces in southern Tunisia. The stubborn resistance and Axis counterattacks that took place between Tebega and Gabès allowed the predominately non-mobile Italian forces to successfully pull out of the *Mareth Line* and move north covered by the *90th Light*. That evening, as the Regiment pulled back in the face of overwhelming pressure, they did so with less than twenty operational panzers. The losses for the Regiment that day totaled six panzers destroyed or damaged, seven soldiers killed, and twelve wounded.[30] Adolf Lamm wrote on Saturday, 27.3.43:

"Stand-by of the alarm zugs. The previous evening was the celebration of the birthday of Uffz Grall. The Combat supply line returns from Gabès and distributes great passwords! The Kampfstaffel is in Gabès and seems not to get back to the Zug. Probably the English broke through the Mareth-position. Olt Tschech was taken prisoner with the field kitchen of the 1st Company."

As dawn broke over the battlefield on the 28th the Allies again renewed their attacks on the Axis forces defending around El Hamma and Djebel Halouga. The British attacks should have crushed all resistance on the previous day, but they had once again been thwarted in their attempts by determined resistance. Finally an attack on the southern flank of the *15th Panzer* by a British armored column succeeded in forcing back that flank, and the British were able to capture the area east of Djebel Halouga. This move now threatened to cut off and trap those forces of the *164th Light* that had been holding firm near El Hamma. It was in this area that the majority of the Regiment's panzers were located, attempting to block and hold the British and New Zealanders as their comrades to the south continued to make their way through Gabès. It was also during that Sunday morning at about 0830hrs when OGefr Wilhelm Bühler, a former gunner in the *1st Company*, was captured about 20km southwest of Gabès. Bühler had been with the Regiment since December 1940, and he was one of the first men of the Regiment to arrive in Africa in 1941. On 17 June 1941 he was seriously wounded and spent the next six months in hospital before finally getting back to Germany in January 1942. He served for some time with *Reserve Battalion 7* in Böblingen, but returned to Africa in early 1943 in time for the last bitter battles in Tunisia. After being taken prisoner, Buhler was to spend until April 1948 as a British PoW in Egypt working under harsh conditions in *POW Camp 306* along the Suez Canal. He remembers:

"On 15.1.43 I landed again for my second time on African soil and was connected with my unit the 1st Company I./Abteilung near Gabès in Tunisia. Because of my Reich's driving license of II and III class, I was posted to the combat supply troops. The column started in the early morning with munitions, fuel, water, provisions, etc and was brought for the combat troops in the desert. An Oberleutnant lead the column. Because of the sandstorm we could not see too well and we came to an area of an armored unit of the forces from New Zealand. Defense was not possible. We had only pistols and rifles and to resist was suicide. So we gave up without firing a shot. While in the PoW Camp from 1943-45 our rations were minimal from 1946-48 they were a little better. For eating we had beans with cockroaches, we called them motorized beans. We were given black corn noodle bread with baked cockroaches and a greasy spread we called knee grease. We would say we are eating motorized beans and knee grease. The rice was never cleaned; we had one loaf of black bread for 10 men, 800 men to one water pipe. The summer temperatures were 45-48 C degrees in the night and 15-20 degrees at night. We had one small tent for 10 men, there was no green and we worked building barracks and roads, our main place was the Suez Canal Zone."[31]

As Wilhelm Bühler was being led away to the prisoner of war cages in Tripoli, a different situation was befalling Uffz Hermann Eckardt, a panzer commander in an Mk IV. Eckardt was one of those who was lucky enough to manage to get out of Africa before the end came. Eckardt was due home leave, and so he was sent back towards Tunis, where he was able to catch a flight on a *Ju-52* a few days later and flew out to Naples. As he left Africa, he was one of the very few individuals that had managed to fight in all of the Regiment's battles since May 1941. As a gunner and panzer commander, he had a total of six panzers shot out from underneath him, while being able to claim twenty-five tanks by the time his service in Africa came to an end. This would be only the beginning for this panzer ace, as later during the *Russian Campaign* he would be credited with the destruction of seventy-eight Russian tanks. He would later be decorated with the *Deutsches Kreuz in Gold* and *Ritterkreuz* for his actions there. What is almost unbelievable is that Eckardt was not wounded until the last day of February 1945. This wound was to ensure that he spent the remainder of the war in a military hospital near the family's farm and miss those last terrible days of the war in the east. He had this to say about his last days in Africa:

"I did not think I would ever be able to get out of Afrika, many of the crews of the panzers had been interchanged and only a few of the crews and technical personnel were able to be released, possibly because they needed us urgently or somewhere else, but it was a surprise and so we went back from the Mareth position and this was the last combat for me in Afrika."[32]

The night of the 28/29th, under a bright moon, a hail of bombs fell on the Axis positions around Gabès and El Hamma, and the remaining Axis forces were ordered to withdraw north of those locations. Adolf Lamm's diary notes:

"On Monday the 29th of March saw the heaviest, uninterrupted bombing and Tiefflieger-attack during the whole day. The enemy probably broke through at Gafsa and Mareth. The alarm was given at 2400hrs, and the men ordered to break down their tents and prepare to move out. Some parts of the company drive with hitchhikers."

The following day both towns were occupied by the British and New Zealanders. On the following evening a further withdrawal was ordered to the *Chott Position*. On the 30th, while the men took the brief opportunity to rest, plans were being made for later that day, when they would depart to a new assembly area located some 25km south of Sfax in a beautiful olive grove. Even though the British had been slow in their pursuit, their pressure continued to be felt, as the Axis forces began to settle into their new positions, and once again the mobile formations were tasked with providing a rearguard to hold back the British.

The Defense of Wadi Akarit

The *AOK 1* had just been able to make its way into the *Akarit Position*, where it awaited the last remnants of the German rearguards, which were still full of fight and putting up stiff resistance. However, as the *AOK 1* moved into its new positions along the wadi, it did so without a large number of its men and machines. Almost 7,000 men had been lost, most of them from Italian non-mobile units that had surrendered to the *Eighth Army* since the battle at the *Mareth Line*; it is fortunate that more were not lost, as once again the *Eighth Army* had been all too slow in its pursuit of a beaten and scattered foe.[33] As for combat power, the majority of the Axis mobile forces had managed to escape capture and bring out with them what they could. The *Akarit Position* was initially held by the remnants of two Italian Corps, the *XX* and *XXI*, with a standard corseting of German units interspersed among them, and so it fell to the *15th Panzer* and *90th Light* and a few additional ad hoc formations to stiffen the Axis lines at Akarit. The Wadi Akarit position was a short natural line of defense that stretched some 15km from the Mediterranean coast to the Djebel Fatnassa (Hill 275) and the Chott el Fedjadj. In the middle of the line was the Djebel Roumana (Hill 170), which afforded the defender a clear field of observation along the coastal sector, and also to the Tunis highway over to the west. The wadi itself was quite deep for the first 5km from the coast to the Gabès-Sfax highway, but from that point on the wadi began to even out, and was in some locations shallow enough to negotiate by tanks. From the highway to the Djebel Roumana the wadi and other natural defenses were reinforced by an anti-tank ditch, and supplemented with a double belted minefield and a number of smaller minefields located near critical points. The western section of the line was made up of a series of low hills that rose to the highest point at Ras Zouai (1,000ft) and were more than a mile in depth. It was a good position, with the Mediterranean securing one flank and a vast swamp securing the other, which would require any opposing force to attack the position head on, or be forced to traverse the chott, or conduct an amphibious assault. Both of those options were out of the question at this point in the campaign. The greatest problem that faced those Axis forces emplaced along the Wadi Akarit was that, although the position was not of great length, there was almost nothing left (both men and materiel) with which to defend this line. The position also lacked the depth and reserves necessary to strengthen and reinforce weak points, and to seal off any breakthrough attempts. By now the *D.A.K.* and Italian *First Army (AOK1)* were all but emasculated, with the *10th* and *21st Panzer Divisions* having been recalled farther to the north to face the U.S. *II Corps* attacks against El Guettar and Maknassy. Fortunately, there was the support of nine batteries of 88mm guns from the *19th Flak Division* that had formed a gun line just north of the main line of defense in order to provide both anti-aircraft and anti-tank defense. There were also an additional four batteries placed further north as anti-aircraft protection, and all of these batteries were also prepared for the dual ground and air roles. The Axis defensive alignment took on a somewhat familiar disposition, with the *Young Fascists* occupying positions that stretched from the coast eastwards to the positions manned by the *90th Light*, which was assigned the defense of the vital Gabès-Sfax highway. The *XX Corps' Trieste* Division held positions along the western flank of the *90th* towards Djebel Roumana (Hill 170), and from there the *Spezia* Division extended the line between that djebel to the Djebel Fatnassa (Hill 275). Moving west into the *XXI Corps* area was the *Pistoia* Division, followed by the remnants of the *164th Light*, which was centered on Hill 285. The last element in line was the Italian *Saharan Group*, which had taken up positions on the extreme western flank. The *15th Panzer*, which represented the only true mobile reserve, was located just north of the *XX/XXI Corps* boundary. One might think that given this position and the number of divisions available to defend it the expectations of holding this line would be good. However, at this point in the Tunisian campaign, those Italian forces previously mentioned were so badly demoralized that they would be more likely to surrender than fight. In addition to this, most of the units within the *Panzerarmee* and *D.A.K.* were now down to about battalion strength. Only the *90th Light* had any semblance of a division left, and was the strongest of all the German divisions facing the British at this time. For the Regiment, by this time it was now down to approximately twenty-two operational panzers. Since there were more veteran panzer crews than panzers available, many of the men were either sent back to Germany and Italy or placed into the line as infantrymen. According to Kurt Kathe:

"In North Africa, at the end when there were no more panzers, all of the panzer troops; commander, gunners, loaders and drivers all went off [to serve] as infantry."

On the night of the 31st the Axis defensive alignments were tested when a number of small reconnaissance patrols were sent out in order to probe and test the strength of the Axis positions in order to determine the possibility of conducting a frontal attack. The *Eighth Army*'s plan of attack was nothing new, as it called for a breech being made in the Axis line by the infantry heavy *XXX Corps*, and once that had been achieved and secured, the armored formations of the *X Corps*, with almost 500 tanks, would be used to exploit the gap and drive the Axis out. It was thought that this time the *AOK 1* would be finished once and for all. To Axis planners, it was no secret that Montgomery always took his time and planned out his set piece battles, which he preferred to launch on moonlit nights. He had already done so on numerous occasions, but this time that was not possible, because the next moon phase that would allow him to have those conditions would not come any earlier than the 15th. Montgomery was now able to take advantage of this thinking and was talked into hitting his adversary, and launched his attack quickly and on a moonless night. The date of the attack was set for the night of 5/6 April. In the meantime, the tired and exhausted panzer crews and maintenance personnel tried to grab what sleep they could. With the *DAF* as active as ever the men took the time to set up their shelter halves and tents to protect them from the cold nights, but they also took the time to build slit trenches for protection against bombing and strafing attacks. The first days of April passed by uneventfully, but by Saturday the 3rd, the Regiment was ordered that evening to move from its present location the following morning and transfer its assembly area to the other side of the Gabès-Sfax road. After this move took place, on the 4th Lt Thamphald turned over command of the *2nd Company* to Lt Schuberski. The men had been settled into an assembly area along the Gabès-Sfax road in an olive grove that offered some protection against the incessant *DAF* air attacks.[34] On the night of 5/6 April the British struck. The attack was launched by the *4th Indian Division* (Tuker), and came at the most unexpected place, the Djebel Fatnassa. Montgomery's plan had called for all of the divisions in the *XXX Corps* to be aligned to the west of the coastal road in the sectors manned by the *Trieste*, *Spezia*, and *Pistoia* Divisions, since it was expected that any attacks launched here would be met by less resistance. Another factor for this alignment was that, despite the hills, the terrain obstacles west of the Gabès-Sfax highway consisted of much smaller stream beds, and the wadis were less deep. The initial attack against Djebel Fatnassa was launched by a tough *Gurka Battalion* that went forward up the slopes in the pitch-black darkness. By the early morning of the 6th the Gurkas had captured most of the hill, and had driven off the Italian troops manning positions there. As soon as the hill was

Chapter 14: The Final Battles of the Afrika Korps, March-April 1943

secured, British sappers then began to clear that portion of the anti-tank ditch that ran up to the bottom of the hill so that the tanks and armored vehicles from the *50th Northumbrian Division* and *3rd RTR* could get through. The main attack began at around 0500hrs, when British artillery fired a heavy bombardment by some 450 guns into the Axis line near Djebel Roumana. It was this bombardment that would lead the way for the *XXX Corps*. Following the artillery, the *51st Highland Division's 152nd Brigade* led the advance towards Djebel Roumana. As the *50th* and *51st Divisions* were moving forward, the *201st Guards Brigade* pushed a short distance up the Gabès-Sfax highway in order to prevent any Axis counterattacks, and to be ready to exploit any Allied gains. Farther to the west, additional elements from the *X Corps* were to be sent in closer to Chott el Fedjadj in order to launch a feint attack there. The attacks were making good progress, and by 0800hrs Djebel Roumana had been taken by the *152nd Brigade*. Even though the two key hills had been taken, elements of the *50th Division's 69th Brigade* were being held up on the anti-tank ditch and Pak gun line that lay between the two hills; they would not reach their objectives until after midday.[35] By 0930hrs the situation was becoming clear to the *D.A.K.*, which then released its reserves to General Messe in the hope that he could contain the attacks by the *XXX Corps* with the small number of panzers and grenadiers available. By midday, von Arnim had arrived at the headquarters of *AOK 1* in order to speak with Messe and determine whether the situation was hopeless or not. Arnim determined that it was not yet time for another withdrawal, and so he ordered in some reinforcements from the *Fifth Panzerarmee* in the form of *Panzergrenadier Regiment 47*. Arnim also ordered Messe to give all his available vehicles to the remnants of von Liebenstein's *164th Light* so that it could respond when and where he needed them to. Orders were then issued for elements of the *15th Panzer* and *90th Light* to launch counterattacks against Djebel Roumana in order to retake the hill. By midday, the attack launched by the *90th Light's Grenadier Regiment 200* was successful in retaking a portion of the eastern edge of Djebel Roumana. Also that afternoon the Regiment's panzers and supporting grenadiers had succeeded in reaching the northern portion of the hill in the *Trieste* Divisions sector, where they were able to push some of the *152nd Brigade's* infantry off of the djebel. However, the British infantry continued to hold on to a good portion of the hill when the *Valentine* tanks of the *40th RTR* arrived. It now looked as if the British would retake the hill and overrun those scant reserves that had been sent in to help; however, the panzers held their ground and succeeded in knocking out almost all of the *40th RTR* tanks. Unfortunately, this was about the only victory that could be achieved that day, as the pressure by the *X* and *XXX Corps* was beginning to show. By mid-afternoon, with fuel and ammunition running desperately low for both the panzers and grenadiers, they were forced to withdraw, which allowed the British infantry to retake the hill. It looked as if the game was up until a bit of good news arrived, when some of the panzer and grenadier elements that had been utilized in containing the U.S. *II Corps* attack near El Guettar began to arrive in the area. Those forces were now on their way south to assist *AOK 1*, and would soon be attacking the western flank of the British advance. That attack was to be launched by the panzers and grenadiers of the *Centauro* and *21st Panzer Divisions*, and was aimed at hitting the infantry of the *4th Indian Division* near Djebel Fatnassa and Point 152. Unfortunately, the attack was plagued by time and mechanical difficulty, as well as *DAF* fighter and dive-bomber attacks, which turned what should have been a counterattack into more of a demonstration. By the late afternoon the situation looked all but over, despite the fact that the Axis infantry was still holding out along the majority of the line. The situation was almost too great, as the British had captured two key pieces of terrain, fuel and ammunition was almost gone, almost all of the attempts to halt the British advance had failed, and now there were a number of dangerous gaps beginning to open in the Axis lines, which despite all attempts could not be straightened out. To von Arnim and his staff the situation looked critical but not terminal, so he prepared to issue orders to Messe informing him that the formations in *AOK 1* were to conduct a limited withdrawal to the north of Wadi Akarit. However Messe, after speaking with his senior commanders at around 1700hrs and hearing from them that their men were too exhausted, and that the ammunition was so low that neither was capable of holding on for another day, issued orders for the withdrawal to begin at 2000hrs. This time the withdrawal was ordered for the positions at Enfidaville, and once again it would fall to the mobile elements to cover the retreat and protect the slower infantry formations as they trudged the 150 miles there. The British planned on a continuation of the attack on the 7th, but during the night the final rearguards withdrew, leaving the battlefield to the British. With the Axis forces falling back the British began their pursuit the following morning, but were slowed when they ran into the 88mm guns of the *19th Flak Division*, which were able to check the follow-on advance for a short time. The 150 miles to Enfidaville would take five days to cover, and as they fell back the *90th Light* was responsible for covering the eastern flank closest to the coast, while the *164th Light* took over the center sector. The *15th Panzer* was responsible for covering the inland flank, where its left flank was covered by the elements of the *D.A.K.* under Hans Cramer. Even though this was a very short battle, in terms of the number of actual fighting days, the loss of over 5,000 Axis soldiers was almost as high as those suffered in the Mareth battle. The Germans had suffered the loss of only 125 men captured, while the Italians had over 5,200 men taken prisoner; these numbers go a long way in pointing out that the Italians were about finished as an effective fighting force, and their ability to withstand further actions was suspect.[36] On Wednesday the 7th, the *DAF* again carried out numerous bombing attacks on the retreating Axis forces, and these attacks came both during the day and night. Even though the attacks did little in terms of damage and casualties inflicted, they did much to worsen the morale, especially in the Italian ranks, who would continue to surrender in large groups and hamper efforts in attempting to maintain unit cohesion and discipline. On the following day a sand storm blew up that aided the Germans and Italians as they attempted to make their way back to Enfidaville. With the retreat of *AOK 1*, the supply dumps of Sfax were cleaned out and evacuated north, all the while under a hail of bombs from the *DAF*. The 8th also saw the loss of *Olt* Max Keil, commander of the *1st Company*, who was killed in action along with his crew defending the retreat of *AOK 1* north of Wadi Akarit. Kiel had been a long serving member of the *1st Company*, and had served in the company while it was under the command of such noted figures as Hans Kümmel and Otto Stiefelmayer. And like his former commanders, Kiel too was awarded a *Ritterkreuz*, although posthumously, on 20 April for his actions as company commander, and for engaging and destroying numerous Allied vehicles during the battles of March and April 1943. It was Kiel who had replaced Hermann Eckardt as the panzer commander in his Mk IV. Unfortunately, Kiel's name is missing from many of the lesser works detailing the exploits of these highly decorated men.[37] Hermann Eckardt, who was replaced by Kiel as the commander of a Mk IV, mentioned that he always seemed to have a "scratchy throat." This was the common term used by those veteran soldiers when describing young and ambitious officers who longed for action and glory. As the retreat continued it crossed the Sfax-Faïd road on the 9th, while later that Friday, the Regiment's *2nd Company* moved off at 1500hrs to march the dozen miles north to El Djem (El Jem) until it was approximately 15km from Sousse (Susa). Adolf Lamm remembered:

"At around midday on the 10th the remaining elements of the commando arrived and joined up with the advanced elements. It had

barely escaped from the British and when it arrived was in need of almost everything. At 1800hrs again the panzers marched off, where the men began to set up the tents and make themselves as comfortable as possible. The British were pushing very hard and right on their heels."

It was also during this time that there was a link-up near Kairouan between the British *Eighth* and *Eighteenth Armies*, which had been driving east in its attempts to cut off the retreating *AOK 1*. On 11 April the first troops arrived at the Enfidaville position, but this was a position only in name, as little had been done in the previous months, and terrain surrounding the position was not the best on which to halt the British. The previous day, *General* Messe had made the recommendation to von Arnim that the defensive line be moved back to some foothills to the north, but was refused permission to do so until the 14th, when Arnim was finally able to pay a visit to the area and see for himself the terrain on which the line was to be formed. During the retreat, the Regiment had been deployed as a rearguard in order to launch quick strikes against those leading British elements that came too close to the *AOK 1*. Since the order to withdraw had been issued, the mobile formations had moved off to their pre-designated defensive points, while much of the non-mobile elements were forced to walk back. The plan again was a repeat of previous withdrawal plans, whereby the Italians would disengage first and move back while the German formations covered their retreat. Along the way some of the Regiment's rearguard elements fought off attacks by their old nemesis, the "Highlanders" of the *51st Division*. During these attacks the losses to both sides were minimal, as neither had time for a set piece battle. During the final days of the retreat the Regiment was forced to retreat to a new defense position, which was located near the heights of Di Zaghouan (Hill 1295). After a march of over 250km, which was often interrupted in order to receive fuel, the Regiment reached its assembly area located in the area of Pont du Fahs on the 12th with fifteen operational panzers.[38] The British had kicked off their pursuit at 1000hrs on the 7th by sending the *XXX Corps* along the coast and the *X Corps* inland towards Gafsa. During this point in the campaign, all German formations within *AOK 1* were now being controlled by *Generalmajor* Fritz Bayerlein, the *AOK 1* Chief of Staff; *General* Messe was still in command of the army, but he issued orders to only those Italian formations still fighting. The *D.A.K.*, still under the command of Hans Cramer, was busy to the north and west holding off the Americans and moving back into the hills of the western dorsal just a step ahead of the pursuing *Eighth Army*. Along the coast the *90th* and *164th Light* fought off the *XXX Corps' 7th Armored* and *51st Divisions*, while the *15th Panzer* fought off attacks by the *X Corps' 1st Armored* and *2nd New Zealand Divisions*. The race was truly on, as the Axis forces attempted to make their way to Enfidaville with the *Eighth Army* nipping at their heels the entire way. On the 9th the *Eighth Army* occupied Maharès, fifty miles north of Gabès, while the Sfax-Faïd road was reached by midday. The following day Sfax fell to the *Eighth Army*, while the British *IX Corps* was able to move out of the Fondouk Pass, but they had exited just a bit too late in order to help bag the fast moving rearguards. On the 11th, the British *First Army* took Kairouan, which was located just one hundred miles south of Tunis, and on the 12th the *Eighth Army* was able to capture Sousse.

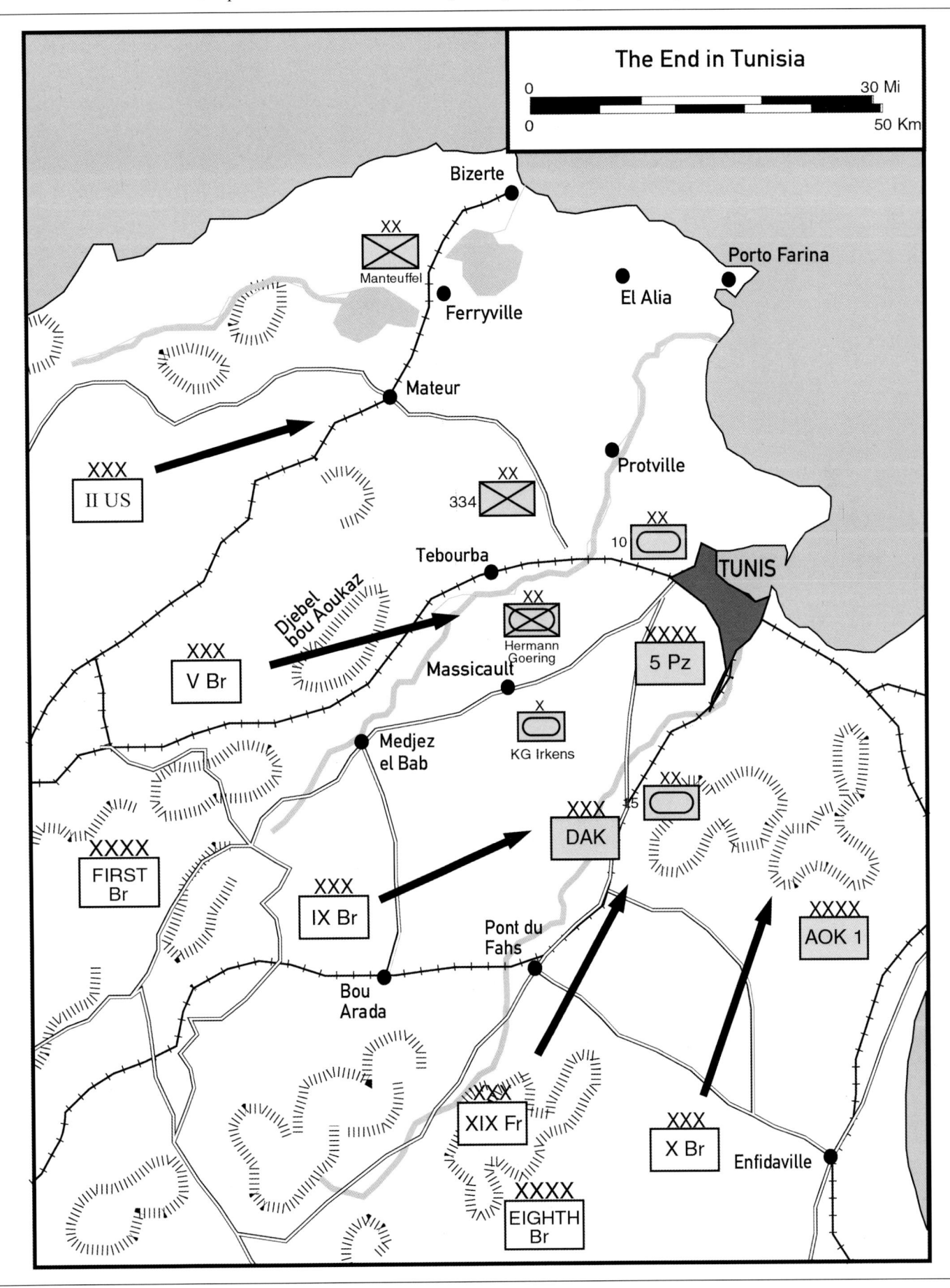

Chapter 14: The Final Battles of the Afrika Korps, March-April 1943

253

15

The End in North Africa
April-May 1943

By mid-April, *Armeegruppe Afrika* (Arnim) and the remaining Axis forces in Tunisia had been pushed back into their final line of defense. This perimeter stretched for approximately 80 miles from Enfidaville to the northwest coast near Cape Serrat. The line was manned from east to west by the *AOK 1* (Messe with Bayerlein), with the Italian *XX* and *XXI Corps*, with the *Trieste, Pistoia, Spezia,* and *Young Fascist Divisions*. The German *15th Panzer, 90th Light,* and *164th Light Divisions* were next in line, followed by the *D.A.K.* (Cramer), which was responsible for covering the area between *AOK 1* and the *Fifth Panzerarmee*; the *D.A.K.* had the *10th* (Broich) and *21st* (Hildebrandt) *Panzer Divisions*, in addition to the remains of the *Italian XXX Corps* (Sogno), with the *Superga Division* (Lorenzelli) and *50th Special Brigade* (Imperiali). The sector assigned to the *Fifth Panzerarmee* (Vaerst) began north of Pont du Fahs, and moving west was covered by the *Hermann Göring Division* (Schmid), the *334th Infantry Division* (Krause), and finally the *Manteuffel Division* (Bülowius), which was augmented by personnel from the *999th Division* (Wolff). Those divisions were backed up by the Flak guns of the *19th* (Frantz) and *20th* (Neuffer) *Flak Divisions*. There were also the remains of *Luftwaffe* and *Heer* units, which had been formed into various adhoc fighting groups. In addition there the remnants of the *Aufklärungs Gruppe, 5th Fallschirmjäger Regiment, Gebirgstruppen,* and panzer battalions like the *190th Panzer Battalion* and the *501st Heavy Panzer Battalion*.[1] Allied intelligence sections now placed the estimated fighting strength of those formations to be severely depleted, with the Italian *Young Fascist Division* down to five battalions and twenty-five guns, the *Trieste* Division at four battalions and thirty guns, and the *Pistoia* Division with only two battalions and thirty guns, while the *Centauro* and *Spezia* Divisions were considered all but destroyed. The German *90th Light* had about 6,000 effectives, while the *164th Light* had approximately 3,000; together they could form one weak division. The *15th Panzer* had about 5,600, which equaled about one kampfgruppe. The *21st Panzer* also had about 5,600, while in the *Fifth Panzerarmee* the *Manteuffel Division* had about 4,500 men, the *334th* about 9,500, the *999th* 5,800, and the *Hermann Göring* and *10th Panzer Divisions* had about 10,000 each. The *19th* and *20th Flak Divisions* had a combined strength of 13,000, and the adhoc battalions had a combined strength of approximately 15,000.[2] Opposing them was the *Eighteenth Army Group* (Alexander), with the British *First* (Anderson) and *Eighth* (Montgomery) Armies. Under command of *First Army* was the *U.S. II Corps* (Bradley), with the *1st Armored* (Harmon), *1st Infantry* (Allen), *9th Infantry* (Eddy), and *34th Infantry* (Ryder) Divisions. In addition to these U.S. divisions, there was the addition of a few augmented French battalions and some other smaller formations like Tank Destroyer, Airborne, and Ranger Units. British and French formations within the *First Army* included the British *V Corps* (Allfrey), with the *1st Infantry* (Clutterbuck), *4th Infantry* (Hawkesworth), and *78th Infantry* (Evelegh) Divisions, augmented by the *25th Tank Brigade* less its *51st RTR*. The British *IX Corps* (Crocker) had with it the *1st Armored* (Briggs), *6th Armored* (Keightley), and *46th Infantry* (Freeman) Divisions, as well as the *51st RTR*. The French had the *XIX Corps* (Koeltz) with the *Moroccan, Algerian,* and *Oran* Divisions, along with an attached armored battalion and guards group. The *First Army* was facing those formations from the *5th Panzerarmee*, while facing the *AOK 1* was the British *Eighth Army* with the *X Corps* (Horrocks) and *XXX Corps* (Leese) and the *New Zealand Corps* (Freyberg). As those Axis forces further west were seen as a greater threat to the *First Army*, the *Eighth Army* was soon ordered to detach the *4th Indian* Division (Tuker), *7th Armored Division* (Erskine), and *201st Guards Brigade* to the *First Army* by 30 April. The *Eighth* still retained the *50th Infantry* (Nichols), *51st Infantry* (Whimberley), *2nd New Zealand Division*, and the French "L" Force (LeClerc). There was also the arrival of the British *56th (London) Infantry Division* from Iraq, but it was not a veteran division, and would arrive almost too late to influence the battle.[3]

The plan and orders issued by *Armeegruppe Afrika* now centered on gathering all available resources and grouping them under the command of the *Armeegruppe*. The defensive lines were to be developed in depth, and German battalions were once again placed in between Italian formations to act as corsets. All remaining panzers were grouped together, and the *15th* and *21st Panzer Divisions* were placed in reserve. These formations came under the direct control of the *D.A.K.*, while the Italians grouped their tanks under the *Centauro* Division, which was then attached to a German panzer division. In the opinion of *Field Marshal* Kesselring, *Commander in Chief (South)*, the line looked acceptable, and appeared to be lacking in just two sectors: the area around Medjez el Bab, and along the coastal plain near Enfidaville. Thanks to Messe's proposal earlier in April, the *AOK 1* lines were now being withdrawn north to more defensible positions. The *Luftwaffe* was able to fly men, equipment, and supplies into the Tunis bridgehead from their airfields in Sicily and Italy. On average, 1800-2000 men were flown in daily aboard *Luftwaffe Ju-52* transport planes and the huge *Me-323* gliders. This system worked for a while, but on 18 April the squadrons of the *DAF* intercepted a mixed group of approximately 100 transports and gliders that had been flying low and destroyed almost half of them before they reached the coast. The following day another attempt to again fly in troops ended in disaster, although on a smaller scale, when a

254

Chapter 15: The End in North Africa, April-May 1943

number of aircraft were shot down. On the 22nd another attempt was made, and again losses were high, as thirty-nine *Luftwaffe* aircraft were brought down. After these attacks the *Luftwaffe* halted almost all daylight flights and switched to flying at night, but again the *DAF* was there waiting for them.[4] These disasters were a clear signal to the *OKW* that there was now little hope of getting the required amount of men and materiel to Africa in order to reinforce the *D.A.K.* In the days following the Regiment's movement into positions supporting the Enfidaville line, the workshops, and *I-Staffel* attempted to make improvements in the Regiment's ability to operate. It was now no longer possible to count on any new vehicles reaching the Regiment, because at this time only a few small ships and *Siebel ferries* were able to reach Tunis. The larger freighters were prevented from unloading their cargos in Tunis due to the air and naval superiority of the Allied navies and air forces. *OFw* Kurt Kathe of the 5th company remembers the situation:

"I was sent to Tunis in March 1943 to receive five new panzers [Tigers] from the harbor, I went there with 25 men and I slept in the Hotel Retzi. At around 0200hrs I held a formation with my soldiers and made a speech regarding the panzers and if they would come or not come. After waiting two weeks my commander came and told me 'you don't need to wait any longer your panzers were sunk'... the tigers were gone I thought. I then brought the soldiers to the Marshal Foch Kaserne and I returned to my hotel. Later I went to the commander and for me and my soldiers wrote a letter [telegraph] to my Spieskrate Bauergeiger who was located some 42km away where the group was located and we were in Tunis. After 3-4 days a reply came back granting us, me and the soldiers, vacation [leave]. In two days we were in Italy then sent back to Böblingen for 4 weeks vacation."[5]

Kurt Kathe was able to escape the end in Tunis, and was sent to the Grafenwöhr training center to train new panzer troops; he was later posted to the *21st Panzer Division* and fought for a short time at the end of the war in Western Europe before finally making his way home to Böblingen. As the remnants of the Axis armies continued to fall back into the Tunis bridgehead they established a new defensive line that ran from Cape Serrat, through Jefna, Sid Nisr, Medjez-el-Bab, and Enfidaville. The position was stretched for over two hundred kilometers, and there were few quality troops remaining to effectively hold that line. In order to take advantage of all its resources, the *Armeegruppe* ordered the *10th Panzer Division* to the Medjerda plain, west of Tunis, in order to act as the reserve for the *Fifth Panzerarmee*. The remaining elements of the *15th Panzer* were placed under immediate control of *Armeegruppe Afrika*, and they were ordered to take up positions southeast of Zarhouan. Luckily for the Regiment, the *Eighth Army* was again slow in its pursuit of *AOK 1*, and the Regiment was able to use this time to improve its operational ability and reorganize what meager forces remained into effective combat groups. Hampering these efforts were the Allied air forces, which were able to inflict serious damage on the logistics tail of the Regiment, so that there was now very little fuel and ammunition remaining for the panzers to operate on. Even though some of the most basic provisions were now at extremely low levels, the troops made do and found or took what they needed to carry on fighting. As the *Eighteenth Army Group* consolidated and prepared itself for the final battle, Alexander did not want to waste time, as his corps and divisions were reorganized for the main attack. No time was to be lost allowing the Axis defenders the time they needed to resupply themselves and further prepare and strengthen their defensive positions. So a number of preliminary attacks were launched against the Axis lines, and the first of these attacks fell on the *AOK 1* sector, when the *Eighth Army* attacked during the night of 19/20 April. Wilhelm Hagios remembers:

"On 20 April, Oberst Irkens made a speech to the entire regiment. During the night we went into positions. In the morning we were there; the radio car, my vehicle and the [command] panzer. Oberst Irkens said to me that I should take care of the panzer because during the night its tracks had been damaged. So I stayed at the panzer and fixed the track. Shortly afterwards we received fire from the British. I saw there was a 20mm gun that I had overlooked and quickly checked the wind and how to avoid it. Then the next load came directly at us, fired from the whole battery. I thought 'But they can't see us' and then one round hit directly on my vehicle but I was in the panzer so nothing happened to me. But if I hadn't been in the vehicle, that would have been it for me. The one vehicle on the right of me was still intact. I reported that my vehicle was completely wrecked but that the radio car stationed a few meters away was intact. The Oberst had ordered to the stabs that the radio car should drive 250m away in order to report and they had ignored it. The British knew 100% where we were and directed the attack on it."[6]

This British attack was initially able to gain some ground, but it was a costly affair, and was finally checked when *Generalmajor* Fritz Bayerlein moved forward and coordinated the Axis defense by moving in German troops in order to contain the attack. Elsewhere, the Germans too launched a number of spoiling attacks in the *First Army* sector; these attacks made some small gains, but like the *Eighth Army*'s attack, they were halted and pushed back, giving up ground as they did so. One of the largest Allied attacks came on the 23rd when the British *6th Armored Division* hit a section of the line around the Pont du Fahs-Tunis road. This attack caused some concern, and the *D.A.K.* was quickly ordered to shift its forces in order to cover the threatened sector; this was done with the help of the *10th* and *21st Panzer Divisions* with support from the Italian *Superga* Division and *Kampfgruppe Schmid* (the non-mobile elements from the *10th* and *21st Panzer Divisions*). In the actions fought from 20-26 April, *Armeegruppe Afrika* reported the destruction of 162 tanks, twenty-four guns, sixty-seven vehicles, and twenty-three planes. After the first two days of battle, the *10th Panzer Division* had been reduced to twenty-five panzers. But reinforcements drawn from *AOK 1* and the *15th Panzer* raised the number of operational panzers to fifty-five panzers and ten Italian tanks. Another fifteen panzers were being held by *Fifth Panzerarmee* in support of the *334th Infantry*'s sector.[7] The British *IX Corps' 46th Infantry Division* attacked on 22 April against the positions of the *Hermann Göring Division* near Sebkret el Kourzia as part of *Operation Vulcan*, but that attack failed to gain its objectives when it progressed over difficult terrain and came up against defenders that were alert and waiting for them. In the end, these British attacks fell short of their objectives, but in doing so they had forced the *Armeegruppe* to use up almost all of its mobile reserves.[8] On 21 April, *Oberst* Josef Irkens was awarded the *Deutsches Kreuz in Gold* for his actions as the regimental commander during the previous four months of fighting; it was a well deserved award, but unfortunately he would have little time for celebrations.[9] On the 24th, *Armeegruppe Afrika* realized that the main Allied effort against the Tunis bridgehead would come from the critically important sector around the Djebel Bou Aoukaz, with the attack coming from the south of the Medjerda River. That attack began on 23 and 24 April when the British *1st* and *4th Infantry Divisions* attacked east of Medjerda. The *1st Division* went northward to the area around Djebel Bou Aoukaz, while the *4th Division* attacked east of the djebel, but both units made little progress, and continued to fight a see-saw battle for the next few days. As soon as the attacks by the British *V* and *IX Corps'* near Sebkret el Kourzia were halted, von Arnim ordered the reorganization of all the remaining panzers into one combined force, and that force was to be entrusted to the most senior and capable panzer leader. The man selected to lead this force was Josef Irkens, who was named "*Panzerführer Afrika*" and overall commander of all the remaining panzers in Africa. "*Panzergruppe Irkens*" was to initially consist of the remaining panzers from the *5th*, *7th*, and *8th Panzer Regiments*, and the remaining *Tigers* from the *501st Heavy Panzer Battalion*. In addition to the panzers, Irkens' force contained *Grenadier Regiment 47*, one German artillery battalion, one Italian artillery battalion, and two flak battalions, in addition to the remnants of *Kampfgruppe Audorff*.[10] The *panzergruppe* had approximately seventy panzers ranging from the 50mm Mk IIIs to the dreaded Mk VI *Tigers* with their 88mm guns. As the Germans were ordered to consolidate their panzers the same was also done with the Italians, as they grouped all of their remaining tanks and an assault gun battalion under the *Centauro* Division. This force was commanded by *Major* Piscelli, and fell under the direct command of *Armeegruppe Afrika*. With these last few panzers, commanders like Irkens and Piscelli were supposed to bring about a change in Axis fortunes and halt the Allied armored armada.[11] At this point it is important to point out that although the word "Regiment" is used to indicate or describe the actions of *Panzer Regiment 8*, the reader should understand that the Regiment ceased to exist when *Panzergruppe Irkens* was formed. The actual number of panzers and personnel assigned to the Regiment by this time had become so widely distributed over the entire Tunis bridgehead that tracing their movement and locations is all but impossible. However, whenever there is a written or verbal account of a specific action that took place with the men and machines from the Regiment they will be referred to as such. Additionally, it is important to mention that as the *abteilungs*, companies, platoons, and sections moved off to various locations in order to counter any Allied threats, those forces became separated, and although the officers and *unteroffiziers* attempted to maintain unit integrity as best they could, many groups were faced with joining up with whatever formation was closest to them, and could offer the best form of protection or chance of survival and escape. In the end, the men of the Regiment became so separated that they were forced to surrender in a number of different locations scattered between Cape Bon and Tunis, Protville, Porto Farina, and El Alia. The remaining panzers from the Regiment were now located in the center of the line near the town of Tébourba, roughly 20km north of Djebel Bou Aoukaz on the Medjerda River. On the 27th, the British were finally able to take the Djebel Bou Aoukaz and Longstop Hill in the center of the Medjerda valley. On the 28th and 29th *Panzergruppe Irkens*, under the direct command of the *Fifth Panzerarmee* and now equipped with just over sixty-eight panzers, was ordered to attack the Djebel Bou Aoukaz. In the heavy fighting that followed, the *Panzergruppe* was able to throw the British off the djebel. In one of the last major panzer assaults undertaken in the North African Campaign, the cream of the *D.A.K.* and the Regiment fought themselves to exhaustion, and they were able to halt the British *V Corps*. The next two descriptions come from two different books; both give an overall picture of the attack and how it must have proceeded that day. However, both descriptions exaggerate overall numbers and claims, as well as dates and locations, and the overall gallantry of the attack. They give to the reader an almost mythical description of the attack, but I have included them because both of them surely came from speaking with the veterans of this battle. The first account is from Volkmar Kühn's book:

"*Irken's few panzers threw themselves against the wave of allied armor. Just north of the point of penetration were 30 German panzers [probably closer to 20], mostly from PR 8, which was led by Hptm Schnelle. Irkens decided on his own to launch a counter-attack against the northern wing and north flank of the enemy forces which had broken through. Once again the battle tested panzer commanders proved themselves, halting the enemy penetration for a short time. When the last 20 panzers broke contact with the enemy that afternoon they had destroyed 90 enemy tanks [this number seems highly inflated] at a cost of 10 of their own. During the night and the following day they drove back towards the airfield at El Alia.*"[12]

The second description is from Erwan Bergot's *The Afrika Korps*:

"*Irkens force' moved off at dawn. It was a suicide operation, a last desperate charge. Every man was determined to demonstrate for the last time that the spirit of the Afrika Korps was not dead. Even at odds of one to a hundred, even though they were only a handful of men they would never surrender. 'Through to the end!' Away they went in their worn-out old tanks with the yellow paint peeling off, old hits half patched, and cracks in their armor plate covered by bits of tank track secured to the cowlings. They were the tanks of Tobruk and El Alamein of Gazala and Benghazi. Von Arnim lead them from Lieutenant Paschy's tank. He too had wished to be present as had von Thoma for the final charge at El Alamein. They climbed the mountain, pennants flying turrets open. The weather was fine. The mountain shone green and red with here and there narrow goat tracks or shady olive groves. The tanks of the Afrika Korps were going into the assault. The dust flew, thicker and redder than that of the desert. 'Heia Safari!' It was the old war-cry. For the last time the Afrika Korps had hoisted its battle flag. The fight began at 10:00 am and it was brief. The British tanks guarding the flank of the Eighth Army were swept away in the attack, the violence of which reminded the old hands of Sidi Rezegh. The Mark IIIs and IVs together with a few 'Tigers' available penetrated into the heart of the British Army which gave way and began to disintegrate. The Afrika Korps now had only a few thousand men and very few tanks but what did it matter. It charged on, forestalling a counter-attack which threatened from the flank. In two hours it had topped the mountain and was flooding down into the valley. Without artillery or air support it charged across the plain. By mid-afternoon the Afrika Korps had advanced four miles, driving two enemy armored brigades before it. Losses were fearful. Half the Germans tanks were destroyed in this offensive. But this did not diminish the fury of the survivors. They fired and then moved on from tree to bush, from ridge to hedge, moving by bounds and dealing out the blows referred to by Paschy. The 'old man' [Rommel] would have been pleased. Paschy said.*"[13]

The account goes on to mention Lt Paschy and four others lying wounded at the foot of a tree waiting to be picked up by either side; to them it did not matter, but as the account continues it mentions Paschy's wound, and that he died that night. Fortunately for Lt Paschy he did not die that night, and was taken prisoner by the Americans, and did not pass away until 2003. When the battle was over *Panzergruppe Irkens* was able to claim the destruction of ninety British tanks; they also reported a total panzer strength of approximately sixty-nine panzers, including four Mk VI Tigers.[14] For the men of the Regiment who participated in the battle, they claimed some twenty-three of those enemy tanks. The losses they suffered in doing so amounted to some six panzers listed as total write offs. The human toll amounted to just three dead and sixteen wounded. By that evening the attack had indeed succeeded, and the djebel was in German hands. In a letter that might have been written from this djebel, and definitely during this time period, Adolf Lamm wrote one of his last diary notes:

"*These were my last entries [in a diary]. I remember still, that some days later we had the tent camp on the hill in front of Enfidaville. Fw Honecker was there. We were holding our breath day and night due to bombers and Tiefffliegers (Fighter-Bombers). They mostly attacked the road which led to Tunis, and shot down the small transport, even the single*

Chapter 15: The End in North Africa, April-May 1943

vehicles. We were able to watch it precisely from our hill. Down there was the hell! One evening came the order to march off. I drove in somebody's company vehicle. Luckily we went by Enfidaville and on the shore road to a large extend unmolested and in three hours we reached Tunis. I didn't know where in the city we were located. It was a large square, full of vehicles, slit-trenches against aircraft attacks. I was completely frozen and crouched in one of these dugouts. One could only sit in an 'L' and it was impossible to sleep due to the coldness."[15]

With the failure of *Operation Vulcan* and the loss of Djebel Bou Aoukaz, Alexander and his commanders met to discuss their next series of moves against the *Panzerarmee*. The plan that they came up with was given the name Strike. *Operation Strike* was scheduled to kick off on 6 May, and was to focus along the First Army's central front. The plan called for the transfer of the two and a half divisions from the *Eighth Army* to the First, and once the First Army was strong enough, break through the Axis line and capture Tunis. In the first days of May, both sides reorganized and maneuvered their forces into various positions along the hills and valleys near Tunis in anticipation for the final showdown. Although the *Panzerarmee* had achieved a small victory in halting British operations around Djebel Bou Aoukaz, and the cost in terms of overall panzer losses had been few, the fighting in the central sector had all but crippled the rest of *Armeegruppe Afrika*, as it had taken almost all of the remaining stocks of fuel from the other divisions to keep the *kampfgruppe* in action. Up until this point, small amounts of fuel had been able to be flown in by air, but it was nowhere near enough to keep the fuel hungry panzers in action as they attempted to move from hot spot to hot spot. On 4 May, a small amount of fuel and ammunition was landed by small ships and flown into the bridgehead, but by this time those combat units were so scattered, and the required transportation was so limited, that barely any of it reached the men and machines on the front lines that needed it most. By the 28th, the British, supported by a couple of weak French divisions of the French *XIX Corps*, had managed to push forward, and now stood in front of the area around Pont du Fahs. Unfortunately, much of their supporting armor was still to the rear, and had yet to move up over this difficult terrain. Shortly after that, the transfer of the *4th Indian* and *7th Armored Divisions* and *201st Guards Brigade* from *Eighth Army* to *First Army* sector took place. Von Arnim was sure that the British would be exhausted from the previous two weeks of heavy fighting, and their moves towards the center had convinced him that the British were assembling forces there for an attack. After securing the line near Djebel Bou Aoukaz, von Arnim and von Vaerst then ordered the *Panzergruppe* into the most critical sector between the Medjerda River and the Medjez el Bab–Tunis highway. At this point, *Kampfgruppe Irkens* was reinforced with the remaining elements from the *15th Panzer Division*, and he had approximately sixty operational panzers on hand. Other moves also took place at this time to reinforce and adjust the lines of defense, and one of those moves was for elements of the *Hermann Göring Division* to bolster the *Manteuffel Division's* sector, while the *10th Panzer Division* was held in reserve as the *Armeegruppe's* only reserve. While the fighting was heavy in the central and western sectors, in the east *AOK 1* was under continued attack by the *Eighth Army* near Enfidaville. The *AOK 1* was surprisingly able to hold on along its sector of the line, despite being under heavy pressure. Further in the west, the American *II Corps* was launching attacks to the northwest around Cape Serrat, Mateur, and Bizerte. After the battles around Djebel Bou Aoukaz the remaining panzers from the *kampfgruppe* were deployed as the *Armeegruppe's* "Fire Brigade," and were employed whenever the Allies threatened a breakthrough. That, of course, was easier said than done, because at that time there was very little fuel reaching Tunisia, and the supplies that did make it in had to be flown in by the *Luftwaffe*; not a very practical or expedient means with which to support armored forces.

The German supply services struggled to get what fuel and ammunition had arrived to the troops then fighting forward. *Panzergruppe Irkens* found itself having to scrounge what supplies it could from other formations, and unfortunately many of the panzers were never able to be recovered when the fuel tanks ran dry and the crews were forced to destroy the panzers, rather than have them fall into the hands of the enemy. At this time two Mk IIIs were reported lost due to mechanical breakdowns, but more than likely they ran out of fuel. The workshop was still busy, as it made all efforts to improve the *kampfgruppe's* ability to operate. There are some reports that state on 1 May the *Panzergruppe* had some sixty-nine operational panzers remaining, but this number is doubtful at best, considering the losses suffered over the past week and lack of fuel that immobilized a number of them. There is one report that claims there were just twenty-one panzers remaining, and this number seems to be more accurate. Finally, on 5 May, the *15th Panzer Division* headquarters issued orders that all non-committed personnel, many of which were panzer crews who no longer had a panzer with which to fight, were ordered to an assembly area near Porto Farina. This was an attempt to get out many of the experienced troops and panzer crews. By the end of April, the *OKW* had halted all further deployments of men to Africa, and the "*German Dunkirk*," as Rommel and so many others had envisioned many months beforehand, finally began to take shape, as *Ju-52s* and *Siebel* ferries, along with a few smaller ships attempted to make their way to Africa and remove what troops they could. But as he had done at Stalingrad in late 1942, and would soon become infamous for, Hitler and his staff cronies in Berlin waited until it was too late before giving their permission to evacuate. The feeble rescue attempt had been far too little and far too late, as there was now little possibility in conducting any type of organized withdrawal of forces from Africa. Alfred Toppe wrote after the war about the decisions being made at the top levels:

"Even Kesselring, the Commander in Chief South, had intended consolidating all staffs and withdrawing all specialists-such as gunners, radio specialists, tank crews, armorer artificers, and so forth-in order to fly them to Europe and thus prevent the capture of at least the more important personnel. He was supported in this intention by the Italian Supreme Command but was prevented from putting his plan into effect by the deputy chief of the Wehrmacht operations staff, who intervened in April."[16]

On 5 May, the British *1st Infantry Division* succeeded in capturing Djebel Bou Aoukaz for the final time. That evening the *IX Corps* began its move forward in order to launch *Operation Strike*. On the morning of 6 May, at around 0300hrs the British infantry of the *4th Indian* and *4th British Infantry Divisions*, supported by the *25th Tank Brigade*, advanced along both sides of the Massicault-Tunis highway behind a massive aerial and artillery barrage. Alexander was now launching his *First Army* up the Medjerda Valley, while the *Eighth Army* moved up from Enfidaville. The attacks went well in the face of stubborn resistance; the bombs and artillery fell upon the positions of the German infantry and remaining *Fallschirmjägers*, which effectively smashed their lines and created huge gaps through which the British infantry poured through. These bombardments had all but destroyed what remained of *Panzergrenadier Regiment 115*, which had lost its two remaining battalions. By 0730hrs the first tanks from the British *6th* and *7th Armored Divisions*, along with the *201st Guards Brigade* had begun moving through the first minefields in order to widen the gaps made previously by the infantry and artillery. By 1030hrs, the British tanks had passed through the minefields and were beginning

257

to move forward towards Massicault. At this point the line of defense of the Tunis bridgehead had been effectively broken wide open; however, as the British advanced, those few remaining German formations began to recover their senses and throw up a hasty defensive front that succeeded in slowing down the British. In one last attempt to hold back this flood, the last twenty panzers of *Kampfgruppe Irkens* were led forward from their positions near Massicault and into combat. In this final attack the panzers were assembled and made combat ready before they pushed forward to take the fight to the British. The sudden appearance of these panzers caught some of the British infantry by surprise, and they quickly fled to safer locations in the rear, and by doing so abandoned sixteen of their halftracks and antitank guns. Irkens and his panzers continued forward and began to engage the tanks of the two British armored divisions for the final time. A fierce firefight soon developed between the Regiment and its old nemesis, the *7th Armored Division*. After forty minutes of intense combat, twenty-three British tanks were left burning on the battlefield for the loss of twelve panzers. This small victory was short-lived, however, when supporting *DAF* fighter-bombers pounced all over the *kampfgruppe*, and were able to catch one of the panzers out in the open, attacking it and setting it on fire. The panzer crew, however, was not able to escape the burning wreck, and as a panzer from the *4th Company* was coming to its rescue in an attempt to free the trapped crew, it too was hit and disabled. The loss of those two panzers caused the remaining panzers to break off the engagement and withdraw from the fight with their wounded. Wilhelm Hagios remembers that day:

"On 4 May there was a counter-attack at Massicault from our side. I was behind the column and saw the bombs. I was in the village and hid under the wall in that village, and the vehicle survived and I survived too. And in the morning as soon as we were on the road here came the bombers again. The division commander, the Oberst and I were in the abandoned ruins and went from one position to the next, one here, one there, the whole stabs was this way. So because my vehicle was shot up, I went to the workshop and thought that I could now rest a little and the next day came the order over the radio for me to return to the Regiment stab. I was told that I should take over the vehicle from officer so-and-so, who will give me his car and he will go to the workshop and take over my vehicle when it is fixed. That probably never happened as the vehicle couldn't be repaired. The next day there was again a bombing attack and I discovered that on my vehicle there was a missing liquid container [radiator/coolant system] on the front. I said that it's not possible to drive this way and on my other vehicle this container was intact, so I went to the workshop and while I was driving I almost went under the bomb, just one bomb was dropped and it hit right in front of me so that if I had been driving under that mark it would have hit me."

More than anything else, Irkens' final attack led the British to believe that they were still in for a long and costly fight, and so they decided to halt for the remainder of the day and resume the advance on the 7th. After halting the British armor, and instead of maintaining their hasty line of defense, the remaining panzers and grenadiers were withdrawn during the night to the northeast near St. Cyprien and Sebkret es Sedjoumi. As the day ended so did the formidable combat record of the *15th Panzer Division*, as it was all but destroyed and ceased to exist as a viable fighting force. Wilhelm Hagios has these memories of how those final days went:

"On 5 May, this is also by the way nowhere written, we were with Oberst Irkens, Olt Pashy and Uffz Schaeffer were there also, with them we drove to Tunis. In Tunis there was a delivery such that he had to go back to Europe with the Regiments' documents. The Army commander was in Tunis and we also visited the Bay of Tunis and then went back to Massicault. On the way there a stray round hit in our proximity, we didn't know if we were under attack or what it was, but nothing happened to us. From the AOK in Tunis we received the new terrain map with the circles. On this map there were circles around each town and the number, if we were given the order to go to a certain place, then it would be called by its number and the man who had a map would find out the area by the number where they were to go. I was told that if something happens to us, that I should destroy the map, but nothing happened. In the evening we came back to Massicault but we didn't stay in the combat position, but went on the side and drove through the place where we had gone a few days ago. There was a French farm, we got from them something for dinner and overnighted there. He [Irkens] slept in the house and I slept in the back seat. Since I had the vehicle, I had no tent in there. From the summer of 1942 until my imprisonment, I hadn't seen any beds. I was either in the panzer in the seat, or in the jeep in the backseat."

Since 5 May, elements of the *U.S. II Corps' 1st Armored Division* had been pushing forward against the defensive line of Bizerte-Ferryville-Mateur. There were few panzers in the west, and *Armeegruppe Afrika* was aware of the threat that the Americans poised to holding onto the Tunis bridgehead. Orders were then issued that the road from Mateur to Tunis must be held for as long as possible, and so a few of the remaining panzers of *Panzergruppe Irkens* were deployed in order to hold this key line of communication. Of course, this was easier said that done, for at that time the Americans had already managed to cross the roadway and were holding positions along the flank. The *panzergruppe* was not the only unit tasked with holding this road; the *Fallschirmjägers* of the *5th Fallschirmjäger Regiment* had already deployed to the threatened sector with whatever weapons were on hand, and doggedly attacked the American tanks and halftracks in their attempts to halt them. As the panzers moved up into the sector they began to engage the Americans, and in this engagement the *panzergruppe* lost four panzers, but they had succeeded in temporarily halting any further deployment by the Americans. Of course, by this time there was no chance of stopping the Americans, and before long they were able to call on their artillery, which fired a heavy concentration into the area now being held by the panzers and forced them to break off the engagement and withdraw to the rear. Fuel was now the main priority, and without it the panzers were to go no farther; at this point in the battle the discovery of a jerry can or two could make all the difference between surrendering and fighting on. Men combed through abandoned and wrecked trucks, tents, and any abandoned supply bases in order to find precious fuel. Occasionally a can or two was found and brought immediately to the panzers, which allowed the continued movement of only a few kilometers. While fuel was being procured, the remainder of the "I" *Staffel* was busy cannibalizing abandoned and wrecked panzers in its attempts to repair the few slightly damaged panzers so that they could carry on the fight.

Surrender

Early on 7 May, the British *6th* and 7th Armored Divisions were able to overcome the stout resistance around Massicault, and break through the thin defensive lines along the Tébourba-Massicault road, while south of Ferryville the U.S. *1st Armored Division* broke through the thinly held defense lines there and drove on towards Bizerte. By the afternoon the Americans were in Bizerte, and the British had been able to speed two of their armored car regiments forward in order to take Tunis. A short time after these attacks began the final seven panzers were able to withdraw, but due to the lack of fuel they could barely reach the HKL. Wilhelm Hagios remembers:

Chapter 15: The End in North Africa, April-May 1943

"We saw during the night that British and Americans had used their artillery to shoot at our positions, but nothing happened. On the next afternoon we wanted to go back to the combat squadron. We drove from the place over to Macedon, and during this time the British had started their attack. The artillery fired from all tubes and the tanks drove and shot at us like crazy and in this present situation I had to drive. There was an olive grove and so I drove in there to take cover. In Djedeida we arrived around mid-day, in the evening Kaiser said that everyone was to become infantry. General Borowietz was there and we overnighted there and the next morning we saw the British tanks to the south of Tunis. I thought that if they gave it the gas they would be able to reach there by the next morning. Believe me I had not seen a single soldier between Tunis and Massicault, it was about 41km. We went slowly upwards, until Porto Farina. El Alia was the first on the way, we drove by the workshop of some Tiger tanks and there was no one to be seen, the airport in the field was also deserted and left behind in the retreat."

At that point all the bravery of the panzer crews was useless for preventing the *7th Armored* from entering Tunis. Those panzers that were still battle-worthy and with fuel still left in their gas tanks moved up the Tunis-Bizerte road towards the town of Protville, and after a short halt continued on towards Porto Farina. It was here that the last remaining panzers had to be destroyed due to the lack of fuel; amongst them was the panzer of Lt Ballhaus, the last Mk IV panzer of the once proud *4th Company*. There are some accounts that mention that these last remaining panzers were driven over a cliff and destroyed, while another account states that they fired their remaining ammunition at the enemy and then were destroyed by their crews. Regardless of how they were destroyed, the fighting was over for the Regiment and *Panzergruppe Irkens*. With the destruction of these final few panzers the end had finally come for the Regiment, as its ability to engage the enemy was lost. So after almost four years of continuous combat and participation in numerous campaigns from Poland to Africa, the Regiment sent out its final situation report:

"The fuel is gone, ammunition expended, weapons and equipment destroyed."[17]

On 9 May, the U.S. *1st Armored Division* was poised in front of Porto Farina. At 1200hrs the remnants of *Panzer Regiment 8* entered into American captivity. Wilhelm Hagios, who was with his commander *Oberst* Irkens, recalls these last few days:

"On the Bizerte-Tunis road came the order to stop fighting. On the nearby hilltop there was a French fortress and we drove up and there was no one around. I thought hopefully that the Americans wouldn't notice us from below; otherwise all hell would break loose on us. But they didn't notice us, so in the evening we came to Porto Farina, on the evening of the 8th the division commander was there, they wanted to award decorations but they had no paperwork with them and decided not to do it. The next morning we drove in the direction of Cape Bon but we returned back to the place. Around 1100hrs appeared the first Sherman tanks, and the division commander and Oberst Irkens were present, I observed it all from my Kfz-15 vehicle I was in. The two Americans upfront followed by the two officers and Oberst Irkens in the rear. There was some talking and then I followed one of their carriers and I drove to their combat positions. There was an armored division but I don't know which one. There we were interrogated; the one who interrogated us was speaking perfect German as he had studied in Jena. He told General Borowietz that they didn't expect to meet us there; he was counting on another couple of days. But by then they had captured his driver, that is why Borowietz didn't have a car at that time and they found his general's uniform, and they thought that the driver was a general. So we were all interrogated there, everyone who I knew and the whole stabs had been cracked open. I had not escaped, because in the vehicle which I had taken over since mine was broken there was a compartment in which I still had egg hand grenades among other things. I also found in the vehicle the machine pistol with a magazine and more hand grenades. As a kamikaze I could blow up the whole stabs, I wanted to do it, but they hit me with the machine gun without me knowing what was going on. I wanted to do it again and told this to Oberst Irkens and he told me to give up. That was the end."

On the 10th, the commanding general of the *D.A.K.*, Hans Cramer, was informed that the commander of the *15th Panzer Division*, *Generalmajor* Willibald Borowietz, had been awarded the *Ritterkreuz*, and that the commander of the *I./Abteilung*, *Panzer Regiment 8*, Hptm Hans-Günther Stotten, had been awarded the Oak leaves to his Knight's Cross. Shortly beforehand Stotten had been wounded again in the final days of the campaign and evacuated to a hospital in Germany. He would later recover and continue his heroic service, but unfortunately his life came to an end in the final days of the war when he was killed near Vienna, Austria, in April 1945. One interesting point to mention is that there was no such award for the Regimental and *Panzergruppe Afrika* commander, Josef Irkens, who over the previous five months had fought and worked hard to ensure the continued success of the Regiment and that of the entire *Armeegruppe*. By 10 May all organized resistance had ceased. Those German and Italian troops that could crowd together on the Cape Bon peninsula in the hope of a last minute miracle to pluck them from Africa, but for over 250,000 of them, half of whom were German, only the barbed wire of Allied prison camps awaited them. However, some men were saved in those final hours and brought out in the last plane or ferry, and some even attempted to row back to Italy or improvise a way out, but these were the true exception. For the majority of them, their fate had been sealed many months ago. Karl Halverscheidt, now working as the adjutant to *Generalmajor* Borowietz, was with the general and others in the hills north of El Alia when the surrender terms were being negotiated. Since they had been separated earlier by the attacks up the Tunis highway, they had been holding out until elements of the U.S. *II Corps* finally reached their positions:

"After destroying our last four panzers the Regiment was taken prisoner of war on 10 May 43. Our division commander Generalmajor Borowietz ordered me to go from our dayroom to a street. It was known that an armistice was being negotiated, there was still some shooting and above us American bombers were still circling they did not drop any bombs and at the same time were not shot at. Arriving in the street I met three American soldiers in a jeep driving carefully towards me, I walked up to the jeep and told the NCO 'You can capture a German general here and maybe you will be promoted or get a medal for this.' But the NCO did not believe me and spoke with his unit for additional orders. I finally got into the jeep and drove with them to our camp area. A couple of days earlier we had captured an American captain whom we carried around with us as we did not know what else to do with him. This proved to be very helpful now. He grabbed the walkie-talkie from the jeep and talked to the unit's commander. Shortly afterwards the commander arrived leading twelve Sherman tanks. It was Colonel Benson from the 1st Armored Division I remembered his name because it was on his helmet. During the surrender with all honors, we had no incidents. Finally we all conversed and joked and passed the wine and liquor bottles around. Why didn't we only a few hours ago fight each other? I was then taken in the vicinity of Bizerte where I reported with eight other officers from the Regiment to a British PoW Camp commanded by a Scottish Colonel. He was in charge

of 4,000 men from our division and we were in charge of their food and sanitary installations and etc. After all these arrangements were made we were later relocated. At first we were considered to be 'Supermen' and at that time I thought this was pronounced 'Suppermen' until I was told what it meant. Today I would say this meaning could not have been any better. After we stayed four weeks in Oran in Algeria we were shipped to England and from Liverpool we crossed the Atlantic in a large American ship the 'Alexander' which in 1920 had been turned over to the Americans by the Germans. I was the adjutant of 172 German officers among them ten colonels, which were more difficult than girls in a boarding school. I had my first conversation with a tall Captain from Texas, a real southerner, I learned right away that he couldn't stand the Yankees much like the Prussians and Bavarians and we talked about Margaret Mitchell's Gone with the Wind. He complimented me and said 'Boys you are O.K.!' and we received many cartons of cigarettes. Then the Captain took me to the chief mess steward, well he must have liked me too and he ordered that all German officers we authorized to eat a la carte! During that ten-day journey I gained three kilos (7lbs). Additionally there was a Chaplain who took care of us and we had many long discussions with him and succeeded in reducing his cigar supply. After landing in New York close to the Waldorf Astoria we were greeted by Generals and Admirals there were camera teams from movies and news and newspaper representatives. Then, by train to Camp Crossville, Tennessee, which would be our home for the next two years."[18]

Adolf Lamm of the *2nd Company* was with the groups of men who had been able to reach the perimeter being formed around the Cape Bon peninsula. He recalled his last few days and the surrender:

"We stayed in Tunis probably one or two days. My memory remembers a large gate, behind it the streets, where we didn't dare to go. I saw two covered-up Arabian women approaching me; they had white gowns and a veil over their mouths and across their faces. One could only see their nose, the eyes, the forehead and the roots of black hair. This little was of such groomed beauty and witness of so much culture, that I froze standing. What an opposite to the rough face of the war, probably these were the women from the palace of Bay of Tunis. From Tunis we were transported to Kelibia [on the eastern side] on the semi-island of Cape Bon. We became the small accumulation of men. God knows how many we have lost on our hitchhiker's way. In the proximity of the airfield we were camping on the heights alongside the street. No tents anymore. In the afternoon, around 1600hrs arrived troops from the other side of the street. It was the 10th of May 1943 and we still hoped to be transported by airplanes out. Some, who returned from the airfield, had reported that there was almost no chance of it. They told us that there was a wrestle for the places in aircraft and how some had cleared their way with pistols. We had an inspection, we came in as torn out as we were. Hauptmann Lindner informed us that the Army had surrendered and thanked us for our effort. We didn't know that he himself was badly ill. He shook hands with each of us, called us by name as we fought back the tears. Then back over the street to the old place. I don't know how long it lasted. Probably one day, afterwards in the afternoon at around 1600hrs, came an English Panzerspähwagens [Armored Car] with white flags from the direction of Cape Bon. The loudspeaker demanded us not to shoot and that the Army had surrendered. Not to shoot? Why should we? I still had my Army revolver attached to me. I took it in front of me, dismantled it and threw the parts together with a small amount of ammunition far away. That was the end."[19]

Gotthilf Haidt remembers;

"There was nothing left, we were forced to capitulate at Cape Bon nearby Tunis to the British. We were in Cap Bon and loaded on to the truck, with a German driver, an English soldier, young guy was with us and we drove off. We went through Tunis in one column, it was endless, and we went on as a single vehicle so long on the way to Algeria 400km from Cap Bon to the first camp. That morning before we went into the camp, the British halted us and told us the camp was too full and asked us to drive further. We went to another camp and there it was all finished."[20]

Rommel, who at that time was recovering in Austria and anxiously following the news from Africa every day by radio, received a text message from Cramer via his aides that stated to Rommel that at least his "*Afrikaans*" that were going into captivity would be spared the coming holocaust in Europe. As the headquarters of both von Arnim and Cramer gathered together in the hills near Tunis, they were, unlike many of their men, determined to carry on the resistance to a point of lunacy. Unable to accept their fate, and lowering themselves to pettiness that did not befit the professionalism of the *D.A.K.*, they haggled with British officers, and in the end were escorted by a Gurka officer, which set von Arnim into a rage. On the afternoon of 12 May, von Arnim requested surrender terms for *Armeegruppe Afrika* and the *D.A.K.*, while Mussolini promoted *General* Messe to the rank of *Field Marshal* in the hopes of prolonging the struggle in Africa, but the following day Messe ordered the surrender of all remaining German and Italian troops under his command. The fighting in Tunisia had cost the Axis forces over 290,000 prisoners, over 50,000 killed, 1,000 guns, 250 tanks, and 520 aircraft, along with stores of ammunition and supplies. In the two year campaign, the Axis had lost a total of over 600,000 men: 250,000 Germans and 350,000 Italians.[21] *Generalleutnant* Hans Cramer, the first commander of *Panzer Regiment 8* in Africa, and befittingly the last commander of the *Deutsches Afrika Korps*, made a final, if somewhat defiant, radio broadcast:

"To OKH, Ammunition shot off. Arms and equipment destroyed. In accordance with orders received D.A.K. has fought itself to the condition where it can fight no more. The Deutsches Afrika Korps must rise again. Heia Safari, Cramer, General Commanding."[22]

Epilogue

The war for many had ended; many of those fortunate enough to have survived would soon be on their way into American PoW camps scattered throughout the United States. For these men the life they would live was far better than the harsh conditions they had experienced; they were treated accordingly, and few perished in the camps, but the war was to go on, and it would be another bloody two years before the killing stopped. Those that had survived North Africa and been able to make it out, or were recovering from wounds in Böblingen, were formed into a new formation, the *8th Panzer Abteilung*. The history of this *abteilung* takes too long to cover in the space of these remaining pages, but the *abteilung* would be retrained in France and Holland on the *Sturmgeschütze III* and assigned to the *20th Panzer Grenadier Division*. After spending some time in Holland the *Abteilung* was posted to the Eastern Front, where it was to see a different kind of combat that would seem foreign to them, but which they had to quickly adapt to if they did not wish to perish. The *Abteilung* would fight in some of the hardest defensive battles on the front, as the once mighty German *Wehrmacht* was pushed back to the borders of Germany. In places like Krivoi Rog, Kirovgrad, the Dnieper bridgehead, Kamenets-Podolsk, Ternopol, Lvov, the Oder bridgehead, and Berlin the men would continue to win victories, albeit small ones. Others, like Kummel, Spohn, Huttenlocher, and Ludwig were sent to fight in Italy with the *15th Panzer Grenadier Division*, where a number of them were to fall. Many did not return, but are remembered today by those that did every September when the last small group of veterans hold their regimental reunions. They are also remembered in November during the World War I remembrance of *Volkstrauertag*, when a few veterans still living around Böblingen come to visit the small remembrance stone located on their old training kaserne, which is now the home of the *1st Battalion, 10th Special Forces Group*. These remembrances last only a short time, but they serve their purpose for these old veterans, who now have the constant companion of walking sticks, and do not need too much time to remember their old comrades. The memories and nightmares from the days of their youth are horrors that will just not disappear, and are still with them and will always be. Unlike American, British, Australian, and the many other nations who fought in this climatic struggle, many of the German veterans never put their memories on paper, for to them they had lost, and to them nobody is interested in the vanquished stories. We do, however, have numerous photographs and combat reports which, keeping with good German traditions, are plentiful and detailed.

Appendix 1: German Award Definitions

Knights Cross (with Oak leaves, Swords, Diamonds) – Awarded for actions or accomplishments of extreme bravery or in high command.

German Cross in Gold – Awarded to recognize bravery above which was required for the Iron Cross I Class, but not up to that required for the Knights Cross.

Iron Cross First Class – Awarded for outstanding service and bravery and to have distinguished oneself three or more times than required for the second class award.

Iron Cross Second Class - Awarded for outstanding service and bravery in the face of the enemy.

Silver Tank Assault Badge – Awarded to tank commanders, drivers, gunners, loaders and radio operators that have taken part in three armored assaults on three different days, been wounded in an assault or won a decoration for bravery in an assault. A separate award was given for 25, 50, 75, 100, 200 assaults.

Tank Assault Badge – Awarded to the crews of armored vehicles, other than tanks, which comprised self propelled gunners, panzergrenadiers, support units and medical personnel that have taken part in three armored assaults on three different days, been wounded in an assault, or won a decoration for bravery in an assault. A separate award was given for 25, 50, 75, 100, 200 assaults.

Infantry Assault Badge – Silver awarded to service members who have taken part in three or more infantry assaults, counterattacks, reconnaissance operations, hand to hand combat in assault positions or three days in the reconstitution of combat positions operations. A Bronze award met the same requirements, but was awarded to the motorized infantry.

General Assault Badge - Awarded to members of the artillery, anti-aircraft, anti-tank, engineers and medical personnel who served with infantry or armor in the auxiliary role during three assaults on three different days, been wounded in an assault, or won a decoration for bravery in an assault. A separate award was given for 25, 50, 75, 100 assaults.

Wound Badge (three grades) - Awarded to service members wounded in combat; Black, 1-2 wounds, Silver, 3-5 wounds or the loss of limb, eye, deafness, Gold, five or more wounds or one wound causing total disability, permanent blindness or loss of manhood.

Africa Cuff Title or Arm Band - Authorized for wear on 18 July 1941 to those members of the D.A.K. who fought in North Africa. Service members must have had a minimum of six months in the theater of operations, this was later changed to four months or awarded decorations in theater or killed in action.

Italian-German African Campaign Medal – Awarded to German members of the D.A.K. by the Italian government for service in Africa. The medal was instituted by the Italian Government to reward the achievements of the German D.A.K. The medal was awarded in 1942 to only German troops. German soldiers were allowed to wear the award but there were no regulations specifying a particular method. Later in 1944, due to Italy's surrender the wearing of all Italian awards and decorations was prohibited.

Appendix 2: Regimental Commanders and Award Holders

Panzer Regiment 8
HAARDE, Hans   Oberst   08/10/36-08/10/38
ELSTER, Botho   Oberstlt   08/10/38-25/03/41
CRAMER, Hans   Oberst   25/03/41-01/03/42
TEEGE, Willi   Oberstlt   01/03/42-02/11/42
MILDEBRATH, Werner   Oberstlt   16/07/42-06/09/42
TEEGE, Willi   Oberstlt   06/09/42-02/11/42 (KIA)
IRKENS, Joseph   Oberst   27/12/42-12/05/43

Knights Cross Recipients with Oak leaves in Panzer Regiment 8
CRAMER, Hans, Generalmajor on 08/05/43 as the Commanding officer D.A.K.
KÜMMEL, Johannes, Major on 11/10/42 as the Commanding Officer I./Abteilung
STOTTEN, Hans-Gunther, Hauptmann on 10/5/43 as the Commanding Officer I./Abteilung

Knights Cross Recipients in Panzer Regiment 8
CRAMER, Hans, Oberst on 27/06/41 as the Commanding Officer Panzer Regiment 8
KÜMMEL, Johannes, Oberleutnant on 09/07/41 as the Commander 1st Company
FENSKI, Günther, Major (Posthumously) on 31/12/41 as the Commander I./Abteilung
WAHL, Wolfgang, Hauptmann on 06/01/42 as Commander II./Abteilung
STIEFELMAYER, Otto, Oberleutnant on 12/07/42 as Commander 1st Company
KEIL, Max, Oberleutnant (Posthumously) on 20/04/43 as Commander 1st Company

Panzer Regiment 8 German Cross in Gold Recipients (DKiG)
BASTIGKEIT, Heinrich, Leutnant 26/08/42 - Regt 8
BOCK, Hans, Oberleutnant 01/05/42 - Regt 8
BRILL, Albert, Feldwebel 26/08/42 – II./Regt 8
CRAMER, Hans, Oberst 05/03/42 - Regt 8
DÖWLING, Heinz, Oberfeldwebel 08/08/42 - Regt 8
GEIGER, Paul, Feldwebel 09/10/42 - 5./Regt 8
HESS, Heinz, Oberleutnant 21/02/42 – II./Regt 8
IRKENS, Josef, Oberst 21/04/43 - Regt 8
PRION, Hilmar, Oberleutnant 01/05/42 - Regt 8
SCHELLHAUS, Heinrich, Oberleutnant 14/04/43 - 2./Regt 8
SCHUBERT, Hugo, Oberleutnant 02/04/42 - Regt 8
SPOHN, Walter, Oberfeldwebel 07/02/43 - 5./Regt 8
STOTTEN, Hans-Günther, Hauptmann 14/03/43 - Regt 8
TRETTIN, Rudi, Feldwebel 10/05/43 - 6./Regt. 8
WEBER, Helmut, Unteroffizer 21/02/42 - 6./Regt. 8
WEISS, Richard, Oberleutnant 08/08/42 - Regt 8
ZÜGNER, Josef, Hauptmann 09/10/42 - Regt 8

Appendix 3: Glossary

A.P.	Artillery registration point	Funker	Radio operator
Abholkommando	Retrieval detail or party	Fw	Feldwebel or Staff Sergeant
Abteilung	Battalion size unit, refers to close combat support formations	Gefrieter	Corporal
		Generalkommando	Level of Command of an Army Corps or Group
Abt.	see Abteilung	Gepkfz.	Gepanzertes kraftfahrzeug, armed vehicle
Alam	Rock cairn	GDIR	Grossdeutschland Infantry Regiment
Angriff	Attack	Gympy Tummy	British term for Dysentery
Anthrazit	Light grey or blue black (coal) color	H-39	French light tank, Hotchkiss model 39
AOK 1	First German-Italian Army	HE/AP	High Explosive/Armor Piercing tank round
AP	Armor Piercing ammunition	HFw	Hauptfeldwebel (Senior Sergeant)
Arty.	Artillery	Hinterhangstellung	A reverse slope position
Arzt.	Doctor	HKL	abbreviation for Hauptkriegslinie or main line of resistance
Aufklärung	Reconnaissance		
Ausf	Model or version	Honey	British name for the U.S. produced tank also known as a Stuart
Bab	Pass		
Battalion	a specific unit composed of approximately 500-700 personnel	Hptm	Hauptmann or Captain
		Hurricane	British Hawker Hurricane fighter plane
B.E.F.	British Expeditionary Force	Ia	Division Chief or Staff, or 1st General Staff officer
Befehl	Command or Order		
Befehlswagen	Command vehicle	Ib (kfz)	Division Motor officer
Bir	Cistern or native water wells found in the desert	Ib (WuG)	Division Armorer officer
Bn.	see Battalion	Ib	Division Quartermaster, 2nd General Staff officer
Casino	Officers club	Ic	Division Intelligence officer or 3rd General Staff officer (Enemy Intel)
Cdr.	Abbreviation for Commander		
Char-B	French heavy tank	Igel	German word for a hedgehog
Chef	German for company commander	iG	General Staff officer in service on General Staff
Chief	a company commander	IIa	Division Adjutant (G-1)
Chott	Salt Marsh	IIb	Division Adjutant (enlisted affairs) (CSM)
CO	Commanding Officer	Inf.	Infantry
Crusader	British battle tank	Ing.	Engineer
D-2	Renault model D-2 Tank	I-Staffel	Engineer section
DAF	Desert Air Force comprised of U.S., British, Australian and S.African forces	Jabos	Nickname for Fighter Bombers
		Jäger	Hunter, refers to Light infantry and Anti-tank formations
D.A.K.	Deutsches Afrika Korps		
DCR	French Armored Division	Ju-52	German transport plane
Deir	Depression	Ju-87	German dive bomber
DIM	French Motorized Infantry Division	Kampfgruppe	a combat or battle group
Div.	Division	Kampfstaffel	combat sections or squadrons
Djebels	Rocky hills in the desert	Kar-98	Carbine or standard German bolt action rifle of WWII
DKiG	Deutsches Kreuz in Gold		
DLC	French Light Cavalry Division	Karetten	a small trailer
DLM	French Cavalry or Light Mechanized Division	Kaserne	Barracks or Military Camp/Post
EK I	Eisernes Kreuz or Iron Cross First Class	Kfz	Kraftfahrzug or 4x4 type military vehicle/command car
EK II	Eisernes Kreuz or Iron Cross Second Class		
Erkzug	Erkundungszug or Reconnaissance Platoon	KIA	Killed in Action
Ersatz	Reserve	Kittyhawk	British version of the American made Curtis P-40 fighter
FCM	French light tank		
Feldpost	Field post office	KOB	Kriegsofficerbeweber or Officers Candidate School
Flak	Fliegerabwehrkanone or Anti-aircraft gun		
Flitzer	a small fast vehicle, car or bike	Kradmelder	Motorcycle courier
FT-17	Renault WWI era tank		

Appendix 3: Glossary

KTB	abbreviation for German kriegstagbuch or daily war diary	RAF	Royal Air Force
KV-1	Russian battle tank	Ras	Cape
Kwk	Kampfwagenkanone or tank main gun	Regt	Abbreviation for regiment
Ladeschütze	gun loader	Rgt	Abbreviation for regiment
Lade	short for ladeschütze	Richtschützen	Gunner or Gun layer
Lazaret	Hospital	Ritterkreuz	Knights Cross, the highest award given to German soldiers
Lehr	Training	RTR	Royal Tank Regiment, a battalion size armored formation
LeKol	Leiche Kolonne or Transport supply unit or column	S-35/40	Soumua Model 35/40 tank
LKW	Ladekraftwagen (Lkw) or truck type vehicle	Sanka	Short name for a medical field ambulance
LNO	Liaison Officer	Schützen	Early term for infantry forces later known as grenadiers
Lt	Leutnant or Lieutenant		
M-13	Italian battle tank	Schwere	Heavy
M-14	Italian Semovente assault gun	Sdf	Sonderführer or special leader
Matilda	British Mk II infantry tank	Sdl	Selbstfahrlafette or self propelled vehicle
Me-109	German fighter plane manufactured by Messerschmitt	Sfl	see Sdl
		Sherman	U.S. made battle tank mounting a 75mm gun
MG	Machine gun, as in MG-34, MG-42	Souma	French heavy tank
MIA	Missing in Action	Speiss	Company First Sergeant
Mk I	German light tank	Sperrverbande	Blocking detachment
Mk II	German light tank	Spitzenkompanie	Lead Company
Mk III	German medium battle tank	Sprenggranaten	Hi-Explosive round known as HE
Mk IV	German medium battle tank	Sprengkommando	Demolitions Squads
MP-40	German sub machine gun commonly known as the Schmeisser	SP	Abbreviation for a Self-Propelled Gun, like the British 2-Pounder
MTW	Manschafts transport wagen, personnel carrier (armed)	SPW	Schützenpanzerwagen or half tracked vehicle
		Stabs	Staff or Headquarters
Nachrichten	Signals and Communications	StKp	Stabs Company or Headquarters Company
Nebelwerfer	Six barreled rocket launcher	Stoss	Assault or storm group
Oberkommando	Level of Command of a Field Army or Army Group	Stug	Abbreviation for Sturmgeschütze
		Stuka	Sturzkampfbomber or dive bomber
Oberst	Colonel	Sturmgeschütz	German assault gun
Oberstlt	Oberstleutnant or Lieutenant Colonel	StZmstr	Stabszahlmeister or Paymaster
Ofumstr	Oberfunkmeister (main radio master)	T-34	Russian main battle tank
OFw	Oberfeldwebel or Master Sergeant	Tel	Mound
OKH	Oberkommando Heeres or Army High Command	Tieflader	Low loading vehicle tank transport
OKL	Oberkommando Luftwaffe or air force High Command	Tieflieger	Dive-bomber
		Tiele	German for tank wedge
OKW	Oberkommando Wehrmacht or Supreme High Command	Tiger	German heavy tank or Mk VI
		Trigh	Impermanent firm surface tracks in the desert
Olt	Oberleutnant or 1st Lieutenant	Tross	Supply troop or trains
OO	Assistant Adjutant or Ordnance Orderly	Uffz	Unteroffizier or Junior Sergeant
Pak	Panzerabwehrkanone or Anti-tank gun	Valentine	British battle tank
Panzerarmee	German Tank Army	Via	A hard paved all weather surface
Panzerjäger	Tank hunters or anti-tank guns	Wadi	Dried-up river bed or deep ravine
Pilot	German word used to describe the M-3 Grant tank	Warter	Tank mechanic
		Warte	Watch tower, observatory
Piste	Off-road trail or dirt track	WIA	Wounded in Action
Poilus	French term for an infantryman or soldier	Zahlmeister	Paymaster
PoW	Abbreviation for Prisoner of War	zbV	an abbreviation used to designate a special grouping
Pzr	Panzer or Tank		
PzKpfw	abbreviation for Panzerkampfwagen or tank	Zeltbahn	Tent or Shelter half
Qaret	Low hill	Zgkw	Zugkraftwagen or truck
R-35	Renault Model 35 tank	Zug	Platoon or Section

Appendix 4: Regimental Role

ABELE, Eugen, 1st Kp, STW
ADAM, Lt., KIA Nov 41
ADE, OGefr, StKp, I./Abt.
AICH, Karl Lt, STW
ALBERS, OGefr, 1st Kp.
ALDINGER, Fritz
ALLGÖWER, Otto, OGefr, 5th Kp, MIA
ALTDÖRFER, Albert, STW
AMENT, Hermann, OFw, STW
ANGERSTEIN, Josef, STW
ARENTSCHILDT von, Alexander
ARMBRÜSTER, Küno, Gefr. 5th Kp.
ARNBERGE, OGefr, 7th Kp.
ARNDT, Gefr.
ARNDT, Günter, OZm, STW
ARNOLD, Hans, 8th Kp, STW
ARNOLD, Lt/Olt, 1st Kp, WIA in Africa
ASKANI, Uffz, 5th Kp.
ASTER, Hptm, 3rd Kp.
AUERBACHER, Winfried, OFw, STW
BACH,
BACH, Hptm, StKp II./Abt.
BACH, Walter, HFw, STW
BACHHOFER, Walter, OFw, STW
BÄCK,
BADER, Hermann, STW
BAHNERT, Paul, Lt.
BALLHAUS, Hermann, Lt, 4th Kp, PoW, STW
BALSER, Willi, STW
BÄNGER,
BANHOLZER, Max, STW
BANZHAF, Hans, STW
BARLOG, Stanislaus, OGefr.
BARTENSCHLAGER, Hptm, Rgt LeKol.
BASSLER, Willi, Fw, Pioneer Zug, II Abt, STW
BASTIGKEIT, Heinrich, Lt,
BAUCH, Uffz, II Abt.
BAUDERT,
BAUER, Hans, Olt, Pioneer Zug, 4th Kp, STW
BAUER, Helmut, HFw, STW
BAUER, Johann, OFw, STW
BAUER, Lt, 4th Kp.
BAUER, Uffz, 7th Kp.
BAUER, Walter, Ofw.
BAUERGEIGER, Fw, 5th Kp.
BAUERUND, Lt, 3rd Kp.
BAUMAN, L.
BAUMANN, Heinz, Olt.
BAUMANN, Uffz, II./Abt.
BAUMBÄRTL, Helmut, Maj, STW
BAUMGARTEN, Uffz, II Abt.

BAUMGÄRTNER, Wilhelm, 6th Kp, STW
BAUSCH, Ernst, Uffz, 7th Kp.
BAYER, Ernst, Fw.
BAYLÄNDER, Enrico, STW
BAYLÄNDER, Heinrich, Gefr, Rgt H.Q.
BECHTHOLD, Karl, Uffz, 7th Kp, MIA 1945
BECK, Ernst, STW
BECKER, Fw.
BECKER, FwOa /Lt, 1st Kp.
BECKER, Rudolf, Dr, STW
BECKERS, Fw, Rgt Stabs Kp.
BECKERS, Josef
BEER, Uffz, I./Abt.
BEHR, Uffz, II./Abt, KIA Nov 41
BEHRENSMANN, Gefr,
BENECKE, Martin, KIA May 1941
BENKE, Willi, 1st Kp, STW
BENNEMANN, Hans STW
BENTEL, Hans, STW
BENZ, Albert, 7th Kp, STW
BENZ, Franz, 2nd Kp, STW
BENZ, Gerhard, Schutze, 7th Kp, MIA Sep 42
BERG, Hans, 1st Kp, STW
BERGER, Gefr, 7th Kp.
BERGMANN, Horst, HFw, STW
BERKEMER, OGefr,4th Kp.
BERKER, Ludwig
BERMANN, Anton, 4th Kp, STW
BERNAU, Joachim, Olt, 1st Kp.
BERTSCH, Eugen
BETZ, Hptm, I./Abt.
BETZEL,
BEYEN, Dr. STW
BEYER, Gunner, KIA in Africa
BEZ, Jakob, 2nd Kp, STW
BIALAS, 3rd Kp.
BIELMAYER, OGefr, KIA Jun 40
BIRBALD, H., Gefr, KIA Jun 41
BISCHOFF, Erwin, Olt,
BISSBART, Reinhard, STW
BITTER Von, Rudolf, StKp, I./Abt.
BLANK, Kurt, Lt, POW
BLEIBER, Helmut OFw, Rgt H.Q., STW
BLIDSCHUN, Artur, Olt, WkStKp
BLUM, Otto, STW
BOCK, Hans Olt, I./Abt
BÖCKEL, Walter, OFw, 5th Kp. KIA Sep 39 (1st Regimental KIA)
BODENHAUSEN, Frhr Von
BOECKELMANN, Johannes
BOEHM, Gefr, Rgt H.Q.
BOEKELMANN, Johann, STW

Appendix 4: Regimental Role

BOESER, Emil, STW
BOHLAND, KIA,
BOHM, Helmut, 2nd Kp, STW
BOHMANN, Uffz.
BOHR, Franz-Joseph, Lt.
BOKELRIG, Uffz, KIA 1940
BÖLTZ, Karl
BONGARD, Leo, STW
BÖNISCH, Heinz, Lt.
BÖSEBECK, Karl-Heinz Lt, STW
BÖSEKES, Wolfgang, Hptm
BÖSER, Emil, STW
BÖTTGER, Werner, STW
BÖTTGER, Karl-Heinz, STW
BOZETTI, Heribert, 7th Kp. STW
BRÄCKER, Egon
BRAÜHERR, Josef, Rgt HQ, STW
BRAUN, II./Abt, KIA Nov 41
BRAUN, Walter, StKp, STW
BRECHT, Karl, STW
BREITER, Uffz, KIA Jun 40
BREITINGER, Heinz, Fw, STW
BREKER, Egon, STW
BRENNER, Johannes, Gefr, KIA Jun 42
BREUNINGER, Fritz, 7th Kp, STW
BRILL, Albert, Fw, II./Abt. StKp
BROSS, Fritz, STW
BRUCK, Ernst, Uffz, STW
BRUCKER, Heinrich, STW
BRÜGGEMANN, Fritz, STW
BRUHN, Hermann, StKp I./Abt, STW
BRUNN, von, Albrecht, Gefr/Lt, 7th Kp, POW
BRUNS, Hptm.
BUCH, Helmut, STW
BUCHOFER, Paul, Gefr, 4th Kp, MIA Dec 41
BÜCHIN, Erwin, STW
BÜHL, Josef, 2nd Kp, STW
BÜHLER, Wilhelm, Uffz, POW, STW
BÜRKLE, Herbert, STW
BÜRKLE, Karl, STW
BÜTTENWEG, Johann, 6th Kp, STW
BULLA, OFm,
BULOW von Fhr, Hptm.
BUTHENHOFF, Gerhard, Uffz, 7th Kp, MIA 1945
BUTZ, Ernst, 2nd Kp, STW
CHRESTIN, Herbert, Rgt Stabs, STW
CONZE, Wilhelm, Major, I./Abt.
CRAMER, Hans, Oberst Rgt HQ, later General der Panzertruppen, STW
CROHN, Major I./Abt
CROOMENBROEK, Albert, STW
DAEBICH, Walter, OGefr 4th Kp.
DAIS, Karl, STW
DANNER, Hermann, 4th Kp, STW
DANZ, Walter, Lt, 8th Kp KIA Jun 42
DAST, Karl, STW
DAUNER, Hermann
DECKER, Lt.
DEGNER, Gefr, 7th Kp.
DENNICKE, Fw, I./Abt.
DEPPE Ernst, HFw.

DICKMANN, Rudolf, 5th Kp, STW
DIETRICH, Uffz, II./Abt.
DIETRICH, Uffz.
DIEZ, Alfred, STW
DITTRICH, Karl, 5th Kp, STW
DORNEN, Gerhard, Schutze, 8th Kp, MIA Dec 44
DÖWLING, Heinz, Fw.
DRÄGER, later Maj,
DREHER, Karl, Soldat, 3rd Kp MIA May 42
DRETTIGEN, Fw.
DREWS, Ludwig, Fw, STW
DROHNENFELS, von Lt. 4th Kp.
DUCKGEISEL, Karl, 7th Kp, STW
DÜRR, Alfred, OGefr, 2nd Kp, STW
EBERSPÄCHER,
ECKARDT, Hermann, Uffz, STW
ECKARDT, Kurt, STW
ECKERT, Uffz, KIA May 41
ECKLE, Erwin, STW
EGER, Max, Gefr, S-Kp, STW
EHNINGER, Hans, STW
EHRBECK, Wilhelm., Hptm, 4th Kp.
EHRET, Georg, 4th Kp, STW
EICHBERG, Lt later Hptm
EINSIEDLER, Kurt, STW
EISELE, STW
EISENLOHR, Herbert, STW
ELLESER, Fritz, 2nd Kp, STW
ELLWANGER, Helmut, STW
ELSTER, Botho Oberstlt, GenMaj, POW, STW
EMMERLING, Fritz
EMMERLING, Friedrich, 7th Kp, STW
ERB, Siegfried, STW
ERDMANN, OGefr.
ERHART, Uffz, 5th Kp.
ERLENMAIER, Wilhelm, 4th Kp, STW
ERTL, Rudolf, STW
ESCH, Peter, 6th Kp, STW
ESSER, Gefr, S-Kp.
ESTOR, Dr.
ETZEL, Paul, Uffz, StKp I./Abt.
FAIGLE, Karl, Lt, 3rd Kp, POW, STW
FASS, Uffz, KIA Nov 41
FAUSER, Hermann, 7th Kp, STW
FAUTER, Emil, Fw, 1st Kp, KIA May 42
FECHTIG, Emil, Lt, KIA Nov 42
FECKLER, Gottfried, Gefr, 8th Kp, MIA Feb 1945
FEIGL, Toni, Uffz, 2nd Kp.
FELITZER, Gefr, II./Abt.
FELLER, Roger, Regt Dr.
FENSKI, Günther, II./Abt KIA Nov 41
FISCHER, Erich, II./Abt, STW
FISCHER, Johann, 6th Kp, STW
FISCHER, Ogefr, 7th Kp.
FISCHER, Siegfried, Lt, II./Abt, POW, STW
FISCHER-LAMPE, Hptm.
FLAD, Gottlob, STW
FLATT, Walter, 7th Kp, STW
FLEISCHMANN, Georg 3rd Kp II./Abt, STW
FLICK, Karl, Dr., STW

FLOD, Uffz, II./Abt, KIA Nov 41
FLÖSS, K, Gefr, KIA Jun 40
FLÜHRER, Gefr, 7th Kp.
FODERS, Olt, LeZug StKp I./Abt.
FOELLMER, Lt, 7th Kp.
FOLLMANN, Matthias, STW
FÖRSTER, Klaus, Africa, POW, STW
FRANK, Heinrich, WkKp, STW
FRANKE, Olt, KIA Nov 41
FRANKENBERG U PROSCHLITZ, Von Hptm,
FRÄNKLE, Wilhelm, STW
FRAUENHOFER, Josef, 6th Kp, STW
FRECKSMEYER, Bruno, STW
FREI, Alois, STW
FREY, Eugen, STW
FREY, Otto, STW
FRIEDLE, Kurt, STW
FRIEDRICH,
FRIEDRICH, Heinrich, 5th Kp, STW
FRIES, Hans, STW
FRIESSINGER, Ofw.
FRINGSKARTE, Gefr II./Abt WIA Nov 41
FUCHS, Günter
FUNK, HELMUT
FUSSMAUL, OGefr, KIA Jun 40
GABRIEL, Walter, 7th Kp, STW
GAISER, Karl, Gefr, 2nd Kp.
GAMPER, Josef, Gefr, 7th Kp, MIA Jan 1945
GANDERT, Horst, Fw, Stabs I./Abt.
GAUERMANN, August, STW
GAUSS, Gefr, I./Abt.
GAYDE, Karl, STW
GEBERT, Fritz, 5th Kp, STW
GECKELER, Heinrich, Rgt HQ, STW
GEIER, Josef, 5th Kp, STW
GEIGER, Karl, STW
GEIGER, Paul, Fw, 5th Kp.
GEIGIS, Alois, 7th Kp, STW
GEILENBRAUN, Fw, KIA Feb 43
GENZ, Ewald
GENZLER, Oberfähnrich
GERBERT, Fritz, STW
GERDER, Fw, II./Abt.
GERDES, Uffz, 7th Kp.
GERHARD,
GERIES,
GERLACH, Ewald, Fw, 3rd Kp, STW
GERSDORFF, von, Joachim, Maj, STW
GESSER, KIA in Africa
GESSNER, Hans, STW
GESSWEIN, Walter, STW
GFRÖHRER, Josef, STW
GIERK, Gerhard, Fw, STW
GIESSER, Gefr, 2nd Kp, KIA Apr 42
GILCHER, Rudolf, OFw, STW
GISY, Fritz, II./Abt, STW
GITZER, II./Abt.
GLIESE, Siegfried, Fw, LeZug StKp, STW
GLÜCK, Hans, STW
GMÄHLE, Georg, STW

GÖB, Erich, Fw, 3rd Kp, STW
GOHL, Eugen, 8th Kp, STW
GOLD, Willibald, STW
GOLINSKI, Heinz, Lt, II./Abt, POW, STW
GONSCHOREK, Paul, 2nd Kp, STW
GOTTFRIED, Lt, Pi Zug II./Abt KIA May 42
GÖTZE, Georg, Uffz, 7th Kp KIA May 1940
GRABIS, Uffz, Rgt HQ
GRAF, Adolf, 5th Kp STW
GRAF, Rudi, STW
GRÄFE, Gefr, 7th Kp.
GRALL, Helmut, Uffz, 2nd Kp, STW
GRAMÜLLER, Erich, HFw, STW
GREIFF, Peter, Lt, STW
GRIEF, Theodor, Uffz, II./Abt, STW
GRIESINGER, Georg, STW
GROH, Uffz, KIA, France 1940
GROSS, Uffz, 7th Kp, KIA May 1940
GROSS, Uffz, II./Abt.
GROTH, Eckart, Lt, 2nd Kp.
GRUBER, Hermann, Lt, Africa, POW
GRUNDIG, Walter, STW
GRUNOW, Erich 7th Kp, STW
GSTREIN, Sdf (G) 1st Kp.
GUGGEMOS, Otto, 2nd Kp, STW
GUNDELACH, Lt., 8th Kp.
GUTEKUNST, Ernst, STW
HAAG, Willi, Lt, LeKol, POW, STW
HAAR, Josef, STW
HAARDE, Friedrich, Oberstlt, I./Abt, STW
HAARDE, Hans, Oberst, STW
HAARER, Karl, STW
HAAS, Friedrich, 2nd Kp, KIA Sep 39
HAAS, Karl, Gefr, I./Abt, KIA Jun 40
HAAS, Walter, STW
HABERMANN, Emil, 1st Kp, STW
HABICH, Karl, STW
HABISREITINGER, Fritz, Workshop Kp, STW
HABLITZEL, Hans, StKp II./Abt, STW
HADLER, Oberzahlmstr, KIA Jan 43
HÄFNER,
HAGEN, Uffz, 7th Kp.
HAGIOS, Wilhelm, Fw, I./Abt, POW, STW
HAHN, Helmut, 1st Kp, STW
HAHN, Lt, 2nd Kp, KIA May 40
HAHN, Mannfried, Lt.
HAHNEN, Uffz, II./Abt.
HAIDT, Gotthilf, OGefr, Werkstadt Kp, STW
HAKE, von, Hans-Joachim, STW
HALVERSCHEIDT, Karl, Lt, 6th Kp, POW, STW
HAMPEL, Paul, STW
HANAGARTH, Wilhelm, 1st Kp, STW
HANEMANN, Horst, 3rd Kp, STW
HANSKE, Fw, 2nd Kp.
HÄRCHER, Ogefr, 7th Kp.
HARDTER, Kurt, STW
HARMGARTH, 2nd Kp, KIA Nov 41
HÄRTE, Gefr, 5th Kp.
HÄRTHER, Gustav, STW
HARTMANN, Kurt, Dr, STW

Appendix 4: Regimental Role

HARTSCHEN, Peter Gefr, II./Abt KIA May 40
HASCHE, Otto, 1st Kp, STW
HASS, Walter, STW
HATSCHER, Hans, STW
HAUERWAS, Emil, Rgt HQ
HAUSER, Arno, STW
HAUSKA, OFw
HAUSMANN, OGefr.
HAUSSELS, Hugo, STW
HÄUSSER, Kurt, STW
HAUSTEIN, Fritz, Fw, STW
HECKEL, Lt, 5th Kp.
HECKMANN, Ogefr, 7th Kp.
HEHRING, Tech Insp, II./Abt.
HEIDBACH Friedrich, STW
HEILER, STW
HEILMANN Helmut, STW
HEIM, Kurt, Lt, 5th Kp, POW, STW
HEIMBERGER, Wilhelm, Fw, 6th Kp, KIA May 1940
HEINRICH, Lt, 7th Kp,
HEINS, Fw, 7th Kp, KIA Jun 40
HEINTZ, Fw, KIA Jun 40
HEINZ, Otto, Fw, 7th Kp, KIA France 1940
HEINZMANN Franz, Lt, Rgt HQ, POW, STW
HEISS, Oskar 4th Kp, STW
HELGER, Sdf (G) 2nd Kp.
HELLMIGK, Uffz.
HELLSTERN, Hfw, KIA June 41
HENN, Manfred, Olt, STW
HERDE, Willi, 6th Kp.
HERDER, Hans, OFw, STW
HERDTER, Hermann, 4th Kp.
HERING, Ing Off.
HERTHER, Gustav, STW
HESS, Heinz, Lt, II./Abt, POW, STW
HETTICH, Gefr, KIA Jun 40
HETZEL, Lt, 5th Kp, KIA
HEUSCHER, Werner Lt, I./Abt, STW
HEYDEBRECK, von, Georg-Henning, I.Abt, STW
HILDEBRAND, Heinz, OFw, STW
HILLE, Karl, Fw, STW
HIMMELREICH, Fw, II./Abt.
HIMMIGHÖFER, Otto, STW
HIRSCHFELD, Hptm, KIA 1943
HOCHSTETTER, Helmut Dr ObFeldArzt II./Abt, STW
HOFFER, Uffz, 1st Kp.
HOFFMANN, Alois, STW
HOFFMANN, Friedrich, 6th Kp, STW
HOFMANN, Artur, Fw, STW
HOFMANN, Heinrich, 8th Kp, STW
HOFMANN, Walter, OGefr, 8th Kp, MIA Oct 42
HOHNECKER, Hugo, Lt, POW, STW
HOLCHIG, Uffz, KIA May 40
HOLL, Walter, OGefr, 4th Kp
HOLLACK, Uffz, II./Abt.
HOLTEY, von, Lt, I./Abt
HOLZWARTH, Adolf, STW
HONECKER, Fw 2nd Kp.
HÖNEMANN, August, STW
HÖNICH, Michel, STW

HONOLD, Willi, 7th Kp, STW
HORN, Uffz, I./Abt.
HORNIKEL, Uffz, 5th Kp.
HORNUNG, Edelbert
HÖRR, Otto, Gefr, 3rd Kp, MIA Oct 42
HOSS, Karl, 7th Kp, STW
HÖSS, Walter, STW
HOSSFELD, Uffz
HOUWALDT, Freiherr von, Lt, 2nd Kp, KIA Mar 43
HUBBUCH, Klaus Gefr, II./Abt, POW, STW
HUBER, Josef, Gefr, 1st Kp.
HÜMMELCHEN, Ogefr.
HUMBERT, Emil, OFw, STW
HUND, Ofw.
HUNZELMANN, Gefr, 7th Kp.
HURLEBAUS, Walter, STW
HUTTENLOCHER, Theo, Gefr, II./Abt, STW
HUTZLER, Gefr.
IHDE, Eberhard, Lt 1st Kp, STW
ILL, Karl, STW
IRKENS, Josef, Oberst, POW, STW
IRMISCH, Oberstlt, I./Abt.
ISENSEE, Ernst StFw Rgt HQ, STW
JACKOBS, Uffz.
JACOB, Gerhard, StKp, STW
JÄGER, Hptm.
JAHN, Gunther, Uffz, 7th Kp.
JAHNS, Rudi, Oblt, II./Abt.
JAKOB, Gerhard, STW
JANDO, Paul, STW
JATTKOWSKI, Helmut, Hptm 5th Kp, STW
JENNER, Jakob
JENZER, Uffz, 7th Kp.
JEUTHER, Robert, 6th Kp, STW
JOHANNSEN, Franz, Sonderführer, Rgt HQ, STW
JOHN, Günter, Gefr, 7th Kp, STW
JOHNER, Wilhelm, 6th Kp, STW
JOOS, Hermann, Gefr, 1st Kp.
JÖRGER, Karl, 6th Kp, STW
KADURA, Fw 7th Kp, KIA Jun 42
KAHMEIER, Karl, OFw.
KAISER, Gustav, 5th Kp.
KAISER, Karl OGefr.
KAISER, Marbold, OFw, STW
KAJA, Paul, 7th Kp, STW
KALINSKI, Fw, 2nd Kp.
KANT, OGefr.
KAPPENBERGER, Herbert, STW
KARWEHL, Karl, 4th Kp, STW
KATHE, Kurt. OFw, 5th Kp, STW
KAUDEL, Willi, STW
KAUFFMANN, Kurt, Olt, 3rd Kp.
KAUFMANN, Erich, 1st Kp, STW
KAULBARS, OGefr, 7th Kp.
KAUPP, Eugen, STW
KECK, Fritz, STW
KECK, Walter, STW
KEHRER, Arthur, Lt, STW
KEIL, Max, Lt, 1st Kp, KIA Apr 43
KELLER, von Heinrich, Lt, 2nd Kp, POW, STW

KEMPKES, Ernst,
KENTEL, Hptm.
KERN, Erich, Uffz, 4th Kp, MIA Mar 43
KERTSCHER, Gerd, Lt, 3rd Kp, STW
KESSEL, Han-Georg, Gefr, I./Abt.
KESSLER, Georg, STW
KIEFER, Manfred, Hptm, STW
KIELMANN, Gefr.
KIELWEIN, Gefr.
KIENZLE, Gerhard, Uffz, 4th Kp, STW
KILLERMANN, Hans, Uffz, 3rd Kp, STW
KIRCHBERG, OFw, 5th Kp, KIA Nov 41
KIRCHNER, Eugen, STW
KISTNER, Albert, 2nd Kp, STW
KLAMEREK, Siegfried, Uffz 2nd Kp.
KLEFF, Theo, OGefr, 1st Kp.
KLEIN, Karl-Heinz, Maj, STW
KLEMEREK, Siegfried, Gefr.
KLIENS, Hptm, StKp, KIA Africa
KLINGAUF, Karl, 8th Kp, STW
KLINGLER, Alfred STW
KLINK, Otto,
KLINKE, Günter, STW
KLOSS, Lothar, STW
KNAUSS, Gustav, 5th Co, STW
KNOBELSPEIS, Gefr, 8th Kp, KIA Sep 42
KNÖDEL, Robert, 8th Kp, STW
KNOPP, Richard, STW
KNORR, Carl-Heinz, Olt, I./Abt, STW
KNOTH, Hans, 2nd Kp, STW
KNOTH, Sdf (G), Rgt HQ.
KOCH, Erwin, Gefr, 7th Kp, KIA Jun 40
KOCH, Karl, Fw, 7th Kp.
KOCH, Uffz, II./Abt.
KOCH, Gefr, 8th Kp, KIA, Sep 42
KÖGL, Hans, Gefr, 7th Kp.
KOHLEN, Oskar
KOHLER, Ewald, 7th Kp, STW
KOHLER, H, Dr, Uffz, STW
KOHLER, Oskar, 7th Kp, STW
KOHLMANN, Uffz,
KOLBE, Heinz, STW
KOLBE, Wilhelm, Fw, I./Abt.
KOLESCH, August, STW
KOLINSKI, Heinz
KOLK, Günter, Artz, POW, STW
KOMOROWSKI, OGefr, 7th Kp.
KÖNIG, Kurt, STW
KONZ, Uffz, 8th Kp.
KOPPE, Uffz, 7th Kp.
KOPPE, Gefr, 8th Kp, KIA Feb 43
KÖRBEL, Lt, STW
KÖRNER, Olt.
KÖRNER, Teodor, Olt, 5th Kp, KIA Nov 41
KOSCHIG, Uffz, 7th Kp, KIA May 40
KOSER, Olt, KIA Nov 41
KRAFT, Gefr, I./Abt.
KRAFT, Hans, 1st Kp, STW
KRAFT, Kuno, STW
KRAMER, Max, Gefr, 5th Kp, MIA Nov 42

KRAMER, Stefan, Fw, Africa, STW
KRANZ, Hugo, Lt, Africa, POW
KRANZ, Olt, Rgt HQ.
KRAPF, Hans, STW
KRATSCHMER, Sepp, KIA Sep 39
KRATZ, Hermann, Gefr, 5th Kp, MIA Nov 41
KRAUS, Fw, KIA, Jun 40
KRAUS, Uffz.
KRAUSS, Eugen, STW
KRAUSS, Friedrich, I./Abt, STW
KRAUSS, Gustav, 5th Kp, STW
KRIEGER, Willy, II./Abt, STW
KRIES, Ogefr, LeZug I./Abt.
KROMER, Eugen, STW
KROMER, Stefan, 7th Kp, STW
KRONAUER, Josef, 1st Kp, STW
KRÖNER, Konrad, Uffz, 8th Kp, MIA Feb 45
KRUCK, Ferdinand, OFw, I./Abt, KIA Dec 41
KRÜGER, Dr.,
KRÜGER, Kurt, Olt, KIA 1945
KRÜPAR, Franz Dr. I./Abt, STW
KRUGEL, Helmet, 7th Kp, KIA May 41
KRUMHOLZ, August, Gefr, 7th Kp, MIA Jun 42
KRUSCHINSKI, Toni, Fw, 1st Kp.
KSIS, Gefr, 4th Kp.
KUCH, Erich OGefr, 2nd Kp, STW
KUECK, Gefr, 2nd Kp, STW
KÜCKLICH, Hptm Dr, Lekol.
KÜHN, Fw,
KÜHNE, Paul, Uffz, 1st Kp.
KÜMMEL, Johannes, Maj, I./Abt. KIA 1944
KUGLER, Artur Sonderführer, 5th Kp.
KUHLHOFF, Alois, Lt, POW, STW
KUNZMANN, Erich, STW
KUPPINGER, I./Abt, KIA Jan 43
KURS, Lt.
KURZ, Jakob, Fw.
KURZ, Werner, 8th Kp, STW
KUSCHKA, Driver, 8th Co,
KUSSMAUL, G, Uffz, 2nd Kp, KIA Jun 40
KYNAST, Fw, LeZug, StKp.
LADENDOFF, Fw, KIA in Sep 39
LAHUSEN, Lt, 6th Kp.
LAMM, Adolf, Uffz, 2nd Kp, POW, STW
LAMMEK, Karl-Heinz, 6th Kp, STW
LÄMMLE, Erwin 5th Kp, STW
LAMPE, Heinrich, Lt/OInsp, STW
LANDTHALER, Siegfried, Gefr, 7th Kp, STW
LANG, Fritz, Uffz, StKp I./Abt.
LANGENBACH, Helmut, Lt.
LANGHANS, Karl, Sonderführer, Rgt HQ.
LATENDORFF, OFw 7th Kp.
LAUBENSTEIN, Hans, STW
LAUER, August, STW
LAUN, Otto, Uffz 2nd Kp, KIA Jun 40
LEBOLD, Max Uffz, 5th Kp, POW, STW
LEHN, Olt, 5th Kp, KIA May/Jun 42
LEIDIG, Rgt HQ
LEINMÜLLER, Hugo, 7th Kp, STW
LENZ, Erwin, 1st Kp, STW

LENZ, Oswald, OGefr, 7th Kp, MIA May 42
LEULE, Lt.
LIEBIG, Helmut, STW
LIESTMANN, Heinz, Lt, 8th Kp, KIA Nov 41
LIESTMANN, Kurt, Lt, 3rd Kp, STW
LINDNER, Georg, Lt.
LINKE, Hptm.
LOETZ, Erwin, Lt, 7th Kp.
LÖFFLER, Anton, I./Abt, STW
LÖFFLER, Josef, STW
LÖFFLER, Martin, STW
LÖFFLER, Wilhelm, STW
LOHSS, Martin, STW
LÖNS, Hermann, KIA Sep 39
LÖSSER, Horst, Olt, STW
LÖTZ, "Speck" Fw.
LÖW, Gustav, 7th Kp, STW
LUDWIG, Wilhelm. Uffz, 5th Kp, STW
LUDWIGKEIT, 2nd Kp, KIA Sep 39
LÜDERS, Fw, 7th Kp, KIA Jun 40
LUETHLE Emil, STW
LÜTTICH, Lt.
LUIPPOLD, Ludwig, STW
LUITTLE, Emil, 2nd Kp, STW
MACK, GERT, Olt, STW
MAGDEBURG, Ernst, 3rd Kp, POW, STW
MAHLEBRINK, Gefr, 5th Kp.
MAIER, August, 3rd Kp.
MAIER, Erwin, 8th Kp, STW
MAIER, Hans, 6th Kp, STW
MAINKEL-SCHMITT, OGefr.
MAISCH, Dieter, Dr., Hptm, STW
MALENBREY, OGefr, 5th Kp.
MÄNIKE, Kurt, 2nd Kp, STW
MANZ, Otto, STW
MARKERT, Hermann, STW
MARQUARDT, Paul, Olt 8th Kp, POW, STW
MARSCHALL, Hermann, Gefr, Rgt HQ.
MATTHES, Benno, STW
MATTHIAS, Jürgen, Rgt HQ, Lt, STW
MATTHIAS, Wolfgang, KIA in Africa
MAURER, Kurt, Soldat, 4th Kp, MIA Nov 41
MÄURER, Oskar, 4th Kp, STW
MAYER, Gotthilf, 8th Kp, STW
MAYER, Johannes, STW
MAYER, Josef, STW
MAYER, Klaus, STW
MAYER, Olt, 1st Kp.
MAYLÄNDER, Lt.
MEHL, Erich, II./Abt, STW
MEHLIG, OFw, 6th Kp.
MEHRER, Fw, Rgt HQ.
MEISER, F, Gefr, 2nd Kp KIA Jun 40
MEISNEST, Helmut, 2nd Kp, STW
MELBER, Hans, Lt, 8th Kp, POW, STW
MELENK, Hans, Soldat, 7th Kp, MIA Dec 44
MELZER, Erwin, STW
MENDELSCHMIDT,
MERKATZ, von, Lt.
MERTENS, Paul, STW

MERZ, A, OGefr 2nd Kp, KIA Jun 40
MERZ, Otto, 1st Kp, STW
METZE, Gefr, KIA Jun 40
METZGER, Georg, STW
MEYER Alfred, II./Abt, STW
MEYER, August, STW
MEYER, Berthold, 1st Kp, STW
MEYER, Erwin, STW
MEYER, Gerhard, 4th Kp, STW
MEYER, Hans, STW
MEYER, Wilhelm, Fw.
MICHAELIS, Harald, 4th Kp, STW
MICHEL, Walter, 1st Kp, STW
MICHELT, Uffz, 7th Kp, KIA 15 May 40
MIELEBACHER, Albert, II./Abt, STW
MIELKE, Willi, 1st Kp, STW
MILDE, Egon, Uffz, 1st Kp.
MILDEBRATH, Werner Oberstlt.
MINDER, Josef, 1st Kp, STW
MITTELMAYER, KIA
MITTERREITER, Uffz, I./Abt.
MOEST, Richard, Hptm.
MOHR, Uffz, II./Abt, KIA Nov 41
MOLZEN, Sdf (G) 3rd Kp.
MORLACH, August, I./Abt, STW
MOSER, Karl, II./Abt, STW
MOSER, Wilhelm, 5th Kp, STW
MOTSCH, I./Abt.
MUCKENFUSS, Helmut, STW
MÜLLER, Franz, STW
MÜLLER, Hans, STW
MÜLLER, Helmut, 3rd Kp, STW
MÜLLER, Karl, STW
MÜLLER, Rudolf, Gefr, 2nd Kp, MIA Aug 42
MÜLLER, Uffz,
MÜLLER, Werner, Dr., STW
MÜLLER-WENK, Rolf, 7th Kp, STW
MÜNCH, Fritz, 3rd Kp, STW
MÜNCH, Karl, STW
MÜNDIGE, Matthias,
MULLER, Rolf, STW
MUNDT, Erich, 7th Kp, STW
MUNZ, Karl, Rgt HQ, STW
MURSZAT, Heinz, STW
MUSSENBROCK, B, Gefr, 7th Kp, MIA Mar 1945
NACKE, I./Abt.
NAGEL, Fw, 7th Kp.
NÄGELIN, Walter, 8th Kp, STW
NÄGLER, Gerhard, 6th Kp, STW
NAUMANN, Christian, STW
NEBEL, Siegfried, 6th Kp, STW
NEFF, Olt.
NEUGEBAUER, Karl-Heinz, STW
NEULICHEDL, Sdf (G) Rgt HQ.
NEUMANN, Olt, 1st Kp, KIA Jun 40
NEUSTEIN, Fritz, Fw, 4th Kp, STW
NICKEL, Kurt, OFw, STW
NIER, Erich, STW
NILKE, Willi, STW
NINTZ, Arnold, STW

NOAK, Kurt, STW
NOLD, Stabartz Dr.
NOLL, Helmut, I./Abt, STW
NÜRNBERGER, Gerhard, Lt, II./Abt, POW, STW
NÜSSLE, Hermann, 3rd Kp, STW
OCKER, Uffz, 2nd Kp, KIA Africa
ODENTHAL, Hilarius, STW
OHLENHAUT, Lt.
OHR, Uffz, 8th Kp, KIA Nov 41
OKER, Uffz.
OLSBERG, Uffz, 3rd Kp, KIA Jun 41
OPPOLD, Fw, 2nd Kp, KIA Feb 43
ORB, Albert, Gefr, Rgt HQ,
OSTER, Gefr.
OTT, Herbert, OGefr, 7th Kp, KIA May 40
OTTENS, Hptm.
OTTO, Herbert, later Maj, STW
PACKEISEN, Uffz, 7th Kp, KIA Nov 41
PAPST, Fritz, 4th Kp, STW
PASCHY, Hans, Lt, STW
PAUL, Fw, 7th Kp.
PAULUS, Gefr, 3rd Kp, MIA Jul 42
PEINTINGER, Karl, Gefr, 4th Kp, MIA 1944
PERSIKOWSKI, Ernst, Uffz, 7th Kp, STW
PETER, August, STW
PETERS, Fw, 2nd Kp.
PETERS, Lt.
PETERS, Schutze, KIA France 1940
PFÄFFLE, Helmut, STW
PFEFFER, Walter, STW
PFEIFER, Fw, I./Abt, KIA 1943
PFEIFFER, Max, Fw, STW
PICKEL, Willy, Olt, StKp, POW, STW
PIERATH, FwOa.
PIERSCHEL, Helmut, STW
PIRATH, Lt.
PISAT, Lt, KIA Nov 41
PITTORF, Wolf, Hptm, STW
PITZKE, Artur, STW
PLAASAN, Heinrich, Fw, 8th Kp, MIA Oct 42
PLETZ, Willi, STW
PLEYL, Walter, 2nd Kp, STW
PLINZNER, Peter-Paul, Lt, KIA 1941
PORT, Julius, Dr, STW
PORTATIUS, Von, Lt.
POSSECKEL, Ofw, STW
POSSEKEL, Günter, II./Abt, STW
PRAÜER, Gabriel, Fw, Rgt HQ.
PRECK, Otto-Ernst, 5th Kp, STW
PREID, Leni,
PREK, Uffz, 5th Kp.
PRESTEL, Karl 4th Kp, STW
PRION, Hilmar, Lt, Stkp, KIA
PROBST, Lt.
PROKESCH, Uffz,
PROSCH, Sdf (G), I./Abt.
PRÜFER, Heinz, Uffz, 7th Kp, KIA, Jun 40
PUSSE, Hans, Uffz, 5th Kp, KIA in Africa
RAASCH, Gefr, WIA France
RAISCH, Gottfried, 4th Kp.

RALL, Heinz, STW
RAMMKE, Le Kol.
RAMSAUER, Oskar, Maj, STW
RASEN, Hubert, STW
RATHGEBER, Paul, Fw, MIA Mar 1945
RATHSACK, Fw, 2nd Kp.
RATZEL, Emil, 2nd Kp, STW
RAULFS, Hermann, STW
REBEL, Gefr, 2nd Kp.
REBSCHER, Uffz, 7th Kp.
REHM, Willi 8th Kp, STW
REHMET, Paul STW
REICH, Gefr, 7th Kp.
REICHEL, OGefr, Rgt HQ.
REICHERT, Uffz, II./Abt, KIA Nov 41
REICHMANN, Hans-Joachim, Fahnenjunker, KIA Jun 40
REINBOLD, Andreas, 6th Kp, STW
REINER, Helmut, OGefr, 3rd Kp, STW
RENNER, Franz, Workshop Kp, STW
RENZ, Manfred, Uffz, STW
RICHTER, Hermann, Uffz, Stabs Kp, STW
RIEDESSER, Sepp, STW
RIEHLE, Hans, STW
RIESE, Paul, STW
RIESTER, Hans Fw, 3rd Kp, STW
RIMMELE, Anton, STW
RING, Uffz, 8th Kp, KIA Nov 41
RINK, Uffz, II./Abt, KIA Nov 41
RINKUNBÜRGER, Otto, Lt, POW, STW
RISCH, Dieterich, Lt, 7th Kp, KIA May 40
RISCH, Lt.
RITTER, Lt.
RITTER, Otmar, STW
RITZER, Carl, STW
ROLL, Fritz, STW
ROLLER, STW
ROLLKA, Wolf-Dieter, Fw, STW
ROLLPETZ, Franz, Obersoldat
ROMBACH, Oskar, STW
ROMER, Anton, STW
ROMPEL, Olt, 6th Kp.
RÖSCH, Lt.
RÖSCH, OGefr, STW
ROSSGODERER, Hans, 8th Kp, STW
ROSSHADERER, Gefr, II./Abt.
RÖSSLER, S., STW
ROSSNER, Walter, II./Abt, STW
ROSSWAG, Adolf, STW
ROTHER, I./Abt.
ROTHFUSS Karl, STW
ROTHLÄNDER, Uffz, 2nd Kp.
ROUPETZ, Franz, Oberschütze Rgt HQ.
RÜCKDESCHEL, Ernst, STW
RUETE, STW
RUMMLER, Erwin, Uffz, 2nd Kp, STW
RUPPERT, Fritz, 7th Kp, STW
RUSSOW, Lt.
SAHMEL, Otto, Olt, I./Abt.
SANDER, Josef, 7th Kp, STW
SANNWALD, Adolf

Appendix 4: Regimental Role

SASS, Heinz, 7th Kp, STW
SAUTER, Oberstabsintendant
SAUTTER, Hans, Uffz, Kradmelder I./Abt, KIA 1945
SCHAAF, August, STW
SCHAEFFER, Uffz.
SCHÄFER, Albert, STW
SCHAICH, Wilhelm, 7th Kp, STW
SCHARPF, Erwin, 2nd Kp, STW
SCHARY, Lt.
SCHATZ, Heinz, STW
SCHAUPP Alfred. II./Abt. STW
SCHEFOLD, Wolf. Lt, Rgt Stabs, STW
SCHEIB Willi, Uffz, StKp I./Abt, STW
SCHEIBER, Adalbert, Sonderführer, Rgt HQ
SCHEIDLE, Karl, STW
SCHEIKERT, Otto, 7th Kp, STW
SCHELLHAUS, Heinrich, Olt, 2nd Kp.
SCHENK, Anton, 7th Kp, STW
SCHERENBACHER, Karl, STW
SCHEUFFELE, Wilhelm, STW
SCHICK, Erwin, I./Abt, STW
SCHIED, Günter, 8th Kp, STW
SCHIEFER, Rudi, STW
SCHIEGER, Wilhelm, STW
SCHIESSL, Erich, OFw, STW
SCHILD, Günther, OGefr, II./Abt, 8th Kp
SCHISSLER, Helmuth, STW
SCHLAGENHAUF, Fritz STW
SCHLANDERER, Gustav, STW
SCHLEEHUBER, Helmut, STW
SCHLEGAL, Martin, STW
SCHLEGAL, Siegfried, Fw, STW
SCHLEGAL, Wilhelm, 7th Kp, STW
SCHLEICHER, Paul, 1st Kp, STW
SCHLEMPP, Günter, 6th Kp, STW
SCHLERTH, Konrad, 5th Kp, STW
SCHLIEBS, Gunter, OGefr, 2nd Kp, STW
SCHLIPF, Gefr, 7th Kp.
SCHMANDER, Ernst, 1st Kp, STW
SCHMID, Anton, Uffz, I./Abt.
SCHMID, Bruno, Fw, STW
SCHMID, Gottfried, STW
SCHMID, Hans, STW
SCHMID, Kurt OGefr, Rgt HQ, MIA May 42
SCHMID, Willibald, 6th Kp, STW
SCHMIDT, Ernst, STW
SCHMIDT, I./Abt.
SCHMIDT, Richard, II./Abt, STW
SCHMIDT, Uffz, KIA Jun 41
SCHMIDT, Wilhelm, STW
SCHNAIDT, Lt, 7th Kp.
SCHNEIDER, Adolf, OFw, STW
SCHNELL, Julius, Maj, STW
SCHNELLE, Wolfgang, Hptm, II./Abt
SCHNIER, Fw.
SCHOCK, Max, 8th Kp, STW
SCHÖFFLER, Otto 7th Kp, STW
SCHÖNAU, Willi, 7th Kp.
SCHÖNFELD, Gefr, KIA May 42
SCHOPP, Robert, II./Abt, STW

SCHÖPPLER, Uffz, 7th Kp.
SCHRAMM, Albert, 8th Kp, STW
SCHREIBER, Rudolf, STW
SCHRÖDER, Heinz, STW
SCHUBERSKI, Ernst, Lt, 2nd Kp POW, STW
SCHUBERT, Helmut, STW
SCHUBERT, Hugo, Olt, 3rd Kp.
SCHÜSSLER, Helmut, STW
SCHULER, Herbert, Uffz, STW
SCHULTZ, I./Abt.
SCHULTZ, OFw, 6th Kp.
SCHUMACHER, Ernst, STW
SCHUMACHER, Kurt, STW
SCHUNDER, Franz, STW
SCHURR, Hermann, 7th Kp, STW
SCHWABE, Günter, HFw, STW
SCHWAN, Bernhard, HFw, STW
SCHWARZENBERG, Alfred, Uffz.
SCHWARZENFELD, von, I./Abt.
SCHWARZHAUPT, Lt.
SCHWEDE, Uffz, 7th Kp, KIA May 40
SCHWEGLER, Erwin, STW
SCHWEINGER, Richard, 3rd Kp, STW
SCHWEIZER, Gerhard, Zug Fhr, 5th Kp.
SCHWEIZER, Rudolf, STW
SCHWENGER, Richard, 3rd Kp, STW
SCHWÖRER, Joseph, II./Abt, STW
SEEGER, Jakob, 6th Kp, STW
SEEMÜLLER, Alexander, POW, STW
SEIDLER, Olt, 8th Kp, KIA May 42
SEMERAK, Olt, 6th Kp, KIA Sep 39
SEUFFERT, Walter, 4th Kp, STW
SEYFERT,
SIEBMANN, HFw, 5th Kp.
SIEBOLD, Oskar, Gefr, Werkshop Kp.
SIEFERS, I./Abt.
SIEGL, STW
SIEMENS, Horst-Hennig, Hptm 5th Kp.
SINGER, Martin, 7th Kp, STW
SOBIREI, Uffz, KIA Jun 40
SÖHNER, Ludwig, 4th Kp, STW
SOLAR, Gerhard, STW
SÖLLER, Josef, StKp, POW, STW
SOMMER, I./Abt.
SONN, Richard, Gefr, 2nd Kp, KIA Jun 40
SONNENKALB, Horst, Fw, 7th Kp, STW
SONTON, Burkhard, OFw, STW
SONTOWSKI, Olt, KIA 1941
SPATHELF, Ernst, Fkm, I./Abt.
SPOHN, Walter, Ofw, II./Abt.
SPRINGORUM, Olt, II./Abt, KIA 1941
STACKELBERG, von, Gefr, 7th Kp, KIA Jun 40
STADTER, Josef, 8th Kp, STW
STAHL, Walter, STW
STÄHLE,
STÄNGEL, Hans-Eberhard Olt, 3rd Kp, KIA Oct 42
STARK, STW
STEFFENS, Josef, Uffz, 7th Kp, MIA Jan 45
STEGELMANN, Max, Uffz.
STEGEMANN, Gerd, Lt, STW

STEGMAIER, Walter, STW
STEIFELMAYER, Otto. Hptm, I./Abt, KIA Nov 42
STEIN, Uffz, II./Abt.
STEINBACH, Fritz, 7th Kp, STW
STEINEL, Lt,
STEINGRABER, Gefr, KIA Jun 40
STELZER,
STEPHEN, I./Abt.
STETTEN, Matthias, Uffz, STW
STIEFL, Anton, STW
STIEGEL, Karl, STW
STIERLE, Franz, 4th Kp, STW
STOCKER, Rolf, STW
STOCKHAMMER, Josef, Rgt HQ.
STOHLMEYER, Hermann, OFw, 8th Kp, STW
STÖHR, August, Fw.
STÖRNER, Gefr, 7th Kp.
STOTTEN, Han-Gunther, Hptm, I./Abt, KIA Apr 45
STOTZ, Eberhard, Lt, STW
STOTZ, Erwin, 7th Kp, STW
STRACK, Walter, OFMstr, I./Abt, STW
STRAUB, Josef, STW
STRIEBEL,
STRIEGEL, Karl 2nd Kp, STW
STROBEL, Emil, STW
STROHÄCKER, Reinhold, I./Abt, STW
STROHMEIER, Wilhelm, STW
STROHMENGER, Sdf (G) II./Abt.
STROMAIER, Wilhelm, STW
STUBER, Reinhard Uffz, STW
STÜLPNAGEL, von, Jurgen, Lt.
STUMPP, Eugen, 1st Kp, STW
STUMPP, Gottlieb, Ogefr.
STUNZNER, von, Olt, StKp.
SÜLZLE, Helmut, Gefr, 4th Kp, MIA Nov 42
SUND, Kurt, STW
SWOBODA, Josef, STW
TANKE, Walter, FW, 4th Kp, MIA Apr 43
TEEGE, Willi, Oberst, Regiment Cdr, KIA Nov 42
TEUBER, Reinhard, STW
THAMPHALD, Heinz, HFw, 2nd Kp.
THOM, Herbert Fw, Rgt HQ, STW
THROM, Tilo, Hptm, STW
THÜROW, Jürgen, Olt, 1st Kp, POW, STW
THUMM, Gerhard, STW
THUMM, Karl STW
THURER, Jürgen
THUST, Fw, 6th Kp KIA Sep 39
TISCHNER, Albert, Zahlmstr, I./Abt
TOFFERT, Hans-Erich, Dr, Lt.
TOMASZEWSKI, Max, Olt, 1st Kp.
TONDOCK, Leni, STW
TRAUNER, Helmut, Fw, STW
TREML, Rudi, STW
TRETTIN, Rudi, OFw, KIA 1943
TREUENFELS, von.
TSCHECH, Rudolf, Olt, STW
ÜBELE, Heinrich, STW
UEBERSCHÄR, STW
UHLENHAUT, Olt, Kradmelder, KIA May 40

UHLMANN, Wilhelm, II./Abt, STW
ULMER, Ernst, 2nd Kp STW
ULMER, Ludwig, 4th Kp, STW
UNBESCHEIDT, Fw.
VETTER, Ernst, I./Abt, STW
VOGEL, Heinz, STW
VOGES, Gefr, KIA Jun 40
VOGT, Rudolf, Uffz, 7th Kp.
VOIGT, Viktor, Lt, 8th Kp, MIA Jun 42
VOLZ, Ludwig, OGefr, 7th Kp, STW
WACHSMANN, Karl, OGefr, 5th Kp, STW
WAGNER, Norbert, 6th Kp, STW
WAHL, Erich, STW
WAHL, Karl, STW
WAHL, Wolfgang, Hptm, II./Abt, STW
WALD, Karl, STW
WALD, Uffz, 7th Kp.
WALDMÜLLER, Wolf-Dieter, 2nd Kp, STW
WALSER, Karl, STW
WALTER, Hans, 6th Kp, STW
WALZ, Fritz, 7th Kp, STW
WANDRUSZKA, Olt, II./Abt.
WARNKE, OFw, 4th Kp.
WEBER, Hans, Gefr, 5th Kp, STW
WEBER, Helmut, Uffz, 6th Kp.
WEBER, Lt, 1st Kp, KIA Sep 39
WEBER, Siegfried, STW
WEBER, Uffz.
WEGST, Hermann, 7th Kp, STW
WEIDLICH, HFw, 7th Kp.
WEIDELENER, Gerhard, Fw, 8th Kp, STW
WEIMANN, Olt, LeKol.
WEINERT,
WEINGÄRTNER, Karl-Heinz, STW
WEINHARDT, Eugen, STW
WEISINGER, Josef, Fw, STW
WEISS, Franz, I./Abt, STW
WEISS, Richard, Lt,
WEISSCHUH, Sdf (G), 7th Kp.
WEIZ, Uffz, 7th Kp.
WELLMER, Ernst, STW
WENDLAND, Gerhard, II./Abt, STW
WENGEL,
WENZEL, Wolfgang, Fw, 5th Kp, STW
WENZLER, Wilhelm, HQ I./Abt, STW
WERNER, Ernst, 1st Kp, STW
WICKENHÄUSER, Hans, Lt, POW, STW
WIDMANN, Rudolf, Uffz, 1st Kp.
WIEGELS, Hans Lt, I./Abt, STW
WILFS, Hermann, Gefr, 4th Kp.
WILPART, Klaus, Olt, STW
WINTERS, Rudolf, Gefr, Rgt HQ.
WIRTH, Heinz, STW
WITKOWSKI, Olt, Pioneer, 7th Kp.
WITZKY, Hans Dr.
WÖHL, Volker, Lt, STW
WÖHRMANN, Paul, Lt, STW
WOLDSEN,
WOLF, Erich, Olt, I./Abt, STW
WOLF, Karl, 1st Kp, STW

WOLFF, Lt.
WOLLENBERG, Paul, STW
WOLPERT, Otto, 7th Kp, STW
WÖRNER, Gustav, 1st Kp, STW
WÖRNER, Karl, STW
WURSTER, Emil, Uffz, II./Abt, STW
WUTH, Wolfgang Olt, 8th Kp, KIA Nov 41
ZANGLE Ogefr, 7th Kp.
ZECHIEL, Erwin, Uffz, II./Abt, STW
ZEPF, Wolfgang, OGefr, 5th Kp, STW
ZESSNER, Hans, Rgt HQ.
ZEUKE, Werner, Lt.
ZIEGELMUELLER, Erwin, 6th Kp, STW
ZIEGELSCHMIED, Josef, STW

ZIEGENER, Maj, MIA
ZIEGESAR, von Frh, Wolfgang, 4th Kp, STW
ZIEGLER, Erich, STW
ZIEGLER, Hermann, Uffz, 4th Kp, STW
ZIEGLER, Reinhold, 5th Kp, STW
ZIEMER, Uffz.
ZIETZ, Gerhard, Uffz, KIA in Russia
ZIMMER, Gefr, 1st Kp.
ZIMMERMANN, Erich, OFw, STW
ZINNT, Franz, 4th Kp.
ZOELLER, Dr, Unterartz.
ZÜGNER, Josef, Hptm.
ZÜNKLEY, Gefr, 1st Kp.
ZUGMANTEL, Fritz, Gefr, STW

Appendix 5:
Rank Equivalent Guide

Wehrmacht	Abbreviation	U.S. Army
Schütze	None	Private
Gefreiter	Gefr	Private First Class
Obergefreiter	OGefr	Corporal
Unterofficer	Uffz	Sergeant
Feldwebel	Fw	Staff Sergeant
Stabsfeldwebel	SFw	Staff Sergeant
Oberfeldwebel	OFw	Sergeant First Class
Hauptfeldwebel	HFw	First Sergeant
Fahnrich/Junker	None	Warrant Officer
Leutnant	Lt	Second Lieutenant
Oberleutnant	Olt	First Lieutenant
Hauptmann	Hptm	Captain
Major	Maj	Major
Oberstleutnant	Oberstlt	Lieutenant Colonel
Oberst	None	Colonel
Generalmajor	None	Brigadier General
Generalleutnant	None	Major General
General der Panzertruppen	None	Lieutenant General
Generaloberst	None	General
Generalfeldmarshal	G.F.M.	General of the Army

Endnotes

Chapter One, The Early Years, 1936-1939
[1] Roger Edwards, *Panzer*, Brockhampton, 1998, p.16
[2] Ibid, p.19
[3] Ibid, p.19
[4] Ibid, p.20
[5] Heinz Guderian, *Panzer Leader*, Noontide Press, 1988, p.24
[6] Kurt Kathe, interview, 2003
[7] Thomas Jentz, *Panzer Truppen*, Schiffer, 1996, p.26
[8] Ibid, p.49
[9] H.F. Beckmann, *Panzerkampf in zwei Kontinenten 1936-1943*, 1994, p.3
[10] Ibid, p.3
[11] Ibid, p.3
[12] Ibid, p.3
[13] Thomas Jentz, *Panzer Truppen*, Schiffer, 1996, p.52
[14] Kurt Kathe, interview, 2003
[15] H.F. Beckmann, *Panzerkampf in zwei Kontinenten 1936-1943*, 1994, p.4
[16] Kurt Liestmann, unpublished diary courtesy BBN Archive
[17] Unknown, unpublished article, courtesy BBN Archive
[18] Kurt Liestmann, unpublished diary courtesy BBN Archive
[19] Karl Halverscheidt, letter courtesy of Fr Dorit Halverscheidt
[20] Kurt Liestmann, unpublished diary courtesy BBN Archive
[21] Wilhelm Ludwig, interview, 2003
[22] Kurt Kathe, interview, 2003
[23] H.F. Beckmann, *Panzerkampf in zwei Kontinenten 1936-1943*, 1994, p.5
[24] Thomas Jentz, *Panzer Truppen*, Schiffer, 1996, p.49
[25] W.J.K. Davies, *Panzer Regiments*, Almark, 1978, pp.16-28
[26] Thomas Jentz, *Panzer Truppen*, Schiffer, 1996, p.70
[27] Kurt Liestmann, unpublished diary courtesy BBN Archive
[28] Ibid
[29] Thomas Jentz, *Panzer Truppen*, Schiffer, 1996, p.65
[30] Kurt Liestmann, unpublished diary courtesy BBN Archive
[31] Fritz Hausstein, interview, 2003
[32] Kurt Liestmann, unpublished diary courtesy BBN Archive
[33] Ibid
[34] H.F. Beckmann, *Panzerkampf in zwei Kontinenten 1936-1943*, 1994, p.7
[35] Thomas Jentz, *Panzer Truppen*, Schiffer, 1996, p.91
[36] H.F. Beckmann, *Panzerkampf in zwei Kontinenten 1936-1943*, 1994, p.6

Chapter Two, The Polish Campaign, September 1939-May 1940

[1] Words and Music by Norbert Schultz
[2] Steven Zaloga, *Poland 1939*, Osprey, 2002, pp.9-10
[3] Ibid, pp.22-23
[4] Ibid, p.23
[5] Ibid, p.39
[6] Kurt Kathe, interview, 2003
[7] H.F. Beckmann, *Panzerkampf in zwei Kontinenten 1936-1943*, 1994, p.7
[8] Kurt Liestmann, unpublished diary courtesy BBN Archive
[9] Ibid
[10] Ibid
[11] Ibid
[12] Ibid
[13] Ibid
[14] Ibid
[15] H.F. Beckmann, *Panzerkampf in zwei Kontinenten 1936-1943*, 1994, p.8
[16] Kurt Liestmann, unpublished diary courtesy BBN Archive
[17] Ibid
[18] H.F. Beckmann, *Panzerkampf in zwei Kontinenten 1936-1943*, 1994, p.9
[19] Jews rounded up see material BBN Archive and letters and accounts
[20] Botho Elster, unpublished Combat Report, courtesy of BBN Archive
[21] Ibid
[22] Ibid
[23] Ibid
[24] H.F. Beckmann, *Panzerkampf in zwei Kontinenten 1936-1943*, 1994, p.10
[25] Weber, unpublished Combat Report, courtesy of BBN Archive
[26] Wolf Schefold, interview, 2006
[27] Botho Elster, unpublished Combat Report, courtesy of BBN Archive
[28] H.F. Beckmann, *Panzerkampf in zwei Kontinenten 1936-1943*, 1994, p.10
[29] Botho Elster, unpublished Combat Report, courtesy of BBN Archive
[30] Ibid
[31] H.F. Beckmann, *Panzerkampf in zwei Kontinenten 1936-1943*, 1994, p.11
[32] Botho Elster, unpublished Combat Report, courtesy of BBN Archive
[33] H.F. Beckmann, *Panzerkampf in zwei Kontinenten 1936-1943*, 1994, p.11
[34] Ibid, pp.11-12
[35] Carl-Heinz Knorr, various papers and articles courtesy BBN Archive and Frau M. Knorr
[36] H.F. Beckmann, *Panzerkampf in zwei Kontinenten 1936-1943*, 1994, p.12
[37] Steven Zaloga, *Poland 1939*, Osprey, 2002, p.86
[38] Thomas Jentz, *Panzer Truppen*, Schiffer, 1996, pp.101-2
[39] Ibid, p.102
[40] Ibid, p.104
[41] Ibid, p.106
[42] Ibid, pp.106-9
[43] H.F. Beckmann, *Panzerkampf in zwei Kontinenten 1936-1943*, 1994, p.14
[44] Ibid, p.14

Chapter Three, The French Campaign, May-July 1940
[1] Alistair Horne, *To Lose a Battle*, Little Brown, 1969, pp.158-9
[2] H.F. Beckmann, *Panzerkampf in zwei Kontinenten 1936-1943*, 1994, p.14
[3] Alistair Horne, *To Lose a Battle*, Little Brown, 1969, pp.125-28
[4] Ibid, pp.186-7
[5] Kurt Liestmann, unpublished diary courtesy BBN Archive
[6] Ibid
[7] Alistair Horne, *To Lose a Battle*, Little Brown, 1969, p.309
[8] Kurt Liestmann, unpublished diary courtesy BBN Archive
[9] Alistair Horne, *To Lose a Battle*, Little Brown, 1969, p.328
[10] Adolphe Goutard, *The battle of France, 1940*, Ives Washburn, 1959, p.139
[11] Heinz Guderian, *Panzer Leader*, Noontide Press, 1988, p.99
[12] Alistair Horne, *To Lose a Battle*, Little Brown, 1969, pp.296-7
[13] H.F. Beckmann, *Panzerkampf in zwei Kontinenten 1936-1943*, 1994, p.15
[14] Kurt Liestmann, unpublished diary courtesy BBN Archive
[15] Bruce Quarrie, *Panzer-Grenadier Division Gorssdeutschland*, Squadron, 1977, p.3
[16] John Williams, *France, Summer 1940*, Ballantine, 1969, p.52
[17] Alistair Horne, *To Lose a Battle*, Little Brown, 1969, pp.182-3
[18] H.F. Beckmann, *Panzerkampf in zwei Kontinenten 1936-1943*, 1994, p.16
[19] Kurt Liestmann, unpublished diary courtesy BBN Archive
[20] Koch, written account, 7th Company diary, courtesy of BBN Archive
[21] Julian Jackson, *The fall of France*, Oxford Press, 2003, p.50
[22] Koch, written account, 7th Company diary, courtesy of BBN Archive
[23] Alistair Horne, *To Lose a Battle*, Little Brown, 1969, p.362

[24] H.F. Beckmann, *Panzerkampf in zwei Kontinenten 1936-1943*, 1994, p.17
[25] Guy Chapman, *Why France Fell*, Holt, Rhinehart & Winston, 1968 p.145
[26] Adolphe Goutard, *The battle of France, 1940*, Ives Washburn, 1959, pp.146-7
[27] Kurt Liestmann, unpublished diary courtesy BBN Archive
[28] Alistair Horne, *To Lose a Battle*, Little Brown, 1969, p.425
[29] Kurt Liestmann, unpublished diary courtesy BBN Archive
[30] Alistair Horne, *To Lose a Battle*, Little Brown, 1969, p.435
[31] Kurt Liestmann, unpublished diary courtesy BBN Archive
[32] Ibid
[33] Ibid
[34] Seidler, written account on 6.8.40, unpublished, courtesy BBN Archive
[35] Reich, written account on 6.8.40, unpublished, courtesy BBN Archive
[36] Harcher, written account on 6.8.40, unpublished, courtesy BBN Archive
[37] Kurt Liestmann, unpublished diary, courtesy BBN Archive
[38] H.F. Beckmann, *Panzerkampf in zwei Kontinenten 1936-1943*, 1994, p.17
[39] Heinz Guderian, *Panzer Leader*, Noontide Press, 1988, p.117
[40] Alistair Horne, *To Lose a Battle*, Little Brown, 1969, p.522
[41] Heinz Guderian, *Panzer Leader*, Noontide Press, 1988, p.119
[42] Phillip Warner, *The Battle of France*, Cassell, 1990, p.168
[43] Adolphe Goutard, *The Battle of France, 1940*, Ives Washburn, 1959, pp.237-244
[44] S-Company unpublished diary, courtesy of BBN Archive
[45] Alistair Horne, *To Lose a Battle*, Little Brown, 1969, p.556
[46] John Williams, *France Summer 1940*, Ballantine, 1969, p.148
[47] Alistair Horne, *To Lose a Battle*, Little Brown, 1969, p.556
[48] H.F. Beckmann, *Panzerkampf in zwei Kontinenten 1936-1943*, 1994, p.19
[49] Thomas Jentz, *Panzer Truppen*, Schiffer, 1996, p.135
[50] S-Company, unpublished diary courtesy BBN Archive
[51] Spathelf, written account on 4.6.40, unpublished, courtesy BBN Archive
[52] Schöppler, written account, 7th Company diary courtesy BBN Archive
[53] Kaulbars, written account, 7th Company diary courtesy BBN Archive
[54] Zängle, written account, 7th Company diary courtesy BBN Archive
[55] Von Brunn, written account, 7th Company diary courtesy BBN Archive
[56] Alistair Horne, *To Lose a Battle*, Brown Little, 1969, p.558
[57] Combat report, I Abteilung, NARA T315/559
[58] Wilhelm Ludwig, interview, 2003
[59] H.F. Beckmann, *Panzerkampf in zwei Kontinenten 1936-1943*, 1994, p.20
[60] Ibid, p.21
[61] Spathelf, written account on 4.6.40, unpublished, courtesy BBN Archive
[62] Schlipf, written account, 7th Company diary courtesy BBN Archive
[63] S-Company unpublished diary, courtesy of BBN Archive
[64] Koppe, written account, 7th Company diary courtesy BBN Archive
[65] Spathelf, written account on 4.6.40, unpublished, courtesy BBN Archive
[66] Kurt Liestmann, unpublished diary courtesy BBN Archive
[67] Schlipf, written account, 7th Company diary courtesy BBN Archive
[68] S-Company unpublished diary, courtesy of BBN Archive
[69] Bauer, written account, 7th Company diary courtesy BBN Archive
[70] Degner, written account, 7th Company diary courtesy BBN Archive
[71] S-Company unpublished diary, courtesy of BBN Archive
[72] Schöppler, written account, 7th Company diary courtesy BBN Archive
[73] S-Company unpublished diary, courtesy of BBN Archive
[74] Rebscher, written account, 7th Company diary courtesy BBN Archive
[75] Baumann, written account, 7th Company diary courtesy BBN Archive
[76] Himmelreich, written account, 7th Company diary courtesy BBN Archive
[77] Landthaler, written account, 7th Company diary courtesy BBN Archive
[78] S-Company unpublished diary, courtesy of BBN Archive
[79] Ibid
[80] Alistair Horne, *To Lose a Battle*, Little Brown, 1969, pp.564-5
[81] Guy Chapman, *Why France Fell*, Holt, Rhinehart & Winston, 1968 p.332
[82] S-Company unpublished diary, courtesy of BBN Archive
[83] Landthaler, written account, 7th Company diary courtesy BBN Archive
[84] Bohnish, written account, 7th Company diary courtesy BBN Archive
[85] Baumann, written account, 7th Company diary courtesy BBN Archive
[86] Alistair Horne, *To Lose a Battle*, Little Brown, 1969, p.581
[87] S-Company unpublished diary, courtesy of BBN Archive
[88] Ibid

Chapter Four, Between Campaigns, August 1940-April 1941
[1] Alistair Horne, *To Lose a Battle*, Brown Little, 1969, p.584
[2] Thomas Jentz, *Panzer Truppen*, Schiffer, 1996, p.141
[3] Heinz Guderian, *Panzer Leader*, Noontide Press, 1988, p.469
[4] Fritz Haustein, interview, 2003
[5] H.F. Beckmann, *Panzerkampf in zwei Kontinenten 1936-1943*, 1994, p.23
[6] Alfred Toppe, *The German Army in Desert*, U.S. Army, 1952, p.3
[7] Wilhelm Hagios, interview, 2007
[8] Horst Sonnenkalb, Part I, courtesy of Die Oase Magazine
[9] H.F. Beckmann, *Panzerkampf in zwei Kontinenten 1936-1943*, 1994, p.23
[10] Alfred Toppe, *The German Army in Desert*, U.S. Army, 1952, p.4
[11] Kurt Liestmann, unpublished diary courtesy BBN Archive
[12] H.F. Beckmann, *Panzerkampf in zwei Kontinenten 1936-1943*, 1994, pp.23-4
[13] Reconstructed by author but based on part by Beckmann article
[14] H.F. Beckmann, *Panzerkampf in zwei Kontinenten 1936-1943*, 1994, p.23
[15] Wilhelm Bühler, in letter to author, 2006
[16] Kurt Liestmann, unpublished diary courtesy BBN Archive
[17] Ibid
[18] Kurt Kathe, interview, 2004
[19] H.F. Beckmann, *Panzerkampf in zwei Kontinenten 1936-1943*, 1994, p.24
[20] Thomas Jentz, *Tank Combat in North Africa*, Schiffer, 1998, p.16
[21] Kurt Liestmann, unpublished diary courtesy BBN Archive
[22] Thomas Jentz, *Tank Combat in North Africa*, Schiffer, 1998, p.216
[23] Wilhelm Hagios, interview, 2007
[24] Thomas Jentz, *Tank Combat in North Africa*, Schiffer, 1998, p.216
[25] Fritz Haustein, interview, 2003
[26] Hermann Eckardt, interview, 2004
[27] Schubert, unpublished diary, courtesy of BBN Archive
[28] Kurt Kathe, interview, 2004
[29] Horst Sonnenkalb, Part I, courtesy of Die Oase Magazine

Chapter Five, North Africa, May 1941
[1] Words from an unknown soldier music from Norbert Schultze
[2] Erwin Rommel, *The Rommel Papers*, Harcourt Brace, 1953, p.101
[3] W.G.F. Jackson, *The Battle for North Africa*, Mason/Charter,1975, pp.117-19
[4] Ibid, p.120
[5] H.F. Beckmann, *Panzerkampf in zwei Kontinenten 1936-1943*, 1994, p.25
[6] Kurt Liestmann, unpublished diary, courtesy of BBN Archive
[7] Schubert, unpublished diary notes, courtesy of BBN Archive
[8] Kurt Liestmann unpublished diary, courtesy of BBN Archive
[9] Hermann Eckardt, interview, 2005
[10] Horst Sonnenkalb, Part I, courtesy of Die Oase Magazine
[11] Alfred Toppe, *The German Army in Desert*, U.S. Army, 1952, p.52
[12] Kurt Liestmann, unpublished diary, courtesy of BBN Archive
[13] Ibid
[14] Horst Sonnenkalb, Part I, courtesy of Die Oase Magazine
[15] Hermann Eckardt, interview, 2005
[16] 3rd Company diary, unpublished, courtesy of the BBN Archive
[17] Horst Sonnenkalb, Part I, courtesy of Die Oase Magazine
[18] 3rd Company diary, unpublished, courtesy of BBN Archive
[19] Ibid
[20] Alfred Toppe, *The German Army in Desert*, U.S. Army, 1952, p.36
[21] Kurt Kathe, interview, 2003
[22] Gotthilf Haidt, interview, 2005
[23] Thomas Jentz, *Panzer Truppen*, Schiffer, 1996, p.160
[24] Horst Sonnenkalb, Part I, courtesy of Die Oase Magazine
[25] Klaus Hubbuch, unpublished letters courtesy BBN Archive
[26] H.F. Beckmann, *Panzerkampf in zwei Kontinenten 1936-1943*, 1994, p.26
[27] B.H. Liddell Hart, *The Tanks, Vol. II*, Praeger, 1959, p.80
[28] Kurt Liestmann, unpublished diary, courtesy of BBN Archive
[29] Wilhelm Hagios, interview, 2007
[30] Erwin Rommel, *The Rommel Papers*, Harcourt Brace, 1953, p.136
[31] Ibid, p.136
[32] Horst Sonnenkalb, Part I, courtesy of Die Oase Magazine
[33] Kurt Kathe, interview, 2003
[34] Fritz Haustein, interview, 2003

Endnotes

[35] 15th Panzer Division KTB, Herff Combat Report, NARA, T315, Roll 665
[36] Kurt Liestmann, unpublished diary, courtesy of BBN Archive
[37] Horst Sonnenkalb Part I, courtesy of Die Oase Magazine
[38] H.F. Beckmann, *Panzerkampf in zwei Kontinenten 1936-1943*, 1994, p.27
[39] Thomas Jentz, *Tank Combat in North Africa*, Schiffer, 1998, p.142
[40] Schubert, unpublished diary notes, courtesy of BBN Archive
[41] Hermann Danner, unpublished written account, courtesy of BBN Archive
[42] 3rd Company diary, unpublished, courtesy of BBN Archive
[43] Kurt Liestmann, unpublished diary, courtesy of BBN Archive
[44] Ibid
[45] Kurt Kathe, interview, 2003
[46] Horst Sonnenkalb, Part I, courtesy of Die Oase Magazine
[47] 15th Panzer Division, KTB, Herff Combat Report NARA, T315, Roll 665
[48] Kurt Liestmann, unpublished diary, courtesy of BBN Archive
[49] Wilhelm Hagios, interview, 2007
[50] 15th Panzer Division, KTB, May 1941, NARA, T315, Roll 665
[51] Kurt Liestmann, unpublished diary, courtesy of BBN Archive
[52] Hermann Eckardt, interview, 2004
[53] Kurt Kathe, interview, 2003
[54] Kurt Liestmann, unpublished diary, courtesy of BBN Archive
[55] Horst Sonnenkalb, Part I, courtesy of Die Oase Magazine
[56] H.F. Beckmann, *Panzerkampf in zwei Kontinenten 1936-1943*, 1994, p.27

Chapter Six, The Summer Battles, June-September 1941
[1] Francois de Lannoy, *Afrikakorps*, Heimdal, 2002, p.73
[2] Kurt Kathe, interview, 2004
[3] H.F. Beckmann, *Panzerkampf in zwei Kontinenten 1936-1943*, 1994, p..28
[4] Kurt Liestmann, unpublished diary, courtesy of BBN Archive
[5] Schubert unpublished diary notes, courtesy of BBN Archive
[6] B.H. Liddell Hart, *The Tanks, Vol. II*, Praeger, 1959, p.81
[7] Ibid, p.81
[8] Hans Kümmel, unpublished after action report courtesy of the BBN Archive
[9] Ibid
[10] H.F. Beckmann, *Panzerkampf in zwei Kontinenten 1936-1943*, 1994, p.28
[11] B.H. Liddell Hart, *The Tanks, Vol. II*, Praeger, 1959, pp.83-4
[12] Ibid, p.84
[13] Ibid, p.85
[14] Thomas Jentz, *Tank Combat in North Africa*, Schiffer, 1998, pp.164-5
[15] Ibid, p.166
[16] Hans Kümmel, unpublished after action report courtesy of BBN Archive
[17] Ibid
[18] Thomas Jentz, *Tank Combat in North Africa*, Schiffer, 1998, p.173
[19] Wilhelm Hagios, interview, 2007
[20] Hans Kümmel, unpublished after action report courtesy of BBN Archive
[21] Ibid
[22] Hermann Eckardt, interview, 2005
[23] B.H. Liddell Hart, *The Tanks, Vol. II*, Praeger, 1959, p.86
[24] Horst Sonnenkalb, Part I, courtesy of Die Oase Magazine
[25] Thomas Jentz, *Tank Combat in North Africa*, Schiffer, 1998, p.170
[26] Schubert, unpublished diary notes courtesy of BBN Archive
[27] W.G.F. Jackson, *The Battle for North Africa*, Mason/Charter,1975, p.162
[28] Kurt Liestmann, unpublished diary, courtesy of BBN Archive
[29] H.F. Beckmann, *Panzerkampf in zwei Kontinenten 1936-1943*, 1994, p.29
[30] W.G.F. Jackson, *The Battle for North Africa*, Mason/Charter, 1975, p.162
[31] Kurt Liestmann, unpublished diary, courtesy of BBN Archive
[32] W.G.F. Jackson, *The Battle for North Africa*, Mason/Charter, 1975, p.162
[33] Franz Kurowski, *Panzer Aces II*, Stackpole, 2000, p.225
[34] Kurt Liestmann, unpublished diary, courtesy of BBN Archive
[35] Franz Kurowski, *Panzer Aces II*, Stackpole, 2000, p.226
[36] Kurt Liestmann, unpublished diary, courtesy of BBN Archive
[37] Klaus Hubbuch, unpublished diary and letters, courtesy of BBN Archive
[38] Hermann Eckardt, interview, 2004
[39] Schubert, unpublished diary notes courtesy of BBN Archive
[40] Thomas Jentz, *Panzer Truppen*, Schiffer, 1996, p.167
[41] Thomas Jentz, *Tank Combat in North Africa*, Schiffer, 1998, p.177
[42] H.F. Beckmann, *Panzerkampf in zwei Kontinenten 1936-1943*, 1994, p.29
[43] Heinz Liestmann, unpublished combat report courtesy of BBN Archive
[44] Horst Sonnenkalb, Part I, courtesy of Die Oase Magazine
[45] Schubert, unpublished diary notes courtesy of BBN Archive
[46] Heinz Liestmann unpublished combat report courtesy of BBN Archive
[47] 15th Panzer Division, KTB, May 1941, NARA, T315, Roll 665
[48] Heinz Liestmann unpublished combat report courtesy of BBN Archive
[49] Hermann Eckardt, interview, 2004
[50] H.F. Beckmann, *Panzerkampf in zwei Kontinenten 1936-1943*, 1994, p.30
[51] Ibid, p.30
[52] Ibid, p.30
[53] Franz Kurowski, *Knights Cross Holders of the Afrika Korps*, Schiffer, 1996, p.83
[54] James Lucas, *Panzer Army Africa*, Jove, 1986, appendix p.238
[55] Erwin Rommel, *The Rommel Papers*, Harcourt Brace, 1953, p.143
[56] 3rd Company diary, unpublished, courtesy of BBN Archive
[57] Klaus Hubbuch, unpublished diary and letters, courtesy of BBN Archive
[58] Wilhelm Hagios, interview, 2007
[59] H.F. Beckmann, *Panzerkampf in zwei Kontinenten 1936-1943*, 1994, p.31
[60] Franz Kurowski, *Knights Cross Holder of the Afrika Korps*, Schiffer, 1996, p.203
[61] Kurt Kathe, verbal account, 2004
[62] Alfred Toppe, *The German Army in Desert*, U.S. Army, 1952, p.53
[63] Klaus Hubbuch, unpublished diary and letters, courtesy of BBN Archive
[64] 15th Panzer Division, KTB, May 1941, NARA, T315, Roll 665
[65] 15th Panzer Division, KTB, May 1941, NARA, T315, Roll 665
[66] 15th Panzer Division, KTB, May 1941, NARA, T315, Roll 665
[67] Horst Sonnenkalb, Part I, courtesy of Die Oase Magazine
[68] Wilhelm Hagios, interview, 2007
[69] Horst Sonnenkalb, Part I, courtesy of Die Oase Magazine
[70] Kurt Kathe, interview, 2003
[71] Unknown letter, courtesy of BBN Archive
[72] Klaus Hubbuch, unpublished diary and letters courtesy of BBN Archive
[73] Volkmar Kühn, *Rommel in the Desert*, Schiffer, 1991, p.61
[74] H.W. Schmidt, *With Rommel in the Desert*, Bantam, 1979, p.103
[75] H.F. Beckmann, *Panzerkampf in zwei Kontinenten 1936-1943*, 1994, p.31
[76] Ibid, p.31

Chapter Seven, The Crusader Battles, October-November 1941
[1] W.G.F. Jackson, *The Battle for North Africa*, Mason/Charter, 1975, p.54
[2] Ronald Lewin, *The Life and Death of the Afrika Korps*, Pen and Sword, 2003, p.81
[3] B.H. Liddell Hart, *The Tanks, Vol. II*, Praeger, 1959, p.102
[4] Rainer Kreibel, *Inside the Afrika Korps*, Greenhill, 1999, p.31
[5] F.W. Mellenthin, *Panzer Battles*, Oklahoma Press, 1956, p.54
[6] H.F. Beckmann, *Panzerkampf in zwei Kontinenten 1936-1943*, 1994, p.32
[7] Ibid, p.32
[8] 15th Panzer Division, KTB, May 1941, NARA, T315, Roll 665
[9] Klaus Hubbuch letters and diary courtesy of BBN Archives
[10] Gliese, combat report dated February 1942
[11] Horst Sonnenkalb, Part I, courtesy of Die Oase Magazine
[12] Klaus Hubbuch, unpublished diary and letters courtesy of BBN Archive
[13] Gliese, combat report dated February 1942
[14] B.H. Liddell Hart, *The Tanks, Vol. II*, Praeger, 1959, p.107-9
[15] Ibid, p.100
[16] Rainer Kreibel, *Inside the Afrika Korps*, Greenhill, 1999, p.69
[17] H.F. Beckmann, *Panzerkampf in zwei Kontinenten 1936-1943*, 1994, p.32
[18] Gliese, combat report dated February 1942
[19] Horst Sonnenkalb, Part I, courtesy of Die Oase Magazine
[20] Rainer Kreibel, *Inside the Afrika Korps*, Greenhill, 1999, p.77
[21] Ibid, p.77
[22] B.H. Liddell Hart, *The Tanks, Vol. II*, Praeger, 1959, pp.110-11
[23] Ibid, pp.111-12
[24] 15th Panzer Division, KTB, May 1941, NARA, T315, Roll 665
[25] Gliese, combat report dated February 1942
[26] Hubbuch cont Hubbuch, unpublished diary and letters courtesy of BBN Archive
[27] B.H. Liddell Hart, *The Tanks, Vol. II*, Praeger, 1959, p.115
[28] Rainer Kreibel, *Inside the Afrika Korps*, Greenhill, 1999, p.82

[29] Gliese, combat report dated February 1942
[30] Wilhelm Hagios, interview, 2007
[31] Gliese, combat report dated February 1942
[32] H.F. Beckmann, *Panzerkampf in zwei Kontinenten 1936-1943*, 1994, p.33
[33] Wilhelm Hagios, interview, 2007
[34] Gliese, combat report dated February 1942
[35] Horst Sonnenkalb, Part I, courtesy of Die Oase Magazine
[36] H.F. Beckmann, *Panzerkampf in zwei Kontinenten 1936-1943*, 1994, p.33
[37] 15th Panzer Division, KTB, May 1941, NARA, T315, Roll 665
[38] Author note: I've found in some books that historians say that *Panzer Regiment 5* which was raised from men from the Berlin area and was not as aggressive as its sister regiment, which had been formed in Baden Wurttemburg
[39] Etzel, combat report dated 22.2.42 courtesy of BBN Archives
[40] Ibid
[41] Ibid
[42] Ibid
[43] Rainer Kreibel, *Inside the Afrika Korps*, Greenhill, 1999, p.87
[44] Ibid, p.88
[45] 15th Panzer Division, KTB, May 1941, NARA, T315, Roll 665
[46] Klaus Hubbuch, unpublished diary and letters courtesy of BBN Archive
[47] Ibid
[48] Klaus Hubbuch, report as related by Uffz Konz to Hubbuch, unpublished diary and letters courtesy of BBN Archive
[49] 15th Panzer Division, KTB, May 1941, NARA, T315, Roll 665
[50] Wilhelm Hagios, interview, 2007
[51] Klaus Hubbuch, unpublished diary and letters courtesy of BBN Archive
[52] H.F. Beckmann, *Panzerkampf in zwei Kontinenten 1936-1943*, 1994, p.35
[53] Wilhelm Hagios, interview, 2007
[54] Ronald Lewin, *The Life and Death of the Afrika Korps*, Pen and Sword, 2003, p.98
[55] Karl Alman, *Panzer Vor*, Verlaghaus, 2006, p.382
[56] Author's Note: The 3rd and 7th Companies had yet to arrive in Africa and had not been activated at this time.
[57] Klaus Hubbuch, unpublished diary and letters courtesy of BBN Archive
[58] Ibid
[59] James Lucas, *Panzer Army Africa*, Jove, 1986, p.103
[60] 15th Panzer Division, KTB, May 1941, NARA, T315, Roll 665
[61] Klaus Hubbuch, unpublished diary and letters courtesy of BBN Archive
[62] Ibid
[63] 15th Panzer Division, KTB, May 1941, NARA, T315, Roll 665
[64] Philip Warner, *Auchinleck*, Cassell, 2001, p.103
[65] Klaus Hubbuch, unpublished diary and letters courtesy of BBN Archive
[66] Ibid
[67] Ibid
[68] 15th Panzer Division, KTB, May 1941, NARA, T315, Roll 665
[69] Kurt Kathe, interview, 2002
[70] Paul Carrell, *The Foxes of the Desert*, Bantam, 1962, pp.80-1
[71] B.H. Liddell Hart, *The Tanks, Vol. II*, Praeger, 1959, p.133
[72] H.F. Beckmann, *Panzerkampf in zwei Kontinenten 1936-1943*, 1994, p.36
[73] Rainer Kreibel, *Inside the Afrika Korps*, Greenhill, 1999, p.115
[74] Ibid, p.115
[75] Volkmar Kühn, *Rommel in the Desert*, Schiffer 1991, p.83
[76] Klaus Hubbuch, unpublished diary and letters courtesy of BBN Archive
[77] Gotthilf Haidt, interview, 2005
[78] H.F. Beckmann, *Panzerkampf in zwei Kontinenten 1936-1943*, 1994, p.36
[79] Klaus Hubbuch, unpublished diary and letters courtesy of BBN Archive
[80] 15th Panzer Division, KTB, May 1941, NARA, T315, Roll 665
[81] Fritz Lang, written account, courtesy of BBN Archives
[82] H.F. Beckmann, *Panzerkampf in zwei Kontinenten 1936-1943*, 1994, p.36
[83] Klaus Hubbuch, unpublished diary and letters courtesy of BBN Archive
[84] Rainer Kreibel, *Inside the Afrika Korps*, Greenhill, 1999, p.128
[85] Klaus Hubbuch, unpublished diary and letters courtesy of BBN Archive
[86] 15th Panzer Division, KTB, May 1941, NARA, T315, Roll 665
[87] H.F. Beckmann, *Panzerkampf in zwei Kontinenten 1936-1943*, 1994, p.36
[88] 15th Panzer Division, KTB, May 1941, NARA, T315, Roll 665
[89] 15th Panzer Division, KTB, May 1941, NARA, T315, Roll 665
[90] Klaus Hubbuch, unpublished diary and letters courtesy of BBN Archive
[91] Ibid
[92] W.G.F. Jackson, *The Battle for North Africa*, Mason/Charter, 1975, p.221
[93] H.F. Beckmann, *Panzerkampf in zwei Kontinenten 1936-1943*, 1994, p.36
[94] Klaus Hubbuch, unpublished diary and letters courtesy of BBN Archive

Chapter Eight, Withdrawal from Cyrenaica, December 1941
[1] Rainer Kreibel, *Inside the Afrika Korps*, Greenhill, 1999, p.133-4
[2] H.F. Beckmann, *Panzerkampf in zwei Kontinenten 1936-1943*, 1994, p.37
[3] Klaus Hubbuch, unpublished diary and letters courtesy of BBN Archive
[4] Horst Sonnenkalb, Part I, courtesy of Die Oase Magazine
[5] 15th Panzer Division, KTB, May 1941, NARA, T315, Roll 665
[6] Rainer Kreibel, *Inside the Afrika Korps*, Greenhill, 1999, p.136
[7] Klaus Hubbuch, unpublished diary and letters courtesy of BBN Archive
[8] 15th Panzer Division, KTB, May 1941, NARA, T315, Roll 665
[9] Klaus Hubbuch, unpublished diary and letters courtesy of BBN Archive
[10] 15th Panzer Division, KTB, May 1941, NARA, T315, Roll 665
[11] Klaus Hubbuch, unpublished diary and letters courtesy of BBN Archive
[12] Ibid
[13] James Lucas, *Panzer Army Africa*, Jove, 1986, p.110
[14] 15th Panzer Division, KTB, Dec 1941, NARA, T315, Roll 665
[15] 15th Panzer Division, KTB, Dec 1941, NARA, T315, Roll 665
[16] Klaus Hubbuch, unpublished diary and letters courtesy of BBN Archive
[17] James Lucas, *Panzer Army Africa*, Jove, 1986, p.110
[18] B.H. Liddell Hart, *The Tanks, Vol. II*, Praeger, 1959, p.139
[19] Erwin Rommel, *The Rommel Papers*, Harcourt Brace, 1953, p.171
[20] H.F. Beckmann, *Panzerkampf in zwei Kontinenten 1936-1943*, 1994, p.38
[21] 15th Panzer Division, KTB, May 1941, NARA, T315, Roll 665
[22] 15th Panzer Division, KTB, May 1941, NARA, T315, Roll 665
[23] 15th Panzer Division, KTB, May 1941, NARA, T315, Roll 665
[24] Franz Kurowski, *Panzer Aces II*, Stackpole, 2004, pp.256-7
[25] Klaus Hubbuch, unpublished diary and letters courtesy of BBN Archive
[26] Rainer Kreibel, *Inside the Afrika Korps*, Greenhill, 1999, p.158
[27] 15th Panzer Division, KTB, May 1941, NARA, T315, Roll 665
[28] Klaus Hubbuch, unpublished diary and letters courtesy of BBN Archive
[29] Rainer Kreibel, *Inside the Afrika Korps*, Greenhill, 1999, p.158-9
[30] Horst Sonnenkalb, Part I, courtesy of Die Oase Magazine
[31] Klaus Hubbuch, unpublished diary and letters courtesy of BBN Archive
[32] Rainer Kreibel, *Inside the Afrika Korps*, Greenhill, 1999, p.171
[33] Klaus Hubbuch, unpublished diary and letters courtesy of BBN Archive
[34] 15th Panzer Division, KTB, 13 Dec 1941, NARA, T315, Roll 665
[35] H.F. Beckmann, *Panzerkampf in zwei Kontinenten 1936-1943*, 1994, p.39
[36] Rainer Kreibel, *Inside the Afrika Korps*, Greenhill, 1999, p.175
[37] 15th Panzer Division, KTB, May 1941, NARA, T315, Roll 665
[38] Klaus Hubbuch, unpublished diary and letters courtesy of BBN Archive
[39] Erwin Rommel, *The Rommel Papers*, Harcourt Brace 1953, p.174
[40] Klaus Hubbuch, unpublished diary and letters courtesy of BBN Archive
[41] 15th Panzer Division, KTB, May 1941, NARA, T315, Roll 665
[42] Klaus Hubbuch, unpublished diary and letters courtesy of BBN Archive
[43] Philip Warner, *Auchinleck*, Cassell, 2001, p.115
[44] Hans Killermann, interview, 2004
[45] 15th Panzer Division, KTB, Dec 1941, NARA, T315, Roll 665
[46] Scheib, combat report, courtesy of BBN Archive
[47] H.F. Beckmann, *Panzerkampf in zwei Kontinenten 1936-1943*, 1994, p.40
[48] 15th Panzer Division, KTB, Dec 1941, NARA, T315, Roll 665
[49] H.F. Beckmann, *Panzerkampf in zwei Kontinenten 1936-1943*, 1994, p.40
[50] Göb, combat report, courtesy of BBN Archive
[51] 15th Panzer Division, KTB, 29 Dec 1941, NARA, T315, Roll 665
[52] H.F. Beckmann, *Panzerkampf in zwei Kontinenten 1936-1943*, 1994, p.40
[53] Christian Federl, *Die Ritterkreuzträger der Deutschen Panzerdivision*, VDM, 2000, p.80
[54] B.H. Liddell Hart, *The Tanks, Vol. II*, Praeger, 1959, p.147
[55] Erwin Rommel, *The Rommel Papers*, Harcourt Brace, 1953, p.180
[56] Horst Sonnenkalb, Part I, courtesy of Die Oase Magazine
[57] Christian Federl, *Die Ritterkreuzträger der Deutschen Panzerdivision*, VDM, 2000, p.315

[58] Kurt Kathe, interview, 2004
[59] H.F. Beckmann, *Panzerkampf in zwei Kontinenten 1936-1943*, 1994, p.40
[60] Volkmar Kühn, *Rommel in the Desert*, Schiffer, 1991, p.95
[61] F.W. Mellenthin, *Panzer Battles*, Oklahoma Press, 1956, pp.86-87
[62] H.F. Beckmann, *Panzerkampf in zwei Kontinenten 1936-1943*, 1994, p.41

Chapter Nine, Back from Tripolitania, January-April 1942
[1] Volkmar Kühn, *Rommel in the Desert*, Schiffer, 1991, p.102
[2] H.F. Beckmann, *Panzerkampf in zwei Kontinenten 1936-1943*, 1994, p.41
[3] Rainer Kreibel, *Inside the Afrika Korps*, Greenhill, 1999, p.228
[4] Ibid, p.231
[5] Franz Kurowski, *Panzer Aces II*, Stackpole, 2004, p.257
[6] K.J. Macksey, *Afrika Korps*, Ballantine, 1968, p.62
[7] Rainer Kreibel, *Inside the Afrika Korps*, Greenhill, 1999, p.235
[8] Paul Carrell, *The Foxes of the Desert*, Bantam, 1962, p.129
[9] H.F. Beckmann, *Panzerkampf in zwei Kontinenten 1936-1943*, 1994, p.41
[10] Rainer Kreibel, *Inside the Afrika Korps*, Greenhill, 1999, pp.235-6
[11] Kneck, unpublished combat report courtesy of the BBN Archive
[12] Gaiser, unpublished combat report courtesy of the BBN Archive
[13] H.F. Beckmann, *Panzerkampf in zwei Kontinenten 1936-1943*, 1994, p.41
[14] Rainer Kreibel, *Inside the Afrika Korps*, Greenhill, 1999, p.236
[15] Ronald Lewin, *The Life and Death of the Afrika Korps*, Pen and Sword, 2003, p.122
[16] H.F. Beckmann, *Panzerkampf in zwei Kontinenten 1936-1943*, 1994, p.41
[17] Ibid, p.42
[18] 15th Panzer Division, KTB, Jan 1942, NARA, T315, Roll 665/667
[19] H.F. Beckmann, *Panzerkampf in zwei Kontinenten 1936-1943*, 1994, p.42
[20] 15th Panzer Division, KTB, Feb 1942, NARA, T315, Roll 665/667
[21] 15th Panzer Division, KTB, Feb 1942, NARA, T315, Roll 665/667
[22] 15th Panzer Division, KTB, Feb 1942, NARA, T315, Roll 665/667
[23] Horst Scheibert, *Die Träger des Deutschen Kreuzes in Gold*, Podzun-Pallas, 1992, p.152
[24] 15th Panzer Division, KTB, Feb 1942, NARA, T315, Roll 665/667
[25] Horst Scheibert, *Die Träger des Deutschen Kreuzes in Gold*, Podzun-Pallas, 1992, p.69
[26] Franz Kurowski, *Panzer Aces II*, Stackpole, 2004, p.259
[27] H.F. Beckmann, *Panzerkampf in zwei Kontinenten 1936-1943*, 1994, p.42
[28] Ibid, p.42
[29] Alfred Toppe, *The German Army in Desert*, U.S. Army, 1952, p.24
[30] 15th Panzer Division, KTB, Mar 1942, NARA, T315, Roll 665
[31] 15th Panzer Division, KTB, Apr 1942, NARA, T315, Roll 665
[32] Wilhelm Hagios, interview, 2007
[33] H.F. Beckmann, *Panzerkampf in zwei Kontinenten 1936-1943*, 1994, p.42
[34] Horst Sonnenkalb, Part II, courtesy of Die Oase Magazine
[35] Ibid
[36] Hans Killermann, interview, 2005
[37] Kurt Liestmann, unpublished diary courtesy of BBN Archive
[38] Ibid

Chapter Ten, Gazala and Tobruk, May-August 1942
[1] W.G.F. Jackson, *The Battle for North Africa*, Mason/Charter, 1975, pp.250-53
[2] Thomas Jentz, *Panzer Truppen*, Schiffer, 1996, p.177
[3] 15th Panzer Division, KTB, May 1942, NARA, T315, Roll 665/667
[4] Thomas Jentz, *Panzer Truppen*, Schiffer, 1996, p.178
[5] H.F. Beckmann, *Panzerkampf in zwei Kontinenten 1936-1943*, 1994, p.43
[6] Horst Sonnenkalb, Part II, courtesy of Die Oase Magazine
[7] Ibid
[8] Ibid
[9] Volkmar Kühn, *Rommel in the Desert*, Schiffer, 1991, p.121
[10] Ibid, p.121
[11] Ibid, p.121
[12] Ibid, p.122
[13] Ibid, p.122
[14] B.H. Liddell Hart, *The Tanks, Vol. II*, Praeger, 1959, p.155
[15] Ibid, p.176
[16] Horst Sonnenkalb, Part II, courtesy of Die Oase Magazine
[17] Wilhelm Hagios, interview, 2007
[18] Thomas Jentz, *Panzer Truppen*, Schiffer, 1996, p.178
[19] Hermann Eckardt, interview, 2005
[20] Thomas Jentz, *Panzer Truppen*, Schiffer, 1996, p.178
[21] Hans Killermann, interview, 2004
[22] H.F. Beckmann, *Panzerkampf in zwei Kontinenten 1936-1943*, 1994, p.44
[23] Erwin Rommel, *The Rommel Papers*, Harcourt Brace 1953, pp.210-11
[24] Thomas Jentz, *Panzer Truppen*, Schiffer, 1996, p.178
[25] H.F. Beckmann, *Panzerkampf in zwei Kontinenten 1936-1943*, 1994, p.44
[26] Ibid, p.44
[27] Wilhelm Hagios, interview, 2007
[28] W.G.F. Jackson, *The Battle for North Africa*, Mason/Charter, 1975, pp.274-5
[29] B.H. Liddell Hart, *The Tanks, Vol. II*, Praeger, 1959, p.174
[30] Gerhart Kienzle, written letter to the author, 2005
[31] Wilhelm Hagios, interview, 2007
[32] Erwin Rommel, *The Rommel Papers*, Harcourt Brace 1953, p.217
[33] Gerhart Kienzle, written account to the author, 2005
[34] Wilhelm Hagios, interview, 2007
[35] H.F. Beckmann, *Panzerkampf in zwei Kontinenten 1936-1943*, 1994, p.45
[36] Ibid, p.45
[37] Ibid, p.45
[38] Horst Sonnenkalb, Part II, courtesy of Die Oase Magazine
[39] Franz Kurowski, *Panzer Aces II*, Stackpole 2004, p.264
[40] Hans Killermann, interview, 2004
[41] Kurt Kathe, interview, 2002
[42] F.W. Mellenthin, *Panzer Battles*, Oklahoma Press, 1956, pp.117-8
[43] 15th Panzer Division, KTB, Jun 1942, NARA, T315, Roll 665/667
[44] Horst Sonnenkalb, Part II, courtesy of Die Oase Magazine
[45] 15th Panzer Division, KTB, Jun 1942, NARA, T315, Roll 665/667
[46] Hermann Eckardt, interview, 2005
[47] Wilhelm Hagios, interview, 2007
[48] H.F. Beckmann, *Panzerkampf in zwei Kontinenten 1936-1943*, 1994, p.47
[49] Max Lebold, interview, 2004
[50] Erwin Rommel, *The Rommel Papers*, Harcourt Brace 1953, p.232
[51] Ibid, p.235
[52] Philip Warner, *Auchinleck*, Cassell, 1981, p.149-50
[53] 15th Panzer Division, KTB, Jun 1942, NARA, T315, Roll 665/667
[54] H.F. Beckmann, *Panzerkampf in zwei Kontinenten 1936-1943*, 1994, p.48
[55] Wilhelm Hagios, interview, 2007
[56] B.H. Liddell Hart, *The Tanks, Vol. II*, Praeger, 1959, pp.188-9
[57] 15th Panzer Division, KTB, Jun 1942, NARA, T315, Roll 665/667
[58] B.H. Liddell Hart, *The Tanks, Vol. II*, Praeger, 1959, p.187
[59] 15th Panzer Division, KTB, Jun 1942, NARA, T315, Roll 665/667
[60] 15th Panzer Division, KTB, Jun 1942, NARA, T315, Roll 665/667
[61] H.F. Beckmann, *Panzerkampf in zwei Kontinenten 1936-1943*, 1994, p.48
[62] Erwin Rommel, *The Rommel Papers*, Harcourt Brace 1953, p.239
[63] Horst Sonnenkalb, Part II, courtesy of Die Oase Magazine
[64] F.W. Mellenthin, *Panzer Battles*, Oklahoma Press, 1956, pp.130-1
[65] Wilhelm Hagios, interview, 2007
[66] F.W. Mellenthin, *Panzer Battles*, Oklahoma Press, 1956, p.132
[67] Wilhelm Hagios, interview, 2007
[68] H.F. Beckmann, *Panzerkampf in zwei Kontinenten 1936-1943*, 1994, p.49
[69] Ibid, p.49
[70] Wilhelm Hagios, interview, 2007
[71] Kurt Kathe, interview, 2003
[72] F.W. Mellenthin, *Panzer Battles*, Oklahoma Press, 1956, p.134
[73] Ibid, p.134
[74] Hagios, but it is doubtful that Teege was captured, he may have thought it was Wahl
[75] W.G.F. Jackson, *The Battle for North Africa*, Mason/Charter, 1975, p.321-22
[76] Christian Federl, *Die Ritterkreuzträger der deutschen Panzerdivision*, VDM, 2000, p.283
[77] Gotthilf Haidt, interview, 2005
[78] W.G.F. Jackson, *The Battle for North Africa*, Mason/Charter, 1975, p.322
[79] H.F. Beckmann, *Panzerkampf in zwei Kontinenten 1936-1943*, 1994, p.50
[80] F.W. Mellenthin, *Panzer Battles*, Oklahoma Press, 1956, p.138

[81] W.G.F. Jackson, *The Battle for North Africa*, Mason/Charter, 1975, p.325
[82] H.F. Beckmann, *Panzerkampf in zwei Kontinenten 1936-1943*, 1994, p.50
[83] 15th Panzer Division, KTB, Jul 1942, NARA, T315, Roll 665/667
[84] B.H. Liddell Hart, *The Tanks, Vol. II*, Praeger, 1959, pp.214-15
[85] Gotthilf Haidt, interview, 2005
[86] Thomas Jentz, *Panzer Truppen*, Schiffer, 1996, pp.180-82
[87] Kurt Kathe, interview, 2002
[88] Horst Sonnenkalb, Part II, courtesy of Die Oase Magazine
[89] W.G.F. Jackson, *The Battle for North Africa*, Mason/Charter, 1975, pp.330-1
[90] Bierman and Smith, *Alamein*, Penguin, 2003, p.232
[91] B.H. Liddell Hart, *The Tanks, Vol. II*, Praeger, 1959, pp.214-5
[92] Alfred Toppe, *The German Army in Desert*, U.S. Army, 1952, p.28
[93] Horst Sonnenkalb, Part II, courtesy of Die Oase Magazine
[94] The author's best guess at reconstructing the chain of command

Chapter Eleven, The Battle of Alam Halfa, August-September 1942

[1] F.W. Mellenthin, *Panzer Battles*, Oklahoma Press, 1956, p.142
[2] Fritz Bayerlein CGSC report on Alam Halfa
[3] Erwin Rommel, *The Rommel Papers*, Harcourt Brace, 1959, p.272-75
[4] Barrie Pitt, *Year of Alamein 1942*, Paragon, 1990, p.222
[5] Ronald Lewin, *The Life and Death of the Afrika Korps*, Pen and Sword, 2003, p.157
[6] Barrie Pitt, *Year of Alamein 1942*, Paragon, 1990, pp.212-13
[7] B.H. Liddell Hart, *The Tanks Vol. II*, Praeger, 1959, p.215
[8] G.P.B. Roberts, CSI Battlefield Reports, Alam Halfa and El Alamein, from U.S. Army CGSC, 1955
[9] H.F. Beckmann, *Panzerkampf in zwei Kontinenten 1936-1943*, 1994, p.51
[10] Thomas Jentz, *Panzer Truppen*, Schiffer, 1996, p.183
[11] Combat report II./Abteilung courtesy of BBN Archives
[12] 15th Panzer Division KTB Aug 1942, NARA T312, Roll 667
[13] Fritz Bayerlein, CSI Battlefield Reports, Alam Halfa and El Alamein, from U.S. Army CGSC, 1955
[14] H.F. Beckmann, *Panzerkampf in zwei Kontinenten 1936-1943*, 1994, p.51
[15] Klaus Hubbuch, Combat Report, 23.11.42 courtesy of BBN Archive
[16] Fritz Bayerlein, CSI Report, CGSC, 1955
[17] G.P.B. Roberts, CSI Report, CGSC, 1955
[18] Klaus Hubbuch, Combat Report, 23.11.42, courtesy of BBN Archive
[19] Ibid
[20] Ibid
[21] Ibid
[22] Ibid
[23] Ibid
[24] Ibid
[25] Horst Scheibert, *Die Träger des Deutschen Kreuzes in Gold*, Podzun-Pallas, 1992, p.420. He was awarded the DKiG on 9 Oct 42
[26] Klaus Hubbuch Ibid p
[27] Franz Kurowski, *Knights Cross Holders of the Afrika Korps*, Schiffer, 1996, p.219
[28] Kurt Kathe, interview, 2002
[29] Gerhard Weidelener, interview, 2007
[30] H.F. Beckmann, *Panzerkampf in zwei Kontinenten 1936-1943*, 1994, p.52
[31] Gotthilf Haidt, interview, 2005
[32] H.F. Beckmann, *Panzerkampf in zwei Kontinenten 1936-1943*, 1994, p.52
[33] Klaus Hubbuch, Combat Report, 23.11.42, courtesy of BBN Archive
[34] 15th Panzer Division, KTB, Sep 1942, NARA, T315, Roll 666
[35] H.F. Beckmann, *Panzerkampf in zwei Kontinenten 1936-1943*, 1994, p.53
[36] Jon Latimer, *Alamein*, Murray, 2003, p.114
[37] H.F. Beckmann, *Panzerkampf in zwei Kontinenten 1936-1943*, 1994, p.53
[38] Ibid, p.53
[39] Fritz Bayerlein, CSI Battlefield Reports, Alam Halfa and El Alamein, from U.S. Army CGSC, 1955
[40] Thomas Jentz, *Panzer Truppen*, Schiffer, 1996, p.185
[41] 15th Panzer Division, KTB, Sep 1942, NARA, T315, Roll 666
[42] Gotthilf Haidt, interview, 2004
[43] Kurt Kathe, interview, 2003

[44] Horst Sonnenkalb, Part II, courtesy of Die Oase Magazine
[45] Adolf Lamm diary courtesy of the BBN Archives
[46] Franz Kurowski, *Knights Cross Holders of the Afrika Korps*, Schiffer, 1996, p.204
[47] Kurt Kathe, interview, 2003
[48] C.E. Lucas-Phillips, *Alamein*, Heinemann, 1962, p.123
[49] Gotthilf Haidt, interview, 2005
[50] Horst Sonnenkalb, Part II, courtesy of Die Oase Magazine
[51] Barrie Pitt, *Year of Alamein 1942*, Paragon House, 1990, p.222
[52] John Lucas Phillips, according to official British war office p.123
[53] In Jul 42 the infantry or schützen regiments were re-designated as panzergrenadiers regiments see Ronald Lewin p.73N
[54] Jon Latimer, *Alamein*, Murray, 2003, p320 Appendix
[55] 15th Panzer Division, KTB, Sep 1942, NARA, T315, Roll 666
[56] Kurt Kathe, interview, 2003
[57] H.F. Beckmann, *Panzerkampf in zwei Kontinenten 1936-1943*, 1994, pp.53-4

Chapter Twelve, The Battle of El Alamein, October-December 1942

[1] Ronald Lewin, *The Life and Death of the Afrika Korps*, Pen and Sword, 2003, p.162
[2] Wilhelm Hagios interview 2007
[3] Gerhard Weidelener, interview, 2007
[4] Jon Latimer, *Alamein*, Murray, 2003, p.176
[5] 15th Panzer Division KTB Oct 1942, NARA, T315, Roll 666/667
[6] Barrie Pitt, *Year of Alamein 1942*, Paragon House, 1990, pp.340-41
[7] Jon Latimer, *Alamein*, Murray, 2003, p.179
[8] C.E. Lucas-Phillips, *Alamein*, Heinemann, 1962, p.123
[9] Jon Latimer, *Alamein*, Murray, 2003, p.324 Appendix
[10] Adolf Lamm, unpublished diary, courtesy BBN Archive
[11] 15th Panzer Division, KTB, map extracts, Oct 1942, NARA, T315, Roll 666/667
[12] Bierman and Smith, *Alamein*, Penguin, 2003, p.290
[13] Barrie Pitt, Year of *Alamein* Paragon House, 1990, 1942 p.342
[14] H.F. Beckmann, *Panzerkampf in zwei Kontinenten 1936-1943*, 1994, p.54
[15] 15th Panzer Division, KTB, Oct 1942, NARA, T315, Roll 666/667
[16] 15th Panzer Division, KTB, Oct 1942, NARA, T315, Roll 666/667
[17] H.F. Beckmann, *Panzerkampf in zwei Kontinenten 1936-1943*, 1994, p.55
[18] 15th Panzer Division, KTB, Oct 1942, NARA, T315, Roll 666/667
[19] H.F. Beckmann, *Panzerkampf in zwei Kontinenten 1936-1943*, 1994, p.55
[20] Ibid, p.55
[21] Wilhelm Hagios, interview, 2007
[22] Klaus Hubbuch, unpublished letter courtesy of BBN Archive
[23] Horst Sonnenkalb, Part III, courtesy of Die Oase Magazine
[24] H.F. Beckmann, *Panzerkampf in zwei Kontinenten 1936-1943*, 1994, p.55
[25] B.H. Liddell Hart, *The Tanks, Vol. II*, Praeger, 1959, p.232
[26] W.G.F. Jackson, *The Battle for North Africa*, Mason/Charter, 1975, p.369
[27] Jon Latimer, *Alamein*, Murray, 2003, pp.234-5
[28] Bierman and Smith *Alamein* p.310-11
[29] Jon Latimer *Alamein*, Murray, 2003, p.242
[30] Ibid, p.243
[31] Ibid, p.245
[32] H.F. Beckmann, *Panzerkampf in zwei Kontinenten 1936-1943*, 1994, p.56
[33] Jon Latimer, *Alamein*, Murray, 2003, p.245
[34] C.E. Lucas Phillips, *Alamein*, Heinemann, 1962, p.277
[35] Jon Latimer, *Alamein*, Murray, 2003, p.247
[36] C.E. Lucas Phillips, *Alamein*, Heinemann, 1962, p.282
[37] Ibid, p.283
[38] Ibid, p.285
[39] Ibid, p.286
[40] Jon Latimer, *Alamein*, Murray, 2003p254 and Lucas Phillips p.278
[41] H.F. Beckmann, *Panzerkampf in zwei Kontinenten 1936-1943*, 1994, p.56
[42] 15th Panzer Division, KTB, Oct 1942, NARA, T315, Roll 666/667
[43] Gerhard Weidelener, interview, 2007
[44] H.F. Beckmann, *Panzerkampf in zwei Kontinenten 1936-1943*, 1994, p.56
[45] Klaus Hubbuch, unpublished letter courtesy of BBN Archive
[46] H.F. Beckmann, *Panzerkampf in zwei Kontinenten 1936-1943*, 1994, p.56
[47] Jon Latimer, *Alamein*, Murray, 2003, p.277

[48] H.F. Beckmann, *Panzerkampf in zwei Kontinenten 1936-1943*, 1994, p.56
[49] Karl Halversheidt, unpublished letter
[50] Wilhelm Hagios, interview, 2007
[51] Karl Halverscheidt, unpublished letter
[52] H.F. Beckmann, *Panzerkampf in zwei Kontinenten 1936-1943*, 1994, p.47
[53] W.G.F. Jackson, *The Battle for North Africa*, Mason/Charter, 1975, p.372
[54] Barrie Pitt, *Year of Alamein 1942*, Paragon House, 1990, p.393
[55] Jon Latimer *Alamein*, Murray, 2003, p.276
[56] H.F. Beckmann, *Panzerkampf in zwei Kontinenten 1936-1943*, 1994, p.56
[57] Adolf Lamm, unpublished diary, courtesy BBN Archive
[58] 15th Panzer Division, KTB, Nov 1942, NARA, T315, Roll 666/667
[59] Wilhelm Hagios, interview, 2007
[60] 15th Panzer Division, KTB, Nov 1942, NARA, T315, Roll 666/667
[61] W.G.F. Jackson, *The Battle for North Africa*, Mason/Charter, 1975, p.375
[62] Hermann Eckardt, interview, 2004
[63] Gerhard Weidelener, interview, 2007
[64] B.H. Liddell-Hart, *The Tanks, Vol. II*, Praeger, 1959, p.234
[65] 15th Panzer Division, KTB, Nov 1942, NARA, T315, Roll 666
[66] 15th Panzer Division, KTB, Nov 1942, NARA, T315, Roll 666
[67] 15th Panzer Division, KTB, Nov 1942, NARA, T315, Roll 666
[68] Jon Latimer, *Alamein*, Murray, 2003, p.290
[69] 15th Panzer Division, KTB, Nov 1942, NARA, T315, Roll 666
[70] W.G.F. Jackson, *The Battle for North Africa*, Mason/Charter, 1975, p.376
[71] Erwin Rommel, *The Rommel Papers*, Harcourt Brace, 1953, p.321
[72] 15th Panzer Division, KTB, Nov 1942, NARA, T315, Roll 666
[73] 15th Panzer Division, KTB, Nov 1942, NARA, T315, Roll 666
[74] 15th Panzer Division, KTB, Nov 1942, NARA, T315, Roll 666
[75] Ronald Lewin, *The Life and Death of the Afrika Korps*, Pen and Sword, 2003, p.177
[76] Paul Carrell, *The Foxes of the Desert*, Bantam, 1962, pp.288-89
[77] Kurt Kathe, interview, 2003
[78] 15th Panzer Division KTB, Nov 1942, NARA, T315, Roll 666
[79] H.F. Beckmann, *Panzerkampf in zwei Kontinenten 1936-1943*, 1994, p.57
[80] 15th Panzer Division, KTB, Nov 1942, NARA, T315, Roll 666
[81] Wilhelm Hagios, interview, 2007
[82] 15th Panzer Division, KTB, Nov 1942, NARA, T315, Roll 666
[83] Adolf Lamm, unpublished diary, courtesy BBN Archive
[84] 15th Panzer Division, KTB, Nov 1942, NARA, T315, Roll 666
[85] Report found in NARA Archives and 15th Panzer Division, KTB
[86] Adolf Lamm, unpublished diary, courtesy BBN Archive
[87] Alfred Toppe, *The German Army in Desert*, U.S. Army, 1952, p.31
[88] 15th Panzer Division, KTB, Nov 1942, NARA, T315, Roll 666
[89] 15th Panzer Division, KTB, Nov 1942, NARA, T315, Roll 666
[90] Klaus Hubbuch, unpublished diary, courtesy BBN Archive
[91] H.F. Beckmann, *Panzerkampf in zwei Kontinenten 1936-1943*, 1994, p.57
[92] 15th Panzer Division, KTB, Nov 1942, NARA, T315, Roll 666
[93] Alfred Toppe, *The German Army in Desert*, U.S. Army, 1952, p.28
[94] W.G.F. Jackson, *The Battle for North Africa*, Mason/Charter, 1975, p.393 and 404
[95] Alfred Toppe, *The German Army in Desert*, U.S. Army, 1952, p.31
[96] 2nd Company diary, unpublished, courtesy BBN Archive
[97] Adolf Lamm, unpublished diary, courtesy BBN Archive
[98] K.J. Macksey, *Afrika Korps*, Ballantine, 1962, p.126
[99] Erwin Rommel, *The Rommel Papers*, Harcourt Brace, 1953, p.373
[100] B.H. Liddell-Hart, *The Tanks, Vol. II*, Praeger, 1959, p.242
[101] W.G.F. Jackson, *The Battle for North Africa*, Mason/Charter, 1975, p.410
[102] Wilhelm Hagios, interview, 2007
[103] Ronald Lewin, *The Life and Death of the Afrika Korps*, Pen and Sword, 2003, p.182
[104] Adolf Lamm, unpublished diary courtesy of BBN Archive
[105] 15th Panzer Division, KTB, Dec 1942, NARA, T315, Roll 667
[106] Unknown author, unpublished letter, courtesy BBN Archive BBN
[107] Klaus Hubbuch, unpublished diary, courtesy BBN Archive
[108] Hermann Eckardt, interview, 2005
[109] Ronald Lewin, *The Life and Death of the Afrika Korps*, Pen and Sword, 2003, p.184
[110] Horst Scheibert, *Die Träger des Deutschen Kreuzes in Gold*, Podzun-Pallas, 1992, p.332
[111] 15th Panzer Division, KTB, Dec 1942, NARA, T315, Roll 667
[112] H.F. Beckmann, *Panzerkampf in zwei Kontinenten 1936-1943*, 1994, p.58
[113] 15th Panzer Division, KTB, Dec 1942, NARA, T315, Roll 667
[114] 15th Panzer Division, KTB, Dec 1942, NARA, T315, Roll 667

Chapter Thirteen, Fighting for time in Tunisia, January-February 1943
[1] 15th Panzer Division, KTB, Jan 1943, NARA, T315, Roll 667
[2] 15th Panzer Division, KTB, Jan 1943, NARA, T315, Roll 667
[3] 15th Panzer Division, KTB, Jan 1943, NARA, T315, Roll 667
[4] 15th Panzer Division, KTB, Jan 1943, NARA, T315, Roll 667
[5] 15th Panzer Division, KTB, Jan 1943, NARA, T315, Roll 667
[6] 15th Panzer Division, KTB, Jan 1943, NARA, T315, Roll 667
[7] 15th Panzer Division, KTB, Jan 1943, NARA, T315, Roll 667
[8] Gottholf Haidt, interview, 2005
[9] 15th Panzer Division, KTB, Jan 1943, NARA, T315, Roll 667
[10] Ronald Lewin, *The Life and Death of the Afrika Korps*, Pen and Sword, 2003, p.185
[11] H.F. Beckmann, *Panzerkampf in zwei Kontinenten 1936-1943*, 1994, p.58
[12] Hermann Eckardt, interview, 2005
[13] 15th Panzer Division, KTB, Jan 1943, NARA, T315, Roll 667
[14] Adolf Lamm, unpublished diary, courtesy BBN Archive
[15] 15th Panzer Division, KTB, Jan 1943, NARA, T315, Roll 667
[16] 15th Panzer Division, KTB, Jan 1943, NARA, T315, Roll 667
[17] 2nd Company diary, unpublished, courtesy BBN Archive
[18] 15th Panzer Division, KTB, Jan 1943, NARA, T315, Roll 667
[19] 15th Panzer Division, KTB, Jan 1943, NARA, T315, Roll 667
[20] Adolf Lamm, unpublished diary, courtesy BBN Archive
[21] 15th Panzer Division, KTB, Jan 1943, NARA, T315, Roll 667
[22] 2nd Company diary, unpublished, courtesy BBN Archive
[23] 15th Panzer Division, KTB, Jan 1943, NARA, T315, Roll 667
[24] 15th Panzer Division, KTB, Jan 1943, NARA, T315, Roll 667
[25] Adolf Lamm, unpublished diary, courtesy BBN Archive
[26] 15th Panzer Division, KTB, Jan 1943, NARA, T315, Roll 667
[27] 15th Panzer Division, KTB, Jan 1943, NARA, T315, Roll 667
[28] James Lucas, *Panzer Army Africa*, Jove 1986, p.202
[29] W.G.F. Jackson, *The Battle for North Africa*, Mason/Charter, 1975, p.414
[30] 15th Panzer Division, KTB, Jan 1943, NARA, T315, Roll 667
[31] 15th Panzer Division, KTB, Jan 1943, NARA, T315, Roll 667
[32] George Howe, *Northwest Africa: Seizing the initiative in the West*, CMH, USA, 1957, p.388
[33] Ibid, pp.390-1
[34] Ibid, p.392
[35] Gerhard Weidelener, interview, 2007
[36] H.F. Beckmann, *Panzerkampf in zwei Kontinenten 1936-1943*, 1994, p.59
[37] George Howe, *Northwest Africa: Seizing the initiative in the West*, CMH, USA, 1957, p.406
[38] Ibid, p.425n
[39] 15th Panzer Division, KTB, Jan 1943, NARA, T315, Roll 667
[40] 15th Panzer Division, KTB, Feb 1943, NARA, T315, Roll 667
[41] 15th Panzer Division, KTB, Feb 1943, NARA, T315, Roll 667
[42] Adolf Lamm, unpublished diary, courtesy BBN Archive
[43] Gerhard Weidelener, interview, 2007
[44] George Howe, *Northwest Africa: Seizing the initiative in the West*, CMH, USA, 1957, p.418
[45] Erwin Rommel, *The Rommel Papers*, Harcourt Brace, 1953, p.401
[46] Adolf Lamm, unpublished diary, courtesy BBN Archive
[47] H.F. Beckmann, *Panzerkampf in zwei Kontinenten 1936-1943*, 1994, p.59
[48] Gerhard Weidelener, interview, 2007
[49] George Howe, *Northwest Africa: Seizing the initiative in the West*, CMH, USA, 1957, p.422n
[50] Ibid, p.424
[51] K.J. Macksey, *Afrika Korps*, Ballantine Books, 1968, p.129
[52] Wilhelm Hagios, interview, 2007

[53] George Howe, *Northwest Africa: Seizing the initiative in the West*, CMH, USA, 1957, p.435n
[54] Ibid, p.437
[55] Adolf Lamm, unpublished diary, courtesy BBN Archive
[56] Erwin Rommel, *The Rommel Papers*, Harcourt Brace, 1953, p.400
[57] Ibid, pp.401-2
[58] Adolf Lamm, unpublished diary, courtesy BBN Archive
[59] H.F. Beckmann, *Panzerkampf in zwei Kontinenten 1936-1943*, 1994, p.59
[60] George Howe claims A.A. 33 while Rommel and Luck claim A.A. 3
[61] Kampfgruppe Menton was known by a number of different titles; Sonderverband z.b.V. 288, Special Unit 288 or Special Group Menton. The unit was assigned to the 90th Light Division and formed in approximately regimental strength with three battalions containing; infantry, panzerjägers, engineer and mountain troops. The unit was commanded by an old friend of Rommel's, Oberst Otto Menton and appears in various reports and diaries as SV Menton or its most noted title as Panzergrenadier Regiment "Afrika". By this time in the campaign the regiment's strength was down to just two strong battalions and was the unit of former Rommel aide Heinz-Werner Schmidt.
[62] George Howe, *Northwest Africa: Seizing the initiative in the West*, CMH, USA, 1957, pp.448-50
[63] Adolf Lamm, unpublished diary, courtesy BBN Archive
[64] Gerhard Weidelener, interview, 2007
[65] George Howe, *Northwest Africa: Seizing the initiative in the West*, CMH, USA, 1957, pp.454-5
[66] Ibid, p.459
[67] Ibid, pp.455-6
[68] Adolf Lamm, unpublished diary, courtesy BBN Archive
[69] George Howe, *Northwest Africa: Seizing the initiative in the West*, CMH, USA, 1957, p.466
[70] Gerhard Weidelener, interview, 2007
[71] H.F. Beckmann, *Panzerkampf in zwei Kontinenten 1936-1943*, 1994, p.59
[72] George Howe, *Northwest Africa: Seizing the initiative in the West*, CMH, USA, 1957, pp.464-66
[73] Adolf Lamm, unpublished diary, courtesy BBN Archive
[74] Erwin Rommel, *The Rommel Papers*, Harcourt Brace, 1953, p.406
[75] George Howe, *Northwest Africa: Seizing the initiative in the West*, CMH, USA, 1957, pp.463-4
[76] Ibid, p.477
[77] 15th Panzer Division, KTB, Feb 1943, NARA, T315, Roll 667
[78] Hermann Eckardt, interview, 2005
[79] Horst Sonnenkalb, Part III, courtesy of Die Oase Magazine
[80] George Howe, *Northwest Africa: Seizing the initiative in the West*, CMH, USA, 1957, p.470
[81] Christian Federl, *Die Ritterkreuzträger der Deutschen Panzerdivision*, VDM, 2000, p.284
[82] James Lucas, *Panzer Army Africa*, Jove 1986, p.239
[83] Erwin Rommel, *The Rommel Papers*, Harcourt Brace, 1953, p.408
[84] 15th Panzer Division, KTB, Feb 1943, NARA, T315, Roll 669
[85] George Howe, *Northwest Africa: Seizing the initiative in the West*, CMH, USA, 1957, pp.486-7 chart
[86] 15th Panzer Division, KTB, Feb 1943, NARA, T315, Roll 667
[87] 15th Panzer Division, KTB, Feb 1943, NARA, T315, Roll 667

Chapter Fourteen, The Final Battles of the Afrika Korps, March-April 1943
[1] George Howe, *Northwest Africa: Seizing the initiative in the West*, CMH, USA, 1957, p.514
[2] 15th Panzer Division, KTB, Mar 1943, NARA, T315, Roll 667
[3] Adolf Lamm, unpublished diary, courtesy BBN Archive
[4] 15th Panzer Division, KTB, Mar 1943, NARA, T315, Roll 667
[5] W.G.F. Jackson, *The Battle for North Africa*, Mason/Charter, 1975, p.435-6
[6] Adolf Lamm, unpublished diary, courtesy BBN Archive
[7] H.F. Beckmann, *Panzerkampf in zwei Kontinenten 1936-1943*, 1994, p.60
[8] Volkmar Kühn, *Rommel in the Desert*, Schiffer, 1991, p.198
[9] Kurt Kathe, interview, 2004
[10] 15th Panzer Division, KTB, Mar 1943, NARA T315, Roll 667
[11] Klaus Hubbuch diary letters courtesy of BBN Archive
[12] 15th Panzer Division, KTB, Mar 1943, NARA, T315, Roll 667
[13] H.F. Beckmann, *Panzerkampf in zwei Kontinenten 1936-1943*, 1994, p.60
[14] Adolf Lamm, unpublished diary, courtesy BBN Archive
[15] Klaus Hubbuch, unpublished letter, courtesy BBN Archive
[16] Karl Halverscheidt letter, courtesy of Fr Dorit Halverscheidt
[17] Adolf Lamm, unpublished diary, courtesy BBN Archive
[18] 15th Panzer Division, KTB, Mar 1943, NARA T315, Roll 667
[19] 15th Panzer Division, KTB, Mar 1943, NARA T315, Roll 667, numbers represent: Actual/Out of place/Ready/Ready for combat operations.
[20] Horst Scheibert, *Die Träger des Deutschen Kreuzes in Gold*, Podzun-Pallas, 1992, p.365
[21] Klaus Hubbuch, unpublished letters, courtesy of BBN Archives
[22] George Howe, *Northwest Africa: Seizing the initiative in the West*, CMH, USA, 1957, pp.527-30
[23] Ibid, p.526
[24] B.H. Liddell Hart, *The Tanks, Vol. II*, Praeger, 1959, p.249
[25] Wilhelm Hagios interview, 2007
[26] H.F. Beckmann, *Panzerkampf in zwei Kontinenten 1936-1943*, 1994, p.61
[27] Horst Sonnenkalb, Part III, courtesy of Die Oase Magazine
[28] Volkmar Kühn, *Rommel in the Desert*, Schiffer, 1991, p.202
[29] Kurt Kathe, interview, 2004
[30] H.F. Beckmann, *Panzerkampf in zwei Kontinenten 1936-1943*, 1994, p.61
[31] Wilhelm Bühler, interview and written accounts, 2006
[32] Hermann Eckardt, interview, 2006
[33] George Howe, *Northwest Africa: Seizing the initiative in the West*, CMH, USA, 1957, p.537
[34] 2nd Company diary, unpublished, courtesy BBN Archive
[35] W.G.F. Jackson, *The Battle for North Africa*, Mason/Charter, 1975, pp.464-66
[36] Coggins, Jack. *The Campaign for North Africa*, Doubleday & Co, 1980, p.150
[37] Christian Federl, *Die Ritterkreuzträger der Deutschen Panzerdivision*, VDM, 2000, p.146
[38] H.F. Beckmann, *Panzerkampf in zwei Kontinenten 1936-1943*, 1994, p.61

Chapter Fifteen, The end in North Africa, April-May 1943
[1] George Howe, *Northwest Africa: Seizing the initiative in the West*, CMH, USA, 1957, p.542
[2] Ibid, pp.603-4
[3] Ibid, p.601
[4] Ibid, p.601n
[5] Kurt Kathe, interview, 2003
[6] Wilhelm Hagios, interview, 2007
[7] George Howe, *Northwest Africa: Seizing the initiative in the West*, CMH, USA, 1957, p.611
[8] Ibid, p.611
[9] Horst Scheibert, *Die Träger des Deutschen Kreuzes in Gold*, Podzun-Pallas, 1992, p.169
[10] George Howe, *Northwest Africa: Seizing the initiative in the West*, CMH, USA, 1957, p.612
[11] Ibid, pp.612-13
[12] Volkmar Kühn, *Rommel in the Desert*, Schiffer, 1991, pp.204-5
[13] Erwan Bergot, *Afrika Korps*, Charter, 1971, pp.239-41
[14] George Howe, *Northwest Africa: Seizing the initiative in the West*, CMH, USA, 1957, p.613
[15] Adolf Lamm, unpublished diary courtesy of BBN Archive
[16] Alfred Toppe, *The German Army in Desert*, U.S. Army, 1952, p.35
[17] H.F. Beckmann, *Panzerkampf in zwei Kontinenten 1936-1943*, 1994, p.62
[18] Halverscheidt letter courtesy of the BBN Archive and Fr Dorit Halverscheidt
[19] Adolf Lamm, unpublished diary, courtesy BBN Archive
[20] Gotthilf Haidt, interview, 2005
[21] Arthur Whitehouse, *Tank*, Doubleday, 1960, p.257
[22] John Strawson, *The Battle for North Africa*, Scribner's Sons, 1969, p.207

Bibliography

Ailsby, Christopher. *Combat Medals of the Third Reich*, Patrick Stephens, Wellingborough Northhamptonshire, UK, 1987

Alman, Karl. *Panzer vor*, Verlagshaus Würzburg GmbH, Würzburg Germany, 2006

Atkinson, Rick. *An Army at Dawn*, Henry Holt, New York, 2002

Baldwin, Hanson. *The Crucial Years 1939-1941*, Harper Row, New York, N.Y., 1976

Barnett, Correlli. *The Desert Generals*, Indiana University Press Bloomington, Indiana, 1982

Battistelli, Pier Paolo. *Rommel's Afrika Korps*, Osprey Publishing, New York, N.Y., 2006

Beckman, H. F. *Panzerregiment 8 Panzerkampf in zwei kontinenten 1936-1943*, Die Schwarze Barett, 1994

Bergot, Erwan. *The Afrika Korps*, Charter Books, New York, N.Y., 1971

Bierman John and Smith Colin. *The Battle of Alamein*, Viking Penguin Putnam Inc., New York, N.Y., 2002

Carell, Paul. *The Foxes of the Desert*, E. P. Dutton and Co., New York, N.Y., 1961

Carse, Robert. *Dunkirk 1940*, Prentice-Hall, Englewood Cliffs, N.J., 1970

Carver, Michael. *Dilemmas of the Desert War*, Indiana University Press, Bloomington and Indianapolis, Indiana, 1986

Carver, Michael. *El Alamein*, MacMillian Company, New York N.Y., 1962

Chapman, Guy. *Why France Fell*, Holt, Rhinehart & Winston, New York, N.Y., 1968

Coggins, Jack. *The Campaign for North Africa*, Doubleday & Co. New York, 1980

Collier, Richard. *The War in the Desert*, Time-Life Books Inc, 1979

Cooper Matthew. *The German Army 1933-1945*, Bonaza Books New York, N.Y., 1978

Crisp, Robert. *Brazen Chariots*, Ballantine Books New York, N. Y., 1961

CSI Battlefield Reports Alam Halfa and El Alamein, from U.S. Army Command and General Staff College, Ft. Leavenworth, Kansas, 1955

Culver, Bruce and Murphy, Bill. *Panzers Colors, Camouflage of the German Army Panzer Forces 1939-45*, Squadron / Signal Publication Inc. Carrollton, Texas, 1976

Culver, Bruce. *Panzer Colors II, Markings of German Army Panzer Forces 1939-45*, Squadron / Signal Publication Inc. Warren, Michigan, 1978

Davies, W.J.K. *Panzer Regiments Equipment and Organization*, Almark Publishing Co Ltd. London, 1978

Deighton, Len. *Blitzkrieg*, Alfred A. Knopf, New York, N.Y., 1980

D'Este, Carlo. *World War II in the Mediterranean 1942-1945*, Algonquin Books, Chapel Hill, N.C., 1990

Doughty, Robert Allan. *The Breaking Point*, Archon Books, Hamden, Connecticut, 1990

Downing, David. *Devil's Virtuosos*, St Martin's Press, New York, N.Y. 1977

Edwards, Roger. *Panzer A Revolution in Warfare 1939-1945*, Arms and Armour Press, London, 1989

Eggenberger, David. *A Dictionary of Battles*, Thomas Crowell Co., New York, N.Y., 1967

Fellgiebel, Walther-Peer. *Die Trägers des Ritterkreuzes des Eisernen Kreuzes 1939-1945*, Podzun-Pallas Verlag, Wölferseim-Berstadt Germany, 2000

Finegold, Jonathan, *The Battle of Sedan*, All Empires

Forty, George. *Afrika Korps at War Vol 1. The Road to Alexandria*, Ian Allan Pub, Shepperton, Surrey U.K., 1978

Forty, George. *Afrika Korps at War Vol 2. The Long Road Back*, Ian Allan Pub, Shepperton, Surrey U.K., 1978

Forty, George. *German Tanks of WWII in Action*, Blandford Press, London, 1988

Forty, George. *The Armies of Rommel*, Cassell, London, 1997

Funk, Erwin. *Böblingen-Fliegerstadt und Garnison*, Herausgeber, Böblingen Germany, 1974

Gelb, Norman. *Desperate Venture*, William Morrow and Co Inc., New York, N.Y., 1992

Gelb, Norman. *Dunkirk*, William Morrow and Co Inc., New York, N.Y., 1989

Goutard, Adolphe. *The battle of France 1940*, Ives Washburn Inc, New York, N.Y., 1959

Goralski, Robert. *World War II Almanace 1931-1945*, G.P. Putnam's Sons, New York, N.Y., 1981

Grove Eric. *German Armor 1939-1940 Poland and France*, Almark Pub. LTD, London, 1976

Guderian, Heinz. *Panzer Leader*, Michael Joseph, London, 1952

Harmon, Nicholas. *Dunkirk*, Simon and Schuster, New York, N.Y., 1980

Heckmann, Wolf. *Rommel's War in Africa*, Doubleday and Company Inc, Garden City, N.Y. 1981

Holmes, Richard. *Bir Hakim Desert Citadel*, Ballantine Books, New York, N.Y., 1971

Horne, Alistar. *To Lose a Battle, France 1940*, Little Brown & Co., Boston, MA., 1969

Howe, George. *The battle history of the 1st Armored Division "Old Ironsides"*, Combat Forces Press, Washington, D.C., 1954

Howe, George F. *The US Army in WWII, The Mediterranean Theater of Operations Northwest Africa: Seizing the Initiative in the West*, CMH Pub 6-1, Center of Military History, Washington, D.C. 1957

Howe, George F. *To Bizerte with the II Corps 23 April-13 May 1943*, CMH Pub 100-6, Center of Military History, U.S. Army, Washington, D.C. 1990

Hubbuch, Klaus. Various Letters and Diary entries.

Icks, Robert J. *Famous Tank Battles*, Doubleday Co Inc, Garden City, N.Y., 1972

Irving, David. *The Trail of the Fox*, Thomas Congdon Books, New York, N.Y., 1977

Jackson, Julian. *The fall of France*, Oxford University Press, England, 2003

Jackson, WGF. *The Battle for North Africa 1940-43*, Mason/Charter Pub Inc New York, N.Y., 1975

Jentz, Thomas L. *Panzer Truppen*, Schiffer Military History, Atglen, PA., 1996

Jentz, Thomas L. *Tank Combat in North Africa, the Opening Rounds*, Schiffer Military History, Atglen, PA., 1998

Kennedy, Robert M. *The German Campaign in Poland 1939*, DA PAM 20-255, Government Printing Office, Washington D.C., 1956

Kriebel, Rainer. *Inside the Afrika Korps The Crusader Battles 1941-1942*, Greenhill Books, London, 1999

Kriegstagebuch (KTB) War Diary of the 15th Panzer Division, various rolls from U.S. National Archives

Kühn, Volkmar. *Mit Rommel in der Wüste*, Motorbuch Verlag, Stuttgart 1999

Kurowski, Franz. *Panzer Aces II*, Stackpole Books, Mechanicsburg, PA., 2004

Kurowski, Franz. *Knight's Cross Holders of the Afrikakorps*, Schiffer Publishing, Atglen, PA., 1996

Lande, D.A. *Rommel in North Africa*, MBI Publishing Co., Osceola, WI., 1999

Lamm, Adolf. Various diaries entries of, unpublished

Lannoy de Francois. *Afrikakorps the Libya-Egypt Campaign*, Heimdal Pub, Bayeux, France

Latimer, Jon. *Alamein*, John Murray, London 2002

Lewin, Ronald. *The Life and Death of the Afrika Korps*, Quadrangle New York Times Book Co. New York, N.Y., 1977

Liddell Hart, B.H. *The Tanks The History of the Royal Tank Regiment Vol II*, Frederick A. Praeger Pub, New York, N.Y., 1959

Lucas, James. *Panzer Army Africa*, Jove Books/Presidio Press, New York, N.Y., 1968

Lucas, James. *War in the Desert, The 8th Army at El Alamein*, Beaufort Books Inc., New York, N.Y., 1982

Lucas, Philips C.E. *Alamein*, William Heinemann Ltd, London, 1962

Lukacs, John. *The Last European War September 1939- December 1941*, Anchor Dress/Doubleday, Garden City, N.Y., 1976

Macksey, Kenneth. *Beda Fomm the classic victory*, Ballantine Books, New York, N.Y., 1971

Macksey, Kenneth. *Afrika Korps*, Ballantine Books, New York, N.Y., 1968

Macksey, Kenneth. *Guderian, Creator of the Blitzkrieg*, Stein and Day Publishers, New York, N.Y., 1975

Macksey, Kenneth. *Panzer Division*, Ballantine Books, New York, N.Y., 1968

Macksey, Kenneth. *Rommel Battles and Campaigns*, Mayflower Books New York, N.Y., 1979

Macksey, Kenneth. *The Tank Pioneers*, Jane's Publishing Co. LTD., London, 1981

Macksey, Kenneth. *Tank versus Tank*, Salem House Publishers, Topsfield, MA 1988

Majdalany, Fred. *The Battle of El Alamein*, J.B. Lippincott Company, Philadelphia, PA., 1965

Mellenthin von F.W. *Panzer Battles*, University of Oklahoma, Norman, Oklahoma, 1956

Messenger, Charles. *Blitzkrieg Story*, Charles Scribner's Sons, New York, N.Y., 1976

Messenger, Charles. *The Tunisian Campaign*, Ian Allan LTD, London, 1982

Mitcham, Samuel W. *Triumphant Fox*, Stein & Day, New York, N.Y., 1984

Moorehead, Alan. *The March to Tunis*, Harper Row, New York, N.Y., 1965

National Archives. Collection of Records of German Field Commands: Divisions, Microfilm Publication T315, 2,379 rolls. 10th Panzer Division: rolls, 558 and 559.

National Archives. Collection of Records of German Field Commands: Divisions, Microfilm Publication T315, 2,379 rolls. 15th Panzer Division: rolls; 664-667.

Neillands, Robin. *Eighth Army*, Overlook Press New York, N.Y., 2004

Perrett, Bryan. *Knights of the Black Cross*, St. Martin's Press, New York, N.Y., 1986

Perrett, Bryan. *The Valentine in North Africa 1942-43*, Ian Allen Ltd., London, 1972

Piekalkiewicz, Janusz. *Tank Warfare 1939-1945*, Blandford Press, Poole-Dorset, UK, 1986

Pitt, Barrie. *The Crucible of War, Year of Alamein 1942*, Jonathan Cape Ltd, London, 1982

Quarrie, Bruce. *Panzer-Grenadier Division Grossdeutschland*, Squadron/Signals Publications Inc., Warren, MI, 1977

Bibliography

Rommel, Erwin. *The Rommel Papers*, edited by B.H. Liddell Hart, Harcourt Brace Co. New York, N.Y. 1953

Rutherford, Ward. *Rommel*, Hamlyn Publishing Group Ltd, London, 1981

Rutherford, Ward. *Blitzkrieg 1940*, Bison Books Ltd, London, 1979

Scheibert, Horst. *Die Träger des Deutschen Kreuzes in Gold, Das Heer*, Podzun-Pallas Verlag, Friedberg, Germany, 1992

Schmidt, Heinz-Werner. *With Rommel in the Desert*, George Harrap & Co Ltd, England, 1979

Shanahan, Edward P. The *XIX Panzer Corps Lightening Advance in France May 1940, Chapter 29 of Combined Arms in Battle Since 1939*, CGSC Research Library

Sheppard, Alan. *Poland 1939*, Osprey Publishing, Oxford, England, 1990

Snyder, Louis L. *The War a Concise History 1939-1945*, Julian Messner Inc. New York N.Y., 1960

Sonnenkalb, Horst. *Wie uns die Jugendjahre gestolen wurden parts I/II/III*, OASE Magazine articles Aug/Oct/ 2002

Stolfi, R.H.S. *German Panzers on the Offensive*, Schiffer Publishing, Atglen, PA., 2003

Strawson, John. *The Battle for North Africa*, Ace Books, New York, N.Y., 1969

Toppe, Alfred. *Desert Warfare: German Army in Desert*, Combat Studies Institute, Foreign Studies Series by Historical Division U.S. Army Europe, 1952

Turnbull, Patrick. *Dunkirk, Anatomy of Disaster*. Holmes and Meier Publishers, New York, 1978

Uhle-Wettler, Franz, Dr. *Westfeldzug Ein glänzender ins Leere (2)*, Soldat im Volk, Number 5/05, Germany, Dec, 2005

UNKNOWN *Die Hindenburg und Ludendorff Kasernen*

Various After Action and Combat Reports. 26 May 1940; 4 Jun 1940; 5-9 Jun 1940; 7 Jun 1940; Attack on Brest-Litovsk; 15-17 Jun 1941; 30 Aug - 6 Sep 1942; 27 Oct 1942;

Warner, Philip. *Panzer*, Arthur Baker Ltd, London

Warner, Philip. *The Battle of France*, Cassell & Co, London, 1990

Watson, Bruce Allen. *Exit Rommel*, Stackpole Books, Mechanicsburg PA., 1999

Weeks, John. *Men against Tanks*, Mason/Charter New York, N.Y., 1975

Weinberg, Gerhard. *A World at Arms*, Cambridge University Press, England, 1994

White, B.T. *Tanks and other AFVs of the Blitzkrieg Era 1939-41*, Blandford Press, Poole-Dorset, UK, 1972

Whitehouse, Arthur. *Tank*, Doubleday, New York, N.Y., 1960

Williams, John. *The Ides of May*, Alfred A. Knopf, New York N.Y., 1968

Zaloga, Steven. *Poland 1939*, Osprey Publishing, Oxford, England, 2002

Index

A
A-9, British cruiser tank: 90
A-10, British cruiser tank: 90
A-13, British cruiser tank: 90
Aa Canal: 46-47
Abbeville: 45, 50
Aberdeen, Operation: 161
Acroma: 73-74, 76, 92, 133-135, 154, 159-160, 164
Agedabia: 70-73, 136-137, 139, 141-148, 213
Akarit, Wadi: 247, 249-251
Alam Halfa: 5, 8, 178-187, 189, 191, 212, 282, 285
Alam Halfa Ridge: 178, 180, 182, 185-186
Alarm Piste: 189, 194
Alamein Position: 171, 178, 184, 208, 210, 213
Alexander, Harold: 175-176, 192, 239, 254-255, 257, 260
Algeria: 212, 225, 227, 235, 239, 260
Allen, Terry: 254
Alter Mann (A.M.): 99-100
Amiens: 12, 45, 48, 50-57, 107
Anderson, Kenneth: 225, 239, 254
Ardennes: 34, 36, 38-39, 41
Ankara, ship: 65, 138
Arco de Fileni: 139
Armistice: 12, 57-60, 259
Arnim von, Hans-Jurgen: 96, 212-213, 25-227, 229-231, 235-237, 241, 245, 247, 251-252, 254-257, 260
Arras: 45-46
Atlantic Charter: 96
Auchinleck, Claude: 96, 102, 118, 131, 168, 172, 175
Australian Forces:
    7th Australian Division: 71
    9th Australian Division: 71, 102, 173, 194, 197
    24th Infantry Brigade: 192
    70th Division: 102
Auxerre: 57

B
Bach, Wilhelm: 80, 86
Badoglio, Pietro: 58
Barbarossa: 96
Barce: 71, 74, 76, 150, 211
Bardia: 62, 71, 75-77, 80-83, 85-88, 90-93, 97-98, 103, 106, 116-121, 132-134, 143, 151, 166, 169, 190, 210
Bastico, Ettore: 103
Battleaxe, Operation: 8, 83, 95-97
Bayerlein, Fritz: 96, 115, 119, 178, 181, 186, 205-206, 252, 254-255, 282
Beda Fomm: 62, 70-71, 147
Belgium: 34, 36-37, 43, 47, 51
Belhamed: 108, 119, 122, 128-31, 154, 164, 166

Ben Gardane: 216, 219, 224, 226-7
Benghazi: 71-76, 92-95, 115-117, 137-143, 147, 150, 168, 175, 188, 201, 210-211, 220, 240, 256
Beni Ulid: 216, 220-223
Benson, Clarence: 260
Berlin: 9, 14-15, 24-27, 38, 62, 71, 75, 96, 149, 189, 219, 224, 249, 257, 280
Bertin-Boussu: 39, 41-42
Bielsk: 26, 30
Billotte: 36, 41-42
Bir el Chetla: 115
Bir Creimisa: 122, 128
Bir el Gubi: 103-107, 110-112, 128, 132-134, 154, 158
Bir el Hafey: 229
Bir Recha: 210
Bir Temrad: 137, 152
Bismarck, Georg: 16, 154, 180-1
Bizerte: 225, 257-259, 260, 286
Blaskowitz, Johannes: 22
Blenheim, RAF bombers: 171
Blitzkrieg: 13, 18, 26, 31, 37, 52, 56
Böblingen: 15-20, 24, 31-32, 63, 77, 97, 101, 115, 138, 152, 158, 176, 187-188, 249, 255, 261
Bock, von Fedor: 22, 48, 50
Bordj Chambi: 232
Borowietz, Willibald: 210, 216, 220, 225, 238, 240-241, 244-245, 259
Böttcher, Karl: 121-122, 128, 144
Bou Arada: 225
Bou Chebka: 235-6
Bradley, Omar: 254
Bransk: 26
Breda Plan: 36
Brenner Pass: 62, 64, 67, 153
Bren Gun Carrier: 149, 166, 172, 174, 197, 199-200, 206, 219
Brest-Litovsk: 9, 26-31, 58, 287
Brevity, Operation: 75, 79, 86
Brindisi: 152-153
British Force:
    British Expeditionary Force (B.E.F.): 36, 46-47, 264
    First Army: 225, 239, 245, 252, 254-255, 257
    Fourth Army: 12
    Eighth Army: 96, 154, 168, 176, 209, 237, 241, 254
    Eighteenth Army: 239, 254-255
    V Corps: 256
    IX Corps: 239, 252, 254-257
    X Corps: 168, 170, 194, 202, 210, 239, 245, 250-252, 254
    XIII Corps: 85-86, 102-103, 105-106, 116-118, 143, 151, 154, 160, 164, 168-170, 178, 180, 185, 194, 197, 200
    XXX Corps: 102-105, 110, 114-119, 135, 137, 139, 148, 154, 168, 174, 180-181, 194-196, 198, 201, 239, 242, 245-248, 250-252, 254

Index

1st Armored Division: 143-144, 146-148, 160-161, 169-170, 172, 174, 194, 197-199, 202, 204, 248
1st Infantry Division: 257
3rd Infantry Division: 47
6th Armored Division: 232, 234, 239, 255
7th Armored Division: 85, 90, 93-94, 102, 106, 108-111, 114-115, 122, 128, 132-133, 141, 147, 154, 161, 180, 185-186, 213, 215-216, 219, 242-243, 254, 257
10th Armored Division: 175, 180, 194, 199, 200, 205, 208
51st Infantry (Highland) Division: 48, 198, 200, 242-244, 251
56th Infantry (London) Division: 254
78th Infantry Division: 254
1st Army Tank Brigade: 102, 117, 151, 154, 159-160, 161
1st Royal Buffs Regiment: 86
1st RTR: 182, 184
2nd Armored Brigade: 154, 159, 194, 198-199, 248
2nd Cameron Highlanders: 86
2nd Hussars: 145
2nd Rifle Brigade: 76
2nd RTR: 76, 78, 90, 107-108
2nd Scots Guards: 86
3rd Coldstream Guards: 81, 86
4th Armored Brigade: 85-88, 90-91, 93-94, 101-102, 104-110, 114, 116, 130, 132-133, 142, 154, 157-159, 163, 166, 170, 180
4th Light Armored Brigade: 180, 242
4th RTR: 76, 85-86, 92, 119
6th RTR: 90, 93, 107, 117
7th Armored Brigade: 76, 85, 90-91, 93, 104-107, 117
7th Hussars: 107, 164
7th Motor Brigade: 154, 159, 181, 197-198
7th RTR: 85-86, 88-89, 91-93, 166
7th Support Group: 76, 85, 101, 107-108
8th Armored Brigade: 180, 183, 185, 202, 242, 246, 248
8th Hussars: 105, 109, 112-113, 158-159
9th Lancers Regiment: 160
10th Royal Buffs Regiment: 234
22nd Armored Brigade: 102, 104-108, 110, 112, 114, 120, 136, 139, 147, 154, 158-161, 163, 170-171, 180-182, 242
22nd Guards Brigade: 76, 79, 85-86, 91, 102
23rd Armored Brigade: 174, 180-181, 184, 201, 247
24th Armored Brigade: 197-199
32nd Army Tank Brigade: 102, 119, 154, 159, 161-162, 167
41st RTR: 199
44th Infantry (Home Counties) Division: 182, 186
44th RTR: 119, 161
47th RTR: 198-199
50th Infantry (Northumbrian) Division: 154, 201, 246-247, 251
50th RTR: 186, 246-247
51st RTR: 254
60th Rifles: 197-198
69th Brigade: 201, 251
132nd Brigade: 186
133rd Rifle Brigade: 182-183, 197-198
150th Brigade: 154, 160-161
151st Brigade: 154, 201
152nd Brigade: 201, 251
201st Guards Brigade: 154, 158, 164, 166-167, 242, 245, 251, 254, 257
239th Battery, 76th A.T. Regiment: 198-199
County of London Yeomanry (CLY): 180, 182
Irish Hussars: 105
KRRC: 197
Brocard: 39, 41-42
Broich, von: 236
Brooke, Sir Alan: 175
Brown House: 98
Brzesc: 27
Buerat Position: 72, 212-217, 220
Bug River: 25-31
Bulson: 37-38, 41-43

C
Calais: 42-48
Cambrai: 12, 43
Cap Bon: 260
Cap Farina (Porto): 256-7, 259
Cape Serrat: 254-255, 257
Capri, Operation: 241, 245
Capuzzo Fort: 71, 76-78, 80, 82-83, 85-87, 89, 90, 91, 96-97, 118
Casablanca: 210
Case Yellow (Fall Gelb): 34, 36
Cavallero: 178, 186
Chamberlain, Neville: 36
Char-B, French tank: 39-43, 264
Chinon: 41, 61
Chlef, wadi el: 219
Chott Fedjadj: 250-251
Chott Position: 244, 247-248
Churchill, British tank: 208, 225
Churchill, Winston: 36, 42, 56, 95-96, 102, 175, 197
Citadel, Brest Litovsk: 27-31
Clark, Mark: 239
Commando Supremo: 144, 178, 215, 219, 227, 231, 237
Commonwealth Forces: 82, 96, 99, 102, 132, 186
Condor Legion: 17-18
Connage: 37
Contay: 45, 50
Cramer, Hans: 64, 82, 95-96, 101, 104, 109, 112, 115, 119, 129, 146, 151, 241, 251-252, 259-260
Crete: 70, 115, 122, 143, 152-153, 167, 187, 200
Crohn, Major: 75, 82, 91, 94-95, 101, 267
Crüwell, Ludwig: 96, 102, 105-106, 108, 110, 115-120, 122, 128-129, 132, 136, 138, 144, 154, 160
Cruiser tanks: 76, 85, 90, 93, 102, 107
Crusader, British tank: 75, 90, 97, 117, 120, 139, 150, 167, 173, 176
Crusader, Operation: 8, 103
Cunningham, Alan: 96, 102, 118
Cyrenaica: 8, 62, 70-74, 79, 103-104, 128-133, 135, 137, 139, 141, 143, 150, 152, 189, 210, 280
Czechoslovakia: 20

D

D-2, French tank: 42-43, 264
Danzig, Corridor: 24
De Gaulle Group: 153
De Gaulle, Charles: 42
Deir el Shein: 171, 173-174
Derna: 62, 71-74, 85, 92, 95, 115, 134-138, 148-153, 163, 176, 190, 210
Desert Air Force (DAF): 176, 180, 188-190, 213, 246-248, 250-251, 254-255, 264
Deutsches Kreuz im Gold (DkiG): 151, 183, 216, 263-264
Devil's Gardens: 189, 195-196
Directive, Fuhrer No 22: 62
Dirschau: 24-25
Djebel Akhdar: 74, 149
Djebel Zebbeus: 232, 235-236
Do-17 German bomber: 37
Dora, Special Detachment: 62
Dunkirk: 45-48, 210, 245, 257
Dyle Plan: 34, 36

E

Eastern Dorsal: 225-227
Eben-Emael, Fort: 36
Eddy, Manton: 254
Eilbote, Operations: 225-226
Eisenhower, Dwight D: 210, 225, 227, 239
El Adem Box: 163, 166
El Adem: 73-74, 76-78, 85, 98, 103, 105, 113, 115, 119, 121-124, 129, 132-133, 139, 154, 157, 159, 162-164, 166
El Agheila: 70, 72-73, 139, 141, 143, 210, 211-215, 221
El Alamein Box:
El Alamein: 168-171, 174, 178, 184-188, 190, 192, 195, 197, 199, 201, 203, 205, 208-209, 211, 213, 215
El Alia: 256, 259
El Duda: 76, 104, 119, 122-124, 128-132, 135, 160, 164, 166
El Guettar: 230, 248, 250-51
El Hamma: 247-249
El Hamra: 81, 235
El Mireir: 171-174
El Wishka: 196, 200-201
Elster, Botho: 18, 21, 27, 29-30, 33, 46, 52, 54, 60-61, 64
Enfidaville: 251-252, 254-255, 257
Escaut Plan: 34
Esebeck, von Hans-Karl: 71, 83
Essertaux: 53-54

F

Faïd Pass: 225-226, 229
Fall Blau
Fall Gelb: 34
Fall Rot: 48
Fall Weiss: 22
Fallschirmjägers: 36, 153, 216, 257-258
FCM: French tank, 21, 264
Fenski, Günther: 101, 103, 109-111, 115, 139, 143, 141-142, 263, 267
Fériana: 227, 229-232, 237
Ferryville: 258
Field Maintenance Centers, FMC-62 and 65: 116

Fieseler-Storch: 122, 142
Flaba: 40-42
Flavigny: 39, 41-42
Flers: 12, 50, 54
Fort Maddalena: 103-105, 168
Fredendall Lloyd: 225, 227
Free French Forces: 154, 194
French Campaign: 5, 34-35, 37, 39, 41, 43, 45, 47, 49, 51, 53, 55, 57, 59, 60, 97
French Forces:

    First Army Group: 36
    Second Army Group: 36, 48
    Third Army Group: 36, 48
    Fourth Army Group: 48
    Army of the Alps: 58
    First Army: 36
    Second Army: 36
    Third Army: 36
    Fourth Army: 36
    Fifth Army: 36
    Seventh Army: 36
    Eighth Army: 36
    Ninth Army: 36, 42
    X Corps: 37
    XIX Corps: 225, 229, 234, 239, 254, 257
    XXI Corps: 39
    1st Armored Division: 54
    1st Colonial Division: 41
    2nd DLC, Light Cavalry: 41, 264
    3rd DCR, Armored: 39-43, 264
    3rd DIM Motorized Infantry: 39-41, 264
    3rd North African Division: 37
    4th DCR: 42-43, 264
    9th Division: 50
    16th Division: 42, 50
    24th Division: 53
    55th Division: 38
    71st Division: 38
    Algerian Division: 254
    Constantine Division: 226
    Moroccan Division: 254
    Oran Division: 254
    51st Infantry Regiment: 40-41
    67th Infantry Regiment: 40-41
    205th Infantry Regiment: 37
    213th Infantry Regiment: 37
    4th Tank Battalion: 37, 41
    7th Tank Battalion: 37
    41st Tank Battalion: 41
    45th Tank Battalion: 40-41
    49th Tank Battalion: 41

French Foreign Legion: 103
Freyberg, Bernard: 102, 143, 168, 180, 186, 194, 202, 204, 239, 245-247, 254
Frühlingswind, Operation: 227, 229
FT-17, tanks: 24, 28-29, 264
Fuka: 170, 205-206, 208
Fuka Position: 170, 206, 208

Index

G
Gabès: 219, 225-230, 237-239, 242, 245, 248-252
Gabr Saleh: 103-107, 114, 133
Gafsa: 226-232, 237-239, 247, 249, 252
Gaillac: 41
Gambut: 85-86, 99, 101-105, 108, 119-121, 132-135, 164, 166
Gariboldi, Italo: 71
Gauleiters: 30
Gause, Alfred: 96, 115-116, 119
Gazala Line: 135, 149, 154, 163-164, 166
German Forces:
- Armeegruppe A: 34, 36, 39, 48
- Armeegruppe B: 34, 36, 48, 50
- Armeegruppe C: 34, 48
- Armeegruppe Nord: 22, 24, 30
- Armeegruppe Sud: 22
- Armeegruppe Afrika: 237, 239, 241, 254-260
- First Armee: 34
- Third Armee: 24
- Fourth Armee: 24, 30, 34
- Fifth Panzerarmee: 212-213, 219, 225-226, 237, 239, 241, 245-246, 251, 254-256
- Sixth Armee: 34
- Seventh Armee: 34
- Eighth Armee: 22
- Tenth Armee: 22
- Twelfth Armee: 34
- Fourteenth Armee: 22
- Sixteenth Armee: 34
- Eighteenth Armee: 48
- Panzerarmee Afrika: 141, 147, 150, 180
- III Armee Korps: 20
- XC Korps: 212
- XIV Motorized Korps: 34, 38
- XIX Armee Korps: 25
- XIX Panzer Korps: 34, 50
- XLI Panzer Korps: 34, 50
- XV Panzer Korps: 50
- XVI Panzer Korps: 48
- XXXIX Panzer Korps: 50
- D.A.K. Assault Gruppe: 137
- D.A.K. Gruppe: 227, 230-232, 234-237
- Gruppe Falkenhorst: 25
- Panzergruppe Afrika: 96, 102-104, 119, 131, 137, 145, 147, 259
- Panzergruppe Guderian: 36-37, 45
- Panzergruppe Kliest: 34, 46, 50
- 1st Panzer Division: 14, 18, 45
- 2nd Panzer Division: 13, 36, 38-39, 42-43, 45, 45-47
- 3rd Light Division: 18
- 3rd Panzer Division: 14-15, 18, 26-27, 29-30, 62
- 5th Light Division: 62, 65, 71, 85
- 7th Flieger Division: 36
- 7th Panzer Division: 15, 62, 189
- 8th Panzer Division: 83
- 9th Panzer Division: 9
- 10th Panzer Division: 18-20, 24-25, 27, 32, 34, 36-39, 41-42, 45, 48, 50, 52-53, 55, 58, 61, 64, 216, 225, 227, 229-232, 235, 237, 241, 254-255, 257
- 15th Panzer Division: 62, 64-65, 70-71, 74-75, 80, 83, 85-86, 91, 93, 104-108, 110, 112, 115-116, 122, 128, 131, 133-136, 143, 145-148, 150-153, 156, 161-163, 167, 169, 170,174, 180, 186, 188, 190, 192, 194-195, 197, 200-203, 206, 208, 210-211, 214-217, 219, 220-221, 225-227, 234, 236-237, 239, 242, 245-248, 257-259
- 19th Flak Division: 225, 245, 250-251, 254
- 20th Flak Division: 254
- 20th Infantry Division (Motorized): 19, 26-27, 29-30
- 21st Panzer Division: 6, 72, 101, 103, 105, 107, 108, 110-111, 14-116, 118-119, 122, 128, 133-134, 145-147, 149, 153-154, 157, 160-161, 163-164, 166, 168-170, 174, 176, 178, 181, 196, 199, 200, 203-205, 216, 219, 225-227, 229, 231-232, 234-235, 243, 245, 250-251, 254-255, 263
- 22nd Luftlande Division: 36
- 29th Infantry Division (Motorized): 38, 43
- 90th Light Division: 103, 144-145, 154, 169-171, 178, 190, 194, 202-203, 225, 232, 284
- 164th Light Division: 173, 176, 178, 180, 197, 202, 212, 217, 221, 225, 227, 247-248, 254
- 207th Infantry Division: 24
- 334th Infantry Division: 225
- 999th Infantry Division: 254
- Herman Goring Division: 225, 237, 254-255
- Manteuffel Division: 254, 257
- Von Broich Division: 225
- Panzer Brigade 4: 14-15, 18, 20, 32, 36, 38-42, 47, 52-54, 56, 59, 61
- Schützen Brigade 10: 46, 53-54
- Schützen Brigade 15: 106, 108, 134, 150, 152, 154
- Afrika Regiment 361: 103, 114
- Artillery Regiment 33: 80, 93, 98, 104, 112, 118, 137, 140, 152, 158-159, 161, 167, 190, 194-195, 203-206, 208, 216-217, 220, 223, 225, 227, 238, 242-244
- Artillery Regiment 37: 39
- Artillery Regiment 75:
- Flak Regiment 18: 104, 136
- Flak Regiment 135: 161, 231
- Flak Regiment 33: 88, 90, 113, 238-239
- Flak Regiment 35: 129
- Flak Regiment 43: 206, 216-217, 223, 238, 244
- Flak Regiment 46: 227
- Grenadier Regiment 47: 251, 256
- Jager Brigade (Luftwaffe): 224, 227
- Luftwaffe Field Brigade: 227
- Panzer Regiment 1: 14
- Panzer Regiment 2: 14
- Panzer Regiment 3: 212
- Panzer Regiment 6: 14, 29-30
- Panzer Regiment 7: 14, 19-20, 52-54, 56, 61, 63, 216, 235, 242
- Panzer Regiment 10: 101
- Panzer Regiment 25: 15
- Panzer Regiment 26: 188
- Panzer Regiment 33: 9
- Panzergrenadier Regiment 104: 205, 229, 231
- Panzergrenadier Regiment 115: 185, 190, 194-196, 198, 202-203, 205, 217, 219-220, 244, 257
- Panzergrenadier Regiment 200: 203, 251
- Panzergrenadier Regiment Afrika: 223

Schützen Regiment 104: 80-81, 86, 102-103, 108, 114, 143, 161
Schützen Regiment 115: 74, 80, 93, 104, 107, 112, 118, 120, 124, 128, 134, 151-152, 156, 159, 166-167, 170-172, 174
Schützen Regiment 155: 143-144
Schützen Regiment 200: 103-104, 106-107, 112, 120, 129, 167, 168
Schützen Regiment 69: 29, 37-38, 41-42, 46
Schützen Regiment 71: 41
Schützen Regiment 86: 26, 29-30, 37-38, 46
Sondergruppe 288: 190, 210, 214-215, 284
Werfer Regiment 71: 216, 234, 243
Aufklärungs Abteilung 3: 80, 101, 105, 108, 133, 149
Aufklärungs Abteilung 33: 93, 105, 108, 133, 147, 150, 152, 156, 227, 235, 242
Aufklärungs Abteilung 580: 226, 235
Flak Battalion 617: 190, 217
Kradschutzen Battalion 15: 80-81, 86, 93, 103, 108, 129, 174
Machine Gun Battalion 2: 103-104, 122, 129, 136-137, 140, 146
Panzerjäger Abteilung 33: 104, 108, 111, 139, 152, 161, 163, 167, 170, 172, 174, 184-185, 190, 195-196, 200, 205, 217, 219, 225, 227, 238
Panzerjäger Abteilung 605: 156, 190, 205-206
Panzer Battalion 501 (Heavy): 211, 229, 254, 256
Panzer Battalion 190: 254
Pioneer Battalion 33: 104, 120, 152, 190, 198, 205-206, 208, 216-217, 219, 225, 241
Pioneer Battalion 39: 29
Pioneer Battalion 49: 38, 46
Oasis Battalion 300: 143
Oasis Company 10: 143
Oasis Company 12: 143

Giraud, Henri: 36
Gleecol: 169
Godwin-Austin: 102
Gott, W.H.E.: 76-77, 102, 143, 154, 168, 170, 175
Grattepanche: 52-54
Graziani: 62
Greek Brigade: 194
Grossdeutschland Regiment: 36, 38-42, 47-48, 53, 264
Guderian, Heinz: 12-13, 18, 25, 27, 30, 34, 37-38, 43, 45-46, 50, 61, 189
Gurkas: 250
Gympy Tummy: 97, 264

H
H-39, French tank: 39-42, 264
Haarde, Friedrich: 7, 15, 65
Haarde, Hans: 14-16, 18, 64
Hafid Ridge: 83, 90-91, 93
Halfaya Pass: 71, 75, 77, 79-83, 85-87, 90-91, 93-98, 103-104, 116, 134, 143, 168-169, 210
Hallouf, wadi: 238, 241-243
Hatab River: 232, 235
Hauvillers: 41
He-111, German bomber: 166
Heidelberg: 62, 64
Herff: 76-77, 80
Heydte von: 227

Hildebrandt, Hans-Georg: 225, 241, 247, 254
Himmler, Operation: 24
Hitler, Adolf: 12-13, 16, 18, 22, 24, 32, 34, 36, 46, 48, 61-62, 70-71, 99, 102, 149, 168, 175, 178, 189, 197, 206, 208, 212, 215, 219, 231, 245, 257
Holland: 34, 36, 261
Homs: 72, 215, 220
Honeys, British tank, M-3: 102, 106, 109, 111
Horrocks, Brian: 180, 185, 194, 239, 245, 254
Hurricane RAF fighter: 75, 77, 94, 96, 120-121, 174, 264

I
Indian Forces:
    4th Indian Division: 85, 90, 93, 102, 119, 128, 132-133, 143, 147, 149, 194, 248, 250-251, 254
    5th Indian Division: 161
    5th Indian Brigade: 173, 248
    7th Indian Brigade: 149, 248
    9th Indian Brigade: 154, 161-162
    10th Indian Brigade: 161-162
    11th Indian Brigade: 85, 148, 166-167
    18th Indian Brigade: 171
    29th Indian Brigade: 154, 166
Irkens, Josef: 215-217, 219, 220-225, 237-244, 246, 248, 255-259, 263, 269
Italian Forces:
    AOK1: 225, 227, 237, 239, 241-246, 248-252, 244, 255, 257, 264
    First Army: 58, 250
    X Corps: 154, 171, 173, 178, 190
    XX Corps: 144-147, 149, 169, 171, 225, 245, 250
    XXI Corps: 103, 132, 144, 154, 168-169, 171, 176, 190, 221, 245, 247, 250, 254
    XXX Corps: 254
    Ariete (132nd): 103-105, 110-113, 116, 120-122, 124, 128-129, 133, 136-137, 154, 157, 159-161, 164, 166-168, 172-173, 180-181, 190, 213, 216
    Bersaglieri: 190, 203, 205, 234, 236
    Bologna (25th): 103, 178, 190
    Brescia (27th): 103, 166, 172-173, 178, 190
    Centauro: 213, 217, 221-222, 225, 227, 230, 232, 234-236, 251, 254, 256
    Folgore (185th): 176, 180, 190
    Giovanni Young Fascists: 245-246, 250
    Littorio (133rd): 168, 173, 180, 187, 190, 192, 197, 202, 203-204, 211, 216
    Pavia (17th): 103, 154, 159-160, 166, 173, 190
    Pistoia: 190, 225, 241, 245, 250, 254
    Sabratha: 154, 166, 173
    Sahara Group: 245
    Savona (55th): 103, 143
    Special Brigade (50th): 226, 254
    Superga Division (1st): 227, 254-255
    Trento (102nd): 86, 154, 173, 174, 197
    Trieste (101st): 103, 110, 136, 154, 159-160, 173, 180, 197, 204, 250-251, 254
    Bersaglieri Regiment 5: 234, 236
        Bersaglieri Regiment 12: 190, 203
        Jager Regiment 65: 203-205
Tank Regiment 113: 194-195

Index

J
Japan: 135
Jews: 277
Ju-52: 18, 77, 92, 143, 162, 176, 187, 190, 249, 254, 257, 264
Jussy: 44-45

K
Kairouan: 225, 234, 252
Kal Basie: 26
Kampfgruppe Audorff: 256
Kampfgruppe Baade: 152, 162
Kampfgruppe Bach: 80, 81
Kampfgruppe Böttcher: 119, 121, 122-123, 128
Kampfgruppe Cramer: 80-81, 146
Kampfgruppe D.A.K.: 227
Kampfgruppe Ebert: 185
Kampfgruppe Geissler: 150, 152
Kampfgruppe Gerhardt: 227, 229-231
Kampfgruppe Grün: 226
Kampfgruppe Herff: 76-77
Kampfgruppe Irkens: 219, 224, 239, 241-241, 257-258
Kampfgruppe Knabe: 80-81, 172
Kampfgruppe Kümmel: 137-139
Kampfgruppe Lang: 227
Kampfgruppe Lindemann: 217, 220, 224
Kampfgruppe Lindner: 217
Kampfgruppe Marcks: 144-145, 147, 149
Kampfgruppe Menny: 152, 166
Kampfgruppe Menton: 225, 230, 232, 234, 236, 284
Kampfgruppe Mickl: 128
Kampfgruppe Mitte: 190, 192, 194-196, 203
Kampfgruppe Nord: 190, 206
Kampfgruppe Patzold: 217
Kampfgruppe Pfeiffer: 226, 231
Kampfgruppe Reimann: 227, 229
Kampfgruppe Schemmel: 194
Kampfgruppe Schmid: 255
Kampfgruppe Schneider-Eicke: 217, 220-223
Kampfgruppe Schuette: 227, 229, 231
Kampfgruppe Siemens: 208
Kampfgruppe Stenkhoff: 227, 229-231
Kampfgruppe Stephan: 101, 105-106
Kampfgruppe Stiefelmayer: 198
Kampfgruppe Stotten: 217, 220, 223, 230, 232, 234-237
Kampfgruppe Sud: 190, 192, 195-196, 199, 206
Kampfgruppe Thinkel: 238
Kampfgruppe Wechmar: 80-81
Kampfgruppe Wissmann: 242
Kasserine Pass: 8, 232, 234-235, 237, 241, 245
Kesselring, Albert: 122, 168, 176, 178, 186, 208, 227, 231, 236, 254, 257
Kidney Ridge: 194, 197-200
Kittyhawk: 264
Kleemann: 154, 178, 181
Kleist, von: 34, 37, 43, 46, 48, 50
Kluge: 24, 34, 46, 48
Knabe: 132
Knights Cross: 9, 10, 141-143, 152, 237, 262-263, 265
Knightsbridge Box: 154, 158-159, 163-164

Krause, Fritz: 241, 254
Kriebel: 78-79, 130, 140
Krupp: 13, 15, 31
Ksaira: 230
Kümmel, Hans: 52, 85, 87, 97, 111, 123, 151-152, 161-162, 167, 170, 174-175, 188, 251

L
La Besece: 38-39
Landau, Operation: 76
Le Kef: 231, 234, 236
Le Kol (Light Column): 14, 20, 66, 78, 91, 94, 109, 150, 272
Leathercol: 169
Leese, Oliver: 180, 194, 239, 242, 245, 254
Lessouda: 229-230
Libya: 62, 67, 72-73, 77-78, 82, 99, 101, 153
Liebenstein von: 227, 230-231, 241, 245, 251
Lightfoot, Operation: 192, 201
Lomza: 29
Long Range Desert Group (LRDG): 101
Low Countries: 34
Luftwaffe: 15-18, 24-26, 37, 45-46, 50, 62-63, 66, 71-72, 134-5, 141, 153, 161, 166, 168 -169, 172, 175, 181, 188-89, 199, 209, 213, 216, 221, 224-227, 229-230, 232, 236-238, 254- 255, 257, 265
Lumsden, Herbert: 154, 194
Lyons: 58-59

M
M-13: 103, 199, 213, 230, 265
M-14: 213, 265
Maas (Meuse) River: 34, 36, 38, 42, 43
Magic Fire, Operation: 17
Maginot Line: 32, 34, 36-38, 40, 48, 60
Maisoncelle: 38, 41-42
Maïzila Pass: 226, 229
Maknassy: 225-226, 247, 250
Malta: 66, 151-154, 168, 175-176, 190
Mammoth: 101, 117, 119
Manstein, Erich: 34
Maori: 170, 201
Marada Line: 143-144
Marcks, Werner: 143-145, 147, 149
Mareth Line: 224-227, 236-240, 242, 245, 250
Marle: 43-44
Marne River: 56, 61
Marosczek anti-tank rifle: 25
Marsa el Brega: 70. 72-73, 142, 210-212
Martuba Oasis: 74
Massicault: 257-259
Mateur: 257-258
Matilda, tanks: 32, 75-76, 78-81, 85-88, 90-95, 99, 101-102, 114, 117, 119, 123-124, 128-130, 137, 141, 161-163, 167, 172, 194, 265
Matmata Hills: 225, 239, 241-242, 244-245, 248
Me-109: 45-46, 162, 181, 265
Me-110: 65-66, 76, 153, 166
Mechili: 71, 73-74, 85, 138-139, 147-150, 152
Médenine: 225, 227, 237-239, 241-242, 245, 247
Medjerda River: 255-257

Medjerda Valley: 255-257
Medjez el Bab: 225, 241, 254, 255, 257
Mellenthin, von: 172, 178
Menton, Otto: 223, 284
Menton, Sondergruppe (SV): 231, 284
Mersa Matruh: 168-170, 190
Messe, Giovanni: 225, 237, 241, 245, 247, 251-252, 254, 260
Messervy: 85, 102, 143, 154, 161
Metameur: 237-239, 241-242, 244
Midsummer Night's Dream, Operation: 101
Mildebrath, Werner: 117, 175, 177, 185-186, 263, 271
Milowitz: 20, 22, 24
Misurata: 71-73
Miteiriya Ridge: 174, 194, 196-197, 200
Mont Dieu: 38-39
Montcornet: 42-43
Montgomery, Bernard: 47, 175-176, 180, 185-186, 189, 192, 199, 202, 227, 236, 239, 241-242, 245, 247-248, 250, 254
Morane MS-406 fighter: 45, 58
Morgenluft, Operation: 227, 230
Morocco: 225
Msus: 73, 143, 147-149
Mt Damion: 38, 40
Mussolini, Benito: 55, 58, 62, 71, 75, 168, 178, 212, 231, 260

N
Naples: 64-67, 105, 152, 163, 249
Narew Army (Polish): 26-27
Narew River: 25-27
Nebelwerfers: 216, 234, 265
Nehring, Walther: 154, 163, 181, 212-213
Neumann-Silkow, Walter: 83, 97, 102, 110, 113, 122, 128-130, 132, 134
New Zealand Forces:
    New Zealand Corps: 239, 245-248, 254
    2nd New Zealand Division: 102, 115, 119, 122, 128, 131, 143, 169, 170, 180, 186, 194-195, 200-201, 213-214, 216, 219, 239, 242, 248, 252, 254
    4th New Zealand Brigade: 119, 170, 173-174
    5th New Zealand Brigade: 118-119, 132, 172, 186
    6th New Zealand Brigade: 114, 128, 174
Nicholson, Cameron: 46, 234
Nickforce: 234-235
Nofilia: 72, 76, 213-215
Norway: 32, 100
Noyers: 37-38

O
O'Connor, Richard: 70
O'Moore-Creagh: 85
Oberkommando der Heer (OKH): 14, 30, 34, 45, 61-62, 71, 237, 260, 265
Oberkommando der Luftwaffe (OKL): 265
Oberkommando der Wehrmacht (OKW): 18, 34, 45, 48, 62, 70-71, 102, 138, 189, 192, 197, 212, 219, 241, 255, 257, 265
Oise, River: 43, 54, 56
Oran: 210, 254, 260
Oresmaux: 52-54
Otto Piste: 189, 194, 196, 198, 202-204

Ox Head, (Ochsenkopf) Operation: 241
Oxalic Line: 194, 197, 199-200

P
Pain de Sucre: 38, 41
Panzer Mk III Specials: 152, 156, 159, 161, 174-175, 180, 183, 186, 211, 217, 223, 226, 236, 238, 244-245
Panzer Mk IV Specials: 161, 163, 175, 180, 182-183, 186, 198, 199, 211, 217, 223, 226, 236, 238, 245
Panzer Mk VI Tiger: 227, 229, 235, 255-256
Panzerführer Afrika: 256
Panzergruppe Irkens: 256-259
Panzerwaffe: 18, 22, 61, 75
Paris: 34, 42-43, 45, 50-53, 56, 59-61
Péronne: 43, 45, 50, 56
Petain: 57-58
Pioneergruppe Perser: 217
Phony War: 32, 36
Point 206: 77-80, 86-87, 90-91, 94
Point 208: 77, 87, 90, 93, 242
Polish Air Force: 24, 26
Polish Army: 24-25
Polish Campaign: 5, 18, 22-23, 25, 27, 29-33, 97, 99
Polish Forces: 22, 24-31
    Modlin Army: 27
    Narew Army: 26-27
    18th Division: 25-26
    33rd Infantry Division (Reserve): 26
    Podlaska Cavalry Brigade: 25-26
    Suwalska Cavalry Brigade: 25-26
Prittwitz-Gaffron, Heinrich: 62, 65, 71
Proserpina, ship: 197, 200

Q
Qattara Depression: 171, 177-178, 180, 186-190
Quala: 78

R
Rahman Track: 174, 201-206
Ramcke Brigade: 178, 185, 190, 206, 212
Ramcke, Bernhard: 176
Ramsauer, Otto: 20-21, 27, 33, 53, 56, 64, 82, 92, 95, 150, 272
Randow, Heinz: 190, 203
Ranger Battalions (US): 229
Raucourt: 40-42
Ravenstein, Johann: 85, 101-102, 116, 124
Renault R-35: 30, 42-43, 265
Retma: 154, 157
Rhine River: 48, 32, 70, 98
Rhineland: 22
Rigel Ridge: 159, 163-164
Ritchie, Neil: 118, 143, 154, 168
Royal Air Force (RAF):
Royal Navy: 46, 65, 153, 175, 177-178, 188, 197
Rundstedt, von Gerd: 22, 34, 43, 46, 48
Russian anti-tank gun 7.62: 198, 200, 238
Russian, forces: 26, 30

Index

Ruweisat Ridge: 170-174, 181, 187
Ryder: 254

S
Saunnu: 145-147
Sbeïtla: 226-232, 234
Sbiba: 232, 234, 236
Schaal, Generalmajor: 24, 27, 34, 38
Sciaf Sciaf: 108, 110, 120
Schleswig-Holstein: 24
Schlieffen Plan: 34
Scorpion, flail tanks: 246
Sedada: 217, 219-223
Sedan: 8, 34, 36-40, 42-43, 97
Seeckt von, Hans: 12
Semovette: 199, 265
Sened Station: 226
Sfax: 226, 249-252
Sherman, tanks: 159, 176, 188, 195, 197, 199-202, 204, 208-209, 219, 225, 230, 235, 239, 243, 259, 260, 265
Sicily: 65-67
Sidi Abd el Rahman: 189
Sidi Azeiz: 76-78, 81-85, 90, 93, 97, 105-106, 117-120, 132, 135
Sidi Barrani: 62, 78, 95, 209
Sidi Bou Zid: 226-227, 229-230
Sidi Muftah: 106-108, 110, 112, 121-122, 154, 160
Sidi Omar: 91, 93, 98, 103-106, 115-117, 119, 132, 151, 168, 210
Sidi Rezegh: 105-108, 110-111, 114-116, 118-122, 124, 128-129, 164, 166, 256
Sidi Suleiman: 77-78, 80, 86, 91, 93, 95, 97-98
Sidra Ridge: 160-162
Siebel ferries: 255, 257
Siegfried Line: 16, 34
Sirte: 70, 72, 76, 213, 215-216
Sitzkrieg: 32
Siwa Oasis: 169
Snipe, position: 197-199
Sollum: 80-86, 91, 93-97, 100, 103, 105-106, 115-119, 131-135, 143, 166, 168-169, 190, 210
Somme: 43, 45
Somme River: 45, 48, 50
Souma S-40: 52
South African Forces:
    1st South African Division: 102, 107, 115, 143, 149, 163-164, 194
    2nd South African Division: 154, 166
    1st South Brigade: 110
    3rd South African Brigade: 154, 173
    5th South African Brigade: 108, 110-112, 114, 173
    6th South African Brigade: 154, 166, 171
SS and SD troops: 24, 27
St. Fuscien: 50-52
St. Just: 43, 54-55
St. Quentin: 12, 43-45
Stonne: 38-43, 107
Stotten, Hans-Gunther:
Streich, Johannes: 70-71
Stuart, tanks: 109-110, 161, 163-164, 170, 180
Stuka Ju-87: 46, 166, 173, 264

Stuka: 24-25, 38, 43, 45-46, 50, 53-54, 66, 70, 133, 138, 140-141, 153, 161, 166-167, 173, 181, 199, 238-239, 242-244, 265
Stumme, Georg: 189, 192, 194, 206
Sturmgeschwader: 46
Sturmgeschutze: 18, 211, 261, 265
Suez Canal: 18, 102, 171, 175, 178, 249
Summermann, Max: 103
Supercharge, Operation: 201-202, 204
Surrender, France: 54
Swinton, E.D.: 12
Syria: 96, 168, 173

T
Tadjera: 238, 243
Tarhuna: 215-216, 220-221, 223-224
Task Force Stark: 226
Tebega Gap: 246-249
Tébessa: 225, 232, 234-236
Tébourba: 256-258
Teege, Willi: 151, 163, 166, 175, 190, 195-196, 200, 203-205, 211
Tel el Aqqaqir: 171, 202, 206
Tel el Eisa: 173, 178, 201
Telegraph Piste: 201, 203-05
Thala: 231-232, 234-236
Thélepte: 227, 231-232, 237
Thoma, von Wilhelm: 194, 197, 203-204, 206, 225, 256
Tiger Convoy: 25, 83, 85, 102
Tmimi: 73, 150-152, 212
Tobruk: 62, 65-68, 71-76, 80-86, 89-92, 98-100, 102-108, 114-124, 128-35, 143, 147, 151-152, 154-155, 157, 159-166, 168-173, 175-177, 187-188, 197, 210, 212, 256
Toppe, Alfred: 62-63, 72, 74, 98, 151, 176, 210, 212, 257
Torch, Operation: 210
Totensonntag: 110, 112-113, 115, 118, 131, 134, 139, 141, 152, 211
Tours: 56, 59-60
Treaty of Versailles: 12, 22
Trigh Capuzzo: 74, 76, 83, 101-103, 105-108, 115, 118-122, 128-133, 154-158, 160, 163, 210
Trigh el Abd: 74, 103-106, 110, 114-118, 142, 150, 157, 159-161
Tripoli: 65-67, 70-77, 83, 95, 101, 138-139, 142, 148, 168, 175, 213, 215-216, 219-220, 224, 226, 242, 249
Tripolitania: 5, 62, 71-72, 99, 103, 145, 147, 149, 151, 153, 219, 225
Tuker: 143, 168, 194, 245, 250, 254
Tunis: 104, 210, 213, 215, 219, 225, 245, 247, 249-250, 254-260, 286
Tunisia: 66, 72, 187, 210-212, 215, 217, 219, 221, 224-227, 229, 231, 233, 235-237, 239-241, 245-246, 249-250, 254, 257, 260, 283

U
Ultra: 101, 178
United States: 96, 135, 261
United States Forces:
    Fifth Army: 239
    I Corps: 239
    II Corps: 225, 227, 229-230, 234, 239, 246, 248, 250-251, 254, 257, 289, 286
    VI Corps: 239
    1st Armored Division: 226, 229-231, 234-236, 258-260

CCA: 226, 229
CCB: 231, 235-236
CCC: 226, 230
13th Armored Regiment: 235
1st Infantry Division: 254
9th Infantry Division: 232, 234, 254
DIVARTY: 234-235
34th Artillery Battalion: 235
60th Artillery Battalion: 235
84th Artillery Battalion: 235
34th Infantry Division: 229, 232, 234, 239, 254
39th Infantry Regiment: 232
168th Infantry Regiment: 229-230
1st Ranger Battalion: 229
81st Reconnaissance Battalion: 229
United States Army Air Forces (USAAF): 200

V
Vadencourt: 45
Vaerst, von Gustav: 144, 154, 158-159, 180, 190, 210, 215, 245, 254, 257
Veith, Richard: 144
Venizia, Case:
Via Balbia: 72-74, 76, 78, 83, 86, 92, 97, 101, 105, 119-120, 132-133, 138-139, 143-146, 148, 150, 157, 159, 164, 166, 168-170, 173, 188, 212-213, 215
Vichy: 56, 96
Vistula River: 22, 25

W
Wadelincourt: 37-39
Wahl, Wolfgang: 15, 18, 51, 64, 82, 95, 103, 116-117, 123, 130, 133, 136-137, 142, 156, 170, 173-174, 190, 263
Wavell: 83-85, 96
Weber: 225
Western Desert Force: 70, 75, 96, 102
Western Dorsal: 225-226, 252
Western Front: 12-13
Westphal, Siegfried:
Weygand Line: 8, 48, 50-52, 97
Weygand Maxime: 48
Wizna: 25-26, 31
Woodcock: 197-198
Wünsdorf: 14-16
Wysokie-Mazowieckie: 26, 31

Y
Yellow, Case: 32, 34, 36

Z
Zaafria: 229
Zarat: 246-248
Zebeus, djebel: 224, 231
Zem Zem, wadi: 217
Zemlet el Lebene: 238, 242-243
Ziegler, Heinz: 100, 227, 230, 241
Zigzaou, wadi: 225, 246
Zurzur, wadi: 220-221

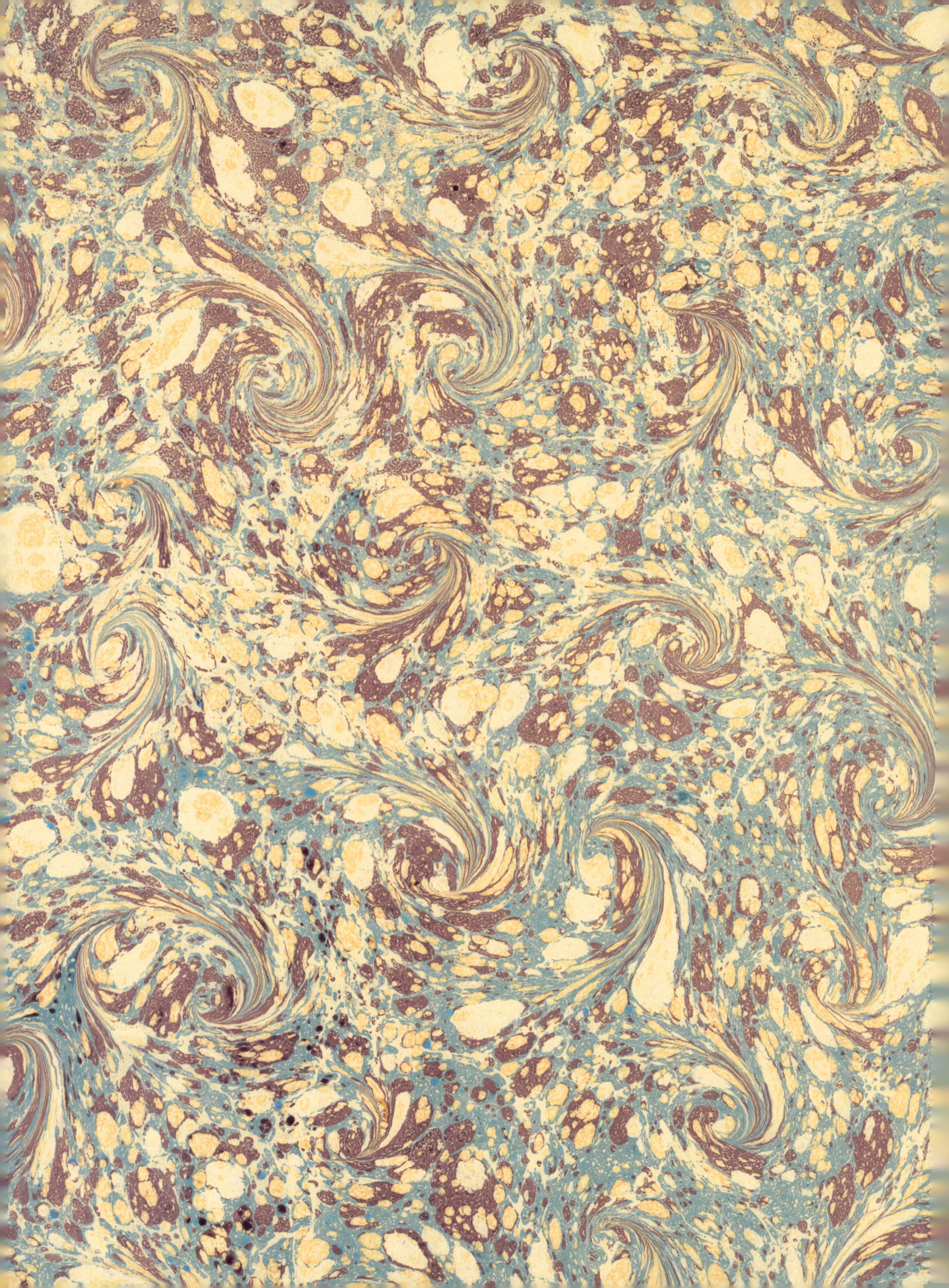